MW00709758

# *Golf*

# GREAT BRITAIN
# *and* IRELAND

A TRAVELER'S GUIDE TO MORE THAN 2,500 COURSES
IN ENGLAND, SCOTLAND, WALES, NORTHERN IRELAND,
AND IRELAND

CONTEMPORARY BOOKS
A TRIBUNE COMPANY

**Library of Congress Cataloging-in-Publication Data**

Golf Great Britain and Ireland : a traveler's guide to more than 2,500
  courses in England, Scotland, Northern Ireland, and Ireland.
      p.    cm.
      Published in England by the Automobile Association under the
  title: Sunday express guide to golf courses.
      Includes index.
      ISBN 0-8092-3122-0
      1. Golf courses—Great Britain—Directories.    2. Golf courses—
  Ireland—Directories.    3. Great Britain—Guidebooks.    4. Ireland—
  Guidebooks.    I. Automobile Association (Great Britain)    II. Sunday
  express (London, England)
      GV984.G65    1996
      796.352'025'41—dc20                                              96-9297
                                                                          CIP

Published simultaneously by AA Publishing as *Sunday Express Guide to
Golf Courses 1997*, copyright © The Automobile Association 1996.

AA Publishing is a trading name of Automobile Association Developments
Limited whose registered office is Norfolk House, Priestly Road,
Basingstoke, Hampshire RG24 9NY, England.

Cover design by Monica Baziuk
Cover photograph of 8th hole, Turnberry Golf Course, Scotland,
copyright © Aldo Torelli/Tony Stone Images

Copyright © 1996 by The Automobile Association
All rights reserved
Published by Contemporary Books, Inc.
Two Prudential Plaza, Chicago, Illinois 60601-6790
International Standard Book Number: 0-8092-3122-0
10    9    8    7    6    5    4    3    2    1

# CONTENTS

# LOOKING FOR SOMEWHERE DIFFERENT TO STAY OR EAT?

*Try one of the 4000 inspected hotels on offer in*

## AA The Hotel Guide

- Country house hotels, town houses, busy city hotels or cliff-top seaside hotels

- Whatever you fancy – whether you are on holiday or on business the wide range of hotels has something for everyone

*You can be sure of a delicious meal if you use*

## AA Best Restaurants in Britain

- The Abbey Well guide to AA recommended restaurants

- With 1500 AA Rosette-awarded restaurants, the excellence of the food is assured

- With over 20 national cuisines represented, there should be something for every palate

# HOW TO USE THIS
# GUIDE

 his guide contains about 2800 golf courses in Britain and Ireland most of which welcome visiting golfers. This includes many newly-built courses.

## ALL YOU NEED TO KNOW

We have endeavoured to supply all the information you need to know before your visit by telling you what kind of course you can expect, what club facilities are available, including catering, any leisure facilities and the green fees you can expect to pay. We have also included AA-recommended accommodation - whether it be at the course itself or slightly further away.

## ARRANGING A VISIT

Some courses want advance notice of any visit, and possibly a letter of introduction from your own club. They may also require a handicap certificate. If this is the case the directory will include this information. However, it is always a good idea to check with any course in advance as **details in the directory can change,** particularly green fees, during the currency of the guide.

## COURSES OF NOTE

Courses that are considered to be of particular merit or interest have been placed within a shaded box. They may be very historic clubs or they may have been chosen because their courses are particularly testing or enjoyable to play. Some have been included because they are in holiday areas and have proved popular with visiting golfers. Such a selection cannot be either exhaustive or totally objective, and these courses do not represent any formal category on quality or other grounds.

Major Championship courses have special treatment with a full page entry, including a selection of places at which to eat as well as to stay.

## THE DIRECTORY

The directory is arranged in countries: England, Northern Ireland and the Republic of Ireland are listed in alphabetical location within each county. Scotland and Wales are listed in alphabetical location within regions - the counties that comprise each region are listed below the region heading. If you are not sure where your chosen course may be, there is an alphabetical index of courses at the end of the directory. The maps at the end of the book will also help to locate any golf course.

## MAP REFERENCES

Should you be travelling in an unfamiliar part of the country and want to know the choice of courses available to you, consult the atlas at the end of the book. In its directory entry, each course has a map number and National Grid reference and there are directions to the course giving the nearest place located on the map. The grid references for the Irish Republic are unique to the atlas at the back of this book.

## SYMBOLS AND ABBREVIATIONS

In order to maximise the space available, we have used certain symbols and abbreviations within the directory entries and these are explained in the panel below.

| | |
|---|---|
| 04 TQ21 | atlas page and National Grid reference |
| ☎ | telephone number |
| IR£ | Irish Punts (Republic only - the rates of exchange between Punts and pounds sterling are liable to fluctuate) |
| ⊗ | lunch |
| ⅲ | dinner |
| 🍴 | bar snacks |
| ☕ | tea/coffee |
| ⅄ | bar open midday and evenings |
| 🛏 | accommodation at club |
| 🔺 | changing rooms |
| 🏠 | well-stocked shop |
| ⍑ | clubs for hire |
| ʃ | professional at club |
| ★ | hotel classification |
| ❀ | restaurant classification (applicable to championship course entry only) |
| Q | Guest house classification |
| B | AA Branded group hotels |
| TH | Town House hotels |

5

## Entries in Bold Italics

**NB** Although we make every effort to obtain up-to-date information from golf clubs, in some cases we have been unable to verify details with the club's management. Where this is the case the course name is shown in bold italics and you would be strongly advised to check with the club in advance of your visit

## Telephone Codes

The area codes shown against telephone numbers under Republic of Ireland courses are applicable within the Republic only. Similarly the area codes shown for entries in Great Britain and Northern Ireland cannot be used direct from the Republic. Check your telephone directory for details.

## Accommodation

For each course listed, we recommend a nearby AA-appointed hotel, giving its classification, full name and address, telephone number and total number of bedrooms, including the number with private bath or shower. In some cases the hotel will be within the grounds of the golf course itself. The hotels recommended in the Golf Guide are mostly in the ★★, ★★★, and ★★★★ star categories. Where there is no AA-appointed hotel nearby, we have recommended an AA-inspected Listed Establishment These are classified by a quality assessment, or Q rating, of 1-5 Q's.

## Club Accommodation

Some courses offer accommodation at their club. Where this facility exists, the 'bed' symbol (🛏) will appear in the entry under club facilities. This has been listed as a further option for those who might wish to stay at the course. However, unless the club accommodation has an AA star-rating, the only accommodation recommended by the AA is the star-rated hotel that appears at the foot of each entry.

## Key to Hotel Classification

The AA system of star rating from one to five stars is the market leader in hotel classifications and has long been universally recognised as an accurate, objective indication of the facilities one can expect to find at any hotel in the AA scheme.

★ Black stars indicate the level of facilities and services available at a hotel. One-star hotels are generally small hotels and inns, with good but often simple furnishings, facilities and food.

★★ Small to medium-sized hotels offering more facilities(telephones and televisions etc), and at least half the bedrooms will have en-suite bath or shower.

★★★ Medium-sized hotels with more spacious accommodation and a greater range of facilities and services; all rooms have en-suite bath or shower.

★★★★ Large hotels with spacious accommodation and high standards od comfort, service and food; all rooms have full en suite facilities.

★★★★★ Large luxury hotels offering the highest international standards of accommodation, facilities, services and cuisine.

🏠 This denotes an AA Country House hotel with a relaxed informal atmosphere and offering a personal welcome. Often secluded, they are not always rurally situated but are quiet.

**Branded Hotels** Hotels belonging to large groups do not carry star ratings as they reach a common level of comfort and facilities. They are indicated by a B prior to the hotel name.

## Percentage Ratings for Quality

Our inspectors give percentage scores to hotels with black stars as a way of comparing hotels of the same star rating in terms of quality. This covers all aspects of a hotel's operation, including hospitality, service, cleanliness, food, and overall presentation of bedrooms and public areas. A high percentage score indicates superior standards within the star rating.

## Red Stars

The AA recognises hotels that consistently provide outstanding levels of hospitality, service, food and comfort through its prestigious red-star award scheme. These are given to a select group of hotels considered to be of the very best within their star rating. In such cases, a percentage score for quality is considered unnecessary. Red-star hotels in this guide are indicated by the word 'red' after the star classification.

## Rosettes

🏵 Rosettes are awarded to hotels and restaurants achieving notable excellence for quality of cuisine, from one rosette – indicating carefully prepared food reflecting a high level of culinary skill – to a maximum of five rosettes, indicating outstanding cuisine reaching the highest international standards.

# STUFF of DREAMS

From any viewpoint, the United Kingdom is a golfing jewel, set among wild seas, created by nature, basic and pure and often oblivious to modern trends. Some of the great links, famed throughout the world, remain mercifully undisturbed and unspoiled. The passage of time has, obviously, produced 'modifications' but we ordinary mortals can still walk old gems, sinking our shoes into the spike-marks of champions long gone. These classic tests are available to the traveller who makes an early request for admission. But there can be problems!

Our golfing kingdom is divided into four quite different countries - but all of them speak the same language. However, it is true that knocking on the door of an exclusive club does not guarantee a round. A well-written letter of introduction can work wonders, particularly if you stress that a game at an off-peak time is what you have in mind. It is important to bear in mind though that famous courses near big cities usually refuse casual visitors.

Britain's golf population is guessed at almost 4 million people and I am assured by Bernard Pendry, Chief Executive of the Golf Club Great Britain, that there are 1.3 million players who belong to no club, being nomads of a huge sporting fraternity.

So let's grasp the nettle and name Britain's clubs that must be played. A daunting task, I'm sure you'll agree.

# ENGLAND

*'Seek out England's golf heritage. Those stretches are the old established classics with no artificial lakes, or whopping clubhouses.......'*

Where better to start than at the headquarters of the English Golf Union which bases itself at one of the finest inland courses you'll ever find, at Woodhall Spa in Lincolnshire. Without doubt this test is one of my top 10 favourites in England. Play it, you must!

Many of the classic English courses are close to the seaside. These links are selected by the R&A for the Open, and not just because they have sufficient space to park thousands of cars! Raw and basic, exposed to the elements and close to the ancient town of Sandwich in Kent, any American visitor accustomed to manicured excellences at Augusta will find the whopping, breezey links course of Royal St George's a culture shock. Nearby, ships heave their way through the choppy seas of the English Channel in winter, while on a still, summer day, high-climbing skylarks accompany your every shot with an unforgettable chorus. Arnold Palmer won a professional event here in 1970s and I bought him the champagne, while Greg Norman collected an Open Championship here, as did Sandy Lyle, Harry Vardon, Walter Hagen, Sir Henry Cotton - and many other legendary names.

If you wish to join those at the 19th hole talking about the qualities of English golf, your entry ticket must include the Sandwich experience. But there are others, of course!

## HERE'S A HIDDEN GEM

Moving inland, nearer London, one finds world class stretches like West Sussex (Pulborough) and Sunningdale (both Old and New), not to mention the splendid Berkshire course, near Ascot. Playing the marvellous and expansive Walton Heath courses is a joy and, also in Surrey, Hankley Common is a hidden gem while Woking, West Hill, Swinley Forest and Worplesdon are all 5-star. I also rate the North Hants course at Fleet and usually enjoy Wentworth, although I once competed in the English Amateur Championship there with no distinction as, from the back tees, it is designed with the Toyota World Match-Play Championship, and Ernie Els in mind!

Heading cross country, try the 18-holes of Royal West Norfolk at Brancaster before the tide claims it, and sink to your knees to beg to play Royal Worlington, the home of Cambridge University golfers and a challenge accepted as the best 9-holer in Europe. Mentioning excellent golf courses by name is

fatal because of the ones you leave out, including my own home course at Royal Wimbledon, designed by the great Colt.

But travel north and tackle three other 'Royal' courses - Birkdale, Liverpool and Lytham St Anne's. These Lancashire challenges are known far and wide. However, if you are in that neck of the woods, also seek out and enjoy Formby and Hillside which I know to be good from personal experience. And in Yorkshire, I boast about shots hit across the Moortown course (Leeds), and the sporty Pannal test near Harrogate.

## IMPORTED COPIES

But what, you cry, about the new and wondrous courses, such as the ones constructed recently alongside castles, in the parkland grounds belonging to some Lord who has fallen on hard times - aren't they worthy? And why leave out newish tests like East Sussex National, or the huge Oxfordshire, built with no Japanese money spared? These have magnificent facilities, the greens are automatically watered and the artificial lakes are certainly not dyed. They fulfil everything their millionaire designers intended. But are they, I ask, what you call English courses, or imported copies of some stretch that is forever un-English?

On this subject, you are the jury and finding out will provide years of endless pleasure. Believe me, I know........

# ENGLAND

---

## BEDFORDSHIRE

---

### ASPLEY GUISE        Map 04 SP93

**Aspley Guise & Woburn Sands** West Hill MK17 8DX
☎ 01908 583596
A fine undulating course in expansive heathland
interspersed with many attractive clumps of gorse, broom
and bracken. Some well-established silver birch are a
feature. The 7th, 8th and 9th are really tough holes to
complete the first half.
*18 holes, 6135yds, Par 71, SSS 70, Course record 67.*
*Club membership 600.*
**Visitors**     with member only at weekends.
**Societies**    normally booked 12 mths ahead.
**Green Fees** £28 per day; £22 per round.
**Facilities**    ⊗ ⅏ ⅃ ☕ ♀ ⚲ ☎ ꞓ David Marsden.
**Leisure**     trolley for hire, putting green, practice area.
**Location**    2m W of M1 junc 13
**Hotel**       ★★★ 69% Moore Place Hotel, The Square,
           ASPLEY GUISE
           ☎ 01908 282000 39 ⇋ ꞓ Annexe15 ⇋ ꞓ

### BEDFORD        Map 04 TL04

*Bedford & County* Green Ln, Clapham MK41 6ET
☎ 01234 352617
Pleasant parkland course with views over Bedford and
surrounding countryside. The 15th is a testing par 4.
*18 holes, 6347yds, Par 70, SSS 70.*
*Club membership 600.*
**Visitors**     handicap certificate required, weekends with
           member only.
**Societies**    welcome Mon,Tue,Thu & Fri, telephone in
           advance.
**Green Fees** not confirmed.
**Facilities**    ♀ ⚲ ☎ ꞓ E Bullock.
**Location**    2m N off A6
**Hotel**       ★★★ 72% Woodlands Manor Hotel, Green Ln,
           Clapham, BEDFORD
           ☎ 01234 363281 22 ⇋ ꞓ Annexe3 ⇋ ꞓ

*Bedfordshire* Bromham Rd, Biddenham MK40 4AF
☎ 01234 261669
An easy walking, parkland course with tree hazards.
*18 holes, 6196yds, Par 70, SSS 69, Course record 63.*
*Club membership 700.*
**Visitors**     may not play at weekends except with member.
**Societies**    must telephone in advance/confirm in writing.
**Green Fees** not confirmed.
**Facilities**    ♀ ⚲ ☎ ꞓ
**Leisure**     putting green, practice area, trolley hire.
**Location**    1m W on A428
**Hotel**       ★★★ 72% Woodlands Manor Hotel, Green Ln,
           Clapham, BEDFORD
           ☎ 01234 363281 22 ⇋ ꞓ Annexe3 ⇋ ꞓ

*Mowsbury* Cleat Hill, Kimbolton Rd MK41 8DQ
☎ 01234 771041 & 216374
Parkland municipal course in rural surroundings. Long and
testing 14-bay driving range and squash facilities.
*18 holes, 6514yds, Par 72, SSS 71, Course record 66.*
*Club membership 800.*
**Visitors**     no restrictions.
**Societies**    apply in writing.
**Green Fees** not confirmed.
**Facilities**    ♀ ⚲ ☎ ☎ ꞓ Malcolm Summers.
**Leisure**     squash, driving range.
**Location**    2m N of town centre on B660
**Hotel**       ★★★ 72% Woodlands Manor Hotel, Green Ln,
           Clapham, BEDFORD
           ☎ 01234 363281 22 ⇋ ꞓ Annexe3 ⇋ ꞓ

### COLMWORTH        Map 04 TL15

**Colmworth & North Bedfordshire** New Rd MK44 2BY
☎ 01234 378181
An easy walking course with well-bunkered greens, opened
in 1991. The course is often windy and plays longer than the
yardage suggests. Water comes into play on 3 holes.
*18 holes, 6459yds, Par 71, SSS 71, Course record 69.*
*9 holes, 611yds, Par 27.*
*Club membership 230.*
**Visitors**     advisable to contact in advance, tee reserved for
           members Sat & Sun until 9.30 am & between
           12.30 & 2pm.
**Societies**    telephone in advance.
**Green Fees** £10 per 18 holes (£15 weekends); £6 per 9 holes
              (£8 weekends).
**Facilities**    ⊗ ⅏ ⅃ ☕ ♀ ⚲ ☎ ☎ ꞓ Steve Brydon.
**Leisure**     fishing, trolley for hire, putting green, practice
           area, snooker.
**Location**    7m NE of Bedford, off B660
**Hotel**       ★★★ 68% The Barns Hotel, Cardington Rd,
           BEDFORD ☎ 01234 270044 49 ⇋ ꞓ

### DUNSTABLE        Map 04 TL02

**Dunstable Downs** Whipsnade Rd LU6 2NB
☎ 01582 604472
A fine downland course set on two levels with far-
reaching views and frequent sightings of graceful gliders.
The 9th hole is one of the best short holes in the country.
There is a modernised clubhouse.
*18 holes, 6255yds, Par 70, SSS 70, Course record 64.*
*Club membership 600.*
**Visitors**     weekends with member only. Handicap
           certificate required.
**Societies**    apply in advance.
**Green Fees** £28 per round/day.
**Facilities**    ⊗ ⅏ ⅃ ☕ ♀ ⚲ ☎ ꞓ Michael Weldon.
**Leisure**     trolley for hire, putting green, practice area.
**Location**    2m S off B4541
**Hotel**       ★★★ 66% Old Palace Lodge Hotel,
           Church St, DUNSTABLE
           ☎ 01582 662201 50 ⇋ ꞓ

*Griffin* Chaul End Rd, Caddington LU1 4AX
☎ 01582 415573
A new challenging 18-hole course with a SSS of 69.
*18 holes, 6161yds, Par 71, SSS 69.*
*Club membership 450.*            ▶

| | |
|---|---|
| Visitors | with member only after 3pm & at weekends. |
| Societies | apply in writing. |
| Green Fees | not confirmed. |
| Facilities | ♀ ⚲ 🖼 |
| Location | Off A505 Luton/Dunstable |
| Hotel | ★★★ 60% Luton Gateway, Dunstable Rd, LUTON ☎ 01582 575955 117 ⇔ ♠ |

## LEIGHTON BUZZARD                              Map 04 SP92

**Leighton Buzzard** Plantation Rd LU7 7JF
☎ 01525 373811/2
Parkland course with easy walking. The 17th and 18th holes are challenging tree-lined finishing holes with tight fairways.
*18 holes, 6101yds, Par 71, SSS 70, Course record 66.*
*Club membership 700.*

| | |
|---|---|
| Visitors | may not play Tue (Ladies Day). May only play with member weekends and bank holidays. Handicap certificate required. Must contact in advance and have an introduction from own club. |
| Societies | prior booking required. |
| Green Fees | £27 per day; £20 per round. |
| Facilities | ⊗ �𝍤 ⓑ ⚑ ♀ ⚲ 🖼 ⚐ ⓘ Lee Scarbrow. |
| Leisure | trolley for hire, putting green, practice area. |
| Location | 1.5m N of town centre off A4146 |
| Hotel | ★★★ 58% Swan Hotel, High St, LEIGHTON BUZZARD ☎ 01525 372148 38 ⇔ ♠ |

## LOWER STONDON                                Map 04 TL13

***Mount Pleasant*** Station Rd SG16 6JL ☎ 01462 850999
A 9-hole course which, when played over 18 totals some 5644 yards. The course is undulating meadowland and there is a significant ditch in play on 2,7,8,9th holes. The 5th hole plays long in a prevailing West wind. Alternative tees for all holes are planned for the end of 1996 which will change the par and SSS.
*9 holes, 3086yds, Par 72, SSS 69, Course record 70.*
*Club membership 300.*

| | |
|---|---|
| Visitors | no restrictions, can book 1 day in advance, booking advisable weekends & evenings May-Sep. |
| Societies | telephone or apply in writing. |
| Green Fees | not confirmed. |
| Facilities | ♀ ⚲ 🖼 ⚐ ⓘ Zac Thompson. |
| Location | 0.75m W of A600 |
| Hotel | ★★★ 75% Flitwick Manor Hotel, Church Rd, FLITWICK ☎ 01525 712242 15 ⇔ ♠ |

## LUTON                                          Map 04 TL02

**South Beds** Warden Hill LU2 7AA ☎ 01582 591500
27-hole downland course, slightly undulating.
*Galley Course: 18 holes, 6389yds, Par 71, SSS 71, Course record 64.*
*Warden Course: 9 holes, 2500yds, Par 32.*
*Club membership 1000.*

| | |
|---|---|
| Visitors | must contact in advance. |
| Societies | telephone for details. |
| Green Fees | Galley Course; £28 per day; £18 per round (£36.50/£25 weekends & bank holidays). Warden Course; £7 (£10 weekends & bank holidays). |
| Facilities | ⊗ �𝍤 ⓑ ⚑ ♀ ⚲ 🖼 ⓘ Eddie Cogle. |

| | |
|---|---|
| Leisure | trolley for hire, putting green, practice area. |
| Location | 2m N of Luton on A6 |
| Hotel | ★★★ 71% Strathmore Thistle, Arndale Centre, LUTON ☎ 01582 34199 150 ⇔ ♠ |

**Stockwood Park** London Rd LU1 4LX ☎ 01582 413704
Well laid out municipal parkland course with established trees and several challenging holes.
*18 holes, 6049yds, Par 69, SSS 69, Course record 67.*
*Club membership 800.*

| | |
|---|---|
| Visitors | no restrictions. |
| Societies | Mon, Tue & Thu only, telephone for application. |
| Green Fees | £7.30 per round (£9.60 weekends). |
| Facilities | ⊗ ⓘ ⓑ ⚑ ♀ ⚲ 🖼 ⚐ ⓘ Glyn McCarthy. |
| Leisure | motorised carts for hire, buggies for hire, trolley for hire, driving range, putting green, practice area. |
| Location | 1m S |
| Hotel | ★★★ 62% The Chiltern, Waller Av, Dunstable Rd, LUTON ☎ 01582 575911 91 ⇔ ♠ |

## MILLBROOK                                     Map 04 TL03

**Millbrook** Millbrook Village MK45 2JB ☎ 01525 840252
Long parkland course, on rolling countryside high above the Bedfordshire plains, with several water hazards. Laid out on well-drained sandy soil with many fairways lined with silver birch, pine and larch.
*18 holes, 7100yds, Par 74, SSS 73, Course record 68.*
*Club membership 550.*

| | |
|---|---|
| Visitors | must contact in advance, may not play after 11am on Thu. |
| Societies | telephone for details. |
| Green Fees | £15 (£25 weekends & bank holidays). |
| Facilities | ⊗ ⓘ ⓑ ⚑ ♀ ⚲ 🖼 ⓘ David Armour. |
| Leisure | trolley for hire, practice area. |
| Location | E side of village off A507 |
| Hotel | ★★★ 75% Flitwick Manor Hotel, Church Rd, FLITWICK ☎ 01525 712242 15 ⇔ ♠ |

## SANDY                                          Map 04 TL14

**John O'Gaunt** Sutton Park SG19 2LY ☎ 01767 260360
Two magnificent parkland courses - John O'Gaunt and Carthagena - covering a gently undulating and tree-lined terrain. The John O'Gaunt course makes the most of numerous natural features, notably a river which crosses the fairways of four holes. The Carthagena course has larger greens, longer tees and from the back tees is a challenging course. Fine clubhouse.
*John O'Gaunt Course: 18 holes, 6513yds, Par 71, SSS 71, Course record 64.*
*Carthagena Course: 18 holes, 5869yds, Par 69, SSS 69, Course record 62.*
*Club membership 1500.*

| | |
|---|---|
| Visitors | must contact in advance. |
| Societies | must pre-book. |
| Green Fees | £42 per day/round (£50 weekends & bank holidays). |
| Facilities | ⊗ ⓘ ⓑ ⚑ ♀ ⚲ 🖼 ⓘ Peter Round. |
| Leisure | motorised carts for hire, buggies for hire, trolley for hire, putting green, practice area. |
| Location | 3m NE of Biggleswade on B1040 |
| Hotel | ★★ 65% Abbotsley Golf Hotel, Eynesbury Hardwicke, ST NEOTS ☎ 01480 474000 15 ⇔ ♠ |

## SHEFFORD

Map 04 TL13

***Beadlow Manor Hotel & Golf & Country Club*** SG17 5PH
☎ 01525 861292 & 860800 Hotel
A 36-hole golf and leisure complex. The Baroness Manhattan and the Baron Manhattan golf courses are undulating with water hazards on numerous holes. The parkland course are good challenging gourses of the beginner and low handicap player.
*Baroness Course: 18 holes, 6072yds, Par 71, SSS 69, Course record 67.*
*Baron Course: 18 holes, 6619yds, Par 73, SSS 72, Course record 66.*
*Club membership 600.*

| | |
|---|---|
| **Visitors** | must adhere to dress code. |
| **Societies** | apply in writing or telephone in advance. |
| **Green Fees** | not confirmed. |
| **Facilities** | ♀ ♨ 🏠 ⛴ ✦ ⛳ Dale Brightman. |
| **Leisure** | sauna, solarium, gymnasium, range, putting, motor cart/trolley hire. |
| **Location** | 2m W on A507 |
| **Hotel** | ★★★ 75% Flitwick Manor Hotel, Church Rd, FLITWICK ☎ 01525 712242 15 ⇆ ⧫ |

## TILSWORTH

Map 04 SP92

**Tilsworth** Dunstable Rd LU7 9PU ☎ 01525 210721/2
An undulating parkland course upgraded from 9 to 18 holes in 1992. 30-bay floodlit driving range.
*18 holes, 5306yds, Par 69, SSS 66, Course record 66.*
*Club membership 400.*

| | |
|---|---|
| **Visitors** | may book up to 7 days in advance. |
| **Societies** | apply in advance. |
| **Green Fees** | £8 per 18 holes; £5 per 9 holes (£10/£6 weekends & bank holidays). |
| **Facilities** | ⊗ ⅲ ▌ ⬛ ♀ ♨ 🏠 ⛴ ⛳ Nick Webb. |
| **Leisure** | buggies for hire, trolley for hire, floodlit driving range, practice area. |
| **Location** | 0.5m NE off A5 |
| **Hotel** | ★★★ 66% Old Palace Lodge Hotel, Church St, DUNSTABLE ☎ 01582 662201 50 ⇆ ⧫ |

## WHIPSNADE

Map 04 TL01

**Whipsnade Park** Studham Ln, Dagnall HP4 1RH
☎ 01442 842330 & 842310
Parkland course situated on downs overlooking the Chilterns adjoining Whipsnade Zoo. Easy walking, good views.
*18 holes, 6800yds, Par 73, SSS 72, Course record 69.*
*Club membership 600.*

| | |
|---|---|
| **Visitors** | with member only at weekends. Must contact in advance. |
| **Societies** | by prior arrangement. |
| **Green Fees** | Weekdays: £32 per 36 holes; £21 per 18 holes. |
| **Facilities** | ⊗ ⅲ ▌ ⬛ ♀ ♨ 🏠 ⛴ ⛳ Michael Lewendon. |
| **Leisure** | motorised carts for hire, buggies for hire, trolley for hire, putting green, practice area. |
| **Location** | 1m E off B4506 |
| **Hotel** | ★★★ 66% Old Palace Lodge Hotel, Church St, DUNSTABLE ☎ 01582 662201 50 ⇆ ⧫ |

## WOBURN

Map 04 SP93

For Woburn Golf Course see Bow Brickhill, Buckinghamshire.

## WYBOSTON

Map 04 TL15

**Wyboston Lakes** MK44 3AL ☎ 01480 223004
Parkland course, with narrow fairways, small greens, set around four lakes and a river which provide the biggest challenge on this very scenic course.
*18 holes, 5803yds, Par 69, SSS 69, Course record 65.*
*Club membership 300.*

| | |
|---|---|
| **Visitors** | a booking system is in operation at weekends, book no more than 8 days in advance. |
| **Societies** | telephone in advance. |
| **Green Fees** | £10 per 18 holes; £5 per 9 holes (£14/£7 weekends & bank holidays) Twilight round £7. |
| **Facilities** | ⊗ ⅲ ▌ ⬛ ♀ ♨ 🏠 ⛴ ⛳ Paul Ashwell. |
| **Leisure** | fishing, motorised carts for hire, buggies for hire, trolley for hire, driving range, putting green, practice area. |
| **Location** | NE side of village off A1 |
| **Hotel** | ★★★ 72% Woodlands Manor Hotel, Green Ln, Clapham, BEDFORD ☎ 01234 363281 22 ⇆ ⧫Annexe3 ⇆ ⧫ |

---

# BERKSHIRE

## ASCOT

Map 04 SU96

**Berkshire** Swinley Rd SL5 8AY ☎ 01344 21496
Two heathland courses with splendid tree-lined fairways.
*Red Course: 18 holes, 6369yds, Par 72, SSS 71.*
*Blue Course: 18 holes, 6260yds, Par 71, SSS 71.*
*Club membership 1000.*

| | |
|---|---|
| **Visitors** | weekdays only on application to secretary. |
| **Societies** | applications in writing only. |
| **Green Fees** | £65 per day; £50 per round. |
| **Facilities** | ⊗ ▌ ⬛ ♀ ♨ 🏠 ⛴ ⛳ P Anderson. |
| **Leisure** | motorised carts for hire, buggies for hire, trolley for hire, putting green, practice area. |
| **Location** | 2.5m NW of M3 jct 3 on A332 |
| **Hotel** | ★★★★ 68% The Berystede, Bagshot Rd, Sunninghill, ASCOT ☎ 01344 23311 91 ⇆ ⧫ |

**Lavender Park** Swinley Rd SL5 8BD
☎ 01344 890940 & 886096
Public parkland course, ideal for the short game featuring challenging narrow fairways. Driving range with 9-hole par 3 course, floodlit until 22.30 hrs.
*9 holes, 1102yds, Par 27, SSS 28.*

| | |
|---|---|
| **Visitors** | no restrictions. |
| **Societies** | welcome, notice prefered. |
| **Green Fees** | £4.50 per 18 holes; £3.25 per 9 holes (£7/£4.50 weekends & bank holidays). |
| **Facilities** | ⬛ ♀ 🏠 ⛴ ⛳ Wayne Ower/Andy Piper. |
| **Leisure** | floodlit driving range, snooker hall. |
| **Location** | 3.5m SW of Ascot, on A332 ▶ |

**Hotel** ★★★★ 68% The Berystede, Bagshot Rd, Sunninghill, ASCOT ☎ 01344 23311 91 ⊨ ℟

---

**Mill Ride** Mill Ride Estate SL5 8LT ☎ 01344 886777
Opened for play in 1991, this 18-hole course combines good golfing country and attractive surroundings with a challenging design. The holes require as much thinking as playing.
*18 holes, 6752yds, Par 72, SSS 72, Course record 64.*
*Club membership 400.*
**Visitors** must contact in advance.
**Societies** apply in advance.
**Green Fees** prices on application.
**Facilities** ⊗ ⅋ ♭ ♥ ♀ ♨ 🖮 ↑ ﬂ ℓ Mark Palmer.
**Leisure** sauna, trolley for hire, driving range, putting green, practice area.
**Location** 2m W of Ascot
**Hotel** ★★★★ 68% The Berystede, Bagshot Rd, Sunninghill, ASCOT ☎ 01344 23311 91 ⊨ ℟

---

**Royal Ascot** Winkfield Rd SL5 7LJ ☎ 01344 25175
Heathland course inside Ascot racecourse and exposed to weather.
*18 holes, 5716yds, Par 68, SSS 68, Course record 65.*
*Club membership 620.*
**Visitors** must be guest of member.
**Societies** telephone for provisional booking.
**Green Fees** on request.
**Facilities** ⊗ ⅋ ♭ ♥ ♀ ♨ 🖮 ℓ Garry Malia.
**Leisure** trolley for hire, putting green, practice area.
**Location** 0.5m N on A330
**Hotel** ★★★★ 68% The Berystede, Bagshot Rd, Sunninghill, ASCOT ☎ 01344 23311 91 ⊨ ℟

---

**Swinley Forest** Coronation Rd SL5 9LE
☎ 01344 874979 (Secretary) & 874811 (Pro)
An attractive and immaculate course of heather and pine situated in the heart of Swinley Forest. The 17th is as good a short hole as will be found, with a bunkered plateau green and the 12th hole is one of the most challenging par 4's.
*18 holes, 6100yds, Par 68, SSS 69, Course record 62.*
*Club membership 275.*
**Visitors** by invitation only.
**Societies** must contact in writing.
**Green Fees** £60 per day.
**Facilities** ⊗ ♭ ♥ ♀ ♨ 🖮 ↑ ℓ R C Parker.
**Leisure** motorised carts for hire, buggies for hire, trolley for hire, putting green.
**Location** 1.5m S, off A330
**Hotel** ★★★★ 68% The Berystede, Bagshot Rd, Sunninghill, ASCOT ☎ 01344 23311 91 ⊨ ℟

---

## BINFIELD

Map 04 SU87

**Blue Mountain Golf Centre** Wood Ln RG42 4EX
☎ 01344 300200
An 18-hole Pay and Play course with many testing holes with water hazards. Greens are large, undulating and strategically placed bunkers provide a fair challenge.
*18 holes, 6097yds, Par 70, SSS 70, Course record 63.*
*Club membership 1250.*
**Visitors** tee times bookable in person at the Golf Shop up to 9 days in advance.

---

**Societies** must contact in advance.
**Green Fees** £14 per 18 holes; £7 per 9 holes (£18/£9 weekends).
**Facilities** ⊗ ⅋ ♭ ♥ ♀ ♨ 🖮 ↑ ℓ Neil Dainton.
**Leisure** motorised carts for hire, trolley for hire, driving range, putting green, practice area.
**Location** 2m from junct 10 of the M4
**Hotel** ★★★★ 64% Reading Moat House, Mill Ln, Sindlesham, WOKINGHAM ☎ 01734 499988 96 ⊨ ℟

---

## CHADDLEWORTH

Map 04 SU47

**West Berkshire** RG16 0HS ☎ 01488 638574 & 638851
Challenging and interesting downland course with testing 635 yds 5th hole, one of the longest par 5's in southern England.
*18 holes, 7059yds, Par 73, SSS 74.*
*Club membership 650.*
**Visitors** must contact in advance, may play weekends pm only.
**Societies** telephone in advance
**Green Fees** £24 per day; £16 per round (£20 per round weekends pm only).
**Facilities** ⊗ ⅋ ♭ ♥ ♀ ♨ 🖮 ↑ ℓ Wraith Grant.
**Leisure** buggies for hire, trolley for hire, putting green, practice area.
**Location** 1m S of village off A338
**Hotel** ★★★ 62% The Chequers, Oxford St, NEWBURY ☎ 01635 38000 45 ⊨ ℟Annexe11 ⊨ ℟

---

## COOKHAM

Map 04 SU88

**Winter Hill** Grange Ln SL6 9RP
☎ 01628 527613 (Secretary) 527610 (Pro)
Parkland course set in a curve of the Thames with wonderful views across the river to Cliveden.
*18 holes, 6408yds, Par 72, SSS 71, Course record 69.*
*Club membership 850.*
**Visitors** not permitted weekends.
**Societies** welcome Wed & Fri, telephone initially.
**Green Fees** £25 per day; summer £15 after 2pm; winter £12 after noon.
**Facilities** ⊗ ♭ ♥ ♀ ♨ 🖮 ↑ ℓ David Hart.
**Leisure** trolley for hire, driving range, putting green, practice area.
**Location** 1m NW off B4447
**Hotel** ★★★★ 72% The Compleat Angler, Marlow Bridge, MARLOW ☎ 01628 484444 62 ⊨ ℟

---

## CROWTHORNE

Map 04 SU86

**East Berkshire** Ravenswood Ave RG45 6BD
☎ 01344 772041
An attractive heathland course with an abundance of heather and pine trees. Walking is easy and the greens are exceptionally good. Some fairways become tight where the heather encroaches on the line of play. The course is testing and demands great accuracy.
*18 holes, 6344yds, Par 69, SSS 70.*
*Club membership 766.*
**Visitors** must contact in advance and have a handicap certificate; must play with member at weekends & bank holidays.

| | |
|---|---|
| **Societies** | telephone for availability. |
| **Green Fees** | £35 per day. |
| **Facilities** | ⊗ ⅢⅢ ⅃⅄ ☐⌒♈ ⟨ Arthur Roe. |
| **Leisure** | trolley for hire, putting green, practice area. |
| **Location** | W side of town centre off B3348 |
| **Hotel** | ★★★★(red)⚬ Pennyhill Park Hotel, London Rd, BAGSHOT ☎ 01276 471774 22 ⇆ ⟨Annexe54 ⇆ ⟨ |

## DATCHET
Map 04 SU97

*Datchet* Buccleuch Rd SL3 9BP
☎ 01753 543887 & 541872
Meadowland course, easy walking.
*9 holes, 5978yds, Par 70, SSS 69, Course record 63.*
*Club membership 405.*

| | |
|---|---|
| **Visitors** | may play weekdays before 3pm. |
| **Societies** | Tue only. |
| **Green Fees** | not confirmed. |
| **Facilities** | ⅃⅄ ☐⌒♈ ⟨ Bill Mainwaring. |
| **Leisure** | trolleys. |
| **Location** | NW side of Datchet off B470 |
| **Hotel** | ★★★ 69% The Castle, High St, WINDSOR ☎ 01753 851011 104 ⇆ ⟨ |

## MAIDENHEAD
Map 04 SU88

*Bird Hills* Drift Rd, Hawthorn Hill SL6 3ST
☎ 01628 771030
A gently undulating course with easy walking and many water hazards. Some challenging holes are the Par 5 6th dogleg, Par 3 9th surrounded by water and bunkers, and the 16th which is a long uphill Par 4 and a two-tier green.
*18 holes, 6176yds, Par 72, SSS 69, Course record 65.*
*Club membership 400.*

| | |
|---|---|
| **Visitors** | to book ring 7 days in advance. |
| **Societies** | write or telephone in advance. |
| **Green Fees** | not confirmed. |
| **Facilities** | ⅃⅄ ☐⌒♈ ⟨ Nick Slimming/Adam Bishop. |
| **Location** | 4m SW of Bray on A330 |
| **Hotel** | ★★★ 70% Stirrups Country House, Maidens Green, BRACKNELL ☎ 01344 882284 24 ⇆ |

*Castle Royle Golf & Country Club* Knowl Hill RG10 9XA
☎ 01628 829252
Designed by Neil Coles to championship standard, Castle Royle has six lakes and is well drained and irrigated. In attractive countryside with views of Windsor Castle, the course is very well bunkered with wide fairways and there are Par 3's with all four aspects to the prevailing wind as each faces a different direction. Visitors are usually only permitted as a guest of a member but it is suitable for low or high handicappers.
*18 holes, 6828yds, Par 72, SSS 73.*
*Club membership 400.*

| | |
|---|---|
| **Visitors** | with member only. |
| **Green Fees** | Members Guests: £20 per round. |
| **Facilities** | ⊗ ⅢⅢ ⅃⅄ ☐⌒♈ ⟨ Paul Stanwick. |
| **Leisure** | fishing, trolley for hire, putting green, practice area. |
| **Location** | Bath road A4 |
| **Hotel** | ★★★★ 78% Fredrick's Hotel, Shoppenhangers Rd, MAIDENHEAD ☎ 01628 35934 37 ⇆ ⟨ |

*Maidenhead* Shoppenhangers Rd SL6 2PZ
☎ 01628 24693 & 24067
A pleasant parkland course on level ground with easy walking to good greens. Perhaps a little short but there are many natural features and some first-rate short holes.
*18 holes, 6364yds, Par 70, SSS 70.*
*Club membership 650.*

| | |
|---|---|
| **Visitors** | may not play after noon on Fri or at weekends. Must contact in advance and have a handicap certificate. |
| **Societies** | must contact in writing. |
| **Green Fees** | not confirmed. |
| **Facilities** | ⅃⅄ ☐⌒♈ ⟨ Steve Geary. |
| **Leisure** | putting green,carts,trolley hire. |
| **Location** | S side of town centre off A308 |
| **Hotel** | ★★★★ 78% Fredrick's Hotel, Shoppenhangers Rd, MAIDENHEAD ☎ 01628 35934 37 ⇆ ⟨ |

*Temple* Henley Rd, Hurley SL6 5LH
☎ 01628 824795
An open parkland course with many excellent, fast greens relying on natural slopes rather than heavy bunkering. On one 'blind' punchbowl hole there is actually a bunker on the green. Good drainage assures play when many other courses are closed.
*18 holes, 6207yds, Par 70, SSS 70, Course record 63.*
*Club membership 480.*

| | |
|---|---|
| **Visitors** | must contact in advance, limited weekend access. |
| **Societies** | apply in writing for formal bookings. |
| **Green Fees** | £40 per 36 holes; £25 per 18 holes (£40 Sun & bank holidays). |
| **Facilities** | ⊗ ⅢⅢ ⅃⅄ ☐⌒♈ ⟨ James Whiteley. |
| **Leisure** | squash, motorised carts for hire, buggies for hire, trolley for hire, putting green, practice area. |
| **Location** | Exit M4 junct 8/9 and take A404 and then A423 |
| **Hotel** | ★★★★ 72% The Compleat Angler, Marlow Bridge, MARLOW ☎ 01628 484444 62 ⇆ ⟨ |

## NEWBURY
Map 04 SU46

*Donnington Valley* Old Oxford Rd, Donnington RG14 3AG
☎ 01635 551199
Undulating, short, but testing course with mature trees and elevated greens, some protected by water.
*18 holes, 4000yds, Par 61, SSS 60, Course record 59.*
*Club membership 500.*

| | |
|---|---|
| **Visitors** | booking system up to 7 days in advance, members have priority weekends. |
| **Societies** | write or telephone in advance. |
| **Green Fees** | £13 per round (£17 weekends). |
| **Facilities** | ⊗ ⅢⅢ ⅃⅄ ☐⌒♈⇆⟨ Nick Mitchell. |
| **Leisure** | hard tennis courts, trolley for hire, putting green, practice area. |
| **Location** | 2m N of Newbury |
| **Hotel** | ★★★★ 76% Donnington Valley Hotel & Golf Course, Old Oxford Rd, Donnington, NEWBURY ☎ 01635 551199 58 ⇆ ⟨ |

*Newbury & Crookham* Bury's Bank Rd, Greenham RG19 8BZ ☎ 01635 40035
A well-laid out, attractive course running mostly through woodland, and giving more of a challenge than its length suggests.
*18 holes, 5880yds, Par 68, SSS 68.*
*Club membership 800.*

| | |
|---|---|
| **Visitors** | must play with member on weekends & bank holidays. Handicap certificate required. |
| **Societies** | must contact in advance. |
| **Green Fees** | not confirmed. |
| **Facilities** | ♀ ♣ 🏠 ⌊ David Harris. |
| **Leisure** | putting,trolley hire,practice area. |
| **Location** | 2m SE off A34 |
| **Hotel** | ★★★ 62% The Chequers, Oxford St, NEWBURY ☎ 01635 38000 45 ⇆ 🐾Annexe11 ⇆ 🐾 |

## READING                              Map 04 SU77

**Calcot Park** Bath Rd, Calcot RG31 7RN
☎ 01734 427124
A delightfully sporting parkland course just outside the town. Hazards include a lake and many trees. The 6th is the longest, 497 yard par 5, with the tee-shot hit downhill over cross-bunkers to a well-guarded green. The 13th (188 yards) requires a big carry over a gully to a plateau green.
*18 holes, 6283yds, Par 70, SSS 70, Course record 65.*
*Club membership 730.*

| | |
|---|---|
| **Visitors** | must have handicap certificate or letter of introduction from club. May play weekdays only, excluding bank holidays. |
| **Societies** | must apply in writing. |
| **Green Fees** | £33 per day/round; £20 after 4pm Apr-Sep, noon Oct to Mar. |
| **Facilities** | ⊗ ⋔ ♣ ♟ ♀ ♣ 🏠 ⌐ ⌊ Albert MacKenzie. |
| **Leisure** | motorised carts for hire, trolley for hire, putting green, practice area. |
| **Location** | 1.5m from M4 junct 4 on A4 towards Reading |
| **Hotel** | ★★★ 55% The Copper Inn, Church Rd, PANGBOURNE ☎ 01734 842244 14 ⇆ 🐾Annexe8 ⇆ 🐾 |

**Hennerton** Crazies Hill Rd, Wargrave RG10 8LT
☎ 01734 401000
Overlooking the Thames Valley, this Par 68 course has many of existing natural features and an good number of hazards such as bunker, mature trees and two small lakes. The most memorable hole is probably the 7th which is a par 3, 183 yards crossing a sharp valley to the green from which there are spectacular views of the whole course.
*9 holes, 5460yds, Par 68, SSS 67, Course record 66.*
*Club membership 430.*

| | |
|---|---|
| **Visitors** | telephone in advance. |
| **Societies** | telephone or write for information. |
| **Green Fees** | £12 per 18 holes; £9 per 9 holes (£18/£14 weekends). |
| **Facilities** | ⊗ ♣ ♟ ♀ ♣ 🏠 ⌐ ⌊ William Farrow. |
| **Leisure** | trolley for hire, floodlit driving range, putting green, practice area. |
| **Hotel** | ★★★ 66% Red Lion Hotel, Hart St, HENLEY-ON-THAMES ☎ 01491 572161 26rm(23 ⇆ 🐾) |

**Mapledurham** Chazey Heath, Mapledurham RG4 7UD
☎ 01734 463353
18-hole course designed by Bob Sandow. Flanked by hedgerows and mature woods, it is testing for players of all levels.
*18 holes, 5750yds, Par 69, SSS 68 or 57 holes.*
*Club membership 600.*

| | |
|---|---|
| **Visitors** | no restrictions. |
| **Societies** | must contact in advance. |
| **Green Fees** | £19 per day; £14 per 18 holes (£23/£17 weekends). |
| **Facilities** | ⊗ ⋔ ♣ ♟ ♀ ♣ 🏠 ⌐ ⌊ Symon O'Keefe. |
| **Leisure** | trolley for hire, putting green, practice area, video tuition. |
| **Location** | On A4074 to Oxford |
| **Hotel** | ★★★★ 61% Holiday Inn, Caversham Bridge, Richfield Av, READING ☎ 01734 259988 111 ⇆ 🐾 |

**Reading** 17 Kidmore End Rd, Emmer Green RG4 8SG
☎ 01734 472909 (Manager) & 476115 (Pro)
Pleasant tree-lined parkland course, part hilly and part flat with interesting views and several challenging par 3's.
*18 holes, 6212yds, Par 70, SSS 70, Course record 67.*
*Club membership 700.*

| | |
|---|---|
| **Visitors** | contact the professional. With member only weekends. |
| **Societies** | apply by telephone. |
| **Green Fees** | £27 per day. |
| **Facilities** | ⊗ ⋔ ♣ ♟ ♀ ♣ 🏠 ⌊ Andrew Wild. |
| **Leisure** | trolley for hire, putting green, practice area. |
| **Location** | 2m N off B481 |
| **Hotel** | ★★★ 61% Ship Hotel, 4-8 Duke St, READING ☎ 01734 583455 31rm(21 ⇆ 🐾) |

## SINDLESHAM                            Map 04 SU76

**Bearwood** Mole Rd RG41 5DB ☎ 01734 760060
Flat parkland course with one water hazard, the 40 lake which features on the challenging 6th and 7th holes. Also 9-hole pitch and putt.
*9 holes, 5610yds, Par 70, SSS 68, Course record 66.*
*Club membership 500.*

| | |
|---|---|
| **Visitors** | with member only on weekends. |
| **Societies** | apply in writing. |
| **Green Fees** | £15 per 18 holes; £8 per 9 holes. |
| **Facilities** | ⊗ ⋔ ♣ ♟ ♀ ♣ 🏠 |
| **Leisure** | trolley for hire, putting green, practice area, pitch & putt. |
| **Location** | 1m SW on B3030 |
| **Hotel** | ★★★★ 64% Reading Moat House, Mill Ln, Sindlesham, WOKINGHAM ☎ 01734 499988 96 ⇆ 🐾 |

## SONNING                               Map 04 SU77

*Sonning* Duffield Rd RG4 6GJ ☎ 01734 693332
A quality parkland course and the scene of many county championships. Wide fairways, not overbunkered, and very good greens. Holes of changing character through wooded belts.
*18 holes, 6366yds, Par 70, SSS 70, Course record 65.*

| | |
|---|---|
| **Visitors** | weekdays only. Handicap certificate required. |
| **Societies** | must apply in writing. ▶ |

# SUNNINGDALE

**SUNNINGDALE** *Berks* ☎ 01344 21681          Map 04 SU96

*John Ingham writes:* Many famous golfers maintain that Sunningdale, on the borders of Berkshire, is the most attractive inland course in Britain. The great Bobby Jones once played the 'perfect' round of 66 made up of threes and fours on the Old Course. Later, Norman von Nida of Australia shot a 63 while the then professional at the club, Arthur Lees, scored a 62 to win a huge wager.

To become a member of this club takes years of waiting. Maybe it is the quality of the courses, maybe the clubhouse atmosphere and perhaps the excellence of the professionals shop has something to do with it; but added up, it has to be the most desirable place to spend a day.

Founded just over ninety years ago, the Old Course was designed by Willie Park, while H.S. Colt created the New Course in 1923. Most golfers will agree that there isn't one indifferent hole on either course. While the Old Course, with silver birch, heather and perfect turf, is lovely to behold, the New Course alongside is considered by many to be its equal. But just as golfers want to play the Old Course at St Andrews, and miss the redesigned Jubilee, so visitors to Sunningdale opt for the Old, and fail to realise what they are overlooking by not playing the New.

The classic Old Course is not long, measuring just 6341 yards, and because the greens are normally in excellent condition, anyone with a 'hot' putter can have an exciting day, providing they keep teeshots on the fairway and don't stray into the gorse and the pine trees that lie in wait. On a sunny day, if you had to be anywhere in the world playing well, then we opt for the elevated 10th tee on the Old. What bliss!

| | |
|---|---|
| **Visitors** | May not play Fri, Sat, Sun or public holidays. Must contact in advance and have a handicap certificate and letter of introduction |
| **Societies** | Tue, Wed, Thu by arrangement. |
| **Green fees** | £88 per day |
| **Facilities** | ⊗ 🏌 🍺 ♀ ⅄ 🏠 ⛳ 𝄢 (Keith Maxwell) practice area, trolleys |
| **Location** | Ridgemount Rd Sunningdale, Ascot SL5 9RR (1m S of Sunningdale, off A30) |

**36 holes. Old Course: 18 holes, 6341yds, Par 70, SSS 70, Course record 62 (Nick Faldo) New Course: 18 holes 6703yds, Par 70, SSS 72, Course record 62 (C. Challen)**

## WHERE TO STAY AND EAT NEARBY

**HOTELS:**

**ASCOT**
★★★★⊕ 68% The Berystede, Bagshot Rd, Sunninghill. ☎ 01344 23311.
91 (1 🛏 90 🛏 🐾)

★★ 71% Highclere, 19 Kings Rd, Sunninghill. ☎ 01344 25220. 11 🛏 🐾

**BAGSHOT**
★★★★(Red)⊕⊕⊕ ♨ Pennyhill Park, London Rd. ☎ 01276 471774
22 🛏 🐾 Annexe 54 🛏 🐾

**RESTAURANTS:**

**BRAY**
⊕⊕⊕⊕ Waterside Inn, River Cottage, Ferry Road. ☎ 01628 20691.

**Green Fees** not confirmed.
**Facilities** ♀ ⚐ 🏠 🍴 R McDougall.
**Location** 1m S off A4
**Hotel** ★★★ 68% The French Horn, SONNING
☎ 01734 692204 12 ⇆ 🏠 Annexe4 ⇆ 🏠

## STREATLEY       Map 04 SU58

**Goring & Streatley** RG8 9QA
☎ 01491 873229 & 873715
A parkland/moorland course that requires 'negotiating'.
Four well-known first holes lead up to the heights of the
5th tee, to which there is a 300ft climb. Wide fairways,
not overbunkered, with nice rewards on the way home
down the last few holes.
*18 holes, 6320yds, Par 71, SSS 70, Course record 65.*
*Club membership 740.*
**Visitors** must contact in advance, with member only
at weekends.
**Societies** must telephone in advance.
**Green Fees** £30 per day; £20 per round.
**Facilities** ⊗ ⅲ ⅃ 🍺 ♀ ⚐ 🏠 🍴 🍴 Roy Mason.
**Leisure** trolley for hire, putting green, practice area.
**Location** N of village off A417
**Hotel** ★★★★ 66% Swan Diplomat Hotel, High St,
STREATLEY ☎ 01491 873737 46 ⇆ 🏠

## SUNNINGDALE       Map 04 SU96

**SUNNINGDALE** See page 15

***Sunningdale Ladies*** Cross Rd SL5 9RX ☎ 01344 20507
A short 18-hole course with a typical Surrey heathland
layout. A very tight course, making for a challenging game.
*18 holes, 3616yds, Par 60, SSS 60.*
*Club membership 350.*
**Visitors** telephone in advance.
**Societies** Ladies societies only.
**Green Fees** not confirmed.
**Facilities** ♀ ⚐
**Location** 1m S off A30
**Hotel** ★★★★ 68% The Berystede, Bagshot Rd,
Sunninghill, ASCOT ☎ 01344 23311 91 ⇆ 🏠

## WOKINGHAM       Map 04 SU86

**Downshire** Easthampstead Park RG40 3DH
☎ 01344 302030
Beautiful municipal parkland course with mature trees. Water
hazards come into play on the 14th and 18th holes, and
especially on the short 7th, a testing downhill 169 yards over
the lake. Pleasant easy walking. Challenging holes: 7th (par
4), 15th (par 4), 16th (par 3).
*18 holes, 6383yds, Par 73, SSS 70.*
*Club membership 1000.*
**Visitors** must book six days in advance by telephone or
seven days in person, weekend times available.
**Societies** must telephone in advance.
**Green Fees** £12.50 per 18 holes (£15.50 weekends).
**Facilities** ⊗ ⅲ ⅃ 🍺 ♀ ⚐ 🏠 🍴 🍴 Warren Humphries.
**Leisure** motorised carts for hire, buggies for hire, trolley
for hire, floodlit driving range, putting green,
practice area.

**Location** 3m SW of Bracknell
**Hotel** ★★★★ 75% Coppid Beech, John Nike Way,
BRACKNELL
☎ 01344 303333 205 ⇆ 🏠

**Sand Martins** Finchampstead Rd RG40 3RQ
☎ 01734 770265 & 792711
Two different 9-hole loops: the front nine is mostly tree-lined
with ponds and the back nine is similar to a links course.
*18 holes, 6204yards, Par 70, SSS 70, Course record 65.*
*Club membership 750.*
**Visitors** no restrictions, but with member only at
weekends.
**Societies** prior arrangement by telephone.
**Green Fees** £35 per day (£20 per 18 holes).
**Facilities** ⊗ ⅲ ⅃ 🍺 ♀ ⚐ 🏠 🍴 🍴 Andrew Hall.
**Leisure** motorised carts for hire, buggies for hire, trolley
for hire, driving range, putting green.
**Location** 1m S of Wokingham
**Hotel** ★★★★ 64% Reading Moat House, Mill Ln,
Sindlesham, WOKINGHAM
☎ 01734 499988 96 ⇆ 🏠

# BRISTOL

## BRISTOL       Map 03 ST57

**Bristol and Clifton** Beggar Bush Ln, Failand BS8 3TH
☎ 01275 393474
A downland course with splendid turf and fine tree-lined
fairways. The 222-yard (par 3) 13th with the green well
below, and the par 4 16th, with its second shot across an
old quarry, are outstanding. There are splendid views
over the Bristol Channel towards Wales.
*18 holes, 6316yds, Par 70, SSS 70, Course record 65.*
*Club membership 968.*
**Visitors** must contact in advance & have a handicap
certificate. Weekends restricted.
**Societies** telephone to enquire.
**Green Fees** £30 per day (£38 weekends).
**Facilities** ⊗ ⅃ 🍺 ♀ ⚐ 🏠 🍴 🍴 Peter Mawson.
**Leisure** trolley for hire, putting green, practice area.
**Location** 4m W on B3129 off A369
**Hotel** ★★★ 66% Redwood Lodge Hotel, Country
Club Resort, Beggar Bush Ln, Failand,
BRISTOL ☎ 01275 393901 108 ⇆ 🏠

**Filton** Golf Course Ln, Filton BS12 7QS ☎ 0117 969 4169
Challenging parkland course situated on high ground in a
pleasant suburb to the north of the city. Extensive views can
be enjoyed from the course, especially from the second tee
and the clubhouse, where on a clear day the Cotswold Hills
and the Brecon Beacons can be seen. Good par 4 testing hole
'dog-leg' 383 yds.
*18 holes, 6310yds, Par 70, SSS 70, Course record 68.*
*Club membership 730.*
**Visitors** advisable to contact in advance for availability,
may not play at weekends unless with member.
**Societies** apply in writing Nov/Dec for following year.
**Green Fees** £25 per day; £20 per round.
**Facilities** ⊗ ⅲ ⅃ 🍺 ♀ ⚐ 🏠 🍴 🍴 J C N Lumb.

| | |
|---|---|
| **Leisure** | motorised carts for hire, buggies for hire, trolley for hire, putting green, practice area. |
| **Location** | 5m NW off A38 |
| **Hotel** | B Forte Posthouse Bristol, Filton Rd, Hambrook, BRISTOL ☎ 0117 956 4242 197 ⇔ ⁂ |

---

**Henbury** Henbury Hill, Westbury-on-Trym BS10 7QB
☎ 0117 950 0044
A parkland course tree-lined and on two levels. The River Trym comes into play on the 7th drop-hole with its green set just over the stream. The last nine holes have the beautiful Blaise Castle woods for company.
*18 holes, 6039yds, Par 70, SSS 70, Course record 64.*
*Club membership 760.*

| | |
|---|---|
| **Visitors** | with member only weekends. Advisable to contact in advance for availability. |
| **Societies** | apply in writing or telephone well in advance. |
| **Green Fees** | £21 per round; £28 per 18+ holes. |
| **Facilities** | ⊗ �𝄞 ⚐ ♨ ♀ ♣ 🖢 ⵟ ⟨ Nick Riley. |
| **Leisure** | trolley for hire, putting green, practice area. |
| **Location** | 3m NW of city centre on B4055 off A4018 |
| **Hotel** | ★★★ 65% Henbury Lodge Hotel, Station Rd, Henbury, BRISTOL ☎ 0117 950 2615 11 ⇔ ⁂Annexe8 ⇔ ⁂ |

---

**Knowle** West Town Ln, Brislington BS4 5DF
☎ 0117 977 0660
A parkland course with nice turf. The first five holes climb up and down hill but the remainder are on a more even plane.
*18 holes, 6016yds, Par 69, SSS 69.*
*Club membership 700.*

| | |
|---|---|
| **Visitors** | must have handicap certificate. Must play with member at weekends. |
| **Societies** | Thu only, apply in writing. |
| **Green Fees** | £27 per day; £22 per round. |
| **Facilities** | ⊗ �𝄞 by prior arrangement ⚐ ♨ ♀ ♣ 🖢 ⟨ Gordon Brand Snr. |
| **Leisure** | buggies for hire, trolley for hire, putting green, practice area. |
| **Location** | 3m SE of city centre off A37 |
| **Hotel** | ★★★(red)♨♨ Hunstrete House Hotel, CHELWOOD ☎ 01761 490490 13 ⇔ ⁂Annexe11 ⇔ ⁂ |

---

**Mangotsfield** Carsons Rd, Mangotsfield BS17 3LW
☎ 0117 956 5501
An easy hilly parkland course. Caravan site.
*18 holes, 5337yds, Par 68, SSS 66, Course record 61.*
*Club membership 400.*

| | |
|---|---|
| **Visitors** | no restrictions. |
| **Societies** | bookings in advance to Craig Trewin. |
| **Green Fees** | £9 (£11 weekends & bank holidays). |
| **Facilities** | ⊗ ⚐ ♨ ♀ ♣ 🖢 ⵟ ⟨ Craig Trewin. |
| **Leisure** | sauna, motorised carts for hire, buggies for hire, trolley for hire, putting green, practice area. |
| **Location** | 6m NE of city centre off B4465 |
| **Hotel** | B Forte Posthouse Bristol, Filton Rd, Hambrook, BRISTOL ☎ 0117 956 4242 197 ⇔ ⁂ |

---

*Shirehampton Park* Park Hill, Shirehampton BS11 0UL
☎ 0117 982 2083
A lovely course in undulating parkland comprising two loops. There are views over the Portway beside the River Avon,

where sliced balls at the opening hole are irretrievable.
*18 holes, 5600yds, Par 67, SSS 68.*
*Club membership 600.*

| | |
|---|---|
| **Visitors** | with member only at weekends. |
| **Societies** | Mon (if booked). |
| **Green Fees** | not confirmed. |
| **Facilities** | ♀ ♣ 🖢 ⵟ ⟨ Brent Ellis. |
| **Location** | 4m NW of city centre on A4 |
| **Hotel** | ★★★ 66% Redwood Lodge Hotel, Country Club Resort, Beggar Bush Ln, Failand, BRISTOL ☎ 01275 393901 108 ⇔ ⁂ |

---

**Woodlands** Woodlands Ln, Almondsbury BS12 4JZ
☎ 01454 619319 & 618121
Situated on the edge of the Severn Valley, bordered by Hortham Brook and Shepherds Wood this interesting parkland course, features five testing par 3's set around the course's five lakes, notably the 206 yd 5th hole which extends over water.
*18 holes, 6068yds, Par 69, SSS 67.*
*Club membership 101.*

| | |
|---|---|
| **Visitors** | no restrictions. |
| **Societies** | telephone in advance. |
| **Green Fees** | £12 per round (£15 weekends & bank holidays). |
| **Facilities** | ⊗ ⚐ ♨ ♀ ♣ 🖢 ⵟ |
| **Leisure** | fishing, trolley for hire, putting green, practice area. |
| **Location** | N of Bristol off A38 |
| **Hotel** | B Forte Posthouse Bristol, Filton Rd, Hambrook, BRISTOL ☎ 0117 956 4242 197 ⇔ ⁂ |

---

# BUCKINGHAMSHIRE

**Aylesbury**          Map 04 SP81

**Aylesbury Golf Centre** Hulcott Ln, Bierton HP22 5GA
☎ 01296 393644
A parkland course with magnificent views to the Chiltern Hills. The course is tight with out of bounds coming into play on the 1st, 2nd, 6th 7th and 8th.
*9 holes, 2744yds, Par 68, SSS 67.*

| | |
|---|---|
| **Visitors** | no restrictions, but booking advisable. |
| **Societies** | telephone for details. |
| **Green Fees** | £9 per 18 holes; £6 per 9 holes (£10/£7 weekends). |
| **Facilities** | ⊗ ⚐ ⚑ ♨ ♀ ♣ 🖢 ⵟ ⟨ Mitch Kierstenson. |
| **Leisure** | trolley for hire, driving range, putting green, practice area. |
| **Location** | 1m N of Aylesbury on A418 |
| **Hotel** | B Forte Posthouse Aylesbury, Aston Clinton Rd, AYLESBURY ☎ 01296 393388 94 ⇔ ⁂ |

---

**Ellesborough** Butlers Cross HP17 0TZ
☎ 01296 622114
Once part of the property of Chequers, and under the shadow of the famous monument at the Wendover end of the Chilterns. A downland course, it is rather hilly with most holes enhanced by far-ranging views over the Aylesbury countryside.
*18 holes, 6283yds, Par 71, SSS 71, Course record 64.*
*Club membership 700.* ▶

**Visitors** contact for details.
**Societies** Wed & Thu only, by prior arrangement with General Manager.
**Green Fees** fees on application.
**Facilities** ⊗ ▥ ♨ ⬛ ♥ ♀ ♨ 📷 ℓ Mike Squires.
**Leisure** trolley for hire, putting green, practice area.
**Location** 1m E of Ellesborough on B4010
**Hotel** ★★★ 75% The Bell Inn, ASTON CLINTON
☎ 01296 630252 6 ➡ ℛ Annexe15 ➡ ℛ

## BEACONSFIELD                          Map 04 SU99

**Beaconsfield** Seer Green HP9 2UR ☎ 01494 676545
An interesting and, at times, testing tree-lined and parkland course which frequently plays longer than appears on the card! Each hole differs to a considerable degree and here lies the charm. Walking is easy, except perhaps to the 6th and 8th. Well bunkered.
*18 holes, 6487yds, Par 72, SSS 71, Course record 63.*
*Club membership 850.*
**Visitors** must contact in advance and have a handicap certificate. May not play weekends.
**Societies** phone for details
**Green Fees** £48 per day; £36 per round.
**Facilities** ⊗ ▥ by prior arrangement ⬛ ♥ ♀ ♨ 📷 ⭐ ℓ Michael Brothers.
**Leisure** trolley for hire, driving range, putting.
**Location** 2m E,S of Seer Green
**Hotel** ★★★★ 62% Bellhouse Hotel, Oxford Rd, BEACONSFIELD
☎ 01753 887211 136 ➡ ℛ

# The Bell Inn Woburn

★ ★
69%

**Bedford Street, Woburn, Beds MK17 9QD**
**Telephone: 01525 290280 Fax: 01525 290017**

This friendly Inn is a mixture of Tudor, Georgian and Victorian architecture. The beamed Elizabethan restaurant serves excellent food and wine or try real ale and bar food with the locals in our pub. Bedrooms are individual with tasteful fabrics and furnishings. Woburn Abbey with its beautiful park is close by, as is Woburn Golf Club. Special rates for golfing breaks.

*Egon Ronay listed*

## BLETCHLEY                             Map 04 SP83

**Windmill Hill** Tattenhoe Ln MK3 7RB ☎ 01908 378623
Long, open-parkland course designed by Henry Cotton and opened in 1972. Municipal.
*18 holes, 6773yds, Par 73, SSS 72, Course record 68.*
*Club membership 400.*
**Visitors** booking system in operation up to 7 days in advance.
**Societies** packages available, contact for details.
**Green Fees** £8.50 per 18 holes (£11.85 weekends).
**Facilities** ⊗ ▥ ♨ ⬛ ♥ ♀ ♨ 📷 ℓ Colin Clingan.
**Leisure** buggies for hire, trolley for hire, driving range, putting green.
**Location** W side of town centre on A421
**Hotel** ★★ 71% Shenley Church Inn, Burchard Crescent, Shenley Church End, MILTON KEYNES ☎ 01908 505467 50 ➡ ℛ

## BOW BRICKHILL                         Map 04 SP93

**BOW BRICKHILL** See page 19

## BUCKINGHAM                            Map 04 SP63

**Buckingham** Tingewick Rd MK18 4AE
☎ 01280 815566 & 815210
Undulating parkland course with a stream and river affecting 8 holes.
*18 holes, 6082yds, Par 70, SSS 69, Course record 67.*
*Club membership 690.*
**Visitors** welcome Mon-Fri, with member only at weekends.
**Societies** by prior arrangement.
**Green Fees** £28 (weekdays).
**Facilities** ⊗ ▥ ♨ ⬛ ♥ ♀ ♨ 📷 ℓ Tom Gates.
**Leisure** trolley for hire, putting green, practice area.
**Location** 1.5m W on A421
**Hotel** ★★★ 66% Buckingham Four Pillars Hotel, Ring Rd South, BUCKINGHAM
☎ 01280 822622 70 ➡ ℛ

## BURNHAM                               Map 04 SU98

**Burnham Beeches** Green Ln SL1 8EG
☎ 01628 661448
In the centre of the lovely Burnham Beeches countryside. Wide fairways, carefully maintained greens, some hills, and some devious routes to a few holes. A good finish.
*18 holes, 6449yds, Par 70, SSS 71.*
*Club membership 670.*
**Visitors** must contact in advance. May play on weekdays only.
**Societies** welcome Apr-Oct, write or telephone for information.
**Green Fees** £42 per day; £28 per round (£37.50/£25 in winter).
**Facilities** ⊗ ▥ ♨ ⬛ ♥ ♀ ♨ 📷 ⭐ ℓ Ronnie Bolton.
**Leisure** motorised carts for hire, buggies for hire, trolley for hire, putting green, practice area.
**Location** 0.5m NE of Burnham ▶

# WOBURN

### BOW BRICKHILL *Bucks* ☎ 01908 370756   Map O4 SP93

*John Ingham writes:* Come off the M1 motorway at Junction 13 and you are quickly at Woburn, with its magnificent stately home, wildlife safari park and surrounding echoes of Henry VIII and the Dukes of Bedford. Within the last 20 years two new attractions have been added - two golf courses designed by the famed Charles Lawrie of Cotton Pennink.

To create these beautiful courses, the bulldozers got among pine and chestnut and literally cut fairways through some of the most picturesque country in all England - but it had been country seen by very few. From the very back tees, both courses are somewhat long for the weekend amateur. The Duke's measures 69461 yards and makes for a stiff test for any class of golfer, while the 'easier' Duchess, measuring a very respectable 6651 yards, requires a high degree of skill on its fairways guarded by towering pines.

Today, under the direction of Alex Hay, a Scottish TV golf commentator, the Dukes course has become the home of the increasingly popular Weetabix Women's British Open. It has been held at Woburn since 1990.

The town of Woburn and the Abbey are both within Bedfordshire, while the golf and country club actually lie over the border in Buckinghamshire. Although just 45 miles from London, you will feel very much in the wilds and the local pubs and people, plus some wonderful countryside, make this area an excellent place to stay for a few days.

And, if you can hit the ball straight, you might get near the course record of 63 achieved by Peter Baker and Ian Woosnam!

| | |
|---|---|
| **Visitors** | must play with a member at weekends. Must contact in advance and have an introduction from own club |
| **Societies** | must telephone in advance |
| **Green fees** | on application |
| **Facilities** | ⊗ ≣ by prior arrangement (groups only) ☙ ♀ ⚲ 🖼 ⊺ 𝄐 driving range, putting green. (Luther Blacklock) motor carts, buggies, trolleys, practice area |
| **Leisure** | outdoor swimming pool (heated) |
| **Location** | Bow Brickhill, nr Milton Keynes MK17 9LJ. 0.5 miles SE of Bow Brickhill |

36 holes. Dukes Course: 18 holes, 6961 yds, Par 72, SSS 74
Duchess Course: 18 holes, 6651 yds, Par 72, SSS 72

## WHERE TO STAY AND EAT NEARBY

**HOTELS:**

**ASPLEY GUISE**
★★★69% Moore Place, The Square ☎ 01908 282000, 39 ⊨ 🐾 Annexe 15 ⊨ 🐾

**Flitwick**
★★★ ⚘⚘⚘ 75% Flitwick Manor, Church Rd. ☎ 01525 712242. 15 (2 🐾12 ⊨ 1 ⊨ 🐾)

**WOBURN**
★★ ⚘ 69% The Bell Inn, 34 Bedford St ☎ 01525 290280
21 (3 🐾 18 ⊨) Annexe 6 (1 🐾 3 ⊨)

**RESTAURANTS:**

**WOBURN**
⚘⚘ Paris House, Woburn Park ☎ 01525 290692.

| Hotel | ★★★ 68% Burnham Beeches Hotel, Grove Rd, BURNHAM ☎ 01628 429955 75 ⇄ ﾙ |
|---|---|

**Lambourne** Dropmore Rd SL1 8NF
☎ 01628 666755 & 662936
A championship standard 18-hole parkland course. Undulating terrain with many trees and several lakes, notably on the tricky 7th hole which has a tightly guarded green reached via a shot over a lake.
*18 holes, 6764yds, Par 72, SSS 72.*
*Club membership 600.*
**Visitors** must contact in advance.
**Green Fees** £30 per day (£40 weekends).
**Facilities** ⊗ ⅷ ﾑ 💺 ♀ 🏌 🍴 ﾙ 𝆏 David Mart.
**Leisure** sauna, motorised carts for hire, buggies for hire, trolley for hire, driving range, putting green, practice area.
**Hotel** ★★ 66% Chequers Inn, Kiln Ln, Wooburn, WOOBURN COMMON ☎ 01628 529575 17 ⇄ ﾙ

## CHALFONT ST GILES          Map 04 SU99

**Harewood Downs** Cokes Ln HP8 4TA
☎ 01494 762308 & 762184
A testing undulating parkland course with sloping greens and plenty of trees.
*18 holes, 5958yds, Par 69, SSS 69, Course record 64.*
**Visitors** must contact in advance.
**Societies** apply in writing or telephone.
**Green Fees** £25 (£30 weekends & bank holidays).
**Facilities** ⊗ ⅷ ﾑ 💺 ♀ 🏌 🍴 𝆏 G C Morris.
**Leisure** trolley for hire, putting green, practice area.
**Location** 2m E of Amersham on A413
**Hotel** ★★★★ 62% Bellhouse Hotel, Oxford Rd, BEACONSFIELD ☎ 01753 887211 136 ⇄ ﾙ

## CHARTRIDGE          Map 04 SP90

**Chartridge Park** HP5 2TF ☎ 01494 791772
A family, easy walking parkland course set high in the beautiful Chiltern Hills, affording breathtaking views.
*18 holes, 5516yds, Par 69, SSS 67.*
*Club membership 600.*
**Visitors** no restrictions.
**Societies** must telephone in advance.
**Green Fees** £20 per 18/36 holes (£25 per round weekends and bank holidays).
**Facilities** ⊗ ⅷ ﾑ 💺 ♀ 🏌 🍴 ﾙ 𝆏 Peter Gibbins.
**Leisure** motorised carts for hire, buggies for hire, trolley for hire.
**Location** 3m NW of Chesham
**Hotel** ★★★ 62% The Crown Hotel, High St, AMERSHAM ☎ 01494 721541 19 ⇄ ﾙAnnexe4 ⇄ ﾙ

## CHESHAM          Map 04 SP90

**Chesham & Ley Hill** Ley Hill Common HP5 1UZ
☎ 01494 784541
Heathland course on hilltop with easy walking. Subject to wind.
*9 holes, 5296yds, Par 66, SSS 65, Course record 62.*
*Club membership 400.*

**Visitors** may play Mon & Thu all day, Wed after noon, Fri up to 4pm.
**Societies** subject to approval, Thu only.
**Green Fees** £12 per 18 holes.
**Facilities** ⊗ ⅷ ﾑ 💺 ♀ 🏌
**Leisure** putting green.
**Location** 2m E of Chesham
**Hotel** ★★★ 62% The Crown Hotel, High St, AMERSHAM ☎ 01494 721541 19 ⇄ ﾙAnnexe4 ⇄ ﾙ

## DENHAM          Map 04 TQ08

**Buckinghamshire** Denham Court Dr UB9 5BG
☎ 01895 835777
A John Jacobs designed championship-standard course. Visitors only welcome as guests of members to this beautiful course in 269 acres of lovely grounds including mature trees, five lakes and two rivers. The testing 7th hole requires a 185 yd carry over a stream, followed by a second shot over a river to a green guarded by a lake.
*18 holes, 6880yds, Par 72, SSS 73, Course record 70.*
*Club membership 500.*
**Visitors** with member only or introduced by member. Weekdays only.
**Societies** must contact in advance.
**Green Fees** on application.
**Facilities** ⊗ ⅷ ﾑ 💺 ♀ 🏌 🍴 ﾙ 𝆏 John O'Leary.
**Leisure** sauna, trolley for hire, driving range, putting green, practice area.
**Hotel** ★★★★ 62% Bellhouse Hotel, Oxford Rd, BEACONSFIELD ☎ 01753 887211 136 ⇄ ﾙ

**Denham** Tilehouse Ln UB9 5DE ☎ 01895 832022
A beautifully maintained parkland/heathland course, home of many county champions. Slightly hilly and calling for good judgement of distance in the wooded areas.
*18 holes, 6440yds, Par 70, SSS 71, Course record 66.*
*Club membership 550.*
**Visitors** must contact in advance & have handicap certificate. Must play with member Fri-Sun.
**Societies** must book in advance.
**Green Fees** not confirmed.
**Facilities** ♀ 🏌 🍴 ﾙ 𝆏 John Sheridan.
**Location** 2m NW
**Hotel** ★★★★ 62% Bellhouse Hotel, Oxford Rd, BEACONSFIELD ☎ 01753 887211 136 ⇄ ﾙ

## FLACKWELL HEATH          Map 04 SU89

**Flackwell Heath** Treadaway Rd, High Wycombe HP10 9PE
☎ 01628 520929
Open sloping heath and tree-lined course on hills overlooking Loudwater and the M40. Some good challenging par 3's and a several testing small greens.
*18 holes, 6207yds, Par 71, SSS 70, Course record 63.*
*Club membership 800.*
**Visitors** with member only at weekends.
**Societies** Wed & Thu only, by prior booking.
**Green Fees** £27 per day.
**Facilities** ⊗ ⅷ by prior arrangement ﾑ 💺 ♀ 🏌 🍴 𝆏 Paul Watson.
**Leisure** trolley for hire, putting green, practice area.

**Location**   NE side of town centre
**Hotel**   ★★★★ 62% Bellhouse Hotel, Oxford Rd,
BEACONSFIELD ☎ 01753 887211 136 ⇄ ⋒

## GERRARDS CROSS Map 04 TQ08

**Gerrards Cross** Chalfont Park SL9 0QA
☎ 01753 883263
A wooded parkland course which has been modernised in recent years and is now a very pleasant circuit with infinite variety. The best part lies on the plateau above the clubhouse where there are some testing holes.
*18 holes, 6295yds, Par 69, SSS 70, Course record 65.*
*Club membership 773.*
**Visitors**   must contact professional in advance, a handicap certificate is required, may not play Tuesday, weekends or public holidays.
**Societies**   booking well in advance necessary, handicap certicates required, packages to suit.
**Green Fees**   £36 per day; £29 per round.
**Facilities**   ⊗ ⍓ by prior arrangement ⓛ ⬤ ♀ ⅄ 🖻 ⍑ ⋒ Matthew Barr.
**Leisure**   trolley for hire, putting green, practice area.
**Location**   NE side of town centre off A413
**Hotel**   ★★★★ 62% Bellhouse Hotel, Oxford Rd, BEACONSFIELD ☎ 01753 887211 136 ⇄ ⋒

## HALTON Map 04 SP81

**Chiltern Forest** Aston Hill HP22 5NQ
☎ 01296 630899 & 631817
Extended to 18 holes in 1992, this very hilly wooded parkland course is on two levels. It is a true test of skill to the low handicap golfer, as well as being a fair challenge to higher handicap golfers. The surrounding woodland makes the course very scenic.
*18 holes, 5765yds, Par 70, SSS 70, Course record 69.*
*Club membership 600.*
**Visitors**   must play with member at weekends.
**Societies**   contact in advance for booking form.
**Green Fees**   £23 per day weekdays only.
**Facilities**   ⊗ ⍓ ⓛ ⬤ ♀ ⅄ 🖻 ⋒ C Skeet.
**Leisure**   trolley for hire, putting green.
**Location**   1m NE off A4011
**Hotel**   ★★★ 64% Rose & Crown Hotel & Restaurant, High St, TRING ☎ 01442 824071 27 ⇄ ⋒

## HIGH WYCOMBE Map 04 SU89

**Hazlemere Golf & Country Club** Penn Rd, Hazlemere HP15 7LR ☎ 01494 714722 & 718298
Undulating parkland course in beautiful countryside with water hazards in play on some holes. Two long par 5s and a fine par 4 closing hole.
*18 holes, 5873yds, Par 70, SSS 68, Course record 62.*
*Club membership 700.*
**Visitors**   weekdays all day. Weekends in the afternoon by prior arrangement through Pro. shop telephone 01494 718298.
**Societies**   by prior telephone arrangement.
**Green Fees**   £35 per day; £26 per round (£40 per round subject to availability at weekends).

**Facilities**   ⊗ ⍓ ⓛ ⬤ ♀ ⅄ 🖻 ⍑ ⋒ Steve Morvell.
**Leisure**   motorised carts for hire, buggies for hire, trolley for hire, putting green, practice area.
**Location**   2m NE, A404 towards Amersham
**Hotel**   ★★★ 62%´ The Crown Hotel, High St, AMERSHAM
☎ 01494 721541 19 ⇄ ⋒Annexe4 ⇄ ⋒

## IVER Map 04 TQ08

**Iver** Hollow Hill Ln, Langley Park Rd SL0 0JJ
☎ 01753 655615
Fairly flat, pay and play parkland course with challenging par 5s, plenty of hazards - water and ditches - and strong crosswinds to contend with.
*9 holes, 6288yds, Par 72, SSS 72, Course record 68.*
*Club membership 200.*
**Visitors**   competitions at weekends, telephone to pre book tee times.
**Societies**   telephone in advance.
**Green Fees**   £9 per 18 holes; £5.30 per 9 holes (£12.50/£7 weekends).
**Facilities**   ⊗ ⓛ ⬤ ♀ ⅄ 🖻 ⍑ ⋒ Karl Teschner.
**Leisure**   trolley for hire, driving range, putting green, practice area.
**Location**   1.5m SW off B470
**Hotel**   B Marriott Hotel, Ditton Road, Langley, SLOUGH
☎ 01753 544244 350 ⇄ ⋒

## IVINGHOE Map 04 SP91

**Ivinghoe** Wellcroft LU7 9EF ☎ 01296 668696
Testing parkland course with water on three holes. Easy walking on rolling countryside.
*9 holes, 4508yds, Par 62, SSS 62, Course record 57.*
*Club membership 250.*
**Visitors**   may only play after 8am.
**Societies**   must contact in advance.
**Green Fees**   not confirmed.
**Facilities**   ♀ ⅄ 🖻 ⍑ ⋒ Bill Garrad.
**Leisure**   putting,bunker practice,trolley hire.
**Location**   N side of village
**Hotel**   ★★★ 75% The Bell Inn, ASTON CLINTON
☎ 01296 630252 6 ⇄ ⋒Annexe15 ⇄ ⋒

## LITTLE CHALFONT Map 04 SU99

**Little Chalfont** Lodge Ln HP8 4AJ
☎ 01494 764877
Gently undulating flat course surrounded by woods.
*9 holes, 5852yds, Par 68, SSS 68, Course record 66.*
*Club membership 300.*
**Visitors**   no restrictions, please phone to ensure there are no competitions in progress.
**Societies**   please telephone in advance.
**Green Fees**   £10 per 18 holes (£12 weekends).
**Facilities**   ⊗ ⍓ ⓛ ⬤ ♀ ⅄ 🖻 ⍑ ⋒ David Hawes.
**Leisure**   trolley for hire, putting green, practice area, one motorised cart for hire by arrangement.
**Location**   Between Little Chalfont & Chorleywood
**Hotel**   ★★★ 62% The Crown Hotel, High St, AMERSHAM
☎ 01494 721541 19 ⇄ ⋒Annexe4 ⇄ ⋒

## LOUDWATER Map 04 SU89

**Wycombe Heights Golf Centre** Rayners Ave HP10 9SW
☎ 01494 816686
Opened in 1991 and designed by the John Jacobs Partnership.
The golf centre includes a 24-bay driving range.
*18 holes, 6253yds, Par 70, SSS 72, Course record 69.*
*Club membership 1070.*
**Visitors** booking advisable 6 days in advance.
**Societies** telephone in advance & confirm in writing.
**Green Fees** £17.95 per day; £10.95 per round (£14.35 per
round weekends) Twilight fee available.
**Facilities** ⊗ ⅋ ⅃ ⅃ ⅃ ⅃ ⅃ ⅃ Adam Bishop.
**Leisure** motorised carts for hire, buggies for hire, trolley
for hire, driving range, putting green, 18 hole par
3 course.
**Hotel** B Forte Posthouse High Wycombe, Handy
Cross, HIGH WYCOMBE
☎ 01494 442100 106 ⇔ ↾

## MENTMORE Map 04 SP91

**Mentmore Golf & Country Club** LU7 0UA
☎ 01296 662020
Two 18-hole courses - Roseberry and Rothschild - set within
the wooded estate grounds of Mentmore Towers. Gently
rolling parkland course with mature trees and lakes and two
interesting feature holes; the long par 5 (606 yds) 9th on the
Roseberry course with fine views of the Chilterns and the par
4 (340yd) 5th on the Rothschild course, in front of the hall.
*Roseberry Course: 18 holes, 6777yds, Par 72, SSS 72.*
*Rothschild Course: 18 holes, 6763yds, Par 72, SSS 72.*
*Club membership 1100.*
**Visitors** must contact in advance, may not play weekends
before 11am.
**Societies** by prior arrangement.
**Green Fees** £45 per day; £30 per round (£45/35 weekends).
**Facilities** ⊗ ⅋ ⅃ ⅃ ⅃ ⅃ ⅃ ⅃ ⅃ Pip Elson.
**Leisure** hard tennis courts, heated indoor swimming
pool, fishing, sauna, gymnasium, motorised carts
for hire, buggies for hire, trolley for hire, driving
range, putting green, practice area, jacuzzi.
**Location** 4m S of Leighton Buzzard
**Hotel** ★★★ 58% Swan Hotel, High St, LEIGHTON
BUZZARD ☎ 01525 372148 38 ⇔ ↾

## MILTON KEYNES Map 04 SP83

*Abbey Hill* Two Mile Ash MK8 8AA ☎ 01908 563845
Undulating municipal course within the new city. Tight
fairways and well-placed bunkers. Stream comes into play on
five holes. Also Par 3 course.
*18 holes, 6177yds, Par 68, SSS 69.*
*Club membership 600.*
**Visitors** no restrictions.
**Societies** must telephone (01908) 562408 in advance.
**Green Fees** not confirmed.
**Facilities** ⅃ ⅃ ⅃ ⅃ ⅃ Gary George.
**Leisure** pool table, darts.
**Location** 2m W of new town centre off A5
**Hotel** ★★★ 62% Quality Friendly Hotel, Monks
Way, Two Mile Ash, MILTON KEYNES
☎ 01908 561666 88 ⇔ ↾

**Three Locks** Great Brickhill MK17 9BH
☎ 01525 270470 & 270050
Parkland course offering a challenge to beginners and
experienced golfers, with water coming into play on ten
holes. Magnificent views.
*18 holes, 5850yds, Par 69, SSS 68, Course record 69.*
*Club membership 350.*
**Visitors** telephone 01525 270050 to book tee times.
**Societies** write or telephone for details.
**Green Fees** £16 per day; £10 per round; £7.50 twilight
(£20/£12.50/£8 weekends)
**Facilities** ⊗ ⅃ ⅃ ⅃ ⅃ ⅃ ⅃ ⅃
**Leisure** fishing, motorised carts for hire, buggies for hire,
trolley for hire, putting green, practice area.
**Location** A4146 between Leighton Buzzard/Bletchley
**Hotel** ★★ 71% Shenley Church Inn, Burchard
Crescent, Shenley Church End, MILTON
KEYNES ☎ 01908 505467 50 ⇔ ↾

## PRINCES RISBOROUGH Map 04 SP80

**Whiteleaf** Whiteleaf HP27 0LY
☎ 01844 343097 & 274058
Short, hilly and tricky 9-hole parkland course, requiring great
accuracy, set high in the Chilterns with beautiful views.
*9 holes, 5391yds, Par 66, SSS 66, Course record 64.*
*Club membership 400.*
**Visitors** advisable to contact in advance, with member
only at weekends.
**Societies** on Thu only, must contact the secretary in
advance.
**Green Fees** £25 per day; £18 per round.
**Facilities** ⊗ ⅃ ⅃ ⅃ ⅃ ⅃ ⅃ ⅃ Ken Ward.
**Leisure** trolley for hire, putting green, practice area.
**Location** 1m NE off A4010
**Hotel** ★★★ 75% The Bell Inn, ASTON CLINTON
☎ 01296 630252 6 ⇔ ↾Annexe15 ⇔ ↾

## STOKE POGES Map 04 SU98

**Farnham Park** Park Rd SL2 4PJ ☎ 01753 643332
Fine, public parkland course in pleasing setting.
*18 holes, 6172yds, Par 71, SSS 70, Course record 68.*
*Club membership 600.*
**Visitors** telephone in advance for tee times.
**Societies** apply in writing.
**Green Fees** £8 per round (£11 weekends and bank holidays).
**Facilities** ⊗ ⅃ ⅃ ⅃ ⅃ ⅃ ⅃ ⅃ Paul Warner.
**Leisure** trolley for hire, putting green.
**Location** W side of village off B416
**Hotel** B Marriott Hotel, Ditton Road, Langley,
SLOUGH ☎ 01753 544244 350 ⇔ ↾

**Stoke Poges** Stoke Park, North Dr SL2 4PG
☎ 01753 717171
Judgement of the distance from the tee is all important on
this first-class parkland course. There are 8 outstanding
par 4's of around 440 yards, several calling for much
thought. Fairways are wide and the challenge seemingly
innocuous.
*18 holes, 6654yds, Par 71, SSS 72, Course record 65.*
*Club membership 564.*
**Visitors** must contact in advance.
**Societies** apply in writing or telephone in advance.

**Green Fees** £65 per day; £45 per round; £30 after 5pm (£100 per round; £50 after 4pm weekends).
**Facilities** ⊗ ⋔ ♭ ⚑ ♀ ♨ 🖿 ♏ ( Tim Morrison.
**Leisure** hard and grass tennis courts, sauna, motorised carts for hire, buggies for hire, trolley for hire, driving range, putting green, practice area, snooker room,croquet lawn.
**Location** 2m N of Slough
**Hotel** B Marriott Hotel, Ditton Road, Langley, SLOUGH ☎ 01753 544244 350 ⇄ ♞

## WAVENDON                                    Map 04 SP93

**Wavendon Golf Centre** Lower End Rd MK17 8DA
☎ 01908 281811
Pleasant parkland course set within mature oak and lime trees and incorporating several small lakes as water hazards. Easy walking.
*18 holes, 5540yds, Par 67, SSS 67.*
*Club membership 300.*
**Visitors** must book 3 days in advance.
**Societies** must contact in advance by telephone.
**Green Fees** £10 per 18 holes (£13.50 weekends). Par3 £3.75 (£4.75 weekends).
**Facilities** ⊗ ⋔ ♭ ⚑ ♀ ♨ 🖿 ♏ ( Greg Iron.
**Leisure** trolley for hire, driving range, 9 hole Par 3 course, putting green, practice area.
**Location** Just off A421
**Hotel** ★★★ 69% Moore Place Hotel, The Square, ASPLEY GUISE
☎ 01908 282000 39 ⇄ ♞Annexe15 ⇄ ♞

## WESTON TURVILLE                                Map 04 SP81

**Weston Turville Golf & Squash Club** New Rd HP22 5QT
☎ 01296 24084 & 25949
Parkland course situated at the foot of the Chiltern Hills and providing an excellent challenge for the accomplished golfer, yet not too daunting for the higher handicap player. Flat easy walking with water hazards and many interesting holes, notably the testing dog-leg 5th (418yds).
*18 holes, 6008yds, Par 69, SSS 69, Course record 71.*
*Club membership 600.*
**Visitors** no restrictions.
**Societies** must contact in advance.
**Green Fees** £15 per round (£20 weekends & bank holidays).
**Facilities** ⊗ ⋔ by prior arrangement ♭ ⚑ ♀ ♨ 🖿 ♏ ( Gary George.
**Leisure** squash, buggies for hire, trolley for hire, putting green.
**Location** 2m SE of Aylesbury, off A41
**Hotel** ★★★ 75% The Bell Inn, ASTON CLINTON
☎ 01296 630252 6 ⇄ ♞Annexe15 ⇄ ♞

## WEXHAM STREET                                Map 04 SU98

**Wexham Park** SL3 6ND ☎ 01753 663271
Gently undulating parkland course. Two courses.
*18 holes, 5836yds, Par 69, SSS 68 or 9 holes, 2283yds, Par 32, SSS 32.*
*Club membership 500.*
**Visitors** no restrictions.
**Societies** may not play at weekends; must contact in advance.

**Green Fees** not confirmed.
**Facilities** ♀ ♨ 🖿 ♏ (
**Location** 0.5m S
**Hotel** B Marriott Hotel, Ditton Road, Langley, SLOUGH ☎ 01753 544244 350 ⇄ ♞

## WING                                    Map 04 SP82

**Aylesbury Vale** Stewkley Rd LU7 0UJ ☎ 01525 240196
The course, which is gently undulating and played over water, was opened in the autumn of 1991. There are five ponds to add interest, notably on the par 4 420 yd 13th - unlucky for some - where the second shot is all downhill with an inviting pond spanning the approach to the green. In addition there is a 10-bay driving range, a practice fairway and practice putting green as well as an In-Golf Simulator.
*18 holes, 6622yds, Par 72, SSS 72, Course record 65.*
*Club membership 545.*
**Visitors** must adhere to dress regulations. Must contact in advance.
**Societies** telephone to book in advance.
**Green Fees** £16 per day; £10 per round; £6 per 9 holes (£28/£18.50/£10 weekends and bank holidays).
**Facilities** ⊗ ⋔ ♭ ⚑ ♀ ♨ 🖿 ♏ ( Richard Hodgson.
**Leisure** trolley for hire, covered driving range, putting green.
**Location** 2m NW on unclassified Stewkley road
**Hotel** ★★★ 58% Swan Hotel, High St, LEIGHTON BUZZARD ☎ 01525 372148 38 ⇄ ♞

# CAMBRIDGESHIRE

## BAR HILL                                    Map 05 TL36

**Cambridgeshire Moat House** Moat House Hotel
CB3 8EU ☎ 01954 780098 & 780555
Undulating parkland course with lake and water hazards, easy walking. Many leisure facilities. Course record holders, Paul Way and Peter Townsend.
*18 holes, 6734yds, Par 72, SSS 72.*
*Club membership 500.*
**Visitors** must book in advance.
**Societies** must telephone in advance.
**Green Fees** not confirmed.
**Facilities** ♀ ♨ 🖿 ♏ ⊨ ( David Vernon.
**Leisure** hard tennis courts, heated indoor swimming pool, squash, sauna, solarium, gymnasium, buggies.
**Location** 5m NW of Cambridge on A604
**Hotel** ★★★ 64% Cambridgeshire Moat House, BAR HILL ☎ 01954 249988 99 ⇄ ♞

## BRAMPTON                                    Map 04 TL27

**Brampton Park** Buckden Rd PE18 8NF ☎ 01480 434700
Set in truly attractive countryside, bounded by the River Great Ouse and bisected by the River Lane. Great variety with mature trees, lakes and water hazards. One of the most difficult holes is the 4th, a Par 3 island green, named 'Fowler's Folly'.                                    ▶

*18 holes, 6403yds, Par 72, SSS 73, Course record 69.*
*Club membership 700.*

**Visitors**    must contact in advance.
**Societies**    apply in advance.
**Green Fees** £24 per day; £18 per round (£36 per day weekend, includes meal voucher); Nov-Mar £15 day (including light lunch).
**Facilities**    ⊗ ⅢⅢ ⓑ ♥ ♀ ♨ 🖱 🏌 ℓ Alisdair Currie.
**Leisure**    fishing, trolley for hire, putting green, practice area.
**Hotel**    ★★ 64% Grange Hotel, 115 High St, Brampton, HUNTINGDON
     ☎ 01480 459516 9rm(1 ⇄7 📷)

## CAMBRIDGE      Map 05 TL45

**Gog Magog** Shelford Bottom CB2 4AB
☎ 01223 247626
Situated just outside the centre of the university town, Gog Magog, established in 1901, is known as the nursery of Cambridge undergraduate golf. The course is on high ground, and it is said that if you stand on the highest point and could see far enough to the east the next highest ground would be the Ural Mountains! The courses (there are two of them) are open but there are enough trees and other hazards to provide plenty of problems. Views from the high parts are superb. The nature of the ground ensures good winter golf.
*Old Course: 18 holes, 6400yds, Par 70, SSS 70, Course record 64.*
*New Course: 9 holes, 2979yds, Par 69, SSS 68.*
*Club membership 1130.*
**Visitors**    must contact in advance.
**Societies**    Tue & Thu by reservation.
**Green Fees** Old Course: £37.50 per day; £30 per round. New Course £19 per day/round.
**Facilities**    ⊗ ⅢⅢ ⓑ ♥ ♀ ♨ 🖱 🏌 ℓ Ian Bamborough.
**Leisure**    trolley for hire, putting green, practice area.
**Location**    3m SE on A1307
**Hotel**    ★★★ 71% Gonville Hotel, Gonville Place, CAMBRIDGE ☎ 01223 366611 64 ⇄ 📷

## ELY      Map 05 TL58

**Ely City** Cambridge Rd CB7 4HX
☎ 01353 662751 (Office) & 663317 (Pro)
Parkland course slightly undulating with water hazards formed by lakes and natural dykes. Demanding par 4 5th hole (467yds), often into a headwind, and a testing par 3 2nd hole (160yds) played over 2 ponds Magnificent views of Cathedral. Lee Trevino is the professional record holder.
*18 holes, 6627yds, Par 72, SSS 72, Course record 66.*
*Club membership 850.*
**Visitors**    advisable to contact the club in advance.
**Societies**    Tue to Fri, advisable to contact club well in advance.
**Green Fees** £25 per day; £20 per round (£32/£25 weekends & bank holidays).
**Facilities**    ⊗ ⅢⅢ ⓑ ♥ ♀ ♨ 🖱 🏌 ℓ Andrew George.
**Leisure**    trolley for hire, putting green, practice area.
**Location**    SW side of city centre on A10
**Hotel**    ★★ 64% Lamb Hotel, 2 Lynn Rd, ELY
     ☎ 01353 663574 32 ⇄ 📷

## GIRTON      Map 05 TL46

**Girton** Dodford Ln CB3 0QE ☎ 01223 276169
Flat, open parkland course with many trees and ditches. Easy walking.
*18 holes, 6085yds, Par 69, SSS 69, Course record 66.*
*Club membership 800.*
**Visitors**    with member only at weekends. Contact professional in advance (01223 276991).
**Societies**    apply writing.
**Green Fees** £16 per day.
**Facilities**    ⊗ ⅢⅢ ⓑ ♥ ♀ ♨ 🖱 🏌 ℓ Scott Thomson.
**Leisure**    trolley for hire, putting green, practice area.
**Location**    NW side of village
**Hotel**    B Forte Posthouse Cambridge, Lakeview, Bridge Rd, Impington, CAMBRIDGE
     ☎ 01223 237000 118 ⇄ 📷

## HEMINGFORD ABBOTS      Map 04 TL27

*Hemingford Abbots* Cambridge Rd PE18 9HQ
☎ 01480 495000 & 493900
Interesting 9-hole course featuring a par 5 dog-leg 4th with a testing tapering fairway, two ponds at the entrance to the 8th green and an island green on the 9th.
*9 holes, 5468yds, Par 68, SSS 68.*
*Club membership 170.*
**Visitors**    advisable to phone in advance, particularly for weekends.
**Societies**    advise in writing or telephone.
**Green Fees** not confirmed.
**Facilities**    ⊗ ⅢⅢ ⓑ ♥ ♀ ♨ 🖱 🏌 ℓ Craig Watson.
**Leisure**    trolley for hire, driving range, putting green.
**Location**    A14 Hemingford Abbots turning
**Hotel**    ★★★ 73% The Old Bridge Hotel, HUNTINGDON ☎ 01480 052681 26 ⇄ 📷

## MARCH      Map 05 TL49

**March** Frogs Abbey, Grange Rd PE15 0YH
☎ 01354 52364
Nine-hole parkland course with a particularly challenging par 3 9th hole, with out of bounds on the left and high hedges to the right.
*9 holes, 6204yds, Par 70, SSS 70, Course record 65.*
*Club membership 413.*
**Visitors**    contact in advance, with member only at weekends.
**Societies**    apply in writing.
**Green Fees** £15 per day.
**Facilities**    ⊗ ⅢⅢ ♥ ♀ ♨ 🖱 ℓ Jason Hadland.
**Leisure**    trolley for hire, putting green, practice area.
**Location**    0.5m off A141, March bypass
**Hotel**    ★★ 66% Olde Griffin Hotel, High St, MARCH
     ☎ 01354 52517 20rm(19 ⇄ 📷)

## PETERBOROUGH      Map 04 TL19

**Elton Furze** Bullock Rd, Haddon PE7 3TT
☎ 01832 280189
A new course opened in 1993. Wooded parkland 18-hole course in lovely surroundings.
*18 holes, 6289yds, Par 70, SSS 70, Course record 69.*
*Club membership 388.*

**Visitors** weekends only with prior permission.
**Societies** by prior arrangement telephone for details.
**Green Fees** not confirmed.
**Facilities** ⊗ ⅲ ⅊ 🍷 ♀ ⅄ 🛆 ⟡ *Frank Kiddie.
**Leisure** sauna, trolley for hire, putting green, practice area.
**Location** 4m SW of Peterborough, off A605
**Hotel** ★★★★ 65% Swallow Hotel, Peterborough Business Park, Lynchwood, PETERBOROUGH
☎ 01733 371111 163 ⇥ 🐾

---

**Orton Meadows** Ham Ln, Orton Waterville PE2 0UU
☎ 01733 237478
Pretty municipal parkland course set within the Nene Valley Country Park with large lakes and water hazards. Challenging 3rd hole (616yards from white tee) incorporating lots of water and 'out of bounds' areas. Also 12-hole pitch and putt course.
*18 holes, 5664yds, Par 67, SSS 68, Course record 71.*
*Club membership 520.*
**Visitors** no restrictions.
**Societies** apply in advance.
**Green Fees** £9 per round (£11.50 weekends & bank holidays).
**Facilities** 🍷 ⅄ 🛆 ⟡ *Neil Grant.
**Leisure** trolley for hire, putting green, practice area.
**Location** 3m W of town on A605
**Hotel** ★★★ 68% Orton Hall Hotel, Orton Longueville, PETERBOROUGH
☎ 01733 391111 49 ⇥ 🐾

---

**Peterborough Milton** Milton Ferry PE6 7AG
☎ 01733 380489 & 380793
Designed by James Braid, this well-bunkered parkland course is set in the grounds of the Earl Fitzwilliam's estate, many of the holes being played in full view of Milton Hall. Challenging holes are the difficult dog-leg 10th and 15th. Easy walking.
*18 holes, 6198yds, Par 71, SSS 70.*
*Club membership 800.*
**Visitors** must contact in advance.
**Societies** bookings in writing to secretary.
**Green Fees** £30 per day; £20 per round (£25 per round weekends).
**Facilities** ⊗ ⅲ ⅊ 🍷 ♀ ⅄ 🛆 ⟡ *Michael Gallagher.
**Leisure** motorised carts for hire, buggies for hire, trolley for hire, driving range, putting green, practice area.
**Location** 2m W of Peterborough on A47
**Hotel** ★★★ 66% Butterfly Hotel, Thorpe Meadows, Off Longthorpe Parkway, PETERBOROUGH
☎ 01733 64240 70 ⇥ 🐾

---

**Thorpe Wood** Thorpe Wood, Nene Parkway PE3 6SE
☎ 01733 267701
Gently undulating, municipal parkland course designed by Peter Alliss and Dave Thomas. Challenging holes include the 5th, the longest hole usually played with prevailing wind and the 14th, entailing a difficult approach shot over water to a two-tier green.
*18 holes, 7086yds, Par 73, SSS 74, Course record 71.*
*Club membership 750.*
**Visitors** phone for reservations.
**Societies** must telephone in advance, bookings taken up to year ahead.
**Green Fees** £9 per round (£11.50 weekends & bank holidays).

**Facilities** ⊗ ⅲ ⅊ 🍷 ♀ ⅄ 🛆 ⟡
*Dennis & Roger Fitton.
**Leisure** trolley for hire, putting green, practice area.
**Location** 3m W of city centre on A47
**Hotel** ★★★ 67% Peterborough Moat House, Thorpe Wood, PETERBOROUGH
☎ 01733 260000 125 ⇥ 🐾

---

## PIDLEY
Map 05 TL37

**Lakeside Lodge** Fen Rd PE17 3DD
☎ 01487 740540 & 741541
A well designed, spacious course incorporating eight lakes, 12,000 trees and a modern clubhouse. The 9th and 18th holes both finish dramatically alongside a lake in front of the clubhouse. Also 9-hole Par 3 and 25-bay driving range.
*18 holes, 6821yds, Par 72, SSS 73, Course record 72.*
*Club membership 350.*
**Visitors** no restrictions.
**Societies** must telephone in advance.
**Green Fees** £9 per 18 holes (£15 weekends).
**Facilities** ⊗ ⅲ ⅊ 🍷 ♀ ⅄ 🛆 ⟡ *Alistair Headley.
**Leisure** fishing, motorised carts for hire, buggies for hire, trolley for hire, driving range, par 3 course, hot-air ballooning, bowling.
**Hotel** ★★★ 64% Slepe Hall Hotel, Ramsey Rd, ST IVES ☎ 01480 463122 16rm(15 ⇥ 🐾)

---

## RAMSEY
Map 04 TL28

**Old Nene Golf & Country Club** Muchwood Ln, Bodsey PE17 1XQ ☎ 01487 813519
A flat well-drained course with water hazards and boundaries. There are excellent greens and the 8th and 9th holes are challenging across water in either a head wind or cross wind.
*9 holes, 2762yds, Par 68, SSS 67, Course record 66.*
*Club membership 200.*
**Visitors** book in advance especially evenings & weekends.
**Societies** arrange in advance with Secretary.
**Green Fees** £10 per 18 holes; £7 per 9 holes (£13/£9 weekends & bank holidays).
**Facilities** ⊗ ⅲ by prior arrangement 🍷 ♀ ⅄ 🛆 ⟡
*Ken McKechnie.
**Leisure** fishing, motorised carts for hire, buggies for hire, trolley for hire, driving range, practice area.
**Location** 0.75m N of Ramsey
**Hotel** ★★★ 73% The Old Bridge Hotel, HUNTINGDON ☎ 01480 052681 26 ⇥ 🐾

---

**Ramsey** 4 Abbey Ter PE17 1DD ☎ 01487 812600
Flat, parkland course with water hazards.
*18 holes, 6123yds, Par 71, SSS 70, Course record 66.*
*Club membership 750.*
**Visitors** contact professional in advance (01487 813022), may only play with member at weekends & bank holidays.
**Societies** apply in writing.
**Green Fees** £22 per day/round.
**Facilities** ⊗ ⅲ ⅊ 🍷 ♀ ⅄ 🛆 ⟡ *Stuart Scott.
**Leisure** trolley for hire, putting green, practice area.
**Location** 12m SE of Peterborough on B1040
**Hotel** ★★★ 73% The Old Bridge Hotel, HUNTINGDON
☎ 01480 052681 26 ⇥ 🐾

## St Ives                                Map 05 TL37

**St Ives (Cambs)** Westwood Rd PE17 4RS
☎ 01480 468392
Picturesque parkland course.
*9 holes, 6100yds, Par 70, SSS 69.*
*Club membership 500.*
Visitors     must contact in advance, may not play
             weekends.
Societies    welcome Wednesday & Fridays.
Green Fees   £20 per day.
Facilities   ⊗ 🍽 ⓑ ♨ ♀ ⚒ 🛆 ☎ ⚑ ( Darren Glasby.
Leisure      trolley for hire, putting green, practice area.
Location     W side of town centre off A1123
Hotel        ★★★ 64% Slepe Hall Hotel, Ramsey Rd,
             ST IVES
             ☎ 01480 463122 16rm(15 ⇄ ↾)

## St Neots                              Map 04 TL16

**Abbotsley Golf & Squash Club** PE19 4XN
☎ 01480 474000 & 215153
Two courses - main Abbotsley course featuring mature
parkland with tree-lined fairways, plenty of water hazards and
a particularly testing par 3 2nd hole - the 'Mousehole'.
Cromwell course, opened in 1991, is less demanding with
tricky driving holes and sloping greens. Courses surround
moated country house and hotel. Residential golf schools 30
weeks of the year plus floodlit, covered driving range.
*Abbotsley Course: 18 holes, 6311yds, Par 73, SSS 71, Course*
*record 69.*
*Cromwell Course: 18 holes, 6087yds, Par 70, SSS 69.*
*Club membership 500.*
Visitors     welcome all times advisable to book weekends.
Societies    prior booking for large parties.
Green Fees   Abbotsley: £20 per round (£25 weekends).
             Cromwell: £9 per round (£13 weekends).
Facilities   ⊗ 🍽 ⓑ ♨ ♀ ⚒ 🛆 ☎ ⚑ 🏄 ( Vivien Saunders.
Leisure      squash, motorised carts for hire, buggies for hire,
             trolley for hire, driving range, putting green,
             practice area.
Location     2m SE off B1046
Hotel        ★★ 65% Abbotsley Golf Hotel, Eynesbury
             Hardwicke, ST NEOTS
             ☎ 01480 474000 15 ⇄ ↾

**St Neots** Crosshall Rd PE19 4AE
☎ 01480 472363
Undulating and very picturesque parkland course with lake
and water hazards and exceptional greens, close to the Kym
and Great Ouse rivers. Easy, level walking.
*18 holes, 6074yds, Par 69, SSS 69, Course record 64.*
*Club membership 630.*
Visitors     must book in advance. with member only at
             weekends.
Societies    must contact in advance.
Green Fees   £30 per day; £20 per round.
Facilities   ⊗ 🍽 ⓑ ♨ ♀ ⚒ 🛆 ☎ ⚑ ( Graham Bithrey.
Leisure      motorised carts for hire, buggies for hire, trolley
             for hire, putting green, practice area.
Location     W side of town centre on A428
Hotel        ★★ 64% Grange Hotel, 115 High St, Brampton,
             HUNTINGDON
             ☎ 01480 459516 9rm(1 ⇄7 ↾)

## Thorney                               Map 04 TF20

**Thorney** English Drove, Thorney PE6 0TJ
☎ 01733 270570
The 18-hole Fen course is ideal for the beginner, while the
Lakes course, opened in June 1995, has a challenging links-
style layout with eight holes around water.
*Fen Course: 18 holes, 6104yds, Par 70, SSS 69, Course*
*record 66.*
*Lakes Course: 18 holes, 6400yds, Par 71, SSS 71, Course*
*record 72 or 9 holes, 990yds, Par 27.*
*Club membership 400.*
Visitors     book in advance for Fen course, limited
             weekend play Lakes course.
Societies    contact in advance.
Green Fees   Fen: £5.75 (£7.75 weekends & bank holidays).
             Lakes: £10 (£16 weekends & bank holidays).
             Day tickets available.
Facilities   ⊗ 🍽 ⓑ ♨ ♀ ⚒ 🛆 ☎ ⚑ ( Mark Templeman.
Leisure      motorised carts for hire, buggies for hire, trolley
             for hire, driving range, par 3 course, putting
             green, practice area.
Location     Off A47, 7m NE of Peterborough
Hotel        ★★★ 66% Butterfly Hotel, Thorpe Meadows,
             Off Longthorpe Parkway, PETERBOROUGH
             ☎ 01733 64240 70 ⇄ ↾

## Toft                                  Map 05 TL35

**Cambridge Meridian** Comberton Rd CB3 7RY
☎ 01223 264700
Opened in 1993. Set in 207 acres to a Peter Allis/Clive Clark
design with sweeping fairways, lakes and well bunkered
greens. The 4th hole with bunker complexes, a sharp dog-leg
and a river with the green heavily guarded by bunkers.
*18 holes, 6651yds, Par 73, SSS 72, Course record 72.*
*Club membership 600.*
Visitors     must contact in advance.
Societies    telephone for provisional booking
Green Fees   £25 per day; £16 per round (£30/£18 weekends).
Facilities   ⊗ 🍽 ⓑ ♨ ♀ ⚒ 🛆 ☎ ⚑ ( Michael Clemons.
Leisure      motorised carts for hire, buggies for hire, trolley
             for hire, putting green, practice area.
Location     3m W of Cambridge, on B1046
Hotel        ★★ 65% Abbotsley Golf Hotel, Eynesbury
             Hardwicke, ST NEOTS
             ☎ 01480 474000 15 ⇄ ↾

# CHESHIRE

## Alderley Edge                         Map 07 SJ87

**Alderley Edge** Brook Ln SK9 7RU
☎ 01625 585583
Well-wooded, undulating pastureland course. A stream
crosses 7 of the 9 holes.
*9 holes, 5823yds, Par 68, SSS 68, Course record 62.*
*Club membership 400.*
Visitors     by arrangement on Thu.
Societies    Thu only, apply in writing or telephone.

**Green Fees** £18 per day; (£22 weekends).
**Facilities** ⊗ ⫴ ⓛ ⚑ ♀ ♨ 🏠 ℓ Peter Bowring.
**Leisure** trolley for hire, putting green, small practice area.
**Location** 1m NW on B5085
**Hotel** ★★★ 70% Alderley Edge Hotel, Macclesfield Rd, ALDERLEY EDGE
☎ 01625 583033 32 ⇥ ℟

## ALSAGER                                   Map 07 SJ75

**Alsager Golf & Country Club** Audley Rd ST7 2UR
☎ 01270 875700
An 18-hole parkland course situated in rolling Cheshire countryside and offering a challenge to all golfers whatever their standard. Clubhouse is well appointed with good facilities and a friendly atmosphere.
*18 holes, 6200yds, Par 70, SSS 70.*
*Club membership 640.*
**Visitors** must contact in advance, can only play with member at weekends.
**Societies** must contact in advance.
**Green Fees** £25 per round Mon-Fri.
**Facilities** ⊗ ⫴ ⓛ ⚑ ♀ ♨ 🏠 ⚑ ℓ Paul Preston.
**Leisure** motorised carts for hire, buggies for hire, trolley for hire, putting green, practice area, bowls, snooker.
**Location** 2m NE of M6 junct 16
**Hotel** ★★★ 66% Manor House Hotel, Audley Rd, ALSAGER
☎ 01270 884000 57 ⇥ ℟

## CHESTER                                   Map 07 SJ46

**Carden Park Hotel** Carden Park CH3 9DQ
☎ 01829 731000
Currently under construction and scheduled to open in May 1997, this championship course, designed by Jack and Steve Nicklaus, will enjoy a splendid setting within a magnificent country estate. Teaching Academy headed by the former Ryder Cup player John Garner. Excellent leisure facilities at adjacent Country Club.
*18 holes, 6775yds, Par 72, SSS 73, Course record 74.*
**Visitors** must contact in advance.
**Societies** contact for details.
**Green Fees** £25 per 18 holes (£30 weekends).
**Facilities** ⊗ ⫴ ⓛ ⚑ ♀ ♨ ⚑ 🏠

**Chester** Curzon Park CH4 8AR
☎ 01244 677760
Meadowland course on two levels contained within a loop of the River Dee. The car park overlooks the racecourse across the river.
*18 holes, 6500yds, Par 72, SSS 71, Course record 66.*
*Club membership 820.*
**Visitors** must contact in advance.
**Societies** must telephone or write in advance.
**Green Fees** £23 per day (£26 weekends).
**Facilities** ⊗ ⫴ ⓛ ⚑ ♀ ♨ 🏠 ⚑ ℓ George Parton.
**Leisure** trolley for hire, putting green, practice area.
**Location** 1m W of city centre
**Hotel** ★★★★ 65% Chester Moat House, Trinity St, CHESTER
☎ 01244 899988 150 ⇥

**Upton-by-Chester** Upton Ln, Upton-by-Chester CH2 1EE
☎ 01244 381183
Pleasant, tree-lined, parkland course. Not easy for low-handicap players to score well. Testing holes are 2nd (par 4), 14th (par 4) and 15th (par 3).
*18 holes, 5808yds, Par 69, SSS 68, Course record 63.*
*Club membership 800.*
**Visitors** must contact in advance.
**Societies** apply in writing.
**Green Fees** £20 per day (£25 per round weekends).
**Facilities** ⊗ ⫴ ⓛ ⚑ ♀ ♨ 🏠 ℓ P A Gardner.
**Leisure** motorised carts for hire, buggies for hire, trolley for hire, putting green.
**Location** N side off A5116
**Hotel** ★★★★ 65% Mollington Banastre Hotel, Parkgate Rd, CHESTER
☎ 01244 851471 63 ⇥

**Vicars Cross** Tarvin Rd, Great Barrow CH3 7HN
☎ 01244 335174
Tree-lined parkland course, with undulating terrain.
*18 holes, 6243yds, Par 72, SSS 70, Course record 64.*
*Club membership 750.*
**Visitors** advisable to contact in advance, visitors may not play competition days.
**Societies** Tue & Thu only.
**Green Fees** £22 per day.
**Facilities** ⊗ ⫴ ⓛ ⚑ ♀ ♨ 🏠 ℓ J A Forsythe.
**Leisure** buggies for hire, trolley for hire, putting green, practice area.
**Location** 4m E on A51
**Hotel** ★★★ 66% Rowton Hall Hotel, Whitchurch Road,Rowton, CHESTER
☎ 01244 335262 42 ⇥ ℟

## CONGLETON                                 Map 07 SJ86

**Astbury** Peel Ln, Astbury CW12 4RE ☎ 01260 272772
Parkland course in open countryside, bisected by a canal. The testing 12th hole involves a long carry over a tree-filled ravine. Large practice area.
*18 holes, 6296yds, Par 71, SSS 70.*
**Visitors** with member only at weekends, contact for further details.
**Societies** contact for details.
**Green Fees** £25 per day.
**Facilities** ⊗ ⫴ ⚑ ♀ ♨ 🏠 ℓ Ashley Salt.
**Leisure** trolley for hire, putting green, practice area.
**Location** 1.5m S between A34 and A527
**Hotel** ★★★ 65% Lion & Swan Hotel, Swan Bank, CONGLETON ☎ 01260 273115 21 ⇥ ℟

*Congleton* Biddulph Rd CW12 3LZ ☎ 01260 273540
Superbly-manicured parkland course with views over three counties from the balcony of the clubhouse.
*9 holes, 5103yds, Par 68, SSS 65.*
*Club membership 400.*
**Visitors** may not play during competitions.
**Societies** must apply in writing to Secretary.
**Green Fees** not confirmed.
**Facilities** ♀ ♨ 🏠 ℓ John Colclough.
**Location** 1.5m SE on A527
**Hotel** ★★★ 65% Lion & Swan Hotel, Swan Bank, CONGLETON
☎ 01260 273115 21 ⇥ ℟

## CREWE
Map 07 SJ75

**Crewe** Fields Rd, Haslington CW1 1TB ☎ 01270 584099
Undulating parkland course.
*18 holes, 6259yds, Par 70, SSS 69, Course record 65.*
*Club membership 674.*
**Visitors** contact for details.
**Societies** Tue only, prior arrangement with the secretary.
**Green Fees** not confirmed.
**Facilities** ⊗ �X ⌶ ⌷ ♀ ⚲ 🏠 ℓ Mike Booker.
**Leisure** trolley for hire, putting green, practice area.
**Location** 2.25m NE off A534
**Hotel** ★★★ 64% Hunters Lodge Hotel, Sydney Rd,
Sydney, CREWE
☎ 01270 583440 & 588216 42 ⇋ ℟

**Queen's Park** Queen's Park Dr CW2 7SB ☎ 01270 666724
A short but testing municipal course, the 9 holes are
highlighted by the tight dogleg 4th holes and 450yard Par 4
7th hole. There is a testing Par 4 on finishing hole with a
bomb crater on left and outerbounds on the right.
*9 holes, 4920yds, Par 68, SSS 64, Course record 67.*
*Club membership 400.*
**Visitors** booking for weekends, cannot play Wed or Sun
before 10.30am.
**Societies** must book at least 2 weeks in advance.
**Green Fees** £4.60 per 18 holes; £3.60 per per 9 holes
(£6.10/£4.60 weekends & bank holidays).
**Facilities** ⊗ �X ⌶ ⌷ ♀ ⚲ 🏠 ⅋
**Leisure** hard tennis courts, putting green, bowling green.
**Hotel** ★★★ 64% Hunters Lodge Hotel, Sydney Rd,
Sydney, CREWE
☎ 01270 583440 & 588216 42 ⇋ ℟

## DELAMERE
Map 07 SJ56

**Delamere Forest** Station Rd CW8 2JE
☎ 01606 883264 & 883307
Played mostly on undulating open heath there is great
charm in the way this course drops down into the
occasional pine sheltered valley. Six of the first testing
nine hole are between 420 and 455 yards in length.
*18 holes, 6305yds, Par 69, SSS 70, Course record 63.*
**Visitors** must contact in advance.
**Societies** apply in writing.
**Green Fees** £35 per day; £25 per round (£30 per round
weekends and bank holidays).
**Facilities** ⊗ by prior arrangement �X by prior
arrangement ⌶ ⌷ ♀ ⚲ 🏠 ℓ Ellis B Jones.
**Leisure** motorised carts for hire, buggies for hire,
trolley for hire, putting green, practice area.
**Location** 1.5m NE, off B5152
**Hotel** ★★★(red)⚏ Nunsmere Hall Country
House Hotel, Tarporley Rd, Oakmere,
SANDIWAY ☎ 01606 889100 32 ⇋ ℟

## DISLEY
Map 07 SJ98

**Disley** Stanley Hall Ln, Jacksons Edge SK12 2JX
☎ 01663 762071
Parkland/moorland course with trees. Often breezy. Good
views. Testing hole: 3rd (par 5).
*18 holes, 6015yds, Par 71, SSS 69, Course record 63.*
*Club membership 500.*

**Visitors** contact in advance, may not normally play at
weekends.
**Societies** by prior arrangement.
**Green Fees** £25 per day (£30 weekends).
**Facilities** ⊗ ⌷ ♀ ⚲ 🏠 ⅋ ℓ Andrew Esplin.
**Leisure** trolley for hire, putting green, practice area.
**Location** NW side of village off A6
**Hotel** ★★★ 67% Bramhall Moat House, Bramhall Ln
South, BRAMHALL
☎ 0161 439 8116 65 ⇋ ℟

## ELLESMERE PORT
Map 07 SJ47

**Ellesmere Port** Chester Rd, Hooton L66 1QF
☎ 0151 339 7689
Municipal parkland course with natural hazards of woods,
brook and ponds.
*18 holes, 6432yds, Par 71, SSS 71, Course record 66.*
*Club membership 300.*
**Visitors** must book with professional & send a deposit.
**Societies** by arrangement with professional.
**Green Fees** not confirmed.
**Facilities** ♀ ⚲ 🏠 ⅋ ℓ David Yates.
**Leisure** squash, putting green,practice area,trolley hire.
**Location** NW side of town centre on A41
**Hotel** ★★★ 66% Woodhey Hotel, Welsh Rd, Little
Sutton, WIRRAL ☎ 0151 339 5121 53 ⇋ ℟

## FRODSHAM
Map 07 SJ57

**Frodsham** Simons Ln WA6 6HE ☎ 01928 732159
Undulating parkland course with pleasant views from all
parts. Emphasis on accuracy over the whole course, the long
and difficult par 5 18th necessitating a drive across water to
the green. Crossed by two footpaths so extreme care needed.
*18 holes, 6298yds, Par 70, SSS 70.*
*Club membership 600.*
**Visitors** must contact in advance.
**Societies** telephone for bookings.
**Green Fees** £18 per day (£25/£20 weekends & bank
holidays).
**Facilities** ⊗ ⌷ ⌶ ⌷ ♀ ⚲ 🏠 ⅋ ℓ Graham Tonge.
**Leisure** motorised carts for hire, buggies for hire, trolley
for hire, putting green, practice area.
**Location** 1.5m SW
**Hotel** ★★★ 66% Forest Hills Hotel & Leisure
Complex, Bellemonte Rd, Overton Hill,
FRODSHAM ☎ 01928 735255 57 ⇋ ℟

## HELSBY
Map 07 SJ47

**Helsby** Towers Ln WA6 0JB ☎ 01928 722021
Quiet parkland course with many trees, natural hazards and a
very challenging final three holes.
*18 holes, 6229yds, Par 70, SSS 70.*
*Club membership 590.*
**Visitors** weekends and bank holidays with member only.
**Societies** Tue & Thu. Booking through Hon Secretary.
**Green Fees** £27 per day; £20 per round.
**Facilities** ⊗ ⌷ ⌶ ⌷ ♀ ⚲ 🏠 ⅋ ℓ Matthew Jones.
**Leisure** trolley for hire, putting green, practice area.
**Location** 1m S off A56
**Hotel** ★★★★(red) The Chester Grosvenor Hotel,
Eastgate, CHESTER
☎ 01244 324024 86 ⇋ ℟

## KNUTSFORD     Map 07 SJ77

**Heyrose** Budworth Rd, Tabley WA16 0HY
☎ 01565 733664
An 18-hole course in wooded and gently undulating terrain.
The par 3 16th (237yrds), bounded by a small river in a
wooded valley, is an interesting and testing hole - one of the
toughest par 3s in Cheshire. Both the course and the
comfortable clubhouse have attractive views.
*18 holes, 6510yds, Par 73, SSS 71, Course record 66.*
*Club membership 600.*

| | |
|---|---|
| **Visitors** | not before 3pm Sat, ladies priority Wed and seniors priority Thu am. |
| **Societies** | must contact in advance. |
| **Green Fees** | £24 per day; £19 per round (£29/£24 weekends & bank holidays). |
| **Facilities** | ⊗ ⓑ 🏌 ♀ ⚑ 🏠 ☂ Martin Redrup. |
| **Leisure** | trolley for hire, putting green, practice area & bunker. |
| **Location** | 1.5m from junc 19 on M6 |
| **Hotel** | ★★★★ 64% Cottons Hotel, Manchester Rd, KNUTSFORD ☎ 01565 650333 82 ⇔ ☛ |

---

**Knutsford** Mereheath Ln WA16 6HS ☎ 01565 633355
Parkland course set in a beautiful old deer park. It demands
some precise iron play.
*9 holes, 6288yds, Par 70, SSS 70.*
*Club membership 230.*

| | |
|---|---|
| **Visitors** | are not permitted weekends and restricted Wed. Must contact in advance. |
| **Green Fees** | not confirmed. |
| **Facilities** | ♀ ⚑ |
| **Location** | N side of town centre off A50 |
| **Hotel** | ★★★★ 64% Cottons Hotel, Manchester Rd, KNUTSFORD ☎ 01565 650333 82 ⇔ ☛ |

---

*Mere Golf & Country Club* Chester Rd, Mere
WA16 6LJ ☎ 01565 830155
A gracious parkland championship course designed by
James Braid in the Cheshire sand belt, with several holes
close to a lake. The round has a tight finish with four
testing holes.
*18 holes, 6817yds, Par 71, SSS 73, Course record 64.*
*Club membership 540.*

| | |
|---|---|
| **Visitors** | must contact in advance. |
| **Societies** | Mon,Tue & Thu only by prior arrangement. |
| **Green Fees** | not confirmed. |
| **Facilities** | ♀ ⚑ 🏠 ☂ Peter Eyre. |
| **Leisure** | hard tennis courts, heated indoor swimming pool, squash, fishing, sauna, solarium, gymnasium, floating ball drive range, petrol buggies. |
| **Location** | 1m E of junc 19 of M6 |
| **Hotel** | ★★★★ 64% Cottons Hotel, Manchester Rd, KNUTSFORD ☎ 01565 650333 82 ⇔ ☛ |

## LYMM     Map 07 SJ68

**Lymm** Whitbarrow Rd WA13 9AN
☎ 01925 752177 & 755020
First ten holes are gently undulating with the Manchester
Ship Canal running alongside the 9th hole. The remaining
holes are comparatively flat.
*18 holes, 6304yds, Par 71, SSS 70.*
*Club membership 650.*

| | |
|---|---|
| **Visitors** | may not play at weekends except with member. Must contact in advance. |
| **Societies** | Wed only, must contact in advance. |
| **Green Fees** | £20 per day. |
| **Facilities** | ⊗ ⓜ ⓑ 🏌 ♀ ⚑ 🏠 ☂ Steve McCarthy. |
| **Leisure** | trolley for hire, putting green, practice area. |
| **Location** | 0.5m N off A6144 |
| **Hotel** | ★★★ 61% Lymm Hotel, Whitbarrow Rd, LYMM ☎ 01925 752233 22 ⇔ ☛Annexe47 ⇔ ☛ |

## MACCLESFIELD     Map 07 SJ97

**Macclesfield** The Hollins SK11 7EA
☎ 01625 615845 (Secretary) & 616952 (Pro)
Very hilly heathland course situated on the edge of the
Pennines with excellent views across the Cheshire Plain. A
pleasant course providing a good test for players of all
abilities..
*18 holes, 5769yds, Par 70, SSS 68.*
*Club membership 620.*

| | |
|---|---|
| **Visitors** | apply in advance. |
| **Societies** | telephone initially. |
| **Green Fees** | £17 per day (£20 weekends & bank holidays). |
| **Facilities** | ⊗ ⓜ ⓑ 🏌 ♀ ⚑ 🏠 ☂ Tony Taylor. |
| **Leisure** | motorised carts for hire, trolley for hire, putting green, practice area. |
| **Location** | SE side of town centre off A523 |
| **Hotel** | ★★★ 63% Belgrade Hotel & Restaurant, Jackson Ln, Kerridge, Bollington, MACCLESFIELD ☎ 01625 573246 54 ⇔ ☛ |

---

**Tytherington** Dorchester Way, Tytherington SK10 2JP
☎ 01625 434562
Modern championship course in beautiful, mature
parkland setting with numerous water features. Testing
holes, notably the signature 12th hole (par 5), played
from an elevated tee with adjacent snaking ditch and a
lake guarding the green. Headquarters of the Women's
European Tour and venue of the WPGET English Open
and County matches. Country club facilities.
*18 holes, 6750yds, Par 72, SSS 72.*
*Club membership 3100.*

| | |
|---|---|
| **Visitors** | advisable to contact in advance and be of handicap standard. |
| **Societies** | weekdays only by prior arrangement. |
| **Green Fees** | £35 per day; £25 per 18 hole (£40/£30 weekends). Prices under review. |
| **Facilities** | ⊗ ⓜ ⓑ 🏌 ♀ ⚑ 🏠 ☂ John Garner. |
| **Leisure** | motorised carts for hire, buggies for hire, trolley for hire, driving range, putting green, practice area. |
| **Location** | 1m N of Macclesfield off A523 |
| **Hotel** | ★★★★ 60% Shrigley Hall Golf & Country Club, Shrigley Park, POTT SHRIGLEY ☎ 01625 575757 156 ⇔ ☛ |

## NANTWICH     Map 07 SJ65

**Reaseheath Research Course** Reaseheath College CW5 6DF
☎ 01270 625131
The course at Reaseheath is attached to Reaseheath College,
which is one of the major centres of greenkeeper training in
the UK. It is a short 9-hole which can only be played with a
member. ▶

*9 holes, 1618yds, Par 60, SSS 55, Course record 62.*
*Club membership 250.*

| | |
|---|---|
| **Societies** | by prior arrangement, apply in writing. |
| **Location** | 1.5m NE of Nantwich, off A51 |

## POTT SHRIGLEY                                    Map 07 SJ97

***Shrigley Hall Hotel*** Shrigley Park SK10 5SB
☎ 01625 575755 & 575757
Parkland course set in 262-acre estate with breathtaking views
over the Peak District and Cheshire Plain. Designed by Donald
Steel, this championship standard course provides a real
sporting challenge while the magnificent hotel provides a
wealth of sporting facilities as well as accommodation and food.
*18 holes, 6305yds, Par 71, SSS 71, Course record 68.*

| | |
|---|---|
| **Visitors** | must contact in advance by telephone. |
| **Societies** | contact in advance. |
| **Green Fees** | not confirmed. |
| **Facilities** | ♀ ♨ 🏠 ⛳ 🚩 𝌆 Granville Ogden. |
| **Leisure** | hard tennis courts, heated indoor swimming pool, squash, fishing, sauna, solarium, gymnasium. |
| **Hotel** | ★★★★ 60% Shrigley Hall Golf & Country Club, Shrigley Park, POTT SHRIGLEY ☎ 01625 575757 156 ➡ ❦ |

## POYNTON                                          Map 07 SJ98

***Davenport*** Worth Hall, Middlewood Rd SK12 1TS
☎ 01625 876951
Undulating parkland course. Extensive view over Cheshire
Plain from elevated 5th tee. Testing 17th hole, par 4.
*18 holes, 6027yds, Par 69, SSS 69, Course record 64.*
*Club membership 700.*

| | |
|---|---|
| **Visitors** | contact professional in advance (01625 858387). May not play Wed or Sat. |
| **Societies** | Tue and Thu only. Must apply in advance. |
| **Green Fees** | £24 (£30 weekends). |
| **Facilities** | ⊗ ⅷ ♨ 💪 ♀ ♨ 🏠 ⛳ 𝌆 Wyn Harris. |
| **Leisure** | trolley for hire, putting green, practice area. |
| **Location** | 1m E off A523 |
| **Hotel** | ★★★ 67% Bramhall Moat House, Bramhall Ln South, BRAMHALL ☎ 0161 439 8116 65 ➡ ❦ |

## PRESTBURY                                        Map 07 SJ97

**Prestbury** Macclesfield Rd SK10 4BJ
☎ 01625 828241 & 829388
Rather strenuous parkland course, undulating hills, with
many plateau greens looked after by one of only 7 Master
Greenkeepers in the world. The 9th hole has a
challenging uphill 3-tier green and the 17th is over a
valley. Host to county and inter-county championships as
well as England v USA competitions.
*18 holes, 6359yds, Par 71, SSS 71, Course record 64.*
*Club membership 702.*

| | |
|---|---|
| **Visitors** | must contact in advance and have an introduction from own club, with member only at weekends. |
| **Societies** | apply in writing, Thu only. |
| **Green Fees** | £32 per day. |
| **Facilities** | ⊗ ⅷ ♨ 💪 ♀ ♨ 🏠 ⛳ 𝌆 Nick Summerfield. |
| **Leisure** | motorised carts for hire, trolley for hire, driving range, putting green, practice area. |

| | |
|---|---|
| **Location** | S side of village off A538 |
| **Hotel** | ★★★★ 64% Mottram Hall Hotel, Wilmslow Rd, Prestbury, WILMSLOW ☎ 01625 828135 133 ➡ ❦ |

## RUNCORN                                          Map 07 SJ58

**Runcorn** Clifton Rd WA7 4SU ☎ 01928 574214
Parkland course with tree-lined fairways and easy walking.
Fine views over Mersey and Weaver valleys. Testing holes:
7th par 5; 14th par 5; 17th par 4.
*18 holes, 6035yds, Par 69, SSS 69, Course record 58.*
*Club membership 570.*

| | |
|---|---|
| **Visitors** | weekends restricted to playing with member only. |
| **Societies** | telephone in advance. |
| **Green Fees** | £18 per day. |
| **Facilities** | ⊗ ⅷ ♨ 💪 ♀ ♨ 🏠 𝌆 Steve Dooley. |
| **Leisure** | putting green. |
| **Location** | 1.25m S of Runcorn Station |
| **Hotel** | B Forte Posthouse Warrington/Runcorn, Wood Ln, Beechwood, RUNCORN ☎ 01928 714000 135 ➡ ❦ |

## SANDBACH                                         Map 07 SJ76

***Malkins Bank*** Betchton Rd, Malkins Bank CW11 0XN
☎ 01270 765931
Parkland course. Tight 13th hole with stream running through.
*18 holes, 6071yds, Par 70, SSS 69, Course record 65.*
*Club membership 500.*

| | |
|---|---|
| **Visitors** | no restrictions. Advisable to book in advance. |
| **Societies** | apply for booking form to course professional |
| **Green Fees** | not confirmed. |
| **Facilities** | ♀ ♨ 🏠 ⛳ 𝌆 David Wheeler. |
| **Leisure** | practice area, putting green, trolley hire. |
| **Location** | 1.5m SE off A533 |
| **Hotel** | ★★★ 63% Saxon Cross Hotel, Holmes Chapel Rd, SANDBACH ☎ 01270 763281 52 ➡ ❦ |

***Sandbach*** Middlewich Rd CW11 9BT ☎ 01270 762117
Meadowland, undulating course with easy walking. Limited
facilities.
*9 holes, 5598yds, Par 68, SSS 67.*
*Club membership 570.*

| | |
|---|---|
| **Visitors** | weekdays except Tue, and with member only weekends & bank holidays. Must contact in advance. |
| **Societies** | apply by letter. |
| **Green Fees** | not confirmed. |
| **Facilities** | ♀ ♨ |
| **Location** | 0.5m W on A533 |
| **Hotel** | ★★★ 63% Saxon Cross Hotel, Holmes Chapel Rd, SANDBACH ☎ 01270 763281 52 ➡ ❦ |

## SANDIWAY                                         Map 07 SJ67

**Sandiway** Chester Rd CW8 2DJ
☎ 01606 883247 (Secretary) & 883180 (Pro)
Delightful undulating woodland and heath golf with long
hills up to the 8th, 16th and 17th holes. Many dog-legged
and tree-lined holes give opportunities for the deliberate
fade or draw.

*18 holes, 6435yds, Par 70, SSS 72, Course record 65.*
*Club membership 700.*

| | |
|---|---|
| **Visitors** | book through professional, members have reserved tees 8.30-9.30 and 12.30-1.30 (11.30-12.30 winter). |
| **Societies** | book in advance through Secretary/Manager. |
| **Green Fees** | £35 per day; £30 per round (£40/£35 weekends and bank holidays). |
| **Facilities** | ⊗ ⅧⅢ ᴸ ⬛ ♀ ♐ 📷 ⛳ ℂ William Laird. |
| **Leisure** | trolley for hire, putting green, practice area. |
| **Location** | 1m E on A556 |
| **Hotel** | ★★★ 64% Hartford Hall Hotel, School Ln, Hartford, NORTHWICH ☎ 01606 75711 20 ⇆ |

## TARPORLEY
Map 07 SJ56

**Portal Golf & Country Club** Cobbler's Cross Ln CW6 0DJ
☎ 01829 733933 & 733884
Opened in 1991, there are two 18-hole courses here - Championship and Premier - and one 9-hole course - Arderne. They are set in mature, wooded parkland. There are fine views over the Cheshire Plain and numerous water hazards. The Championship 13th is just a short iron through trees, but its green is virtually an island surrounded by water.
*Championship Course: 18 holes, 7037yds, Par 73, SSS 74, Course record 64.*
*Premier Course: 18 holes, 6508yds, Par 71, SSS 72.*
*Arderne Course: 9 holes, 1724yds, Par 30.*
*Club membership 250.*

| | |
|---|---|
| **Visitors** | must contact in advance. |
| **Societies** | must pre-book. |
| **Green Fees** | Championship: £30 per round Mon-Sun. Premier: £22 per round (£25 weekends). |
| **Facilities** | ⊗ ⅧⅢ ᴸ ⬛ ♀ ♐ 📷 ⛳ ℂ David Clare. |
| **Leisure** | hard tennis courts, motorised carts for hire, buggies for hire, trolley for hire, driving range, putting green, practice area. |
| **Location** | Off A49 |
| **Hotel** | ★★★ 67% The Wild Boar, Whitchurch Rd, Beeston, TARPORLEY ☎ 01829 260309 37 ⇆ ℝ |

## WARRINGTON
Map 07 SJ68

**Birchwood** Kelvin Close, Birchwood WA3 7PB
☎ 01925 818819 & 816574
Very testing parkland course with many natural water hazards and the prevailing wind creating a problem on each hole. The 11th hole is particularly challenging.
*18 holes, 6727yds, Par 71, SSS 73, Course record 67.*
*Club membership 675.*

| | |
|---|---|
| **Visitors** | advisable to check with the professional to determine if course is being used. |
| **Societies** | Mon, Wed & Thu. Apply in writing, or telephone. |
| **Green Fees** | £26 per day; £19 per round (£34 Sat and bank holidays). |
| **Facilities** | ⊗ ⅧⅢ ᴸ ⬛ ♀ ♐ 📷 ℂ Paul McEwan. |
| **Leisure** | sauna, trolley for hire, putting green, practice area. |
| **Location** | 4m NE on A574 |

**Hotel** B Forte Posthouse Haydock, Lodge Ln, Newton-Le-Willows, HAYDOCK
☎ 01942 717878 136 ⇆ ℝ

**Leigh** Kenyon Hall, Broseley Ln, Culcheth WA3 4BG
☎ 01925 762943 (Secretary) & 762013 (Pro)
A pleasant, well-wooded parkland course. Any discrepancy in length is compensated by the wide variety of golf offered here. The course is well maintained and there is a comfortable clubhouse.
*18 holes, 5853yds, Par 69, SSS 68, Course record 64.*
*Club membership 550.*

| | |
|---|---|
| **Visitors** | contact professional for details. |
| **Societies** | Mon (ex bank holidays) & Tue, apply by telephone. |
| **Green Fees** | £26 per day/round (£33 weekends & bank holidays). |
| **Facilities** | ⊗ ⅧⅢ ᴸ ⬛ ♀ ♐ 📷 ℂ Andrew Baguley. |
| **Leisure** | trolley for hire, putting green, practice area. |
| **Location** | 5m NE off A579 |
| **Hotel** | ★★★ 65% Fir Grove Hotel, Knutsford Old Rd, WARRINGTON ☎ 01925 267471 40 ⇆ ℝ |

**Poulton Park** Dig Ln, Cinnamon Brow, Padgate WA2 0SH
☎ 01925 822802
Tight, flat parkland course with good greens and many trees. A straight drive off each tee is important. The 4/13th has a fairway curving to the left with water and out-of-bounds on left and trees on right.
*9 holes, 4978metres, Par 68, SSS 66, Course record 66.*
*Club membership 350.*

| | |
|---|---|
| **Visitors** | contact professional for details (01925 825220). |
| **Societies** | apply in advance. |
| **Green Fees** | £17 per day (£19 weekends). |
| **Facilities** | ⊗ ⅧⅢ ᴸ ⬛ ♀ ♐ 📷 ℂ Darren Newing. |
| **Leisure** | practice area, putting green. |
| **Location** | 3m from Warrington on A574 |
| **Hotel** | ★★★ 65% Fir Grove Hotel, Knutsford Old Rd, WARRINGTON ☎ 01925 267471 40 ⇆ ℝ |

**Walton Hall** Warrington Rd, Higher Walton WA4 5LU
☎ 01925 263061
A quiet, wooded, municipal parkland course on Walton Hall estate.
*18 holes, 6801yds, Par 72, SSS 73, Course record 70.*
*Club membership 400.*

| | |
|---|---|
| **Visitors** | must book 6 days in advance. |
| **Societies** | must contact in writing. |
| **Green Fees** | not confirmed. |
| **Facilities** | ♀ ♐ 📷 ⛳ ℂ Peter Maton. |
| **Leisure** | putting, trolley hire, driving range. |
| **Location** | 2m from junct 11 of M56 |
| **Hotel** | ★★★ 65% Fir Grove Hotel, Knutsford Old Rd, WARRINGTON ☎ 01925 267471 40 ⇆ ℝ |

**Warrington** Hill Warren, London Rd, Appleton WA4 5HR
☎ 01925 261775 (Secretary) & 265431 (Pro)
Meadowland, with varied terrain and natural hazards. Major work has recently been carried out on both the clubhouse and the course to ensure high standards. The course is a constant challenge with with ponds, trees and bunkers threatening the errant shot!
*18 holes, 6305yds, Par 72, SSS 70, Course record 61.*
*Club membership 840.*

▶

**Visitors**    contact in advance.
**Societies**    by prior arrangement with Secretary.
**Green Fees** £25 per day (£38 weekends & bank holidays).
**Facilities** ⊗ ⅢⅢ 🏌 💺 ♀ 👥 🛍 ⛳ ⚑ Reay Mackay.
**Leisure**    trolley for hire, putting green, practice area.
**Location**    2.5m S on A49
**Hotel**    ★★ 70% Rockfield Hotel, Alexandra Rd,
Grappenhall, WARRINGTON
☎ 01925 262898 6 ⇄ ⮕Annexe6 ⇄ ⮕

## WAVERTON      Map 07 SJ46

**Eaton** Guy Ln CH3 7PH ☎ 01244 335885 & 335826
Eaton Golf Club has moved to a new course. Designed by
Donald Steel, the course was opened in 1993 and is parkland
with a liberal covering of both mature trees and new planting
enhanced by natural water hazards. The old course at
Eccleston has been returned to nature.
*18 holes, 6562yds, Par 72, SSS 71, Course record 69.*
*Club membership 550.*
**Visitors**    must contact in advance particularly for
weekends.
**Societies**    must contact in advance. May not play weekends
or Wednesdays.
**Green Fees** £21 per round/day (£27 weekends & bank
holidays).
**Facilities** ⊗ ⅢⅢ 🏌 💺 ♀ 👥 🛍 ⚑ Neil Dunroe.
**Leisure**    motorised carts for hire, buggies for hire, trolley
for hire, putting, practice area.
**Location**    3m SE of Chester off A41
**Hotel**    ★★★★(red) The Chester Grosvenor Hotel,
Eastgate, CHESTER
☎ 01244 324024 86 ⇄ ⮕

## WIDNES      Map 07 SJ58

*St Michael Jubilee* Dunalk Rd WA8 8BS
☎ 0151 424 6230
Municipal parkland course dominated by the 'Stewards
Brook'. It is divided into two sections which are split by the
main road and joined by an underpass.
*18 holes, 2648yds, Par 69, SSS 68.*
**Visitors**    must be accompanied by member, contact in
advance and have an introduction from own
club.
**Societies**    must contact in writing.
**Green Fees** not confirmed.
**Facilities** ♀ 👥 🛍 ⚑
**Location**    W side of town centre off A562
**Hotel**    ★★★ 61% Everglades Park Hotel, Derby Rd,
WIDNES ☎ 0151 495 2040 32 ⇄ ⮕

*Widnes* Highfield Rd WA8 7DT ☎ 0151 424 2440
Parkland course, easy walking.
*18 holes, 5719yds, Par 69, SSS 68.*
**Visitors**    may play after 9am & after 4pm on competition
days. Must contact in advance.
**Societies**    must contact in writing.
**Green Fees** not confirmed.
**Facilities** ♀ 👥 🛍 ⚑ S Forster.
**Hotel**    ★★★ 61% Everglades Park Hotel, Derby Rd,
WIDNES
☎ 0151 495 2040 32 ⇄ ⮕

## WILMSLOW      Map 07 SJ88

**Mottram Hall** Wilmslow Rd, Mottram St Andrew SK10
4QT ☎ 01625 828135
Championship standard course with flat meadowland on the
front nine and undulating woodland on the back with well
guarded greens. The course was designed in 1989 and opened
in May 1991. The course is unusual as each half opens and
closes with Par 5's. The hotel offers many leisure facilities.
*18 holes, 7006yds, Par 72, SSS 74, Course record 65.*
*Club membership 500.*
**Visitors**    must contact in advance.
**Societies**    must contact in advance.
**Green Fees** £35 (£40 weekends).
**Facilities** ⊗ ⅢⅢ 🏌 💺 ♀ 👥 🛍 ⛳ ⚑ Tim Rastall.
**Leisure**    hard tennis courts, heated indoor swimming
pool, squash, sauna, solarium, gymnasium,
motorised carts for hire, buggies for hire, trolley
for hire, driving range, putting green, practice
area, clay pigeon shooting.
**Location**    On A538 between Wilmslow and Preston
**Hotel**    ★★★★ 64% Mottram Hall Hotel, Wilmslow
Rd, Prestbury, WILMSLOW
☎ 01625 828135 133 ⇄ ⮕

**Wilmslow** Great Warford, Mobberley WA16 7AY
☎ 01565 872148
A fine parkland championship course, of middle length,
fair to all classes of player and almost in perfect
condition.
*18 holes, 6607yds, Par 72, SSS 72, Course record 62.*
*Club membership 800.*
**Visitors**    must contact in advance.
**Societies**    Tue & Thu only application in writing.
**Green Fees** £40 per day; £30 per round (£50/£40
weekends).
**Facilities** ⊗ ⅢⅢ 🏌 💺 ♀ 👥 🛍 ⚑ John Nowicki.
**Leisure**    trolley for hire, putting green, practice area.
**Location**    2m SW off B5058
**Hotel**    ★★★ 70% Alderley Edge Hotel,
Macclesfield Rd, ALDERLEY EDGE
☎ 01625 583033 32 ⇄ ⮕

## WINSFORD      Map 07 SJ66

**Knights Grange** Grange Ln CW7 2PT
☎ 01606 552780
Municipal parkland course with water hazards.
*9 holes, 2719yds, Par 33, SSS 68.*
**Visitors**    24 hr booking system for weekly play, after
10am Wed for weekend bookings.
**Societies**    apply in writing.
**Green Fees** £3.50 per 18 holes; £2.70 per 9 holes
(£5.10/£3.95 weekends). Prices under review..
**Facilities** 💺 👥 ⚑ Graham Moore.
**Leisure**    hard and grass tennis courts, trolley for hire,
putting green, practice area, bowls.
**Location**    N side of town off A54
**Hotel**    ★★★ 64% Hartford Hall Hotel, School Ln,
Hartford, NORTHWICH
☎ 01606 75711 20 ⇄

# CORNWALL & ISLES OF SCILLY

## BODMIN
Map 02 SX06

**Lanhydrock** Lostwithiel Rd, Lanhydrock PL30 5AQ
☎ 01208 73600
Championship standard parkland/moorland course adjacent to
the National Trust property Lanhydrock house. Nestling in a
picturesque wooded valley of oak and birch, this undulating
course provides an exciting and enjoyable challenge to all
abilities with discreet use of water and bunkers.
*18 holes, 6185yds, Par 71, SSS 69.*
*Club membership 300.*
**Visitors**     no restrictions.
**Societies**    please telephone in advance.
**Green Fees** £33 per 36 holes; £23 per 18 holes. 7 Day ticket
            £100.
**Facilities**   ⊗ ⅷ ⅃ ▤ ♀ ⚘ 🏠 ⛳ 🛒 ℓ Jason Broadway.
**Leisure**     motorised carts for hire, buggies for hire, trolley
            for hire, putting green, practice area.
**Location**    1m S of Bodmin from B3268
**Hotel**       ★★★ 65% Restormel Lodge Hotel, Hillside
            Gardens, LOSTWITHIEL
            ☎ 01208 872223 21 ⇆ ℟Annexe12 ⇆

## BUDE
Map 02 SS20

**Bude & North Cornwall** Burn View EX23 8DA
☎ 01288 352006
Seaside links course with natural sand bunkers, superb greens
and breathtaking views. Club established in 1893.
*18 holes, 6205yds, Par 71, SSS 70.*
*Club membership 1000.*
**Visitors**     book by telephone 6 days in advance for starting
            time - or before 6 days with a deposit.
**Societies**    apply in writing or telephone.
**Green Fees** £20 per day (£25 per round weekends & bank
            holidays).
**Facilities**   ⊗ ⅷ ⅃ ▤ ♀ ⚘ 🏠 ℓ John Yeo.
**Leisure**     trolley for hire, putting green, practice area.
**Location**    N side of town
**Hotel**       ★★ 66% Camelot Hotel, Downs View, BUDE
            ☎ 01288 352361 21 ⇆ ℟

## BUDOCK VEAN
Map 02 SW73

**Budock Vean Golf & Country House Hotel** Mawnan Smith
TR11 5LG ☎ 01326 250288
Set in 65 acres of mature grounds with a private foreshore to
the Helford River, this undulating parkland course has a
tough par 4 5th hole (456yds) which dog-legs at halfway
around an oak tree.
*9 holes, 2657yds, Par 68, SSS 65, Course record 61.*
*Club membership 200.*
**Visitors**     must contact in advance.
**Societies**    apply in writing or telephone in advance.
**Green Fees** £14 per day (£18 Sun & bank holidays).
**Facilities**   ⊗ ⅷ ⅃ ▤ ♀ ⚘ 🏠 ⛳ 🛒
**Leisure**     hard tennis courts, heated indoor swimming
            pool, motorised carts for hire, buggies for hire,
            trolley for hire, putting green, practice area.
**Location**    1.5m SW

**Hotel**       ★★★ 73% Budock Vean Hotel, MAWNAN
            SMITH ☎ 01326 250288 58 ⇆ ℟

## CAMBORNE
Map 02 SW64

**Tehidy Park** TR14 0HH ☎ 01209 842208
A well-maintained parkland course providing good holiday golf.
*18 holes, 6241yds, Par 72, SSS 71, Course record 65.*
*Club membership 850.*
**Visitors**     must contact in advance and have a handicap
            certificate.
**Societies**    telephone followed by letter.
**Green Fees** £22 per day; £16 per round (£32/£27 weekends).
**Facilities**   ⊗ ⅷ ⅃ ▤ ♀ ⚘ 🏠 ⛳ ℓ James Dumbreck.
**Leisure**     motorised carts for hire, trolley for hire, putting
            green, practice area.
**Location**    On Portreath/Pool road, 2m S of Camborne
**Hotel**       ★★★ 66% Penventon Hotel, REDRUTH
            ☎ 01209 214141 50 ⇆ ℟

## CARLYON BAY
Map 02 SX05

**Carlyon Bay Hotel** Sea Rd PL25 3RD
☎ 01726 814250
Championship-length, cliff-top course moving into
parkland. Magnificent views surpassed only by the
quality of the course. The 230-yard (par 3) 18th with
railway and road out-of-bounds, holds the player's
interest to the end.
*18 holes, 6549yds, Par 72, SSS 71, Course record 66.*
*Club membership 500.*
**Visitors**     no restrictions.
**Societies**    must contact in advance.
**Green Fees** £20 per round £5 per extra round.
**Facilities**   ⊗ ⅷ by prior arrangement ⅃ ▤ ♀ ⚘ 🏠
            ⛳ 🛒 ℓ Nigel Sears.
**Leisure**     hard tennis courts, outdoor and indoor
            heated swimming pools, sauna, solarium,
            motorised carts for hire, buggies for hire,
            trolley for hire, putting green, practice area.
**Hotel**       ★★★★ 73% Carlyon Bay Hotel, Sea Rd,
            Carlyon Bay, ST AUSTELL
            ☎ 01726 812304 73 ⇆ ℟

## CONSTANTINE BAY
Map 02 SW87

**Trevose** PL28 8JB ☎ 01841 520208
A pleasant holiday seaside course with early holes close
to the sea on excellent springy turf. A championship
course affording varying degrees of difficulty appealing
to both the professional and higher handicap player. It is
a good test with well-positioned bunkers, and a
meandering stream, and the wind playing a decisive role
in preventing low scoring. Self-catering accommodation
is available at the club.
*Championship Course: 18 holes, 6461yds, Par 71, SSS
71, Course record 67.*
*Short Course: 9 holes, 1360yds, Par 29, SSS 29.*
*New Course: 9 holes, 3031yds, Par 35, SSS 35.*
*Club membership 1200.*
**Visitors**     must contact in advance.
**Societies**    telephone or write to the secretary.
**Green Fees** contact for details.
**Facilities**   ⊗ ⅷ ⅃ ▤ ♀ ⚘ 🏠 ⛳ 🛒 ℓ Gary Alliss. ▶

| Leisure | hard tennis courts, heated outdoor swimming pool, motorised carts for hire, buggies for hire, trolley for hire, putting green, practice area. |
|---|---|
| Location | N of Constantine Bay, off B3276 |
| Hotel | ★★★ 77% Treglos Hotel, CONSTANTINE BAY ☎ 01841 520727 44 ⇥ ℟ |

## FALMOUTH Map 02 SW83

*Falmouth* Swanpool Rd TR11 5BQ ☎ 01326 311262
Seaside/parkland course with outstanding coastal views. Sufficiently bunkered to punish any inaccurate shots. Five acres of practice grounds.
*18 holes, 5680yds, Par 70, SSS 68, Course record 61.*
*Club membership 600.*

| Visitors | restricted play on competition days. Must contact in advance. |
|---|---|
| Societies | must contact in advance. |
| Green Fees | not confirmed. |
| Facilities | ♀⊼🏠⚲ℓ David J Short. |
| Leisure | practice fields, putting green,trolleys. |
| Location | SW side of town centre |
| Hotel | ★★★⚑ 76% Penmere Manor, Mongleath Rd, FALMOUTH ☎ 01326 211411 38 ⇥ ℟ |

## HOLYWELL BAY Map 02 SW75

*Holywell Bay* TR8 5PW ☎ 01637 830095
Holywell Golf Club is situated beside a family fun park with many amenities. The course is an 18 hole Par 3 with excellent sea views. Fresh Atlantic winds make the course hard to play and there are several tricky holes, particularly the 18th over the trout pond. The site also has and excellent 18 hole Pitch & Putt course for the whole family.
*18 holes, 2784yds, Par 61, Course record 58.*
*Club membership 100.*

| Visitors | no restrictions. |
|---|---|
| Societies | telephone in advance. |
| Green Fees | £7, £3.90 pitch & putt. |
| Facilities | ⊗🕭 ▟⚲🏠⚲ |
| Leisure | hard tennis courts, heated outdoor swimming pool, fishing, putting green, practice area, 18 hole pitch & putt, fun park. |
| Location | Off A3075 Newquay/Perranporth road |
| Hotel | ★★ 67% Crantock Bay Hotel, West Pentire, CRANTOCK ☎ 01637 830229 34 ⇥ ℟ |

## LAUNCESTON Map 02 SX38

*Launceston* St Stephens PL15 8HF ☎ 01566 773442
Undulating parkland course with views over Tamar Valley to Dartmoor and Bodmin Moor. Dominated by the 'The Hill' up which the 8th and 11th fairways rise, and on which the 8th, 9th, 11th and 12th greens sit.
*18 holes, 6407yds, Par 70, SSS 71, Course record 65.*
*Club membership 800.*

| Visitors | must contact in advance, may not play weekends Apr-Oct. |
|---|---|
| Societies | telephone in first instance. |
| Green Fees | £20 per day. |
| Facilities | ⊗∭🕭 ▟⚲⊼🏠⚲ℓ John Tozer. |
| Leisure | trolley for hire, putting green. |

| Location | NW side of town centre on B3254 |
|---|---|
| Hotel | ★★ 60% Eagle House, Castle St, LAUNCESTON ☎ 01566 772036 14 ⇥ ℟ |

## LELANT Map 02 SW53

*West Cornwall* TR26 3DZ ☎ 01736 753319 753401
A seaside links with sandhills and lovely turf adjacent to the Hayle estuary and St Ives Bay. A real test of the player's skill, especially 'Calamity Corner' starting at the 5th on the lower land by the River Hayle. A small (3 hole) course is available for practice.
*18 holes, 5884yds, Par 69, SSS 69, Course record 63.*
*Club membership 748.*

| Societies | must apply in writing. |
|---|---|
| Green Fees | £20 per day (£25 weekends and bank holidays). |
| Facilities | ⊗∭🕭 ▟⚲⊼🏠⚲ℓ Paul Atherton. |
| Leisure | trolley for hire, putting green, practice area. |
| Location | N side of village off A3074 |
| Hotel | ★★ 66% Boskerris Hotel, Boskerris Rd, Carbis Bay, ST IVES ☎ 01736 795295 13rm(11 ⇥ ℟)Annexe5 ⇥ ℟ |

## LOOE Map 02 SX25

*Looe* Widegates PL13 1PX ☎ 01503 240239
Exposed and somewhat windy course on high moorland; designed by Harry Vardon in 1935. Easy walking. Fine views over Looe coastline.
*18 holes, 5940yds, Par 70, SSS 68.*
*Club membership 600.*

| Visitors | booking must be made in advance, no limitations subject to availability. |
|---|---|
| Societies | telephone in advance, booking to be confirmed in writing. |
| Green Fees | £24 per 36/27 holes; £18 per 18 holes. |
| Facilities | 🕭 ▟⚲⊼🏠⚲ℓ Alistair Macdonald. |
| Leisure | motorised carts for hire, buggies for hire, trolley for hire, putting green, practice area. |
| Location | 3.5m NE off B3253 |
| Hotel | ★★ 68% Commonwood Manor Hotel, St Martin's Rd, LOOE ☎ 01503 262929 11 ⇥ ℟ |

## LOSTWITHIEL Map 02 SX15

*Lostwithiel Golf & Country Club* Lower Polscoe PL22 0HQ ☎ 01208 873550
An undulating, parkland course with water hazards. Overlooked by Restormel Castle and the Rover Fowey flows alongside the course. Driving range.
*18 holes, 5984yds, Par 72, SSS 71.*
*Club membership 500.*

| Visitors | must contact in advance. |
|---|---|
| Societies | contact in advance. |
| Green Fees | summer £18 per round (£20 weekend). |
| Facilities | ⊗∭🕭 ▟⚲⊼🏠⚲⛳❤ℓ Tony Nash. |
| Leisure | hard tennis courts, heated indoor swimming pool, fishing, sauna, gymnasium, trolley for hire, driving range, putting green, practice area. |
| Location | 1m outside Lostwithiel off A390 |
| Hotel | ★★ 66% Lostwithiel Golf & Country Club, Lower Polscoe, LOSTWITHIEL ☎ 01208 873550 18 ⇥ ℟ |

# LOSTWITHIEL
## Hotel
### GOLF & COUNTRY CLUB

*Set in richly wooded hills above the banks of the River Fowey. An 18 - hole parkland golf course, tennis courts, heated indoor swimming pool, bar and restaurant facilities. Eighteen bedrooms of great charm and character converted from Cornish stone farm buildings.*

## 50% OFF GREEN FEES
Concessionary rates at surrounding courses. Any golfing itinerary arranged.

**Full leisure inc. tennis, swimming & gym.
Riding & fishing nearby**

# Tel : 01208 873550
**Lostwithiel, Cornwall. PL22 0HQ**

## MAWGAN PORTH      Map 02 SW86

**Merlin** TR8 4AD ☎ 01841 540222
A heathland course. The most challenging hole is the Par 5 3rd with out of bounds along the lefthand side.
*18 holes, 5227yds, Par 67, SSS 67.*
**Visitors**     no restrictions.
**Societies**    telephone in advance.
**Green Fees** £10 per day.
**Facilities**   ⊗ ⅷ ⤢ ♨ ♀ ⚘ 🏠 ⚑
**Leisure**      motorised carts for hire, trolley for hire, driving range, putting green, practice area.
**Hotel**       ★★ 66% Tredragon Hotel, MAWGAN PORTH ☎ 01637 860213 27 ⇥ ↾

## MAWNAN SMITH      See **Budock Vean**

## MULLION      Map 02 SW61

**Mullion** Cury TR12 7BP ☎ 01326 240685
Founded in 1895, a clifftop and links course with panoramic views over Mounts Bay. A steep downhill slope on 6th and the 10th descends to the beach with a deep ravine alongside the green. Most southerly course in the British Isles.
*18 holes, 6022yds, Par 69, SSS 69, Course record 69.*
*Club membership 654.*
**Visitors**     preferable to contact in advance, restricted during club competitions.
**Societies**    must contact in advance.

**Green Fees** £20 per day/round.
**Facilities**   ⊗ ⅷ ⤢ ♨ ♀ ⚘ 🏠 ⚑ ⛄ Phil Blundell.
**Leisure**      motorised carts for hire, buggies for hire, trolley for hire, putting green, practice area.
**Location**   1.5m NW of Mullion, off A3083
**Hotel**       ★★★ 74% Polurrian Hotel, MULLION ☎ 01326 240421 39 ⇥ ↾

## NEWQUAY      Map 02 SW86

**Newquay** Tower Rd TR7 1LT
☎ 01637 874354 & 872091
Gently undulating seaside course running parallel to the beach and open to wind. Breathtaking views.
*18 holes, 6140yds, Par 69, SSS 69, Course record 63.*
*Club membership 700.*
**Visitors**     please telephone in advance.
**Societies**    apply in writing or telephone.
**Green Fees** £20 per round/day.
**Facilities**   ⊗ ⅷ ⤢ ♨ ♀ ⚘ 🏠 ⚑ ⛄ Anfrew J Cullen.
**Leisure**      hard tennis courts, trolley for hire, putting green, practice area.
**Location**   W side of town
**Hotel**       ★★ 63% Philema Hotel, 1 Esplanade Rd, Pentire, NEWQUAY ☎ 01637 872571 27 ⇥ ↾

**Treloy** TR8 4JN ☎ 01637 878554
An Executive course constructed in 1991 to American specifications with large contoured and mounded greens. Offers an interesting round for all categories of player.
*9 holes, 2143yds, Par 32, SSS 31.*
**Visitors**     no restrictions.
**Societies**    telephone in advance.
**Green Fees** £11.50 per 18 holes; £7.50 per 9 holes.
**Facilities**   ⤢ ♨ ♀ ⚘ 🏠 ⚑
**Location**   On A3059 Newquay to St Columb Major Road
**Hotel**       ★★ 70% Whipsiderry Hotel, Trevelgue Road, Porth, NEWQUAY ☎ 01637 874777 24rm(5 ⇥ 14 ↾)

## PADSTOW      See **Constantine Bay**

## PERRANPORTH      Map 02 SW75

**Perranporth** Budnick Hill TR6 0AB ☎ 01872 573701
There are three testing par 5 holes on the links course (2nd, 5th, 11th) and a fine view over Perranporth Beach from all holes.
*18 holes, 6288yds, Par 72, SSS 72, Course record 63.*
*Club membership 618.*
**Visitors**     no reserved tee times.
**Societies**    by prior arrangement.
**Green Fees** £20 per day (£25 weekends & bank holidays).
**Facilities**   ⊗ ⅷ ⤢ ♨ ♀ ⚘ 🏠 ⚑ ⛄ D Michell.
**Leisure**      trolley for hire, putting green, practice area.
**Location**   0.75m NE on B3285
**Hotel**       ★★ 63% Beach Dunes Hotel, Ramoth Way, Reen Sands, PERRANPORTH ☎ 01872 572263 6rm(5 ⇥ ↾)Annexe3 ⇥ ↾

## PRAA SANDS                          Map 02 SW52

**Praa Sands** Germoe Cross Roads TR20 9TQ
☎ 01736 763445
A beautiful parkland course with outstanding sea views from
every tee and green.
*9 holes, 4104yds, Par 62, SSS 60, Course record 59.*
*Club membership 220.*
**Visitors**    restricted Sun 8-12.30pm.
**Societies**   telephone for details.
**Green Fees** £14 per 18 holes.
**Facilities**  ⊗ ⫼ ﹗ ⬛ ♥ ⚲ ⚵ ⛿ ☂
**Leisure**     trolley for hire, putting green, practice area.
**Location**    (A394 midway between Penzance/Helston)
**Hotel**       ★★▲▲ 76% Nansloe Manor Hotel, Meneage
                Rd, HELSTON ☎ 01326 574691 7rm(6 ⇌ ☏)

## ROCK                               Map 02 SW97

*St Enodoc* PL27 6LB ☎ 01208 863216
Classic links courses with huge sand hills and rolling
fairways. James Braid laid out the original 18 holes in
1907 and changes were made in 1922 and 1935. English
County Final and English Ladies Closed Amateur
Championships held recently. On the Church, the 10th is
the toughest par 4 on the course and on the 6th is a truly
enormous sand hill known as the Himalayas.
*Church Course: 18 holes, 6207yds, Par 69, SSS 70,*
*Course record 65.*
*Holywell Course: 18 holes, 4142yds, Par 63, SSS 61.*
*Club membership 1500.*
**Visitors**    may not play on bank holidays. Must have a
                handicap certificate of 24 or below for
                Church Course. Must contact in advance.
**Societies**   must contact in writing.
**Green Fees** not confirmed.
**Facilities**  ♀ ⚲ ⚵ ⛿ ☂ ⛿ Nick Williams.
**Leisure**     putting, buggies/trolleys hire.
**Location**    W side of village
**Hotel**       ★★ 63% St Enodoc Hotel, ROCK
                ☎ 01208 863394 13 ⇌ ☏

## ST AUSTELL                         Map 02 SX05

*Porthpean* Porthpean PL26 6AY ☎ 01726 64613
A challenging 9-hole course which plays out at over 6500
yards. There are spectacular views over St Austell Bay. There
is also an 8-bay covered and floodlit driving range.
*9 holes, 3266yds, Par 37, SSS 37.*
*Club membership 180.*
**Visitors**    no restrictions
**Societies**   telephone in advance.
**Green Fees** not confirmed.
**Facilities**  ♀ ⚲ ⚵ ☂
**Leisure**     8 bay covered & floodlit driving range.
**Location**    1.5m from St Austell by-pass
**Hotel**       ★★ 66% The Pier House, Harbour Front,
                Charlestown, ST AUSTELL
                ☎ 01726 67955 12 ⇌ ☏Annexe13 ☏

**St Austell** Tregongeeves Ln PL26 7DS ☎ 01726 72649
Very interesting inland parkland course designed by James
Braid and offering glorious views of the surrounding
countryside. Undulating, well-covered with tree plantations

and well-bunkered. Notable holes are 8th (par 4) and 16th
(par 3).
*18 holes, 6089yds, Par 69, SSS 69, Course record 67.*
*Club membership 700.*
**Visitors**    advisable to contact in advance, weekend play is
                limited.
**Societies**   must apply in writing.
**Green Fees** £15 per round (£18 weekends & bank holidays).
**Facilities**  ⊗ ⫼ ﹗ ⬛ ♥ ⚲ ⚵ ⛿ Mark Rowe.
**Leisure**     trolley for hire, putting green, practice area.
**Location**    1m W of St Austell on A390
**Hotel**       ★★★ 65% Porth Avallen Hotel, Sea Rd,
                Carlyon Bay, ST AUSTELL
                ☎ 01726 812802 24 ⇌ ☏

## ST IVES                            Map 02 SW54

**Tregenna Castle Hotel, Golf & Country Club** TR26 2DE
☎ 01736 797381
Parkland course surrounding a castellated hotel and
overlooking St Ives Bay and harbour.
*18 holes, 3464, Par 59, SSS 57.*
*Club membership 150.*
**Visitors**    no booking needed.
**Societies**   telephone for details.
**Green Fees** £17.50 per day; £12.50 per round.
**Facilities**  ⊗ ⫼ by prior arrangement ♥ ⚲ ⚵ ☂ ⇌
**Leisure**     trolley for hire.
**Location**    From A30 Penzance road turn off just past Hayle
                onto A3074
**Hotel**       ★★★ 69% Carbis Bay Hotel, Carbis Bay,
                ST IVES ☎ 01736 795311 30 ⇌ ☏

## ST JUST (NEAR LAND'S END)          Map 02 SW33

*Cape Cornwall Golf & Country Club* Cape Cornwall
TR19 7NL ☎ 01736 788611
Coastal parkland, walled course. The walls are an integral
part of its design. Country club facilities.
*18 holes, 5650yds, Par 70, SSS 68, Course record 69.*
*Club membership 700.*
**Visitors**    may not play before 11.30am at weekends.
**Societies**   must contact in advance.
**Green Fees** not confirmed.
**Facilities**  ♀ ⚲ ⚵ ☂ ⇌ ⛿ Bob Hamilton.
**Leisure**     heated indoor swimming pool, sauna, solarium,
                gymnasium, trolley for hire, driving range,
                children's area.
**Location**    1m W of St Just
**Hotel**       ★★★▲▲ 61% Higher Faugan Hotel, Newlyn,
                PENZANCE ☎ 01736 62076 11 ⇌ ☏

## ST MARY'S

*Isles of Scilly* TR21 0NF ☎ 01720 422692
Links course, glorious views.
*9 holes, 6001yds, Par 73, SSS 69.*
*Club membership 300.*
**Visitors**    only with member on Sun.
**Societies**   must apply in writing
**Green Fees** not confirmed.
**Facilities**  ♀ ⚲ ⚵ ☂
**Leisure**     putting,trolley hire,practice area.
**Location**    1m N of Hugh Town                          ▶

# St Mellion

## ST MELLION *Cornwall*
☎ 01579 351351

**Map 02 SX36**

*John Ingham writes:* Five miles north west of Saltash, St Mellion is set in Sherlock Holmes country, not far from the famous moor. Opened in 1986, the big course was created by two farming brothers, Martin and Hermon Bond who decided the Tamar Valley, not far from Plymouth, deserved a golf course – and they were prepared to sacrifice their farm to achieve that end.

The first problem was to get hold of an architect who would not be overwhelmed by the problem of converting the rugged countryside into eighteen holes. They had set their hearts on a Jack Nicklaus layout and to ensure he would take on the task, they sent him a letter and a cheque, said to be for £1 million and their determination concentrated the mind of Nicklaus comprehensively!

I have known Tony Moore, the one-time professional here, for thirty odd years and he suggested I play the course, with his long-hitting son Bobby. But first we were to enjoy a dinner at the heart of this St Mellion International Golf & Country Club, which they thought, would be the ideal preparation for the task of facing a course with four holes in excess of 500 yards!

Tony's son Bobby was one of those strapping lads who lashed the ball miles. But in the first few holes he was missing the fairway, and lost four balls fairly quickly, putting me in what I thought was an unbeatable position. But his erratic play did not last, neither did my lead despite a birdie two at the short 11th, a delightful hole across water from a tee almost overlooked by the ancient church in the background. The two courses are both rugged tests. and St Mellion is home of the Benson & Hedges tournament.

When Jack Nicklaus played here he said: 'I knew it was going to be good, but not this good – it's everything I had hoped for and more ... St Mellion is potentially the finest course in Europe'. This may be true. But it is a tough one, and for some it's too severe a challenge.

| Visitors | no restrictions but dress code to be observed |
|---|---|
| Societies | please apply in writing |
| Green fees | on application; telephone 01579 351182 |
| Facilities | ⊗ ⅷ ᴸ ♣ ♀ ⇔ ᴧ ⌂ ⟟ driving range, putting green, ℓ (Andrew Milton/David Moon) motor carts, buggies, trolleys, caddy cars, practice area |
| Leisure | tennis courts, indoor swimming (heated), squash, snooker, health spa |
| Location | Saltash PL12 6SD 0.5m NW off A388 |

**36 holes. Nicklaus Course: 18 holes, 6651yds, Par72 SSS 72 Course record 63 (Carl Mason)**
**The Old Course: 18 holes, 5782yds, Par 68 SSS 68 Course record 64 (David Russell)**

### WHERE TO STAY AND EAT NEARBY

**HOTELS:**
**ST MELLION**
★★★ 65% St Mellion Hotel, ☎ 01579 351351. Annexe 24 ⇔ ↾

**LISKEARD**
★★ (Red)⬤⬤⬤ ≝ Well House, St Keyne ☎ 01579 342001. 7 ⇔ ↾

**RESTAURANTS:**
**CALSTOCK**
⬤⬤ Danescombe Valley, Lower Kelly ☎ 01822 832414

**Hotel**    ★★ 73% Tregarthens Hotel, Hugh Town, ST
MARY'S
☎ 01720 422540 28 ⇄ 🐾Annexe1 ⇄ 🐾

## ST MELLION                               Map 02 SX36

**ST MELLION**   See page 37

## SALTASH                                 Map 02 SX45

**China Fleet Country Club** PL12 6LJ ☎ 01752 848668
A parkland course with river views. The 14th tee shot has to
carry a lake of approximately 150yards.
*18 holes, 6551yds, Par 72, SSS 72, Course record 69.*
*Club membership 550.*
**Visitors**    may play anytime and can book up to 7 days in
advance.
**Societies**   telephone for provisional booking.
**Green Fees** £20 per day (£25 weekends).
**Facilities**  ⊗ ⅷ ⅃ 🍷 ♀ ⚐ 🐾 🏵 🛡 Robert Moore.
**Leisure**     hard tennis courts, heated indoor swimming
pool, squash, sauna, solarium, gymnasium,
trolley for hire, driving range, putting green,
practice area.
**Location**    1m from the Tamar Bridge
**Hotel**       B Granada Lodge, Callington Rd, Carkeel,
SALTASH
☎ Central Res 0800 555300 32 ⇄ 🐾

## TORPOINT                                Map 02 SX45

**Whitsand Bay Hotel Golf & Country Club** Portwrinkle
PL11 3BU ☎ 01503 230276 & 230900
Testing seaside course laid-out on cliffs overlooking
Whitsand Bay. Easy walking after 1st hole. The par 3 (3rd)
hole is acknowledged as one of the most attractive holes in
Cornwall.
*18 holes, 5796yds, Par 69, SSS 68, Course record 62.*
*Club membership 400.*
**Visitors**    visitors welcome.
**Societies**   must contact in advance.
**Green Fees** £15 per day/round (£17.50 weekends & bank
holidays).
**Facilities**  ⊗ ⅷ ⅃ 🍷 ♀ ⚐ 🐾 🏵 🛡 Stephen Poole.
**Leisure**     heated indoor swimming pool, sauna, solarium,
motorised carts for hire, buggies for hire, trolley
for hire, putting green, practice area.
**Location**    5m W off B3247
**Hotel**       ★★ 64% Whitsand Bay Hotel, Golf & Country
Club, Portwrinkle, TORPOINT
☎ 01503 230276 34rm(32 ⇄ 🐾)

## TRURO                                   Map 02 SW84

*Killiow Park* Killiow, Kea TR3 6AG ☎ 01872 70246
Picturesque parkland course with mature oaks and woodland
and five holes played across or around water hazards.
Floodlit, all-weather driving range.
*18 holes, 3542yds, Par 60.*
*Club membership 500.*
**Visitors**    may not play until after 10.30am at weekends.
**Societies**   apply in writing, limited catering facilities at
present.

**Green Fees** not confirmed.
**Facilities**  ♂ ⚐ 🛡
**Location**    3m SW of Truro, off A39
**Hotel**       ★★★ 66% Brookdale Hotel, Tregolls Rd,
TRURO ☎ 01872 73513 & 79305 22 ⇄

**Truro** Treliske TR1 3LG ☎ 01872 78684
Undulating parkland course with small greens requiring
accurate play. Lovely views over the cathedral city of Truro.
*18 holes, 5306yds, Par 66, SSS 66.*
*Club membership 900.*
**Visitors**    must have handicap certificate.
**Societies**   telephone for details.
**Green Fees** £18 per day (£22 weekends & bank holidays).
**Facilities**  ⊗ ⅷ ⅃ 🍷 ♀ ⚐ 🐾 🛡 Nigel Bicknell.
**Leisure**     motorised carts for hire, buggies for hire, trolley
for hire, putting green, small practice area.
**Location**    1.5m W on A390
**Hotel**       ★★★ 66% Brookdale Hotel, Tregolls Rd,
TRURO ☎ 01872 73513 & 79305 22 ⇄

## WADEBRIDGE                             Map 02 SW97

**St Kew** St Kew Highway PL30 3EF ☎ 01208 814500
An interesting, well-laid out 9-hole parkland course with 6
holes with water and 15 bunkers. In a picturesque setting
there are 10 par 4s and 8 par 3s. No handicap certificate
required but some experience of the game is essential.
*9 holes, 4543yds, Par 64, SSS 62.*
*Club membership 200.*
**Visitors**    no restrictions. Start time system in operation
allowing prebooking.
**Societies**   apply in writing, telephone or fax (same as
phone number).
**Green Fees** £12 per 18 holes; £7.50 per 9 holes. Weekly
ticket £50. Two weeks £80.
**Facilities**  ⊗ ⅷ ⅃ 🍷 ♀ ⚐ 🐾 🛡 Tony Pitts.
**Leisure**     fishing, buggies for hire, trolley for hire, driving
range, putting, pony trekking.
**Location**    2m N, main A39
**Hotel**       ★★ 69% Port Gaverne Hotel, PORT
GAVERNE
☎ 01208 880244 16 ⇄ 🐾Annexe3 ⇄ 🐾

# CUMBRIA

## ALSTON                                  Map 12 NY74

**Alston Moor** The Hermitage, Middleton in Teesdale Rd
CA9 3DB ☎ 01434 381675 & 381354
Parkland course with lush fairways and naturally interesting
greens.
*10 holes, 5518yds, Par 68, SSS 66, Course record 67.*
*Club membership 150.*
**Visitors**    usually turn up and play but some weekends
busy with competitions.
**Societies**   telephone or write in advance.
**Green Fees** £8 per day (£10 weekends and bank holidays).
**Facilities**  ⊗ by prior arrangement ⅷ by prior arrangement
♀ ⚐
**Leisure**     practice area.
**Location**    1 S of Alston on B6277

Hotel ★★ 68% Lowbyer Manor Country House
Hotel, ALSTON
☎ 01434 381230 8 ⊷ ♟Annexe4 ⊷

## APPLEBY-IN-WESTMORLAND    Map 12 NY62

**Appleby** Brackenber Moor CA16 6LP
☎ 01768 351432
This remotely situated heather and moorland course
offers interesting golf with the rewarding bonus of
several long par-4 holes that will be remembered. There
are superb views.
*18 holes, 5901yds, Par 68, SSS 68, Course record 63.*
*Club membership 800.*
Visitors    phone for details.
Societies    must contact in advance by letter.
Green Fees £12 per day (£16 weekends & bank holidays).
Facilities    ⊗ ⊪ ⊾ ⬛ ♀ ⚎ 📠 ⓵ Paul Jenkinson.
Leisure    trolley for hire, putting green, practice area.
Location    1m E of Appleby 0.5m off A66
Hotel    ★★★⚏ 73% Appleby Manor Country
House Hotel, Roman Rd, APPLEBY-IN-
WESTMORLAND
☎ 017683 51571 23 ⊷ ♟Annexe7 ⊷ ♞

## ASKAM-IN-FURNESS    Map 07 SD27

**Dunnerholme** Duddon Rd LA16 7AW ☎ 01229 462675
Unique 10-hole (18 tee) links course with view of Lakeland
hills, and a stream running through.
*10 holes, 6154yds, Par 72, SSS 70.*
*Club membership 450.*

# Swim, Bubble and Golf!

**Enjoy your par 68 round on
Appleby's eighteen beautiful
moorland holes (5915 yds), then it's
five-minutes by car to return to your
favourite Country House Hotel for a
refreshing swim and a relaxing
jacuzzi in the indoor leisure club,
followed by a superb meal in the
award-winning restaurant.**

*Phone 017683 51571 now for a free
colour brochure with full details of
the hotel, leisure club and prices.*

Best Western
★★★
73% ⊛ APPLEBY·MANOR
COUNTRY HOUSE HOTEL
*Roman Road
Appleby-in-Westmorland
Cumbria  CA16 6JB*
*Telephone: 017683 51571*

Visitors    restricted times on Sun.
Societies    apply in writing to the secretary.
Green Fees £12 per day (£15 weekends & bank holidays).
Facilities    ⊾ ⬛ ♀ ⚎
Leisure    putting green, practice area.
Location    1m N on A595
Hotel    ★★ 64% Lisdoonie Hotel, 307/309 Abbey Rd,
BARROW-IN-FURNESS
☎ 01229 827312 12 ⊷ ♞

## BARROW-IN-FURNESS    Map 07 SD26

**Barrow** Rakesmoor Ln, Hawcoat LA14 4QB
☎ 01229 825444
Pleasant course laid out two levels on meadowland with
extensive views of the nearby Lakeland fells. Upper level is
affected by easterly winds.
*18 holes, 6209yds, Par 71, SSS 70, Course record 66.*
*Club membership 620.*
Visitors    must be a member of a recognised golf club,
advisable to contact the professional regarding
tee time.
Societies    small groups ring professional for details, groups
over 12 apply to the secretary in advance.
Green Fees £15 per day/round (£25 weekends & bank
holidays).
Facilities    ⊗ ⊪ by prior arrangement ⊾ ⬛ ♀ ⚎ 📠
⓵ Neale Hyde.
Leisure    putting green, practice area.
Location    2m N off A590
Hotel    ★★ 64% Lisdoonie Hotel, 307/309 Abbey Rd,
BARROW-IN-FURNESS
☎ 01229 827312 12 ⊷ ♞

**Furness** Central Dr LA14 3LN ☎ 01229 471232
Links golf with a fairly flat first half but a much sterner
second nine played across subtle sloping ground. There are
good views of the Lakes, North Wales and the Isle of Man.
*18 holes, 6363yds, Par 71, SSS 71, Course record 65.*
*Club membership 630.*
Visitors    must contact the secretary in advance.
Societies    apply in writing, must be member of recognised
club with handicap certificate.
Green Fees £17 per day.
Facilities    ⊗ ⊪ ⊾ ⬛ ♀ ⚎ 📠
Leisure    trolley for hire, putting green, practice area.
Location    1.75 W of town centre off A590
Hotel    ★★ 64% Lisdoonie Hotel, 307/309 Abbey Rd,
BARROW-IN-FURNESS
☎ 01229 827312 12 ⊷ ♞

## BOWNESS-ON-WINDERMERE    Map 07 SD49

**Windermere** Cleabarrow LA23 3NB ☎ 015394 43123
Enjoyable holiday golf on a short, slightly hilly but
sporting course in this delightful area of the Lake District
National Park, with superb views of the mountains as the
backcloth to the lake and the course.
*18 holes, 5006yds, Par 67, SSS 65, Course record 58.*
*Club membership 1043.*
Visitors    contact pro shop 7 days before day of play,
9-12 & 2-4.30 by arrangement.
Societies    by arrangement contact the secretary.
Green Fees £23 per day (£28 weekends & bank
holidays). ▶

## TARN END HOUSE HOTEL    AA ★★

**Talkin Tarn, Brampton, Cumbria CA8 1LS    Tel: 016977 2340**

Comfortable traditional family-run hotel set in own secluded grounds. All public rooms and bedrooms overlook the lovely tarn. All bedrooms are en-suite with tea/coffee & colour TV. Restaurant offers both à la carte and table d'hôte menus freshly prepared to order.

Special inclusive terms for golf parties, and a prize is given for the best round on the local course which runs alongside the hotel. Concessionary green fees available to our guests. We can also arrange visits etc. to the many other good golf courses in the area.

**Please write or telephone for colour brochure & full details.**

---

**Facilities** ⊗ � 🍴 ♨ ♀ ⛾ 🏠 🏌 ♟ W S M Rooke.
**Leisure** motorised carts for hire, trolley for hire, putting green, practice area.
**Location** B5284 1.5m from Bowness
**Hotel** ★★★ 71% Wild Boar Hotel, Crook, WINDERMERE ☎ 015394 45225 36 ⇔ ♠
*See advertisement on page 43.*

### BRAMPTON              Map 12 NY56

**Brampton** Talkin Tarn CA8 1HN
☎ 016977 2255 & 2000
Challenging golf across glorious rolling fell country demanding solid driving and many long second shots. A number of particularly fine holes, the pick of which may arguably be, the 3rd and 11th. The course offers unrivalled panoramic views from its hilly position.
*18 holes, 6407yds, Par 72, SSS 71, Course record 66.*
*Club membership 800.*
**Visitors** visitors intending to play at weekends are recommended to telephone in advance.
**Societies** apply in writing to M Ogilvie (Hon Commercial Sec), 3 Warwick St, Carlisle, Cumbria CA3 8QW or telephone 01228 401996.
**Green Fees** Apr-Oct '96; £20 per day (£23 weekends & bank holidays). Nov-Mar '96 £13 per day (£17 weekends & bank holidays).
**Facilities** ⊗ website 🍴 ♨ ♀ ⛾ 🏠 🏌 ♟ Stephen Harrison.
**Leisure** trolley for hire, putting green, practice area.
**Location** 1.5m SE of Brampton on B6413
**Hotel** ★★ 63% The Tarn End House Hotel, Talkin Tarn, BRAMPTON ☎ 016977 2340 7 ⇔ ♠

### CARLISLE              Map 11 NY35

**Carlisle** Aglionby CA4 8AG ☎ 01228 513303 & 513241
Majestic looking parkland course with great appeal. A complete but not too severe test of golf, with fine turf,

natural hazards, a stream and many beautiful trees.
*18 holes, 6278yds, Par 71, SSS 70, Course record 63.*
*Club membership 800.*
**Visitors** may not play before 9am and between 12-1.30 and when tee is reserved. With member on Sat.
**Societies** Mon, Wed & Fri, contact in advance for details.
**Green Fees** £30 per day; £20 per round (Sun £35).
**Facilities** ⊗ website 🍴 ♨ ♀ ⛾ 🏠 🏌 ♟ John Smith More.
**Leisure** trolley for hire, practice area.
**Location** On A69 1m E of M6 junc 43
**Hotel** ★★★ 60% Central Plaza Hotel, Victoria Viaduct, CARLISLE ☎ 01228 20256 84 ⇔ ♠

*Stony Holme Municipal* St Aidans Rd CA1 1LS
☎ 01228 34856
Municipal parkland course, bounded on three sides by the River Eden.
*18 holes, 5783yds, Par 69, SSS 68, Course record 68.*
*Club membership 350.*
**Visitors** must contact in advance.
**Societies** must telephone in advance.
**Green Fees** not confirmed.
**Facilities** ♀ ⛾ 🏠 🏌 ♟ S Ling.
**Location** 3m E off A69
**Hotel** B Forte Posthouse Carlisle, Parkhouse Rd, Kingstown, CARLISLE ☎ 01228 31201 93 ⇔ ♠

### COCKERMOUTH         Map 11 NY13

**Cockermouth** Embleton CA13 9SG ☎ 017687 76223
Fell-land course, fenced, with exceptional views and a hard climb on the 3rd and 11th holes. Testing holes: 10th and 16th (rearranged by James Braid).
*18 holes, 5496yds, Par 69, SSS 67, Course record 62.*
*Club membership 600.*
**Visitors** restricted Wed, Sat & Sun.
**Societies** apply in writing to the secretary.

# Stony Holme Golf Course Carlisle

## St. Aldans Rd, Carlisle, Cumbria, CA1 1LS

For superb value Society packages on an excellent course with great food to follow call the pro-shop on:

**B B C** GOLF MAGAZINE RECOMMENDED

# 01228 34856

Please quote ref : GAA

**Green Fees** £15 per day/round (£20 weekends & bank holidays).
**Facilities** ⊗ by prior arrangement 〗 by prior arrangement ⓛ ⚑ ♀ ⚐
**Leisure** putting green.
**Location** 3m E off A66
**Hotel** ★★★ 65% The Trout Hotel, Crown St, COCKERMOUTH ☎ 01900 823591 23 ⇌ ฿

## CROSBY-ON-EDEN      Map 12 NY45

**Eden** CA6 4RA ☎ 01228 573003 & 573013
Open, championship-length parkland course following the River Eden. A large number of water hazards, including the river on certain holes, demands acuracy, as do the well designed raised greens. Flood-lit driving range and excellent clubhouse facilities.
*18 holes, 6368yds, Par 72, SSS 72.*
*Club membership 500.*
**Visitors** contact in advance.
**Societies** telephone to check availability.
**Green Fees** £15 per day (£20 weekends and bank holidays).
**Facilities** ⊗ 〗 ⓛ ⚑ ♀ ⚐ 🏠 ⚑ ฿
**Leisure** trolley for hire, driving range, putting green, practice area.
**Location** 5m from M6 junc 44,on A689 towards Brampton
**Hotel** ★★★♨ 73% Crosby Lodge Country House Hotel, High Crosby, CROSBY-ON-EDEN ☎ 01228 573618 9 ⇌ ฿Annexe2 ⇌ ฿

## GRANGE-OVER-SANDS      Map 07 SD47

**Grange Fell** Fell Rd LA11 6HB ☎ 015395 32536
Hillside course with magnificent views over Morecambe Bay and the surrounding Lakeland mountains.
*9 holes, 5278yds, Par 70, SSS 66, Course record 67.*
*Club membership 400.*
**Visitors** may normally play Mon-Sat.
**Green Fees** £15 per day (£20 weekends & bank holidays).
**Facilities** ⚑ ♀ ⚐
**Leisure** putting green.
**Location** 1m W
**Hotel** ★★★ 65% Netherwood Hotel, Lindale Rd, GRANGE-OVER-SANDS ☎ 015395 32552 29 ⇌ ฿

**Grange-over-Sands** Meathop Rd LA11 6QX
☎ 015395 33180 or 33754
Interesting parkland course with well sited tree plantations, ditches and water features. The four par 3s are considered to be some of the best in the area.

*18 holes, 5958yds, Par 70, SSS 69, Course record 68.*
*Club membership 570.*
**Visitors** must contact in advance for play at weekends.
**Societies** apply in writing but may not play weekends and bank holidays.
**Green Fees** £20 per day; £15 per round (£25/£20 weekends & bank holidays).
**Facilities** ⊗ 〗 ⓛ ⚑ ♀ ⚐ 🏠 ฿ Steve Sumner-Roberts.
**Leisure** trolley for hire, putting green, practice area.
**Location** NW of town centre off B5277
**Hotel** ★★★ 64% Grange Hotel, Station Square, GRANGE-OVER-SANDS ☎ 015395 33666 41 ⇌ ฿

## KENDAL      Map 07 SD59

**Kendal** The Heights LA9 4PQ ☎ 01539 724079 & 733708
Elevated moorland course affording breathtaking views of Lakeland fells and surrounding district.
*18 holes, 5515yds, Par 66, SSS 67, Course record 60.*
*Club membership 737.*
**Visitors** must have a handicap certificate, weekends subject to availability.
**Societies** must contact in advance.
**Green Fees** £16 per day (£20 weekends).
**Facilities** ⊗ 〗 ⓛ ⚑ ♀ ⚐ 🏠 ⚑ ฿ D J Turner.
**Leisure** trolley for hire, putting green, practice area.
**Location** W side of town centre
**Hotel** ★★ 71% Garden House Hotel, Fowl-ing Ln, KENDAL ☎ 01539 731131 10 ⇌ ฿

## KESWICK      Map 11 NY22

**Keswick** Threlkeld Hall CA12 4SX
☎ 017687 79324 & 79010
Varied fell and tree-lined course with commanding views of Lakeland scenery.
*18 holes, 6225yds, Par 71, SSS 72, Course record 69.*
*Club membership 900.*
**Visitors** must book tee 7 days in advance 017687 79010. Restricted on competition days.
**Societies** apply in writing to secretary.
**Green Fees** £15 per day (£20 weekends & bank holidays).
**Facilities** ⊗ 〗 by prior arrangement ⓛ ⚑ ♀ ⚐ 🏠 ⚑ ฿ Craig Hamilton.
**Leisure** fishing, trolley for hire, putting green, practice area.
**Location** 4m E of Keswick, off A66
**Hotel** ★★★★ 62% Keswick Country House Hotel, Station Rd, KESWICK ☎ 017687 72020 66 ⇌ ฿
**Additional hotel** ★★ 68% Chaucer House Hotel, Derwentwater Place, KESWICK ☎ 017687 72318 & 73223 35rm(28 ⇌ ฿)

# Chaucer House Hotel
ETB   Ashley   AA ★★
🌺🌺🌺   Courtney   BHA
**Derwentwater Place, Keswick.**
**Tel: 017687 72318 Fax: 017687 75551**
Just 5 mins drive away from the challenging 71 par Keswick Golf Club. A happy, friendly, comfortable, relaxing Victorian House Hotel. 35 rooms, most en-suite, all with central heating, tea & coffee making facilities, electric blanket, hairdryer. Satellite TV. FREE MIDWEEK GOLF & SPECIAL BREAKS. Superb table d'hote and a la carte meals. A place you like to return to time and time again. Drying room, lift, car park. Also self catering

## KIRKBY LONSDALE                    Map 07 SD67

**Kirkby Lonsdale** Scaleber Ln, Barbon LA6 2LE
☎ 015242 76365
Parkland course on the east bank of the River Lune and
crossed by Barbon Beck. Mainly following the lie of the land,
the gently undulating course uses the beck to provide water
hazards.
*18 holes, 6472yds, Par 72, SSS 72, Course record 68.*
*Club membership 600.*
**Visitors**   restricted on Sunday, must telephone in advance
          or call in at pro shop.
**Societies**  apply in writing for society package.
**Green Fees** £16 per day (£20 weekends).
**Facilities** ⊗ ⅷ Ⅼ ☕ ♀ ⚹ 🖰 ⚲ ⚡ Chris Barret.
**Leisure**    trolley for hire, putting green, practice area.
**Location**   6m S of Sedbergh
**Hotel**      ★★ 67% Pheasant Inn, CASTERTON
          ☎ 015242 71230 10 ⇄ ⚶

## MARYPORT                           Map 11 NY03

**Maryport** Bank End CA15 6PA
☎ 01900 812605 & 815626
A tight seaside links course exposed to Solway breezes. Fine
views across Solway Firth.
*18 holes, 6088yds, Par 70, SSS 69, Course record 70.*
*Club membership 400.*
**Visitors**   no restrictions.
**Societies**  must apply in writing.
**Green Fees** £15 per day/round (£20 weekends & bank
          holidays).
**Facilities** ⊗ ⅷ Ⅼ ☕ ♀ ⚹
**Leisure**    putting green, practice area.
**Location**   1m N on B5300
**Hotel**      ★★ 64% Ellenbank Hotel, Birkby,
          MARYPORT ☎ 01900 815233 26 ⇄ ⚶

## PENRITH                            Map 12 NY53

**Penrith** Salkeld Rd CA11 8SG ☎ 01768 891919
A beautiful and well-balanced course, always changing
direction, and demanding good length from the tee. It is
set on rolling moorland with occasional pine trees and
some fine views.
*18 holes, 6047yds, Par 69, SSS 69, Course record 63.*
*Club membership 850.*
**Visitors**   contact in advance.
**Societies**  telephone in advance.
**Green Fees** £25 for 2 rounds; £20 per round (£30/£25
          weekends).
**Facilities** ☕ ♀ ⚹ 🖰 ⚲ ⚡ Garry Key.
**Leisure**    trolley for hire, driving range, putting green,
          practice area.
**Location**   0.75m N off A6
**Hotel**      ★★ 68% George Hotel, Devonshire St,
          PENRITH ☎ 01768 862696 31 ⇄ ⚶

## ST BEES                            Map 11 NX91

*St Bees* CA27 0EJ ☎ 01946 824300
Links course, down hill and dale, with sea views.
*9 holes, 5082yds, Par 64, SSS 65.*
*Club membership 275.*

**Visitors**   no restrictions.
**Green Fees** not confirmed.
**Location**   0.5m W of village off B5345
**Hotel**      ★★★ 58% Blackbeck Bridge Inn,
          EGREMONT ☎ 01946 841661 22 ⇄ ⚶

## SEASCALE                           Map 06 NY00

**Seascale** The Banks CA20 1QL ☎ 019467 28202
A tough links requiring length and control. The natural
terrain is used to give a variety of holes and considerable
character. Undulating greens add to the challenge. Fine
views over the Western Fells, the Irish Sea and Isle of Man.
*18 holes, 6416yds, Par 71, SSS 71, Course record 65.*
*Club membership 670.*
**Visitors**   must contact in advance.
**Societies**  telephone to make provisional booking.
**Green Fees** £25 per day; £20 per round (£30/£25
          weekends & bank holidays).
**Facilities** ⊗ ⅷ Ⅼ ☕ ♀ ⚹ 🖰 ⚲
**Leisure**    motorised carts for hire, trolley for hire,
          driving range, putting green, practice area.
**Location**   NW side of village off B5344
**Hotel**      ★★★ 58% Blackbeck Bridge Inn,
          EGREMONT ☎ 01946 841661 22 ⇄ ⚶

## SEDBERGH                           Map 07 SD69

**Sedbergh** Catholes, Abbot Holme LA10 5SS
☎ 015396 21551 & 20993
A tree-lined grassland course with superb scenery in the
Yorkshire Dales National Park. Feature hole is the par 3 2nd
(110yds) where the River Dee separates the tee from the
green.
*9 holes, 5588yds, Par 70, SSS 68, Course record 66.*
*Club membership 300.*
**Visitors**   must book to play on weekends & bank
          holidays.
**Societies**  must contact in advance.
**Green Fees** £20 per day; £14 per 18 holes (£25/£18
          weekends and bank holidays).
**Facilities** ⊗ ⅷ Ⅼ ☕ ♀ ⚹ 🖰 ⚲
**Leisure**    trolley for hire, practice area.
**Location**   1m S off A683
**Hotel**      ★★ 71% Garden House Hotel, Fowl-ing Ln,
          KENDAL ☎ 01539 731131 10 ⇄ ⚶

## SILECROFT                          Map 06 SD18

**Silecroft** LA18 4NX ☎ 01229 774250
Seaside links course parallel to the coast of the Irish Sea.
Often windy. Easy walking. Spectacular views inland of
Lakeland hills.
*9 holes, 5877yds, Par 68, SSS 68, Course record 67.*
*Club membership 300.*
**Visitors**   may be restricted competition days & bank
          holidays,
**Societies**  must contact in writing.
**Green Fees** £10 per day (£15 weekends).
**Facilities** ☕ ♀ ⚹
**Leisure**    practice area.
**Location**   1m SW
**Hotel**      ★ 59% Old King's Head Hotel, Station Rd,
          BROUGHTON IN FURNESS
          ☎ 01229 716293 5rm(1 ⚶)

## SILLOTH                                        Map 11 NY15

**Silloth on Solway** CA5 4BL
☎ 016973 31304 & 32440
Billowing dunes, narrow fairways, heather and gorse and
the constant subtle problems of tactics and judgement
make these superb links on the Solway an exhilarating
and searching test. The 13th is a good long hole. Superb
views.
*18 holes, 6614yds, Par 72, SSS 72, Course record 65.*
*Club membership 700.*
**Visitors**      must contact in advance.
**Societies**    telephone for times available.
**Green Fees** £25 per day (£30 per round weekends &
                bank holidays). Weekday package incl meal
                £35.
**Facilities**    ⊗ ℣ ⌶ ♨ ♕ ♁ ⚑ ☏ ♪ Carl Weatherhead.
**Leisure**      trolley for hire, putting green, practice area.
**Location**    S side of village off B5300
**Hotel**        ★★ 62% Golf Hotel, Criffel St, SILLOTH
                ☎ 016973 31438 22 ⇥ ♜

## ULVERSTON                                   Map 07 SD27

**Ulverston** Bardsea Park LA12 9QJ ☎ 01229 582824
Inland golf with many medium length holes on
undulating parkland. The 17th is a testing par 4.
Overlooking Morecambe Bay the course offers extensive
views to the Lakeland Fells.
*18 holes, 6201yds, Par 71, SSS 70, Course record 67.*
*Club membership 750.*

# Birdie, Eagle, Albatross ...
### ... or even if you're looking for the elusive 'hole in one', Windermere is the place.

Situated only a mile from this challenging
18 hole golf course, The Wild Boar Hotel
situated in the tranquil Gilpin Valley, with its
olde worlde charme offers you a friendly and
welcome atmosphere.

Reflect, whilst sampling the excellent cuisine
of our award winning restaurant on your 67 par
round. Enjoy free use of extensive leisure
facilities during your stay.

Discounted Green Fees for Residents

AA★★★
71%

## Wild Boar Hotel
Crook, Nr. Windermere, Cumbria LA23 3NF.
Tel: Windermere (015 394) 45225
Fax: Windermere (015 394) 42498

**Visitors**      must contact in advance, be a member of an
                accredited golf club with a handicap
                certificate. May not play on Sat competition
                days or on Tue Ladies day.
**Societies**    by arrangement in writing.
**Green Fees** Summer: £25 per day; £20 per round
                (£30/£25 weekends & bank holidays).
                Winter: £18 per day; £14 per round
                (£20/£18 weekends & bank holidays), Nov-
                Feb.
**Facilities**    ⊗ ℣ ⌶ ♨ ♕ ♁ ⚑ ☏ ♪ M R Smith.
**Leisure**      trolley for hire, putting green, practice area.
**Location**    2m S off A5087
**Hotel**        ★★★ 69% Whitewater Hotel, The
                Lakeland Village,  NEWBY BRIDGE
                ☎ 015395 31133 35 ⇥ ♜

## WINDERMERE          See **Bowness-on-Windermere**

## WORKINGTON                               Map 11 NX92

**Workington** Branthwaite Rd CA14 4SS ☎ 01900 67828
Meadowland course, undulating, with natural hazards created
by stream and trees. Good views of Solway Firth and
Lakeland Hills. 10th, 13th and 15th holes are particularly
testing.
*18 holes, 6217yds, Par 72, SSS 70.*
*Club membership 735.*
**Visitors**      advisable to contact pro for weekday, weekends
                are generally very busy.
**Societies**    booking required for over 8 people.
**Green Fees** Summer: £19 per day; £15 per round (£25/£18
                weekends & bank holidays).
**Facilities**    ⊗ ℣ ⌶ ♨ ♕ ♁ ⚑ ♪ Aidrian Drabble.
**Leisure**      buggies for hire, trolley for hire, putting green,
                practice area.
**Location**    1.75m E off A596
**Hotel**        ★★★ 68% Washington Central Hotel,
                Washington St,  WORKINGTON
                ☎ 01900 65772 40 ⇥ ♜

# DERBYSHIRE

## ALFRETON                                     Map 08 SK45

**Alfreton** Wingfield Rd, Oakerthorpe DE66 7LH
☎ 01773 832070 & 831901
A small parkland course with tight fairways and many natural
hazards.
*9 holes, 5074yds, Par 66, SSS 65, Course record 60.*
*Club membership 300.*
**Visitors**      must contact in advance, with member only
                weekends.
**Societies**    apply in writing or telephone in advance.
**Green Fees** £18 per day; £13 per round (18 holes).
**Facilities**    ⊗ ℣ by prior arrangement ♨ ♕ ♁ ⚑
                ♪ Julian Mellors.
**Leisure**      putting green, practice area.
**Location**    1m W on A615                              ▶

**Hotel**      ★★★★ 65%  Swallow Hotel, Carter Ln East,
              SOUTH NORMANTON
              ☎ 01773 812000 161 ⇄ ₪

---

## ASHBOURNE                                                    Map 07 SK14

**Ashbourne** Clifton DE6 1BN ☎ 01335 342078
Undulating parkland course.
*9 holes, 5359yds, Par 66, SSS 66.*
*Club membership 350.*
**Visitors**    may not play on competition days. With member
              only at weekends.
**Societies**   telephone in advance.
**Green Fees** not confirmed.
**Facilities**  ♀⚄
**Location**    1.5m SW on A515
**Hotel**       ★★★⚘ 75%  Callow Hall, Mappleton Rd,
              ASHBOURNE
              ☎ 01335 343403 & 342412 16 ⇄ ₪

---

## BAKEWELL                                                     Map 08 SK26

**Bakewell** Station Rd DE45 1GB ☎ 01629 812307
Parkland course, hilly, with plenty of natural hazards to test
the golfer. Magnificent views across the Wye Valley.
*9 holes, 5240yds, Par 68, SSS 66.*
*Club membership 360.*
**Visitors**    with members only weekends.
**Societies**   apply in writing.
**Green Fees** not confirmed.
**Facilities**  ⊗ ⅏ ⅃ ⅄ ♀ (ex Mon) ⚄ 🏠
**Leisure**     putting green, practice area.
**Location**    E side of town off A6
**Hotel**       ★★ 67%  Milford House Hotel, Mill St,
              BAKEWELL ☎ 01629 812130 12 ⇄ ₪

---

## BAMFORD                                                      Map 08 SK28

**Sickleholme** Saltergate Ln S30 2BH ☎ 01433 651306
Undulating downland course in the lovely Peak District, with
rivers and ravines and spectacular scenery.
*18 holes, 6064yds, Par 69, SSS 69, Course record 62.*
*Club membership 700.*
**Visitors**    must contact in advance, restricted weekends.
**Societies**   telephone in advance.
**Green Fees** £25 per day (£32 weekends & bank holidays).
**Facilities**  ⊗ ⅏ ⅃ ⅄ ♀ ⚄ 🏠 ₵ P H Taylor.
**Location**    0.75m SW on A6013
**Hotel**       ★★ 69%  Yorkshire Bridge Inn, Ashopton Rd,
              Yorkshire Bridge, BAMFORD
              ☎ 01433 651361 10 ⇄ ₪

---

## BREADSALL                                                    Map 08 SK33

**Breadsall Priory Hotel, Golf & Country Club** Moor Rd,
Morley DE7 6DL ☎ 01332 832235
Set in 200 acres of mature parkland, the Old Course is built
on the site of a 13th-century priory. Full use had been made
of natural features and fine old trees. In contrast the Moorland
Course, opened in Spring 1992, designed by Donald Steel and
built by Brian Piersen, features Derbyshire stone walls and
open moors heavily affected by winds.
*Priory Course: 18 holes, 6201yds, Par 72, SSS 70, Course
record 66.*

*Moorland Course: 18 holes, 6028yds, Par 70, SSS 69.*
*Club membership 900.*
**Visitors**    must contact in advance.
**Societies**   telephone in advance.
**Green Fees** Priory: £50 per day; £44 per round (£45 per
              round weekends & bank holidays). Moorland:
              £50 per day; £30 per round (£45 per round
              weekends & bank holidays).
**Facilities**  ⊗ ⅏ ⅃ ⅄ ♀ ⚄ 🏠 ₸ ⅋ ₵ Andrew Smith.
**Leisure**     hard tennis courts, heated indoor swimming
              pool, buggies for hire, trolley for hire, putting
              green, practice area.
**Location**    0.75m W
**Hotel**       ★★★★ 64%  Breadsall Priory Hotel, Country
              Club Resort, Moor Rd,  MORLEY
              ☎ 01332 832235 14 ⇄ ₪Annexe77 ⇄ ₪

---

## BUXTON                                                       Map 07 SK07

**Buxton & High Peak** Townend, Waterswallows Rd
SK17 7EN ☎ 01298 23453 & 26263
Bracing, well-drained meadowland course; the highest in
Derbyshire. Challenging course where wind direction is a
major factor on some holes; others require blind shots to
sloping greens.
*18 holes, 5966yds, Par 69, SSS 69, Course record 65.*
*Club membership 670.*
**Visitors**    contact Mrs S Arnfield.
**Societies**   apply in writing to Mrs S Arnfield.
**Green Fees** £20 per day (£25 weekends & bank holidays).
**Facilities**  ⊗ ⅏ ⅃ ⅄ ♀ ⚄ 🏠 ₸ ₵ Gary Brown.
**Leisure**     buggies for hire, trolley for hire, putting green,
              practice area, snooker.
**Location**    1m NE off A6
**Hotel**       ★★★ 66%  Palace Hotel, Palace Rd,  BUXTON
              ☎ 01298 22001 122 ⇄

---

**Cavendish** Gadley Ln SK17 6XD
   ☎ 01298 25052 & 79708
This parkland/moorland course with its comfortable
clubhouse nestles below the rising hills. Generally open
to the prevailing west wind, it is noted for its excellent
surfaced greens which contain many deceptive subtleties.
Designed by Dr Alastair McKenzie, good holes include
the 8th, 9th and 18th.
*18 holes, 5833yds, Par 68, SSS 68, Course record 61.*
*Club membership 650.*
*Visitors*      must contact in advance, weekends are
              restricted by competitions.
**Societies**   telephone professional on 01298 25052.
**Green Fees** £20 per round (£35 weekends & bank
              holidays).
**Facilities**  ⊗ ⅏ ⅃ ⅄ ♀ ⚄ 🏠 ₸ ₵ Paul Hunstone.
**Leisure**     trolley for hire, practice area.
**Location**    0.75m W of town centre off A53
**Hotel**       ★★★ 73%  Lee Wood Hotel, 13
              Manchester Rd,  BUXTON
              ☎ 01298 23002 36 ⇄ ₪Annexe2 ⇄ ₪

---

## CHAPEL-EN-LE-FRITH                                           Map 07 SK08

**Chapel-en-le-Frith** The Cockyard, Manchester Rd
SK12 6UH ☎ 01298 812118
Scenic parkland course, with testing holes at the 15th (par 4)
and 17th (517 yds), par 5. Good views.

*18 holes, 6054yds, Par 70, SSS 69.*
*Club membership 641.*
| | |
|---|---|
| **Visitors** | must contact professional in advance. |
| **Societies** | apply in advance to Secretary. |
| **Green Fees** | £20 per day (£30 weekends & bank holidays). |
| **Facilities** | ⊗ ⅷ ☘ ☕ ♀ ♨ 🕿 ⛳ David J Cullen. |
| **Leisure** | trolley for hire, putting green, practice area, snooker. |
| **Location** | On B5470 |
| **Hotel** | ★★★ 73% Lee Wood Hotel, 13 Manchester Rd, BUXTON 🕿 01298 23002 36 ⇄ ⋒Annexe2 ⇄ ⋒ |

---

## CHESTERFIELD            Map 08 SK37

**Chesterfield** Walton S42 7LA 🕿 01246 279256
A varied and interesting, undulating parkland course with trees picturesquely adding to the holes and the outlook alike. Stream hazard on back nine. Views over four counties.
*18 holes, 6326yds, Par 71, SSS 70, Course record 65.*
*Club membership 500.*
| | |
|---|---|
| **Visitors** | must contact in advance and must play with member at weekends and bank holidays. A handicap certificate is generally required. |
| **Societies** | apply in writing. |
| **Green Fees** | not confirmed. |
| **Facilities** | ♀ ♨ ☕ ⛳ M McLean. |
| **Location** | 2m SW off A632 |
| **Hotel** | ★★★ 61% Chesterfield, Malkin St, CHESTERFIELD 🕿 01246 271141 73 ⇄ ⋒ |

**Grassmoor Golf Centre** North Wingfield Rd, Grassmoor S41 5EA 🕿 01246 856044
An 18-hole heathland course with interesting and challenging water features. 26-bay floodlit driving range, practice bunkers and putting area.
*18 holes, 5723yds, Par 69, SSS 69, Course record 67.*
*Club membership 420.*
| | |
|---|---|
| **Visitors** | contact Manager in advance. |
| **Societies** | telephone in Manager in advance. |
| **Green Fees** | £7.50 (£9 weekends). |
| **Facilities** | ⊗ ⅷ ☘ ☕ ♀ ♨ 🕿 ⛳ Peter Goldthorpe. |
| **Leisure** | sauna, trolley for hire, floodlit driving range, putting green. |
| **Location** | Between Chesterfield & Grassmoor, off B6038 |
| **Hotel** | ★★★ 61% Chesterfield, Malkin St, CHESTERFIELD 🕿 01246 271141 73 ⇄ ⋒ |

**Stanedge** Walton Hay Farm S45 0LW 🕿 01246 566156
Moorland course in hilly situation open to strong winds. Some tricky short holes with narrow fairways, so accuracy is paramount. Magnificent views over four counties.
*9 holes, 4867yds, Par 64, SSS 64, Course record 64.*
*Club membership 310.*
| | |
|---|---|
| **Visitors** | with member only Sat & Sun, and may not play after 2pm weekdays. |
| **Societies** | apply in writing. |
| **Green Fees** | £15 per round (18 holes). |
| **Facilities** | ☕ ♀ ♨ |
| **Leisure** | putting green, practice area. |
| **Location** | 5m SW off B5057 nr Red Lion public house |
| **Hotel** | ★★★ 61% Chesterfield, Malkin St, CHESTERFIELD 🕿 01246 271141 73 ⇄ ⋒ |

**Tapton Park Municipal** Tapton Park, Tapton S41 0EQ
🕿 01246 239500
Municipal parkland course with some fairly hard walking. The 620 yd (par 5) 5th is a testing hole.
*Tapton Main: 18 holes, 6013yds, Par 71, SSS 69.*
*Dobbin Clough: 9 holes, 2613yds, Par 34.*
*Club membership 750.*
| | |
|---|---|
| **Visitors** | must contact in advance. No caddies allowed. |
| **Societies** | apply in writing. |
| **Green Fees** | not confirmed. |
| **Facilities** | ♀ ♨ ☕ ⛳ Fraser Scott. |
| **Leisure** | putting, practice area, trolley hire. |
| **Location** | 0.5m E of Chesterfield Station |
| **Hotel** | ★★★ 61% Chesterfield, Malkin St, CHESTERFIELD 🕿 01246 271141 73 ⇄ ⋒ |

---

## CODNOR           Map 08 SK44

**Ormonde Fields Golf & Country Club** Nottingham Rd DE5 9RG 🕿 01773 570043 (Secretary) & 742987 (Pro)
Parkland course with undulating fairways and natural hazards. The par 4 (4th) and the par 3 (11th) are notable. There is a practice area.
*18 holes, 6011yds, Par 69, SSS 69, Course record 68.*
*Club membership 500.*
| | |
|---|---|
| **Visitors** | must contact in advance. |
| **Societies** | telephone in advance. |
| **Green Fees** | £15 per day (£20 per round weekends). |
| **Facilities** | ⊗ ⅷ ☘ ☕ ♀ ♨ ⛳ Peter Buttifant. |
| **Leisure** | trolley for hire, putting green, practice area. |
| **Location** | 1m SE on A610 |
| **Hotel** | ★★★ 75% Makeney Hall Country House Hotel, Makeney, Milford, BELPER 🕿 01332 842999 27 ⇄ ⋒Annexe18 ⇄ ⋒ |

---

## DERBY           Map 08 SK33

**Allestree Park** Allestree Hall DE22 2EU
🕿 01332 550616
Municipal parkland course in rather hilly country.
*18 holes, 5749yds, Par 68, SSS 68, Course record 66.*
*Club membership 275.*
| | |
|---|---|
| **Visitors** | restricted weekends & bank holidays. |
| **Societies** | restricted at weekends & bank holidays. |
| **Green Fees** | not confirmed. |
| **Facilities** | ♀ ♨ ☕ ⛳ Colin Henderson. |
| **Leisure** | fishing. |
| **Location** | 3m N on A6 |
| **Hotel** | ★★ 69% Kedleston Country House Hotel, Kedleston Rd, DERBY 🕿 01332 559202 & 556507 14 ⇄ ⋒ |

**Derby** Shakespeare St, Sinfin DE24 9HD 🕿 01332 766323
Municipal parkland course. The front nine holes are rather difficult.
*18 holes, 6144yds, Par 70, SSS 69.*
*Club membership 450.*
| | |
|---|---|
| **Visitors** | starting time must be booked at weekends. |
| **Societies** | apply in writing in advance. |
| **Green Fees** | not confirmed. |
| **Facilities** | ♨ ☕ ⛳ |
| **Location** | 3.5m S of city centre |
| **Hotel** | ★★★ 63% International Hotel, Burton Rd (A5250), DERBY 🕿 01332 369321 41 ⇄ ⋒Annexe21 ⇄ ⋒ |

**Mickleover** Uttoxeter Rd, Mickleover DE3 5AD
☎ 01332 512092
Undulating parkland course in pleasant setting, affording splendid country views. Some attractive par 3s and a number of elevated greens..
*18 holes, 5708yds, Par 68, SSS 68, Course record 64.*
*Club membership 800.*
**Visitors** must contact in advance.
**Societies** apply in writing.
**Green Fees** £22 per day/round (£25 weekends & bank holidays).
**Facilities** ⊗ ⅷ � ■ ♀ ⅄ 🖻 ⅋ ℓ Tim Coxon.
**Leisure** trolley for hire, putting green, practice area, snooker.
**Location** 3m W off A516/B5020
**Hotel** B Forte Posthouse Derby/Burton, Pastures Hill, Littleover, DERBY
☎ 01332 514933 62 ⇄ ₨

## DRONFIELD                Map 08 SK37

**Hallowes** Hallowes Ln S18 6UA
☎ 01246 413734
Attractive moorland/meadowland course set in the Derbyshire hills. Several testing par 4's and splendid views.
*18 holes, 6342yds, Par 71, SSS 70, Course record 64.*
*Club membership 630.*
**Visitors** may only play with member at weekends. Must contact in advance.
**Societies** must contact in advance.
**Green Fees** £27 per day; £20 per round.
**Facilities** ⊗ ⅷ ⅃ ■ ♀ ⅄ 🖻 ℓ Philip Dunn.
**Leisure** trolley for hire, putting green, practice area.
**Location** S side of town
**Hotel** ★★ 64% Chantry Hotel, Church St, DRONFIELD ☎ 01246 413014 7 ⇄ ₨

## DUFFIELD                Map 08 SK34

**Chevin** Golf Ln DE56 4EE
☎ 01332 841864
A mixture of parkland and moorland, this course is rather hilly which makes for some hard walking. The 8th calls for a very hard drive, possibly the hardest in the area.
*18 holes, 6057yds, Par 69, SSS 69, Course record 65.*
*Club membership 750.*
**Visitors** not before 9.30am or off first tee between 12.30 and 2pm. Proof of handicap required.
**Societies** contact in advance.
**Green Fees** £27 per day.
**Facilities** ⊗ ⅷ ⅃ ■ ♀ ⅄ 🖻 ⅋ ℓ Willie Bird.
**Leisure** motorised carts for hire, trolley for hire, driving range, putting green, practice area, snooker.
**Location** N side of town off A6
**Hotel** ★★ 69% Kedleston Country House Hotel, Kedleston Rd, DERBY
☎ 01332 559202 & 556507 14 ⇄ ₨

## GLOSSOP                Map 07 SK09

***Glossop and District*** Hurst Ln, off Sheffield Rd SK13 9PU
☎ 01457 865247
Moorland course in good position, excellent natural hazards.
*11 holes, 5800yds, Par 68, SSS 68.*
*Club membership 250.*

**Visitors** may not play on bank holidays.
**Societies** must apply in writing to professional.
**Green Fees** not confirmed.
**Facilities** ♀ (ex Mon) ⅄ 🖻 ℓ Gary S Brown.
**Location** 1m E off A57
**Hotel** ★★ 69% York House Hotel, York Place, Richmond St, ASHTON-UNDER-LYNE
☎ 0161 330 5899 24 ⇄ ₨ Annexe10 ⇄ ₨

## HORSLEY                Map 08 SK34

**Horsley Lodge** Smalley Mill Rd DE21 5BL
☎ 01332 780838 & 781400
This course, opened in 1991 and set in 100 acres of Derbyshire countryside, has some challenging holes. Also Par 3 course and floodlit driving range.
*18 holes, 6400yds, Par 72, SSS 71, Course record 72.*
*Club membership 600.*
**Visitors** must contact professional in advance and have handicap. May not play weekends.
**Societies** must telephone in advance.
**Green Fees** £18 per 18 holes.
**Facilities** ⊗ ⅷ ⅃ ■ ♀ ⅄ 🖻 ⅋ ♨ ℓ
**Leisure** fishing, sauna, solarium, motorised carts for hire, buggies for hire, trolley for hire, driving range, putting green, practice area.
**Location** 4m NE of Derby, off A38
**Hotel** ★★★★ 64% Breadsall Priory Hotel, Country Club Resort, Moor Rd, MORLEY
☎ 01332 832235 14 ⇄ ₨ Annexe77 ⇄ ₨

## KEDLESTON                Map 08 SK34

**Kedleston Park** DE22 5JD ☎ 01332 840035
The course is laid out in flat mature parkland with fine trees and background views of historic Kedleston Hall (National Trust). Many testing holes are included in each nine and there is an excellent modern clubhouse.
*18 holes, 6583yds, Par 71, SSS 72, Course record 63.*
*Club membership 868.*
**Visitors** must contact in advance. With member only at weekends.
**Societies** weekdays only, apply in writing.
**Green Fees** £35 per day; £27 per round weekdays only.
**Facilities** ⊗ ⅷ ⅃ ■ ♀ ⅄ 🖻 ⅋ ℓ Jim Hetherington.
**Leisure** sauna, trolley for hire, putting green, practice area.
**Location** Signposted Kedleston Hall from A38
**Hotel** ★★ 69% Kedleston Country House Hotel, Kedleston Rd, DERBY
☎ 01332 559202 & 556507 14 ⇄ ₨

## MATLOCK                Map 08 SK36

**Matlock** Chesterfield Rd DE4 5LF
☎ 01629 582191 & 584934
Moorland course with fine views of the beautiful Peak District.
*18 holes, 5991yds, Par 70, SSS 68, Course record 64.*
*Club membership 700.*
**Visitors** with member only weekends & bank holidays. Members only weekdays 12.30-1.30pm.
**Societies** prior arrangement with Secretary.
**Green Fees** £25 per day/round.
**Facilities** ⊗ by prior arrangement ⅷ by prior arrangement ⅃ ■ ♀ ⅄ 🖻 ℓ M A Whithorn.

**Leisure**   trolley for hire, putting green, practice area.
**Location**   1.5m NE of Matlock on A632
**Hotel**   ★★★ 66% New Bath Hotel, New Bath Rd,
MATLOCK ☎ 01629 583275 55 ⇋ ↑

---

## MICKLEOVER                    Map 08 SK33

*Pastures* Pastures Hospital DE3 5DQ ☎ 01332 521074
Small course laid-out on undulating meadowland in the
grounds of a psychiatric hospital, with good views across the
Trent valley. Fishing and snooker.
*9 holes, 5005yds, Par 64, SSS 64, Course record 62.*
*Club membership 320.*
**Visitors**   must be accompanied by a member, may not
play on Sun. Must contact in advance.
**Societies**   must contact in advance.
**Green Fees** not confirmed.
**Facilities**   ♀↘
**Leisure**   fishing, bowls, table tennis.
**Location**   1m SW off A516
**Hotel**   ★★★ 63% International Hotel, Burton Rd
(A5250), DERBY
☎ 01332 369321 41 ⇋ ↑Annexe21 ⇋ ↑

---

## NEW MILLS                     Map 07 SK08

*New Mills* Shaw Marsh SK12 4QE ☎ 01663 743485
Moorland course with panoramic views and first-class greens.
*9 holes, 5633yds, Par 68, SSS 67.*
*Club membership 350.*
**Visitors**   must play with member on Sunday & special
days.
must contact in advance.
**Green Fees** not confirmed.
**Facilities**   ♀↘☎↑↑
**Leisure**   putting green, practice area, trolley hire.
**Location**   0.5m N off B6101
**Hotel**   ★★ 70% Red Lion Inn, 112 Buxton Rd, High
Ln, STOCKPORT
☎ 01663 765227 6 ⇋ ↑

---

## RENISHAW                      Map 08 SK47

*Renishaw Park* Club House S31 9UZ ☎ 01246 432044
Part parkland and part meadowland with easy walking.
*18 holes, 6253yds, Par 71, SSS 70, Course record 65.*
*Club membership 750.*
**Visitors**   must contact in advance. Visitors not allowed
Thu, weekends or competition days.
**Societies**   must contact in advance.
**Green Fees** £28 per day; £20 per round (£33 per round/day
weekends & bank holidays).
**Facilities**   ⊗ ℳ ⓛ ⛴ ♀↘☎↑ John Oates.
**Leisure**   trolley for hire, putting green, practice area.
**Location**   0.5m NW on A616
**Hotel**   ★★★ 57% Sitwell Arms Hotel, Station Rd,
RENISHAW ☎ 01246 435226 30 ⇋ ↑

---

## RISLEY                        Map 08 SK43

*Maywood* Rushy Ln DE72 3ST ☎ 0115 030 2306
Wooded parkland course with numerous water hazards.
*18 holes, 6424yds, Par 72, SSS 71, Course record 70.*
*Club membership 450.*

**Visitors**   advisable to contact in advance during summer,
may not play during competitions.
**Societies**   by prior arrangement.
**Green Fees** £15 per round (£20 weekends).
**Facilities**   ⊗ ℳ ⓛ ⛴ ♀↘☎↑ Colin Henderson.
**Leisure**   trolley for hire, putting green, practice area.
**Hotel**   ★★★ 70% Risley Hall Hotel, Derby Rd,
RISLEY ☎ 01159 399000 16rm

---

## SHIRLAND                      Map 08 SK45

*Shirlands* Lower Delves DE55 6AU ☎ 01773 834935
Rolling parkland and tree-lined course with extensive views
of Derbyshire countryside.
*18 holes, 6072yds, Par 71, SSS 70, Course record 71.*
*Club membership 600.*
**Visitors**   contact professional in advance.
**Societies**   contact Professional.
**Green Fees** £25 per day; £15 per round (£20 per round
weekends).
**Facilities**   ⊗ ℳ ⓛ ⛴ ♀↘☎↑↑ Neville Hallam.
**Leisure**   trolley for hire, putting green, practice area.
**Location**   S side of village off A61
**Hotel**   ★★★★ 65% Swallow Hotel, Carter Ln East,
SOUTH NORMANTON
☎ 01773 812000 161 ⇋ ↑

---

## STANTON-BY-DALE                Map 08 SK43

*Erewash Valley* DE7 4QR ☎ 0115 932 3258
Parkland/meadowland course overlooking valley and M1.
Unique 4th and 5th in Victorian quarry bottom: 5th-testing
par 3.
*18 holes, 6487yds, Par 72, SSS 71, Course record 67.*
*Club membership 860.*
**Visitors**   no restrictions
**Societies**   contact in advance.
**Green Fees** not confirmed.
**Facilities**   ♀↘☎↑↑ M J Ronan.
**Leisure**   bowling green.
**Location**   1m W
**Hotel**   ★★★ 70% Risley Hall Hotel, Derby Rd,
RISLEY ☎ 01159 399000 16rm

---

# DEVON

---

## AXMOUTH                       Map 03 SY29

*Axe Cliff* EX12 4AB ☎ 01297 24371
Undulating links course with coastal views.
*18 holes, 5057yds, Par 67, SSS 65.*
*Club membership 400.*
**Visitors**   may only play after 11am on Wed & Sun.
**Societies**   must contact in advance.
**Green Fees** not confirmed.
**Facilities**   ↘☎↑ Mark Dack.
**Location**   0.75m S on B3172
**Hotel**   ★★ 64% Anchor Inn, BEER
☎ 01297 20386 8rm(5 ⇋ ↑)

## BIGBURY-ON-SEA                    Map 03 SX64

**Bigbury** TQ7 4BB ☎ 01548 810557
Clifftop, heathland course with easy walking. Exposed to
winds, but with fine views over the sea and River Avon. 7th
hole particularly tricky.
*18 holes, 6048yds, Par 70, SSS 69, Course record 65.*
*Club membership 850.*
**Visitors**      must have handicap certificate.
**Societies**     must apply in writing.
**Green Fees** £20 per day (£24 weekends & bank holidays).
                  Half price after 4pm.
**Facilities**    ⊗ ⊼ ⅃ ♨ ♀ ♨ 🏠 ⚐ 🏌 Simon Lloyd.
**Leisure**       motorised carts for hire, buggies for hire, trolley
                  for hire, putting green, practice area.
**Location**      1m S on B3392
**Hotel**         ★ 69% Henley Hotel, BIGBURY-ON-SEA ☎
                  01548 810240 8 ⇌ ♟

## BLACKAWTON                       Map 03 SX85

**Dartmouth Golf & Country Club** TQ9 7DQ
☎ 01803 712686 & 712650
The 9-hole Club course and the 18-hole Championship course
are both worth a visit and not just for the beautiful views. The
Championship is one of the most challenging courses in the
West Country with a 4th hole visitors will always remember.
*Championship Course: 18 holes, 6663yds, Par 72, SSS 72.*
*Club Course: 9 holes, 5166yds, Par 66, SSS 65.*
*Club membership 800.*
**Visitors**      must contact in advance, visitors welcome
                  subject to availability.
**Societies**     telephone in advance.
**Green Fees** Championship: £32 per day; £26 per round
                  (£35/£32 weekends). Club: £15 per 18 holes;
                  £10 per 10 holes.
**Facilities**    ⊗ ⊼ ⅃ ♨ ♀ ♨ 🏠 ⚐ 🏌 Peter Laugher.
**Leisure**       heated indoor swimming pool, sauna, solarium,
                  gymnasium, buggies for hire, trolley for hire,
                  driving range, putting green.
**Location**      On A3122 Totnes/Dartmouth road
**Hotel**         ★★★ 65% Stoke Lodge Hotel, Stoke Fleming,
                  DARTMOUTH ☎ 01803 770523 24 ⇌ ♟

## BUDLEIGH SALTERTON                Map 03 SY08

*East Devon* North View Rd EX9 6DQ ☎ 01395 443370
An interesting course with downland turf, much heather
and gorse, and superb views over the bay. The early
holes climb to the cliff edge. The downhill 17th has a
heather section in the fairway, leaving a good second to
the green.
*18 holes, 6239yds, Par 70, SSS 70, Course record 64.*
*Club membership 850.*
**Visitors**      no visitors before 10am and between 12.30-
                  2pm. Visitors must be member of a
                  recognised club and must produce proof of
                  handicap.
**Societies**     must contact in advance. Large parties 16+
                  only on Thu.
**Green Fees** not confirmed.
**Facilities**    ♀ ♨ 🏠 ⚐ 🏌 Trevor Underwood.
**Leisure**       putting green, practice area, trolley hire.
**Location**      W side of town centre

**Hotel**         ★★★ 63% The Imperial, The Esplanade,
                  EXMOUTH ☎ 01395 274761 57 ⇌ ♟

## CHITTLEHAMHOLT                    Map 03 SS62

**Highbullen Hotel** EX37 9HD ☎ 01769 540561
Mature parkland course with water hazards and outstanding
scenic views to Exmoor and Dartmoor. Excellent facilities
offered by the hotel.
*18 holes, 5700yds, Par 67, SSS 66.*
*Club membership 100.*
**Visitors**      to book tee time telephone 01769 540530
                  daytime, 01769 540561 evenings.
**Green Fees** £12-£14 (£14-£17 weekends and bank holidays).
**Facilities**    ⊼ ⅃ ♨ ♀ ♨ 🏠 ⚐ 🏒 Paul Weston.
**Leisure**       hard tennis courts, outdoor and indoor heated
                  swimming pools, squash, fishing, sauna,
                  solarium, gymnasium, motorised carts for hire,
                  trolley for hire, putting green, indoor tennis,
                  beauty treatments.
**Location**      0.5m SE of village
**Hotel**         ★★★⚜ 70% Highbullen Hotel,
                  CHITTLEHAMHOLT
                  ☎ 01769 540561 12 ⇌Annexe25 ⇌ ♟

## CHULMLEIGH                        Map 03 SS61

**Chulmleigh** Leigh Rd EX18 7BL ☎ 01769 580519
Situated in a scenic area with views to distant Dartmoor, this
undulating meadowland course offers a good test for the most
experienced golfer and a challenge to newcomers to the
game. Short 18 hole summer course with a tricky 1st hole; in
winter the course is changed to 9 holes and made longer for
players to extend their game.
*Summer Short Course: 18 holes, 1450yds, Par 54, Course
record 51.*
*Winter Course: 9 holes, 2372yds, Par 58.*
*Club membership 77.*
**Visitors**      welcome anytime, closed on Mon from mid
                  Dec-1 Apr.
**Societies**     telephone in advance.
**Green Fees** £10 per day; £5.50 per 18 holes.
**Facilities**    ⅃ ♨ ♀ ♨ 🏠 ⚐
**Location**      SW side of village just off A377
**Hotel**         ★★★⚜ 70% Northcote Manor,
                  BURRINGTON ☎ 01769 560501 12 ⇌ ♟

## CHURSTON FERRERS                  Map 03 SX95

**Churston** Dartmouth Rd TQ5 0LA
☎ 01803 842751 & 842218
A cliff-top downland course with splendid views over
Brixham harbour and Tor Bay. There is some gorse with a
wooded area inland. A variety of shot is called for, with
particularly testing holes at the 3rd, 9th and 15th, all par 4.
*18 holes, 6219yds, Par 70, SSS 70, Course record 64.*
*Club membership 700.*
**Visitors**      must telephone in advance and be a member
                  of recognised golf club with a handicap
                  certificate.
**Societies**     apply in writing or telephone.
**Green Fees** £22 per round (£27 weekends).
**Facilities**    ⊗ ⊼ ⅃ ♨ ♀ ♨ 🏠 ⚐ 🏌 Neil Holman.
**Location**      NW side of village on A379

| Hotel | ★★ 63% Dainton Hotel, 95 Dartmouth Rd, Three Beaches, Goodrington, PAIGNTON ☎ 01803 550067 11 ⇌ ♠ |

## CREDITON
Map 03 SS80

**Downes Crediton** Hookway EX17 3PT
☎ 01363 773025 & 774464
Converted farmhouse course with lovely views. Parkland with hilly back nine.
*18 holes, 5859yds, Par 69, SSS 68.*
*Club membership 700.*

| | |
|---|---|
| Visitors | handicap certificate required, must contact in advance, restricted at weekends. |
| Societies | must contact in advance. |
| Green Fees | not confirmed. |
| Facilities | ♀ ⚑ ☎ ✦ ℓ Howard Finch. |
| Leisure | putting,practice area,trolley hire. |
| Location | 1.5m SE off A377 |
| Hotel | ★★★ 72% Barton Cross Hotel & Restaurant, Huxham, STOKE CANON ☎ 01392 841245 7 ⇌ ♠ |

## CULLOMPTON
Map 03 ST00

**Padbrook Park** EX15 1RU
☎ 01884 38286
A 9-hole, 18 tee parkland course with many water and woodland hazards and spectacular views. The dog-leg 2nd and pulpit 2nd are of particular challenge to golfers of all standards.
*9 holes, 6108yds, Par 70, SSS 70.*
*Club membership 250.*

| | |
|---|---|
| Visitors | welcome at all times, tee may be reserved by telephoning in advance. |
| Societies | apply in writing or telephone. |
| Green Fees | £10 per 18 holes; £7 per 9 holes (£16/£8 weekends). |
| Facilities | ⊗ ∭ ♭ ☎ ♀ ⚑ ☎ ✦ ℓ Stewart Adwick. |
| Leisure | fishing, trolley for hire, putting green, practice area. |
| Location | Southern edge of Cullompton on B3181 |
| Hotel | ★★★ 62% The Tiverton Hotel, Blundells Rd, TIVERTON ☎ 01884 256120 75 ⇌ ♠ |

## DAWLISH WARREN
Map 03 SX97

**Warren** EX7 0NF ☎ 01626 862255 & 864002
Typical flat, genuine links course lying on spit between sea and Exe estuary. Picturesque scenery, a few trees but much gorse. Testing in windy conditions. The 7th hole provides the opportunity to go for the green across a bay on the estuary.
*18 holes, 5965yds, Par 69, SSS 69.*
*Club membership 600.*

| | |
|---|---|
| Visitors | must contact in advance & have handicap certificate. |
| Societies | prior arrangement essential. |
| Green Fees | £21 (£24 weekends & bank holidays). |
| Facilities | ⊗ ∭ ♭ ☎ ♀ ⚑ ☎ ✦ ℓ Andrew Naldrett. |
| Leisure | trolley for hire, practice area. |
| Location | E side of village |
| Hotel | ★★★ 65% Langstone Cliff Hotel, Dawlish Warren, DAWLISH ☎ 01626 865155 64 ⇌ ♠Annexe4 ⇌ ♠ |

## DOWN ST MARY
Map 03 SS70

**Waterbridge** EX17 5LG ☎ 01363 85111
A testing course of 9-holes set in a gently sloping valley. The Par of 31 will not be easily gained with 4 par-4's and 5 par-3's, although the course record holder has Par 29! The 3rd hole which is a raised green is surrounded by water and the 4th (439 yards) is demanding for beginners.
*9 holes, 3908yds, Par 62, SSS 62.*

| | |
|---|---|
| Visitors | no restrictions. |
| Societies | no restrictions. |
| Green Fees | not confirmed. |
| Facilities | ☎ ✦ ℓ David Ridyard. |
| Leisure | trolley for hire. |
| Location | From Exeter on A377 towards Barnstaple |
| Hotel | ★★★★⚑ 70% Northcote Manor, BURRINGTON ☎ 01769 560501 12 ⇌ ♠ |

## EXETER
Map 03 SX99

**Exeter Golf & Country Club** Topsham Rd, Countess Wear EX2 7AE ☎ 01392 874139
A sheltered parkland course with some very old trees and known as the flattest course in Devon. 15th & 17th are testing par 4 holes.
*18 holes, 6000yds, Par 69, SSS 69.*
*Club membership 800.*

| | |
|---|---|
| Visitors | visitors welcome but may not play during match or competitions, very busy pre booking needed up to 1 week in advance. |
| Societies | welcome Thu only, booking available by telephone to starter tel 01392 876303. |
| Green Fees | £22 per day. |
| Facilities | ⊗ ∭ ♭ ☎ ♀ ⚑ ☎ ℓ Mike Rowlett. |
| Leisure | hard tennis courts, heated indoor plus outdoor swimming pool, squash, sauna, solarium, gymnasium, trolley for hire, putting green, practice area. |
| Location | SE side of city centre off A379 |
| Hotel | B Travel Inn, R98 Topsham Rd, Countess Wear Roundabout, Exeter Bypass, EXETER ☎ 01392 875441 44 ⇌ ♠ |

**Woodbury Park** Woodbury Castle, Woodbury EX5 1JJ
☎ 01395 233382
Two courses set in the lovely wooded parkland of Woodbury Castle.The 18-hole championship Oaks course is host to professional Championships and the 9-hole is a championship-standard training course.
*Oaks: 18 holes, 6707yds, Par 72, SSS 72.*
*Acorn: 9 holes, 4582yds, Par 69, SSS 62.*
*Club membership 400.*

| | |
|---|---|
| Visitors | advisable to contact in advance. |
| Societies | contact in advance. |
| Green Fees | not confirmed. |
| Facilities | ♀ (Mon-Sat) ⚑ ☎ ✦ |
| Leisure | fishing. |
| Hotel | ★★★ 67% Ebford House Hotel, Exmouth Rd, EBFORD ☎ 01392 877658 16 ⇌ ♠ |

Entries with a shaded background identify courses that are considered to be particularly interesting

## HIGH BICKINGTON       Map 02 SS52

**Libbaton** EX37 9BS ☎ 01769 560269 & 560167
Parkland course on undulating land with no steep slopes.
Floodlit driving range.
*18 holes, 6494yds, Par 73, SSS 72, Course record 72.*
*Club membership 500.*
**Visitors**     book in advance.
**Societies**    telephone to book in advance.
**Green Fees** £22 per day; £18 per round (£26/£22 bank
            holidays & weekends).
**Facilities**    ⊗ ⊁ ⊾ ⛳ ♀ ♨ 🏠 ⛵ 📧 ⁆ John Phillips.
**Leisure**     fishing, gymnasium, motorised carts for hire,
            buggies for hire, trolley for hire, driving range,
            putting green, practice area.
**Hotel**        ★★★♨ 70% Highbullen Hotel,
            CHITTLEHAMHOLT
            ☎ 01769 540561 12 ⇌Annexe25 ⇌ ↝

## HOLSWORTHY       Map 02 SS30

**Holsworthy** Killatree EX22 6LP ☎ 01409 253177
Pleasant parkland course with gentle slopes and numerous
trees..
*18 holes, 6062yds, Par 70, SSS 69, Course record 64.*
*Club membership 600.*
**Visitors**     may not play Sun am.
**Societies**    by arrangement with secretary or professional.
**Green Fees** £15 per day/round (£20 weekends & bank
            holidays).
**Facilities**    ⊗ ⊁ ⊾ ⛳ ♀ ♨ 🏠 ⛵ 📧 ⁆ Simon Chapman.
**Leisure**     trolley for hire, putting green, practice area.
**Location**    1.5m W on A3072
**Hotel**        ★★♨ 71% Court Barn Country House Hotel,
            CLAWTON ☎ 01409 271219 8rm(7 ⇌ ↝)

## HONITON       Map 03 ST10

**Honiton** Middlehills EX14 8TR
☎ 01404 44422 & 42943
Level parkland course on a plateau 850ft above sea level.
Easy walking and good views. The 4th hole is a testing par 3.
The club was founded in 1896.
*18 holes, 5902yds, Par 69, SSS 68.*
*Club membership 800.*
**Visitors**     must contact in advance.
**Societies**    society bookings on Thursdays.
**Green Fees** £20 per day (£25 weekends).
**Facilities**    ⊗ ⊁ ⊾ ⛳ ♀ ♨ 🏠 ⛵ ⁆ Adrian Cave.
**Leisure**     trolley for hire, putting green, practice area,
            touring caravan site.
**Location**    1.25m SE of Honiton
**Hotel**        ★★ 71% Home Farm Hotel, Wilmington,
            HONITON
            ☎ 01404 831278 6 ⇌Annexe7 ⇌ ↝

## ILFRACOMBE       Map 02 SS54

**Ilfracombe** Hele Bay EX34 9RT ☎ 01271 862176
A sporting, clifftop, heathland course with views over the
Bristol Channel and moors from every tee and green.
*18 holes, 5893yds, Par 69, SSS 69, Course record 66.*
*Club membership 642.*

**Visitors**     recommended to make tee reservation prior to
            visit, member only 12-2 daily and before 10 am
            on weekends.
**Societies**    telephone in advance.
**Green Fees** £17 per day (£20 weekends & bank holidays).
**Facilities**    ⊗ ⊁ ⊾ ⛳ ♀ ♨ 🏠 ⛵ ⁆ David Hoare.
**Leisure**     trolley for hire, driving range, putting, practice
            area.
**Location**    1.5m E off A399
**Hotel**        ★★ 69% Elmfield Hotel, Torrs Park,
            ILFRACOMBE
            ☎ 01271 863377 11 ⇌ ↝Annexe2 ⇌ ↝

## IPPLEPEN       Map 03 SX86

**Dainton Park** Totnes Rd, Ipplepen TQ12 5TN
☎ 01803 83812
The first full-length pay and play course serving the Torbay
area. A challenging parkland type course in typical Devon
countryside, with gentle contours, tree-lined fairways and
raised tees. Water hazards make the two opening holes
particularly testing. The 8th, a dramatic 180yard drop hole
totally surrounded by sand, is one of four tough Par 3's on the
course. It is advisable to book start times.
*18 holes, 6207yds, Par 71, SSS 70, Course record 71.*
*Club membership 500.*
**Visitors**     prior booking by phone advisable to guarantee
            start time.
**Societies**    apply in writing.
**Green Fees** £20 per day; £12 per round (£24/£15 weekends
            & bank holidays).
**Facilities**    ⊗ ⊁ ⊾ ⛳ ♀ ♨ 🏠 ⛵ ⁆ Martin Tyson.
**Leisure**     motorised carts for hire, trolley for hire, driving
            range, putting green, practice area.
**Location**    2m S of Newton Abbot on A381
**Hotel**        ★★ 63% Old Church House Inn, Torbryan,
            IPPLEPEN ☎ 01803 812372 6 ⇌ ↝

## IVYBRIDGE       Map 02 SX65

**Dinnaton Sporting & Country Club** Blachford Rd
PL21 9HU ☎ 01752 892512 & 892452
Challenging 9-hole moorland course overlooking the South
Hams. Mainly par 3 but with four recently added par 4 holes,
three lakes and tight fairways; excellent for improving the
short game Floodlit driving range.
*9 holes, 4089yds, Par 64, SSS 60.*
*Club membership 275.*
**Visitors**     no restrictions.
**Societies**    telephone in advance.
**Green Fees** weekdays £10 per day (£12.50 weekends & bank
            holidays).
**Facilities**    ⊗ ⊁ ⊾ ⛳ ♀ ♨ 🏠 ⛵ 📧 ⁆ David Ridyard.
**Leisure**     hard tennis courts, heated indoor swimming
            pool, squash, sauna, solarium, gymnasium,
            driving range, practice area.
**Location**    Just off main A38
**Hotel**        ★★★♨ 74% Glazebrook House Hotel &
            Restaurant, SOUTH BRENT
            ☎ 01364 73322 10 ⇌ ↝

---

Entries with a shaded background identify
courses that are considered to be particularly
interesting

# No Ordinary Golfing Hotel

Set on the edge of beautiful Dartmoor, the luxury and comfort of the Manor House Hotel complements a par 69 Championship course of stunning beauty, renowned as one of England's finest courses.

Enjoy a challenging game, modern facilities and the traditional comfort of our fine country house hotel. In addition, with 4 spacious meeting rooms and easy access to the M5, we are the ideal conference and team building venue. Ask about our self contained and luxurious North Lodge.

**Book now on 01647 440355**

## MANOR HOUSE HOTEL & GOLF COURSE ★★★★
MORETONHAMPSTEAD, DEVON, TQ13 8RE.

*A PRINCIPAL HOTEL*

---

## MORETONHAMPSTEAD　　　　　Map 03 SX78

**Manor House Hotel** TQ13 8RE ☎ 01647 440998
This enjoyable parkland course is a sporting circuit with just enough hazards (most of them natural) to make any golfer think. The Rivers Bowden and Bovey meander through the first eight holes. Driving range.
*18 holes, 6016yds, Par 69, SSS 69, Course record 65.*
*Club membership 120.*

| | |
|---|---|
| Visitors | must contact in advance and pre-arrange starting times. |
| Societies | must telephone for reservation in advance. |
| Green Fees | £28 per day; £22.50 per round (£35/£28 weekends). |
| Facilities | ⊗ ⅶ ▮ 🖢 ♀ ♨ 🖻 ⌖ 🏌 ☎ Richard Lewis. |
| Leisure | hard tennis courts, fishing, motorised carts for hire, buggies for hire, trolley for hire, putting green, practice area. |
| Location | 3m W of Moretonhampstead, off B3212 |
| Hotel | ★★★★ 63% Manor House Hotel, MORETONHAMPSTEAD ☎ 01647 440355 89 ⇄ ⮝ |

## MORTEHOE　　　　　　　　　　Map 02 SS44

**Mortehoe & Woolacombe** EX34 7EH
☎ 01271 870225 & 870745
Attached to a camping and caravan site, this 9-hole course has 2 par 3s and 7 par 4s. The gently sloping clifftop course has spectacular views across Morte Bay.
*9 holes, 4690yds, Par 66, SSS 63, Course record 69.*
*Club membership 233.*

| | |
|---|---|
| Visitors | no restrictions. |
| Societies | must telephone or write in advance. |
| Green Fees | £10 per 18 holes; £6 per 9 holes. |
| Facilities | ⊗ ⅶ ▮ 🖢 ♀ ♨ 🖻 ⌖ |
| Leisure | heated indoor swimming pool, trolley for hire, putting green, practice nets, camping & caravan site. |
| Location | 0.25m before Mortehoe on station road |
| Hotel | ★★★ 76% Watersmeet Hotel, Mortehoe, WOOLACOMBE ☎ 01271 870333 23 ⇄ ⮝ |

## NEWTON ABBOT　　　　　　　　Map 03 SX87

**Newton Abbot (Stover)** Bovey Rd TQ12 6QQ
☎ 01626 52460 (Secretary) & 62078 (Pro)
Wooded parkland course with a stream coming into play on eight holes. Fairly flat.
*18 holes, 5862yds, Par 69, SSS 68, Course record 63.*
*Club membership 800.*

| | |
|---|---|
| Visitors | must have proof of membership of recognised club or current handicap certificate. |

---

| | |
|---|---|
| Societies | by arrangement on Thu only. |
| Green Fees | £22 per day. |
| Facilities | ⊗ ⅶ ▮ 🖢 ♀ ♨ 🖻 ☎ Malcolm Craig. |
| Leisure | trolley for hire, putting green, practice area. |
| Location | 3m N on A382 |
| Hotel | ★★ 63% Queens Hotel, Queen St, NEWTON ABBOT ☎ 01626 63133 & 54106 22rm(19 ⇄ ⮝) |

## OKEHAMPTON　　　　　　　　　Map 02 SX59

**Okehampton** Tors Rd EX20 1EF ☎ 01837 52113
A good combination of moorland, woodland and river make this one of the prettiest, yet testing courses in Devon.
*18 holes, 5243yds, Par 68, SSS 67, Course record 66.*
*Club membership 600.*

| | |
|---|---|
| Visitors | advance booking recommended, limited times available at weekends. |
| Societies | by prior arrangement. |
| Green Fees | £16 per day (£22 Sat, £18 Sun). |
| Facilities | ⊗ ⅶ ▮ 🖢 ♀ ♨ 🖻 ⌖ ☎ Simon Jefferies. |
| Leisure | trolley for hire, putting green, practice area. |
| Location | 1m S off A30 |
| Hotel | ★★ 65% Oxenham Arms, SOUTH ZEAL ☎ 01837 840244 & 840577 8rm(7 ⇄ ⮝) |

## PLYMOUTH　　　　　　　　　　Map 02 SX45

**Elfordleigh** Plympton PL7 5EB ☎ 01752 336428
Charming, saucer-shaped parkland course with alternate tees for 18 holes. Tree-lined fairways and three lakes. Fairly hard walking.
*9 holes, 5664yds, Par 68, SSS 67.*
*Club membership 450.*

| | |
|---|---|
| Visitors | must contact in advance & have handicap certificate. |
| Societies | by arrangement. |
| Green Fees | not confirmed. |
| Facilities | ♀ ♨ 🖻 ⌖ 🏌 ☎ Andrew Rickard. |
| Leisure | hard tennis courts, outdoor and indoor heated swimming pools, squash, sauna, solarium, gymnasium, games room, jacuzzi, croquet. |
| Location | 8m NE off B3416 |
| Hotel | ★★★ 68% Elfordleigh Hotel & Country Club, Colebrook, Plympton, PLYMOUTH ☎ 01752 336428 18 ⇄ ⮝ |

**Staddon Heights** Plymstock PL9 9SP
☎ 01752 402475 & 492630
Seaside course affording spectacular views across Plymouth Sound, Dartmoor and Bodmin Moor. Testing holes include the par 3 17th with its green cut into a hillside and the par 4 14th across a road. Easy walking.　▶

*18 holes, 5869yds, Par 68, SSS 68, Course record 66.*
*Club membership 655.*

**Visitors** must have handicap certificate and contact the pro or secretary.
**Societies** apply by telephone in advance.
**Green Fees** £20 per day (£25 weekends).
**Facilities** ⊗ ⵊ ⅏ ⬤ ♀ ⅄ ⬙ ⚑ ⚐ Ian Marshall.
**Leisure** trolley for hire, putting green, practice area.
**Location** 5m SW of city centre
**Hotel** B Forte Posthouse Plymouth, Cliff Rd, The Hoe, PLYMOUTH ☎ 01752 662828 106 ⇆ ☏

## SAUNTON
Map 02 SS43

**Saunton** EX33 1LG ☎ 01271 812436
Two traditional links courses (one championship). Windy, with natural hazards.
*East Course: 18 holes, 6708yds, Par 73, SSS 73, Course record 65.*
*West Course: 18 holes, 6356yds, Par 71, SSS 71, Course record 68.*
*Club membership 1100.*
**Visitors** prior booking recommended and must have handicap certificate.
**Societies** must apply in advance, handicap certificates required.
**Green Fees** £35 per day (£40 weekends & bank holidays).
**Facilities** ⊗ ⵊ ⅏ ⬤ ♀ ⅄ ⬙ ⚑ ⚐ J A McGhee.
**Leisure** trolley for hire, putting green, practice area, snooker.
**Location** S side of village off B3231
**Hotel** ★★★★ 69% Saunton Sands Hotel, SAUNTON ☎ 01271 890212 92 ⇆ ☏

## SIDMOUTH
Map 03 SY18

**Sidmouth** Cotmaton Rd, Peak Hill EX10 8SX
☎ 01395 513451 & 516407
Situated on the side of Peak Hill, offering beautiful coastal views. Club founded in 1889.
*18 holes, 5100yds, Par 66, SSS 65, Course record 59.*
*Club membership 700.*
**Visitors** by prior arrangement.
**Societies** by prior arrangement with the secretary.
**Green Fees** £20 per day.
**Facilities** ⊗ ⵊ ⅏ ⬤ ♀ ⅄ ⬙ ⚑ ⚐ Haydn Barrell.
**Leisure** trolley for hire, putting green, limited practice area.
**Location** W side of town centre
**Hotel** ★★★★ 71% Victoria Hotel, Esplanade, SIDMOUTH ☎ 01395 512651 61 ⇆ ☏

## SOUTH BRENT
Map 03 SX66

**Wrangaton (S Devon)** Golf Links Rd, Wrangaton TQ10 9HJ
☎ 01364 73229
Moorland/parkland course within Dartmoor National Park. Spectacular views towards sea and rugged terrain. Natural fairways and hazards include bracken, sheep and ponies.
*18 holes, 6041yds, Par 69, SSS 69, Course record 63.*
*Club membership 700.*
**Visitors** play any time.
**Societies** write or telephone.
**Green Fees** £17 per day (£23 weekends & bank holidays).

**Facilities** ⊗ ⵊ ⅏ ⬤ ♀ ⅄ ⬙ ⚑ ⚐ Adrian Whitehead.
**Leisure** practice facilities.
**Location** 2.25 m SW off A38
**Hotel** ★★★ 74% Glazebrook House Hotel & Restaurant, SOUTH BRENT ☎ 01364 73322 10 ⇆ ☏

## SPARKWELL
Map 02 SX55

**Welbeck Manor & Sparkwell Golf Course** Blacklands PL7 5DF ☎ 01752 837219
A mature parkland course with several challenging holes, it features fairway and greenside bunkers, mature trees and streams. The house on the site, now the hotel, was built by Isambard Kingdom Brunel. Several of the holes have been named to commemorate some of his famous works - the 6th being The Great Western.This is a very challenging Par 5 tee which is out of bounds all the way up the left.
*9 holes, 2886yds, Par 68, SSS 68, Course record 68.*
*Club membership 200.*
**Visitors** no restrictions.
**Societies** telephone in advance.
**Green Fees** £9 per 18 holes; £5 per 9 holes (£11/£6 weekends).
**Facilities** ⊗ ⵊ ⅏ ⬤ ♀ ⅄ ⬙ ⚑ ⚐
**Leisure** trolley for hire, pitch & putt.
**Location** 1m N of A38 Plymouth/Ivybridge road
**Hotel** ★★★ 68% Boringdon Hall, Colebrook, Plympton, PLYMOUTH ☎ 01752 344455 41 ⇆ ☏

## TAVISTOCK
Map 02 SX47

**Hurdwick** Tavistock Hamlets PL19 8PZ
☎ 01822 612746
This Executive parkland course with many bunkers and fine views opened in 1990. The idea of Executive golf originated in America and the concept is that a round should take no longer than 3 hours whilst offering solid challenge, thus suiting the busy business person.
*18 holes, 4553yds, Par 67, SSS 64, Course record 69.*
*Club membership 180.*
**Visitors** no restrictions.
**Societies** must contact in advance.
**Green Fees** £12 per day.
**Facilities** ⅏ ⬤ ♀ ⅄ ⬙ ⚑
**Leisure** buggies for hire, trolley for hire, putting green, practice area.
**Location** 1m N of Tavistock
**Hotel** ★★★ 62% Bedford Hotel, Plymouth Rd, TAVISTOCK ☎ 01822 613221 31rm(30 ⇆ ☏)

**Tavistock** Down Rd PL19 9AQ ☎ 01822 612344
Set on Whitchurch Down in south-west Dartmoor with easy walking and magnificent views over rolling countryside into Cornwall. Downland turf with some heather, and interesting holes on undulating ground.
*18 holes, 6230yds, Par 70, SSS 70, Course record 64.*
*Club membership 700.*
*Visitors* advisable to contact in advance.
**Societies** by arrangement with secretary.
**Green Fees** £18 per round/day (£23 weekends).
**Facilities** ⊗ ⵊ ⅏ ⬤ ♀ ⅄ ⬙ ⚐ D Rehaag.
**Leisure** trolley for hire, putting green, practice area.

| Location | 1m SE of town centre |
| Hotel | ★★★ 62% Bedford Hotel, Plymouth Rd, TAVISTOCK ☎ 01822 613221 31rm(30 ⇄ ℟) |

## TEDBURN ST MARY
Map 03 SX89

**Fingle Glen** EX6 6AF ☎ 01647 61817
9-hole course containing six par 4's and three par 3's set in 52 acres of rolling countryside. Testing 4th, 5th and 9th holes. 12-bay floodlit driving range.
*9 holes, 4818yds, Par 66, SSS 63, Course record 63.*
*Club membership 400.*

| Visitors | must contact in advance. |
| Societies | write or telephone in advance. |
| Green Fees | Summer: £13.50 per 18 holes; £9 per 9 holes (£16/£11.50 weekends). Winter: £6 per 9 holes (£8 weekends). |
| Facilities | ⊗ ℳ ⓑ ♥ ♀ ⚑ ☎ ⚐ ☂ ⚑ ℓ Stephen Gould. |
| Leisure | trolley for hire, driving range, practice area. |
| Location | 5m W of Exeter, off A30 |
| Hotel | B Travel Inn, R98 Topsham Rd, Countess Wear Roundabout, Exeter Bypass, EXETER ☎ 01392 875441 44 ⇄ ℟ |

## TEIGNMOUTH
Map 03 SX97

**Teignmouth** Haldon Moor TQ14 9NY
☎ 01626 774194
This fairly flat heathland course is high up with a fine seascape from the clubhouse. Good springy turf with some heather and an interesting layout makes for very enjoyable holiday golf.
*18 holes, 6200yds, Par 71, SSS 70, Course record 65.*
*Club membership 900.*

| Visitors | groups must contact in advance, restricted tee off times at weekends. |
| Societies | telephone in advance and confirm in writing. |
| Green Fees | £22 per day/round (£25 weekends). |
| Facilities | ⊗ ℳ ⓑ ♥ ♀ ⚑ ☎ ⚐ ℓ Peter Ward. |
| Leisure | trolley for hire, putting green, practice area. |
| Location | 2m NW off B3192 |
| Hotel | ★★ 68% Ness House Hotel, Marine Dr, Shaldon, TEIGNMOUTH ☎ 01626 873480 7 ⇄ ℟Annexe5 ⇄ ℟ |

## THURLESTONE
Map 03 SX64

**Thurlestone** TQ7 3NZ ☎ 01548 560405
Situated on the edge of the cliffs with typical downland turf and good greens. The course, after an interesting opening hole, rises to higher land with fine seaviews, and finishes with an excellent 502-yard downhill hole to the clubhouse.
*18 holes, 6340yds, Par 71, SSS 70, Course record 65.*
*Club membership 770.*

| Visitors | must contact in advance & have handicap certificate from a recognised club. |
| Green Fees | £24 per day/round. £90 7 consecutive days. |
| Facilities | ⊗ ℳ by prior arrangement ⓑ ♥ ♀ ⚑ ☎ ⚐ ℓ Neville Whitley. |
| Leisure | hard and grass tennis courts, trolley for hire, putting green, practice area. |
| Location | S side of village |

| Hotel | ★★★★ 70% Thurlestone Hotel, THURLESTONE ☎ 01548 560382 68 ⇄ ℟ |

## TIVERTON
Map 03 SS91

**Tiverton** Post Hill EX16 4NE ☎ 01884 252187
A parkland course where the many different species of tree are a feature and where the lush pastures ensure some of the finest fairways in the south-west. There are a number of interesting holes which visitors will find a real challenge.
*18 holes, 6236yds, Par 71, SSS 71, Course record 65.*
*Club membership 725.*

| Visitors | must have a current handicap certificate. |
| Societies | apply in writing or telephone. |
| Green Fees | £21 (£27 weekends). |
| Facilities | ⊗ ℳ ⓑ ♥ ♀ ⚑ ☎ ℓ David Sheppard. |
| Leisure | trolley for hire, putting green, practice area. |
| Hotel | ★★ 65% Hartnoll Hotel, Bolham, TIVERTON ☎ 01884 252777 11 ⇄ ℟Annexe5 ℟ |

## TORQUAY
Map 03 SX96

**Torquay** 30 Petitor Rd, St Marychurch TQ1 4QF
☎ 01803 329113
Unusual combination of cliff and parkland golf, with wonderful views over the sea and Dartmoor.
*18 holes, 6175yds, Par 69, SSS 70, Course record 66.*
*Club membership 700.*

| Visitors | must contact in advance. |
| Societies | must apply in writing. |
| Green Fees | £20 per day/round (£25 weekends & bank holidays). |
| Facilities | ⊗ ℳ ⓑ ♥ ♀ ⚑ ☎ ⚐ ℓ Martin Ruth. |
| Leisure | motorised carts for hire, buggies for hire, trolley for hire, putting green. |
| Location | 1.25m N |
| Hotel | ★★ 60% Norcliffe Hotel, 7 Babbacombe Downs Rd, Babbacombe, TORQUAY ☎ 01803 328456 27 ⇄ ℟ |

## TORRINGTON
Map 02 SS41

**Torrington** Weare Trees, Great Torrington EX38 7EZ
☎ 01805 622229
Hard walking on hilly commonland 9 hole course. Challenging par 3 4th hole with a sloping green and difficult crosswinds. Small greens and outstanding views.
*9 holes, 4419yds, Par 64, SSS 62, Course record 58.*
*Club membership 420.*

| Visitors | cannot play Sat & Sun before noon. |
| Societies | by arrangement. |
| Green Fees | £10 per day/round. |
| Facilities | ⊗ ℳ by prior arrangement ⓑ ♥ ♀ ⚑ ⚐ |
| Leisure | trolley for hire, putting green, practice area. |
| Location | 1m W of Torringdon |
| Hotel | ★★ 63% Beaconside Hotel, LANDCROSS ☎ 01237 477205 8rm(6 ⇄ ℟) |

# CULLODEN HOUSE HOTEL
## WESTWARD HO! (01237) 479421
Victorian elegance – modern comforts – most rooms en-suite – views across Bideford Bay and Atlantic – friendly and comfortable atmosphere.

SPECIAL GOLFING HOLIDAYS AVAILABLE
– CHOICE OF 8 COURSES

AA ★★

---

## UPOTTERY
Map 03 ST20

**Otter Valley Golf Centre**
☎ 01404 861266 (5m NW of Honiton off A30, on U pottery Rd) This Golf School set in beautiful Devon c ountryside was established in 1969. There are practice facilities with driving range, approach green, chipping green with bunkers and 5 practice holes. Weekend an d 5 day courses are available and there is self catering accommodation, telephone for details. All coaching is given personally by Andrew Thompson P.G.A.

## WESTWARD HO!
Map 02 SS42

**Royal North Devon** EX39 1HD
☎ 01237 473817
Links course with sea views.
*18 holes, 6644yds, Par 71, SSS 72.*
*Club membership 1100.*
| | |
|---|---|
| **Visitors** | advisable to telephone and book tee time, must have handicap certificate or letter of introduction from club. |
| **Societies** | apply in writing or telephone. |
| **Green Fees** | £28 per day; £24 per round. |
| **Facilities** | ⊗ ⅀ by prior arrangement ⓛ ⬛ ♀ ⚲ ⌂ ⚐ Ⓕ Graham Johnston. |
| **Leisure** | trolley for hire, driving range, putting green, practice area. |
| **Location** | N side of village off B3236 |
| **Hotel** | ★★ 62% Culloden House Hotel, Fosketh Hill, WESTWARD HO! ☎ 01237 479421 9rm(2 ⇄5 ⓘ) |

## WOOLFARDISWORTHY
Map 02 SS32

**Hartland Forest** Woolsery, Bideford EX39 5RA
☎ 01237 431442
This course is affected by winds and can be very windy at times.
*18 holes, 6015yds, Par 71, SSS 69.*
*Club membership 240.*
| | |
|---|---|
| **Visitors** | no restrictions. |
| **Societies** | apply in writing. |
| **Green Fees** | not confirmed. |
| **Facilities** | ♀ ⚲ ⚐ ⌂ |
| **Leisure** | hard tennis courts, heated indoor swimming pool, fishing, sauna, solarium, gymnasium. |
| **Location** | 4m E of A39 |
| **Hotel** | ★★★⚑ 74% Penhaven Country House, PARKHAM ☎ 01237 451388 12 ⇄ ⓘ |

## YELVERTON
Map 02 SX56

**Yelverton** Golf Links Rd PL20 6BN
☎ 01822 852824
An excellent course on the moors with virtually no trees. It is exposed to high winds. The fairways are tight but there is plenty of room. The longest hole is the 8th, a 569-yard, par 5. Outstanding views.
*18 holes, 6363yds, Par 71, SSS 70.*
*Club membership 650.*
| | |
|---|---|
| **Visitors** | subject to availability, advisable to contact in advance. |
| **Societies** | must be booked in advance, by telephone initially. |
| **Green Fees** | £22 per day/round (£25 weekends). |
| **Facilities** | ⊗ ⅀ ⓛ ⬛ ♀ ⚲ ⌂ ⚐ Ⓕ Tim McSherry. |
| **Leisure** | trolley for hire, putting green, practice area. |
| **Location** | 1m S of Yelverton, off A386 |
| **Hotel** | ★★★ 69% Moorland Links Hotel, YELVERTON ☎ 01822 852245 45 ⇄ ⓘ |

---

# YELVERTON GOLF CLUB
**Golf Links Road, Yelverton, Devon PL20 6BN.**
**Telephone: (01822) 852824**

18 Hole moorland course within the Dartmoor National Park
8 miles north of Plymouth on the A386 road
Green Fee £22w/day £25 w/end; 6363 yards; S.S.S. 70; fully licensed with catering facilities

# DORSET

## BEAMINSTER
Map 03 ST40

**Chedington Court** South Perrott DT8 3HU
☎ 01935 891413
At present 9 holes, though due to be extended to 18, this course is laid out in parkland using the natural features of the rolling countryside. The Par 5 4th is 596yards and looks daunting but it is downhill from the tee to the green. The Par 4 9th is a tricky final hole with its hidden small lake waiting for the errant second shot. Preservation of wildlife and the natural flora are of prime concern in managing the course.
*9 holes, 6754yds, Par 74, SSS 72, Course record 72.*
*Club membership 260.*
**Visitors**    must book tee time.
**Societies**    apply in writing or telephone.
**Green Fees** £13 per 18 holes; £8 per 9 holes (£16/£10 weekends & bank holidays).
**Facilities**    ⊗ ⓑ ⲙ ♀ ⤳ 🏠 ⛳ 🏄
**Leisure**    trolley for hire, practice ground, pitch & putt.
**Location**    5m NE of Beaminster
**Hotel**    ★★★ 68%  Bridge House Hotel, 3 Prout Bridge, BEAMINSTER
☎ 01308 862200 9 ⇆ ᴿAnnexe4 ⇆ ᴿ

## BELCHALWELL
Map 03 ST70

**Mid-Dorset** DT11 0EG ☎ 01258 861386
Set in an area of outstanding natural beauty, rich in wildlife, which provides a picturesque backdrop to this stimulating, undulating course. Modern clubhouse with magnificent views.
*18 holes, 6162yds, Par 70, SSS 70, Course record 69.*
*Club membership 270.*
**Visitors**    no restrictions.
**Societies**    must telephone in advance.
**Green Fees** £20 per day; £12 per round (£28/£17 weekends & bank holidays).
**Facilities**    ⊗ ⫰ ⓑ ⲙ ♀ ⤳ 🏠 ⛳ ᴿ Spencer Taylor.
**Leisure**    trolley for hire, driving range, putting green, practice area.
**Hotel**    ★★★ 68%  Crown Hotel, 8 West St, BLANDFORD FORUM
☎ 01258 456626 32 ⇆

## BLANDFORD FORUM
Map 03 ST80

**Ashley Wood** Wimborne Rd DT11 9HN ☎ 01258 452253
Undulating and well drained downland course with superb views over the Tarrant and Stour Valleys.
*18 holes, 6335yds, Par 70, SSS 70, Course record 69.*
*Club membership 550.*
**Visitors**    phone professional in advance (01258 480379).
**Societies**    apply to Secretary.
**Green Fees** £17 per day (£24 weekends).
**Facilities**    ⊗ ⫰ ⓑ ⲙ ♀ ⤳ 🏠 ᴿ Spencer Taylor.
**Leisure**    motorised carts for hire, buggies for hire, trolley for hire, putting green, practice area.
**Location**    2m E on B3082
**Hotel**    ★★★ 68%  Crown Hotel, 8 West St, BLANDFORD FORUM
☎ 01258 456626 32 ⇆

## BOURNEMOUTH
Map 04 SZ09

**Bournemouth & Meyrick** Central Dr, Meyrick Park BH2 6LH ☎ 01202 292425
Picturesque muncipal parkland course founded in 1890.
*18 holes, 5852yds, Par 70, SSS 69, Course record 64.*
*Club membership 500.*
**Visitors**    advance booking is essential.
**Societies**    telephone in advance.
**Green Fees** £12.50 per round (£13.50 weekends & bank holidays).
**Facilities**    ♀ ⤳ 🏠 ⛳ ᴿ Lee Thompson.
**Leisure**    squash, trolley for hire, putting green, practice area.
**Hotel**    ★★★ 63%  Burley Court Hotel, Bath Rd, BOURNEMOUTH
☎ 01202 552824 & 556704 38 ⇆ ᴿ

**Knighton Heath** Francis Av, West Howe BH11 8NX
☎ 01202 572633
Undulating heathland course on high ground inland from Bournemouth.
*18 holes, 6064yds, Par 70, SSS 69.*
*Club membership 700.*
**Visitors**    may not play weekend. Phone for availability.
**Societies**    must book in advance.
**Green Fees** £25 per day or round.
**Facilities**    ⊗ ⫰ ⓑ ⲙ ♀ ⤳ 🏠 ᴿ Jane Miles.
**Leisure**    trolley for hire, putting green, practice area.
**Location**    N side of town centre off A348
**Hotel**    ★★★ 63%  Bridge House Hotel, 2 Ringwood Rd, Longham,  FERNDOWN
☎ 01202 578828 37 ⇆ ᴿ

*Queen's Park* Queens Park Dr West BH8 9BY
☎ 01202 396198
Undulating parkland course of pine and heather, with narrow, tree-lined fairways. Public course played over by 'Boscombe Golf Club' and 'Bournemouth Artisans Golf Club'.
*18 holes, 6505yds, Par 72, SSS 72.*
**Visitors**    must contact in advance.
**Societies**    must contact in advance.
**Green Fees** not confirmed.
**Facilities**    ♀ ⤳ 🏠 ᴿ Richard Hill.
**Location**    2m NE of town centre off A338
**Hotel**    ★★ 66%  Hotel Riviera, West Cliff Gardens, BOURNEMOUTH
☎ 01202 552845 34 ⇆ ᴿ

## BRIDPORT
Map 03 SY49

**Bridport & West Dorset** East Cliff, West Bay DT6 4EP
☎ 01308 421491 & 421095
Seaside links course on the top of the east cliff, with fine views over Lyme Bay and surrounding countryside. A popular feature is the pretty and deceptive 14th hole, its sunken green lying 90 feet below the tee and guarded by natural hazards and bunkers. New course layout from June 1996.
*18 holes, 6500yds, Par 71, SSS 69.*
*Club membership 700.*
**Visitors**    must contact in advance.
**Societies**    must contact in writing in advance.
**Green Fees** £25 per day (£18 after 2pm).
**Facilities**    ⊗ ⓑ ⲙ ♀ ⤳ 🏠 ᴿ David Parsons.    ▶

## Bridport Arms Hotel
### West Bay, Bridport, Dorset DT6 4EN
### Tel: 01308 422994

A 16th century thatched hotel on the beach at West Bay. The Restaurant specialising in local sea foods is open to non residents. Bar meals are also available throughout the year. Very close to Bridport and West Dorset Golf Course.

*Please contact for brochure.*

**Leisure**    trolley for hire, putting green, pitch & putt (holiday season).
**Location**    2m S of Bridport
**Hotel**    ★★ 67% Ullswater Hotel, West Cliff Gardens, BOURNEMOUTH
    ☎ 01202 555181 42 ⇄ 🏌
**Additional hotel**    ★★★ 59% Grosvenor Hotel, Bath Rd, East Cliff, BOURNEMOUTH
    ☎ 01202 558858 40 ⇄ 🏌

### BROADSTONE      Map 04 SZ09

**Broadstone (Dorset)** Wentworth Dr BH18 8DQ
☎ 01202 692595
Undulating and demanding heathland course with the 2nd, 7th, 13th and 16th being particularly challenging holes.
*18 holes, 6315yds, Par 70, SSS 70. Course record 66.*
*Club membership 700.*
**Visitors** restricted at weekends & bank holidays. Must contact in advance.
**Societies** contact in advance.
**Green Fees** £36 per day; £28 per round (£40 per round weekends & bank holidays).
**Facilities** ⊗ �🀆 🏌 🍴 ♀ ⛳ 🏧 🏌 ⚑ Nigel Tokely.
**Leisure** motorised carts for hire, trolley for hire, driving range, putting green, practice area.
**Location** N side of village off B3074
**Hotel** ★★★ 60% King's Head Hotel, The Square, WIMBORNE
    ☎ 01202 880101 27 ⇄ 🏌

### CERNE ABBAS      Map 03 ST60

*Lyons Gate* Lyons Gate Farm, Lyons Gate DT2 7AZ
☎ 01300 345239
Since this course was opened in 1990, it has gained a reputation as 'the toughest 9-hole course in English golf' and the most spcetacular. Up to the time of publication no contender has reached par.
*9 holes, 4000yds, Par 30, SSS 30, Course record 32.*
*Club membership 200.*
**Visitors** no restrictions.
**Societies** telephone for details.
**Green Fees** not confirmed.
**Facilities** ⛳ 🏧 ⚑
**Location** On A352, 11m N of Dorchester
**Guesthouse** QQQ Old Bakehouse Hotel, PIDDLETRENTHIDE
    ☎ 01300 348305 2 ⇄ Annexe7 ⇄ 🏌

### CHRISTCHURCH      Map 04 SZ19

**Dudmoor Farm** Dudmoor Farm Rd BH23 6AQ
☎ 01202 483980
A non-membership golf course with tree-lined par 3 and 4 fairways.
*9 holes, 1428mtrs, Par 31.*
**Visitors** no restrictions.
**Societies** telephone in advance.
**Green Fees** £4.50 per 18 holes.
**Facilities** 🏌 ⛳ ⚑ 🏡
**Leisure** squash, fishing.
**Hotel** ★★★ 75% Waterford Lodge Hotel, 87 Bure Ln, Friars Cliff, Mudeford, CHRISTCHURCH
    ☎ 01425 272948 17 ⇄

*Iford Bridge* Barrack Rd BH23 2BA ☎ 01202 473817
Parkland course with the River Stour running through. Driving range.
*9 holes, 2377yds, Par 34, SSS 32.*
*Club membership 350.*
**Visitors** no restrictions.
**Societies** must contact in advance.
**Green Fees** not confirmed.
**Facilities** ♀ ⛳ ⚑ ⚑ Peter Troth.
**Leisure** hard and grass tennis courts, driving range,bowls,trolley hire.
**Location** W side of town centre on A35
**Hotel** ★★★ 75% Waterford Lodge Hotel, 87 Bure Ln, Friars Cliff, Mudeford, CHRISTCHURCH
    ☎ 01425 272948 17 ⇄

### DORCHESTER      Map 03 SY69

**Came Down** Came Down DT2 8NR
☎ 01305 813494 & 812670
Scene of the West of England Championships on several occasions, this fine course lies on a high plateau commanding glorious views over Portland. Three par 5 holes add interest to a round. The turf is of the springy, downland type.
*18 holes, 6244yds, Par 70, SSS 71.*
*Club membership 750.*
**Visitors** advisable to phone in advance, must have handicap certificate. May play after 9am weekdays & after noon Sun.
**Societies** by arrangement on Wed only.
**Green Fees** £20 per day (£25 per day weekends & bank holidays).
**Facilities** ⊗ �🀆 🏌 🍴 ♀ ⛳ 🏧 ⚑ ⚑ Robert Preston.
**Leisure** buggies for hire, trolley for hire, driving range, putting green, practice area.

| | |
|---|---|
| **Location** | 2m S off A354 |
| **Guesthouse** | QQQQQ Yalbury Cottage Hotel & Restaurant, Lower Bockhampton, DORCHESTER ☎ 01305 262382 8 ⇆ ﹫ |

## FERNDOWN                                      Map 04 SU00

**Dudsbury** Christchurch Rd BH22 8ST
☎ 01202 593499 & 594488 pro shop
Set in 150 acres of beautiful Dorset countryside rolling down to the River Stour. Wide variety of interesting and challenging hazards, notably water which comes into play on 14 holes.
*Main Course: 18 holes, 6508yds, Par 71, SSS 71, Course record 64.*
*Academy Course: 5 holes, 680yds, Par 16.*
*Club membership 650.*

| | |
|---|---|
| **Visitors** | welcome by arrangement with secretary or golf professional. |
| **Societies** | telephone in advance. |
| **Green Fees** | Main: £40 per day; £30 per 18 holes. |
| **Facilities** | ⊗ ⅏ ﹢ ⬛ ♀ ⚶ 🕮 ﹖ Kevin Spurgeon. |
| **Leisure** | fishing, motorised carts for hire, buggies for hire, trolley for hire, driving range, putting green, practice area. |
| **Location** | 3m N of Bournemouth on B3073, between Parley and Longham |
| **Hotel** | ★★★★ 66% The Dormy, New Rd, FERNDOWN ☎ 01202 872121 128 ⇆ ﹫ |

| | |
|---|---|
| **Ferndown** 119 Golf Links Rd BH22 8BU ☎ 01202 874602 | |
| Fairways are gently undulating amongst heather, gorse and pine trees giving the course a most attractive appearance. There are a number of dog-leg holes and, on a clear day, there are views across to the Isle of Wight. | |
| *Championship Course: 18 holes, 6452yds, Par 71, SSS 71, Course record 64.* | |
| *Presidents Course: 9 holes, 2797yds, Par 35, SSS 68.* | |
| *Club membership 700.* | |
| **Visitors** | must contact in advance & have handicap certificate, no visitors on Thursdays except on Presidents course, numbers restricted at weekends. |
| **Societies** | welcome Tue & Fri only, telephone in advance. |
| **Green Fees** | Championship: £40 (£45 weekends). Presidents: £15 (£20 weekends and bank holidays). |
| **Facilities** | ⊗ ⅏ ﹢ ⬛ ♀ ⚶ 🕮 ﹖ Iais Parker. |
| **Leisure** | buggies for hire, trolley for hire, putting green, practice area. |
| **Location** | S side of town centre off A347 |
| **Hotel** | ★★★★ 66% The Dormy, New Rd, FERNDOWN ☎ 01202 872121 128 ⇆ ﹫ |

## HALSTOCK                                      Map 03 ST50

**Halstock** Common Ln BA22 9SF ☎ 01935 891689
Halstock is a short tight course, but challenging. There are plenty of trees and water hazards.
*18 holes, 4351yds, Par 65, SSS 63, Course record 65.*
*Club membership 120.*

| | |
|---|---|
| **Visitors** | no restrictions. |
| **Societies** | telephone in advance. |

| | |
|---|---|
| **Green Fees** | £9.50 per 18 holes; £5.50 per 9 holes (£11.50/£7 weekends). |
| **Facilities** | ⬛ ⚶ 🕮 ﹖ |
| **Leisure** | trolley for hire, driving range, putting green, practice area. |
| **Location** | 6m S of Yeovil |
| **Hotel** | ★★★(red)⚘ Summer Lodge, EVERSHOT ☎ 01935 83424 11 ⇆ ﹫Annexe6 ⇆ ﹫ |

## HIGHCLIFFE                                    Map 04 SZ29

**Highcliffe Castle** 107 Lymington Rd BH23 4LA
☎ 01425 272210
Picturesque parkland course with easy walking.
*18 holes, 4762yds, Par 64, SSS 63, Course record 58.*
*Club membership 500.*

| | |
|---|---|
| **Visitors** | must have handicap certificate or be a member of recognised club. |
| **Societies** | write or telephone in advance. |
| **Green Fees** | not confirmed. |
| **Facilities** | ♀ ⚶ 🕮 ﹖ ﹖ R E Crockford. |
| **Leisure** | putting green, practice area, trolley hire. |
| **Location** | SW side of town on A337 |
| **Hotel** | ★★★ 75% Waterford Lodge Hotel, 87 Bure Ln, Friars Cliff, Mudeford, CHRISTCHURCH ☎ 01425 272948 17 ⇆ |

## LYME REGIS                                    Map 03 SY39

**Lyme Regis** Timber Hill DT7 3HQ ☎ 01297 442963
Undulating cliff-top course with magnificent views of Golden Cap and Lyme Bay.
*18 holes, 6220yds, Par 71, SSS 70, Course record 65.*
*Club membership 575.*

| | |
|---|---|
| **Visitors** | must contact in advance & have handicap certificate or be a member of recognised golf club. No play on Thu & Sun mornings. |
| **Societies** | Tue, Wed & Fri; must contact in writing. |
| **Green Fees** | not confirmed. |
| **Facilities** | ♀ ⚶ 🕮 ﹖ Andrew Black. |
| **Leisure** | trolley hire, putting, practice area. |
| **Location** | 1.5m N on A3052 |
| **Hotel** | ★★★ 69% Alexandra Hotel, Pound St, LYME REGIS ☎ 01297 442010 27 ⇆ ﹫ |

## LYTCHETT MATRAVERS                            Map 03 SY99

**Bulbury Woods** Halls Rd BH16 6EP ☎ 01929 459574
Parkland course in 40 acres of woodland, with well guarded greens, tight fairways and extensive views over the Purbecks, Poole Bay and Wareham Forest. Not too hilly.
*18 holes, 6065yds, Par 70, SSS 69, Course record 68.*
*Club membership 600.*

| | |
|---|---|
| **Visitors** | must contact in advance. |
| **Societies** | must contact in advance. |
| **Green Fees** | £28 per day; £18 per round. |
| **Facilities** | ⊗ ⬛ ⬛ ♀ ⚶ 🕮 ﹙ ﹖ John Sharkey. |
| **Leisure** | buggies for hire, trolley for hire, putting green, practice area. |
| **Location** | A35 Poole to Dorchester, 1m from Bakers Arms roundabout |
| **Hotel** | ★★★(red)⚘ Priory Hotel, Church Green, WAREHAM ☎ 01929 551666 15 ⇆ ﹫Annexe4 ⇆ ﹫ |

## AA 3 star & 80% rating – 2 AA Rosettes

Superb Waterside hotel with outstanding food. 20 beautifully furnished bedrooms overlooking Poole Harbour and Brownsea Island. Many top national awards presented for exceptionally high of customer care and outstanding service.
Only a pitch and a put away (¼ mile) from Parkstone Golf Club!

**38 Salterns Way, Lilliput, Poole, Dorset, BH14 8JR Tel: 01202 707321**

---

### POOLE      Map 04 SZ09

**Parkstone** Links Rd, Parkstone BH14 9QS
☎ 01202 707138
Very scenic heathland course with views of Poole Bay.
Club founded in 1910.
*18 holes, 6250yds, Par 72, SSS 70, Course record 63.*
*Club membership 700.*
**Visitors**    must contact in advance and have handicap certificate.
**Societies**    apply in writing.
**Green Fees** £36 per day; £27 per round (£42/£32 weekends and bank holidays).
**Facilities** ⊗ ⊪ ⅃ 🝙 ♀ ⅄ 🕭 ᵮ ʅ Mark Thomas.
**Leisure**    trolley for hire, putting green, practice area.
**Location**    E side of town centre off A35
**Hotel**    ★★★ 80% Salterns Hotel, 38 Salterns Way, Lilliput, POOLE
       ☎ 01202 707321 20 ⇔ ℝ

### SHERBORNE      Map 03 ST61

**Sherborne** Higher Clatcombe DT9 4RN
☎ 01935 814431
A sporting course of first-class fairways with far-reaching views over the lovely Blackmore Vale and the Vale of Sparkford. Parkland in character, the course has many well-placed bunkers. The dog-leg 2nd calls for an accurately placed tee shot, and another testing hole is the 7th, a 194-yard, par 3. There is a practice area.
*18 holes, 5882yds, Par 70, SSS 68, Course record 63.*
*Club membership 900.*

---

**Visitors**    must contact in advance & have handicap certificate.
**Societies**    prior booking only.
**Green Fees** £25 per day (£30 weekends and bank holidays).
**Facilities** ⊗ ⊪ ⅃ 🝙 ♀ ⅄ 🕭 ʅ Stewart Wright.
**Leisure**    trolley for hire, putting green, practice area.
**Location**    2m N off B3145
**Hotel**    ★★★ 60% Sherborne Hotel, Horsecastles Ln, SHERBORNE
       ☎ 01935 813191 59 ⇔ ℝ

### STURMINSTER MARSHALL      Map 03 ST90

**Sturminster Marshall** Moor Ln BH21 4BD
☎ 01258 858444
Opened in June 1992, this 9-hole is Pay-and-Play. A membership scheme allows players to gain an official handicap. Course was designed by John Sharkey.
*9 holes, 4650yds, Par 68, SSS 63.*
*Club membership 350.*
**Visitors**    no restrictions.
**Societies**    welcome.
**Green Fees** not confirmed.
**Facilities** ⅄ 🕭 ᵮ ʅ John Sharkey.
**Hotel**    ★★★ 68% Crown Hotel, 8 West St, BLANDFORD FORUM
       ☎ 01258 456626 32 ⇔

### SWANAGE      Map 04 SZ07

**Isle of Purbeck** BH19 3AB ☎ 01929 450361
A heathland course sited on the Purbeck Hills with grand views across Swanage, the Channel and Poole Harbour. Holes of note include the 5th, 8th, 14th, 15th, and 16th where trees, gorse and heather assert themselves. The very attractive clubhouse is built of the local stone.
*Purbeck Course: 18 holes, 6295yds, Par 70, SSS 71.*
*Dene Course: 9 holes, 4014yds, Par 60.*
*Club membership 500.*
**Visitors**    advisable to telephone.
**Societies**    must contact in advance.
**Green Fees** Purbeck: £32.50 per day; £25 per round (£37.50/£30 weekends). Dene: £10 (£12 weekends).
**Facilities** ⊗ ⊪ by prior arrangement ⅃ 🝙 ♀ ⅄ 🕭 ᵮ ʅ Ian Brake.
**Leisure**    motorised carts for hire, buggies for hire, trolley for hire, putting green.
**Location**    2.5m N on B3351
**Hotel**    ★★★ 67% The Pines Hotel, Burlington Rd, SWANAGE ☎ 01929 425211 51rm(49 ⇔ ℝ)

### VERWOOD      Map 04 SU00

**Crane Valley** BH31 7LE ☎ 01202 814088
Two secluded parkland courses set amid rolling Dorset countryside and mature woodland - a 9-hole Pay and Play and an 18-hole Valley course for golfers holding a handicap certificate.The 6th nestles in the bend of the River Crane and there are 4 long Par 5's ranging from 499 to 545 yards.
*Valley: 18 holes, 6445yds, Par 72, SSS 72, Course record 69.*
*Woodland: 9 holes, 2090yds, Par 33.*
*Club membership 650.*

# EAST DORSET 🦌 GOLF CLUB
### Calling Group Golf Organisers.
Recently opened The Dorchester Golf Lodge en-suite accommodation for 32 golfers.
An invitation to stage your Society or Corporate Golf Day at Dorsets golfing gem!
Attractive 18-hole Lakeland course with casual water features and 9-hole Woodland course set amongst trees
and rhododendrons. Floodlit 22-bay driving range. Visitors should contact in advance to book tee time.
**For details call: Brian Lee, Telephone: 01929-472244**
**East Dorset Golf Club, Hyde, Wareham, Dorset BH20 7NT**

| | |
|---|---|
| **Visitors** | must have handicap certificate for Valley course. |
| **Societies** | telephone in advance. |
| **Green Fees** | Valley, £20 per round (£30 per round weekends). Woodland, £5.50 per 9 holes (£6.50 weekends). |
| **Facilities** | ⊗ 🎵 ⓑ 🍷 ♀ ⅄ 🏠 ⚑ 🏌 ℓ Paul Cannings. |
| **Leisure** | motorised carts for hire, buggies for hire, trolley for hire, driving range, putting green, practice area. |
| **Location** | 6m N of Ferndown on B3081 |
| **Hotel** | ★★★★ 66% The Dormy, New Rd, FERNDOWN<br>☎ 01202 872121 128 ⇌ 🐾 |

## WAREHAM                                                     Map 03 SY98

**East Dorset** Bere Regis BH20 7NT
☎ 01929 472244
Long 18-hole parkland course with natural water features. A second 9-hole, 18-tee course is set amongst trees and rhododendrons. Floodlit 22-bay driving range, club fitting centre, indoor putting area and extensive golf shop.
*Lakeland Course: 18 holes, 6580yds, Par 72, SSS 73, Course record 68.*
*Woodland Course: 9 holes, 4887yards, Par 66, SSS 64.*
*Club membership 650.*

| | |
|---|---|
| **Visitors** | must contact in advance and handicap certificate required for Lakeland course. |
| **Societies** | apply in advance. |
| **Green Fees** | Lakeland: £28 per day; £23 per round (£33/£28 weekends). Woodland: £19 per day; £16 per round (£23/£20 weekends). |
| **Facilities** | ⊗ 🎵 ⓑ 🍷 ♀ ⅄ 🏠 ⚑ 🏌<br>ℓ Derwynne Honan. |
| **Leisure** | motorised carts for hire, buggies for hire, trolley for hire, covered and floodlit driving range, putting green, practice area. |
| **Location** | 5m NW on unclass Puddletown Rd,off A352 |
| **Hotel** | ★★ 65% Kemps Country House Hotel, East Stoke, WAREHAM<br>☎ 01929 462563 5rm(4 ⇌ 🐾)Annexe10<br>⇌ 🐾 |

**Wareham** Sandford Rd BH20 4DH
☎ 01929 554147 & 554156
Heathland/parkland course. The club was founded in 1926.
*18 holes, 5603yds, Par 69, SSS 67, Course record 66.*
*Club membership 500.*

| | |
|---|---|
| **Visitors** | must contact the club in advance. Must be accompanied by a member at weekends & bank holidays. |
| **Societies** | must contact in advance. |

| | |
|---|---|
| **Green Fees** | £20 per day; £15 per round. |
| **Facilities** | ⊗ ⓑ 🍷 ♀ ⅄ |
| **Leisure** | trolley for hire, putting green, practice area. |
| **Location** | Adjacent to A351, nr Wareham railway station |
| **Hotel** | ★★★ 71% Springfield Country Hotel & Leisure Club, Grange Rd, WAREHAM<br>☎ 01929 552177 32 ⇌ 🐾 |

## WEYMOUTH                                                   Map 03 SY67

**Weymouth** Links Rd DT4 0PF
☎ 01305 773981 (Secretary) & 773997 (Pro)
Seaside parkland course. The 5th is played off an elevated green over copse.
*18 holes, 5976yds, Par 70, SSS 69, Course record 63.*
*Club membership 750.*

| | |
|---|---|
| **Visitors** | must contact in advance. |
| **Societies** | Tue & Thu, apply in writing. |
| **Green Fees** | £25 per day; £20 per round (£30/£26 weekends). |
| **Facilities** | ⊗ 🎵 ⓑ 🍷 ♀ ⅄ 🏠 ℓ Des Lochrie. |
| **Leisure** | putting green, practice area. |
| **Location** | N side of town centre off B3157 |
| **Hotel** | ★★ 66% Hotel Rex, 29 The Esplanade, WEYMOUTH<br>☎ 01305 760400 31 ⇌ 🐾 |

## CO DURHAM

## BARNARD CASTLE                                            Map 12 NZ01

**Barnard Castle** Marwood DL12 8QN
☎ 01833 638355 & 631980
Perched high on the steep bank of the River Tees, the extensive remains of Barnard Castle with its splendid round tower dates back to the 12th and 13th centuries, when this was the main fortress of the Baliol family.
*18 holes, 6406yds, Par 73, SSS 71.*
*Club membership 630.*

| | |
|---|---|
| **Visitors** | must contact in advance. |
| **Societies** | apply in writing. |
| **Green Fees** | £18 per day; £15 per round (£24 weekends). |
| **Facilities** | ⊗ 🎵 ⓑ 🍷 ♀ ⅄ 🏠 ⚑ ℓ Darren Pearce. |
| **Leisure** | trolley for hire, putting green, practice area. |
| **Location** | 1m N of town centre on B6278 |
| **Hotel** | ★★ 73% Rose & Crown Hotel, ROMALDKIRK<br>☎ 01833 650213 7 ⇌ 🐾Annexe5 ⇌ 🐾 |

## BEAMISH                              Map 12 NZ25

**Beamish Park** DH9 0RH ☎ 0191 370 1382
Parkland course. Designed by Henry Cotton and W Woodend.
*18 holes, 6204yds, Par 71, SSS 70, Course record 64.*
*Club membership 630.*
**Visitors**     must contact in advance and may not play
                 weekends.
**Societies**    telephone in advance.
**Green Fees**   £20 per day; £16 per round.
**Facilities**   ⊗ 川 ╚ ♥ ♀ ♠ 🛖 ʅ Chris Cole.
**Leisure**      trolley for hire, putting green, practice area.
**Location**     1m NW off A693
**Hotel**        ★★★ 66% Beamish Park Hotel, Beamish Burn
                 Rd, MARLEY HILL
                 ☎ 01207 230666 47 ⇄ 📠

## BILLINGHAM·                          Map 08 NZ42

**Billingham** Sandy Ln TS22 5NA
☎ 01642 533816 & 554494
Parkland course on edge of urban-rural district, with hard
walking and water hazards; testing 15th hole.
*18 holes, 6460yds, Par 73, SSS 71, Course record 63.*
*Club membership 1050.*
**Visitors**     contact professional in advance.
**Societies**    apply in writing to Secretary/Manager.
**Green Fees**   £20 per day (£33 weekends).
**Facilities**   ⊗ 川 ╚ ♥ ♀ ♠ 🛖 ⚐ ʅ Michael Ure.
**Leisure**      trolley for hire, putting green, practice area.
**Location**     1m W of town centre E of A19
**Hotel**        ★★★ 59% Billingham Arms Hotel, The
                 Causeway, Billingham, STOCKTON-ON-TEES
                 ☎ 01642 553661 & 360880 69 ⇄ 📠

## BISHOP AUCKLAND                      Map 08 NZ22

**Bishop Auckland** High Plains, Durham Rd DL14 8DL
☎ 01388 602198 & 663648
A rather hilly parkland course with many well-
established trees offering a challenging round. A small
ravine adds interest to several holes including the short
7th, from a raised tee to a green surrounded by a stream,
gorse and bushes. Pleasant views down the Wear Valley.
*18 holes, 6420yds, Par 72, SSS 71, Course record 64.*
*Club membership 950.*
**Visitors**     must contact in advance. Handicap
                 certificate advisable. Dress rules apply.
**Societies**    weekdays only; must contact in advance.
**Green Fees**   £24 per day; £20 per round (£26 per round
                 weekends).
**Facilities**   ⊗ 川 ╚ ♥ ♀ ♠ 🛖 ʅ David Skiffington.
**Leisure**      trolley for hire, driving range, putting green,
                 practice area, snooker.
**Location**     1m NE on A689
**Hotel**        ★★★ 64% Park Head Hotel, New
                 Coundon, BISHOP AUCKLAND
                 ☎ 01388 661727 8 ⇄ 📠Annexe7 ⇄

## BURNOPFIELD                         Map 12 NZ15

**Hobson Municipal** Hobson NE16 6BZ ☎ 01207 271605
Meadowland course opened in 1981.
*18 holes, 6403yds, Par 69, SSS 68.*
*Club membership 700.*
**Visitors**     no restrictions.
**Societies**    must contact in advance.
**Green Fees**   £9 per round (£12 weekends & bank holidays).
**Facilities**   ⊗ 川 ╚ ♥ ♀ ♠ 🛖 ⚐ ʅ Jack Ord.
**Leisure**      trolley for hire, putting green, practice area.
**Location**     0.75m S on A692
**Hotel**        ★★★ 66% Swallow Hotel, High West St,
                 GATESHEAD ☎ 0191 477 1105 103 ⇄ 📠

## CHESTER-LE-STREET                    Map 12 NZ25

**Chester-le-Street** Lumley Park DH3 4NS
☎ 0191 388 3218 (Secretary) & 389 0157 (Pro)
Parkland course in castle grounds, good views, easy walking.
*18 holes, 6437yds, Par 71, SSS 71, Course record 71.*
*Club membership 650.*
**Visitors**     must contact in advance and have an introduction
                 from own club or handicap certificate.
**Societies**    must apply in writing.
**Green Fees**   £20 per day/round (£25 weekends & bank
                 holidays).
**Facilities**   ⊗ 川 ╚ ♥ ♀ ♠ 🛖 ⚐ ʅ David Fletcher.
**Leisure**      motorised carts for hire, trolley for hire, putting
                 green, practice area.
**Location**     0.5m E off B1284
**Hotel**        ★★★ 72% Ramside Hall Hotel, Carrville,
                 DURHAM ☎ 0191 386 5282 82 ⇄ 📠

**Roseberry Grange** Grange Villa DH2 3NF
☎ 0191 370 0670 & 370 0660
Testing holes on this parkland course include the uphill par 3
12th (147yds) and the par 4 8th (438yds) with a ditch
crossing the fairway.
*18 holes, 5628yds, Par 70, SSS 67.*
*Club membership 550.*
**Visitors**     after 11.30am summer weekends, pay and play
                 Mon-Fri.
**Societies**    booking form available on request.
**Green Fees**   £14 per day; £10 per round.
**Facilities**   ⊗ 川 ╚ ♥ ♀ ♠ 🛖 ʅ Alan Hartley.
**Leisure**      trolley for hire, driving range, putting green.
**Hotel**        ★★★ 67% Washington Moat House, Stone
                 Cellar Rd, District 12, High Usworth,
                 WASHINGTON ☎ 0191 402 9988 105 ⇄ 📠

## CONSETT                             Map 12 NZ15

**Consett & District** Elmfield Rd DH8 5NN
☎ 01207 502186
Undulating parkland/moorland course with views across the
Derwent Valley to the Cheviot Hills.
*18 holes, 6013yds, Par 71, SSS 69.*
*Club membership 900.*
**Visitors**     advised to contact in advance.
**Societies**    apply in writing.
**Green Fees**   £15 per day (£22 weekends & bank holidays).
**Facilities**   ⊗ 川 ╚ ♥ ♀ ♠ 🛖 ʅ Craig Dilley.
**Leisure**      putting green, practice area.

| | |
|---|---|
| Location | N side of town on A691 |
| Hotel | ★★★ 67% The Raven Hotel, Broomhill, EBCHESTER ☎ 01207 560367 28 ⇄ ☘ |

## CROOK

Map 12 NZ13

**Crook** Low Jobs Hill DL15 9AA ☎ 01388 762429
Meadowland/parkland course in elevated position with
natural hazards, varied holes and terrain. Panoramic views
over Durham and Cleveland Hills.
*18 holes, 6102yds, Par 70, SSS 69, Course record 64.*
*Club membership 660.*

| | |
|---|---|
| Visitors | must contact Secretary for weekend play, limited availability. |
| Societies | apply in writing to Secretary. |
| Green Fees | £12 per day (£20 weekends). |
| Facilities | ⊗ ℿ ⅃ ■ ♀ ⚵ |
| Leisure | putting green, practice area. |
| Location | 0.5m E off A690 |
| Hotel | ★★ 65% Kensington Hall Hotel, Kensington Ter, WILLINGTON ☎ 01388 745071 10 ⇄ ☘ |

## DARLINGTON

Map 08 NZ21

**Blackwell Grange** Briar Close, Blackwell DL3 8QX
☎ 01325 464458
Pleasant parkland course with good views, easy walking.
*18 holes, 5621yds, Par 68, SSS 67, Course record 63.*
*Club membership 700.*

| | |
|---|---|
| Visitors | restricted Wed & weekends. |
| Societies | welcome weekdays except Wed (Ladies Day). |
| Green Fees | £22 per day; £16 per round (£20 per round weekends & bank holidays). |
| Facilities | ⊗ ℿ ⅃ ■ ♀ ⚵ ☎ ⚒ ⚑ Ralph Givens. |
| Leisure | trolley for hire, putting green. |
| Location | 1m SW off A66, turn into Blackwell, signposted |
| Hotel | ★★★ 68% Swallow King's Head Hotel, Priestgate, DARLINGTON ☎ 01325 380222 85 ⇄ ☘ |

**Darlington** Haughton Grange DL1 3JD ☎ 01325 355324
Fairly flat parkland course with tree-lined fairways, and large
first-class greens. Championship standard.
*18 holes, 6271yds, Par 71, SSS 70, Course record 64.*
*Club membership 850.*

| | |
|---|---|
| Visitors | may not play weekends unless accompanied by member. |
| Societies | by prior arrangement with the Secretary but not at weekends. |
| Green Fees | £22 per day weekdays. |
| Facilities | ⊗ ℿ ⅃ ■ ♀ ⚵ ☎ ⚒ ⚑ Mark Rogers. |
| Leisure | motorised carts for hire, buggies for hire, trolley for hire, putting green, practice area. |
| Location | N side of town centre off A1150 |
| Hotel | ★★★⚴ 68% Headlam Hall Hotel, Headlam, Gainford, DARLINGTON ☎ 01325 730238 17 ⇄ ☘Annexe9 ⇄ ☘ |

**Hall Garth Golf & Country Club Hotel** Coatham
Mundeville DL1 3LU ☎ 01325 300400
A 6900yard course with mature trees and Victorian deer
folly. Three greens have been newly laid. The challenging
165 yard Par 3 3rd requires teeing over water, whilst the 500
yard Par 5 6th hole features the picturesque River Swale
running alongside the fairway and the green.

*9 holes, 6621yds, Par 72, SSS 72.*

| | |
|---|---|
| Visitors | advisable to book at least 1 week in advance. |
| Societies | prior booking by telephone. |
| Green Fees | £15 per day all week; £10 per 18 holes (£12.50 weekends). |
| Facilities | ⊗ ℿ ⅃ ■ ♀ ⚵ ☎ ⚒ ⚑ |
| Leisure | grass tennis courts, heated indoor swimming pool, sauna, solarium, gymnasium, putting green, practice area. |
| Location | 0.5m from A1(M) off A167 |
| Hotel | ★★★ 70% Hall Garth Golf and Country Club Hotel, Coatham Mundeville, DARLINGTON ☎ 01325 300400 38 ⇄ ☘Annexe4 ⇄ ☘ |

**Stressholme** Snipe Ln DL2 2SA
☎ 01325 461002
Picturesque municipal parkland course, long but wide, with
98 bunkers and a par 3 hole played over a river.
*18 holes, 6511yds, Par 71, SSS 71.*
*Club membership 650.*

| | |
|---|---|
| Visitors | must contact in advance. |
| Societies | apply to the steward or professional. |
| Green Fees | not confirmed. |
| Facilities | ♀ ⚵ ☎ ⚒ ⚑ Tim Jenkins. |
| Location | SW side of town centre on A67 |
| Hotel | ★★★ 68% Swallow King's Head Hotel, Priestgate, DARLINGTON ☎ 01325 380222 85 ⇄ ☘ |

## DURHAM

Map 12 NZ24

**Brancepeth Castle** Brancepeth Village DH7 8EA
☎ 0191 378 0075
Parkland course overlooked at the 9th hole by beautiful
Brancepeth Castle.
*18 holes, 6300yds, Par 70, SSS 70, Course record 64.*
*Club membership 780.*

| | |
|---|---|
| Visitors | may be restrictions at weekends for parties. |
| Societies | must contact in advance. |
| Green Fees | not confirmed. |
| Facilities | ♀ ⚵ ☎ ⚒ ⚑ David Howdon. |
| Leisure | putting green,practice area,trolley hire. |
| Location | 4.5m SW on A690 |
| Hotel | ★★★★ 70% Royal County Hotel, Old Elvet, DURHAM ☎ 0191 386 6821 150 ⇄ ☘ |

**Durham City** Littleburn, Langley Moor DH7 8HL
☎ 0191 378 0806 & 378 0029
Undulating parkland course bordered on several holes by the
River Browney.
*18 holes, 6321yds, Par 71, SSS 70.*
*Club membership 750.*

| | |
|---|---|
| Visitors | restricted on competition days. |
| Societies | apply in writing or telephone the club professional. |
| Green Fees | £20 per day (£30 weekends & bank holidays). |
| Facilities | ⊗ ℿ ⅃ ■ ♀ ⚵ ☎ ⚑ Steve Corbally. |
| Leisure | trolley for hire, putting green, practice area. |
| Location | 2m W of Durham City, turn left off A690into Littleburn Ind Est |
| Hotel | ★★★ 70% Three Tuns Hotel, New Elvet, DURHAM ☎ 0191 386 4326 47 ⇄ ☘ |

# R·A·M·S·I·D·E
# H·A·L·L H·O·T·E·L

### THE NORTH EAST'S PREMIER PRIVATELY OWNED HOTEL
### • WITH GOLF •

*This marvellous 80-bedroomed hotel renowned for its popular bars and good food is now surrounded by 27 holes of golf with range and practice area.*

For details of the North East's best kept secret, contact:

## Ramside Hall Hotel,
## Carrville Durham DH1 1TD

### Phone: 0191-386 5282   Fax: 0191-386 0399

---

**Mount Oswald** South Rd DH1 3TQ ☎ 0191 386 7527
Flat, wooded parkland course with a Georgian clubhouse and good views of Durham cathedral on the back nine.
*18 holes, 6101yds, Par 71, SSS 69.*
*Club membership 120.*

| | |
|---|---|
| Visitors | must contact in advance for weekends but may not play before 10am on Sun. |
| Societies | must contact in advance. |
| Green Fees | £10 per round (£12 weekends & bank holidays). |
| Facilities | ⊗ ⑂ ⓛ ♨ ♀ ♨ ♐ |
| Leisure | trolley for hire, putting green, practice area. |
| Location | On A181 |
| Hotel | ★★ 65% Bridge Toby Hotel, Croxdale, DURHAM ☎ 0191 378 0524 46 ⇔ ⋒ |

**Ramside Hall** Carrville DH1 1TD ☎ 0191 386 9514
Three recently constructed 9-hole parkland courses - Princes, Bishops, Cathedral - with 14 lakes and panoramic views surrounding an impressive hotel. Excellent golf academy and driving range.
*Princes: 9 holes, 3235yds, Par 36, SSS 36.*
*Bishops: 9 holes, 3285yds, Par 36, SSS 36.*
*Cathedral: 9 holes, 2874yds, Par 34, SSS 34.*
*Club membership 400.*

| | |
|---|---|
| Visitors | open at all times subject to tee availability. |
| Societies | telephone in advance. |
| Green Fees | £30 per day; £25 per 18 holes; £13.50 per 9 holes (£37.50/£30/£16 weekends & bank holidays). |
| Facilities | ⊗ ⑂ ⓛ ♨ ♀ ♨ 🏠 ♐ ⋈ |
| Leisure | motorised carts for hire, buggies for hire, trolley for hire, driving range, putting green, practice area. |

| | |
|---|---|
| Location | 500m from A1/A690 interchange |
| Hotel | ★★★ 72% Ramside Hall Hotel, Carrville, DURHAM ☎ 0191 386 5282 82 ⇔ ⋒ |

## EAGLESCLIFFE                               Map 08 NZ41

**Eaglescliffe and District** Yarm Rd TS16 0DQ ☎ 01642 780098 & 790122
This hilly course offers both pleasant and interesting golf to all classes of player. It lies in a delightful setting on a rolling plateau, shelving to the River Tees. There are fine views to the Cleveland Hills.
*18 holes, 6275yds, Par 72, SSS 70, Course record 60.*
*Club membership 550.*

| | |
|---|---|
| Visitors | restricted Tue, Thu, Fri & weekends. |
| Societies | must contact in advance, apply to secretary on 01642 780238 |
| Green Fees | £24 per day (£30 weekends & bank holidays). |
| Facilities | ⊗ ⑂ ⓛ ♨ ♀ ♨ 🏠 ♐ ℓ Paul Bradley. |
| Leisure | trolley for hire, putting green, practice area. |
| Location | E side of village off A135 |
| Hotel | ★★★★ 63% Swallow Hotel, John Walker Square, STOCKTON-ON-TEES ☎ 01642 679721 125 ⇔ ⋒ |

## HARTLEPOOL                                 Map 08 NZ53

*Castle Eden & Peterlee* Castle Eden TS27 4SS
☎ 01429 836510
Beautiful parkland course alongside a nature reserve. Hard walking but trees provide wind shelter.

*18 holes, 6262yds, Par 70, SSS 69.*
*Club membership 750.*
**Visitors** with member only during 12-1.30pm & 4-6.30pm. Must contact in advance.
**Societies** must contact in advance tel: 01429 836689.
**Green Fees** not confirmed.
**Facilities** ♀ ♣ 🏠 🍴 ⚲ Graham J Laidlaw.
**Leisure** putting,practice,cart/buggy/trolley hire.
**Location** 2m S of Peterlee on B1281 off A19
**Hotel** ★★ 69% Hardwicke Hall Manor Hotel, HESLEDEN ☎ 01429 836326 11 ⇔ ℝ

---

**Hartlepool** Hart Warren TS24 9QF ☎ 01429 274398
A seaside course, half links, overlooking the North Sea. A good test and equally enjoyable to all handicap players. The 10th, par 4, demands a precise second shot over a ridge and between sand dunes to a green down near the edge of the beach, alongside which several holes are played.
*18 holes, 6215yds, Par 70, SSS 70, Course record 64.*
*Club membership 700.*
**Visitors** with member only on Sun.
**Societies** must apply in writing in advance.
**Green Fees** £20 per day (£30 weekends and bank holidays).
**Facilities** ⊗ 🍴 🍺 ⚫ ♀ ♣ 🏠 🍴 ⚲ Malcolm E Cole.
**Leisure** trolley for hire, putting green, practice area.
**Location** N of Hartlepool, off A1086
**Hotel** ★★ 68% Ryedale Moor, 3 Beaconsfield St, Headland, HARTLEPOOL ☎ 01429 231436 14 ⇔ ℝ

---

## MIDDLETON ST GEORGE  Map 08 NZ31

**Dinsdale Spa** Neasham Rd DL2 1DW
☎ 01325 332297
A mainly flat, parkland course on high land above the River Tees with views of the Cleveland Hills. Water hazards front the 8th, 9th and 18th tees and the prevailing west wind affects the later holes. There is a practice area by the clubhouse.
*18 holes, 6090yds, Par 71, SSS 69, Course record 65.*
*Club membership 850.*
**Visitors** contact for further details.
**Societies** bookings through office, no weekends or Tue.
**Green Fees** not confirmed.
**Facilities** ⊗ 🍴 🍺 ⚫ ♀ ♣ 🏠 🍴 ⚲ Craig Imlah.
**Leisure** motorised carts for hire, trolley for hire, putting green, practice area.
**Location** 1.5m SW
**Hotel** ★★★ 64% St George, Middleton St George, TEES-SIDE AIRPORT ☎ 01325 332631 59 ⇔ ℝ

---

## NEWTON AYCLIFFE  Map 08 NZ22

**Aycliffe** School Aycliffe Ln DL5 4EF
☎ 01325 312994
A parkland course in a country setting.
*18 holes, 5430yds, Par 68, SSS 66, Course record 63.*
*Club membership 100.*
**Visitors** must contact in advance (01325 310820).
**Societies** apply in writing.
**Green Fees** not confirmed.

---

**Facilities** ♀ ♣ 🏠 🍴 ⚲ Clive Burgess.
**Leisure** squash, cart/buggy/trolley hire,driving range.
**Location** 6m N of Darlington, off A6072
**Hotel** ★★★★ 72% Redworth Hall Hotel & Country Club, REDWORTH ☎ 01388 772442 100 ⇔ ℝ

---

## SEAHAM  Map 12 NZ44

**Seaham** Dawdon SR7 7RD
☎ 0191 581 2354 & 581 1268
Heathland links course with several holes affected by strong prevailing winds.
*18 holes, 6017yds, Par 70, SSS 69, Course record 64.*
*Club membership 600.*
**Visitors** with member only weekends until 3.30pm.
**Societies** must apply in advance.
**Green Fees** £11 (£15 weekends).
**Facilities** ⊗ by prior arrangement 🍴 by prior arrangement 🍺 by prior arrangement ⚫ ♀ ♣ 🏠 🍴 ⚲ Glyn Jones.
**Leisure** trolley for hire, putting green, practice area.
**Location** 3m E of A19, exit for Seaham
**Hotel** ★★★★ 60% Swallow Hotel, Queen's Pde, Seaburn, SUNDERLAND ☎ 0191 529 2041 65 ⇔ ℝ

---

## SEATON CAREW  Map 08 NZ52

**Seaton Carew** Tees Rd TS25 1DE
☎ 01429 261040 & 266249
A championship links course taking full advantage of its dunes, bents, whins and gorse. Renowned for its par 4 (17th); just enough fairway for an accurate drive followed by another precise shot to a pear-shaped, sloping green that is severely trapped.
*The Old Course: 18 holes, 6604yds, Par 72, SSS 72.*
*Brabazon Course: 18 holes, 6849yds, Par 73, SSS 73.*
*Club membership 650.*
**Visitors** restricted until after 10am at weekends & bank holidays.
**Societies** must apply in writing.
**Green Fees** not confirmed.
**Facilities** ♀ ♣ 🏠 ⚲ W Hector.
**Leisure** putting green,cart/trolley hire.
**Location** SE side of village off A178
**Hotel** ★★ 68% Ryedale Moor, 3 Beaconsfield St, Headland, HARTLEPOOL ☎ 01429 231436 14 ⇔ ℝ

---

## SEDGEFIELD  Map 08 NZ32

**Knotty Hill Golf Centre** TS21 2BB ☎ 01740 620320
The 18-hole Princes course is rolling parkland with many holes routed through shallow valleys. Several holes are set wholly or partially within woodland. Water hazards abound. Bishops, a new 18-hole was due to be completed in 1996.
*Princes Course: 18 holes, 6517yds, Par 72, SSS 71.*
**Visitors** no restrictions.
**Societies** package available on request.
**Green Fees** £12 per 18 holes; £7 per 9 holes.
**Facilities** ⊗ 🍴 🍺 ⚫ ♀ ♣ 🏠 🍴 ⚲ Nick Todd.
**Leisure** motorised carts for hire, buggies for hire, trolley for hire, floodlit driving range, putting green, practice area. ▶

| Location | 1m N of Sedgefield on A177 |
|---|---|
| Hotel | ★★★ 64% Hardwick Hall Hotel, SEDGEFIELD ☎ 01740 20253 17 ⇌ ‣ |

## ESSEX

## STANLEY
Map 12 NZ15

**South Moor** The Middles, Craghead DH9 6AG
☎ 01207 232848
Moorland course with natural hazards designed by Dr Alistair McKenzie in 1926 and remains on of the most challenging of its type in north east England. Out of bounds features on 11 holes from the tee and the testing par 5 12th hole is uphill and usually against a strong headwind.
*18 holes, 6445yds, Par 72, SSS 71, Course record 66.*
*Club membership 650.*

| Visitors | must contact in advance but may only play Sun with member. |
|---|---|
| Societies | apply in writing to Secretary. |
| Green Fees | £21 per day; £14 per round (£25 per day/round weekends & bank holidays). Reduced winter fees end Oct-Mar. |
| Facilities | ⊗ ⅷ ⅃ ♥ ♀ ⚘ ⌂ ⚑ ⚏ Shaun Cowell. |
| Leisure | buggies for hire, trolley for hire, putting green, practice area, snooker. |
| Location | 1.5m SE on B6313 |
| Hotel | ★★★ 66% Beamish Park Hotel, Beamish Burn Rd, MARLEY HILL ☎ 01207 230666 47 ⇌ ‣ |

## STOCKTON-ON-TEES
Map 08 NZ41

**Norton** Norton TS20 1SU ☎ 01642 676385
An interesting parkland course with long drives from the 7th and 17th tees. Several water hazards.
*18 holes, 5855yds, Par 70.*

| Visitors | no restrictions. |
|---|---|
| Societies | apply in advance. |
| Green Fees | £13 per 27 holes; £8.50 per 18 holes (£15/£9 weekends). |
| Facilities | ⊗ ⅷ ⅃ ♥ ♀ ⚘ ⌂ ⚏ Terry Myles. |
| Leisure | trolley for hire, putting green, practice area. |
| Location | At Norton 2m N off A19 |
| Hotel | ★★★ 59% Billingham Arms Hotel, The Causeway, Billingham, STOCKTON-ON-TEES ☎ 01642 553661 & 360880 69 ⇌ ‣ |

*Teesside* Acklam Rd, Thornaby TS17 7JS
☎ 01642 676249
Flat parkland course, easy walking.
*18 holes, 6472yds, Par 72, SSS 71.*
*Club membership 600.*

| Visitors | with member only weekdays after 4.30pm, weekends after 11am. |
|---|---|
| Societies | must contact in writing. |
| Green Fees | not confirmed. |
| Facilities | ♀ ⚘ ⌂ ⚏ |
| Location | 1.5m SE on A1130 |
| Hotel | B Forte Posthouse Teeside, Low Ln, Stainton Village, Thornaby, STOCKTON-ON-TEES ☎ 01642 591213 135 ⇌ ‣ |

> Entries with a shaded background identify courses that are considered to be particularly interesting

## ABRIDGE
Map 05 TQ49

**Abridge Golf and Country Club** Epping Ln, Stapleford Tawney RM4 1ST ☎ 01708 688396
A parkland course with easy walking. The quick drying course is by no means easy to play. This has been the venue of several professional tournaments. Abridge is a Golf and Country Club and has all the attendant facilities.
*18 holes, 6692yds, Par 72, SSS 72, Course record 67.*
*Club membership 600.*

| Visitors | must have current handicap certificate, contact in advance. Play with member only at weekends. |
|---|---|
| Societies | telephone in advance. |
| Green Fees | £30 per day/round. |
| Facilities | ⊗ ⅷ ⅃ ♥ ♀ ⚘ ⌂ ⚑ ⚏ Mike Herbert. |
| Leisure | heated outdoor swimming pool, sauna, motorised carts for hire, buggies for hire, trolley for hire, driving range, putting green, practice area. |
| Location | 1.75m NE |
| Hotel | B Forte Posthouse Epping, High Rd, Bell Common, EPPING ☎ 01992 573137 Annexe79 ⇌ ‣ |

## BASILDON
Map 05 TQ78

**Basildon** Clay Hill Ln, Kingswood SS16 5JP
☎ 01268 533297
Undulating municipal parkland course. Testing 13th hole (par 4).
*18 holes, 6153yds, Par 71, SSS 69, Course record 64.*
*Club membership 300.*

| Visitors | contact professional in advance 01268 533532. |
|---|---|
| Societies | may contact for details. |
| Green Fees | £8.70 (£14.50 weekends). |
| Facilities | ⊗ ⅷ ⅃ ♥ ♀ ⚘ ⌂ ⚑ ⚏ W Paterson. |
| Location | 1m S off A176 |
| Hotel | B Forte Posthouse Basildon, Cranes Farm Rd, BASILDON ☎ 01268 533955 110 ⇌ ‣ |

*Pipps Hill Country Club* Cranes Farm Rd SS14 3DG
☎ 01268 523456
Flat course with ditches and pond.
*9 holes, 2829yds, Par 34, SSS 34.*
*Club membership 400.*

| Visitors | no restrictions. |
|---|---|
| Societies | must contact in advance. |
| Green Fees | not confirmed. |
| Facilities | ♀ ⚘ |
| Location | N side of town centre off A127 |
| Hotel | B Forte Posthouse Basildon, Cranes Farm Rd, BASILDON ☎ 01268 533955 110 ⇌ ‣ |

## BENFLEET
Map 05 TQ78

**Boyce Hill** Vicarage Hill, South Benfleet SS7 1PD
☎ 01268 793625 & 752565
Hilly parkland course with good views.
*18 holes, 5956yds, Par 68, SSS 68, Course record 61.*
*Club membership 700.*

**Visitors** must have a handicap certificate, must contact 24hrs in advance, may not play at weekends.
**Societies** Thu only, book well in advance by telephone.
**Green Fees** £25 per day/round.
**Facilities** ⊗ ⅶ ⓛ ☟ ♀ ⚑ ☎ Graham Burroughs.
**Leisure** motorised carts for hire, trolley for hire, putting green.
**Location** 0.75m NE of Benfleet Station
**Hotel** B Forte Posthouse Basildon, Cranes Farm Rd, BASILDON ☎ 01268 533955 110 ↩ ♜

---

## BILLERICAY Map 05 TQ69

**The Burstead** Tythe Common Rd, Little Burstead CM12 9SS ☎ 01277 631171
The Burstead is an attractive parkland course set amidst some of the most attractive countryside in south Essex. It is an excellent test of golf to players of all standards with the greens showing maturity beyond their years. Challenging holes include the Par 4 13th hole which at 342yds requires an accurate tea shot to leave a second shot played over a lake protecting an attractive contoured green. The 9th is the longest hole on the course.
*18 holes, 6177yds, Par 71, SSS 69, Course record 67.*
*Club membership 900.*
**Visitors** must have handicap certificate and may only play weekdays.
**Societies** apply in writing or telephone for reservation.
**Green Fees** £18 per 18 holes; £9 per 9 holes.
**Facilities** ⊗ ⅶ ⓛ ☟ ♀ ⚑ ☎ ☂ ☎ Keith Bridges.
**Leisure** motorised carts for hire, buggies for hire, trolley for hire, putting green, practice area.
**Hotel** ★★★ 66% Chichester Hotel, Old London Rd, Wickford, BASILDON
☎ 01268 560555 2 ↩ ♜Annexe32 ↩ ♜

**Stock Brook Manor Golf & Country Club** Queens Park Av, Stock CM12 0SP ☎ 01277 653616
Three gently undulating 9-hole parkland courses offering the challenge of water on a large number of holes. Any combination can be played, but the Stock and Brook courses make the 18-hole championship course. Manor Course is the easier 9 holes.
*Stock & Brook Courses: 18 holes, 6728yds, Par 72, SSS 72, Course record 66.*
*Manor Course: 9 holes, 2997yds, Par 35.*
*Club membership 750.*
**Visitors** must contact 24hrs in advance.
**Societies** apply in writing or telephone.
**Green Fees** £25 per day (£30 per round weekends).
**Facilities** ⊗ ⅶ ⓛ ☟ ♀ ⚑ ☎ ☂ ☎ Kevin Merry.
**Leisure** sauna, trolley for hire, driving range, putting green, practice area.
**Hotel** ★★★ 64% The Heybridge Hotel, Roman Rd, INGATESTONE ☎ 01277 355355 22 ↩ ♜

---

## BRAINTREE Map 05 TL72

**Braintree** Kings Ln, Stisted CM7 8DA
☎ 01376 346079
Parkland course with many unique mature trees. Good par 3s with the 14th -'Devils Lair'-regarded as one of the best in the county.
*18 holes, 6199yds, Par 70, SSS 69, Course record 65.*
*Club membership 850.*

**Visitors** weekdays only, contact the pro shop in advance 01376 343465.
**Societies** society days Wed & Thu early booking advised.
**Green Fees** £25 per day; £18 per round.
**Facilities** ⊗ ⅶ ⓛ ☟ ♀ ⚑ ☎ Tony Parcell.
**Leisure** trolley for hire, putting green, practice area.
**Location** 1m E, off A120
**Hotel** ★★★ 61% White Hart Hotel, Bocking End, BRAINTREE ☎ 01376 321401 31 ↩ ♜

---

**Towerlands** Panfield Rd CM7 5BJ ☎ 01376 326802
Undulating, grassland course. Driving range and sports hall.
*9 holes, 2703yds, Par 34, SSS 66.*
*Club membership 300.*
**Visitors** must not play before 12.30pm weekends. Correct dress at all times.
**Societies** must contact in advance by telephone.
**Green Fees** 18 holes £12.50; 9 holes £9 (18 holes weekends & bank holidays £15).
**Facilities** ⊗ ⅶ ⓛ ☟ ♀ ⚑ ☎ ☂
**Leisure** trolley for hire, driving range, putting green, practice area, sportshall, indoor bowls.
**Location** On B1053
**Hotel** ★★★ 61% White Hart Hotel, Bocking End, BRAINTREE ☎ 01376 321401 31 ↩ ♜

---

## BRENTWOOD Map 05 TQ59

**Bentley** Ongar Rd CM15 9SS ☎ 01277 373179
Parkland course with water hazards.
*18 holes, 6709yds, Par 72, SSS 72.*
*Club membership 600.*
**Visitors** should contact in advance, may not play at weekends.
**Societies** must write or telephone in advance.
**Green Fees** £27 per 27-36 holes; £21 per round.
**Facilities** ⊗ ⅶ by prior arrangement ⓛ ☟ ♀ ⚑ ☎
☎ Nick Garrett.
**Leisure** trolley for hire, putting, practice area.
**Location** 3m NW on A128
**Hotel** B Forte Posthouse Brentwood, Brook St, BRENTWOOD ☎ 01277 260260 111 ↩

---

**Hartswood** King George's Playing Fields, Ingrave Rd CM14 5AE ☎ 01277 218850 & 214830
Municipal parkland course, easy walking.
*18 holes, 6160yds, Par 70, SSS 69.*
*Club membership 500.*
**Visitors** pre-booking usually essential am.
**Societies** must contact in advance.
**Green Fees** not confirmed.
**Facilities** ♀ ⚑ ☎ ☂ ☎
**Leisure** putting green,trolley hire.
**Location** 0.75m SE on A128
**Hotel** B Forte Posthouse Brentwood, Brook St, BRENTWOOD ☎ 01277 260260 111 ↩

---

**Warley Park** Magpie Ln, Little Warley CM13 3DX
☎ 01277 224891
Parkland course with reasonable walking. Numerous water hazards. There is also a golf-practice ground.
*1st & 2nd: 18 holes, 5967yds, Par 69, SSS 68, Course record 68.*
*1st & 3rd: 18 holes, 6232yds, Par 71, SSS 69, Course record 67.*
*2nd & 3rd: 18 holes, 6223yds, Par 70, SSS 69, Course record 70.*
*Club membership 800.* ▶

**Visitors** must have handicap certificate and contact in advance. May not play at weekends.
**Societies** telephone in advance for provisional booking.
**Green Fees** £36 per day; £24 per 18 holes.
**Facilities** ⊗ ⅲ ℡ ☺ ♀ ⚲ ☎ ℓ Jason Groat.
**Leisure** motorised carts for hire, buggies for hire, trolley for hire, driving range, putting green, practice area.
**Location** 2.5m S off B186
**Hotel** B Forte Posthouse Brentwood, Brook St, BRENTWOOD ☎ 01277 260260 111 ⇆

## BULPHAN                                          Map 05 TQ68

**Langdon Hills Hotel & Golf Complex** Lower Dunton Rd RM14 3TY ☎ 01268 548444
The complex is the base of the European School of Golf. The 18-hole course is of championship standard and there is also a 9-hole public course. Practice facilities include a 22-bay covered floodlit driving range, short game practice area with greens and bunkers and three-hole practice course.
*Langdon Course: 18 holes, 6485yds, Par 72.*
*Horndon Course: 9 holes, 2941yds, Par 36.*
*Club membership 620.*
**Visitors** may not play at weekends before 1pm in summer before noon in winter.
**Societies** apply in writing or telephone.
**Green Fees** Langdon £17.80 per day; £10.80 per round (£15.80 per round weekends). Horndon £5.90 per 18 holes (£7.50 weekends).
**Facilities** ⊗ ⅲ ℡ ☺ ♀ ⚲ ☎ ℓ Andrew Lavers.
**Leisure** motorised carts for hire, buggies for hire, trolley for hire, driving range, putting green, practice area.
**Hotel** ★★★★ 68% Marygreen Manor, London Rd, BRENTWOOD ☎ 01277 225252 3 ⇆ ☞Annexe30 ⇆ ☞

## BURNHAM-ON-CROUCH                         Map 05 TQ99

**Burnham-on-Crouch** Ferry Rd, Creeksea CM0 8PQ ☎ 01621 782282 & 785508
Undulating meadowland course, easy walking, windy.
*18 holes, 6056yds, Par 70, SSS 69, Course record 66.*
*Club membership 534.*
**Visitors** must contact in advance, may not play weekends.
**Societies** apply in writing.
**Green Fees** £22 per day (weekdays only).
**Facilities** ⊗ ⅲ ℡ ☺ ♀ ⚲ ☎
**Leisure** motorised carts for hire, practice area.
**Location** 1.25m W off B1010
**Hotel** ★★ 64% Blue Boar Hotel, Silver St, MALDON ☎ 01621 852681 21 ⇆ ☞Annexe8 ⇆ ☞

## CANEWDON                                       Map 05 TQ99

**Ballards Gore** Gore Rd SS4 2DA ☎ 01702 258917
A parkland course with several lakes.
*18 holes, 7062yds, Par 73, SSS 74, Course record 69.*
*Club membership 500.*
**Visitors** may not play at weekends.
**Societies** weekdays only, apply in advance.
**Green Fees** £22 per day; £16 per round.

**Facilities** ⊗ ⅲ by prior arrangement ℡ ☺ ♀ ⚲ ☎ ℓ Andrew Curry.
**Leisure** buggies for hire, trolley for hire, putting green, practice area.
**Location** 2m NE of Rochford
**Hotel** ★★★ 66% Hotel Renouf, Bradley Way, ROCHFORD ☎ 01702 541334 24 ⇆ ☞

## CANVEY ISLAND                                  Map 05 TQ78

**Castle Point** Somnes Av SS8 9FG ☎ 01268 510830
A flat seaside links and part parkland course with water hazards on 13 holes and views of the estuary and Hadleigh Castle. Always a test for any golfer when the wind starts to blow.
*18 holes, 6176yds, Par 71, SSS 69, Course record 69.*
*Club membership 275.*
**Visitors** must book for weekends.
**Societies** phone or write for details.
**Green Fees** £8.10 per round (£12.20 weekends).
**Facilities** ⊗ ⅲ ℡ ☺ ♀ ⚲ ☎ ℓ Paul Joiner.
**Leisure** buggies for hire, trolley for hire, driving range, putting green.
**Location** SE of Basildon, A130 to Canvey Island
**Hotel** ★★★ 66% Chichester Hotel, Old London Rd, Wickford, BASILDON ☎ 01268 560555 2 ⇆ ☞Annexe32 ⇆ ☞

## CHELMSFORD                                     Map 05 TL70

**Channels** Belstead Farm Ln, Little Waltham CM3 3PT ☎ 01245 440005
Built on land from reclaimed gravel pits, 18 very exciting holes with plenty of lakes providing an excellent test of golf.
*Channels Course: 18 holes, 6272yds, Par 71, SSS 71.*
*Belsteads: 18 holes, 4779yds, Par 67, SSS 63.*
*Club membership 650.*
**Visitors** Channels Course; must contact in advance and may only play with member at weekends. Belsteads Course; available anytime.
**Societies** telephone starter on 01245 443311.
**Green Fees** Channels £30 per day; £16 per rouund. Belsteads £15 per 18 holes; £9 per 9 holes.
**Facilities** ⊗ ⅲ ℡ ☺ ♀ ⚲ ☎ ℓ Ian Sinclair.
**Leisure** fishing, motorised carts for hire, buggies for hire, trolley for hire, driving range, putting green, practice area.
**Location** 2m NE on A130
**Hotel** ★★★ 58% South Lodge Hotel, 196 New London Rd, CHELMSFORD ☎ 01245 264564 25 ⇆ ☞Annexe16 ⇆ ☞

**Chelmsford** Widford Rd CM2 9AP ☎ 01245 256483
An undulating parkland course, hilly in parts, with 3 holes in woods and four difficult par 4's. From the reconstructed clubhouse there are fine views over the course and the wooded hills beyond.
*18 holes, 5981yds, Par 68, SSS 69, Course record 66.*
*Club membership 650.*
**Visitors** must contact in advance. Society days Wed/Thu, Ladies Day Tue. With member only at weekends.
**Societies** must contact in advance.
**Green Fees** £35 per day; £25 per round.
**Facilities** ⊗ ⅲ ℡ ☺ ♀ ⚲ ☎ ℓ Dennis Bailey.

| Leisure | motorised carts for hire, buggies for hire, trolley for hire, putting green, practice area. |
| Location | 1.5m S of town centre off A12 |
| Hotel | ★★★ 58% South Lodge Hotel, 196 New London Rd, CHELMSFORD ☎ 01245 264564 25 ⇌ ♪Annexe16 ⇌ ♪ |

## CHIGWELL

Map 05 TQ49

**Chigwell** High Rd IG7 5BH ☎ 0181 500 2059
A course of high quality, mixing meadowland with parkland. For those who believe 'all Essex is flat' the undulating nature of Chigwell will be a refreshing surprise. The greens are excellent and the fairways tight with mature trees.
*18 holes, 6279yds, Par 71, SSS 70, Course record 66.*
*Club membership 674.*

| Visitors | must contact in advance & have handicap certificate, but must be accompanied by member at weekends. |
| Societies | recognised societies welcome by prior arrangement. |
| Green Fees | £39 per day (£20 Dec-Feb). £28 per round (£20 Dec-Feb). |
| Facilities | ⊗ ⅊⅂ ⅃ 🍺 ♀ ⌆ ⌂ ♪ Ray Beard. |
| Leisure | trolley for hire, putting green, practice area. |
| Location | 0.5m S on A113 |
| Hotel | ★★ 62% Roebuck Hotel, North End, BUCKHURST HILL ☎ 0181 505 4636 29 ⇌ ♪ |

## CHIGWELL ROW

Map 05 TQ49

*Hainault Forest* Romford Rd, Chigwell Row IG7 4QW
☎ 0181 500 2047
Club playing over Borough of Redbridge public courses; hilly parkland subject to wind. Two courses, driving range.
*No 1 Course: 18 holes, 5744yds, Par 70, SSS 67, Course record 65.*
*No 2 Course: 18 holes, 6600yds, Par 71, SSS 71.*
*Club membership 600.*

| Visitors | no restrictions. |
| Societies | must contact in writing. |
| Green Fees | not confirmed. |
| Facilities | ♀ ⌂ ⌂ ♪ ♪ T Dungate. |
| Location | 0.5m S on A1112 |
| Hotel | ★★★ 65% Epping Forest Moat House, Oak Hill, WOODFORD GREEN ☎ 0181 787 9988 99 ⇌ ♪ |

## CLACTON-ON-SEA

Map 05 TM11

*Clacton* West Rd CO15 1AJ ☎ 01255 421919
Windy, seaside course.
*18 holes, 6494yds, Par 71, SSS 69.*
*Club membership 650.*

| Visitors | must contact in advance. |
| Societies | must contact in writing. |
| Green Fees | not confirmed. |
| Facilities | ♀ ⌂ ⌂ ♪ ♪ S J Levermore. |
| Leisure | putting green,buggy/trolley hire. |
| Location | 1.25m SW of town centre |
| Hotel | ★★ 63% Maplin Hotel, Esplanade, FRINTON-ON-SEA ☎ 01255 673832 12rm(9 ⇌1 ♪) |

## COLCHESTER

Map 05 TL92

**Birch Grove** Layer Rd, Kingsford CO2 0HS
☎ 01206 734276
A pretty, undulating course surrounded by woodland - small but challenging with excellent greens. Challenging 6th hole cut through woodland with water hazards and out of bounds.
*9 holes, 4038yds, Par 62, SSS 60, Course record 58.*
*Club membership 250.*

| Visitors | restricted Sun mornings. |
| Societies | apply in writing or telephone. |
| Green Fees | £10 per day; £7 per 9 holes. |
| Facilities | ⊗ ⅊⅂ 🍺 ♀ ♀ ⌂ ⌂ |
| Leisure | trolley for hire, putting green, practice area. |
| Location | 2.5m S on B1026 |
| Hotel | ★★ 70% Kingsford Park Hotel, Layer Rd, COLCHESTER ☎ 01206 734301 10 ⇌ ♪ |

**Colchester** Braiswick CO4 5AU
☎ 01206 853396 & 853920
A fairly flat, yet scenic, parkland course with tree-lined fairways and small copses. Mainly level walking.
*18 holes, 6319yds, Par 70, SSS 69, Course record 64.*
*Club membership 700.*

| Visitors | weekends by prior arrangement. |
| Societies | apply in writing or by telephone, Mon, Thu & Fri only. |
| Green Fees | £25 per day; £20 per round (£30 per round weekends). |
| Facilities | ⊗ ⅊⅂ by prior arrangement 🍺 ♀ ♀ ⌂ ⌂ ♪ Mark Angel. |
| Leisure | trolley for hire, driving range, putting green, practice area. |
| Location | 1.5m NW of town centre on B1508 |
| Hotel | ★★★ 66% George Hotel, 116 High St, COLCHESTER ☎ 01206 578494 47 ⇌ ♪ |

**Stoke-by-Nayland** Keepers Ln, Leavenheath CO6 4PZ
☎ 01206 262836
Two undulating courses (Gainsborough and Constable) situated in Dedham Vale. Some water hazards and hedges. On Gainsborough the 10th (par 4) takes 2 shots over a lake; very testing par 3 at 11th.
*Gainsborough Course: 18 holes, 6581yds, Par 72, SSS 71, Course record 63.*
*Constable Course: 18 holes, 6544yds, Par 72, SSS 71, Course record 68.*
*Club membership 1400.*

| Visitors | write or telephone for details. |
| Societies | write or telephone for brochures and booking forms. |
| Green Fees | £29.50 per 36 holes (incl £1.50 meal voucher ); £20 per 18 holes (£30/£24 weekends, 10-2pm). |
| Facilities | ⊗ ⅊⅂ 🍺 ♀ ♀ ⌂ ⌂ ♪ Kevin Lovelock. |
| Leisure | motorised carts for hire, buggies for hire, trolley for hire, driving range, putting green, practice area. |
| Location | 1.5m NW of Stoke-by-Nayland on B1068 |
| Hotel | ★★★(red)⚑ Maison Talbooth, Stratford Rd, DEDHAM ☎ 01206 322367 10 ⇌ ♪ |

## EARLS COLNE
Map 05 TL82

*Colne Valley* Station Rd CO6 2LT ☎ 01787 224233
An 18-hole course along the valley of the River Colne.
Opened in 1991.
*18 holes, 6272yds, Par 71, SSS 70.*
*Club membership 600.*

| | |
|---|---|
| Visitors | only after 10am at weekends, must dress correctly,no sharing of clubs. |
| Societies | apply in writing, minimum of 12 persons. |
| Green Fees | not confirmed. |
| Facilities | ♀♨☎ℓ Mrs Kimberley Martin. |
| Leisure | sauna, range,putting,practice area,trolley hire. |
| Location | Off A604 |
| Hotel | ★★★ 67% White Hart Hotel, Market End, COGGESHALL ☎ 01376 561654 18 ⇥ ♠ |

**Earls Colne Golf & Leisure Centre** CO6 2NS
☎ 01787 224466
Created on the site of a World War II airfield, this
challenging public course contains 14 lakes. Also 9-hole
course and 4-hole instruction course as well as a variety of
leisure facilities.
*County Course: 18 holes, 6800yds, Par 73, SSS 73, Course
record 69.*
*Garden Course: 9 holes, 2190yds, Par 34, SSS 34.*
*Club membership 500.*

| | |
|---|---|
| Visitors | contact the pro shop. |
| Societies | apply in writting to the Society Secretary. |
| Green Fees | £16 (£20 weekends). |
| Facilities | ⊗♨♨♠♥♀♨☎ℓ♥ℓ Owen Mckenna. |
| Leisure | hard tennis courts, heated indoor swimming pool, fishing, sauna, solarium, gymnasium, motorised carts for hire, buggies for hire, trolley for hire, driving range, putting green, practice area. |
| Location | Off the A120 onto the B1024 |
| Hotel | ★★★ 67% White Hart Hotel, Market End, COGGESHALL ☎ 01376 561654 18 ⇥ ♠ |

## EPPING
Map 05 TL40

**Nazeing** Middle St, Nazeing EN9 2LW
☎ 01992 893798 & 893915
Parkland course built with American sand based greens and
tees and five strategically placed lakes. One of the most
notable holes is the difficult par 3 13th with out of bounds
and a large lake coming into play.
*18 holes, 6598yds, Par 72, SSS 71, Course record 65.*
*Club membership 500.*

| | |
|---|---|
| Visitors | not compulsory to contact, weekends only restricted times. |
| Societies | prior arrangement required in writing. |
| Green Fees | £35 per day; £20 Tue-Fri; £16 Mon (£28 after midday weekends and bank holidays). |
| Facilities | ⊗♨♨♠♥♀♨☎♥ℓ Robert Green. |
| Leisure | motorised carts for hire, buggies for hire, trolley for hire, driving range, practice area. |
| Location | Just outside Waltham Abbey |
| Hotel | ★★★ 63% Harlow Moat House, Southern Way, HARLOW ☎ 01279 829988 118 ⇥ ♠ |

## FRINTON-ON-SEA
Map 05 TM22

**Frinton** 1 The Esplanade CO13 9EP
☎ 01255 674618 & 671618
Deceptive, flat seaside links course providing fast, firm and
undulating greens that will test the best putters and tidal
ditches that cross many of the fairways, requiring careful
placement of shots. Its open character means that every shot
has to be evaluated with both wind strength and direction in
mind. Easy walking.
*Long Course: 18 holes, 6265yds, Par 71, SSS 70, Course
record 64.*
*Short Course: 9 holes, 1367yds, Par 29.*
*Club membership 850.*

| | |
|---|---|
| Visitors | must contact in advance. |
| Societies | by arrangement, apply in writing to the secretary, Wed, Thu and some Fri. |
| Green Fees | £22 per round, adjusted seasonally.. |
| Facilities | ⊗♨ by prior arrangement ♠♥♀♨☎♥♥ ℓ Peter Taggart. |
| Leisure | motorised carts for hire, buggies for hire, trolley for hire, driving range, putting green, practice area. |
| Location | SW side of town centre |
| Hotel | ★★ 63% Maplin Hotel, Esplanade, FRINTON-ON-SEA ☎ 01255 673832 12rm(9 ⇥1 ♠) |

## GOSFIELD
Map 05 TL72

**Gosfield Lake** The Manor House, Hall Dr CO9 1SE
☎ 01787 474747
Parkland course with bunkers, lake and water hazards.
Designed by Sir Henry Cotton/Mr Howard Swan and opened
in 1988. Also 9-hole course; ideal for beginners and
improvers.
*Lakes Course: 18 holes, 6707yds, Par 72, SSS 72, Course
record 68.*
*Meadows Course: 9 holes, 4180yds, Par 64, SSS 61.*
*Club membership 650.*

| | |
|---|---|
| Visitors | Lakes Course: must contact in advance, handicap certificate required, Sat & Sun from noon only. Meadows Course: restricted during competitions, handicap certificate not required, advisable to contact. |
| Societies | welcome Mon-Fri by arrangement, telephone or write. |
| Green Fees | Lakes: £25 per day; £20 per round (£25 per round weekends). Meadows: £10 per day; £8 per round. |
| Facilities | ⊗♨♠♥♀♨☎ℓ Richard Wheeler. |
| Leisure | sauna, trolley for hire, putting green, practice area. |
| Location | 1m W of Gosfield off B1017 |
| Hotel | ★★★ 61% White Hart Hotel, Bocking End, BRAINTREE ☎ 01376 321401 31 ⇥ ♠ |

## HARLOW
Map 05 TL40

**Canons Brook** Elizabeth Way CM19 5BE
☎ 01279 421482 & 418357
Challenging parkland course designed by Henry Cotton in
1963. Accuracy is the key requiring straight driving from the
tees, especially on the par 5 11th to fly a gap with out of
bounds left and right before setting up the shot to the green.

*18 holes, 6800yds, Par 73, SSS 72, Course record 65.*
*Club membership 850.*

| | |
|---|---|
| **Visitors** | may not play at weekends. |
| **Societies** | welcome Mon, Wed and Fri, must book in advance by telephone. |
| **Green Fees** | £25 per day; £18 per round. |
| **Facilities** | ⊗ ⍏ ⓛ ♥ ♀ ⚘ 🏠 ⚐ ⚭ Alan McGinn. |
| **Leisure** | buggies for hire, trolley for hire, putting green, practice area. |
| **Location** | 3m S of M11 |
| **Hotel** | ★★★ 74% Churchgate Manor Hotel, Churchgate St, Old Harlow, HARLOW ☎ 01279 420246 85 ⇄ |

## HARWICH                    Map 05 TM23

**Harwich & Dovercourt** Station Rd, Parkeston CO12 4NZ
☎ 01255 503616
Flat moorland course with easy walking.
*9 holes, 5900yds, Par 70, SSS 69, Course record 58.*
*Club membership 420.*

| | |
|---|---|
| **Visitors** | visitors with handicap certificate may play by prior arrangement, with member only at weekends. |
| **Societies** | prior arrangement essential. |
| **Green Fees** | on application. |
| **Facilities** | ⊗ by prior arrangement ⍏ by prior arrangement ⓛ ♥ ♀ ⚘ 🏠 |
| **Leisure** | trolley for hire, putting green, practice area. |
| **Location** | Off A120 near Ferry Terminal |
| **Hotel** | ★★ 72% The Pier at Harwich, The Quay, HARWICH ☎ 01255 241212 6 ⇄ |

## INGRAVE                    Map 05 TQ69

**Thorndon Park** Ingrave Rd CM13 3RH
☎ 01277 811666 & 810345
Among the best of the Essex courses with a fine new
purpose-built clubhouse and a lake. The springy turf is easy
on the feet. Many newly planted young trees now replace
the famous old oaks that were such a feature of this course.
*18 holes, 6492yds, Par 71, SSS 71.*
*Club membership 670.*

| | |
|---|---|
| **Visitors** | must contact in advance, at weekends with member only. |
| **Societies** | welcome n Tue and Fri but must apply in writing. |
| **Green Fees** | £45 per day; £30 per round. |
| **Facilities** | ⊗ ⓛ ♥ ♀ ⚘ 🏠 ⚐ ⚭ Brian White. |
| **Leisure** | trolley for hire, putting green, practice area. |
| **Location** | W side of village off A128 |
| **Hotel** | B Forte Posthouse Brentwood, Brook St, BRENTWOOD ☎ 01277 260260 111 ⇄ |

## LOUGHTON                    Map 05 TQ49

**High Beech** Wellington Hill IG10 4AH ☎ 0181 508 7323
Short 9-hole course set in Epping Forest.
*9 holes, Par 27, Course record 25 or 9 holes, Par 27, Course
record 23.*

| | |
|---|---|
| **Visitors** | welcome. |
| **Green Fees** | Yellow; £3 per 9 holes. Red; £2.60 per 9 holes. |
| **Facilities** | ♥ 🏠 ⚐ ⚭ Clark Baker. |
| **Leisure** | trolley for hire, putting green, practice nets. |
| **Location** | Close to M25 Waltham Abbey junct |

**Loughton** Clays Ln, Debden Green IG10 2RZ
☎ 0181 502 2923
Hilly 9-hole parkland course on the edge of Epping Forest.
*9 holes, 4652yds, Par 64, SSS 63, Course record 65.*
*Club membership 180.*

| | |
|---|---|
| **Visitors** | must contact in advance. |
| **Societies** | telephone in advance. |
| **Green Fees** | £8 per 18 holes; £5 per 9 holes (£10/£6 weekends & bank holidays). |
| **Facilities** | ⓛ ♥ ♀ ⚘ 🏠 ⚐ ⚭ Stuart Layton. |
| **Leisure** | trolley for hire, practice area. |
| **Location** | 1.5m SE of Theydon Bois |
| **Hotel** | B Forte Posthouse Epping, High Rd, Bell Common, EPPING ☎ 01992 573137 Annexe79 ⇄ ♜ |

## MALDON                    Map 05 TL80

**Forrester Park** Beckingham Rd, Great Totham CM9 8EA
☎ 01621 891406
Tight, undulating parkland course with tree-lined fairways
and good views over the Blackwater estuary. Easy walking.
Attractive 16th-century clubhouse.
*18 holes, 6073yds, Par 71, SSS 69, Course record 69.*
*Club membership 1000.*

| | |
|---|---|
| **Visitors** | must contact in advance but may not play before noon weekends & bank holidays. |
| **Societies** | must apply in advance. |
| **Green Fees** | £17 per round; £22 per day (£17 weekends). |
| **Facilities** | ⊗ ⓛ ♥ ♀ ⚘ 🏠 ⚭ Gary Pike. |
| **Leisure** | hard tennis courts, trolley for hire, putting green, practice area. |
| **Location** | 3m NE of Maldon off B1022 |
| **Hotel** | ★★ 64% Blue Boar Hotel, Silver St, MALDON ☎ 01621 852681 21 ⇄ ♜Annexe8 ⇄ ♜ |

**Maldon** Beeleigh, Langford CM9 6LL ☎ 01621 853212
Flat, parkland course in a triangle of land by the River
Chelmer, the Blackwater Canal and an old railway
embankment. Alternate tees on 2nd nine holes. Testing par 3
14th (166yds) demanding particular accuracy to narrow green
guarded by bunkers and large trees.
*9 holes, 6197yds, Par 71, SSS 69.*
*Club membership 450.*

| | |
|---|---|
| **Visitors** | telephone to check availability, may only play with member at weekends. |
| **Societies** | intially telephone then confirm in writing. |
| **Green Fees** | £20 per day; £15 per round (Mon-Fri). |
| **Facilities** | ⊗ ⍏ ⓛ ♥ ♀ ⚘ 🏠 |
| **Leisure** | trolley for hire, practice area. |
| **Location** | 1m NW off B1018 |
| **Hotel** | ★★ 64% Blue Boar Hotel, Silver St, MALDON ☎ 01621 852681 21 ⇄ ♜Annexe8 ⇄ ♜ |

## ORSETT                    Map 05 TQ68

**Orsett** Brentwood Rd RM16 3DS
☎ 01375 891352 & 891226
A very good test of golf - this heathland course with its
sandy soil is quick drying and provides easy walking.
Close to the Thames estuary it is seldom calm and the
main hazards are the prevailing wind and thick gorse.
Any slight deviation can be exaggerated by the wind ▶

and a lost ball in the gorse results. The clubhouse has
been modernised.
*18 holes, 6614yds, Par 72, SSS 72, Course record 68.*
*Club membership 800.*
**Visitors** restricted weekends & bank holidays. Must
contact in advance and have a handicap
certificate.
**Societies** must contact in advance.
**Green Fees** £30 per day (£20 after 1pm).
**Facilities** ⊗ ⍦ ⃞ ⌷ ⅋ ⚲ ⛊ ⅌ Robert Newberry.
**Leisure** buggies for hire, trolley for hire, putting.
**Location** 1.5m SE off A128
**Hotel** B Forte Posthouse Basildon, Cranes Farm
Rd, BASILDON
☎ 01268 533955 110 ⇔ ⌘

## PURLEIGH                                      Map 05 TL80

**Three Rivers** Stow Rd CM3 6RR ☎ 01621 828631
Wooded parkland course with ponds, dog-legs and fine rural
views.
*Kings Course: 18 holes, 6536yds, Par 73, SSS 71.*
*Queens Course: 9 holes, 1071yds, Par 27.*
*Club membership 800.*
**Visitors** telephone before visit.
**Societies** apply in writing or telephone.
**Green Fees** Kings Course: £25 per day; £19 per round
(£29/£24 weekends). Queens Course: £7.50 per
day (£8.50 weekends).
**Facilities** ⊗ ⍦ ⃞ ⌷ ⅋ ⚲ ⛊ ⅌ Graham Packer.
**Leisure** hard tennis courts, squash, sauna, motorised
carts for hire, buggies for hire, trolley for hire,
putting green, practice area.
**Location** 1m from Purleigh on B1012
**Hotel** ★★ 64% Blue Boar Hotel, Silver St, MALDON
☎ 01621 852681 21 ⇔ ⌘Annexe8 ⇔ ⌘

## ROCHFORD                                      Map 05 TQ89

*Rochford Hundred* Hall Rd SS4 1NW
☎ 01702 544302
Parkland course with ponds and ditches as natural hazards.
*18 holes, 6292yds, Par 72, SSS 70, Course record 64.*
*Club membership 800.*
**Visitors** must have handicap certificate. Visitors may not
play Tue morning (Ladies) or Sun without a
member.
**Societies** must contact in writing.
**Green Fees** not confirmed.
**Facilities** ⅋ ⚲ ⛊ ⅌ Graham Hill.
**Leisure** putting green,cart/buggy/trolley hire.
**Location** W on B1013
**Hotel** ★★★ 66% Hotel Renouf, Bradley Way,
ROCHFORD ☎ 01702 541334 24 ⇔ ⌘

## SAFFRON WALDEN                               Map 05 TL53

*Saffron Walden* Windmill Hill CB10 1BX
☎ 01799 522786
Undulating parkland course, beautiful views.
*18 holes, 6585yds, Par 72, SSS 72.*
*Club membership 950.*
**Visitors** must contact in advance and have a handicap
certificate. With member only at weekends.

**Societies** must contact in advance.
**Green Fees** not confirmed.
**Facilities** ⅋ ⚲ ⛊ ⅌ Philip Davis.
**Leisure** putting green,practice,cart/trolley hire.
**Location** NW side of town centre off B184
**Hotel** ★★ 65% Saffron Hotel, 10-18 High St,
SAFFRON WALDEN
☎ 01799 522676 20rm(17 ⇔ ⌘)

## SOUTHEND-ON-SEA                              Map 05 TQ88

*Belfairs* Eastwood Rd North, Leigh on Sea SS9 4LR
☎ 01702 525345
Municipal parkland course run by the Borough Council. Tight
second half through thick woods, easy walking.
*18 holes, 5795yds, Par 70, SSS 68.*
*Club membership 300.*
**Visitors** restricted weekends & bank holidays.
**Green Fees** not confirmed.
**Facilities** ⛊ ⅌ ⌘
**Leisure** hard tennis courts.
**Location** 3m W, N of A13
**Hotel** ★★★ 62% Balmoral Hotel, 34 Valkyrie Rd,
Westcliffe-on-Sea, SOUTHEND-ON-SEA
☎ 01702 342947 22 ⇔ ⌘

*Thorpe Hall* Thorpe Hall Av, Thorpe Bay SS1 3AT
☎ 01702 582205
Parkland course with narrow fairways where placement rather
than length is essential.
*18 holes, 6286yds, Par 71, SSS 71, Course record 64.*
*Club membership 995.*
**Visitors** must contact in advance, with member only
weekends & bank holidays.
**Societies** apply in writing, only a certain number a year.
**Green Fees** £30 per day/round.
**Facilities** ⊗ ⍦ ⃞ ⌷ ⅋ ⚲ ⛊ ⅌ ⅌ Bill McColl.
**Leisure** squash, sauna, motorised carts for hire, buggies
for hire, trolley for hire, putting green, practice
area.
**Location** 2m E off A13
**Hotel** ★★★ 62% Balmoral Hotel, 34 Valkyrie Rd,
Westcliffe-on-Sea, SOUTHEND-ON-SEA
☎ 01702 342947 22 ⇔ ⌘

## SOUTH OCKENDON                              Map 05 TQ58

*Belhus Park Municipal* Belhus Park RM15 4PX
☎ 01708 854260
Municipal parkland type course with easy walking.
*18 holes, 5450yds, Par 68, SSS 67.*
*Club membership 250.*
**Visitors** no restrictions. Must have proper golf shoes and
shirts to be worn at all times.
**Societies** must contact in writing.
**Green Fees** not confirmed.
**Facilities** ⅋ ⚲ ⛊ ⅌ ⅌
**Leisure** heated indoor swimming pool, squash, sauna,
solarium, gymnasium, 11 bay floodlit driving
range.
**Location** 2m SW off B1335
**Hotel** ★★★ 64% Stifford Moat House, High Rd,
North Stifford, GRAYS
☎ 01708 719988 96 ⇔ ⌘

**Top Meadow** Fen Ln, North Ockendon RM14 3PR
☎ 01708 852239
Set in the Essex countryside with a panoramic view of the
area. Some holes are very difficult with the variable wind
directions, especially 1st, 6th, 7th and 13th.
*New Course: 18 holes, 5909yds, Par 69, SSS 68, Course
record 67.*
*Old Course: 9 holes, 2010yds, Par 30, SSS 30, Course record
27.*
*Club membership 600.*
**Visitors**      New Course Mon-Fri, Old Course all week.
**Societies**    telephone in advance.
**Green Fees** New Course: £12. Old Course: £5.
**Facilities**    ⊗ ⅢⅬ ♨ ♉ ♈ 曲 ⊁ ⋈ ⌱ Paul King.
**Leisure**      fishing, motorised carts for hire, buggies for hire,
                 trolley for hire, driving range, putting green,
                 practice area.
**Hotel**        B Forte Travelodge,  EAST HORNDEN
                 ☎ 01277 810819 22 ⇔ ⌱

---

### STAPLEFORD ABBOTTS                           Map 05 TQ59

**Stapleford Abbotts** Horsemanside, Tysea Hill RM14 1JU
☎ 01708 381108 & 381278
Two championship 18-hole courses and a 9-hole par 3. The
main features of the Priors course are the numerous lakes and
large sloping greeen. Abbots course has many hazards and
will test players of all standards. It is rapidly maturing into
one of the best in Essex.
*Abbotts Course: 18 holes, 6501yds, Par 72, SSS 71.*
*Priors Course: 18 holes, 5720yds, Par 69, SSS 69.*
*Friars Course: 9 holes, 1140yds, Par 27, SSS 27.*
*Club membership 600.*
**Visitors**      may only play on Priors and par 3 Friars ,
                 advisable to telephone starter on 01277 373344.
**Societies**    apply in writing, must be pre booked.
**Green Fees** Priors £10 (£15 weekends); Par 3 £5 (£8
                 weekends).
**Facilities**    ⊗ Ⅼ ♉ ♈ 曲 ⊁ ⌱ Dominic Eagle.
**Leisure**      fishing, sauna, gymnasium, buggies for hire,
                 trolley for hire, putting green, practice area.
**Location**     1m E of Stapleford Abbotts, off B175
**Hotel**        ★★★★ 68% Marygreen Manor, London Rd,
                 BRENTWOOD ☎ 01277 225252 3 ⇔
                 ⌱Annexe30 ⇔ ⌱

---

### THEYDON BOIS                                  Map 05 TQ49

**Theydon Bois** Theydon Rd CM16 4EH
☎ 01992 812460 & 83054
The course was originally a nine-hole built into Epping
Forest. It was later extendend to 18-holes which were
well-planned and well-bunkered but are situated out in
the open on the hillside. The old nine in the Forest are
short and have three bunkers among them, but even so a
wayward shot can be among the trees. The autumn
colours here are truly magnificent.
*18 holes, 5480yds, Par 68, SSS 68, Course record 64.*
*Club membership 600.*
**Visitors**      may not play Wed, Thu, Sat & Sun
                 mornings, ring 01992 812460 in advance to
                 be sure tee is available.
**Societies**    book through the secretary.
**Green Fees** £23 per round (£20 weekends after 2pm).
**Facilities**    ⊗ ⅢⅬ ♉ ♈ 曲 ⊁ ⌱ R Hall.

---

**Leisure**     trolley for hire, putting green, practice area.
**Location**    1m N
**Hotel**       B Forte Posthouse Epping, High Rd, Bell
                Common,  EPPING
                ☎ 01992 573137 Annexe79 ⇔ ⌱

### TOLLESHUNT KNIGHTS                            Map 05 TL91

**Five Lakes Hotel Golf & Country Club** Colchester Rd
CM9 8HX ☎ 01621 868888 & 862307
Two 18-hole courses. The Links is a seaside course with a
number of greenside ponds and strategically placed bunkers,
while the Lakes is a championship course with large water
features and mounding between fairways.
*Links Course: 18 holes, 6250yds, Par 71, SSS 70, Course
record 67.*
*Lakes Course: 18 holes, 6767yds, Par 72, SSS 72, Course
record 63.*
*Club membership 600.*
**Visitors**      must contact in advance.
**Societies**    must contact in advance.
**Green Fees** Links: £25 per day; £18 per round (£30/£22.50
                 weekends & bank holidays). Lakes: £37.50 per
                 day; £25 per round (£45/£30 weekends and bank
                 holidays) prices due to be reviewed.
**Facilities**    ⊗ ⅢⅬ ♉ ♈ ♊ 曲 ⊁ ⋈ ⌱ Gary Carter.
**Leisure**      hard tennis courts, heated indoor swimming
                 pool, squash, sauna, solarium, gymnasium,
                 motorised carts for hire, buggies for hire, trolley
                 for hire, driving range, putting green.
**Location**     1.75m NE on B1026
**Hotel**        ★★★★ 71% Five Lakes Hotel, Colchester Rd,
                 Whitehouse Hill,  TOLLESHUNT Knights
                 ☎ 01621 868888 114 ⇔ ⌱

### TOOT HILL                                     Map 05 TL50

**Toot Hill** School Rd CM5 9PU ☎ 01277 365523
Pleasant course with several water hazards and sand greens.
*18 holes, 6053yds, Par 70, SSS 69, Course record 65.*
*Club membership 450.*
**Visitors**      welcome but may not play at weekends.
**Societies**    Society days Tue & Thu contact in advance.
**Green Fees** £35 per day; £25 per round.
**Facilities**    ⊗ ⅢⅬ ♉ ♈ ♊ 曲 ⊁ ⌱ Geoff Bacon.
**Leisure**      motorised carts for hire, buggies for hire, trolley
                 for hire, driving range, putting green, practice
                 area.
**Location**     7m SE of Harlow, off A414
**Hotel**        B Forte Posthouse Epping, High Rd, Bell
                 Common,  EPPING
                 ☎ 01992 573137 Annexe79 ⇔ ⌱

### WITHAM                                        Map 05 TL81

**Braxted Park** Braxted Park Estate CM8 3EN
☎ 01376 572372
A Pay and Play course in ancient parkland, surrounded by
lakes and extremely pretty countryside. Suitable for beginners
and average players.
*9 holes, 2940yds, Par 35.*
*Club membership 71.*
**Visitors**      welcome weekdays from 7.30am onwards.
**Societies**    telephone to arrange.                          ▶

**Green Fees** £12 per 18 holes; £9 per 9 holes.
**Facilities** ⊗ ⓑ ▆ ♀ ⚏ 🏠 🍴 ⓒ Michael Woollett.
**Leisure** fishing, trolley for hire, practice area.
**Location** 2m from A12 near Kelvedon
**Hotel** ★★★ 65% Jarvis Rivenhall Hotel, Rivenhall End, WITHAM
☎ 01376 516969 7 ⇔ ⓒAnnexe48 ⇔ ⓒ

## WOODHAM WALTER
Map 05 TL80

*Bunsay Downs* Little Baddow Rd CM9 6RU
☎ 01245 222648
Attractive 9-hole public course. Also Par 3 course.
*9 holes, 2932yds, Par 70, SSS 68.*
*Badgers: 9 holes, 1319yds, Par 54.*
*Club membership 400.*
**Visitors** no restrictions.
**Societies** Mon-Fri only. Must contact in advance.
**Green Fees** not confirmed.
**Facilities** ♀ ⚏ 🏠 🍴 ⓒ Mickey Walker.
**Leisure** putting, practice, cart/buggy/trolley hire.
**Hotel** ★★ 64% Blue Boar Hotel, Silver St, MALDON
☎ 01621 852681 21 ⇔ ⓒAnnexe8 ⇔ ⓒ

*Warren* CM9 6RW ☎ 01245 223258 & 223198
Attractive parkland course with natural hazards and good views.
*18 holes, 6229yds, Par 70, SSS 70, Course record 65.*
*Club membership 765.*
**Visitors** contact in advance, weekend pm only, Wed pm only.
**Societies** arrange by telephone, confirm in writing, weekdays ex Wed.
**Green Fees** £30 per day; £25 per round.
**Facilities** ⊗ ⓜ by prior arrangement ⓑ ▆ ♀ ⚏ 🏠 🍴 ⓒ Mickey Walker.
**Leisure** motorised carts for hire, buggies for hire, trolley for hire, driving range, putting green, practice area, teaching academy.
**Location** 0.5m SW
**Hotel** ★★ 64% Blue Boar Hotel, Silver St, MALDON
☎ 01621 852681 21 ⇔ ⓒAnnexe8 ⇔ ⓒ

# GLOUCESTERSHIRE

## CHELTENHAM
Map 03 SO92

*Cotswold Hills* Ullenwood GL53 9QT ☎ 01242 515264
A gently undulating course with open aspects and views of the Cotswolds.
*18 holes, 6889yds, Par 71, SSS 74.*
*Club membership 750.*
**Visitors** telephone in advance, handicap certificate preferred.
**Societies** must apply in writing or telephone.
**Green Fees** £26 per day; £21 per round (£31/£26 weekends).
**Facilities** ⊗ ⓜ ⓑ ▆ ♀ ⚏ 🏠 ⓒ Noel Boland.
**Leisure** buggies for hire, trolley for hire, putting green, practice area.

**Location** 3m SE on A435 and A436
**Hotel** B Forte Posthouse Gloucester, Crest Way, Barnwood, GLOUCESTER
☎ 01452 613311 123 ⇔ ⓒ

*Lilley Brook* Cirencester Rd, Charlton Kings GL53 8EG
☎ 01242 526785
Undulating parkland course. Magnificent views over Cheltenham and surrounding coutryside.
*18 holes, 6212yds, Par 69, SSS 70, Course record 63.*
*Club membership 800.*
**Visitors** advisable to enquire of availability.
**Societies** apply in writing.
**Green Fees** £25 per day; £20 round (£30/£25 weekends).
**Facilities** ⊗ ⓜ ⓑ ▆ ♀ ⚏ 🏠 🍴 ⓒ Forbes Hadden.
**Leisure** motorised carts for hire, buggies for hire, trolley for hire, putting green, practice area.
**Location** 2m S of Cheltenham on A435
**Hotel** ★★★★ 64% Cheltenham Park Hotel, Cirencester Rd, Charlton Kings, CHELTENHAM ☎ 01242 222021 144 ⇔ ⓒ

## CHIPPING SODBURY
Map 03 ST78

*Chipping Sodbury* BS17 6PU ☎ 01454 319042
Parkland courses of Championship proportions. The old course may be seen from the large opening tee by the clubhouse at the top of the hill. Two huge drainage dykes cut through the course and form a distinctive hazard on eleven holes.
*New Course: 18 holes, 6912yds, Par 73, SSS 73, Course record 65.*
*Old Course: 9 holes, 6184yds, Par 70, SSS 69.*
*Club membership 800.*
**Visitors** no restriction on Old Course, must have a handicap certificate and may only play until after noon at weekends on New Course.
**Societies** must contact in writing.
**Green Fees** £30 per day; £25 per 27 holes (£35/£30 weekends and bank holidays).
**Facilities** ⊗ ⓜ ⓑ ▆ ♀ ⚏ 🏠 🍴 ⓒ Mike Watts.
**Leisure** motorised carts for hire, buggies for hire, trolley for hire, putting green, practice area.
**Location** 0.5m N
**Hotel** ★★ 61% Cross Hands Hotel, OLD SODBURY
☎ 01454 313000 24rm(3 ⇔17 ⓒ)

## CIRENCESTER
Map 04 SP00

*Cirencester* Cheltenham Rd, Bagendon GL7 7BH
☎ 01285 652465 & 656124 pro shop
Undulating Cotswold course.
*18 holes, 6020yds, Par 70, SSS 69.*
**Visitors** restricted play at weekends, contact professional shop in advance.
**Societies** telephone Secretary/Manager.
**Green Fees** £20 per day (£25 weekends & bank holidays).
**Facilities** ⊗ ⓜ ⓑ ▆ ♀ ⚏ 🏠 🍴 ⓒ Geoff Robbins.
**Leisure** buggies for hire, trolley for hire, putting green, practice area.
**Location** 2 N on A435
**Hotel** ★★★ 68% Stratton House Hotel, Gloucester Rd, CIRENCESTER
☎ 01285 651761 41 ⇔ ⓒ

## CLEEVE HILL                    Map 03 SO92

**Cleeve Hill** GL52 3PW ☎ 01242 672025
Undulating and open heathland course affected by
crosswinds.
*18 holes, 6411yds, Par 72, SSS 71, Course record 69.*
*Club membership 450.*
**Visitors**     bookings taken 7 days in advance. Limited play
                 weekends.
**Societies**    telephone in advance.
**Green Fees**   £8 (£10 weekends & bank holidays).
**Facilities**   ⊗ ⅷ ᛒ ☕ ♀ ♨ 🏠 ⛳ ℓ Richard Jenkins.
**Leisure**      trolley for hire, putting green, practice area.
**Location**     1m NE on B4632
**Hotel**        ★★★ 57% Hotel De La Bere, Southam,
                 CHELTENHAM
                 ☎ 01242 237771 32 ⇄ ℟Annexe25 ⇄

## COLEFORD                      Map 03 SO51

**Forest Hills** Mile End Rd GL16 7BY ☎ 01594 810620
A parkland course on a plateau with panoramic views of
Coleford and Forest of Dean. Some testing holes with the par-
5 13th hole sitting tight on a water hazard, and the
challenging 18th with 2nd shot over large pond to a green
protected by another pond and bunker - all in front of the
clubhouse.
*18 holes, 6740yds, Par 68, SSS 68, Course record 66.*
**Visitors**     no restrictions.
**Societies**    contact in advance.
**Green Fees**   £20 per day; £13 per round (£25/£15 weekends).
**Facilities**   ⊗ ⅷ ᛒ ☕ ♀ ♨ 🏠 ⛳ ℓ J Nicholl.
**Leisure**      motorised carts for hire, buggies for hire, trolley
                 for hire, driving range, putting green, practice
                 area.
**Hotel**        ★★★ 65% The Speech House, Forest of Dean,
                 COLEFORD ☎ 01594 822607 14 ⇄ ℟

**Forest of Dean** Lords Hill GL16 8BD ☎ 01594 832583
Established in 1973 and now matured into an extremely
pleasant parkland course. Well bunkered with light rough, a
few blind tee shots and water in play on several holes.
*18 holes, 5813yds, Par 69, SSS 68.*
*Club membership 500.*
**Visitors**     are required to book tee-off times.
**Societies**    must telephone in advance.
**Green Fees**   £13 per round (£15 weekends & bank holidays).
**Facilities**   ⊗ ⅷ ᛒ ☕ ♀ ♨ 🏠 ⛳ 🎳 ℓ Philip Worthing.
**Leisure**      hard tennis courts, outdoor swimming pool,
                 motorised carts for hire, buggies for hire, trolley
                 for hire, putting green, practice area, bowling
                 green.
**Hotel**        ★★★ 65% The Speech House, Forest of Dean,
                 COLEFORD ☎ 01594 822607 14 ⇄ ℟

## DURSLEY                       Map 03 ST79

**Stinchcombe Hill** Stinchcombe Hill GL11 6AQ
☎ 01453 542015
High on the hill with splendid views of the Cotswolds,
the River Severn and the Welsh hills. A downland course
with good turf, some trees and an interesting variety of
greens. Protected greens make this a challenging course
in windy conditions.

*18 holes, 5734yds, Par 68, SSS 68, Course record 63.*
*Club membership 550.*
**Visitors**     restricted at weekends. Must contact
                 professional in advance 01453 543878.
**Societies**    must apply in advance.
**Green Fees**   £20 per day; £12.50 per round (£25 per
                 round/day weekends & bank holidays,
                 winter weekends £15 per round).
**Facilities**   ⊗ ⅷ ᛒ ☕ ♀ ♨ 🏠 ⛳ ℓ Paul Bushell.
**Leisure**      trolley for hire, putting green, practice area.
**Location**     1m W off A4135
**Hotel**        ★★ 65% Prince Of Wales Hotel,
                 BERKELEY ROAD
                 ☎ 01453 810474 41 ⇄ ℟

## GLOUCESTER                    Map 03 SO81

**Jarvis Gloucester Hotel & Country Club** Matson Ln,
Robinswood Hill GL4 6EA ☎ 01452 411331
Undulating, wooded course, built around a hill with superb
views over Gloucester and the Cotswolds. The 12th is a
drive straight up a hill, nicknamed 'Coronary Hill'.
*18 holes, 6170yds, Par 70, SSS 69, Course record 65.*
*Club membership 600.*
**Visitors**     can book up to 7 days in advance.
**Societies**    telephone in advance.
**Green Fees**   £25 per day; £19 per round (£25 per round
                 weekends).
**Facilities**   ⊗ ⅷ ᛒ ☕ ♀ ♨ 🏠 ⛳ 🚗 ℓ Peter Darnell.
**Leisure**      hard tennis courts, heated indoor swimming
                 pool, squash, sauna, solarium, gymnasium,
                 buggies for hire, trolley for hire, practice
                 area, running track.
**Location**     2m SW off M5
**Hotel**        ★★★ 69% Jarvis Bowden Hall Hotel &
                 Country Club, Bondend Ln, Upton St
                 Leonards, GLOUCESTER
                 ☎ 01452 614121 72 ⇄ ℟

**Rodway Hill** Newent Rd, Highnam GL2 8DN
☎ 01452 384222
A challenging 18-hole course with superb panoramic views.
Testing front 5 holes and the par 3 13th and par 5 16th being
affected by strong croswinds off the River Severn.
*18 holes, 5860yds, Par 70, SSS 68, Course record 72.*
*Club membership 400.*
**Visitors**     no restrictions.
**Societies**    telephone in advance.
**Green Fees**   £8 per 18 holes; £5 per 9 holes (£10/£6
                 weekends).
**Facilities**   ⊗ ᛒ ☕ ♨ 🏠 ⛳ ℓ Tony Grubb.
**Leisure**      putting green, practice area.
**Location**     2m outside Gloucester on B4215
**Hotel**        ★★★ 62% Hatherley Manor Hotel, Down
                 Hatherley Ln, GLOUCESTER
                 ☎ 01452 730217 56 ⇄ ℟

## LYDNEY                        Map 03 SO60

**Lydney** Lakeside Av GL15 5QA ☎ 01594 842614
Flat parkland/meadowland course with prevailing wind along
fairways.
*9 holes, 5298yds, Par 66, SSS 66, Course record 63.*
*Club membership 350.*                              ▶

**Visitors**   with member only at weekends & bank holidays.
**Societies**  apply in writing to the Secretary.
**Green Fees** £12 per day.
**Facilities** ⓑ ⬛ ♀ ⅄
**Leisure**    practice area.
**Location**   SE side of town centre
**Hotel**      ★★★ 65% The Speech House, Forest of Dean, COLEFORD ☎ 01594 822607 14 ⇆ ⋔

## MINCHINHAMPTON                                  Map 03 SO80

**Minchinhampton (New Course)** New Course GL6 9BE
☎ 01453 833866 & 833840 bookings
The course is on an upland Cotswold plateau. It is level and open in design. Very good golf is needed to achieve par of 72.
*Avening: 18 holes, 6244yds, Par 70, SSS 70, Course record 65.*
*Cherington: 18 holes, 6320yds, Par 71, SSS 70, Course record 66.*
*Club membership 1100.*
**Visitors**   must contact in advance.
**Societies**  must contact by telephone.
**Green Fees** £25 per day; (£30 weekends & bank holidays).
**Facilities** ⊗ ⅏ ⓑ ⬛ ♀ ⅄ 📠 ⋔ ⋔ Chris Steele.
**Leisure**    trolley for hire, driving range, putting green, practice area.
**Location**   2m E
**Hotel**      ★★★ 65% Burleigh Court, Minchinhampton, STROUD ☎ 01453 883804 11 ⇆ ⋔Annexe6 ⇆ ⋔

**Minchinhampton (Old Course)** Old Course GL6 9AQ
☎ 01453 832642 & 836382
An open grassland course 600 feet above sea level. There is a prevailing west wind that affects most holes. Panoramic Cotswold views.
*18 holes, 6205yds, Par 71, SSS 70, Course record 64.*
*Club membership 600.*
**Visitors**   must contact in advance.
**Societies**  must contact by telephone.
**Green Fees** £10 per day/round (£13 weekends & bank holidays).
**Facilities** ⊗ ⅏ ⓑ ⬛ ♀ ⅄ 📠
**Leisure**    trolley for hire, practice area.
**Location**   1m NW
**Hotel**      ★★★ 65% Burleigh Court, Minchinhampton, STROUD ☎ 01453 883804 11 ⇆ ⋔Annexe6 ⇆ ⋔

## NAUNTON                                         Map 04 SP12

**Naunton Downs** GL54 3AE ☎ 01451 850090
New in 1993, Naunton Downs course plays over beautiful Cotswold countryside. A valley running through the course is one of the main features, creating 3 holes that cross over it. The prevailing wind adds extra challenge to the par 5's (which play into the wind), combined with small undulating greens.
*18 holes, 6078yds, Par 71, SSS 69, Course record 73.*
*Club membership 1000.*
**Visitors**   must contact in advance.
**Societies**  telephone for details.
**Green Fees** £19.95 per day.
**Facilities** ⊗ ⅏ ⓑ ⬛ ♀ ⅄ 📠 ⋔ ⋔ Martin Seddon.
**Leisure**    motorised carts for hire, buggies for hire, trolley for hire, putting green, practice area.

**Location**   B4068 Stow/Cheltenham
**Hotel**      ★★★⅃⅃ 79% Lords of the Manor, UPPER SLAUGHTER ☎ 01451 820243 28 ⇆ ⋔

## PAINSWICK                                       Map 03 SO80

*Painswick* GL6 6TL ☎ 01452 812180
Downland course set on Cotswold Hills at Painswick Beacon, with fine views. Short course more than compensated by natural hazards and tight fairways.
*18 holes, 4895yds, Par 67, SSS 64.*
*Club membership 420.*
**Visitors**   with member only on Sun.
**Societies**  must apply in writing.
**Green Fees** not confirmed.
**Facilities** ♀ ⅄ 📠
**Location**   1m N on A46
**Hotel**      ★★★ 76% Painswick Hotel, Kemps Ln, PAINSWICK ☎ 01452 812160 19 ⇆ ⋔

## TEWKESBURY                                      Map 03 SO83

**Puckrup Hall Hotel** Puckrup GL20 6EL
☎ 01684 296200
Set in 140 acres of undulating parkland with lakes, existing trees and marvellous views of the Malvern hills. There are water hazards at the 5th and a cluster of bunkers on the long 9th before the challnging tee shot across the water to the par-3 18th.
*18 holes, 6431yds, Par 71, SSS 71.*
*Club membership 250.*
**Visitors**   must be a regular golfer familiar with rules and etiquette, must book a tee time, may book up to 6 days in advance.
**Societies**  telephone in advance.
**Green Fees** £25 per day; £20 per round (£33/£25 weekends & bank holidays).
**Facilities** ⊗ ⅏ ⓑ ⬛ ♀ ⅄ 📠 ⋔ ⋈ ⋔ Kevin Pickett.
**Leisure**    heated indoor swimming pool, sauna, solarium, gymnasium, motorised carts for hire, buggies for hire, trolley for hire, driving range, putting green, practice area, aerobics hall.
**Location**   4m N, on main A38
**Hotel**      ★★★ 74% Puckrup Hall Hotel and Golf Club, Puckrup, TEWKESBURY ☎ 01684 296200 84 ⇆ ⋔

**Tewkesbury Park Hotel Golf & Country Club** Lincoln Green Ln GL20 7DN ☎ 01684 295405
A parkland course in a sheltered situation beside the River Severn. The par 3, 5th is an exacting hole calling for accurate distance judgment. The hotel and country club offer many sports facilities.
*18 holes, 6533yds, Par 73, SSS 72.*
**Visitors**   may play weekdays only.
**Societies**  telephone initially.
**Green Fees** £25 weekdays.
**Facilities** ⊗ ⅏ ⓑ ⬛ ♀ ⅄ 📠 ⋔ ⋈ ⋔ Robert Taylor.
**Leisure**    hard tennis courts, heated indoor swimming pool, squash, sauna, solarium, gymnasium, motorised carts for hire, buggies for hire, trolley for hire, driving range, putting green, practice area.
**Location**   1m SW off A38

| Hotel | ★★★ 68% Tewkesbury Park Hotel, Country Club Resort, Lincoln Green Ln, TEWKESBURY ☎ 01684 295405 Annexe78 ⇆ ⋒ |
|---|---|

## THORNBURY                   Map 03 ST69

**Thornbury Golf Centre** Bristol Rd BS12 2XL
☎ 01454 281144
Two 18 hole pay & play courses designed by Hawtree and set in undulating terrain with estensive views towards the Severn estuary. The Low 18 is a Par 3 with holes ranging from 80 to 207 yards and is ideal for beginners. The High course puts to test the more experienced golfer. Excellent 25 bay floodlit driving range.
*High Course: 18 holes, 6154yds, Par 71, SSS 69.*
*Low Course: 18 holes, 2195yds, Par 54.*
*Club membership 420.*

| | |
|---|---|
| Visitors | must contact in advance. |
| Societies | apply in writing for brochure. |
| Green Fees | £21 per day; £13 per round; £7.50 par 3 course. |
| Facilities | ⊗ ⫟ ᒪ ☑ ♀ ⚚ 亼 ♈ ⋈ ⋒ Nicholas Lamb. |
| Leisure | trolley for hire, driving range, putting green, practice area. |
| Location | Off A38 |
| Hotel | ★★★(red)⚫⚫ Thornbury Castle Hotel, THORNBURY ☎ 01454 281182 18 ⇆ ⋒ |

## PUCKRUP HALL HOTEL and GOLF CLUB

**Puckrup, Tewkesbury, Gloucestershire GL20 6EL**
**Telephone: (01684) 296200**
**Fax: (01684) 850788**

Puckrup Hall Hotel and Golf Club is set amidst 140 acres of rolling parkland between the Cotswolds and Malvern Hills, just a few minutes from junction 8 of the M5. The 18 hole par 71 championship golf course, with the addition of lakes to the natural water sources and astute use of specimen trees, will satisfy the most discerning golfer. The 84 luxury bedrooms, superb cuisine and extensive conference and private dining facilities are all complemented by "Generations" Leisure Club which hosts swimming pool, spa bath and crêche. Altogether the ideal location for a touring base, golfing break or management retreat.

## WESTONBIRT                 Map 03 ST88

**Westonbirt** Westonbirt School GL8 8QG
☎ 01666 880242
A parkland course with good views.
*9 holes, 4504yds, Par 64, SSS 64.*
*Club membership 150.*

| | |
|---|---|
| Visitors | no restrictions. |
| Societies | no reserved tees. |
| Green Fees | not confirmed. |
| Facilities | 亼 |
| Leisure | practice area. |
| Location | E side of village off A433 |
| Hotel | ★★★ 65% Hare & Hounds Hotel, Westonbirt, TETBURY ☎ 01666 880233 22 ⇆ ⋒Annexe8 ⇆ ⋒ |

## WICK                          Map 03 ST77

**Tracy Park** Tracy Park, Bath Rd BS15 5RN
☎ 0117 937 2251
Three undulating 9-hole parkland courses situated on the south-western escarpment of the Cotswolds, affording fine views. Whichever 18-hole combination is played, the variety of holes will ensure an enjoyable and interesting challenge to all levels of handicap. Natural water hazards affect a number of holes. The clubhouse dates back to 1600 and is a building of great beauty and elegance, set in the 220 acre estate of this golf and country club.
*Avon Course: 9 holes, 3091yds, Par 35, SSS 35.*
*Bristol Course: 9 holes, 3332yds, Par 35, SSS 35.*
*Cotswold Course: 9 holes, 3098yds, Par 35, SSS 35.*
*Club membership 900.*

| | |
|---|---|
| Visitors | no restrictions. |
| Societies | must telephone or write to P A Murphy. |
| Green Fees | £30 per day; £20 per round (£30 weekends). |
| Facilities | ⊗ ⫟ ᒪ ☑ ♀ 亼 ♈ ⋒ Richard Berry. |
| Leisure | hard tennis courts, squash, motorised carts for hire, buggies for hire, trolley for hire, driving range, putting green, practice area. |
| Location | S side of village off A420 |
| Hotel | ★★★ 79% The Queensberry Hotel, Russel St, BATH ☎ 01225 447928 22 ⇆ ⋒ |

## WOTTON-UNDER-EDGE      Map 03 ST79

**Cotswold Edge** Upper Rushmire GL12 7PT
☎ 01453 844167
Meadowland course situated in a quiet Cotswold valley with magnificent views. First half flat and open, second half more varied.
*18 holes, 6170yds, Par 71, SSS 70.*
*Club membership 800.*

| | |
|---|---|
| Visitors | preferable to contact in advance, at weekends may only play with member. |
| Societies | must contact in writing or telephone in advance. |
| Green Fees | £15.50. |
| Facilities | ⊗ ᒪ ☑ ♀ 亼 ♈ ⋒ David Gosling. |
| Leisure | buggies for hire, trolley for hire, putting green, practice area. |
| Location | N of town on B4058 Wotton-Tetbury road |
| Hotel | ★★ 66% Egypt Mill Hotel, NAILSWORTH ☎ 01453 833449 & 835449 6 ⇆ ⋒Annexe8 ⇆ ⋒ |

# GREATER LONDON

Those courses which fall within the confines of the London Postal District area (ie have London postcodes - W1, SW1 etc) are listed under the county heading of **London** in the gazetteer (see page 147).

## ADDINGTON
Map 05 TQ36

**The Addington** 205 Shirley Church Rd, Addington CR0 5AB ☎ 0181 777 1055
A world of heather, bracken, silver birch and pine referred to by Henry Longhurst as his favourite inland course. It is one where thought is required at every hole.
*18 holes, 6242yds, Par 71, SSS 71, Course record 66.*
Visitors      may not play weekends. Must be recognised of recognised club.
Societies     weekdays only, telephone for prior arrangement.
Green Fees £30 per round or day weekdays only.
Facilities    ⊗ ▮ ♀ ♣ 🏠 ⛳ ℄ E Campbell.
Leisure       trolley for hire.
Hotel         ★★★★ 68% Croydon Park Hotel, 7 Altyre Rd, CROYDON
              ☎ 0181 680 9200 212 ⇥ ℟

*Addington Court* Featherbed Ln CR0 9AA
☎ 0181 657 0281
Challenging, well-drained courses designed by F. Hawtree. Two 18-hole courses, 9-hole course and a pitch-and-putt course.
*Old Course: 18 holes, 5577yds, Par 67, SSS 67, Course record 60.*
*New Falconwood Course: 18 holes, 5360yds, Par 66, SSS 66.*
*Club membership 350.*
Visitors      no restrictions.
Societies     must telephone in advance.
Green Fees not confirmed.
Facilities    ♀ ♣ 🏠 ⛳ ℄ Geoffrey A Cotton.
Leisure       putting green, practice area, trolley hire.
Location      1m S off A2022
Hotel         ★★★★ 65% Selsdon Park Hotel, Addington Rd, Sanderstead, CROYDON
              ☎ 0181 657 8811 170 ⇥ ℟

**Addington Palace** Addington Park, Gravel Hill CR0 5BB
☎ 0181 654 3061
Hard-walking parkland course, with two (par 4) testing holes (2nd and 10th).
*18 holes, 6286yds, Par 71, SSS 71, Course record 63.*
*Club membership 700.*
Visitors      telephone in advance, must play with member at weekends & bank holidays.
Societies     Tue, Wed & Fri only, telephone in advance.
Green Fees £30 per day/round.
Facilities    ⊗ 🕱 by prior arrangement ▮ ♥ ♀ ♣ 🏠 ℄ Roger Williams.
Leisure       trolley for hire, putting green, practice area.
Location      0.5m SW on A212
Hotel         ★★★★ 65% Selsdon Park Hotel, Addington Rd, Sanderstead, CROYDON
              ☎ 0181 657 8811 170 ⇥ ℟

## BARNEHURST
Map 05 TQ57

*Barnehurst* Mayplace Rd East DA7 6JU ☎ 01322 523746
Parkland course, easy walking.
*9 holes, 5320yds, Par 66, SSS 66.*
*Club membership 300.*
Visitors      restricted Tue, Thu, Sat (pm) & Sun.
Societies     by arrangement.
Green Fees not confirmed.
Facilities    ♀ ♣ 🏠 ⛳ ℄ Tudor Morgan.
Leisure       practice area, trolley hire.
Location      0.75m NW of Crayford off A2000
Hotel         B Forte Posthouse Bexley, Black Prince Interchange, Southwold Rd, BEXLEY
              ☎ 01322 526900 103 ⇥ ℟

## BARNET
Map 04 TQ29

**Arkley** Rowley Green Rd EN5 3HL ☎ 0181 449 0394
Wooded parkland course situated on highest spot in Hertfordshire with fine views.
*9 holes, 6045yds, Par 69, SSS 69.*
*Club membership 450.*
Visitors      may play weekdays only (ex Tue).
Societies     must contact in advance.
Green Fees £20 per day.
Facilities    ⊗ ▮ ♥ ♀ ♣ 🏠 ℄ Mark Squire.
Leisure       trolley for hire, putting green, practice area.
Location      2m W off A411
Hotel         ★★★ 74% Edgwarebury Hotel, Barnet Ln, ELSTREE ☎ 0181 953 8227 47 ⇥ ℟

*Dyrham Park Country Club* Galley Ln EN5 4RA
☎ 0181 440 3361
Parkland course.
*18 holes, 6369yds, Par 71, SSS 70, Course record 65.*
*Club membership 1200.*
Visitors      must be guest of member.
Societies     Wed only, must book in advance.
Green Fees not confirmed.
Facilities    ♀ (all day) ♣ 🏠 ⛳ ℄ Bill Large.
Leisure       hard tennis courts, heated outdoor swimming pool, fishing.
Location      3m NW off A1081
Hotel         B Forte Posthouse South Mimms, SOUTH MIMMS ☎ 01707 643311 120 ⇥ ℟

**Old Fold Manor** Old Fold Ln, Hadley Green EN5 4QN
☎ 0181 440 9185
Heathland course, good test of golf.
*18 holes, 6481yds, Par 71, SSS 71, Course record 66.*
*Club membership 520.*
Visitors      with member only weekends & bank holidays.
Societies     must apply in writing.
Green Fees £20 per round; Mon & Wed public days £11 per round.
Facilities    ⊗ 🕱 ▮ ♥ ♀ (ex Mon & Wed) ♣ 🏠 ⛳ ℄ Daniel Fitzsimmons.
Leisure       trolley for hire, putting green, practice area.
Location      Off A1000 between Barnet/Potters Bar
Hotel         ★★★★♨ 69% West Lodge Park Hotel, Cockfosters Rd, HADLEY WOOD
              ☎ 0181 440 8311 43 ⇥ ℟Annexe2 ⇥ ℟

## BECKENHAM
Map 05 TQ36

*Beckenham Place* The Mansion BR3 2BP
☎ 0181 650 2292
Picturesque course in the grounds of a public park. The
course is played over by the Braeside Golf Club.
*18 holes, 5722yds, Par 68, SSS 68.*
*Club membership 200.*
**Visitors**     no restrictions.
**Societies**    must contact in advance.
**Green Fees** not confirmed.
**Facilities** ♀♨️🏠⛳🍸
**Location**    0.5m N on B2015
**Hotel**       ★★★ 69% Bromley Court Hotel, Bromley Hill,
                BROMLEY ☎ 0181 464 5011 118 ⇥ 🐾

**Langley Park** Barnfield Wood Rd BR6 2SZ
☎ 0181 658 6849
This is a pleasant, but difficult, well-wooded, parkland
course with natural hazards including a lake at the 18th
hole.
*18 holes, 6488yds, Par 69, SSS 71, Course record 65.*
*Club membership 700.*
**Visitors**     must contact in advance and may not play
                 weekends.
**Societies**    Wed & Thu only, telephone to book.
**Green Fees** £35 per day/round (concessionary rate
                 winter).
**Facilities** ⊗ ⅲ 📢 🍺 ♀♨️🏠⛳🍸 Colin Staff.
**Leisure**     trolley for hire, putting green, practice area.
**Location**    0.5 N on B2015
**Hotel**       ★★★ 69% Bromley Court Hotel, Bromley
                Hill, BROMLEY
                ☎ 0181 464 5011 118 ⇥ 🐾

## BEXLEYHEATH
Map 05 TQ47

**Bexleyheath** Mount Rd DA6 8JS ☎ 0181 303 6951
Undulating course.
*9 holes, 5162yds, Par 66, SSS 66, Course record 65.*
*Club membership 330.*
**Visitors**     must contact Secretary in advance, may not play
                 weekends.
**Societies**    telephone in advance.
**Green Fees** £20 per day.
**Facilities** ⊗ ⅲ 📢 🍺 ♀♨️
**Leisure**     putting green.
**Location**    1m SW
**Hotel**       B Forte Posthouse Bexley, Black Prince
                Interchange, Southwold Rd, BEXLEY
                ☎ 01322 526900 103 ⇥ 🐾

## BIGGIN HILL
Map 05 TQ45

*Cherry Lodge* Jail Ln TN16 3AX ☎ 01959 572250
Undulating parkland course with good views, 600feet above
sea level and affected by wind. 14th is 434 yards across a
valley and uphill. Requires two good shots to reach the green.
*18 holes, 6652yds, Par 72, SSS 73.*
*Club membership 700.*
**Visitors**     must contact in advance but may not play at
                 weekends.
**Societies**    must telephone in advance.
**Green Fees** not confirmed.

**Facilities** ♀♨️🏠⛳ Nigel Child.
**Leisure**     sauna, putting, practice area, buggy/trolley hire.
**Location**    1m E
**Hotel**       ★★★ 68% Kings Arms Hotel, Market Square,
                WESTERHAM ☎ 01959 562990 16 ⇥ 🐾

## BROMLEY
Map 05 TQ46

**Bromley** Magpie Hall Ln BR2 8JF ☎ 0181 462 7014
Flat course, ideal for beginners.
*9 holes, 2745yds, Par 70, SSS 67.*
**Visitors**     no restrictions.
**Societies**    apply in writing.
**Green Fees** £4.85 per 9 holes (£6.15 weekends and bank
                 holidays).
**Facilities** ⊗ 📢 ♀🏠⛳🍸 Peter Remy.
**Leisure**     trolley for hire, putting green, practice area.
**Location**    2m SE off A21
**Hotel**       ★★★ 69% Bromley Court Hotel, Bromley Hill,
                BROMLEY ☎ 0181 464 5011 118 ⇥ 🐾

*Shortlands* Meadow Rd, Shortlands BR2 0PB
☎ 0181 460 2471
Easy walking parkland course with a brook as a natural
hazard.
*9 holes, 5261yds, Par 65, SSS 66, Course record 59.*
*Club membership 410.*
**Visitors**     must be guest of member.
**Green Fees** not confirmed.
**Facilities** ♨️🏠⛳ Jamie Bates.
**Location**    0.75m W off A222
**Hotel**       ★★★ 69% Bromley Court Hotel, Bromley Hill,
                BROMLEY ☎ 0181 464 5011 118 ⇥ 🐾

**Sundridge Park** Garden Rd BR1 3NE
☎ 0181 460 0278
The East course is longer than the West but many think
the shorter of the two courses is the more difficult. The
East is surrounded by trees while the West is more hilly,
with good views. Both are certainly a good test of golf.
*East Course: 18 holes, 6516yds, Par 70, SSS 71, Course
record 63.*
*West Course: 18 holes, 6016yds, Par 68, SSS 69, Course
record 65.*
*Club membership 1200.*
**Visitors**     may only play on weekdays. Must contact in
                 advance and must have a handicap certificate.
**Societies**    must contact well in advance.
**Green Fees** £36 per day.
**Facilities** ⊗ ⅲ 📢 🍺 ♀♨️🏠⛳ Bob Cameron.
**Leisure**     trolley for hire, putting green.
**Location**    N side of town centre off A2212
**Hotel**       ★★★ 69% Bromley Court Hotel, Bromley
                Hill, BROMLEY
                ☎ 0181 464 5011 118 ⇥ 🐾

## CARSHALTON
Map 04 TQ26

**Oaks Sports Centre** Woodmansterne Rd SM5 4AN
☎ 0181 643 8363
Public parkland course with floodlit, covered driving range.
*18 holes, 6025yds, Par 70, SSS 69, Course record 65 or 9
holes, 1443yds, Par 28, SSS 28.*
*Club membership 864.*
**Visitors**     no restrictions.                           ▶

Societies  must apply in writing.
Green Fees £11 per round (£13 weekends). 9 hole: £5.20 per round (£6 weekends).
Facilities  ⊗ ⑉ ⓛ 🍺 ♀ ♨ 🏠 ℓ G Horley/P Russell/M Pilkinton.
Leisure  squash, trolley for hire, driving range, putting green.
Location  0.5m S on B278
Hotel  B Forte Posthouse Croydon, Purley Way, CROYDON ☎ 0181 688 5185 83 ⇔ ℝ

---

## CHESSINGTON                             Map 04 TQ16

*Chessington* Garrison Ln KT9 2LW ☎ 0181 391 0948
Tree-lined parkland course designed by Patrick Tallack.
*9 holes, 1400yds, Par 27, SSS 28.*
*Club membership 250.*
Visitors  must book 7.30am-noon weekends only.
Societies  must telephone 1 month in advance.
Green Fees not confirmed.
Facilities  ♀ ♨ 🏠 ♈ ℓ
Location  Opp Chessington South Station nr Zoo
Hotel  ★★ 65% Haven Hotel, Portsmouth Rd, ESHER ☎ 0181 398 0023 16 ⇔ ℝAnnexe4 ⇔ ℝ

---

## CHISLEHURST                            Map 05 TQ47

**Chislehurst** Camden Park Rd BR7 5HJ ☎ 0181 467 2782
Pleasantly wooded undulating parkland/heathland course.
Magnificent clubhouse with historical associations.
*18 holes, 5106yds, Par 66, SSS 65, Course record 61.*
*Club membership 800.*
Visitors  with member only weekends.
Societies  weekdays only.
Green Fees £25 per round/day.
Facilities  ⊗ ⑉ by prior arrangement ⓛ 🍺 ♀ ♨ 🏠 ♈ ℓ Mark Lawrence.
Leisure  trolley for hire, putting green.
Hotel  ★★★ 69% Bromley Court Hotel, Bromley Hill, BROMLEY ☎ 0181 464 5011 118 ⇔ ℝ

---

## COULSDON                               Map 04 TQ25

**Coulsdon Manor Hotel** Coulsdon Court Rd CR5 2LL ☎ 0181 660 6083
A public parkland course with good views. Clubhouse formerly owned by the Byron family.
*18 holes, 6037yds, Par 70, SSS 68.*
Visitors  must telephone up to 5 days in advance.
Societies  by arrangement.
Green Fees £13 per round (£16 weekends & bank holidays).
Facilities  ⊗ ⑉ ⓛ 🍺 ♀ ♨ 🏠 ♈ 🍴 ℓ David Copsey.
Leisure  hard tennis courts, squash, sauna, solarium, gymnasium, trolley for hire, putting green, practice area.
Location  0.75m E off A23 on B2030
Hotel  ★★★★ 73% Coulsdon Manor Hotel, Coulsdon Court Rd, Coulsdon, CROYDON ☎ 0181 668 0414 35 ⇔ ℝ

**Woodcote Park** Meadow Hill, Bridle Way CR5 2QQ ☎ 0181 668 2788
Slightly undulating parkland course.
*18 holes, 6669yds, Par 71, SSS 72, Course record 66.*
*Club membership 650.*

Visitors  contact professional for details. Visitors may not play weekends.
Societies  must contact Secretary in advance.
Green Fees £25 per round (Mon-Fri only).
Facilities  ⊗ ⑉ ⓛ 🍺 ♀ ♨ 🏠 ℓ D Hudspith.
Leisure  trolley for hire, putting green, practice area.
Location  1m N of town centre off A237
Hotel  B Forte Posthouse Croydon, Purley Way, CROYDON ☎ 0181 688 5185 83 ⇔ ℝ

---

## CROYDON                                Map 04 TQ36

**Croham Hurst** Croham Rd CR2 7HJ ☎ 0181 657 5581
Parkland course with tree-lined fairways and bounded by wooded hills. Easy walking.
*18 holes, 6274yds, Par 70, SSS 70.*
*Club membership 800.*
Visitors  must contact in advance & have handicap certificate. With member only weekends & bank holidays.
Societies  must book 1 year in advance.
Green Fees £32 per day/round (£42 weekends & bank holidays).
Facilities  ⊗ ⑉ by prior arrangement ⓛ 🍺 ♀ ♨ 🏠 ♈ ℓ Eric Stillwell.
Leisure  trolley for hire, putting green, practice area.
Location  (1.5m SE)
Hotel  ★★★★ 65% Selsdon Park Hotel, Addington Rd, Sanderstead, CROYDON ☎ 0181 657 8811 170 ⇔ ℝ

---

**Selsdon Park** Addington Rd, Sanderstead CR2 8YA ☎ 0181 657 8811
Parkland course. Full use of hotel's sporting facilities by residents.
*18 holes, 6473yds, Par 73, SSS 71.*
Visitors  booking advisable.
Societies  telephone in advance.
Green Fees £25 per round; £15 early birdie/twilight (£30/£20 weekends & bank holidays).
Facilities  ⊗ ⑉ ⓛ 🍺 ♀ ♨ 🏠 ♈ 🍴 ℓ Tom O'Keefe.
Leisure  hard and grass tennis courts, outdoor and indoor heated swimming pools, squash, sauna, solarium, gymnasium, motorised carts for hire, buggies for hire, trolley for hire, driving range, putting green, practice area, other leisure facilities for residents of hotel only.
Location  3m S on A2022
Hotel  ★★★★ 65% Selsdon Park Hotel, Addington Rd, Sanderstead, CROYDON ☎ 0181 657 8811 170 ⇔ ℝ

---

**Shirley Park** 194 Addiscombe Rd CR0 7LB ☎ 0181 654 1143
This parkland course lies amid fine woodland with good views of Shirley Hills. The more testing holes come in the middle section of the course. The remarkable 7th hole calls for a 187-yard iron or wood shot diagonally across a narrow valley to a shelved green set right-handed into a ridge.
*18 holes, 6210yds, Par 71, SSS 70, Course record 66.*
*Club membership 600.*
Visitors  should contact in advance. With member only at weekends.
Societies  by arrangement.

Addington Road, Sanderstead,
S. Croydon, Surrey CR2 8YA
Tel: 0181 657 8811  Fax: 0181 651 6171

In a magnificent parkland settting, designed by J. H. Taylor and opened in 1929, this challenging 18 hole, 6,473 yards course has now been brought up to championship standard.
The Selsdon Park Golf Academy is located here and provides excellent tuition along with master classes and special privileges. An annual season ticket is available.
The course is open to green fee players. Golf societies welcome.

**Green Fees** £29 weekdays only.
**Facilities** ⊗ ⅢⅢ ㋿ 및 ♀ ♨ 🏠 ⛳ ♭ Nick Allen.
**Leisure** trolley for hire, putting green, practice area.
**Location** E side of town centre on A232
**Hotel** ★★★★ 68% Croydon Park Hotel, 7 Altyre Rd, CROYDON
☎ 0181 680 9200 212 ⇆ 🐾

## DOWNE                                    Map 05 TQ46

**High Elms** High Elms Rd BR6 7JL
☎ 01689 853232 & 858175 bookings
Municipal parkland course. Very tight 13th, 230 yds (par 3).
*18 holes, 6210yds, Par 71, SSS 70, Course record 68.*
*Club membership 450.*
**Visitors** no restrictions.
**Societies** telephone to book. Tel 01689 861813.
**Green Fees** £9.75 per 18 holes (£12.80 weekends and bank holidays).
**Facilities** ⊗ ⅢⅢ ㋿ 및 ♀ ♨ 🏠 ⛳ ♭ Peter Remy.
**Leisure** motorised carts for hire, buggies for hire, trolley for hire, putting green, practice area.
**Location** 1.5m NE
**Hotel** ★★★ 69% Bromley Court Hotel, Bromley Hill, BROMLEY
☎ 0181 464 5011 118 ⇆ 🐾

**West Kent** West Hill BR6 7JJ ☎ 01689 851323
Partly hilly downland course.
*18 holes, 6399yds, Par 70, SSS 70.*
*Club membership 700.*
**Visitors** with member only at weekends. Must contact in advance.
**Societies** must apply in writing.
**Green Fees** £40 per 36 holes; £26 per round.
**Facilities** ⊗ ⅢⅢ ㋿ 및 ♀ ♨ 🏠 ♭ Roger Fidler.
**Leisure** trolley for hire, practice area.
**Location** 0.75m SW
**Hotel** ★★★ 69% Bromley Court Hotel, Bromley Hill, BROMLEY ☎ 0181 464 5011 118 ⇆ 🐾

## ENFIELD                                   Map 04 TQ39

**Crews Hill** Cattlegate Rd, Crews Hill EN2 8AZ
☎ 0181 363 6674
Parkland course in country surroundings.
*18 holes, 6250yds, Par 70, SSS 70, Course record 65.*
*Club membership 603.*
**Visitors** must play with member at weekends. Handicap certificate required.
**Societies** Wed-Fri; must apply in writing.
**Green Fees** on application.

**Facilities** ⊗ ⅢⅢ ㋿ 및 ♀ ♨ 🏠 ♭ John Reynolds.
**Leisure** motorised carts for hire, buggies for hire, trolley for hire, putting green.
**Location** 3m NW off A1005
**Hotel** ★★★ 57% Enfield Hotel, 52 Rowantree Rd, ENFIELD ☎ 0181 366 3511 34 ⇆ 🐾

**Enfield** Old Park Rd South EN2 7DA
☎ 0181 363 3970
Parkland course. Salmons Brook crosses 7 holes.
*18 holes, 6154yds, Par 72, SSS 70, Course record 61.*
*Club membership 700.*
**Visitors** must contact in advance & have handicap certificate.
**Societies** must contact the secretary in advance.
**Green Fees** £30 per day; £22 per round.
**Facilities** ⊗ ⅢⅢ ㋿ 및 ♀ ♨ 🏠 ♭ Lee Fickling.
**Leisure** trolley for hire, putting green.
**Location** W side of town centre off A110
**Hotel** ★★★ 57% Enfield Hotel, 52 Rowantree Rd, ENFIELD ☎ 0181 366 3511 34 ⇆ 🐾

*Whitewebbs Municipal* Beggars Hollow, Clay Hill EN2 9JW
☎ 0181 363 4454
Flat wooded parkland course. 9th hole is a left-hand dog-leg with second shot over a brook.
*18 holes, 5755yds, Par 68, SSS 68.*
*Club membership 350.*
**Visitors** must play with member.
**Societies** must apply in writing to the secretary.
**Green Fees** not confirmed.
**Facilities** 🏠 ⛳ ♭ David Lewis.
**Location** N side of town centre
**Hotel** ★★★ 57% Enfield Hotel, 52 Rowantree Rd, ENFIELD ☎ 0181 366 3511 34 ⇆ 🐾

## GREENFORD                                 Map 04 TQ18

**C & L Golf & Country Club** Westend Rd, Northolt UB5 6RD ☎ 0181 845 5662
Parkland course.
*18 holes, 4438yds, Par 64, SSS 63.*
*Club membership 150.*
**Visitors** welcome, but may not play Sun mornings.
**Societies** contact for details.
**Green Fees** £8 per 18 holes; £5 per 9 holes (£10/£6 weekends).
**Facilities** ⊗ ⅢⅢ ㋿ 및 ♀ ♨ ♭ Richard Kelly.
**Leisure** hard tennis courts, outdoor swimming pool, squash, sauna, solarium, gymnasium.
**Location** Junct Westend Road/A40
**Hotel** ★★★ 70% The Bridge Hotel, Western Av, GREENFORD ☎ 0181 566 6246 68 ⇆ 🐾

*Ealing* Perivale Ln UB6 8SS ☎ 0181 997 0937
Flat, parkland course relying on natural hazards; trees, tight
fairways, and the River Brent which affects 9 holes.
*18 holes, 6216yds, Par 70, SSS 70, Course record 64.*
*Club membership 700.*
**Visitors**  Mon-Fri only on application to pro shop.
**Societies**  Mon, Wed & Thu only by arrangement.
**Green Fees**  not confirmed.
**Facilities**  ♀ ♣ 🏠 ⬧ Arnold Stickley.
**Leisure**  putting, practice, buggy/trolley hire.
**Hotel**  ★★★ 70% The Bridge Hotel, Western Av,
GREENFORD ☎ 0181 566 6246 68 ⇄ 🏳

*Horsenden Hill* Whitten Av, Woodland Rise UB6 0RD
☎ 0181 902 4555
A well-kept, tree-lined short course.
*9 holes, 1618yds, Par 28, SSS 28.*
*Club membership 135.*
**Visitors**  no restrictions.
**Societies**  telephone for details.
**Green Fees**  not confirmed.
**Facilities**  ♀ ♣ 🏠 ⬧ ⬧ Anthony Ferrier.
**Location**  3m NE on A4090
**Hotel**  ★★★ 70% The Bridge Hotel, Western Av,
GREENFORD ☎ 0181 566 6246 68 ⇄ 🏳

**Lime Trees Park** Ruislip Rd, Northolt UB5 6QZ
☎ 0181 842 0442
Parkland course.
*9 holes, 5836yds, Par 71, SSS 69.*
*Club membership 300.*
**Visitors**  no restrictions, but advisable to book for
weekends.
**Societies**  contact for details.
**Green Fees**  £10.50 per 18 holes; £5.50 per 9 holes.
**Facilities**  ⊗ 🍴 ☕ ♀ ♣ 🏠 ⬧ ⬧ Ian Godleman.
**Leisure**  trolley for hire, driving range, putting green.
**Location**  300yds off A40 at Polish War Memorial/A4180
towards Hayes
**Hotel**  ★★★ 70% The Bridge Hotel, Western Av,
GREENFORD ☎ 0181 566 6246 68 ⇄ 🏳

*Perivale Park* Stockdove Way UB6 8TJ
☎ 0181 575 7116
Parkland course.
*9 holes, 2600yds, Par 68, SSS 65.*
*Club membership 250.*
**Visitors**  no restrictions.
**Green Fees**  not confirmed.
**Facilities**  ♣ 🏠 ⬧ ⬧ Peter Bryant.
**Leisure**  trolleys.
**Location**  E side of town centre, off A40
**Hotel**  ★★★ 69% Carnarvon Hotel, Ealing Common,
LONDON ☎ 0181 992 5399 145 ⇄ 🏳

### HADLEY WOOD
Map 04 TQ29

**Hadley Wood** Beech Hill EN4 0JJ
☎ 0181 449 4328 & 4486
A parkland course on the northwest edge of London. The
gently undulating fairways have a friendly width inviting
the player to open his shoulders, though the thick rough
can be very punishing to the unwary. The course is
pleasantly wooded and there are some admirable views.
*18 holes, 6457yds, Par 72, SSS 71, Course record 66.*
*Club membership 600.*

**Visitors**  may not play Tue mornings & Sat. Must
book in advance Sun.
**Societies**  must contact in advance.
**Green Fees**  £40 per day; £30 per round (£35 Sun).
**Facilities**  ⊗ 🍴 🍴 ☕ ♀ ♣ 🏠 ⬧ ⬧ Peter Jones.
**Leisure**  trolley for hire, driving range, putting green,
practice area.
**Location**  E side of village
**Hotel**  ★★★★🏵 69% West Lodge Park Hotel,
Cockfosters Rd, HADLEY WOOD
☎ 0181 440 8311 43 ⇄ 🏳Annexe2 ⇄ 🏳

### HAMPTON
Map 04 TQ17

*Fulwell* Wellington Rd, Hampton Hill TW12 1JY
☎ 0181 977 3844 & 081-977 2733
Championship-length parkland course with easy walking. The
575-yd, 17th, is notable.
*18 holes, 6544yds, Par 71, SSS 71.*
*Club membership 750.*
**Visitors**  may not play Tue & weekends. Must contact in
advance and have a handicap certificate.
**Societies**  must apply in writing.
**Green Fees**  not confirmed.
**Facilities**  ♀ ♣ 🏠 ⬧ ⬧ David Haslam.
**Location**  1.5m N on A311
**Hotel**  ★★★ 70% Richmond Hill, Richmond Hill,
RICHMOND UPON THAMES
☎ 0181 940 2247 & 0181 940 5466 124 ⇄ 🏳

### HAMPTON WICK
Map 04 TQ16

**Home Park** KT1 4AD ☎ 0181 977 2423
Flat, parkland course with easy walking.
*18 holes, 6611yds, Par 71, SSS 71.*
*Club membership 550.*
**Visitors**  welcome all week subject to club competitions.
**Societies**  apply in writing.
**Green Fees**  £30 per 36 holes; £20 per 18 holes (£25 per 18
holes weekends & bank holidays).
**Facilities**  ⊗ 🍴 🍴 ☕ ♀ ♣ 🏠 ⬧ Len Roberts.
**Leisure**  putting green, practice area.
**Location**  Off A308 on W side of Kingston Bridge
**Hotel**  ★★★ 70% Richmond Hill, Richmond Hill,
RICHMOND UPON THAMES
☎ 0181 940 2247 & 0181 940 5466 124 ⇄ 🏳

### HILLINGDON
Map 04 TQ08

*Hillingdon* Dorset Way, Vine Ln UB10 0JR
☎ 01895 233956
Parkland course west of London.
*9 holes, 5490yds, Par 68, SSS 67.*
*Club membership 400.*
**Visitors**  may not play Thu, weekends, or bank holidays.
Must have an introduction from own club.
**Societies**  must apply in writing.
**Green Fees**  not confirmed.
**Facilities**  ♀ ♣ 🏠 ⬧
**Location**  W side of town off A4020
**Hotel**  ★★★ 63% Master Brewer Hotel, Western Av,
HILLINGDON
☎ 01895 251199 106 ⇄ 🏳

## HOUNSLOW
Map 04 TQ17

**Airlinks** Southall Ln TW5 9PE
☎ 0181 561 1418
Meadowland/parkland course designed by P. Allis and D. Thomas.
*18 holes, 6000yds, Par 72, SSS 68, Course record 63.*
*Club membership 500.*
**Visitors** may not play before noon at weekends.
**Societies** must apply in writing.
**Green Fees** not confirmed.
**Facilities** ♀ ⚑ 曲 ⚐ ⁅ Chris Woodcocks.
**Leisure** flood lit driving range,cart/buggy hire.
**Location** W of Hounslow off M4 junc 3
**Hotel** ★★★ 63% Master Robert Hotel, Great West Rd, HOUNSLOW
☎ 0181 570 6261 94 ⇄ ₨

**Hounslow Heath Municipal** Staines Rd TW4 5DS
☎ 0181 570 5271
Parkland course in a conservation area, planted with an attractive variety of trees. The 15th hole lies between the fork of two rivers.
*18 holes, 5901yds, Par 69, SSS 68, Course record 62.*
*Club membership 300.*
**Visitors** pay & play, bookings taken for weekends & bank holidays seven days in advance.
**Societies** must telephone and confirm at least 14 days in advance.
**Green Fees** £7.50 per day (£10.50 weekends & bank holidays).
**Facilities** ⊗ ⚑ 曲 ⚐
**Leisure** trolley for hire, putting green, practice area.
**Hotel** B The Heathrow Crest, Sipson Rd, WEST DRAYTON
☎ 0181 759 2323 569 ⇄ ₨

## ILFORD
Map 05 TQ48

**Ilford** Wanstead Park Rd IG1 3TR
☎ 0181 554 2930
Fairly flat parkland course intersected five times by a river.
*18 holes, 5308yds, Par 67, SSS 66, Course record 61.*
*Club membership 700.*
**Visitors** must contact in advance, book with pro on 0181 554 0094.
**Societies** telephone for provisional date and booking form.
**Green Fees** £13.50 per round (£16 weekends).
**Facilities** ⊗ ℳ ⚑ ♟ ♀ ⚑ 曲 ⁅ S Dowsett.
**Location** NW side of town centre off A12
**Hotel** ★★★ 65% Epping Forest Moat House, Oak Hill, WOODFORD GREEN
☎ 0181 787 9988 99 ⇄ ₨

## ISLEWORTH
Map 04 TQ17

**Wyke Green** Syon Ln TW7 5PT
☎ 0181 560 8777 & 847 0685
Fairly flat parkland course.
*18 holes, 6211yds, Par 69, SSS 70, Course record 64.*
*Club membership 500.*
**Visitors** may not play before 3pm weekends and bank holidays, must have a handicap certificate required.

**Societies** must apply in writing or telephone in advance, Tue & Thu only.
**Green Fees** £25 per day (£42 weekends, after 3pm).
**Facilities** ⊗ ℳ ⚑ ♟ ♀ ⚑ 曲 ⁅ David Holmes.
**Leisure** motorised carts for hire, buggies for hire, trolley for hire, putting green, practice area.
**Location** 1.5m N on B454 off A4
**Hotel** ★★★ 63% Master Robert Hotel, Great West Rd, HOUNSLOW
☎ 0181 570 6261 94 ⇄ ₨

## KINGSTON UPON THAMES
Map 04 TQ16

**Coombe Hill** Golf Club Dr, Coombe Ln West KT2 7DG
☎ 0181 942 2284
A splendid course in wooded terrain. The undulations and trees make it an especially interesting course of great charm. And there is a lovely display of rhododendrons in May and June.
*18 holes, 6293yds, Par 71, SSS 71, Course record 67.*
*Club membership 600.*
**Visitors** must contact in advance. With member only at weekends.
**Societies** must book in advance.
**Green Fees** £50 per day/round; £30 after 3pm (weekdays).
**Facilities** ⊗ ℳ ⚑ ♟ ♀ ⚑ 曲 ⚐ ⁅ Craig Defoy.
**Leisure** sauna, buggies for hire, trolley for hire, putting green, practice area, snooker.
**Location** 1.75m E on A238
**Hotel** ★★★ 68% Kingston Lodge Hotel, Kingston Hill, KINGSTON UPON THAMES ☎ 0181 541 4481 62 ⇄ ₨

**Coombe Wood** George Rd, Kingston Hill KT2 7NS
☎ 0181 942 0388
Parkland course.
*18 holes, 5210yds, Par 66, SSS 66.*
*Club membership 630.*
**Visitors** must contact in advance & play with member at weekends.
**Societies** Wed, Thu & Fri; must contact in advance.
**Green Fees** £32 per day; £21 per 18 holes; £13 after 6pm.
**Facilities** ⊗ ℳ by prior arrangement ⚑ ♟ ♀ ⚑ 曲 ⁅ David Butler.
**Leisure** trolley for hire, putting green, practice area.
**Location** 1.25m NE on A308
**Hotel** ★★★ 68% Kingston Lodge Hotel, Kingston Hill, KINGSTON UPON THAMES
☎ 0181 541 4481 62 ⇄ ₨

## MITCHAM
Map 04 TQ26

**Mitcham** Carshalton Rd CR4 4HN ☎ 0181 648 4280
A wooded heathland course on a gravel base.
*18 holes, 5935yds, Par 69, SSS 68, Course record 65.*
*Club membership 500.*
**Visitors** must telephone & book in advance.
**Societies** must phone in advance.
**Green Fees** not confirmed.
**Facilities** ♀ ⚑ 曲 ⁅ Jeff Godfrey.
**Leisure** putting green,trolley hire.
**Location** 1m S
**Hotel** B Forte Posthouse Croydon, Purley Way, CROYDON ☎ 0181 688 5185 83 ⇄ ₨

## NEW MALDEN
Map 04 TQ26

**Malden** Traps Ln KT3 4RS ☎ 0181 942 0654
Parkland course with the hazard of the Beverley Brook which
affects 4 holes (3rd, 7th, 8th and 12th).
*18 holes, 6295yds, Par 71, SSS 70.*
*Club membership 800.*
**Visitors**     restricted weekends and bank holidays.
Advisable to telephone.
**Societies**     must apply in writing.
**Green Fees** on application.
**Facilities**     ⊗ ⅷ ⅃ ⬛ ♀ ⚑ ⚐ ℓ Robert Hunter.
**Leisure**     buggies for hire, trolley for hire, putting green.
**Location**     N side of town centre off B283
**Hotel**     ★★★ 68% Kingston Lodge Hotel, Kingston
Hill, KINGSTON UPON THAMES
☎ 0181 541 4481 62 ⇄ ℟

## NORTHWOOD
Map 04 TQ09

*Haste Hill* The Drive HA6 1HN
☎ 01923 822877 & 825224
Parkland course with stream running through. Excellent
views.
*18 holes, 5787yds, Par 68, SSS 68.*
*Club membership 350.*
**Visitors**     no restrictions.
**Societies**     must apply in advance.
**Green Fees** not confirmed.
**Facilities**     ♀ ⚑ ⚐ ⚐
**Leisure**     putting, cart/buggy/trolley hire.
**Location**     0.5m S off A404
**Hotel**     ★★ 69% Harrow Hotel, Roxborough Bridge,
12-22 Pinner Rd, HARROW
☎ 0181 427 3435 57 ⇄ ℟Annexe23 ⇄ ℟

**Northwood** Rickmansworth Rd HA6 2QW
☎ 01923 821384
A very old club to which, it is said, golfers used to drive
from London by horse-carriage. They would find their
golf interesting as present-day players do. The course is
relatively flat although there are some undulations, and
trees and whins add not only to the beauty of the course
but also to the test of golf.
*18 holes, 6553yds, Par 71, SSS 71, Course record 67.*
*Club membership 650.*
*Visitors*     must contact in advance. May not play
weekends.
**Societies**     must apply in writing.
**Green Fees** £24 per round.
**Facilities**     ⊗ ⅷ ⅃ ⬛ ♀ ⚑ ⚐ ⚐ ℓ C J Holdsworth.
**Leisure**     trolley for hire, putting green, practice area.
**Location**     SW side of village off A404
**Hotel**     ★★ 69% Harrow Hotel, Roxborough
Bridge, 12-22 Pinner Rd, HARROW
☎ 0181 427 3435 57 ⇄ ℟Annexe23 ⇄ ℟

**Sandy Lodge** Sandy Lodge Ln HA6 2JD
☎ 01923 825429
A links-type, very sandy, heathland course.
*18 holes, 6080yds, Par 71, SSS 70, Course record 64.*
*Club membership 780.*
*Visitors*     must contact in advance.
**Societies**     must telephone in advance.

**Green Fees** on application.
**Facilities**     ⊗ ⅷ ⅃ ⬛ ♀ ⚑ ⚐ ℓ Jeff Pinsent.
**Leisure**     trolley for hire, putting green, practice area.
**Location**     N side of town centre off A4125
**Hotel**     ★★★ 62% The White House, Upton Rd,
WATFORD
☎ 01923 237316 60 ⇄ ℟Annexe26 ⇄ ℟

## ORPINGTON
Map 05 TQ46

**Chelsfield Lakes Golf Centre** Court Rd BR6 9BX
☎ 01689 896266
A downland course but some holes are played through the
orchards which used to occupy the site. The 9th and 18th
holes are separated by a hazardous lake.
*18 holes, 6077yds, Par 71, SSS 69, Course record 64.*
*Club membership 438.*
**Visitors**     must book in advance.
**Societies**     telephone in advance.
**Green Fees** £14 per round (£17 weekends & bank holidays).
9 hole par 3 £5.50 (£6 weekends).
**Facilities**     ⊗ ⅷ ⅃ ⬛ ♀ ⚑ ⚐ ⚐
ℓ N Lee/B Hodkin/D Clark.
**Leisure**     trolley for hire, floodlit driving range, putting
green, par 3 course.
**Location**     Exit M25 junct 4, on A224 Court Rd
**Hotel**     ★★★ 69% Bromley Court Hotel, Bromley Hill,
BROMLEY ☎ 0181 464 5011 118 ⇄ ℟

*Cray Valley* Sandy Ln BR5 3HY
☎ 01689 39677 & 31927
An open parkland course with two man-made lakes and open
ditches.
*18 holes, 5400yds, Par 70, SSS 67.*
*Club membership 640.*
**Visitors**     no restrictions.
**Societies**     by arrangement.
**Green Fees** not confirmed.
**Facilities**     ♀ ⚑ ⚐ ⚐ ℓ John Gregory.
**Location**     1m off A20
**Hotel**     ★★★ 69% Bromley Court Hotel, Bromley Hill,
BROMLEY ☎ 0181 464 5011 118 ⇄ ℟

**Lullingstone Park** Parkgate, Chelsfield BR6 7PX
☎ 01959 533793
Popular 27-hole public course set in 690 acres of undulating
parkland. Championship length 18-holes, plus 9-hole course
and a further 9-hole pitch and putt.
*Main Lullingstone Park Golf Course: 18 holes, 6759yds, Par
72, SSS 72, Course record 71 or 9 holes, 2432yds, Par 33,
SSS 33.*
**Visitors**     telephone for details.
**Societies**     must telephone in advance.
**Green Fees** £9.30 per 18 holes; £5.80 per 9 holes (£11.70-
£14.30/£7.80 weekends).
**Facilities**     ⊗ ⅷ ⅃ ⬛ ♀ ⚑ ⚐ ⚐ ℓ Alan Hodgson.
**Leisure**     motorised carts for hire, buggies for hire, trolley
for hire, driving range, putting green, practice
area, pitch & putt.
**Location**     Leave M25 junct 4 and take Well Hill turn
**Hotel**     ★★★ 69% Bromley Court Hotel, Bromley Hill,
BROMLEY ☎ 0181 464 5011 118 ⇄ ℟

**Ruxley Park Golf Centre** Sandy Ln, St Paul's Cray
BR5 3HY ☎ 01689 871490
Parkland course with public, floodlit driving range. Difficult
6th hole, par 4. Easy walking and good views.
*18 holes, 5703yds, Par 70, SSS 68.*
*Club membership 450.*
**Visitors**      book in advance.
**Societies**    telephone for details 01689 839677.
**Green Fees** telephone for details.
**Facilities**    ⊗ ⅷ ⅃ ⅃ ♀ ♨ 🗃 ⚑ ⅃ Richard Pilbury.
**Leisure**       motorised carts for hire, buggies for hire, trolley
                  for hire, covered and floodlit driving range,
                  putting green, practice area, 9 hole par 3 course.
**Location**     2m NE on A223
**Hotel**          ★★★ 69% Bromley Court Hotel, Bromley Hill,
                  BROMLEY
                  ☎ 0181 464 5011 118 ⇌ ⅋

---

## PINNER                                    Map 04 TQ18

**Grims Dyke** Oxhey Ln, Hatch End HA5 4AL
☎ 0181 428 4539
Pleasant, undulating parkland course.
*18 holes, 5600yds, Par 69, SSS 67, Course record 62.*
*Club membership 580.*
**Visitors**      must contact in advance, may not play
                  weekends.
**Societies**    by arrangement, booked in advance.
**Green Fees** £25 per day; £20 per round.
**Facilities**    ⊗ ⅷ by prior arrangement ⅃ ♀ ♀ ♨ 🗃 ⚑
                  ⅃ John Rule.
**Leisure**       trolley for hire, putting green, practice area.
**Location**     3m N of Harrow on A4008
**Hotel**          ★★ 69% Harrow Hotel, Roxborough Bridge,
                  12-22 Pinner Rd, HARROW
                  ☎ 0181 427 3435 57 ⇌ ⅋Annexe23 ⇌ ⅋

---

*Pinner Hill* Southview Rd, Pinner Hill HA5 3YA
☎ 0181 866 0963 & 081-866 2109
A hilly, wooded parkland course.
*18 holes, 6266yds, Par 72, SSS 70, Course record 63.*
*Club membership 770.*
**Visitors**      are required to have handicap certificate on Mon,
                  Tue & Fri. Public days Wed & Thu. Contact in
                  advance.
**Societies**    Mon, Tue & Fri only, by arrangement.
**Green Fees** not confirmed.
**Facilities**    ♀ ♨ 🗃 ⚑ ⅃ Mark Grieve.
**Location**     2m NW off A404
**Hotel**          ★★ 69% Harrow Hotel, Roxborough Bridge,
                  12-22 Pinner Rd, HARROW
                  ☎ 0181 427 3435 57 ⇌ ⅋Annexe23 ⇌ ⅋

---

## PURLEY                                    Map 05 TQ36

*Purley Downs* 106 Purley Downs Rd CR2 0RB
☎ 0181 657 8347
Hilly downland course. Notable holes are 6th and 12th.
*18 holes, 6020yds, Par 70, SSS 69, Course record 64.*
*Club membership 700.*
**Visitors**      must have a handicap certificate, & play on
                  weekdays only with member.
**Societies**    must contact in advance.
**Green Fees** not confirmed.
**Facilities**    ♀ ♨ 🗃 ⅃ Graham Wilson.

**Leisure**       putting,trolley hire,practice area.
**Location**     E side of town centre off A235
**Hotel**          B Forte Posthouse Croydon, Purley Way,
                  CROYDON ☎ 0181 688 5185 83 ⇌ ⅋

---

## RICHMOND UPON THAMES              Map 04 TQ17

*Richmond* Sudbrook Park, Petersham TW10 7AS
☎ 0181 940 4351
A beautiful and historic wooded, parkland course on the
edge of Richmond Park, with six par-3 holes. The 4th is
often described as the best short hole in the south of
England. Low scores are uncommon because cunningly
sited trees call for great accuracy. The clubhouse is one
of the most distinguished small Georgian mansions in
England.
*18 holes, 6007yds, Par 70, SSS 69.*
*Club membership 700.*
**Visitors**      may not play weekends.
**Societies**    must apply in writing.
**Green Fees** not confirmed.
**Facilities**    ♀ ♨ 🗃 ⚑ ⅃ Nick Job.
**Location**     1.5m S off A307
**Hotel**          ★★★ 70% Richmond Hill, Richmond Hill,
                  RICHMOND UPON THAMES
                  ☎ 0181 940 2247 & 0181 940 5466 124 ⇌ ⅋

---

*Royal Mid-Surrey* Old Deer Park TW9 2SB
☎ 0181 940 1894
A long playing parkland course. The flat fairways are
cleverly bunkered. The 18th provides an exceptionally
good par 4 finish with a huge bunker before the green to
catch the not quite perfect long second.
*Outer Course: 18 holes, 6343yds, Par 69, SSS 70.*
*Inner Course: 18 holes, 5544yds, Par 67.*
*Club membership 1250.*
**Visitors**      may not play at weekends. Must contact in
                  advance and bring a handicap certificate.
**Societies**    must apply in writing.
**Green Fees** not confirmed.
**Facilities**    ⊗ ⅃ ♀ ♀ ♨ 🗃 ⚑ ⅃ David Talbot.
**Leisure**       motorised carts for hire, trolley for hire.
**Location**     0.5m N of Richmond upon Thames off
                  A316
**Hotel**          ★★★ 70% Richmond Hill, Richmond Hill,
                  RICHMOND UPON THAMES
                  ☎ 0181 940 2247 & 0181 940 5466 124 ⇌ ⅋

---

## ROMFORD                                   Map 05 TQ58

*Maylands Golf Club & Country Park* Colchester Rd, Harold
Park RM3 0AZ ☎ 01708 346466
Picturesque undulating parkland course.
*18 holes, 6351yds, Par 71, SSS 70, Course record 67.*
*Club membership 700.*
**Visitors**      proof of membership or handicap certificate
                  required, with member only at weekends.
**Societies**    Mon, Wed & Fri only, by arrangement.
**Green Fees** not confirmed.
**Facilities**    ♀ ♨ 🗃 ⚑ ⅃ John Hopkin.
**Leisure**       putting, practice, cart/buggy/trolley hire.
**Hotel**          B Forte Posthouse Brentwood, Brook St,
                  BRENTWOOD ☎ 01277 260260 111 ⇌

**Risebridge Golf Centre** Risebridge Chase, Lower Bedfords Rd RM1 4DG ☎ 01708 741429
A well matured parkland golf course, with many challenging holes especially the long 12th, the Par 4 13th and Par 5 14th with water and a two tiered green.
*18 holes: 18 holes, 6000yds, Par 71, SSS 70, Course record 66.*
*9 holes: 9 holes, 459yds, Par 27, SSS 27.*
*Club membership 300.*
Visitors     no restrictions.
Societies    must telephone in advance.
Green Fees £10 per round (£12 weekends & bank holidays) reduced rate twilight rounds on request.
Facilities    ⊗ ⽇ ⮟ ⮜ ♀ ⛳ ⮝ ⌁ ⌇ Paul Jennings.
Leisure      trolley for hire, driving range, putting green, practice area.
Location     Between Colier Row and Harold Hill
Hotel        ★★★ 61% Palms Hotel, Southend Arterial Rd, HORNCHURCH ☎ 01708 346789 137 ⇆ ⌁

*Romford* Heath Dr, Gidea Park RM2 5QB
☎ 01708 740986
A many-bunkered parkland course with easy walking. It is said there are as many bunkers as there are days in the year. The ground is quick drying making a good course for winter play when other courses might be too wet.
*18 holes, 6374yds, Par 72, SSS 70.*
*Club membership 693.*
*Visitors* with member only weekends & bank holidays. Must contact in advance & have handicap certificate.
Societies    must telephone in advance.
Green Fees not confirmed.
Facilities    ♀ ⮜ ⛳ ⌇ Harry Flatman.
Location     1m NE on A118
Hotel        B Forte Posthouse Brentwood, Brook St, BRENTWOOD ☎ 01277 260260 111 ⇆

## RUISLIP                      Map 04 TQ08

**Ruislip** Ickenham Rd HA4 7DQ ☎ 01895 638081
Municipal parkland course. Many trees.
*18 holes, 5700yds, Par 69, SSS 68, Course record 65.*
*Club membership 500.*
Visitors     advised to telephone in advance.
Societies    must contact in advance.
Green Fees £10 per day (£15 weekends & bank holidays).
Facilities    ⊗ ⽇ ⮟ ⮜ ♀ ⮜ ⛳ ⮝ ⌇ Paul Glozier.
Leisure      motorised carts for hire, buggies for hire, trolley for hire, driving range, putting green, pool tables, snooker.
Location     0.5m SW on B466
Hotel        ★★★ 63% Master Brewer Hotel, Western Av, HILLINGDON ☎ 01895 251199 106 ⇆ ⌁

## SIDCUP                     Map 05 TQ47

**Sidcup** 7 Hurst Rd DA15 9AE ☎ 0181 300 2150
Easy walking parkland course with natural water hazards.
*9 holes, 5722yds, Par 68, SSS 68.*
*Club membership 380.*
Visitors     contact in advance and may not play weekends.
Societies    must apply in writing.
Green Fees £18 per day/round.
Facilities    ⊗ ⽇ ⮟ ⮜ ♀ ⮜ ⌇ John Murray.
Leisure      putting green, practice area.

Location     N side of town centre off A222
Hotel        ★★★★ 71% Swallow Hotel, 1 Broadway, BEXLEYHEATH ☎ 0181 298 1000 142 ⇆ ⌁

## SOUTHALL                Map 04 TQ17

**West Middlesex** Greenford Rd UB1 3EE ☎ 0181 574 3450
Gently undulating parkland course.
*18 holes, 6242yds, Par 69, SSS 70, Course record 64.*
*Club membership 700.*
Visitors     must contact in advance and may not play at weekends.
Societies    must apply in advance.
Green Fees £15.50 per round; £10 Mon & Wed.
Facilities    ⊗ ⮟ ⮜ ♀ ⮜ ⛳ ⌇ I P Harris.
Leisure      trolley for hire, putting green, practice area.
Location     W side of town centre on A4127 off A4020
Hotel        ★★★ 63% Master Robert Hotel, Great West Rd, HOUNSLOW ☎ 0181 570 6261 94 ⇆ ⌁

## STANMORE                Map 04 TQ19

**Stanmore** 29 Gordon Av HA7 2RL ☎ 0181 954 2599
North London parkland course.
*18 holes, 5860yds, Par 68, SSS 68, Course record 61.*
*Club membership 560.*
Visitors     may not play weekends. Contact professional (0181 954 2646).
Societies    phone in advance for booking sheet.
Green Fees Mon & Fri £13 per day; £10 per round. Tue-Thu £32 per day; £25 per round.
Facilities    ⊗ ⽇ ⮟ ⮜ ♀ ⮜ ⌇ V Law.
Leisure      trolley for hire, practice area.
Location     S side of town centre, between Stanmore & Belmont
Hotel        ★★ 69% Harrow Hotel, Roxborough Bridge, 12-22 Pinner Rd, HARROW ☎ 0181 427 3435 57 ⇆ ⌁Annexe23 ⇆ ⌁

## SURBITON                Map 04 TQ16

**Surbiton** Woodstock Ln KT9 1UG
☎ 0181 398 3101 (Secretary) & 398 6619 (Pro)
Parkland course with easy walking.
*18 holes, 6055yds, Par 70, SSS 69, Course record 63.*
*Club membership 700.*
Visitors     with member only at weekends & bank holidays. No visitors Tue am (Ladies Day).
Societies    Mon & Fri only. Apply year in advance.
Green Fees £40.50 per day; £27 per round.
Facilities    ⊗ ⽇ ⮟ ⮜ ♀ ⮜ ⛳ ⮝ ⌇ Paul Milton.
Leisure      trolley for hire, putting green, practice area.
Location     2m S off A3
Hotel        ★★ 65% Haven Hotel, Portsmouth Rd, ESHER ☎ 0181 398 0023 16 ⇆ ⌁Annexe4 ⇆ ⌁

## TWICKENHAM             Map 04 TQ17

**Strawberry Hill** Wellesley Rd, Strawberry Hill TW2 5SD
☎ 0181 894 0165
Parkland course with easy walking.
*9 holes, 4762yds, Par 64, SSS 62, Course record 59.*
*Club membership 300.*

**Visitors** must contact in advance.
**Societies** must apply in writing.
**Green Fees** £26 per day; £20 per round.
**Facilities** ⓑ ⚑ ♀ ♨ ☎ ℓ Peter Buchan.
**Leisure** trolley for hire, putting green, practice area.
**Location** S side of town centre off A311
**Hotel** ★★★ 70% Richmond Hill, Richmond Hill, RICHMOND UPON THAMES
☎ 0181 940 2247 & 0181 940 5466 124 ⇄ ℟

---

**Twickenham** Staines Rd TW2 5JD
☎ 0181 783 1748 & 1698
Municipal commonland course.
*9 holes, 3180yds, Par 36, SSS 69.*
**Visitors** must book in advance for weekends & bank holidays.
**Societies** apply in advance
**Green Fees** £12 per 18 holes; £6 per 9 holes (£14/£7 weekends & bank holidays).
**Facilities** ⊗ ⅶ ⓑ ⚑ ♀ ♨ ☎ ℓ Steve LLoyd.
**Leisure** trolley for hire, floodlit driving range, putting green.
**Location** 2m W on A305
**Hotel** ★★★ 70% Richmond Hill, Richmond Hill, RICHMOND UPON THAMES
☎ 0181 940 2247 & 0181 940 5466 124 ⇄ ℟

## UPMINSTER                              Map 05 TQ58

**Upminster** 114 Hall Ln RM14 1AU
☎ 01708 222788 (Secretary) 220000 (Pro)
Situated adjacent to a river, which features on several holes, this wooded parkland course provides a range of challenges for golfers of all abilities. Clubhouse is a beautiful Grade II listed building.
*18 holes, 6076yds, Par 69, SSS 69, Course record 66.*
*Club membership 1000.*
**Visitors** contact in advance. Must have an introduction from own club.
**Societies** telephone initially.
**Green Fees** £30 per day; £25 per round weekdays.
**Facilities** ⊗ ⅶ ⓑ ⚑ ♀ ♨ ☎ ℓ Neil Carr.
**Leisure** trolley for hire, putting green.
**Location** 2m W from A127 junct with M25
**Hotel** ★★★ 61% Palms Hotel, Southend Arterial Rd, HORNCHURCH
☎ 01708 346789 137 ⇄ ℟

## UXBRIDGE                               Map 04 TQ08

**Stockley Park** Stockley Park UB11 1AQ
☎ 0181 813 5700
Hilly and challenging parkland championship course designed by Trent Jones in 1993 and situated within two miles of Heathrow Airport.
*18 holes, 6548yds, Par 72, SSS 71.*
**Visitors** 6 day in advance reservation facility.
**Societies** please contact corporate Sales Manager.
**Green Fees** £27 (£35 weekends).
**Facilities** ⊗ ⅶ ⓑ ⚑ ♀ ♨ ☎ ℓ Alex Knox.
**Leisure** trolley for hire, putting green.
**Hotel** ★★★ 63% Master Brewer Hotel, Western Av, HILLINGDON
☎ 01895 251199 106 ⇄ ℟

---

*Uxbridge* The Drive, Harefield Place UB10 8PA
☎ 01895 237287
Municipal parkland course, undulating and tricky.
*18 holes, 5750yds, Par 68, SSS 68, Course record 66.*
*Club membership 700.*
**Visitors** no restrictions.
**Societies** Thu by arrangment.
**Green Fees** not confirmed.
**Facilities** ♀ ♨ ☎ ʏ ℓ Phil Howard.
**Leisure** buggies.
**Location** 2m N off B467
**Hotel** ★★★ 63% Master Brewer Hotel, Western Av, HILLINGDON ☎ 01895 251199 106 ⇄ ℟

## WEMBLEY                                Map 04 TQ18

*Sudbury* Bridgewater Rd HA0 1AL ☎ 0181 902 3713
Undulating parkland course very near centre of London.
*18 holes, 6282yds, Par 69, SSS 70.*
*Club membership 650.*
**Visitors** must have handicap certificate. With member only at weekends.
**Societies** must apply in writing.
**Green Fees** not confirmed.
**Facilities** ♀ ♨ ☎ ℓ Neil Jordan.
**Location** SW side of town centre on A4090
**Hotel** ★★★ 70% The Bridge Hotel, Western Av, GREENFORD ☎ 0181 566 6246 68 ⇄ ℟

## WEST DRAYTON                           Map 04 TQ07

*Holiday* Stockley Rd UB7 9BW ☎ 01895 444232
Fairly large, testing, hilly par 3 course suitable both for beginners and scratch players.
*9 holes, 1618yds, Par 28, Course record 50.*
*Club membership 120.*
**Visitors** restricted Sun morning.
**Societies** by arrangement.
**Green Fees** not confirmed.
**Facilities** ♀ ♨ ☎ ʏ ⇔
**Leisure** heated indoor swimming pool, sauna, solarium, gymnasium.
**Location** 1m SE off A408
**Hotel** ★★★★ 72% Holiday Inn Crowne Plaza, Stockley Rd, WEST DRAYTON
☎ 01895 445555 374 ⇄ ℟

## WOODFORD GREEN                         Map 05 TQ49

*Woodford* Sunset Av IG8 0ST
☎ 0181 504 3330 & 504 0553
Forest land course on the edge of Epping Forest. Views over the Lea Valley to the London skyline.
*9 holes, 5806yds, Par 70, SSS 68, Course record 66.*
*Club membership 420.*
**Visitors** advisable to contact in advance. May not play Sat or Sun afternoon.
**Societies** telephone for details.
**Green Fees** £15 per day (£10 after 1pm in winter).
**Facilities** ⊗ ⓑ ⚑ ♀ ♨ ☎ ℓ Ashley Johns.
**Location** NW side of town centre off A104
**Hotel** ★★★ 65% Epping Forest Moat House, Oak Hill, WOODFORD GREEN
☎ 0181 787 9988 99 ⇄ ℟

# GREATER MANCHESTER

## ALTRINCHAM                    Map 07 SJ78

*Altrincham* Stockport Rd WA15 7LP ☎ 0161 928 0761
Municipal parkland course with easy walking, water on many
holes, rolling contours and many trees. Driving range in
grounds.
*18 holes, 6162yds, Par 71, SSS 69.*
*Club membership 350.*
**Visitors**     must book in advance.
**Societies**    by prior arrangement.
**Green Fees**   not confirmed.
**Facilities**   ⛏ 🏠 ⛳ ( John Jackson.
**Leisure**      driving range.
**Location**     0.75 E of Altrincham on A560
**Hotel**        ★★★ 66% Cresta Court Hotel, Church St,
                 ALTRINCHAM ☎ 0161 927 7272 138 ⇆ 🐾

**Dunham Forest** Oldfield Ln WA14 4TY
☎ 0161 928 2605 & 928 2727
Attractive parkland course cut through magnificent beech
woods.
*18 holes, 6636yds, Par 72, SSS 72.*
*Club membership 680.*
**Visitors**     may not play weekends & bank holidays.
**Societies**    apply in writing or telephone in advance.
**Green Fees**   £32 per day; £27 per round (£32 per round
                 weekends and bank holidays).
**Facilities**   ⊗ 🗠 by prior arrangement ⛏ 🍺 ♀ ⛏ 🏠 ⛳
                 ( Ian Wrigley.
**Leisure**      hard tennis courts, squash, motorised carts for
                 hire, buggies for hire, trolley for hire, putting
                 green, practice area.
**Location**     1.5m W off A56
**Hotel**        ★★★ 60% Bowdon Hotel, Langham Rd,
                 Bowdon, ALTRINCHAM
                 ☎ 0161 928 7121 82 ⇆ 🐾

**Ringway** Hale Mount, Hale Barns WA15 8SW
☎ 0161 904 9609
Parkland course, with interesting natural hazards. Easy
walking, good views.
*18 holes, 6494yds, Par 71, SSS 71, Course record 67.*
*Club membership 700.*
**Visitors**     may not play before 9.30am or between 1-2pm,
                 play restricted Tue, Fri & Sat.
**Societies**    Thu only May-Sep.
**Green Fees**   £28 Mon-Thu (£34 weekends & bank holidays).
**Facilities**   ⊗ 🗠 ⛏ 🍺 ♀ ⛏ 🏠 ⛳ ( Nick Ryan.
**Leisure**      trolley for hire, putting green.
**Location**     2.5m SE on A538
**Hotel**        ★★★ 66% Cresta Court Hotel, Church St,
                 ALTRINCHAM ☎ 0161 927 7272 138 ⇆ 🐾

## ASHTON-IN-MAKERFIELD          Map 07 SJ59

*Ashton-in-Makerfield* Garswood Park, Liverpool Rd
WN4 0YT ☎ 01942 727267 & 719330
Well-wooded parkland course. Easy walking.
*18 holes, 6250yds, Par 70, SSS 70.*
*Club membership 800.*

**Visitors**     with member only weekends & bank holidays.
                 No visitors Wed.
**Societies**    apply in writing.
**Green Fees**   not confirmed.
**Facilities**   ♀ ⛏ 🏠 ⛳ ( Peter Allan.
**Leisure**      putting green, practice area, trolley hire.
**Location**     0.5m W of M6 (Junc 24) on A58
**Hotel**        B Forte Posthouse Haydock, Lodge Ln, Newton-
                 Le-Willows, HAYDOCK
                 ☎ 01942 717878 136 ⇆ 🐾

## ASHTON-UNDER-LYNE              Map 07 SJ99

*Ashton-under-Lyne* Gorsey Way, Higher Hurst OL6 9HT
☎ 0161 330 1537
A testing, varied moorland course, with large greens. Easy
walking. Three new holes have improved the course.
*18 holes, 6209yds, Par 70, SSS 70, Course record 68.*
*Club membership 550.*
**Visitors**     must contact in advance, with member only
                 weekends & bank holidays.
**Societies**    apply ihn advance.
**Green Fees**   £24 per day.
**Facilities**   ⊗ 🗠 ⛏ 🍺 ♀ ⛏ 🏠 ( Colin Boyle.
**Leisure**      trolley for hire, putting green, practice area.
**Location**     N off B6194
**Hotel**        ★★ 69% York House Hotel, York Place,
                 Richmond St, ASHTON-UNDER-LYNE
                 ☎ 0161 330 5899 24 ⇆ 🐾Annexe10 ⇆ 🐾

**Dukinfield** Lyne Edge, Yew Tree Ln SK16 5DF
☎ 0161 338 2340
Recently extended, tricky hillside course with several
difficult Par 3s and a very long par 5.
*18 holes, 5303yds, Par 67, SSS 66.*
*Club membership 250.*
**Visitors**     may not play on Wed afternoons & must play
                 with member at weekends, advisable to contact
                 in advance.
**Societies**    apply in writing or telephone.
**Green Fees**   £16.50 per day.
**Facilities**   ⊗ 🗠 ⛏ 🍺 ♀ ⛏ 🏠 ( Jason Peel.
**Leisure**      trolley for hire, practice area.
**Location**     S off B6175
**Hotel**        ★★ 69% York House Hotel, York Place,
                 Richmond St, ASHTON-UNDER-LYNE
                 ☎ 0161 330 5899 24 ⇆ 🐾Annexe10 ⇆ 🐾

## BOLTON                        Map 07 SD70

**Bolton** Lostock Park, Chorley New Rd BL6 4AJ
☎ 01204 843067 & 843278
This well maintained heathland course is always a
pleasure to visit. The 12th hole should be treated with
respect and so too should the final four holes which have
ruined many a card.
*18 holes, 6233yds, Par 70, SSS 70, Course record 66.*
*Club membership 612.*
**Visitors**     not able to play Tue before 2.30pm or on
                 competition days.
**Societies**    write or telephone in advance, not accepted
                 Tue, Sat or Sun.
**Green Fees**   £34 per day; £28 per round (£38/£32 Wed,
                 bank holidays and weekends).
**Facilities**   ⊗ 🗠 ⛏ 🍺 ♀ ⛏ 🏠 ( R Longworth.

**Leisure** trolley for hire, putting green, practice area.
**Location** 3m W of Bolton, on A673
**Hotel** ★★★★ 64% Georgian House Hotel, Manchester Rd, Blackrod, BOLTON
☎ 01942 814598 100 ➡ ℟

**Breightmet** Red Bridge, Ainsworth BL2 5PA
☎ 01204 527381
Long parkland course.
*9 holes, 6416yds, Par 72, SSS 71, Course record 68.*
*Club membership 350.*
**Visitors** may not play Wed or weekends.
**Societies** welcome Tue & Thu only, apply in advance in writing.
**Green Fees** not confirmed.
**Facilities** ♀⅄
**Leisure** putting green,practice area.
**Location** E side of town centre off A58
**Hotel** ★★★ 65% Egerton House Hotel, Blackburn Rd, Egerton, BOLTON
☎ 01204 307171 32 ➡ ℟

**Deane** Broadford Rd, Deane BL3 4NS
☎ 01204 61944 & 651808
Undulating parkland course with small ravines on approaches to some holes.
*18 holes, 5583yds, Par 68, SSS 67, Course record 64.*
*Club membership 470.*
**Visitors** must be a member of a golf club or member's guest. Restricted weekends.
**Societies** must telephone in advance and confirm in writing.
**Green Fees** £20 per day (£25 weekends).
**Facilities** ⊗ ⅏ ᒪ ⬛ ♀⅄ ⌂ ℓ David Martindale.
**Leisure** trolley for hire, putting green, practice area.
**Location** 1m from exit 5 on M61 towards Bolton
**Hotel** ★★★ 64% Beaumont Hotel, Beaumont Rd, BOLTON ☎ 01204 651511 96 ➡ ℟

**Dunscar** Longworth Ln, Bromley Cross BL7 9QY
☎ 01204 303321
A scenic moorland course with panoramic views. A warm friendly club.
*18 holes, 6085yds, Par 71, SSS 69, Course record 65.*
*Club membership 600.*
**Visitors** must telephone 01204 592992 in advance.
**Societies** must apply in writing.
**Green Fees** £20 (£30 weekends & bank holidays).
**Facilities** ⊗ ⅏ ᒪ ⬛ ♀⅄ ⌂ ℓ Gary Treadgold.
**Leisure** trolley for hire, putting green, practice area.
**Location** 2m N off A666
**Hotel** ★★★ 65% Egerton House Hotel, Blackburn Rd, Egerton, BOLTON
☎ 01204 307171 32 ➡ ℟

**Great Lever & Farnworth** Plodder Ln, Farnworth BL4 0LQ
☎ 01204 656137
Downland course with easy walking.
*18 holes, 5986yds, Par 70, SSS 69, Course record 67.*
*Club membership 600.*
**Visitors** must contact in advance.
**Societies** apply in writing.
**Green Fees** £15 per day (£25 weekends & bank holidays).
**Facilities** ⊗ ⅏ ᒪ ⬛ ♀⅄ ⌂ ℓ David Clarke.
**Leisure** trolley for hire, putting green, practice area.
**Location** SW side of town centre off A575

**Hotel** ★★★ 64% Beaumont Hotel, Beaumont Rd, BOLTON ☎ 01204 651511 96 ➡ ℟

**Harwood** Springfield, Roading Brook Rd, Harwood BL2 4JD ☎ 01204 522878
Mainly flat parkland course.
*9 holes, 5993yds, Par 71, SSS 69, Course record 62.*
*Club membership 430.*
**Visitors** must be members of a golf club and hold a current handicap cartificate. May not play at weekends.
**Societies** contact in writing.
**Green Fees** £15.
**Facilities** ᒪ ⬛ ♀⅄ ⌂ ℓ M Dance.
**Leisure** putting green, practice area.
**Location** 2.5m NE off B6196
**Hotel** ★★★ 65% Egerton House Hotel, Blackburn Rd, Egerton, BOLTON
☎ 01204 307171 32 ➡ ℟

**Old Links** Chorley Old Rd, Montserrat BL1 5SU
☎ 01204 842307
Championship moorland course.
*18 holes, 6406yds, Par 72, SSS 72.*
*Club membership 600.*
**Visitors** must contact in advance.
**Societies** apply by letter or telephone.
**Green Fees** £25 per day (£35 weekends and bank holidays).
**Facilities** ⊗ ⅏ ᒪ ⬛ ♀⅄ ⌂ ℓ Paul Horridge.
**Leisure** trolley for hire, putting green, practice area.
**Location** NW of town centre on B6226
**Hotel** ★★★★ 64% Georgian House Hotel, Manchester Rd, Blackrod, BOLTON
☎ 01942 814598 100 ➡ ℟

**Regent Park** Links Rd, Chorley New Rd BL2 9XX
☎ 01204 844170
Parkland course.
*18 holes, 6130yds, Par 70, SSS 69, Course record 67.*
*Club membership 200.*
**Visitors** must book 6 days in advance.
**Societies** must telephone 01204 495421 in advance.
**Green Fees** £8 per round (£10 weekends).
**Facilities** ⊗ ⅏ ᒪ ⬛ ♀⅄ ⌂ ℮ ℓ Bob Longworth.
**Leisure** trolley for hire, putting green, practice area.
**Location** 3.5m W off A673
**Hotel** ★★★ 64% Beaumont Hotel, Beaumont Rd, BOLTON
☎ 01204 651511 96 ➡ ℟

## BRAMHALL                                  Map 07 SJ88

**Bramall Park** 20 Manor Rd SK7 3LY ☎ 0161 485 3119
Well-wooded parkland course with splendid views of the Pennines.
*18 holes, 6043yds, Par 70, SSS 69.*
*Club membership 600.*
**Visitors** must contact in advance.
**Societies** apply in writing.
**Green Fees** not confirmed.
**Facilities** ♀⅄ ⌂ ℓ
**Location** NW side of town centre off B5149
**Hotel** ★★★ 67% Bramhall Moat House, Bramhall Ln South, BRAMHALL
☎ 0161 439 8116 65 ➡ ℟

**Bramhall** Ladythorn Rd SK7 2EY ☎ 0161 439 6092
Undulating parkland course, easy walking.
*18 holes, 6340yds, Par 70, SSS 70.*
*Club membership 700.*
**Visitors** must contact in advance.
**Societies** apply in writing.
**Green Fees** £27 per day; £23 per round (£37/30 weekends).
**Facilities** ⊗ ⅷ ⅼ ⅶ ⅼ ⅔ ⅾ ⅼ Richard Green.
**Leisure** motorised carts for hire, trolley for hire, driving range, putting green, practice area.
**Location** E side of town centre off A5102
**Hotel** ★★★ 67% Bramhall Moat House, Bramhall Ln South, BRAMHALL
☎ 0161 439 8116 65 ⇔ ⅼ

## BROMLEY CROSS Map 07 SD71

**Turton** Wood End Farm, Chapeltown Rd BL7 9QH
☎ 01204 852235
Moorland course.
*18 holes, 5690yds, Par 68, SSS 68.*
*Club membership 450.*
**Visitors** avoid 11.30-2pm Wed Ladies day. Sat tee available after last competition.
**Societies** must contact in writing.
**Green Fees** £16 per day (£20 per day weekends).
**Facilities** ⊗ ⅷ ⅼ ⅶ ⅼ ⅔
**Leisure** putting green, practice area.
**Location** 3m N on A676
**Hotel** ★★★ 65% Egerton House Hotel, Blackburn Rd, Egerton, BOLTON
☎ 01204 307171 32 ⇔ ⅼ

## BURY Map 07 SD81

**Bury** Unsworth Hall, Blackford Bridge BL9 9TJ
☎ 0161 766 2213 & 766 4897
Hard walking on hilly moorland course.
*18 holes, 5961yds, Par 69, SSS 69, Course record 64.*
*Club membership 450.*
**Visitors** must contact in advance.
**Societies** telephone 0161 766 4897.
**Green Fees** £22 per day (£28.50 weekends).
**Facilities** ⊗ ⅷ ⅼ ⅶ ⅼ ⅔ ⅾ ⅼ S Crake.
**Leisure** trolley for hire, putting green, practice area.
**Location** 2m S on A56
**Hotel** ★★★ 63% Bolholt Country Park Hotel, Walshaw Rd, BURY
☎ 0161 764 5239 38 ⇔ ⅼAnnexe9rm(8 ⇔ ⅼ)

**Lowes Park** Hilltop, Lowes Rd BL9 6SU ☎ 0161 764 1231
Moorland course, with easy walking. Usually windy.
*9 holes, 6009yds, Par 70, SSS 69, Course record 65.*
*Club membership 400.*
**Visitors** may not play Wed & Sat, by appointment Sun. Must contact in advance.
**Societies** apply in writing.
**Green Fees** £15 per round (£20 Sun and bank holidays).
**Facilities** ⊗ ⅷ ⅼ ⅶ ⅼ ⅔ ⅾ
**Leisure** practice area.
**Location** N side of town centre off A56
**Hotel** ★★★ 63% Bolholt Country Park Hotel, Walshaw Rd, BURY
☎ 0161 764 5239 38 ⇔ ⅼAnnexe9rm(8 ⇔ ⅼ)

**Walmersley** Garretts Close, Walmersley BL9 6TE
☎ 0161 764 1429
Moorland hillside course, with wide fairways, large greens and extensive views. Testing holes: 2nd (484 yds) par 5; 4th (444 yds) par 4.
*18 holes, 5341yds, Par 69, SSS 67.*
*Club membership 475.*
**Visitors** welcome Mon & Tue after 5.30pm. With member only wed-Sun.
**Societies** must apply in writing.
**Green Fees** £20 per day.
**Facilities** ⊗ ⅷ ⅼ ⅶ ⅼ ⅔ ⅾ ⅼ S Craike.
**Leisure** putting green, small practice area.
**Location** 2m N off A56
**Hotel** ★★★ 63% Old Mill Hotel, Springwood, RAMSBOTTOM
☎ 01706 822991 36 ⇔

## CHEADLE Map 07 SJ88

**Cheadle** Cheadle Rd SK8 1HW ☎ 0161 491 4452
Parkland course with hazards on every hole, from sand bunkers and copses to a stream across six of the fairways.
*9 holes, 5006yds, Par 64, SSS 65.*
*Club membership 425.*
**Visitors** may not play Tue & Sat, & restricted Sun. Must contact in advance and have a handicap certificate and be member of a bona-fide golf club.
**Societies** apply in writing to secretary
**Green Fees** £15 per round 18 holes (£23 Sun & bank holidays).
**Facilities** ⊗ ⅷ ⅼ ⅶ ⅼ ⅔ ⅾ ⅼ G J Norcott.
**Leisure** trolley for hire, putting green, practice area.
**Location** S side of village off A5149
**Hotel** ★★ 67% Wycliffe, 74 Edgeley Rd, Edgeley, STOCKPORT
☎ 0161 477 5395 20 ⇔ ⅼ

## DENTON Map 07 SJ99

**Denton** Manchester Rd M34 2NU
☎ 0161 336 3218
Easy, flat parkland course with brook running through. Notable hole is one called 'Death and Glory'.
*18 holes, 6541yds, Par 72, SSS 71, Course record 66.*
*Club membership 585.*
**Visitors** must contact in advance & may not play summer weekends.
**Societies** apply in advance.
**Green Fees** £22 (£27 weekends & bank holidays).
**Facilities** ⊗ ⅷ ⅼ ⅶ ⅼ ⅔ ⅾ ⅼ M Hollingworth.
**Leisure** trolley for hire, putting green, practice area.
**Location** 1.5m W on A57
**Hotel** ★★ 69% York House Hotel, York Place, Richmond St, ASHTON-UNDER-LYNE
☎ 0161 330 5899 24 ⇔ ⅼAnnexe10 ⇔ ⅼ

## FAILSWORTH Map 07 SD80

**Brookdale** Medlock Rd M35 9WQ ☎ 0161 681 4534
Undulating parkland course, with river crossed 5 times in play. Hard walking.
*18 holes, 5841yds, Par 68, SSS 68, Course record 64.*
*Club membership 600.*

| | |
|---|---|
| **Visitors** | advisable to contact in advance. May only play as guest of member at weekends. |
| **Societies** | must contact in advance. |
| **Green Fees** | £25 per day; £20 per round. |
| **Facilities** | ⊗ by prior arrangement 🍴 by prior arrangement 🏐 ⬛ ♀ ⛳ 🏠 ℓ Jason Spibey. |
| **Leisure** | trolley for hire, putting green, practice area. |
| **Location** | N side of Manchester |
| **Hotel** | ★★ 69% York House Hotel, York Place, Richmond St, ASHTON-UNDER-LYNE ☎ 0161 330 5899 24 ⇋ ℝAnnexe10 ⇋ ℝ |

## FLIXTON
Map 07 SJ79

**William Wroe Municipal** Pennybridge Ln, Flixton Rd M41 5DX ☎ 0161 748 8680
Parkland course, with easy walking.
*18 holes, 4395yds, Par 68, SSS 65.*

| | |
|---|---|
| **Visitors** | must book in advance. |
| **Societies** | contact for details. |
| **Green Fees** | £6.50 (£8.70 weekends & bank holidays). |
| **Facilities** | ⛳ 🏠 🍴 ℓ Scott Partington. |
| **Leisure** | putting green, practice area. |
| **Location** | E side of village off B5158 |
| **Hotel** | ★ 64% Beaucliffe Hotel, 254 Eccles Old Rd, Pendleton, SALFORD ☎ 0161 789 5092 21rm(2 ⇋15 ℝ) |

## GATLEY
Map 07 SJ88

*Gatley* Waterfall Farm, Styal Rd, Heald Green SK8 3TW ☎ 0161 437 2091
Parkland course. Moderately testing.
*9 holes, 5934yds, Par 68, SSS 68.*
*Club membership 400.*

| | |
|---|---|
| **Visitors** | may not play Tue & Sat. With member only weekends.Handicap certificate required. |
| **Societies** | apply in writing. |
| **Green Fees** | not confirmed. |
| **Facilities** | ♀ ⛳ 🏠 ℓ |
| **Leisure** | squash. |
| **Location** | S side of village off B5166 |
| **Hotel** | ★★★★ 62% Belfry Hotel, Stanley Rd, HANDFORTH ☎ 0161 437 0511 80 ⇋ ℝ |

## HALE
Map 07 SJ78

**Hale** Rappax Rd WA15 0NU ☎ 0161 980 4225 & 904 0835
Beautiful, undulating parkland course, with the River Bollin winding round fairways.
*9 holes, 5780yds, Par 70, SSS 68, Course record 65.*
*Club membership 300.*

| | |
|---|---|
| **Visitors** | may not play before 4.30pm Thu; with member only weekends. |
| **Societies** | apply in writing or telephone in advance. |
| **Green Fees** | £20 per day/round. |
| **Facilities** | ⊗ 🍴 by prior arrangement 🏐 ⬛ ♀ ⛳ 🏠 ℓ Joy Jackson. |
| **Leisure** | putting green, practice area. |
| **Location** | 1.25m SE |
| **Hotel** | ★★★ 60% Bowdon Hotel, Langham Rd, Bowdon, ALTRINCHAM ☎ 0161 928 7121 82 ⇋ ℝ |

## HAZEL GROVE
Map 07 SJ98

**Hazel Grove** Buxton Rd SK7 6LU ☎ 0161 483 3978
Testing parkland course with tricky greens and water hazards coming into play on several holes.
*18 holes, 6310yds, Par 71, SSS 71.*
*Club membership 600.*

| | |
|---|---|
| **Visitors** | must contact in advance (0161 483 7272). |
| **Societies** | must apply in writing, Thu & Fri only. |
| **Green Fees** | £25 per day (£30 Fri/Sun & bank holidays). |
| **Facilities** | ⊗ 🍴 🏐 ⬛ ♀ ⛳ 🏠 🍴 ℓ M E Hill. |
| **Leisure** | trolley for hire, putting green, practice area, snooker room. |
| **Location** | 1m E off A6 |
| **Hotel** | ★★★ 67% Bramhall Moat House, Bramhall Ln South, BRAMHALL ☎ 0161 439 8116 65 ⇋ ℝ |

## HINDLEY
Map 07 SD60

**Hindley Hall** Hall Ln WN2 2SQ ☎ 01942 255131
Parkland course with mostly easy walking.
*18 holes, 5913yds, Par 69, SSS 68, Course record 64.*
*Club membership 430.*

| | |
|---|---|
| **Visitors** | must contact in advance and may not play weekends. |
| **Societies** | apply in advance to Secretary |
| **Green Fees** | £20 per day. |
| **Facilities** | ⊗ 🍴 🏐 ⬛ ♀ ⛳ 🏠 ℓ Neil Brazell. |
| **Leisure** | trolley for hire, putting green, practice area. |
| **Location** | 1m N off A58 |
| **Hotel** | ★★★ 65% Oak Hotel, Riverway, WIGAN ☎ 01942 826888 88 ⇋ ℝ |

## HYDE
Map 07 SJ99

**Werneth Low** Werneth Low Rd, Gee Cross SK14 3AF ☎ 0161 368 2503
Hard walking but good views from this moorland course. Exposed to wind.
*11 holes, 6113yds, Par 70, SSS 70, Course record 69.*
*Club membership 375.*

| | |
|---|---|
| **Visitors** | may not play Tue mornings or Sun and by prior arrangement on Sat. |
| **Societies** | must contact in at least 14 days in advance. |
| **Green Fees** | £18 per round (weekdays). |
| **Facilities** | ⊗ 🍴 🏐 ⬛ ♀ ⛳ 🏠 ℓ Tony Bacchus. |
| **Leisure** | putting green, practice area. |
| **Location** | 2m S of town centre |
| **Hotel** | ★★ 70% Red Lion Inn, 112 Buxton Rd, High Ln, STOCKPORT ☎ 01663 765227 6 ⇋ ℝ |

## LEIGH
Map 07 SD60

*Pennington* St Helen's Rd WN7 4HW ☎ 01942 682852
Municipal parkland course, with natural hazards of brooks, ponds and trees, and easy walking.
*9 holes, 2919yds, Par 35, SSS 34.*
*Club membership 200.*

| | |
|---|---|
| **Visitors** | no restrictions. |
| **Societies** | must contact in advance. |
| **Green Fees** | not confirmed. ▶ |

**Facilities** 🏠 ⛳ ⚑ Tim Kershaw.
**Leisure** trolleys for hire.
**Location** SW side of town centre off A572
**Hotel** ★★ 65% Kirkfield Hotel, 2/4 Church St, NEWTON LE WILLOWS
☎ 01925 228196 14 ⇔ ♪

## LITTLEBOROUGH                                          Map 07 SD91

*Whittaker* Whittaker Ln OL15 0LH ☎ 01706 378310
Moorland 9-hole course.
*9 holes, 5632yds, Par 68, SSS 67, Course record 61.*
*Club membership 150.*
**Visitors** welcome except for Tue pm and Sun.
**Societies** apply to Secretary.
**Green Fees** not confirmed.
**Facilities** ⚲ ⚹
**Leisure** putting green,practice area.
**Location** 3m NE of Rochdale, along A58
**Hotel** ★★★ 66% Norton Grange Hotel, Manchester Rd, Castleton, ROCHDALE
☎ 01706 30788 50 ⇔ ♪

## MANCHESTER                                             Map 07 SJ89

**Blackley** Victoria Ave East, Blackley M9 6HW
☎ 0161 643 2980 & 654 7770
Parkland course. Course crossed by footpath.
*18 holes, 6237yds, Par 70, SSS 70.*
*Club membership 730.*
**Visitors** with member only Thu, weekends and bank holidays.
**Societies** apply in advance.
**Green Fees** not confirmed.
**Facilities** ⊗ ⥾ ㏑ ♥ ⚲ ⚹ 🏠 ⚑ Martin Barton.
**Leisure** trolley for hire, putting green, practice area.
**Location** 4m N of city centre, on Rochdale Rd
**Hotel** ★★★ 61% Bower Hotel, Hollinwood Av, Chadderton, OLDHAM
☎ 0161 682 7254 66 ⇔ ♪

*Chorlton-cum-Hardy* Barlow Hall, Barlow Hall Rd, Chorlton-cum-Hardy M21 7JJ
☎ 0161 881 5830 & 061-881 3139
Meadowland course with trees, stream and several ditches.
*18 holes, 5980yds, Par 70, SSS 69, Course record 63.*
*Club membership 780.*
**Visitors** handicap certificate required.
**Societies** on Thu only by prior booking.
**Green Fees** not confirmed.
**Facilities** ⚲ ⚹ 🏠 ⚑ ⛳ ⚑ David Screeton.
**Leisure** putting,trolley hire,practice area.
**Location** 4m S of Manchester A5103/A5145
**Hotel** ★★★ 61% Willow Bank Hotel, 340-342 Wilmslow Rd, Fallowfield, MANCHESTER
☎ 0161 224 0461 116 ⇔ ♪

**Davyhulme Park** Gleneagles Rd, Davyhulme M41 8SA
☎ 0161 748 2260
Parkland course.
*18 holes, 6237yds, Par 72, SSS 70, Course record 65.*
**Visitors** must contact in advance, may not play Wed, weekends by prior notice. Must have an introduction from own club.
**Societies** telephone in advance.

**Green Fees** £25 per day; £21 per round.
**Facilities** ⊗ ⥾ ㏑ ♥ ⚲ ⚹ 🏠 ⚑ Dean Butler.
**Leisure** trolley for hire, putting green, practice area.
**Location** 8m S adj to Park Hospital
**Hotel** ★ 64% Beaucliffe Hotel, 254 Eccles Old Rd, Pendleton, SALFORD
☎ 0161 789 5092 21rm(2 ⇔ 15 ♪)

**Didsbury** Ford Ln, Northenden M22 4NQ
☎ 0161 998 9278 (Secretary) & 998 2811 (Pro)
Parkland course.
*18 holes, 6273yds, Par 70, SSS 70, Course record 63.*
*Club membership 750.*
**Visitors** advised to check dates/times with professional.
**Societies** Thu & Fri, must contact in advance.
**Green Fees** £24 per day (£28 weekends & bank holidays).
**Facilities** ⊗ ⥾ ㏑ ♥ ⚲ ⚹ 🏠 ⚑ Peter Barber.
**Leisure** trolley for hire, putting green, practice area.
**Location** 6m S of city centre off A5145
**Hotel** B Forte Posthouse Manchester, Palatine Rd, Northenden, MANCHESTER
☎ 0161 998 7090 190 ⇔ ♪

**Fairfield** "Boothdale", Booth Rd, Audenshaw M34 5GA
☎ 0161 370 1641
Parkland course set around a reservoir. Course demands particularly accurate placing of shots.
*18 holes, 5654yds, Par 70, SSS 68.*
*Club membership 450.*
**Visitors** may not play mornings at weekends & may be restricted on Wed & Thu.
**Societies** prior booking through Secretary.
**Green Fees** £17 per round (£23 weekends & bank holidays).
**Facilities** ⊗ ⥾ ㏑ ♥ ⚲ ⚹ 🏠 ⚑ Nick Harding.
**Leisure** trolley for hire, sailing.
**Location** 1.5m W of Audenshaw off A635
**Hotel** ★★ 69% York House Hotel, York Place, Richmond St, ASHTON-UNDER-LYNE
☎ 0161 330 5899 24 ⇔ ♪Annexe10 ⇔ ♪

**Northenden** Palatine Rd, Northenden M22 4FR
☎ 0161 998 4738
Parkland course surrounded by the River Mersey.
*18 holes, 6503yds, Par 72, SSS 71, Course record 64.*
*Club membership 700.*
**Visitors** Must contact in advance.
**Societies** Tue & Fri only, apply in advance to Secretary.
**Green Fees** £25 per day (£27.50 weekends & bank holidays).
**Facilities** ⊗ ⥾ ㏑ ♥ ⚲ ⚹ 🏠 ⚑ P A Scott.
**Leisure** trolley for hire, putting green, practice area.
**Location** 6.5m S of city centre on B1567 off A5103
**Hotel** B Forte Posthouse Manchester, Palatine Rd, Northenden, MANCHESTER
☎ 0161 998 7090 190 ⇔ ♪

*Pike Fold* Cooper Ln, Victoria Av, Blackley M9 6QQ
☎ 0161 740 1136
Picturesque, hilly course. Good test of golf.
*9 holes, 5785yds, Par 70, SSS 68, Course record 66.*
*Club membership 200.*
**Visitors** may not play Sun. Must be with member Sat & bank holidays.
**Societies** apply in writing.
**Green Fees** not confirmed.
**Facilities** ⚲ ⚹
**Location** 4m N of city centre off Rochdale Rd

**Hotel** ★★★ 61% Bower Hotel, Hollinwood Av,
Chadderton, OLDHAM
☎ 0161 682 7254 66 ⇌ 📷

**Withington** 243 Palatine Rd, West Didsbury M20 8UD
☎ 0161 445 9544
Flat parkland course.
*18 holes, 6410yds, Par 71, SSS 71.*
*Club membership 600.*
**Visitors** welcome except Thu, must contact in advance,
restricted at weekends.
**Societies** telephone in advance, welcome except Thu, Sat
& Sun.
**Green Fees** not confirmed.
**Facilities** ♀ ♨ 🏠 ℓ R J Ling.
**Location** 4m SW of city centre off B5167
**Hotel** B Forte Posthouse Manchester, Palatine Rd,
Northenden, MANCHESTER
☎ 0161 998 7090 190 ⇌ 📷

**Worsley** Stableford Av, Worsley M30 8AP
☎ 0161 789 4202
Well-wooded parkland course.
*18 holes, 6252yds, Par 72, SSS 70, Course record 65.*
*Club membership 600.*
**Visitors** no restrictions except during club competitions.
**Societies** apply in advance.
**Green Fees** £25 per day (£30 weekends & bank holidays).
**Facilities** ⊗ 🏮 🛍 ♨ ♀ ♨ 🏠 🍴 ℓ Ceri Cousins.
**Leisure** trolley for hire, putting green, practice area.
**Location** 6.5m NW of city centre off A572
**Hotel** ★★★ 61% Novotel, Worsley Brow,
WORSLEY
☎ 0161 799 3535 119 ⇌ 📷

## MELLOR　　　　　　　　　　　Map 07 SJ98

**Mellor & Townscliffe** Gibb Ln, Tarden SK6 5NA
☎ 0161 427 2208
Scenic parkland and moorland course, undulating with some
hard walking. Good views. Testing 200 yd, 9th hole, par 3.
*18 holes, 5925yds, Par 70, SSS 69.*
*Club membership 650.*
**Visitors** with member only Sun.
**Societies** apply by letter.
**Green Fees** not confirmed.
**Facilities** ♀ ♨ 🏠 ℓ Gary R Broadley.
**Location** 0.5m S
**Hotel** ★ 74% Springfield Hotel, Station Rd,
MARPLE ☎ 0161 449 0721 6 ⇌ 📷

## MIDDLETON　　　　　　　　　Map 07 SD80

**Manchester** Hopwood Cottage, Rochdale Rd M24 2QP
☎ 0161 643 3202
Moorland golf of unique character over a spaciously laid
out course with generous fairways sweeping along to
large greens. A wide variety of holes will challenge the
golfer's technique, particularly the testing last three
holes.
*18 holes, 6519yds, Par 72, SSS 70, Course record 65.*
*Club membership 650.*
**Visitors** must contact in advance, may not play Wed
and limited play weekends.
**Societies** telephone in advance.

**Green Fees** £40 per day; £30 per round (£45 weekends
& bank holidays).
**Facilities** ⊗ by prior arrangement 🏮 by prior
arrangement 🛍 ♨ ♀ ♨ 🏠 ℓ Brian Connor.
**Leisure** motorised carts for hire, buggies for hire,
trolley for hire, driving range, putting green,
practice area.
**Location** 2.5m N off A664
**Hotel** ★★ 57% Midway Hotel, Manchester Rd,
Castleton, ROCHDALE
☎ 01706 32881 24 ⇌ 📷

**North Manchester** Rhodes House, Manchester Old Rd
M24 4PE ☎ 0161 643 9033
A long, tight heathland course with natural water hazards.
Excellent views of the Yorkshire Wolds.
*18 holes, 6527yds, Par 72, SSS 72, Course record 66.*
*Club membership 800.*
**Visitors** no restrictions.
**Societies** telephone in advance.
**Green Fees** not confirmed.
**Facilities** ♀ ♨ 🏠 🍴 ℓ Peter Lunt.
**Leisure** putting green, trolley hire, practice area.
**Location** W side of town centre off A576
**Hotel** ★★★ 61% Bower Hotel, Hollinwood Av,
Chadderton, OLDHAM
☎ 0161 682 7254 66 ⇌ 📷

## MILNROW　　　　　　　　　　Map 07 SD91

**Tunshill** Kiln Ln OL16 3TS
☎ 01706 342095
Testing moorland course, particularly 6th and 15th (par 5's).
*9 holes, 5804yds, Par 70, SSS 68.*
*Club membership 275.*
**Visitors** must contact in advance, restricted weekends &
evenings.
**Societies** apply in writing.
**Green Fees** not confirmed.
**Facilities** ♀ ♨
**Leisure** pool table.
**Location** 1m NE M62 exit junc 21 off B6225
**Hotel** ★★★ 66% Norton Grange Hotel, Manchester
Rd, Castleton, ROCHDALE
☎ 01706 30788 50 ⇌ 📷

## OLDHAM　　　　　　　　　　Map 07 SD90

**Crompton & Royton** Highbarn OL2 6RW
☎ 0161 624 0986
Undulating moorland course.
*18 holes, 6214yds, Par 70, SSS 70, Course record 65.*
*Club membership 500.*
**Visitors** must contact in advance and may not play Tue or
Sat, limited play Sun pm and Wed.
**Societies** apply in advance
**Green Fees** £24 (£30 weekends & bank holidays).
**Facilities** ⊗ 🏮 🛍 ♨ ♀ ♨ 🏠 ℓ David Melling.
**Leisure** trolley for hire, putting green, practice area.
**Location** 0.5m NE of Royton
**Hotel** ★★★ 61% Bower Hotel, Hollinwood Av,
Chadderton, OLDHAM
☎ 0161 682 7254 66 ⇌ 📷

**Oldham** Lees New Rd OL4 5PN
☎ 0161 624 4986
Moorland course, with hard walking.
*18 holes, 5122yds, Par 66, SSS 65, Course record 62.*
*Club membership 370.*
**Visitors**  no restrictions.
**Societies**  must contact in advance.
**Green Fees** £16 (£22 weekends & bank holidays).
**Facilities**  ⊗ ⅏ ⅃ 🍴 ♀ ⅄ 🖻 ⅂ Gavin Peter Mutch.
**Leisure**  trolley for hire, putting green.
**Location**  2.5m E off A669
**Hotel**  ★★ 69%  York House Hotel, York Place,
Richmond St, ASHTON-UNDER-LYNE
☎ 0161 330 5899 24 ⇆ ⅏Annexe10 ⇆ ⅄

---

*Werneth* Green Ln, Garden Suburb OL8 3AZ
☎ 0161 624 1190
Semi-moorland course, with a deep gulley and stream
crossing eight fairways. Testing hole: 3rd (par 3).
*18 holes, 5363yds, Par 68, SSS 66.*
*Club membership 460.*
**Visitors**  may not play on Tue or Thu and weekends. Must
contact in advance.
**Societies**  must contact in advance.
**Green Fees** not confirmed.
**Facilities**  ♀ ⅄ 🖻 ⅂
**Location**  S side of town centre off A627
**Hotel**  ★★ 69%  York House Hotel, York Place,
Richmond St, ASHTON-UNDER-LYNE
☎ 0161 330 5899 24 ⇆ ⅏Annexe10 ⇆ ⅄

---

## PRESTWICH
Map 07 SD80

*Heaton Park Municipal M25 2SW*
☎ 0161 798 0295
A hilly parkland municipal course with lakes to cross,
including the 12th which requires an 183yd carry across the
water.
*18 holes, 5766yds, Par 70, SSS 68.*
*Club membership 190.*
**Visitors**  restricted to club members only between 8-10am
Sat & Sun.
**Societies**  apply in writing to John Andrew.
**Green Fees** not confirmed.
**Facilities**  ⅄ 🖻 ⅂ ⅂ Terry Morley.
**Hotel**  ★★★★ 63%  Bolton Moat House, 1 Higher
Bridge St, BOLTON
☎ 01204 879988 128 ⇆ ⅄

---

**Prestwich** Hilton Ln M25 9XB  ☎ 0161 773 2544
Parkland course, near to Manchester city centre.
*18 holes, 4806yds, Par 64, SSS 63, Course record 60.*
*Club membership 507.*
**Visitors**  weekdays by arrangement.
**Societies**  apply in writing or telephone.
**Green Fees** not confirmed.
**Facilities**  ⊗ ⅏ ⅃ ♀ ⅄ 🖻 ⅂ ⅂ Anthony Sposton.
**Leisure**  trolley for hire, putting green practice area.
**Location**  N side of town centre on A6044
**Hotel**  ★ 64%  Beaucliffe Hotel, 254 Eccles Old Rd,
Pendleton, SALFORD
☎ 0161 789 5092 21rm(2 ⇆ 15 ⅄)

## ROCHDALE
Map 07 SD81

**Castle Hawk** Chadwick Ln, Castleton OL11 3BY
☎ 01706 40841
Two parkland courses, with challenging par 3s, and a driving
range.
*New Course: 9 holes, 2699yds, Par 34, SSS 34, Course*
*record 30.*
*Old Course: 18 holes, 3460yds, Par 55, SSS 55, Course*
*record 54.*
*Club membership 350.*
**Visitors**  no restrictions.
**Societies**  must contact in advance.
**Green Fees** £6 per day (£8 weekends & bank holidays).
**Facilities**  ⊗ ⅏ ⅃ ♀ ⅄ 🖻 ⅂ ⅂ Mike Vipond.
**Leisure**  fishing, trolley for hire, driving range, putting
green, practice area.
**Location**  S of Rochdale, nr junc 20 (M62)
**Hotel**  ★★★ 66%  Norton Grange Hotel, Manchester
Rd, Castleton, ROCHDALE
☎ 01706 30788 50 ⇆ ⅄

---

**Rochdale** Edenfield Rd OL11 5YR  ☎ 01706 43818
Parkland course with enjoyable golf and easy walking.
*18 holes, 6050yds, Par 71, SSS 69, Course record 65.*
*Club membership 750.*
**Visitors**  must telephone in advance.
**Societies**  apply in writing.
**Green Fees** £23 per day (£27 weekends & bank holidays).
**Facilities**  ⊗ ⅏ by prior arrangement ⅃ ⅃ ♀ ⅄ 🖻 ⅂
⅂ Andrew Laverty.
**Leisure**  trolley for hire, putting green, practice area.
**Location**  1.75m W on A680
**Hotel**  ★★ 57%  Midway Hotel, Manchester Rd,
Castleton, ROCHDALE
☎ 01706 32881 24 ⇆ ⅄

---

**Springfield Park** Springfield Park, Bolton Rd OL11 4RE
☎ 01706 56401 (weekend only)
Parkland-moorland course situated in a valley. The River
Roch adds an extra hazard to the course.
*18 holes, 5237yds, Par 67, SSS 66, Course record 64.*
*Club membership 300.*
**Visitors**  must contact professional in advance.
**Societies**  telephone in advance.
**Green Fees** under review.
**Facilities**  🖻 ⅂ ⅂ David Wills.
**Location**  1.5m SW off A58
**Hotel**  ★★ 57%  Midway Hotel, Manchester Rd,
Castleton, ROCHDALE
☎ 01706 32881 24 ⇆ ⅄

## ROMILEY
Map 07 SJ99

**Romiley** Goose House Green SK6 4LJ  ☎ 0161 430 2392
Semi-parkland course on the edge of the Derbyshire Hills,
providing a good test of golf with a number of outstanding
holes, notably the 6th, 9th, 14th and 16th. The latter enjoys
magnificent views from the tee.
*18 holes, 6454yds, Par 70, SSS 71, Course record 66.*
*Club membership 700.*
**Visitors**  are advised to contact in advance, may not play
Thu or Sat before 4pm.
**Societies**  Tue & Wed, must book in advance.

**Green Fees** £30 per day; £24 per round (£44/£33 weekends & bank holidays).
**Facilities** ⊗ ⫟ ⯑ ⯑ ⯑ ⯑ ⯑ ⯑ Garry Butler.
**Leisure** trolley for hire, putting green.
**Location** E side of town centre off B6104
**Hotel** ★★ 70% Red Lion Inn, 112 Buxton Rd, High Ln, STOCKPORT ☎ 01663 765227 6 ⇥ ↰

---

## SALE                                          Map 07 SJ79

**Ashton on Mersey** Church Ln M33 5QQ ☎ 0161 973 3220
Parkland course with easy walking.
*9 holes, 6146yds, Par 72, SSS 69.*
*Club membership 450.*
**Visitors** with member only Sun & bank holidays, not Sat.
**Societies** Thu only. Apply in writing.
**Green Fees** not confirmed.
**Facilities** ⯑ ⯑ ⯑ ⯑ Mike Williams.
**Leisure** sauna, putting green,trolley hire.
**Location** 1m W of M63 junc 7
**Hotel** ★★★ 66% Cresta Court Hotel, Church St, ALTRINCHAM ☎ 0161 927 7272 138 ⇥ ↰

---

**Sale** Golf Rd M33 2XU
☎ 0161 973 1638 (Gen Man) & 973 1730 (Pro)
Tree-lined parkland course. Feature holes are the 13th - Watery Gap - and the par 3 (117yd) 17th.
*18 holes, 6352yds, Par 71, SSS 70.*
*Club membership 700.*
**Visitors** contact professional in advance.
**Societies** apply by letter.
**Green Fees** £25 per round weekdays.
**Facilities** ⊗ ⫟ ⯑ ⯑ ⯑ ⯑ ⯑ ⯑ Mike Stewart.
**Leisure** trolley for hire, putting green, practice area.
**Location** NW side of town centre off A6144
**Hotel** ★★★ 66% Cresta Court Hotel, Church St, ALTRINCHAM ☎ 0161 927 7272 138 ⇥ ↰

---

## SHEVINGTON                                     Map 07 SD50

**Gathurst** 62 Miles Ln WN6 8EW
☎ 01257 255235 (Secretary) & 254909 (Pro)
Testing parkland course, slightly hilly.
*18 holes, 6016yds, Par 70, SSS 69, Course record 65.*
*Club membership 550.*
**Visitors** may play anytime except competition days.
**Societies** welcome Mon, Tue, Thu & Fri. Apply in writing to Secretary.
**Green Fees** £20 weekdays.
**Facilities** ⊗ ⫟ ⯑ ⯑ ⯑ ⯑ ⯑ ⯑ David Clarke.
**Leisure** trolley for hire, putting green, practice area.
**Location** W side of village B5375 off junc 27 of M6
**Hotel** ★★★ 65% Wigan/Standish Moat House, Almond Brook Rd, STANDISH ☎ 01257 499988 113 ⇥ ↰

---

## STALYBRIDGE                                    Map 07 SJ99

**Stamford** Oakfield House, Huddersfield Rd SK15 3PY
☎ 01457 832126 & 834829
Undulating moorland course.
*18 holes, 5701yds, Par 70, SSS 68, Course record 62.*
*Club membership 600.*
**Visitors** limited play at weekends.
**Societies** apply in writing.

---

**Green Fees** £20 per day (£25 weekends).
**Facilities** ⊗ ⫟ ⯑ ⯑ ⯑ ⯑ ⯑
**Leisure** trolley for hire, putting green.
**Location** 2m NE off A635
**Hotel** ★★ 69% York House Hotel, York Place, Richmond St, ASHTON-UNDER-LYNE ☎ 0161 330 5899 24 ⇥ ↰Annexe10 ⇥ ↰

---

## STOCKPORT                                      Map 07 SJ89

**Heaton Moor** Heaton Mersey SK4 3NX ☎ 0161 432 2134
Parkland course, easy walking.
*18 holes, 5907yds, Par 70, SSS 69, Course record 66.*
*Club membership 400.*
**Visitors** restricted Tue & bank holidays.
**Societies** apply in writing.
**Green Fees** not confirmed.
**Facilities** ⯑ ⯑ ⯑ ⯑ ⯑ C Loydall.
**Location** N of town centre off B5169
**Hotel** ★★ 67% Saxon Holme Hotel, 230 Wellington Rd, STOCKPORT ☎ 0161 432 2335 33 ⇥ ↰

---

**Houldsworth** Houldsworth Park, Reddish SK5 6BN
☎ 0161 442 9611 & 0161 442 1712
Flat parkland course, tree-lined and with water hazards.
Testing holes 9th (par 5) and 13th (par 5).
*18 holes, 6209yds, Par 71, SSS 70.*
*Club membership 680.*
**Visitors** may not play weekends & bank holidays unless by prior arrangement with professional.
**Societies** by prior arrangement.
**Green Fees** not confirmed.
**Facilities** ⯑ ⯑ ⯑ ⯑ David Naylor.
**Leisure** putting,trolley hire,practice area.
**Location** 4m SE of city centre off A6
**Hotel** ★★★ 61% Willow Bank Hotel, 340-342 Wilmslow Rd, Fallowfield, MANCHESTER ☎ 0161 224 0461 116 ⇥ ↰

---

**Marple** Barnsfold Rd, Hawk Green, Marple SK6 7EL
☎ 0161 427 2311
Parkland course.
*18 holes, 5552yds, Par 68, SSS 67, Course record 66.*
*Club membership 640.*
**Visitors** restricted Thu afternoon & weekend competition days.
**Societies** apply in writing to professional.
**Green Fees** £20 per day (£30 weekends & bank holidays).
**Facilities** ⊗ ⫟ ⯑ ⯑ ⯑ ⯑ ⯑ ⯑ Nick Hamilton.
**Leisure** putting green.
**Location** S side of town centre
**Hotel** ★★ 70% Red Lion Inn, 112 Buxton Rd, High Ln, STOCKPORT ☎ 01663 765227 6 ⇥ ↰

---

**Reddish Vale** Southcliffe Rd, Reddish SK5 7EE
☎ 0161 480 2359
Undulating heathland course designed by Dr. A Mackenzie and situated in the River Thame valley.
*18 holes, 6100yds, Par 69, SSS 69, Course record 64.*
*Club membership 550.*
**Visitors** must play with member at weekends.
**Societies** must contact in writing.
**Green Fees** not confirmed.
**Facilities** ⯑ ⯑ ⯑ ⯑ Richard Brown.
**Location** 1.5m N off Reddish road                    ▶

**Hotel**  ★★ 67% Wycliffe, 74 Edgeley Rd, Edgeley, STOCKPORT ☎ 0161 477 5395 20 ⇔ ℩

---

**Stockport** Offerton Rd, Offerton SK2 5HL
☎ 0161 427 8369 (Secretary) & 427 2421 (Pro)
A beautifully situated course in wide open countryside with views of the Cheshire and Derbyshire hills. It is not too long but requires that the player plays all the shots, to excellent greens. Demanding holes include the dog-leg 3rd and 12th, and the 460 yard opening hole is among the toughest on the course.
*18 holes, 6326yds, Par 71, SSS 71, Course record 66.*
*Club membership 500.*

**Visitors**  must contact professional in advance, limited play weekends.
**Societies**  Wed & Thu only, apply in writing to Secretary.
**Green Fees** £35 per day (£45 per round weekends & bank holidays).
**Facilities**  ⊗ ℳ ▙ ☏ ♀ ☖ 🏠 ⚑ ℩ Mike Peel.
**Leisure**  trolley for hire.
**Location**  4m SE on A627
**Hotel**  ★★ 70% Red Lion Inn, 112 Buxton Rd, High Ln, STOCKPORT ☎ 01663 765227 6 ⇔ ℩

---

## SWINTON  Map 07 SD70

**Swinton Park** East Lancashire Rd M27 5LX
☎ 0161 794 0861
One of Lancashire's longest inland courses. Clubhouse extensions have greatly improved the facilities.
*18 holes, 6726yds, Par 73, SSS 72, Course record 66.*
*Club membership 600.*

**Visitors**  may not play weekends or Thu. Must contact in advance and have handicap certificate.
**Societies**  by letter.
**Green Fees** £25 per day.
**Facilities**  ⊗ ℳ ▙ ☏ ♀ ☖ 🏠 ℩ James Wilson.
**Leisure**  trolley for hire, putting green, practice area.
**Location**  1m W off A580
**Hotel**  ★★★ 61% Novotel, Worsley Brow, WORSLEY ☎ 0161 799 3535 119 ⇔ ℩

---

## UPPERMILL  Map 07 SD90

**Saddleworth** Mountain Ash OL3 6LT ☎ 01457 873653
Moorland course, with superb views of Pennines.
*18 holes, 5976yds, Par 71, SSS 69, Course record 65.*
*Club membership 800.*

**Visitors**  must contact in advance, restricted at weekends.
**Societies**  contact in advance.
**Green Fees** £23 per day (£26 weekends & bank holidays).
**Facilities**  ⊗ ℳ ▙ ☏ ♀ ☖ 🏠 ⚑ ℩ Tom Shard.
**Leisure**  motorised carts for hire, buggies for hire, trolley for hire, putting green, practice area.
**Location**  E side of town centre off A670
**Hotel**  ★★★ 70% Hotel Smokies Park, Ashton Rd, Bardsley, OLDHAM ☎ 0161 624 3405 47 ⇔ ℩

---

## URMSTON  Map 07 SJ79

**Flixton** Church Rd, Flixton M41 6EP ☎ 0161 748 2116
Meadowland course bounded by River Mersey.
*9 holes, 6410yds, Par 71, SSS 71.*
*Club membership 400.*

**Visitors**  contact professional in advance, with member only weekends & bank holidays.
**Societies**  apply in writing.
**Green Fees** £15 per day.
**Facilities**  ⊗ ℳ by prior arrangement ▙ ☏ ♀ ☖ 🏠 ℩ John Watson.
**Leisure**  trolley for hire, putting green, practice area, snooker.
**Location**  S side of town centre on B5213
**Hotel**  ★ 64% Beaucliffe Hotel, 254 Eccles Old Rd, Pendleton, SALFORD ☎ 0161 789 5092 21rm(2 ⇔ 15 ℩)

---

## WALKDEN  Map 07 SD70

**Brackley Municipal** M38 9TR ☎ 0161 790 6076
Mostly flat course.
*9 holes, 3003yds, Par 35, SSS 69.*
**Visitors**  no restrictions.
**Green Fees** not confirmed.
**Facilities**  🏠 ℩
**Location**  2m NW on A6
**Hotel**  ★★★ 61% Novotel, Worsley Brow, WORSLEY ☎ 0161 799 3535 119 ⇔ ℩

---

## WESTHOUGHTON  Map 07 SD60

**Westhoughton** Long Island, School St BL5 2BR
☎ 01942 811085 & 840545
Compact downland course.
*9 holes, 2886yds, Par 70, SSS 68, Course record 64.*
*Club membership 280.*
**Visitors**  with member only at weekends.
**Societies**  telephone in advance or apply in writing.
**Green Fees** not confirmed.
**Facilities**  ⊗ ℳ by prior arrangement ▙ ☏ ♀ ☖ 🏠 ℩ Jason Seed.
**Leisure**  putting green, practice area, pool & snooker table.
**Location**  0.5m NW off A58
**Hotel**  ★★★ 64% Beaumont Hotel, Beaumont Rd, BOLTON ☎ 01204 651511 96 ⇔ ℩

---

## WHITEFIELD  Map 07 SD80

**Stand** The Dales, Ashbourne Grove M45 7NL
☎ 0161 766 3197
A semi-parkland course with five moorland holes. A fine test of golf with a very demanding finish.
*18 holes, 6411yds, Par 72, SSS 71, Course record 67.*
*Club membership 500.*
**Visitors**  must contact professional in advance.
**Societies**  Wed & Fri, apply by telephone.
**Green Fees** £25 per day (£30 weekends).
**Facilities**  ⊗ ℳ ▙ ☏ ♀ ☖ 🏠 ⚑ ℩ Mark Dance.
**Leisure**  trolley for hire, putting green, practice area.
**Location**  1m W off A667
**Hotel**  ★★★ 63% Bolholt Country Park Hotel, Walshaw Rd, BURY ☎ 0161 764 5239 38 ⇔ ℩Annexe9rm(8 ⇔ ℩)

---

**Whitefield** Higher Ln M45 7EZ ☎ 0161 766 2904 & 2728
Fine sporting parkland course with well-watered greens.
*18 holes, 6045yds, Par 69, SSS 69, Course record 64.*

**Visitors** must contact in advance, play restricted weekends.
**Societies** must contact in advance.
**Green Fees** £25 (£35 weekends & bank holidays).
**Facilities** ⊗ ⅢⅢ ⓛ ⓛ ♀ ♔ 🖼 ℓ Paul Reeves.
**Leisure** hard tennis courts, motorised carts for hire, buggies for hire, trolley for hire, putting green, practice area.
**Location** N side of town centre on A665
**Hotel** ★★★★ 57% Portland Thistle, 3/5 Portland St, Piccadilly Gdns, MANCHESTER ☎ 0161 228 3400 205 ⇆ ℝ

## WIGAN  Map 07 SD50

**Haigh Hall** Haigh Country Park, Aspull WN2 1PE ☎ 01942 831107
Municipal parkland course, with hard walking, and a canal forms the west boundary. Adjacent to 'Haigh Country Park' with many facilities.
*18 holes, 6423yds, Par 70, SSS 71, Course record 65.*
*Club membership 250.*
**Visitors** must contact professional in advance.
**Societies** apply in writing to professional.
**Green Fees** £5.90 (£8.50 weekends).
**Facilities** ⓛ ♀ 🖼 ⌐ℓ Ian Lee.
**Leisure** trolley for hire, putting green, practice area.
**Location** 2m NE off B5238
**Hotel** ★★ 64% Bel-Air Hotel, 236 Wigan Ln, WIGAN ☎ 01942 241410 12 ⇆ ℝ

**Wigan** Arley Hall, Haigh WN1 2UH ☎ 01257 421360
Among the best of Lancashire's 9-hole courses. The fine old clubhouse is the original Arley Hall, and is surrounded by a moat.
*9 holes, 6036yds, Par 70, SSS 69.*
*Club membership 200.*
**Visitors** must contact in advance.
**Societies** apply by telephone.
**Green Fees** £25 per day (£30 weekends & bank holidays).
**Facilities** ⊗ ⅢⅢ ⓛ ♀ ♀ ⚘
**Leisure** putting green.
**Location** 3m NE off B5238
**Hotel** ★★★ 65% Wigan/Standish Moat House, Almond Brook Rd, STANDISH ☎ 01257 499988 113 ⇆ ℝ

## WOODFORD  Map 07 SJ88

*Avro* Old Hall Ln SK7 1QR ☎ 0161 439 2709
An attractive, tight and challenging 9-hole course.
*9 holes, 5735yds, Par 69, SSS 68.*
*Club membership 400.*
**Visitors** restricted weekends and competition days.
**Societies** must contact The Hon Secretary, c/o 23 Meadowbank Avenue, Atherton, Manchester M49 9LB.
**Green Fees** not confirmed.
**Facilities** ⚘
**Location** W side of village on A5102
**Hotel** ★★★ 67% Bramhall Moat House, Bramhall Ln South, BRAMHALL ☎ 0161 439 8116 65 ⇆ ℝ

## WORSLEY  Map 07 SD70

**Ellesmere** Old Clough Ln M28 7HZ ☎ 0161 799 0554
Parkland course with natural hazards. Testing holes: 3rd (par 5), 9th (par 3), 13th (par 4). Hard walking.
*18 holes, 6248yds, Par 70, SSS 70, Course record 67.*
*Club membership 600.*
**Visitors** welcome except club competition days & bank holidays.
**Societies** apply in advance.
**Green Fees** £24 per day; £18 per round (£25 per day/round weekends).
**Facilities** ⊗ ⅢⅢ ⓛ ♀ ♀ ⚘ 🖼 ℓ Terry Morley.
**Leisure** trolley for hire, putting green.
**Location** N side of village off A580
**Hotel** ★★★ 61% Novotel, Worsley Brow, WORSLEY ☎ 0161 799 3535 119 ⇆ ℝ

# ● HAMPSHIRE ●

## ALDERSHOT  Map 04 SU85

**Army** Laffans Rd GU11 2HF ☎ 01252 540638
Picturesque heathland course with three par 3's, over 200 yds.
*18 holes, 6550yds, Par 71, SSS 71, Course record 67.*
*Club membership 750.*
**Visitors** may not play weekends.
**Societies** apply in writing.
**Green Fees** £22 per round; £30 per day.
**Facilities** ⊗ ⅢⅢ ⓛ ♀ 🖼 ℓ Graham Cowley.
**Leisure** putting green, practice area.
**Location** 1.5m N of town centre off A323/A325
**Hotel** ★★★ 69% Potters International Hotel, 1 Fleet Rd, ALDERSHOT ☎ 01252 344000 101 ⇆ ℝ

## ALRESFORD  Map 04 SU53

**Alresford** Cheriton Rd, Tichborne Down SO24 0PN ☎ 01962 733746
A testing downland course on well drained chalk.Now expanded to 18 holes, incorporating the original 12, but changing direction of play to give two starting points and two closing greens near clubhouse.
*18 holes, 5905yds, Par 69, SSS 68, Course record 65.*
*Club membership 720.*
**Visitors** must contact in advance but must play with member weekends & bank holidays.
**Societies** must telephone in advance.
**Green Fees** £30 per day; £18 per round (£37 per round weekends & bank holidays).
**Facilities** ⊗ ⅢⅢ ⓛ ♀ ♀ ⚘ 🖼 ⌐ℓ Malcolm Scott.
**Leisure** trolley for hire, putting green, practice area.
**Location** 1m S on B3046
**Hotel** ★★ 61% Swan Hotel, 11 West St, ALRESFORD ☎ 01962 732302 & 734427 23rm(10 ⇆)

## ALTON
Map 04 SU73

**Alton** Old Odiham Rd GU34 4BU ☎ 01420 82042
Undulating meadowland course.
*9 holes, 5744yds, Par 68, SSS 68, Course record 64.*
*Club membership 350.*
**Visitors** must contact in advance and must have a handicap certificate to play at weekends.
**Societies** must contact in advance.
**Green Fees** not confirmed.
**Facilities** ⊗ ⅢⅬ ⚑ ♀ ⚒ 🖻 ᒥ Paul Brown.
**Leisure** trolley for hire, putting green, practice area.
**Location** 2m N off A32
**Hotel** ★★★ 66% Alton House Hotel, Normandy St, ALTON ☎ 01420 80033 39 ➪ ℞

**Worldham Park** Cakers Ln, Worldham GU34 3AG
☎ 01420 543151
The course is in a picturesque woodland setting with an abundance of challenging holes (doglegs, water and sand). Increased to 18-holes in the summer of 1995.
*18 holes, 5800yds, Par 71, SSS 68.*
*Club membership 450.*
**Visitors** normally may play Mon-Fri.
**Societies** Mon-Fri only. Must contact in advance.
**Green Fees** £10 per round (£12 weekends).
**Facilities** ⊗ Ⅲ Ⅼ ⚑ ♀ 🖻 ᒥ
**Leisure** driving range, putting green.
**Location** B3004, 2mins from Alton
**Hotel** ★★★ 66% Grange Hotel, London Rd, ALTON ☎ 01420 86565 26 ➪ ℞Annexe4 ➪ ℞

## AMPFIELD
Map 04 SU42

**Ampfield Par Three** Winchester Rd SO51 9BQ
☎ 01794 368480
Pretty parkland course designed by Henry Cotton in 1963. Well-bunkered greens.
*18 holes, 2478yds, Par 54, SSS 53, Course record 49.*
*Club membership 470.*
**Visitors** must contact in advance & have a handicap certificate to play at weekends & bank holidays.
**Societies** must contact in advance.
**Green Fees** £15 per day; £9 per round (£15.50 per round weekends & bank holidays).
**Facilities** ⊗ Ⅲ by prior arrangement Ⅼ ⚑ ♀ ⚒ 🖻 ᒥ ᒥ Richard Benfield.
**Leisure** trolley for hire, putting green.
**Location** 4m NE of Romsey on A31
**Hotel** ★★★ 70% Potters Heron Hotel, Winchester Rd, AMPFIELD ☎ 01703 266611 54 ➪ ℞

## ANDOVER
Map 04 SU34

**Andover** 51 Winchester Rd SP10 2EF
☎ 01264 358040
Undulating downland course combining a good test of golf for all abilities with breathtaking views across Hampshire countryside. Well guarded greens and a notable par 3 9th (225yds) with the tee perched on top of a hill, 100ft above the green.
*9 holes, 6096yds, Par 70, SSS 69, Course record 66.*
*Club membership 450.*

# South Lawn Hotel & Restaurant ★★★ ◉

Milford-on-Sea, Lymington, Hampshire SO41 0RF
Tel: Lymington (01590) 643911 Fax: (01590) 644820

*Delightful Country House Hotel in peaceful surroundings where comfort and good food predominate. Owner/Chef Ernst Barten supervises excellent cuisine. Specially imported wines from Germany.*

*All rooms en-suite, colour TV, phone and trouser press. Facilities nearby include windsurfing and sailing from Keyhaven, Golf at Brockenhurst and Barton-on-Sea, the Beach at Milford and walking or riding in the beautiful New Forest.*

**Visitors** must contact in advance.
**Societies** Mon-Wed only. Must contact in advance.
**Green Fees** £15 per day; £10 per round; (£22 Sun & bank holidays).
**Facilities** ⊗ Ⅲ Ⅼ ⚑ ♀ ⚒ 🖻 ᒥ ᒥ D Lawrence.
**Leisure** trolley for hire, putting green, practice area.
**Location** 0.5m S on A3057
**Hotel** ★★ 61% Danebury Hotel, High St, ANDOVER ☎ 01264 323332 23 ➪ ℞

## ASHLEY HEATH
Map 04 SU10

**Moors Valley** Moors Valley Country Park, Horton Rd BH24 2ET ☎ 01425 479776
This municipal course is set in the beautiful surroundings of a country park. It offers a test for all standards. It is gently undulating, with water hazards on six holes.
*18 holes, 6200yds, Par 72, SSS 70.*
*Club membership 250.*
**Visitors** must contact in advance.
**Societies** telephone for availability.
**Green Fees** £8.50 per 18 holes; £5 per 11 holes (£11/£6 weekends).
**Facilities** ⊗ Ⅲ Ⅼ ⚑ ♀ ⚒ 🖻 ᒥ ᒥ Michael Torrens.
**Leisure** driving range.
**Location** Signposted from A31 Ashley Heath roundabout
**Hotel** ★★★ 66% St Leonards Hotel, ST LEONARDS ☎ 01425 471220 33 ➪ ℞

## BARTON-ON-SEA                    Map 04 SZ29

**Barton-on-Sea** Milford Rd BH25 5PP
☎ 01425 615308
Though not strictly a links course, it is right on a cliff
edge with views over the Isle of Wight and Christchurch
Bay. On a still day there is nothing much to it - but when
it blows the course undergoes a complete change in
character. Recently reconstructed to create 27 holes.
*Becton-Needles: 18 holes, 6505yds, Par 72, SSS 71.*
*Needles-Stroller: 18 holes, 6444yds, Par 72, SSS 71.*
*Stroller-Becton: 18 holes, 6289yds, Par 72, SSS 70.*
*Club membership 920.*

| | |
|---|---|
| Visitors | must contact in advance and have a handicap certificate. |
| Societies | must telephone oin advance. |
| Green Fees | £25 per day (£30 weekends & bank holidays). |
| Facilities | ⊗ ⅷ ⅃ ☂ ♀ ⅄ 🏠 ⛳ ⅃ Pat Coombs. |
| Leisure | motorised carts for hire, buggies for hire, trolley for hire, putting green, practice area, snooker. |
| Location | B3058 E side of town |
| Hotel | ★★★★★(red)🏨 Chewton Glen Hotel, Christchurch Rd, NEW MILTON ☎ 01425 275341 55 ⇄ ⻏Annexe2 ⇄ ⻏ |
| Additional hotel | ★★★ 74% South Lawn Hotel, Lymington Rd, MILFORD ON SEA ☎ 01590 643911 24 ⇄ ⻏ |

## BASINGSTOKE                    Map 04 SU65

**Basingstoke** Kempshott Park RG23 7LL
☎ 01256 465990
A well-maintained parkland course with wide and
inviting fairways. You are inclined to expect longer
drives than are actually achieved - partly on account of
the trees. There are many two-hundred-year-old beech
trees, since the course was built on an old deer park.
*18 holes, 6350yds, Par 70, SSS 70, Course record 67.*
*Club membership 700.*

| | |
|---|---|
| Visitors | must contact in advance and play Mon-Fri only (ex bank holidays). |
| Societies | must contact in advance. |
| Green Fees | £32 per day; £21 per round. |
| Facilities | ⊗ ⅷ ⅃ ☂ ♀ ⅄ 🏠 ⛳ ⅃ Ian Hayes. |
| Leisure | motorised carts for hire, buggies for hire, trolley for hire, putting green, practice area. |
| Location | 3.5m SW on A30 M3 exit 7 |
| Hotel | B Forte Posthouse Basingstoke, Grove Rd, BASINGSTOKE ☎ 01256 468181 84 ⇄ ⻏ |

*Dummer* Nr Basingstoke RG25 2AR
☎ 01256 397888
Opened in July 1993 and designed by Peter Alliss/Clive Clark
to consist of two 9-hole loops with water hazards. Gentle
terrain makes the course suitable for players of all ages.
*18 holes, 6556yds, Par 72.*
*Club membership 830.*

| | |
|---|---|
| Visitors | must contact in advance, handicap card required, limited at weekends. |
| Societies | contact in advance. |
| Green Fees | not confirmed. |
| Facilities | ⅄ 🏠 ⛳ ⅃ |

| | |
|---|---|
| Leisure | sauna. |
| Location | Off junc 7 of M3 towards Dummer village |
| Hotel | ★★★ 56% Wheatsheaf Hotel, NORTH WALTHAM ☎ 01256 398282 28 ⇄ ⻏ |

**Weybrook Park** Aldermaston Rd, Sherborne St John
RG24 9ND ☎ 01256 20347
A course designed to be enjoyable for all standards of player.
*18 holes, 5988yds, Par 70, SSS 69.*
*Club membership 530.*

| | |
|---|---|
| Visitors | telephone for availability. |
| Societies | telephone in advance for availability and confirm in writing. |
| Green Fees | £15 per 18 holes (£25 weekends & bank holidays; £20 Nov-Mar). |
| Facilities | ⊗ ⅃ ☂ ♀ ⅄ |
| Leisure | putting green, practice area. |
| Location | 2m W of town centre, entrance via A339 |
| Hotel | ★★★ 61% Ringway Hotel, Popley Way, Aldermaston Roundabout, Ringway North (A339), BASINGSTOKE ☎ 01256 20212 134 ⇄ ⻏ |

## BORDON                    Map 04 SU73

**Blackmoor** Firgrove Rd, Whitehill GU35 9EH
☎ 01420 472775
A first-class moorland course with a great variety of
holes. Fine greens and wide pine tree-lined fairways are a
distinguishing feature. The ground is mainly flat and
walking easy.
*18 holes, 6300yds, Par 69, SSS 70, Course record 65.*
*Club membership 750.*

| | |
|---|---|
| Visitors | must contact in advance and may not play at weekends. |
| Societies | must telephone in advance. |
| Green Fees | £30 per round. |
| Facilities | ⊗ ⅷ ⅃ ☂ ♀ ⅄ 🏠 ⅃ Stephen Clay. |
| Leisure | trolley for hire, putting green, practice area. |
| Hotel | ★★★ 62% Swan Hotel, High St, ALTON ☎ 01420 83777 36 ⇄ ⻏ |

## BOTLEY                    Map 04 SU51

*Botley Park Hotel & Country Club* Winchester Rd, Boorley
Green SO32 2UA ☎ 01489 780888
Pleasantly undulating course with water hazards. Driving
range and country club facilities.
*18 holes, 6026yds, Par 70, SSS 70.*
*Club membership 750.*

| | |
|---|---|
| Visitors | must play with member. Must contact in advance & have handicap certificate. |
| Societies | contact in advance. |
| Green Fees | not confirmed. |
| Facilities | ♀ ⅄ 🏠 ⛳ ⊠ ⅃ Tim Barter. |
| Leisure | hard tennis courts, heated indoor swimming pool, squash, sauna, solarium, gymnasium, croquet lawn & petanque. |
| Location | 1m NW of Botley on B3354 |
| Hotel | ★★★★ 68% Botley Park Hotel & Country Club, Winchester Rd, Boorley Green, BOTLEY ☎ 01489 780888 100 ⇄ ⻏ |

## ★★
# The Watersplash Hotel
### Brockenhurst in the New Forest

The Watersplash Hotel is recommended for its excellent food, friendly service and accommodation. Brokenhurst Manor Golf Club, situated just half a mile away, is one of ten courses within easy reach of the hotel. Personally supervised by resident proprietors Robin and Judy Foster who specialise in catering for the individual and small golf parties. Well-stocked bar and extensive wine list. All 23 bedrooms have private bathroom, colour TV, tea and coffee making facilities, direct dial telephone and radio. Heated outdoor pool in season. For further details ask for our colour brochure.

**The Watersplash Hotel, The Rise, Brockenhurst, Hampshire SO42 7ZP.**
**Tel: (01590) 622344  Fax: (01590) 624047**

---

**BROCKENHURST**　　　　　　　　Map 04 SU20

**Brokenhurst Manor** Sway Rd SO41 7SG
☎ 01590 623332 (Secretary) & 623092 (Pro Shop)
An attractive woodland/heathland course set at the edge of the New Forest, with the unusual feature of three loops of six holes each to complete the round. Fascinating holes include the short 5th and 12th, and the 4th and 17th, both dog-legged. A stream also features on seven of the holes.
*18 holes, 6222yds, Par 70, SSS 70, Course record 63.*
*Club membership 700.*
Visitors　　　must contact in advance, numbers limited.
Societies　　Thu only, apply in writing.
Green Fees　£35 per day; £28 per round (£40 weekends & bank holidays).
Facilities　　⊗ ⅲ by prior arrangement ᒪ ⬛ ♀ ㅿ 🏠 𝄢 John Lovell.
Leisure　　　trolley for hire, driving range, putting green, practice area.
Location　　1m S on B3055
Hotel　　　★★★ 66% Balmer Lawn Hotel, Lyndhurst Rd, BROCKENHURST
　　　　　　☎ 01590 623116 55 ⇥ 𝄖
Additional hotel　★★ 67% Watersplash Hotel, The Rise, BROCKENHURST
　　　　　　☎ 01590 622344 23 ⇥ 𝄖

---

**BURLEY**　　　　　　　　　　　Map 04 SU20

**Burley** Cott Ln BH24 4BB
☎ 01425 402431
Undulating heather and gorseland. The 7th requires an accurately placed tee shot to obtain par 4. Played off different tees on second nine.
*9 holes, 6149yds, Par 71, SSS 69, Course record 68.*
*Club membership 520.*
Visitors　　　must contact in advance & have a handicap certificate. May not play before 4pm Sat.
Green Fees　£14 per round/day (£16 weekends).
Facilities　　⊗ ᒪ ⬛ ♀ ㅿ
Leisure　　　trolley for hire, putting green, practice area.
Location　　E side of village
Hotel　　　★★★ 60% Moorhill House, BURLEY
　　　　　　☎ 01425 403285 24 ⇥ 𝄖

---

**CORHAMPTON**　　　　　　　　Map 04 SU62

**Corhampton** Sheep's Pond Ln SO32 3LP
☎ 01489 877279 & 877638
Free draining downland course situated in the heart of the picturesque Meon Valley.
*18 holes, 6444yds, Par 71, SSS 71.*
*Club membership 800.*
Visitors　　　weekdays only and must contact in advance.
Societies　　Mon & Thu only, contact in writing or telephone.
Green Fees　£30 per day; £20 per round.
Facilities　　⊗ ⅲ ᒪ ⬛ ㅿ 🏠 𝄢 Ian Roper.
Leisure　　　motorised carts for hire, buggies for hire, trolley for hire, driving range, putting green, practice area.
Location　　1m W of Corhampton, off B3035
Hotel　　　★★ 74% Old House Hotel, The Square, WICKHAM
　　　　　　☎ 01329 833049 9 ⇥ 𝄖Annexe3 ⇥ 𝄖

---

**CRONDALL**　　　　　　　　　Map 04 SU74

**Oak Park** Heath Ln GU10 5PB
☎ 01252 850880
Gently undulating course overlooking pretty village. 16-bay floodlit driving range, practice green and practice bunker. An additional 9-holes are due to be opened in Spring 1996.
*Woodland: 18 holes, 6240yds, Par 70, SSS 70.*
*Village: 9 holes, 3279yds, Par 36.*
*Club membership 600.*
Visitors　　　no restrictions for Village Course. Must book in advance and have a handicap certificate for Woodland Course.
Societies　　must telephone in advance.
Green Fees　Woodland: £25 per day; £16 per round (£40/£22.50 weekends & public holidays). Village: £8.50 per round.
Facilities　　⊗ ⅲ ᒪ ⬛ ♀ ㅿ 🏠 𝄚 𝄢 Simon Coaker.
Leisure　　　motorised carts for hire, trolley for hire, driving range, putting green, practice area.
Location　　0.5m E of village off A287
Hotel　　　★★★🏌 60% Farnham House Hotel, Alton Rd, FARNHAM
　　　　　　☎ 01252 716908 20 ⇥ 𝄖

## DIBDEN              Map 04 SU40

**Dibden** Main Rd SO45 5TB
☎ 01703 207508 & 845596
Municipal parkland course with views over Southampton
Water. A pond guards the green at the par 5, 3rd hole.
Twenty-bay driving range.
*Course 1: 18 holes, 5900yds, Par 70, SSS 69, Course record
63.*
*Course 2: 9 holes, 1400yds, Par 29.*
*Club membership 600.*
**Visitors**     must book in advance.
**Societies**    must contact in writing.
**Green Fees** 18 holes: £7.25 (£10.50 weekends); 9 holes:
               £3.40 (£4.75 weekends).
**Facilities**    ⊗ ⅏ ⓛ ▆ ♀ ♨ 🏠 ⚓ ℂ Alan Bridge.
**Leisure**      trolley for hire, driving range, putting green,
               practice area.
**Location**    2m NW of Dibden Purlieu
**Hotel**        ★★★ 65% Forest Lodge Hotel, Pikes Hill,
               Romsey Rd, LYNDHURST
               ☎ 01703 283677 23 ⇥ ℟

## EASTLEIGH           Map 04 SU41

*Fleming Park* Magpie Ln SO50 9LS
☎ 01703 612797
Parkland course with stream-'Monks Brook'-running
through.
*18 holes, 4436yds, Par 65, SSS 62.*
*Club membership 300.*
**Visitors**     no restrictions.
**Societies**    must contact in advance.
**Green Fees** not confirmed.
**Facilities**    ♀ ♨ 🏠 ⚓ ℂ Chris Strickett.
**Leisure**      putting green,trolley hire.
**Location**    E side of town centre
**Hotel**        ★★★ 63% Southampton Park Hotel,
               Cumberland Place, SOUTHAMPTON
               ☎ 01703 343343 72 ⇥ ℟

## EAST WELLOW        Map 04 SU32

**Wellow** Ryedown Ln SO51 6BD
☎ 01794 323833 & 322872
Three 9-hole courses set in 217 acres of parkland surrounding
Embley Park, former home of Florence Nightingale.
*Ryedown: 9 holes, 2745yds, Par 34.*
*Embley: 9 holes, 3221yds, Par 36.*
*Blackwater: 9 holes, 3099, Par 36.*
*Club membership 500.*
**Visitors**     advisable to contact in advance weekdays and
               weekends.
**Societies**    apply in writing or telephone, Mon-Fri not bank
               holidays.
**Green Fees** £17 per day; £15 per 18 holes; £9 per 9 holes
               (£20/£18/£11 weekends & bank holidays).
**Facilities**    ⊗ ⅏ ⓛ ▆ ♀ ♨ 🏠 ℂ Neil Bratley.
**Leisure**      motorised carts for hire, buggies for hire, trolley
               for hire, putting green, practice area.
**Location**    1m N from A36 to Salisbury then 1m right
**Hotel**        ★★★ 62% White Horse Hotel, Market Place,
               ROMSEY
               ☎ 01794 512431 33 ⇥ ℟

## FAREHAM             Map 04 SU50

**Cams Hall** Porchester Rd PO16 8UP
☎ 01329 827222 & 827732
Two Peter Alliss/Clive Clark designed golf courses opened in
1993. The Historic is in parkland and the Coastal has lakes
and undulating hills.
*Creek Course: 18 holes, 6244yds, Par 71, SSS 71, Course
record 69.*
*Park Course: 9 holes, 3059yds, Par 36, SSS 71.*
*Club membership 940.*
**Visitors**     must contact in advance, tee times available any
               time.
**Societies**    telephone for details and society golf day pack.
**Green Fees** £23.50 per 27 holes; £15 per 18 holes; £9.50 per
               9 holes (£30/£25/£12 weekends and bank
               holidays).
**Facilities**    ⊗ ⅏ ⓛ ▆ ♀ ♨ 🏠 ⚓ ℂ Jason Neve.
**Leisure**      sauna, motorised carts for hire, buggies for hire,
               trolley for hire, driving range, putting green.
**Location**    M27 exit 11 to A27
**Hotel**        ★★★ 67% Lysses House Hotel & Conference
               Centre, 51 High St, FAREHAM
               ☎ 01329 822622 21 ⇥ ℟

## FARNBOROUGH       Map 04 SU85

**Southwood** Ively Rd, Cove GU14 0LJ ☎ 01252 548700
Municipal parkland course with stream running through.
*18 holes, 5738yds, Par 69, SSS 68, Course record 61.*
*Club membership 650.*
**Visitors**     must book in advance.
**Societies**    must contact in advance.
**Green Fees** Summer: £11.50 (£14 weekends). Winter £7.50
               (£10.50 weekends).
**Facilities**    ⊗ ⅏ ⓛ ▆ ♀ ♨ 🏠 ⚓ ℂ Bob Hammond.
**Leisure**      motorised carts for hire, buggies for hire, trolley
               for hire, putting green, practice area.
**Location**    0.5m W
**Hotel**        B Forte Posthouse Farnborough, Lynchford Rd,
               FARNBOROUGH
               ☎ 01252 545051 110 ⇥ ℟

## FLEET                  Map 04 SU85

**North Hants** Minley Rd GU13 8RE ☎ 01252 616443
Picturesque tree-lined course with much heather and
gorse close to the fairways. A comparatively easy par-4
first hole may lull the golfer into a false sense of security,
only to be rudely awakened at the testing holes which
follow. The ground is rather undulating and, though not
tiring, does offer some excellent 'blind' shots, and more
than a few surprises in judging distance.
*18 holes, 6257yds, Par 69, SSS 70, Course record 65.*
*Club membership 600.*
**Visitors**     must contact at least 48 hours in advance.
               Must play with member at weekends.
**Societies**    Tue & Wed only. Must telephone in
               advance.
**Green Fees** £26 per round; £33 two rounds. With
               member only at weekends.
**Facilities**    ⊗ ⅏ ⓛ ▆ ♀ ♨ 🏠 ℂ Steve Porter.
**Leisure**      trolley for hire, driving range, putting green,
               practice area.                 ▶

> **Location** 0.25m N of Fleet station on B3013
> **Hotel** ★★★ 59% Lismoyne Hotel, Church Rd,
> FLEET ☎ 01252 628555 42 ⇔ ♠

## GOSPORT
Map 04 SZ69

**Gosport & Stokes Bay** Off Fort Rd, Haslar PO12 2AT
☎ 01705 527941
A testing links course overlooking the Solent, with plenty of gorse and short rough. Changing winds.
*9 holes, 5999yds, Par 70, SSS 69, Course record 65.*
*Club membership 460.*
**Visitors** may not play at weekends & Thu.
**Societies** must contact in writing.
**Green Fees** £15 per round (£20 weekends).
**Facilities** ⊗ ⋔ ⓛ ♥ ♀ ♨ 🏠 ✦
**Leisure** trolley for hire, putting green, practice area.
**Location** A32 S from Fareham,E on Fort rd to Haslar
**Hotel** ★★★ 60% Belle Vue Hotel, 39 Marine Pde East, LEE-ON-THE-SOLENT
☎ 01705 550258 24 ⇔ ♠Annexe3 ⇔ ♠

## HARTLEY WINTNEY
Map 04 SU75

**Hartley Wintney** London Rd RG27 8PT ☎ 01252 844211
Easy walking, parkland course in pleasant countryside.
Played off different tees on back nine, with testing par 4s at 4th and 13th.
*9 holes, 6096yds, Par 70, SSS 69.*
**Visitors** must contact in advance.
**Societies** Tue & Thu only by prior arrangement.
**Green Fees** £17 per round; £25 per day (£20.25/£31.25 weekends).
**Facilities** ⊗ ⋔ by prior arrangement ⓛ ♥ ♀
**Location** NE side of village on A30
**Hotel** ★★★ 59% Lismoyne Hotel, Church Rd, FLEET ☎ 01252 628555 42 ⇔ ♠

## HAYLING ISLAND
Map 04 SU70

> **Hayling** Links Ln PO11 0BX
> ☎ 01705 464446 & 464491
> A delightful links course among the dunes offering fine sea-scapes and views across to the Isle of Wight. Varying sea breezes and sometimes strong winds ensure that the course seldom plays the same two days running. Testing holes at the 12th and 13th, both par 4. Club selection is important.
> *18 holes, 5521yds, Par 71, SSS 71, Course record 65.*
> *Club membership 800.*
> **Visitors** must contact in advance and have a handicap certificate, no jeans or denims allowed.
> **Societies** welcome Tue & Wed, or half days Mon & Thu, apply in writing or telephone.
> **Green Fees** £30 per day (£40 weekends).
> **Facilities** ⊗ ⋔ ⓛ ♥ ♨ 🏠 ✦ ✦ Raymond Gadd.
> **Leisure** trolley for hire, putting green, practice area.
> **Location** SW side of island at West Town
> **Hotel** B Forte Posthouse Havant, Northney Rd, HAYLING ISLAND
> ☎ 01705 465011 92 ⇔ ♠

## KINGSCLERE
Map 04 SU55

> **Sandford Springs** Wolverton RG26 5RT
> ☎ 01635 297881
> The course has unique variety in beautiful surroundings and offers three distinctive loops of 9 holes. There are water hazards, woodlands and gradients to negotiate, providing a challenge for all playing categories. From its highest point there are extensive views.
> *The Park: 9 holes, 2963yds, Par 34.*
> *The Lakes: 9 holes, 3180yds, Par 36.*
> *The Wood: 9 holes, 3042yds, Par 35.*
> *Club membership 650.*
> **Visitors** must contact in advance. Restricted at weekends.
> **Societies** must contact in advance.
> **Green Fees** £23 per 18 holes, £15 per 9 holes.
> **Facilities** ⊗ ⋔ ⓛ ♥ ♀ ♨ 🏠 ✦
> ✦ Gary Edmunds/Kim Brake.
> **Leisure** buggies for hire, trolley for hire, putting green, practice ground.
> **Location** On A339
> **Hotel** ★★★ 61% Millwaters Hotel & Restaurant, London Rd, NEWBURY
> ☎ 01635 528838 30 ⇔ ♠

## KINGSLEY
Map 04 SU73

**Dean Farm** GU35 9NG ☎ 01420 489478 & 472313
Undulating downland course.
*9 holes, 1500yds, Par 29.*
**Visitors** no restrictions.
**Societies** must contact in writing.
**Green Fees** £6.50 per 18 holes; £4 per 9 holes.
**Facilities** ⓛ ♥ 🏠 ✦
**Leisure** hard tennis courts, putting green.
**Location** W side of village off B3004
**Hotel** ★★★ 66% Grange Hotel, London Rd, ALTON
☎ 01420 86565 26 ⇔ ♠Annexe4 ⇔ ♠

## LECKFORD
Map 04 SU33

*Leckford* SO20 6JG ☎ 01264 810320
A testing downland course with good views.
*9 holes, 6444yds, Par 70, SSS 71.*
*Club membership 200.*
**Visitors** must be accompanied by member and contact in advance.
**Green Fees** not confirmed.
**Facilities** ♨
**Location** 1m SW off A3057
**Hotel** ★★★ 62% Grosvenor Hotel, High St, STOCKBRIDGE ☎ 01264 810606 25 ⇔ ♠

## LEE-ON-THE-SOLENT
Map 04 SU50

**Lee-on-Solent** Brune Ln PO13 9PB ☎ 01705 551170
A modest parkland/heathland course, yet a testing one. The five short holes always demand a high standard of play and the 13th is rated one of the best in the country.
*18 holes, 5755yds, Par 69, SSS 69, Course record 64.*
*Club membership 750.*
**Visitors** may not play before 9am. Handicap certificate required.

**Societies**   must contact in advance.
**Green Fees**  £25 per day/round (£35 weekends).
**Facilities**  ⊗ 🎮 ⅊ ♟ ♀ ♨ 🏠 𝆑 John Richardson.
**Leisure**     trolley for hire, driving range, putting green,
                practice area.
**Location**    1m N off B3385
**Hotel**       ★★★ 60% Belle Vue Hotel, 39 Marine Pde
                East, LEE-ON-THE-SOLENT
                ☎ 01705 550258 24 ⇆ 𝆑Annexe3 ⇆ 𝆑

## LIPHOOK                                          Map 04 SU83

**Liphook** Wheatsheaf Enclosure GU30 7EH
☎ 01428 723271
Heathland course with easy walking and fine views.
*18 holes, 6247yds, Par 70, SSS 70, Course record 67.*
*Club membership 800.*
**Visitors**    must contact in advance; may not play Tue,
                competition days etc.
**Societies**   Wed-Fri only. Must contact in advance.
**Green Fees**  £37 per day; £29 per round (£47/£37 Sat,
                £47 per round Sun).
**Facilities**  ⊗ ⅊ ♟ ♀ ♨ 🏠 𝆑 Ian Large.
**Leisure**     trolley for hire, putting green, practice area.
**Location**    1m S on B2030 (old A3)
**Hotel**       ★★★★ 72% Lythe Hill Hotel, Petworth
                Rd, HASLEMERE
                ☎ 01428 651251 40 ⇆ 𝆑

*Old Thorns* Griggs Green GU30 7PE ☎ 01428 724555
A challenging 18-hole championship-standard course
designed around magnificent oaks, beeches and Scots
pine.
*18 holes, 6041yds, Par 72, SSS 70.*
**Visitors**    no restrictions.
**Societies**   must telephone in advance.
**Green Fees**  not confirmed.
**Facilities**  ♟ 🏠 𝆑 ♨ 𝆑
**Leisure**     hard tennis courts, heated indoor swimming
                pool, sauna, solarium, caddy cars.
**Location**    1m W on B2131
**Hotel**       ★★★ 76% Old Thorns Golf Course Hotel
                & Restaurant, Longmoor Rd, Griggs Green,
                LIPHOOK
                ☎ 01428 724555 28 ⇆ 𝆑Annexe5 𝆑
                *See advertisement on page 198*

## LYNDHURST                                        Map 04 SU20

**Bramshaw** Brook SO43 7HE ☎ 01703 813433
Two 18-hole courses. The Manor Course is landscaped
parkland with excellent greens, and features mature trees
and streams. The Forest course is set amidst beautiful
open forest. Easy walking. The Bell Inn Hotel, attached to
the club, provides fine accommodation just a wedge shot
from the first tee, and reserved tee times for its guests.
*Manor Course: 18 holes, 6517yds, Par 71, SSS 71.*
*Forest Course: 18 holes, 5925yds, Par 69, SSS 68.*
*Club membership 950.*
**Visitors**    must be accompanied by member at
                weekends and bank holidays.
**Societies**   apply in writing or telephone in advance.
**Green Fees**  £30 per day; £20 per round.
**Facilities**  ⊗ 🎮 ⅊ ♟ ♀ ♨ 🏠 𝆑 ♨ 𝆑 Clive Bonner.
**Leisure**     motorised carts for hire, buggies for hire,
                trolley for hire, putting, golfing rates at Bell
                Inn.
**Location**    On B3079 1m W of M27 junc 1
**Hotel**       ★★★ 67% Bell Inn, BROOK
                ☎ 01703 812214 22 ⇆

*New Forest* Southampton Rd SO43 7BU
☎ 01703 282450
This picturesque heathland course is laid out in a typical
stretch of the New Forest on high ground a little above
the village of Lyndhurst. Natural hazards include the
inevitable forest ponies. The first two holes are somewhat
teasing, as is the 485-yard (par 5) 9th. Walking is easy.
*18 holes, 5742yds, Par 69, SSS 68.*
*Club membership 900.*
**Visitors**    must contact in advance.
**Societies**   must contact in advance.
**Green Fees**  not confirmed.
**Facilities**  ♀ ♨ 🏠 𝆑 A Sackley.
**Leisure**     putting green,trolley hire.
**Location**    0.5m NE off A35
**Hotel**       ★★★ 71% Crown Hotel, High St,
                LYNDHURST ☎ 01703 282922 39 ⇆ 𝆑
**Additional**  QQQ The Penny Farthing Hotel, Romsey
**hotel**       Rd, LYNDHURST
                ☎ 01703 284422 11rm(10 ⇆ 𝆑)

## NEW MILTON                                       Map 04 SZ29

**Chewton Glen Hotel** Christchurch Rd BH25 6QS
☎ 01425 275341
A 9-hole, Par 3 course with the hotel grounds plus a practice
area. ONLY open to residents of the hotel or as a guest of a
member of the club.                                         ▶

🏵 English Tourist Board COMMENDED
ᵂᵂ ᵂᵂ

# THE PENNY FARTHING HOTEL  *AA*

### Romsey Road, Lyndhurst, Hampshire SO43 7AA
### Telephone: 01703 284422 Facsimile: 01703 284488

Ideally situated a moments walk from Lyndhurst High Street this smart family run Hotel offers centrally
heated rooms with ensuite, colour TV and tea/coffee facilities. There is a comfortable residents
lounge/Bar with Satellite TV and large private car park to the rear. Lyndhurst is the centre of the New
Forest and provides the main visitor information centre as well as a fine selection of shops, cafes,
restaurants and inns.

*9 holes, 854yds, Par 27.*
*Club membership 150.*
**Visitors** non residents must play with member.
**Societies** must contact in advance.
**Green Fees** £10 (non residents).
**Facilities** ⊗ ⅢⅢ ⅃⅄ ⬛ ♀ ☺ ⚑ ⋈
**Leisure** hard tennis courts, outdoor and indoor heated swimming pools, sauna, solarium, gymnasium, driving range, putting, practice area.
**Hotel** ★★★★★(red)⚘ Chewton Glen Hotel, Christchurch Rd, NEW MILTON
☎ 01425 275341 55 ⇥ 🐾Annexe 2 ⇥ 🐾

## OVERTON                                Map 04 SU54

**Test Valley** Micheldever Rd RG25 3DS ☎ 01256 771737
A new inland links course with fine turf fairways and greens laid out in traditonal links style with pot bunkers as a feature. There is strategic bunkering and ponds on this easy walking course on a well drained chalk subsoil. The 2nd, 4th, 12th, 14th and 17th holes are particularly challenging but every hole has its own appealing individual character.
*18 holes, 6811yds, Par 72, SSS 73, Course record 66.*
*Club membership 500.*
**Visitors** advisable to ring in advance.
**Societies** apply in writing or telephone in advance.
**Green Fees** £22 per day; £14 per 18 holes (£32/£20 weekends).
**Facilities** ⊗ ⅢⅢ ⅃⅄ ⬛ ♀ ⅄ ☺ ⚑ ⋈ ⋌ Terry Notley.
**Leisure** motorised carts for hire, buggies for hire, trolley for hire, putting green, practice area.
**Location** 1.5m N of A303
**Hotel** ★★★ 56% Wheatsheaf Hotel, NORTH WALTHAM ☎ 01256 398282 28 ⇥ 🐾

## OWER                                   Map 04 SU31

**Paultons Golf Centre** Old Salisbury Rd SO51 6AN
☎ 01703 813992 & 813345
A Pay and Play 18-hole course built within the original Paultons parkland which was laid out by 'Capability' Brown. There is also a 9-hole academy course, ideal for beginners or players wishing to improve their short games as well as a 20-bay floodlit driving range.
*18 holes, 6238yds, Par 71, SSS 70, Course record 72.*
*Academy: 9 holes, 1324yds, Par 27, SSS 27, Course record 24.*
**Visitors** pay & play.
**Societies** telephone for details.
**Green Fees** £17.50 per 18 holes; £6.50 per 9 holes (£18.50 per 18 holes weekends).
**Facilities** ⊗ ⅢⅢ ⅃⅄ ⬛ ♀ ⅄ ☺ ⚑
⋌ John Cave & Heath Teschner.
**Leisure** motorised carts for hire, buggies for hire, trolley for hire, floodlit driving range, putting green, practice area.
**Hotel** ★★★ 60% Bartley Lodge, Lyndhurst Rd, CADNAM ☎ 01703 812248 20 ⇥ 🐾

## PETERSFIELD                           Map 04 SU72

**Petersfield** Heath Rd GU31 4EJ
☎ 01730 262386 & 267732
Level part-heath and part-parkland course with a lake, two par 5s, 5 par 3s and good views.
*18 holes, 5603yds, Par 69, SSS 67, Course record 65.*
*Club membership 750.*

**Visitors** advisable to contact in advance for weekdays, must contact for weekends.
**Societies** booking form must be completed & deposit paid.
**Green Fees** £15 per round (£21 weekends & bank holidays), £21 Mon-Fri 36 holes.
**Facilities** ⊗ ⅃⅄ ⬛ ♀ ⅄ ☺ ⋌ Greg Hughes.
**Leisure** trolley for hire, practice area.
**Location** E side of town centre off A3
**Hotel** ★★★ 73% Spread Eagle Hotel, South St, MIDHURST
☎ 01730 816911 37 ⇥ 🐾Annexe 4 🐾

## PORTSMOUTH & SOUTHSEA              Map 04 SU60

**Great Salterns Public Course** Eastern Rd PO3 5HH
☎ 01705 664549 & 699519
Easy walking, seaside course with open fairways and testing shots onto well-guarded, small greens. Testing 13th hole, par 4, requiring 130yd shot across a lake.
*18 holes, 5610yds, Par 69, SSS 66, Course record 64.*
*Club membership 700.*
**Visitors** no restrictions.
**Societies** must contact in advance.
**Green Fees** not confirmed.
**Facilities** ♀ ☺ ⚑ ⋈ ⋌ Terry Healy.
**Location** NE of town centre on A2030
**Hotel** ★★★ 65% Hospitality Inn, St Helens Pde, SOUTHSEA
☎ 01705 731281 115 ⇥ 🐾

**Southsea** The Mansion, Great Salterns, Eastern Rd PO3 6QB
☎ 01705 664549
Municipal, meadowland course.
*18 holes, 5800yds, Par 71, SSS 68, Course record 64.*
*Club membership 400.*
**Visitors** no restrictions.
**Societies** must contact in advance, tel: 01705 664549.
**Green Fees** £10 per round.
**Facilities** ⊗ ⅢⅢ ⅃⅄ ⬛ ♀ ⅄ ☺ ⚑ ⋈ ⋌ Terry Healy.
**Leisure** trolley for hire, driving range, practice area.
**Location** 0.5m off M27
**Hotel** ★★★ 65% Hospitality Inn, St Helens Pde, SOUTHSEA ☎ 01705 731281 115 ⇥ 🐾

## ROMSEY                                 Map 04 SU32

**Dunwood Manor** Shootash Hill SO51 0GF
☎ 01794 340549
Undulating parkland course with fine views. Testing 1st hole: Reynolds Leap (par 4).
*18 holes, 5925yds, Par 69, SSS 68.*
*Club membership 720.*
**Visitors** always welcome advisable to contact in advance but not essential.
**Societies** must contact in advance.
**Green Fees** £28 per day; £20 per round (weekends subject to availability).
**Facilities** ⊗ ⅢⅢ ⅃⅄ ⬛ ♀ ⅄ ☺ ⚑ ⋈
⋌ Johnathan Simpson.
**Leisure** motorised carts for hire, buggies for hire, trolley for hire, putting green, practice area.
**Location** 4m W off A27
**Hotel** ★★★ 67% Bell Inn, BROOK
☎ 01703 812214 22 ⇥

**Romsey** Romsey Rd, Nursling SO16 0XW
☎ 01703 734637
Parkland/woodland course with narrow tree-lined fairways.
Six holes are undulating, rest are sloping. There are superb
views over the Test valley.
*18 holes, 5851yds, Par 69, SSS 68.*
*Club membership 900.*
**Visitors**      must play with member weekends and bank
                 holidays.
**Societies**    Mon, Tue & Thu, must contact in advance.
**Green Fees** £25 per day; £20 per round.
**Facilities**   ⊗ ⅶ ᴇ ♥ ♀ ♨ 🏠 ℓ Mark Desmond.
**Leisure**     trolley for hire, putting green, practice area.
**Location**    3m S on A3057
**Hotel**        ★★★ 62% New Forest Heathlands, Romsey
                 Rd, Ower, ROMSEY
                 ☎ 01703 814333 52 ⇄ 🐾

## ROTHERWICK                        Map 04 SU75

**Tylney Park** RG27 9AY ☎ 01256 762079
Parkland course. Practice area.
*18 holes, 6109yds, Par 70, SSS 69, Course record 67.*
*Club membership 730.*
**Visitors**      must be with member at weekends or have a
                 handicap certificate.
**Societies**    must apply by phone in advance.
**Green Fees** £23 per day; £18 per round (£28 per round
                 weekends).
**Facilities**   ⊗ ⅶ ᴇ ♥ ♀ ♨ 🏠 ℓ Chris De Bruin.
**Leisure**     motorised carts for hire, buggies for hire, trolley
                 for hire, putting green, practice area.
**Location**    0.5m SW
**Hotel**        ★★★★(red)♨ Tylney Hall Hotel,
                 ROTHERWICK
                 ☎ 01256 764881 35 ⇄ Annexe56 ⇄

## ROWLANDS CASTLE               Map 04 SU71

**Rowlands Castle** 31 Links Ln PO9 6AE
☎ 01705 412784
Exceptionally dry in winter, the flat parkland course is a
testing one with a number of tricky dog-legs and bunkers
much in evidence. The 7th, at 522yds, is the longest hole
on the course and leads to a well-guarded armchair green.
*18 holes, 6618yds, Par 72, SSS 72, Course record 69.*
*Club membership 800.*
**Visitors**      may not play Sat; must contact in advance.
**Societies**    Tue & Thu only; must contact in writing.
**Green Fees** £25 per round (£30 weekends and bank
                 holidays).
**Facilities**   ⊗ ⅶ ᴇ ♥ ♀ ♨ 🏠 ℓ Peter Klepacz.
**Leisure**     motorised carts for hire, buggies for hire,
                 trolley for hire, driving range, putting green,
                 practice area.
**Location**    W side of village off B2149
**Hotel**        ★★★ 69% Brookfield Hotel, Havant Rd,
                 EMSWORTH
                 ☎ 01243 373363 & 376383 40 ⇄ 🐾

## SHEDFIELD                        Map 04 SU51

**Meon Valley Hotel** Sandy Ln SO32 2HQ
☎ 01329 833455
It has been said that a golf course architect is as good as
the ground on which he has to work. Here Hamilton Stutt
had magnificent terrain at his disposal and a very good
and lovely parkland course is the result. There are three
holes over water. The hotel provides many sports
facilities.
*Meon Course: 18 holes, 6519yds, Par 71, SSS 71, Course
record 67.*
*Valley Course: 9 holes, 5770yds, Par 70, SSS 68.*
*Club membership 910.*
**Visitors**      may book up to seven days in advance, no
                 available am weekends and bank holidays.
**Societies**    telephone in advance, written confirmation.
**Green Fees** Meon Course: £30 per round (£40 weekends
                 & bank holidays). Valley Course: £10 per
                 round (£12 weekends & bank holidays).
**Facilities**   ⊗ ⅶ ᴇ ♥ ♀ ♨ 🏠 ✦ 🐾 ℓ Peter Green.
**Leisure**     hard tennis courts, heated indoor swimming
                 pool, squash, sauna, solarium, gymnasium,
                 motorised carts for hire, buggies for hire,
                 trolley for hire, driving range, putting green,
                 practice area.
**Location**    Off A334 between Botley and Wickham
**Hotel**        ★★★ 64% Meon Valley Hotel, Country
                 Club Resort, Sandy Ln, SHEDFIELD
                 ☎ 01329 833455 83 ⇄ 🐾

## SOUTHAMPTON                  Map 04 SU41

**Chilworth** Main Rd, Chilworth SO16 7JP
☎ 01703 733166
A course with two loops of nine holes, with a restricted
booking system to allow undisturbed play.
*Manor Golf Course: 18 holes, 5740yds, Par 69, SSS 69,
Course record 68.*
*Club membership 700.*
**Visitors**      must book in advance.
**Societies**    telephone in advance and complete booking
                 form, various packages available.
**Green Fees** £12 per 18 holes; £6 per 9 holes (£18/£9
                 weekends and bank holidays).
**Facilities**   ⊗ ⅶ ᴇ ♥ ♀ 🏠 ℓ Martin Butcher/Jon Barnes.
**Leisure**     trolley for hire, driving range, floodlit driving
                 range with 31 bays.
**Location**    A27 towards Romsey
**Hotel**        ★★★ 61% County Hotel, Highfield Ln,
                 Portswood, SOUTHAMPTON
                 ☎ 01703 359955 66 ⇄ 🐾

*Southampton* Golf Course Rd, Bassett SO16 7LE
☎ 01703 760478
This beautiful municipal parkland course always ensures a
good game, fast in summer, slow in winter. Three par 4's
over 450 yds.
*18 holes, 6213yds, Par 69, SSS 70.*
*Club membership 500.*
**Visitors**      no restrictions.
**Societies**    welcome.
**Green Fees** not confirmed.
**Facilities**   ♀ ♨ 🏠 ✦ ℓ
**Location**    4m N of city centre off A33           ▶

**Hotel**  ★★ 61% Star Hotel, High St,
SOUTHAMPTON
☎ 01703 339939 45rm(38 ⇶ ⁿ)

---

**Stoneham** Monks Wood Close, Bassett SO16 3TT
☎ 01703 769272
A hilly, heather course with sand or peat sub-soil; the
fairways are separated by belts of woodland and gorse to
present a varied terrain. The interesting 4th is a difficult
par 4 and the fine 11th has cross-bunkers about 150 yards
from the tee.
*18 holes, 6310yds, Par 72, SSS 69, Course record 63.*
*Club membership 800.*
**Visitors**       advisable to contact in advance.
**Societies**     Mon, Thu & Fri only. Must telephone in
advance.
**Green Fees**  £27 per day/round (£30 weekends & bank
holidays).
**Facilities**     ⊗ ⋔ ⓑ ☕ ♀ ᗢ 盒 ⌇ ℓ Ian Young.
**Location**     4m N of city centre off A27
**Hotel**         ★★★ 61% County Hotel, Highfield Ln,
Portswood, SOUTHAMPTON
☎ 01703 359955 66 ⇶ ⁿ

---

## SOUTHWICK                                    Map 04 SU60

*Southwick Park Naval Recreation Centre* Pinsley Dr
PO17 6EL  ☎ 01705 380131
Set in 100 acres of parkland.
*18 holes, 5972yds, Par 69, SSS 69.*
*Club membership 700.*
**Visitors**       must contact in advance and may play weekday
mornings only.
**Societies**     Tue only, telephone in advance.
**Green Fees**  not confirmed.
**Facilities**     ♀ ᗢ 盒 ⌇ ℓ John Green.
**Leisure**       pitch & putt, skittle alley.
**Location**     0.5m SE off B2177
**Hotel**         ★★ 74% Old House Hotel, The Square,
WICKHAM
☎ 01329 833049 9 ⇶ ⁿAnnexe3 ⇶ ⁿ

---

## TADLEY                                          Map 04 SU66

**Bishopswood** Bishopswood Ln RG26 4AT  ☎ 01734 812200
Wooded course, fairly tight, with stream and natural water
hazards.
*9 holes, 6474yds, Par 72, SSS 71, Course record 66.*
*Club membership 485.*
**Visitors**       must contact in advance. No play weekends or
bank holidays.
**Societies**     must contact by telephone.
**Green Fees**  £8 per 9 holes, £13 per 18 holes.
**Facilities**     ⊗ ⋔ ⓑ ☕ ♀ ᗢ 盒 ⌇ ℓ Steve Ward.
**Leisure**       floodlit driving range, putting green.
**Location**     1m W off A340
**Hotel**         ★★★ 73% Romans Hotel, Little London Rd,
SILCHESTER
☎ 01734 700421 11 ⇶ ⁿAnnexe14 ⇶ ⁿ

---

Entries with a shaded background identify
courses that are considered to be particularly
interesting

---

## WATERLOOVILLE                            Map 04 SU60

**Portsmouth** Crookhorn Ln, Purbrook PO7 5QL
☎ 01705 372210
Hilly, challenging course with good views of Portsmouth
Harbour. Rarely free from the wind and the picturesque 6th,
17th and 18th holes can test the best.
*18 holes, 6139yds, Par 69, SSS 70, Course record 64.*
*Club membership 700.*
**Visitors**       must book in advance.
**Societies**     must book in advance, in writing or by
telephone.
**Green Fees**  Apr-Oct: £16 per day; £9.90 per 18 holes; £6 per
9 holes. Nov-Dec: £7.60 per 18 holes; £4.40 per
9 holes.
**Facilities**     ⊗ ⋔ ⓑ ☕ ♀ ᗢ 盒 ⌇
ℓ Jason Banting/Mike Holman.
**Leisure**       putting green, practice area, lessons available.
**Location**     2m S, off A3
**Hotel**         ★★★ 61% The Bear Hotel, East St,  HAVANT
☎ 01705 486501 42 ⇶ ⁿ

---

*Waterlooville* Cherry Tree Av, Cowplain PO8 8AP
☎ 01705 263388
Parkland course, easy walking.
*18 holes, 6647yds, Par 72, SSS 72.*
*Club membership 800.*
**Visitors**       must contact in advance & may only play on
weekdays.
**Societies**     Thu only; apply by letter.
**Green Fees**  not confirmed.
**Facilities**     ♀ ᗢ 盒 ⌇ ℓ John Hay.
**Leisure**       putting green,practice area,trolley hire.
**Location**     NE side of town centre off A3
**Hotel**         B Forte Posthouse Havant, Northney Rd,
HAYLING ISLAND
☎ 01705 465011 92 ⇶ ⁿ

---

## WINCHESTER                                  Map 04 SU42

**Hockley** Twyford SO21 1PL  ☎ 01962 713165
High downland course with good views.
*18 holes, 6296yds, Par 71, SSS 70, Course record 69.*
*Club membership 650.*
**Visitors**       are advised to phone in advance.
**Societies**     must telephone in advance and confirm in
writing with deposit.
**Green Fees**  £28.
**Facilities**     ⊗ ⋔ ⓑ ☕ ♀ ᗢ 盒 ⌇ ℓ Terry Lane.
**Leisure**       trolley for hire, driving range, putting green,
practice area.
**Location**     2m S via junct 12 on M27
**Hotel**         B Forte Posthouse Winchester, Paternoster Row,
WINCHESTER ☎ 01962 861611 94 ⇶ ⁿ

---

*Royal Winchester* Sarum Rd SO22 5QE
☎ 01962 852462
The Royal Winchester course is a sporting downland
course centred on a rolling valley, so the course is hilly in
places. After a disastrous fire in 1994, a new clubhouse
was built (opened August 1995). Royal Winchester must
be included in any list of notable clubs, because of its age
(it dates from 1888) and also because the club was
involved in one of the very first professional matches.

*18 holes, 6212yds, Par 71, SSS 70, Course record 7.*
*Club membership 772.*

| | |
|---|---|
| Visitors | must play with member at weekends. Must contact in advance and have a handicap certificate. |
| Societies | must contact in writing. |
| Green Fees | not confirmed. |
| Facilities | ♀ ⚘ 🏠 ⚑ ⌾ Steven Hunter. |
| Leisure | practice area, trolley hire. |
| Location | 1.5m W off A3090 |
| Hotel | ★★★★🏨 78% Lainston House Hotel, Sparsholt, WINCHESTER ☎ 01962 863588 38 ⇌ ✿ |

**South Winchester** Pitt SO22 5QW
☎ 01962 877800 & 840469
Opened in September 1993, this Peter Alliss/Clive Clark course incorporates downland, meadows and seven lakes. Visitors are only welcome if playing with a memember.
*18 holes, 7086yds, Par 72, SSS 74.*
*Club membership 750.*

| | |
|---|---|
| Visitors | members guests only. |
| Societies | must contact in advance. |
| Green Fees | with member only £15 (£24 weekends). |
| Facilities | ⊗ ⅲ ᴽ 🐦 ♀ ⚘ 🏠 ⚑ ⌾ Richard Adams. |
| Leisure | motorised carts for hire, driving range, putting green, practice area. |
| Location | toff A3090) |
| Hotel | ★★★ 70% Royal Hotel, Saint Peter St, WINCHESTER ☎ 01962 840840 75 ⇌ ✿ |

# HEREFORD & WORCESTER

## ALVECHURCH           Map 07 SP07

**Kings Norton** Brockhill Ln, Weatheroak B48 7ED
☎ 01564 826706 & 826789
An old club with three, 9-hole courses; the Blue, Red and Yellow. Parkland with some exacting water hazards, it has housed important events. There is also a 12-hole, par 3 course.
*Red Course: 9 holes, 3372yds, Par 36, SSS 36.*
*Blue Course: 9 holes, 3382yds, Par 36, SSS 36.*
*Yellow Course: 9 holes, 3290yds, Par 36, SSS 36.*
*Club membership 1000.*

| | |
|---|---|
| Visitors | must contact in advance. No visitors at weekends |
| Societies | must telephone in advance. |
| Green Fees | £29.50 per 27 holes; £27 per 18 holes. |
| Facilities | ⊗ ⅲ 🐦 ᴽ ♀ ⚘ 🏠 ⌾ Kevan Hayward. |
| Leisure | trolley for hire, putting green, practice area. |
| Location | M42 junct3, off A435 |
| Hotel | ★★★ 73% Pine Lodge Hotel, Kidderminster Rd, BROMSGROVE ☎ 01527 576600 114 ⇌ ✿ |

★★★★ ◎◎

# LAINSTON HOUSE HOTEL

*where English Tradition remains our hallmark*

Set in sixty three acres of tranquil Hampshire downland, just 2½ miles from the Historic Cathedral City of Winchester. Lainston House is an elegant William and Mary House with thirty eight individually designed bedrooms and suites. The charm of the reception rooms is enhanced by the peace and serenity of this period house. The highly praised restaurant offers gourmet food freshly prepared with local ingredients and the superb service is complemented by breathtaking views over the tranquil parkland. Lainston House offers weekend tariffs and special events throughout the year.

*Golf can be arranged at The Royal Winchester Golf Club which is 2 miles away*

**Lainston House Hotel & Restaurant, Sparsholt, Winchester, Hampshire SO21 2LT**
**Telephone: (01962) 863588  Fax: (01962) 776672.**
*Situated on the A272 Stockbridge Road out of Winchester*

## BEWDLEY                               Map 07 SO77

**Little Lakes Golf and Country Club** Lye Head DY12 2UZ
☎ 01299 266385
A pleasant undulating parkland course extended to 18 holes
in April 1995. The course offers some pleasing views and
several demanding holes.
*18 holes, 5812yds, Par 69.*
*Club membership 500.*
**Visitors**      must contact in advance.
**Societies**     must telephone in advance.
**Green Fees** not confirmed.
**Facilities**    ♀ ♨ 🏠 𝐶 Mark A Laing.
**Leisure**       hard tennis courts, outdoor swimming pool,
                  fishing, putting green, cart/buggy/trolley hire.
**Location**      2.25m W off A456
**Hotel**         ★★ 64% The George Hotel, Load St,
                  BEWDLEY
                  ☎ 01299 402117 13rm(2 ⇌8 🏠)

**Wharton Park** Longbank DY12 2QW
☎ 01299 405222 & 405163
18-hole championship-standard course in 140 acres of
countryside. Some long Par 5s on the 6th (577yds) and the
9th (525yds)as well as superb par 3 holes at 3rd, 7th, 12th
make this a very challenging course.
*18 holes, 6603yds, Par 73, SSS 72, Course record 66.*
*Club membership 330.*
**Visitors**      must contact in advance.
**Societies**     prior booking required.
**Green Fees** £25 per day; £15 per round (£32/£22 weekends
                  and bank holidays).
**Facilities**    ⊗ Ⓧ Ꮟ ▬ ♀ ♨ 🏠 𝐶 Angus Hoare.
**Leisure**       fishing, motorised carts for hire, buggies for hire,
                  trolley for hire, driving range, putting green.
**Location**      Off A456 Bewdley bypass
**Hotel**         ★★ 64% The George Hotel, Load St,
                  BEWDLEY
                  ☎ 01299 402117 13rm(2 ⇌8 🏠)

## BISHAMPTON                            Map 03 SO95

**Vale Golf & Country Club** Hill Furze Rd WR10 2LZ
☎ 01386 462781
Opened in 1991 this course offers an American-style layout,
with large greens, trees and bunkers and several water
hazards. Its rolling fairways provide a testing round, as well
as superb views of the Malvern Hills. Picturesque and
peaceful. Also 9-hole course and 20-bay driving range.
*International Course: 18 holes, 7114yds, Par 74, SSS 74.*
*Lenches Course: 9 holes, 2759yds, Par 35, SSS 34.*
*Club membership 650.*
**Visitors**      may play International course after 10.30am
                  weekends. Booking in advance.
**Societies**     must apply in advance.
**Green Fees** International: £18 (£24 weekends). Lenches: 18
                  holes £12; 9 holes £7.50 (£16/£9.50 weekends).
**Facilities**    ⊗ Ⓧ Ꮟ ▬ ♀ ♨ 🏠 𝐶 Caroline Griffiths.
**Leisure**       fishing, motorised carts for hire, buggies for hire,
                  trolley for hire, driving range, putting green,
                  practice area, archery, clay pigeon shooting.
**Location**      Signposted off A4538
**Hotel**         ★★ 65% The Chequers Inn, Chequers Ln,
                  FLADBURY
                  ☎ 01386 860276 & 860527 8 ⇌ 🏠

## BLAKEDOWN                             Map 07 SO87

**Churchill and Blakedown** Churchill Ln DY10 3NB
☎ 01562 700018
Pleasant course on hilltop with extensive views.
*9 holes, 6472yds, Par 72, SSS 71, Course record 63.*
*Club membership 380.*
**Visitors**      with member only weekends & bank holidays.
                  Handicap certificate required.
**Societies**     by arrangement through secretary.
**Green Fees** £17.50 per day/round.
**Facilities**    ⊗ Ⓧ Ꮟ ▬ ♀ ♨ 🏠 𝐶 K Wheeler.
**Leisure**       trolley for hire, putting green, practice area.
**Location**      W side of village off A456
**Hotel**         ★★★★ 59% Stone Manor Hotel, Stone,
                  KIDDERMINSTER
                  ☎ 01562 777555 52 ⇌ 🏠

## BRANSFORD                            Map 03 SO75

**Bank House Hotel Golf & Country Club** WR6 5JD
☎ 01886 833551
Designed by Bob Sandow, the Pine Lakes course is in the
'Florida' style with fairways weaving between water courses,
13 lakes and sculptured mounds with colourful plant displays.
The 6,210yd course has doglegs, island greens and tight
fairways to challenge all standards of player. The 10th, 16th
and 18th (TheDevil's Elbow) are particularly tricky.
*18 holes, 6101yds, Par 72, SSS 70.*
*Club membership 350.*
**Visitors**      all tee times must be booked, no play before
                  9.30am.
**Societies**     contact the secretary, all tee times must be
                  booked in advance.
**Green Fees** not confirmed.
**Facilities**    ♀ ♨ 🏠 ⍾ ▣ 𝐶 Craig George.
**Leisure**       outdoor swimming pool, fishing, sauna,
                  solarium, gymnasium, caddy cars, elec trolleys,
                  practice area.
**Location**      3m S of Worcester, A4103
**Hotel**         ★★★ 68% Fownes Hotel, City Walls Rd,
                  WORCESTER
                  ☎ 01905 613151 61 ⇌ 🏠

## BROADWAY                             Map 04 SP03

**Broadway** Willersey Hill WR12 7LG
☎ 01386 853683
At the edge of the Cotswolds this downland course lies at an
altitude of 900 ft above sea level, with extensive views.
*18 holes, 6216yds, Par 72, SSS 70, Course record 65.*
*Club membership 850.*
**Visitors**      may not play Sat between Apr-Sep before 3pm.
                  Restricted play Sun. Must contact in advance.
**Societies**     Wed-Fri, must contact in advance.
**Green Fees** £33 per day; £27 per round (£33 per round/day
                  weekends & bank holidays).
**Facilities**    ⊗ Ⓧ Ꮟ ▬ ♀ ♨ 🏠 ⍾ 𝐶 Martyn Freeman.
**Leisure**       trolley for hire, putting green, practice area.
**Location**      1.5m E on A44
**Hotel**         ★★★ 68% Dormy House Hotel, Willersey Hill,
                  BROADWAY
                  ☎ 01386 852711 26 ⇌ 🏠Annexe23 ⇌

## BROMSGROVE
Map 07 SO97

**Blackwell** Blackwell B60 1PY ☎ 0121 445 1994
Pleasantly undulating parkland with a variety of trees. Laid out in two 9-hole loops.
*18 holes, 6202yds, Par 70, SSS 71, Course record 63.*
**Visitors** must contact in advance, must have handicap certificate.
**Societies** must contact in advance.
**Green Fees** not confirmed.
**Facilities** ♀ ♣ 🏠 ⛳ Nigel Blake.
**Leisure** putting green,cart/trolley hire.
**Location** 2m W of Alvechurch
**Hotel** ★★★ 73% Pine Lodge Hotel, Kidderminster Rd, BROMSGROVE ☎ 01527 576600 114 ⇄ ⋒

**Bromsgrove Golf Centre** Stratford Rd B60 1LD ☎ 01527 575886
Gently undulating parkland course with large contoured greens, generous tee surfaces and superb views over Worcestershire. Tricky par 3 16th across a lake. Also 41 bay floodlit driving range, floodlit practice bunker and new clubhouse with conference facilities.
*18 holes, 5366mtrs, Par 68, SSS 68.*
*Club membership 900.*
**Visitors** dress restriction, no T-shirts, jeans, tracksuits etc. 7 day booking facilities available.
**Societies** weekdays only, apply in writing or telephone.
**Green Fees** £11 per 18 holes; £6.50 per 9 holes (£13.50/£8 weekends & bank holidays).
**Facilities** ⊗ ⅷ ▐ ▆ ♀ ♣ 🏠 ⛳ Graeme Long.
**Leisure** trolley for hire, floodlit driving range, putting green, practice area.
**Location** E side of Bromsgrove, 6m W of Alvechurch
**Hotel** ★★★ 73% Pine Lodge Hotel, Kidderminster Rd, BROMSGROVE ☎ 01527 576600 114 ⇄ ⋒

## DROITWICH
Map 03 SO86

**Droitwich** Ford Ln WR9 0BQ ☎ 01905 774344 (Secretary) & 770207 (Pro)
Undulating parkland course.
*18 holes, 6058yds, Par 70, SSS 69, Course record 62.*
*Club membership 732.*
**Visitors** with member only weekends & bank holidays.
**Societies** must apply by telephone or letter.
**Green Fees** £24 per day.
**Facilities** ⊗ ⅷ ▐ ▆ ♀ ♣ 🏠 ⛳ C Thompson.
**Leisure** trolley for hire, putting green, practice area.
**Location** 1.5m N off A38
**Hotel** ★★★★ 66% Chateau Impney Hotel, DROITWICH ☎ 01905 774411 67 ⇄ ⋒

**Ombersley** Bishops Wood Rd, Lineholt, Ombersley WR9 0LE ☎ 01905 620747
Undulating course in beautiful countryside high above the edge of the Severn Valley. Covered driving range and putting green.
*18 holes, 6139yds, Par 72, SSS 69.*
*Club membership 750.*
**Visitors** suitable dress expected, no jeans.
**Societies** telephone in advance.
**Green Fees** £13.30 per 18 holes (£10 off peak).

**Facilities** ⊗ ⅷ ▐ ▆ ♀ ♣ 🏠 ⛳ Graham Glenister.
**Leisure** motorised carts for hire, buggies for hire, trolley for hire, driving range, putting green, practice area.
**Location** 3m W of Droitwich, off A449
**Hotel** ★★★★ 61% Raven Hotel, St Andrews St, DROITWICH ☎ 01905 772224 72 ⇄ ⋒

## FLADBURY
Map 03 SO94

**Evesham** Craycombe Links, Old Worcester Rd WR10 2QS ☎ 01386 860395
Parkland, heavily wooded, with the River Avon running alongside 5th and 14th holes. Good views. Nine greens played from eighteen different tees.
*9 holes, 6415yds, Par 72, SSS 71, Course record 68.*
*Club membership 383.*
**Visitors** must contact in advance. With members only at weekends.
**Societies** must apply by letter.
**Green Fees** £15 per day/round.
**Facilities** ⊗ by prior arrangement ⅷ by prior arrangement ▐ ▆ ♀ ♣ 🏠 ⛳ Charles Haynes.
**Leisure** motorised carts for hire, trolley for hire, driving range, putting green, practice area.
**Location** 0.75m N on A4538
**Hotel** ★★★ 69% The Evesham Hotel, Coopers Ln, off Waterside, EVESHAM ☎ 01386 765566 & 0800 716969 (Res) 40 ⇄ ⋒
**Additional** ★★ 65% The Chequers Inn, Chequers Ln,
**hotel** FLADBURY ☎ 01386 860276 & 860527 8 ⇄ ⋒

# THE
# CHEQUERS
# INN

AA
★★

English Tourist Board
COMMENDED

An old English village Inn offering exceptional accommodation, good food and hospitality. Eight en suite rooms all with colour TV/Sky and tea/coffee facilities.
**Golf Breaks – 3 days Dinner, Bed & Breakfast, 4 days golf (different courses) – £225 per person.**
**FLADBURY, PERSHORE, WORCESTERSHIRE WR10 2PZ
TELEPHONE: (01386) 860276**

## HEREFORD
Map 03 SO53

**Belmont Lodge** Belmont HR2 9SA ☎ 01432 352666
Partly wooded course, the second half of which is on the banks of the River Wye.
*18 holes, 6490yds, Par 71.*
*Club membership 550.*
**Visitors** advised to contact in advance at weekends.
**Societies** must telephone in advance.
**Green Fees** summer: £22 per day; £15 per round (£30/£25 weekends). winter: £18 per day; £10 per round (£20/£16 weekends.
**Facilities** ⊗ ⅷ � ⬛ ♀ ⛳ 🏌 ⛳ 𝔣 Mike Welsh.
**Leisure** hard tennis courts, fishing, buggies for hire, trolley for hire, putting green, practice area, bowling green.
**Location** 2m S off A465
**Hotel** ★★★ 62% Belmont Lodge & Golf Course, Belmont, HEREFORD
☎ 01432 352666 30 ⇔ 𝔣

**Burghill Valley** Tillington Rd, Burghill HR4 7RW
☎ 01432 760456
The course is situated in typically beautiful Herefordshire countryside. The walking is easy on gently rolling fairways with a background of hills and woods and in the distance, the Welsh mountains. Some holes have been constructed through mature cider orchards and there are two lakes to negotiate. A fair but interesting test for players of all abilities.
*18 holes, 6239yds, Par 71, SSS 70.*
*Club membership 600.*
**Visitors** contact in advance.
**Societies** apply in writing or telephone in advance.
**Green Fees** £15 per round (£18 weekends & bank holidays).
**Facilities** ⊗ ⅷ � ⬛ ♀ ⛳ 𝔣 Nigel Clarke.
**Leisure** buggies for hire, trolley for hire, putting green, practice area.
**Location** 4m NW of Hereford
**Hotel** ★★★ 62% The Green Dragon, Broad St, HEREFORD ☎ 01432 272506 87 ⇔ 𝔣

**Hereford Municipal** Hereford Leisure Centre, Holmer Rd HR4 9UD ☎ 01432 344376
This municipal parkland course is more challenging than first appearance. The well-drained greens are open all year round with good drainage for excellent winter golf.
*9 holes, 3060yds, Par 35, SSS 69.*
*Club membership 85.*
**Visitors** restrictions on race days.
**Societies** telephone in advance.
**Green Fees** £5.35 per 18 holes; £3.30 per 9 holes (£7.20/£4.50 weekends).
**Facilities** ⊗ ⅷ � ⬛ ♀ ⛳ 𝔣 Philip Brookes.
**Leisure** squash, sauna, gymnasium, trolley for hire, putting green, practice area.
**Location** Adjacent to race course & leisure centre
**Hotel** ★★ 64% The Merton Hotel & Governors Restaurant, 28 Commercial Rd, HEREFORD ☎ 01432 265925 19 ⇔ 𝔣

## HOLLYWOOD
Map 07 SP07

**Gay Hill** Hollywood Ln B47 5PP
☎ 0121 430 8544 & 6523
A meadowland course, some 7m from Birmingham.

*18 holes, 6532yds, Par 72, SSS 71, Course record 64.*
*Club membership 740.*
**Visitors** must contact in advance.
**Societies** telephone in advance.
**Green Fees** £28.50 per day (weekdays).
**Facilities** ⊗ ⅷ � ⬛ ♀ ⛳ 🏌 𝔣 Andrew Hill.
**Leisure** trolley for hire, putting green, practice area.
**Location** N side of village
**Hotel** ★★★★ 61% Regency Hotel, Stratford Rd, Shirley, SOLIHULL
☎ 0121 745 6119 112 ⇔ 𝔣

## KIDDERMINSTER
Map 07 SO87

**Habberley** Low Trimpley DY11 5RG
☎ 01562 745756
Very hilly, wooded parkland course.
*9 holes, 5481yds, Par 69, Course record 62.*
*Club membership 300.*
**Visitors** may only play weekends with a member,
**Societies** telephone initially.
**Green Fees** on application.
**Facilities** ⊗ ⅷ � ⬛ ♀ ⛳
**Location** 2m NW
**Hotel** ★★★★ 59% Stone Manor Hotel, Stone, KIDDERMINSTER
☎ 01562 777555 52 ⇔ 𝔣

**Kidderminster** Russell Rd DY10 3HT ☎ 01562 822303
Parkland course with natural hazards and some easy walking.
*18 holes, 6405yds, Par 72, SSS 71, Course record 66.*
*Club membership 800.*
**Visitors** with member only weekends & bank holidays.
**Societies** Thu only, apply in advance.
**Green Fees** £30 per day; £22 per round.
**Facilities** ⊗ ⅷ � ⬛ ♀ ⛳ 𝔣 Nick Underwood.
**Leisure** trolley for hire, putting green, practice area.
**Location** 0.5m SE of town centre, signposted off A449
**Hotel** ★★★★ 59% Stone Manor Hotel, Stone, KIDDERMINSTER
☎ 01562 777555 52 ⇔ 𝔣

## KINGTON
Map 03 SO25

**Kington** Bradnor Hill HR5 3RE
☎ 01544 230340 & 231320
The highest 18-hole course in England, with magnificent views over seven counties. A natural heathland course with easy walking on mountain turf cropped by sheep. There is bracken to catch any really bad shots but no sand traps.
*18 holes, 5980yds, Par 70, SSS 68, Course record 65.*
*Club membership 640.*
**Visitors** contact the professional.
**Societies** must book in advance through the Hon Secretary.
**Green Fees** £18 per day; £13 per round (£22/£16 weekends & bank holidays).
**Facilities** ⊗ ⅷ � ⬛ ♀ ⛳ 🏌 𝔣 Dean Oliver.
**Leisure** trolley for hire, driving range, putting green, practice area.
**Location** 0.5m N of Kington, off B4355
**Hotel** ★★ 67% Talbot Hotel, West St, LEOMINSTER
☎ 01568 616347 20 ⇔ 𝔣

★★

*West Street - Leominster - Herefordshire - HR6 8EP*

*A coaching inn originating from the 15th century, oak beams, log fire and traditional hospitality. Leominster lies in an 'undiscovered' corner of England – memorable for its beautiful countryside, black and white villages and wealth of antique shops – an easy drive to Wye Valley, Malvern Hills, Welsh Marches and Ironbridge, home of the industrial revolution.*

\* \* \* \* \* \* \* \* \* \* \* \*

**The Talbot Hotel Offers A Two Day Golfing Break**
*Dinner, Bed and Breakfast PLUS two days golf at Leominster 18 hole course – £127 per person*
**OR**
*Kington Golf Course £133 per person*
**Enquiries, Hotel Brochure and Further Information**
**Telephone 01568 616347**

## LEOMINSTER
Map 03 SO45

**Leominster** Ford Bridge HR6 0LE
☎ 01568 611402 & 610055
Sheltered parkland course alongside River Lugg with undulating land for nine holes.
*18 holes, 6029yds, Par 70, SSS 69.*
*Club membership 550.*
**Visitors**    must contact in advance.
**Societies**    must telephone in advance.
**Green Fees** £18 per day; £14.50 per round (£21 per day weekends & bank holidays).
**Facilities**    ⊗ ⅶ Ⅱ ❤ ♀ ⚐ ⛳ ✆ Andrew Ferriday.
**Leisure**    fishing, trolley for hire, driving range, putting green.
**Location**    3m S on A49
**Hotel**    ★★ 57% Royal Oak Hotel, South St, LEOMINSTER
☎ 01568 612610 17 ⇆ ℝAnnexe1 ⇆ ℝ
**Additional**    ★★ 67% Talbot Hotel, West St,
**hotel**    LEOMINSTER ☎ 01568 616347 20 ⇆ ℝ

## MALVERN WELLS
Map 03 SO74

**Worcestershire** Wood Farm, Hanley Rd WR14 4PP
☎ 01684 575992 & 573905
Fairly easy walking on windy downland course with trees, ditches and other natural hazards. Outstanding views of Malvern Hills and Severn Valley. 17th hole (par 5) is approached over small lake.
*18 holes, 6449yds, Par 71, SSS 71, Course record 65.*
*Club membership 770.*

**Visitors**    only after 10am at weekends or with a member. Must contact in advance.
**Societies**    Thu & Fri only, apply in writing.
**Green Fees** £25 per day (£30 weekends & bank holidays).
**Facilities**    ⊗ ⅶ Ⅱ ❤ ♀ ⚐ ✆ Grahame Harris.
**Leisure**    trolley for hire, putting green, practice area.
**Location**    2m S of Gt Malvern on B4209
**Hotel**    ★★★⚑ 70% The Cottage in the Wood Hotel, Holywell Rd, Malvern Wells, MALVERN
☎ 01684 575859 8 ⇆ ℝAnnexe12 ⇆ ℝ

## REDDITCH
Map 07 SP06

**Abbey Park Golf & Country Club** Dagnell End Rd B98 9BE
☎ 01527 68006
Young parkland course opened in 1985, with rolling fairways. A 'Site of Special Scientific Interest', the course includes two fly-fishing lakes and is pleasant to play.
*18 holes, 6411yds, Par 71, SSS 71, Course record 69.*
*Club membership 1000.*
**Visitors**    no restrictions.
**Societies**    must apply in writing.
**Green Fees** not confirmed.
**Facilities**    ♀ ⚐ ⚑ ⛳ ✆ R K Cameron.
**Leisure**    heated indoor swimming pool, fishing, sauna, solarium, gymnasium, driving range, trolley hire, practice area.
**Location**    1.25m N off A441 on B4101
**Hotel**    ★★★ 62% Southcrest Hotel, Pool Bank, Southcrest, REDDITCH
☎ 01527 541511 58 ⇆ ℝ

**Pitcheroak** Plymouth Rd B97 4PB
☎ 01527 541054 & 541043
Woodland course, hilly in places.There is also a putting green and a practice ground.
*9 holes, 4561yds, Par 65, SSS 62.*
*Club membership 200.*
**Visitors**    no restrictions.
**Societies**    telephone to book.
**Green Fees** £6 per 18 holes; £4.50 per 9 holes (£7/£5 weekends).
**Facilities**    ⊗ ⅶ Ⅱ ❤ ♀ ⚐ ⚑ ✆ David Stewart.
**Leisure**    trolley for hire, putting green, practice area.
**Location**    SW side of town centre off A448
**Hotel**    ★★★ 62% Southcrest Hotel, Pool Bank, Southcrest, REDDITCH
☎ 01527 541511 58 ⇆ ℝ

**Redditch** Lower Grinsty, Green Ln, Callow Hill B97 5PJ
☎ 01527 543079
Parkland course, the hazards including woods, ditches and large ponds. The par 4, 14th is a testing hole.
*18 holes, 6671yds, Par 72, SSS 72, Course record 68.*
*Club membership 650.*
**Visitors**    with member only weekends & bank holidays.
**Societies**    telephone Secretary.
**Green Fees** £27.50 per day; £20 per 18 holes.
**Facilities**    ⊗ ⅶ Ⅱ ❤ ♀ ⚐ ⚑ ✆ Frank Powell.
**Leisure**    motorised carts for hire, buggies for hire, trolley for hire, putting green, practice area.
**Location**    2m SW
**Hotel**    ★★★ 62% Southcrest Hotel, Pool Bank, Southcrest, REDDITCH
☎ 01527 541511 58 ⇆ ℝ

## Pengethley Manor

### GEORGIAN COUNTRY HOTEL & RESTAURANT

Nr. Ross-on-Wye, Herefordshire HR9 6LL
Tel: (01989) 730211 Fax: (01989) 730238

This delightful hotel and restaurant is quietly situated in 15 acres of gardens and grounds, has its own vineyard, with lovely views of the Herefordshire countryside. The attractive, elegant restaurant features fresh local produce and fresh herbs. A la Carte and Table d'hôte menus are available.

A separate Conference Centre provides everything you need for meetings 'away from it all'.

To help you relax, we have a heated outdoor swimming pool, 9 hole golf improvement course, designer walks, trout pond, croquet and snooker.

AA ★★★ 72% ☜☜      Egon Ronay
BTA Commended Country House Hotel
Derek Johansen Recommended Hotels

## Cadmore Lodge

### COUNTRY HOTEL ★★

**Berrington Green, Tenbury Wells, WR15 8TQ**
**Tel/Fax: 01584 810044**

Located 2½ miles west of Tenbury Wells, just off A4112 to Leominster. Brook Valley with lake and streams in constant play. **Green fees weekdays £7.00, weekends &10.00.** Hotel bar and restaurant – all meals catered for. 10 ensuite bedrooms. Visitors welcome. Society meetings welcome.
**Secretary: Mr R. Farr,**
**Telephone: 01584 810306**

---

### ROSS-ON-WYE                     Map 03 SO62

**Ross-on-Wye** Two Park, Gorsley HR9 7UT
☎ 01989 720267
The undulating, parkland course has been cut out of a silver birch forest; the fairways being well-screened from each other. The fairways are tight, the greens good.
*18 holes, 6451yds, Par 72, SSS 73, Course record 68.*
*Club membership 760.*

| | |
|---|---|
| Visitors | must contact professional in advance 01989 720439. |
| Societies | must telephone in advance. |
| Green Fees | £35 day; £30 per 18 holes. |
| Facilities | ⊗ ∭ ⊾ ☕ ⚑ ♀ ⚖ ⛳ ⚓ 𝆑 |
| Leisure | trolley for hire, driving range, putting green, practice area. |
| Location | On B4221 N side of M50 junc 3 |
| Hotel | ★★★⚬⚬ 72% Pengethley Manor, ROSS-ON-WYE ☎ 01989 730211 11 ⇔ 𝄢Annexe14 ⇔ 𝄢 |

### TENBURY WELLS                    Map 07 SO56

**Cadmore Lodge Hotel & Country Club** Berrington Green WR15 8TQ ☎ 01584 810044
A picturesque 9-hole course in a brook valley. Challenging holes include the 1st and 6th over the lake, 8th over the valley and 9th over hedges.

*9 holes, 5129yds, Par 68, SSS 65.*
*Club membership 120.*

| | |
|---|---|
| Visitors | no restrictions but check availability. |
| Societies | telephone in advance. |
| Green Fees | not confirmed. |
| Facilities | ♀ ⚖ 𝄢 |
| Leisure | hard tennis courts, fishing, practice net, bowling green. |
| Hotel | ★★ 65% Cadmore Lodge Hotel & Country Club, Berrington Green, Tenbury Wells ☎ 01584 810044 8 ⇔ 𝄢 |

### UPPER SAPEY                      Map 03 SO66

**Sapey** WR6 6XT ☎ 01886 853288
Parkland course with views of the Malvern Hills. Trees, lakes and water hazards. Not too strenuous a walk.
*18 holes, 5935yds, Par 69, SSS 68, Course record 63.*
*Club membership 520.*

| | |
|---|---|
| Visitors | must contact in advance. |
| Societies | must contact in advance. |
| Green Fees | £22 per day; £15 per round (£25/£20 weekends & bank holidays). |
| Facilities | ⊗ ∭ ⊾ ☕ ⚑ ♀ ⚖ 𝄢 ⛳ 𝆑 Chris Knowles. |
| Leisure | motorised carts for hire, buggies for hire, trolley for hire, driving range, putting green, practice area, bowling green. |
| Location | B4203 Bromyard/Whitley Rd |
| Hotel | ★★★ 70% The Elms, ABBERLEY ☎ 01299 896666 16 ⇔ 𝄢Annexe9 ⇔ 𝄢 |

## WORCESTER      Map 03 SO85

**Tolladine** Tolladine Rd WR4 9BA ☎ 01905 21074
Parkland course, hilly and very tight, but with excellent views
of the surrounding hills and Worcester city.
*9 holes, 2813yds, Par 68, SSS 67.*
*Club membership 350.*
**Visitors**    with member only weekend & bank holidays.
**Societies**    must apply in writing.
**Green Fees** not confirmed.
**Facilities** ⛇⛳☎ Clare George.
**Location**    1.5m E
**Hotel**    ★★★ 61% The Giffard, High St,
       WORCESTER ☎ 01905 726262 103 ⇌ ↾

**Worcester Golf & Country Club** Boughton Park WR2 4EZ
☎ 01905 422555 & 422044 (Pro)
Fine parkland course with many trees, a lake, and views of
the Malvern Hills.
*18 holes, 6251yds, Par 70, SSS 70, Course record 67.*
*Club membership 1000.*
**Visitors**    with member only weekends. Must contact
       professional in advance.
**Societies**    telephone in advance.
**Green Fees** £25 per day.
**Facilities** ⛇♨⛳☎ Colin Colenso.
**Leisure**    hard and grass tennis courts, squash, putting
       green, practice area.
**Location**    1½m from city centre on A4103
**Hotel**    ★★★ 61% The Giffard, High St,
       WORCESTER ☎ 01905 726262 103 ⇌ ↾

## WORMSLEY      Map 03 SO44

**Herefordshire** Ravens Causeway HR4 8LY
☎ 01432 830219
Undulating parkland course with expansive views.
*18 holes, 6036yds, Par 70, SSS 69, Course record 61.*
*Club membership 800.*
**Visitors**    must contact in advance.
**Societies**    must apply in advance.
**Green Fees** £20 per day; £15 per round (£18 per round
       weekends; £26 per day bank holidays).
**Facilities** ⛇♨⛳☎ David Hemming.
**Leisure**    motorised carts for hire, buggies for hire, trolley
       for hire, putting green, practice area.
**Location**    E side of village
**Hotel**    ★★★ 62% The Green Dragon, Broad St,
       HEREFORD ☎ 01432 272506 87 ⇌ ↾

## WYTHALL      Map 07 SP07

**Fulford Heath** Tanners Green Ln B47 6BH
☎ 01564 824758
A mature parkland course encompassing two classic par
threes. The 11th, a mere 149 yards, shoots from an elevated
tee through a channel of trees to a well protected green. The
16th, a 166 yard par 3, elevated green, demands a 140 yard
carry over an imposing lake.
*18 holes, 5971yds, Par 70, SSS 69.*
*Club membership 700.*
**Visitors**    with member only weekend & bank holidays.
**Societies**    must apply in advance.
**Green Fees** £30 day/round weekdays.

**Facilities** ⛇♨⛳☎ David Down.
**Leisure**    trolley for hire, putting green, practice area.
**Location**    1m SE off A435
**Hotel**    ★★★ 65% St John's Swallow Hotel, 651
       Warwick Rd, SOLIHULL
       ☎ 0121 711 3000 177 ⇌ ↾

# HERTFORDSHIRE

## ALDBURY      Map 04 SP91

**Stocks Hotel Golf & Country Club** Stocks Rd HP23 5RX
☎ 01442 851341 & 851586
An 18-hole parkland course is one of the many facilities at
this country club. The course plays off blue, white (6,804
yards), yellow and red tees. There is also a driving range.
*18 holes, 6804yds, Par 72, SSS 73, Course record 68.*
**Visitors**    must contact in advance and have a handicap
       certificate. May not play before 2pm at
       weekends.
**Societies**    must contact well in advance.
**Green Fees** £30 per round (£40 weekends by arrangement).
**Facilities** ⛇♨⛳☎ Peter Lane.
**Leisure**    hard tennis courts, heated outdoor swimming
       pool, sauna, solarium, gymnasium, motorised
       carts for hire, buggies for hire, trolley for hire,
       driving range, putting green, practice area,
       snooker, croquet, table tennis, steam room.
**Location**    2m from A41 at Tring
**Hotel**    ★★★★ 61% Pendley Manor, Cow Ln, TRING
       ☎ 01442 891891 71 ⇌ ↾

## ALDENHAM      Map 04 TQ19

**Aldenham Golf and Country Club** Church Ln WD2 8AL
☎ 01923 853929
Undulating parkland course.
*Old Course: 18 holes, 6480yds, Par 70, SSS 71.*
*New Course: 9 holes, 2350yds, Par 33.*
*Club membership 550.*
**Visitors**    Old Course restricted weekends before noon.
       New Course no restrictions.
**Societies**    must contact in advance.
**Green Fees** not confirmed.
**Facilities** ⛳☎ Murray White.
**Leisure**    putting green,buggy/trolley hire.
**Location**    W side of village
**Hotel**    ★★★ 58% Dean Park Hotel, 30-40 St Albans
       Rd, WATFORD ☎ 01923 229212 90 ⇌ ↾

## BERKHAMSTED      Map 04 SP90

**Berkhamsted** The Common HP4 2QB
☎ 01442 865832
There are no sand bunkers on this Championship
heathland course but this does not make it any easier to
play. The natural hazards will test the skill of the most
able players, with a particularly testing hole at the 11th,
568 yards, par 5. Fine Greens, long carries and heather
and gorse. The clubhouse is very comfortable.  ▶

*18 holes, 6605yds, Par 71, SSS 72, Course record 65.*
*Club membership 700.*

| | |
|---|---|
| **Visitors** | must contact in advance. |
| **Societies** | must contact in advance. |
| **Green Fees** | £35 per day; £22.50 per round (£35 weekends after 11.30am). Winter: £30 per day; £22.50 per round (£30 weekends after 11.30am). |
| **Facilities** | ⊗ Ⅻ ⮬ ⬛ ♀ ⚎ 🛏 ( Basil Proudfoot. |
| **Leisure** | trolley for hire, putting green, practice area. |
| **Location** | 1.5m E |
| **Hotel** | ★★★★ 61% Pendley Manor, Cow Ln, TRING ☎ 01442 891891 71 ⇌ ℟ |

## BISHOP'S STORTFORD                Map 05 TL42

**Bishop's Stortford** Dunmow Rd CM23 5HP
☎ 01279 654715
Parkland course, fairly flat.
*18 holes, 6404yds, Par 71, SSS 71.*
*Club membership 850.*

| | |
|---|---|
| **Visitors** | must play with member at weekends. |
| **Societies** | must contact in writing. |
| **Green Fees** | £22 per day. |
| **Facilities** | ⊗ Ⅻ ⮬ ⬛ ♀ ⚎ 🛏 ( Vince Duncan. |
| **Leisure** | motorised carts for hire, buggies for hire, trolley for hire, putting green, practice area. |
| **Location** | 0.5m W of M11 junc 8 on A1250 |
| **Hotel** | ★★★★ 69% Down Hall Country House Hotel, Hatfield Heath, BISHOP'S STORTFORD ☎ 01279 731441 103 ⇌ ℟ |

**Great Hadham** Great Hadham Rd, Much Hadham SE10 6JE
☎ 01279 843558
An undulating open parkland course offering excellent country views and a challenge with its ever present breeze.
*18 holes, 6854yds, Par 72, SSS 73.*
*Club membership 700.*

| | |
|---|---|
| **Visitors** | welcome all times except am Mon, Wed, Sat & Sun. |
| **Societies** | by advance booking in writing. |
| **Green Fees** | £16 per 18 holes (£23 weekends & bank holidays). |
| **Facilities** | ⊗ Ⅻ ⮬ ⬛ ♀ ⚎ 🛏 ⛳ ( Kevin Lunt. |
| **Leisure** | motorised carts for hire, buggies for hire, trolley for hire, driving range, putting green, practice area. |
| **Location** | On the B1004, 3m SW of Bishop's Stortford |
| **Hotel** | ★★★★ 69% Down Hall Country House Hotel, Hatfield Heath, BISHOP'S STORTFORD ☎ 01279 731441 103 ⇌ ℟ |

## BRICKENDON                Map 05 TL30

*Brickendon Grange* SG13 8PD
☎ 01992 511258
Parkland course.
*18 holes, 6349yds, Par 71, SSS 70, Course record 66.*
*Club membership 680.*

| | |
|---|---|
| **Visitors** | must have handicap certificate. With member only at weekends & bank holidays. |
| **Societies** | by arrangement. |
| **Green Fees** | not confirmed. |
| **Facilities** | ♀ ⚎ 🛏 ( John Hamilton. |

| | |
|---|---|
| **Leisure** | putting,practice area,buggy/trolley hire. |
| **Location** | W side of village |
| **Hotel** | ★★★ 63% White Horse, Hertingfordbury, HERTFORD ☎ 01992 586791 42 ⇌ ℟ |

## BROOKMANS PARK                Map 04 TL20

**Brookmans Park** Golf Club Rd AL9 7AT
☎ 01707 652487
Brookman's Park is an undulating parkland course, with several cleverly constructed holes. But it is a fair course, although it can play long. The 11th, par 3, is a testing hole which plays across a lake.
*18 holes, 6460yds, Par 71, SSS 71, Course record 66.*
*Club membership 750.*

| | |
|---|---|
| **Visitors** | must contact professional in advance 01707 652468 and have a handicap certificate; must play with member at weekends & bank holidays. |
| **Societies** | must telephone in advance. |
| **Green Fees** | £35 per day; £27 per round. |
| **Facilities** | ⊗ ⮬ ⬛ ♀ ⚎ 🛏 ( Ian Jelley. |
| **Leisure** | putting green, practice area. |
| **Location** | N side of village off A1000 |
| **Hotel** | B Forte Posthouse South Mimms, SOUTH MIMMS ☎ 01707 643311 120 ⇌ ℟ |

## BUNTINGFORD                Map 05 TL32

**East Herts** Hamels Park SG9 9NA ☎ 01920 821922 (Pro)
An attractive undulating parkland course with magnificent specimen trees.
*18 holes, 6485yds, Par 71, SSS 71.*
*Club membership 750.*

| | |
|---|---|
| **Visitors** | must contact in advance & have handicap certificate, but may not play on Wed & weekends. |
| **Societies** | apply in writing. |
| **Green Fees** | £24 per round. |
| **Facilities** | ⊗ Ⅻ ⮬ ⬛ ♀ ⚎ 🛏 ⛳ ( S Bryan. |
| **Location** | 1m N of Puckeridge off A10 |
| **Hotel** | ★★★ 61% Vintage Court Hotel, Vintage Corner, PUCKERIDGE ☎ 01920 822722 25 ⇌ ℟ |

## BUSHEY                Map 04 TQ19

**Bushey Golf & Country Club** High St WD2 1BJ
☎ 0181 950 2283
Undulating parkland with challenging 2nd and 9th holes. The latter has a sweeping dogleg left, playing to a green in front of the club house. For the rather too enthusiatic golfer, Bushey offers its own physiotherapist!
*9 holes, 6000yds, Par 70, SSS 69, Course record 67.*
*Club membership 411.*

| | |
|---|---|
| **Visitors** | must contact in advance. |
| **Societies** | apply in writing or by telephone. |
| **Green Fees** | £10 per round (£14 weekends & bank holidays). |
| **Facilities** | ⊗ Ⅻ ⮬ ⬛ ♀ ⚎ 🛏 ⛳ ( Michael Lovegrove. |
| **Leisure** | squash, motorised carts for hire, buggies for hire, trolley for hire, driving range, putting green, physiotherapy. |
| **Hotel** | ★★★ 74% Edgwarebury Hotel, Barnet Ln, ELSTREE ☎ 0181 953 8227 47 ⇌ ℟ |

**Bushey Hall** Bushey Hall Dr WD2 2EP
☎ 01923 225802 & 222253
Parkland course.
*18 holes, 6099yds, Par 70, SSS 69.*
*Club membership 500.*
Visitors    may book 7 days in advance.
Societies    must contact in writing.
Green Fees    not confirmed.
Facilities    ♀ ♨ 🏌 ⛳ 🍴 ℓ Ken Wickham.
Leisure    practice area.
Location    1.5m NW on A4008
Hotel    ★★★ 58% Dean Park Hotel, 30-40 St Albans
Rd, WATFORD
☎ 01923 229212 90 ⇌ 🐾

**Hartsbourne Golf & Country Club** Hartsbourne Ave
WD2 1JW ☎ 0181 950 1133
Parkland course with good views.
*18 holes, 6305yds, Par 71, SSS 70, Course record 62.*
*Club membership 750.*
Visitors    must be guest of a member.
Societies    phone for details.
Green Fees    not confirmed.
Facilities    ⊗ 🍴 🏌 🍴 ♀ ♨ ⛳ 🍴 ℓ Geoff Hunt.
Leisure    motorised carts for hire, buggies for hire, trolley
for hire, driving range, putting.
Location    5m SE of Watford
Hotel    ★★★ 58% Dean Park Hotel, 30-40 St Albans
Rd, WATFORD
☎ 01923 229212 90 ⇌ 🐾

## CHESHUNT    Map 05 TL30

**Cheshunt** Cheshunt Park, Park Ln EN7 6QD
☎ 01992 629777 & 624009
Municipal parkland course, well-bunkered with ponds, easy
walking.
*18 holes, 6613yds, Par 71, SSS 71.*
*Club membership 350.*
Visitors    must book Tee-times through Pro shop.
Societies    must apply in writing.
Green Fees    not confirmed.
Facilities    ♀ ♨ ⛳ 🍴 ℓ Chris Newton.
Leisure    cart/trolley hire, practice area.
Location    1.5m NW off B156
Hotel    B Marriott Hotel, Halfhide Ln, Turnford,
BROXBOURNE
☎ 01992 451245 150 ⇌ 🐾

## CHORLEYWOOD    Map 04 TQ09

**Chorleywood** Common Rd WD3 5LN
☎ 01923 282009
Heathland course with natural hazards and good views.
*9 holes, 5676yds, Par 68, SSS 67.*
*Club membership 300.*
Visitors    must contact in advance, restricted weekends.
Societies    must apply in writing.
Green Fees    £14 per round; £17.50 weekends & bank
holidays.
Facilities    ⊗ 🍴 🏌 🍴 ♀ ♨ ⛳
Location    E side of village off A404
Hotel    ★★★ 72% Bedford Arms, CHENIES
☎ 01923 283301 10 ⇌ 🐾

## ELSTREE    Map 04 TQ19

**Elstree** Watling St WD6 3AA ☎ 0181 953 6115
Parkland course.
*18 holes, 6603yds, Par 73, SSS 72.*
*Club membership 650.*
Visitors    advisable to contact in advance, no restrictions
weekdays, may not play until after 2pm
weekends unless tee time available day prior.
Societies    telephone in advance.
Green Fees    not confirmed.
Facilities    ♀ ♨ ℓ Marc Warwick.
Leisure    driving range, putting, trolley hire.
Location    E of Bushey, on A5
Hotel    ★★★ 74% Edgwarebury Hotel, Barnet Ln,
ELSTREE ☎ 0181 953 8227 47 ⇌ 🐾

## ESSENDON    Map 04 TL20

**Hatfield London Country Club** Bedwell Park AL9 6JA
☎ 01707 642624
Parkland course with many varied hazards, including ponds, a
stream and a ditch. 19th-century manor clubhouse. 9-hole
pitch and putt.
*18 holes, 6880yds, Par 72, SSS 72.*
*Club membership 250.*
Visitors    must contact in advance.
Societies    must contact in advance.
Green Fees    Tue-Fri: £23 per day ticket; Mon £20 per day,
£11 per round (£19-£27 per round weekends &
bank holidays).
Facilities    ⊗ 🍴 🏌 🍴 ♀ ♨ ⛳ 🍴 ℓ Norman Greer.
Leisure    hard tennis courts, buggies for hire, trolley for
hire, driving range, putting green, practice area.
Location    On B158 1m S
Hotel    ★★★ 57% The Homestead Court, Homestead
Ln, WELWYN GARDEN CITY
☎ 01707 324336 58 ⇌ 🐾

## GRAVELEY    Map 04 TL22

**Chesfield Downs Family Golf Centre** Jack's Hill SG4 7EQ
☎ 01462 482929
A revolutionary new golf course with the emphasis on
facilities for the entire family. Its undulating, open downland
course has an inland links feel. There is a 25-bay floodlit,
covered driving range, a 9-hole Par 3 and many other
facilities.
*Chesfield Downs: 18 holes, 6648yds, Par 71, SSS 72.*
*Lannock Links: 9 holes, 975yds, Par 27, SSS 27.*
*Club membership 500.*
Visitors    no restrictions.
Societies    must telephone in advance.
Green Fees    not confirmed.
Facilities    ♀ ♨ ⛳ 🍴 ℓ Ross Whitehead.
Leisure    putting, driving range, cart/trolley hire.
Hotel    ★★★ 60% Hertfordpark Hotel, Danestrete,
STEVENAGE ☎ 01438 779955 98 ⇌ 🐾

## HARPENDEN    Map 04 TL11

**Harpenden** Hammonds End, Redbourn Ln AL5 2AX
☎ 01582 712580
Gently undulating parkland course, easy walking.   ▶

*18 holes, 6381yds, Par 70, SSS 70, Course record 67.*
*Club membership 800.*
**Visitors** must contact in advance. May not play Thu & weekends.
**Societies** must apply in writing.
**Green Fees** £34 per day; £24 per round (weekdays).
**Facilities** ⊗ ⊮ ⊾ ⬛ ♀ ⚲ 🏠 ⚑ ☏ Peter Cherry.
**Leisure** trolley for hire, driving range, putting green, practice area.
**Location** 1m S on B487
**Hotel** ★★★ 63% Harpenden House Hotel, 18 Southdown Rd, HARPENDEN ☎ 01582 764111 18 ⇄ ☏Annexe35 ⇄ ☏

---

**Harpenden Common** Cravells Rd, East Common AL5 1BL
☎ 01582 715959
Flat, easy walking, good greens, typical common course.
*18 holes, 6214yds, Par 70, SSS 70.*
*Club membership 710.*
**Visitors** must contact in advance.
**Societies** Thu & Fri only. Must apply in writing.
**Green Fees** £27 per day; £22 per round (£27 per round weekdays).
**Facilities** ⊗ ⊾ ⬛ ♀ ⚲ 🏠 ⚑ ☏ Barney Puttick.
**Leisure** trolley for hire, driving range, putting green, practice area.
**Location** 1m S on A1081
**Hotel** ★★★ 68% Glen Eagle Hotel, 1 Luton Rd, HARPENDEN ☎ 01582 760271 50 ⇄ ☏

---

## HEMEL HEMPSTEAD — Map 04 TL00

**Boxmoor** 18 Box Ln, Boxmoor HP3 0DJ
☎ 01442 242434
Challenging, very hilly, moorland course with sloping fairways divided by trees. Fine views. Testing holes: 3rd (par 3), 4th (par 4).
*9 holes, 4812yds, Par 64, SSS 63, Course record 62.*
*Club membership 280.*
**Visitors** may not play on Sun & bank holidays. Restricted some Sat.
**Societies** must contact in advance.
**Green Fees** £10 per day/round (£15 Sat).
**Facilities** ⊗ ⊮ by prior arrangement ⊾ ⬛ ♀ ⚲
**Location** 2m SW on B4505
**Hotel** ★★★ 64% The Two Brewers Inn, The Common, CHIPPERFIELD ☎ 01923 265266 20 ⇄ ☏

---

**Little Hay** Box Ln, Bovingdon HP3 0DQ
☎ 01442 833798
Semi-parkland, inland links.
*18 holes, 6678yds, Par 72, SSS 72.*
**Visitors** advisable to contact in advance.
**Societies** telephone for details.
**Green Fees** £9.50 per round (£13.50 weekends).
**Facilities** ⊗ ⊮ by prior arrangement ⊾ ⬛ ♀ ⚲ 🏠 ⚑ ☏ D Johnson/S Proudfoot.
**Leisure** trolley for hire, floodlit driving range, putting green.
**Location** 1.5m SW on B4505 off A41
**Hotel** B Forte Posthouse Hemel Hempstead, Breakspear Way, HEMEL HEMPSTEAD ☎ 01442 251122 146 ⇄ ☏

---

**Shendish Manor** London Rd, Apsley HP3 0AA
☎ 01442 251806
A hilly course with plenty of trees and good greens. A tough course for any golfer.
*9 holes, 6076yds, Par 70, SSS 69.*
**Visitors** no restrictions.
**Societies** must contact in advance.
**Green Fees** not confirmed.
**Facilities** ♀ ⚲ 🏠 ⚑ ☏ Kevin Hughes.
**Leisure** practice area, trolley hire.
**Hotel** ★★★★ 61% Pendley Manor, Cow Ln, TRING ☎ 01442 891891 71 ⇄ ☏

---

## KNEBWORTH — Map 04 TL22

**Knebworth** Deards End Ln SG3 6NL ☎ 01438 812752
Parkland course, easy walking.
*18 holes, 6492yds, Par 71, SSS 71, Course record 68.*
*Club membership 900.*
**Visitors** must have handicap certificate , but must play with member at weekends.
**Societies** must contact in advance.
**Green Fees** £29 per day/round.
**Facilities** ⊗ ⊮ ⊾ ⬛ ♀ ⚲ 🏠 ☏ Garry Parker.
**Leisure** motorised carts for hire, buggies for hire, trolley for hire, putting green, practice area.
**Location** N side of village off B197
**Hotel** B Forte Posthouse Stevenage, Old London Rd, Broadwater, STEVENAGE ☎ 01438 365444 54 ⇄ ☏

---

## LETCHWORTH — Map 04 TL23

***Letchworth*** Letchworth Ln SG6 3NQ ☎ 01462 683203
Planned more than 50 years ago by Harry Vardon, this adventurous, parkland course is set in a peaceful corner of 'Norman' England. To its variety of natural and artificial hazards is added an unpredictable wind.
*18 holes, 6181yds, Par 70, SSS 69.*
*Club membership 1000.*
**Visitors** with member only at weekends. Must contact in advance and have a handicap certificate.
**Societies** Wed, Thu & Fri only, must telephone in advance.
**Green Fees** not confirmed.
**Facilities** ♀ ⚲ 🏠 ☏ J Mutimer.
**Leisure** putting green, practice area, trolley hire.
**Location** S side of town centre off A505
**Hotel** ★★★ 63% Blakemore Thistle, Blakemore End Rd, Little Wymondley, HITCHIN ☎ 01438 355821 82 ⇄ ☏

---

## LITTLE GADDESDEN — Map 04 SP91

**Ashridge** HP4 1LY ☎ 01442 842244
Good parkland course, challenging but fair. Good clubhouse facilities.
*18 holes, 6547yds, Par 72, SSS 71, Course record 64.*
*Club membership 720.*
**Visitors** must contact in advance , be a member of a recognised club & have handicap certificate, may not play weekends & bank holidays.
**Societies** must apply in writing and complete booking form.

**Green Fees** £50 per day; £35 per round.
**Facilities** ⊗ ⅢⅢ ⓑ ♥ ♀ ⚲ 🏠 🜋 ℂ Andrew Ainsworth.
**Leisure** trolley for hire, putting green, practice area.
**Location** 5m N of Berkhamsted on the B4506
**Hotel** ★★★ 75% The Bell Inn, ASTON CLINTON
☎ 01296 630252 6 ⇋ ℝAnnexe15 ⇋ ℝ

## POTTERS BAR
Map 04 TL20

**Potters Bar** Darkes Ln EN6 1DE ☎ 01707 652020
Undulating parkland course with water in play on many holes.
*18 holes, 6279yds, Par 71, SSS 70.*
*Club membership 500.*
**Visitors** with member only at weekends, Ladies Day
Wed morning.
**Societies** Mon Tue & Fri only, by arrangement with
Secretary.
**Green Fees** £30 per day; £20 per round.
**Facilities** ⊗ ⓑ ♥ ♀ ⚲ 🏠 🜋 ℂ Gary Carver.
**Leisure** motorised carts for hire, buggies for hire, trolley
for hire, putting green, practice area.
**Location** 1m N of M25 junct 24
**Hotel** B Forte Posthouse South Mimms, SOUTH
MIMMS ☎ 01707 643311 120 ⇋ ℝ

## RADLETT
Map 04 TL10

**Porters Park** Shenley Hill WD7 7AZ ☎ 01923 854127
A splendid, undulating parkland course with fine trees
and lush grass. The holes are all different and interesting
- on many accuracy of shot to the green is of paramount
importance.
*18 holes, 6313yds, Par 70, SSS 70, Course record 64.*
*Club membership 820.*
**Visitors** must book 24hrs in advance. With member
only weekends.
**Societies** Wed & Thu only, must apply in writing.
**Green Fees** £44 per day; £29 per round.
**Facilities** ⊗ ⓑ ♥ ♀ ⚲ 🏠 🜋 ℂ David Gleeson.
**Leisure** trolley for hire, driving range, putting green,
practice area.
**Location** NE side of village off A5183
**Hotel** ★★★★ 65% The Noke Thistle, Watford
Rd, ST ALBANS
☎ 01727 854252 111 ⇋ ℝ

## REDBOURN
Map 04 TL11

**Redbourn** Kinsbourne Green Ln AL3 7QA
☎ 01582 793493
Testing parkland course (five par 4's over 400 yds). Also 9-
hole par 3 course.
*Ver Course: 18 holes, 6506yds, Par 70, SSS 71, Course
record 67.*
*Kingsbourne Course: 9 holes, 1361yds, Par 27.*
*Club membership 850.*
**Visitors** must contact up to 3 days in advance for Ver
course. No restrictions for Par 3.
**Societies** must telephone in advance.
**Green Fees** 18 hole: £16 per round (£20 weekends & bank
holidays). 9 hole: £4.50 per round.
**Facilities** ⊗ ⅢⅢ ⓑ ♥ ♀ ⚲ 🏠 🜋 ℂ Martin Wright.
**Leisure** motorised carts for hire, buggies for hire, trolley
for hire, driving range, putting green, practice
area,.

**Location** 1m N off A5183
**Hotel** ★★★ 63% Harpenden House Hotel, 18
Southdown Rd, HARPENDEN
☎ 01582 764111 18 ⇋ ℝAnnexe35 ⇋ ℝ

## RICKMANSWORTH
Map 04 TQ09

**Moor Park** WD3 1QN ☎ 01923 773146
Two parkland courses.
*High Golf Course: 18 holes, 6713yds, Par 72, SSS 72,
Course record 63.*
*West Golf Course: 18 holes, 5815yds, Par 69, SSS 68,
Course record 62.*
*Club membership 1700.*
**Visitors** must contact in advance but may not play at
weekends, bank holidays or before 1pm on
Tue & Thu.
**Societies** must contact in advance.
**Green Fees** High: £40 per round. West: £25 per round.
**Facilities** ⊗ ⅢⅢ ⓑ ♥ ♀ ⚲ 🏠 🜋 ℂ Lawrence Farmer.
**Leisure** hard and grass tennis courts, motorised carts
for hire, buggies for hire, trolley for hire,
putting green, practice area.
**Location** 1.5m SE off A4145
**Hotel** ★★★ 58% Dean Park Hotel, 30-40 St
Albans Rd, WATFORD
☎ 01923 229212 90 ⇋ ℝ

**Rickmansworth Public Course** Moor Ln WD3 1QL
☎ 01923 775278
Undulating, municipal parkland course.
*18 holes, 4469yds, Par 63, SSS 62.*
*Club membership 240.*
**Visitors** must contact the club in advance.
**Societies** must contact in advance.
**Green Fees** £9 (£12.50 weekends).
**Facilities** ⊗ ⓑ ♥ ♀ ⚲ 🏠 🜋 ℂ Alan Dobbins.
**Leisure** motorised carts for hire, buggies for hire, trolley
for hire, pool table.
**Location** 2m S of town off A4145
**Hotel** ★★★ 58% Dean Park Hotel, 30-40 St Albans
Rd, WATFORD
☎ 01923 229212 90 ⇋ ℝ

## ROYSTON
Map 05 TL34

**Barkway Park** Nuthampstead Rd, Barkway SG8 8EN
☎ 01763 849070 & 848215
An undulating course criss-crossed by ditches which come
into play on several holes. The challenging par 3 7th features
a long, narrow green with out of bounds close to the right
edge of the green.
*18 holes, 6997yds, Par 74, SSS 74.*
*Club membership 360.*
**Visitors** telephone for tee times, weekends after 11.30am
only.
**Societies** apply for booking form.
**Green Fees** £18 per 36 holes; £12 per 18 holes; £6 per 9
holes (£17 per 18 holes/£8.50 per 9 holes
weekends).
**Facilities** ⊗ ⅢⅢ ⓑ ♥ ♀ ⚲ 🏠 ℂ Steve Fox.
**Leisure** buggies for hire, trolley for hire, putting green,
practice area.
**Location** Off B1368 from A10 ▶

**Hotel** ★★★ 66% Duxford Lodge Hotel, Ickleton Rd, DUXFORD ☎ 01223 836444 11 ⇆ ✿Annexe4 ⇆ ✿

---

**Kingsway** Cambridge Rd, Melbourn SG8 6EY
☎ 01763 262727 & 262943
Short and deceptively tricky 9-hole course providing a good test for both beginners and experienced golfers. Out of bounds and strategically placed bunkers come into play on several holes, in particular the tough par 3 7th.
*9 holes, 2455yds, Par 33, SSS 32.*
*Club membership 150.*
**Visitors** welcome.
**Societies** telephone for details.
**Green Fees** £9.50 per 18 holes; £5.50 per 9 holes. Pitch & Putt £4.25 per 18 holes; £3 per 9 holes..
**Facilities** ⊗ ┗ ☟ ♀ ⚖ 🏠 ✦✿ Denise Hastings.
**Leisure** trolley for hire, driving range, putting green, practice area.
**Location** Off the A10
**Hotel** ★★★ 66% Duxford Lodge Hotel, Ickleton Rd, DUXFORD ☎ 01223 836444 11 ⇆ ✿Annexe4 ⇆ ✿

---

**Royston** Baldock Rd SG8 5BG ☎ 01763 242696
Heathland course on undulating terrain and fine fairways.The 8th, 9th and 18th are the most notable holes.
*18 holes, 6052yds, Par 70, SSS 69, Course record 65.*
*Club membership 550.*
**Visitors** with member only at weekends. Must contact in advance.
**Societies** by arrangement Mon-Fri.
**Green Fees** £20 per day/round.
**Facilities** ⊗ ℳ ┗ ☟ ♀ ⚖ 🏠 ✦✿ Mark Hatcher.
**Leisure** trolley for hire, putting green, practice area, snooker table.
**Location** 0.5m W of town centre
**Hotel** ★★★ 66% Duxford Lodge Hotel, Ickleton Rd, DUXFORD ☎ 01223 836444 11 ⇆ ✿Annexe4 ⇆ ✿

---

## ST ALBANS Map 04 TL10

**Abbey View** Westminster Lodge Leisure Ctr, Hollywell Hill AL1 2DL ☎ 01727 841973
Abbey View is a public golf course designed for beginners, but is sufficiently challenging for experienced golfers who only have time for a short game. There is a resident professional for assistance and lessons.
*9 holes, 2162yds.*
**Visitors** welcome but no sharing clubs, suitable footwear & wide wheel trolleys.
**Green Fees** not confirmed.
**Facilities** ⚖ ✦✿ Mark Sibley.
**Leisure** swimming pool, leisure centre adjacent to course.
**Hotel** ★★★ 64% Hertfordshire Moat House, London Rd, Markyate, ST ALBANS ☎ 01582 449988 89 ⇆ ✿

---

**Batchwood Hall** Batchwood Dr AL3 5XA
☎ 01727 844250
Municipal parkland course designed by J H Taylor and opened in 1935.
*18 holes, 6487yds, Par 71, SSS 71.*
*Club membership 200.*

**Visitors** must contact in advance, in person.
**Societies** must contact in advance.
**Green Fees** £8.50 per round (£11.50 weekends).
**Facilities** ⊗ ℳ ┗ ☟ ♀ ⚖ 🏠 ✦✿ Jimmy Thompson.
**Leisure** hard tennis courts, squash, solarium, gymnasium, trolley for hire, putting green, practice area, indoor tennis.
**Location** 1m NW off A5183
**Hotel** ★★★ 66% St Michael's Manor Hotel, Fishpool St, ST ALBANS ☎ 01727 864444 24 ⇆ ✿

---

**Verulam** London Rd AL1 1JG ☎ 01727 853327
Parkland course with fourteen holes having out-of-bounds. Water affects the 5th, 6th and 7th holes. Samuel Ryder was Captain here in 1927 when he began the now celebrated Ryder Cup Competition.
*18 holes, 6448yds, Par 72, SSS 71.*
*Club membership 630.*
**Visitors** must contact in advance. With member only at weekends.
**Societies** must contact advance.
**Green Fees** Mon: £20 per 36 holes, £12 per 18 holes. Tue-Fri: £30 per 36 holes, £25 per 18 holes.
**Facilities** ⊗ ℳ by prior arrangement ┗ ☟ ♀ ⚖ 🏠 ✦ ✿ Nick Burch.
**Leisure** motorised carts for hire, trolley for hire, practice area.
**Location** 1m from junc 22 of M25 off A1081
**Hotel** ★★★★ 74% Sopwell House Hotel & Country Club, Cottonmill Ln, Sopwell, ST ALBANS ☎ 01727 864477 92 ⇆ ✿

---

## SAWBRIDGEWORTH Map 05 TL41

**Manor of Groves Golf & Country Club** High Wych CM21 0LA ☎ 01279 722333 & 721486
The 6,280yd, Par 71 course is set out over 150 acres of established parkland and rolling countryside and is a true test of golf for the club golfer.
*18 holes, 6280yds, Par 71, SSS 70, Course record 65.*
*Club membership 450.*
**Visitors** telephone bookings preferred, may not play until after 12 noon at weekends.
**Societies** Mon-Fri by prior arrangement, telephone in advance.
**Green Fees** £20 per round (£25 weekends). Twilight after 6pm £15. Price review Mar'96.
**Facilities** ⊗ ℳ ┗ ☟ ♀ ⚖ 🏠 ✦ 🍴✿ Craig Laurence.
**Leisure** hard tennis courts, outdoor swimming pool, gymnasium, motorised carts for hire, buggies for hire, trolley for hire, putting green, practice area.
**Location** 1.5m on west side of town
**Hotel** ★★★ 74% Churchgate Manor Hotel, Churchgate St, Old Harlow, HARLOW ☎ 01279 420246 85 ⇆

---

## STANSTEAD ABBOTS Map 05 TL31

**Briggens House Hotel** Briggens Park, Stanstead Rd SG12 8LD ☎ 01279 793142
An attractive 9-hole course set in the grounds of a hotel and 80 acres of countryside.
*9 holes, 2793yds, Par 36, SSS 69, Course record 31.*
*Club membership 180.*

| | |
|---|---|
| **Visitors** | may not play Thu 5-6pm and Sun am. No jeans. Must have own clubs. |
| **Societies** | must contact in advance. |
| **Green Fees** | £10.50 per 18 holes (£15 weekends). |
| **Facilities** | ⊗ ⅢⓁ ■ ♡ ♀ ☖ ⛳ ♭ ☏ Sean Carter. |
| **Leisure** | hard tennis courts, heated outdoor swimming pool, fishing, motorised carts for hire, buggies for hire, trolley for hire, practice area, pitch & putt (summer only). |
| **Location** | Off Stanstead road A414 |
| **Hotel** | ★★★ 64% County Hotel, Baldock St, WARE ☎ 01920 465011 50 ⇥ ♟ |

## STEVENAGE Map 04 TL22

**Stevenage Golf Centre** Aston Ln SG2 7EL
☎ 01438 880424
Municipal course designed by John Jacobs, with natural water hazards and some wooded areas.
*18 holes, 6451yds, Par 72, SSS 71.*
*Club membership 600.*

| | |
|---|---|
| **Visitors** | no restrictions. |
| **Societies** | must contact 1 week in advance. Deposit required. |
| **Green Fees** | not confirmed. |
| **Facilities** | ♀ (all day) ☖ ⛳ ♭ ☏ Keith Bond. |
| **Leisure** | floodlit driving range. |
| **Location** | 4m SE off B5169 |
| **Hotel** | B Forte Posthouse Stevenage, Old London Rd, Broadwater, STEVENAGE ☎ 01438 365444 54 ⇥ ♟ |

## WARE Map 05 TL31

**Chadwell Springs** Hertford Rd SG12 9LE
☎ 01920 461447
Quick drying moorland course on high plateau subject to wind. The first two holes are par 5 and notable.
*9 holes, 6418yds, Par 72, SSS 71, Course record 68.*
*Club membership 650.*

| | |
|---|---|
| **Visitors** | with member only at weekends. |
| **Societies** | bookings accepted, Mon, Wed & Fri only. |
| **Green Fees** | £15 per 18 holes. |
| **Facilities** | ⊗ ⅢⓁ ■ ♡ ♀ ☖ ☏ Mark Wall. |
| **Leisure** | trolley for hire. |
| **Location** | 0.75m W on A119 |
| **Hotel** | ★★★ 64% County Hotel, Baldock St, WARE ☎ 01920 465011 50 ⇥ ♟ |

**Hanbury Manor Golf & Country Club** SG12 0SD
☎ 01920 487722
Superb parkland course designed by Jack Nicklaus II. Large oval tees, watered fairways and undulating greens make up the first 9 holes. Attractive lakes and deep-faced bunkers are strategically sited. Second 9 holes offer open panoramas and challenging holes.
*18 holes, 7016yds, Par 72, SSS 74, Course record 70.*
*Club membership 600.*

| | |
|---|---|
| **Visitors** | with handicap certificate, members guest and hotel residents welcome. |
| **Societies** | strictly limited to Mon-Thu and restricted tee times, must be booked in advance. |
| **Green Fees** | Hotel guests £50. |
| **Facilities** | ⊗ ⅢⓁ ■ ♡ ♀ ☖ ☏ ⛳ ♭ Peter Blaze. |
| **Leisure** | hard tennis courts, heated indoor swimming pool, squash, sauna, solarium, gymnasium, |

motorised carts for hire, buggies for hire, trolley for hire, putting green, practice area.

| | |
|---|---|
| **Location** | Adjacent to A10 |
| **Hotel** | ★★★★★ 75% Hanbury Manor, WARE ☎ 01920 487722 69 ⇥ ♟Annexe27 ⇥ ♟ |

**Whitehill** Dane End SG12 0JS ☎ 01920 438495
Undulating course providing a good test for both the average golfer and the low handicapper. Several lakes in challenging positions.
*18 holes, 6681yds, Par 72, SSS 72.*
*Club membership 600.*

| | |
|---|---|
| **Visitors** | handicap certificate must be produced or competence test taken (free), appropriate clothing must be worn. |
| **Societies** | telephone or write for booking form. |
| **Green Fees** | £15 per round (£18 weekends). |
| **Facilities** | ⊗ ⅢⓁ ■ ♡ ♀ ☖ ☏ ⛳ ♭ David Ling. |
| **Leisure** | motorised carts for hire, buggies for hire, trolley for hire, driving range, putting green, practice area. |
| **Hotel** | ★★★ 64% County Hotel, Baldock St, WARE ☎ 01920 465011 50 ⇥ ♟ |

## WATFORD Map 04 TQ19

**West Herts** Cassiobury Park WD1 7SL
☎ 01923 236484
Another of the many clubs that were inaugurated in the 1890's when the game of golf was being given a tremendous boost by the the performances of the first star professionals, Baird, Vardon and Taylor. The West Herts course is close to Watford but its tree-lined setting is beautiful and tranquil. Set out on a plateau the course is exceedingly dry. It also has a very severe finish with the 17th, a hole of 378 yards, the toughest on the course. The last hole measures over 480 yards.
*18 holes, 6400yds, Par 72, SSS 71, Course record 66.*
*Club membership 700.*

| | |
|---|---|
| **Visitors** | must contact in advance. No play at weekends. |
| **Societies** | must telephone in advance and confirm in writing. |
| **Green Fees** | £30 per day; £20 per round weekdays. |
| **Facilities** | ⊗ ⅢⓁ ■ ♡ ♀ ☖ ☏ ⛳ ♭ Charles Gough. |
| **Leisure** | motorised carts for hire, buggies for hire, trolley for hire, putting green, practice area. |
| **Location** | W side of town centre off A412 |
| **Hotel** | ★★★ 58% Dean Park Hotel, 30-40 St Albans Rd, WATFORD ☎ 01923 229212 90 ⇥ ♟ |

## WELWYN GARDEN CITY Map 04 TL21

**Mill Green** Gypsy Ln AL6 4TY
☎ 01707 276900 & 270542 (Pro)
Opened in autumn 1993, the 18-hole, Peter Alliss/Clive Clark designed, Mill Green course makes use of woodland and meadows. The par 3 9-hole gives a good test for improving the short game.
*18 holes, 6615yds, Par 72, SSS 72, Course record 68.*
*Club membership 700.*

| | |
|---|---|
| **Visitors** | must contact in advance. |
| **Societies** | apply in writing for details. |
| **Green Fees** | £27.50 per round (£32.50 weekends & bank holidays); Mon £12. |

▶

**Facilities** ⊗ ⵢ ⵏ ⵡ ⵟ ⴷ ⴼ ⴼ Alan Hall.
**Leisure** motorised carts for hire, buggies for hire, trolley
for hire, driving range, putting green.
**Location** Exit 4 of A1(M), A414 to Mill Green
**Hotel** ★★★ 57% The Homestead Court, Homestead
Ln, WELWYN GARDEN CITY
☎ 01707 324336 58 ⇄ ⟲

---

**Panshanger Golf & Squash Complex** Old Herns Ln
AL7 2ED ☎ 01707 333350
Municipal parkland course overlooking Mimram Valley.
Squash.
*18 holes, 6347yds, Par 72, SSS 70, Course record 65.*
*Club membership 600.*
**Visitors** no restrictions.
**Societies** telephone for details.
**Green Fees** £20 per day; £11 per round (£15 per round
weekends).
**Facilities** ⊗ ⵏ ⵡ ⵟ ⴷ ⴼ ⴼ
ⴼ Bryan Lewis/Mick Corlass.
**Leisure** squash, motorised carts for hire, buggies for hire,
trolley for hire, putting green, practice area, pitch
& putt.
**Location** N side of town centre off B1000
**Hotel** ★★★ 57% The Homestead Court, Homestead
Ln, WELWYN GARDEN CITY
☎ 01707 324336 58 ⇄ ⟲

---

**Welwyn Garden City** Mannicotts, High Oaks Rd AL8 7BP
☎ 01707 325243
Undulating parkland course with a ravine. Course record
holder is Nick Faldo.
*18 holes, 6074yds, Par 70, SSS 69.*
*Club membership 975.*
**Visitors** must contact in advance but may not play Sun
am.
**Societies** must contact in advance.
**Green Fees** £25 (£35 weekends).
**Facilities** ⊗ ⵢ ⵏ ⵡ ⵟ ⴷ ⴼ ⴼ Richard May.
**Leisure** motorised carts for hire, buggies for hire, trolley
for hire, putting green, practice area.
**Location** W side of city, exit 6 off A1
**Hotel** ★★★ 57% The Homestead Court, Homestead
Ln, WELWYN GARDEN CITY
☎ 01707 324336 58 ⇄ ⟲

---

## WHEATHAMPSTEAD Map 04 TL11

**Mid Herts** Lamer Ln, Gustard Wood AL4 8RS
☎ 01582 832242
Commonland, wooded with heather and gorse-lined fairways.
*18 holes, 6060yds, Par 69, SSS 69.*
*Club membership 760.*
**Visitors** may not play Tue, Wed afternoons & weekends.
**Societies** must contact in writing.
**Green Fees** on application.
**Facilities** ⊗ ⵢ ⵏ ⵡ ⵟ ⴷ ⴼ ⴼ Nick Brown.
**Leisure** trolley for hire, putting green, practice area.
**Location** 1m N on B651
**Hotel** ★★★ 63% Harpenden House Hotel, 18
Southdown Rd, HARPENDEN
☎ 01582 764111 18 ⇄ ⟲Annexe35 ⇄ ⟲

---

# KENT

## ADDINGTON Map 05 TQ65

**West Malling** London Rd ME19 5AR ☎ 01732 844785
Two 18-hole parkland courses.
*Spitfire Course: 18 holes, 6142yds, Par 70, SSS 70, Course
record 67.*
*Hurricane Course: 18 holes, 6268yds, Par 70, SSS 70,
Course record 69.*
**Visitors** must contact in advance, may not play weekends
until 2pm.
**Societies** prior booking required.
**Green Fees** £30 per day; £20 per round (£30 per round after
2pm weekends).
**Facilities** ⊗ ⵢ ⵏ ⵡ ⵟ ⴷ ⴼ ⴼ Jonathan Foss.
**Leisure** squash, motorised carts for hire, buggies for hire,
trolley for hire, putting green, practice area,
snooker, table tennis.
**Location** 1m S off A20
**Hotel** ★★★ 64% Larkfield Priory Hotel, London Rd,
LARKFIELD
☎ 01732 846858 52rm(51 ⇄ ⟲)

---

## ASH Map 05 TQ66

**The London** South Ash Manor Estate TN15 7EN
☎ 01474 879899
Visitors may only play the courses at LGC as guests of
members or prospective members by invitation.The courses,
the Heritage and the International were designed by Jack
Nicklaus: both include a number of lakes, generous fairways
framed with native grasses and many challenging holes. A
state-of-the-art drainage system ensures continuous play.
*Heritage Course: 18 holes, 6771yds, Par 72, Course record 68.*
*International Course: 18 holes, 6574yds, Par 72.*
*Club membership 350.*
**Visitors** guest of member & prospective members invited
by the membership office only.
**Societies** companies only by application.
**Green Fees** Guest of member. Heritage: £50 per round (£60
weekend & bank holidays). International: £40
per round (£45 weekend & bank holiday).
**Facilities** ⊗ ⵢ ⵏ ⵡ ⵟ ⴷ ⴼ ⴼ Keith Morgan.
**Leisure** sauna, motorised carts for hire, buggies for hire,
trolley for hire, driving range, putting green,
practice area.
**Location** A20, 2m from Brands Hatch
**Hotel** ★★★ 64% Larkfield Priory Hotel, London Rd,
LARKFIELD
☎ 01732 846858 52rm(51 ⇄ ⟲)

---

## ASHFORD Map 05 TR04

**Ashford** Sandyhurst Ln TN25 4NT
☎ 01233 622655
Parkland course with good views and easy walking. Narrow
fairways and tightly bunkered greens ensure a challenging
game.
*18 holes, 6263yds, Par 71, SSS 70, Course record 65.*
*Club membership 650.*
**Visitors** must contact in advance & have handicap
certificate.

Societies   Tue & Thu only, by arrangement.
Green Fees  £30 per day; £20 per round weekdays.
Facilities  ⊗ ⫙ ᛒ ⬛ ♀⅄ 🏠 ℓ Hugh Sherman.
Leisure     putting green.
Location    1.5m NW off A20
Hotel       ★★★★ 66% Ashford Moat House, Simone
            Weil Av, ASHFORD
            ☎ 01233 219988 200 ⇋ ℝ
Additional  QQQQ Elvey Farm Country Hotel, PLUCKLEY
hotel       ☎ 01233 840442 10 ⇋ ℝ

**Homelands Bettergolf Centre** Ashford Rd, Kingsnorth
TN26 1NJ ☎ 01233 661620
Challenging 9-hole course designed by Donald Steel to
provide a stern test for experienced golfers and for others to
develop their game. With 4 par 3s and 5 par 4s it demands
accuracy rather than length. Floodlit driving range.
*9 holes, 2205yds, Par 32, SSS 31.*
Visitors    no restrictions, but booking recommended for
            weekend and summer evenings.
Societies   prior arrangements are essential.
Green Fees  £10.50 per 18 holes; £7 per 9 holes (£14/£8
            weekends and bank holidays).
Facilities  ⊗ ᛒ ⬛ ♀⅄ 🏠 ⚲ ℓ Johnathan Callister.
Leisure     trolley for hire, driving range, putting green,
            practice area, 4 hole academy teaching course.
Hotel       ★★★ 62% Master Spearpoint Hotel,
            Canterbury Rd, Kennington, ASHFORD
            ☎ 01233 636863 35 ⇋ ℝ

## BARHAM                                           Map 05 TR25

**Broome Park** CT4 6QX ☎ 01227 831701
Championship standard parkland course in a valley, with a
350-year-old mansion clubhouse.
*18 holes, 6610yds, Par 72, SSS 72, Course record 66.*
*Club membership 500.*
Visitors    advisable to contact in advance, must have
            handicap certificate, but may not play Sat/Sun
            mornings.
Societies   Mon-Fri only, apply in writing or by telephone.
Green Fees  £26 per round (£32 weekends & bank holidays).
            Dusk ticket £15 after 6pm.
Facilities  ⊗ ⫙ ᛒ ⬛ ♀⅄ 🏠 ⚲ 🏌 ℓ Tienne Britz.
Leisure     heated outdoor swimming pool, squash, sauna,
            solarium, gymnasium, motorised carts for hire,
            buggies for hire, trolley for hire, driving range,
            putting green, practice area.
Location    1.5m SE on A260
Hotel       ★★★ 64% Chaucer Hotel, Ivy Ln,
            CANTERBURY
            ☎ 01227 464427 42 ⇋ ℝ

## BEARSTED                                          Map 05 TQ85

**Bearsted** Ware St ME14 4PQ ☎ 01622 738198
Parkland course with fine views of the North Downs.
*18 holes, 6437yds, Par 72, SSS 71.*
*Club membership 720.*
Visitors    must have handicap certificate and may not play
            weekends unless with member. Must contact in
            advance.
Societies   write for reservation forms.
Green Fees  £32 per day; £24 per round (£30 per round
            weekends).
Facilities  ⊗ ⫙ ᛒ ⬛ ♀⅄ 🏠 ℓ Tim Simpson.
Leisure     trolley for hire, putting green, practice area.
Location    2.5m E of Maidstone off A20
Hotel       ★★★★ 61% Tudor Park Hotel, Country Club
            Resort, Ashford Rd, Bearstead, MAIDSTONE
            ☎ 01622 734334 117 ⇋ ℝ

## BIDDENDEN                                         Map 05 TQ83

**Chart Hills** Weeks Ln TN27 8JX ☎ 01580 292222
Created by Nick Faldo and completed in 1993, this huge
course of grand design measures 7,000 yards from the back
tees. Facilities include a David Leadbetter Golf Academy.
*18 holes, 7086yds, Par 72, SSS 74.*
*Club membership 280.*
Visitors    contact for details.
Societies   telephone for details.
Green Fees  not confirmed.
Facilities  ⊗ ⫙ ᛒ ⬛ ♀⅄ 🏠 ⚲ ℓ William Easdale.
Leisure     sauna, solarium, gymnasium, motorised carts for
            hire, buggies for hire, driving range, putting
            green, practice area.
Location    1m N of Biddenden off A274
Hotel       ★★ 67% Jarvis White Lion Hotel, High St,
            TENTERDEN
            ☎ 01580 765077 15 ⇋ ℝ

## BOROUGH GREEN                                     Map 05 TQ65

**Wrotham Heath** Seven Mile Ln TN15 8QZ
☎ 01732 884ᶜ )0
Parkland course, hilly, good views.
*18 holes, 5954yds, Par 70, SSS 69.*
*Club membership 550.*
Visitors    must contact in advance, may not play
            weekends.
Societies   Thu & Fri only, by arrangement.
Green Fees  £32 per day; £22 per round.
Facilities  ⊗ ⫙ ᛒ ⬛ ♀⅄ 🏠 ℓ Harry Dearden.          ▶

# Elvey Farm Country Hotel
**Pluckley, Nr. Ashford, Kent TN27 0SU**
**Tel: Pluckley (01233) 840442    Fax/Guest Tel: (01233) 840726**

Situated right in the heart of 'Darling Buds of May' country, we offer delux accommodation in our
Oast House, converted stables and 15thC. Kent Barn. Traditional English breakfast is served in
our unique dining room, dinner available when booked in advance, fully licensed. Ten double and
family rooms all with private bath/shower and colour T.V. Special rates for groups and societies,
many local courses including Faldo's designed Chart Hills.

*Junction 9, M20 only 12 minutes
away. Channel Tunnel 20 minutes*

**Leisure** trolley for hire, putting green, practice area.
**Location** 2.25m E on B2016
**Hotel** B Forte Posthouse Maidstone/Sevenoaks,
London Rd, Wrotham Heath, WROTHAM
☎ 01732 883311 106 ⇔ ℾ

## BRENCHLEY Map 05 TQ64

**Moatlands** Watermans Ln TN12 6ND
☎ 01892 724400
A rolling parkland course with dramatic views over the
Weald of Kent. The challenging holes are the Par 4 8th with
its tough dogleg, the 10th where there is a wooded copse with
a Victorian bath-house to be avoided and the 14th where the
approach to the green is guarded by oak trees.
*18 holes, 6693yds, Par 72, SSS 72, Course record 71.*
*Club membership 453.*
**Visitors** must book in advance.
**Societies** apply in writing or telephone.
**Green Fees** £45 per day; £29 per round (£55/£39 weekends).
Day prices summer only.
**Facilities** ⊗ ℳ ℔ ▆ ♀ ⚘ 🖻 ℾ ℓ Simon Wood.
**Leisure** hard tennis courts, heated indoor swimming
pool, sauna, gymnasium, motorised carts for
hire, buggies for hire, trolley for hire, driving
range, putting green, practice area.
**Location** 3m N of Brenchley off B2160
**Hotel** ★★★ 67% Jarvis Pembury Hotel, 8 Tonbridge
Rd, Pembury, TUNBRIDGE WELLS
(ROYAL) ☎ 01892 823567 80 ⇔ ℾ

## BROADSTAIRS Map 05 TR36

**North Foreland** Convent Rd, Kingsgate CT10 3PU
☎ 01843 862140
A picturesque course situated where the Thames Estuary
widens towards the sea. North Foreland always seems to
have a breath of tradition of golf's earlier days about it.
Perhaps the ghost of one of its earlier professionals, the
famous Abe Mitchell, still haunts the lovely turf of the
fairways. Walking is easy and the wind is deceptive. The
8th and 17th, both par 4, are testing holes. There is also
an approach and putting course.
*18 holes, 6430yds, Par 71, SSS 71, Course record 65.*
*Short Course: 18 holes, 1752yds, Par 54, Course record 47.*
*Club membership 1200.*
**Visitors** for Main course are required to book in
advance & have handicap certificate. May
play afternoons only Mon and Tue,
weekends restricted and no visitors Sun
morning. Short course has no restrictions.
**Societies** Wed & Fri only, by arrangement.
**Green Fees** Main course £35 per day; £25 per round
(£35 per round weekends). Short course
£5.50/£6.50 per day.
**Facilities** ⊗ ℳ by prior arrangement ℔ ▆ ♀ ⚘ 🖻
ℾ ℓ Neil Hansen.
**Leisure** hard tennis courts, motorised carts for hire,
buggies for hire, trolley for hire, putting
green, practice area.
**Location** 1.5m N off B2052
**Hotel** ★★★ 60% Royal Albion Hotel, Albion St,
BROADSTAIRS
☎ 01843 868071 19 ⇔ ℾ

## CANTERBURY Map 05 TR15

**Canterbury** Scotland Hills, Littlebourne Rd CT1 1TW
☎ 01227 453532
Undulating parkland course, densely wooded in places, with
elevated trees and difficult drives on several holes.
*18 holes, 6249yds, Par 70, SSS 70, Course record 64.*
*Club membership 650.*
**Visitors** may only play after 3pm weekends & bank
holidays. Must have a handicap certificate.
**Societies** by arrangement.
**Green Fees** £36 per day; £27 per round (£36 per round
weekends and bank holidays).
**Facilities** ⊗ ℳ ℔ ▆ ♀ ⚘ 🖻 ℓ Paul Everard.
**Leisure** trolley for hire, putting green, practice area.
**Location** 1.5m E on A257
**Hotel** ★★★ 64% Chaucer Hotel, Ivy Ln,
CANTERBURY
☎ 01227 464427 42 ⇔ ℾ

## CHART SUTTON Map 05 TQ84

**The Ridge** Chartway St, East Sutton ME17 3DL
☎ 01622 844382
Opened in 1993, the course was designed by Patrick Dawson
around mature orchards to challenge all levels of player. The
par 5, 18th has two lakes to negotiate.
*18 holes, 6254yds, Par 71, SSS 70, Course record 68.*
*Club membership 650.*
**Visitors** weekdays only, must have handicap certificate.
**Societies** Tue & Thu, by arrangement.
**Green Fees** £25 per day; £18 per round.
**Facilities** ⊗ ℳ ℔ ▆ ♀ ⚘ 🖻 ℾ ℓ Matthew Rackham.
**Leisure** solarium, gymnasium, trolley for hire, driving
range, putting green, practice area.
**Location** 5m S of Bearsted, off A274
**Hotel** ★★★★ 61% Tudor Park Hotel, Country Club
Resort, Ashford Rd, Bearstead, MAIDSTONE
☎ 01622 734334 117 ⇔ ℾ

## CRANBROOK Map 05 TQ73

**Cranbrook** Benenden Rd TN17 4AL
☎ 01580 712833
Scenic, parkland course with easy terrain, backed by
Hemstead Forest and close to Sissinghurst Castle (1m) and
Bodiam Castle (6m). The most testing hole is the 12th (530
yds par 5). Venue for the County Championships.
*18 holes, 6351yds, Par 70, SSS 70.*
*Club membership 480.*
**Visitors** may not play at weekends before 11am. Phone to
book tee time up to one week in advance.
**Societies** minimum of 12 write or telephone to book.
**Green Fees** £30 per 36 holes; £20 per 18 holes (£27.50 per
18 holes weekends).
**Facilities** ⊗ ℳ ℔ ▆ ♀ ⚘ 🖻 ℓ Alan Gillard.
**Leisure** trolley for hire, driving range, extensive practice
area.
**Location** 2m E
**Hotel** ★★ 69% Hartley Mount Country House,
Hartley Rd, CRANBROOK
☎ 01580 712230 6 ⇔ ℾ

## DARTFORD
Map 05 TQ57

**Birchwood Park** Birchwood Rd, Wilmington DA2 7HJ
☎ 01322 662038 & 660554
18-hole course of two separate nines, reasonably demanding for good golfers. Last four holes very interesting. Additional 9-hole simple beginners/practice course and 38-bay floodlit driving range.
*18 holes, 6364yds, Par 71, SSS 70, Course record 64 or 9 holes, 1259yds, Par 28.*
*Club membership 630.*
**Visitors** must contact in advance.
**Societies** telephone for details.
**Green Fees** £14 (£23 weekends). 9 hole course £4 (£5 weekends).
**Facilities** ⊗ ⅶ ⅃ ♨ ☾ ⅂ ☖ ☎ ☏ ☾ Martyn Hirst.
**Leisure** floodlit driving range, putting green.
**Location** B258 between Dartford & Swanley
**Hotel** ★★★★ 71% Swallow Hotel, 1 Broadway, BEXLEYHEATH
☎ 0181 298 1000 142 ⇆ ☏

**Dartford** Upper Heath Ln, Dartford Heath DA1 2TN
☎ 01322 226455
Heathland course.
*18 holes, 5914yds, Par 69, SSS 69, Course record 65.*
*Club membership 700.*
**Visitors** may not play at weekends. Must have a handicap certificate.
**Societies** Mon & Fri only by prior arrangement with Secretary.
**Green Fees** £28 per day; £20 per round.
**Facilities** ⊗ ⅶ by prior arrangement ♨ ☾ ⅂ ☖ ☎ ☏ Gary Cooke.
**Leisure** trolley for hire, putting green, practice area.
**Hotel** B Forte Posthouse Bexley, Black Prince Interchange, Southwold Rd, BEXLEY
☎ 01322 526900 103 ⇆ ☏

## DEAL
Map 05 TR35

*Royal Cinque Ports* Golf Rd CT14 6RF
☎ 01304 374007
Famous championship seaside links, windy but with easy walking. Outward nine is generally considered the easier, inward nine is longer and includes the renowned 16th, perhaps the most difficult hole. On a fine day there are wonderful views across the Channel.
*18 holes, 6785yds, Par 72, SSS 72.*
*Club membership 850.*
**Visitors** restricted Wed mornings, weekends & bank holidays. Must contact in advance and have a handicap certificate.
**Societies** must contact in advance.
**Green Fees** not confirmed.
**Facilities** ⅂ ☖ ☎ ☏ ☾ Andrew Reynolds.
**Leisure** putting,motor cart/buggy/trolley hire.
**Location** Along seafront at N end of Deal
**Hotel** B Forte Posthouse Dover, Singledge Ln, Whitfield, DOVER
☎ 01304 821222 67 ⇆ ☏

## EDENBRIDGE
Map 05 TQ44

**Edenbridge Golf & Country Club** Crouch House Rd TN8 5LQ ☎ 01732 865097 & 867381
Gently undulating course with a driving range.
*Old Course: 18 holes, 6646yds, Par 73.*
*Skeynes Course: 18 holes, 5698yds, Par 67.*
*Club membership 1300.*
**Visitors** must contact in advance for Old Course.
**Societies** contact in advance.
**Green Fees** Old Course: £15 (£20 weekends). Skeynes Course: £10 (£14 weekends, £12 after noon).
**Facilities** ⊗ ⅶ ♨ ☾ ⅂ ☖ ☎ ☏ ☾ Keith Burkin.
**Leisure** hard tennis courts, gymnasium, motorised carts for hire, buggies for hire, trolley for hire, driving range, putting green, practice area, pitch & putt.
**Location** 1m W of town centre, signposted 'Golf Course'
**Hotel** ★★★(red)♨♨ Gravetye Manor Hotel, EAST GRINSTEAD ☎ 01342 810567 18 ⇆ ☏

## EYNSFORD
Map 05 TQ56

*Austin Lodge* Eynsford Station DA4 0HU
☎ 01322 868944
A well drained course designed to lie naturally in three secluded valleys in rolling countryside. Over 7000 yds from the medal tees. Practice ground, nets and a putting green add to the features.
*18 holes, 6600yds, Par 73, SSS 71.*
*Club membership 600.*
**Visitors** must contact in advance, may not play until after 1pm on weekends and bank holidays.
**Societies** telephone for bookings.
**Green Fees** not confirmed.
**Facilities** ⅂ ☖ ☎ ☏ Nigel Willis.
**Leisure** putting,cart/buggy/trolley hire.
**Location** 6m S of Dartford
**Hotel** ★★★★ 61% Brands Hatch Thistle, BRANDS HATCH ☎ 01474 854900 137 ⇆ ☏

## FAVERSHAM
Map 05 TR06

*Faversham* Belmont Park ME13 0HB
☎ 01795 890561
A beautiful inland course laid out over part of a large estate with pheasants walking the fairways quite tamely. Play follows two heavily wooded valleys but the trees affect only the loose shots going out of bounds. Fine views.
*18 holes, 6030yds, Par 70, SSS 69.*
*Club membership 800.*
**Visitors** must have handicap certificate. With member only at weekends. Contacting the club in advance is advisable.
**Societies** must contact in advance.
**Green Fees** not confirmed.
**Facilities** ⅂ ☖ ☎ ☏ Stuart Rokes.
**Location** 3.5m S
**Hotel** ★★★★♨♨ 75% Eastwell Manor, Eastwell Park, Boughton Lees, ASHFORD
☎ 01233 219955 23 ⇆ ☏

## FOLKESTONE

Map 05 TR23

**Etchinghill** Canterbury Rd, Etchinghill CT18 8FA
☎ 01303 863863
A varied course incorporating parkland on the outward 9 holes and an interesting downland landscape with many challenging holes on the back 9.
*18 holes, 6174yds, Par 70, SSS 69, Course record 67.*
*Club membership 600.*
**Visitors** advisable to reserve tee time in advance.
**Societies** telephone or write, packages available.
**Green Fees** £15 (£20 weekends & bank holidays).
**Facilities** ⊗ ⋙ ⓛ 💺 ♀ 🕿 🏠 ⛳ ⌁ Trevor Dungate.
**Leisure** buggies for hire, trolley for hire, floodlit driving range, putting green, practice area, par 3 course.
**Location** N of M20, access from junct 11 or 12
**Hotel** ★★ 67% Wards Restaurant & Hotel, 39 Earls Ave, FOLKESTONE
☎ 01303 245166 10 ⇆ ℝ

## GILLINGHAM

Map 05 TQ76

**Gillingham** Woodlands Rd ME7 2AP
☎ 01634 853017
Parkland course.
*18 holes, 5347yds, Par 67, SSS 65.*
*Club membership 800.*
**Visitors** contact in advance, weekends only with member.
**Societies** must apply in writing.
**Green Fees** £25 per day; £18 per round (£15/£10 weekends).
**Facilities** ⊗ ⋙ ⓛ 💺 ♀ 🕿 🏠 ⛳ ⌁ Brian Impett.
**Leisure** trolley for hire, driving range, putting green, practice area.
**Location** 1.5m SE on A2
**Hotel** B Forte Posthouse Rochester, Maidstone Rd, ROCHESTER ☎ 01634 687111 105 ⇆ ℝ

## GRAVESEND

Map 05 TQ67

**Mid Kent** Singlewell Rd DA11 7RB ☎ 01474 568035
A well-maintained downland course with some easy walking and some excellent greens. The first hole is short, but nonetheless a real challenge. The slightest hook and the ball is out of bounds or lost.
*18 holes, 6199yds, Par 69, SSS 69, Course record 60.*
*Club membership 900.*
**Visitors** must contact in advance & have handicap certificate. May not play weekends.
**Societies** Tue only, apply in writing.
**Green Fees** £30 per day; £20 per round.
**Facilities** ⊗ ⋙ ⓛ 💺 ♀ 🕿 🏠 ⛳ ⌁ Mark Foreman.
**Leisure** trolley for hire, putting green, practice area.
**Location** S side of town centre off A227
**Hotel** ★★★ 61% Overcliffe Hotel, 15-16 The Overcliffe, GRAVESEND
☎ 01474 322131

## HAWKHURST

Map 05 TQ73

**Hawkhurst** High St TN18 4JS ☎ 01580 752396
Undulating parkland course.
*9 holes, 5751yds, Par 70, SSS 68, Course record 69.*
*Club membership 508.*

**Visitors** may play weekdays and after 4pm weekends except with member.
**Societies** must apply in advance.
**Green Fees** £12 per round; £9 per 9 holes (£12 per round weekends after 4pm).
**Facilities** ⊗ ⋙ by prior arrangement ⓛ 💺 ♀ 🕿 🏠 ⛳ ⌁ Tony Collins.
**Leisure** squash, buggies for hire, trolley for hire, driving range, putting green, practice area.
**Location** W side of village off A268
**Hotel** ★★★ 68% Tudor Court Hotel, Rye Rd, HAWKHURST ☎ 01580 752312 18 ⇆ ℝ

## HERNE BAY

Map 05 TR16

**Herne Bay** Eddington CT6 7PG ☎ 01227 373964
Parkland course with bracing air.
*18 holes, 4966yds, Par 65, SSS 64.*
*Club membership 500.*
**Visitors** may not play mornings at weekends. Temporary course pending road works.
**Societies** apply in advance.
**Green Fees** £18 (£25 weekends and bank holidays).
**Facilities** ⊗ ⋙ by prior arrangement ⓛ 💺 ♀ 🕿 🏠 ⛳ ⌁ D Lambert.
**Leisure** trolley for hire, practice area.
**Location** 1m S on A291
**Hotel** ★★★ 66% Falstaff Hotel, St Dunstans St, Westgate, CANTERBURY
☎ 01227 462138 24 ⇆ ℝ

## HEVER

Map 05 TQ44

**Hever** TN8 7NG ☎ 01732 700771
The newly established Hever course has recently been voted one of the top ten developments in the British Isles. The 18-hole parkland course is set in 210 acres with water hazards and outstanding holes like the Par 3 12th which is similar to the 12th at Augusta.
*18 holes, 7002yds, Par 72, SSS 75, Course record 69.*
*Club membership 620.*
**Visitors** must book tee times Mon-Fri.
**Societies** telephone for details.
**Green Fees** not confirmed.
**Facilities** ♀ 🕿 🏠 ⛳ ⌁ John Powell.
**Hotel** ★★★ 76% Spa Hotel, Mount Ephraim, TUNBRIDGE WELLS
☎ 01892 520331 76 ⇆ ℝ

## HILDENBOROUGH

Map 05 TQ54

**Nizels** Nizels Ln TN11 8NX ☎ 01732 833138
Woodland course with many mature trees, wildlife and lakes that come into play on several holes. The 2nd hole is a 553yd Par 5, the green being guarded by bunkers hidden by a range of hillocks. The Par 4 7th has water on both sides of the fairway and a pitch over water to the green. The 10th is 539yd Par 5 with a sharp dogleg to the right, followed by a very narrow entry between trees for the 2nd shot.
*18 holes, 6408yds, Par 72, SSS 71, Course record 68.*
*Club membership 650.*
**Visitors** telephone professional shop for tee reservation 01732 838926.
**Societies** weekdays only, telephone initially.
**Green Fees** £35 all day, £25 per 18 holes (after 2pm).

| Facilities | ⊗ ⅶ ⅃ ⅃ ♀ ♨ ⌂ ☂ ꙭ Ⅽ Richard Tinworth. |
|---|---|
| Leisure | motorised carts for hire, buggies for hire, trolley for hire, putting green, practice area. |
| Location | Off B245 |
| Hotel | ★★★ 58%  Rose & Crown Hotel, 125 High St, TONBRIDGE ☎ 01732 357966 48 ⇄ ꜰ |

## HOO
Map 05 TQ77

**Deangate Ridge** ME3 8RZ ☎ 01634 251180
Parkland, municipal course designed by Fred Hawtree. 18-hole pitch and putt.
*18 holes, 6300yds, Par 71, SSS 70.*
*Club membership 700.*

| Visitors | no restrictions. |
|---|---|
| Societies | must apply in writing. |
| Green Fees | not confirmed. |
| Facilities | ♀ ♨ ⌂ ☂ Ⅽ Richard Fox. |
| Leisure | hard tennis courts, buggy/trolley hire, practice area. |
| Location | 4m NE of Rochester off A228 |
| Hotel | B Forte Posthouse Rochester, Maidstone Rd, ROCHESTER ☎ 01634 687111 105 ⇄ ꜰ |

## HYTHE
Map 05 TR13

**Hythe Imperial** Princes Pde CT21 6AE
☎ 01303 267441
A 9-hole links course played off alternative tees on the second nine. Flat but interesting and testing. Hotel provides many leisure and sports facilities.
*9 holes, 5560yds, Par 68, SSS 66, Course record 61.*
*Club membership 300.*

| Visitors | course closed some Sun until 11am. |
|---|---|
| Societies | must apply in writing. |
| Green Fees | not confirmed. |
| Facilities | ♀ ♨ ⌂ ☂ ꙭ Ⅽ Gordon Ritchie. |
| Leisure | hard and grass tennis courts, heated indoor swimming pool, squash, sauna, solarium, gymnasium, boule, bowling, croquet, health & beauty spa. |
| Location | SE side of town |
| Hotel | ★★★★ 73% The Hythe Imperial Hotel, Princes Pde, HYTHE ☎ 01303 267441 100 ⇄ ꜰ |
| Additional hotel | ★★★ 69% Stade Court Hotel, West Pde, HYTHE ☎ 01303 268263 42 ⇄ ꜰ |

**Sene Valley** Sene CT18 8BL
☎ 01303 268513 (Manager) & 268514 (Pro)
A two-level downland course which provides interesting golf over an undulating landscape with sea views.
*18 holes, 6196yds, Par 71, SSS 69, Course record 61.*
*Club membership 650.*

| Visitors | must contact professional in advance. |
|---|---|
| Societies | telephone in advance. |
| Green Fees | £30 per day; £20 per round (£32/£25 weekends). |
| Facilities | ⊗ ⅶ ⅃ ⅃ ♀ ♨ ⌂ Ⅽ Paul Moger. |
| Leisure | trolley for hire, driving range, putting green, practice hire. |
| Location | 1m NE off B2065 |
| Hotel | ★★★★ 73% The Hythe Imperial Hotel, Princes Pde, HYTHE ☎ 01303 267441 100 ⇄ ꜰ |

## KINGSDOWN
Map 05 TR34

**Walmer & Kingsdown** The Leas CT14 8EP
☎ 01304 373256
This course near Deal has through the years been overshadowed by its neighbours at Deal and Sandwich, yet it is a testing circuit with many undulations. The course is famous as being the one on which, in 1964, Assistant Professional, Roger Game became the first golfer in Britain to hole out in one at two successive holes; the 7th and 8th. The course is situated on top of the cliffs, with fine views.
*18 holes, 6437yds, Par 72, SSS 71, Course record 66.*
*Club membership 600.*

| Visitors | must contact in advance. Not before 9.30am weekdays and noon weekends & bank holidays. |
|---|---|
| Societies | apply in writing. |
| Green Fees | £28 per day; £22 per round (£30/£24 weekends & bank holidays). |
| Facilities | ⊗ ⅶ ⅃ ⅃ ♀ ♨ ⌂ Ⅽ Matthew Paget. |
| Leisure | trolley for hire, putting green, practice area. |
| Location | 0.5m S off B2057 |
| Hotel | B Forte Posthouse Dover, Singledge Ln, Whitfield, DOVER ☎ 01304 821222 67 ⇄ ꜰ |

## LAMBERHURST
Map 05 TQ63

**Lamberhurst** Church Rd TN3 8DT ☎ 01892 890591
Parkland course crossing river twice. Fine views.
*18 holes, 6345yds, Par 72, SSS 70, Course record 65.*
*Club membership 700.*

| Visitors | may only play after noon weekends unless with member, handicap certificate required. |
|---|---|
| Societies | Tue, Wed & Thu only from Apr-Oct, by arrangement. |
| Green Fees | £30 per day; £20 per round (£36 weekends after noon, £20 Oct-Mar). |
| Facilities | ⊗ ⅶ by prior arrangement ⅃ ♀ ♀ ♨ ⌂ Ⅽ Mike Travers. |
| Leisure | motorised carts for hire, buggies for hire, trolley for hire, putting green, practice area. |
| Location | N side of village on B2162 |
| Hotel | ★★★ 67% Jarvis Pembury Hotel, 8 Tonbridge Rd, Pembury, TUNBRIDGE WELLS (ROYAL) ☎ 01892 823567 80 ⇄ ꜰ |

## LITTLESTONE
Map 05 TR02

**Littlestone** St Andrew's Rd TN28 8RB
☎ 01797 363355
Located on the Romney Marshes, this flattish seaside links course calls for every variety of shot. The 8th, 15th, 16th and 17th are regarded as classics by international golfers. Allowance for wind must always be made. Extensive practice area.
*18 holes, 6460yds, Par 71, SSS 72, Course record 67.*
*Club membership 550.*

| Visitors | must contact in advance, no visitors before 3pm weekends and bank holidays. |
|---|---|
| Societies | must apply in advance. |
| Green Fees | £36 per day; £26 per round (£45/£40 weekends). ▶ |

**Facilities** ⊗ ⊪ ⓛ ⓨ ♀ ⏃ 🕿 ʃ Stephen Watkins.  ·
**Leisure** trolley for hire, putting green, practice area.
**Location** N side of village
**Hotel** ★★★★ 73% The Hythe Imperial Hotel,
Princes Pde, HYTHE
🕿 01303 267441 100 ⇋ ʕ

**Romney Warren** St Andrews Rd TN28 8RB
🕿 01797 362231
A traditional links course, newly developed alongside the 9-
hole course at Littlestone.
*18 holes, 5126yds, Par 67, SSS 65.*
*Club membership 340.*
**Visitors** contact professional in advance.
**Societies** contact in advance.
**Green Fees** £18 per day; £10 per round (£25/£15 weekends
& bank holidays).
**Facilities** ⊗ ⊪ ⓛ ⓨ ♀ ⏃ 🕿 ʃ Stephen Watkins.
**Leisure** trolley for hire, putting green, practice area.
**Location** N side of Littlestone
**Hotel** ★★★★ 73% The Hythe Imperial Hotel, Princes
Pde, HYTHE 🕿 01303 267441 100 ⇋ ʕ

---

## MAIDSTONE                                    Map 05 TQ75

---

***Cobtree Manor Park*** Chatham Rd, Sandling ME14 3AZ
🕿 01622 681560
An undulating parkland course with some water hazards.
*18 holes, 5716yds, Par 69, SSS 68, Course record 67.*
*Club membership 550.*
**Visitors** no restrictions.
**Societies** Mon-Fri only, by arrangement.
**Green Fees** not confirmed.
**Facilities** ♀ ⏃ 🕿 ʃ Martin Drew.
**Location** On A229 0.25m N of M20 junc 6
**Hotel** ★★ 61% Boxley House Hotel, The Street,
Boxley, MAIDSTONE
🕿 01622 692269 11 ⇋ ʕAnnexe7 ⇋ ʕ

---

**Leeds Castle** Ashford Rd ME17 1PL 🕿 01622 880467
Situated around Leeds Castle, this is one of the most
picturesque courses in Britain. Re-designed in the 1980s by
Neil Coles, it is a challenging 9-hole course with the added
hazard of the Castle moat. 18-holes may be played on
weekdays.
*9 holes, 2880yds, Par 34, SSS 34, Course record 32.*
**Visitors** booking must be made. Bookings taken from 6
days in advance.
**Societies** apply in advance.
**Green Fees** £15 per 18 holes; £9 per 9 holes (£10 per 9 holes
weekends).
**Facilities** ⊗ ⊪ ⓛ ⓨ ♀ ⏃ 🕿
**Leisure** trolley for hire, putting green, practice area.
**Location** On A20, 4m E of Maidstone
**Hotel** ★★★★ 61% Tudor Park Hotel, Country Club
Resort, Ashford Rd, MAIDSTONE
🕿 01622 734334 117 ⇋ ʕ

---

**Tudor Park Country Club** Ashford Rd, Bearsted
ME14 4NQ 🕿 01622 734334
The course is set in a 220 acre former deerpark with the
pleasant undulating Kent countryside as a backdrop. The
natural features of the land have been incorporated into this
picturesque course to form a challenge for those of both high
and intermediate standard. The Par 5 14th is particularly

interesting. It can alter your score dramatically should you
gamble with a drive to a narrow fairway. This hole has to be
carefully thoughtout from tee to green depending on the wind
direction.
*18 holes, 6041yds, Par 70, SSS 69, Course record 63.*
*Club membership 750.*
**Visitors** may not play Sat & Sun before noon. Contact
pro shop 01622 739412 for bookings.
**Societies** please call the Golf Manager.
**Green Fees** £18 per round (£24 weekends & bank holidays).
**Facilities** ⊗ ⊪ ⓛ ⓨ ♀ ⏃ 🕿 ⚐ ⛳ ʃ John Slinger.
**Leisure** hard tennis courts, heated indoor swimming
pool, sauna, solarium, gymnasium, motorised
carts for hire, buggies for hire, trolley for hire,
driving range, putting green, practice area.
**Location** On A20, 1.25m W of M20 junct 8
**Hotel** ★★★★ 61% Tudor Park Hotel, Country Club
Resort, Ashford Rd, Bearstead, MAIDSTONE
🕿 01622 734334 117 ⇋ ʕ

---

## RAMSGATE                                    Map 05 TR36

---

**St Augustine's** Cottington Rd, Cliffsend CT12 5JN
🕿 01843 590333
A comfortably flat course in this famous bracing
Championship area of Kent. Neither as long nor as
difficult as its lordly neighbours, St Augustine's will
nonetheless extend most golfers. Dykes run across the
course.
*18 holes, 5197yds, Par 69, SSS 65, Course record 61.*
*Club membership 670.*
**Visitors** must contact in advance.
**Societies** must contact in advance.
**Green Fees** £20.50 per day/round (£22.50 weekends and
bank holidays). Afternoons £12.50 (£15
weekends).
**Facilities** ⊗ ⓛ ⓨ ♀ ⏃ 🕿 ʃ Derek Scott.
**Leisure** buggies for hire, trolley for hire, putting
green, practice area.
**Hotel** ★★ 66% Jarvis Marina Hotel, Harbour Pde,
RAMSGATE 🕿 01843 588276 59 ⇋ ʕ

---

## ROCHESTER                                    Map 05 TQ76

---

**Rochester & Cobham Park** Park Pale ME2 3UL
🕿 01474 823411
A first-rate course of challenging dimensions in
undulating parkland. All holes differ and each requires
accurate drive placing to derive the best advantage. The
clubhouse and course are situated a quarter of a mile
from the western end of the M2. The club was formed in
1891.
*18 holes, 6440yds, Par 72, SSS 71, Course record 66.*
*Club membership 720.*
**Visitors** must contact in advance & have handicap
certificate. No visitors weekends.
**Societies** apply in advance.
**Green Fees** £36 per day; £26 per round.
**Facilities** ⊗ ⊪ ⓛ ⓨ ♀ ⏃ 🕿 ʃ Joe Blair.
**Leisure** trolley for hire, putting green, practice area.
**Location** 2.5m W on A2
**Hotel** ★★★★ 75% Bridgewood Manor Hotel,
Bridgewood Roundabout, Maidstone Rd,
ROCHESTER
🕿 01634 201333 100 ⇋ ʕ

# ROYAL ST. GEORGE'S

SANDWICH *Kent* ☎ 01304 613090          Map 05 TR35

*John Ingham writes:* Sandwich is one of the most beautiful and unspoiled towns in southern England. Driving to this part of Kent is much like stepping back into history. The big golf course here, Royal St George's, is where Sandy Lyle won the Open Championship in 1985 by one shot from that colourful American, Payne Stewart.

Like the region, the clubhouse is old-fashioned and the seats near the window in the bar seem to have been there forever. The bar staff may know as much about fishing or lifeboats as they know about beer, and make a visit there a delight, providing you are not looking for modern sophistication.

The course itself is the truest links you will find in all England and the Royal & Ancient, in its wisdom, choose Royal St George's for major championships knowing it will find the pedigree player at the end of a week. Close to the sea, overlooking Pegwell Bay, any kind of wind can make this man-size test even tougher. The sweeping rough at the 1st can be daunting, so can the bunkers and the huge sandhills. But there are classic shots here.

Off-sea breezes can turn to incredible gales, and it is possible to find the course virtually unplayable. A smooth swing can be blown inside out and stories of three good woods to reach certain greens, into wind, are commonplace. Often the problem in high winds is simply to stand up and address the ball. Putting, too, can be almost impossible, with the ball blown off the surface and maybe into the sand. Christy O'Connor Jnr put together a 64 here, and no wonder it's the record!

| | |
|---|---|
| **Visitors** | must contact in advance and have a handicap certificate. May not play at weekends or BHs |
| **Societies** | must apply in writing |
| **Green fees** | Midweek only £55 (18 holes); day £75 |
| **Facilities** | ⊗ ⚊ ⚑ ♀ ⚒ 🍴 ⛳ ∫ (Andrew Brooks) motor carts, tolleys, caddy cars, putting green, practice area |
| **Location** | Sandwich CT13 9PB 1.5m E of town |

**18 holes, 6565yds, Par 70, SSS 72.**
**Course record 64 (N. Faldo/P Stewart/Christy O'Connor)**

## WHERE TO STAY AND EAT NEARBY

**HOTELS:**
**CANTERBURY**
★★★ 66% Falstaff, St Dunstans St.
☎ 01227 462138. 24 (2 ♠ 22 ⇄ ℝ)
★★★ 64% Chaucer, Ivy Lane
☎ 01227 464427. 42 (1 ℝ 41 ⇄ ℝ)

**DOVER**
Forte Posthouse Dover, Singledge Ln, Whitfield (3m NW jct A2/A256)
☎ 01304 821222. 67 ⇄ ℝ

**RAMSGATE**
★★ 66% Jarvis Marina Hotel, Harbour Pde. ☎ 01843 588276. 59 ⇄ ℝ

**RESTAURANTS:**
**CANTERBURY**
❀ Ristorante Tuo e Mio, 16 The Borough. ☎ 01227 761471

**ST MARGARET'S AT CLIFFE**
❀❀❀ Wallets Court, West Cliffe
☎ 01304 852424

## SANDWICH                                    Map 05 TR35

**Prince's** Prince's Dr, Sandwich Bay CT13 9QB
☎ 01304 611118
A 27 hole championship links of the highest calibre built
in three loops of nine holes from a modern clubhouse.
The course represents all that is best in traditional links
golf in the use of depression ridges and broken ground on
a predominantly flat surface with as little protection from
the wind as possible. The three 18 hole combinations all
demand the highest standard of distance judgement.
*Dunes: 9 holes, 3343yds, Par 36, SSS 36.*
*Himalayas: 9 holes, 3163yds, Par 35, SSS 35.*
*Shore: 9 holes, 3347yds, Par 36, SSS 36.*
*Club membership 350.*
**Visitors**       must contact in advance.
**Societies**      must contact in advance.
**Green Fees**   £42 per day; £36 per round (£47/£39 Sat,
                 £52/£40 Sun).
**Facilities**     ⊗ 🎿 ⅃ ♨ ♀ ⚒ 🏠 ⚐ ( Chris Evans.
**Leisure**        motorised carts for hire, buggies for hire,
                   trolley for hire, driving range, putting green,
                   practice area, snooker.
**Location**       2m E via toll road
**Hotel**          ★★ 66% Jarvis Marina Hotel, Harbour Pde,
                   RAMSGATE ☎ 01843 588276 59 ⇌ ♺

**ROYAL ST GEORGES** See page 125

## SEVENOAKS                                   Map 05 TQ55

**Knole Park** Seal Hollow Rd TN15 0HJ
☎ 01732 452150
The course is set in a majestic park with many fine trees
and deer running loose. It has a wiry turf seemingly
impervious to rain. Certainly a pleasure to play on.
Excellent views of Knole House and the North Downs.
Outstanding greens.
*18 holes, 6259yds, Par 70, SSS 70, Course record 64.*
*Club membership 800.*
**Visitors**       may not play at weekends or bank holidays.
                   Must contact Secretary in advance.
**Societies**      telephone initially.
**Green Fees**   £42 per 36 holes; £32 per 18 holes.
**Facilities**     ⊗ ⅃ ♨ ♀ ⚒ 🏠 ( P E Gill.
**Leisure**        squash, trolley for hire, putting green,
                   practice area, snooker.
**Location**       SE side of town centre off B2019
**Hotel**          ★★★ 65% Royal Oak Hotel, Upper High
                   St, SEVENOAKS
                   ☎ 01732 451109 21 ⇌ ♺Annexe16 ⇌ ♺

## SHEERNESS                                   Map 05 TQ97

**Sheerness** Power Station Rd ME12 3AE
☎ 01795 662585
Marshland/meadowland course, few bunkers, but many
ditches and water hazards. Often windy.
*18 holes, 6460yds, Par 72, SSS 71, Course record 66.*
*Club membership 750.*
**Visitors**       with member only at weekends.
**Societies**      Tue-Thu only, telephone in advance.
**Green Fees**   £20 per day; £15 per round.

**Facilities**     ⊗ 🎿 by prior arrangement ♨ ♀ ♀ ⚒ 🏠
                   ( W Evans.
**Leisure**        trolley for hire, putting green, practice area.
**Location**       1.5m E off A249
**Hotel**          ★★★★ 75% Bridgewood Manor Hotel,
                   Bridgewood Roundabout, Maidstone Rd,
                   ROCHESTER
                   ☎ 01634 201333 100 ⇌ ♺

## SHOREHAM                                    Map 05 TQ56

**Darenth Valley** Station Rd TN14 7SA
☎ 01959 522944
Easy walking parkland course in beautiful valley. Testing
12th hole, par 4.
*18 holes, 6327yds, Par 72, SSS 71, Course record 64.*
**Visitors**       must contact in advance.
**Societies**      contact in advance.
**Green Fees**   £12 per round (£17 weekends).
**Facilities**     ⊗ 🎿 ♨ ♀ ♀ ⚒ 🏠 ⚐ ( Scott Fotheringham.
**Leisure**        fishing, trolley for hire, putting green, practice
                   area.
**Location**       1m E on A225
**Hotel**          ★★★ 65% Royal Oak Hotel, Upper High St,
                   SEVENOAKS
                   ☎ 01732 451109 21 ⇌ ♺Annexe16 ⇌ ♺

## SITTINGBOURNE                               Map 05 TQ96

**The Oast Golf Centre** Church Rd, Tonge ME9 9AR
☎ 01795 473527
A Par 3 Approach course of 9 holes with 18 tees augmented
by a 17-bay floodlit driving range and a putting green.
*9 holes, 1664yds, Par 54, SSS 54.*
**Visitors**       no restrictions.
**Societies**      telephone in advance.
**Green Fees**   £5.50 per 18 holes; £4 per 9 holes.
**Facilities**     ⊗ 🎿 ♨ ♀ ⚐
**Leisure**        driving range, putting green, practice area,
                   bowls.
**Location**       2m NE
**Hotel**          ★★★★ 75% Bridgewood Manor Hotel,
                   Bridgewood Roundabout, Maidstone Rd,
                   ROCHESTER
                   ☎ 01634 201333 100 ⇌ ♺

**Sittingbourne & Milton Regis** Wormdale, Newington
ME9 7PX ☎ 01795 842261
A downland course with pleasant vistas. There are a few
uphill climbs, but the course is far from difficult. The 166-
yard, 2nd hole is a testing par 3.
*18 holes, 6279yds, Par 71, SSS 70, Course record 64.*
*Club membership 670.*
**Visitors**       must contact in advance & may not play at
                   weekends.
**Societies**      Tue & Thu, apply in advance.
**Green Fees**   £32 per 36 holes; £20 per 18 holes.
**Facilities**     ⊗ 🎿 ♨ ♀ ♀ ⚒ 🏠 ( John Hearn.
**Leisure**        motorised carts for hire, buggies for hire, trolley
                   for hire, putting green, practice area.
**Location**       Turn off A249 at Dalaway
**Hotel**          ★★★★ 75% Bridgewood Manor Hotel,
                   Bridgewood Roundabout, Maidstone Rd,
                   ROCHESTER
                   ☎ 01634 201333 100 ⇌ ♺

## SNODLAND
Map 05 TQ76

**Oastpark** Malling Rd ME6 5LG
☎ 01634 242661
A challenging parkland course for golfers of all abilities. The course has water hazards, orchards and views across the Valley of Dean.
*18 holes, 6173yds, Par 69, SSS 69, Course record 71.*
*Club membership 620.*
**Visitors** may book 3 days in advance.
**Societies** early booking with deposits required.
**Green Fees** £8.50 per 18 holes; £6 per 9 holes (£12/£7 weekends).
**Facilities** ⊗ ⽊ ⱔ ⤵ ⱒ ⋏ 🖻 ⋲ John Gregory.
**Leisure** trolley for hire, buggy for handicapped golfers.
**Hotel** ★★★ 64% Larkfield Priory Hotel, London Rd, LARKFIELD
☎ 01732 846858 52rm(51 ⇄ ⋔)

## TENTERDEN
Map 05 TQ83

**Tenterden** Woodchurch Rd TN30 7DR
☎ 01580 763987
Attractive parkland course, last 3 holes are hilly.
*18 holes, 6050yds, Par 70, SSS 69, Course record 65.*
*Club membership 600.*
**Visitors** contact professional shop. May only play with member weekends and bank holidays.
**Societies** must apply in writing.
**Green Fees** £20 per day.
**Facilities** ⊗ ⽊ ⱔ ⤵ ⱒ ⋏ 🖻 ⋲ Andrew Scullion.
**Leisure** motorised carts for hire, buggies for hire, trolley for hire, driving range, putting green, practice area.
**Location** 0.75m E on B2067
**Hotel** ★★ 67% Jarvis White Lion Hotel, High St, TENTERDEN
☎ 01580 765077 15 ⇄ ⋔

## TONBRIDGE
Map 05 TQ54

**Poultwood** Higham Ln TN11 9QR
☎ 01732 364039
With the opening of a 9-hole course in the summer of 1994 there are now two public 'pay and play' parkland courses in an idyllic woodland setting. The courses are ecologically designed, offering varied walking, water hazards, natural and interesting playing opportunities for all standards of golfer.
*18 holes, 5569yds, Par 68, SSS 67 or 9 holes, 1281yds, Par 28.*
**Visitors** non registered golfers may book up to 2 days in advance for 18 hole course, or take available tee times, pay and play system on 9 hole.
**Societies** apply in advance to the clubhouse manager.
**Green Fees** £10.50 (£15.50 weekends). 9 hole course £6.90 per 18 holes; £4.60 per 9 holes (£8.60/£5.70 weekends).
**Facilities** ⊗ ⽊ ⱔ ⤵ ⱒ ⋏ 🖻 ⱦ ⋲ Chris Miller.
**Leisure** squash, trolley for hire, putting green, practice area.
**Location** Off A227, 3m N of Tonbridge
**Hotel** ★★★ 58% Rose & Crown Hotel, 125 High St, TONBRIDGE
☎ 01732 357966 48 ⇄ ⋔

## TUNBRIDGE WELLS (ROYAL)
Map 05 TQ53

**Nevill** Benhall Mill Rd TN2 5JW
☎ 01892 525818
Just within Sussex, the county boundary with Kent runs along the northern perimeter of the course. Open undulating ground, well-wooded with much heather and gorse for the first half. The second nine holes slope away from the clubhouse to a valley where a narrow stream hazards two holes.
*18 holes, 6349yds, Par 71, SSS 70, Course record 63.*
*Club membership 900.*
**Visitors** must contact 48 hours in advance, handicap certificate required, permission from secretary for weekends play.
**Societies** must apply in writing one month in advance.
**Green Fees** £33 per day; £25 per round (£46 per day/round weekends and bank holidays).
**Facilities** ⊗ ⽊ ⱔ ⤵ ⱒ ⋏ 🖻 ⱦ ⋲ Paul Huggett.
**Leisure** buggies for hire, trolley for hire, putting green, practice area.
**Location** S of Tunbridge Wells, off forest road
**Hotel** ★★★ 76% Spa Hotel, Mount Ephraim, TUNBRIDGE WELLS
☎ 01892 520331 76 ⇄ ⋔

**Tunbridge Wells** Langton Rd TN4 8XH ☎ 01892 523034
Somewhat hilly, well-bunkered parkland course with lake; trees form natural hazards.
*9 holes, 4560yds, Par 65, SSS 62, Course record 59.*
*Club membership 450.*
**Visitors** must contact in advance, limited availability weekends.
**Societies** weekdays, apply in advance.
**Green Fees** £15 per 18 holes; £10 per 9 holes (£25 per 19 holes weekend).
**Facilities** ⊗ ⱔ ⤵ ⱒ ⋏ 🖻 ⱦ ⋲ Keith Smithson.
**Leisure** trolley for hire, putting green.
**Location** 1m W on A264
**Hotel** ★★★ 76% Spa Hotel, Mount Ephraim, TUNBRIDGE WELLS
☎ 01892 520331 76 ⇄ ⋔

## WESTGATE ON SEA
Map 05 TR37

**Westgate and Birchington** 176 Canterbury Rd CT8 8LT
☎ 01843 831115
Seaside course.
*18 holes, 4926yds, Par 64, SSS 64.*
*Club membership 310.*
**Visitors** must contact in advance & have handicap certificate, restricted at weekends.
**Societies** must contact three months in advance.
**Green Fees** not confirmed.
**Facilities** ⱒ ⋏ 🖻 ⋲ Roger Game.
**Location** E side of town centre off A28
**Hotel** ★★ 60% Ivyside Hotel, 25 Sea Rd, WESTGATE ON SEA
☎ 01843 831082 75rm(73 ⇄ ⋔)

Entries with a shaded background identify courses that are considered to be particularly interesting

## WEST KINGSDOWN                Map 05 TQ56

**Woodlands Manor** Woodlands TN15 6AB
☎ 01959 523806
Interesting, undulating parkland course with testing 1st, 9th
and 15th holes.
*18 holes, 6100yds, Par 69, SSS 68.*
*Club membership 650.*
Visitors        with member only weekend afternoons.
Societies       apply in writing.
Green Fees      not confirmed.
Facilities      ⛄ 🏠 ⛳ ℓ Andrew Brooks.
Leisure         hard tennis courts, driving range, putting green,
                trolley hire.
Location        2m S off A20
Hotel           ★★★★ 61% Brands Hatch Thistle, BRANDS
                HATCH
                ☎ 01474 854900 137 ⇔ ℮

## WHITSTABLE                    Map 05 TR16

**Chestfield (Whitstable)** 103 Chestfield Rd CT5 3LU
☎ 01227 794411
Gently undulating parkland course with sea views. The Par 3
3rd is generally played into the wind and the Par 4th has a
difficult lefthand dogleg.
*18 holes.*
*Club membership 650.*
Visitors        with member weekends. Due to road works
                passing through the course the details on yardage
                cannot be given as the course is also undergoing
                changes to its structure.
Societies       must apply in writing.
Green Fees      £28 per day; £18 per round.
Facilities      ⊗ ⚑ ℙ ♀ ⛄ 🏠 ℓ John Brotherton.
Leisure         motorised carts for hire, buggies for hire, trolley
                for hire, putting green, practice area.
Location        2m SE off A299
Hotel           ★★★ 64% Chaucer Hotel, Ivy Ln,
                CANTERBURY
                ☎ 01227 464427 42 ⇔ ℮

**Whitstable & Seasalter** Collingwood Rd CT5 1EB
☎ 01227 272020
Links course.
*9 holes, 5314yds, Par 66, SSS 63, Course record 62.*
*Club membership 300.*
Visitors        must contact in advance. Must play with
                member at weekends.
Green Fees      £12 per round.
Facilities      ⚑ ℙ ♀ ⛄ 🏠
Leisure         putting green.
Location        W side of town centre off B2205
Hotel           ★★★ 64% Chaucer Hotel, Ivy Ln,
                CANTERBURY
                ☎ 01227 464427 42 ⇔ ℮

---

A golf course name printed in ***bold italics***
means we have been unable to verify
information with the club's management for
the current year

---

# LANCASHIRE

## ACCRINGTON                    Map 07 SD72

**Accrington & District** Devon Av, Oswaldtwistle BB5 4LS
☎ 01254 381614 & 232734
Moorland course with pleasant views of the Pennines and
surrounding areas.
*18 holes, 6044yds, Par 70, SSS 69, Course record 64.*
*Club membership 600.*
Visitors        must contact in advance.
Societies       contact in advance.
Green Fees      £15 Mon-Thu (£20 Fri-Sun & bank holidays).
Facilities      ⊗ ⅏ ⚑ ℙ ♀ ⛄ 🏠 ⛳ ℓ Bill Harling.
Leisure         motorised carts for hire, buggies for hire, trolley
                for hire, driving range, putting green, practise
                area.
Location        Mid way between Accrington & Blackburn
Hotel           ★★★ 66% Dunkenhalgh Hotel, Blackburn Rd,
                Clayton le Moors, ACCRINGTON
                ☎ 01254 398021 37 ⇔ ℮Annexe42 ⇔ ℮

**Baxenden & District** Top o' th' Meadow, Baxenden
BB5 2EA ☎ 01254 234555
Moorland course.
*9 holes, 5740yds, SSS 68.*
Visitors        may not play Sat, Sun and bank holidays except
                with member.
Societies       must contact in advance.
Green Fees      not confirmed.
Facilities      ♀ ⛄
Location        1.5m SE off A680
Hotel           ★★★ 66% Dunkenhalgh Hotel, Blackburn Rd,
                Clayton le Moors, ACCRINGTON
                ☎ 01254 398021 37 ⇔ ℮Annexe42 ⇔ ℮

**Green Haworth** Green Haworth BB5 3SL
☎ 01254 237580
Moorland course dominated by quarries and difficult in
windy conditions.
*9 holes, 5556yds, Par 68, SSS 67, Course record 65.*
*Club membership 360.*
Visitors        may not play Sun, Mar-Oct.
Societies       apply in writing. Weekdays only before 5pm. Or
                contact secretary on above telephone number.
Green Fees      not confirmed.
Facilities      ♀ ⛄
Leisure         putting green, practice area.
Location        2m S off A680
Hotel           ★★★ 59% Blackburn Moat House, Preston
                New Rd, BLACKBURN
                ☎ 01254 899988 98 ⇔ ℮

## BACUP                        Map 07 SD82

**Bacup** Maden Rd OL13 8HY ☎ 01706 873170
Moorland course, predominantly flat except climbs to 1st and
10th holes.
*9 holes, 6008yds, Par 70, SSS 69.*
*Club membership 350.*
Visitors        no restrictions.
Societies       must contact in writing.
Green Fees      not confirmed.

**Facilities** ⊗ 〗Ⅲ ♭ 💄 ♀ ⚘

**Location** W side of town off A671

**Hotel** ★★ 65% Comfort Friendly Inn, Keirby Walk, BURNLEY ☎ 01282 427611 48 ⇥ ♜

## BARNOLDSWICK
Map 07 SD84

**Ghyll** Skipton Rd BB8 6JQ ☎ 01282 842466
Excellent, parkland course with outstanding views, especially from the 8th tee where you can see the Three Peaks. Testing 3rd hole is an uphill par 4.
*9 holes, 5790yds, Par 68, SSS 66, Course record 62.*
*Club membership 345.*

**Visitors** may not play Tue, Fri after 4.30pm & Sun.

**Societies** must contact in writing.

**Green Fees** £14 per day (£18 weekends & bank holidays).

**Facilities** ⊗ by prior arrangement 〗Ⅲ by prior arrangement ♭ by prior arrangement ♀ evenings only ⚘

**Leisure** putting green.

**Location** 1m NE on B6252

**Hotel** ★★★ 64% Stirk House Hotel, GISBURN ☎ 01200 445581 36 ⇥ ♜Annexe12 ⇥ ♜

## BLACKBURN
Map 07 SD62

**Blackburn** Beardwood Brow BB2 7AX
☎ 01254 51122
Parkland course on a high plateau with stream and hills. Superb views of Lancashire coast and the Pennines.
*18 holes, 6144yds, Par 71, SSS 70.*
*Club membership 550.*

**Visitors** must contact professional in advance.

**Societies** must contact in advance.

**Green Fees** £19.50 per day (£22.50 weekends).

**Facilities** ⊗ 〗Ⅲ ♭ 💄 ♀ ⚘ 🏠 ⚲ † ♜ Alan Rodwell.

**Leisure** motorised carts for hire, buggies for hire, trolley for hire, putting green, practice area.

**Location** 1.25m NW of town centre off A677

**Hotel** ★★★ 59% Blackburn Moat House, Preston New Rd, BLACKBURN ☎ 01254 899988 98 ⇥ ♜

## BLACKPOOL
Map 07 SD33

**Blackpool North Shore** Devonshire Rd FY2 0RD
☎ 01253 352054
Undulating parkland course.
*18 holes, 6400yds, Par 71, SSS 71.*
*Club membership 900.*

**Visitors** may not play Thu & Sat. Advisable to contact in advance.

**Societies** must contact in advance.

**Green Fees** not confirmed.

**Facilities** ⚘ 🏠 ⚲ † ♜ Brendan Ward.

**Location** On A587 N of town centre

**Hotel** ★★ 70% Brabyns Hotel, Shaftesbury Av, North Shore, BLACKPOOL ☎ 01253 354263 22 ⇥ ♜Annexe3 ⇥ ♜

**Herons Reach De Vere Hotel** East Park Dr FY3 8LL
☎ 01253 766156 & 838866
The course was designed by Peter Alliss and Clive Clarke. There are 10 man-made lakes and several existing ponds. Built to a links design, well mounded but fairly easy walking. Water comes into play on 9 holes, better players can go for

the carry or shorter hitters can take the safe route. The course provides an excellent and interesting challenge for golfers of all standards.
*18 holes, 6431yds, Par 72, SSS 71, Course record 67.*
*Club membership 500.*

**Visitors** can book up to 4 days in advance by tel 01253 766156, or if staying in hotel or a visiting society, there is no limit to how far in advance bookings can be made.

**Societies** telephone or write to golf sales office 01253 838866 ext 573.

**Green Fees** £20 per 18 holes (£30 weekends & bank holidays).

**Facilities** ♀ ⚘ 🏠 ⚲ † 🍴 ♜ Richard Hudson.

**Leisure** hard tennis courts, heated indoor swimming pool, squash, sauna, solarium, gymnasium, driving range,buggies.

**Location** Off A587 adjacent to Stanley Park & Zoo

**Hotel** ★★★★ 59% De Vere Hotel, East Park Dr, BLACKPOOL ☎ 01253 838866 166 ⇥ ♜

**Stanley Park Municipal** North Park Dr FY3 8LS
☎ 01253 397916
The golf course, situated in Stanley Park is municipal. The golf club (Blackpool Park) is private but golfers may use the clubhouse facilities if playing the course.
*18 holes, 6060yds, Par 70, SSS 69, Course record 64.*
*Club membership 600.*

**Visitors** must apply to Mrs A Hirst, Town Hall, Talbot Square, Blackpool.

**Societies** must apply in writing to Mrs A Hirst, Blackpool Borough Council, Town Hall, Talbot Square, Blackpool.

**Green Fees** £9 per 18 holes (£10.50 weekends & bank holidays).

**Facilities** ⊗ 〗Ⅲ 💄 ♀ ⚘ 🏠 † 🍴 Brian Purdie.

**Leisure** trolley for hire, driving range, putting green, practice area.

**Location** 1m E of Blackpool Tower

**Hotel** ★★★ 58% Clifton Hotel, Talbot Square, BLACKPOOL ☎ 01253 21481 77 ⇥ ♜

## BURNLEY
Map 07 SD83

**Burnley** Glen View BB11 3RW
☎ 01282 421045 & 451281
Moorland course with hilly surrounds.
*18 holes, 5899yds, Par 69, SSS 69, Course record 65.*
*Club membership 750.*

**Visitors** must contact in advance. May not play on Saturdays.

**Societies** must apply in writing.

**Green Fees** £20 per day (£25 weekends & bank holidays).

**Facilities** ⊗ 〗Ⅲ ♭ 💄 ♀ ⚘ 🏠 ♜ William Tye.

**Leisure** trolley for hire, putting green, practice area, snooker.

**Location** 1.5m S off A646

**Hotel** ★★ 65% Comfort Friendly Inn, Keirby Walk, BURNLEY ☎ 01282 427611 48 ⇥ ♜

**Towneley** Towneley Park, Todmorden Rd BB11 3ED
☎ 01282 38473
Parkland course, with other sporting facilities.
*18 holes, 5811yds, Par 70, SSS 68, Course record 67.*
*Club membership 290.*

**Visitors** must contact in advance. ▶

**Societies** must contact in advance in writing.
**Green Fees** £7.50 (£8.50 weekends & bank holidays).
**Facilities** ⊗ ⊞ ⓛ ⬛ ♀ ♨ 🏠 ⚐
**Leisure** trolley for hire, practice area.
**Location** 1m SE of town centre on A671
**Hotel** ★★★ 72% Oaks Hotel, Colne Rd, Reedley,
BURNLEY ☎ 01282 414141 54 ⇄ ⋒

## CHORLEY                                   Map 07 SD51

**Chorley** Hall o' th' Hill, Heath Charnock PR6 9HX
☎ 01257 480263
A splendid moorland course with plenty of fresh air. The
well-sited clubhouse affords some good views of the
Lancashire coast and of Angelzarke, a local beauty spot.
Beware of the short 3rd hole with its menacing out-of-
bounds.
*18 holes, 6307yds, Par 71, SSS 70, Course record 63.*
*Club membership 550.*
**Visitors** must contact in advance and may not play
weekends or bank holidays.
**Societies** must contact in advance. Tue-Fri only.
**Green Fees** £25 day/round Mon-Fri.
**Facilities** ⊗ ⊞ ⓛ ⬛ ♀ ♨ 🏠 ⚐ Mark Tomlinson.
**Leisure** buggies for hire, trolley for hire, putting
green, practice area.
**Location** 2.5m SE on A673
**Hotel** ★★★ 65% Pines Hotel, CLAYTON-LE-
WOODS ☎ 01772 38551 39 ⇄ ⋒

**Duxbury Jubilee Park** Duxbury Hall Rd PR7 4AS
☎ 01257 265380 & 241634
Municipal parkland course.
*18 holes, 6390yds, Par 71, SSS 70.*
*Club membership 250.*
**Visitors** must contact in advance.
**Societies** must contact in advance.
**Green Fees** £6.40 per round (£8.50 weekends & bank
holidays).
**Facilities** ⊗ ⓛ ⬛ ♨ 🏠 ⚐ S Middelman.
**Leisure** trolley for hire, putting green, practice area.
**Location** 2.5m S off A6
**Hotel** B Forte Travelodge, Mill Ln, CHARNOCK
RICHARD ☎ 01257 791746 100 ⇄

**Shaw Hill Hotel Golf & Country Club** Preston Rd,
Whittle-Le-Woods PR7 7PP ☎ 01257 269221
A fine course designed by one of Europe's most
prominent golf architects and offering a considerable
challenge as well as tranquillity and scenic charm. Seven
lakes guard par 5 and long par 4 holes.
*18 holes, 6405yds, Par 72, SSS 71, Course record 65.*
*Club membership 500.*
**Visitors** denims and trainers not allowed on course or
in clubhouse. Jacket and tie required in
restaurant.
**Societies** must telephone in advance.
**Green Fees** not confirmed.
**Facilities** ♀ ♨ 🏠 ⚐ ⋈ ⚐ David Clark.
**Leisure** putting,cart/buggy/trolley hire.
**Location** On A6 1.5m N
**Hotel** ★★★ 68% Shaw Hill Hotel Golf &
Country Club, Preston Rd, Whittle-le-
Woods, CHORLEY
☎ 01257 269221 18 ⇄ ⋒ Annexe4 ⇄ ⋒

## CLITHEROE                                 Map 07 SD74

**Clitheroe** Whalley Rd, Pendleton BB7 1PP
☎ 01200 22292
One of the best inland courses in the country. Clitheroe is
a parkland-type course with water hazards and good
scenic views, particularly on towards Longridge, and
Pendle Hill. The Club has been the venue for the
Lancashire Amateur Championships.
*18 holes, 6326yds, Par 71, SSS 71, Course record 67.*
*Club membership 725.*
**Visitors** must contact in advance.
**Societies** must telephone in advance.
**Green Fees** £27 per day (£32 weekends & bank
holidays).
**Facilities** ⊗ ⊞ ⓛ ⬛ ♀ ♨ 🏠 ⚐ ⚐ John Twissell.
**Leisure** trolley for hire, driving range, putting green,
practice area.
**Location** 2m S on A671
**Hotel** ★★ 68% Shireburn Arms Hotel,
HURST GREEN
☎ 01254 826518 16 ⇄ ⋒

## COLNE                                     Map 07 SD84

**Colne** Law Farm, Skipton Old Rd BB8 7EB
☎ 01282 863391
Moorland course.
*9 holes, 5961yds, Par 70, SSS 69, Course record 63.*
*Club membership 356.*
**Visitors** restricted Thu. Must contact in advance.
**Societies** must contact in advance.

**Whittle-le-Woods, near Chorley, Lancashire, PR6 7PP.**
**Telephone: Chorley (01257) 269221**
**Fax: Chorley (01557) 261223**

*Idyllic Georgian Mansion, set in the midst of a
mature 18 hole golf course, Shaw Hill's magnificent
Georgian exterior is matched only by the beauty of
the many original features, and lavish furnishings
inside the building. Complementing this gracious
building and unsurpassed surroundings is superb
cuisine of mouthwatering excellence.*

*MINI-BREAKS
From £99.00 per person
Comprising of two days, dinner, bed and breakfast
and three complimentary rounds of golf.*

*CORPORATE & SOCIETY GOLF DAYS
A SPECIALITY*

**Telephone 01257 269221
for full colour brochure**

**Green Fees** £15 per round (£20 weekends).
**Facilities** ⊗ ⅲ ㋮ ♥ ♀ ⚲
**Leisure** putting green, practice area, snooker.
**Location** 1m E off A56
**Hotel** ★★★ 64% Stirk House Hotel, GISBURN
☎ 01200 445581 36 ⇆ ⚑Annexe12 ⇆ ⚑

## DARWEN                                    Map 07 SD62

*Darwen* Winter Hill BB3 0LB ☎ 01254 701287
Moorland course.
*18 holes, 5752yds, Par 68, SSS 68.*
*Club membership 600.*
**Visitors** may not play on Sat.
**Societies** must telephone in advance.
**Green Fees** not confirmed.
**Facilities** ♀ ⚲ ⚑ ⚑ Wayne Lennon.
**Leisure** driving range,putting green,practice.
**Location** 1m NW
**Hotel** ★★★ 64% Whitehall Hotel, Springbank,
Whitehall, DARWEN
☎ 01254 701595 15 ⇆ ⚑

## FLEETWOOD                                 Map 07 SD34

*Fleetwood* Princes Way FY7 8AF
☎ 01253 873661 & 773573
Championship length, flat seaside links where the player
must always be alert to changes of direction or strength
of the wind.
*18 holes, 6723yds, Par 72, SSS 72.*
*Club membership 600.*
**Visitors** may not play on competition days.
**Societies** must contact in advance. A deposit of £5 per
player is required.
**Green Fees** not confirmed.
**Facilities** ♀ ⚲ ⚑ ⚑ S McLaughlin.
**Leisure** putting green,trolley hire.
**Location** W side of town centre
**Guesthouse** QQQQQ The Victorian House, Trunnah Rd,
THORNTON-CLEVELEYS
☎ 01253 860619 3 ⇆ ⚑

## GREAT HARWOOD                             Map 07 SD73

**Great Harwood** Harwood Bar, Whallwy Rd BB6 7TE
☎ 01254 884391
Flat parkland course with fine views of the Pendle region.
*9 holes, 6415yds, Par 73, SSS 71, Course record 68.*
*Club membership 320.*
**Visitors** must contact in advance.
**Societies** welcome mid-week only, apply in writing.
**Green Fees** £16 per round (£22 weekends & bank holidays).
**Facilities** ⊗ ⅲ ㋮ ♥ ♀ ⚲
**Leisure** putting green, practice area.
**Location** E side of town centre on A680
**Hotel** ★★★ 66% Dunkenhalgh Hotel, Blackburn Rd,
Clayton le Moors, ACCRINGTON
☎ 01254 398021 37 ⇆ ⚑Annexe42 ⇆ ⚑

## HASLINGDEN                                Map 07 SD72

**Rossendale** Ewood Ln Head BB4 6LH ☎ 01706 831339
Testing, and usually windy meadowland course.

*18 holes, 6293yds, Par 72, SSS 70, Course record 64.*
*Club membership 700.*
**Visitors** must contact in advance. Must play with
member on Sat.
**Societies** must telephone in advance & confirm in writing.
**Green Fees** £22.50 per day (£27.50 weekends & bank
holidays).
**Facilities** ⊗ ⅲ ㋮ ♥ ♀ (ex Mon) ⚲ ⚑
⚑ Stephen Nicholls.
**Leisure** trolley for hire, putting green, practice area.
**Location** 1.5m S off A56
**Hotel** ★★★ 63% Old Mill Hotel, Springwood,
RAMSBOTTOM ☎ 01706 822991 36 ⇆

## HEYSHAM                                   Map 07 SD46

**Heysham** Trumacar Park, Middleton Rd LA3 3JH
☎ 01524 851011
Seaside parkland course, partly wooded. The 15th is a 459
yard Par 4 hole nearly always played into the prevailing south
west wind.
*18 holes, 6258yds, Par 69, SSS 70, Course record 64.*
*Club membership 1100.*
**Visitors** restricted at weekends.
**Societies** must contact in advance.
**Green Fees** £20 per day; £15 per round (£25 weekends).
**Facilities** ⊗ ⅲ ㋮ ♥ ♀ ⚲ ⚑ ⚑ Ryan Done.
**Leisure** motorised carts for hire, trolley for hire, putting
green, practice area, snooker.
**Location** 0.75m S off A589
**Hotel** ★★ 59% Clarendon Hotel, Marine Rd West,
West End Promenade, MORECAMBE
☎ 01524 410180 31rm(28 ⇆ ⚑)

## KNOTT END-ON-SEA                          Map 07 SD34

**Knott End** Wyreside FY6 0AA ☎ 01253 810576
Pleasant, undulating parkland course on banks of River Wyre.
Open to sea breezes.
*18 holes, 5789yds, Par 69, SSS 68, Course record 63.*
*Club membership 500.*
**Visitors** must contact in advance. May not play
weekends.
**Societies** must contact in advance.
**Green Fees** £21 per day; £18 per round (£24 per day
weekends).
**Facilities** ⊗ ⅲ ㋮ ♥ ♀ ⚲ ⚑ ⚑ Paul Walker.
**Leisure** trolley for hire, putting green, practice area.
**Location** W side of village off B5377
**Guesthouse** QQQQQ The Victorian House, Trunnah Rd,
THORNTON-CLEVELEYS
☎ 01253 860619 3 ⇆ ⚑

## LANCASTER                                 Map 07 SD46

*Lancaster Golf & Country Club* Ashton Hall, Ashton-
with-Stodday LA2 0AJ ☎ 01524 751247
This course is unusual for parkland golf as it is exposed
to the winds coming off the Irish Sea. It is situated on the
Lune estuary and has some natural hazards and easy
walking. There are however several fine holes among
woods near the old clubhouse.
*18 holes, 6282yds, Par 71, SSS 71.*
*Club membership 925.*                              ▶

| Visitors | residential visitors only at weekends. Must contact in advance and have a handicap certificate. |
| Societies | Mon-Fri only. Must contact in advance. Handicap certificate required. |
| Green Fees | not confirmed. |
| Facilities | ♀ ⚐ 🖎 ♨ ⎷ David Sutcliffe. |
| Leisure | putting,trolley hire,practice area. |
| Location | 3m S on A588 |
| Hotel | ★★★★ 68% Lancaster House Hotel, Green Ln, Ellel, LANCASTER ☎ 01524 844822 80 ⇆ ♟ |

*Lansil* Caton Rd LA1 3PE ☎ 01524 61233
Parkland course.
*9 holes, 5608yds, Par 70, SSS 67.*
*Club membership 375.*

| Visitors | may not play before 1pm at weekends. |
| Societies | weekdays only; must contact in writing. |
| Green Fees | not confirmed. |
| Facilities | ♀ (eves & weekends) ⚐ |
| Location | N side of town centre on A683 |
| Hotel | B Forte Posthouse Lancaster, Waterside Park, Caton Rd, LANCASTER ☎ 01524 65999 115 ⇆ ♟ |

## LANGHO
Map 07 SD73

**Mytton Fold Farm Hotel** Whalley Rd BB6 8AB
☎ 01254 240662
The course has panoramic views across the Ribble Valley and Pendle Hill. Tight fairways and water hazards are designed to make this a challenging course for any golfer.
*18 holes, 6217yds, Par 72, SSS 70.*
*Club membership 200.*

| Visitors | must contact in advance. |
| Societies | telephone in advance. |
| Green Fees | £12 per day (£12 weekends & bank holidays). |
| Facilities | ⊗ ∭ ⓑ ♥ ♀ ⚐ ⎷ Gary P Coope. |
| Leisure | motorised carts for hire, trolley for hire, putting green, practice area, pool table. |
| Location | On A59 between Langho and Whalley |
| Hotel | ★★★ 65% Mytton Fold Farm Hotel, Whalley Rd, LANGHO ☎ 01254 240662 27 ⇆ ♟ |

## LEYLAND
Map 07 SD52

**Leyland** Wigan Rd PR5 2UD
☎ 01772 436457 & 423425
Parkland course, fairly flat and usually breezy.
*18 holes, 6123yds, Par 69, SSS 60, Course record 64.*
*Club membership 650.*

| Visitors | must contact in advance. With member only at weekends. |
| Societies | must contact in advance. |
| Green Fees | £25. |
| Facilities | ⊗ ∭ ⓑ ♥ ♀ ⚐ ⎷ Colin Burgess. |
| Leisure | trolley for hire, putting green, practice area. |
| Location | E side of town centre on A49 |
| Hotel | ★★★ 65% Pines Hotel, CLAYTON-LE-WOODS ☎ 01772 38551 39 ⇆ ♟ |

## LONGRIDGE
Map 07 SD63

**Longridge** Fell Barn, Jeffrey Hill PR3 3TU
☎ 01772 783291
Moorland course 850 ft high with views of the Ribble Valley, Trough of Bowland, The Fylde and Welsh Mountains.
*18 holes, 5975yds, Par 70, SSS 69, Course record 65.*
*Club membership 700.*

| Visitors | welcome. |
| Societies | welcome by prior arrangement. |
| Green Fees | £18 per day (£21 weekends and bank holidays). |
| Facilities | ⊗ ∭ ⓑ ♥ ♀ ⚐ ⎷ Neil James. |
| Leisure | trolley for hire, putting green, practice area. |
| Location | 8m NE of Preston off B6243 |
| Hotel | ★★ 68% Shireburn Arms Hotel, HURST GREEN ☎ 01254 826518 16 ⇆ ♟ |

## LYTHAM ST ANNES
Map 07 SD32

**Fairhaven** Lytham Hall Park, Ansdell FY8 4JU
☎ 01253 736741 (Secretary) 736976 (Pro)
A flat, but interesting parkland links course of good standard. There are natural hazards as well as numerous bunkers and players need to produce particularly accurate second shots.
*18 holes, 6883yds, Par 74, SSS 73, Course record 66.*
*Club membership 750.*

| Visitors | telephone professional in advance. |
| Societies | must contact in advance. |
| Green Fees | £35 per day; £30 per round (£35 per round weekends). |
| Facilities | ⊗ ∭ ⓑ ♥ ♀ ⚐ ⎷ Brian Plucknett. |
| Leisure | trolley for hire, putting green, practice area. |
| Location | E side of town centre off B5261 |
| Hotel | ★★★ 65% Bedford Hotel, 307-311 Clifton Dr South, LYTHAM ST ANNES ☎ 01253 724636 36 ⇆ ♟ |

**Lytham Green Drive** Ballam Rd FY8 4LE
☎ 01253 737390
Pleasant parkland course, ideal for holidaymakers.
*18 holes, 6157yds, Par 70, SSS 69, Course record 64.*
*Club membership 740.*

| Visitors | must contact in advance. May not play at weekends. |
| Societies | must apply in writing. |
| Green Fees | £30 per day; £24 per round. |
| Facilities | ⊗ ∭ ⓑ ♥ ♀ ⚐ ⎷ Andrew Lancaster. |
| Leisure | trolley for hire, putting green, practice area. |
| Location | E side of town centre off B5259 |
| Hotel | ★★★★ 61% Clifton Arms, West Beach, Lytham, LYTHAM ST ANNES ☎ 01253 739898 44 ⇆ ♟ |

**ROYAL LYTHAM ST ANNES** See page 133

*St Annes Old Links* Highbury Rd FY8 2LD
☎ 01253 723597
Seaside links, qualifying course for Open Championship; compact and of very high standard, particularly greens. Windy, very long 5th, 17th and 18th holes. Famous hole: 9th (171 yds), par 3. Excellent club facilities.
*18 holes, 6616yds, Par 72, SSS 72.*
*Club membership 950.*

▶

# ROYAL LYTHAM AND ST ANNES

**LYTHAM ST ANNES** *Lancs*

☎ 01253 724206          Map 07 SD32

*John Ingham writes:* Venue for many Open Championships, the most famous winner here was amateur Bobby Jones who, in 1926, put together a four-round total of 291 using wooden clubs and the old-fashioned ball. In the last round, when level with Al Watrous with two to play, Jones bunkered his teeshot at the 17th while Watrous hit a perfect drive and then a fine second on to the green. Jones climbed into the bunker, decided a 175-yard shot was needed if he had any chance, and hit a club similar to today's 4-iron. The shot was brilliant and finished, not only on the green, but nearer than his rival. Shaken, Watrous 3-putted, Jones got his four and finished with a perfect par while Watrous, rattled, had taken six. The club placed a plaque by the famous bunker and it's there to this day.

Since that time the course, which runs close to the railway but slightly inland from the sea, has staged other historic Opens. Bob Charles of New Zealand became the only left-hander to win the title while Tony Jacklin, in 1969, signalled the re-awakening of British golf by winning.

This huge links, founded in 1886 not far from Blackpool, is not easy. When the wind gets up it can be a nightmare. And not everyone approves a championship course that starts with a par 3 hole and it is, in fact, a rare thing in Britain. Some object to the close proximity of red-bricked houses, and aren't keen on trains that rattle past. Now there is an additional nine-hole course and a driving range.

But it's a test full of history and deserves to be played.

---

**Visitors**    weekdays only (unless guest at Dormy House). Must contact in advance, and have a handicap certificate

**Societies**    must apply to Secretary (large groups Mon & Thur only

**Green fees**    £75 per round (includes lunch)

**Facilities**    ⊗ ⅲ ⅼ ⅼ ⬝ ♀ ⌂ ⚲ ⬚ ⌕ (E.Birchenough) driving range, putting, practice area, trollies

**Leisure**    snooker

**Location**    Links Gate, Lytham FY8 3LQ (0.5m E of St Annes town)

**18 holes, 6334 yds, Par 71, SSS 74,**

## WHERE TO STAY AND EAT NEARBY

**HOTELS:**

**LYTHAM ST ANNES**

★★★ 65% Bedford, 307-311 Clifton Drive South. ☎ 01253 724636. 36 (15 ⋔ 21 ⇄ ⋔)

★★★ 67% Chadwick, South Promenade. ☎ 01253 720061. 72 (7 ⋔ 65 ⇄ ⋔)

★★ 66% Glendower, North Promenade. ☎ 01253 723241. 60 ⇄

★★ 65% St Ives, 7-9 South Promenade. ☎ 01253 720011. 70 (3 ⋔ 60 ⇄)

**RESTAURANT:**

**THORNTON**

⚜⚜ The Victorian House, ☎ 01253 860619

**Visitors** may not play on Sat or before 9.15am & between noon-2pm. Sundays by prior arrangement only. Handicap certificate requested.
**Societies** must contact in advance.
**Green Fees** not confirmed.
**Facilities** ♀ ♣ 🏠 ⌂ G Hardiman.
**Leisure** putting,trolley hire,practice area.
**Location** N side of town centre
**Hotel** ★★★ 65% Bedford Hotel, 307-311 Clifton Dr South, LYTHAM ST ANNES
☎ 01253 724636 36 ⇔ ♞

## MORECAMBE                                    Map 07 SD46

**Morecambe** Bare LA4 6AJ
☎ 01524 412841 & 415596
Holiday golf at its most enjoyable. The well-maintained, wind-affected seaside parkland course is not long but full of character. Even so the panoramic views across Morecambe Bay and to the Lake District and Pennines make concentration difficult. The 4th is a testing hole.
*18 holes, 5770yds, Par 67, SSS 68, Course record 63.*
*Club membership 850.*
**Visitors** must contact in advance.
**Societies** must contact in advance.
**Green Fees** on application.
**Facilities** ⊗ ∭ ♭ ♟ ♀ ♣ 🏠 ⌂ Simon Fletcher.
**Leisure** trolley for hire, practice area, putting green.
**Location** N side of town centre on A5105
**Hotel** ★★★ 66% Elms Hotel, Bare Village, MORECAMBE
☎ 01524 411501 40 ⇔ ♞

## NELSON                                        Map 07 SD83

**Marsden Park** Nelson Municipal Golf Course, Townhouse Rd BB9 8DG ☎ 01282 67525
Hilly, parkland course open to the wind.
*18 holes, 5806yds, Par 70, SSS 68, Course record 66.*
*Club membership 320.*
**Visitors** must telephone in advance at weekends.
**Societies** may not play on Sat. Must contact in writing.
**Green Fees** not confirmed.
**Facilities** ♀ (weekends or by prior arrangement) ♣ 🏠 ⌐
⌂ Nick Brown.
**Location** E side of town centre off A56
**Hotel** ★★★ 72% Oaks Hotel, Colne Rd, Reedley, BURNLEY ☎ 01282 414141 54 ⇔ ♞

**Nelson** King's Causeway, Brierfield BB9 0EU
☎ 01282 611834
Hilly moorland course, usually windy, with good views. Testing 8th hole, par 4.
*18 holes, 5967yds, Par 70, SSS 69, Course record 63.*
*Club membership 500.*
**Visitors** must telephone 01282 617000 in advance.
**Societies** must contact in writing.
**Green Fees** £25 per day (£30 weekends & bank holidays).
**Facilities** ⊗ ∭ ♭ ♟ ♀ ♣ 🏠 ⌐ ⌂ Nigel Sumner.
**Leisure** trolley for hire, putting green, practice area.
**Location** 1.5m SE
**Hotel** ★★★ 72% Oaks Hotel, Colne Rd, Reedley, BURNLEY ☎ 01282 414141 54 ⇔ ♞

## ORMSKIRK                                      Map 07 SD40

*Ormskirk* Cranes Ln, Lathom L40 5UJ
☎ 01695 572112
A pleasantly secluded, fairly flat, parkland course with much heath and silver birch. Accuracy from the tees will provide an interesting variety of second shots.
*18 holes, 6358yds, Par 70, SSS 70, Course record 63.*
*Club membership 300.*
**Visitors** restricted Sat.
**Societies** must contact in writing.
**Green Fees** not confirmed.
**Facilities** ♀ ♣ 🏠 ⌂ Jack Hammond.
**Leisure** putting,practice,cart/buggy/trolley hire.
**Location** 1.5m NE
**Hotel** ★★★ 64% Holland Hall Hotel, 6 Lafford Ln, UPHOLLAND
☎ 01695 624426 28 ⇔ ♞ Annexe6 ⇔ ♞

## PLEASINGTON                                   Map 07 SD62

**Pleasington** BB2 5JF ☎ 01254 202177
Plunging and rising across lovely moorland turf this course tests judgement of distance through the air to greens of widely differing levels. The 11th and 17th are testing holes.
*18 holes, 6417yds, Par 71, SSS 71.*
*Club membership 700.*
**Visitors** may play Mon & Wed-Fri only.
**Societies** must contact in advance.
**Green Fees** not confirmed.
**Facilities** ⊗ ∭ ♭ ♟ ♀ ♣ 🏠 ⌂ Ged Furey.
**Leisure** trolley for hire, putting green, snooker.
**Location** W side of village
**Hotel** ★★★ 59% Blackburn Moat House, Preston New Rd, BLACKBURN
☎ 01254 899988 98 ⇔ ♞

## POULTON-LE-FYLDE                              Map 07 SD33

**Poulton-le-Fylde** Breck Rd FY6 7HJ
☎ 01253 892444 & 893150
Municipal parkland course, with easy walking.
*9 holes, 3028yds, Par 70, SSS 68.*
*Club membership 300.*
**Visitors** no restrictions.
**Societies** contact in advance.
**Green Fees** £5.50 (£7.50 weekends & bank holidays).
**Facilities** ⊗ ♭ ♟ ♀ ♣ 🏠 ⌐ ⌂ Lewis Ware.
**Leisure** heated indoor swimming pool, trolley for hire, driving range, putting green, practice area.
**Location** N side of town
**Guesthouse** QQQQQ The Victorian House, Trunnah Rd, THORNTON-CLEVELEYS
☎ 01253 860619 3 ⇔ ♞

## PRESTON                                        Map 07 SD52

**Ashton & Lea** Tudor Av, Lea PR4 0XA
☎ 01772 726480 & 735282
Heathland/parkland course with pond and streams, offering pleasant walks and some testing holes.
*18 holes, 6346yds, Par 71, SSS 70, Course record 65.*
*Club membership 825.*

**Visitors**     must contact professional on 01772 724370.
**Societies**    must contact in writing or by telephone.
**Green Fees** £20 per day (£23 weekends & bank holidays).
**Facilities**    ⊗ ⅷ ৳ ☕ ♀ ⚘ 🏳 ⚑ ⚐ M Greenough.
**Leisure**      trolley for hire, putting green, practice area.
**Location**     3m W on A5085
**Hotel**        B Forte Posthouse Preston, Ringway,
                PRESTON ☎ 01772 259411 121 ⇌ ⚐

---

**Fishwick Hall** Glenluce Dr, Farringdon Park PR1 5TD
☎ 01772 798300 & 795870
Meadowland course overlooking River Ribble. Natural
hazards.
*18 holes, 6092yds, Par 70, SSS 69, Course record 66.*
*Club membership 750.*
**Visitors**     advisable to contact in advance.
**Societies**    must contact in advance.
**Green Fees** £20 per day (£25 weekends & bank holidays).
**Facilities**    ⊗ ⅷ ৳ ☕ ♀ ⚘ 🏳 ⚐ Stuart Bence.
**Leisure**      trolley for hire, putting green, practice area.
**Hotel**        B Forte Posthouse Preston, Ringway,
                PRESTON ☎ 01772 259411 121 ⇌ ⚐

---

*Ingol* Tanterton Hall Rd, Ingol PR2 7BY ☎ 01772 734556
Long, high course with natural water hazards.
*18 holes, 6296yds, Par 72, SSS 70, Course record 67.*
*Club membership 800.*
**Visitors**     must contact in advance but may not play on
                competition days.
**Societies**    must contact in writing.
**Green Fees** not confirmed.
**Facilities**    ♀ ⚘ 🏳 ⚐
**Leisure**      squash.
**Location**     2m NW junc 32 of M55 off B5411
**Hotel**        B Forte Posthouse Preston, Ringway,
                PRESTON ☎ 01772 259411 121 ⇌ ⚐

---

**Penwortham** Blundell Ln, Penwortham PR1 0AX
☎ 01772 744630
A progressive golf club set close to the banks of the
River Ribble. The course has tree-lined fairways,
excellent greens, and provides easy walking. Testing
holes include the 178-yd, par 3 third, the 480-yd, par 5
sixth, and the 398-yd par 4 sixteenth.
*18 holes, 6056yds, Par 69, SSS 69.*
*Club membership 975.*
*Visitors*      must contact in advance; restricted Sun.
**Societies**    must apply in writing.
**Green Fees** £25 per day; £22 per round (£28 weekends).
**Facilities**    ⊗ ⅷ ৳ ☕ ♀ ⚘ 🏳 ⚐ John Wright.
**Leisure**      trolley for hire, putting green, practice area.
**Location**     1.5m W of town centre off A59
**Hotel**        ★★★ 66% Tickled Trout, Preston New Rd,
                Samlesbury, PRESTON
                ☎ 01772 877671 72 ⇌ ⚐

---

**Preston** Fulwood Hall Ln, Fulwood PR2 8DD
☎ 01772 700011
Pleasant inland golf at this course set in very agreeable
parkland. There is a well-balanced selection of holes,
undulating amongst groups of trees, and not requiring great
length.
*18 holes, 6233yds, Par 71, SSS 70.*
*Club membership 800.*
**Visitors**     may play midweek only. Must contact in
                advance and have a handicap certificate.

**Societies**    must contact in writing/telephone.
**Green Fees** £27 per day; £22 per round.
**Facilities**    ⊗ ⅷ ৳ ☕ ♀ ⚘ 🏳 ⚐ Pat Wells.
**Leisure**      trolley for hire, putting green, practice area.
**Location**     N side of town centre
**Hotel**        ★★★★ 66% Broughton Park Hotel, Garstang
                Rd, Broughton, PRESTON
                ☎ 01772 864087 98 ⇌ ⚐

---

## RISHTON                            Map 07 SD73

**Rishton** Eachill Links, Hawthorn Dr BB1 4HG
☎ 01254 884442
Undulating moorland course.
*9 holes, 6097yds, Par 70, SSS 69, Course record 68.*
*Club membership 270.*
**Visitors**     must play with member on weekends and bank
                holidays.
**Societies**    must contact in writing.
**Green Fees** £13 per day.
**Facilities**    ⊗ ⅷ ৳ ☕ ♀ by arrangement ⚘
**Leisure**      putting green, practice area.
**Location**     S side of town off A678
**Hotel**        ★★★ 66% Dunkenhalgh Hotel, Blackburn Rd,
                Clayton le Moors, ACCRINGTON
                ☎ 01254 398021 37 ⇌ ⚐Annexe42 ⇌ ⚐

---

## SILVERDALE                      Map 07 SD47

**Silverdale** Redbridge Ln LA5 0SP ☎ 01524 701300
Difficult heathland course with rock outcrops. Excellent
views.
*12 holes, 5463yds, Par 69, SSS 67.*
*Club membership 500.*
**Visitors**     may only play on Sun in summer if accompanied
                by a member.
**Societies**    must contact in writing.
**Green Fees** £12 per day (£17 weekends & bank holidays).
**Facilities**    ⊗ ⅷ ৳ ☕ ♀ ⚘ 🏳 ⚐ S Sumner Roberts.
**Leisure**      putting green.
**Location**     Opposite Silverdale Station
**Hotel**        ★ 62% Wheatsheaf Hotel, BEETHAM
                ☎ 015395 62123 6 ⇌ ⚐

---

## UPHOLLAND                     Map 07 SD50

**Beacon Park** Beacon Ln WN8 7RU
☎ 01695 622700
Undulating/hilly parkland course, designed by Donald Steel,
with magnificent view of the Welsh hills and Blackpool
Tower. Twenty-four-bay floodlit driving range.
*18 holes, 6000yds, Par 72, SSS 69, Course record 68.*
*Club membership 200.*
**Visitors**     may book 6 days in advance.
**Societies**    must contact in advance.
**Green Fees** £6 (£8 weekends & bank holidays).
**Facilities**    ⊗ ⅷ by prior arrangement ৳ by prior
                arrangement ☕ ♀ ⚘ 🏳 ⚑ ⚐ Ray Peters.
**Leisure**      trolley for hire, driving range, putting green,
                practice area.
**Location**     S of Ashurst Beacon Hill
**Hotel**        ★★★ 64% Holland Hall Hotel, 6 Lafford Ln,
                UPHOLLAND
                ☎ 01695 624426 28 ⇌ ⚐Annexe6 ⇌ ⚐

**Dean Wood** Lafford Ln WN8 0QZ ☏ 01695 622219
This parkland course has a varied terrain - flat front nine, undulating back nine. Beware the par 4, 11th and 17th holes, which has ruined many a card. If there were a prize for the best maintained course in Lancashire, Dean Wood would be a strong contender.
*18 holes, 6179yds, Par 71, SSS 71, Course record 66.*
*Club membership 800.*
**Visitors**     must play with member Tue, Wed & weekends. Must contact in advance.
**Societies**    must contact in advance.
**Green Fees** £24 per day.
**Facilities**   ⊗ ⅲ ᴎ 🛌 ♀ ♁ 🏠 ⚑ ℓ Tony Coop.
**Leisure**      trolley for hire, putting green, practice area.
**Location**     0.5m NE off A577
**Hotel**        ★★★ 64% Holland Hall Hotel, 6 Lafford Ln, UPHOLLAND
                 ☏ 01695 624426 28 ⇆ ℟Annexe6 ⇆ ℟

---

## WHALLEY                                    Map 07 SD73

**Whalley** Long Leese Barn, Portfield Ln BB7 9DR
☏ 01254 822236
Parkland course on Pendle Hill, overlooking the Ribble Valley. Superb views. Ninth hole over pond.
*9 holes, 6258yds, Par 72, SSS 70.*
*Club membership 400.*
**Visitors**     must telephone 01254 824766 in advance.
**Societies**    must apply in writing.
**Green Fees** £15 per day (£20 weekends & bank holidays).
**Facilities**   ⊗ ⅲ ᴎ 🛌 ♀ ♁ 🏠 ℓ H Smith.
**Leisure**      trolley for hire, putting green, practice area.
**Location**     1m SE off A671
**Hotel**        ★★★★ 67% Foxfields Country Hotel & Restaurant, Whalley Rd, BILLINGTON
                 ☏ 01254 822556 28 ⇆ ℟Annexe16 ⇆ ℟

---

## WHITWORTH                                  Map 07 SD81

**Lobden** Lobden Moor OL12 8XJ ☏ 01706 343228
Moorland course, with hard walking. Windy.
*9 holes, 5697yds, Par 70, SSS 68, Course record 67.*
*Club membership 250.*
**Visitors**     must contact in advance. May not play Sat.
**Societies**    must apply in writing to Secretary.
**Green Fees** £10 per day (£15 weekends & bank holidays).
**Facilities**   ⊗ ⅲ ᴎ 🛌 ♀ ♁
**Leisure**      putting, snooker.
**Location**     E side of town centre off A671
**Hotel**        ★★ 57% Midway Hotel, Manchester Rd, Castleton, ROCHDALE
                 ☏ 01706 32881 24 ⇆ ℟

---

## WILPSHIRE                                  Map 07 SD63

**Wilpshire** Whalley Rd BB1 9LF ☏ 01254 248260
Semi-moorland course. Testing 17th hole (229 yds) par 3. Extensive views of Ribble Valley, the coast and the Yorkshire Dales.
*18 holes, 5921yds, Par 69, SSS 66, Course record 61.*
*Club membership 500.*
**Visitors**     must contact in advance.
**Societies**    must contact by telephone and confirm in writing.

**Green Fees** £25 per day/round (£30 weekends & bank holidays).
**Facilities**   ⊗ ⅲ ᴎ 🛌 ♀ ♁ 🏠 ⚑ ℓ Walter Slaven.
**Leisure**      trolley for hire, putting green, practice area.
**Hotel**        ★★★ 59% Blackburn Moat House, Preston New Rd, BLACKBURN
                 ☏ 01254 899988 98 ⇆ ℟

---

# LEICESTERSHIRE

---

### ASHBY-DE-LA-ZOUCH                         Map 08 SK31

**Willesley Park** Measham Rd LE65 2PF
☏ 01530 414596
Undulating heathland and parkland course with quick draining sandy sub-soil.
*18 holes, 6304yds, Par 70, SSS 70, Course record 64.*
*Club membership 600.*
**Visitors**     Must contact in advance. Restricted weekends.
**Societies**    Wed-Fri only. Must apply in writing.
**Green Fees** £28 per day (£33 weekends & bank holidays).
**Facilities**   ⊗ ⅲ by prior arrangement ᴎ 🛌 ♀ ♁ 🏠 ℓ C J Hancock.
**Leisure**      buggies for hire, trolley for hire, snooker.
**Location**     SW side of town centre on A453
**Hotel**        ★★★ 63% The Fallen Knight, Kilwardby St, Ashby-de-la-Zouch
                 ☏ 01530 412230 24 ⇆ ℟

---

### BIRSTALL                                  Map 04 SK50

**Birstall** Station Rd LE4 3BB ☏ 0116 267 4322
Parkland course with trees, shrubs, ponds and ditches.
*18 holes, 6222yds, Par 70, SSS 70.*
*Club membership 650.*
**Visitors**     with member only weekends; may not play Tue.
**Societies**    apply in writing.
**Green Fees** £25 per day; £20 per round.
**Facilities**   ⊗ ⅲ ᴎ 🛌 ♀ ♁ 🏠 ℓ David Clarke.
**Leisure**      trolley for hire, putting green, practice area.
**Location**     2m N of Leicester on A6
**Hotel**        ★★★ 58% Hotel Saint James, Abbey St, LEICESTER
                 ☏ 0116 251 0666 73 ⇆ ℟

---

### BOTCHESTON                                Map 04 SK40

*Forest Hill* Markfield Ln LE9 9FJ ☏ 01455 824800
Parkland course with many trees, four Par 4s, but no steep gradients.
*18 holes, 6111yds, Par 72, SSS 69, Course record 72.*
*Club membership 450.*
**Visitors**     must contact in advance for weekends.
**Societies**    must telephone in advance.
**Green Fees** not confirmed.
**Facilities**   ♀ ♁ 🏠 ⚑ ℓ Martin Wing.
**Leisure**      driving range.
**Hotel**        ★★★ 63% Field Head Hotel, Markfield Ln, MARKFIELD
                 ☏ 01530 245454 28 ⇆ ℟

## COSBY                                                                                    Map 04 SP59

**Cosby** Chapel Ln, Broughton Rd LE9 1RG
☎ 0116 286 4759
Undulating parkland course with a number of tricky, tight driving holes.
*18 holes, 6417yds, Par 71, SSS 71, Course record 68.*
*Club membership 750.*
**Visitors**     restricted weekdays before 4pm. May not play at weekends. Recommended to telephone in advance.
**Societies**    book with secretary.
**Green Fees**   £26 per day; £22 per round.
**Facilities**   ⊗ ⅏ ⅃ 🍺 ♀ ⅄ 🛍 ⅏ ♪ Martin Wing.
**Leisure**      trolley for hire, putting green, practice area.
**Location**     S side of village
**Hotel**        B Forte Posthouse Leicester, Braunstone Ln East, LEICESTER
                 ☎ 0116 263 0500 164 ⇥ ⋔

## ENDERBY                                                                                  Map 04 SP59

**Enderby** Mill Ln LE9 5HL  ☎ 0116 2849 388
A gently undulating 9-hole course at which beginners are especially welcome. The longest hole is the 2nd at 407 yards and there are 5 Par 3's.
*9 holes, 2133yds, Par 31, SSS 31, Course record 27.*
*Club membership 150.*
**Visitors**     no restrictions.
**Societies**    must telephone in advance.
**Green Fees**   £5.25 per 18 holes; £4.25 per 9 holes (£7.25/£5.25 weekends).
**Facilities**   ⊗ ⅏ ⅃ 🍺 ♀ ⅄ 🛍 ⅏ ♪ Chris D'Araujo.
**Leisure**      heated indoor swimming pool, squash, sauna, solarium, gymnasium, trolley for hire.
**Hotel**        ★★ 63% Charnwood Hotel, 48 Leicester Rd, NARBOROUGH ☎ 0116 286 2218 20 ⇥ ⋔

## HINCKLEY                                                                                 Map 04 SP49

*Hinckley* Leicester Rd LE10 3DR  ☎ 01455 615124
Rolling parkland with lake features, and lined fairways.
*18 holes, 6517yds, Par 71, SSS 71.*
*Club membership 1000.*
**Visitors**     with member only weekends and bank holidays. Must contact in advance and have a handicap certificate.
**Societies**    apply by letter.
**Green Fees**   not confirmed.
**Facilities**   ♀ ⅄ 🛍 ♪ Richard Jones.
**Leisure**      putting,practice area,buggy/trolley hire.
**Location**     1.5m NE on A47
**Hotel**        ★★ 67% Longshoot Toby Hotel, Watling St, NUNEATON
                 ☎ 01203 329711 Annexe47 ⇥ ⋔

## KETTON                                                                                   Map 04 SK90

**Luffenham Heath** PE9 3UU
☎ 01780 720205 & 720298
This undulating heathland course with low bushes, much gorse and many trees, lies in a conservation area for flora and fauna. From the higher part of the course there is a magnificent view across the Chater Valley.

*18 holes, 6273yds, Par 70, SSS 70, Course record 64.*
*Club membership 550.*
**Visitors**     must contact in advance.
**Societies**    write or telephone in advance.
**Green Fees**   £30 per day/round (£35 weekends & bank holidays).
**Facilities**   ⊗ by prior arrangement ⅏ by prior arrangement ⅃ 🍺 ♀ ⅄ 🛍 ⅏ ♪ Ian Burnett.
**Leisure**      trolley for hire, putting green, practice area.
**Location**     1.5m SW on A6121
**Hotel**        ★★★ 75% George of Stamford Hotel, St Martins, STAMFORD
                 ☎ 01780 55171 47 ⇥ ⋔

## KIBWORTH                                                                                 Map 04 SP69

**Kibworth** Weir Rd, Beauchamp LE8 0LP
☎ 0116 279 2301
Parkland course with easy walking. A brook affects a number of fairways
*18 holes, 6333yds, Par 71, SSS 70, Course record 65.*
*Club membership 700.*
**Visitors**     must contact in advance. With member only weekends.
**Societies**    must contact in advance.
**Green Fees**   £28 per day; £22 per round.
**Facilities**   ⊗ ⅏ ⅃ 🍺 ♀ ⅄ 🛍 ⅏ ♪ Bob Larratt.
**Leisure**      trolley for hire, driving range, putting green, practice area, snooker.
**Location**     S side of village
**Hotel**        ★★★ 68% Three Swans Hotel, 21 High St, MARKET HARBOROUGH
                 ☎ 01858 466644 20 ⇥ ⋔Annexe16 ⇥ ⋔

## KIRBY MUXLOE                                                                             Map 04 SK50

**Kirby Muxloe** Station Rd LE9 2EP  ☎ 0116 239 3457
Pleasant parkland course with a lake in front of the 17th green and a short 18th.
*18 holes, 6351yds, Par 70, SSS 70, Course record 65.*
*Club membership 750.*
**Visitors**     must contact in advance and a handicap certificate is required. No visitors on Tue or at weekends.
**Societies**    must contact in advance.
**Green Fees**   £25 per day; £20 per round.
**Facilities**   ⊗ ⅏ ⅃ 🍺 ♀ ⅄ 🛍 ♪ Robert Stephenson.
**Leisure**      trolley for hire, driving range, putting green, practice area, snooker.
**Location**     S side of village off B5380
**Hotel**        ★★★★ 60% Holiday Inn, St Nicholas Circle, LEICESTER ☎ 0116 253 1161 188 ⇥ ⋔

## LEICESTER                                                                                Map 04 SK50

**Humberstone Heights** Gypsy Ln LE5 0TB
☎ 0116 276 4674 & 276 3680
Municipal parkland course with 9 hole pitch and putt.
*18 holes, 6343yds, Par 70, SSS 70, Course record 66.*
*Club membership 400.*
**Visitors**     must contact in advance.
**Societies**    must telephone in advance.
**Green Fees**   £6 per round (£9 weekends).
**Facilities**   ⊗ ⅏ ⅃ 🍺 ♀ ⅄ 🛍 ⅏ ♪ Philip Highfield.          ▶

**Leisure** trolley for hire, driving range, putting green, practice area.
**Location** 2.5m NE of city centre
**Hotel** ★★★ 72% Belmont House Hotel, De Montfort St, LEICESTER
☎ 0116 254 4773 44 ⇔ 🐾Annexe21 ⇔ 🐾

**Leicestershire** Evington Ln LE5 6DJ
☎ 0116 273 8825
Pleasantly undulating parkland course.
*18 holes, 6312yds, Par 68, SSS 70, Course record 63.*
*Club membership 800.*
**Visitors** must contact in advance.
**Societies** must contact in advance.
**Green Fees** £28 per day; £23 per round (£34/£29 weekends & bank holidays).
**Facilities** ⊗ 🍴 🛒 🍺 ♀ ⚲ 🏠 🐾 John R Turnbull.
**Leisure** trolley for hire, putting green, practice area.
**Location** 2m E of city off A6030
**Hotel** ★★★ 64% Hermitage Hotel, Wigston Rd, Oadby, LEICESTER
☎ 0116 271 9441 57 ⇔ 🐾

**Western** Scudamore Rd, Braunstone Frith LE3 1UQ
☎ 0116 287 2339 & 287 6158
Pleasant, undulating parkland course with open aspect fairways in two loops of nine holes.Not too difficult but a good test of golf off the back tees.
*18 holes, 6518yds, Par 72, SSS 71.*
*Club membership 400.*
**Visitors** must contact in advance.
**Societies** must contact the secretary in advance.
**Green Fees** on application.
**Facilities** ⊗ 🍴 🛒 🍺 ♀ ⚲ 🏠 🐾 🐾 Bruce Whipham.
**Leisure** trolley for hire, driving range, putting green, practice area.
**Location** 1.5m W of city centre off A47
**Hotel** B Forte Posthouse Leicester, Braunstone Ln East, LEICESTER
☎ 0116 263 0500 164 ⇔ 🐾

## LOUGHBOROUGH
Map 08 SK51

**Longcliffe** Snell's Nook Ln, Nanpantan LE11 3YA
☎ 01509 239129
A re-designed course of natural heathland with outcrops of granite forming natural hazards especially on the 1st and 15th. The course is heavily wooded and has much bracken and gorse. There are a number of tight fairways and one blind hole.
*18 holes, 6611yds, Par 72, SSS 72.*
*Club membership 660.*
**Visitors** must contact in advance. With member only at weekends.
**Societies** telephone for availability, handicap certificate required.
**Green Fees** £30 per day; £22 per round.
**Facilities** ⊗ 🍴 🛒 🍺 ♀ ⚲ 🏠 🐾 Ian D Bailey.
**Leisure** trolley for hire, putting green, practice area.
**Location** 3m SW off B5350
**Hotel** ★★★ 65% Quality Friendly Hotel, New Ashby Rd, LOUGHBOROUGH
☎ 01509 211800 94 ⇔ 🐾

## LUTTERWORTH
Map 04 SP58

**Kilworth Springs** South Kilworth Rd, North Kilworth LE17 6HJ ☎ 01858 575082 & 575974
An 18-hole course of two loops of 9: the front 9 are links style while the back 9 are in parkland with 4 lakes. On a windy day it is a very challenging course and the 6th hole is well deserving of its nickname 'the Devil's Toenail'.
*18 holes, 6543yds, Par 72, SSS 71, Course record 66.*
*Club membership 800.*
**Visitors** welcome subject to availability.
**Societies** contact in advance.
**Green Fees** not confirmed.
**Facilities** ♀ ⚲ 🏠 🐾 N Melvin.
**Leisure** driving range, buggies, caddys, trollies.
**Location** 4m E of M1 junc 20, A427 to Mkt Harborough
**Hotel** ★★★ 64% Denbigh Arms Hotel, High St, LUTTERWORTH
☎ 01455 553537 31 ⇔ 🐾

**Lutterworth** Rugby Rd LE17 4HN ☎ 01455 552532
Hilly course with River Swift running through.
*18 holes, 6431yds, Par 71, SSS 71.*
*Club membership 700.*
**Visitors** must play with member at weekends.
**Societies** must contact in advance.
**Green Fees** £24 per day; £18 per round.
**Facilities** ⊗ 🍴 🛒 🍺 ♀ ⚲ 🏠 🐾 🐾 Roland Tisdall.
**Leisure** motorised carts for hire, buggies for hire, trolley for hire, putting green, practice area.
**Location** 0.5m S on A426
**Hotel** ★★★ 64% Denbigh Arms Hotel, High St, LUTTERWORTH
☎ 01455 553537 31 ⇔ 🐾

## MARKET HARBOROUGH
Map 04 SP78

**Langton Park Golf & Country Club** Langton Hall, West Langton LE16 7TY ☎ 01858 545374
Set in the grounds of a former stately home, this attractive 9-hole course offers sufficient challenge to make it worthwhile playing them a second time.
*9 holes, 3362yds, Par 72, SSS 72.*
*Club membership 135.*
**Visitors** preferred on weekdays, preceedence given to members competitions at weekends.
**Societies** telephone enquiries welcome.
**Green Fees** £13.50 per 18 hole; £9 per 9 holes (£24/£12 weekends).
**Facilities** ⊗ 🍴 🛒 🍺 ♀ ⚲ 🐾 Michael Balderstone.
**Leisure** trolley for hire, putting green, practice area.
**Location** Just off B6047, approx 5m N of Market Harborough
**Hotel** ★★★ 60% The Angel Hotel, 37 High St, MARKET HARBOROUGH
☎ 01858 462702 30 ⇔ 🐾

**Market Harborough** Oxendon Rd LE16 8NF
☎ 01858 463684
A parkland course situated close to the town. There are wide-ranging views over the surrounding countryside.
*18 holes, 6022yds, Par 70, SSS 69, Course record 63.*
*Club membership 600.*
**Visitors** must contact in advance and must play with member at weekends.

**Societies** must apply in writing.
**Green Fees** £22 per day; £16 per round.
**Facilities** ⊗ )Ⅲ ㄴ ♥ ♀ ♣ 🖻 ₹ Frazer Baxter.
**Leisure** trolley for hire, putting green, practice area.
**Location** 1m S on A508
**Hotel** ★★★ 68% Three Swans Hotel, 21 High St, MARKET HARBOROUGH
☎ 01858 466644 20 ➥ ☏Annexe16 ➥ ☏

---

## MELTON MOWBRAY      Map 08 SK71

**Melton Mowbray** Waltham Rd, Thorpe Arnold LE14 4SD
☎ 01664 62118
Downland but flat course providing easy walking. Open to the wind.
*18 holes, 6222yds, Par 70, SSS 70.*
*Club membership 600.*
**Visitors** must contact professional on 01664 69629.
**Societies** must contact in advance.
**Green Fees** £25 per day; £20 per round.
**Facilities** ⊗ )Ⅲ ㄴ ♥ ♀ ♣ 🖻 ₹ ₹ Tony Westwood.
**Leisure** trolley for hire, putting green, practice area.
**Location** 2m NE on A607
**Hotel** ★★ 68% Sysonby Knoll Hotel, Asfordby Rd, MELTON MOWBRAY
☎ 01664 63563 23 ➥ ☏Annexe1 ➥ ☏

---

## OADBY      Map 04 SK60

**Glen Gorse** Glen Rd LE2 4RF ☎ 0116 271 4159
Fairly flat 18-hole parkland course with some strategically placed mature trees, new saplings and ponds affecting play on 6 holes. Ridge and furrow is a feature of 5 holes.
*18 holes, 6603yds, Par 72, SSS 72, Course record 65.*
*Club membership 600.*
**Visitors** must contact in advance. Must play with member at weekends.
**Societies** must telephone secretary in advance.
**Green Fees** £27 per day; £23 per round.
**Facilities** ⊗ )Ⅲ ㄴ ♥ ♀ ♣ 🖻 ₹ Simon Ward.
**Leisure** trolley for hire, putting green, practice area, snooker.
**Location** On A6 trunk road between Oadby/Great Glen
**Hotel** ★★★ 64% Hermitage Hotel, Wigston Rd, Oadby, LEICESTER
☎ 0116 271 9441 57 ➥ ☏

**Oadby** Leicester Rd LE2 4AJ ☎ 0116 270 9052
Municipal parkland course.
*18 holes, 6376yds, Par 72, SSS 70, Course record 60.*
*Club membership 500.*
**Visitors** no restrictions.
**Societies** by arrangement contact pro shop.
**Green Fees** £6 per round (£9 weekends and bank holidays).
**Facilities** ⊗ )Ⅲ ㄴ ♥ ♀ ♣ 🖻 ₹ ₹ Alan Kershaw.
**Leisure** trolley for hire, putting green, practice area.
**Location** West of Oadby, off A6
**Hotel** ★★★ 64% Hermitage Hotel, Wigston Rd, Oadby, LEICESTER
☎ 0116 271 9441 57 ➥ ☏

---

## ROTHLEY      Map 08 SK51

**Rothley Park** Westfield Ln LE7 7LH ☎ 0116 230 2809
Parkland course in picturesque situation.

*18 holes, 6477yds, Par 71, SSS 71, Course record 67.*
*Club membership 600.*
**Visitors** must contact professional on 0116 230 3023.
**Societies** apply in writing to secretary.
**Green Fees** £30 per day; £25 per round.
**Facilities** ⊗ )Ⅲ ㄴ ♥ ♀ ♣ 🖻 ₹ ₹ Andrew Collins.
**Location** 0.75m W on B5328
**Hotel** ★★★ 61% Rothley Court Hotel, Westfield Ln, ROTHLEY
☎ 0116 237 4141 14 ➥ ☏Annexe21 ➥ ☏

---

## SCRAPTOFT      Map 04 SK60

**Scraptoft** Beeby Rd LE7 9SJ ☎ 0116 241 8863
Pleasant, inland country course.
*18 holes, 6166yds, Par 69, SSS 69.*
*Club membership 550.*
**Visitors** with member only weekends. Handicap certificate required.
**Societies** apply in writing.
**Green Fees** not confirmed.
**Facilities** ♀ ♣ 🖻 ₹ ₹
**Location** 1m NE
**Hotel** ★★★ 64% Hermitage Hotel, Wigston Rd, Oadby, LEICESTER
☎ 0116 271 9441 57 ➥ ☏

---

## SEAGRAVE      Map 08 SK61

**Park Hill** Park Hill LE12 7NG ☎ 01509 815454
A new rolling parkland course with views over Charnwood Forest. The opening hole is 420yards with a forced water carry 100yards short of the green. The 10th is a 610yard Par 5 against the prevailing wind and there are 2 Par 5's to finish.
*18 holes, 7219yds, Par 73, SSS 74.*
*Club membership 340.*
**Visitors** must contact in advance.
**Societies** apply in writing.
**Green Fees** £24 per 36 holes; £20 per 27 holes; £16 per 18 holes (£32/£26/£20 weekends and bank holidays).
**Facilities** ⊗ )Ⅲ ㄴ ♥ ♀ ♣ 🖻 ₹ David C Mee.
**Leisure** trolley for hire, practice area.
**Location** 6m N of Leicester on A46
**Hotel** ★★★ 65% Quality Friendly Hotel, New Ashby Rd, LOUGHBOROUGH
☎ 01509 211800 94 ➥ ☏

---

## ULLESTHORPE      Map 04 SP58

**Ullesthorpe** Frolesworth Rd LE17 5BZ ☎ 01455 209023
Parkland course. Many leisure facilities.
*18 holes, 6650yds, Par 72, SSS 72, Course record 67.*
*Club membership 650.*
**Visitors** must contact in advance.
**Societies** contact well in advance.
**Green Fees** £21.50 per day, £13.50 per round.
**Facilities** ⊗ )Ⅲ ㄴ ♥ ♀ ♣ 🖻 🏊 ₹ David Bowring.
**Leisure** hard tennis courts, heated indoor swimming pool, sauna, solarium, gymnasium, motorised carts for hire, buggies for hire, trolley for hire, putting.
**Location** 0.5m N off B577
**Hotel** ★★★ 64% Denbigh Arms Hotel, High St, LUTTERWORTH ☎ 01455 553537 31 ➥ ☏

## WHETSTONE                                    Map 04 SP59

*Whetstone* Cambridge Rd, Cosby LE9 1SJ
☎ 0116 286 1424
Small and very flat parkland course adjacent to motorway.
*18 holes, 5795yds, Par 68, SSS 68.*
*Club membership 500.*
**Visitors**    limited times at weekends
**Societies**   must contact in advance.
**Green Fees** not confirmed.
**Facilities**  ♀ ⅄ 🏠 ໒ David Raitt.
**Leisure**    driving range.
**Location**   1m S of village
**Hotel**      ★★★ 65% Time Out Hotel & Leisure, Enderby
               Rd, Blaby, LEICESTER
               ☎ 0116 278 7898 25 ⇌ ໒

## WILSON                                       Map 08 SK42

*Breedon Priory* Green Ln DE73 1AT
☎ 01332 863081
A relatively short and forgiving course set in undulating
countryside with magnificent views from several holes.
*18 holes, 5530yds, Par 70, SSS 67, Course record 66.*
*Club membership 760.*
**Visitors**    may play any time if tee available, must book for
               weekends.
**Societies**   apply in writing or telephone for booking form.
**Green Fees** £16 per day; £14 per round (£16 per round
               weekends).
**Facilities**  ⅃ ▀ ♀ ⅄ 🏠
**Leisure**    motorised carts for hire, buggies for hire, trolley
               for hire, driving range, putting green, practice
               area, teaching bays.
**Location**   4m W of A42/M1 junct 24
**Hotel**      ★★★ 66% The Priest House, Kings Mills,
               CASTLE DONINGTON
               ☎ 01332 810649 27 ⇌ ໒Annexe18 ⇌ ໒

## WOODHOUSE EAVES                              Map 08 SK51

*Charnwood Forest* Breakback Ln LE12 8TA
☎ 01509 890259
Hilly heathland course with hard walking, but no bunkers.
*9 holes, 5960yds, Par 69, SSS 69, Course record 64.*
*Club membership 210.*
**Visitors**    must contact in advance.
**Societies**   Wed & Thu only. Must contact in advance.
**Green Fees** £25 per day; £15 per 18 holes (£25 weekends &
               bank holidays); £10 per 9 holes.
**Facilities**  ⊗ ℜ ⅃ ▀ ♀⅄
**Leisure**    putting green.
**Location**   0.75m NW off B591
**Hotel**      ★★★★ 71% Quorn Country Hotel, Charnwood
               House, Leicester Rd, QUORN
               ☎ 01509 415050 19 ⇌ ໒

*Lingdale* Joe Moore's Ln LE12 8TF
☎ 01509 890703
Parkland course located in Charnwood Forest with some hard
walking at some holes. The par 3, (3rd) and par 5, (8th) are
testing holes. The 4th and 5th have water hazards.
*18 holes, 6545yds, Par 71, SSS 71, Course record 68.*
*Club membership 610.*

**Visitors**    must telephone professional in advance.
**Societies**   must contact in advance.
**Green Fees** £21 per day; £18 per round (£24 weekends).
**Facilities**  ⊗ ℜ ⅃ ▀ ♀⅄ 🏠 ໒ Peter Sellears.
**Leisure**    putting green, practice ground.
**Location**   1.5m S off B5330
**Hotel**      ★★★★ 71% Quorn Country Hotel, Charnwood
               House, Leicester Rd, QUORN
               ☎ 01509 415050 19 ⇌ ໒

---

# LINCOLNSHIRE

---

## BELTON                                       Map 08 SK93

*Belton Woods Hotel* NG32 2LN
☎ 01476 593200
Two challenging 18-hole courses, a 9-hole Par 3 and a
driving range. The Lakes Course has 13 lakes, while The
Woodside boasts the third longest hole in Europe at 613
yards. Many leisure facilities.
*The Lakes Course: 18 holes, 6808yds, Par 72, SSS 73,*
*Course record 68.*
*The Woodside Course: 18 holes, 6834yds, Par 73, SSS 73.*
*Spitfire Course: 9 holes, 1164yds, Par 27.*
*Club membership 500.*
**Visitors**    available at all times, for further informatiom or
               reservation telephone the sales office.
**Societies**   welcome all week, reservations to be made by
               telephone or letter.
**Green Fees** Lakes or Woodside: Apr-Oct, £35 per day; £25
               per round. Nov-Mar, £18 per round. Spitfire £5
               per round all year.
**Facilities**  ⊗ ℜ ⅃ ▀ ♀ ⅄ 🏠 ⅃ ໒ Tony Roberts.
**Leisure**    hard tennis courts, heated indoor swimming
               pool, squash, sauna, solarium, gymnasium,
               motorised carts for hire, buggies for hire, trolley
               for hire, driving range, putting green, practice
               area.
**Location**   On A607, 2m N of Grantham
**Hotel**      ★★★★ 75% Belton Woods Hotel, BELTON
               ☎ 01476 593200 136 ⇌ ໒

## BLANKNEY                                     Map 08 TF06

*Blankney* LN4 3AZ ☎ 01526 320263
Open parkland course with mature trees; fairly flat.
*18 holes, 6479yds, Par 72, SSS 71, Course record 66.*
*Club membership 640.*
**Visitors**    must contact in advance, may not play Wed
               mornings, restricted at weekends.
**Societies**   not Wed mornings, booking required.
**Green Fees** £25 per day; £17 per round (£30/£25 weekends
               & bank holidays).
**Facilities**  ⊗ ℜ ⅃ ▀ ♀⅄ 🏠 ⅃ ໒ Graham Bradley.
**Leisure**    squash, motorised carts for hire, trolley for hire,
               putting green, practice area.
**Location**   1m SW on B1188
**Hotel**      ★★★ 60% Moor Lodge Hotel, Sleaford Rd,
               BRANSTON
               ☎ 01522 791366 26 ⇌ ໒

## BOSTON

Map 08 TF34

**Boston** Cowbridge, Horncastle Rd PE22 7EL
☎ 01205 350589
Parkland course many water hazards in play on ten holes.
*18 holes, 6490yds, Par 72, SSS 71, Course record 69.*
*Club membership 650.*
**Visitors**    contact in advance for tee time.
**Societies**    apply in writing.
**Green Fees** £22 per day; £17 per round (£30/£20 weekends
         & bank holidays).
**Facilities**   ⊗ �🍴 🍺 ☕ ♀ ♨ 🏠 🛈 ₹ Terry Squires.
**Leisure**    trolley for hire, driving range, putting green,
         practice area.
**Location**   2m N of Boston on B1183
**Hotel**     ★★★ 59% New England, 49 Wide Bargate,
         BOSTON ☎ 01205 365255 25 ⇋ ℝ

**Kirton Holme** Holme Rd, Kirton Holme PE20 1SY
☎ 01205 290669
A young parkland course designed for mid to high
handicappers. It is flat but has 2500 young trees, two natural
water course plus water hazards. The 2nd is a challenging,
386yard Par 4 dogleg.
*9 holes, 5768yds, Par 70, SSS 68, Course record 71.*
*Club membership 350.*
**Visitors**    no restrictions but booking advisable for
         weekends & summer evenings.
**Societies**    weekdays only, by prior arrangement.
**Green Fees** £7.70 per day; £4.40 per round (£8.80/£5.50
         weekends & bank holidays).
**Facilities**   ⊗ �🍴 🍺 ☕ ♀ ♨ 🏳
**Leisure**    trolley for hire, practice area.
**Location**   4m W of Boston off A52
**Hotel**     ★★ 66% Comfort Friendly Inn, Bonnington Rd,
         Bicker Bar, BOSTON
         ☎ 01205 820118 55 ⇋ ℝ

## BOURNE

Map 08 TF02

**Toft Hotel** Toft PE10 0JT
☎ 01778 590614 & 590615
Parkland course on the verge of the Lincoln Edge. Includes
lake and uses contours of the hills to full effect.
*18 holes, 6486yds, Par 72, SSS 71, Course record 63.*
*Club membership 550.*
**Visitors**    advisable to book for weekends.
**Societies**    apply in advance by telephone.
**Green Fees** £18 per day; £10 per round (£25/£15 weekends
         & bank holidays).
**Facilities**   ⊗ �🍴 🍺 ☕ ♀ ♨ 🏠 🏳 ⊨ ₹ Mark Jackson.
**Leisure**    motorised carts for hire, buggies for hire, trolley
         for hire, driving range, putting green, practice
         area.
**Location**   On A6121 Bourne/Stamford road
**Hotel**     ★★ 60% Angel Hotel, Market Place,
         BOURNE ☎ 01778 422346 14 ⇋ ℝ

## CLEETHORPES

Map 08 TA30

**Cleethorpes** Kings Rd DN35 0PN ☎ 01472 814060
Flat meadowland seaside course intersected by large dykes.
*18 holes, 6018yds, Par 70, SSS 69, Course record 64.*
*Club membership 760.*

**Visitors**    restricted Wed afternoons.
**Societies**    Tue,Thu or Fri only. Must contact in advance.
**Green Fees** not confirmed.
**Facilities**   ♀ ♨ 🏠 ₹ Eric Sharp.
**Location**   1.5m S off A1031
**Hotel**     ★★★ 69% Kingsway Hotel, Kingsway,
         CLEETHORPES
         ☎ 01472 601122 50 ⇋ ℝ

## ELSHAM

Map 08 TA01

**Elsham** Barton Rd DN20 0LS
☎ 01652 680291
Parkland course in country surroundings. Easy walking.
*18 holes, 6411yds, Par 71, SSS 71, Course record 67.*
*Club membership 650.*
**Visitors**    with member only weekends & bank holidays.
         Must contact in advance.
**Societies**    must apply in writing.
**Green Fees** £24 per day/round.
**Facilities**   ⊗ �🍴 🍺 ☕ ♀ ♨ 🏠 ₹ Stuart Brewer.
**Leisure**    motorised carts for hire, buggies for hire, trolley
         for hire, putting green, practice area.
**Location**   2m SW on B1206
**Hotel**     ★★★ 65% Wortley House Hotel, Rowland Rd,
         SCUNTHORPE
         ☎ 01724 842223 38 ⇋ ℝ

## GAINSBOROUGH

Map 08 SK88

**Gainsborough** Thonock DN21 1PZ
☎ 01427 613088
Scenic parkland course. Floodlit driving range.
*18 holes, 6620yds, Par 73, SSS 72, Course record 66.*
*Club membership 600.*
**Visitors**    welcome weekdays. Must contact in advance.
         Ladies Day Thu morning.
**Societies**    must telephone in advance.
**Green Fees** not confirmed.
**Facilities**   ♀ ♨ 🏠 ₹ Stephen Cooper.
**Leisure**    driving range,putting,trolley hire.
**Location**   1m N off A159
**Hotel**     ★★ 65% Hickman-Hill Hotel, Cox's Hill,
         GAINSBOROUGH
         ☎ 01427 613639 8rm(3 ⇋3 ℝ)

## GEDNEY HILL

Map 08 TF31

**Gedney Hill** West Drove PE12 0NT
☎ 01406 330922 & 330183
Flat parkland course similar to a links course. Made testing
by Fen winds and small greens. Also a 10-bay driving range.
*18 holes, 5493yds, Par 70, SSS 66, Course record 67.*
*Club membership 300.*
**Visitors**    no restrictions.
**Societies**    telephone in advance.
**Green Fees** not confirmed.
**Facilities**   ♀ ♨ 🏠 🏳 ₹ David Creek.
**Leisure**    10 bay driving range.
**Location**   5m SE of Spalding
**Hotel**     ★★ 63% Queens Hotel, South Brink,
         WISBECH
         ☎ 01945 583933 11 ⇋ ℝAnnexe6 ⇋ ℝ

## GRANTHAM                    Map 08 SK93

**Belton Park** Belton Ln, Londonthorpe Rd NG31 9SH
☎ 01476 67399
Three 9-hole courses set in classic mature parkland of Lord
Brownlow's country seat, Belton House. Gently undulating
with streams, ponds, plenty of trees and beautiful scenery,
including a deer park. Famous holes: 5th, 12th, 16th and 18th.
Combine any of the three courses for a testing 18-hole round.
*Bronnlow: 18 holes, 6412yds, Par 71, SSS 71, Course record
66.*
*Ancaster: 18 holes, 6109yds, Par 70, SSS 69.*
*Belmont: 18 holes, 5857yds, Par 69, SSS 68.*
*Club membership 900.*
**Visitors**      contact for tee booking.
**Societies**     apply in writing.
**Green Fees**    £27.50 per 36 holes; £22 per round (£33/£27
                  weekends & bank holidays).
**Facilities**    ⊗ ⅷ ⅃ ⏾ ♀ ⅄ 🖻 ⚐ ʈ Brian McKee.
**Leisure**       buggies for hire, trolley for hire, practice area.
**Location**      1.5m NE of Grantham
**Hotel**         ★★★ 64% Kings Hotel, North Pde,
                  GRANTHAM
                  ☎ 01476 590800 22rm(21 ⇆ ♞)

**Sudbrook Moor** Charity St, Carlton Scroop NG32 3AT
☎ 01400 250796
A testing 9-hole parkland course in open countryside.
*9 holes, 4566yds, Par 66, SSS 61, Course record 69.*
**Visitors**      welcome by arrangement.
**Green Fees**    £5 per day (£7 weekends and bank holidays).
**Facilities**    ⊗ ⅃ ⏾ ♀ ⅄ 🖻 ⚐ ʈ Tim Hutton.
**Leisure**       trolley for hire, putting green, practice area.
**Location**      6m NE of Grantham on A607
**Hotel**         ★★★ 64% Kings Hotel, North Pde,
                  GRANTHAM
                  ☎ 01476 590800 22rm(21 ⇆ ♞)

## GRIMSBY                     Map 08 TA21

**Grimsby** Littlecoates Rd DN34 4LU ☎ 01472 342630
Parkland course with easy walking.
*18 holes, 6098yds, Par 70, SSS 69, Course record 66.*
*Club membership 730.*
**Visitors**      contact in advance.
**Societies**     by prior arrangement with secretary.
**Green Fees**    £25 per day; £18 per 18 holes (£25 per round
                  weekends).
**Facilities**    ⊗ ⅷ ⅃ ⏾ ♀ ⅄ 🖻 ʈ Richard Smith.
**Leisure**       trolley for hire, putting green, practice area.
**Location**      W side of town centre off A1136
**Hotel**         B Forte Posthouse Grimsby, Littlecoates Rd,
                  GRIMSBY ☎ 01472 350295 52 ⇆ ♞

## HORNCASTLE                  Map 08 TF26

**Horncastle** West Ashby LN9 5PP ☎ 01507 526800
Heathland course with many water hazards and bunkers; very
challenging. There is a 25-bay floodlit driving range.
*18 holes, 5717yds, Par 70, SSS 70, Course record 71.*
*Par 3: 9 holes, 4025yds, Par 27, SSS 27.*
*Club membership 250.*
**Visitors**      dress code must be adhered to, welcome
                  anytime, may contact in advance.
**Societies**     apply in writing or telephone in advance.
**Green Fees**    £18 per day; £12 per round (£20/£15 weekends
                  and bank holidays).
**Facilities**    ⊗ ⅷ ⅃ ⏾ ♀ ⅄ ⚐ ʈ E C Wright.
**Leisure**       fishing, trolley for hire, driving range, putting
                  green, practice area.
**Location**      Off A158 Lincoln/Skegness road at Edlington
**Hotel**         ★★ 65% Admiral Rodney Hotel, North St,
                  HORNCASTLE ☎ 01507 523131 32 ⇆ ♞

## IMMINGHAM                   Map 08 TA11

**Immingham** St Andrews Ln, off Church Ln DN40 2EU
☎ 01469 575298
Parkland course with some water hazards and a public
footpath across holes 1, 2 & 8.
*18 holes, 6191yds, Par 71, SSS 69.*
*Club membership 700.*
**Visitors**      telephone in advance.
**Societies**     telephone (am) to arrange date.
**Green Fees**    £20 per day; £15 per round (£20 weekend and
                  bank holidays).
**Facilities**    ⊗ ⅷ by prior arrangement ⅃ ⏾ ♀ ⅄ 🖻 ⚐
                  ʈ Geoffrey Norton.
**Leisure**       trolley for hire, putting green, practice area.
**Location**      7m NW off Grimsby
**Hotel**         ★★ 63% Old Chapel Hotel & Restaurant, 50
                  Station Rd, IMMINGHAM
                  ☎ 01469 572377 14 ⇆ ♞

## LACEBY                      Map 08 TA20

**Manor** Barton St, Laceby Manor DN37 7EA
☎ 01472 873468
Upgraded to 18 holes in the summer of 1995. The first nine
holes as a parkland course, all the fairways lined with young
trees. The newly created second nine are mainly open
fairways. The 18th hole green is surrounded by water.
*18 holes, 6354yds, Par 71, SSS 70.*
*Club membership 470.*
**Visitors**      welcome but requested to book tee times.
**Societies**     telephone in advance.
**Green Fees**    £18 per day; £12 per round; Twilight £8.

# Admiral Rodney Hotel ★ ★
### North Street, Horncastle, Lincoln LN9 5DX
### Telephone: 01507 523131
### Fax: 01507 523104
The Admiral Rodney Hotel is situated in the market town of Horncastle, this luxuriously refurbished
hotel has 32 comfortable bedrooms with all facilities.
Excellent rates – special weekend rates available. The challenging Horncastle Golf Club is only a 5
minute drive away and Woodhall Spa a 15 minute drive.

**Facilities** ☕ ♀ ⚲ 🏠
**Leisure** fishing, solarium, trolley for hire, driving range, putting green, practice area.
**Location** A18 Barton St - Laceby/Louth
**Hotel** ★★★ 63% Oaklands Hotel, Barton St, LACEBY ☎ 01472 872248 46 ⇥ ⋔

## LINCOLN                                    Map 08 SK97

**Canwick Park** Canwick Park, Washingborough Rd LN4 1EF
☎ 01522 522166 & 542912
Parkland course. Testing 14th hole (par 3).
*18 holes, 6257yds, Par 70, SSS 70, Course record 66.*
*Club membership 700.*
**Visitors** with member only Sat also Sun before 3pm.
**Societies** weekdays only by prior arrangement in writing.
**Green Fees** £19 per day; £13.50 per round Tue-Fri, £9.50 per round Mon.
**Facilities** ⊗ ⅏ ⅃ ☕ ♀ ⚲ 🏠 ⛏ ⋔ S Williamson.
**Leisure** trolley for hire, putting green, practice area.
**Location** 1m E of Lincoln
**Hotel** B Forte Posthouse Lincoln, Eastgate, LINCOLN ☎ 01522 520341 70 ⇥ ⋔

**Carholme** Carholme Rd LN1 1SE ☎ 01522 523725
Parkland course where prevailing west winds can add interest. Good views.
*18 holes, 6243yds, Par 71, SSS 70, Course record 69.*
*Club membership 825.*
**Visitors** must contact in advance. Weekends may no play before 2.30pm.
**Societies** apply in writing.
**Green Fees** £18 per day; £14 per round (£17 per round weekends and bank holidays,when available).
**Facilities** ⊗ ⅏ ⅃ ☕ ♀ ⚲ 🏠 ⛏ ⋔ Gary Leslie.
**Leisure** trolley for hire, practice area.
**Location** 1m W of city centre on A57
**Hotel** ★★★★ 63% The White Hart, Bailgate, LINCOLN ☎ 01522 526222 48 ⇥

## LOUTH                                      Map 08 TF38

**Louth** Crowtree Ln LN11 9LJ ☎ 01507 603681
Undulating parkland course, fine views.
*18 holes, 6424yds, Par 72, SSS 71.*
*Club membership 700.*
**Visitors** must contact in advance to make sure tee is not reserved for competition.
**Societies** a booking form will be sent on request.
**Green Fees** £20 day; £16 per round (£30/£25 weekends and bank holidays).
**Facilities** ⊗ ⅏ ⅃ ☕ ♀ ⚲ 🏠 ⛏ ⋔ A Blundell.
**Leisure** squash, motorised carts for hire, buggies for hire, trolley for hire, putting green, practice area.
**Location** W side of Louth between A157/A153
**Hotel** ★★★ 62% Beaumont Hotel, 66 Victoria Rd, LOUTH ☎ 01507 605005 17 ⇥ ⋔

## MARKET RASEN                               Map 08 TF18

**Market Rasen & District** Legsby Rd LN8 3DZ
☎ 01673 842319
Picturesque, well-wooded heathland course, easy walking, breezy with becks forming natural hazards. Good views of Lincolnshire Wolds.

*18 holes, 6045yds, Par 70, SSS 69, Course record 65.*
*Club membership 565.*
**Visitors** must play with member at weekends and must contact in advance.
**Societies** Tue & Fri only; must contact in advance.
**Green Fees** £24 per day; £16 per round.
**Facilities** ⊗ ⅏ ⅃ ☕ ♀ ⚲ 🏠 ⋔ A M Chester.
**Leisure** trolley for hire, putting, practice area.
**Location** 1m E, off A46
**Hotel** ★★★ 62% Beaumont Hotel, 66 Victoria Rd, LOUTH ☎ 01507 605005 17 ⇥ ⋔

**Market Rasen Race Course (Golf Course)** Legsby Rd LN8 3EA ☎ 01673 843434 & 842307
This is a public course set within the bounds of Market Rasen race course - the entire racing area is out of bounds. The longest hole is the 4th at 454yards with the race course providing a hazard over the whole length of the drive.
*9 holes, 2532yds, Par 32.*
**Visitors** closed racedays apart from evening meetings when open until noon.
**Societies** telephone in advance to arrange.
**Green Fees** £6 per 18 holes; £4 per 9 holes (£8/£5 weekends).
**Facilities** ⋔
**Location** 2m E of Market Rasen
**Hotel** ★★★ 62% Beaumont Hotel, 66 Victoria Rd, LOUTH ☎ 01507 605005 17 ⇥ ⋔

## NORMANBY                                   Map 08 SE81

**Normanby Hall** Normanby Park DN15 9HU
☎ 01724 720226
Parkland course.
*18 holes, 6548yds, Par 72, SSS 71.*
*Club membership 770.*
**Visitors** book in advance by contacting professional.
**Societies** must contact in advance: Manager, Scunthorpe Leisure Centre, Carlton St, Scunthorpe, DN15 6TA.
**Green Fees** £16 per day; £10 per round (£12 per round weekends & bank holidays). Twilight ticket £5 (£6 weekends).
**Facilities** ⊗ ⅃ ☕ ♀ ⚲ 🏠 ⛏ ⋔ Christopher Mann.
**Leisure** motorised carts for hire, buggies for hire, trolley for hire, putting green, practice area.
**Location** 3m N of Scunthorpe adj to Normanby Hall
**Hotel** ★★★ 62% Royal Hotel, Doncaster Rd, SCUNTHORPE ☎ 01724 282233 33 ⇥ ⋔

## SCUNTHORPE                                 Map 08 SE81

**Ashby Decoy** Burringham Rd DN17 2AB
☎ 01724 866561 (Office) & 868972 (Pro)
Very tight parkland course.
*18 holes, 6281yds, Par 71, SSS 71, Course record 65.*
*Club membership 650.*
**Visitors** may not play Sun or Tue. Sat with member only.
**Societies** apply in advance.
**Green Fees** £21 per day; £16 per round.
**Facilities** ⊗ ⅏ ⅃ ☕ ♀ ⚲ 🏠 ⋔ A Miller.
**Leisure** putting, practice area.
**Location** 2.5m SW on B1450 nr Asda Superstore
**Hotel** ★★★ 62% Royal Hotel, Doncaster Rd, SCUNTHORPE ☎ 01724 282233 33 ⇥ ⋔

**Forest Pines - Briggate Lodge Inn Hotel** Ermine St,
Broughton DN20 0AQ ☎ 01652 650770 & 650756
Set in 185 acres of mature parkland and open heathland and
constructed in a similar design to that of Wentworth or
Sunningdale, Forest Pines offers three challenging 9-hole
courses - Forest, Pines and Beeches. Any combination can be
played. Facilities include a 17-bay driving range and a
spacious clubhouse.
*Forest Course: 9 holes, 3291yds, Par 35.*
*Pines Course: 9 holes, 3591yds, Par 37.*
*Beeches: 9 holes, 3102yds, Par 35.*
**Visitors** must contact in advance.
**Societies** telephone in advance.
**Green Fees** £35 per day; £25 per round (£40/£30 weekends
and bank holidays). 9 holes £15.
**Facilities** ⊗ ⅲ ⅃ ♨ ♀ ♨ 🖿 ⅂ 🖿 ⅂ David Edwards.
**Leisure** motorised carts for hire, buggies for hire, trolley
for hire, floodlit driving range, putting green,
practice area.
**Location** 200yds from junct 4 M180
**Hotel** ★★★ 68% Briggate Lodge Inn, Ermine St,
Broughton, SCUNTHORPE
☎ 01652 650770 50 ⇆ ⸙

---

*Holme Hall* Holme Ln, Bottesham DN16 3RF
☎ 01724 862078
Heathland course with sandy subsoil. Easy walking.
*18 holes, 6475yds, Par 71, SSS 71.*
*Club membership 724.*
**Visitors** must play with member at weekends & bank
holidays. Must contact in advance.
**Societies** must contact in advance.
**Green Fees** not confirmed.
**Facilities** ♀ ♨ 🖿 ⅂ Richard McKiernan.
**Leisure** putting,trolley hire,practice area.
**Location** 3m SE
**Hotel** ★★★ 62% Royal Hotel, Doncaster Rd,
SCUNTHORPE
☎ 01724 282233 33 ⇆ ⸙

---

*Kingsway* Kingsway DN15 7ER ☎ 01724 840945
Parkland course with many par 3's.
*9 holes, 1915yds, Par 29, Course record 28.*
**Visitors** no restrictions.
**Green Fees** £2.95 per 9 holes (£3.45 weekends).
**Facilities** ♨ 🖿 ⅂ Chris Mann.
**Leisure** trolley for hire, putting green, practice area,
facilities for handicapped.
**Location** W side of town centre off A18
**Hotel** ★★★ 62% Royal Hotel, Doncaster Rd,
SCUNTHORPE
☎ 01724 282233 33 ⇆ ⸙

---

SKEGNESS Map 09 TF56

---

**North Shore Hotel & Golf Club** North Shore Rd PE25 1DN
☎ 01754 763298
A half-links, half-parkland course designed by James Braid in
1910. Easy walking and good sea views.
*18 holes, 6200yds, Par 71, SSS 71, Course record 67.*
*Club membership 450.*
**Visitors** tee times must be booked.
**Societies** write or telephone in advance.
**Green Fees** £24 per day; £17 per round (£35/£25 weekdays).
**Facilities** ⊗ ⅲ ⅃ ♨ ♀ ♨ 🖿 ⅂ J Cornelius.
**Leisure** trolley for hire, practice area.

**Location** 1m N of town centre off A52
**Hotel** ★★ 62% North Shore Hotel, North Shore Rd,
SKEGNESS
☎ 01754 763298 30 ⇆ ⸙Annexe3 ⇆ ⸙

**Seacroft** Drummond Rd, Seacroft PE25 3AU
☎ 01754 763020
A typical seaside links with flattish fairways separated by
low ridges and good greens. Easy to walk round. To the
east are sandhills leading to the shore. Southward lies
'Gibraltar Point Nature Reserve'.
*18 holes, 6479yds, Par 71, SSS 71, Course record 67.*
*Club membership 590.*
**Visitors** must be a member of an affiliated golf club.
**Societies** contact in advance.
**Green Fees** £35 per day; £25 per round (£40/£30
weekends & bank holidays).
**Facilities** ⊗ ⅲ ⅃ ♨ ♀ 🖿 ⅂ Robin Lawie.
**Leisure** trolley for hire, putting green, practice area.
**Location** S side of town centre
**Hotel** ★★★ 62% Crown Hotel, Drummond Rd,
Seacroft, SKEGNESS
☎ 01754 610760 27 ⇆ ⸙

---

SLEAFORD Map 08 TF04

---

**Sleaford** Willoughby Rd NG34 8PL ☎ 01529 488273
Inland links-type course, moderately wooded and fairly flat.
*18 holes, 6443yds, Par 72, SSS 71, Course record 66.*
*Club membership 650.*
**Visitors** may not play Sun in winter.
**Societies** telephone enquiry to fixture secretary.
**Green Fees** £21 per round/day (£28 weekends & bank
holidays).
**Facilities** ⊗ ⅲ ⅃ ♨ ♀ ♨ 🖿 ⅂ James Wilson.
**Leisure** trolley for hire, putting green, practice area.
**Location** 2m W of Sleaford, off A153
**Hotel** ★★★ 62% Angel & Royal Hotel, High St,
GRANTHAM ☎ 01476 65816 30 ⇆ ⸙

---

SOUTH KYME Map 08 TF14

---

**South Kyme** Skinners Ln LN4 4AT
☎ 01526 861113
A challenging fenland course described as an 'Inland links'.
More water hazards, trees and fairway hazards added during
1995 so the course is improving all the time.
*18 holes, 6597yds, Par 71, SSS 71, Course record 67 or 6*
*holes, 895yds.*
*Club membership 250.*
**Visitors** telephone for advise on tee times.
**Societies** telephone for booking form.
**Green Fees** £15 per day; £10 per round (£18/£12 weekends).
Fees due to be revised.
**Facilities** ⊗ ⅲ ⅃ ♨ ♀ ♨ 🖿 ⅂ Peter Chamberlain.
**Leisure** trolley for hire, putting green, practice area.
**Location** Off B1395 in South Kyme village
**Hotel** B Forte Travelodge, Holdingham, SLEAFORD
☎ 01529 414752 40 ⇆ ⸙

---

Entries with a shaded background identify
courses that are considered to be particularly
interesting

# WOODHALL SPA

**WOODHALL SPA** *Lincs* ☎ **01526 352511   Map 08 TF16**

*John Ingham writes:* Opened in 1905 and regarded as the finest inland course in the British Isles, it has been purchased for £8 million by the English Golf Union to use as a headquarters. Many miles from the nearest towns, the heathland course is covered with silver birch and the fairways are made up of dry, springy turf and several big competitions have been played here.

In the 1960s I played in the Central England Mixed Foursomes and enjoyed the hospitality of the then owner, Neil Hotchkin, who had somehow helped create a wonderful clubhouse atmosphere, with country people behind the bar, giving the place a friendly glow. It remains the same today.

Although 18 miles south-east of Lincoln, I now understand it is wise to telephone to see whether the course can receive visitors for the day. If the answer is 'yes' then be prepared for a treat. Tony Jacklin brought his friend Tom Weiskopf to play and the American was thrilled with the shot-making that is required.

Designed by the great Harry Vardon, the course is a pleasant and fairly flat walk but because of the clever shaping of the holes, and the delightful isolation of almost each hole, hidden like a corridor through a stately home, the course becomes a most private place for a friendly four-ball. Measuring 6942 yards, it doesn't appear that long because of the fast-running fairways. The club don't like men visitors to have a handicap above 20 or the women above 30 and since the course is renowned for its huge bunkers, it is to the advantage of players to know how to escape from sand traps. In many ways, Woodhall Spa is like Sunningdale and as those who know that course would readily admit, there is no greater compliment.

| | |
|---|---|
| **Visitors** | must be a member of a golf club affiliated to the appropriate Golf Union, max handicap-gentlemen 20, ladies 30. Handicap certificate must be produced |
| **Societies** | must book in advance |
| **Green fees** | £35 per round, £55 per day. |
| **Facilities** | ⊗ ⅷ ⅊ ↳ ⬤ ♀ ⚑ 🛅 ⌧ (C C Elliot) driving range putting green, practice area, trollies |
| **Leisure** | pitch & putt course |
| **Location** | The Broadway LN10 6PU (NE side of village B1191) |

**18 holes, 6947yards, Par 73 SSS 73
Course record 67**

### WHERE TO STAY NEARBY

**HOTELS:**
**WOODHALL SPA**
★★★ 65% Petwood House Hotel, Stixwould Rd ☎ 01526 352411. 46 ⇄ ↾

★★★ 63% Golf Hotel, The Broadway ☎ 01526 353535.   50 (14 ↾ 36 ⇄ ↾)

## SPALDING                                     Map 08 TF22

**Spalding** Surfleet PE11 4EA ☎ 01775 680386 & 680234
A pretty, well laid-out course in a fenland area. The River
Glen runs beside the 1st and 2nd holes, and streams, ponds
and new tree plantings add to the variety of this well-
maintained course.
*18 holes, 6478yds, Par 72, SSS 71.*
*Club membership 750.*
**Visitors**      must contact in advance.
**Societies**     write to the secretary, Societies on Thu all day
                  and Tue pm.
**Green Fees**    £24 per day (£30 weekends & bank holidays).
**Facilities**    ⊗ ⫲ ᛒ ☕ ♀ ♨ 🏠 ⏱ John Spencer.
**Leisure**       putting green, practice area.
**Location**      4m N of Spaldingadjacent to A16
**Hotel**         ★★ 60% Cley Hall Hotel, 22 High St,
                  SPALDING
                  ☎ 01775 725157 4 ⇄ 🏌Annexe7 🏌

## STAMFORD                                     Map 08 TF00

**Burghley Park** St Martins PE9 3JX
☎ 01780 62100 due to change to 762100
Open parkland course with superb greens, many new trees,
ponds and bunkers. Situated in the grounds of Burghley
House.
*18 holes, 6238yds, Par 70, SSS 70, Course record 64.*
*Club membership 805.*
**Visitors**      with member only weekends. Must contact in
                  advance & have handicap certificate.
**Societies**     prior arrangement in writing, preferably by 1st
                  Dec previous year.
**Green Fees**    £20 per day weekdays only.
**Facilities**    ⊗ ⫲ ᛒ ☕ ♀ ♨ 🏠 ⏱ Glenn Davies.
**Leisure**       motorised carts for hire, buggies for hire, trolley
                  for hire, putting green, practice area.
**Location**      1m S of town on B1081
**Hotel**         ★★★ 75% George of Stamford Hotel, St
                  Martins, STAMFORD
                  ☎ 01780 55171 47 ⇄ 🏌

## STOKE ROCHFORD                               Map 08 SK92

*Stoke Rochford* NG33 5EW ☎ 01476 530275
Parkland course designed by C. Turner.
*18 holes, 6251yds, Par 70, SSS 70, Course record 65.*
*Club membership 525.*
**Visitors**      must contact in advance, restricted to 9am
                  weekdays, 10.30am weekends & bank holidays.
**Societies**     contact one year in advance, in writing.
**Green Fees**    not confirmed.
**Facilities**    ♀ ♨ 🏠 ⏱ Angus Dow.
**Leisure**       putting,cart/buggy/trolley hire.
**Location**      Off A1 5m S of Grantham
**Hotel**         ★★★ 64% Kings Hotel, North Pde,
                  GRANTHAM ☎ 01476 590800 22rm(21 ⇄ 🏌)

---

A golf course name printed in ***bold italics***
means we have been unable to verify
information with the club's management for
the current year

---

## SUTTON BRIDGE                                Map 09 TF42

**Sutton Bridge** New Rd PE12 9RQ ☎ 01406 350323
Parkland course.
*9 holes, 5724yds, Par 70, SSS 68.*
*Club membership 350.*
**Visitors**      may not play competition days, weekends &
                  bank holidays, must contact in advance.
**Societies**     write or telephone in advance.
**Green Fees**    £15 per day.
**Facilities**    ⊗ ⫲ ᛒ ☕ ♀ ♨ 🏠 ⏱ L Rawlings.
**Leisure**       trolley for hire, putting green, practice area.
**Location**      E side of village off A17
**Hotel**         ★★★ 65% The Duke's Head, Tuesday Market
                  Pl, KING'S LYNN
                  ☎ 01553 774996 71 ⇄ 🏌

## SUTTON ON SEA                                Map 09 TF58

**Sandilands** Roman Bank LN12 2RJ ☎ 01507 441432
Flat links course on the sea shore.
*18 holes, 5995yds, Par 70, SSS 69.*
*Club membership 230.*
**Visitors**      no restrictions.
**Societies**     telephone in advance.
**Green Fees**    £20 per day; £15 per round (£20 per round
                  weekends & bank holidays).
**Facilities**    ⊗ ⫲ ☕ ♀ ♨ 🏠 ⏱ 🏌
**Leisure**       grass tennis courts, trolley for hire, putting
                  green, practice area.
**Location**      1.5m S off A52
**Hotel**         ★★★ 68% Grange & Links Hotel, Sea Ln,
                  Sandilands, MABLETHORPE
                  ☎ 01507 441334 24 ⇄ 🏌

## TORKSEY                                      Map 08 SK87

**Lincoln** LN1 2EG ☎ 01427 718210
A testing inland course with quick-drying sandy subsoil and
easy walking.
*18 holes, 6438yds, Par 71, SSS 71, Course record 66.*
*Club membership 650.*
**Visitors**      accepted on non event days.
**Societies**     apply in writing or telephone.
**Green Fees**    £28 per day; £22 per round.
**Facilities**    ⊗ ⫲ ᛒ ☕ ♀ ♨ 🏠 ⏱ Ashley Carter.
**Leisure**       trolley for hire, putting green, practice field.
**Location**      SW side of village
**Hotel**         ★★★★ 63% The White Hart, Bailgate,
                  LINCOLN ☎ 01522 526222 48 ⇄

---

*Millfield* Sandfield Farm, Laughterton LN1 2LB
☎ 01427 718255
There is an unusual set-up at Millfield with a 15 hole 4,201
yard Family course on which anyone can play, as well as a 9-
hole Par 3 and an 18-hole course of nearly 6,000 yards. Due
to its location in flat Lincolnshire the courses are affected by
winds, which change every day.
*18 holes, 5974yds, Par 69, SSS 69.*
*Family 15: 15 holes, 4201yds, Par 56.*
**Visitors**      18 hole; shoes must be worn, no jeans etc.
                  Family 15 hole no restrictions.
**Societies**     welcome on weekdays.
**Green Fees**    not confirmed.

Facilities ⚐ 🏠 ⌖
Location On A1133 1m N of A57
Hotel ★★★★ 63% The White Hart, Bailgate, LINCOLN
☎ 01522 526222 48 ⇆

---

**WOODHALL SPA** See page 145

---

## WOODTHORPE                                 Map 09 TF48

**Woodthorpe Hall** LN13 0DD
☎ 01507 463664
Parkland course.
*18 holes, 5010yds, Par 66, SSS 65.*
*Club membership 400.*
Visitors contact in advance for weekends.
Societies Mon-Fri, telephone in first instance at least one month prior to visit.
Green Fees £10 per day.
Facilities ⊗ ⅏ ⓑ 🍺 ♀ 🏠 ⌖ ⌖
Leisure fishing, trolley for hire.
Location 3m NNW of Alford on B1373
Hotel ★★★ 68% Grange & Links Hotel, Sea Ln, Sandilands, MABLETHORPE
☎ 01507 441334 24 ⇆ ⓕ

---

# LONDON

**Courses within the London Postal District area (ie those that have London Postcodes - W1, SW1 etc) are listed here in postal district order commencing East then North, South and West.** Courses outside the London Postal area, but within Greater London are to be found listed under the county of **Greater London** in the gazetteer (see page 76).

---

## E4 CHINGFORD

**Royal Epping Forest** Forest Approach, Chingford E4 7AZ
☎ 0181 529 2195
Woodland course. 'Red' garments must be worn.
*18 holes, 6342yds, Par 71, SSS 70.*
*Club membership 400.*
Visitors booking system in operation.
Societies must contact secretary in advance.
Green Fees £9.50 per round (£13 weekends).
Facilities 🍺 ♀ (members only) 🏠 ⌖
⌖ R Gowers/J Francis.
Leisure trolley for hire.
Location 300 yds S of Chingford Station
Hotel ★★★ 65% Epping Forest Moat House, Oak Hill, WOODFORD GREEN
☎ 0181 787 9988 99 ⇆ ⓕ

---

*West Essex* Bury Rd, Sewardstonebury E4 7QL
☎ 0181 529 7558
Testing parkland course within Epping Forest. Notable holes are 8th (par 4), 16th (par 4), 18th (par 5).
*18 holes, 6289yds, Par 71, SSS 70.*
*Club membership 645.*
Visitors must contact in advance & have handicap certificate but may not play on Tue morning, Thu afternoon & weekends.
Societies must contact in advance.
Green Fees not confirmed.
Facilities ♀ ⚐ 🏠 ⌖ Robert Joyce.
Leisure buggies for hire.
Location Off N Circular Rd at Chingford on M25
Hotel ★★ 62% Roebuck Hotel, North End, BUCKHURST HILL
☎ 0181 505 4636 29 ⇆ ⓕ

---

## E11 LEYTONSTONE

**Wanstead** Overton Dr, Wanstead E11 2LW
☎ 0181 989 3938
A flat, picturesque parkland course with many trees and shrubs and providing easy walking. The par 3, 16th, involves driving across a lake.
*18 holes, 6004yds, Par 69, SSS 69, Course record 62.*
*Club membership 600.*
Visitors must contact in advance and may only play Mon, Tue & Fri.
Societies by prior arrangement.
Green Fees £25 per day.
Facilities ⊗ ⅏ ⓑ 🍺 ♀ ⚐ 🏠 ⌖ David Hawkins.
Leisure fishing, trolley for hire, putting green, practice area.
Location From central London A11 NE to Wanstead
Hotel ★★★ 65% Epping Forest Moat House, Oak Hill, WOODFORD GREEN
☎ 0181 787 9988 99 ⇆ ⓕ

---

## N2 EAST FINCHLEY

**Hampstead** Winnington Rd N2 0TU ☎ 0181 455 0203
Undulating parkland course.
*18 holes, 5822yds, Par 68, SSS 68.*
*Club membership 526.*
Visitors restricted Tue and weekends.
Societies small societies by prior arrangements.
Green Fees £30 all day; £25 per 18 holes (£32 per 18 holes weekends and bank holidays).
Facilities ⊗ ⓑ 🍺 ♀ ⚐ 🏠 ⌖ Peter Brown.
Leisure trolley for hire, putting green, practice area.
Location Off Hampstead Lane
Hotel B Forte Posthouse Hampstead, 215 Haverstock Hill, LONDON ☎ 0171 794 8121 140 ⇆ ⓕ

---

## N6 HIGHGATE

*Highgate* Denewood Rd N6 4AH ☎ 0181 340 1906
Parkland course.
*18 holes, 5985yds, Par 69, SSS 69, Course record 66.*
*Club membership 800.*
Visitors may not play Wed & weekends.
Societies by arrangement.
Green Fees not confirmed.
Facilities ♀ ⚐ 🏠 ⌖ ⌖ Robin Turner. ▶

**Hotel** ★★★★ 69% Marriott Hotel, 128 King Henry's Rd, LONDON ☎ 0171 722 7711 303 ⇆ 🏤

## N9 LOWER EDMONTON

**Lee Valley Leisure** Picketts Lock Sports Centre, Meridian Way, Edmonton N9 0AS ☎ 0181 803 3611
Tricky municipal parkland course with some narrow fairways and the River Lea providing a natural hazard.
*18 holes, 4902yds, Par 66, SSS 64, Course record 66.*
*Club membership 200.*
**Visitors** may telephone for advance bookings.
**Societies** must telephone in advance.
**Green Fees** £10 per round (£13 weekends).
**Facilities** ⊗ ⅏ ⅃ ⵣ ♀ ♨ 🏠 ⵜ ⸋ R Gerken.
**Leisure** heated indoor swimming pool, squash, sauna, solarium, gymnasium, trolley for hire, floodlit driving range, putting green, practice area.
**Hotel** ★★★ 57% Enfield Hotel, 52 Rowantree Rd, ENFIELD ☎ 0181 366 3511 34 ⇆ 🏤

## N14 SOUTHGATE

**Trent Park** Bramley Rd, Oakwood N14 4UW
☎ 0181 366 7432
Parkland course set in 150 acres of green belt area. Seven holes played across Merryhills brook. Testing holes are 2nd (423 yds) over brook, 190 yds from the tee, and up to plateau green; 7th (463 yds) dog-leg, over brook, par 4.
*18 holes, 6085yds, Par 70, SSS 69, Course record 68.*
*Club membership 1200.*
**Visitors** must contact 7 days in advance.
**Societies** must telephone in advance.
**Green Fees** £10.60 (£13.50 weekends).
**Facilities** ⊗ ⅏ ⅃ ⵣ ♀ ♨ 🏠 ⵜ ⸋ Mike Plumbridge.
**Leisure** trolley for hire, floodlit driving range, putting green.
**Location** Opposite Oakwood underground station
**Hotel** ★★★★⬥ 69% West Lodge Park Hotel, Cockfosters Rd, HADLEY WOOD
☎ 0181 440 8311 43 ⇆ 🏤Annexe2 ⇆ 🏤

## N20 WHETSTONE

**North Middlesex** The Manor House, Friern Barnet Ln, Whetstone N20 0NL ☎ 0181 445 1604 & 0181 445 3060
Short parkland course renowned for its tricky greens.
*18 holes, 5625yds, Par 69, SSS 67, Course record 64.*
*Club membership 580.*
**Visitors** advisable to contact in advance, contact professional shop.
**Societies** bookings in advance, winter offers & summer packages by prior arrangement.
**Green Fees** £27.50 per day; £22 per round (£30 per round, £25 after 3pm, weekends).
**Facilities** ⊗ ⅏ ⅃ ⵣ ♀ ♨ 🏠 ⵜ ⸋ Steve Roberts.
**Leisure** trolley for hire, putting green.
**Hotel** ★★★ 74% Edgwarebury Hotel, Barnet Ln, ELSTREE ☎ 0181 953 8227 47 ⇆ 🏤

**South Herts** Links Dr, Totteridge N20 8QU
☎ 0181 445 2035
An open undulating parkland course officially in Hertfordshire, but now in a London postal area. It is,

---

perhaps, most famous for the fact that two of the greatest of all British professionals, Harry Vardon and Dai Rees, CBE were professionals at the club. The course is testing, over rolling fairways, especially in the prevailing southwest wind.
*18 holes, 6432yds, Par 72, SSS 71, Course record 65.*
*Club membership 850.*
**Visitors** must be members of recognised golf club & have handicap certificate of 24 or less.
**Societies** Wed-Fri only, must apply in writing.
**Green Fees** £30 per round/day.
**Facilities** ⊗ ⅏ ⅃ ⵣ ♀ ♨ 🏠 ⵜ ⸋ Bobby Mitchell.
**Leisure** motorised carts for hire, buggies for hire, trolley for hire, putting green, practice area.
**Hotel** B Forte Posthouse South Mimms, SOUTH MIMMS ☎ 01707 643311 120 ⇆ 🏤

## N21 WINCHMORE HILL

**Bush Hill Park** Bush Hill, Winchmore Hill N21 2BU
☎ 0181 360 5738
Pleasant parkland course surrounded by trees.
*18 holes, 5809yds, Par 70, SSS 68.*
*Club membership 700.*
**Visitors** may not play Wed mornings or weekends & bank holidays.
**Societies** by arrangement.
**Green Fees** not confirmed.
**Facilities** ⵣ ♀ ♨ 🏠 ⸋
**Hotel** ★★★ 57% Enfield Hotel, 52 Rowantree Rd, ENFIELD ☎ 0181 366 3511 34 ⇆ 🏤

## N22 WOOD GREEN

**Muswell Hill** Rhodes Av, Wood Green N22 4UT
☎ 0181 888 1764
Narrow parkland course featuring numerous water hazards.
*18 holes, 6438yds, Par 71, SSS 71, Course record 65.*
*Club membership 560.*
**Visitors** must contact in advance, restricted weekends.
**Societies** apply in writing or telephone.
**Green Fees** telephone for current rates.
**Facilities** ⊗ ⅏ ⅃ ⵣ ♀ ♨ 🏠 ⵜ ⸋ David Wilton.
**Leisure** motorised carts for hire, buggies for hire, trolley for hire, putting green, practice area.
**Location** Off N Circular Rd at Bounds Green
**Hotel** ★★★ 67% Raglan Hall Hotel, 8-12 Queens Ave, Muswell Hill, LONDON
☎ 0181 883 9836 46 ⇆ 🏤

## NW7 MILL HILL

**Finchley** Nether Court, Frith Ln, Mill Hill NW7 1PU
☎ 0181 346 2436 & 346 5086
Easy walking on wooded parkland course.
*18 holes, 6411yds, Par 72, SSS 71.*
*Club membership 500.*
**Visitors** must contact in advance.
**Societies** must apply in writing.
**Green Fees** £30 per day; £24 per round (£36/£30 weekends and bank holidays).
**Facilities** ⊗ ⅃ ⵣ ♀ ♨ 🏠 ⵜ ⸋ David Brown.
**Leisure** motorised carts for hire, buggies for hire, trolley for hire, putting green.

**Location** Near Mill Hill East Tube Station
**Hotel** ★★★ 74% Edgwarebury Hotel, Barnet Ln,
ELSTREE ☎ 0181 953 8227 47 ⇌ ♦

---

**Hendon** Sanders Ln, Devonshire Rd, Mill Hill NW7 1DG
☎ 0181 346 6023
Easy walking, parkland course with a good variety of trees,
and providing testing golf.
*18 holes, 6266yds, Par 70, SSS 70.*
*Club membership 540.*
**Visitors** must contact in advance. Restricted weekends &
bank holidays.
**Societies** Tue-Fri. Must contact in advance.
**Green Fees** £30 per day; £25 per round (£35 per round
weekends & bank holidays).
**Facilities** ⊗ ℳ by prior arrangement ⓑ 🍺 ♀ ⚘ 🏠 ⛳
ℓ Stuart Murray.
**Leisure** trolley for hire, putting green, practice area.
**Location** 10 mins from junc 2 of M1 southbound
**Hotel** ★★★ 74% Edgwarebury Hotel, Barnet Ln,
ELSTREE ☎ 0181 953 8227 47 ⇌ ♦

---

*Mill Hill* 100 Barnet Way, Mill Hill NW7 3AL
☎ 0181 959 2339
Undulating parkland course with all holes separated by good
tree and shrub cover.
*18 holes, 6247yds, Par 69, SSS 70, Course record 65.*
*Club membership 550.*
**Visitors** restricted weekends & bank holidays. Must
contact in advance.
**Societies** must contact in advance.
**Green Fees** not confirmed.
**Facilities** ♀ ⚘ 🏠 ⛳ ℓ Alex Daniel.
**Location** 0n A1 S bound carriageway
**Hotel** ★★★ 74% Edgwarebury Hotel, Barnet Ln,
ELSTREE ☎ 0181 953 8227 47 ⇌ ♦

## SE9 ELTHAM

**Eltham Warren** Bexley Rd, Eltham SE9 2PE
☎ 0181 850 4477 & 0181 850 1166
Parkland course with narrow fairways and small greens. The
course is bounded by the A210 on one side and Eltham Park
on the other.
*9 holes, 5840yds, Par 69, SSS 68, Course record 66.*
*Club membership 440.*
**Visitors** may not play at weekends. Must contact in
advance and have a handicap certificate.
**Societies** must book in advance. Deposit required.
**Green Fees** £25 per day.
**Facilities** ⊗ ℳ ⓑ 🍺 ♀ ⚘ 🏠 ℓ Ross Taylor.
**Leisure** trolley for hire, putting green, practice area,
snooker.
**Hotel** ★★★ 69% Bromley Court Hotel, Bromley Hill,
BROMLEY ☎ 0181 464 5011 118 ⇌ ♦

**Royal Blackheath** Court Rd SE9 5AF
☎ 0181 850 1795
A pleasant, parkland course of great character as befits
the antiquity of the Club; the clubhouse dates from the
17th century. Many great trees survive and there are two
ponds. The 18th requires a pitch to the green over a thick
clipped hedge, which also crosses the front of the 1st tee.
*18 holes, 6219yds, Par 70, SSS 70.*
*Club membership 720.*

---

**Visitors** must contact in advance but may play mid-
week only, handicap certificate is required.
**Societies** must apply in writing.
**Green Fees** £40 per day; £30 per round.
**Facilities** ⊗ ⓑ 🍺 ♀ ⚘ 🏠 ⛳ ℓ Ian McGregor.
**Leisure** motorised carts for hire, buggies for hire,
trolley for hire, putting green, golf museum.
**Hotel** ★★★ 69% Bromley Court Hotel, Bromley
Hill, BROMLEY
☎ 0181 464 5011 118 ⇌ ♦

## SE18 WOOLWICH                                    Map 05 TQ47

**Shooters Hill** Eaglesfield Rd, Shooters Hill SE18 3DA
☎ 0181 854 6368
Hilly and wooded parkland course with good view and
natural hazards.
*18 holes, 5721 yds, Par 69, SSS 68, Course record 63.*
*Club membership 900.*
**Visitors** must have handicap certificate and be a member
of a recognised golf club but may not play at
weekends.
**Societies** Tue & Thu only, by arrangement.
**Green Fees** £25 per day; £20 per round.
**Facilities** ⊗ ℳ ⓑ 🍺 ♀ ⚘ 🏠 ℓ Michael Ridge.
**Leisure** motorised carts for hire, buggies for hire, trolley
for hire, putting green.
**Location** Shooters Hill Rd from Blackheath
**Hotel** B Forte Posthouse Bexley, Black Prince
Interchange, Southwold Rd, BEXLEY
☎ 01322 526900 103 ⇌ ♦

## SE21 DULWICH

**Dulwich & Sydenham Hill** Grange Ln, College Rd
SE21 7LH ☎ 0181 693 3961 & 693 8491
Parkland course overlooking London. Hilly with narrow
fairways.
*18 holes, 6008yds, Par 69, SSS 69, Course record 63.*
*Club membership 850.*
**Visitors** must contact in advance and have a handicap
certificate. May not play weekends or bank
holidays.
**Societies** must telephone in advance & confirm in writing.
**Green Fees** £30 per day; £25 per round.
**Facilities** ⊗ ℳ ⓑ 🍺 ♀ ⚘ 🏠 ⛳ ℓ David Baillie.
**Leisure** motorised carts for hire, buggies for hire, trolley
for hire, putting green, practice area.
**Hotel** ★★★ 69% Bromley Court Hotel, Bromley Hill,
BROMLEY ☎ 0181 464 5011 118 ⇌ ♦

## SE22 EAST DULWICH

**Aquarius** Marmora Rd, Honor Oak, Off Forest Hill Rd
SE22 0RY ☎ 0181 693 1626
Course laid-out on two levels around and over covered
reservoir; hazards include vents and bollards.
*9 holes, 5246yds, Par 66, SSS 66, Course record 66.*
*Club membership 350.*
**Visitors** must be accompanied by member and have a
handicap certificate.
**Green Fees** £10 per day/round.
**Facilities** ⊗ ℳ by prior arrangement ⓑ 🍺 ♀ ⚘ 🏠
ℓ Frederick Private.                              ▶

**Hotel**    ★★★ 69% Bromley Court Hotel, Bromley Hill, BROMLEY ☎ 0181 464 5011 118 ⇔ ♠

## SE28 WOOLWICH

**Riverside** Summerton Way, Thamesmead SE28 8PP
☎ 0181 310 7975
A delightful undulating course with a mix of mature trees, new trees and water hazards. The 4th hole is a challenging 515yards down a narrow fairway.
*9 holes, 5462yds, Par 70, SSS 66.*
*Club membership 150.*
**Visitors**    no restrictions.
**Societies**    book by telephone or in writing.
**Green Fees** £8.50 per 18 holes; £5 per 9 holes (£10.50/£6.50 weekends).
**Facilities**   ⊗ ⓑ ⌷ ♀ ⚒ 🕾 ⚐ ℓ Paul Jolner.
**Leisure**    driving range, putting green.
**Hotel**    ★★ 67% Bardon Lodge Hotel, Stratheden Rd, LONDON ☎ 0181 853 4051 32rm(27 ⇔ ♠)

## SW15 PUTNEY

**Richmond Park** Roehampton Gate, Priory Ln
SW15 5JR ☎ 0181 876 1795
Two public parkland courses.
*Princes Course: 18 holes, 5868yds, Par 69, SSS 68.*
*Dukes Course: 18 holes, 6036yds, Par 68, SSS 68.*
**Visitors**    must contact in advance or pay and play.
**Societies**    must contact in advance.
**Green Fees** £4-£13 (£4-£16 weekends).
**Facilities**   ⊗ ⽰ ⓑ ⌷ ♀ 🕾 ⚐
       ℓ Stuart Hill & David Brown.
**Leisure**    motorised carts for hire, buggies for hire, trolley for hire, driving range, putting green, practice area.
**Hotel**    ★★★ 70% Richmond Hill, Richmond Hill, RICHMOND UPON THAMES
       ☎ 0181 940 2247 & 0181 940 5466 124 ⇔ ♠

## SW18 WANDSORTH

**Springfield Park** Burntwood Ln, Wandsworth SW18 0AT
☎ 0181 871 2468
Attractive flat parkland course in the middle of London. The longest drive is the 430 yard 3rd to one of the course's superb greens. Well placed bunkers trap the careless shot and the course rewards the accurate player.
*9 holes, 2250yds, Par 62, SSS 62.*
*Club membership 100.*
**Visitors**    must contact in advance.
**Societies**    telephone or write to the secretary.
**Green Fees** £11 per 18 holes; £6 per 9 holes (£13/£8 weekends & bank holidays).
**Facilities**   ⊗ ⽰ ⓑ ⌷ ♀ ⚒ 🕾 ⚐ ℓ Jeremy Robson.
**Leisure**    trolley for hire, putting green, practice area.
**Hotel**    ★★★★ 76% Cannizaro House, West Side, Wimbledon Common, LONDON
       ☎ 0181 879 1464 46 ⇔ ♠

Entries with a shaded background identify
courses that are considered to be particularly
interesting

## SW19 WIMBLEDON

**Royal Wimbledon** 29 Camp Rd SW19 4UW
☎ 0181 946 2125
A club steeped in the history of the game, it is also of great age, dating back to 1865. Of sand and heather like so many of the Surrey courses its 12th hole (par 4) is rated as the best on the course.
*18 holes, 6300yds, Par 70, SSS 70.*
*Club membership 1050.*
**Visitors**    must be guests of current club member.
**Societies**    welcome Wed-Thu. Must apply in writing.
**Green Fees** not confirmed.
**Facilities**   ⚒ 🕾 ⚐ ℓ
**Hotel**    ★★★★ 76% Cannizaro House, West Side, Wimbledon Common, LONDON
       ☎ 0181 879 1464 46 ⇔ ♠

*Wimbledon Common* Camp Rd SW19 4UW
☎ 0181 946 0294
Quick-drying course on Wimbledon Common. Well wooded, with tight fairways, challenging short holes but no bunkers.The course isalso played over by London Scottish Golf Club (0181 788 0135). All players must wear plain red upper garments.
*18 holes, 5438yds, Par 68, SSS 66.*
*Club membership 250.*
**Visitors**    with member only at weekends.
**Societies**    must telephone in advance.
**Green Fees** not confirmed.
**Facilities**   ♀ ⚒ 🕾 ℓ J S Jukes.
**Hotel**    ★★★★ 76% Cannizaro House, West Side, Wimbledon Common, LONDON
       ☎ 0181 879 1464 46 ⇔ ♠

*Wimbledon Park* Home Park Rd, Wimbledon SW19 7HR
☎ 0181 946 1250
Easy walking on parkland course. Sheltered lake provides hazard on 3 holes.
*18 holes, 5465yds, Par 66, SSS 66.*
*Club membership 700.*
**Visitors**    restricted weekends & bank holidays. Must contact in advance and have handicap certificate or letter of introduction.
**Societies**    must apply in writing.
**Green Fees** not confirmed.
**Facilities**   ♀ ⚒ 🕾 ℓ Dean Wingrove.
**Leisure**    putting green,trolley hire.
**Location**    400 yds from Wimbledon Park Station
**Hotel**    ★★★ 70% Richmond Hill, Richmond Hill, RICHMOND UPON THAMES
       ☎ 0181 940 2247 & 0181 940 5466 124 ⇔ ♠

## W7 HANWELL

*Brent Valley* 138 Church Rd, Hanwell W7 3BE
☎ 0181 567 1287
Municipal parkland course with easy walking. The River Brent winds through the course.
*18 holes, 5426yds, Par 67, SSS 66.*
*Club membership 350.*
**Visitors**    no restrictions.
**Societies**    one month's notice required.
**Green Fees** not confirmed.
**Facilities**   ♀ ⚒ 🕾 ⚐ ℓ Peter Byrne.
**Hotel**    ★★★ 63% Master Robert Hotel, Great West Rd, HOUNSLOW ☎ 0181 570 6261 94 ⇔ ♠

# MERSEYSIDE

**Hotel** ★★★ 68% Bowler Hat Hotel, 2 Talbot Rd,
Oxton, BIRKENHEAD
☎ 0151 652 4931 32 ⇄ ✎

## BEBINGTON
Map 07 SJ38

*Brackenwood* Brackenwood Park L63 2LY
☎ 0151 608 3093
Municipal parkland course with easy walking.
*18 holes, 6285yds, Par 70, SSS 70.*
*Club membership 320.*
**Societies** must apply in advance.
**Green Fees** not confirmed.
**Facilities** ⬛ ↱ ʄ
**Location** 0.75m N of M53 junc 4 on B5151
**Hotel** ★★★ 68% Thornton Hall Hotel, Neston Rd,
THORNTON HOUGH
☎ 0151 336 3938 5 ⇄ ✎Annexe58 ⇄ ✎

## BIRKENHEAD
Map 07 SJ38

*Arrowe Park* Woodchurch L49 5LW ☎ 0151 677 1527
Pleasant municipal parkland course.
*18 holes, 6435yds, Par 72, SSS 71, Course record 68.*
*Club membership 220.*
**Visitors** no restrictions.
**Societies** must telephone in advance.
**Green Fees** not confirmed.
**Facilities** ♀⬛ ↱ ʄ Clive Scanlon.
**Leisure** putting green, trolley hire.
**Location** 1m from M53 junc 3 on A551
**Hotel** ★★★ 68% Bowler Hat Hotel, 2 Talbot Rd,
Oxton, BIRKENHEAD
☎ 0151 652 4931 32 ⇄ ✎

*Prenton* Golf Links Rd, Prenton L42 8LW
☎ 0151 608 1053
Parkland course with easy walking and views of the Welsh
Hills.
*18 holes, 6411yds, Par 71, SSS 71.*
*Club membership 610.*
**Visitors** must contact in advance.
**Societies** must telephone in advance and confirm in
writing.
**Green Fees** £25 per day (£30 weekends & bank holidays).
**Facilities** ⊗ ⅏ by prior arrangement ⬛ ♥ ♀⬛ ↱
ʄ Robin Thompson.
**Leisure** trolley for hire, putting green, practice area,
snooker.
**Location** S side of town centre off B5151
**Hotel** ★★ 64% Riverhill Hotel, Talbot Rd, Oxton,
BIRKENHEAD ☎ 0151 653 3773 16 ⇄ ✎

*Wirral Ladies* 93 Bidston Rd, Oxton L43 6TS
☎ 0151 652 1255
Heathland course with heather and birch.
*18 holes, 4966yds, SSS 70.*
*Club membership 450.*
**Visitors** may not play over Christmas and Easter
holidays.
**Societies** must telephone in advance.
**Green Fees** not confirmed.
**Facilities** ♀⬛ ⬛ ʄ Philip Chandler.
**Location** W side of town centre on B5151

## BLUNDELLSANDS
Map 07 SJ39

*West Lancashire* Hall Rd West L23 8SZ
☎ 0151 924 1076
Challenging, traditional links with sandy subsoil
overlooking the Mersey Estuary. The course provides
excellent golf throughout the year. The four short holes
are very fine.
*18 holes, 6763yds, Par 72, SSS 73.*
*Club membership 650.*
**Visitors** may not play on competition days; must
have a handicap certificate.
**Societies** must contact in advance.
**Green Fees** not confirmed.
**Facilities** ♀⬛ ⬛ ʄ David Lloyd.
**Location** N side of village
**Hotel** ★★★ 64% Blundellsands Hotel, The
Serpentine, BLUNDELLSANDS
☎ 0151 924 6515 41 ⇄ ✎

## BOOTLE
Map 07 SJ39

*Bootle* 2 Dunnings Bridge Rd L30 2PP ☎ 0151 928 6196
Municipal seaside course, with prevailing north-westerly
wind. Testing holes: 5th (200 yds) par 3; 7th (415 yds) par 4.
*18 holes, 6362yds, Par 70, SSS 70, Course record 64.*
*Club membership 380.*
**Visitors** must contact in advance.
**Societies** must apply in writing.
**Green Fees** on application.
**Facilities** ⊗ ⅏ ⬛ ♥ ♀⬛ ↱ ʄ Alan Bradshaw.
**Leisure** hard tennis courts, trolley for hire, putting green.
**Location** 2m NE on A5036
**Hotel** ★★★ 64% Blundellsands Hotel, The
Serpentine, BLUNDELLSANDS
☎ 0151 924 6515 41 ⇄ ✎

## BROMBOROUGH
Map 07 SJ38

*Bromborough* Raby Hall Rd L63 0NW ☎ 0151 334 2155
Parkland course.
*18 holes, 6650yds, Par 72, SSS 73, Course record 67.*
*Club membership 800.*
**Visitors** are advised to contact professional on 0151 334
4499 in advance.
**Societies** normal society day Wed ; must apply in
advance.
**Green Fees** £26 per day (£30 weekends).
**Facilities** ⊗ ⅏ ⬛ ♥ ♀⬛ ⬛ ʄ Geoff Berry.
**Leisure** motorised carts for hire, trolley for hire, putting
green.
**Location** 0.5m W of Station
**Hotel** B Travel Inn, High St, BROMBOROUGH
☎ 0151 334 2917 31 ⇄ ✎

Entries with a shaded background identify
courses that are considered to be particularly
interesting

## CALDY                          Map 07 SJ28

*Caldy* Links Hey Rd L48 1NB
☎ 0151 625 5660
A parkland course situated on the estuary of the River
Dee with many of the fairways running parallel to the
river. Of Championship length, the course offers
excellent golf all year, but is subject to variable winds
that noticeably alter the day to day playing of each hole.
There are excellent views of North Wales and
Snowdonia.
*18 holes, 6675yds, Par 72, SSS 73, Course record 68.*
*Club membership 800.*
Visitors       may play on weekdays only. Must contact in
               advance and have an introduction from own
               club.
Societies      must telephone in advance.
Green Fees     not confirmed.
Facilities     ⚑ ⚘ 🏠 ℓ K Jones.
Location       SE side of village
Hotel          ★★★ 68% Thornton Hall Hotel, Neston
               Rd, THORNTON HOUGH
               ☎ 0151 336 3938 5 ⇄ ℓ Annexe58 ⇄ ℟

## EASTHAM                        Map 07 SJ38

Eastham Lodge 117 Ferry Rd L62 0AP
☎ 0151 327 3003 & 327 3008
A 15-hole parkland course with many trees. Three holes
played twice to make 18, but restricted to 15 holes in winter.
*18 holes, 5953yds, Par 69, SSS 69, Course record 67.*
*Club membership 800.*
Visitors       with member only at weekends.
Societies      welcome Tue. Must apply in writing.
Green Fees     £22 per day/round.
Facilities     ⊗ ⅲ by prior arrangement ⚏ ⚑ ⚘ 🏠
               ℓ R Boobyer.
Leisure        trolley for hire, putting green, small practice
               area.
Location       1.5m N
Hotel          B Travel Inn, High St, BROMBOROUGH
               ☎ 0151 334 2917 31 ⇄ ℟

## FORMBY                         Map 07 SD30

Formby Golf Rd L37 1LQ
☎ 01704 872164
Championship seaside links through sandhills and partly
through pine trees.It plays well throughout the year.
*18 holes, 6496yds, Par 72, SSS 72, Course record 66.*
*Club membership 680.*
Visitors       must contact in advance.
Societies      must contact well in advance.
Green Fees     £50 per day/round.
Facilities     ⊗ ⅲ ⚏ ⚐ ⚑ ⚘ 🏠 ℐ ⌂
               ℓ Clive Harrison.
Leisure        trolley for hire, putting green, practice area.
Location       N side of town
Hotel          ★★★ 64% Blundellsands Hotel, The
               Serpentine, BLUNDELLSANDS
               ☎ 0151 924 6515 41 ⇄ ℟

*Formby Ladies* Golf Rd L37 1YH ☎ 01704 873493
Seaside links - one of the few independent ladies clubs in the
country. The course has contrasting hard-hitting holes in flat
country and tricky holes in sandhills and woods.
*18 holes, 5374yds, Par 71, SSS 71.*
*Club membership 423.*
Visitors       must contact in advance and may not play Thu
               or before noon Sat & Sun.
Societies      must apply in advance.
Green Fees     not confirmed.
Facilities     ⚑ ⚘ 🏠 ℓ
Leisure        driving range,putting,trolley hire.
Location       N side of town
Hotel          ★★★ 64% Blundellsands Hotel, The
               Serpentine, BLUNDELLSANDS
               ☎ 0151 924 6515 41 ⇄ ℟

## HESWALL                        Map 07 SJ28

Heswall Cottage Ln L60 8PB ☎ 0151 342 1237
A pleasant parkland course in soft undulating country
over-looking the estuary of the River Dee. There are
excellent views of the Welsh hills and coastline, and a
good test of golf. The clubhouse is modern and well-
appointed with good facilities.
*18 holes, 6492yds, Par 72, SSS 72, Course record 62.*
*Club membership 940.*
Visitors       must contact in advance.
Societies      must apply in advance.
Green Fees     £40 per day; £30 per round (£45/35
               weekends).
Facilities     ⊗ ⅲ ⚏ ⚐ ⚑ ⚘ 🏠 ℓ Alan Thompson.
Leisure        trolley for hire, putting green, practice area.
Location       1m S off A540
Hotel          ★★★ 68% Thornton Hall Hotel, Neston
               Rd, THORNTON HOUGH
               ☎ 0151 336 3938 5 ⇄ ℓ Annexe58 ⇄ ℟

## HOYLAKE                        Map 07 SJ28

*Hoylake* Carr Ln, Municipal Links L47 4BG
☎ 0151 632 2956
Flat, generally windy semi-links course. Tricky fairways.
*18 holes, 6313yds, Par 70, SSS 70, Course record 67.*
*Club membership 303.*
Societies      must telephone 0151 632 4883 M E Down club
               steward or 0151 632 2956 club professional.
Green Fees     not confirmed.
Facilities     ⚑ (ex Fri) ⚘ 🏠 ⅌ ℓ Simon Hooton.
Leisure        practice ground no charge.
Location       SW side of town off A540
Hotel          ★★★ 66% Leasowe Castle Hotel, Leasowe Rd,
               MORETON ☎ 0151 606 9191 47 ⇄ ℟

Royal Liverpool Meols Dr L47 4AL ☎ 0151 632 3101
A world famous, windswept seaside links course.
*18 holes, 6162yds, Par 71, SSS 71.*
*Club membership 650.*
Visitors       must contact in advance & have a handicap
               certificate. Restricted before 9.30am &
               between 1-2pm. No play Thu am (ladies
               day). Limited play weekends.
Societies      must contact in advance.
Green Fees     £65 per day; £47.50 per round (£95/£60
               weekends).

| Facilities | ⊗ 🄱 ☂ ♀ ⚲ 🄰 ⼻ ( John Heggarty. |
| Leisure | trolley for hire, putting green, practice area. |
| Location | SW side of town on A540 |
| Hotel | ★★★ 66% Leasowe Castle Hotel, Leasowe Rd, MORETON ☎ 0151 606 9191 47 ⇌ ( |

## HUYTON                                    Map 07 SJ49

**Bowring** Bowring Park, Roby Rd L36 4HD
☎ 0151 489 1901
Flat parkland course.
*9 holes, 2796yds, Par 34.*
*Club membership 80.*
Visitors    no restrictions.
Green Fees not confirmed.
Facilities   ⚲ 🄰 (
Location    On A5080 adjacent M62 junc 5
Hotel       ★ 59% Rockland Hotel, View Rd, RAINHILL
            ☎ 0151 426 4603 10rm(9 ⇌)

**Huyton & Prescot** Hurst Park, Huyton Ln L36 1UA
☎ 0151 489 3948
An easy walking, parkland course providing excellent golf.
*18 holes, 5779yds, Par 68, SSS 68.*
*Club membership 700.*
Visitors    must contact in advance. Must play with
            member at weekends.
Societies   must apply in writing.
Green Fees  £22.
Facilities  ⊗ ⼞ 🄱 ☂ ♀ ⚲ 🄰 ( Malcolm Harrison.
Leisure     trolley for hire, putting green, practice area.
Location    1.5m NE off B5199
Hotel       ★ 59% Rockland Hotel, View Rd, RAINHILL
            ☎ 0151 426 4603 10rm(9 ⇌)

## LIVERPOOL                                 Map 07 SJ39

**Allerton Park** Allerton Manor Golf Estate, Allerton Rd
L18 3JT ☎ 0151 428 1046
Parkland course.
*18 holes, 5459yds, Par 67, SSS 67.*
*Club membership 300.*
Visitors    must book with professional in advance.
Green Fees not confirmed.
Facilities  ♀ 🄰 ⼻ ( Barry Large.
Leisure     putting green,trolley hire.
Location    5.5m SE of city centre off A562 and B5180
Hotel       ★★★★ 55% Atlantic Tower, Chapel St,
            LIVERPOOL ☎ 0151 227 4444 226 ⇌ (

**The Childwall** Naylors Rd, Gateacre L27 2YB
☎ 0151 487 0654
Parkland golf is played here over a testing course, where
accuracy from the tee is well-rewarded. The course is
very popular with visiting societies for the clubhouse has
many amenities. Course designed by James Braid.
*18 holes, 6425yds, Par 72, SSS 71, Course record 66.*
*Club membership 650.*
Visitors    must contact in advance.
Societies   must apply in writing.
Green Fees  £23 per day (£33 weekends).
Facilities  ⊗ ⼞ 🄱 ☂ ♀ ⚲ 🄰 ⼻ ( Nigel M Parr.

| Leisure | trolley for hire, driving range, putting green, practice area. |
| Location | 7m E of city centre off B5178 |
| Hotel | ★ 59% Rockland Hotel, View Rd, RAINHILL ☎ 0151 426 4603 10rm(9 ⇌) |

**Kirkby-Liverpool Municipal** Ingoe Ln, Kirkby L32 4SS
☎ 0151 546 5435
Flat, easy course.
*18 holes, 6588yds, Par 72, SSS 71, Course record 70.*
*Club membership 150.*
Visitors    must contact in advance.
Societies   must contact 1 week in advance.
Green Fees not confirmed.
Facilities  ♀ ⚲ 🄰 ⼻ ( Dave Weston.
Location    7.5m NE of city centre on A506
Hotel       ★★★★ 57% Liverpool Moat House Hotel,
            Paradise St, LIVERPOOL
            ☎ 0151 709 0181 251 ⇌ (

**Lee Park** Childwall Valley Rd L27 3YA ☎ 0151 487 3882
Flat course with ponds in places.
*18 holes, 5508mtrs, Par 71, SSS 69.*
*Club membership 600.*
Visitors    must dress acceptably.
Societies   must contact in advance.
Green Fees not confirmed.
Facilities  ♀ ⚲
Leisure     putting green,practice area.
Location    7m E of city centre off B5178
Hotel       ★★★★ 57% Liverpool Moat House Hotel,
            Paradise St, LIVERPOOL
            ☎ 0151 709 0181 251 ⇌ (

**West Derby** Yew Tree Ln, West Derby L12 9HQ
☎ 0151 228 1540 & 0151 254 1034
A parkland course always in first-class condition, and so
giving easy walking. The fairways are well-wooded. Care
must be taken on the first nine holes to avoid the brook
which guards many of the greens. A modern well-
designed clubhouse with many amenities, overlooks the
course.
*18 holes, 6333yds, Par 72, SSS 70.*
*Club membership 550.*
Visitors    may not play before 9.30am.
Societies   may not play on Sat, Sun & bank holidays;
            must contact in advance.
Green Fees not confirmed.
Facilities  ♀ ⚲ 🄰 ( Nick Brace.
Location    4.5m E of city centre off A57
Hotel       ★★★★ 55% Atlantic Tower, Chapel St,
            LIVERPOOL ☎ 0151 227 4444 226 ⇌ (

**Woolton** Speke Rd, Woolton L25 7TZ ☎ 0151 486 2298
Parkland course providing a good round of golf for all
standards.
*18 holes, 5717yds, Par 69, SSS 68.*
*Club membership 700.*
Visitors    must contact in advance. Restricted at weekends.
Societies   must contact in advance.
Green Fees  £20 per day (£30 weekends).
Facilities  ⊗ ⼞ 🄱 ☂ ♀ ⚲ 🄰 ( Alan Gibson.
Leisure     motorised carts for hire, putting green.
Location    7m SE of city centre off A562          ▶

Hotel    ★★★★ 55%  Atlantic Tower, Chapel St,
         LIVERPOOL
         ☎ 0151 227 4444 226 ⇌ ⋔

## NEWTON-LE-WILLOWS                  Map 07 SJ59

**Haydock Park** Newton Ln WA12 0HX
☎ 01925 228525
A well-wooded parkland course, close to the well-known
racecourse, and always in excellent condition. The
pleasant undulating fairways offer some very interesting
golf and the 6th, 11th and 13th holes are particularly
testing. The clubhouse is very comfortable.
*18 holes, 6043yds, Par 70, SSS 69, Course record 65.*
*Club membership 560.*
Visitors    with member only weekends & bank
            holidays. Must contact in advance.
Societies   must contact in advance.
Green Fees  £25 per day/round.
Facilities  ⊗ ⤣ ⬛ ⬛ ⚲ ⅄ 🏠 ⋔ ⅃ Peter Kenwright.
Leisure     trolley for hire, putting green, practice area.
Location    0.75m NE off A49
Hotel       B Forte Posthouse Haydock, Lodge Ln,
            Newton-Le-Willows, HAYDOCK
            ☎ 01942 717878 136 ⇌ ⋔

## ST HELENS                          Map 07 SJ59

**Grange Park** Prescot Rd WA10 3AD
☎ 01744 26318
A course of Championship length set in plesant country
surroundings - playing the course it is hard to believe that
industrial St Helens lies so close at hand. The course is a
fine test of golf and there are many attractive holes liable
to challenge all grades.
*18 holes, 6422yds, Par 72, SSS 71, Course record 65.*
*Club membership 730.*
Visitors    play allowed any day except public
            holidays. Advisable to contact professional
            in advance (01744 28785)
Societies   phone initially.
Green Fees  £29 per 36 holes; £23 per 27 holes (£35 per
            27 holes weekends).
Facilities  ⊗ ⤣ ⬛ ⬛ ⚲ ⅄ 🏠 ⋔ ⅃ Paul Roberts.
Leisure     motorised carts for hire, trolley for hire,
            putting, snooker.
Location    1.5m SW on A58
Hotel       ★★★★ 65%  Chalon Court, Chalon Way,
            Linkway West, ST HELENS
            ☎ 01744 453444 84 ⇌ ⋔

*Sherdley Park* Sherdley Rd WA9 5DE
☎ 01744 813149
Fairly hilly course with ponds in places.
*18 holes, 5941yds, Par 70, SSS 69.*
*Club membership 160.*
Visitors    no restrictions.
Green Fees  not confirmed.
Facilities  ⅄ 🏠 ⋔ ⅃
Location    2m S off A570
Hotel       ★★★★ 65%  Chalon Court, Chalon Way,
            Linkway West, ST HELENS
            ☎ 01744 453444 84 ⇌ ⋔

## SOUTHPORT                          Map 07 SD31

*The Hesketh* Cockle Dick's Ln, off Cambridge Rd
PR9 9QQ  ☎ 01704 536897
Hesketh is the senior club in Southport, founded in 1885.
The Championship course comprises much of the
original territory plus a large area of reclaimed land on
the seaward side - essentially 'Links' in character.
*18 holes, 6407yds, Par 71, SSS 72, Course record 66.*
*Club membership 600.*
Visitors    must have a handicap certificate. May not
            play Tue mornings (Ladies) or 12.30-2pm
            daily.
Green Fees  not confirmed.
Facilities  ⚲ ⅄ 🏠 ⋔ ⅃ John Donoghue.
Location    1m NE of town centre off A565
Hotel       ★★ 65%  Bold Hotel, 585 Lord St,
            SOUTHPORT
            ☎ 01704 532578 23 ⇌ ⋔

**Hillside** Hastings Rd, Hillside PR8 2LU
☎ 01704 567169 & 568360
Championship links course with natural hazards open to
strong wind.
*18 holes, 6850yds, Par 72, SSS 74.*
*Club membership 700.*
Visitors    must contact in advance.
Societies   must apply to secretary in advance.
Green Fees  £45 per day; £35 per round (£45 per round
            Sun).
Facilities  ⊗ ⤣ ⬛ ⬛ ⚲ ⅄ 🏠 ⋔ ⅃ Brian Seddon.
Leisure     motorised carts for hire, buggies for hire,
            trolley for hire, driving range, putting green,
            practice area.
Location    3m S of town centre on A565
Hotel       ★★★ 68%  Royal Clifton Hotel,
            Promenade, SOUTHPORT
            ☎ 01704 533771 107 ⇌ ⋔

## ROYAL BIRKDALE    See page 155

*Southport & Ainsdale* Bradshaws Ln, Ainsdale PR8 3LG
☎ 01704 578000
'S and A', as it is known in the North is another of the
fine Championship courses for which this part of the
country is famed. This Club has staged many important
events and offers golf of the highest order.
*18 holes, 6603yds, Par 72, SSS 73.*
*Club membership 815.*
Visitors    welcome except Thu am, weekends & bank
            holidays. Must contact club in advance &
            have handicap certificate.
Societies   must apply in advance.
Green Fees  not confirmed.
Facilities  ⚲ ⅄ 🏠 ⋔ ⅃ M Houghton.
Leisure     putting green,practice area,trolley hire.
Location    3m S off A565
Hotel       ★★★ 68%  Royal Clifton Hotel,
            Promenade, SOUTHPORT
            ☎ 01704 533771 107 ⇌ ⋔

# THE ROYAL BIRKDALE

## SOUTHPORT *Lancs* ☎ 01704 567920     Map 07 SD31

*John Ingham writes:* There are few seaside links in the world that can be described as 'great', but Royal Birkdale, with its expanse of towering sandhills and willow scrub, is one of them. There have been some changes since the club was founded in 1889 and they have hosted everything that matters here, including the Open (which returns in 1998) and the Ryder Cup. Some changes have been made even since Arnold Palmer hit that wondrous recovery shot that helped him win an Open in the early sixties, and led to a plaque being erected at the spot from which the divot was taken.

Well bunkered, the sandhills run along the edges of the fairways and make ideal platforms from which to view the Open Championship - played frequently here because the examination is supreme in the United Kingdom.

The links, in a wind, may be too difficult for the weekender. Certainly it found out Dai Rees in 1961 when he was chasing Palmer for the title. In the last round the course struck at the very first hole. Rees had hit his teeshot a might to the left, and then had to wait for the players to hole out on the green ahead, before attempting a powerful shot with a lofted wood from the fairway. The ball smacked into the back of a bunker, and fell back into sand. Rees took an awful seven and Palmer beat him for the trophy - by one shot. The Welshman had stormed back in 31 but his chance to win an Open had gone forever. But Rees still touched his hat to the links, and held it in great respect as, indeed, does Arnold Palmer.

But for the amateur, another problem is simply hitting the ball far enough. If you play this terrific course from the Open Championship back tees, it measures 6690 yards and par 72 takes some getting, even with your handicap allowance!

**Visitors** must contact in advance, and have a handicap certificate. Normally not Fri & Sat; only Sun am. Play off yellow tees

**Societies** must apply in advance. Principle days: Wed, Thur

**Green fees** Weekdays £75 per day, £55 per round. Sun am only £75

**Facilities** ⊗ ℼ ⬧ ♨ ♥ ♀ ⛳ ⌂ ⛳ ♪ (Richard Bradbeer) putting green, practice area

**Location** Waterloo Road, Birkdale, Southport PR8 2LX (2m S of town on A565)

18 holes, 6690yds, Par 72, SSS 73, Course record 63 (1991 Open, Jodie Mudd, USA)

### WHERE TO STAY AND EAT NEARBY

**HOTELS:**
**SOUTHPORT**
★★★✿ 68% Royal Clifton, Promenade. ☎ 01704 533771. 107 (6 ♪ 101 ⇌ ♪)

★★★ 67% Scarisbrick, Lord St. ☎ 01704 543000. 77 (2 ♪ 75 ⇌ ♪)

★★ 70% Balmoral Lodge, 41 Queens Rd. ☎ 01704 544298. 15 ⇌ ♪

★★★ 65% Stutelea Hotel & Leisure Club, Alexandra Rd. ☎ 01704 544220. 22(3 ♪ 19 ⇌ ♪)

**RESTAURANT:**
**WRIGHTINGTON**
✿ High Moor Inn, Highmoor Ln (jct 27 off M6, take B5239). ☎ 01257 252364

**Southport Municipal** Park Rd West PR9 0JR
☎ 01704 535286
Municipal seaside links course. Played over by Southport
Municipal, Alt and Park golf clubs.
*18 holes, 6400yds, Par 70, SSS 69, Course record 66.*
*Club membership 750.*
Visitors     no restrictions.
Societies    must telephone 6 days in advance.
Green Fees not confirmed.
Facilities   ♀ ⚒ 🏠 ⛳ ♟ Bill Fletcher.
Location     N side of town centre off A565
Hotel        ★★★ 68% Royal Clifton Hotel, Promenade,
             SOUTHPORT ☎ 01704 533771 107 ⇄ ♜

**Southport Old Links** Moss Ln, Churchtown PR9 7QS
☎ 01704 28207
Seaside course with tree-lined fairways and easy walking.
One of the oldest courses in Southport, Henry Vardon won
the 'Leeds Cup' here in 1922.
*9 holes, 6244yds, Par 72, SSS 71, Course record 68.*
*Club membership 450.*
Visitors     advisable to contact in advance.
Societies    apply in writing.
Green Fees £25.50 per day; £18.50 per round (£25.50 per
             round weekends).
Facilities   ⊗ ⎷ ⚒ ⬛ ♀ ⚒
Leisure      putting green.
Location     NW side of town centre off A5267
Hotel        ★★ 65% Bold Hotel, 585 Lord St,
             SOUTHPORT ☎ 01704 532578 23 ⇄ ♜

## WALLASEY   Map 07 SJ29

**Bidston** Bidston Link Rd L44 2HR ☎ 0151 638 3412
Parkland course, with westerly winds.
*18 holes, 5827yds, Par 70, SSS 71, Course record 66.*
*Club membership 650.*
Visitors     must contact in advance, restricted weekends.
Societies    must apply in writing.
Green Fees not confirmed.
Facilities   ♀ ⚒ 🏠 ♟ J Law.
Leisure      putting green, practice area.
Location     0.5m W of M53 junc 1 entrance off A551
Hotel        ★★★ 66% Leasowe Castle Hotel, Leasowe Rd,
             MORETON ☎ 0151 606 9191 47 ⇄ ♜

**Leasowe** Moreton L46 3RD ☎ 0151 677 5852
Rather flat, semi-links, seaside course.
*18 holes, 6227yds, Par 71, SSS 71.*
*Club membership 602.*
Visitors     telephone professional (0151 678 5460).
             Handicap certificate required.
Societies    contact in advance.
Green Fees £20 per day (£25 weekends & bank holidays).
Facilities   ⊗ ⎷ ⚒ ⬛ ♀ ⚒ 🏠 ♟ ♟ Neil Sweeney.
Leisure      trolley for hire, putting green, practice area.
Location     2m W on A551
Hotel        ★★★ 66% Leasowe Castle Hotel, Leasowe Rd,
             MORETON ☎ 0151 606 9191 47 ⇄ ♜

> **Wallasey** Bayswater Rd L45 8LA ☎ 0151 691 1024
> A well-established sporting links, adjacent to the Irish
> Sea, with huge sandhills and many classic holes where
> the player's skills are often combined with good fortune.
> Large, firm greens and fine views but not for the faint-
> hearted.

> *18 holes, 6607yds, Par 72.*
> *Club membership 605.*
> Visitors     must contact one month in advance.
> Societies    must apply in writing or telephone.
> Green Fees £32 per day; £27 per round (£37/£32
>              weekends & bank holidays).
> Facilities   ⊗ ⚒ ⬛ ♀ 🏠 ⛳ ♟ Mike Adams.
> Leisure      trolley for hire, putting green, practice area.
> Location     N side of town centre off A554
> Hotel        ★★★ 66% Leasowe Castle Hotel, Leasowe
>              Rd, MORETON ☎ 0151 606 9191 47 ⇄ ♜

**Warren** Grove Rd L45 0JA ☎ 0151 639 8323
Short, undulating links course with first-class greens and
prevailing winds off the sea.
*9 holes, 5854yds, Par 72, SSS 68.*
*Club membership 150.*
Visitors     except Sun until 10.30.am.
Green Fees not confirmed.
Facilities   🏠 ⛳ ♟ Ken Lamb.
Location     N side of town centre off A554
Hotel        ★★★ 66% Leasowe Castle Hotel, Leasowe Rd,
             MORETON ☎ 0151 606 9191 47 ⇄ ♜

# ● NORFOLK ●

## BARNHAM BROOM   Map 05 TG00

> **Barnham Broom Hotel Golf and Country Club**
> Honingham Rd NR9 4DD
> ☎ 01603 759393
> Attractive river valley courses with modern hotel and
> leisure complex.
> *Hill Course: 18 holes, 6470yds, Par 71, SSS 71.*
> *Valley Course: 18 holes, 6628yds, Par 72, SSS 72.*
> *Club membership 500.*
> Visitors     must contact in advance. With member only
>              at weekends.
> Societies    must contact in advance.
> Green Fees £33 per day; £27 per round.
> Facilities   ⊗ ⎷ ⚒ ⬛ ♀ ⚒ 🏠 ⛳ ⊞
>              ♟ Stephen Beckham.
> Leisure      hard tennis courts, heated indoor swimming
>              pool, squash, sauna, solarium, gymnasium,
>              motorised carts for hire, buggies for hire,
>              trolley for hire, putting green, practice area,
>              snooker.
> Location     1m N, S of A47
> Hotel        ★★★ 69% Barnham Broom Hotel
>              Conference & Leisure, Centre, BARNHAM
>              BROOM ☎ 01603 759393 52 ⇄ ♜
>              *See advetisement on page 159.*

## BAWBURGH   Map 05 TG10

**Bawburgh** Glen Lodge, Marlingford Rd NR9 3LU
☎ 01603 740404
An open-links. Driving range available.
*18 holes, 6224yds, Par 70, SSS 70.*
*Club membership 700.*

**Visitors** must contact in advance.
**Societies** must contact in advance.
**Green Fees** £20 per 36 holes; £15 per 18 holes (£20 per 18 holes weekends).
**Facilities** ⊗ ⍿ ⓑ 🍺 ♀ ⚶ 🏠 ⓒ Chris Potter.
**Leisure** motorised carts for hire, buggies for hire, trolley for hire, driving range, putting green, practice area.
**Location** S of Royal Norfolk Showground, on A47
**Hotel** ★★★ 68% Hotel Norwich, 121-131 Boundary Rd, NORWICH
    ☎ 01603 787260 107 ⇌ ⓡ

## BRANCASTER        Map 09 TF74

**Royal West Norfolk PE31 8AX**
☎ 01485 210223 & 210616
If you want to see what golf courses were like years ago, then go to the Royal West Norfolk where tradition exudes from both clubhouse and course. Close by the sea, the links are laid out in the grand manner and are characterised by sleepered greens, superb cross-bunkering and salt marshes.
*18 holes, 6428yds, Par 71, SSS 71, Course record 66.*
*Club membership 700.*
**Visitors** must contact in advance.
**Societies** must contact Secretary in advance.
**Green Fees** £37.50 (£46.50 weekends).
**Facilities** ⊗ ⍿ ⓑ 🍺 ♀ ⚶ 🏠 ⍿ ⓒ R E Kimber.
**Leisure** trolley for hire, putting green, practice area.
**Hotel** ★★ 72% Titchwell Manor Hotel, TITCHWELL
    ☎ 01485 210221 11rm(7 ⇌ ⓡ)Annexe4 ⇌ ⓡ

## CROMER        Map 09 TG24

**Royal Cromer** 145 Overstrand Rd NR27 0JH
☎ 01263 512884
Seaside course set out on cliff edge, hilly and subject to wind.
*18 holes, 6447yds, Par 71, SSS 71, Course record 67.*
*Club membership 650.*
**Visitors** must contact in advance & have handicap certificate. Restricted at weekends.
**Societies** must contact in advance.
**Green Fees** £27 per day (£32 weekends & bank holidays).
**Facilities** ⊗ ⍿ ⓑ 🍺 ♀ ⚶ 🏠 ⓒ Robin Page.
**Leisure** trolley for hire, putting green, practice area.
**Location** 1m E on B1159
**Hotel** ★★ 69% Red Lion, Brook St, CROMER
    ☎ 01263 514964 12 ⇌ ⓡ

## DENVER        Map 05 TF60

**Ryston Park** PE38 0HH ☎ 01366 382133
Parkland course.
*9 holes, 6310yds, Par 70, SSS 70, Course record 66.*
*Club membership 330.*
**Visitors** must contact in advance. May not play weekends or bank holidays.
**Societies** must apply in writing.
**Green Fees** £20 per day.
**Facilities** ⊗ ⍿ ⓑ 🍺 ♀ ⚶ 🏠

**Leisure** putting green, practice area.
**Location** 0.5m S on A10
**Hotel** ★★ 65% Castle Hotel, High St, DOWNHAM MARKET ☎ 01366 384311 12rm(9 ⇌ ⓡ)

## DEREHAM        Map 09 TF91

**Dereham** Quebec Rd NR19 2DS
☎ 01362 695900 & 685631
Parkland course.
*9 holes, 6225yds, Par 71, SSS 70, Course record 64.*
*Club membership 400.*
**Visitors** must contact in advance and have a handicap certificate; must play with member at weekends.
**Societies** must apply in writing.
**Green Fees** £20 per day.
**Facilities** ⊗ ⍿ ⓑ 🍺 ♀ ⚶ 🏠 ⓒ Robert Curtis.
**Leisure** trolley for hire, putting green, practice area.
**Location** N side of town centre off B1110
**Hotel** ★★ 63% King's Head Hotel, Norwich St, DEREHAM
    ☎ 01362 693842 & 693283 10rm(4 ⇌ 2 ⓡ)Annexe5 ⇌ ⓡ

**Reymerston** Hingham Rd, Reymerston NR9 4QQ
☎ 01362 850297
The course was opened in June 1993 with large tees and greens which drain very well. Created from open farmland, it has many ditches and hedges and room for the 18th green to be over 1000sq.yds. The 17th green is protected by two large trees in front.
*18 holes, 6609yds, Par 72, SSS 72, Course record 74.*
*Club membership 400.*
**Visitors** must book tee times.
**Societies** telephone or write to arrange tee times.
**Green Fees** £30 per day; £20 per round (£35/£25 weekends).
**Facilities** ⊗ ⍿ ⓑ 🍺 ♀ ⚶ 🏠 ⓒ Alison Sheard.
**Leisure** motorised carts for hire, buggies for hire, trolley for hire, 9 hole pitch & putt, putting green, practice area.
**Location** 12m W of Norwich, off B1135
**Hotel** ★★ 63% King's Head Hotel, Norwich St, DEREHAM
    ☎ 01362 693842 & 693283 10rm(4 ⇌ 2 ⓡ)Annexe5 ⇌ ⓡ

## DISS        Map 05 TM18

*Diss* Stuston IP22 3JB ☎ 01379 642847
Commonland course with natural hazards.
*18 holes, 6238yds, Par 73, SSS 70.*
*Club membership 650.*
**Visitors** must contact in advance but may not play weekends & bank holidays.
**Societies** by arrangement.
**Green Fees** not confirmed.
**Facilities** ♀ ⚶ 🏠 ⓒ
**Location** 1.5m SE on B1118
**Hotel** ★★★ 64% Cornwallis Arms, BROME
    ☎ 01379 870326 11 ⇌ ⓡ

---

Entries with a shaded background identify courses that are considered to be particularly interesting

## FAKENHAM

Map 09 TF92

**Fakenham** Gallow Sports Centre, The Race Course
N21 7NY ☎ 01328 820316 & 862867
A well-wooded 9-hole course.
*9 holes, 6000yds, Par 71, SSS 69, Course record 67.*
*Club membership 520.*
**Visitors** any time with member, restricted until after noon
weekends and bank holidays.
**Societies** apply in writing.
**Green Fees** not confirmed.
**Facilities** ♀ ⅄ 🏠 ⬩ J Westwood.
**Leisure** hard tennis courts, squash.
**Hotel** ★★ 63% Crown Hotel, Market Place,
FAKENHAM ☎ 01328 851418 11 ⇄ 🐾

## GORLESTON-ON-SEA

Map 05 TG50

**Gorleston** Warren Rd NR31 6JT
☎ 01493 661911 & 662103
Seaside course.
*18 holes, 6391yds, Par 71, SSS 71, Course record 68.*
*Club membership 860.*
**Visitors** advisable to contact in advance.
**Societies** must apply in writing.
**Green Fees** £21 per day/round (£25 weekends & bank
holidays).
**Facilities** ⊗ ⅲ ⅃ ⬩ ♀ ⅄ 🏠 ⬩ ⬩ Nick Brown.
**Leisure** trolley for hire, putting green, practice area.
**Location** S side of town centre
**Hotel** ★★★ 72% Cliff Hotel, Gorleston, GREAT
YARMOUTH ☎ 01493 662179 39 ⇄ 🐾

## GREAT YARMOUTH

Map 05 TG50

**Great Yarmouth & Caister** Beach House, Caister-on-
Sea NR30 5TD ☎ 01493 728699
This great old club, which celebrated its centenary in
1982, has played its part in the development of the game.
It is a fine old-fashioned links where not many golfers
have bettered the SSS in competitions. The 468-yard 8th
(par 4), is a testing hole.
*18 holes, 6330yds, Par 70, SSS 70, Course record 67.*
*Club membership 770.*
**Visitors** must contact in advance. Restricted
weekends.
**Societies** must apply in writing or telephone.
**Green Fees** £23.50 per day (£28 weekends).
**Facilities** ⊗ ⅲ ⅃ ⬩ ♀ ⅄ 🏠 ⬩ Robert Foster.
**Leisure** motorised carts for hire, trolley for hire,
putting green, practice area, snooker.
**Location** 0.5m N off A149
**Hotel** ★★★ 66% Imperial Hotel, North Dr,
GREAT YARMOUTH
☎ 01493 851113 39 ⇄ 🐾

## HUNSTANTON

Map 09 TF64

**Hunstanton** Golf Course Rd PE36 6JQ
☎ 01485 532811
A championship links course set among some of the most
natural golfing country in East Anglia. Known for its fast
and true greens. The wind is usually a factor in play and
it is a real test to play to handicap.

*18 holes, 6735yds, Par 72, SSS 73, Course record 65.*
*Club membership 675.*
**Visitors** must contact in advance and be a club
member with current handicap certificate.
Restricted at weekends & may not play bank
holiday weekends. Play in two ball format ie
singles or foursomes.
**Societies** apply in advance.
**Green Fees** £40 per day (£50 weekends).
**Facilities** ⊗ ⅲ ⅃ ⬩ ♀ ⅄ 🏠 ⬩ ⬩ John Carter.
**Leisure** caddies available, motorised carts for hire,
buggies for hire, trolley for hire, putting
green, practice area.
**Location** Off A149 in Old Hunstanton Village
signposted
**Hotel** ★★ 69% Caley Hall Motel, Old
Hunstanton Rd, HUNSTANTON
☎ 01485 533486 Annexe33 ⇄

## KING'S LYNN

Map 09 TF62

**Eagles** 39 School Rd, Tilney All Saints PE34 4RS
☎ 01553 827147
Parkland course with plenty of water hazards and bunkers.
Also Par-3 course and floodlit, covered driving range.
*9 holes, 4284yds, Par 64, SSS 61, Course record 64.*
*Club membership 300.*
**Visitors** no restrictions.
**Societies** must contact in advance.
**Green Fees** £11.50 per 18 holes, £5.75 per 9 holes
(£13.50/£6.75 weekends and bank holidays).
**Facilities** ⊗ ⅲ ⅃ ⬩ ♀ ⅄ 🏠 ⬩ ⬩ Nigel Pickerell.
**Leisure** trolley for hire, driving range, par 3, putting
green, practice area.
**Hotel** ★★★ 65% The Duke's Head, Tuesday Market
Pl, KING'S LYNN
☎ 01553 774996 71 ⇄ 🐾

**King's Lynn** Castle Rising PE31 6BD ☎ 01553 631654
Challenging, wooded parkland course.
*18 holes, 6609yds, Par 72, SSS 72.*
*Club membership 1000.*
**Visitors** must contact in advance.
**Societies** must contact in advance.
**Green Fees** £32 per day/round (£40 weekends).
**Facilities** ⊗ ⅲ ⅃ ⬩ ♀ ⅄ 🏠 ⬩ Chris Hanlon.
**Leisure** motorised carts for hire, trolley for hire, putting
green, practice area, snooker.
**Location** 4m NE off A149
**Hotel** ★★★ 65% The Duke's Head, Tuesday Market
Pl, KING'S LYNN ☎ 01553 774996 71 ⇄ 🐾

## MATTISHALL

Map 09 TG01

**Mattishall** South Green NR20 3JZ ☎ 01362 850111
Mattishall has the distinction of having the longest hole in
Norfolk at a very demanding 615yds.
*9 holes, 3109yds, Par 35, SSS 69.*
*Club membership 120.*
**Visitors** no restrictions.
**Societies** welcome.
**Green Fees** £5 per 9 holes.
**Facilities** ⅃ ♀ ⅄ ⬩
**Leisure** trolley for hire, putting green.

**Hotel**    ★★ 63% King's Head Hotel, Norwich St,
DEREHAM
☎ 01362 693842 & 693283 10rm(4 ⇌2
ſ↘)Annexe5 ⇌ ſ↘

## MIDDLETON       Map 09 TF61

*Middleton Hall* PE32 1RH ☎ 01553 841800
The 9-hole King's course (played off 18 tees) is a pleasant
parkland course constructed with conservation in mind
around numerous mature trees, pond and reservoir.
Additional Par 3 pitch and putt course.
*9 holes, 5570yds, Par 68, SSS 67, Course record 69.*
*Club membership 300.*
**Visitors**    no restrictions.
**Societies**    must contact in advance.
**Green Fees** not confirmed.
**Facilities**    ⚑⚑⚑⚑⚑ Brian McKee.
**Leisure**    driveing range,putting,trolley hire.
**Location**    4m from King's Lynn off A47
**Hotel**    ★★★ 66% Butterfly Hotel, Beveridge Way,
Hardwick Narrows, KING'S LYNN
☎ 01553 771707 50 ⇌ ſ↘

## MUNDESLEY       Map 09 TG33

*Mundesley* Links Rd NR11 8ES ☎ 01263 720279
Seaside course, good views, windy.
*9 holes, 5410yds, Par 68, SSS 66.*
*Club membership 400.*
**Visitors**    restricted Wed & weekends. Must contact in
advance.

AA
★ ★ ★

# BARNHAM BROOM HOTEL

GOLF • CONFERENCE • LEISURE

## Barnham Broom, Norwich NR9 4DD
## Tel: (01603) 759393
## Fax: (01603) 758224

In a beautiful valley, this modern hotel and leisure
complex has 52 bedrooms all with private bathrooms; a
spacious lounge with open log fire; two bars; and a host
of leisure facilities including two 18 hole championship
golf courses (one par 71, one par 72), practice holes
and putting green areas.
Inside the leisure centre are a heated indoor swimming
pool; sauna; solarium; steam room; a beauty and
hairdressing salon and a fully equipped gymnasium.
Other sports facilities include four squash courts, 3 all-
weather tennis courts and a full size snooker table.
The complex also contains a spacious and
comprehensively equipped conference centre.

**Prices include full English breakfast.**
**Children charged for meals as taken.**
**Host: Richard Bond.**

*Access: From London and the South via A11; from Midlands and the*
*North via A47. 10 miles west of Norwich. Norwich Airport 10 miles.*

---

**Societies**    must contact one month in advance.
**Green Fees** not confirmed.
**Facilities**    ⚑⚑⚑⚑ T G Symmons.
**Leisure**    putting green,practice area,trolley hire.
**Location**    W side of village off B1159
**Hotel**    ★★ 69% Red Lion, Brook St, CROMER
☎ 01263 514964 12 ⇌ ſ↘

## NORWICH       Map 05 TG20

*Costessy Park* Old Costessy NR8 5AL
☎ 01603 746333 & 747085
*18 holes, 6104yds, Par 72, SSS 69.*
*Club membership 600.*
**Visitors**    may not play competition days, prior booking
required for weekends.
**Societies**    welcome by prior arrangement.
**Green Fees** £15 (£18 weekends).
**Facilities**    ⊗⚑⚑⚑⚑⚑⚑⚑ Simon Cook.
**Leisure**    trolley for hire, putting green, practice area.
**Hotel**    ★★★ 64% Norwich Sport Village & Hotel in
Broadland, Drayton High Rd, Hellesdon,
NORWICH ☎ 01603 789469 55 ⇌ ſ↘

*Eaton* Newmarket Rd NR4 6SF
☎ 01603 451686 & 452881
An undulating, tree-lined parkland course with excellent
trees.
*18 holes, 6135yds, Par 70, SSS 69, Course record 64.*
*Club membership 800.*
**Visitors**    restricted before 11.30am weekends. Advised to
contact in advance.
**Societies**    must contact in advance.
**Green Fees** £28 per day; £15 per round (£35/£20 weekends).
**Facilities**    ⊗⚑⚑⚑⚑⚑⚑⚑ Nigel Bundy.
**Leisure**    trolley for hire, putting green, practice area.
**Location**    2.5m SW of city centre off A11
**Hotel**    ★★★ 64% Norwich Sport Village & Hotel in
Broadland, Drayton High Rd, Hellesdon,
NORWICH ☎ 01603 789469 55 ⇌ ſ↘

*Royal Norwich* Drayton High Rd, Hellesdon NR6 5AH
☎ 01603 429928
Undulating heathland course.
*18 holes, 6603yds, Par 72, SSS 72, Course record 67.*
*Club membership 700.*
**Visitors**    must contact in advance. Restricted weekends &
bank holidays.
**Societies**    must contact in advance.
**Green Fees** £26 per day (£30 weekends & bank holidays).
**Facilities**    ⊗⚑⚑⚑⚑⚑⚑⚑ Gary Potter.
**Leisure**    trolley for hire, putting green, practice area.
**Location**    2.5m NW of city centre on A1067
**Hotel**    ★★★ 68% Hotel Norwich, 121-131 Boundary
Rd, NORWICH ☎ 01603 787260 107 ⇌ ſ↘

*Sprowston Park* Wroxham Rd NR7 8RP ☎ 01603 410657
A Pay & Play course set in 100 acres of parkland. A very
tight course, so accuracy is required for good golf. The
facilities include a 27-bay driving range, a practice area and
tuition from a team of professionals.
*18 holes, 5921yds, Par 70, SSS 69, Course record 64.*
*Club membership 550.*
**Visitors**    no restrictions.
**Societies**    must contact in advance.
**Green Fees** £14 per round (£17 weekends).    ▶

**Facilities** ⊗ ⫴ ⛳ ♣ ♀ ♨ 🏠 🏴 ( Philip J Grice.
**Leisure** motorised carts for hire, buggies for hire, trolley for hire, driving range, putting green, practice area.
**Location** 4m NE from city centre on A1151
**Hotel** ★★★★ 74% Sprowston Manor, Sprowston Park, Wroxham Road, Sprowston, NORWICH ☎ 01603 410871 87 ⇆ 🏴

**Wensum Valley** Beech Av, Taverham NR8 6HP
☎ 01603 261012
An undulating, picturesque golf course situated on the side of a valley. The greens in particular are very undulating and always give the average golfer a testing time. The 12th hole from a raised tee provides a blind and windy tee shot and a very slopey green.
*Valley Course: 18 holes, 6059yds, Par 71, SSS 69, Course record 67.*
*Wensum Course: 9 holes, 2824yds, Par 35.*
*Club membership 900.*
**Visitors** no restrictions but advisable to book tee times at weekends.
**Societies** apply in writing or by telephone.
**Green Fees** £12 day ticket (£15 weekends).
**Facilities** ⊗ ⫴ ⛳ ♣ ♀ ♨ 🏠 🏴 🥤( Tony Varney.
**Leisure** fishing, trolley for hire, driving range, putting green, practice area, bowling green, snooker.
**Location** 5m NE of Norwich
**Hotel** ★★★ 68% Hotel Norwich, 121-131 Boundary Rd, NORWICH ☎ 01603 787260 107 ⇆ 🏴

## SHERINGHAM                          Map 09 TG14

**Sheringham** Weybourne Rd NR26 8HG
☎ 01263 823488 & 822038
Splendid cliff-top links with gorse, good 'seaside turf' and plenty of space. Straight driving is essential for a low score. The course is close to the shore and can be very windswept, but offers magnificent views.
*18 holes, 6464yds, Par 70, SSS 71, Course record 65.*
*Club membership 680.*
**Visitors** must contact in advance & have handicap certificate. Restricted weekends.
**Societies** must apply in writing.
**Green Fees** £32.50 per day/round (£37.50 weekends & bank holidays).
**Facilities** ⊗ ⫴ ⛳ ♣ ♀ ♨ 🏠( R H Emery.
**Leisure** trolley for hire, practice area.
**Location** W side of town centre on A149
**Hotel** ★★ 66% Beaumaris Hotel, South St, SHERINGHAM ☎ 01263 822370 23 ⇆ 🏴

## SWAFFHAM                           Map 05 TF80

**Swaffham** Cley Rd PE37 8AE ☎ 01760 721611
Heathland course.
*9 holes, 6252yds, Par 72, SSS 70.*
*Club membership 475.*
**Visitors** must contact in advance. With member only at weekends.
**Societies** must contact in advance.
**Green Fees** £18 per day/round.
**Facilities** ⊗ ⫴ ⛳ ♣ ♀ ♨ 🏠 🏴( Peter Field.
**Leisure** trolley for hire, putting green, practice area.
**Location** 1.5m SW

**Hotel** ★★★ 62% George Hotel, Station Rd, SWAFFHAM
☎ 01760 721238 27rm(24 ⇆1 🏴)

## THETFORD                           Map 05 TL88

**Feltwell** Thor Ave, Feltwell IP26 4AY
☎ 01842 827762 & 827644
In spite of being an inland links, this 9-hole course is still open and windy.
*9 holes, 6175yds, Par 70, SSS 69.*
*Club membership 400.*
**Visitors** dress restriction, no jeans,tracksuits or collarless shirts, golf shoes to be worn.
**Societies** apply in writing or telephone in advance.
**Green Fees** not confirmed.
**Facilities** ♀ (closed Mon) ♨ 🏠
**Leisure** trolleys for hire.
**Hotel** ★★★ 59% Bell Hotel, King St, THETFORD ☎ 01842 754455 47 ⇆ 🏴

**Thetford** Brandon Rd IP24 3NE ☎ 01842 752169
This is a course with a good pedigree. It was laid-out by a fine golfer, C.H. Mayo, later altered by James Braid and then again altered by another famous course designer, Mackenzie Ross. It is a testing heathland course with a particularly stiff finish.
*18 holes, 6879yds, Par 72, SSS 73, Course record 66.*
*Club membership 850.*
**Visitors** pre booking advisable, may not play weekends or bank holidays except with member.
**Societies** must contact in advance, Wed-Fri only.
**Green Fees** £30 per day/round (weekdays).
**Facilities** ⊗ ⫴ ⛳ ♣ ♀ ♨ 🏠 🏴( Gary Kitley.
**Leisure** trolley for hire, putting green, practice area.
**Location** 2m W of Thetford on B1107
**Hotel** ★★★ 59% Bell Hotel, King St, THETFORD ☎ 01842 754455 47 ⇆ 🏴

## WATTON                            Map 05 TF90

**Richmond Park** Saham Rd IP25 6EA ☎ 01953 881803
Meadowland course dotted with newly planted trees and set on either side of the Little Wissey River.
*18 holes, 6289yds, Par 71, SSS 70, Course record 69.*
*Club membership 600.*
**Visitors** must contact in advance.
**Societies** must contact in advance.
**Green Fees** £20 per day; £15 per round (£20 per day/round weekends).
**Facilities** ⊗ ⫴ ⛳ ♣ ♀ ♨ 🏠( Alan Hemsley.
**Leisure** gymnasium, trolley for hire, driving range, putting green, practice area.
**Location** 500yds NW of town centre
**Hotel** ★★★ 62% George Hotel, Station Rd, SWAFFHAM
☎ 01760 721238 27rm(24 ⇆1 🏴)

## WESTON LONGVILLE                   Map 09 TG11

**Weston Park** NR9 5JW ☎ 01603 872363
Testing course set in 200 acres of mature parkland with specimen trees.
*18 holes, 6603yds, Par 72, SSS 72.*
*Club membership 250.*

**Visitors** must telephone for tee times.
**Societies** must telephone for prices and tee times.
**Green Fees** £30 per day; £20 per 18 holes (£35/£25 weekends).
**Facilities** ⊗ ⅷ ⅃ 坐 Ϙ ᠘ 龠 ᵬ Michael Few.
**Leisure** motorised carts for hire, buggies for hire, trolley for hire, putting green, practice area.
**Location** Off the A1067 Norwich/Fakenham road
**Hotel** ★★★ 65% Quality Friendly Hotel, 2 Barnard Rd, Bowthorpe, NORWICH
☎ 01603 741161 80 ⇔ ᖾ

---

## WEST RUNTON            Map 09 TG14

**Links Country Park Hotel & Golf Club** NR27 9QH
☎ 01263 837691
Parkland course 500 yds from the sea, with superb views overlooking West Runton. The hotel offers extensive leisure facilities.
*9 holes, 4814yds, Par 66, SSS 64.*
*Club membership 250.*
**Visitors** must have a handicap certificate.
**Societies** must telephone in advance.
**Green Fees** not confirmed.
**Facilities** Ϙ ᠘ 龠 ᵬ ⊭ ᵬ Mike Jubb.
**Leisure** hard tennis courts, heated indoor swimming pool, sauna, solarium.
**Location** S side of village off A149
**Hotel** ★★ 71% Dormy House Hotel, Cromer Rd, WEST RUNTON
☎ 01263 837537 16 ⇔ ᖾ

---

# ● NORTHAMPTONSHIRE ●

## CHACOMBE            Map 04 SP44

**Cherwell Edge** OX17 2EN ☎ 01295 711591
Parkland course open since 1980.
*18 holes, 5800yds, Par 70, SSS 68.*
*Club membership 650.*
**Visitors** no restrictions but golf shoes to be worn (can be hired) and tidy appearance expected.
**Societies** must apply in writing.
**Green Fees** not confirmed.
**Facilities** Ϙ ᠘ 龠 ᵬ ᵬ Richard Jefferies.
**Leisure** putting green,cart/buggy/trolley hire,driving range,practice area.
**Location** 0.5m S off B4525
**Hotel** ★★★ 67% Whately Hall Hotel, Banbury Cross, BANBURY ☎ 01295 263451 74 ⇔ ᖾ

---

## COLD ASHBY            Map 04 SP67

**Cold Ashby** Stanford Rd NN6 6EP
☎ 01604 740548 & 740099
Undulating parkland course, nicely matured, with superb views. The 27 holes consist of three loops of nine which can be interlinked with each other. All three loops have their own challenge - the Ashby and the Winwick are Par 3's of 200 yards and the start of the Elkington offfers five holes of scenic beauty and testing golf.

*Ashby-Elkington: 18 holes, 6250yds, Par 70, SSS 70, Course record 66.*
*Winwick-Ashby: 18 holes, 6004yds, Par 70, SSS 69.*
*Elkington-Winwick: 18 holes, 6308yds, Par 72, SSS 70.*
*Club membership 650.*
**Visitors** restricted weekends.
**Societies** must contact in advance.
**Green Fees** £14 per round (£16 weekends).
**Facilities** ⊗ ⅷ ⅃ 坐 Ϙ ᠘ 龠 ᵬ ᵬ Shane Rose.
**Leisure** motorised carts for hire, trolley for hire, putting green, practice area.
**Location** 1m W
**Hotel** B Forte Posthouse Northampton/Rugby, CRICK
☎ 01788 822101 88 ⇔ ᖾ

---

## COLLINGTREE            Map 04 SP75

**Collingtree Park** Windingbrook Ln NN4 0XN
☎ 01604 700000
Superb 18-hole resort course designed by former U.S. and British Open champion Johnny Miller. Stunning island green at the 18th hole. Green fee includes buggy cart and range balls. The Golf Academy includes a driving range, practice holes, indoor video teaching room, golf custom-fit centre.
*18 holes, 6695yds, Par 72, SSS 72, Course record 66.*
**Visitors** must contact in advance & have handicap certificate.
**Societies** contact in advance.
**Green Fees** £30 per round (£40 weekends and bank holidays).
**Facilities** ⅃ 坐 Ϙ ᠘ 龠 ᵬ ᵬ Geoff Pook.
**Leisure** fishing, motorised carts for hire, buggies for hire, trolley for hire, driving range, putting green, practice area.
**Location** M1-junc 15 on A508 to Northampton
**Hotel** ★★★★ 67% Swallow Hotel, Eagle Dr, NORTHAMPTON
☎ 01604 768700 120 ⇔ ᖾ

---

## CORBY            Map 04 SP88

**Corby Public** Stamford Rd, Weldon NN17 3JH
☎ 01536 260756
Municipal course laid out on made-up quarry ground and open to prevailing wind. Wet in winter. Played over by Priors Hall Club.
*18 holes, 6677yds, Par 72, SSS 72.*
*Club membership 600.*
**Visitors** are advised to book in advance.
**Societies** must contact in advance.
**Green Fees** £7 per round (£9 weekends).
**Facilities** ⊗ by prior arrangement ⅃ 坐 Ϙ ᠘ ᵬ
**Leisure** putting green, practice area.
**Location** 4m NE on A43
**Hotel** ★★★ 66% The Talbot, New St, OUNDLE
☎ 01832 273621 39 ⇔ ᖾ

---

## DAVENTRY            Map 04 SP56

**Daventry & District** Norton Rd NN11 5LS
☎ 01327 702829
A hilly course with hard walking.
*9 holes, 5555yds, Par 69, SSS 67, Course record 68.*
*Club membership 360.* ▶

**Visitors** restricted Sun mornings & weekends (Oct-Mar).
**Societies** contact the club professional.
**Green Fees** not confirmed.
**Facilities** ♀ ♣ 🏠 🍴 ( Michael Higgins.
**Leisure** putting,trolley hire,practice area.
**Location** 1m NE
**Hotel** ★★★ 69% The Daventry Hotel, Ashby Rd
(A361), DAVENTRY ☎ 01327 301777 138 ⇆ ↟

## FARTHINGSTONE                              Map 04 SP65

**Farthingstone Hotel & Golf Course** NN12 8AH
☎ 01327 361533
Pleasant rambling course with open aspect and widespread
views.
*18 holes, 6248yds, Par 71, SSS 71, Course record 67.*
*Club membership 500.*
**Visitors** must contact in advance.
**Societies** must contact in advance.
**Green Fees** £10 per round (£15 weekends).
**Facilities** ⊗ ⅏ ⅃ 🝙 ♀ ♣ 🏠 🍴 ⊨ ( Tom Jones.
**Leisure** squash, motorised carts for hire, buggies for hire,
trolley for hire, putting green, indoor practice area.
**Location** 1m W
**Hotel** ★★ 64% Globe Hotel, High St, WEEDON
☎ 01327 340336 17 ⇆ ↟

## HELLIDON                                   Map 04 SP55

**Hellidon Lakes Hotel & Country Club** NN11 6LN
☎ 01327 262550
Spectacular parkland course designed by David Snell.
*18 holes, 6691yds, Par 72, SSS 72 or 9 holes, 2791yds,*
*Par 35.*
*Club membership 500.*
**Visitors** 18 hole course; must contact in advance & have
handicap certificate at weekends. 9 hole; open to
beginners.
**Societies** must telephone in advance.
**Green Fees** not confirmed.
**Facilities** ♀ ♣ 🏠 🍴 ⊨ ( Gary Wills.
**Leisure** hard tennis courts, heated indoor swimming
pool, fishing, sauna, solarium, gymnasium,
buggies, driving range, health studio.
**Hotel** ★★★★ 67% Hellidon Lakes Hotel & Country
Club, HELLIDON ☎ 01327 262550 45 ⇆ ↟
*See advertisement on page 221.*

## KETTERING                                  Map 04 SP87

**Kettering** Headlands NN15 6XA ☎ 01536 511104
A very pleasant, mainly flat meadowland course with easy
walking.
*18 holes, 6081yds, Par 69, SSS 69, Course record 65.*
*Club membership 700.*
**Visitors** welcome but with member only weekends &
bank holidays.
**Societies** Wed & Fri only, apply in writing.
**Green Fees** £22.
**Facilities** ⊗ ⅏ 🝙 ⅃ ♀ ♣ 🏠 🍴 ( Kevin Theobald.
**Leisure** trolley for hire, putting green, practice area.
**Location** S side of town centre
**Hotel** ★★★★ 73% Kettering Park Hotel, Kettering
Parkway, KETTERING
☎ 01536 416666 88 ⇆ ↟

## NORTHAMPTON                               Map 04 SP76

**Delapre Golf Complex** Eagle Dr, Nene Valley Way
NN4 7DU ☎ 01604 764036
Rolling parkland course, part of municipal golf complex,
which includes two 9-hole, par 3 courses, pitch-and-putt and
33 bay driving-range.
*Main Course: 18 holes, 6269yds, Par 70, SSS 70, Course*
*record 66.*
*Hardingstone Course: 9 holes, 2109yds, Par 32, SSS 32.*
*Club membership 900.*
**Visitors** no restrictions.
**Societies** must book and pay full green fees 2 weeks in
advance.
**Green Fees** not confirmed.
**Facilities** ⊗ ⅏ 🝙 ⅃ ♀ ♣ 🏠 🍴 ( John Corby.
**Leisure** trolley for hire, driving range, putting green, par
3, pitch & putt.
**Location** 2m SE
**Hotel** ★★★ 61% Westone Hotel, Ashley Way,
Weston Favell, NORTHAMPTON
☎ 01604 739955 31 ⇆ ↟Annexe35 ⇆ ↟

**Kingsthorpe** Kingsley Rd NN2 7BU
☎ 01604 710610 & 711173
A compact, undulating parkland course set within the town
boundary. Not a long course but testing enough to attract a
competitive membership that boasts several County players.
*18 holes, 5918yds, Par 69, SSS 69, Course record 63.*
*Club membership 630.*
**Visitors** must contact in advance and have handicap
certificate. With member only weekends & bank
holidays.
**Societies** must contact in advance.
**Green Fees** £25 per day/round.
**Facilities** ⊗ ⅏ 🝙 ⅃ ♀ ♣ 🏠 ( Paul Armstrong.
**Leisure** trolley for hire, putting green.
**Location** N side of town centre on A5095
**Hotel** ★★★ 61% Westone Hotel, Ashley Way,
Weston Favell, NORTHAMPTON
☎ 01604 739955 31 ⇆ ↟Annexe35 ⇆ ↟

**Northampton** Harlestone NN7 4EF
☎ 01604 845155
New parkland course with water in play on three holes.
*18 holes, 6615yds, Par 72, SSS 71.*
*Club membership 750.*
**Visitors** must contact in advance and have handicap
certificate. With member only at weekends.
**Societies** must contact in advance.
**Green Fees** £25 per day/round.
**Facilities** ⊗ ⅏ 🝙 ⅃ ♀ ♣ 🏠 ( Kevin Dickens.
**Leisure** trolley for hire, putting green, practice area.
**Location** NW of town centre on A428
**Hotel** ★★★ 63% Northampton Moat House, Silver
St, NORTHAMPTON
☎ 01604 739988 140 ⇆ ↟

**Northamptonshire County** Sandy Ln, Church Brampton
NN6 8AZ ☎ 01604 843025
Undulating heathland/woodland course with gorse, heather
and fine pine woods.
*18 holes, 6503yds, Par 70, SSS 71, Course record 65.*
*Club membership 650.*

**Visitors** restricted weekends. Must contact in advance and have a handicap certificate.
**Societies** Wed only, must contact in advance.
**Green Fees** £37.50 per day summer; £27.50 winter.
**Facilities** ⊗ 〲 ⓛ ⬛ ♀ ⚑ 台 ⫩ �𝄆 Tim Rouse.
**Leisure** trolley for hire, driving range, putting green, practice area.
**Location** 5m NW of Northampton, off A50
**Hotel** ★★★ 61% Westone Hotel, Ashley Way, Weston Favell, NORTHAMPTON
☎ 01604 739955 31 ⇥ 𝄆Annexe35 ⇥ 𝄆

---

## OUNDLE                                    Map 04 TL08

**Oundle** Benefield Rd PE8 4EZ
☎ 01832 273267 (Gen Manager) & 272273 (Pro)
Undulating parkland course, shortish but difficult. A small brook affects some of the approaches to the greens.
*18 holes, 6235yds, Par 71, SSS 70, Course record 68.*
**Visitors** may not play Tue (Ladies Day) or before 10am weekends unless with member.
**Societies** must apply in advance.
**Green Fees** £20 per day (£30 weekends); weekdays £12 after 3pm.
**Facilities** ⊗ 〲 ⓛ ⬛ ♀ ⚑ 台 ⫩ �𝄆 Richard Keys.
**Leisure** trolley for hire, putting green, practice area.
**Location** 1m W on A427
**Hotel** ★★★ 66% The Talbot, New St, OUNDLE
☎ 01832 273621 39 ⇥ 𝄆

---

## STAVERTON                                 Map 04 SP56

**Staverton Park** NN11 6JT ☎ 01327 302000
Open course, fairly testing with good views.
*18 holes, 6661yds, Par 71, SSS 72, Course record 65.*
*Club membership 300.*
**Visitors** restricted weekends. Must contact in advance. Handicap certificates preferred.
**Societies** must contact in advance.
**Green Fees** Apr-Oct: £29 per day; £19 per round (£35/£22.50 weekends). Other times: £22 per day; £15 per round (£30/£19.50 weekends).
**Facilities** ⊗ by prior arrangement 〲 by prior arrangement ⓛ ⬛ ♀ ⚑ 台 ⫩ 🖾 𝄆 Richard Mudge.
**Leisure** sauna, gymnasium, motorised carts for hire, buggies for hire, trolley for hire, floodlit driving range, putting green, practice area, pool table.
**Location** 0.75m NE of Staverton on A425
**Hotel** ★★★ 69% The Daventry Hotel, Ashby Rd (A361), DAVENTRY
☎ 01327 301777 138 ⇥ 𝄆

---

## WELLINGBOROUGH                            Map 04 SP86

*Rushden* Kimbolton Rd, Chelveston NN9 6AN
☎ 01933 312581
Parkland course with brook running through the middle.
*10 holes, 6335yds, Par 71, SSS 70.*
*Club membership 400.*
**Visitors** may not play Wed afternoon. With member only weekends.
**Societies** must apply in writing.
**Green Fees** not confirmed.
**Facilities** ♀ (ex Mon) ⅄
**Leisure** putting green, practice area.

---

**Location** 2m E of Higham Ferrers on A45
**Hotel** ★★★ 63% Hind Hotel, Sheep St, WELLINGBOROUGH
☎ 01933 222827 34 ⇥ 𝄆

---

**Wellingborough** Great Harrowden Hall NN9 5AD
☎ 01933 677234 & 678752
An undulating parkland course with many trees. The 514-yd, 14th is a testing hole. The clubhouse is a stately home.
*18 holes, 6617yds, Par 72, SSS 72, Course record 68.*
*Club membership 820.*
**Visitors** may not play at weekends & bank holidays or Tue between 10.30am and 2.30pm.
**Societies** must apply in writing.
**Green Fees** £30 per day; £25 per round.
**Facilities** ⊗ 〲 ⓛ ⬛ ♀ ⚑ 台 𝄆 David Clifford.
**Leisure** outdoor swimming pool, motorised carts for hire, buggies for hire, trolley for hire, putting green, practice area, snooker.
**Location** 2m N on A509
**Hotel** ★★★ 63% Hind Hotel, Sheep St, WELLINGBOROUGH
☎ 01933 222827 34 ⇥ 𝄆

---

## WHITTLEBURY                                Map 04 SP64

**West Park Golf & Country Club** NN12 8XW
☎ 01327 858092
The 36 holes incorporate three loops of tournament-standard nines plus a short course. The 1905 Course is a reconstruction of the original parkland course built at the turn of the century, the Royal Whittlewood is a lakeland course playing around copses and the Grand Prix, next to Silverstone Motor Racing circuit has a strong links feel playing over gently undulating grassland with challenging lake features.
*Grand Prix: 9 holes, 3339yds, Par 36, SSS 72.*
*1905: 9 holes, 3256yds, Par 36, SSS 72.*
*Royal Whittlewood: 9 holes, 3323yds, Par 36, SSS 71.*
*Wedgewood: 9 holes, 1664yds, Par 36, SSS 72.*
*Club membership 650.*
**Visitors** must contact in advance.
**Societies** telephone 01327 857509 in advance.
**Green Fees** £25 per 18 holes (£30 weekends & bank holidays). £5 per extra 9 holes.
**Facilities** ⊗ 〲 ⓛ ⬛ ♀ ⚑ 台 𝄆 Simon Murdoch.
**Leisure** buggies for hire, trolley for hire, driving range, putting green, practice area.
**Hotel** ★★★ 64% The Saracens Head, 219 Watling St, TOWCESTER ☎ 01327 350414 21 ⇥ 𝄆

---

# NORTHUMBERLAND

---

## ALLENDALE                                  Map 12 NY85

**Allendale** High Studdon, Allenheads Rd NE47 9DQ
☎ 01434 683234 & 683237
Challenging and hilly parkland course set 1000 feet above sea level with superb views of Allendale. Holes with interesting features include the 3rd, 7th and 8th.
*9 holes, 5044yds, Par 66, SSS 65, Course record 70.*
*Club membership 170.*

▶

**Visitors** may not play Aug bank holiday.
**Societies** must apply in writing to Secretary.
**Green Fees** £10 per day. Reductions after 5pm.
**Facilities** ⬛ ⛴
**Leisure** putting green.
**Location** 1.5m S on B6295
**Hotel** ★★ 62% County Hotel, Priestpopple,
HEXHAM ☎ 01434 602030 9 ⇆ ⬢

## ALNMOUTH                    Map 12 NU21

**Alnmouth** Foxton Hall, Lesbury NE66 3BE
☎ 01665 830231
Coastal course with pleasant views.
*18 holes, 6500yds, Par 69, SSS 69, Course record 65.*
**Visitors** may not play Wed, Fri, weekends & bank
holidays.
**Societies** Mon, Tue or Thu only.
**Green Fees** £27 per day/round.
**Facilities** ⊗ ⍢ ⓑ ⬛ ♀ ⛴ 🏠 ⛳
**Leisure** trolley for hire, putting green, practice area.
**Location** 1m NE
**Hotel** ★★★ 61% White Swan Hotel, Bondgate
Within, ALNWICK
☎ 01665 602109 58 ⇆ ⬢

*Alnmouth Village* Marine Rd NE66 2RZ ☎ 01665 830370
Seaside course with part coastal view.
*9 holes, 6078yds, Par 70, SSS 70.*
*Club membership 480.*
**Visitors** no restrictions.
**Societies** must contact in advance.
**Facilities** ♀ ⛴
**Location** E side of village
**Hotel** ★★★ 61% White Swan Hotel, Bondgate
Within, ALNWICK
☎ 01665 602109 58 ⇆ ⬢

## ALNWICK                    Map 12 NU11

**Alnwick** Swansfield Park NE66 2AT ☎ 01665 602632
Parkland course offering a fair test of golfing skills.
*18 holes, 6284yds, Par 70, SSS 70.*
*Club membership 550.*
**Visitors** must contact in advance.
**Societies** must contact in advance.
**Green Fees** £15 per day; £12 per round (£20 weekends &
bank holidays).
**Facilities** ⊗ ⍢ ⓑ ⬛ ♀ ⛴
**Leisure** trolley for hire, putting green, practice area.
**Location** S side of town
**Hotel** ★★★ 61% White Swan Hotel, Bondgate
Within, ALNWICK
☎ 01665 602109 58 ⇆ ⬢

## BAMBURGH                    Map 12 NU13

**Bamburgh Castle** NE69 7DE
☎ 01668 214378 & 214321
This is not a long, links course, but there are those who
have played golf all over the world who say that for sheer
breathtaking beauty this northern seaside gem cannot be
bettered. And the course itself is the greatest fun to play.
Magnificent views of Farne Island, Lindisfarne and Holy
Island.

*18 holes, 5621yds, Par 68, SSS 67, Course record 64.*
*Club membership 650.*
**Visitors** must contact in advance. Restricted weekends,
bank holidays and competition days.
**Societies** apply in writing. Weekdays only.
**Green Fees** £24 per day/round (£35 per day;£30 per
round weekends and bank holidays).
**Facilities** ⊗ ⍢ ⓑ ⬛ ♀ ⛴
**Leisure** buggies for hire, trolley for hire, putting
green, practice area.
**Location** 6m E of A1 via B1341 or B1342
**Hotel** ★★ 69% Lord Crewe Arms, Front St,
BAMBURGH
☎ 01668 214243 25rm(20 ⇆ ⬢)

## BEDLINGTON                    Map 12 NZ28

**Bedlingtonshire** Acorn Bank NE22 6AA
☎ 01670 822087 & 822457
Meadowland/parkland course with easy walking. Under
certain conditions the wind can be a distinct hazard.
*18 holes, 6813mtrs, Par 73, SSS 73, Course record 68.*
*Club membership 960.*
**Visitors** must contact in advance.
**Societies** must apply in writing.
**Green Fees** £18 per round.
**Facilities** ⊗ ⍢ ⓑ ⬛ ♀ ⛴ 🏠 ⛳ ⓘ Marcus Webb.
**Leisure** trolley for hire, putting green, practice area.
**Location** 1m SW on A1068
**Hotel** ★★★★ 58% Holiday Inn, Great North Rd,
SEATON BURN ☎ 0191 201 9988 150 ⇆ ⬢

## BELFORD                    Map 12 NU13

**Belford** South Rd NE70 7HY ☎ 01668 213433
On the east coast, this course is often affected by crosswinds
especially the 4th - the compensation is spectacular views of
Holy Island. A number of other holes are affected by mature
trees.
*9 holes, 3152yds, Par 72, SSS 70, Course record 72.*
*Club membership 200.*
**Visitors** no restrictions.
**Societies** must contact in advance.
**Green Fees** £16 per day; £13 per 18 holes; £9 per 9 holes
(£21/£16/£10 weekends and bank holidays).
**Facilities** ⊗ ⍢ ⓑ ⬛ ♀ ⛴ 🏠 ⛳
**Leisure** motorised carts for hire, trolley for hire, driving
range, practice area.
**Location** Off A1 between Alnwick & Berwick on Tweed
**Hotel** ★★★ 64% Blue Bell Hotel, Market Place,
BELFORD ☎ 01668 213543 17 ⇆ ⬢

## BELLINGHAM                    Map 12 NY88

**Bellingham** Boggle Hole NE48 2DT
☎ 01434 220530 (Secretary) & 220152 (Clubhouse)
9-hole downland course with natural hazards and 18 tees.
*9 holes, 5226yds, Par 67, SSS 66, Course record 63.*
*Club membership 450.*
**Visitors** must contact in advance.
**Societies** must contact in advance.
**Green Fees** £10 per day/round (£15 weekends).
**Facilities** ⊗ ⍢ ⓑ ⬛ ♀ ⛴
**Leisure** driving range, putting green, practice area.

Visitors are welcomed at

# Berwick-upon-Tweed (Goswick) Golf Club

Signposted off the A1, south of Berwick, only 10 minutes from the centre.
The club is open all year to non-members
**Anytime weekdays. Bookings weekends. Bar. Service/Catering. Residents Pro**
**Secretary Mr A. E. French (01289) 387256**
Membership available
**Paul Terras, Goswick Golf Club Pro Shop**
**Golf Club Repairs ★ Tuition ★ Sales ★ Tel: 01289 387380**

---

**Location** N side of village on B6320
**Hotel** ★★ 68% Riverdale Hall Hotel,
BELLINGHAM ☎ 01434 220254 20 ⇆ ✆

## BERWICK-UPON-TWEED　　　Map 12 NT95

**Berwick-upon-Tweed (Goswick)** Goswick TD15 2RW
☎ 01289 387256
Natural seaside links course, with undulating fairways,
elevated tees and good greens.
*18 holes, 6425yds, Par 72, SSS 71, Course record 69.*
*Club membership 575.*
**Visitors** must contact in advance for weekends,
advisable at other times.
**Societies** must telephone in advance (apply in writing
Apr-Sep).
**Green Fees** £24 per day; £18 per round (£32/£24
weekends).
**Facilities** ⊗ ⛥ �ⓑ ♥ ♀ ♨ 🏠 ⚐ ⏃ Paul Terras.
**Leisure** motorised carts for hire, buggies for hire,
trolley for hire, driving range, putting green,
practice area.
**Location** 6m S off A1
**Hotel** ★★★♨♨ 69% Tillmouth Park Hotel,
CORNHILL-ON-TWEED
☎ 01890 882255 12 ⇆ ✆Annexe2 ⇆ ✆

**Magdalene Fields** Magdalene Fields TD15 1NE
☎ 01289 306384
Seaside course with natural hazards formed by sea bays. Last
9 holes open to winds. Testing 18th hole over bay (par 3).
*18 holes, 6407yds, Par 72, SSS 71, Course record 66.*
*Club membership 400.*
**Visitors** must contact in advance for weekend play.
**Societies** must contact in advance.
**Green Fees** £20 per day; £15.50 per round (£22/£17.50
weekends).
**Facilities** ⊗ ⛥ ⓑ ♥ ♀ ♨
**Leisure** putting green.
**Location** E side of town centre
**Hotel** ★★★♨♨ 69% Tillmouth Park Hotel,
CORNHILL-ON-TWEED
☎ 01890 882255 12 ⇆ ✆Annexe2 ⇆ ✆

## BLYTH　　　　　　　　　　　Map 12 NZ38

**Blyth** New Delaval, Newsham NE24 4DB
☎ 01670 367728
Course built over old colliery. Parkland with water hazards.
*18 holes, 6430yds, Par 72, SSS 71, Course record 66.*
*Club membership 820.*
**Visitors** with member only after 3pm & at weekends.
Must contact in advance.

**Societies** apply in writing.
**Green Fees** £20 per day; £18 per round.
**Facilities** ⊗ ⛥ ⓑ ♥ ♀ ♨ 🏠 ⏃ Brian Rumney.
**Leisure** trolley for hire, putting green, practice area.
**Location** 6m N of Whitley Bay
**Hotel** ★★★ 64% Windsor Hotel, South Pde,
WHITLEY BAY ☎ 0191 251 8888 64 ⇆ ✆

## CRAMLINGTON　　　　　　Map 12 NZ27

**Arcot Hall** NE23 7QP ☎ 0191 236 2794 & 236 2147
A wooded parkland course, reasonably flat.
*18 holes, 6380yds, Par 70, SSS 70, Course record 65.*
*Club membership 660.*
**Visitors** must contact in advance. May not play
weekends.
**Societies** must contact in advance.
**Green Fees** £25 per day; £20 per round (£28 weekends).
**Facilities** ⊗ ⛥ ⓑ ♥ ♀ ♨ 🏠 ⚐ ⏃ Graham Cant.
**Leisure** trolley for hire, putting green, practice area.
**Location** 2m SW off A1
**Hotel** ★★★★ 58% Holiday Inn, Great North Rd,
SEATON BURN ☎ 0191 201 9988 150 ⇆ ✆

## EMBLETON　　　　　　　　Map 12 NU22

**Dunstanburgh Castle** NE66 3XQ ☎ 01665 576562
Rolling links designed by James Braid, with castle and bird
sanctuary either side. Superb views.
*18 holes, 6298yds, Par 70, SSS 69, Course record 69.*
*Club membership 390.*
**Visitors** advisable to contact in advance at weekends and
holiday periods.
**Societies** must contact in advance.
**Green Fees** £15 per day (£22 per day; £18 per round
weekends & bank holidays).
**Facilities** ⊗ ⛥ ⓑ ♥ ♀ ♨ 🏠 ⚐
**Location** 0.5m E
**Hotel** ★★ 72% Beach House Hotel, Sea Front,
SEAHOUSES ☎ 01665 720337 14 ⇆ ✆

## GREENHEAD　　　　　　　Map 12 NY66

*Haltwhistle* Banktop CA6 7HL
☎ 016977 47367 & 01434 320337 sec
Interesting course with panoramic views of Northumberland
National Park. The 515yard Par 5 8th hole is a real test of
golf skill, played from the highest point of the course through
an undulating fairway to a viciously sloping green. The
188yard Par 3 10th hole, played uphill, is particularly difficult
playing into the prevailing west wind.
*12 holes, 5986yds, Par 71, SSS 69, Course record 78.*
*Club membership 287.*　　　　　　　　　　　　　　　　▶

**Visitors**   course played over 18 holes, no visitors Sun
mornings.
**Societies**   apply in writing to: Hon Secretary, W E Barnes,
Croftlynn, Haltwhistle, Northumberland NE49
9JR.
**Green Fees** not confirmed.
**Facilities**   ♀ ☕
**Hotel**        ★★ 66%  Kirby Moor Country House Hotel,
Longtown Rd,  BRAMPTON
☎ 016977 3893 6rm(5 ♠)

## HEXHAM                                    Map 12 NY96

*Hexham* Spital Park NE46 3RZ ☎ 01434 603072
A very pretty undulating parkland course with interesting
natural contours. From parts of the course, particularly
the elevated 6th tee, there are the most exquisite views of
the valley below. As good a parkland course as any in the
North of England.
*18 holes, 6000yds, Par 70, SSS 68, Course record 64.*
*Club membership 700.*
**Visitors**      advance booking advisable.
**Societies**     welcome weekdays, contact in advance.
**Green Fees**  not confirmed.
**Facilities**     ♀ ☕ 🏠 ⛳ ∫ Martin Forster.
**Leisure**       squash, putting,trolley hire,practice area.
**Location**     1m NW on B6531
**Hotel**          ★★★ 65%  Beaumont Hotel, Beaumont St,
HEXHAM ☎ 01434 602331 23 ⇆ ♠

*Slaley Hall* Slaley NE47 OBY ☎ 01434 673350 & 673154
Measuring 7021yds from the championship tees, this Dave
Thomas designed course incorporates forest, parkland and
moorland with an abundance of lakes and streams. The
challenging par 4 9th (452yds) is played over water through a
narrow avenue of towering trees and dense rhododendrons.
*18 holes, 6759yds, Par 72, SSS 73, Course record 65.*
*Club membership 350.*
**Visitors**      must contact in advance, times subject to
availability, restricted weekends, must provide
proof of official handicap Gentlemen max28,
Ladies max36.
**Societies**     apply in writing to bookings co-ordinator, small
groups 8 or less may book through pro shop.
**Green Fees** £55 per 36 holes; £45 per 27 holes; £35 per 18
holes (Standby rate £40/£35/£25). Twilight rate
£25 per 18 holes (£22.50 winter).
**Facilities**     ⊗ 🍽 🍺 🌂 ♀ ☕ 🏠 ⛳ 🎣 ∫ To be appointed.
**Leisure**       heated indoor swimming pool, fishing, sauna,
solarium, gymnasium, motorised carts for hire,
buggies for hire, trolley for hire, putting green,
practice area.
**Location**     8m S of Hexham off A68

*Tynedale* Tyne Green NE46 3HQ ☎ 01434 608154
Flat, easy moorland course. Bounded by river and railway.
*9 holes, 5643yds, Par 69, SSS 67, Course record 67.*
*Club membership 421.*
**Visitors**      may not play Sun mornings.
**Societies**     must contact in advance.
**Green Fees**  not confirmed.
**Facilities**     ♀ ☕ 🏠 ⛳ ∫ Claire Brown.
**Leisure**       practice net,pool table,darts.
**Location**     N side of town
**Hotel**          ★★★ 65%  Beaumont Hotel, Beaumont St,
HEXHAM ☎ 01434 602331 23 ⇆ ♠

AA ★★★

# The Beaumont Hotel,
### Hexham, Northumberland
## NE46 3LT
## (01434) 602331
The perfect base for 3 of the North
East's finest Golf Courses: Slaley,
Hexham & Matfen Hall.
23 Bedrooms, with full facilities,
excellent food and choice of bars
make a wonderful 'Golfing Hotel'.
Special Golf Rates on Request

## MORPETH                                    Map 12 NZ28

*Morpeth* The Common NE61 2BT ☎ 01670 504942
Parkland course with views of the Cheviots.
*18 holes, 6206yds, Par 71, SSS 69.*
*Club membership 700.*
**Visitors**      restricted weekends & bank holidays. Must
contact in advance and have a handicap
certificate.
**Societies**     apply in writing.
**Green Fees**  not confirmed.
**Facilities**     ♀ ☕ 🏠 ∫
**Leisure**       snooker.
**Location**     S side of town centre on A197
**Hotel**          ★★★★ 66%  Longhirst Hall, Longhirst,
MORPETH ☎ 01670 791348 75 ⇆ ♠

## NEWBIGGIN-BY-THE-SEA                        Map 12 NZ38

**Newbiggin-by-the-Sea** Prospect Close NE64 6DW
☎ 01670 817344
Seaside-links course.
*18 holes, 6452yds, Par 72, SSS 71, Course record 65.*
*Club membership 570.*
**Visitors**      must contact professional on arrival and may not
play before 10am.
**Societies**     must apply in writing.
**Green Fees** £14 per day/round (£19 weekends).
**Facilities**     ⊗ 🍽 🍺 🌂 ♀ ☕ 🏠 ⛳ ∫ Marcus Webb.
**Leisure**       trolley for hire, putting green, practice area,
snooker.

**Location** N side of town
**Hotel** ★★★★ 66% Longhirst Hall, Longhirst,
MORPETH ☎ 01670 791348 75 ⇄ ☞

## PONTELAND Map 12 NZ17

**Ponteland** 53 Bell Villas NE20 9BD ☎ 01661 822689
Open parkland course offering testing golf and good views.
*18 holes, 6524yds, Par 72, SSS 71, Course record 66.*
*Club membership 720.*
**Visitors** with member only Fri, weekends & bank
holidays.
**Societies** welcome Tue & Thu only. Must contact in
advance.
**Green Fees** £22.50 per day/round.
**Facilities** ⊗ ⅶ ⅃ ♥ ♀ ⅃ 🏠 ⅂ Alan Crosby.
**Leisure** trolley for hire, putting, practice area.
**Location** 0.5m E on A696
**Hotel** ★★★ 64% Newcastle Airport Moat House,
Woolsington, NEWCASTLE UPON TYNE
AIRPORT ☎ 0191 401 9988 100 ⇄ ☞

## PRUDHOE Map 12 NZ06

**Prudhoe** Eastwood Park NE42 5DX
☎ 01661 832466
Parkland course with natural hazards and easy walking along
undulating fairways.
*18 holes, 5812yds, Par 69, SSS 68, Course record 63.*
*Club membership 700.*
**Visitors** must contact in advance. Weekends after 4.30pm
**Societies** must contact in writing.
**Green Fees** not confirmed.
**Facilities** ♀ ⅃ 🏠 ⅂ John Crawford.
**Location** E side of town centre off A695
**Hotel** ★★ 62% County Hotel, Priestpopple,
HEXHAM ☎ 01434 602030 9 ⇄ ☞

## ROTHBURY Map 12 NU00

**Rothbury** Old Race Course NE65 7TR
☎ 01669 620718 & 621271
Very flat parkland course alongside the River Coquet.
*9 holes, 5681yds, Par 68, SSS 68, Course record 65.*
*Club membership 400.*
**Visitors** may play at weekends by arrangement only.
**Societies** may not play at weekends. Must contact in
advance.
**Green Fees** not confirmed.
**Facilities** ♀ ⅃
**Location** S side of town off B6342
**Hotel** ★★★ 61% White Swan Hotel, Bondgate
Within, ALNWICK
☎ 01665 602109 58 ⇄ ☞

## SEAHOUSES Map 12 NU23

**Seahouses** Beadnell Rd NE68 7XT ☎ 01665 720794
Typical links course with many hazards, including the famous
10th, 'Logans Loch', water hole.
*18 holes, 5462yds, Par 67, SSS 67, Course record 63.*
*Club membership 750.*
**Visitors** must contact in advance.
**Societies** must contact in advance. May not play Sun.

**Green Fees** £16 per day (£20 weekends & bank holidays).
**Facilities** ⊗ ⅶ ⅃ ♥ ♀ ⅃
**Leisure** trolley for hire, putting green, practice area.
**Location** S side of village on B1340
**Hotel** ★★ 72% Olde Ship Hotel, SEAHOUSES
☎ 01665 720200 12 ⇄ ☞Annexe4 ⇄ ☞

## STOCKSFIELD Map 12 NZ06

**Stocksfield** New Ridley Rd NE43 7RE
☎ 01661 843041 & 843101
Challenging course: parkland (9 holes), woodland (9 holes).
*18 holes, 5978yds, Par 68, SSS 68.*
*Club membership 900.*
**Visitors** welcome except Wed & weekends until 4pm.
Must contact in advance.
**Societies** must contact in advance.
**Green Fees** £16-£19 (£24 weekends).
**Facilities** ⊗ by prior arrangement ⅶ by prior arrangement
⅃ ♥ ♀ ⅃ 🏠 ⅂ ⅂ Steven McKenna.
**Leisure** motorised carts for hire, trolley for hire, putting
green, practice area.
**Location** 2.5m SE off A695
**Hotel** ★★★ 65% Beaumont Hotel, Beaumont St,
HEXHAM
☎ 01434 602331 23 ⇄ ☞

## SWARLAND Map 12 NU10

**Swarland Hall** Coast View NE65 9JG
☎ 01670 787010 & 787940
Parkland course set in mature woodland. There are seven Par
4 holes in excess of 400 yards.
*18 holes, 6628yds, Par 72, SSS 72.*
*Club membership 400.*
**Visitors** restricted on competition days.
**Societies** apply in writing.
**Green Fees** £17.50 per day; £12.50 per round (£15 per round
weekends & bank holidays).
**Facilities** ⊗ ⅶ ⅃ ♥ ♀ ⅃ ⅂
⅂ David Fletcher/Linzi Hardy.
**Leisure** motorised carts for hire, buggies for hire, trolley
for hire, putting green, practice area, snooker.
**Location** Approx 1m W of A1
**Hotel** ★★★★♨ 71% Linden Hall Hotel and Health
Spa, LONGHORSLEY
☎ 01670 516611 50 ⇄ ☞

## WARKWORTH Map 12 NU20

**Warkworth** The Links NE65 0SW ☎ 01665 711596
Seaside links course, with good views and alternative tees for
the back nine.
*9 holes, 5856yds, Par 70, SSS 68, Course record 66.*
*Club membership 470.*
**Visitors** welcome except Tue & Sat.
**Societies** must contact in advance.
**Green Fees** £12 per day (£20 weekends & bank holidays).
**Facilities** ⊗ ⅃ ♥ ♀ ⅃
**Leisure** practice area.
**Location** 0.5m E of village off A1068
**Hotel** ★★★ 61% White Swan Hotel, Bondgate
Within, ALNWICK
☎ 01665 602109 58 ⇄ ☞

## WOOLER                                    Map 12 NT92

**Wooler** Dod Law, Doddington NE71 6EA
☎ 01668 281137
Hilltop, moorland course with spectacular views over the
Glendale valley. Nine greens played from 18 tees. A very
challenging course when windy with one Par 5 of 580 yards.
The course is much under used during the week so is always
available.
*9 holes, 6358yds, Par 72, SSS 70.*
*Club membership 300.*
**Visitors**      normally no restrictions.
**Societies**     by prior arrangement with secretary.
**Green Fees**  £10 (£15 weekends & bank holidays).
**Facilities**    ⊗ 〼 ⅄ ♨ ♀ ⅄
**Leisure**       motorised carts for hire, buggies for hire, trolley
                  for hire, putting green, practice area.
**Location**     At Doddington on B6525 Wooler/Berwick Rd
**Hotel**         ★★ 62% Tankerville Arms Hotel, Cottage Rd,
                  WOOLER
                  ☎ 01668 281581 16 ⇄ ⌀

---

# ● 
# NOTTINGHAMSHIRE
# ●

---

## CALVERTON                                Map 08 SK64

**Ramsdale Park Golf Centre** Oxton Rd, Calverton
NG14 6NU ☎ 0115 965 5600
The High course is a challenging and comprehensive test for
any standard of golfer. A relatively flat front nine is followed
by an undulating back nine that is renowned as one of the
best 9 holes of golf in the county. The Low course comprises
contoured and bunkered greens that is ideal for both beginner
and established golfer who wants to improve his iron and shot
play.
*High Course: 18 holes, 6546yds, Par 71, SSS 71, Course
record 70.*
*Low Course: 18 holes, 2844yds, Par 54.*
*Club membership 400.*
**Visitors**      may book up to 6 days in advance with credit
                  card.
**Societies**     welcome midweek, apply in writing or
                  telephone.
**Green Fees** High: £13; Low: £7.20.
**Facilities**    ⊗ 〼 ⅄ ♨ ♀ ⅄ ♨ ⌀ ⌀ Robert Macey.
**Leisure**       driving range, video teaching bay.
**Location**     8m NE of Nottingham, off B6386
**Hotel**         ★★★ 65% Saracen's Head Hotel, Market
                  Place, SOUTHWELL
                  ☎ 01636 812701 27 ⇄ ⌀

---

## EAST LEAKE                                Map 08 SK52

**Rushcliffe** Stocking Ln LE12 5RL
☎ 01509 852959
Hilly, tree-lined and picturesque parkland course.
*18 holes, 6013yds, Par 70, SSS 69, Course record 63.*
*Club membership 700.*
**Visitors**      restricted weekends & bank holidays 9.30-11am
                  & 3-4.30pm.

---

**Societies**     must apply in advance.
**Green Fees** £22 per day (£25 weekends).
**Facilities**    ⊗ 〼 ⅄ ♨ ♀ ⌀ ⌀ Chris Hall.
**Leisure**       trolley for hire, putting green, practice area.
**Location**     1m N
**Hotel**         ★★★ 63% Yew Lodge, 33 Packington Hill,
                  KEGWORTH
                  ☎ 01509 672518 54 ⇄ ⌀

---

## KEYWORTH                                 Map 08 SK63

**Stanton on the Wolds** NG12 5BH
☎ 0115 937 2044
Parkland course, fairly flat with stream running through four
holes.
*18 holes, 6437yds, Par 73, SSS 71, Course record 67.*
*Club membership 705.*
**Visitors**      must play with member at weekends.
**Societies**     must apply in writing.
**Green Fees** £25/£20 per day/round.
**Facilities**    ⊗ 〼 ⅄ ♨ ♀ ⅄ ♨ ⌀ ⌀ Nick Hernon.
**Leisure**       trolley for hire, putting green, practice area.
**Location**     E side of village
**Hotel**         ★★ 65% Rufford Hotel, 53 Melton Road, West
                  Bridgford, NOTTINGHAM
                  ☎ 0115 981 4202 35 ⌀

---

## KIRKBY IN ASHFIELD                       Map 08 SK55

**Notts** Derby Rd NG17 7QR
☎ 01623 753225
Undulating heathland Championship course.
*18 holes, 7030yds, Par 72, SSS 74, Course record 64.*
*Club membership 500.*
**Visitors**      must contact in advance & have handicap
                  certificate. With member only weekends &
                  bank holidays.
**Societies**     must apply in advance.
**Green Fees** £45 per day; £35 per round.
**Facilities**    ⊗ 〼 ⅄ ♨ ♀ ⅄ ♨ ⌀ ⌀ Brian Waites.
**Leisure**       trolley for hire, driving range, putting green,
                  practice area.
**Location**     1.5m SE off A611
**Hotel**         ★★★★ 65% Swallow Hotel, Carter Ln
                  East, SOUTH NORMANTON
                  ☎ 01773 812000 161 ⇄ ⌀

---

## LONG EATON                               Map 08 SK43

**Trent Lock Golf Centre** Lock Ln, Sawley NG10 2FY
☎ 0115 9464398 & 9461184
Parkland course.
*18 holes, 6211yds, Par 73, SSS 70, Course record 73.*
*Club membership 400.*
**Visitors**      no restriction Mon-Fri am but booking system
                  12pm Fri-closing Sun.
**Societies**     apply in writing or telephone in advance.
**Green Fees** £13 per day (£10 per 18 holes).
**Facilities**    ⊗ 〼 ⅄ ♨ ♀ ⅄ ♨ ⌀ M Taylor/E McCausland.
**Leisure**       fishing, trolley for hire, driving range, putting
                  green.
**Hotel**         ★★★ 61% Novotel, Bostock Ln, LONG
                  EATON
                  ☎ 0115 946 5111 105 ⇄ ⌀

## MANSFIELD

Map 08 SK56

**Sherwood Forest** Eakring Rd NG18 3EW
☎ 01623 26689
As the name suggests, the Forest is the main feature of
this natural heathland course with its heather, silver birch
and pine trees. The homeward nine holes are particularly
testing. The 11th and 14th are notable par 4 holes on this
well-bunkered course designed by the great James Braid.
*18 holes, 6698yds, Par 71, SSS 73, Course record 68.*
*Club membership 750.*
**Visitors**      weekdays only by prior arrangement with
             the Secretary.
**Societies**     by arrangement with the Secretary.
**Green Fees** on application.
**Facilities**    ⊗ ⅜ ⅃ ♥ ♀ ⅄ 龠 ⌇ Ken Hall.
**Leisure**     trolley for hire, putting green, practice area,
             snooker table.
**Location**    E of Mansfield
**Hotel**       ★★ 65% Pine Lodge Hotel, 281-283
             Nottingham Rd, MANSFIELD
             ☎ 01623 22308 20rm(19 ⇌ ↾)

## MANSFIELD WOODHOUSE

Map 08 SK56

*Mansfield Woodhouse* Leeming Ln North NG19 9EU
☎ 01623 23521
Easy walking on heathland.
*9 holes, 2446yds, Par 68, SSS 64.*
*Club membership 130.*
**Visitors**      no restrictions.
**Societies**     must contact by telephone.
**Green Fees** not confirmed.
**Facilities**    ♀ 龠 ⌇ ⌇ Leslie Highfield.
**Location**    N side of town centre off A60
**Hotel**       ★★ 65% Pine Lodge Hotel, 281-283
             Nottingham Rd, MANSFIELD
             ☎ 01623 22308 20rm(19 ⇌ ↾)

## NEWARK-ON-TRENT

Map 08 SK75

**Newark** Coddington NG24 2QX ☎ 01636 626282
Wooded, parkland course in secluded situation with easy
walking.
*18 holes, 6421yds, Par 71, SSS 71, Course record 66.*
*Club membership 600.*
**Visitors**      must contact in advance and have handicap
             certificate. May not play Tue (Ladies Day).
**Societies**     must contact in advance.
**Green Fees** £27 per day; £22 per round.
**Facilities**    ⊗ ⅜ ⅃ ♥ ♀ ⅄ 龠 ⌇ H A Bennett.
**Leisure**     trolley for hire, putting green, practice area.
**Location**    4m E on A17
**Hotel**       ★★ 71% Grange Hotel, 73 London Rd,
             NEWARK
             ☎ 01636 703399 10 ⇌ ↾Annexe5 ⇌ ↾

## NOTTINGHAM

Map 08 SK53

**Beeston Fields** Old Dr, Wollaton Rd, Beeston NG9 3DD
☎ 0115 925 7062
Parkland course with sandy subsoil and wide, tree-lined
fairways. The par 3, 14th has elevated tee and small bunker-
guarded green.

*18 holes, 6402yds, Par 71, SSS 71, Course record 65.*
*Club membership 750.*
**Visitors**      must contact in advance.
**Societies**     must apply in advance.
**Green Fees** £30 per day; £20 per round (£25 per round
             weekends).
**Facilities**    ⊗ ⅜ ⅃ ♥ ♀ ⅄ 龠 ⌇ ⌇ Alun Wardle.
**Leisure**     trolley for hire, putting green, practice area.
**Location**    4m SW off A52
**Hotel**       B Forte Posthouse Nottingham/Derby, Bostocks
             Ln, SANDIACRE ☎ 0115 9397800 91 ⇌ ↾

**Bramcote Hills** Thoresby Rd, off Derby Rd, Bramcote
NG9 3EP ☎ 0115 928 1880
A Pay and Play, 18-hole Par 3 course with challenging
greens.
*18 holes, 1500yds, Par 54.*
**Visitors**      no restrictions.
**Societies**     telephone in advance.
**Green Fees** £5.40 per 18 holes (£5.90 weekends).
**Facilities**    ♥ 龠 ⌇
**Location**    Off A52 Derby rd
**Hotel**       ★★ 70% Priory Hotel, Derby Rd, Wollaton
             Vale, NOTTINGHAM
             ☎ 0115 922 1691 31 ⇌ ↾

**Bulwell Forest** Hucknall Rd, Bulwell NG6 9LQ
☎ 0115 977 0576
Municipal heathland course with many natural hazards. Very
tight fairways and subject to wind.
*18 holes, 5606yds, Par 68, SSS 67.*
*Club membership 450.*
**Visitors**      restricted weekends. Must contact in advance.
**Societies**     must apply in writing.
**Green Fees** not confirmed.
**Facilities**    ♀ ⅄ 龠 ⌇ ⌇
**Leisure**     putting green.
**Location**    4m NW of city centre on A611
**Hotel**       ★★★ 67% Nottingham Moat House, Mansfield
             Rd, NOTTINGHAM
             ☎ 0115 935 9988 172 ⇌ ↾

**Chilwell Manor** Meadow Ln, Chilwell NG9 5AE
☎ 0115 925 8958
Flat parkland course.
*18 holes, 6379yds, Par 70, SSS 70.*
*Club membership 750.*
**Visitors**      with member only weekends. Must contact in
             advance and have a handicap certificate.
**Societies**     welcome Mon, must apply in advance.
**Green Fees** not confirmed.
**Facilities**    ⅄ 龠 ⌇
**Location**    4m SW on A6005
**Hotel**       ★★ 62% Europa Hotel, 20 Derby Rd, LONG
             EATON ☎ 0115 972 8481 15 ⇌ ↾

**Edwalton Municipal** Wellin Ln, Edwalton NG12 4AS
☎ 0115 923 4775 & 923 1987
Gently sloping, 9-hole parkland course. Also 9-hole Par 3 and
large practice ground.
*9 holes, 3372yds, Par 72, SSS 72, Course record 71.*
*Club membership 900.*
**Visitors**      booking system in operation.
**Societies**     prior booking necessary.
**Green Fees** not confirmed.
**Facilities**    ♀ ⅄ 龠 ⌇ ⌇ John Staples.                 ▶

**Leisure** par 3 course.
**Location** S of Nottingham, off A606
**Hotel** ★★ 65% Rufford Hotel, 53 Melton Road,West
Bridgford, NOTTINGHAM
☎ 0115 981 4202 35 ☾

---

**Mapperley** Central Av, Plains Rd, Mapperley NG3 5RH
☎ 0115 926 5611
Hilly meadowland course but with easy walking.
*18 holes, 6283yds, Par 71, SSS 70, Course record 68.*
*Club membership 650.*
**Visitors** must contact in advance. May not play Sat.
**Societies** must telephone in advance.
**Green Fees** £15 per day; £12 per 18 holes (£21/£18
weekends and bank holidays).
**Facilities** ⊗ ⅢL ⬛ ♀⌂ 🏠⌁ℓ
**Leisure** trolley for hire, putting green, practice area, pool
table.
**Location** 3m NE of city centre off B684
**Hotel** B Forte Posthouse Nottingham, Saint James's St,
NOTTINGHAM ☎ 0115 947 0131 130 ⇄ ☾

---

*Nottingham City* Bulwell Hall Park NG6 8BL
☎ 0115 927 6916 & 927 2767
A pleasant municipal parkland course on the city outskirts.
*18 holes, 6218yds, Par 69, SSS 70, Course record 65.*
*Club membership 425.*
**Visitors** restricted Sat 7am-3pm.
**Societies** welcome except weekends.
**Green Fees** not confirmed.
**Facilities** ♀⌂ 🏠⌁ℓ Cyril Jepson.
**Leisure** putting green,practice area,trolley hire.
**Location** 4m NW of city centre off A6002
**Hotel** ★★★ 67% Nottingham Moat House, Mansfield
Rd, NOTTINGHAM
☎ 0115 935 9988 172 ⇄ ☾

---

**Wollaton Park** Limetree Av, Wollaton Park NG8 1BT
☎ 0115 978 7574
A pleasant, fairly level course set in a park close to the
centre of Nottingham, with red and fallow deer herds.
The fairways are tree-lined. The 502-yd dog-leg 15th is a
notable hole. The stately home - Wollaton Hall - is
situated in the park.
*18 holes, 6445yds, Par 71, SSS 71, Course record 64.*
*Club membership 650.*
**Visitors** may not play Wed or competition days.
**Societies** must apply in advance.
**Green Fees** £35 per day; £21.50 per round (£35/£25
weekends).
**Facilities** ⊗ ⅢL ⬛ ♀⌂ 🏠ℓ John Lower.
**Leisure** trolley for hire, putting green, pitch & putt,
practice area.
**Location** 2.5m W of city centre off A52
**Hotel** ★★★ 63% Swans Hotel & Restaurant, 84-
90 Radcliffe Rd, West Bridgford,
NOTTINGHAM ☎ 0115 981 4042 31 ⇄ ☾

---

## OLLERTON
Map 08 SK66

**Rufford Park Golf Centre** Rufford Ln, Rufford NG22 9DG
☎ 01623 825253
Rufford Park is noted for its pictuesque 18 holes with its
especially challenging Par 3's. From the unique 100yard Par
3 17th to the riverside 585yard 13th, the course offers
everything the golfer needs from beginner to professional.

*18 holes, 5953yds, Par 70, SSS 69.*
*Club membership 650.*
**Visitors** are advised to book in advance.
**Societies** society packages on request, need to be booked
in advance.
**Green Fees** £20 per day; £18 per round.
**Facilities** ⊗ ⅢL ⬛ ♀⌂ 🏠⌁
ℓ John Vaughan/James Thompson.
**Leisure** motorised carts for hire, buggies for hire, trolley
for hire, driving range, putting green, practice
area, 9 hole short course.
**Location** S Of Ollerton off A614
**Hotel** ★★ 65% Hop Pole Hotel, Main St,
OLLERTON
☎ 01623 822573 11rm(10 ⇄ ☾)

---

## OXTON
Map 08 SK65

**Oakmere Park** Oaks Ln NG25 0RH ☎ 0115 965 3545
Set in rolling parkland in the heart of picturesque Robin Hood
country. The par 4 (16th) and par 5 (1st) are notable. Thirty-
bay floodlit driving range.
*North Course: 18 holes, 6617mtrs, Par 72, SSS 72.*
*South Course: 9 holes, 3216mtrs, Par 37, SSS 37.*
*Club membership 450.*
**Visitors** correct golf attire required, please book for
weekends.
**Societies** please apply in writing or telephone.
**Green Fees** not confirmed.
**Facilities** ♀⌂ 🏠⌁ℓ Stephen Meade.
**Leisure** 30 bay floodlit driving range,caddy cars.
**Location** 1m NW off A6097
**Hotel** ★★★ 65% Saracen's Head Hotel, Market
Place, SOUTHWELL
☎ 01636 812701 27 ⇄ ☾

---

## RADCLIFFE-ON-TRENT
Map 08 SK63

**Cotgrave Place Golf & Country Club** Main Rd,
Stragglethorpe NG12 3HB ☎ 01159 333344 & 334686
The course has been designed in three nines to play in three
separate and self-contained styles. The first nine holes are
dotted around a beautiful lake, man-made ponds and a canal.
Water comes into play at every hole, but many are hidden
from the tee waiting to catch the wayward drive. The second
nine are in magnificent parkland with wide, lush fairways and
with huge bunkers. The 13th is protected by enourmous
tiers.The final nine are set amidst hedgerows and coppices
requiring well-placed tee shots.
*Lakeside: 9 holes, 3186yds, Par 36.*
*Parkland: 9 holes, 3117yds, Par 35.*
*Fox Coverts: 9 holes, 2755yds, Par 33.*
*Club membership 700.*
**Visitors** must contact in advance.
**Societies** telephone in advance.
**Green Fees** £22 per day; £15 per 18 holes; £7.50 per 9 holes
(£35/£25/£12.50 weekends).
**Facilities** ⊗ ⅢL ⬛ ♀⌂ 🏠⌁ℓ Greg Towne.
**Leisure** motorised carts for hire, buggies for hire, trolley
for hire, driving range, putting green, practice
area.
**Location** Off A52, 6miles from Nottingham
**Hotel** ★★⚬ 71% Langar Hall, LANGAR
☎ 01949 60559 12 ⇄ ☾

**Radcliffe-on-Trent** Drewberry Ln, Cropwell Rd NG12 2JH
☎ 0115 933 3000
Fairly flat, parkland course with three good finishing holes:
16th (427 yds) par 4; 17th (180 yds) through spinney, par 3;
18th (331 yds) dog-leg par 4. Excellent views.
*18 holes, 6381yds, Par 70, SSS 71, Course record 64.*
*Club membership 620.*

| | |
|---|---|
| Visitors | must contact in advance. |
| Societies | welcome Wed. Must contact in advance. |
| Green Fees | £23 (£28 weekends). |
| Facilities | ⊗ ⅢⅢ ♭ ♣ ♀ ♨ ⌂ ⊤ ℓ Robert Ellis. |
| Leisure | trolley for hire, putting green, practice area. |
| Location | 1m SE off A52 |
| Hotel | ★★★ 63% Swans Hotel & Restaurant, 84-90 Radcliffe Rd, West Bridgford, NOTTINGHAM ☎ 0115 981 4042 31 ⇄ ⋒ |

## RETFORD     Map 08 SK78

**Retford** Brecks Rd, Ordsall DN22 7UA
☎ 01777 860682 (Secretary) & 703733 (Pro)
A wooded, parkland course.
*18 holes, 6301yds, Par 71, SSS 70, Course record 67.*
*Club membership 700.*

| | |
|---|---|
| Visitors | advisable to contact in advance, with member only at weekends and holidays. |
| Societies | apply in writing or telephone. Not welcome Tue morning or bank holidays, limited availability weekends. |
| Green Fees | £23 per day; £19 per round. |
| Facilities | ⊗ ⅢⅢ ♭ ♣ ♀ ♨ ⌂ ⊤ ℓ Stuart Betteridge. |
| Leisure | motorised carts for hire, buggies for hire, trolley for hire, putting green, practice area. |
| Location | 1.5m S A620, between Worksop & Gainsborough |
| Hotel | ★★★ 67% West Retford Hotel, 24 North Rd, RETFORD ☎ 01777 706333 Annexe60 ⇄ ⋒ |

## RUDDINGTON     Map 08 SK53

***Ruddington Grange*** Wilford Rd NG11 6NB
☎ 0115 984 6141
Undulating parkland course with water hazards on 12 holes.
*18 holes, 6543yds, Par 72, SSS 72.*
*Club membership 650.*

| | |
|---|---|
| Visitors | a handicap certificate is required, contact in advance if possible. Play may be restricted Sat & Wed mornings. |
| Societies | must contact in advance. |
| Green Fees | not confirmed. |
| Facilities | ♀ ♨ ⌂ ℓ Richard Daibell. |
| Leisure | putting green,practice area,trolley hire. |
| Location | 5m S of Nottingham, A60 to Ruddington |
| Hotel | ★★★ 63% Swans Hotel & Restaurant, 84-90 Radcliffe Rd, West Bridgford, NOTTINGHAM ☎ 0115 981 4042 31 ⇄ ⋒ |

## SERLBY     Map 08 SK68

***Serlby Park*** DN10 6BA ☎ 01777 818268
Parkland course.
*11 holes, 5325yds, Par 66, SSS 66, Course record 63.*
*Club membership 250.*

| | |
|---|---|
| Visitors | must be introduced by and play with member. |

| | |
|---|---|
| Societies | apply in writing before 31 Dec for following year. |
| Green Fees | not confirmed. |
| Facilities | ♀ ♨ |
| Leisure | putting green & practice area. |
| Location | E side of village off A638 |
| Hotel | ★★★ 63% Charnwood Hotel, Sheffield Rd, BLYTH ☎ 01909 591610 20 ⇄ ⋒ |

## SUTTON IN ASHFIELD     Map 08 SK45

**Coxmoor** Coxmoor Rd NG17 5LF ☎ 01623 557359
Undulating moorland/heathland course with easy walking
and excellent views. The clubhouse is modern with a
well-equipped games room. The course lies adjacent to
Forestry Commission land over which there are several
footpaths and extensive views.
*18 holes, 6571yds, Par 73, SSS 72, Course record 64.*
*Club membership 700.*

| | |
|---|---|
| Visitors | must play with member weekends & bank holidays. Must contact in advance. |
| Societies | must apply in advance. |
| Green Fees | £25 per round. |
| Facilities | ⊗ ⅢⅢ ♭ ♣ ♀ ♨ ⌂ ℓ David Ridley. |
| Leisure | trolley for hire, putting green, practice area. |
| Location | 2m SE off A611 |
| Hotel | ★★★★ 65% Swallow Hotel, Carter Ln East, SOUTH NORMANTON ☎ 01773 812000 161 ⇄ ⋒ |

## WORKSOP     Map 08 SK57

**Bondhay Golf & Country Club** Bondhay Ln, Whitewell
S80 3EH ☎ 01909 724709 & 723608
The wind usually plays quite an active role in making this
pleasantly undulating course testing. Signatures holes are the
10th which requires a 2nd shot over water into a basin of
trees; the 11th comes back over the same expanse of water
and requires a mid to short iron to a long, narrow green; the
18th is a Par 5 with a lake right in lay up distance - the
dilemma is whether to lay up short or go for the carry.
*Devonshire Course: 18 holes, 6720yds, Par 72, SSS 71,
Course record 67.*
*Family Course: 9 holes, 1118yds, Par 27, Course record 23.*
*Club membership 600.*

| | |
|---|---|
| Visitors | must contact in advance. |
| Societies | must telephone in advance. |
| Green Fees | Devonshire: £19.95 per day; £14.95 per round (£24.95 per day weekends). Family: £3.95 per 9 holes. |
| Facilities | ⊗ ⅢⅢ ♭ ♣ ♀ ♨ ⌂ ⊤ ℓ Martin Bell. |
| Leisure | fishing, motorised carts for hire, buggies for hire, trolley for hire, driving range, putting green. |
| Location | 5m W of Worksop, off A616 |
| Hotel | ★★ 62% Regancy Hotel, Carlton Rd, WORKSOP ☎ 01909 474108 13rm(7 ⋒) |

**Kilton Forest** Blyth Rd S81 0TL
☎ 01909 485994 & 486563
Slightly undulating, parkland course on the north edge of
Sherwood Forest. Includes three ponds.
*18 holes, 6424yds, Par 72, SSS 71, Course record 69.*
*Club membership 350.*

| | |
|---|---|
| Visitors | must contact in advance. |
| Societies | must contact in advance. |

▶

**Green Fees** £6.40 £(8.40 weekends).
**Facilities** ⊗ ☰ by prior arrangement ⬛ 🍴 ♀ ⚲ 🛍 ⛳
🏌 Peter W Foster.
**Leisure** trolley for hire, putting green, practice area,
bowling green.
**Location** 1m NE of town centre on B6045
**Hotel** ★★ 72% Lion Hotel, 112 Bridge St,
WORKSOP ☎ 01909 477925 32 ⇄ 🐾

---

**Lindrick** Lindrick Common S81 8BH
☎ 01909 475282
Heathland course with some trees and masses of gorse.
*18 holes, 6486yds, Par 71, SSS 72, Course record 65.*
*Club membership 500.*
**Visitors** must contact in advance. Restricted Tue &
weekends. Handicap certificate required.
**Societies** welcome except Tue (am) & weekends by
prior arrangement with the Secretary.
**Green Fees** £40 per day (£45 weekends); £25 per
day/round winter.
**Facilities** ⊗ ☰ ⬛ 🍴 ♀ ⚲ 🛍 🏌 Peter Cowen.
**Leisure** trolley for hire, putting green, practice area.
**Location** 4m NW on A57
**Hotel** ★★ 72% Lion Hotel, 112 Bridge St,
WORKSOP
☎ 01909 477925 32 ⇄ 🐾

---

*Worksop* Windmill Ln S80 2SQ ☎ 01909 472696
Adjacent to Clumber Park this course has a heathland-type
terrain, with gorse, broom, oak and birch trees. Fast, true
greens, dry all year round.
*18 holes, 6651yds, Par 72, SSS 73.*
*Club membership 500.*
**Visitors** by arrangement with professional tel: 01909
477732. No visitors Nov-Mar without member.
**Societies** must apply in advance.
**Green Fees** not confirmed.
**Facilities** ♀ ⚲ 🛍 🏌 J R King.
**Leisure** putting green, trolley hire, practice area.
**Location** 1.75m S off A620
**Hotel** ★★★ 70% Clumber Park Hotel, Clumber Park,
WORKSOP
☎ 01623 835333 48 ⇄ 🐾

---

# OXFORDSHIRE

---

## ABINGDON
Map 04 SU49

*Drayton Park* Steventon Rd, Drayton Village OX14 2RR
☎ 01235 550607
Set in the heart of the Oxfordshire countryside, an 18-hole
parkland course designed by Hawtree. Five lakes and sand
based greens.
*18 holes, 6500yds, Par 67, SSS 67, Course record 63.*
*Club membership 500.*
**Visitors** may phone to book, must have golf shoes, no
jeans or tracksuits.
**Societies** contact in advance.
**Green Fees** not confirmed.
**Facilities** ♀ ⚲ 🛍 🏌 Dinah Masey,Tony Williams.
**Leisure** putting green,trolley hire,driving range,9 hole
par 3 course.

**Location** Between Oxford & Newbury,off A34 at Didcot
**Hotel** ★★★ 64% The Upper Reaches, Thames St,
ABINGDON ☎ 01235 522311 25rm(19 ⇄ 🐾)

---

## BURFORD
Map 04 SP21

**Burford** Swindon Rd OX18 4JG ☎ 01993 822583
Created out of open-farmland, this parkland course has high
quality fairways and greens.
*18 holes, 6414yds, Par 71, SSS 71, Course record 64.*
*Club membership 830.*
**Visitors** must contact in advance. May not play
weekends.
**Societies** apply in writing.
**Green Fees** £28 per day.
**Facilities** ⊗ ☰ ⬛ 🍴 ♀ ⚲ 🛍 ⛳ 🏌 Norman Allen.
**Leisure** practice area.
**Location** 0.5m S off A361
**Hotel** ★★ 66% Golden Pheasant Hotel, 91 High St,
BURFORD
☎ 01993 823223 & 823417 12rm(11 ⇄ 🐾)

---

## CHESTERTON
Map 04 SP52

**Chesterton Golf & Country Club** OX6 8TE
☎ 01869 242023 & 241204
Laid out over one-time farmland. Well-bunkered, and water
hazards increase the difficulty of the course.
*18 holes, 6229yds, Par 71, SSS 70, Course record 68.*
*Club membership 500.*
**Visitors** must pre-book up to 4 days ahead.
**Societies** must contact in advance.
**Green Fees** £15 per day; £10 per round (£20/£15 weekends
& bank holidays).
**Facilities** ⊗ ⬛ 🍴 ♀ ⚲ 🛍 🏌 J Wilkshire.
**Leisure** trolley for hire, driving range, putting green,
practice area.
**Location** 0.5m W on A4095
**Hotel** ★★ 68% Jersey Arms Hotel, MIDDLETON
STONEY
☎ 01869 343234 & 343505 6 ⇄Annexe10 ⇄

---

## CHIPPING NORTON
Map 04 SP32

**Chipping Norton** Southcombe OX7 5QH ☎ 01608 642383
Pleasant downland course open to winds.
*18 holes, 6241yds, Par 71, SSS 70, Course record 65.*
*Club membership 900.*
**Visitors** with member only at weekends & bank holidays.
**Societies** telephone in advance.
**Green Fees** £17 per round/day.
**Facilities** ⊗ ☰ ⬛ 🍴 ♀ ⚲ 🛍 ⛳ 🏌 Bob Gould.
**Leisure** trolley for hire, putting green, practice area.
**Location** 1.5m E on A44
**Hotel** ★★ 63% The White Hart Hotel, 16 High St,
CHIPPING NORTON
☎ 01608 642572 16 ⇄ 🐾Annexe5 ⇄

---

**Lyneham** Lyneham OX7 6QQ ☎ 01993 831841
Lyneham was designed to use the natural features. It is set in
170 acres on the fringe of the Costwolds and bleds superbly
with its surroundings. Lakes and streams enhance the
challenge of the course with water coming into play on 8 of
the 18 holes. All greens are sand based, built ot USGA
specification.

*18 holes, 6669yds, Par 72, SSS 72.*
*Club membership 600.*
**Visitors** must contact in advance.
**Societies** apply in advance.
**Green Fees** £13 (£16 weekends).
**Facilities** ⊗ ⅫⅬ ♥ ♀ ♨ 🏠 ⚑ ⟨ Mark Stancer.
**Leisure** motorised carts for hire, buggies for hire, trolley for hire, driving range, putting green, practice area.
**Location** Off A361, between Burford/Chipping Norton
**Hotel** ★★ 63% Shaven Crown Hotel, SHIPTON-UNDER-WYCHWOOD
☎ 01993 830330 9rm(8 ⇄ ⟨)

## DIDCOT
Map 04 SU59

**Hadden Hill** Wallingford Rd OX11 9BJ ☎ 01235 510410
A challenging course on undulating terrain with excellent drainage so visitors can be sure of playing no matter what the weather conditions have been. Two loops of nine holes.
*18 holes, 6563yds, Par 71, SSS 71, Course record 65.*
*Club membership 400.*
**Visitors** telephone to book tee times.
**Societies** telephone to arrange times & dates & receive booking form.
**Green Fees** £12 per 18 holes; £7 per 9 holes (£16/£9.50 weekends).
**Facilities** ⊗ ⅫⅬ ♥ ♀ ♨ 🏠 ⚑
⟨ Dean Halford/Adrian Waters.
**Leisure** motorised carts for hire, buggies for hire, trolley for hire, floodlit driving range, putting green, practice area.
**Location** On A4130 1m E of Didcot
**Hotel** ★★★ 64% Abingdon Four Pillars Hotel, Marcham Rd, ABINGDON
☎ 01235 553456 63 ⇄ ⟨

## FRILFORD
Map 04 SU49

**Frilford Heath** Abingdon OX13 5NW
☎ 01865 390864
54 holes of heathland courses. Both the Red and the Green courses are of outstanding interest and beauty. Heather, pine, birch and, in particular, a mass of flowering gorse enhance the terrain.The new Blue course is extremely testing in design, especially the four opening holes.
*Red Course: 18 holes, 6843yds, Par 73, SSS 71, Course record 70.*
*Green Course: 18 holes, 6006yds, Par 69, SSS 68, Course record 64.*
*Blue Course: 18 holes, 6726yds, Par 72, SSS 71, Course record 69.*
*Club membership 1300.*
**Visitors** contact in advance.
**Societies** apply in advance.
**Green Fees** £45 per day (£55 weekends & bank holidays).
**Facilities** ⊗ Ⅼ ♥ ♀ ♨ 🏠 ⚑ ⟨ Derek Craik.
**Leisure** motorised carts for hire, buggies for hire, trolley for hire, putting green, practice area.
**Location** 1m N off A338
**Hotel** ★★★ 64% Abingdon Four Pillars Hotel, Marcham Rd, ABINGDON
☎ 01235 553456 63 ⇄ ⟨

## HENLEY-ON-THAMES
Map 04 SU78

**Aspect Park** Remenham Hill RG9 3EH
☎ 01491 577562 & 578306
Parkland course.
*18 holes, 6643yds, Par 72, SSS 72.*
*Club membership 500.*
**Visitors** must contact in advance.
**Societies** must contact in advance.
**Green Fees** not confirmed.
**Facilities** ♥ ♀ ♨ 🏠 ⟨ Roger Frost.
**Leisure** motorised carts for hire, buggies for hire, trolley for hire, driving range, putting green, practice area, pitch & putt.
**Hotel** ★★★ 66% Red Lion Hotel, Hart St, HENLEY-ON-THAMES
☎ 01491 572161 26rm(23 ⇄ ⟨)

**Badgemore Park** RG9 4NR ☎ 01491 573667 & 572206
Parkland course with many trees and easy walking. The 13th is a very difficult par 3 hole played over a valley to a narrow green.
*18 holes, 6112yds, Par 69, SSS 69, Course record 65.*
*Club membership 600.*
**Visitors** contact professional shop on 01491 574175.
**Societies** contact General Manager to book.
**Green Fees** £27 per day; £21 per round (£30 per round weekends).
**Facilities** ⊗ Ⅼ ♥ ♀ ♨ 🏠 ⚑ ⟨ Jonathon Dunn.
**Leisure** motorised carts for hire, buggies for hire, trolley for hire, putting green.
**Location** 1m W
**Hotel** ★★★ 66% Red Lion Hotel, Hart St, HENLEY-ON-THAMES
☎ 01491 572161 26rm(23 ⇄ ⟨)

**Henley** Harpsden RG9 4HG ☎ 01491 575742
Undulating parkland course. 6th hole, blind (par 4), with steep hill.
*18 holes, 6329yds, Par 70, SSS 70, Course record 65.*
*Club membership 800.*
**Visitors** must contact in advance. Weekend only with a member.
**Societies** Wed & Thu, apply in writing.
**Green Fees** £30 per day/round.
**Facilities** ⊗ ⅫⅬ ♥ ♀ ♨ 🏠 ⚑ ⟨ Mark Howell.
**Leisure** trolley for hire, putting green, practice area.
**Location** 1.25m S off A4155
**Hotel** ★★★ 66% Red Lion Hotel, Hart St, HENLEY-ON-THAMES
☎ 01491 572161 26rm(23 ⇄ ⟨)

## MILTON COMMON
Map 04 SP60

**The Oxfordshire** Rycote Ln OX9 2PU
☎ 01844 278300
Designed by Rees Jones, The Oxfordshire is considered to be one of the most excitng courses in the country. With four man-made lakes and 135 bunkers, it is a magnificent test of shot-making where almost every hole deserves special mention. Unfortunately it is only open to members and their guests.
*18 holes, 6856mtrs, Par 72, SSS 73, Course record 68.*
*Club membership 900.*
**Visitors** Members guests only. ▶

| Facilities | ⊗ ⓑ ☰ ♀ ♨ 🏠 ⚑ ⓒ Ian Mosey. |
|---|---|
| Leisure | motorised carts for hire, buggies for hire, trolley for hire, driving range, putting green. |
| Location | 1.5m from junct 7, M40 |
| Hotel | ★★★ 74% Spread Eagle Hotel, Cornmarket, THAME ☎ 01844 213661 33 ⇥ ⓡ |

## NUFFIELD                    Map 04 SU68

**Huntercombe** RG9 5SL ☎ 01491 641207
This heathland/woodland course overlooks the Oxfordshire plain and has many attractive and interesting fairways and greens. Walking is easy after the 3rd which is a notable hole. The course is subject to wind and grass pot bunkers are interesting hazards.
*18 holes, 6301yds, Par 70, SSS 70, Course record 63.*
*Club membership 900.*

| Visitors | must contact in advance and have a handicap certificate. |
|---|---|
| Societies | must contact in advance. |
| Green Fees | not confirmed. |
| Facilities | ♀ ♨ 🏠 ⓒ John B Draycott. |
| Location | N off A423 |
| Hotel | ★★★ 63% Shillingford Bridge Hotel, Shillingford, WALLINGFORD ☎ 01865 858567 34 ⇥ ⓡAnnexe8 ⇥ ⓡ |

## OXFORD                    Map 04 SP50

**North Oxford** Banbury Rd OX2 8EZ
☎ 01865 54924 & 54415
Gently undulating parkland course.
*18 holes, 5736yds, Par 67, SSS 67, Course record 62.*
*Club membership 700.*

| Visitors | at weekends & bank holidays may only play after 4pm. |
|---|---|
| Societies | must contact in advance. |
| Green Fees | £25 per day/round. |
| Facilities | ⊗ ⓜ ⓑ ☰ ♀ ♨ 🏠 ⚑ ⓒ Robert Harris. |
| Leisure | trolley for hire, putting green. |
| Location | 3m N of city centre on A423 |
| Hotel | ★★★ 63% Oxford Moat House, Godstow Rd, Wolvercote Roundabout, OXFORD ☎ 01865 59933 155 ⇥ |

**Southfield** Hill Top Rd OX4 1PF
☎ 01865 242158
Home of the City, University and Ladies Clubs, and well-known to graduates throughout the world. A challenging course, in varied parkland setting, providing a real test for players.
*18 holes, 5973yds, Par 69, SSS 69.*
*Club membership 850.*

| Visitors | with member only at weekends. |
|---|---|
| Societies | must apply in writing. |
| Green Fees | not confirmed. |
| Facilities | ♀ ♨ 🏠 ⓒ Tony Rees. |
| Leisure | putting,buggy/trolley hire. |
| Location | 1.5m SE of city centre off B480 |
| Hotel | ★★★ 64% Eastgate Hotel, The High, Merton St, OXFORD ☎ 01865 248244 43 ⇥ ⓡ |

## SHRIVENHAM                    Map 04 SU28

**Shrivenham Park** Penny Hooks SN6 8EX
☎ 01793 783853 & 783854
Parkland course with easy walking. The par 4, 17th is a difficult dog-leg.
*18 holes, 5713yds, Par 69, SSS 69.*
*Club membership 450.*

| Visitors | phone in advance. |
|---|---|
| Societies | phone for details. |
| Green Fees | £14.50 per day; £10.50 per round; £6.50 per 10 holes (£16.50/£12.50/£8.50 weekends & bank holidays). |
| Facilities | ⊗ ⓜ ⓑ ☰ ♀ ♨ 🏠 ⚑ ⓒ J McArthur. |
| Leisure | motorised carts for hire, buggies for hire, trolley for hire, putting, practice area. |
| Location | 0.5m NE of town centre |
| Hotel | ★★★ 63% The Crest Hotel, Oxford Rd, Stratton St Margaret, SWINDON ☎ 01793 831333 91 ⇥ ⓡ |

## TADMARTON                    Map 04 SP33

**Tadmarton Heath** OX15 5HL ☎ 01608 737278
A mixture of heath and sandy land, the course, which is open to strong winds, incorporates the site of an old Roman encampment. The clubhouse is an old farm building with a 'holy well' from which the greens are watered. The 7th is a testing hole over water.
*18 holes, 5917yds, Par 69, SSS 69, Course record 63.*
*Club membership 600.*

| Visitors | weekday by appointment, with member only at weekends. |
|---|---|
| Societies | by arrangement with club office. |
| Green Fees | £26 per day; £18 after 2.30pm (Winter £15 per day). |
| Facilities | ⊗ ⓜ ⓑ ☰ ♀ ♨ 🏠 ⚑ ⓒ Les Bond. |
| Leisure | fishing, buggies for hire, trolley for hire, driving range, putting green, practice area. |
| Location | 1m SW of Lower Tadmarton off B4035 |
| Hotel | ★★★ 65% Banbury House, Oxford Rd, BANBURY ☎ 01295 259361 49 ⇥ ⓡ |

## WATERSTOCK                    Map 04 SP60

**Waterstock** Thame Rd OX33 1HT
☎ 01844 338093
A 6,500yard course designed by Donald Steel with USGA greens and tees fully computer irrigated. Four Par 3's facing North, South, East and West. A brook and hidden lake affect six holes, with doglegs being 4th and 10th holes. Five Par 5's on the course, making it a challenge for players of all standards.
*18 holes, 6535yds, Par 73, SSS 71, Course record 70.*
*Club membership 600.*

| Visitors | no restrictions. |
|---|---|
| Societies | apply in writing or telephone. |
| Green Fees | not confirmed. |
| Facilities | ♀ ♨ 🏠 ⚑ ⓒ Andy Wyatt. |
| Leisure | fishing, 22 bay floodlit range, caddy cars. |
| Location | On junc 8 of M40 |
| Hotel | ★★★ 74% Spread Eagle Hotel, Cornmarket, THAME ☎ 01844 213661 33 ⇥ ⓡ |

# RUTLAND

## GREETHAM
Map 08 SK91

**Greetham Valley** Wood Ln LE15 7RG ☎ 01780 460444
Set in 200 acres, including mature woodland and water
hazards, Greetham Valley was opened in spring 1992. The
complex comprises an 18-hole course and clubhouse, a
floodlit 9-hole Par 3 and a 21-bay floodlit driving range.
*18 holes, 6362yds, Par 71, SSS 71.*
*Club membership 850.*
**Visitors**      must contact in advance.
**Societies**    must contact in advance.
**Green Fees** £16 per round (£25 weekends).
**Facilities**   ⊗ ∭ ⓛ ☕ ♀ ♨ 🏠 ⛳ ( Mark Cunningham.
**Leisure**      fishing, motorised carts for hire, buggies for hire,
              trolley for hire, driving range, putting green,
              practice area, pool table, snooker, bowls,
              archery, Par 3 course.
**Location**     Off B668 in Greetham
**Hotel**        ★★ 69% Ram Jam Inn, Great North Rd,
              STRETTON ☎ 01780 410776 Annexe7 ⇥ (

# SHROPSHIRE

## BRIDGNORTH
Map 07 SO79

**Bridgnorth** Stanley Ln WV16 4SF ☎ 01746 763315
A pleasant course laid-out on parkland on the bank of the
River Severn.
*18 holes, 6673yds, Par 73, SSS 72, Course record 65.*
*Club membership 725.*
**Visitors**      must contact in advance but may not play on
              Wed. Restricted weekends.
**Societies**    must contact in writing.
**Green Fees** not confirmed.
**Facilities**   ♀ ♨ 🏠 (
**Leisure**      fishing, putting green,practice area,trolley hire.
**Location**     1m N off B4373
**Hotel**        ★★ 62% Falcon Hotel, Saint John St,
              Lowtown, BRIDGNORTH
              ☎ 01746 763134 15rm(5 ⇥7 (\*)

## CHURCH STRETTON
Map 07 SO49

**Church Stretton** Trevor Hill SY6 6JH ☎ 01694 722281
Hillside course constructed by James Braid on the lower
slopes of the Long Mynd.
*18 holes, 5020yds, Par 66, SSS 65, Course record 63.*
*Club membership 400.*
**Visitors**      Tee reserved for members Sat 9-10.30 & 1-2.30,
              Sun prior to 10.30 & 1-2.30.
**Societies**    must contact in advance.
**Green Fees** £12 per day (£18 weekends & bank holidays).
**Facilities**   ⊗ ∭ ⓛ ☕ ♀ ♨ 🏠 ⇥( P Seal (wknds only).
**Leisure**      putting green.
**Location**     W of the town
**Hotel**        ★★ 71% Mynd House Hotel, Little Stretton,
              CHURCH STRETTON
              ☎ 01694 722212 8 ⇥ (

## HIGHLEY
Map 07 SO78

**Severn Meadows** WV16 6HZ ☎ 01746 862212
Picturesque course set alongside the River Severn and
providing a tight test of golf with much of the course
bordered by mature trees.
*9 holes, 5258yds, Par 68, SSS 67.*
*Club membership 170.*
**Visitors**      booking advisable for weekends.
**Societies**    advance booking necessary.
**Green Fees** £10 per 18 holes; £6 per 9 holes (£12/£7
              weekends and bank holidays).
**Facilities**   ⊗ by prior arrangement ∭ by prior arrangement
              ⓛ by prior arrangement ☕ ♀ ♨ 🏠
**Leisure**      putting green.
**Hotel**        ★★★★ 65% Mill Hotel & Restaurant,
              ALVELEY ☎ 01746 780437 21 ⇥ (

## LILLESHALL
Map 07 SJ71

**Lilleshall Hall** TF10 9AS ☎ 01952 603840
Heavily-wooded parkland course. Easy walking.
*18 holes, 5906yds, Par 68, SSS 68.*
*Club membership 650.*
**Visitors**      must contact in advance and play with member
              at weekends.
**Societies**    must apply in writing by Dec for the following
              year.
**Green Fees** not confirmed.
**Facilities**   ♀ ♨ 🏠 ( Nigel Bramall.
**Location**     3m SE
**Hotel**        ★★ 68% White House Hotel, Wellington Rd,
              Muxton, TELFORD
              ☎ 01952 604276 & 603603 30 ⇥ (

## LUDLOW
Map 07 SO57

**Ludlow** Bromfield SY8 2BT ☎ 01584 856285
A long-established parkland course in the middle of the
racecourse. Very flat, quick drying, with broom and gorse-
lined fairways.
*18 holes, 6277yds, Par 70, SSS 70, Course record 65.*
*Club membership 700.*
**Visitors**      advisable to contact in advance.
**Societies**    apply in advance.
**Green Fees** £18 per day (£24 weekends).
**Facilities**   ⊗ ∭ ⓛ ☕ ♀ ♨ 🏠 ⛳ ( Russell Price.
**Leisure**      motorised carts for hire, trolley for hire, putting
              green, practice area.
**Location**     1m N of Ludlow, off A49
**Hotel**        ★★★ 70% The Feathers at Ludlow, Bull Ring,
              LUDLOW ☎ 01584 875261 39 ⇥ (

## MARKET DRAYTON
Map 07 SJ63

**Market Drayton** Sutton TF9 2HX ☎ 01630 652266
Parkland course in quiet, picturesque surroundings providing
a good test of golf. Bungalow on course is made available for
golfing holidays.
*18 holes, 6400yds, Par 71, SSS 70, Course record 69.*
*Club membership 550.*
**Visitors**      may not play on Sun; must play with member on
              Sat. Must contact in advance.
**Societies**    must contact in advance.          ▶

**Green Fees** not confirmed.
**Facilities** ♀⚐🏠℄ Russel Clewes.
**Location** 1m SW
**Hotel** ★★★♨ 70% Goldstone Hall, Goldstone,
MARKET DRAYTON
☎ 01630 661202 & 661487 8 ⇆ ☏

## MEOLE BRACE Map 07 SJ41

**Meole Brace** SY2 6QQ ☎ 01743 364050
Pleasant municipal course.
*9 holes, 5830yds, Par 68, SSS 68, Course record 66.*
*Club membership 300.*
**Visitors** may not play Wed and must book in advance for weekends & bank holidays.
**Societies** must contact Mr R Wootton, Shrewsbury & Atcham Borough Council on 01743 231456.
**Green Fees** £5.10 per 18 holes; £4 per 9 holes (£6.90/£5.10 weekends and bank holidays).
**Facilities** 🏠❜℄ Ian Doran.
**Leisure** trolley for hire, pitch & putt, practice area.
**Location** NE side of village off A49
**Hotel** ★★★ 62% Lion Hotel, Wyle Cop,
SHREWSBURY ☎ 01743 353107 59 ⇆ ☏

## OSWESTRY Map 07 SJ22

**Mile End** Mile End, Old Shresbury Rd SY11 4JE
☎ 01691 670580 & 671246
A gently undulating parkland-type course now featuring 18 holes, the new 9-holes offering a number of challenging holes for all standards of golfing ability. Well-spaced holes in 70 acres.
*9 holes, 6130yds, Par 70, SSS 69, Course record 71.*
**Visitors** welcome at all times please telephone in advance.
**Societies** must contact in advance.
**Green Fees** £14 per day; £10 per 18 holes (£18/£14 weekends & bank holidays).
**Facilities** ⊗🡇💺♀⚐🏠℄ Scott Carpenter.
**Leisure** trolley for hire, putting green, practice area.
**Location** 1m SE of Oswestry, just off A5
**Hotel** ★★★ 70% Wynnstay Hotel, Church St,
OSWESTRY ☎ 01691 655261 27 ⇆ ☏

**Oswestry** Aston Park SY11 4JJ ☎ 01691 610535
Parkland course laid-out on undulating ground.
*18 holes, 6024yds, Par 70, SSS 69, Course record 62.*
*Club membership 960.*
**Visitors** must contact in advance.
**Societies** must contact in advance.
**Green Fees** £18 per day (£25 weekends and bank holidays).
**Facilities** ⊗🎜🡇💺♀⚐🏠℄ David Skelton.
**Leisure** motorised carts for hire, trolley for hire, putting green, practice area.
**Location** 2m SE on A5
**Hotel** ★★★ 70% Wynnstay Hotel, Church St,
OSWESTRY ☎ 01691 655261 27 ⇆ ☏

## PANT Map 07 SJ22

**Llanymynech** SY10 8LB ☎ 01691 830983 & 830542
Upland course on the site of an early Iron Age/Roman hillfort with far-reaching views. The 4th fairway crosses the Welsh border.

*18 holes, 6114yds, Par 70, SSS 69, Course record 65.*
*Club membership 600.*
**Visitors** must contact in advance, some weekends restricted.
**Societies** must contact Secretary.
**Green Fees** £22 per day; £15 per round (£25/£20 weekends & bank holidays).
**Facilities** ⊗🎜🡇💺♀⚐🏠℄ Andrew P Griffiths.
**Leisure** trolley for hire, putting green, practice area.
**Location** 0.5m SW off A483
**Hotel** ★★★ 70% Wynnstay Hotel, Church St,
OSWESTRY ☎ 01691 655261 27 ⇆ ☏

## SHIFNAL Map 07 SJ70

**Shifnal** Decker Hill TF11 8QL ☎ 01952 460330
Well-wooded parkland course. Walking is easy and an attractive country mansion serves as the clubhouse.
*18 holes, 6468yds, Par 71, SSS 71, Course record 65.*
*Club membership 600.*
**Visitors** must contact in advance, may not play at weekends.
**Societies** must contact in advance.
**Green Fees** £30 per day; £22 per round.
**Facilities** ⊗🎜🡇💺♀⚐🏠℄ Justin Flanagan.
**Leisure** trolley for hire, putting green, practice area.
**Location** 1m N of Shifnal, off B4379
**Hotel** ★★★★ 59% Park House Hotel, Park St,
SHIFNAL
☎ 01952 460128 38 ⇆ ☏Annexe16 ⇆ ☏

## SHREWSBURY Map 07 SJ41

**Arscott** Arscot, Pontesbury SY5 0XP
☎ 01743 860114 & 860881
At 365feet above sea level, the views from Arscott Golf Club of the hills of south Shropshire and Wales are superb. Arscott is a new course, set in parkland with water features and holes demanding all sorts of club choice. A challenge to all golfers both high and low handicap.
*18 holes, 6112yds, Par 70, SSS 69, Course record 65.*
*Club membership 550.*
**Visitors** most times available by prior arrangement.
**Societies** apply in writing for tee reservation.
**Green Fees** £12.50 per day (£20.50 weekends).
**Facilities** ⊗🎜🡇💺♀⚐🏠℄ Gary Sawyer.
**Leisure** fishing, trolley for hire, putting green, practice area.
**Location** Off A488, S of Shrewsbury 3m from A5
**Hotel** ★★★♨ 64% Rowton Castle Hotel, Halfway House, SHREWSBURY
☎ 01743 884044 19 ⇆

**Shrewsbury** Condover SY5 7BL ☎ 01743 872976
Parkland course. First nine flat, second undulating with good views.
*18 holes, 6300yds, Par 70, SSS 70.*
*Club membership 872.*
**Visitors** may only play between 10am-noon and after 2.15pm at weekends. Must contact in advance and have a handicap certificate.
**Societies** must contact in writing.
**Green Fees** not confirmed.
**Facilities** ♀⚐🏠℄ Peter Seal.
**Location** 4m S off A49

**Hotel** ★★★ 68% Prince Rupert Hotel, Butcher Row, SHREWSBURY ☎ 01743 499955 65 ⇥

## TELFORD                                          Map 07 SJ60

**The Shropshire** Muxton Grange, Muxton TF2 8PQ
☎ 01952 677866
Pay and Play, 3 loops of 9-holes. Also tuition hole, practice green, 12 hole pitch and putt and 18-hole contoured putting green.
*Blue Course: 9 holes, 3286yds, Par 35, SSS 35.*
*Silver Course: 9 holes, 3303yds, Par 36, SSS 36.*
*Gold Course: 9 holes, 3334yds, Par 36, SSS 36.*
*Club membership 250.*
**Visitors** must book 7 days in advance.
**Societies** must book in advance.
**Green Fees** not confirmed.
**Facilities** ♀⚲ 🏠 ⚐ ℓ Kevin Craggs.
**Leisure** fishing, caddy car/trolley hire, pitch & putt.
**Hotel** ★★★ 69% Holiday Inn, St Quentin Gate, TELFORD ☎ 01952 292500 100 ⇥ ⍩

**Telford Golf & Country Moat House** Great Hay Dr, Sutton Hill TF7 4DT ☎ 01952 429977
Rolling parkland course with easy walking. Three lakes and large sand traps are hazards to the fine greens.
*18 holes, 6754yds, Par 71, SSS 71, Course record 66.*
*Club membership 400.*
**Visitors** must contact in advance.
**Societies** must book in advance 01952 429977 ext 297
**Green Fees** £25 weekdays (£31 per weekends).
**Facilities** ⊗ ⅢⓀ ⚑ ♥ ♀⚲ 🏠 ⚐ ㊉ℓ Graham Farr.
**Leisure** heated indoor swimming pool, squash, sauna, solarium, gymnasium, motorised carts for hire, buggies for hire, trolley for hire, driving range, putting, clay pigeon, quad bikes.
**Location** 4m S of town centre off A442
**Hotel** ★★★ 68% Telford Golf & Country Moat House, Great Hay Dr, Sutton Hill, TELFORD ☎ 01952 429977 86 ⇥ ⍩

## WELLINGTON                                       Map 07 SJ61

**Wrekin** Ercall Woods TF6 5BX ☎ 01952 244032
Downland course with some hard walking but rewarding views.
*18 holes, 5699yds, Par 67, SSS 66, Course record 44.*
*Club membership 681.*
**Visitors** must contact in advance.
**Societies** must apply in writing.
**Green Fees** £18 (£25 weekends & bank holidays).
**Facilities** ⊗ Ⅲ Ⓚ ⚑ ♥ ♀⚲ 🏠 ℓ K Housden.
**Leisure** trolley for hire, putting green, practice area.
**Location** 1.25m S off B5061
**Hotel** ★★★ 67% Buckatree Hall Hotel, The Wrekin, Wellington, TELFORD ☎ 01952 641821 64 ⇥ ⍩

## WESTON-UNDER-REDCASTLE              Map 07 SJ52

*Hawkstone Park Hotel* SY4 5UY ☎ 01939 200611
In a beautiful setting, with natural hazards and good views, Hawkstone Course has been established for over 50 years and enjoys a superb setting. A new course, the Windmill, is being developed.

*Hawkstone Course: 18 holes, 6465yds, Par 72, SSS 70.*
*Windmill Course: 18 holes, 6655yds, Par 72, SSS 72.*
*Academy Course: 6 holes, 741yds, Par 18.*
*Club membership 750.*
**Visitors** must book 7 days in advance.
**Societies** must contact in advance by telephone.
**Green Fees** not confirmed.
**Facilities** ♀⚲ 🏠 ⚐ ㊉
    ℓ Paul Brown & Damian Tudor.
**Leisure** grass tennis courts, fishing, putting, cart/buggy/trolley hire.
**Location** N side of village 0.75m E of A49

## WHITCHURCH                                       Map 07 SJ54

**Hill Valley** Terrick Rd SY13 4JZ
☎ 01948 663584
Two testing parkland courses ideally suited to the club and scratch golfer alike. The West Course, cleverly designed by Peter Alliss and Dave Thomas, has fairways that thread their way through 160 acres of trees, lakes and streams to American-style greens trapped by sand and water. Shorter East Course with smaller greens requiring accurate approach shots.
*West Course: 18 holes, 6240yds, Par 73, SSS 70, Course record 64.*
*East Course: 18 holes, 4862yds, Par 66, SSS 64.*
*Club membership 600.*
**Visitors** must contact in advance. Restricted weekends.
**Societies** must contact in advance; a deposit will be required.
**Green Fees** West: £19 (£25 weekends); East £9 (£12 weekends). Reductions Jul-Aug.
**Facilities** ⊗ Ⅲ Ⓚ ⚑ ♥ ♀⚲ 🏠 ⚐ ㊉ℓ A R Minshall.
**Leisure** hard tennis courts, sauna, gymnasium, motorised carts for hire, buggies for hire, trolley for hire, putting green, practice area, snooker.
**Location** 1m N
**Hotel** ★★★ 59% Dodington Lodge Hotel, Dodington, WHITCHURCH ☎ 01948 662539 10 ⇥ ⍩

## WORFIELD                                         Map 07 SO79

**Worfield** Roughton WV15 5HE
☎ 01746 716372 & 716357
Opened in 1991, this undulating course with good-sized greens, well placed bunkers and 2 lakes, rated highly in a golf magazine survey.
*18 holes, 6801yds, Par 73, SSS 73, Course record 68.*
**Visitors** must contact in advance, weekends only after 10am.
**Societies** contact in advance.
**Green Fees** £20 per day; £15 per round (£25/£22 weekends).
**Facilities** ⊗ Ⅲ Ⓚ ⚑ ♥ ♀⚲ 🏠 ℓ Steve Russell.
**Leisure** buggies for hire, trolley for hire, driving range, putting green, practice area.
**Location** 3m W of Bridgenorth, off A454
**Hotel** ★★★⭐ 77% Old Vicarage Hotel, WORFIELD ☎ 01746 716497 10 ⇥ ⍩ Annexe4 ⇥ ⍩

---
# SOMERSET
---

## BACKWELL        Map 03 ST46

**Tall Pines** Cooks Bridle Path, Downside BS19 3DJ
☎ 01275 472076
Parkland course with views over the Bristol Channel.
*18 holes, 5827yds, Par 70, SSS 68.*
*Club membership 500.*
| | |
|---|---|
| **Visitors** | must contact in advance. |
| **Societies** | prior arrangement by telephone for details. |
| **Green Fees** | £12 per round; £6 second round (£14 per round; £7 second round weekends & bank holidays). Twilight £8. |
| **Facilities** | ⊗ ⅢⅡ ⅢⅡ ♨ ♀ ⚲ 🏠 ( Terry Murray. |
| **Leisure** | motorised carts for hire, buggies for hire, trolley for hire, putting green, practice field. |
| **Location** | Adjacent to Bristol Airport, 1m off A38 |
| **Hotel** | ★★★ 60% Walton Park Hotel, Wellington Ter, CLEVEDON ☎ 01275 874253 41 ⇆ ℟ |

## BATH        Map 03 ST76

**Bath** Sham Castle, North Rd BA2 6JG
☎ 01225 463834 & 425182
Considered to be one of the finest courses in the west, this is the site of Bath's oldest golf club. An interesting course situated on high ground overlooking the city and with splendid views over the surrounding countryside. The rocky ground supports good quality turf and there are many good holes. The 17th is a dog-leg right past, or over the corner of an out-of-bounds wall, and thence on to an undulating green.
*18 holes, 6429yds, Par 71, SSS 71, Course record 67.*
*Club membership 750.*
| | |
|---|---|
| **Visitors** | advisable to contact in advance. |
| **Societies** | Wed & Fri by prior arrangement. |
| **Green Fees** | £30 per day; £25 per round (£35/£30 weekends & bank holidays). |
| **Facilities** | ⊗ ⅢⅡ ⅢⅡ ♨ ♀ ⚲ 🏠 ⚐ ( Peter J Hancox. |
| **Leisure** | trolley for hire, putting green, practice area. |
| **Location** | 1.5m SE city centre off A36 |
| **Hotel** | ★★★ 65% Francis Hotel, Queen Square, BATH ☎ 01225 424257 94 ⇆ ℟ |

**Entry Hill** BA2 5NA ☎ 01225 834248
*9 holes, 1922yds, Par 33, SSS 30.*
*Club membership 650.*
| | |
|---|---|
| **Visitors** | no restrictions. |
| **Societies** | bookings required in advance. |
| **Green Fees** | not confirmed. |
| **Facilities** | ⚲ 🏠 ⚐ ( Tim Tapley. |
| **Location** | Off A367 |

**Lansdown** Lansdown BA1 9BT ☎ 01225 422138
A flat parkland course situated 800 feet above sea level, providing a challenge to both low and high handicap golfers due to the strong prevailing wind that comes into play at every hole.
*18 holes, 6316yds, Par 71, SSS 70, Course record 65.*
*Club membership 790.*
| | |
|---|---|
| **Visitors** | must contact in advance to ascertain availability. |
| **Societies** | apply in writing or telephone in advance. |

| | |
|---|---|
| **Green Fees** | £24 per day; £18 per round (£30 per round/day weekends; £24 bank holidays). |
| **Facilities** | ⊗ ⅢⅡ ⅢⅡ ♨ ♀ ⚲ 🏠 ( Terry Mercer. |
| **Leisure** | trolley for hire, putting green, practice area. |
| **Location** | 6m SW of exit 18 of M4 |
| **Hotel** | ★★★ 79% The Queensberry Hotel, Russel St, BATH ☎ 01225 447928 22 ⇆ ℟ |

## BRIDGWATER        Map 03 ST23

**Cannington** Cannington College, Cannington TA5 2LS
☎ 01278 652394
Nine hole golf course of 'links-like' appearance, designed by Martin Hawtree of Oxford. The 4th hole is a challenging 464yard Par 4, slightly up hill and into the prevailing wind.
*9 holes, 2929yds, Par 34, SSS 34.*
*Club membership 200.*
| | |
|---|---|
| **Visitors** | pay & play anytime ex Wed evening. |
| **Societies** | apply in writing. |
| **Green Fees** | £10 per 18 holes (£12 weekends). Economy 9 holes £6.50 after 2.30pm winter, 6.30pm summer. |
| **Facilities** | ⊗ ♨ ⚲ 🏠 ⚐ ℟ ( Ron Macrow. |
| **Leisure** | hard tennis courts, trolley for hire, practice area, pitch & putt. |
| **Location** | 4m NW of Bridgwater of A39 |
| **Hotel** | ★★ 67% Friarn Court Hotel, 37 St Mary St, BRIDGWATER ☎ 01278 452859 16 ⇆ ℟ |

## BURNHAM-ON-SEA        Map 03 ST34

**Brean** Coast Rd, Brean Sands TA8 2RF
☎ 01278 751595 office & 751570 pro
Level and open moorland course with water hazards.
Facilities of 'Brean Leisure Park' adjoining.
*18 holes, 5715yds, Par 69, SSS 68, Course record 66.*
*Club membership 350.*
| | |
|---|---|
| **Visitors** | may not play on Sat & Sun before 1pm. Book in advance through professional. |
| **Societies** | contact office or professional in advance. |
| **Green Fees** | £18 per day; £12 per round (£15 per round weekends). |
| **Facilities** | ⊗ ⅢⅡ ⅢⅡ ♨ ♀ ⚲ 🏠 ⚐ ℟ ( G Coombe. |
| **Leisure** | heated indoor swimming pool, fishing, sauna, motorised carts for hire, buggies for hire, trolley for hire. |
| **Location** | 6m N on coast rd |
| **Hotel** | ★★ 63% Royal Clarence Hotel, 31 The Esplanade, BURNHAM-ON-SEA ☎ 01278 783138 19rm(18 ⇆ ℟) |

**Burnham & Berrow** St Christopher's Way TA8 2PE
☎ 01278 785760
Links championship course with large sandhills.
*Championship Course: 18 holes, 6447yds, Par 71, SSS 72.*
*9 Hole Course: 9 holes, 6332yds, Par 72, SSS 70.*
*Club membership 900.*
| | |
|---|---|
| **Visitors** | must contact in advance & have handicap certificate (22 or under gentlemen, 30 or under ladies) to play on the Championship course. |
| **Societies** | telephone in advance. |
| **Green Fees** | £32 per day/round (£44 weekends & bank holidays); 9 hole £8 per day/round. |

# BURNHAM and BERROW GOLF CLUB

Championship links course with panoramic views of the Somerset hills and the Devon coast line sweeping across the reed beds and the Bristol Channel with the islands of Steepholm and Flatholm standing out against the background of the Welsh coast line.

*18 holes. 6447 yards. Par 71, SSS 72, course record 66*
*9 hole course. 6332 yards. Par 72, SSS 70.*

**St Christophers Way, Burnham-on-Sea, Somerset TA8 2PE**
**Telephone: 01278 785760**
*Secretary: Mrs E L Sloman*

| | |
|---|---|
| **Facilities** | ⊗ 🍽 🛍 💺 ♀ 🧍 🏠 ⛳ ⊠ ⓕ Mark Crowther-Smith. |
| **Leisure** | motorised carts for hire, trolley for hire, putting green, practice area. |
| **Location** | 1m N of town on B3140 |
| **Hotel** | ★★ 63% Royal Clarence Hotel, 31 The Esplanade, BURNHAM-ON-SEA ☎ 01278 783138 19rm(18 ⇄ ⓝ) |
| **Additional hotel** | ★★⚄ 65% Batch Farm Country Hotel, LYMPSHAM ☎ 01934 750371 8 ⇄ |

## CHARD                                         Map 03 ST30

**Windwhistle Golf, Squash & Country Club** Cricket St Thomas TA20 4DG ☎ 01460 30231
Parkland course at 735 ft above sea level with outstanding views over the Somerset Levels to the Bristol Channel and South Wales.
*East/West Course: 18 holes, 6500yds, Par 73, SSS 71.*
*Club membership 600.*
**Visitors**     must contact in advance.

| | |
|---|---|
| **Societies** | by prior arrangement. |
| **Green Fees** | not confirmed. |
| **Facilities** | ♀ 🧍 🏠 |
| **Leisure** | squash. |
| **Location** | 3m E on A30 |
| **Hotel** | ★★ 66% Shrubbery Hotel, ILMINSTER ☎ 01460 52108 14 ⇄ ⓝ |

## CLEVEDON                                      Map 03 ST47

**Clevedon** Castle Rd, Walton St Mary BS21 7AA ·
☎ 01275 874057
Situated on the cliff-top overlooking the Severn estuary and with distant views of the Welsh coast. Excellent parkland course in first-class condition overlooking the Severn estuary. Magnificent scenery and some tremendous 'drop' holes. Strong winds.
*18 holes, 6117yds, Par 70, SSS 69, Course record 68.*
*Club membership 640.*

| | |
|---|---|
| **Visitors** | must contact in advance. No play Wed morning. |
| **Societies** | Mon & Tue only (not bank holidays), telephone or apply in writing. |
| **Green Fees** | £22 per 18/36 holes (£35 weekends & bank holidays). |
| **Facilities** | ⊗ 🍽 🛍 💺 ♀ 🧍 🏠 ⛳ ⓕ Martin Heggie. |
| **Leisure** | trolley for hire, putting green, practice area. |
| **Location** | 1m NE of town centre |
| **Hotel** | ★★★ 60% Walton Park Hotel, Wellington Ter, CLEVEDON ☎ 01275 874253 41 ⇄ ⓝ |

## CONGRESBURY                                   Map 03 ST46

**Mendip Spring** Honeyhall Ln BS19 5JT
☎ 01934 852322 & 853337
Set in peaceful countryside with the Mendip Hills as a backdrop, this 18-hole course includes lakes and numerous water hazards covering some 12 acres of the course. The 12th is an island green surrounded by water and there are long drives on the 7th and 13th. The 9-hole Lakeside course is an easy walking course, mainly par 4. Floodlit driving range.
*Brinsea Course: 18 holes, 6328yds, Par 71, SSS 70, Course record 70.*
*Lakeside: 9 holes, 4520yds, Par 68, SSS 68.*
*Club membership 370.*

| | |
|---|---|
| **Visitors** | must contact in advance for Brinsea course, Lakeside is play & pay anytime. |
| **Societies** | booking in advance by arrangement. |
| **Green Fees** | Brinsea: £22 per day; £17 per round (£25/£19 weekends). Lakeside: £6 per round. |
| **Facilities** | ⊗ 🍽 🛍 💺 ♀ 🧍 🏠 ⛳ ⓕ John Blackburn. |
| **Leisure** | buggies for hire, trolley for hire, driving range, putting green, practice area. ▶ |

# BATCH COUNTRY HOUSE HOTEL  AA

**Lympsham, Nr. Weston-super-Mare, Somerset BS24 0EX.** ★★
**Telephone: (01934) 750371 Fax: (01934) 750501**
Family run hotel with long reputation for friendly atmosphere and excellent traditional English food, a la carte menu also available. Fully licensed lounge bar. Situated in own grounds with unlimited parking. Just a short drive from Burnham-on-Sea, Weston-super-Mare and golf courses.
All bedrooms include en suite, colour TV and tea/coffee facilities.
Egon Ronay and Ashley Courtenay recommended.

**Location** 8m E of Weston-Super-Mare
**Hotel** ★★★♨ 69% Daneswood House Hotel, Cuck Hill, SHIPHAM
☎ 01934 843145 & 843945 9
⇌ ⋒Annexe3 ⇌ ⋒

---

## ENMORE
Map 03 ST23

**Enmore Park** TA5 2AN
☎ 01278 671481 & 671519 (Pro)
Hilly, parkland course with water features on foothills of Quantocks. Wooded countryside and views of Quantocks and Mendips. 1st and 10th are testing holes.
*18 holes, 6406yds, Par 71, SSS 71, Course record 64.*
*Club membership 750.*
**Visitors** phone professional for details.
**Societies** must apply in writing.
**Green Fees** £25 per day; £18 per round (£25 weekends).
**Facilities** ⊗ ⅷ �ⓛ ⬤ ♀ ⚲ ⌂ ⚐ ⌀ Nigel Wixon.
**Leisure** motorised carts for hire, buggies for hire, trolley for hire, putting green, practice area.
**Location** A39 to Minehead, at first set of lights trn left to Spaxton, then 1.5m to reservoir and turn left
**Hotel** ★★★ 72% Walnut Tree Hotel, North Petherton, BRIDGWATER
☎ 01278 662255 32 ⇌

---

## FARRINGTON GURNEY
Map 03 ST65

**Farrington** Marsh Ln BS18 5TS
☎ 01761 241274 & 241787
USGA spec greens on both challenging 9 and 18 hole courses. Newly completed 18 hole course with computerised irrigation, six lakes, four tees per hole and excellent views. Testing holes include the 12th (282yds) with the green set behind a lake at the base of a 100ft drop, and the 17th which is played between two lakes.
*Executive Course: 9 holes, 3022yds, Par 54, SSS 53, Course record 57.*
*Main Course: 18 holes, 6693yds, Par 72, SSS 72.*
*Club membership 500.*
**Visitors** starting times at weekends.
**Societies** welcome except for weekends & bank holidays, telephone or write in advance.
**Green Fees** Executive: £10 per day; £6 per round (£12/£8 weekends). Main: £18 per day; £12 per round (£20/£15 weekends).
**Facilities** ⊗ ⅷ ⓛ ⬤ ♀ ⚲ ⌂ ⚐ ⌀ Peter Thompson.
**Leisure** sauna, buggies for hire, trolley for hire, floodlit driving range, putting green, practice area.
**Hotel** ★★ 69% Country Ways Hotel, Marsh Ln, FARRINGTON GURNEY
☎ 01761 452449 6 ⇌ ⋒

---

## FROME
Map 03 ST74

*Orchardleigh* BA11 2PH ☎ 01373 454200
This course is due to open April 1996 so please check any information before visiting. Originally designed by Ryder Cup golfer, Brian Huggett, as two returning nines through mature parkland. Five new lakes bring water into play on seven holes.
*18 holes, 6810yds, Par 72, SSS 73.*
**Visitors** no visitors before 10.30am at weekends and bank holidays.

---

**Societies** apply in writing or telephone in advance.
**Green Fees** not confirmed.
**Facilities** ⚐
**Leisure** fishing, driving range,putting green,practice area,cart/buggy/trolley hire.
**Location** 1m W of Frome on the A362
**Hotel** ★★ 67% The George at Nunney, 11 Church St, NUNNEY
☎ 01373 836458 9 ⇌ ⋒

---

## GURNEY SLADE
Map 03 ST64

**Mendip** BA3 4UT ☎ 01749 840570
Undulating downland course offering an interesting test of golf on superb fairways.
*18 holes, 6330yds, Par 71, SSS 70, Course record 65.*
*Club membership 900.*
**Visitors** must contact in advance.
**Societies** by arrangement with secretary.
**Green Fees** not confirmed.
**Facilities** ⊗ ⅷ ⓛ ⬤ ♀ ⚲ ⌂ ⚐ ⌀ Ron Lee.
**Leisure** motorised carts for hire, buggies for hire, trolley for hire, putting green, practice area.
**Location** 1.5m S off A37
**Hotel** ★★★ 66% Centurion Hotel, Charlton Ln, MIDSOMER NORTON
☎ 01761 417711 44 ⇌ ⋒

---

## KEYNSHAM
Map 03 ST66

**Stockwood Vale** Stockwood Ln BS18 2ER
☎ 0117 986 6505
Undulating and challenging public course in a beautiful setting with interesting well bunkered holes, in particular the superb par 5 556 yrd 7th hole. Good views.
*9 holes, 2760yds, Par 35, SSS 67.*
*Club membership 300.*
**Visitors** no restrictions, but must reserve a start time.
**Societies** telephone in advance.
**Green Fees** £10 per 18 holes; £5.50 per 9 holes (£12/£6 weekends).
**Facilities** ⊗ ⅷ ⓛ ⬤ ♀ ⚲ ⌂ ⌀ Kelvin Aitken.
**Leisure** driving range, putting green.
**Hotel** ★★ 73% Chelwood House Hotel, CHELWOOD
☎ 01761 490730 11 ⇌ ⋒

---

## LANGPORT
Map 03 ST42

**Long Sutton** Long Sutton TA10 9JU
☎ 01458 241017
Gentle, undulating, Pay and Play course.
*18 holes, 6367yds, Par 71, SSS 70, Course record 71.*
*Club membership 500.*
**Visitors** advisable to book in advance.
**Societies** telephone in advance.
**Green Fees** £12 per round (£16 weekends).
**Facilities** ⊗ ⅷ ⓛ ⬤ ♀ ⚲ ⌂ ⚐ ⌀ Michael Blackwell.
**Leisure** trolley for hire, floodlit driving range, putting green, practice area, snooker.
**Location** 5m NW of Yeovil off A372
**Hotel** ★★★ 70% The Hollies, Bower Hinton, MARTOCK
☎ 01935 822232 Annexe30 ⇌ ⋒

## LONG ASHTON        Map 03 ST57

**Long Ashton** The Clubhouse BS18 9DW
☎ 01275 392316 & 392265
Wooded parkland course with nice turf, wonderful views of
Bristol and surrounding areas and a spacious practice area.
Good testing holes, especially the back nine, in prevailing
south-west winds. The short second hole (126yds) cut from
an old quarry and played over a road can ruin many a card!
Good drainage ensures pleasant winter golf.
*18 holes, 6077yds, Par 70, SSS 70, Course record 66.*
*Club membership 700.*
**Visitors** recommended to telephone the professional.
**Societies** must contact the secretary in advance.
**Green Fees** £26 per round (£35 weekends & bank holidays).
**Facilities** ⊗ ▮ ⬛ ♀ ⅄ 🏠 ℓ Denis Scanlan.
**Leisure** trolley for hire, putting green, practice area.
**Location** 0.5m N on B3128
**Hotel** ★★★ 66% Redwood Lodge Hotel, Country
Club Resort, Beggar Bush Ln, Failand,
BRISTOL ☎ 01275 393901 108 ⇥ ℞

**Woodspring Golf & Country Club** Yanley Ln BS18 9LR
☎ 01275 394378
Set in 180 acres of undulating heathland featuring superb
natural water hazards, protected greens and a rising
landscape. Designed by Peter Alliss and Clive Clark and laid
out by Donald Steel, the course has three individual 9-hole
courses, the Avon, Severn & Brunel. The 9th hole on the
Brunel course is a feature hole here, with an elevated tee shot
over a natural gorge. In undulating hills south of Bristol, long
carries to tight fairways, elevated island tees and difficult
approaches to greens make the most of the 27 holes.
*Avon Course: 9 holes, 2960yds, Par 35.*
*Brunel Course: 9 holes, 3261yds, Par 37.*
*Severn Course: 9 holes, 3340yds, Par 36.*
*Club membership 800.*
**Visitors** must contact in advance, weekends may be
limited.
**Societies** must contact Head Professional in advance.
**Green Fees** £20 per 18 holes (£30 weekends & bank
holidays).
**Facilities** ⊗ ℳ ▮ ⬛ ♀ ⅄ 🏠 ⛳ ℓ Mark Pierce.
**Leisure** sauna, motorised carts for hire, buggies for hire,
trolley for hire, driving range, putting green.
**Location** Off A38 Bridgewater Road
**Hotel** ★★★ 66% Redwood Lodge Hotel, Country
Club Resort, Beggar Bush Ln, Failand,
BRISTOL ☎ 01275 393901 108 ⇥ ℞

## MIDSOMER NORTON        Map 03 ST65

**Fosseway Country Club** Charlton Ln BA3 4BD
☎ 01761 412214
Very attractive tree-lined parkland course, not demanding but
with lovely views towards the Mendip Hills.
*9 holes, 4278yds, Par 68, SSS 65.*
*Club membership 400.*
**Visitors** may not play on Wed evenings, Sat & Sun
mornings & competitions days.
**Societies** apply in writing or telephone.
**Green Fees** £8 (£10 weekends & bank holidays).
**Facilities** ⊗ ℳ ▮ ⬛ ♀ ⅄ 🏠 ⋈
**Leisure** heated indoor swimming pool, squash, putting
green, practice area.

*THE IDEAL VENUE*

# CENTURI⊗N
### H O T E L S

20 MINUTES FROM BATH CITY CENTRE
44 LUXURY EN SUITE BEDROOMS
RESTAURANT • CONFERENCE FACILITIES
FULL SIZE 9 HOLE COURSE
BOWLING GREEN • SQUASH COURTS
SWIMMING POOL • INDOOR BOWL GREEN

*Please see entry under*    ★ ★ ★
MIDSOMER NORTON
**(01761) 417711**   ***AA***
FAX (01761) 418357
CHARLTON LANE, MIDSOMER NORTON,
BATH BA3 4BD
*MAJOR CREDIT CARDS ACCEPTED*

**Location** SE of town centre off A367
**Hotel** ★★★ 66% Centurion Hotel, Charlton Ln,
MIDSOMER NORTON
☎ 01761 417711 44 ⇥ ℞

## MINEHEAD        Map 03 SS94

**Minehead & West Somerset** The Warren TA24 5SJ
☎ 01643 702057
Flat seaside links, very exposed to wind, with good turf
set on a shingle bank. The last five holes adjacent to the
beach are testing. The 215-yard 18th is wedged between
the beach and the club buildings and provides a good
finish.
*18 holes, 6228yds, Par 71, SSS 71, Course record 65.*
*Club membership 620.*
**Visitors** must contact secretary in advance.
**Societies** telephone in advance.
**Green Fees** £22 (£25 weekends & bank holidays).
**Facilities** ⊗ ℳ ▮ ⬛ ♀ ⅄ 🏠 ⛳ ℓ Ian Read.
**Leisure** trolley for hire, putting green, practice area.
**Location** E end of esplanade
**Hotel** ★★★ 68% Northfield Hotel, Northfield Rd,
MINEHEAD
☎ 01643 705155 24 ⇥ ℞

## SALTFORD        Map 03 ST66

*Saltford* Golf Club Ln BS18 3AA
☎ 01225 873220 & 872043
Parkland course with easy walking and panoramic views over
the Avon Valley. The par 4, 2nd and 13th are notable. ▶

*18 holes, 6081yds, Par 69, SSS 69.*
*Club membership 800.*
**Visitors** must contact in advance & have handicap certificate.
**Societies** must telephone in advance.
**Green Fees** not confirmed.
**Facilities** ♀ ♣ 🏠 ⛳ ℓ Dudley Millinstead.
**Leisure** caddy cars.
**Location** S side of village
**Hotel** ★★★(red)🏵 Hunstrete House Hotel, CHELWOOD
☎ 01761 490490 13 ⇄ ℓ Annexe11 ⇄ ℓ

### SOMERTON Map 03 ST42

**Wheathill** Wheathill TA11 7HG
☎ 01963 240667
A Par 68 parkland course with nice views in quiet countryside. It is flat lying with the 13th hole along the river.
*18 holes, 5362yds, Par 68, SSS 66.*
*Club membership 300.*
**Visitors** no restrictions.
**Societies** telephone to arrange.
**Green Fees** £12 per day; £10 per round (£15/£13 weekends).
**Facilities** ⊗ ⅢⅢ ⅃ 💺 ♀ ♣ 🏠 ⛳ ℓ A England.
**Leisure** motorised carts for hire, buggies for hire, trolley for hire, practice area.
**Location** 5m E of Somerton off B3153
**Hotel** ★★★ 63% Wessex Hotel, High St, STREET
☎ 01458 443383 50 ⇄ ℓ

### TAUNTON Map 03 ST22

**Oake Manor** Oake TA4 1BA
☎ 01823 461993
A parkland/lakeland course situated in breathtaking Somerset countryside with views of the Quantock, Blackdown and Brendon Hills. Ten holes feature water hazards such as lakes, cascades and a trout stream. The 15th hole (Par 5, 476yds) is bounded by water all down the left with a carry over another lake on to an island green. The course is great fun for all standards of golfer.
*18 holes, 6109yds, Par 70, SSS 69.*
*Club membership 600.*
**Visitors** no restrictions but visitors must book in advance.
**Societies** contact Russell Gardner by telephone.
**Green Fees** £22 per day; £14.50 per round; £8 3´ hours before dark. (£26/£16/£8 weekends).
**Facilities** ⊗ ⅢⅢ ⅃ 💺 ♀ ♣ 🏠 ⛳ ℓ Russell Gardner.
**Leisure** motorised carts for hire, trolley for hire, driving range, putting green, practice area, teaching academy.
**Location** Exit M5 junct 26, take A38 towards Taunton and follow signs to Oake
**Hotel** ★★★ 69% Rumwell Manor Hotel, Rumwell, TAUNTON
☎ 01823 461902 10 ⇄ ℓ Annexe10 ⇄ ℓ

*Taunton & Pickeridge* Corfe TA3 7BY
☎ 01823 421537
Downland course with extensive views.
*18 holes, 5927yds, Par 69, SSS 68, Course record 61.*
*Club membership 600.*
**Visitors** must have a handicap certificate

**Societies** must telephone in advance.
**Green Fees** not confirmed.
**Facilities** ♀ ♣ 🏠 ℓ Gary Milne.
**Leisure** putting green/practice area,trolley hire.
**Location** 4m S off B3170
**Hotel** ★★★ 78% The Mount Somerset Hotel, Henlade, TAUNTON
☎ 01823 442500 11 ⇄ ℓ

**Taunton Vale** Creech Heathfield TA3 5EY
☎ 01823 412220 & 412880
An 18 hole and a 9 hole golf course in a parkland complex occupying 156 acres in the Vale of Taunton. Complex includes a floodlit driving range.
*Charlton Course: 18 holes, 6142yds, Par 70, SSS 69, Course record 66.*
*Durston Course: 9 holes, 2004yds, Par 64, SSS 60.*
*Club membership 640.*
**Visitors** telephone booking essential.
**Societies** must book in advance.
**Green Fees** 18 holes: £20 per day; £14 per round (£25/£17.50 weekends). 9 holes: £10 per day; £7 per round (£13/£8.75 weekends).
**Facilities** ⊗ ⅃ 💺 ♀ ♣ 🏠 ⛳ ℓ Martin Keitch.
**Leisure** trolley for hire, driving range, putting green.
**Location** Off A361 at junct with A38
**Hotel** ★★★ 69% Rumwell Manor Hotel, Rumwell, TAUNTON
☎ 01823 461902 10 ⇄ ℓ Annexe10 ⇄ ℓ

**Vivary Park Municipal** Fons George TA1 3JU
☎ 01823 333875
A parkland course, tight and narrow with ponds.
*18 holes, 4620yds, Par 63, SSS 63, Course record 60.*
*Club membership 700.*
**Visitors** may play anytime except weekends before 10.30, bookings can be made 8 days in advance.
**Societies** apply in writing.
**Green Fees** £7.50 per day.
**Facilities** ⊗ ⅢⅢ ⅃ 💺 ♀ ♣ 🏠 ⛳ ℓ Mike Steadman.
**Leisure** hard tennis courts, trolley for hire, putting green, practice area.
**Location** S side of town centre off A38
**Hotel** ★★ 64% Falcon Hotel, Henlade, TAUNTON
☎ 01823 442502 11 ⇄ ℓ

### WEDMORE Map 03 ST44

**Isle of Wedmore** Lineage BS28 4QT
☎ 01934 713649 (Office) & 712452 (Pro)
Gentle undulating course designed to maintain natural environment. Existing woodland and hedgerow enhanced by new planting. Magnificent panoramic views of Cheddar Valley and Glastonbury Tor.
*18 holes, 5854yds, Par 68, Course record 70.*
*Club membership 560.*
**Visitors** phone professional in advance.
**Societies** weekdays only, telephone in advance.
**Green Fees** £20 per day; £15 per round (£25/£20 weekends).
**Facilities** ⊗ ⅢⅢ ⅃ 💺 ♀ ♣ 🏠 ⛳ ℓ Graham Coombe.
**Leisure** trolley for hire, putting green, practice area.
**Location** Off B3139 between Wells & Burnham-on-Sea
**Hotel** ★★★ 68% Swan Hotel, Sadler St, WELLS
☎ 01749 678877 38 ⇄ ℓ

## AA ★★ 64%

# *Beachlands Hotel*

### *Only a Wedge Shot from the 1st tee!!*

**Commended** 👑👑👑👑

Perhaps it's the Tom Dunne designed Championship course or the fact that the links are practically playable all year. On the othe hand it may be the excellent Hotel & Restaurant and its reputation for quality & service. complete with the 55 malts available in the bar, or the high level of comfort in the 18 ensuite bedrooms. Whatever it is, one thing is for sure – guests of the Beachlands Hotel & Weston-uper-Mare Links Golf Course come back time and time again!! Contact Charles Porter for details on Breaks for individuals, groups & societies from as little as £52.50 per person per day – Dinner, Bed & Breakfast and Green Fees.

*Uphill Road North, Weston-super-Mare BS23 4NG. Tel: (01934) 621401 Fax: (01934) 621966*

## WELLS          Map 03 ST54

**Wells (Somerset)** East Horrington Rd BA5 3DS
☎ 01749 675005
Beautiful wooded course with wonderful views. The prevailing SW wind complicates the 448-yd, 3rd.
*18 holes, 6015yds, Par 70, SSS 69, Course record 66.*
*Club membership 775.*

| | |
|---|---|
| Visitors | must contact in advance & have handicap certificate weekends. Tee times restricted at weekends to after 9.30pm |
| Societies | must apply in advance. |
| Green Fees | £20 per day; £18 per round (£25/£22 weekends & public holidays). |
| Facilities | ⊗ ⊞ ⅃ ♥ ♀ ⚘ 🏠 ⚐ ℓ Adrian Bishop. |
| Leisure | motorised carts for hire, trolley for hire, putting green, practice area. |
| Location | 1.5m E off B3139 |
| Hotel | ★★★ 68% Swan Hotel, Sadler St, WELLS ☎ 01749 678877 38 ⇆ 🐾 |

## WESTON-SUPER-MARE       Map 03 ST36

**Puxton Park** Puxton Ln, Hewish BS24 6TA
☎ 01934 876942
A Pay and Play course built on flat moorland dissected by a network of waterways.
*18 holes, 6636yds, Par 72, SSS 71.*
*Club membership 250.*

| | |
|---|---|
| Visitors | must contact in advance. |
| Societies | apply in advance. |
| Green Fees | not confirmed. |
| Facilities | ♀ ⚘ 🏠 ⚐ ℓ Mike Smedley. |
| Leisure | practice area,trolley hire. |
| Location | 2m junc 21 of M5 on A370 |
| Hotel | ★★★ 68% Commodore Hotel, Beach Rd, Sand Bay, Kewstoke, WESTON-SUPER-MARE ☎ 01934 415778 12 ⇆ 🐾Annexe6 ⇆ 🐾 |

**Weston-super-Mare** Uphill Rd North BS23 4NQ
☎ 01934 626968 & 633360
A compact and interesting layout with the opening hole adjacent to the beach. The sandy, links-type course is slightly undulating and has beautifully maintained turf and greens. The 15th is a testing 455-yard, par 4.
*18 holes, 6300yds, Par 70, SSS 70, Course record 65.*
*Club membership 840.*

| | |
|---|---|
| Visitors | must have handicap certificate to play at weekends. |
| Societies | apply in writing or telephone. |
| Green Fees | £24 per day, £15 after 5pm (£35 per day weekends). |
| Facilities | ⊗ ⊞ ⅃ ♥ ♀ ⚘ 🏠 ℓ Paul Barrington. |
| Leisure | trolley for hire, putting green, practice area. |
| Location | S side of town centre off A370 |
| Hotel | ★★ 64% Beachlands Hotel, 17 Uphill Rd North, WESTON-SUPER-MARE ☎ 01934 621401 17 ⇆ 🐾 |
| Additional hotel | ★★ 64% Rozel Hotel, Madeira Cove, WESTON-SUPER-MARE ☎ 01934 415268 46 ⇆ 🐾 |

**Worlebury** Monks Hill BS22 9SX
☎ 01934 623789 & 623214
Situated on the ridge of Worlebury Hill, this seaside course offers fairly easy walking and extensive views of the Severn estuary and Wales.
*18 holes, 5963yds, Par 70, SSS 69, Course record 66.*
*Club membership 590.*

| | |
|---|---|
| Visitors | must be recognised golfers, handicap certificate or proof of club membership may be required |
| Societies | apply in writing or telephone in advance. |
| Green Fees | £20 per day (£30 weekends, £12 Sun after 2pm). |
| Facilities | ⊗ ⊞ ⅃ ♥ ♀ ⚘ 🏠 ℓ Gary Marks. |
| Leisure | trolley for hire, putting green, practice area. |
| Location | 5m NE off A370 |
| Hotel | ★★★ 59% Royal Pier Hotel, Birnbeck Rd, WESTON-SUPER-MARE ☎ 01934 626644 40 ⇆ 🐾 |

Large Garage and Heated Swimming Pool

# *Rozel Hotel*

Air Conditioned Conference & Banqueting Suite

# Madiera Cove, Weston-super-Mare BS23 2BU
## Telephone: (01934) 415268   Fax: (01934) 644364

The Rozel Hotel is Weston's premier Golf Hotel. A family run hotel for over 70 years which has been sympathetically modernised year after year. All rooms are en-suite with direct dial telephone, colour television, tea and coffee making facilities and computerised alarm call. Tee times and special rates can be organised for all the local courses so your golf days will go by without a hitch. 👑👑👑👑

## and Worlebury & Weston Golf Clubs

Just minutes away from these most enjoyable and quite differing courses, the Commodore caters for the every need of those seeking rest, relaxation and recreation. Stylishly appointed modern bedrooms, traditional bar and a choice of buffet/carvery or modern English cuisine in "Alices" restaurant dedicated to fine food and excellent service. Please telephone our Sales Office for details of year round short breaks and weekly terms plus preferential green fees.

✿  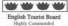 Ashley Courtney
★★★ English Tourist Board    Highly
Highly Commended    Recommended

### The Commodore Hotel
Beach Road, Sand Bay, Kewstoke,
Weston-super-Mare, Avon BS22 9UZ
Telephone Weston-super-Mare
(01934) 415778

---

Additional ★★★ 68% Commodore Hotel, Beach Rd, Sand
hotel    Bay, Kewstoke, WESTON-SUPER-MARE
☎ 01934 415778 12 ⇔ ʀAnnexe6 ⇔ ʀ

---

## YEOVIL    Map 03 ST51

**Yeovil** Sherborne Rd BA21 5BW
☎ 01935 75949
The opener lies by the River Yeo before the gentle climb to high downs with good views. The outstanding 14th and 15th holes present a challenge, being below the player with a deep railway cutting on the left of the green.
*Old Course: 18 holes, 6144yds, Par 72, SSS 69, Course record 64.*
*Newton Course: 9 holes, 4891yds, Par 68, SSS 65.*
*Club membership 1000.*
Visitors    must contact in advance. Members only before 9.30am and 12.30-2.
Societies    telephone in advance.
Green Fees Old Course: £20 per day/round (£25 weekends). Newton Course: £12 per day/round (£15 weekends).
Facilities    ⊗ ⅢⅢ ⅬⅬ ⧫ ⭗ ⚎ 🏠 ⚐ ʄ Geoff Kite.
Leisure    trolley for hire, putting green, practice area.
Location    1m E on A30
Hotel    ★★★ 59% The Manor Hotel, Hendford, YEOVIL
☎ 01935 23116 due to change to 423116 20 ⇔ ʀAnnexe21 ⇔ ʀ

---

## STAFFORDSHIRE

### BARLASTON    Map 07 SJ83

**Barlaston** Meaford Rd ST15 8UX
☎ 01782 372795 & 372867
Picturesque meadowland course designed by Peter Alliss.
*18 holes, 5800yds, Par 69, SSS 68.*
*Club membership 600.*
Visitors    may not play before 10am weekends and bank holidays.
Societies    telephone or apply in writing.
Green Fees not confirmed.
Facilities    ⚎ ⧫ 🏠 ʄ Ian Rogers.
Leisure    putting green.
Hotel    ★★★ 70% Stone House Hotel, Stafford Rd, STONE ☎ 01785 815531 47 ⇔ ʀ

---

### BROCTON    Map 07 SJ91

**Brocton Hall** ST17 0TH
☎ 01785 661901
Parkland course with gentle slopes in places, easy walking.
*18 holes, 6095yds, Par 69, SSS 69, Course record 67.*
*Club membership 665.*
Visitors    not competition days. Must contact in advance.
Societies    must apply in advance.
Green Fees £25 per day (£30 weekends & bank holidays).
Facilities    ⊗ ⅢⅢ ⅬⅬ ⧫ ⚎ ⧫ 🏠 ⚐ ʄ R G Johnson.
Leisure    trolley for hire, putting green, practice area.
Location    NW side of village off A34
Hotel    ★★★ 65% Garth Hotel, Wolverhampton Rd, Moss Pit, STAFFORD
☎ 01785 56124 60 ⇔ ʀ

---

### BURTON-UPON-TRENT    Map 07 SK22

**Branston** Burton Rd, Branston DE14 3DP
☎ 01283 543207 & 512211
Parkland course, adjacent to River Trent, on undulating ground with natural water hazards.
*18 holes, 6632yds, Par 71, SSS 72, Course record 70.*
*Club membership 800.*
Visitors    must contact in advance.
Societies    must telephone in advance.
Green Fees £30 per day; £20 per round.
Facilities    ⊗ ⅢⅢ ⅬⅬ ⧫ ⚎ ⧫ 🏠 ⚐ 🏠 ʄ Gary Prince.
Leisure    heated indoor swimming pool, fishing, sauna, solarium, gymnasium, motorised carts for hire, buggies for hire, trolley for hire, driving range, putting green, practice area.
Location    1.5m SW on A5121
Hotel    ★★★ 68% Riverside Hotel, Riverside Dr, Branston, BURTON UPON TRENT
☎ 01283 511234 22 ⇔ ʀ

---

**Burton-upon-Trent** 43 Ashby Rd East DE15 0PS
☎ 01283 544551 & 562240
Undulating parkland course with trees a major feature. There are testing par 3s at 10th and 12th. The 18th has a lake around its green.
*18 holes, 6579yds, Par 71, SSS 71, Course record 63.*
*Club membership 600.*

**Visitors**   must contact in advance and have a handicap certificate.
**Societies**   must contact in advance.
**Green Fees**   £27 per day; £23 per round (£33 per day; £28 per round weekends & bank holidays).
**Facilities**   ⊗ ⅷ by prior arrangement ⓑ ♨ ♀ ⚏ 🏠 🏌
           𝄽 Gary Stafford.
**Leisure**   trolley for hire, putting green, practice area, snooker.
**Location**   3m E on A50
**Hotel**   ★★★ 68% Riverside Hotel, Riverside Dr, Branston, BURTON UPON TRENT
          ☎ 01283 511234 22 ⇆ ▮

---

**Craythorne** Craythorne Rd, Stretton DE13 0AZ
☎ 01283 564329
A relatively short and challenging parkland course with tight fairways and views of the Trent Valley. Excellent greens. Suits all standards but particularly good for society players.
*18 holes, 5255yds, Par 68, SSS 67, Course record 66.*
*Club membership 480.*
**Visitors**   must contact in advance.
**Societies**   apply in writing or telephone for details.
**Green Fees**   £17 per round (£20 weekends).
**Facilities**   ⊗ ⅷ ⓑ ♨ ♀ ⚏ 🏠 🏌
           𝄽 Steve Hadfield.
**Leisure**   trolley for hire, driving range, putting green, practice area.
**Location**   Off A38 through Stretton village
**Hotel**   ★★★ 68% Riverside Hotel, Riverside Dr, Branston, BURTON UPON TRENT
          ☎ 01283 511234 22 ⇆ ▮

---

**Hoar Cross Hall Health Spa Golf Course** Hoar Cross DE13 8QS ☎ 01283 575671
Newly constructed academy course located in the grounds of a stately home, now a well appointed health spa resort and hotel. Driving range, bunker and practice areas.
*Club membership 300.*
**Visitors**   day guests & residents.
**Societies**   golfing societies that are resident only.
**Green Fees**   on application.
**Facilities**   ⊗ ⅷ ⓑ ♨ ♀ after 6pm ⚏ 🏠 🏌 🥢
           𝄽 Neil Allsebrook.
**Leisure**   hard tennis courts, heated indoor swimming pool, sauna, solarium, gymnasium, driving range, putting green, practice area, health & beauty treatments.
**Hotel**   ★★★★ 67% Hoar Cross Hall Health Spa, Hoar Cross, BURTON UPON TRENT
          ☎ 01283 575671 86 ⇆ ▮

---

**CANNOCK**                                          Map 07 SJ91

**Cannock Park** Stafford Rd WS11 2AL
☎ 01543 578850
Part of a large leisure centre, this parkland-type course plays alongside Cannock Chase. Good drainage, open most of year.
*18 holes, 5149yds, Par 67, SSS 65.*
*Club membership 250.*
**Visitors**   must book in advance.
**Societies**   must contact in advance.
**Green Fees**   £6.50 per round (£7.50 weekends).
**Facilities**   ⊗ ⅷ ⓑ ♨ ♀ ⚏ 🏠 🏌
           𝄽 David Dunk.

**Leisure**   hard tennis courts, heated indoor swimming pool, sauna, solarium, gymnasium, trolley for hire, putting green, indoor bowls, badminton.
**Location**   4m S of Brocton
**Hotel**   ★★★ 66% Roman Way Hotel, Watling St, Hatherton, CANNOCK
          ☎ 01543 572121 56 ⇆ ▮

---

**ENVILLE**                                          Map 07 SO88

**Enville** Highgate Common DY7 5BN
☎ 01384 872047 (Office) & 872585 (Pro shop)
Easy walking on two fairly flat parkland/moorland courses - the 'Highgate' and the 'Lodge'.
*Highgate Course: 18 holes, 6556yds, Par 72, SSS 72, Course record 65.*
*Lodge Course: 18 holes, 6217yds, Par 70, SSS 70, Course record 65.*
*Club membership 900.*
**Visitors**   must play with member at weekends.
**Societies**   phone initially for details.
**Green Fees**   £36 per 36 holes; £30 per 27 holes; £25 per 18 holes.
**Facilities**   ⊗ ⅷ ⓑ ♨ ♀ ⚏ 🏠 𝄽 Sean Power.
**Leisure**   motorised carts for hire, buggies for hire, trolley for hire.
**Location**   Take A458 towards Bridgnorth, after 4.5m turn right. Golf club signposted
**Hotel**   ★★ 65% Talbot Hotel, High St, STOURBRIDGE
          ☎ 01384 394350 25 ⇆ ▮

---

**GOLDENHILL**                                       Map 07 SJ85

**Goldenhill** Mobberley Rd ST6 5SS
☎ 01782 784715
Rolling parkland course with water features on six of the back nine holes.
*18 holes, 5957yds, Par 71, SSS 68.*
*Club membership 400.*
**Visitors**   contact in advance for weekend play.
**Societies**   must apply in writing.
**Green Fees**   not confirmed.
**Facilities**   ♀ ⚏ 🏠 🏌 𝄽 Tony Clingan.
**Location**   On A50, 4m N of Stoke
**Hotel**   ★★★ 66% Manor House Hotel, Audley Rd, ALSAGER
          ☎ 01270 884000 57 ⇆ ▮

---

**HAZELSLADE**                                       Map 07 SK01

**Beau Desert** Ringeley Rd WS12 5PJ
☎ 01543 422626
Woodland course.
*18 holes, 6310yds, Par 70, SSS 71, Course record 64.*
*Club membership 500.*
**Visitors**   are advised to contact in advance.
**Societies**   must contact in advance.
**Green Fees**   £35 per day (£45 weekends).
**Facilities**   ⊗ ⅷ ⓑ ♨ ♀ ⚏ 🏠 🏌 𝄽 Barry Stevens.
**Leisure**   trolley for hire, putting green, practice area.
**Location**   0.5m NE of village
**Hotel**   ★★★ 66% Roman Way Hotel, Watling St, Hatherton, CANNOCK
          ☎ 01543 572121 56 ⇆ ▮

## HIMLEY
Map 07 SO89

**Himley Hall Golf Centre** Log Cabin, Himley Hall Park DY3 4DF ☎ 01902 895207
Parkland course set in grounds of Himley Hall Park, with lovely views. Large practice area including a pitch-and-putt.
*9 holes, 6215yds, Par 72, SSS 70, Course record 69.*
*Club membership 200.*
**Visitors** restricted weekends.
**Green Fees** £7 per 18 holes; £4.80 per 9 holes (£7.50/£5 weekends).
**Facilities** ☵ 🏠
**Leisure** trolley for hire, driving range, putting green, practice area.
**Location** 0.5m E on B4176
**Hotel** ★★★ 59% Himley Country Hotel, School Rd, HIMLEY ☎ 01902 896716 73 ⇌ ⬧

## LEEK
Map 07 SJ95

**Leek** Birchall, Cheddleton Rd ST13 5RE ☎ 01538 384779
Undulating, challenging moorland course.
*18 holes, 6240yds, Par 70, SSS 70, Course record 63.*
*Club membership 750.*
**Visitors** must contact in advance.
**Societies** must apply in advance.
**Green Fees** £24 per day (£30 weekends & bank holidays).
**Facilities** ⊗ ⅏ ⅃ ☵ ♀ ⅄ 🏠 ⅂ Peter A Stubbs.
**Leisure** trolley for hire, putting green, practice area.
**Location** 0.75m S on A520
**Hotel** ★★ 64% Bank End Farm Motel, Leek Old Rd, Longsdon ☎ 01538 383638 10rm(9 ⇌ ⬧)

**Westwood (Leek)** Newcastle Rd ST13 1AA
☎ 01538 398385
A challenging moorland/parkland course.
*18 holes, 6207yds, Par 70, SSS 69.*
*Club membership 700.*
**Visitors** no visitors on Sun and Sat before 1pm.
**Societies** apply by phone or in writing.
**Green Fees** not confirmed.
**Facilities** ⊗ ⅏ ⅃ ☵ ♀ ⅄ 🏠 ⅂ Darren Lewis.
**Leisure** trolley for hire, putting green, practice area.
**Location** On A53, S of Leek
**Hotel** ★★ 64% Bank End Farm Motel, Leek Old Rd, Longsdon ☎ 01538 383638 10rm(9 ⇌ ⬧)

## LICHFIELD
Map 07 SK10

**Seedy Mill** Elmhurst WS13 8HE ☎ 01543 417333
New, gently-rolling parkland course in picturesque rural setting. Lakes and streams are abundant, and there are four challenging Par 3s. Well contoured green, good bunkering. Also a superb 9-hole Par 3 course.
*18 holes, 6308yds, Par 72, SSS 70.*
*Club membership 800.*
**Visitors** must contact in advance. May play weekends after 1pm.
**Societies** phone for details,
**Green Fees** £17 (£22 weekends).
**Facilities** ⊗ ⅏ ⅃ ☵ ♀ ⅄ 🏠 ⅂ Richard O'Hanlon.
**Leisure** motorised carts for hire, buggies for hire, trolley for hire, driving range, 9 hole par 3 course, putting, practice area.

**Location** At Elmhurst, 1.5m N of Lichfield, off A515
**Hotel** ★★★ 65% Little Barrow Hotel, Beacon St, LICHFIELD ☎ 01543 414500 24 ⇌ ⬧

**Whittington Heath** Tamworth Rd WS14 9PW
☎ 01543 432317
18 magnificent holes winding their way through heathland and trees, presenting a good test for the serious golfer. Leaving the fairway can be severely punished. The dog-legs are most tempting, inviting the golfer to chance his arm. Local knowledge is a definite advantage. Clear views of the famous three spires of Lichfield Cathedral.
*18 holes, 6448yds, Par 70, SSS 70, Course record 65.*
*Club membership 660.*
**Visitors** must contact in advance. May not play at weekends.
**Societies** welcome Wed & Thu, must apply in writing.
**Green Fees** £32 per day/round.
**Facilities** ⊗ ⅏ ⅃ ☵ ♀ ⅄ 🏠 ⅂ Adrian Sadler.
**Leisure** trolley for hire, putting green, practice area.
**Location** 2.5m SE on A51
**Hotel** ★★★ 65% Little Barrow Hotel, Beacon St, LICHFIELD
☎ 01543 414500 24 ⇌ ⬧

## NEWCASTLE-UNDER-LYME
Map 07 SJ84

**Newcastle Municipal** Newcastle Rd, Keele ST5 5AB
☎ 01782 627596
Open course on the side of a hill without mature trees.
*18 holes, 6396yds, Par 71, SSS 70, Course record 64.*
*Club membership 297.*
**Visitors** must contact in advance.
**Societies** by prior arrangement to Newcastle-Under-Lyme Borough Council, Civic Offices, Merrial St, Newcastle-Under-Lyme, Staffs.
**Green Fees** £6.40 per round (£8.60 weekends).
**Facilities** ⊗ ⅃ ☵ ♀ 🏠 ⅂ Colin Smith.
**Leisure** trolley for hire, driving range, putting green.
**Location** 2m W on A525
**Hotel** B Forte Posthouse Newcastle under Lyme, Clayton Rd, NEWCASTLE-UNDER-LYME ☎ 01782 717171 119 ⇌ ⬧

**Newcastle-Under-Lyme** Whitmore Rd ST5 2QB ☎ 01782 617006
Parkland course.
*18 holes, 6404yds, Par 72, SSS 71.*
*Club membership 600.*
**Visitors** must contact in advance. With member only weekends.
**Societies** must contact in advance.
**Green Fees** £25 per day/round.
**Facilities** ⊗ ⅏ ⅃ ☵ ♀ ⅄ 🏠 ⅂ Paul Symonds.
**Leisure** trolley for hire, putting green.
**Location** 1m SW on A53
**Hotel** ★★ 63% Comfort Friendly Inn, Liverpool Rd, Cross Heath, NEWCASTLE-UNDER-LYME ☎ 01782 717000 47 ⇌ ⬧Annexe21 ⇌ ⬧

**Wolstanton** Dimsdale Old Hall, Hassam Pde, Wolstanton ST5 9DR ☎ 01782 622413
Meadowland/parkland course in an urban area.
*18 holes, 5807yds, Par 68, SSS 68, Course record 63.*
*Club membership 700.*

**Visitors** must contact in advance. With member only at weekends & bank holidays.
**Societies** must contact in advance.
**Green Fees** £18 per day/round.
**Facilities** ⊗ ⅷ by prior arrangement ⓑ ⅌ ⓠ ⓐ ⓔ ⓕ Colin Smith.
**Leisure** trolley for hire, putting green, snooker.
**Location** Turn off A34 at The Sportsman Inn
**Hotel** B Forte Posthouse Newcastle under Lyme, Clayton Rd, NEWCASTLE-UNDER-LYME
☎ 01782 717171 119 ⇄ ♠

## ONNELEY Map 07 SJ74

**Onneley** CW3 9QF ☎ 01782 750577
A tight, picturesque, hillside parkland course. An ideal test for the short game
*9 holes, 5584yds, Par 70, SSS 67, Course record 67.*
*Club membership 480.*
**Visitors** welcome except during competitions, but may not play on Sun and with member only Sat and bank holidays.
**Societies** packages available apply in writing to secretary.
**Green Fees** £15 per 18 holes.
**Facilities** ⓑ ⅌ ⓠ ⓐ
**Leisure** putting green.
**Location** 2m from Woore on A525
**Hotel** ★★ 69% Wheatsheaf Inn at Onneley, Barhill Rd, ONNELEY ☎ 01782 751581 5 ♠

## PATTINGHAM Map 07 SO89

**Patshull Park Hotel Golf & Country Club** WV6 7HR
☎ 01902 700100
Picturesque course set in 280 acres of glorious Capability Brown landscaped parkland. Designed by John Jacobs, the course meanders alongside trout fishing lakes. Many leisure facilities.
*18 holes, 6700yds, Par 72, SSS 71, Course record 63.*
*Club membership 400.*
**Visitors** must contact in advance.
**Societies** must contact in advance.
**Green Fees** £22.50 per round (£27.50 weekends).
**Facilities** ⊗ ⅷ ⓑ ⅌ ⓠ ⓐ ⓔ ⓕ ⓜ
ⓕ Joe Higgins/Richard Bissell.
**Leisure** heated indoor swimming pool, fishing, sauna, solarium, gymnasium, motorised carts for hire, buggies for hire, trolley for hire, putting green, practice area.
**Location** Off A464
**Hotel** ★★★ 66% Patshull Park Hotel Golf & Country Club, Patshull Park, PATTINGHAM
☎ 01902 700100 49 ⇄ ♠

## PERTON Map 07 SO89

**Perton Park** Wrottesley Park Rd WV6 7HL
☎ 01902 380103 & 380073
Flat meadowland course set in open countryside.
*18 holes, 6620yds, Par 72, SSS 72.*
*Club membership 250.*
**Visitors** must book in advance.
**Societies** must telephone in advance.
**Green Fees** £10 per day; £8 per round (£20/£15 weekends & bank holidays).

**Facilities** ⊗ ⅷ ⓑ ⅌ ⓠ ⓐ ⓔ ⓕ ⓕ Jeremy Harrold.
**Leisure** motorised carts for hire, buggies for hire, trolley for hire, driving range, putting green, bowling green, snooker.
**Location** 6m W of Wolverhampton, on A454
**Hotel** ★★ 68% Ely House Hotel, 53 Tettenhall Rd, WOLVERHAMPTON
☎ 01902 311311 18 ⇄ ♠

## STAFFORD Map 07 SJ92

**Stafford Castle** Newport Rd ST16 1BP ☎ 01785 223821
Parkland type course.
*9 holes, 6382yds, Par 71, SSS 70, Course record 68.*
*Club membership 400.*
**Visitors** must contact in advance. May not play at weekends.
**Societies** must apply in writing.
**Green Fees** £14 per day (£18 weekends & bank holidays).
**Facilities** ⊗ ⅷ ⓑ ⅌ ⓠ ⓐ ⓔ
**Leisure** trolley for hire, putting green, practice area.
**Location** SW side of town centre off A518
**Hotel** ★★★ 65% Tillington Hall Hotel, Eccleshall Rd, STAFFORD
☎ 01785 53531 due to change to 253531 90 ⇄ ♠

## STOKE-ON-TRENT Map 07 SJ84

**Burslem** Wood Farm, High Ln, Tunstall ST6 7JT
☎ 01782 837006
On the outskirts of Tunstall, a moorland course with hard walking.
*9 holes, 5354yds, Par 66, SSS 66.*
*Club membership 250.*
**Visitors** except Sun & with member only Sat & bank holidays.
**Societies** must telephone in advance.
**Green Fees** not confirmed.
**Facilities** ⓐ
**Location** 4m N of city centre on B5049
**Hotel** ★★★ 65% George Hotel, Swan Square, Burslem, STOKE-ON-TRENT
☎ 01782 577544 30 ⇄ ♠

**Greenway Hall** Stanley Rd, Stockton Brook ST9 9LJ
☎ 01782 503158
Moorland course with fine views of the Pennines.
*18 holes, 5678yds, Par 68, SSS 67.*
*Club membership 560.*
**Visitors** may play weekdays only.
**Societies** must apply in writing.
**Green Fees** £14 per round.
**Facilities** ⊗ ⓑ ⅌ ⓠ ⓐ
**Leisure** practice area, snooker.
**Location** 5m NE off A53
**Hotel** ★★★ 65% George Hotel, Swan Square, Burslem, STOKE-ON-TRENT
☎ 01782 577544 30 ⇄ ♠

**Trentham** 14 Barlaston Old Rd, Trentham ST4 8HB
☎ 01782 658109
Parkland course. The par 3, 4th is a testing hole reached over a copse of trees.
*18 holes, 6644yds, Par 72, SSS 72, Course record 63.*
*Club membership 600.*

▶

187

**Visitors** must play with member at weekends.
**Societies** must contact in advance.
**Green Fees** £25 per day.
**Facilities** ⊗ ⅏ 🍴 ☕ ♀ ⚒ 🏠 ⊤ ⸂ Sandy Wilson.
**Leisure** squash, buggies for hire, trolley for hire, driving range, putting green, practice area.
**Location** 3m S off A5035
**Hotel** ★★★ 62% Haydon House Hotel, 1-13 Haydon St, Basford, STOKE-ON-TRENT
☎ 01782 711311 16 ⇆ ⸂Annexe14 ⇆ ⏚

**Trentham Park** Trentham Park ST4 8AE
☎ 01782 658800
Fine woodland course.
*18 holes, 6425yds, Par 71, SSS 71, Course record 67.*
*Club membership 850.*
**Visitors** must contact in advance.
**Societies** Wed & Fri, must apply in advance.
**Green Fees** £25 per day (£30 weekends).
**Facilities** ⊗ ⅏ 🍴 ☕ ♀ ⚒ 🏠 ⸂ Jim McLeod.
**Leisure** trolley for hire, practice area.
**Location** 3m SW off A34
**Hotel** B Forte Posthouse Newcastle under Lyme, Clayton Rd, NEWCASTLE-UNDER-LYME
☎ 01782 717171 119 ⇆ ⏚

## STONE Map 07 SJ93

**Izaak Walton** Eccleshall Rd, Cold Norton ST15 0NS
☎ 01785 760900
Opened in 1992, a gently undulating meadowland course with streams and ponds as features.
*18 holes, 6281yds, Par 72, SSS 72, Course record 66.*
*Club membership 250.*
**Visitors** must contact in advance for weekends play.
**Societies** must telephone in advance.
**Green Fees** £12 per round (£17 weekends).
**Facilities** ⊗ ⅏ 🍴 ☕ ♀ ⚒ 🏠 ⸂ Julie Brown.
**Leisure** driving range, putting green, practice area.
**Hotel** ★★★ 70% Stone House Hotel, Stafford Rd, STONE ☎ 01785 815531 47 ⇆ ⏚

**Stone** Filleybrooks ST15 0NB ☎ 01785 813103
9-hole parkland course with easy walking and 18 different tees.
*9 holes, 6299yds, Par 71, SSS 70, Course record 68.*
*Club membership 310.*
**Visitors** with member only weekends & bank holidays.
**Societies** must apply in writing.
**Green Fees** £15 per day or round.
**Facilities** ⊗ ⅏ 🍴 ☕ ♀ ⚒
**Leisure** practice area.
**Location** 0.5m W on A34
**Hotel** ★★★ 70% Stone House Hotel, Stafford Rd, STONE ☎ 01785 815531 47 ⇆ ⏚

## TAMWORTH Map 07 SK20

**Drayton Park** Drayton Park B78 3TN ☎ 01827 251139
Parkland course designed by James Braid. Club established since 1897.
*18 holes, 6214yds, Par 71, SSS 71, Course record 62.*
*Club membership 450.*
**Visitors** with member only weekends. Must contact in advance.

**Societies** must apply in writing.
**Green Fees** £28 per day/round.
**Facilities** ⊗ ⅏ 🍴 ☕ ♀ ⚒ 🏠 ⸂ M W Passmore.
**Leisure** trolley for hire, putting green, practice area.
**Location** 2m S on A4091, next to Drayton Manor Leisure Park
**Hotel** ★★★★ 72% The Belfry, WISHAW
☎ 01675 470301 219 ⇆ ⏚

**Tamworth Municipal** Eagle Dr, Amington B77 4EG
☎ 01827 53850
First-class municipal, parkland course and a good test of golf.
*18 holes, 6605ydss, Par 73, SSS 72, Course record 63.*
*Club membership 600.*
**Visitors** must book in advance at weekends.
**Societies** must contact in advance.
**Green Fees** £8.50 per 18 holes; £5.60 for 9 holes.
**Facilities** ⊗ ⅏ 🍴 ☕ ♀ ⚒ 🏠 ⊤ ⸂ Barry Jones.
**Leisure** motorised carts for hire, buggies for hire, trolley for hire, putting greens, practice area.
**Location** 2.5m E off B5000
**Hotel** ★★ 62% Angel Croft Hotel, Beacon St, LICHFIELD
☎ 01543 258737 10rm(3 ⇆5 ⏚)Annexe8 ⇆ ⏚

## UTTOXETER Map 07 SK03

**Uttoxeter** Wood Ln ST14 8JR ☎ 01889 565108
Downland course with open aspect.
*18 holes, 5468yds, Par 68, SSS 68, Course record 66.*
*Club membership 750.*
**Visitors** restricted weekends and competition days.
**Societies** must apply in writing.
**Green Fees** £22 per day; £15 per round (£17 per round weekends & bank holidays).
**Facilities** ⊗ ⅏ 🍴 ☕ ♀ ⚒ 🏠 ⸂ John Pearsall.
**Leisure** trolley for hire, putting green, practice area, pool table.
**Location** 1m SE off B5017
**Hotel** ★★ 64% Bank House Hotel, Church St, UTTOXETER
☎ 01889 566922 16 ⇆ ⏚

## WESTON Map 07 SJ92

**Ingestre Park** ST18 0RE ☎ 01889 270845
Parkland course set in the grounds of Ingestre Hall, former home of the Earl of Shrewsbury, with mature trees and pleasant views.
*18 holes, 6334yds, Par 70, SSS 70, Course record 67.*
*Club membership 850.*
**Visitors** with member only weekends & bank holidays. Must play before 3.30pm weekdays . Advance booking preferred.
**Societies** must apply in advance.
**Green Fees** £21 per round.
**Facilities** ⊗ ⅏ 🍴 ☕ ♀ ⚒ 🏠 ⸂ Danny Scullion.
**Leisure** motorised carts for hire, buggies for hire, trolley for hire, driving range, putting green, practice area, snooker.
**Location** 2m SE off A51
**Hotel** ★★★ 65% Tillington Hall Hotel, Eccleshall Rd, STAFFORD
☎ 01785 53531 due to change to 253531 90 ⇆ ⏚

## WHISTON                                    Map 07 SK04

**Whiston Hall** Whiston Hall ST10 2HZ
☎ 01538 266260 & 0850 903815
A challenging 18-hole course in scenic countryside and incorporating many natural obstacles.
*18 holes, 5742yds, Par 71, SSS 69.*
*Club membership 400.*
**Visitors**    reasonable dress on the course. Must telephone
        in advance at weekends.
**Societies**   contact in advance.
**Green Fees** £15 per day; £10 per round (£21/£14 weekends
        & bank holidays).
**Facilities**  ⊗ ⍔ ⓛ ⬤ ♀ ☉
**Leisure**    fishing, trolley for hire, putting green, practice
        area, snooker.
**Location**  Off A52, 3m NE of Cheadle
**Hotel**     ★★(red) Old Beams Restaurant with Rooms,
        Leek Rd, WATERHOUSES
        ☎ 01538 308254 5rm

# SUFFOLK

## ALDEBURGH                                  Map 05 TM45

**Aldeburgh** Saxmundham Rd IP15 5PE
☎ 01728 452890
A most enjoyable and not unduly difficult seaside course; ideal for golfing holidaymakers. A bracing and fairly open terrain with some trees and heathland.
*18 holes, 6330yds, Par 68, SSS 71, Course record 65.*
*River Course: 9 holes, 2114yds, Par 32, SSS 32.*
**Visitors**    must contact in advance.
**Societies**   must contact in advance.
**Green Fees** £33 per day; £22 after noon (£40/£28
        weekends & bank holidays). River Course:
        £12 per day; £10 after noon; £6 after 5pm.
**Facilities**  ⊗ ⓛ ⬤ ♀ ☉ ☎ ⌐
**Leisure**    trolley for hire, putting green, practice area.
**Location**  1m W on A1094
**Hotel**     ★★★ 70% Wentworth Hotel, Wentworth
        Rd, ALDEBURGH
        ☎ 01728 452312 31rm(24 ⇌4 ⌐)Annexe7
        ⇌ ⌐

## BECCLES                                     Map 05 TM49

**Wood Valley** The Common NR34 9YN ☎ 01502 712244
Heathland course with natural hazards and particularly exposed to wind.
*9 holes, 2779yds, Par 68, SSS 67.*
*Club membership 160.*
**Visitors**    must play with member on Sun.
**Societies**   must contact in advance.
**Green Fees** £10 per round (£12 weekends).
**Facilities**  ⊗ ⓛ ⬤ ♀ ☉ ☎ ⌐
**Leisure**    trolley for hire.
**Location**  NE side of town
**Hotel**     ★★★ 64% Hotel Hatfield, The Esplanade,
        LOWESTOFT ☎ 01502 565337 33 ⇌ ⌐

## BUNGAY                                      Map 05 TM38

**Bungay & Waveney Valley** Outney Common NR35 1DS
☎ 01986 892337
Heathland course partly comprising Neolithic stone workings, easy walking.
*18 holes, 6026yds, Par 69, SSS 69.*
*Club membership 730.*
**Visitors**    should contact in advance. With member only
        weekends & bank holidays.
**Societies**   must contact in advance.
**Green Fees** £18 per day/round.
**Facilities**  ⊗ ⍔ ⓛ ⬤ ♀ ☉ ☎ ⌐ ⌐ Nigel Whyte.
**Leisure**    motorised carts for hire, buggies for hire, trolley
        for hire, putting green, practice area.
**Location**  0.5m NW on A143
**Hotel**     ★★★ 64% Hotel Hatfield, The Esplanade,
        LOWESTOFT ☎ 01502 565337 33 ⇌ ⌐

## BURY ST EDMUNDS                             Map 05 TL86

**Bury St Edmunds** Tut Hill IP28 6LG ☎ 01284 755979
Undulating parkland course with easy walking and attractive short holes.
*18 holes, 6678yds, Par 72, SSS 72, Course record 69 or 9*
*holes, 2217yds, Par 62, SSS 62.*
*Club membership 850.*
**Visitors**    with member only at weekends for 18 hole
        course.
**Societies**   must apply in writing.
**Green Fees** 18 hole course: £26 per day ; £24 per round. 9 hole
        course: £11 per 2 rounds (£12 weekends).  ▶

# WENTWORTH
## HOTEL   ★★★
### Aldeburgh, Suffolk
Tel: (01728) 452312  Fax: (01728) 454343

*The Hotel has the comfort and style of a Country House. Two comfortable lounges, with open fires and antique furniture, provide ample space to relax. Each individually decorated bedroom, many with sea views, is equipped with a colour television, radio, hairdryer and tea making facilities. The Restaurant serves a variety of fresh produce whilst a light lunch can be chosen from the Bar menu, eaten outside in the sunken terrace garden. Aldeburgh is timeless and unhurried. There are quality shops, two excellent golf courses within a short distance from the hotel, long walks and some of the best birdwatching at Minsmere Bird reserve. Music and the Arts can be heard at the Internationally famous Snape Malting Concert hall. Lastly, there are miles of beach to sit upon and watch the sea!*

| | |
|---|---|
| **Facilities** | ⊗ 〕⋔ by prior arrangement 🖢 ☕ ♀⚴ 🖻 |
| | ⌡ Mark Jillings. |
| **Leisure** | trolley for hire. |
| **Location** | 2m NW on B1106 off A45 |
| **Hotel** | ★★★ 68% Angel Hotel, Angel Hill, BURY ST |
| | EDMUNDS ☎ 01284 753926 42 ⇥ 🐾 |

*Fornham Park* St John's Hill Plantation, The Street,
Fornham All Saints IP28 6JQ ☎ 01284 706777
Flat parkland course with many water hazards. Also country
club facilities.
*18 holes, 6209yds, Par 71, SSS 70, Course record 67.*
*Club membership 300.*

| | |
|---|---|
| **Visitors** | no restrictions, but must book a tee time. |
| **Societies** | by arrangement. |
| **Green Fees** | not confirmed. |
| **Facilities** | ♀⚴ 🖻 ¶⌡ Sean Clark. |
| **Location** | 2m N off A134 |
| **Hotel** | ★★★🕮 70% Ravenwood Hall Hotel, |
| | Rougham, BURY ST EDMUNDS |
| | ☎ 01359 270345 7 ⇥Annexe7 ⇥ |

## CRETINGHAM        Map 05 TM26

*Cretingham* IP13 7BA ☎ 01728 685275
Parkland course.
*9 holes, 4552yds, Par 66, SSS 64, Course record 61.*
*Club membership 350.*

| | |
|---|---|
| **Visitors** | booking required for weekends. |
| **Societies** | must contact in advance. |
| **Green Fees** | £12 per day; £9 per 18 holes; £7 per 9 holes |
| | (£14/£11/£9 weekends & bank holidays). |
| **Facilities** | ⊗ 🖢 ☕ ♀⚴ 🖻 ¶⌡ Colin Jenkins. |
| **Leisure** | hard tennis courts, outdoor swimming pool, |
| | trolley for hire, driving range, putting green, |
| | practice area, pitch & putt, snooker. |
| **Location** | 2m from A1120 at Earl Soham |
| **Hotel** | ★★ 67% Crown Hotel, Market Hill, |
| | FRAMLINGHAM ☎ 01728 723521 14 ⇥ |

## FELIXSTOWE        Map 05 TM33

*Felixstowe Ferry* Ferry Rd IP11 9RY ☎ 01394 283060
Seaside links course, pleasant views, easy walking. Testing
491-yd, 7th hole.
*18 holes, 6272yds, Par 72, SSS 70.*
*Club membership 800.*

| | |
|---|---|
| **Visitors** | may not play weekends. |
| **Societies** | Tue, Wed & Fri. |
| **Green Fees** | £24 per day. |
| **Facilities** | ⊗ 〕⋔ 🖢 ☕ ♀⚴ 🖻 🖂⌡ Ian MacPherson. |
| **Leisure** | trolley for hire, putting green, practice area. |
| **Location** | NE side of town centre |
| **Hotel** | ★★ 69% Waverley Hotel, 2 Wolsey Gardens, |
| | FELIXSTOWE ☎ 01394 282811 19 ⇥ 🐾 |

## FLEMPTON        Map 05 TL86

*Flempton* IP28 6EQ ☎ 01284 728291
Breckland course.
*9 holes, 6080yds, Par 70, SSS 70.*
*Club membership 500.*

| | |
|---|---|
| **Visitors** | must have handicap certificate. With member |
| | only weekends & bank holidays. |
| **Societies** | must apply in writing. |

| | |
|---|---|
| **Green Fees** | not confirmed. |
| **Facilities** | ♀⚴ 🖻 ⌡ |
| **Location** | 0.5m W on A1101 |
| **Hotel** | ★★ 65% Suffolk Hotel, 38 The Buttermarket, |
| | BURY ST EDMUNDS |
| | ☎ 01284 753995 33 ⇥ 🐾 |

## HALESWORTH        Map 05 TM37

*St Helena* Bramfield Rd IP19 9XA ☎ 01986 875567
A 27-hole professionally designed parkland complex of three
9-hole courses, giving 6 playing options of 3 x 18-hole Par 72
and 3 x Par 36 9-hole.
*Saint Helena: 18 holes, 6580yds, Par 72, SSS 72, Course*
*record 71.*
*Halesworth: 9 holes, 3059yds, Par 36, SSS 36.*
*Club membership 500.*

| | |
|---|---|
| **Visitors** | visitors welcome at all times except for Sunday |
| | before noon on the St Helena course. |
| **Societies** | telephone for booking form. |
| **Green Fees** | £19 per day; £15 per 18 holes; £7.50 per 9 holes |
| | (£21/£18/£7.50 weekends & bank holidays). |
| **Facilities** | ⊗ 〕⋔ 🖢 ☕ ♀⚴ 🖻 ¶⌡ Philip Heil. |
| **Leisure** | motorised carts for hire, buggies for hire, trolley |
| | for hire, driving range, putting green, practice |
| | area, equestrian centre. |
| **Location** | 0.75m S of town, signposted on left of A144 |
| | road to Bramfield |
| **Hotel** | ★★★ 69% Swan Hotel, Market Place, |
| | SOUTHWOLD |
| | ☎ 01502 722186 27 ⇥ 🐾Annexe18 ⇥ |

## HAVERHILL        Map 05 TL64

*Haverhill* Coupals Rd CB9 7UW ☎ 01440 61951
Parkland course with good greens, plenty of trees and a small
river running through three fairways and affecting 6 holes. A
further 9-holes are under constrution and should be playable
Spring 1997..
*9 holes, 5717yds, Par 68, SSS 68, Course record 65.*
*Club membership 500.*

| | |
|---|---|
| **Visitors** | telephone to check for club competitions. |
| **Societies** | must contact in advance. Tue & Thu only. |
| **Green Fees** | £15 per day; £12 per 18 holes (£20/£16 |
| | weekends & bank holidays). |
| **Facilities** | ⊗ 〕⋔ 🖢 ☕ ♀⚴ 🖻 ¶⌡ Simon Mayfield. |
| **Leisure** | buggies for hire, trolley for hire, putting green, |
| | practice area. |
| **Location** | 1m SE off A604 |
| **Hotel** | ★★ 67% Bell Hotel, Market Hill, CLARE |
| | ☎ 01787 277741 9rm(3 ⇥4 🐾)Annexe11 ⇥ |

## HINTLESHAM        Map 05 TM04

*Hintlesham Hall* IP8 3NS ☎ 01473 652761
Magnificent new championship length course blending
harmoniously with the ancient parkland surrounding this
exclusive hotel. The 6630d parkland course was
designed by Hawtree and Son, one of the oldest
established firms of golf course architects in the world.
The course is fair but challenging for low and high
handicappers alike. Hotel offers beautiful
accommodation, excellent cuisine and many facilities.
*18 holes, 6638yds, Par 72, SSS 72, Course record 67.*
*Club membership 350.*

| Visitors | must contact in advance. |
| Societies | must telephone in advance. |
| Green Fees | £45 per day; £26 per round (£75/£45 weekends & bank holidays). |
| Facilities | ⊗ ⫪ ⓑ ⯑ ♀ ⯑ ⯑ ⯑ Ꞓ Alastair Spink. |
| Leisure | hard tennis courts, heated outdoor swimming pool, sauna, solarium, gymnasium, motorised carts for hire, buggies for hire, trolley for hire. |
| Location | In village on A1071 |
| Hotel | ★★★★(red)✿✿ Hintlesham Hall Hotel, HINTLESHAM ☎ 01473 652334 & 652268 33 ⇄ ⓕ |

## IPSWICH                                   Map 05 TM14

**Alnesbourne Priory** Priory Park IP10 0JT
☎ 01473 727393 & 726373
A fabulous outlook facing due south across the River Orwell is one of the many good features of this course set in woodland. All holes run among trees with some fairways requiring straight shots. The 8th green is on saltings by the river.
*9 holes, 1700yds, Par 29.*
*Club membership 50.*

| Visitors | closed on Tuesday. |
| Societies | Tue only, telephone in advance. |
| Green Fees | £10 weekdays, £11 Saturday, £12 Sunday. |
| Facilities | ⊗ ⫪ ⓑ ⯑ ♀ ⯑ ⯑ ⯑ |
| Leisure | hard tennis courts, heated outdoor swimming pool, practice area. |
| Location | 3m SE, off A14 |
| Hotel | ★★★ 69% Suffolk Grange Hotel, The Havens, Ransomes Europark, IPSWICH ☎ 01473 272244 60 ⇄ ⓕ |

---

**Ipswich** Purdis Heath IP3 8UQ
☎ 01473 728941
Many golfers are suprised when they hear that Ipswich has, at Purdis Heath, a first-class golf course. In some ways it resembles some of Surrey's better courses; a beautiful heathland/parkland course with two lakes and easy walking.
*18 holes, 6405yds, Par 71, SSS 71 or 9 holes, 1930yds, Par 31, SSS 59.*
*Club membership 850.*

| Visitors | must contact in advance & have a handicap certificate for 18 hole courses. |
| Societies | must contact in advance. |
| Green Fees | not confirmed. |
| Facilities | ♀ ⯑ ⯑ Ꞓ |
| Location | E side of town centre off A1156 |
| Hotel | ★★★ 69% Marlborough Hotel, Henley Rd, IPSWICH ☎ 01473 257677 22 ⇄ ⓕ |

---

**Rushmere** Rushmere Heath IP4 5QQ ☎ 01473 725648
Heathland course with gorse and prevailing winds. Testing 5th hole - dog leg, 419 yards (par 4).
*18 holes, 6262yds, Par 70, SSS 68, Course record 66.*
*Club membership 792.*

| Visitors | not before 2.30pm weekends & bank holidays. Must have a handicap certificate. |
| Societies | weekdays ex Wed by arrangement. |
| Green Fees | £20 per day/round. |

| Facilities | ⊗ ⓑ ⯑ ♀ ⯑ ⯑ Ꞓ N T J McNeill. |
| Leisure | trolley for hire, putting green, practice area. |
| Location | 3m E off A12 |
| Hotel | ★★★ 69% Marlborough Hotel, Henley Rd, IPSWICH ☎ 01473 257677 22 ⇄ ⓕ |

## LOWESTOFT                               Map 05 TM59

**Rookery Park** Carlton Colville NR33 8HJ ☎ 01502 560380
Parkland course with a 9-hole, Par 3 adjacent.
*18 holes, 6385yds, Par 72, SSS 72.*
*Club membership 1000.*

| Visitors | must have handicap certificate. |
| Societies | by arrangement. |
| Green Fees | not confirmed. |
| Facilities | ♀ ⯑ ⯑ ⯑ Ꞓ |
| Location | 3.5m SW on A146 |
| Hotel | ★★★ 64% Hotel Hatfield, The Esplanade, LOWESTOFT ☎ 01502 565337 33 ⇄ ⓕ |

## NEWMARKET                               Map 05 TL66

**Links** Cambridge Rd CB8 0TG ☎ 01638 663000
Gently undulating parkland.
*18 holes, 6574yds, Par 72, SSS 71, Course record 70.*
*Club membership 780.*

| Visitors | must have handicap certificate, may not play Sun before 11.30am. |
| Societies | telephone secretary in advance. |
| Green Fees | £26 (£30 weekends & bank holidays). |
| Facilities | ⊗ ⫪ ⓑ ⯑ ♀ ⯑ ⯑ ⯑ Ꞓ John Sharkey. |
| Leisure | trolley for hire, putting green, practice area. |
| Location | 1m SW on A1034 |
| Hotel | ★★★ 67% Heath Court Hotel, Moulton Rd, NEWMARKET ☎ 01638 667171 44 ⇄ ⓕ |

## NEWTON                                   Map 05 TL94

**Newton Green** Newton Green CO10 0QN
☎ 01787 377217 & 377501
Flat, 18-hole commonland course.
*18 holes, 5960yds, Par 69, SSS 68.*
*Club membership 575.*

| Visitors | must contact in advance but may not play on Tue or Sat & Sun before 12.30. |
| Societies | apply in advance. |
| Green Fees | £20 per day; £14 per 18 holes. |
| Facilities | ⊗ ⫪ ⓑ ⯑ ♀ ⯑ ⯑ ⯑ Ꞓ Tim Cooper. |
| Leisure | trolley for hire, putting green, practice area. |
| Location | W side of village on A134 |
| Hotel | ★★★ 64% Bull Hotel, Hall St, LONG MELFORD ☎ 01787 378494 25 ⇄ ⓕ |

## RAYDON                                   Map 05 TM03

**Brett Vale** Noakes Rd IP7 5LR ☎ 01473 310718
Brett Vale course takes you through a nature reserve and on lakeside walks. The excellent fairways demand an accurate tee and good approach shots. 1, 2, 3, 8, 10 and 15 are all affected by crosswinds, but once in the valley it is much more sheltered. Although only 5,808yards the course is testing and interesting at all levels of golf.
*18 holes, 5808yds, Par 70, SSS 68, Course record 65.*
*Club membership 300.* ▶

| | |
|---|---|
| **Visitors** | must book tee times and wear appropriate clothing. |
| **Societies** | apply in writing or telephone. |
| **Green Fees** | not confirmed. |
| **Facilities** | ♀♿☎⚐♟ Andrew Boulter. |
| **Leisure** | indoor driving range. |
| **Location** | B1070 at Raydon, 2m from A12 |
| **Hotel** | ★★★(red)♨ Maison Talbooth, Stratford Rd, DEDHAM ☎ 01206 322367 10 ⇋ ⚑ |

## SOUTHWOLD Map 05 TM57

**Southwold** The Common IP18 6TB
☎ 01502 723234 & 723248
Commonland course with 4-acre practice ground and panoramic views of the sea.
*9 holes, 6052yds, Par 70, SSS 69, Course record 67.*
*Club membership 450.*

| | |
|---|---|
| **Visitors** | restricted on competition days (Ladies-Wed, Gents-Sun. |
| **Societies** | must contact in advance. |
| **Green Fees** | £18 per day; £15 per 18 holes (£20 per round or day). |
| **Facilities** | ⊗ �🍴 by prior arrangement ♟ 🍺 ♀ ♿ ☎ ⚐ ⚑ Brian Allen. |
| **Leisure** | motorised carts for hire, trolley for hire, putting green, practice area. |
| **Location** | From A12 - B1140 to Southwold |
| **Hotel** | ★★★ 69% Swan Hotel, Market Place, SOUTHWOLD ☎ 01502 722186 27 ⇋ ⚑Annexe18 ⇋ |

## STOWMARKET Map 05 TM05

**Stowmarket** Lower Rd, Onehouse IP14 3DA
☎ 01449 736473
Parkland course.
*18 holes, 6107yds, Par 69, SSS 69, Course record 66.*
*Club membership 630.*

| | |
|---|---|
| **Visitors** | must contact in advance. |
| **Societies** | Thu or Fri, by arrangement. |
| **Green Fees** | £27 per day; £22 per round (£38/£28 weekends and bank holidays). |
| **Facilities** | ⊗ �🍴 by prior arrangement ♟ 🍺 ♀ ♿ ☎ ⚐ |
| **Leisure** | motorised carts for hire, trolley for hire, driving range, putting green, practice area. |
| **Location** | 2.5m SW off B115 |
| **Hotel** | ★★ 63% Cedars Hotel, Needham Rd, STOWMARKET ☎ 01449 612668 24 ⇋ ⚑ |

## THORPENESS Map 05 TM45

**Thorpeness** IP16 4NH ☎ 01728 452176 & 454926
The holes of this moorland course are pleasantly varied with several quite difficult par 4's. Natural hazards abound. The 15th, with its sharp left dog-leg, is one of the best holes. Designed by James Braid.
*18 holes, 6271yds, Par 69, SSS 71, Course record 66.*
*Club membership 300.*

| | |
|---|---|
| **Visitors** | contact in advance. |
| **Societies** | telephone in advance, deposite required. |
| **Green Fees** | £25 per day (£30 weekends & bank holidays). |

| | |
|---|---|
| **Facilities** | ⊗ �🍴 ♟ 🍺 ♀ ♿ ☎ ⚐ ⚑ Mike Grantham. |
| **Leisure** | motorised carts for hire, buggies for hire, trolley for hire, driving range, putting. |
| **Location** | W side of village off B1353 |
| **Hotel** | ★ 65% White Horse Hotel, Station Rd, LEISTON ☎ 01728 830694 10rm(1 ⇋7 ⚑)Annexe3 ⚑ |

## WALDRINGFIELD Map 05 TM24

**Waldringfield Heath** Newbourne Rd IP12 4PT
☎ 01473 736768 & 736426
Easy walking heathland course with long drives on 1st, 5th (586yds) and 10th tees.
*18 holes, 6141yds, Par 71, SSS 69, Course record 68.*
*Club membership 600.*

| | |
|---|---|
| **Visitors** | welcome Mon-Fri, weekends & bank holidays after noon. |
| **Societies** | weekdays by arrangement. |
| **Green Fees** | £18 per day; £12 per 18 holes (£15 per 18 holes weekends and bank holidays). |
| **Facilities** | ⊗ ♟ 🍺 ♀ ♿ ☎ ⚐ Tony Dobson. |
| **Leisure** | trolley for hire, putting green. |
| **Location** | 3m NE of Ipswich off old A12 |
| **Hotel** | ★★★♨ 73% Seckford Hall Hotel, WOODBRIDGE ☎ 01394 385678 22 ⇋ ⚑Annexe10 ⇋ ⚑ |

## WITNESHAM Map 05 TM15

**Fynn Valley** IP6 9JA ☎ 01473 785267 & 785463
Undulating parkland course plus Par-3 nine-hole and driving range.
*18 holes, 5807yds, Par 69, SSS 68, Course record 64.*
*Club membership 680.*

| | |
|---|---|
| **Visitors** | members only Sun until noon. |
| **Societies** | must apply in advance. |
| **Green Fees** | £18 per day; £14 per 18 holes (£25/£18 weekends and bank holidays). |
| **Facilities** | ⊗ �🍴 ♟ 🍺 ♀ ♿ ☎ ⚐ Robin Mann/Glenn Crane. |
| **Leisure** | buggies for hire, trolley for hire, covered and floodlit driving range, putting green, par 3 course. |
| **Location** | 2m N of Ipswich on B1077 |
| **Hotel** | ★★★ 69% Marlborough Hotel, Henley Rd, IPSWICH ☎ 01473 257677 22 ⇋ ⚑ |

## WOODBRIDGE Map 05 TM24

**Seckford** Seckford Hall Rd, Great Bealings IP13 6NT
☎ 01394 388000
An undulating course interspersed with young tree plantations and undulating greens. The 18th is almost completely surrounded by water.
*18 holes, 5088yds, Par 69, SSS 66, Course record 63.*
*Club membership 300.*

| | |
|---|---|
| **Visitors** | telephone in advance. |
| **Societies** | telephone in advance. |
| **Green Fees** | £14 per day; £12 per 18 holes; £8.50 per 9 holes (£18/£15/£10 weekends). |
| **Facilities** | ⊗ �🍴 ♟ 🍺 ♀ ♿ ☎ ⚐ ⚑ Tony Pennock/J Skinner/S Jay. |

**Leisure**    heated indoor swimming pool, fishing, sauna, solarium, gymnasium, trolley for hire, driving range, putting green, practice area.
**Location**   (3m W of Woodbridge, 0ff A12)
**Hotel**      ★★★▲▲ 73%  Seckford Hall Hotel, WOODBRIDGE ☎ 01394 385678 22 ⇄ ♠Annexe10 ⇄ ♠

---

**Ufford Park Hotel Golf & Leisure** Yarmouth Rd, Ufford IP12 1QW ☎ 01394 383555
A challenging new course opened in autumn 1991. The 18-hole Par 70 course is set in ancient parkland has many natural features including 11 water hazards retaind from the original parkland. There is also an extensive hotel and leisure complex beside the course.
*18 holes, 6300yds, Par 70, SSS 70, Course record 67.*
*Club membership 200.*
**Visitors**   must book tee time from golf shop 01394 382836
**Societies**  contact in advance.
**Green Fees** £20 per day; £14 per 18 holes (£27/£18 weekends & bank holidays).
**Facilities** ⊗ ♉ ╠ ▉ ♀ ▲ 🛍 ✦ ⚔ ♟ Stuart Robertson.
**Leisure**    heated indoor swimming pool, sauna, solarium, gymnasium, motorised carts for hire, buggies for hire, trolley for hire, practice area.
**Hotel**      ★★★ 67% Ufford Park Hotel Golf & Leisure, Yarmouth Rd, Ufford, WOODBRIDGE ☎ 01394 383555 27rm(25 ⇄ ♠)

---

**Woodbridge** Bromeswell Heath IP12 2PF ☎ 01394 382038
A beautiful course, one of the best in East Anglia. It is situated on high ground and in different seasons present golfers with a great variety of colour. Some say that of the many good holes the 14th is the best.
*18 holes, 6299yds, Par 70, SSS 70, Course record 64.*
*also: 9 holes, 2243yds, Par 62, SSS 62.*
*Club membership 900.*
**Visitors**   must play with member at weekends & bank holidays. Must contact in advance and handicap certificate required for 18 hole course.
**Societies**  by prior telephone call or in writing.
**Green Fees** £30 per day/round (18 hole); £14 (9 hole).
**Facilities** ⊗ ♉ ╠ ▉ ♀ ▲ 🛍 ♟ Leslie Jones.
**Leisure**    trolley for hire, putting green, practice area.
**Location**   2.5m NE off A1152
**Hotel**      ★★★▲▲ 73%  Seckford Hall Hotel, WOODBRIDGE ☎ 01394 385678 22 ⇄ ♠Annexe10 ⇄ ♠

---

**WORLINGTON**                                  Map 05 TL67

**Royal Worlington & Newmarket** IP28 8SD ☎ 01638 712216 & 717787
Inland 'links' course. Favourite 9-hole course of many golf writers.
*9 holes, 3105yds, Par 35, SSS 70, Course record 67.*
*Club membership 325.*
**Visitors**   with member only at weekends. Must contact in advance and have a handicap certificate.
**Societies**  must apply in writing.
**Green Fees** not confirmed.
**Facilities** ♀ ▲ 🛍 ✦ ♟ Malcolm Hawkins.
**Leisure**    putting green,practice area,trolley hire.

---

**Location**   0.5m SE
**Hotel**      ★★★ 65%  Riverside Hotel, Mill St, MILDENHALL ☎ 01638 717274 20 ⇄ ♠

# SURREY

---

**ADDLESTONE**                                  Map 04 TQ06

**Abbey Moor** Green Ln KT15 2XV ☎ 01932 570741
A 9-hole course ideal for low or high handicap players, there are enough hazards to trouble the best without being too punishing to the not so good. The 4th is a drive over water to an angled approach to a green well protected by sand and water, usually with a left to right crosswind.
*9 holes, 5150yds, Par 68, SSS 65.*
*Club membership 300.*
**Visitors**   welcome providing they observe smart dress code & course etiquette, tee times should be booked in advance.
**Societies**  apply in writing or by telephone in advance.
**Green Fees** not confirmed.
**Facilities** ♀ 🛍 ✦ ♟ Stephen Carter.
**Leisure**    practice putting green, trolley hire.
**Location**   Off junc 11 of the M25
**Hotel**      ★★★ 71%  Ship Thistle, Monument Green, WEYBRIDGE ☎ 01932 848364 39 ⇄ ♠

---

**New Zealand** Woodham Ln KT15 3QD ☎ 01932 345049
Heathland course set in trees and heather.
*18 holes, 6012yds, Par 68, SSS 69, Course record 66.*
*Club membership 320.*
**Visitors**   must contact in advance.
**Societies**  telephone initially.
**Green Fees** £50 per day; £40 per round (£60 per round/day weekends and bank holidays).
**Facilities** ⊗ ▉ ♀ ▲ 🛍 ✦ ♟ Vic Elvidge.
**Leisure**    motorised carts for hire, buggies for hire, trolley for hire, putting green.
**Location**   1.5m W of Weybridge
**Hotel**      ★★★ 71%  Ship Thistle, Monument Green, WEYBRIDGE ☎ 01932 848364 39 ⇄ ♠

---

**ASHFORD**                                     Map 04 TQ07

**Ashford Manor** Fordbridge Rd TW15 3RT ☎ 01784 252049
Parkland course, looks easy but is difficult.
*18 holes, 6343yds, Par 70, SSS 70, Course record 66.*
*Club membership 700.*
**Visitors**   advisable to telephone in advance, handicap certificate required, with member only at weekends.
**Societies**  welcome weekdays, must contact in advance.
**Green Fees** £25 per day/round.
**Facilities** ⊗ ♉ ╠ ▉ ♀ ▲ 🛍 ♟ Mike Finney.
**Leisure**    trolley for hire, putting green, practice area.
**Location**   2m E of Staines via A308 Staines by-pass
**Hotel**      ★★★ 66%  Thames Lodge Hotel, Thames St, STAINES ☎ 01784 464433 44 ⇄ ♠

## BAGSHOT
Map 04 SU96

**Pennyhill Park Hotel & Country Club** London Rd
GU19 5ET ☎ 01276 471774
A nine-hole course set in 11.4 acres of beautiful parkland. It
is challenging to even the most experienced golfer.
*9 holes, 2095yds, Par 32, SSS 32.*
*Club membership 100.*
Visitors    prior booking must be made.
Societies    telephone in advance.
Green Fees   not confirmed.
Facilities    ⌂ ⛾ ⚑ ⌂
Leisure     hard tennis courts, heated outdoor swimming
            pool, fishing, sauna.
Hotel       ★★★★(red)⚘ Pennyhill Park Hotel, London
            Rd, BAGSHOT
            ☎ 01276 471774 22 ⇆ ⁿ Annexe54 ⇆ ⁿ

**Windlesham** Grove End GU19 5HY
☎ 01276 452220
A parkland course with many tough Par 4 holes over 400
yards.
*18 holes, 6600yds, Par 71, SSS 71, Course record 69.*
*Club membership 800.*
Visitors    handicap certificate required.
Societies    apply in advance.
Green Fees   £30 per round (£40 weekends).
Facilities    ⌂ ⛾ ⌂ ⚑ ⌂ ⚑ ⌂ ⚑ ⌂ Alan Barber.
Leisure     buggies for hire, trolley for hire, driving range,
            putting green.
Location    Junct of A30/A322
Hotel       ★★★★(red)⚘ Pennyhill Park Hotel, London
            Rd, BAGSHOT
            ☎ 01276 471774 22 ⇆ ⁿ Annexe54 ⇆ ⁿ

## BANSTEAD
Map 04 TQ25

**Banstead Downs** Burdon Ln, Belmont, Sutton SM2 7DD
☎ 0181 642 2284
Downland course with narrow fairways and hawthorns.
*18 holes, 6194yds, Par 69, SSS 69, Course record 64.*
*Club membership 835.*
Visitors    must book in advance and have handicap
            certificateor letter of introduction. With member
            only weekends.
Societies    Thu, by prior arrangement
Green Fees   £30 before noon; £20 afternoon.
Facilities    ⌂ ⌂ ⚑ ⚑ ⌂ ⌂ Robert Dickman.
Leisure     trolley for hire, putting green, practice area,
            covered driving nets.
Location    1.5m N on A217
Hotel       ★★ 63% Heathside Hotel, Brighton Rd,
            BURGH HEATH ☎ 01737 353355 73 ⇆ ⁿ

**Cuddington** Banstead Rd SM7 1RD
☎ 0181 393 0952
Parkland course with easy walking and good views.
*18 holes, 6394yds, Par 70, SSS 70, Course record 61.*
*Club membership 694.*
Visitors    must contact in advance and have a handicap
            certificate or letter of introduction.
Societies    welcome Thu, must apply in advance.
Green Fees   £30 per day/round (£35 weekends).
Facilities    ⌂ ⛾ ⌂ ⚑ ⌂ ⌂ ⚑ ⌂ Mark Warner.
Leisure     trolley for hire, putting green, practice area.

Location    N of Banstead station on A2022
Hotel       ★★ 63% Heathside Hotel, Brighton Rd,
            BURGH HEATH ☎ 01737 353355 73 ⇆ ⁿ

## BRAMLEY
Map 04 TQ04

**Bramley** GU5 0AL ☎ 01483 892696
Downland course, fine views from top.
*18 holes, 5990yds, Par 69, SSS 69, Course record 65.*
*Club membership 850.*
Visitors    may not play Tue am (Ladies Morning) and
            must play with member at weekends & bank
            holidays. Must contact in advance.
Societies    must telephone the secretary in advance.
Green Fees   £30 per day; £25 per round.
Facilities    ⌂ ⛾ ⌂ ⚑ ⌂ ⌂ ⌂ ⚑ ⌂ Gary Peddie.
Leisure     motorised carts for hire, buggies for hire, trolley
            for hire, driving range, putting green, practice
            area.
Location    0.5m N on A281
Hotel       B Forte Posthouse Guildford, Egerton Rd,
            GUILDFORD ☎ 01483 574444 111 ⇆ ⁿ

## BROOKWOOD
Map 04 SU95

**West Hill** Bagshot Rd GU24 0BH ☎ 01483 474365
Worplesdon's next-door neighbour and a comparably
great heath-and-heather course. Slightly tighter than
Worplesdon with more opportunities for getting into
trouble - but a most interesting and challenging course
with wonderful greens. Water also provides natural
hazards. The 15th is a testing par 3.
*18 holes, 6368yds, Par 69, SSS 70, Course record 62.*
*Club membership 500.*
Visitors    must contact in advance & have handicap
            certificate, may not play weekends & bank
            holidays.
Societies    weekdays only (ex Wed). Telephone in
            advance.
Green Fees   £45 per day; £35 per round.
Facilities    ⌂ ⛾ ⌂ ⚑ ⌂ ⌂ ⌂ ⚑ ⌂ John A Clements.
Leisure     trolley for hire, putting green, practice area.
Location    E side of village on A322
Hotel       ★★★★(red)⚘ Pennyhill Park Hotel,
            London Rd, BAGSHOT
            ☎ 01276 471774 22 ⇆ ⁿ Annexe54 ⇆ ⁿ

## CAMBERLEY
Map 04 SU86

**Camberley Heath** Golf Dr GU15 1JG
☎ 01276 23258
One of the great 'heath and heather' courses so
frequently associated with Surrey. Several very good
short holes - especially the 8th. The 10th is a difficult and
interesting par 4, as also is the 17th, where the drive must
be held well to the left as perdition lurks on the right.
Course architect Harry Colt.
*18 holes, 6128yds, Par 72, SSS 70, Course record 65.*
*Club membership 600.*
Visitors    may not play at weekends. Must contact in
            advance.
Societies    must apply in advance.
Green Fees   £56 per day; £35 per round.
Facilities    ⌂ ⌂ ⚑ ⌂ ⌂ ⌂ ⚑ ⌂ Gary Smith.

| Leisure | motorised carts for hire, buggies for hire, trolley for hire, driving range, putting green, practice area. |
| Location | 1.25m SE of town centre off A325 |
| Hotel | ★★★★(red)⚇ Pennyhill Park Hotel, London Rd, BAGSHOT ☎ 01276 471774 22 ➪ ʀ̃Annexe54 ➪ ʀ̃ |

## CHERTSEY                                        Map 04 TQ06

**Barrow Hills** Longcross KT16 0DS ☎ 01344 635770
This parkland course with natural hazards is only open to guests of members.
*18 holes, 3090yds, Par 56, SSS 53, Course record 58.*
*Club membership 235.*
Visitors    must play with member at all times.
Green Fees  not confirmed.
Leisure     putting green.
Location    3m W on B386
Hotel       ★★★ 66% Thames Lodge Hotel, Thames St, STAINES ☎ 01784 464433 44 ➪ ʀ̃

**Laleham** Laleham Reach KT16 8RP ☎ 01932 564211
Well-bunkered parkland/meadowland course.
*18 holes, 6211yds, Par 70, SSS 70.*
*Club membership 600.*
Visitors    members guests only at weekends.
Societies   must contact in writing.
Green Fees  £25 per day; £18 per round.
Facilities  ⊗ ▥ by prior arrangement ⬗ 🍺 ♀ ⚘ 🏠
            ℓ Hogan Stott.
Leisure     trolley for hire, putting green, practice area.
Location    1.5m N
Hotel       ★★★ 66% Thames Lodge Hotel, Thames St, STAINES ☎ 01784 464433 44 ➪ ʀ̃

## CHIPSTEAD                                        Map 04 TQ25

**Chipstead** How Ln CR5 3LN ☎ 01737 555781
Hilly parkland course, hard walking, good views. Testing 18th hole.
*18 holes, 5491yds, Par 68, SSS 67, Course record 63.*
*Club membership 650.*
Visitors    must contact in advance. May not play weekends.
Societies   must apply in writing.
Green Fees  £25 per day (£20 after 2pm).
Facilities  ⊗ ▥ by prior arrangement ⬗ 🍺 ♀ ⚘ 🏠 🍴
            ℓ Gary Torbett.
Leisure     trolley for hire, putting green, practice area.
Location    0.5m N of village
Hotel       ★★★★ 65% Selsdon Park Hotel, Addington Rd, Sanderstead, CROYDON
            ☎ 0181 657 8811 170 ➪ ʀ̃

## CHOBHAM                                        Map 04 SU96

**Chobham** Chobham Rd, Knaphill GU21 2TZ
☎ 01276 855584 & 855748 pro
Designed by Peter Allis and CLive Clark, Chobham course sits among mature oaks and tree nurseries offering tree-lined fairways, together with six man-made lakes.
*18 holes, 5821yds, Par 69, SSS 67, Course record 67.*
*Club membership 750.*

Visitors    booking in advance essential.
Societies   by prior arrangement.
Green Fees  £22 (£30 weekends & bank holidays).
Facilities  ⊗ ⬗ 🍺 ♀ ⚘ 🏠 ℓ Richard Thomas.
Leisure     trolley for hire, putting green, practice area.
Hotel       ★★★ 64% Falcon Hotel, 68 Farnborough Rd, FARNBOROUGH ☎ 01252 545378 30 ➪ ʀ̃

## COBHAM                                          Map 04 TQ16

**Silvermere** Redhill Rd KT11 1EF ☎ 01932 866007
Parkland course with many very tight holes through woodland, 17th has 170-yd carry over the lake. Driving range.
*18 holes, 6700yds, Par 73.*
*Club membership 740.*
Visitors    may not play at weekends until 1pm. Must contact in advance.
Societies   must contact by telephone.
Green Fees  £18.50 per round (£25 weekends & bank holidays).
Facilities  ⊗ ▥ ⬗ 🍺 ♀ ⚘ 🏠 🍴 ℓ Doug McClelland.
Leisure     fishing, trolley for hire, driving range, putting green, practice area.
Location    2.25m NW off A245
Hotel       ★★★★ 60% Woodlands Park Hotel, Woodlands Ln, STOKE D'ABERNON
            ☎ 01372 843933 58 ➪ ʀ̃

## CRANLEIGH                                       Map 04 TQ03

**Fernfell Golf & Country Club** Barhatch Ln GU6 7NG
☎ 01483 268855
Scenic woodland/parkland course at the base of the Surrey hills, easy walking. Clubhouse in 400-year-old barn.
*18 holes, 5636yds, Par 68, SSS 67, Course record 64.*
*Club membership 1000.*
Visitors    may only play at weekends after noon. Contact professional in advance 01483 277188
Societies   telephone in advance.
Green Fees  £25 per day (weekday only); £20 per round.
Facilities  ⊗ ▥ by prior arrangement ⬗ 🍺 ♀ ⚘ 🏠 🍴
            ℓ Trevor Longmuir.
Leisure     hard tennis courts, outdoor swimming pool, sauna, trolley for hire, driving range, putting green, practice area.
Location    Off A281 Guildford to Horsham road, signposted Cranleigh
Hotel       ★★★ 61% Gatton Manor Hotel Golf & Country Club, Standon Ln, OCKLEY
            ☎ 01306 627555 14 ➪ ʀ̃

**Wildwood** Horsham Rd, Alfold, Cranleigh GU6 8JE
☎ 01403 753255
Parkland with stands of old oaks dominating several holes, a stream fed by a natural spring winds through a series of lakes and ponds. The greens are smooth, undulating and large. The 5th and 16th are the most challenging holes.
*18 holes, 655yds, Par 72, SSS 73, Course record 65.*
*Club membership 500.*
Visitors    welcome subject to availability & booking.
Societies   apply in writing.
Green Fees  not confirmed.
Facilities  ♀ ⚘ 🏠 🍴 ℓ Nicholas Parfrement.
Leisure     fishing, caddy cars can be booked.                    ▶

| Location | Off A281, approx 9m S of Guildford |
|---|---|
| Hotel | ★★★ 61% Gatton Manor Hotel Golf & Country Club, Standon Ln, OCKLEY ☎ 01306 627555 14 ⇌ 🐾 |

## DORKING
Map 04 TQ14

**Betchworth Park** Reigate Rd RH4 1NZ
☎ 01306 882052
Parkland course, with hard walking on southern ridge of Boxhill.
*18 holes, 6266yds, Par 69, SSS 70, Course record 64.*
*Club membership 725.*

| Visitors | weekend play Sun pm only. Must contact in advance. |
|---|---|
| Societies | apply in writing. |
| Green Fees | weekday £31 per day/round am; £25 per round pm (Sun pm £43 per round). |
| Facilities | ⊗ 🏌 ☕ ♀ ⚒ 🏡 🎯 𝄢 Tocher. |
| Leisure | trolley for hire, putting green, practice area. |
| Location | 1m E on A25 |
| Hotel | ★★★ 62% The White Horse, High St, DORKING ☎ 01306 881138 36 ⇌ 🐾Annexe32 ⇌ 🐾 |

**Dorking** Chart Park, Deepdene Av RH5 4BX
☎ 01306 886917
Undulating parkland course, easy slopes, wind-sheltered.
Testing holes: 5th 'Tom's Puddle' (par 4); 7th 'Rest and Be Thankful' (par 4); 9th 'Double Decker' (par 4).
*9 holes, 5120yds, Par 66, SSS 65, Course record 62.*
*Club membership 408.*

| Visitors | may not play Wed am and with member only weekends & bank holidays. Contact in advance. |
|---|---|
| Societies | Tue & Thu, telephone in advance. |
| Green Fees | £16 per day; £12 per 18 holes. |
| Facilities | ⊗ �🍽 by prior arrangement 🏌 ☕ ♀ ⚒ 🏡 🎯 𝄢 Paul Napier. |
| Leisure | motorised carts for hire, trolley for hire, putting green. |
| Location | 1m S on A24 |
| Hotel | ★★★★ 68% The Burford Bridge, Burford Bridge, Box Hill, DORKING ☎ 01306 884561 48 ⇌ 🐾 |

## EAST HORSLEY
Map 04 TQ05

**Drift** KT24 5HD ☎ 01483 284641
Woodland course with sheltered fairways and many ponds.
*18 holes, 6424yds, Par 73, SSS 72, Course record 71.*
*Club membership 650.*

| Visitors | must contact in advance. With member only weekends & bank holidays. |
|---|---|
| Societies | telephone in advance. |
| Green Fees | £30 per day; £20 per round. |
| Facilities | ⊗ ⍟ 🏌 ☕ ♀ ⚒ 🏡 𝄢 Dominic Tunn. |
| Leisure | motorised carts for hire, buggies for hire, trolley for hire, putting green, practice area. |
| Location | 1.5m N off B2039 |
| Hotel | ★★★ 63% Jarvis Thatchers Hotel, Epsom Rd, EAST HORSLEY ☎ 01483 284291 34 ⇌ 🐾Annexe20 ⇌ 🐾 |

## EFFINGHAM
Map 04 TQ15

**Effingham** Guildford Rd KT24 5PZ ☎ 01372 452203
Easy-walking downland course laid out on 27-acres with tree-lined fairways. It is one of the longest of the Surrey courses with wide subtle greens that provide a provocative but by no means exhausting challenge. Fine views.
*18 holes, 6524yds, Par 71, SSS 71, Course record 64.*
*Club membership 800.*

| Visitors | contact in advance. With member only weekends & bank holidays. |
|---|---|
| Societies | Wed, Thu & Fri only and must book in advance. |
| Green Fees | £35 per day, £27.50 after 2pm. With member only weekends and bank holidays. |
| Facilities | ⊗ 🏌 ☕ ♀ ⚒ 🏡 🎯 𝄢 Steve Hoatson. |
| Leisure | motorised carts for hire, buggies for hire, trolley for hire, driving range, putting green, practice area. |
| Location | W side of village on A246 |
| Hotel | ★★★ 63% Jarvis Thatchers Hotel, Epsom Rd, EAST HORSLEY ☎ 01483 284291 34 ⇌ 🐾Annexe20 ⇌ 🐾 |

## ENTON GREEN
Map 04 SU94

**West Surrey** GU8 5AF ☎ 01483 421275
A good parkland-type course in rolling, well-wooded setting. Some fairways are tight with straight driving at a premium. The 17th is a testing hole with a long hill walk.
*18 holes, 6259yds, Par 71, SSS 70, Course record 65.*
*Club membership 600.*

| Visitors | must contact in advance. |
|---|---|
| Societies | must apply in writing. All players to have a handicap. |
| Green Fees | £38.50 per day; £27 per round (£47.50 all day weekends & bank holidays). |
| Facilities | ⊗ ⍟ 🏌 ☕ ♀ ⚒ 🏡 𝄢 Alister Tawse. |
| Leisure | trolley for hire, putting green, practice area. |
| Location | S side of village |
| Hotel | ★★★ 61% Bush Hotel, The Borough, FARNHAM ☎ 01252 715237 66 ⇌ 🐾 |

## EPSOM
Map 04 TQ26

**Epsom** Longdown Ln South KT17 4JR
☎ 01372 721666
Traditional downland course with many mature trees and well watered greens..
*18 holes, 5701yds, Par 69, SSS 68, Course record 65.*
*Club membership 8900.*

| Visitors | restricted to after midday weekends & bank holidays. |
|---|---|
| Societies | must contact in advance. |
| Green Fees | £25 per day; £16.50 per round (£27/£18.50 weekends & bank holidays). |
| Facilities | ⊗ ⍟ 🏌 ☕ ♀ ⚒ 🏡 𝄢 Ron Goudie. |
| Leisure | trolley for hire, putting green, practice area. |
| Location | SE side of town centre on B288 |
| Hotel | ★★ 63% Heathside Hotel, Brighton Rd, BURGH HEATH ☎ 01737 353355 73 ⇌ 🐾 |

**Horton Park Country Club** Hook Rd KT19 8QG
☎ 0181 394 2626
Parkland course.
*18 holes, 5208yds, Par 69, SSS 65.*
*Club membership 534.*
**Visitors** must book for weekends.
**Societies** must telephone in advance.
**Green Fees** not confirmed.
**Facilities** ♀ ♣ 🏠 ⛳ ⌧ Gary Clements.
**Leisure** golf cart, driving range, putting green.
**Hotel** ★★ 63% Heathside Hotel, Brighton Rd,
BURGH HEATH ☎ 01737 353355 73 ➪ ☏

## ESHER                                    Map 04 TQ16

**Moore Place** Portsmouth Rd KT10 9LN
☎ 01372 463533
Public course on attractive, undulating parkland laid out some
60 years ago by Harry Vardon. Examples of most of the trees
that will survive in the UK are to be found on the course.
Testing short holes at 4th, 5th and 7th.
*9 holes, 2128yds, Par 32, SSS 30, Course record 25.*
*Club membership 300.*
**Visitors** no restrictions.
**Societies** must contact in advance.
**Green Fees** £5.50 (£7.40 weekends & bank holidays).
**Facilities** ⊗ ⛘ ⛳ ⛴ ♀ ♣ 🏠 ⛳ ⌧ David Allen.
**Leisure** trolley for hire, putting green, practice area.
**Location** SW side of town centre on A244
**Hotel** ★★★ 71% Ship Thistle, Monument Green,
WEYBRIDGE ☎ 01932 848364 39 ➪ ☏

*Sandown Golf Centre* Sandown Park, More Ln KT10 8AN
☎ 01372 463340
Flat parkland course in middle of racecourse. Additional
facilities include a driving range, and a pitch-and-putt course.
*New Course: 9 holes, 2828yds, Par 35, SSS 34.*
*Par 3: 9 holes, 1193yds, Par 27.*
*Club membership 650.*
**Visitors** no restrictions.
**Societies** must apply in writing.
**Green Fees** not confirmed.
**Facilities** ♀ ♣ 🏠 ⌧
**Leisure** driving range,putting,trolley hire.
**Location** 1m NW off A307
**Hotel** ★★ 65% Haven Hotel, Portsmouth Rd,
ESHER
☎ 0181 398 0023 16 ➪ ☏Annexe4 ➪ ☏

**Thames Ditton & Esher** Portsmouth Rd KT10 9AL
☎ 0181 398 1551
Commonland course. There is a public right of way across the
course.
*18 holes, 5149yds, Par 66, SSS 65, Course record 63.*
*Club membership 250.*
**Visitors** may not play on Sun mornings. Advisable to
telephone for availability.
**Societies** must contact in advance.
**Green Fees** £10 per round (£12 weekends).
**Facilities** ⊗ ⛘ ⛳ ⛴ by prior arrangement ⛴ ♀ ♣ 🏠
⌧ Mark Rodbard.
**Leisure** trolley for hire, putting green, practice area.
**Location** 1m NE on A307
**Hotel** ★★ 65% Haven Hotel, Portsmouth Rd,
ESHER
☎ 0181 398 0023 16 ➪ ☏Annexe4 ➪ ☏

## FARNHAM                                  Map 04 SU84

**Blacknest** Binsted GU34 4QL ☎ 01420 22888 & 22999
Privately owned pay and play golf centre catering for all ages
and levels of abilities. Facilities include a 20-bay driving
range, gymnasium and a long and testing par 3 9-hole course
with water hazards on 8 of the holes. Extension to 18 holes
during 1997.
*9 holes, 6726yds, Par 72, SSS 72.*
*Club membership 350.*
**Visitors** welcome at all times but should telephone for tee
times especially weekends.
**Societies** prior arrangements necessary telephone or write.
**Green Fees** £13 per 18 holes; £8 per 9 holes (£15/£10
weekends). Par 3 £7.50 per day; £6 per 18 holes;
£3.50 per 9 holes.
**Facilities** ⊗ ⛘ by prior arrangement ⛴ ⛴ ♀ ♣ 🏠 ⌧
⌧ Ian Benson.
**Leisure** gymnasium, driving range, par 3 course.
**Location** 0.5m S of A31 at Bentley
**Hotel** ★★★⬥ 60% Farnham House Hotel, Alton Rd,
FARNHAM ☎ 01252 716908 20 ➪ ☏

**Farnham** The Sands GU10 1PX ☎ 01252 782109
A mixture of meadowland and heath with quick drying
sandy subsoil. Several of the earlier holes have
interesting features, the finishing holes rather less.
*18 holes, 6325yds, Par 72, SSS 70, Course record 66.*
*Club membership 500.*
**Visitors** must be member of recognised club & have
handicap certificate. With member only
weekends.
**Societies** must apply in writing.
**Green Fees** £32 per day; £27 per round.
**Facilities** ⊗ ⛘ ⛳ ⛴ ♀ ♣ 🏠 ⌧ Grahame Cowlishaw.
**Leisure** trolley for hire, putting green, practice area.
**Location** 3m E off A31
**Hotel** ★★★ 61% Bush Hotel, The Borough,
FARNHAM ☎ 01252 715237 66 ➪ ☏

**Farnham Park** Folly Hill, Farnham Park GU9 0AU
☎ 01252 715216
Municipal parkland course in Farnham Park.
*9 holes, 1163yds, Par 27.*
**Visitors** pay and play everyday.
**Societies** telephone in advance.
**Green Fees** 18 holes: £6.50 (£7.75 weekends). 9 holes: £3.75
(£4.25 weekends).
**Facilities** ⊗ ⛘ by prior arrangement ⛴ ⛴ ♀ ♣ ⛳ ⌧ Peter
Chapman.
**Location** N side of town centre on A287
**Hotel** ★★★ 61% Bush Hotel, The Borough,
FARNHAM ☎ 01252 715237 66 ➪ ☏

## GODALMING                                Map 04 SU94

**Broadwater Park** Guildford Rd, Farncombe GU7 3BU
☎ 01483 429955
A Par-3 public course with floodlit driving range.
*9 holes, 1287yds, Par 54, SSS 50.*
*Club membership 160.*
**Visitors** must book for weekends & bank holidays,
**Societies** telephone in advance
**Green Fees** 18 holes £6.25; 9 holes £3.75 (£7.75/£4.25
weekends & bank holidays).                      ▶

**Facilities** ⊗ ⅏ ⓛ ▉ ♀ 🛏 ⚓ 🍴 ╒ Kevin D Milton.
**Leisure** trolley for hire, driving range, putting green.
**Location** 4m SW of Guildford
**Hotel** ★★★ 65% Inn on the Lake, Ockford Rd, GODALMING ☎ 01483 415575 19 ⇔ 🐾

---

**Hurtmore** Hurtmore Rd, Hurtmore GU7 2RN
☎ 01483 426492 & 424440
A Peter Alliss/Clive Clark Pay and Play course with seven lakes and 100 bunkers. The 15th hole is the longest at 540yards. Played mainly into the wind there are 10 bunkers to negotiate. The 3rd hole at 440yds stroke Index 1 is a real test. A dogleg right around a lake and 9 bunkers makes this hole worthy of its stroke index.
*18 holes, 5514yds, Par 70, SSS 67.*
*Club membership 200.*
**Visitors** book by telephone up to 6 days in advance.
**Societies** telephone in advance.
**Green Fees** £14 per 18 holes (£10 weekends).
**Facilities** ⊗ ⓛ ▉ ♀ 🛏 ⚓ 🍴 ╒ Maxine Burton.
**Leisure** trolley for hire.
**Location** 2m NW of Godalming between A3/A3100, access via unclass road
**Hotel** ★★★ 65% Inn on the Lake, Ockford Rd, GODALMING ☎ 01483 415575 19 ⇔ 🐾

---

**Shillinglee Park** Chiddingfold GU8 4TA
☎ 01428 653237 & 708158
Manicured parkland course with many natural features including seven ponds. The 4th and 7th are the signature holes requiring tee shots and second shots over ponds, to well-guarded greens.
*9 holes, 5032yds, Par 64, SSS 64, Course record 65.*

*Club membership 400.*
**Visitors** no restrictions but advisable to book starting times.
**Societies** apply for details.
**Green Fees** £13.50 per day; £11 per 18 holes; £7.50 per 9 holes (£16/£13/£8.50 weekends).
**Facilities** ⊗ ⅏ ⓛ ▉ ♀ 🛏 🍴 ╒ Roger Mace.
**Leisure** motorised carts for hire, buggies for hire, trolley for hire, putting green, practice area.
**Location** 5m S of Godalming, off A283
**Hotel** ★★★ 65% Inn on the Lake, Ockford Rd, GODALMING ☎ 01483 415575 19 ⇔ 🐾

---

## GUILDFORD ................................ Map 04 SU94

**Guildford** High Path Rd, Merrow GU1 2HL
☎ 01483 63941
A downland course but with some trees and much scrub. The holes provide an interesting variety of play, an invigorating experience.
*18 holes, 6090yds, Par 69, SSS 70, Course record 64.*
*Club membership 700.*
**Visitors** must contact in advance. With member only weekends & bank holidays.
**Societies** welcome Mon-Fri. Must apply in advance.
**Green Fees** £35 per day; £25 per round.
**Facilities** ⊗ ⅏ by prior arrangement ⓛ ▉ ♀ 🛏 🍴 ╒ P G Hollington.
**Leisure** motorised carts for hire, trolley for hire, putting green, practice area.
**Location** E side of town centre off A246
**Hotel** ★★★ 70% The Manor, Newlands Corner, GUILDFORD ☎ 01483 222624 19 ⇔ 🐾

# We Welcome Your Company

## KOSAIDO
## OLD THORNS
GOLF COURSE • HOTEL • RESTAURANTS

### Longmoor Road, Griggs Green, Liphook, Hampshire GU30 7PE
### Telephone: 901428 724555    Fax: 01428 725036

Old Thorns golf course, hotel and restaurants complex is an unique combination of old and new. The tranquillity and peace is complemented by the elegant Japanese centre where you can sample authentic Japanese cuisine, experience Japanese baths and enjoy the Natural beauty of the simple Japanese designed gardens. The Fuji Room designed to welcome the traditional Japanese family who prefer tatami matting and paper screens in familiar surroundings. The Clubhouse comprises of an European restaurant offering the finest English cuisine complemented by excellent wines. 28 twin bedded rooms all have their own bathroom, colour television, direct dial telephone, radio and tea making facilities. The adjoining Leisure Complex with its indoor swimming pool and outdoor, all weather, hard tennis courts can provide an alternative to the 18 hole championship golf course, which is a constant challenge for the enthusiastic golfer. Ideally situated in 230 acres of Hampshire countryside within one hour's drive of Heathrow and Gatwick airports just off the A3 at the Griggs Green exit after Liphook.

**Milford** Station Ln, Milford GU8 5HS
☎ 01483 419200
A Peter Alliss/Clive Clark designed course opened summer
1993. The design has cleverly incorporated a demanding
course within an existing woodland and meadow area.
*18 holes, 5916yds, Par 69, SSS 68, Course record 67.*
*Club membership 750.*
Visitors　　telephone 01483 416291 up to 1 week in
　　　　　　advance.
Societies　telephone in advance.
Green Fees £25 per day; £19.50 per round; £10 per 9 holes
　　　　　　(£35/£25/£12.50 weekends).
Facilities　⊗ ⅢⅡ ⴱ ⯅ ♀ ⅄ 🖻 🕈 ℓ Grant Clough.
Leisure　　motorised carts for hire, trolley for hire, buggies
　　　　　　for hire, driving range, putting green, practice
　　　　　　area.
Location　6m SW, leave A3 Milford then A3100 to Enton
Hotel　　　★★★ 65% Inn on the Lake, Ockford Rd,
　　　　　　GODALMING
　　　　　　☎ 01483 415575 19 ⇆ ♟

**Roker Park** Rokers Farm, Aldershot Rd GU3 3PB
☎ 01483 236677
A Pay and Play 9-hole parkland course. A challenging course
with two Par 5 holes.
*9 holes, 3037yds, Par 36, SSS 72.*
*Club membership 200.*
Visitors　　no restrictions, pay & play, phone for
　　　　　　reservations.
Societies　prior arrangement with deposit at least 14 days
　　　　　　before, minimum 12 persons.
Green Fees £11 per 18 holes; £6.50 per 9 holes (£14/£8
　　　　　　weekends).
Facilities　⊗ ⅢⅡ ⴱ ⯅ ♀ ⅄ 🖻 🕈 ℓ Kevin Warn.
Leisure　　motorised carts for hire, buggies for hire, trolley
　　　　　　for hire, driving range, putting green.
Location　A323, 3m from Guildford
Hotel　　　★★★ 75% The Angel Posting House and
　　　　　　Livery, 91 High St, GUILDFORD
　　　　　　☎ 01483 64555 11 ⇆ ♟

## HINDHEAD　　　　　　　　　　Map 04 SU83

**Hindhead** Churt Rd GU26 6HX
☎ 01428 604614
A good example of a Surrey heath-and-heather course,
and most picturesque. Players must be prepared for some
hard walking. The first nine fairways follow narrow
valleys requiring straight hitting; the second nine are
much less restricted.
*18 holes, 6373yds, Par 70, SSS 70, Course record 63.*
*Club membership 850.*
Visitors　　must contact in advance and have a
　　　　　　handicap certificate.
Societies　Wed & Thu only, contact in advance
Green Fees £35 (£42 weekends & bank holidays). 9
　　　　　　holes £27 (£32 weekends & bank holidays).
Facilities　⊗ ⅢⅡ ⴱ ⯅ ♀ ⅄ 🖻 ℓ Neil Ogilvy.
Leisure　　trolley for hire.
Location　1.5m NW on A287
Hotel　　　★★★★ 72% Lythe Hill Hotel, Petworth
　　　　　　Rd, HASLEMERE
　　　　　　☎ 01428 651251 40 ⇆ ♟

## KINGSWOOD　　　　　　　　　　Map 04 TQ25

**Kingswood** Sandy Ln KT20 6NE ☎ 01737 832188
Flat parkland course, easy walking.
*18 holes, 6880yds, Par 72, SSS 73.*
*Club membership 700.*
Visitors　　must contact professional at least 24 hrs in
　　　　　　advance. May not play weekends.
Societies　must apply in advance.
Green Fees £45 per day; £32 per round.
Facilities　⊗ ⴱ ⯅ ♀ ⅄ 🖻 🕈 ℓ James Dodds.
Leisure　　squash, motorised carts for hire, buggies for hire,
　　　　　　trolley for hire, driving range, putting green,
　　　　　　practice area.
Location　5m S of village off A217
Hotel　　　★★ 63% Heathside Hotel, Brighton Rd,
　　　　　　BURGH HEATH ☎ 01737 353355 73 ⇆ ♟

## LEATHERHEAD　　　　　　　　　　Map 04 TQ15

**Leatherhead** Kingston Rd KT22 0EE
☎ 01372 843966 & 843958
Parkland course with numerous ditches and only two hills, so
walking is easy.
*18 holes, 6203yds, Par 71, SSS 69, Course record 67.*
Visitors　　telephone pro shop 01372 843956 up to 10 days
　　　　　　in advance.
Societies　telephone for booking form.
Green Fees £40 per 36 holes; £27.50 per 18 holes (£40 per
　　　　　　18 holes weekends, pm only).
Facilities　⊗ ⅢⅡ ⴱ ⯅ ♀ ⅄ 🖻 🕈 ℓ Richard Hurst.
Leisure　　sauna, buggies for hire, trolley for hire, putting
　　　　　　green, practice area.
Location　0.25m from junct 9 of M25, on A243
Hotel　　　★★★★ 60% Woodlands Park Hotel,
　　　　　　Woodlands Ln, STOKE D'ABERNON
　　　　　　☎ 01372 843933 58 ⇆ ♟

**Pachesham Park Golf Complex** Oaklawn Rd KT22 0BT
☎ 01372 843453
A 9-hole undulating parkland course playing out over 18
holes at 5,400yards.
*9 holes, 2805yds, Par 70, SSS 67.*
*Club membership 385.*
Visitors　　book 2 days in advance by phone. May play
　　　　　　weekends after 12.30pm.
Societies　apply in advance.
Green Fees £12.50 per 18 holes; £7.50 per 9 holes (£15/£9
　　　　　　weekends & bank holidays).
Facilities　⊗ ⅢⅡ by prior arrangement ⴱ ⯅ ♀ ⅄ 🖻 🕈
　　　　　　ℓ Philip Taylor.
Leisure　　trolley for hire, floodlit driving range, putting
　　　　　　green, practice area.
Location　On A244, 0.5m from M25 junct 9
Hotel　　　★★★★ 60% Woodlands Park Hotel,
　　　　　　Woodlands Ln, STOKE D'ABERNON
　　　　　　☎ 01372 843933 58 ⇆ ♟

**Tyrrells Wood** The Drive KT22 8QP ☎ 01372 376025
Parkland course with easy walking. Snooker.
*18 holes, 6234yds, Par 71, SSS 70, Course record 65.*
*Club membership 700.*
Visitors　　must contact in advance. Restricted weekends.
Societies　must apply in advance.
Green Fees £48 per day; £32 per round.　　　　　　▶

| | |
|---|---|
| Facilities | ⊗ 🗲 🖢 💺 ♀ ⚲ 🏠 🔧 ⁅ Max Taylor. |
| Leisure | trolley for hire, putting green & practice area. |
| Location | 2m SE of town, off A24 |
| Hotel | ★★★★ 68% The Burford Bridge, Burford Bridge, Box Hill, DORKING ☎ 01306 884561 48 ⇄ ℟ |

## LIMPSFIELD                                   Map 05 TQ45

**Limpsfield Chart** Westerham Rd RH8 0SL
☎ 01883 723405
Tight heathland course set in National Trust land.
*9 holes, 5718yds, Par 70, SSS 68, Course record 64.*
*Club membership 300.*

| | |
|---|---|
| Visitors | with member only or by appointment weekends & not before 3.30pm Thu (Ladies Day). |
| Societies | must apply in advance. |
| Green Fees | £18 per day/round. £10 four hours before sunset. |
| Facilities | ⊗ by prior arrangement 🗲 by prior arrangement 🖢 💺 ♀ ⚲ |
| Leisure | putting green, practice area. |
| Location | 1m E on A25 |
| Hotel | ★★★ 68% Kings Arms Hotel, Market Square, WESTERHAM ☎ 01959 562990 16 ⇄ ℟ |

## LINGFIELD                                    Map 05 TQ34

**Lingfield Park** Lingfield Rd, Racecourse Rd RH7 6PQ
☎ 01342 834602
Difficult and challenging, tree-lined parkland course set in
210 acres of beautiful Surrey countryside. Driving range.
*18 holes, 6473yds, Par 71, SSS 72, Course record 70.*
*Club membership 750.*

| | |
|---|---|
| Visitors | must be accompanied by member on Sat & Sun. Advisable to telephone first. |
| Societies | must telephone in advance. |
| Green Fees | £25 per round. |
| Facilities | ⊗ 🗲 🖢 💺 ♀ ⚲ 🏠 🔧 ⁅ Christopher Morley. |
| Leisure | motorised carts for hire, buggies for hire, trolley for hire, driving range, putting green, practice area. |
| Location | Entrance next to Lingfield race course |
| Hotel | ★★★ 70% Woodbury House Hotel, Lewes Rd, EAST GRINSTEAD ☎ 01342 313657 13 ⇄ ℟Annexe1 ℟ |

## NEWDIGATE                                    Map 04 TQ14

**Rusper** Rusper Rd RH5 5BX
☎ 01293 871871 & 871456
New course set in mature woodland. The opening two holes
give the golfer an encouraging start with the following holes
demanding accurate playing through the trees. The 5th hole is
a challenging Par 5 from the back tee with a gentle dogleg
tempting the golfer to take a shortcut.
*9 holes, 6069yds, Par 71, SSS 69, Course record 67.*
*Club membership 250.*

| | |
|---|---|
| Visitors | welcome but telephone to reserve time, some restrictions if competitions being played. |
| Societies | telephone for details. |
| Green Fees | £11.50 per 18 holes; £7 per 9 holes (£15.50/£8.50 weekends). |
| Facilities | ⊗ 🗲 by prior arrangement 🖢 💺 ♀ ⚲ 🏠 🔧 ⁅ Karl Spurrier. |

| | |
|---|---|
| Leisure | trolley for hire, driving range, putting green. |
| Location | Between Newdigate/Rusper, off A24 |
| Hotel | ★★★★ 68% The Burford Bridge, Burford Bridge, Box Hill, DORKING ☎ 01306 884561 48 ⇄ ℟ |

## OCKLEY                                       Map 04 TQ14

**Gatton Manor Hotel Golf & Country Club** Standon Ln
RH5 5PQ ☎ 01306 627555
Undulating course through woods and over many challenging
water holes.
*18 holes, 6653yds, Par 72, SSS 72, Course record 68.*
*Club membership 300.*

| | |
|---|---|
| Visitors | must give 2 weeks prior notice. Restricted Sun (am). Tee times to be booked through professional 01306 627557 |
| Societies | must apply in advance. |
| Green Fees | £30 per day; £18 per round;(£50/£25 weekends). Twilight £12 (£15 weekends). |
| Facilities | ⊗ 🗲 🖢 💺 ♀ ⚲ 🏠 🔧 🍴 ⁅ Rae Sargent. |
| Leisure | grass tennis courts, fishing, sauna, solarium, gymnasium, motorised carts for hire, buggies for hire, trolley for hire, driving range, putting green, practice area. |
| Location | 1.5m SW off A29 |
| Hotel | ★★★ 61% Gatton Manor Hotel Golf & Country Club, Standon Ln, OCKLEY ☎ 01306 627555 14 ⇄ ℟ |

# *Gatton Manor Hotel*
### *Golf and Country Club* ★★
### Ockley, Nr. Dorking RH5 5PQ
### Tel: Oakwood Hill (01306) 627555/6
### Fax: (01306) 627713

*Gatton Manor Hotel, Golf & Country Club is an
18th Century manor house set within its own 18-
hole championship length golf course and
offering 14 well appointed en-suite bedrooms,
with an à la carte restaurant serving both
English and Continental cuisine. Adjacent to the
restaurant is a large bar with a superb selection
of wines and spirits.*
*The hotel also offers three tastefully decorated
conference suites available with all the
latest equipment. Other facilities include
tennis, fishing, bowls and purpose built
Gym & Health Suite.*

## OTTERSHAW                     Map 04 TQ06

**Foxhills** Stonehill Rd KT16 0EL ☎ 01932 872050
A pair of parkland courses designed in the grand manner
and with American course-design in mind. One course is
tree-lined, the other, as well as trees, has massive bunkers
and artificial lakes which contribute to the interest. Both
courses offer testing golf and they finish on the same
long 'double green'. Par 3 'Manor' course also available.
*Chertsey Course: 18 holes, 6734yds, Par 73, SSS 72.*
*Longcross Course: 18 holes, 6417yds, Par 72, SSS 71.*
*Manor Course: 9 holes, 1275yds, Par 27.*
**Visitors**        restricted before noon weekends.
**Societies**       welcome Mon-Fri, must apply in advance.
**Green Fees** £65 per day; £45 per 36 holes (£55 per 18
                    holes weekends).
**Facilities**      ⊗ ⍢ ⯘ ⬛ ⛳ ♀ ⚲ 🏠 ⚲ 🏁
                    ✆ A Goode/B Hunt/R Summerscales.
**Leisure**         hard tennis courts, outdoor and indoor
                    heated swimming pools, squash, sauna,
                    solarium, gymnasium, motorised carts for
                    hire, buggies for hire, trolley for hire,
                    driving range, putting green, practice area,
                    health club.
**Location**        1m NW
**Hotel**           ★★★ 66% The Crown Hotel, 7 London St,
                    CHERTSEY
                    ☎ 01932 564657 Annexe30 ⇌ 🏮

## PIRBRIGHT                     Map 04 SU95

**Goal Farm** Gole Rd GU24 0PZ
☎ 01483 473183 & 473205
Beautiful lanscaped parkland 'Pay and Play' course with
excellent greens.
*9 holes, 1273yds, Par 54, SSS 48.*
*Club membership 300.*
**Visitors**        may not play on Sat before 4pm or Thu
                    mornings.
**Societies**       telephone in advance.
**Green Fees** £3.50 per round (£3.75 weekends & bank
                    holidays).
**Facilities**      ⬛ ⛳ ♀ ⚲ 🏠
**Leisure**         putting green, practice area.
**Location**        1.5m NW on B3012
**Hotel**           B Forte Posthouse Farnborough, Lynchford Rd,
                    FARNBOROUGH ☎ 01252 545051 110 ⇌ 🏮

## PUTTENHAM                     Map 04 SU94

**Puttenham** Heath Rd GU3 1AL ☎ 01483 810498
Picturesque tree-lined heathland course offering testing golf,
easy walking.
*18 holes, 6214yds, Par 71, SSS 70.*
*Club membership 650.*
**Visitors**        with member only weekends & public holidays.
                    Must contact in advance.
**Societies**       apply in advance to secretary.
**Green Fees** £30 per day; £23 per round.
**Facilities**      ⊗ ⍢ ⬛ ⯘ ♀ ⚲ 🏠 ✆ Gary Simmons.
**Leisure**         trolley for hire, putting green, practice area.
**Location**        1m SE on B3000
**Hotel**           ★★★ 61% Bush Hotel, The Borough,
                    FARNHAM ☎ 01252 715237 66 ⇌ 🏮

## REDHILL                       Map 04 TQ25

*Redhill & Reigate* Clarence Rd, Pendelton Rd RH1 6LB
☎ 01737 240777
Parkland course.
*18 holes, 5238yds, Par 67, SSS 66.*
*Club membership 600.*
**Visitors**        may not play before 11am weekends or after
                    2pm Sun (Jun-Sep). Must contact in advance.
**Societies**       must apply in writing.
**Green Fees** not confirmed.
**Facilities**      ♀ ⚲ 🏠 ⚲ ✆
**Leisure**         putting, trolley hire.
**Location**        1m S on A23
**Hotel**           ★★★ 65% Reigate Manor Hotel, Reigate Hill,
                    REIGATE ☎ 01737 240125 51 ⇌ 🏮

## REIGATE                       Map 04 TQ25

**Reigate Heath** Flanchford Rd RH2 8QR ☎ 01737 242610
Heathland course.
*9 holes, 5658yds, Par 67, SSS 67, Course record 65.*
*Club membership 550.*
**Visitors**        with member only weekends & bank holidays.
                    Must contact in advance.
**Societies**       must apply in writing.
**Green Fees** £20 per day; £16 morning; £12 afternoon.
**Facilities**      ⊗ ⍢ by prior arrangement ⬛ ⯘ ♀ ⚲ 🏠
                    ✆ Barry Davies.
**Leisure**         trolley for hire, putting green, practice area.
**Location**        1.5m W off A25
**Hotel**           ★★★ 65% Reigate Manor Hotel, Reigate Hill,
                    REIGATE ☎ 01737 240125 51 ⇌ 🏮

**Reigate Hill** Gatton Bottom RH2 0TU ☎ 01737 645577
Championship standard course opened in 1995 with fully
irrigated tees and greens. Feature holes include the 5th which
is divided by four bunkers and the par 5 14th involving a
tricky drive across a lake.
*18 holes, 6175yds, Par 72, SSS 70.*
*Club membership 650.*
**Visitors**        must contact in advance to book tee time, may
                    not play weekends.
**Societies**       welcome Mon-Fri but must book in advance.
**Green Fees** £25 per round.
**Facilities**      ⬛ ⯘ ♀ ⚲ 🏠 ⚲ ✆ Martin Platts.
**Leisure**         trolley for hire, driving range, putting green,
                    practice area.
**Location**        2m from junct 8 of M25
**Hotel**           ★★★ 63% Bridge House Hotel, Reigate Hill,
                    REIGATE
                    ☎ 01737 246801 & 244821 40 ⇌ 🏮

## RIPLEY                        Map 04 TQ05

*Wisley GU23 6QU* ☎ 01483 211022
A 27-hole course designed by Robert Trent Jones Jnr,
and the first that this well-known American golf architect
has designed in the UK. Penncross Bent grasses have
been used to provide a superb playing surface.
*The Church Course: 9 holes, 3355yds, Par 36, SSS 73.*
*The Mill Course: 9 holes, 3473yds, Par 36, SSS 73.*
*The Garden Course: 9 holes, 3385yds, Par 36, SSS 73.*
*Club membership 510.*                                      ▶

**Visitors** may only play with member.
**Green Fees** not confirmed.
**Facilities** ♀ ♣ 🏠 ᵀ ₵ Bill Reid.
**Leisure** fishing, sauna.
**Hotel** ★★★ 63% Jarvis Thatchers Hotel, Epsom
Rd, EAST HORSLEY
☎ 01483 284291 34 ⇌ 🐾Annexe20 ⇌ 🐾

## SHEPPERTON Map 04 TQ06

**Sunbury** Charlton Ln TW17 8QA ☎ 01932 771414
There is a 9-hole course already in use at Sunbury which at
6210 yards, with two Par 5's and two Par 3's, is one of the
longest in the south of England. There is also a new 18-hole
course due to open in September 1996.
*9 holes, 6210yds, Par 72, SSS 72, Course record 70.*
*Club membership 300.*
**Visitors** no restrictions.
**Societies** advance booking necessary.
**Green Fees** 18 holes: £10 £12 weekends & bank holidays). 9
holes: £6 (£7.50 weekends & bank holidays).
Weekends after 4.30pm £5.
**Facilities** ⊗ 圃 ⛳ ♥ ♀ 🏠 ₵ Alistair Hardaway.
**Leisure** floodlit driving range, putting green, practice
area.
**Hotel** ★★★ 65% Shepperton Moat House Hotel,
Felix Ln, SHEPPERTON
☎ 01932 241404 156 ⇌ 🐾

## TANDRIDGE Map 05 TQ35

**Tandridge** RH8 9NQ ☎ 01883 712274
Rolling parkland, Colt designed course; good views.
*18 holes, 6250yds, Par 70, SSS 70.*
*Club membership 750.*
**Visitors** must contact in advance. May play Mon, Wed,
Thu.
**Societies** Mon, Wed & Thu, apply in advance.
**Green Fees** £40 per day; £31 per round (Winter £31/£21).
**Facilities** ⊗ ⛳ ♥ ♀ ♣ 🏠 ᵀ ₵ Allan Farquhar.
**Leisure** motorised carts for hire, trolley for hire, driving
range, putting green, practice area.
**Location** 2m SE junc 6 M25, 1.5m E of Godstone on A25
**Hotel** ★★★ 74% Nutfield Priory, NUTFIELD
☎ 01737 822066 52 ⇌ 🐾

## TILFORD Map 04 SU84

*Hankley Common* GU10 2DD ☎ 01252 792493
A natural heathland course subject to wind. Greens are
first rate. The 18th, a long par 4, is most challenging, the
green being beyond a deep chasm which traps any but the
perfect second shot. The 7th is a spectacular one-shotter.
*18 holes, 6418yds, Par 71, SSS 71.*
*Club membership 700.*
**Visitors** handicap certificate required, restricted to
afternoons at weekends.
**Societies** apply in writing.
**Green Fees** not confirmed.
**Facilities** ♀ ♣ 🏠 ₵ Peter Stow.
**Location** 0.75m SE
**Hotel** ★★★ 61% Bush Hotel, The Borough,
FARNHAM ☎ 01252 715237 66 ⇌ 🐾

## VIRGINIA WATER Map 04 TQ06

## WENTWORTH See page 203

## WALTON-ON-THAMES Map 04 TQ16

**Burhill** Burwood Rd KT12 4BL ☎ 01932 227345
A relatively short and easy parkland course with some
truly magnificent trees. The 18th is a splendid par 4
requiring a well-placed drive and a long firm second.
This course is always in immaculate condition.
*18 holes, 6224yds, Par 69, SSS 70, Course record 64.*
*Club membership 1200.*
**Visitors** may not play Fri-Sun unless introduced by
member. Must contact in advance.
**Societies** apply in writing.
**Green Fees** £44 per day; £30 per round.
**Facilities** ⊗ ⛳ ♥ ♀ ♣ 🏠 ₵ Lee Johnson.
**Leisure** squash, trolley for hire, driving range,
putting green, practice area.
**Location** 2m S
**Hotel** ★★★ 71% Ship Thistle, Monument Green,
WEYBRIDGE ☎ 01932 848364 39 ⇌ 🐾

## WALTON-ON-THE-HILL Map 04 TQ25

## WALTON HEATH See page 205

## WEST BYFLEET Map 04 TQ06

*West Byfleet* Sheerwater Rd KT14 6AA
☎ 01932 343433
An attractive course set against a background of
woodland and gorse. The 13th is the famous 'pond' shot
with a water hazard and two bunkers fronting the green.
No less than six holes of 420 yards or more.
*18 holes, 6211yds, Par 70, SSS 70.*
*Club membership 650.*
**Visitors** with member only weekends. Restricted Thu
(Ladies Day).
**Societies** must apply in writing.
**Green Fees** not confirmed.
**Facilities** ♀ ♣ 🏠 ₵ David Regan.
**Location** W side of village on A245
**Hotel** ★★★ 63% Jarvis Thatchers Hotel, Epsom
Rd, EAST HORSLEY
☎ 01483 284291 34 ⇌ 🐾Annexe20 ⇌ 🐾

## WEST CLANDON Map 04 TQ05

*Clandon Regis* Epsom Rd GU4 7TT ☎ 01483 224888
High quality parkland course with challenging lake holes on
the back nine. European Tour specification tees and greens.
*18 holes, 6412yds, Par 72, SSS 71.*
**Visitors** a visitor is allowed to play 10 times a year mid-
week only.
**Societies** telephone in advance.
**Green Fees** not confirmed.
**Facilities** ♀ ♣ 🏠 ₵ Sean Brady.
**Leisure** sauna, indoor practice area. ▶

# WENTWORTH CLUB

### VIRGINIA WATER *Surrey*

☎ 01344 842201      Map O4 TQO6

*John Ingham writes:* Among the really famous inland courses in England you have to name Wentworth. The challenge, in terms of sheer yards, is enormous. But the qualities go beyond this, and include the atmosphere, the heathland, the silver birch and fairway-side homes.

The West Course is the one every visitor wishes to play. You can't possibly name the best hole. Bernard Gallacher, the course professional, has his view, but you may select the 7th where the drive rolls downhill and the second shot has to be played high up to a stepped green. The closing holes really sort out the best of them too.

The clubhouse offers Country Club facilities not typical of many British golf courses. The pro shop resembles a plush city store; evening hospitality events are frequent and society meetings here are catered for as at few other centres for sport, and it's all done in five-star style. Probably it is during the World Match-Play championship when Wentworth can be seen at its best. The tents are up, the superstars pile in and out of huge cars and the air is one of luxury and opulence.

One of the attractions of Wentworth is that the great players, including Ben Hogan and Sam Snead, have played here. Gary Player has won marvellously at Wentworth, beating Tony Lema after being seven down in the 36-hole match! Great competitors from the past have stamped their mark here. Arnold Palmer, back in the 1960s, beat Neil Coles in the Match-Play final but then, a generation later, faced young Seve Ballesteros. The Spaniard saved his bacon by pitching in for an eagle three at the last against Palmer, to take the clash into extra holes, where he won.

| Visitors | weekdays only. Must contact in advance with letter from own club or a current handicap certificate |
|---|---|
| Societies | apply in advance (handicap restrictions) |
| Green fees | (per round) West Course £120; East Course £85; Edinburgh Course £75 (winter rates cheaper). |
| Facilities | ⊗ ♨ ♨ ♨ ♀ (all day) Breakfast from 7a.m. (private rooms) ♨ ♨ ♨ ♨ (Bernard Gallacher) driving range, putting green, practice area, motor carts caddy/ buggy/ trolley hire. |
| Leisure | tennis (hardcourt & grass), outdoor swimming pool, gym, snooker, private fishing |
| Location | Wentworth Drive, GU25 4LS (Wside of Virginia Water, at jnctn of A30 and A329) |

54 holes. West Course: 18 holes, 6957yds, Par 73, SSS 74, Course record 63 (Wayne Riley) East Course: 18 holes, 6176yds, Par 68, SSS 70, Course record 62 (Doug Sewell) Edinburgh: 18 holes, 6979yds, Par 72, SSS 73, Course record 67 (Gary Orr)

## WHERE TO STAY AND EAT NEARBY

**HOTELS:**

**ASCOT**

★★★★ 🏵🏵 68% The Berystede, Bagshot Rd, Sunninghill. ☎ 01344 23311

91 (1 ♨ 90 ➥ ♨)

★★71% Highclere, 19 Kings Road, Sunninghill. ☎ 01344 25220. 11 ➥ ♨

**BAGSHOT**

★★★★(Red) 🏵🏵🏵 ♨♨ Pennyhill Park, London Rd. ☎ 01276 471774 22 ➥ ♨ Annexe 54 ➥ ♨.

**RESTAURANTS:**

**BRAY**

🏵🏵🏵🏵🏵 Waterside Inn, River Cottage, Ferry Rd. ☎ 01628 20691.

| Location | From A246 Guildford/Leatherhead direction |
|---|---|
| Hotel | ★★★ 63% Jarvis Thatchers Hotel, Epsom Rd, EAST HORSLEY ☎ 01483 284291 34 ⇄ 🐾Annexe20 ⇄ 🐾 |

## WEST END                                 Map 04 SU96

**Windlemere** Windlesham Rd GU24 5LS
☎ 01276 858727
A parkland course, undulating in parts with natural water hazards. There is also a floodlit driving range.
*9 holes, 2673yds, Par 34, SSS 33, Course record 30.*

| Visitors | no restrictions. |
|---|---|
| Societies | advisable to contact in advance. |
| Green Fees | 18 holes £14 (£17 weekends); 9 holes £8 (£9.50 weekends). |
| Facilities | ⊗ 🍴 🍷 ♀ ♨ 🏠 ⛳ 🥢 David Thomas. |
| Leisure | trolley for hire, driving range. |
| Location | N side of village at junct of A319/A322 |
| Hotel | ★★★★(red)🏵 Pennyhill Park Hotel, London Rd, BAGSHOT ☎ 01276 471774 22 ⇄ 🐾Annexe54 ⇄ 🐾 |

## WEYBRIDGE                                 Map 04 TQ06

***St George's Hill*** KT13 0NL ☎ 01932 847758
Comparable and similar to Wentworth, a feature of this course is the number of long and difficult par 4s. To score well it is necessary to place the drive - and long driving pays handsomely. Walking is hard on this undulating, heavily wooded course with plentiful heather and rhododendrons.
*A+B Course: 18 holes, 6569yds, Par 70, SSS 71.*
*A+C Course: 18 holes, 6097yds, Par 70, SSS 69.*
*B+C Course: 18 holes, 6210yds, Par 70, SSS 70.*
*Club membership 600.*

| Visitors | must contact in advance and have a handicap certificate. |
|---|---|
| Societies | must contact in advance. |
| Green Fees | not confirmed. |
| Facilities | ♀ ♨ 🏠 🥢 A C Rattue. |
| Location | 2m S off B374 |
| Hotel | ★★★ 71% Ship Thistle, Monument Green, WEYBRIDGE ☎ 01932 848364 39 ⇄ 🐾 |

## WOKING                                     Map 04 TQ05

**Hoebridge Golf Centre** Old Woking Rd GU22 8JH
☎ 01483 722611
Three public courses set in parkland on Surrey sand belt. 24-bay floodlit driving range.
*Main Course: 18 holes, 6536yds, Par 72, SSS 71, Course record 68.*
*Shey Course: 9 holes, 2294yds, Par 33, SSS 31.*
*Maybury Course: 18 holes, 2230yds, Par 54.*
*Club membership 600.*

| Visitors | welcome every day, course and reservation desk open dawn to dusk. Credit card reservations 6 days in advance. |
|---|---|
| Societies | Mon-Fri only, telephone in advance |
| Green Fees | Main: £22.50 per day; £14 per 18 holes; £7.50 per 9 holes. Shey: £7.50 per 9 holes. Maybury: £7 per 18 holes; £4.25 per 9 holes. Prices under review. |
| Facilities | ⊗ 🍴 🍽 🍷 ♀ ♨ 🏠 ⛳ 🥢 Tim Powell. |

| Leisure | motorised carts for hire, buggies for hire, trolley for hire, floodlit driving range, putting green. |
|---|---|
| Location | On B382 Old Woking to West Byfleet road |
| Hotel | ★★★★(red)🏵 Pennyhill Park Hotel, London Rd, BAGSHOT ☎ 01276 471774 22 ⇄ 🐾Annexe54 ⇄ 🐾 |

**Pyrford** Warren Ln, Pyrford GU22 8XR ☎ 01483 723555
Opened in September 1993 this inland links style course was designed by Peter Alliss and Clive Clark. Set between Surrey woodlands, the fairways weave between 23 acres of water courses while the greens and tees are connected by rustic bridges. The signature hole is the Par 5 9th at 595 yards, with a dogleg and final approach over water and a sand shelf.
*18 holes, 6230yds, Par 72, SSS 70, Course record 69.*
*Club membership 600.*

| Visitors | must book in advance. |
|---|---|
| Societies | must contact in advance. |
| Green Fees | £45 per day; £35 per 18 holes (£50 bank holidays and weekends). £10 per 9 holes. |
| Facilities | ⊗ 🍴 🍽 🍷 ♀ ♨ 🏠 ⛳ 🥢 Jeremy Bennett. |
| Leisure | trolley for hire, driving range, putting green, practice area. |
| Location | Off A3 Ripley to Pyrford |
| Hotel | ★★★★(red)🏵 Pennyhill Park Hotel, London Rd, BAGSHOT ☎ 01276 471774 22 ⇄ 🐾Annexe54 ⇄ 🐾 |

***Woking*** Pond Rd, Hook Heath GU22 0JZ
☎ 01483 760053
An 18-hole course on Surrey heathland with few changes from the original course designed in 1892 by Tom Dunn. Bernard Darwin a past Captain and President has written ' the beauty of Woking is that there is something distinctive about every hole...'.
*18 holes, 6340yds, Par 70, SSS 70, Course record 65.*
*Club membership 550.*

| Visitors | must contact secretary at least 7 days prior to playing. No visitors weekends & bank holidays. |
|---|---|
| Societies | telephone intially then confrim in writing, normally 12 months notice. |
| Green Fees | not confirmed. |
| Facilities | ♀ ♨ 🏠 🥢 John Thorne. |
| Leisure | caddy cars available. |
| Hotel | ★★★★(red)🏵 Pennyhill Park Hotel, London Rd, BAGSHOT ☎ 01276 471774 22 ⇄ 🐾Annexe54 ⇄ 🐾 |

***Worplesdon*** Heath House Rd GU22 0RA
☎ 01483 472277
The scene of the celebrated mixed-foursomes competition. Accurate driving is essential on this heathland course. The short 10th across a lake from tee to green is a notable hole, and the 18th provides a wonderfully challenging par-4 finish.
*18 holes, 6440yds, Par 71, SSS 71, Course record 64.*
*Club membership 590.*

| Visitors | must play with member at weekends & bank holidays. Must contact in advance and have a handicap certificate. |
|---|---|
| Societies | must contact in writing. |
| Green Fees | not confirmed. |
| Facilities | ♨ 🏠 ⛳ 🥢 J Christine. |
| Leisure | trolley hire. |
| Location | 3.5m SW off B380 ▶ |

# WALTON HEATH

**WALTON-ON-THE-HILL** *Surrey*

☎ **01737 812380/812060**　　　　　**Map O4 TQ25**

*John Ingham writes:* Several historic names are etched on the Honours Board at Walton Heath, almost 700 feet above sea level. The rare atmosphere here is justified because these Surrey courses can claim to be the toughest inland examination in Britain. Walton Heath is famous for staging the Ryder Cup and the European Open Championship but older players will remember it best for the Match-Play Championship battles that involved Sir Henry Cotton and Dai Rees as well as huge money matches that brought names such as Bobby Locke and Fred Daly to public prominence.

Once owned by the News of the World newspaper, MP's, Lords and significant members of the press would be invited down to Walton Heath by Sir Emsley Carr, who was one of the first to employ a lady as Secretary and manager of a well-known championship venue.

The courses were designed in 1903 by Herbert Fowler, who used natural hollows and channels for drainage, so the fairways equal the best on any seaside links and quickly dry out, even after a severe storm.

Erratic shots, wide of the prepared surface, are wickedly punished and weekend players are tormented in awful fashion. Nobody escapes undamaged from the gorse and bracken but it is the heather, with those tough stems, that really snarl up any attempt at an over-ambitious recovery shot. So be advised - if you're caught off the fairway, don't attempt anything fancy. Play back on the shortest route to comparative security.

While the Old Course is most frequently played by visitors, the New Course is very challenging and requires all the subtle shots required if you are to get the ball near the hole. And, in the clubhouse, they serve a spectacular lunch.

| | |
|---|---|
| **Visitors** | limited play weekends. Must contact in advance and have a handicap certificate or letter of introduction |
| **Societies** | telephone in advance or apply in writing |
| **Green fees** | per day: £65 before 11.30, £50 after 11.30; weekends £65 |
| **Facilities** | ⊗ (3.30-7pm) 🍴 🍺 ♀ ⛳ 🏌 (Ken Macpherson) practice area, putting green, trolleys |
| **Location** | Tadworth KT20 7TP Deans Lane (SE side of village, off B2032) |

36 holes. Old Course: 18 holes, 6801yds, Par 72, SSS 73, Course record 65 (Peter Townsend) New Course: 18 holes, 6609 yds, Par 72, SSS 72, Course record 64 (Clive Clark)

## WHERE TO STAY AND EAT NEARBY

**HOTELS:**

**BURGH HEATH**
★★ 63% Heathside, Brighton Rd.
☎ 01737 353355. 73 ⇄ ⋔

**DORKING**
★★★★ 66% The Burford Bridge, Burford Bridge, Box Hill (2m NE A24)
☎ 01306 884561.　48 ⇄ ⋔

**REIGATE**
★★★ 64% Reigate Manor, Reigate Hill.
☎ 01737 240125. 51 (11 ⋔ 40 ⇄ ⋔)

**STOKE D'ABERNON**
★★★★❀❀ 60% Woodlands Park, Woodlands Ln.
☎ 01372 843933. 58 ⇄ ⋔

**RESTAURANTS:**

**DORKING**
❀❀Partners West Street, 2-4 West St. ☎ 01306 882826.

**SUTTON**
❀❀Partners Brasserie, 23 Stonecot Hill. ☎ 0181-644 7743.

| Hotel | ★★★★(red)♨ Pennyhill Park Hotel, London Rd, BAGSHOT ☎ 01276 471774 22 ⇄ ‹Annexe54 ⇄ ‹ |

## WOLDINGHAM                                  Map 05 TQ35

**North Downs** Northdown Rd CR3 7AA ☎ 01883 652057
Downland course, 850 ft above sea-level, with several testing holes.
*18 holes, 5843yds, Par 69, SSS 68.*
*Club membership 700.*
Visitors   must play with member at weekends and bank holidays. Must contact in advance and have a handicap certificate.
Societies  must contact in writing.
Green Fees not confirmed.
Facilities ♀⚐🏠‹
Location   0.75m S
Hotel      ★★★ 68%  Kings Arms Hotel, Market Square, WESTERHAM ☎ 01959 562990 16 ⇄ ‹

## SUSSEX, EAST

### BEXHILL                                     Map 05 TQ70

| **Cooden Beach** Cooden Sea Rd TN39 4TR ☎ 01424 842040 The course is close by the sea, but is not real links in character. Despite that, it is dry and plays well throughout the year. There are some excellent holes such as the 4th, played to a built-up green, the short 12th, and three good holes to finish. *18 holes, 6470yds, Par 72, SSS 71, Course record 65.* *Club membership 730.* Visitors   must have a handicap certificate. Restricted at weekends. Book in advance with professional 01424 843938 Societies  must contact in advance by telephoning secretary. Green Fees £29 per day/round, Nov-Mar £26 (£35/£33 weekends & bank holidays). Facilities ⊗⚏🍴🍺♀⚐🏠🏁‹ Jeffrey Sim. Leisure    motorised carts for hire, buggies for hire, trolley for hire, putting green, practice area, snooker. Location   2m W on A259 Hotel      ★★★ 67%  Jarvis Cooden Beach Hotel, COODEN BEACH ☎ 01424 842281 33 ⇄ ‹Annexe8 ⇄ ‹ |

**Highwoods** Ellerslie Ln TN39 4LJ ☎ 01424 212625
Undulating course.
*18 holes, 6218yds, Par 70, SSS 70, Course record 66.*
*Club membership 820.*
Visitors   must play with member on Sun. Must contact in advance and have an introduction from own club. Handicap required.
Societies  must contact 6 months in advance.
Green Fees not confirmed.
Facilities ♀⚐🏠‹ M Andrews.

Location   1.5m NW
Hotel      ★★★ 60%  Grand Hotel, Sea Rd, BEXHILL-ON-SEA ☎ 01424 215437 50 ⇄ ‹

## BRIGHTON & HOVE                              Map 04 TQ30

**Brighton & Hove** Devils Dyke Rd BN1 8YJ
☎ 01273 556482
Downland course with sea views.
*9 holes, 5710yds, Par 68, SSS 68, Course record 65.*
*Club membership 400.*
Visitors   must contact in advance, restricted play Wed, Fri & weekends.
Societies  must contact secretary in advance.
Green Fees Apr-Oct £15 per round (£25 weekends); Nov-Mar £13.50 per round (£23 weekends).
Facilities ⊗⚏ by prior arrangement 🍺♀⚐🏠 ‹ Clive Burgess.
Leisure    trolley for hire, putting green, practice area, snooker.
Location   4m NW
Hotel      ★★ 65%  St Catherines Lodge Hotel, Seafront, Kingsway, Hove ☎ 01273 778181 50rm(40 ⇄ ‹)

| **Dyke** Dyke Rd, Devils Dyke BN1 8YJ ☎ 01273 857296 This downland course has some glorious views both towards the sea and inland. The best hole on the course is probably the 17th; it is one of those teasing short holes of just over 200 yards, and is played across a gully to a high green. *18 holes, 6611yds, Par 72, SSS 72, Course record 66.* *Club membership 750.* Visitors   must contact in advance. Societies  apply by telephone or in writing. Green Fees Winter £31 per day: £21 per round (£31 weekends). Summer £35 per day: £25 per round (£35 weekends). Facilities ⊗⚏🍴🍺♀⚐🏠🏁‹ Martin Ross. Leisure    motorised carts for hire, buggies for hire, trolley for hire, putting green, practice area. Location   4m N of Brighton, between A23 & A27 Hotel      ★★ 65%  St Catherines Lodge Hotel, Seafront, Kingsway, Hove ☎ 01273 778181 50rm(40 ⇄ ‹) |

**East Brighton** Roedean Rd BN2 5RA
☎ 01273 604838
Undulating downland course, overlooking the sea. Windy.
*18 holes, 6346yds, Par 72, SSS 70, Course record 67.*
*Club membership 650.*
Visitors   contact in advance & may only play weekends after 11am.
Societies  must contact in advance, handicap certificate required.
Green Fees £22 per day; £17 per round (£30 per day weekends, £20 after 1pm winter 3pm summer).
Facilities ⊗⚏ by prior arrangement 🍺♀⚐🏠🏁 ‹ Robin S Goodway.
Leisure    trolley for hire, putting green, practice area.
Location   2m E of Palace Pier, overlooking marina
Hotel      ★★★ 54%  Jarvis Norfolk Hotel, 149 Kings Rd, BRIGHTON ☎ 01273 738201 121 ⇄ ‹

**Hollingbury Park** Ditchling Rd BN1 7HS
☎ 01273 552010
Municipal course in hilly situation on the Downs, overlooking the sea.
*18 holes, 6500yds, Par 72, SSS 71, Course record 66.*
*Club membership 300.*
**Visitors**     no restrictions
**Societies**   telephone the secretary for details.
**Green Fees** £11 weekday (£15 weekends & bank holidays).
**Facilities**   ⊗ ଳ ⚑ ♀ ♨ 🏠 ⚐ �î Peter Brown.
**Leisure**     motorised carts for hire, buggies for hire, trolley for hire, putting green, practice area.
**Location**   2m N of town centre
**Hotel**       ★★★ 54% Jarvis Norfolk Hotel, 149 Kings Rd, BRIGHTON ☎ 01273 738201 121 ⇆ ⋒

**Waterhall** Seddlescombe Rd, (Off Devils Dyke Road) BN1 8YN ☎ 01273 508658
Hilly downland course with hard walking and open to the wind. Private club playing over municipal course.
*18 holes, 5773yds, Par 69, SSS 68, Course record 66.*
*Club membership 300.*
**Visitors**     must contact in advance, may not play at start of day.
**Societies**   must contact the secretary in writing.
**Green Fees** £17 per day; £11 per round (£15 per round weekends).
**Facilities**   ⊗ ଳ ⚑ ♀ ♨ 🏠 ⚐ �î Paul Charmon.
**Leisure**     trolley for hire, putting green, practice area.
**Location**   3m N off A27
**Hotel**       ★★ 65% St Catherines Lodge Hotel, Seafront, Kingsway, Hove ☎ 01273 778181 50rm(40 ⇆ ⋒)

*West Hove* Church Farm, Hangleton BN3 8AN
☎ 01273 419738
A downland course designed by Hawtree & Sons.
*18 holes, 6237yds, Par 70, SSS 70.*
*Club membership 700.*
**Visitors**     tee times by arrangement.
**Societies**   by arrangement.
**Green Fees** not confirmed.
**Facilities**   ♀ ♨ 🏠 �î David Mills.
**Leisure**     putting,cart/buggy/trolley hire.
**Hotel**       ★★ 65% St Catherines Lodge Hotel, Seafront, Kingsway, Hove ☎ 01273 778181 50rm(40 ⇆ ⋒)

**CROWBOROUGH**               Map 05 TQ53

**Crowborough Beacon** Beacon Rd TN6 1UJ
☎ 01892 661511
A picturesque course in pleasant heathland. Though most fairways are wide and open, one or two are distinctly

tight where a wayward shot results in a lost ball. By no means an easy course, with testing holes at the 2nd, 6th and 16th.
*18 holes, 6279yds, Par 71, SSS 70, Course record 66.*
*Club membership 700.*
**Visitors**     must contact in advance & have handicap certificate but may not play at weekends & bank holidays.
**Societies**   apply in writing to secretary.
**Green Fees** £40 per day; £25 per round.
**Facilities**   ⊗ ⽊ ⚑ ♀ ♨ 🏠 ⚐ �î D C Newnham.
**Leisure**     trolley for hire, putting green, practice area.
**Location**   1m SW on A26
**Hotel**       ★★★ 76% Spa Hotel, Mount Ephraim, TUNBRIDGE WELLS ☎ 01892 520331 76 ⇆ ⋒

**Dewlands Manor** Cottage Hill, Rotherfield TN6 3JN
☎ 01892 852266
A pretty, moderately hilly, Pay and Play parkland course with water features.
*9 holes, 3186yds, Par 36, SSS 70.*
**Visitors**     must telephone in advance.
**Societies**   telephone for availability.
**Green Fees** not confirmed.
**Facilities**   ⊗ by prior arrangement ଳ by prior arrangement ⚑ ♀ ♨ 🏠 ⚐ �î Nick Godin.
**Leisure**     motorised carts for hire, buggies for hire, trolley for hire, putting green, practice area, indoor teaching facility.
**Location**   0.5m S of Rotherfield
**Inn**         QQQQ The Rose & Crown Inn, Fletching St, MAYFIELD ☎ 01435 872200 4 ⇆ ⋒

**DITCHLING**                Map 05 TQ31

**Mid Sussex** Spatham Ln BN6 8XJ ☎ 01273 846567
Mature parkland course with many trees, water hazards, strategically placed bunkers and superbly contoured greens. The 14th hole, a spectacular par 5, demands accurate shotmaking to avoid the various hazards along its length.
*18 holes, 6431yds, Par 71, SSS 71, Course record 69.*
**Visitors**     telephone in advance to book tee times, members only at weekends.
**Societies**   advance booking required.
**Green Fees** Weekdays only, £30 per day £20 per round.
**Facilities**   ⊗ ⽊ ଳ ⚑ ♀ ♨ 🏠 ⚐ �î Chris Connell.
**Leisure**     motorised carts for hire, buggies for hire, trolley for hire, driving range, putting green, practice area.
**Location**   1m E of Ditchling village
**Hotel**       ★★★ 76% Shelleys, High St, LEWES ☎ 01273 472361 19 ⇆ ⋒

*St Catherines Lodge Hotel*

Seafront, Kingsway, Hove,
Sussex BN3 2RZ
Tel: (01273) 778181
Fax: (01273) 774949

★★
A dozen nearby courses,
(some discount green fees).
Group accommodation bargains.
Fine reputation for good food.
Extensive shopping and
entertainment.

## EASTBOURNE                                        Map 05 TV69

**Eastbourne Downs** East Dean Rd BN20 8ES
☎ 01323 720827
Downland/seaside course.
*18 holes, 6645yds, Par 72, SSS 72, Course record 67.*
*Club membership 650.*
**Visitors**     must contact in advance. A handicap certificate
                 is required for weekend play and may not play
                 weekends before 11am.
**Societies**    must contact secretary in advance.
**Green Fees**   £18 per day, £14 per round (£20/£18 weekends).
**Facilities**   ⊗ ⅢⅢ ፟ዬ ☑ ♀ 📇 ⚑ ⚐ T Marshall.
**Leisure**      trolley for hire, putting green, practice area.
**Location**     1m W of town centre on A259
**Hotel**        ★★★★ 56% Cavendish Hotel, Grand Pde,
                 EASTBOURNE ☎ 01323 410222 112 ⊨ ⌑

---

**Royal Eastbourne** Paradise Dr BN20 8BP
☎ 01323 729738 & 736986
A famous club which celebrated its centenary in 1987.
The course plays longer than it measures. Testing holes
are the 8th, a par 3 played to a high green and the 16th, a
par 5 righthand dogleg.
*Devonshire Course: 18 holes, 6109yds, Par 71, SSS 69,*
*Course record 62.*
*Hartington Course: 9 holes, 2147yds, Par 64, SSS 61.*
*Club membership 800.*
**Visitors**     must contact in advance, may not play
                 weekends except by arrangement.
**Societies**    must apply in advance.
**Green Fees**   Devonshire £20/25; Hartington £8/12.

---

## 7 Courses to choose from!

*Any 2 days - 12 January - 31 December 1997*

Your break includes 2 days' free golf (up to 36 holes
each day), accommodation, newspaper (except Sunday),
full English breakfast, light lunch at the golf club, with
a 4 course Dinner and coffee at the hotel. Guaranteed
tee-off times. Handicap certificates required.

All our 122 rooms are en suite with every modern
facility inc. Satellite TV.

The cost of your golf break from 12 Jan-28 Feb £124:
1-31 Mar £130: 1 Apr-31 May £140: 1 Jun-30 Sep £150:
1 Oct-31 Dec £135. Extra days pro rata.

You may, subject to availability, play at a selection of
7 golf clubs (all 18-hole) in this lovely area.

Please write or telephone for our Golfing Break folder.

## Lansdowne Hotel    AA
                                          ★★★
**King Edward's Parade · Eastbourne BN21 4EE**  75%
**Tel: (01323) 725174      Fax: (01323) 739721**

---

**Facilities**   ⊗ ⅢⅢ by prior arrangement ፟ዬ ☑ ♀ 📇 🖀
                 ⚑ ⊨ ⌑ Richard Wooller.
**Leisure**      motorised carts for hire, buggies for hire,
                 trolley for hire, putting green, practice area.
**Location**     0.5m W of town centre
**Hotel**        ★★★ 75% Lansdowne Hotel, King
                 Edward's Pde, EASTBOURNE
                 ☎ 01323 725174 122 ⊨ ⌑

---

**Willingdon** Southdown Rd, Willingdon BN20 9AA
☎ 01323 410981
Unique, hilly downland course set in oyster-shaped
amphitheatre.
*18 holes, 6118yds, Par 69, SSS 69.*
*Club membership 570.*
**Visitors**     by application, may not play at weekends.
**Societies**    apply in writing.
**Green Fees**   £24 per day/round (£14 winter).
**Facilities**   ⊗ ፟ዬ ☑ ♀ 📇 🖀 ⚑ ⌑ James Debenham.
**Leisure**      motorised carts for hire, buggies for hire, trolley
                 for hire, putting green, practice area.
**Location**     0.5m N of town centre off A22
**Hotel**        ★★★ 60% Wish Tower Hotel, King Edward's
                 Pde, EASTBOURNE
                 ☎ 01323 722676 65 ⊨ ⌑

---

## FOREST ROW                                        Map 05 TQ43

**Ashdown Forest Hotel** Chapel Ln RH18 5BB
☎ 01342 824866
Two natural undulating heathland and woodland courses cut
out of the Ashdown Forest. No sand bunkers, just equally
testing heather dunes with the 14th hole on the Hotel course
being regarded as the best of the 36 holes. The hotel
specialises in catering for golf breaks and societies.
*Hotel Course: 18 holes, 5586yds, Par 68, SSS 67.*
*Old Course: 18 holes, 6477yds, Par 72, SSS 71.*
*Club membership 180.*
**Visitors**     must contact in advance.
**Societies**    must telephone in advance.
**Green Fees**   on request.
**Facilities**   ⊗ ⅢⅢ ፟ዬ ☑ ♀ 📇 🖀 ⚑ ⊨
                 ⌑ Martyn Landsborough.
**Leisure**      trolley for hire, driving range, putting green,
                 practice area.
**Location**     4m S of East Grinstead off A22 & B2110

---

**Royal Ashdown Forest** Chapel Ln RH18 5LR
☎ 01342 822018
Undulating heathland course. Long carries off the tees
and magnificent views over the Forest. Not a course for
the high handicapper.
*Old Course: 18 holes, 6477yds, Par 72, SSS 71, Course*
*record 67.*
*New Course: 18 holes, 5586yds, Par 68, SSS 67.*
*Club membership 450.*
**Visitors**     restricted weekends & Tue. Must have a
                 handicap certificate on Old Course. No
                 restrictions on New Course.
**Societies**    must contact in advance.
**Green Fees**   £36 per day; £30 per round (£42/£36
                 weekends & bank holidays).
**Facilities**   ⊗ ፟ዬ ☑ ♀ 📇 🖀 ⚑
                 ⌑ Martyn Landsborough.

| Leisure | trolley for hire, putting green, practice area. |
|---|---|
| Location | SE side of village, off B2110 |
| Hotel | ★★★ 70% Woodbury House Hotel, Lewes Rd, EAST GRINSTEAD ☎ 01342 313657 13 ⇄ ☞Annexe1 ☞ |

## HAILSHAM                                            Map 05 TQ50

**Wellshurst Golf & Country Club** North St, Hellingly BN27 4EE ☎ 01435 813456 & 813636
There are outstanding views of the South Downs and the Weald Valley from this 18-hole, well-manicured, undulating course. There are varied features and some water hazards. A practice sand bunker, putting green and driving range are available to improve your golf.
*18 holes, 5717yds, Par 70, SSS 68.*
*Club membership 260.*

| Visitors | no restrictions but advisable to book. |
|---|---|
| Societies | telephone in advance to book tee times. |
| Green Fees | £20 per day; £12 per 18 holes (£26/£16/ weekends & bank holidays). |
| Facilities | ⊗ ⅲ ﮩ ♥ ♀ 촌 ☎ 〒 ℓ Matthew Round. |
| Leisure | motorised carts for hire, buggies for hire, trolley for hire, driving range, putting green, practice area. |
| Location | 2.5m N of Hailsham, on A267 |
| Hotel | ★★ 65% The Olde Forge, Magham Down, HAILSHAM ☎ 01323 842893 8rm(6 ⇄ ☞) |

# The Beauport Park Hotel
### Hastings, Sussex TN38 8EA ★★★
### Telephone: 01424 851222
### Fax: 01424 852465

**A Georgian country house hotel set in 33 acres of parkland with its own swimming pool, tennis courts, putting green, croquet lawn, French boules, outdoor chess and country walks. Candle-lit restaurant and open log fires. Adjacent to an 18 hole and 9 hole golf course, floodlight driving range, riding stables and squash courts. Convenient for East Sussex National Golf Course – and many other interesting courses.**

---

**Full inclusive golfing breaks available all year. Please send for our colour brochure and tariff.**

---

## HASTINGS & ST LEONARDS                        Map 05 TQ80

**Beauport Park** St Leonards-on-Sea TN38 0TA
☎ 01424 852977
Played over Hastings Public Course. Undulating parkland with stream and fine views.
*18 holes, 6033yds, Par 70, SSS 70.*
*Club membership 290.*

| Visitors | no restrictions. |
|---|---|
| Societies | must contact in writing. |
| Green Fees | not confirmed. |
| Facilities | ♀ 촌 ☎ 〒 ℓ |
| Location | 3m N of Hastings on A2100 |
| Hotel | ★★★♨ 72% Beauport Park Hotel, Battle Rd, HASTINGS ☎ 01424 851222 23 ⇄ ☞ |

## HEATHFIELD                                         Map 05 TQ52

**Horam Park** Chiddingly Rd, Horam TN21 0JJ
☎ 01435 813477
A woodland course with lakes.
*9 holes, 5965yds, Par 70, SSS 68, Course record 64.*
*Club membership 450.*

| Visitors | contact for tee times. |
|---|---|
| Societies | prior booking required. |
| Green Fees | £15 per day; £12.50 per 18 holes; £8 per 9 holes (£17/£14/£8.50 weekends and bank holidays. |
| Facilities | ⊗ ⅲ ﮩ ♥ ♀ 촌 ☎ 〒 ℓ Mark Jarvis. |
| Leisure | motorised carts for hire, buggies for hire, trolley for hire, driving range, putting green, practice area. |
| Location | Off A267 |
| Hotel | ★★ 62% Horse Shoe Inn, Windmill Hill, HERSTMONCEUX ☎ 01323 833265 13 ⇄ ☞ |

## HOLTYE                                              Map 05 TQ43

**Holtye** TN8 7ED ☎ 01342 850635
Undulating forest/heathland course with tree-lined fairways providing testing golf. Difficult tees on back nine.
*9 holes, 5289yds, Par 66, SSS 66, Course record 65.*
*Club membership 500.*

| Visitors | may not play weekend or Thu mornings. |
|---|---|
| Societies | Tue & Fri only, by arrangement. |
| Green Fees | not confirmed. |
| Facilities | ♀ 촌 ☎ ℓ Kevin Hinton. |
| Location | N side of village on A264 |
| Hotel | ★★★(red)♨ Gravetye Manor Hotel, EAST GRINSTEAD ☎ 01342 810567 18 ⇄ ☞ |

## LEWES                                               Map 05 TQ41

**Lewes** Chapel Hill BN7 2BB ☎ 01273 483474 & 473245
Downland course. Fine views.
*18 holes, 6213yds, Par 71, SSS 70, Course record 65.*
*Club membership 638.*

| Visitors | may not play at weekends before 2pm. Bookings taken up to 7 days in advance. |
|---|---|
| Societies | must contact in advance. |
| Green Fees | £18 (£30 weekends & bank holidays). |
| Facilities | ⊗ ⅲ ﮩ ♥ ♀ 촌 ☎ ℓ Paul Dobson. |
| Leisure | motorised carts for hire, buggies for hire, trolley for hire, putting green, practice area. ▶ |

Location   E side of town centre
Hotel      ★★ 68%  White Hart Hotel, 55 High St,
           LEWES
           ☎ 01273 476694 23rm(19 ⇥ ⋔)Annexe29 ⇥ ⋔

## NEWHAVEN                                    Map 05 TQ40

**Peacehaven** Brighton Rd BN9 9UH
☎ 01273 512571
Downland course, sometimes windy. Testing holes: 1st (par
3), 4th (par 4), 9th (par 3), 10th (par 3), 18th (par 3).
*9 holes, 5305yds, Par 69, SSS 66.*
*Club membership 270.*
Visitors    may not play before 11am weekends.
Societies   telephone in advance.
Green Fees  £11 per 18 holes; £8 per 9 holes (£17/£11
            weekends).
Facilities  ⊗ ⋔ ⓛ ⛑ ⓩ ⚐ ⚑ ⓣ ℓ  Gerry Williams.
Leisure     trolley for hire, putting green.
Location    0.75m W on A259
Hotel       ★★★ 66%  The Star Inn,  ALFRISTON
            ☎ 01323 870495 34 ⇥ ⋔

## RYE                                         Map 05 TQ92

**Rye** New Lydd Rd, Camber TN31 7QS
☎ 01797 225241
Typical links course with superb greens and views.
*Old Course: 18 holes, 6317yds, Par 68, SSS 71.*
*Jubilee Course: 9 holes, 6141yds, Par 71, SSS 70.*
*Club membership 1100.*
Visitors    must be invited/introduced by a member.
Green Fees  contact secretary.
Facilities  ⚐ ⓔ ⚑ ⓣ ℓ  Michael Lee.
Leisure     trolley for hire, putting green, practice area.
Location    2.75m SE off A259
Hotel       ★★★ 62%  George Hotel, High St,  RYE
            ☎ 01797 222114 22 ⇥ ⋔

## SEAFORD                                     Map 05 TV49

**Seaford** Firle Rd, East Blatchington BN25 2JD
☎ 01323 892442
The great H. Taylor did not perhaps design as many
courses as his friend and rival, James Braid, but
Seaford's original design was Taylor's. It is a splendid
downland course with magnificent views and some fine
holes.
*18 holes, 6551yds, Par 69, SSS 71.*
*Club membership 600.*
Visitors    must contact in advance, may not play
            weekends.
Societies   must contact in advance.
Green Fees  Apr-Oct: £35 per day; £25 per round. Nov-
            Mar: £25 per day; £20 per round. Twilight
            after 3.30 £20.
Facilities  ⊗ ⋔ ⓛ ⛑ ⓩ ⚐ ⓓ ℓ  Mark Smith.
Leisure     motorised carts for hire, buggies for hire,
            trolley for hire, driving range, putting green,
            practice area.
Location    Turn inland at war memorial off A259
Hotel       ★★★ 66%  The Star Inn,  ALFRISTON
            ☎ 01323 870495 34 ⇥ ⋔

**Seaford Head** Southdown Rd BN25 4JS
☎ 01323 890139 & 894843
A links type course situated on the cliff edge giving exception
views over the Seven Sisters and coastline. The upper level is
reached via a short hole with elevated green - known as the
'Hell Hole' and the 18th Par 5 tee is on the 'Head' being 300
feet above sea level.
*18 holes, 5848yds, Par 71, SSS 68.*
*Club membership 450.*
Visitors    no restrictions.
Societies   write or telephone the Pro's shop.
Green Fees  not confirmed.
Facilities  ⓩ ⚐ ⓔ ⚑ ℓ  Tony Lowles.
Hotel       ★★★ 63%  Deans Place,  ALFRISTON
            ☎ 01323 870248 36 ⇥ ⋔

## SEDLESCOMBE                                 Map 05 TQ71

**Sedlescombe** Kent St TN33 0SD  ☎ 01424 870898
This course was established in 1989 and is windswept and
challenging. The Par 5 9th holes has a green surrounded by
lakes.
*18 holes, 6359yds, Par 71, SSS 68.*
*Club membership 300.*
Visitors    please telephone and reserve tee times.
Societies   please telephone to reserve tee times.
Green Fees  £15 per day; £12.50 per 18 holes; £8 per 9 holes
            (£17/£14/£8.50). Golf & Food all day £29.50.
Facilities  ⊗ ⋔ ⓛ ⛑ ⓩ ⚐ ⓔ ⚑ ℓ
Leisure     motorised carts for hire, buggies for hire, trolley
            for hire, driving range, putting green, practice
            area.
Location    A21, 4m N of Hastings
Hotel       ★★★ 62%  Brickwall Hotel, The Green,
            SEDLESCOMBE  ☎ 01424 870253 23 ⇥ ⋔

## TICEHURST                                   Map 05 TQ63

**Dale Hill** TN5 7DQ  ☎ 01580 200112
Picturesque course with woodland, water and gently
undulating fairways. Hotel and leisure centre within grounds.
*18 holes, 6106yds, Par 70, SSS 69.*
*Club membership 650.*
Visitors    must play after noon weekends.
Societies   must contact in advance.
Green Fees  £35 per day; £20 per round (£30 per round
            weekends and bank holidays). Twilight
            reductions.
Facilities  ⊗ ⋔ ⓛ ⛑ ⓩ ⚐ ⓔ ⚑ ⓓ ℓ  Liam Greasley.
Leisure     heated indoor swimming pool, sauna, solarium,
            gymnasium, buggies for hire, trolley for hire,
            driving range, putting green, practice area.
Location    N side of village off B2087
Hotel       ★★★ 72%  Dale Hill Hotel & Golf Club,
            TICEHURST  ☎ 01580 200112 32 ⇥ ⋔

## UCKFIELD                                    Map 05 TQ42

**EAST SUSSEX NATIONAL**  See page 211

**Piltdown** Piltdown TN22 3XB  ☎ 01825 722033
Natural heathland course with much heather and gorse. No
bunkers, easy walking, fine views.                       ▶

# EAST SUSSEX NATIONAL

**Uckfield** *East Sussex* ☎ 01825 880088      **Map 05 TQ42**

*John Ingham writes:* Designed by Bob Cupp on a grand championship scale and opened in 1989, East Sussex National presents two massive courses, more than 7000 yards long. Both are ideal for big-hitting professionals and already they have staged the European Open here. Boasting a driving range and a Golf Academy, Bob Cupp, once a designer for Jack Nicklaus, decided to use what they call 'bent' grass from tee to green - and the result is an American-type course to test everyone, depending upon which tee you drive from.

Could either course, brand spanking new, compare with the other Sussex classics of Pulborough (West Sussex) and Royal Ashdown Forest, a gem of a place near Forest Row and a course without a single bunker? When first I drove into the vastness of the car park and eyed the huge redbrick clubhouse, I admit it all looked daunting. The experience is not unlike entering an hotel-country club complex in the United States, signing in as one does at the reception area before walking across a suspended corridor towards the huge and well-stocked professional's shop.

The East Sussex National offers the most modern day's golf in the United Kingdom. The greens on both the East and West courses are immaculate and groomed to perfection. Strike the putt solidly and on-line, and it must go in! While it's true that 50,000 spectators can watch you hole out on the last green, it's just as true that on a quiet day out, you can enjoy letting out plenty of shaft without fear of hitting valuable balls into thick woods.

The West course is reserved for members and their guests, but visitors are welcomed on the other course.

| | |
|---|---|
| **Visitors** | must contact in advance. No handicap certificate required. Must accompany a member on West Course |
| **Societies** | Societies must contact Corporate Hospitality (01825 880230) |
| **Green fees** | £49.50 all day winter inc. lunch or brunch £65 all day summer inc. lunch or brunch, £49.50 18 holes, £29.50 twilight (5 hours) |
| **Facilities** | ⊗ ⅺ ℔ ℔ ☯ ℉ ⋈ 凸 ⓑ ⍗ driving range, putting green, ☏ Philip Lewin motor cart, practice area, buggies, trolleys. 3-hole academy course |
| **Leisure** | hard court tennis, indoor swimming, riding, sauna, croquet |
| **Location** | Little Horsted TN22 5ES (S on A22) |

**36 holes. East Course 18 holes, 7081yds, Par72 SSS 74**
**Course record 65 (Gordon Brand Jr)**
**West Course 18 holes, 7154yds, Par 72, SSS74**

## WHERE TO STAY AND EAT NEARBY

**HOTELS:**

**UCKFIELD**
★★★(Red) ⚘⚘⚘ ♨ 78% Horsted Place, Little Horsted ☎ 01825 750581. 17 ⇌ ℟)

**HALLAND**
★★★ 63% Halland Forge
☎ 01825 840456. Annexe 20 (3 ℟ 17 ⇌ ℟)

AA ★★★
Open 7 days a week

# The ideal 19th hole

Play golf to your heart's content in Sussex.
Then dine in style and stay a while at the
Halland Forge Hotel and Restaurant.
The Forge Restaurant – *à la Carte and Table d'Hôte*
*Luncheon and Dinner*. Coffee Shop/Carvery –
*Open for Breakfast, Lunch and Tea from 8.00am to 6.00pm*
Anvil Lounge Bar – *Fully Licensed*.
20 Bedrooms with private facilities.
▲ We are the ideal golfing centre for South East England ▲

Hotel Restaurant and Coffee
Shop/Carvery
Halland, nr. Lewes, East Sussex
On A22/B2192 roundabout,
4 miles south of Uckfield just
beyond East Sussex National

**Tel: Halland (01825) 840456 Fax: (01825) 840773**

---

*18 holes, 6070yds, Par 68, SSS 69, Course record 67.*
*Club membership 400.*

| | |
|---|---|
| **Visitors** | must telephone pro shop in advance 01825 722389 and have a handicap certificate. Play on Tue, Thu and weekends is restricted. |
| **Societies** | must contact in writing. |
| **Green Fees** | £32 per day; £27.50 per round. Reductions after 4pm.. |
| **Facilities** | ⊗ ℳ by prior arrangement ▮ ♥ ♀ ♨ 🏠 ⚑ ⌂ John Amos. |
| **Leisure** | motorised carts for hire, buggies for hire, trolley for hire, driving range, putting green, practice area. |
| **Location** | 3m NW off A272 |
| **Hotel** | ★★★ 63% Halland Forge Hotel & Restaurant, HALLAND ☎ 01825 840456 Annexe20 ⇆ ☏ |

---

## SUSSEX, WEST

---

### ANGMERING        Map 04 TQ00

**Ham Manor** BN16 4JE ☎ 01903 783288
Two miles from the sea, this parkland course has fine
springy turf and provides an interesting test in two loops
of nine holes each.
*18 holes, 6267yds, Par 70, SSS 70, Course record 64.*
*Club membership 780.*

---

| | |
|---|---|
| **Visitors** | must have a handicap certificate. Telephone pro shop in advance 01903 783732. |
| **Societies** | telephone for details |
| **Green Fees** | £28 (£35 weekends). |
| **Facilities** | ⊗ ℳ ▮ ♥ ♀ ♨ 🏠 ⌂ Simon Buckley. |
| **Leisure** | trolley for hire, putting green, practice area, bowling green, table tennis. |
| **Location** | Off A259 |
| **Hotel** | ★★★ 59% Chatsworth Hotel, Steyne, WORTHING ☎ 01903 236103 107 ⇆ ☏ |

---

### ARUNDEL        Map 04 TQ00

**Avisford Park** Yapton Ln, Walberton BN18 0LS
☎ 01243 554611
Newly extended course - now 18-holes - enjoying a country
hotel complex setting. The course opens with a real challenge
as there is out of bounds water and tree hazards the whole
length of this 414yard drive.
*18 holes, 5703yds, Par 70, SSS 68.*
*Club membership 100.*

| | |
|---|---|
| **Visitors** | must contact in advance for weekend play. |
| **Societies** | apply in writing or telephone. |
| **Green Fees** | Summer rates - Mon-Fri £14 per 18 holes (£16 weekends). |
| **Facilities** | ⊗ ℳ ▮ ♥ ♀ ♨ 🏠 ⚑ ⌂ Richard Beach. |
| **Leisure** | buggies for hire, trolley for hire. |
| **Location** | Off A27 |
| **Hotel** | ★★★ 66% Norfolk Arms Hotel, High St, ARUNDEL ☎ 01903 882101 21 ⇆ Annexe13 ⇆ |

---

### BOGNOR REGIS        Map 04 SZ99

**Bognor Regis** Downview Rd, Felpham PO22 8JD
☎ 01243 821929 (Secretary) & 865867
This flattish, parkland course has more variety than is to be
found on some of the South Coast courses. The club is also
known far and wide for its enterprise in creating a social
atmosphere. The course is open to the prevailing wind.
*18 holes, 6238yds, Par 70, SSS 70, Course record 64.*
*Club membership 700.*

| | |
|---|---|
| **Visitors** | must play with member at weekends Apr-Sep. Must contact in advance (pro shop 01243 865209). |
| **Societies** | phone initially. |
| **Green Fees** | £25 per day or round (£30 weekends & bank holidays). |
| **Facilities** | ⊗ ▮ ♥ ♀ ♨ 🏠 ⌂ |
| **Leisure** | motorised carts for hire, buggies for hire, trolley for hire, putting green,practice area. |
| **Location** | 1.5m NE off A259 |
| **Hotel** | ★★ 67% Black Mill House Hotel, Princess Av, Aldwick, BOGNOR REGIS ☎ 01243 821945 & 865596 22rm(18 ⇆ ☏)Annexe4rm |

---

### BURGESS HILL        Map 04 TQ31

**Burgess Hill** Cuckfield Rd RH15 8RE ☎ 01444 258585
Presently under construction and due to open in February
1997 is an academy course bordered by a tributary of the

River Adur. Facilities currently available for public use include a floodlit driving range and a large sweeping putting green.
*9 holes.*
**Visitors**     details not yet available.
**Societies**     contact in advance.
**Green Fees**     to be advised.
**Facilities**     🏌 ⛳ 🏠 ⛳ ( Steven Dunkley.
**Leisure**     floodlit driving range, putting green, practice area.
**Location**     N of town on B2036
**Hotel**     ★★★⚜ 76% Ockenden Manor, Ockenden Ln, CUCKFIELD ☎ 01444 416111 22 ⇔ ⚑

## CHICHESTER        Map 04 SU80

*Chichester Golf Centre* Hoe Farm, Hunston PO20 6AX
☎ 01243 533833
Set amongst lush farmland, the Tower course has four lakes which bring water into play on seven holes. The Florida-style Cathedral course was opened in spring 1994. There is also a 9-hole par 3 and a floodlit driving range.
*Tower Course: 18 holes, 6174yds, Par 71, SSS 69, Course record 67.*
*Cathedral Course: 18 holes, 6461yds, Par 72, SSS 69, Course record 70.*
*Club membership 300.*
**Visitors**     a strict dress code is in operation. It is advisable to contact in advance.
**Societies**     must contact in advance.
**Green Fees**     not confirmed.
**Facilities**     ♀ ⛳ 🏠 ⛳ ( Carl Rota.
**Leisure**     driving range, putting, buggy/trolley hire.
**Location**     3m S of Chichester, on B2145 at Hunston
**Hotel**     ★★★ 65% The Dolphin & Anchor, West St, CHICHESTER ☎ 01243 785121 49 ⇔ ⚑

## COPTHORNE        Map 05 TQ33

*Copthorne* Borers Arms Rd RH10 3LL
☎ 01342 712033 & 712508
Despite it having been in existence since 1892, this club remains one of the lesser known Sussex courses. It is hard to know why because it is most attractive with plenty of trees and much variety
*18 holes, 6505yds, Par 71, SSS 71, Course record 67.*
*Club membership 550.*
**Visitors**     must contact in advance, may not play weekends before 1pm.
**Societies**     must contact in advance.
**Green Fees**     £35 per day; £27 per round (£30 per round weekends after 1pm).
**Facilities**     ⊗ ⅏ 🍴 🍺 ♀ ⛳ 🏠 ( Joe Burrell.
**Leisure**     trolley for hire, putting green, practice area.
**Location**     E side of village junc 10 of M23 off A264
**Hotel**     ★★★★ 64% The Copthorne, Copthorne Way, COPTHORNE ☎ 01342 714971 227 ⇔ ⚑

*Effingham Park* RH10 3EU ☎ 01342 716528 & 712138
Parkland course.
*9 holes, 1769yds, Par 30, SSS 57, Course record 28.*
*Club membership 390.*
**Visitors**     restricted at weekends after 11am and not after 4pm Apr-Oct.

**Societies**     Mon-Fri, and Sat/Sun after 1pm, must write/telephone in advance.
**Green Fees**     not confirmed.
**Facilities**     ♀ ⛳ 🏠 ⛳ 🍴 ( Duncan Arnold.
**Leisure**     heated indoor swimming pool, sauna, solarium, gymnasium, practice area, putting green, trolley hire.
**Location**     2m E on B2028
**Hotel**     ★★★★ 64% The Copthorne Effingham Park, West Park Rd, COPTHORNE ☎ 01342 714994 122 ⇔ ⚑

## CRAWLEY        Map 04 TQ23

*Cottesmore* Buchan Hill, Pease Pottage RH11 9AT
☎ 01293 528256
The course was originally founded in 1974. The Griffin course is undulating with four holes are over water. The newer Phoenix course is shorter and less testing. But both are lined by silver birch, pine and oak, with rhododendrons ablaze in June.
*Griffin Course: 18 holes, 6280yds, Par 72, SSS 70.*
*Phoenix Course: 18 holes, 5489yds, Par 69, SSS 68.*
*Club membership 1500.*
**Visitors**     may only play after 11am at weekends and bank holidays. Must contact in advance.
**Societies**     weekdays, must telephone in advance.
**Green Fees**     Griffin: £30 per day (£40 weekends); £24 per round (£30 weekends). Phoenix: £20 per day (£26 weekends); £15 per round (£20 weekends).
**Facilities**     ⊗ ⅏ 🍺 ♀ ⛳ 🏠 ⛳ 🍴 ( Andrew Prior.
**Leisure**     hard tennis courts, heated indoor swimming pool, squash, sauna, solarium, gymnasium, motorised carts for hire, buggies for hire, trolley for hire, putting green, practice area.
**Location**     3m SW 1m W of M23 junc 11
**Hotel**     ★★★ 58% George Hotel, High St, CRAWLEY ☎ 01293 524215 86 ⇔ ⚑

*Gatwick Manor* Lowfield Heath RH10 2ST
☎ 01293 538587
Interesting, pay and play short course.
*9 holes, 2492yds, Par 56, SSS 50.*
*Club membership 63.*
**Visitors**     no restrictions.
**Societies**     must telephone in advance.
**Green Fees**     not confirmed.
**Facilities**     ♀ 🏠 ⛳ 🍴 ( C Jenkins.
**Location**     2m N on A23
**Hotel**     B Forte Travelodge, Church Rd, Lowfield Heath, Crawley, CRAWLEY ☎ 01293 533441 121 ⇔ ⚑

*Ifield Golf & Country Club* Rusper Rd, Ifield RH11 0LN
☎ 01293 520222 (Manager) & 523088 (Pro)
Parkland course.
*18 holes, 6330yds, Par 70, SSS 70, Course record 65.*
*Club membership 850.*
**Visitors**     must contact professional in advance. Must be guest of member at weekends.
**Societies**     apply in advance.
**Green Fees**     £30 per day; £20 per round.
**Facilities**     ⊗ ⅏ by prior arrangement 🍺 ♀ ⛳ 🏠 ( Jonathan Earl.
**Leisure**     squash, motorised carts for hire, buggies for hire, trolley for hire, putting green, practice area. ▶

| Location | 1m W side of town centre off A23 |
|---|---|
| Hotel | ★★★ 58% George Hotel, High St, CRAWLEY ☎ 01293 524215 86 ⇌ � |

**Tilgate Forest Golf Centre** Titmus Dr RH10 5EU
☎ 01293 530103
Designed by former Ryder Cup players Neil Coles and Brian Huggett, the course has been carefully cut through a silver birch and pine forest. It is possibly one of th most beautiful public courses in the country. The 17th is a treacherous Par 5 demanding an uphill third shot to a green surrounded by rhododendrons.
*18 holes, 6359yds, Par 72, SSS 69 or 9 holes, 1136yds, Par 27.*

| Visitors | may book up to 7 days in advance. |
|---|---|
| Societies | telephone in advance for details. |
| Green Fees | £11.85 per 18 holes, £4.40 per 9 holes (£16.25/£5.80 weekends). |
| Facilities | ⊗ 🎵 🛍 🍷 ♀ 🏌 🏠 ƒ Sean Trussell. |
| Leisure | trolley for hire, floodlit driving range, putting green. |
| Hotel | ★★★ 58% George Hotel, High St, CRAWLEY ☎ 01293 524215 86 ⇌ 🌴 |

## GOODWOOD                                    Map 04 SU80

**Goodwood** PO18 0PN ☎ 01243 774968
Downland course designed by the master architect, James Braid. Many notable holes, particularly the finishing ones: 17 down an avenue of beech trees and 18 along in front of the terrace. Superb views of the downs and the coast.
*18 holes, 6434yds, Par 72, SSS 71.*
*Club membership 930.*

| Visitors | telephone for details, |
|---|---|
| Societies | Wed & Thu, telephone secretary in advance. |
| Green Fees | £28 per day/round (£38 weekends). |
| Facilities | ⊗ 🎵 🛍 🍷 ♀ 🏌 🏠 ƒ Keith MacDonald. |
| Leisure | trolley for hire, putting green, practice area. |
| Location | 3m NE of Chichester off A27 |
| Hotel | ★★★ 70% Goodwood Park Hotel, Country Club Resort, GOODWOOD ☎ 01243 775537 88 ⇌ 🌴 |

## HAYWARDS HEATH                              Map 05 TQ32

**Haywards Heath** High Beech Ln RH16 1SL
☎ 01444 414457
Pleasant parkland course with several challenging par 4s and 3s.
*18 holes, 6204yds, Par 71, SSS 70, Course record 68.*
*Club membership 770.*

| Visitors | must have a handicap certificate. Must contact in advance. |
|---|---|

| Societies | Wed & Thu only by prior arrangement with the secretary. |
|---|---|
| Green Fees | £36 per 36 holes; £26 per 18 holes (£40/£35 weekends). |
| Facilities | ⊗ 🎵 🛍 🍷 ♀ 🏌 🏠 ƒ Michael Henning. |
| Leisure | trolley for hire, driving range, putting green, practice area. |
| Location | 1.25m N off B2028 |
| Hotel | ★★★🎖 76% Ockenden Manor, Ockenden Ln, CUCKFIELD ☎ 01444 416111 22 ⇌ 🌴 |

**Paxhill Park** East Mascalls Ln, Lindfield RH16 2QN
☎ 01444 484467
A relatively flat parkland course designed by Patrick Tallack.
*18 holes, 6117yds, Par 70, SSS 69.*
*Club membership 375.*

| Visitors | welcome but may not play weekend mornings. |
|---|---|
| Societies | must contact in advance. |
| Green Fees | £20 per day; £15 per round (£20 per round weekend & bank holidays). |
| Facilities | ⊗ 🛍 🍷 ♀ 🏌 🏠 ƒ Steve Dunkerley. |
| Leisure | trolley for hire, putting green, practice area. |
| Hotel | ★★★ 60% The Birch Hotel, Lewes Rd, HAYWARDS HEATH ☎ 01444 451565 53 ⇌ 🌴 |

## HORSHAM                                     Map 04 TQ13

*See also* Slinfold

**Horsham Golf Park** Worthing Rd RH13 7AX
☎ 01403 271525
A short but challenging course with six Par 4s and three Par 3s''s, two of which are played across water. Designed for beginners and intermediates but also challenges better players with a standard scratch of six below par.
*9 holes, 4122yds, Par 33, SSS 30, Course record 55.*
*Club membership 250.*

| Visitors | no restrictions but may not play until after 11am on Sat. |
|---|---|
| Societies | apply in advance. |
| Green Fees | £7 per 18 holes; £6 per 9 holes (£12/£10 weekends & bank holidays). |
| Facilities | ⊗ 🛍 🍷 ♀ 🏌 🏠 ƒ Neil Burke. |
| Leisure | gymnasium, trolley for hire, driving range, putting green. |
| Location | Off A24 rdbt, between Horsham/Southwater, by garage on B2237 |
| Hotel | ★★ 67% Ye Olde King's Head Hotel, HORSHAM ☎ 01403 253126 42rm(41 ⇌ 🌴) |

**SLINFOLD PARK INVITES YOU TO PLAY . . .**
. . . an 18-hole championship course set in established parkland with lakes and streams . . . a challenging 9-hole short course . . . a floodlit driving range . . . two resident golf professionals . . . a luxuriously appointed clubhouse, bar and restaurant . . .
**JUST A SHORT DRIVE AWAY**
**Slinfold Park Golf & Country Club, Stane Street, (A29), Slinfold, West Sussex. Tel: 01403 791555**

*Slinfold Park*
● GOLF & COUNTRY CLUB ●

## HURSTPIERPOINT                 Map 04 TQ21

**Singing Hills** Albourne BN6 9EB
☎ 01273 835353
Three distinct nines (Lake, River & Valley) can be combined to make a truly varied game. Gently undulating fairways and spectacular waterholes make Singing Hills a test of accurate shotmaking. The opening 2 holes of the Rive Nine have long drives, while the second hole on the Lake course is an Island green where the tee is also protected by two bunkers.
*Lake: 9 holes, 3253yds, Par 35.*
*River: 9 holes, 2826yds, Par 34.*
*Valley: 9 holes, 3348yds, Par 36.*
*Club membership 390.*
**Visitors**      no restrictions.
**Societies**    apply in advance.
**Green Fees** £18 per 18 holes (£26 weekends & bank holidays).
**Facilities**    ⊗ ⅏ ♭ ♟ ♀ ⚁ ⌂ ⱦ ⱡ Wallace Street.
**Leisure**      trolley for hire, driving range, putting green.
**Location**    On B2117
**Hotel**        ★★★ 64% The Hickstead Hotel, Jobs Ln, Bolney, ☎ 01444 248023 50 ⇄ ↾

## LITTLEHAMPTON                 Map 04 TQ00

*Littlehampton* Rope Walk, West Beach BN17 5DL
☎ 01903 717170
A delightful seaside links in an equally delightful setting - and the only links course in the area.
*18 holes, 6244yds, Par 70, SSS 70, Course record 66.*
*Club membership 650.*
**Visitors**      must have handicap certificate.
**Societies**    welcome weekdays.
**Green Fees** not confirmed.
**Facilities**    ♀ ⚁ ⌂ ⱡ Guy McQuitty.
**Leisure**      putting,cart/buggy/trolley hire.
**Location**    1m W off A259
**Hotel**        ★★★ 77% Bailiffscourt Hotel, CLIMPING
                  ☎ 01903 723511 10 ⇄ ↾Annexe17 ⇄ ↾

## LOWER BEEDING                 Map 04 TQ22

*Brookfield* Brookfield Farm Hotel, Plummers Plain RH13 6LU ☎ 01403 891568
This is an unusual golf course in that it has only 7 holes par 3 and 4. However, it has been especially designed as an executive course for beginners and those who find it difficult to play a full 18 holes. It is very popular.
*6 holes, 3015yds, Par 57, SSS 53, Course record 53.*
*Club membership 200.*
**Visitors**      no restrictions.
**Societies**    apply in writing or telephone.
**Green Fees** not confirmed.
**Facilities**    ♀ ⚁ ⱦ⛾ⱡ Mike Denny.
**Leisure**      fishing, sauna.
**Farmhouse** QQQ Brookfield Farm Hotel, Winterpit Ln, Plummers Plain, LOWER BEEDING
                  ☎ 01403 891568 20 ⇄ ↾
**Additional** ★★★★≛ 76% South Lodge Hotel, Brighton
**hotel**        Rd, LOWER BEEDING
                  ☎ 01403 891711 39 ⇄

## MANNINGS HEATH                 Map 04 TQ22

**Mannings Heath** Fullers, Hammerpond Rd RH13 6PG
☎ 01403 210228
The course meanders up hill and down dale over heathland with streams affecting 11 of the holes. Wooded valleys protect the course from strong winds. Famous holes at 12th (the 'Waterfall', par 3), 13th (the 'Valley', par 4).
*Waterfall: 18 holes, 6378yds, Par 71, SSS 70, Course record 66.*
*Kingfisher: 18 holes, 6305yds, Par 70, SSS 70.*
*Club membership 760.*
**Visitors**      may book up to 14 days in advance.
**Societies**    must contact in advance.
**Green Fees** £40 per 36 holes; £30 per 18 holes (£55/£40 weekends and bank holidays).
**Facilities**    ⊗ ⅏ ♭ ♟ ♀ ⚁ ⌂ ⱦ ⱡ Clive Tucker.
**Leisure**      hard tennis courts, fishing, sauna, trolley for hire, covered driving range, putting green, practice area, indoor teaching facility.
**Location**    N side of village
**Hotel**        ★★★★≛ 76% South Lodge Hotel, Brighton Rd, LOWER BEEDING
                  ☎ 01403 891711 39 ⇄

## MIDHURST                 Map 04 SU82

**Cowdray Park** Petworth Rd GU29 0BB ☎ 01730 813599
Parkland course, hard walking up to 4th green.
*18 holes, 6212yds, Par 70, SSS 70, Course record 66.*
*Club membership 720.*                                    ▶

## SOUTH LODGE HOTEL

South Lodge Hotel is a fine Victorian Country House set in 93 acres of secluded wooded parkland with views over the South Downs.
Delicious cuisine by Chef Timothy Neal, using local game and fish, with soft fruits and herbs from the hotel's own walled garden.
Superbly appointed bedrooms and suites each individually decorated in true country house style.
Enjoy tennis, croquet, petanque, putting, snooker or golf at our spectacular 18 hole Championship Course at Mannings Heath.
South Lodge is the perfect location for London and the South Coast and for many famous Gardens and National Trust Properties in the area.
For full information please contact:
SOUTH LODGE HOTEL,
Brighton Road, Lower Beeding,
near Horsham, West Sussex RH13 6PS.
Telephone: (01403) 891711 Fax: (01403) 891766

**Visitors** may play after 9.30am or 2pm. Must contact in advance.
**Societies** telephone in advance, mainly Wed & Thu available.
**Green Fees** £20 per day/round (£25 weekends & bank holidays).
**Facilities** ⊗ ⅧⅢ ⤢ ⤢ ♀ ♣ 🏠 ⚑ ⚏ Simon Blanshard.
**Leisure** trolley for hire, putting green, practice area.
**Location** 1m E on A272
**Hotel** ★★★ 73% Spread Eagle Hotel, South St, MIDHURST
☎ 01730 816911 37 ⇆ ⚏Annexe4 ⚏

---

## PULBOROUGH                                     Map 04 TQ01

**West Sussex** Golf Club Ln, Wiggonholt RH20 2EN
☎ 01798 872563
Heathland course.
*18 holes, 6221yds, Par 68, SSS 70, Course record 61.*
*Club membership 850.*
**Visitors** must contact in advance, may not play weekends.
**Societies** Wed & Thu only, apply in writing.
**Green Fees** £42 per 2 rounds; £31.50 per round weekdays.
**Facilities** ⊗ ⤢ ⤢ ♀ ♣ 🏠 ⚑ ⚏ Tim Packham.
**Leisure** trolley for hire, putting green, practice area.
**Location** 1.5m E off A283
**Hotel** ★★★ 71% Roundabout Hotel, Monkmead Ln, WEST CHILTINGTON
☎ 01798 813838 23 ⇆ ⚏

---

## PYECOMBE                                       Map 04 TQ21

**Pyecombe** Clayton Hill BN45 7FF ☎ 01273 845372
Typical downland course on the inland side of the South Downs. Hilly, but magnificent views.
*18 holes, 6278yds, Par 71, SSS 70, Course record 67.*
*Club membership 700.*
**Visitors** must contact in advance and may only play after 9.15am weekdays and after 2.15pm weekends
**Societies** telephone secretary in advance.
**Green Fees** £25 per day; £20 per round (£30/£25 weekends).
**Facilities** ⊗ ⅧⅢ ⤢ ⤢ ♀ ♣ 🏠 ⚑ ⚏ C R White.
**Leisure** trolley for hire, driving range, putting.
**Location** E side of village on A273
**Hotel** ★★★ 64% Courtlands Hotel, 21-27 The Drive, HOVE
☎ 01273 731055 43 ⇆ ⚏Annexe12 ⇆ ⚏

---

## SELSEY                                         Map 04 SZ89

**Selsey** Golf Links Ln PO20 9DR ☎ 01243 602203
Fairly difficult seaside course, exposed to wind and has natural ditches.
*9 holes, 5834yds, Par 68, SSS 68, Course record 64.*
*Club membership 360.*
**Visitors** must contact in advance.
**Societies** must contact in advance.
**Green Fees** £17 per day; £12 per 18 holes; £9 per 9 holes (£20/£15/£10 weekends & bank holidays). Weekly rate £50.
**Facilities** ⊗ ⅧⅢ ⤢ ⤢ ♀ ♣ 🏠 ⚏ Peter Grindley.
**Leisure** hard tennis courts, trolley for hire, putting green, practice area.

---

**Location** 1m N off B2145
**Hotel** ★★★ 65% The Dolphin & Anchor, West St, CHICHESTER
☎ 01243 785121 49 ⇆ ⚏

---

## SLINFOLD                                       Map 04 TQ13

**Slinfold Park Golf & Country Club** Stane St RH13 7RE
☎ 01403 791555
Opened for play in spring 1993, Slinfold course enjoys splendid views among mature trees. The 10th tee is spectacularly located on the centre of one of the two large landscaped lakes. The 166-yard 16th has water running in front of of the tee and everything sloping towards it!
*Championship Course: 18 holes, 6407yds, Par 72, SSS 71, Course record 64.*
*Short Course: 9 holes, 1315yds, Par 28.*
*Club membership 611.*
**Visitors** subject to booking.
**Societies** advance booking required, weekends and bank holidays not available.
**Green Fees** Championship: £30 per day; £20 per round (£35/25 weekends). Short Course £6.50 per 18 holes; £4 per round.
**Facilities** ⊗ by prior arrangement ⅧⅢ by prior arrangement ⤢ ♀ ♣ 🏠 ⚑ ⚏ G McKay.
**Leisure** trolley for hire, driving range, putting green.
**Location** 4m W on the A29
**Hotel** ★★★ 72% Random Hall Hotel, Stane St, Slinfold, HORSHAM
☎ 01403 790558 15 ⇆ ⚏

---

## WEST CHILTINGTON                               Map 04 TQ01

**West Chiltington** Broadford Bridge Rd RH20 2YA
☎ 01798 813574
The Main Course is situated on gently undulating, well-drained greensand and offers panoramic views of the Sussex Downs. Three large double greens provide an interesting feature to this new course. Also 9-hole short course and 13-bay driving range.
*Windmill: 18 holes, 5888yds, Par 70, SSS 69, Course record 66 or 9 holes, 1360yds, Par 28.*
**Visitors** book tee times in advance.
**Societies** by prior arrangement.
**Green Fees** £13 per round (£17.50 weekends, £20 before 11am Sun).
**Facilities** ⊗ ⅧⅢ ⤢ ⤢ ♀ ♣ 🏠 ⚑ ⚏ Giles Downer.
**Leisure** motorised carts for hire, trolley for hire, driving range, putting green.
**Location** On N side of village
**Hotel** ★★★ 71% Roundabout Hotel, Monkmead Ln, WEST CHILTINGTON
☎ 01798 813838 23 ⇆ ⚏

---

## WORTHING                                       Map 04 TQ10

**Hill Barn Municipal** Hill Barn Ln BN14 9QE
☎ 01903 237301
Downland course with views of both Isle of Wight and Brighton.
*18 holes, 6224yds, Par 70, SSS 70.*
*Club membership 1000.*
**Visitors** no restrictions.
**Societies** must telephone in advance.

**Green Fees** not confirmed.
**Facilities** ♀ ♂ 🕯 ⚑ ⚑ A Higgins.
**Leisure** putting,practice,cart/buggy/trolley hire.
**Location** N side of town at junction of A24/A27
**Hotel** ★★★ 59% Chatsworth Hotel, Steyne, WORTHING ☎ 01903 236103 107 ⇄ ↾

**Worthing** Links Rd BN14 9QZ ☎ 01903 260801
The High Course, short and tricky with entrancing views, will provide good entertainment. 'Lower Course' is considered to be one of the best downland courses in the country.
*Lower Course: 18 holes, 6530yds, Par 71, SSS 72, Course record 62.*
*Upper Course: 18 holes, 5243yds, Par 66, SSS 66.*
*Club membership 1200.*
**Visitors** advisable to contact in advance. Only as guest of member at weekends.
**Societies** contact in advance.
**Green Fees** £30 per day both courses; £25 per round Lower Course, £20 per round Upper Course.
**Facilities** ⊗ ⅷ ▮ ▐ ♀ ♂ 🕯 ⚑ ⚑ Stephen Rolley.
**Leisure** trolley for hire, driving range, putting green, practice area.
**Location** N side of town centre off A27
**Hotel** ★★★ 66% Ardington Hotel, Steyne Gardens, WORTHING ☎ 01903 230451 47rm(45 ⇄ ↾)

---

# TYNE & WEAR

## BACKWORTH       Map 12 NZ37

**Backworth** The Hall NE27 0AH ☎ 0191 268 1048
Parkland course with easy walking, natural hazards and good scenery.
*9 holes, 5930yds, Par 71, SSS 69, Course record 64.*
*Club membership 480.*
**Visitors** visitors may not play Tue (Ladies Day) & weekend mornings.
**Societies** apply in writing to secretary.
**Green Fees** £16 per day; £12 per round (£16 per round weekends & bank holidays).
**Facilities** ⊗ ▮ ▐ ♀
**Leisure** putting green, bowls.
**Location** W side of town on B1322
**Hotel** ★★★★ 58% Holiday Inn, Great North Rd, SEATON BURN ☎ 0191 201 9988 150 ⇄ ↾

## BIRTLEY       Map 12 NZ25

**Birtley** Birtley Ln DH3 2LR ☎ 0191 410 2207
Parkland course.
*9 holes, 5660yds, Par 66, SSS 67.*
*Club membership 270.*
**Visitors** must play with member at weekends.
**Societies** apply in writing, must contact 1 month in advance in summer.
**Green Fees** not confirmed.
**Facilities** ♀ ♂
**Leisure** putting green,practice area.

**Hotel** B Forte Posthouse Washington, Emerson District 5, WASHINGTON ☎ 0191 416 2264 138 ⇄ ↾

## BOLDON       Map 12 NZ36

**Boldon** Dipe Ln, East Boldon NE36 0PQ
☎ 0191 536 5360 & 0191 536 4182
Parkland links course, easy walking, distant sea views, windy.
*18 holes, 6362yds, Par 72, SSS 70, Course record 67.*
*Club membership 700.*
**Visitors** may not play after 3.30pm at weekends & bank holidays. Must contact in advance.
**Societies** must contact in advance.
**Green Fees** not confirmed.
**Facilities** ♀ ♂ 🕯 ⚑ ⚑
**Location** S side of village off A184
**Hotel** ★★★ 67% Quality Friendly Hotel, Witney Way, Boldon Business Park, BOLDON ☎ 0191 519 1999 82 ⇄ ↾

## CHOPWELL       Map 12 NZ15

**Garesfield** NE17 7AP ☎ 01207 561309
Undulating parkland course with good views and picturesque woodland surroundings.
*18 holes, 6603yds, Par 72, SSS 72, Course record 68.*
*Club membership 770.*
**Visitors** weekends after 4.30pm only, unless with member. Must contact in advance.
**Societies** must contact secretary in advance.
**Green Fees** not confirmed.
**Facilities** ⊗ ⅷ ▮ ▐ ♀ ♂ 🕯 ⚑ ⚑ David Race.
**Leisure** trolley for hire, putting green, practice area.
**Location** 0.5m N
**Hotel** ★★★ 64% Swallow Hotel, Newgate St, NEWCASTLE UPON TYNE ☎ 0191 232 5025 93 ⇄ ↾

## FELLING       Map 12 NZ26

**Heworth** Gingling Gate, Heworth NE10 8XY
☎ 01632 692137
Fairly flat, parkland course.
*18 holes, 6437yds, Par 71, SSS 71.*
*Club membership 500.*
**Visitors** may not play Sat & before 10am Sun, Apr-Sep.
**Societies** must apply in writing.
**Green Fees** not confirmed.
**Facilities** ♀ ♂
**Leisure** practice area.
**Location** On A195, 0.5m NW of junc with A1(M)
**Hotel** B Forte Posthouse Washington, Emerson District 5, WASHINGTON ☎ 0191 416 2264 138 ⇄ ↾

## GATESHEAD       Map 12 NZ26

**Ravensworth** Moss Heaps, Wrekenton NE9 7UU
☎ 0191 487 2843
Moorland/parkland course 600 ft above sea-level with fine views. Testing 13th hole (par 3).
*18 holes, 5872yds, Par 68, SSS 68.*
*Club membership 600.*       ▶

**Visitors** apply in advance.
**Societies** apply in writing to secretary.
**Green Fees** not confirmed.
**Facilities** ⊗ by prior arrangement ⅋ by prior arrangement ⓛ ⛳ ♀ ⚘ ⬢ ℓ Shaun Cowell.
**Leisure** trolley for hire, putting green, practice area.
**Location** 3m SE off A6127
**Hotel** ★★★ 66% Swallow Hotel, High West St, GATESHEAD ☎ 0191 477 1105 103 ⇥ ℟

## GOSFORTH Map 12 NZ26

**Gosforth** Broadway East NE3 5ER ☎ 0191 285 3495
Parkland course with natural water hazards, easy walking.
*18 holes, 6024yds, Par 69, SSS 68.*
*Club membership 500.*
**Visitors** must contact in advance. Restricted play on competition days.
**Societies** telephone in advance.
**Green Fees** £20 per day.
**Facilities** ⊗ ⅋ ⓛ ⛳ ♀ ⚘ ⬢ ℓ G Garland.
**Leisure** trolley for hire.
**Location** N side of town centre off A6125
**Hotel** ★★★★ 69% Swallow Gosforth Park Hotel, High Gosforth Park, Gosforth, NEWCASTLE UPON TYNE ☎ 0191 236 4111 178 ⇥ ℟

*Parklands* Gosforth Park Golfing Complex, High Gosforth Park NE3 5HQ ☎ 0191 236 4867 & 0191 236 4480
Parklands course is set in pleasant parkland with challenging shots around and sometimes over attractive water hazards. The first 9 holes are easier but the second 9 test even the most experienced golfer.
*18 holes, 6060yds, Par 71, SSS 69, Course record 66.*
*Club membership 750.*
**Visitors** a daily start sheet operates with bookings taken from 4.30pm the previous day during weekdays, and from 8am Fri & Sat for weekends.
**Societies** by prior arrangement with club secretary.
**Green Fees** not confirmed.
**Facilities** ♀ ⚘ ⬢ ℓ Brian Rumney.
**Leisure** 45bay driving range,putting,trolley hire.
**Location** 3m N, at the end A1 Western by Pass
**Hotel** ★★★★ 69% Swallow Gosforth Park Hotel, High Gosforth Park, Gosforth, NEWCASTLE UPON TYNE ☎ 0191 236 4111 178 ⇥ ℟

## HOUGHTON-LE-SPRING Map 12 NZ35

*Elemore* Elemore Ln, Hetton-le-hole DH5 0QB
☎ 0191 526 9020
A new course.
*18 holes, 6000yds, Par 72.*
*Club membership 600.*
**Visitors** no restrictions.
**Societies** apply in writing, telephone enquiries welcome.
**Green Fees** not confirmed.
**Facilities** ⚘ ⬢ ☈
**Leisure** practice area,putting green,trolley hire.
**Location** 3m S
**Hotel** ★★ 58% Chilton Lodge Country Pub & Motel, Black Boy Rd, Chilton Moor, Fencehouses, HOUGHTON-LE-SPRING ☎ 0191 385 2694 18 ⇥ ℟

**Houghton-le-Spring** Copt Hill DH5 8LU
☎ 0191 584 1198 & 584 0048
Hilly, downland course with natural slope hazards.
*18 holes, 6443yds, Par 72, SSS 71, Course record 64.*
*Club membership 600.*
**Visitors** may not play on Sun until 4pm.
**Societies** must contact secretary in advance.
**Green Fees** £25 per day; £18 per round (£30/£25 weekends).
**Facilities** ⊗ ⅋ ⓛ ⛳ ♀ ⚘ ⬢ ℓ Kevin Gow.
**Leisure** putting green, practice area.
**Location** 0.5m E on B1404
**Hotel** ★★ 58% Chilton Lodge Country Pub & Motel, Black Boy Rd, Chilton Moor, Fencehouses, HOUGHTON-LE-SPRING ☎ 0191 385 2694 18 ⇥ ℟

## NEWCASTLE UPON TYNE Map 12 NZ26

**City of Newcastle** Three Mile Bridge NE3 2DR
☎ 0191 285 1775
A well-manicured parkland course in the Newcastle suburbs, subject to wind.
*18 holes, 6508yds, Par 72, SSS 71, Course record 64.*
*Club membership 460.*
**Visitors** no restrictions but advisable to telephone first.
**Societies** telephone in advance
**Green Fees** £20 per day (£25 weekends & bank holidays).
**Facilities** ⊗ ⅋ ⓛ ⛳ ♀ ⚘ ⬢ ℓ Anthony Matthew.
**Leisure** trolley for hire, putting green, practice area.
**Location** 3m N on A1
**Hotel** ★★★ 64% Newcastle Airport Moat House, Woolsington, NEWCASTLE UPON TYNE AIRPORT ☎ 0191 401 9988 100 ⇥ ℟

*Newcastle United* Ponteland Rd, Cowgate NE5 3JW
☎ 0191 286 4693
Moorland course with natural hazards.
*18 holes, 6484yds, Par 72, SSS 71, Course record 68.*
*Club membership 500.*
**Visitors** must play with member at weekends.
**Societies** must contact in writing.
**Green Fees** not confirmed.
**Facilities** ♀ ⚘ ⬢
**Location** 1.25m NW of city centre off A6127
**Hotel** ★★★ 68% Imperial Swallow Hotel, Jesmond Rd, NEWCASTLE UPON TYNE ☎ 0191 281 5511 122 ⇥ ℟

**Northumberland** High Gosforth Park NE3 5HT
☎ 0191 236 2498
Many golf courses have been sited inside racecourses, although not so many survive today. One which does is the Northumberland Club's course at High Gosforth Park. Naturally the course is flat but there are plenty of mounds and other hazards to make it a fine test of golf. It should be said that not all the holes are within the confines of the racecourse, but both inside and out there are some good holes. This is a Championship course.
*18 holes, 6629yds, Par 72, SSS 72, Course record 65.*
*Club membership 580.*
**Visitors** may not play at weekends or competition days. Must contact in advance.
**Societies** must apply in writing.
**Green Fees** £35 per day; £30 per round.
**Facilities** ⊗ ⅋ ⓛ ⛳ ♀ ⚘

| Leisure | trolley for hire, putting green, practice area. |
|---|---|
| Location | 4m N of city centre off A1 |
| Hotel | ★★★★ 69% Swallow Gosforth Park Hotel, High Gosforth Park, Gosforth, NEWCASTLE UPON TYNE ☎ 0191 236 4111 178 ⊨ ⚑ |

**Westerhope** Whorlton Grange, Westerhope NE5 1PP
☎ 0191 286 7636
Attractive parkland course with tree-lined fairways, and easy
walking. Good open views towards the airport.
*18 holes, 6444yds, Par 72, SSS 71, Course record 64.*
*Club membership 778.*
Visitors  with member only at weekends. Must contact in
     advance.
Societies  must contact Secretary in advance.
Green Fees £22 per day; £16 per round.
Facilities  ⊗ ⅢⅢ ᴸᴬ ◗ ♀ ⚶ 🖻 ℓ Nigel Brown.
Leisure  motorised carts for hire, buggies for hire, trolley
     for hire, putting green, practice area, pool table.
Location  4.5m NW of city centre off B6324
Hotel   ★★★★ 69% Swallow Gosforth Park Hotel,
     High Gosforth Park, Gosforth, NEWCASTLE
     UPON TYNE ☎ 0191 236 4111 178 ⊨ ⚑

## RYTON              Map 12 NZ16

**Ryton** Clara Vale NE40 3TD ☎ 0191 413 3737
Parkland course.
*18 holes, 6042yds, Par 70, SSS 69, Course record 68.*
*Club membership 600.*
Visitors  with member only at weekends.
Societies  apply in advance.
Green Fees £20 per day; £15 per round.
Facilities  ⊗ ⅢⅢ ᴸᴬ ◗ ♀ ⚶
Leisure  putting green, practice area.
Location  NW side of town off A695
Hotel   ★★★ 70% Gibside Arms Hotel, Front St,
     WHICKHAM ☎ 0191 488 9292 45 ⊨ ⚑

**Tyneside** Westfield Ln NE40 3QE ☎ 0191 413 2742
Open parkland course, not heavily bunkered. Water hazard,
hilly, practice area.
*18 holes, 6042yds, Par 70, SSS 69, Course record 65.*
*Club membership 900.*
Visitors  must contact in advance to play at weekends.
Societies  must apply in advance.
Green Fees £25 per day; £20 per round (£30 per round
     weekends).
Facilities  ⊗ ⅢⅢ ᴸᴬ ◗ ♀ ⚶ 🖻 ℓ Malcolm Gunn.
Leisure  trolley for hire, putting green, practice area.
Location  NW side of town off A695
Hotel   ★★★ 70% Gibside Arms Hotel, Front St,
     WHICKHAM ☎ 0191 488 9292 45 ⊨ ⚑

## SOUTH SHIELDS         Map 12 NZ36

**South Shields** Cleadon Hills NE34 8EG ☎ 0191 456 8942
A slightly undulating downland course on a limestone base
ensuring good conditions underfoot. Open to strong winds,
the course is testing but fair. There are fine views of the
coastline.
*18 holes, 6264yds, Par 71, SSS 70, Course record 64.*
*Club membership 800.*

Visitors  must contact in advance.
Societies  by arrangement.
Green Fees £20 per day (£25 weekends & bank holidays).
Facilities  ⊗ ⅢⅢ ᴸᴬ ◗ ♀ ⚶ 🖻 ⚑ ℓ Gary Parsons.
Leisure  trolley for hire, putting green, practice area.
Location  SE side of town centre off A1300
Hotel   ★★★ 61% Sea Hotel, Sea Rd, SOUTH
     SHIELDS
     ☎ 0191 427 0999 33 ⊨ ⚑

**Whitburn** Lizard Ln NE34 7AF
☎ 0191 529 4944 & 0191 529 2144
Parkland course.
*18 holes, 5780yds, Par 69, SSS 68, Course record 66.*
*Club membership 650.*
Visitors  restricted weekends. Contact professional in
     advance.
Societies  must apply in writing to secretary
Green Fees £17.50 per day (£22.50 weekends & bank
     holidays).
Facilities  ⊗ ⅢⅢ ᴸᴬ ◗ ♀ ⚶ 🖻 ℓ David Stephenson.
Leisure  trolley for hire, putting green, practice area,
     snooker table.
Location  2.5m SE off A183
Hotel   ★★★★ 60% Swallow Hotel, Queen's Pde,
     Seaburn, SUNDERLAND
     ☎ 0191 529 2041 65 ⊨ ⚑

## SUNDERLAND         Map 12 NZ35

**Ryhope** Leechmore Way, Ryhope SR2 0DH
☎ 0191 523 7333
A municipal course recently extended to 18 holes.
*18 holes, 4601yds, Par 65, SSS 63.*
*Club membership 350.*
Visitors  no restrictions.
Societies  apply in writing, telephone enquiries welcome.
Green Fees not confirmed.
Facilities  ♀ ⚶ 🖻 ⚑
Leisure  trolley hire.
Location  3.5m S of city centre
Hotel   ★★★★ 60% Swallow Hotel, Queen's Pde,
     Seaburn, SUNDERLAND
     ☎ 0191 529 2041 65 ⊨ ⚑

*Wearside* Coxgreen SR4 9JT
☎ 0191 534 2518
Open, undulating parkland course rolling down to the
River Wear and beneath the shadow of the famous
Penshaw Monument. Built on the lines of an Athenian
temple it is a well-known landmark. Two ravines cross
the course presenting a variety of challenging holes.
*18 holes, 6373yds, Par 71, SSS 74.*
*Club membership 729.*
Visitors  may not play before 9.30am & after 4pm.
Societies  must apply in writing.
Green Fees not confirmed.
Facilities  ♀ ⚶ 🖻 ℓ Doug Brolls.
Leisure  putting, trolley hire, practice area.
Location  3.5m W off A183
Hotel   ★★★★ 60% Swallow Hotel, Queen's Pde,
     Seaburn, SUNDERLAND
     ☎ 0191 529 2041 65 ⊨ ⚑

## TYNEMOUTH                                          Map 12 NZ36

**Tynemouth** Spital Dene NE30 2ER ☎ 0191 257 4578
Well-drained parkland/downland course, easy walking.
*18 holes, 6082yds, Par 70, SSS 69.*
*Club membership 824.*
**Visitors**      must play with member weekends & bank
                  holidays.
**Societies**     must contact in writing.
**Green Fees**    not confirmed.
**Facilities**    ♀⅄🏠📫☏ J P McKenna.
**Leisure**       putting,buggy/trolley hire,practice area.
**Location**      0.5m W
**Hotel**         ★★★ 61% Park Hotel, Grand Pde,
                  TYNEMOUTH
                  ☎ 0191 257 1406 49rm(43 ➡ ♠)

## WALLSEND                                          Map 12 NZ26

**Wallsend** Rheydt Av, Bigges Main NE28 8SU
☎ 0191 262 1973
Parkland course.
*18 holes, 6608yds, Par 72, SSS 72, Course record 68.*
*Club membership 750.*
**Visitors**      may not play before 12.30pm weekends.
**Societies**     must apply in writing.
**Green Fees**    not confirmed.
**Facilities**    ♀⅄🏠☏ Ken Phillips.
**Leisure**       putting green,trolley hire,driving range.
**Location**      NW side of town centre off A193
**Hotel**         ★★★ 61% Europa Hotel, Coast Rd,
                  WALLSEND ☎ 0191 202 9955 147 ➡ ♠

## WASHINGTON                                        Map 12 NZ25

**Washington Moat House** Stone Cellar Rd, High Usworth
NE37 1PH ☎ 0191 402 9988
Championship-standard course. Also a 9-hole (par 3) course,
putting green and 21-bay floodlit driving range. 'Bunkers
Bar' at the 10th tee is one of the few 'spike' bars in the
country.
*18 holes, 6267yds, Par 73, SSS 71.*
*Club membership 700.*
**Visitors**      must contact in advance. May not play before
                  10am or between noon & 2pm at weekends.
**Societies**     book in advance.
**Green Fees**    £17 per round (£25 weekends).
**Facilities**    ⊗ 〗⅃ 🍴 ♀⅄🏠📫☏ Warren Marshall.
**Leisure**       heated indoor swimming pool, squash, sauna,
                  solarium, gymnasium, trolley for hire, floodlit
                  driving range, putting green, practice area.
**Hotel**         ★★★ 67% Washington Moat House, Stone
                  Cellar Rd, District 12, High Usworth,
                  WASHINGTON ☎ 0191 402 9988 105 ➡ ♠

## WHICKHAM                                          Map 12 NZ26

**Whickham** Hollinside Park, Fellside Rd NE16 5BA
☎ 0191 488 1576
Parkland course, some uphill walking, fine views.
*18 holes, 5878yds, Par 68, SSS 68, Course record 61.*
*Club membership 630.*
**Visitors**      must contact in advance. Must have an
                  introduction from own club.

**Societies**     by arrangement.
**Green Fees**    £20 per day/round (£25 weekends & bank
                  holidays).
**Facilities**    ⊗ 〗⅃ 🍴 ♀⅄🏠📫☏ Brian Ridley.
**Leisure**       trolley for hire, putting green, practice area.
**Location**      1.5m S
**Hotel**         ★★★ 66% Swallow Hotel, High West St,
                  GATESHEAD ☎ 0191 477 1105 103 ➡ ♠

## WHITLEY BAY                                        Map 12 NZ37

**Whitley Bay** Claremont Rd NE26 3UF
☎ 0191 252 0180 & 252 5568
Downland course close to the sea. A stream runs through the
undulating terrain.
*18 holes, 6600yds, Par 72, SSS 71, Course record 66.*
*Club membership 800.*
**Visitors**      apply in advance for occasional Sun play.
**Societies**     telephone initially.
**Green Fees**    £25 per day; £20 per round (£30 Sun).
**Facilities**    ⊗ 〗⅃ 🍴 ♀⅄🏠☏ Gary Shipley.
**Leisure**       trolley for hire, putting green, practice area.
**Location**      NW side of town centre off A1148
**Hotel**         ★★ 61% Holmedale Hotel, 106 Park Av,
                  WHITLEY BAY
                  ☎ 0191 251 3903 & 0191 253 1162 18 ➡ ♠

# ●
# WARWICKSHIRE
# ●

## ATHERSTONE                                         Map 04 SP39

**Atherstone** The Outwoods, Coleshill Rd CV9 2RL
☎ 01827 713110
Parkland course, established in 1894 and laid out on hilly
ground.
*18 holes, 6006yds, Par 72, SSS 69.*
*Club membership 480.*
**Visitors**      handicap certificate required. With member only
                  weekends and bank holidays. Also with holder
                  of handicap certificate by permission of Club
                  Secretary.
**Societies**     contact in advance.
**Green Fees**    £17 per day/round.
**Facilities**    ⊗ 〗⅃ 🍴 ♀⅄
**Leisure**       putting green.
**Location**      0.5m S on B4116
**Hotel**         ★★ 73% Chapel House Hotel, Friar's Gate,
                  ATHERSTONE ☎ 01827 718949 12 ➡ ♠

## BIDFORD-ON-AVON                                    Map 04 SP15

**Bidford Grange** Stratford Rd B50 4LY ☎ 01789 490319
Designed by Howard Swan & Paul Tillman, this very long,
championship standard course is built to represent a links
course and is fully irrigated. There are water hazards on the
first 7 holes, and particularly challenging holes on the 16th
(223yds,par 3), 8th (600yds, par 5) and an uphill par 4 at the
13th.
*18 holes, 7233yds, Par 72, SSS 74.*
*Club membership 500.*
**Visitors**      no restrictions.

**Societies** apply in writing or phone, minimum 12, maximum 36.
**Green Fees** not confirmed.
**Facilities** ♀ ⅍ 🏠
**Leisure** fishing.
**Location** 4m W of Stratford upon Avon, B439
**Hotel** ★★★ 76% Salford Hall Hotel, ABBOT'S SALFORD
☎ 01386 871300 14 ⇔ ⋔Annexe19 ⇔ ⋔

## BRANDON — Map 04 SP47

**City of Coventry-Brandon Wood** Brandon Ln, Wolston CV8 3GQ ☎ 01203 543141
Municipal parkland course surrounded by fields and bounded by River Avon on east side. Floodlit driving range.
*18 holes, 6610yds, Par 72, SSS 72, Course record 68.*
*Club membership 580.*
**Visitors** telephone for details.
**Societies** telephone secretary for details
**Green Fees** £8.70 per round (£11.60 weekends).
**Facilities** ⊗ ⅍ ⓛ ⓦ ♀ ⅍ 🏠 ⅏ ⚑ Chris Gledhill.
**Leisure** buggies for hire, trolley for hire, driving range, putting green, practice area.
**Location** Off A45 southbound
**Hotel** ★★★ 64% The Brandon Hall, Main St, BRANDON ☎ 01203 542571 60 ⇔ ⋔

## COLESHILL — Map 04 SP28

**Maxstoke Park** Castle Ln B46 2RD ☎ 01675 466743
Parkland course with easy walking. Numerous trees and a lake form natural hazards.
*18 holes, 6442yds, Par 71, SSS 71.*
*Club membership 720.*
**Visitors** with member only at weekends & bank holidays.
**Societies** contact in advance.
**Green Fees** £25 per round.
**Facilities** ⊗ ⅍ ⓛ ⓦ ♀ ⅍ 🏠 ⚑ ⚑ Neil McEwan.
**Leisure** trolley for hire, putting green, practice area.
**Location** 2m E
**Hotel** ★★ 66% Coleshill Hotel, 152 High St, COLESHILL
☎ 01675 465527 15 ⇔ ⋔Annexe8 ⇔ ⋔

## KENILWORTH — Map 04 SP27

**Kenilworth** Crewe Ln CV8 2EA ☎ 01926 858517
Parkland course in open hilly situation. Club founded in 1887.
*18 holes, 6413yds, Par 73, SSS 71, Course record 62.*
*Club membership 725.*
**Visitors** must contact in advance.
**Societies** apply in writing.

**Green Fees** £26 per day/round (£37 weekends).
**Facilities** ⊗ ⅍ by prior arrangement ⓛ ⓦ ♀ ⅍ 🏠 ⚑
⚑ Steven Yates.
**Leisure** motorised carts for hire, trolley for hire, putting green, practice area, par 3 course.
**Location** 0.5m NE
**Hotel** ★★ 64% Clarendon House Hotel, Old High St, KENILWORTH
☎ 01926 57668 Cen. Res. 0800 616883 30 ⇔ ⋔

## LEA MARSTON — Map 04 SP29

*Lea Marston Hotel & Leisure Complex* Haunch Ln B76 0BY ☎ 01675 470468
Par 3, 'pay-and-play' course, with water hazards, out of bounds, and large bunkers. The venue for the past two years of the Midlands Professional Par 3 Competition. Golf driving range.
*9 holes, 783yds, Par 27, SSS 27, Course record 46.*
**Visitors** no restrictions.
**Societies** must telephone in advance.
**Green Fees** not confirmed.
**Facilities** ♀ 🏠 ⚑ ⚑ Andrew Stokes.
**Leisure** hard tennis courts, heated indoor swimming pool, sauna, solarium, gymnasium, driving range,putting green.
**Hotel** ★★★ 69% Lea Marston Hotel & Leisure Complex, Haunch Ln, LEA MARSTON
☎ 01675 470468 49 ⇔ ⋔

## LEAMINGTON SPA — Map 04 SP36

**Leamington & County** Golf Ln, Whitnash CV31 2QA
☎ 01926 425961
Undulating parkland course with extensive views.
*18 holes, 6488yds, Par 71, SSS 71, Course record 65.*
*Club membership 802.*
**Visitors** must contact in advance.
**Societies** telephone in advance.
**Green Fees** £30 per day; £25 per round (£40 per round weekends & bank holidays).
**Facilities** ⊗ ⅍ ⓛ ⓦ ♀ ⅍ 🏠 ⚑ Iain Grant.
**Leisure** buggies for hire, trolley for hire, putting green, practice area, snooker.
**Location** S side of town centre
**Hotel** ★★★ 61% Manor House Hotel, Avenue Rd, LEAMINGTON SPA ☎ 01926 423251 53 ⇔ ⋔

*Newbold Comyn* Newbold Ter East CV32 4EW
☎ 01926 421157
Municipal parkland course with hilly front nine. The par 4, 9th is a 467-yd testing hole.
*18 holes, 6315yds, Par 70, SSS 70, Course record 69.*
*Club membership 420.* ▶

**Where golf is just the beginning . . .**

Nestling into 240 acres of Warwickshire and Northamptonshire countryside, close to the M1 and M40 motorways. Hellidon offers the ultimate in leisure facilities but with that personal touch that only a small, luxury hotel can offer.
Spectacular 18-hole, 6,700 yard championship golf course designed to provide a challenge to both experienced and novice golfers alike, plus new 9 hole course opened 1994. Company and society golfing days. Golfing breaks. Golf tuition. Golf and leisure memberships. Weekend and midweek breaks. Luxury weekends. Gym, sauna, jacuzzi and 2 resident beauty therapists. Indoor swimming pool. Conferences. Corporate entertainment. Wedding receptions. Special celebrations.

**Hellidon Lakes**
HOTEL & COUNTRY CLUB
★★★★ ☺

**The Hellidon Lakes Hotel & Country Club, Hellidon, Daventry, Northants NN11 6LN**
**Tel: (01327) 262550 Fax: (01327) 262559** *See gazetteer under Northamptonshire*

**Visitors** no restrictions.
**Societies** apply to professional.
**Green Fees** not confirmed.
**Facilities** ⛴ 🏠 ⛳ ℓ Don Knight.
**Leisure** heated indoor swimming pool, gymnasium.
**Location** 0.75m E of town centre off B4099
**Hotel** ★★★ 61% Manor House Hotel, Avenue Rd,
LEAMINGTON SPA
☎ 01926 423251 53 ⇆ ⎅

## LEEK WOOTTON    Map 04 SP26

**The Warwickshire** CV35 7QT ☎ 01926 409409
Opened in 1993, this is an unusual championship standard
course. Designed by Karl Litten, the 36 holes are laid out as
four interchangeable loops of 9 holes to create six contrasting
yet superb courses in a parkland and woodland setting.
*South East Course: 18 holes, 7000yds, Par 72, SSS 72,*
*Course record 68.*
*North West Course: 18 holes, 7000yds, Par 72, SSS 72.*
*Par 3: 9 holes, 1133yds, Par 27, SSS 27.*
*Club membership 1100.*
**Visitors** can book up to 7 days in advance.
**Societies** apply to sales office for details.
**Green Fees** £40 per round.
**Facilities** ⊗ ⅶ ⓛ ⬛ ♀ ⛴ 🏠 ⛳ ℓ John Cook.
**Leisure** motorised carts for hire, buggies for hire, trolley
for hire, floodlit driving range, putting, practice
area.
**Location** On B4115
**Hotel** ★★ 56% Warwick Arms Hotel, 17 High St,
WARWICK ☎ 01926 492759 35 ⇆ ⎅

## NUNEATON    Map 04 SP39

*Nuneaton* Golf Dr, Whitestone CV11 6QF
☎ 01203 347810
Undulating moorland and woodland course.
*18 holes, 6429yds, Par 71, SSS 71.*
*Club membership 675.*
**Visitors** with member only at weekends.
**Societies** apply in writing.
**Green Fees** not confirmed.
**Facilities** ⛴ 🏠 ℓ Graham Davison.
**Location** 2m SE off B4114
**Hotel** ★★ 67% Longshoot Toby Hotel, Watling St,
NUNEATON
☎ 01203 329711 Annexe47 ⇆ ⎅

*Oakridge* Arley Ln, Ansley Village CV10 9PH
☎ 01676 541389 & 540542
There are a number of water hazards on the back nine which
add to the natural beauty of the countryside. The undulating
course is affected by winter cross winds on several holes.
Overall it will certainly test golfing skills.
*18 holes, 6242yds, Par 71, SSS 70.*
*Club membership 450.*
**Visitors** contact in advance, with members only at
weekends.
**Societies** apply in writing or telephone in advance.
**Green Fees** £25 per 36 holes: £15 per round.
**Facilities** ⊗ ⅶ ⓛ ⬛ ♀ ⛴ 🏠 ⛳ ℓ Ian Sadler.
**Leisure** buggies for hire, trolley for hire, putting green,
practice area, snooker, games room.
**Location** 4m W

**Hotel** ★★★ 64% Weston Hall, Weston Ln, Weston in
Arden, Bulkington, NUNEATON
☎ 01203 312989 36 ⇆ ⎅

*Purley Chase* Pipers Ln, Ridge Ln CV10 0RB
☎ 01203 393118
Meadowland course with tricky water hazards on eight holes
and undulating greens. 13-bay driving range.
*18 holes, 6772yds, Par 72, SSS 72, Course record 67.*
*Club membership 650.*
**Visitors** welcome except before noon weekends.
**Societies** Telephone for provisional booking.
**Green Fees** £13 per round (£20 weekends & bank holidays).
**Facilities** ⊗ ⅶ ⓛ ⬛ ♀ ⛴ 🏠 ℓ Roy Young.
**Leisure** fishing, motorised carts for hire, trolley for hire,
driving range, putting green.
**Location** 2m NW off B4114
**Hotel** ★★ 67% Longshoot Toby Hotel, Watling St,
NUNEATON
☎ 01203 329711 Annexe47 ⇆ ⎅

## RUGBY    Map 04 SP57

*Rugby* Clifton Rd CV21 3RD ☎ 01788 542306
Parkland course with brook running through the middle and
crossed by a viaduct.
*18 holes, 5457yds, Par 68, SSS 67, Course record 62.*
*Club membership 550.*
**Visitors** weekends & bank holidays with member only.
**Societies** apply in writing.
**Green Fees** not confirmed.
**Facilities** ♀ ⛴ 🏠 ⛳ ℓ Andy Peach.
**Leisure** caddy carts for hire.
**Location** 1m NE on B5414
**Hotel** ★★★ 60% Grosvenor Hotel, Clifton Rd,
RUGBY ☎ 01788 535686 21 ⇆ ⎅

*Whitefields Hotel & Golf Complex* Coventry Rd,
Thurlaston CV23 9JR ☎ 01788 522393 & 521800
Whitefields has superb drainage and has never had to close.
There are four water features and the 12th has a stunnning
dogleg 442yard Par 4 with a superb view across Draycote
Water. The 16th is completely surrounded by water and is
particularly difficult.
*18 holes, 6433yds, Par 71, SSS 71, Course record 69.*
*Club membership 550.*
**Visitors** advisable to book unless hotel guest.
**Societies** contact secretary in advance.
**Green Fees** £18 (£22 weekends & bank holidays).
**Facilities** ⊗ ⅶ ⓛ ⬛ ♀ ⛴ 🏠 ⛳ ⍜
**Leisure** motorised carts for hire, buggies for hire, trolley
for hire, putting green, planned driving range.
**Location** A45 Coventry road

## STONELEIGH    Map 04 SP37

*Stoneleigh* The Old Deer Park, Coventry Rd CV8 3DR
☎ 01203 639991
Parkland course in old deer park with many mature trees. The
River Avon meanders through the course and comes into play
on 4 holes. Also 9-hole course.
*Tantara Course: 18 holes, 6083yds, Par 71, SSS 69.*
*Avon Course: 9 holes, 1251yds, Par 27.*
*Club membership 750.*

| | |
|---|---|
| **Visitors** | must contact in advance, no visitors at weekends except by prior arrangement. |
| **Societies** | by prior arrangement. |
| **Green Fees** | not confirmed. |
| **Facilities** | ♀ ♣ 🏠 ♍ Sid Mouland. |
| **Leisure** | practice area,cart/buggy/trolley hire. |
| **Location** | 3m NE of Kenilworth |
| **Hotel** | ★★★ 64% De Montfort Hotel, The Square, KENILWORTH ☎ 01926 55944 96 ⇔ 🐾 |

## STRATFORD-UPON-AVON                Map 04 SP25

**Stratford Oaks** Bearley Rd, Snitterfield CV37 0EZ
☎ 01789 731571
American styled, parkland course designed by Howard Swan.
*18 holes, 6100yds, Par 71, SSS 69, Course record 66.*
*Club membership 600.*

| | |
|---|---|
| **Visitors** | no restrictions. |
| **Societies** | telephone in advance. |
| **Green Fees** | not confirmed. |
| **Facilities** | ♀ ♣ 🏠 ♍ ♍ Fraser Leek. |
| **Location** | 4m N of Stratford-upon-Avon |
| **Hotel** | ★★★ 74% Stratford Manor, Warwick Rd, STRATFORD-UPON-AVON ☎ 01789 731173 104 ⇔ 🐾 |

**Stratford-upon-Avon** Tiddington Rd CV37 7BA
☎ 01789 205749
Beautiful parkland course. The par 3, 16th is tricky and the
par 5, 17th and 18th, provide a tough end.

*18 holes, 6309yds, Par 72, SSS 70, Course record 64.*
*Club membership 750.*

| | |
|---|---|
| **Visitors** | restricted on Wed. Must contact in advance. |
| **Societies** | must telephone in advance. |
| **Green Fees** | not confirmed. |
| **Facilities** | ♀ ♣ 🏠 ♍ ♍ N D Powell. |
| **Location** | 0.75m E on B4086 |
| **Hotel** | ★★★★ 65% Alveston Manor Hotel, Clopton Bridge, STRATFORD-UPON-AVON ☎ 01789 204581 106 ⇔ 🐾 |

**Welcombe Hotel** Warwick Rd CV37 0NR
☎ 01789 295252
Wooded parkland course of great character and boasting
superb views of the River Avon, Stratford and the Cotswolds.
Set within the hotel's 157-acre estate, it has two lakes and
water features.
*18 holes, 6217yds, Par 70, SSS 68, Course record 65.*
*Club membership 400.*

| | |
|---|---|
| **Visitors** | must contact in advance. |
| **Societies** | booking via Hotel. |
| **Green Fees** | £35 per day; £30 per round (£45/£40 weekends & bank holidays). |
| **Facilities** | ⊗ �🎼 ⬛ 💼 ♀ ♣ 🏠 ♍ 🎣 |
| **Leisure** | hard tennis courts, fishing, motorised carts for hire, buggies for hire, trolley for hire, driving range, putting green, practice area. |
| **Location** | 1.5m NE off A46 |
| **Hotel** | ★★★★ 72% Welcombe Hotel and Golf Course, Warwick Rd, STRATFORD-UPON-AVON ☎ 01789 295252 76 ⇔ 🐾 |

# WELCOMBE
## HOTEL & GOLF COURSE
### STRATFORD-UPON-AVON
### Warwickshire
### Fax:(01789) 414666
### Telephone: (01789) 295252

The Welcombe, a Jacobean-style luxury hotel, is situated within a 157 acre parkland estate with its
own 18-hole Par 70 Golf Course, just 1½ miles from the centre of Stratford-upon-Avon. The club
house facilities include a bar with pub style menu, professional shop and changing facilities and is
a short walk away from the luxury of this superb hotel.

**Special golfing packages throughout the year –**
**Rates and brochure on request.**

## TANWORTH-IN-ARDEN                    Map 04 SP17

**Ladbrook Park** Poolhead Ln B94 5ED
☎ 01564 742264
Parkland course lined with trees.
*18 holes, 6427yds, Par 71, SSS 71, Course record 65.*
*Club membership 700.*
Visitors      with member only weekends. Must contact in
              advance & have handicap certificate.
Societies     apply in advance.
Green Fees    Winter: £20 per day/round. Summer: £35 per
              days, £30 per 27 holes, £25 per round.
Facilities    ⊗ ⅏ ⅃ ℙ ♀ ♧ 🏠 ⫟ 𝄐 Richard Mountford.
Leisure       trolley for hire, putting green, practice area.
Location      2.5m SE of M42 junct 3
Hotel         ★★★(red)⚘ Nuthurst Grange Country House
              Hotel, Nuthurst Grange Ln, HOCKLEY
              HEATH
              ☎ 01564 783972 15 ⇆ ⏴

## UPPER BRAILES                       Map 04 SP32

**Brailes** Sutton Ln, Lower Brailes OX15 5BB
☎ 01608 685336 & 685633
Undulating meadowland on 130 acres of Cotswold
countryside. Sutton brook passes through the course and is
crossed 5 times.The Par 5 17th offers the most spectacular
view of three counties from the tee. There is a prevailing
cross wind.
*18 holes, 6270yds, Par 71, SSS 70, Course record 73.*
*Club membership 420.*
Visitors      advance telephone advisable.
Societies     telephone or write for information to the
              secretary.
Green Fees    £24 per 27/36 holes; £16 per 18 holes (£33/£22
              weekends & bank holidays) Twilight £10 (£13).
Facilities    ⊗ ⅏ ⅃ ℙ ♀ ♧ 🏠 ⫟ 𝄐 Mike Bendall.
Leisure       trolley for hire, putting green, practice area.
Location      4m E of Shipston-on-Stour, on B4035
Hotel         ★★ 63% The Red Lion Hotel, Main St, Long
              Compton, SHIPSTON ON STOUR
              ☎ 01608 684221 5 ⇆ ⏴

## WARWICK                             Map 04 SP26

**Warwick** The Racecourse CV34 6HW
☎ 01926 494316
Parkland course with easy walking. Driving range with
floodlit bays.
*9 holes, 2682yds, Par 34, SSS 66, Course record 67.*
*Club membership 150.*
Visitors      must contact in advance. May not play Sun
              before 12.30pm
Societies     contact in advance.
Green Fees    £4 per 9 holes (£5 weekends).
Facilities    ℙ ♀ ♧ 🏠 ⫟ 𝄐 Phil Sharp.
Leisure       trolley for hire, driving range.
Location      W side of town centre
Hotel         ★★ 56% Warwick Arms Hotel, 17 High St,
              WARWICK
              ☎ 01926 492759 35 ⇆ ⏴

# WEST MIDLANDS

## ALDRIDGE                            Map 07 SK00

**Druids Heath** Stonnall Rd WS9 8JZ
☎ 01922 55595 (Office) & 59523 (Pro)
Testing, undulating heathland course.
*18 holes, 6659yds, Par 72, SSS 73.*
*Club membership 590.*
Visitors      contact in advance recommended. Weekend play
              permitted after 2pm.
Societies     phone initially.
Green Fees    £25 per day (£32 weekends).
Facilities    ⊗ ⅏ ⅃ ℙ ♀ ♧ 🏠 𝄐 Simon Elliott.
Leisure       trolley for hire, putting, practice area.
Location      NE side of town centre off A454
Hotel         ★★★ 70% The Fairlawns at Aldridge, 178
              Little Aston Rd, Aldridge, WALSALL
              ☎ 01922 55122 35 ⇆ ⏴

## BIRMINGHAM                          Map 07 SP08

**Brandhall** Heron Rd, Oldbury, Warley B68 8AQ
☎ 0121 552 2195
Private golf club on municipal parkland course, easy walking,
good hazards. Testing holes: 1st-502 yds (par 5); 10th-455
yds dog-leg (par 5).
*18 holes, 5734yds, Par 70, Course record 66.*
*Club membership 250.*
Visitors      restricted weekends.
Societies     by arrangement.
Green Fees    not confirmed.
Facilities    ♀ 🏠 ⫟ 𝄐
Leisure       practice area.
Location      5.5m W of city centre off A4123
Hotel         B Forte Posthouse Birmingham Great Barr,
              Chapel Ln, GREAT BARR
              ☎ 0121 357 7444 192 ⇆ ⏴

**Cocks Moors Woods Municipal** Alcester Rd South, Kings
Heath B14 4ER ☎ 0121 444 3584
Tree-lined, parkland course.
*18 holes, 5888yds, Par 69, SSS 68.*
*Club membership 250.*
Visitors      no restrictions.
Societies     must contact in advance.
Green Fees    not confirmed.
Facilities    ♀ ♧ 🏠 ⫟
Leisure       heated indoor swimming pool, solarium,
              gymnasium, putting green,trolley hire.
Location      5m S of city centre on A435
Hotel         B Forte Posthouse Birmingham City,
              Smallbrook Queensway, BIRMINGHAM
              ☎ 0121 643 8171 251 ⇆ ⏴

**Edgbaston** Church Rd, Edgbaston B15 3TB
☎ 0121 454 1736
Parkland course in lovely country.
*18 holes, 6106yds, Par 69, SSS 69.*
*Club membership 850.*
Visitors      recommended to contact in advance, must
              have handicap certificate.
Societies     must apply in writing.

> **Green Fees** £42.50 (£50 weekends & bank holidays);
> Winter £35.50/£42.50.
> **Facilities** ⊗ ⚏ ⓛ ▟ ♀ ⚐ 🕭 ⧫ Andrew H Bownes.
> **Leisure** motorised carts for hire, buggies for hire,
> trolley for hire, putting green, practice area.
> **Location** 1m S of city centre on B4217 off A38
> **Hotel** ★★★ 66% Plough & Harrow, 135 Hagley
> Rd, Edgbaston, BIRMINGHAM
> ☎ 0121 454 4111 44 ⇔ ⛵

***Great Barr*** Chapel Ln, Great Barr B43 7BA
☎ 0121 357 5270
Parkland course with easy walking. Pleasant views of Barr
Beacon National Park.
*18 holes, 6523yds, Par 72, SSS 71.*
*Club membership 600.*
**Visitors** restricted at weekends.
**Societies** must contact in writing.
**Green Fees** not confirmed.
**Facilities** ♀ ▟ ⚐ ⧫ ⧫ Richard Spragg.
**Location** 6m N of city centre off A 34
**Hotel** B Forte Posthouse Birmingham Great Barr,
Chapel Ln, GREAT BARR
☎ 0121 357 7444 192 ⇔ ⛵

**Handsworth** 11 Sunningdale Close, Handsworth Wood
B20 1NP ☎ 0121 554 0599 & 554 3387
Undulating parkland course with some tight fairways but
subject to wind.
*18 holes, 6267yds, Par 70, SSS 70, Course record 65.*
*Club membership 800.*
**Visitors** restricted weekends, bank holidays & Xmas.
Must contact in advance and have a handicap
certificate.
**Societies** must contact in advance.
**Green Fees** £30 per day Mon-Fri.
**Facilities** ⊗ ⚏ ⓛ ▟ ♀ ▟ ⚐ ⧫ Lee Bashford.
**Leisure** squash, trolley for hire, putting green, practice
area.
**Location** 3.5m NW of city centre off A4040
**Hotel** ★★★ 67% Birmingham/West Bromwich Moat
House, Birmingham Rd, WEST BROMWICH
☎ 0121 609 9988 171 ⇔ ⛵

**Harborne** 40 Tennal Rd, Harborne B32 2JE
☎ 0121 427 3058 & 427 3512
Parkland course in hilly situation, with brook running
through.
*18 holes, 6230yds, Par 70, SSS 70, Course record 65.*
*Club membership 636.*
**Visitors** must contact in advance, may not play weekends
except with member, Ladies have priority Tue.
**Societies** Mon, Wed-Fri apply to secretary.
**Green Fees** £35 per day; £30 per round.
**Facilities** ⊗ ⚏ ⓛ ▟ ♀ ▟ ⚐ ⧫ ⧫ Alan Quarterman.
**Leisure** trolley for hire, putting green.
**Location** 3.5 m SW of city centre off A4040
**Hotel** ★★★ 66% Plough & Harrow, 135 Hagley Rd,
Edgbaston, BIRMINGHAM
☎ 0121 454 4111 44 ⇔ ⛵

**Harborne Church Farm** Vicarage Rd, Harborne B17 0SN
☎ 0121 427 1204
Parkland course with water hazards and easy walking. Some
holes might prove difficult.

*9 holes, 2457yds, Par 66, SSS 64, Course record 62.*
*Club membership 200.*
**Visitors** must contact in advance.
**Societies** must telephone in advance.
**Green Fees** £7 per 18 holes; £4.50 per 9 holes (£8/£5
weekends).
**Facilities** ⊗ ⚏ ▟ ▟ ⚐ ⧫ ⧫ Mark Hampton.
**Leisure** trolley for hire, putting green.
**Location** 3.5m SW of city centre off A4040
**Hotel** ★★★ 66% Plough & Harrow, 135 Hagley Rd,
Edgbaston, BIRMINGHAM
☎ 0121 454 4111 44 ⇔ ⛵

**Hatchford Brook** Coventry Rd, Sheldon B26 3PY
☎ 0121 743 9821
Fairly flat, municipal parkland course.
*18 holes, 6202yds, Par 69, SSS 70, Course record 69.*
*Club membership 500.*
**Visitors** are restricted early Sat & Sun.
**Societies** must contact in advance.
**Green Fees** £8.50 per round (£9 weekends).
**Facilities** ⊗ ▟ ▟ ⚐ ⧫ ⧫ Paul Smith.
**Leisure** trolley for hire, putting green, practice area.
**Location** 6m E of city centre on A45
**Hotel** B Forte Posthouse Birmingham Airport,
Coventry Rd, BIRMINGHAM
☎ 0121 782 8141 136 ⇔ ⛵

***Hilltop*** Park Ln, Handsworth B21 8LJ ☎ 0121 554 4463
Testing and hilly municipal parkland course.
*18 holes, 6254yds, Par 71, SSS 70.*
*Club membership 400.*
**Visitors** no restrictions but booking recommended.
**Societies** telephone in advance.
**Green Fees** not confirmed.
**Facilities** ▟ ⚐ ⧫ ⧫ Kevin Highfield.
**Leisure** putting green,practice area,trolley hire.
**Location** 3.5m N of city centre off A4040
**Hotel** ★★★ 67% Birmingham/West Bromwich Moat
House, Birmingham Rd, WEST BROMWICH
☎ 0121 609 9988 171 ⇔ ⛵

***Moseley*** Springfield Rd, Kings Heath B14 7DX
☎ 0121 444 2115
Parkland course with a lake, pond and stream to provide
natural hazards. The par-3, 5th goes through a cutting in
woodland to a tree and garden-lined amphitheatre, and the
par-4, 6th entails a drive over a lake to a dog-leg fairway.
*18 holes, 6300yds, Par 70, SSS 70, Course record 64.*
*Club membership 600.*
**Visitors** may only play at weekends by prior
arrangement.
**Societies** by prior arrangement.
**Green Fees** not confirmed.
**Facilities** ♀ ▟ ⚐ ⧫ Gary Edge.
**Leisure** putting,trolley hire,practice area.
**Location** 4m S of city centre on B4146 off A435
**Hotel** ★★ 67% Norwood Hotel, 87-89 Bunbury Rd,
Northfield, BIRMINGHAM
☎ 0121 411 2202 18 ⇔ ⛵

**North Worcestershire** Frankley Beeches Rd, Northfield B31
5LP ☎ 0121 475 1047
Designed by James Braid and established in 1907, this is a
mature parkland course. Tree plantations rather than heavy
rough are the main hazards.　　　　　　　　　　　　▶

*18 holes, 5959yds, Par 69, SSS 68, Course record 64.*
*Club membership 600.*

| | |
|---|---|
| Visitors | by prior arrangement with professional, no visitors before 10.30 or at weekends. All visitors must have an official CONGU handicap. |
| Societies | apply in advance in writing or by telephone to the professional tel: 0121 475 5721. |
| Green Fees | Tue-Fri £25.50 per day; £18.50 per round. Mon £15 per round No visitors weekends. |
| Facilities | ⊗ ⅲ ఏ ☂ ♀ ⚲ 🕭 ⚓ ⌀ Keith Jones. |
| Leisure | trolley for hire, putting green, practice area. |
| Location | 7m SW of Birmingham city centre, off A38 |
| Hotel | ★★ 67% Norwood Hotel, 87-89 Bunbury Rd, Northfield, BIRMINGHAM ☎ 0121 411 2202 18 ⇌ ☏ |

---

***Rose Hill*** Rosehill, Rednal B45 8RR ☎ 0121 453 3159
Hilly municipal course overlooking the city.
*18 holes, 6010yds, Par 69, SSS 69, Course record 64.*
*Club membership 300.*

| | |
|---|---|
| Visitors | may not play between 9 & 10.30am weekends. |
| Societies | must contact in advance. |
| Green Fees | not confirmed. |
| Facilities | ⚲ 🕭 ⚓ ⌀ Mike March. |
| Leisure | tennis courts, putting green.trolley hire,bowls. |
| Location | 10m SW of city centre on B4096 |
| Hotel | ★★ 67% Norwood Hotel, 87-89 Bunbury Rd, Northfield, BIRMINGHAM ☎ 0121 411 2202 18 ⇌ ☏ |

---

**Warley** Lightswood Hill, Warley B67 5ED
☎ 0121 429 2440
Municipal parkland course in Warley Woods.
*9 holes, 5370yds, Par 68, SSS 66, Course record 66.*
*Club membership 200.*

| | |
|---|---|
| Visitors | no restrictions. Advance booking available at reduced cost. |
| Green Fees | £8 per round (£8.50 weekends). |
| Facilities | ⊗ ఏ ☂ ⚲ 🕭 ⚓ ⌀ David Owen. |
| Leisure | trolley for hire, putting green. |
| Location | 4m W of city centre off A456 |
| Hotel | ★★★ 66% Plough & Harrow, 135 Hagley Rd, Edgbaston, BIRMINGHAM ☎ 0121 454 4111 44 ⇌ ☏ |

---

## COVENTRY           Map 04 SP37

***Ansty Golf Centre*** Brinklow Rd, Ansty CV7 9JH
☎ 01203 621341 & 621305
18-hole Pay and Play course of two 9-hole loops.Membership competitions for handicaps. Driving range and putting green.
*18 holes, 5793yds, Par 70, SSS 68, Course record 66.*
*Club membership 300.*

| | |
|---|---|
| Visitors | no restrictions. |
| Societies | welcome. |
| Green Fees | not confirmed. |
| Facilities | ♀ ⚲ 🕭 ⚓ ⌀ John Reay. |
| Leisure | putting/range/practice,cart/trolley hire. |
| Location | 3m from city centre via A4600 |
| Hotel | ★★★ 64% Ansty Hall, ANSTY ☎ 01203 612222 25 ⇌ ☏Annexe6 ⇌ ☏ |

---

**Coventry** St Martins Rd, Finham Park CV3 6PJ
☎ 01203 414152 & 411298
The scene of several major professional events, this undulating parkland course has a great deal of quality.

---

More than that, it usually plays its length, and thus scoring is never easy, as many professionals have found to their cost.
*18 holes, 6613yds, Par 73, SSS 72, Course record 64.*
*Club membership 500.*

| | |
|---|---|
| Visitors | must contact in advance. May not play at weekends and bank holidays. |
| Societies | must apply in writing. |
| Green Fees | £30 per day. |
| Facilities | ⊗ ⅲ ఏ ☂ ♀ ⚲ 🕭 ⚓ ⌀ Philip Weaver. |
| Leisure | trolley for hire, putting green, practice area. |
| Location | 3m S of city centre on A444 |
| Hotel | ★★★ 66% Hylands Hotel, Warwick Rd, COVENTRY ☎ 01203 501600 54 ⇌ ☏ |

---

**Coventry Hearsall** Beechwood Av CV5 6DF
☎ 01203 713470
Parkland course with fairly easy walking. A brook provides an interesting hazard.
*18 holes, 5983yds, Par 70, SSS 69.*
*Club membership 650.*

| | |
|---|---|
| Visitors | with member only at weekends. |
| Societies | apply in writing to secretary. |
| Green Fees | £25 per day. |
| Facilities | ⊗ ⅲ ఏ ☂ ♀ ⚲ 🕭 ⚓ ⌀ Mike Tarn. |
| Leisure | motorised carts for hire, trolley for hire, putting green, practice area. |
| Location | 1.5m SW of city centre off A429 |
| Hotel | ★★★ 66% Hylands Hotel, Warwick Rd, COVENTRY ☎ 01203 501600 54 ⇌ ☏ |

---

***GPT*** The Grange, Copsewood, Binley Rd CV3 1HS
☎ 01203 563127
Flat parkland course with very tight out of bounds on a number of holes, and a river which affects play on five of them. Well-bunkered, with plenty of trees.
*9 holes, 6002yds, Par 72, SSS 69.*
*Club membership 300.*

| | |
|---|---|
| Visitors | may not play after 2pm weekdays or before noon on Sun. No visitors Sat. |
| Societies | must contact in advance. |
| Green Fees | not confirmed. |
| Facilities | ♀ ⚲ |
| Leisure | putting green,practice area. |
| Location | 2m E of city centre on A428 |
| Hotel | ★★★ 60% The Chace Hotel, London Rd, Toll Bar End, COVENTRY ☎ 01203 303398 67 ⇌ ☏ |

---

**Windmill Village** Birmingham Rd, Allesley CV5 9AL
☎ 01203 407241
An 18-hole course over rolling parkland with lakes and ponds. Other leisure facilities available.
*18 holes, 5129yds, Par 70, SSS 67.*
*Club membership 500.*

| | |
|---|---|
| Visitors | welcome except before noon at weekends. Must contact in advance. |
| Societies | telephone and confirm in writing. |
| Green Fees | £10.95 per round (£15 weekends). |
| Facilities | ⊗ ⅲ ఏ ☂ ♀ ⚲ 🕭 ⚓ ⍾ ⌀ Robert Hunter. |
| Leisure | hard tennis courts, heated indoor swimming pool, fishing, sauna, solarium, gymnasium, motorised carts for hire, buggies for hire, trolley for hire, putting green, bowling, beauty salon. |
| Location | On A45 W of Coventry |

**Hotel** ★★★ 72% Brooklands Grange Hotel & Restaurant, Holyhead Rd, COVENTRY
☎ 01203 601601 30 ⇌ ♞

## DUDLEY Map 07 SO99

**Dudley** Turner's Hill, Rowley Regis, Warley B65 9DP
☎ 01384 233877
Exposed and very hilly parkland course.
*18 holes, 6000yds, Par 69, SSS 68.*
*Club membership 550.*
**Visitors** contact in advance, may not play at weekends.
**Societies** must contact in advance.
**Green Fees** £18 per day.
**Facilities** ⊗ �ℿ ㄴ ☕ ♀ ⚖ 🏠 ℓ Paul Taylor.
**Leisure** trolley for hire, putting green, practice area,.
**Location** 2m S of town centre off B4171
**Hotel** ★★★ 59% Himley Country Hotel, School Rd,
HIMLEY ☎ 01902 896716 73 ⇌ ♞

**Swindon** Bridgnorth Rd, Swindon DY3 4PU
☎ 01902 897031 & 895226
Attractive undulating woodland/parkland course, with spectacular views.
*Old Course: 18 holes, 6091yds, Par 71, SSS 69.*
*New Course: 9 holes, 1135yds, Par 27.*
*Club membership 700.*
**Visitors** must contact in advance.
**Societies** must apply in writing.
**Green Fees** £28 per day; £18 per round (£40/£27 weekends & bank holidays).
**Facilities** ⊗ ⍵ ㄴ ☕ ♀ ⚖ 🏠 ℓ Phil Lester.
**Leisure** fishing, buggies for hire, trolley for hire, driving range, putting green, snooker.
**Location** On B4176, 3m from A449 at Himley
**Hotel** ★★★ 59% Himley Country Hotel, School Rd,
HIMLEY ☎ 01902 896716 73 ⇌ ♞

## HALESOWEN Map 07 SO98

**Corngreaves Hall** Corngreaves Rd B64
☎ 01384 567880
Mature course offering a good challenge to the best golfers with American specification greens and most holes holding a testing start. Magnificent views of the Clent Hills.
*Congreaves Hall Golf Course: 9 holes, 2800.*
**Visitors** at anytime by prior arrangement.
**Societies** apply in writing in advance.
**Green Fees** £6.90 per 18 holes; £4.90 per 9 holes (£7.80/£5.50 weekends).
**Facilities** ⊗ ☕ ☞ ℓ S Joyce/C Yates.
**Leisure** trolley for hire, putting green.
**Hotel** ★★ 65% Talbot Hotel, High St,
STOURBRIDGE ☎ 01384 394350 25 ⇌ ♞

**Halesowen** The Leasowes, Leasowes Ln B62 8QF
☎ 0121 501 3606
Parkland course in convenient position.
*18 holes, 5754yds, Par 69, SSS 68.*
**Visitors** may only play weekends or bank holidays with member
**Societies** must apply in writing.
**Green Fees** £25 per day; £18 per round.
**Facilities** ⊗ ⍵ ㄴ ☕ ♀ ⚖ 🏠 ☞ ℓ Jon Nicholas.

**Leisure** trolley for hire, putting green, practice area.
**Location** 1m E
**Hotel** ★★ 65% Talbot Hotel, High St,
STOURBRIDGE ☎ 01384 394350 25 ⇌ ♞

## KNOWLE Map 07 SP17

**Copt Heath** 1220 Warwick Rd B93 9LN
☎ 01564 772650
Parkland course designed by H. Vardon.
*18 holes, 6508yds, Par 71, SSS 71.*
*Club membership 700.*
**Visitors** must contact in advance. May not play weekends & bank holidays.
**Societies** must contact in advance.
**Green Fees** £40 per day; £35 per round.
**Facilities** ⊗ ⍵ ㄴ ☕ ♀ ⚖ 🏠 ℓ Brian J Barton.
**Leisure** motorised carts for hire, buggies for hire, trolley for hire, driving range, putting green, practice area.
**Location** On A4141, 0.50m S of junc 5 of M42
**Hotel** ★★★ 65% St John's Swallow Hotel, 651 Warwick Rd, SOLIHULL
☎ 0121 711 3000 177 ⇌ ♞

## MERIDEN Map 04 SP28

***Forest of Arden Hotel Golf and Country Club***
Shepherd's Ln CV7 7HR
☎ 01676 22335
Two parkland courses, set within the grounds of Packington Park, with extensive water hazards and offering a fine test of golf. On-site hotel with many leisure facilities.
*Arden Course: 18 holes, 6472yds, Par 72, SSS 71, Course record 64.*
*Aylesford Course: 18 holes, 6258yds, Par 72, SSS 69.*
*Club membership 800.*
**Visitors** must have handicap certificate, but may not play weekends (unless hotel resident). Must contact in advance.
**Societies** by arrangement.
**Green Fees** not confirmed.
**Facilities** ♀ ⚖ 🏠 ☞ ⋈ ℓ Mike Tarn.
**Leisure** hard tennis courts, heated indoor swimming pool, squash, fishing, sauna, solarium, gymnasium, steam room, beauty salon.
**Location** 1m SW on B4102
**Hotel** ★★★★ 68% Forest of Arden Hotel, Maxstoke Ln, MERIDEN
☎ 01676 522335 154 ⇌ ♞

**North Warwickshire** Hampton Ln CV7 7LL
☎ 01676 22259
Parkland course with easy walking.
*9 holes, 6390yds, Par 72, SSS 70, Course record 65.*
*Club membership 425.*
**Visitors** must contact in advance.
**Societies** must apply in writing to secretary.
**Green Fees** £18 per round.
**Facilities** ㄴ ☕ ♀ ⚖ 🏠 ℓ David Ingram.
**Leisure** trolley for hire, putting green, practice area.
**Location** 1m SW on B4102
**Hotel** ★★★ 68% Manor Hotel, Main Rd, MERIDEN
☎ 01676 522735 74 ⇌ ♞

## SEDGLEY                                        Map 07 SO99

**Sedgley Golf Centre** Sandyfields Rd DY3 3DL
☎ 01902 880503
Public Pay and Play course. Undulating contours and mature
trees with extensive views over surrounding countryside.
*9 holes, 3147yds, Par 72, SSS 70.*
*Club membership 150.*
**Visitors**    booking advisable for weekends.
**Societies**   must contact in advance.
**Green Fees**  £7 per 18 holes (£7.50 weekends & bank
                holidays); £5 per 9 holes (£5.50 weekends &
                bank holidays).
**Facilities**  ⚑ 🏠 𝑓 Garry Mercer.
**Leisure**     trolley for hire, driving range, putting green,
                practice area, golf lessons.
**Location**    0.5m from town centre off A463
**Hotel**       ★★★ 59% Himley Country Hotel, School Rd,
                HIMLEY ☎ 01902 896716 73 ⇄ 🐾

## SOLIHULL                                       Map 07 SP17

**Olton** Mirfield Rd B91 1JH ☎ 0121 705 1083
Parkland course with prevailing southwest wind.
*18 holes, 6265yds, Par 69, SSS 71, Course record 63.*
*Club membership 600.*
**Visitors**    must contact in advance. No visitors at weekend.
**Societies**   apply in writing.
**Green Fees**  £35 per day.
**Facilities**  ⊗ 🕎 ᴸ ⚑ ♀ ⚘ 🏠 ⚐ 𝑓 Mark Daubney.
**Leisure**     trolley for hire, putting green, practice area.
**Location**    Exit M42 junct 5 and take A41 for 1.5m
**Hotel**       ★★★ 65% St John's Swallow Hotel, 651
                Warwick Rd, SOLIHULL
                ☎ 0121 711 3000 177 ⇄ 🐾

**Robin Hood** St Bernards Rd B92 7DJ ☎ 0121 706 0061
Pleasant parkland course with easy walking and open to good
views.Tree lined fairways and varied holes, culminating in
two excellent finishing holes. Modern clubhouse.
*18 holes, 6635yds, Par 72, SSS 72, Course record 68.*
*Club membership 650.*
**Visitors**    must contact in advance. With member only at
                weekends.
**Societies**   must contact in advance.
**Green Fees**  £35 per day; £29 per round.
**Facilities**  ⊗ 🕎 ᴸ ⚑ ♀ ⚘ 🏠 ⚐ 𝑓 Alan Harvey.
**Leisure**     trolley for hire, driving range, putting green,
                practice area.
**Location**    2m W off B4025
**Hotel**       ★★★ 65% St John's Swallow Hotel, 651
                Warwick Rd, SOLIHULL
                ☎ 0121 711 3000 177 ⇄ 🐾

*Shirley* Stratford Rd, Monkpath B90 4EW
☎ 0121 744 6001
Fairly flat parkland course.
*18 holes, 6510yds, Par 72, SSS 71.*
*Club membership 500.*
**Visitors**    may not play bank holidays & with member only
                at weekends. Handicap certificate is required.
**Societies**   must contact in advance.
**Green Fees**  not confirmed.
**Facilities**  ♀ ⚘ 🏠 𝑓 C J Wicketts.
**Leisure**     putting,practice area,trolley hire.

**Location**    3m SW off A34
**Hotel**       ★★★★ 61% Regency Hotel, Stratford Rd,
                Shirley, SOLIHULL
                ☎ 0121 745 6119 112 ⇄ 🐾

## STOURBRIDGE                                    Map 07 SO98

**Hagley Golf & Country Club** Wassell Grove, Hagley
DY9 9JW ☎ 01562 883701
Undulating parkland course set beneath the Clent Hills; there
are superb views. Testing 15th, par 5, 557 yards.
*18 holes, 6353yds, Par 72, SSS 72, Course record 66.*
*Club membership 700.*
**Visitors**    restricted Wed (Ladies Day) & with member
                only at weekends.
**Societies**   Mon-Fri only, must apply in writing.
**Green Fees**  £25 per day; £20 per round.
**Facilities**  ⊗ 🕎 ᴸ ⚑ ♀ ⚘ 🏠 𝑓 Iain Clark.
**Leisure**     squash, motorised carts for hire, buggies for hire,
                trolley for hire, putting green, practice area.
**Location**    1m E of Hagley off A456
**Hotel**       ★★ 65% Talbot Hotel, High St,
                STOURBRIDGE ☎ 01384 394350 25 ⇄ 🐾

**Stourbridge** Worcester Ln, Pedmore DY8 2RB
☎ 01384 395566
Parkland course.
*18 holes, 6231yds, Par 70, SSS 69, Course record 67.*
*Club membership 857.*
**Visitors**    contact secretary, no casual visitors weekends.
**Societies**   must apply in writing.
**Green Fees**  £25 per day.
**Facilities**  ⊗ 🕎 by prior arrangement ᴸ ⚑ ♀ ⚘ 🏠
                𝑓 W H Firkins.
**Leisure**     trolley for hire, putting green, practice area.
**Location**    2m from town centre
**Hotel**       ★★ 65% Talbot Hotel, High St,
                STOURBRIDGE ☎ 01384 394350 25 ⇄ 🐾

## SUTTON COLDFIELD                              Map 07 SP19

**THE BELFRY** See page 229

**Boldmere** Monmouth Dr B73 6Jl
☎ 0121 354 3379
Established municipal course with 10 par 3s and a lake
coming into play on the 16th and 18th holes.
*18 holes, 4482yds, Par 63, SSS 62, Course record 57.*
*Club membership 300.*
**Visitors**    must contact in advance.
**Societies**   midweek only, apply in writing.
**Green Fees**  £8 per 18 holes; £5 per 9 holes (£8.50/£5.50
                weekends).
**Facilities**  ⊗ ᴸ ⚑ ♀ ⚘ 🏠 ⚐ 𝑓 Trevor Short.
**Leisure**     trolley for hire, putting green.
**Location**    Adjacent to Sutton Park
**Hotel**       ★★★ 69% Moor Hall Hotel, Moor Hall Dr,
                Four Oaks, SUTTON COLDFIELD
                ☎ 0121 308 3751 75 ⇄ 🐾

**Little Aston** Streetly B74 3AN ☎ 0121 353 2942
Parkland course.
*18 holes, 6670yds, Par 72, SSS 73, Course record 64.*
*Club membership 350.*                                    ▶

# THE BELFRY

## SUTTON COLDFIELD *West Midlands*

☎ 01675 470301                    Map 07 SP19

*John Ingham writes:* When professional people are commissioned to turn a piece of farmland into a golf course and hotel complex, they are flattered - and delighted. This happened to Peter Alliss and Dave Thomas, two celebrated tournament competitors. The challenge they were offered: turn an unsympathetic piece of land into a good golf course.The resulting Belfry Golf Club was opened in 1977.

Since that date the two architects have every reason to be proud. The course, set in 370 acres of parkland, has staged more than one of the popular Ryder Cup matches, and the two courses - the Brabazon and the Derby - named after two Lords, have received thousands of visitors. These visitors have been entertained with a kindly reception, enhanced by a really excellent hotel. A third course - the PGA National Course - is due to be completed in Spring 1997. The Belfry is also home to the PGA Training Academy.

In the nineteen years since its establishment, the saplings and newly-created greens have settled down very well and presented a worthwhile face to the world. One of the big challenges of The Belfry are the lakes and many water hazards that gobble up wild shots. Many a famous player, such as Seve Ballesteros, has had balls sinking without trace at the Brabazon's famously testing 18th hole. This monster requires the player to clear the lake twice in its 455-yard drive to reach an uphill, three-tiered, 60-yard long green.

As a public course, The Belfry is open to all-comers every day. This obviously means a great deal of traffic, although there are many other worthwhile courses in the West Midlands such as Hansworth and Little Aston. However, The Belfry is excellently managed and kept in top condition by a team now fully experienced in catering for every golfer. Recently, bunkering and new tees have improved several of the holes and spectator mounding has improved viewing of the golf tournaments.

In its fine parkland setting the club has become well known for its accommodation and fine business facilities and, being so well placed for the NEC, Birmingham and the international airport, it attracts a variety of golfers.

| | |
|---|---|
| **Visitors** | must contact 24 hours in advance. A handicap certificate is required for the Brabazon course |
| **Societies** | must contact in advance |
| **Green fees** | Brabazon £55 per round; Derby £27.50 per round. Reduced fees in winter |
| **Facilities** | ⊗ Ⅲ ⓑ ♥ ♀ ⋈ △ 🖻 🏌 ℓ (P McGovern) putting green, driving range |
| **Leisure** | hard tennis courts, heated indoor swimming pool, squash, snooker, sauna, solarium, gym. Nightclub in grounds |
| **Location** | Sutton Coalfield B76 9PR Lichfield Rd, Wishaw (exit junc 9 M42 4m E) |

36 holes. Brabazon: 18 holes, 7220yds, Par 72, SSS 72. Course record 63
Derby: 18 holes, 6103yds Par70, SSS 70

## WHERE TO STAY AND EAT NEARBY

**HOTELS:**

**WISHAW**
★★★★⊛⊛ 72%The Belfry, Lichfield Rd. ☎ 01675 470301
219 (3 ↰ 216 ⇌ ↰)

★★★58% Moxhull Hall, Holly Lane. ☎ 0121-329 2056.  11(3 ↰ 8 ⇌ ↰) Annex 9

**LEA MARSTON**
★★★69% Lea Marston Hotel and Leisure Complex. ☎ 01675 470468
49  (2 ↰ 47 ⇌ ↰)

**SUTTON COLDFIELD**
★★★ 60% Sutton Court, 60-66 Lichfield Rd. ☎ 0121-355 6071, 56 (9 ↰ 47 ⇌ ↰) Annex 8 ⇌ ↰

★★★★(Red)⊛⊛ ♨ New Hall, Walmley Rd. ☎ 0121-378 2442. 62 ⇌ ↰

## MOXHULL HALL HOTEL

**Holly Lane, Wishaw, Sutton Coldfield, Warwickshire B76 9PD**
**Tel: 0121 329 2056 Fax: 0121 311 1980**

Privately owned ★★★ Country House Hotel set in eight acres of gardens and woodlands. All rooms en-suite, colour television, telephone, etc. Only one mile from international golf at the Belfry.

---

**Visitors** must contact in advance & may not play at weekends.
**Societies** must apply in writing.
**Green Fees** £45 per day.
**Facilities** ⊗ ⅢⅢ ⬛ ♀ ⚘ 🏠 ℓ John Anderson.
**Leisure** trolley for hire, putting green, practice area.
**Location** 3.5m NW off A454
**Hotel** ★★★ 69% Moor Hall Hotel, Moor Hall Dr, Four Oaks, SUTTON COLDFIELD
☎ 0121 308 3751 75 ⇆ ↟

---

**Moor Hall** *Moor Hall Dr B75 6LN* ☎ 0121 308 6130
Parkland course. The 14th is a notable hole.
*18 holes, 6249yds, Par 70, SSS 70.*
*Club membership 600.*
**Visitors** must contact in advance. With member only weekends & bank holidays.
**Societies** must apply in writing.
**Green Fees** not confirmed.
**Facilities** ♀ ⚘ 🏠 ↟ ℓ
**Location** 2.5m N of town centre off A453
**Hotel** ★★★ 69% Moor Hall Hotel, Moor Hall Dr, Four Oaks, SUTTON COLDFIELD
☎ 0121 308 3751 75 ⇆ ↟

---

**Pype Hayes** *Eachel Hurst Rd, Walmley B76 1EP*
☎ 0121 351 1014
Attractive, fairly flat course with excellent greens.
*18 holes, 5996yds, Par 71, SSS 68, Course record 66.*
*Club membership 400.*
**Visitors** phone professional in advance.
**Societies** contact professional in advance.
**Green Fees** £8.50 per round; £5 per 9 holes (£9/£5.50 weekends).
**Facilities** ⊗ ⅢⅢ ⓛ ⬛ 🏠 ↟ ℓ James Bayliss.
**Leisure** trolley for hire, putting green, practice area.
**Location** 2.5m S off B4148
**Hotel** ★★★ 67% Marston Farm Hotel, Bodymoor Heath, SUTTON COLDFIELD
☎ 01827 872133 37 ⇆ ↟

---

**Sutton Coldfield** *110 Thornhill Rd, Streetly B74 3ER*
☎ 0121 353 9633
A fine natural, heathland course, with tight fairways, gorse, heather and trees; which is surprising as the high-rise buildings of Birmingham are not far away.
*18 holes, 6541yds, Par 72, SSS 71, Course record 65.*
*Club membership 550.*
**Visitors** must contact in advance. Restricted at weekends.
**Societies** must apply in writing.
**Green Fees** £35 per day.
**Facilities** ⊗ ⓛ ⬛ ♀ ⚘ 🏠 ℓ Jerry Hayes.
**Leisure** trolley for hire, putting green, practice area.
**Location** 3m NW on B4138

---

**Hotel** ★★★ 69% Moor Hall Hotel, Moor Hall Dr, Four Oaks, SUTTON COLDFIELD
☎ 0121 308 3751 75 ⇆ ↟

---

**Walmley** *Brooks Rd, Wylde Green B72 1HR*
☎ 0121 373 0029 & 377 7272
Pleasant parkland course with many trees. The hazards are not difficult.
*18 holes, 6559yds, Par 72, SSS 72, Course record 67.*
*Club membership 650.*
**Visitors** must contact in advance. May only play weekdays unless guest of member.
**Societies** must contact in advance.
**Green Fees** £30 per day; £25 per round.
**Facilities** ⊗ ⅢⅢ ⓛ ⬛ ♀ ⚘ 🏠 ↟ ℓ M J Skerritt.
**Leisure** trolley for hire.
**Location** 2m S off A5127
**Hotel** ★★★ 67% Marston Farm Hotel, Bodymoor Heath, SUTTON COLDFIELD
☎ 01827 872133 37 ⇆ ↟

---

## WALSALL                                    Map 07 SP09

**Bloxwich** *Stafford Rd, Bloxwich WS3 3PQ*
☎ 01922 405724 & 476593
Undulating parkland course with natural hazards and subject to strong north wind.
*18 holes, 6260yds, Par 71, SSS 70, Course record 68.*
*Club membership 532.*
**Visitors** may not play at weekends.
**Societies** must contact in advance.
**Green Fees** £25 per day; £20 per round.
**Facilities** ⊗ ⅢⅢ ⓛ ⬛ ♀ ⚘ 🏠 ℓ Daryl Scott.
**Leisure** trolley for hire, putting green, practice area.
**Location** 3m N of town centre on A34
**Hotel** ★★★ 70% The Fairlawns at Aldridge, 178 Little Aston Rd, Aldridge, WALSALL
☎ 01922 55122 35 ⇆ ↟

---

**Calderfields** *Aldridge Rd WS4 2JS*
☎ 01922 640540
Parkland course with lake.
*18 holes, 6590yds, Par 73, SSS 72.*
*Club membership 700.*
**Visitors** no restrictions.
**Societies** telephone in advance.
**Green Fees** not confirmed.
**Facilities** ♀ ⚘ 🏠 ↟ ℓ Roger Griffin.
**Leisure** fishing.
**Location** On A454
**Hotel** ★★★ 70% The Fairlawns at Aldridge, 178 Little Aston Rd, Aldridge, WALSALL
☎ 01922 55122 35 ⇆ ↟

**Walsall** The Broadway WS1 3EY ☎ 01922 613512
Well-wooded parkland course with easy walking.
*18 holes, 6300yds, Par 70, SSS 70, Course record 67.*
*Club membership 600.*
| | |
|---|---|
| **Visitors** | must contact in advance. May not play weekends & bank holidays. |
| **Societies** | must apply in writing. |
| **Green Fees** | £40 per day; £33 per round. |
| **Facilities** | ⊗ ⅏ 䑓 ▆ ♀ ♨ 🏠 ⚑ Richard Lambert. |
| **Leisure** | trolley for hire, putting green, practice area. |
| **Location** | 1m S of town centre off A34 |
| **Hotel** | ★★★ 66% Boundary Hotel, Birmingham Rd, WALSALL ☎ 01922 33555 94 ⇆ 🐾 |

## WEST BROMWICH                                        Map 07 SP09

*Dartmouth* Vale St B71 4DW ☎ 0121 588 2131
Meadowland course with undulating but easy walking. The 617 yd (par 5) first hole is something of a challenge.
*9 holes, 6060yds, Par 71, SSS 70, Course record 66.*
*Club membership 350.*
| | |
|---|---|
| **Visitors** | with member only at weekends. May not play bank holidays or medal weekends. |
| **Societies** | must apply in writing. |
| **Green Fees** | not confirmed. |
| **Facilities** | ♀ ♨ 🏠 ⚑ Carl Yates. |
| **Leisure** | practice area, putting green. |
| **Location** | E side of town centre off A4041 |
| **Hotel** | ★★★ 67% Birmingham/West Bromwich Moat House, Birmingham Rd, WEST BROMWICH ☎ 0121 609 9988 171 ⇆ 🐾 |

**Sandwell Park** Birmingham Rd B71 4JJ
☎ 0121 553 4637 & 553 4384
Undulating parkland course situated in the Sandwell Valley.
*18 holes, 6470yds, Par 71, SSS 72, Course record 68.*
*Club membership 550.*
| | |
|---|---|
| **Visitors** | must contact in advance. May not play at weekends. |
| **Societies** | must contact in advance. |
| **Green Fees** | £25 per round. |
| **Facilities** | ⊗ ⅏ 䑓 ▆ ♀ ♨ 🏠 ⚑ Nigel Wylie. |
| **Leisure** | trolley for hire, putting green, practice area. |
| **Location** | SE side of town centre off A4040 |
| **Hotel** | ★★★ 67% Birmingham/West Bromwich Moat House, Birmingham Rd, WEST BROMWICH ☎ 0121 609 9988 171 ⇆ 🐾 |

## WOLVERHAMPTON                                        Map 07 SO99

**Oxley Park** Stafford Rd, Bushbury WV10 6DE
☎ 01902 25892 & 25445
Parklands course with easy walking on the flat.
*18 holes, 6222yds, Par 71, SSS 70, Course record 68.*
*Club membership 550.*
| | |
|---|---|
| **Visitors** | must contact in advance. |
| **Societies** | must contact in advance. |
| **Green Fees** | £24 per day; £20 per round. |
| **Facilities** | ⊗ ⅏ 䑓 ▆ ♀ ♨ 🏠 ⚑ Les Burlison. |
| **Leisure** | buggies for hire, trolley for hire, putting green, snooker. |
| **Location** | N of town centre off A449 |
| **Hotel** | ★★ 68% Ely House Hotel, 53 Tettenhall Rd, WOLVERHAMPTON ☎ 01902 311311 18 ⇆ 🐾 |

**Penn** Penn Common, Penn WV4 5JN
☎ 01902 341142
Heathland course just outside the town.
*18 holes, 6462yds, Par 70, SSS 71, Course record 68.*
*Club membership 650.*
| | |
|---|---|
| **Visitors** | must play with member at weekends. |
| **Societies** | must contact in advance. |
| **Green Fees** | £25 per day. |
| **Facilities** | ⊗ ⅏ 䑓 ▆ ♀ ♨ 🏠 ⚑ A Briscoe. |
| **Leisure** | motorised carts for hire, trolley for hire, putting green. |
| **Location** | SW side of town centre off A449 |
| **Hotel** | ★★★ 60% Jarvis Park Hall, Ednam Rd, Goldthorn Park, WOLVERHAMPTON ☎ 01902 331121 57 ⇆ 🐾 |

**South Staffordshire** Danescourt Rd, Tettenhall WV6 9BQ
☎ 01902 751065 & 754816
A parkland course.
*18 holes, 6513yds, Par 71, SSS 71.*
*Club membership 500.*
| | |
|---|---|
| **Visitors** | must contact in advance but may not play weekends & before 2pm Tue. |
| **Societies** | must apply in writing. |
| **Green Fees** | £37 per day; £32 per round. |
| **Facilities** | ⊗ ⅏ 䑓 ▆ ♀ ♨ 🏠 ⚑ Jim Rhodes. |
| **Leisure** | buggies for hire, trolley for hire, putting green, practice area. |
| **Location** | 3m NW off A41 |
| **Hotel** | ★★ 68% Ely House Hotel, 53 Tettenhall Rd, WOLVERHAMPTON ☎ 01902 311311 18 ⇆ 🐾 |

**Three Hammers Short Course** Old Stafford Rd, Coven WV10 7PP ☎ 01902 790940
Well maintained short course designed by Henry Cotton and providing a unique challenge to golfers of all standards.
*18 holes, 1438yds, Par 54, SSS 54, Course record 43.*
| | |
|---|---|
| **Visitors** | no restrictions. |
| **Societies** | contact for details. |
| **Green Fees** | £5 per day (£6 weekends). |
| **Facilities** | ⊗ ⅏ 䑓 ▆ ♀ ♨ 🏠 ⚑ |
| **Leisure** | driving range. |
| **Location** | On A449 N of junct 2 M54 |
| **Hotel** | ★★★ 66% Roman Way Hotel, Watling St, Hatherton, CANNOCK ☎ 01543 572121 56 ⇆ 🐾 |

**Wergs** Keepers Ln, Tettenhall WV6 8UA
☎ 01902 742225
Open parkland course.
*18 holes, 6949yds, Par 72, SSS 73.*
*Club membership 250.*
| | |
|---|---|
| **Visitors** | are advised to contact in advance. |
| **Societies** | must contact in advance. |
| **Green Fees** | £12.50 per day (£15 weekends & bank holidays). |
| **Facilities** | ⊗ ⅏ 䑓 ▆ ♀ ♨ 🏠 ⚑ Martin Payne. |
| **Leisure** | motorised carts for hire, buggies for hire, trolley for hire, putting green, practice area. |
| **Hotel** | ★★ 68% Ely House Hotel, 53 Tettenhall Rd, WOLVERHAMPTON ☎ 01902 311311 18 ⇆ 🐾 |

Entries with a shaded background identify courses that are considered to be particularly interesting

# WIGHT, ISLE OF

## COWES                                      Map 04 SZ49

**Cowes** Crossfield Av PO31 8HN
☎ 01983 292303
Fairly level, tight parkland course with difficult par 3s and Solent views.
*9 holes, 5934yds, Par 70, SSS 68, Course record 66.*
*Club membership 300.*
**Visitors**      restricted Thu & Sun mornings.
**Societies**     Mon-Wed, must contact in advance.
**Green Fees**   £15 per day/round (£18 weekends).
**Facilities**    ⓑ ☂ ♀ ⌂ ⌁
**Leisure**       trolley for hire, putting green, practice area.
**Location**      NW side of town
**Hotel**         ★★ 62% The Fountain Hotel, High St,
                  COWES ☎ 01983 292397 20 ⇄ ☏

## EAST COWES                               Map 04 SZ59

**Osborne** Osborne House Estate PO32 6JX
☎ 01983 295421
Undulating parkland course in the grounds of Osborne House. Quiet and peaceful situation.
*9 holes, 6372yds, Par 70, SSS 70.*
*Club membership 400.*
**Visitors**      may not play Tue before 1pm, weekends before noon & bank holidays before 11am.
**Societies**     telephone initially.
**Green Fees**   £16 (£19 weekends & bank holidays).
**Facilities**    ⊗ ☶ ⓑ ☂ ♀ ⌂ ⌁
**Leisure**       trolley for hire, putting green, practice area.
**Location**      E side of town centre off A3021
**Hotel**         ★★ 62% The Fountain Hotel, High St,
                  COWES ☎ 01983 292397 20 ⇄ ☏

## FRESHWATER                               Map 04 SZ38

**Freshwater Bay** Afton Down PO40 9TZ
☎ 01983 752955
A downland/seaside links with wide fairways and spectacular coastal views of the Solent and Channel.
*18 holes, 5725yds, Par 69, SSS 68.*
*Club membership 450.*
**Visitors**      may play daily after 9.30 ex Thu & Sun (10.30).
**Societies**     apply to secretary.
**Green Fees**   £20 per day (£24 weekends & bank holidays).
**Facilities**    ⊗ ☶ ⓑ ☂ ♀ ⌂ ⌁
**Leisure**       trolley for hire, putting green, practice area.
**Location**      0.5m E of village off A3055
**Hotel**         ★★★ 64% Albion Hotel, FRESHWATER
                  ☎ 01983 753631 42 ⇄ ☏

## NEWPORT                                  Map 04 SZ58

**Newport** St George's Down, Shide PO30 2JB
☎ 01983 525076
Downland course, fine views.
*9 holes, 5710yds, Par 68, SSS 68.*
*Club membership 350.*

**Visitors**      may not play Wed noon-3.30pm or before 3pm Sat & noon Sun.
**Societies**     contact Secretary in advance.
**Green Fees**   £15 per day (£17.50 weekends & bank holidays).
**Facilities**    ⊗ ☶ by prior arrangement ⓑ ☂ ♀ ⌂ ⌁
**Leisure**       trolley for hire, putting green, practice area.
**Location**      1.5m S off A3020
**Hotel**         ★★ 62% The Fountain Hotel, High St,
                  COWES ☎ 01983 292397 20 ⇄ ☏

## RYDE                                     Map 04 SZ59

**Ryde** Binstead Rd PO33 3NF ☎ 01983 614809
Downland course with wide views over the Solent.
*9 holes, 5287yds, Par 66, SSS 66.*
*Club membership 500.*
**Visitors**      may not play Wed afternoons, Sun mornings or before 10.30 Sat.
**Societies**     must contact in writing.
**Green Fees**   £15 (£20 weekends).
**Facilities**    ⊗ ☶ by prior arrangement ⓑ ☂ ♀ ⌂ ⌁
**Leisure**       trolley for hire, practice area.
**Location**      1m W on A3054
**Hotel**         ★★ 65% Biskra House Beach Hotel, 17 Saint Thomas's St, RYDE
                  ☎ 01983 567913 9 ⇄ ☏

## SANDOWN                                  Map 04 SZ58

**Shanklin & Sandown** The Fairway, Lake PO36 9PR
☎ 01983 403217
Heathland course.
*18 holes, 6063yds, Par 70, SSS 69, Course record 64.*
*Club membership 600.*
**Visitors**      must contact in advance & have handicap certificate.
**Societies**     apply in writing.
**Green Fees**   £22 (£24 weekends).
**Facilities**    ⊗ ☶ by prior arrangement ⓑ ☂ ♀ ⌂ ⌁
                  ☏ Peter Hammond.
**Leisure**       trolley for hire, putting green, practice area.
**Location**      1m NW
**Hotel**         ★★ 58% Birdham Hotel, 1 Steyne Rd,
                  BEMBRIDGE
                  ☎ 01983 872875 14rm(12 ⇄)

## VENTNOR                                  Map 04 SZ57

**Ventnor** Steephill Down Rd PO38 1BP
☎ 01983 853326
Downland course subject to wind. Fine seascapes.
*12 holes, 5767yds, Par 70, SSS 68.*
*Club membership 297.*
**Visitors**      may not play Fri noon-3pm or Sun mornings.
**Societies**     telephone initially.
**Green Fees**   £10-£12 per day (£12-£14 weekends & bank holidays).
**Facilities**    ⊗ by prior arrangement ☶ by prior arrangement ⓑ ☂ ♀ ⌂ ⌁
**Leisure**       trolley for hire.
**Location**      1m NW off B3327
**Hotel**         ★★★ 63% Ventnor Towers Hotel, Madeira Rd, VENTNOR
                  ☎ 01983 852277 27 ⇄ ☏

# WILTSHIRE

## BISHOPS CANNINGS
Map 04 SU06

**North Wilts** SN10 2LP ☎ 01380 860627
High, downland course with fine views.
*18 holes, 6322yds, Par 70, SSS 70, Course record 69.*
*Club membership 800.*
**Visitors** welcome, a handicap certificate is required at weekends.
**Societies** must book in advance.
**Green Fees** not confirmed.
**Facilities** ♀ ♨ 🏠 ↑ ℓ Graham Laing.
**Leisure** putting green,practice,cart/trolley hire.
**Location** 2m NW
**Hotel** ★★★ 61% Bear Hotel, Market Place, DEVIZES ☎ 01380 722444 24 ⇄ ℞

## CALNE
Map 03 ST97

**Bowood Golf & Country Club** Derry Hill SN11 9PQ
☎ 01249 822228
A long, undulating course designed by Dave Thomas. Set in a Grade I listed Capability Brown park full of mature trees and acres of wildflowers, the course is a real test of golf. A 10-bay driving range and grass teeing area are enhanced by a 3-hole Academy course and putting greens
*18 holes, 6890yds, Par 72, SSS 73, Course record 67.*
*Club membership 350.*
**Visitors** welcome except before noon on Sat and Sun. Advisable to book.
**Societies** booking by telephone.
**Green Fees** £40 per 36 holes; £35 per 27 holes; £30 per 18 holes.
**Facilities** ⊗ 〼 ▙ ▆ ♀ ♨ 🏠 ↑ 🛏 ℓ N Blenkarne.
**Leisure** motorised carts for hire, buggies for hire, trolley for hire, driving range, putting green, practice area, croquet.
**Location** Off A6 between Chippenham & Calne
**Hotel** ★★ 62% Lansdowne Strand Hotel & Restaurant, The Strand, CALNE ☎ 01249 812488 21 ⇄ ℞Annexe5 ⇄ ℞

## CASTLE COMBE
Map 03 ST87

**Manor House** SN14 7PL
☎ 01249 782982
Opened in 1992 and set in one of the finest locations in England, this 18-hole Peter Alliss/Clive Clark course was designed to marry neatly with the surrounding conservation area. Many mature trees have been used to great effect giving individuality and challenge to every shot. There are spectacular holes at the 17th & 18th with lakes and waterfalls making them memorable.
*18 holes, 6340yds, Par 73, SSS 71.*
*Club membership 500.*
**Visitors** must have a handicap certificate.
**Societies** contact in advance.
**Green Fees** not confirmed.
**Facilities** ♀ ♨ 🏠 ↑ 🛏 ℓ Chris Smith.
**Leisure** hard tennis courts, heated outdoor swimming pool, fishing, sauna, putting, buggy/trolley hire.

**Location** 5m NW of Chippenham
**Hotel** ★★★★(red)♨ Manor House Hotel, CASTLE COMBE ☎ 01249 782206 16 ⇄ ℞Annexe24 ⇄ ℞

## CHAPMANSLADE
Map 03 ST84

**Thoulstone Park** BA13 4AQ
☎ 01373 832825
A rolling parkland course with natural lakes and mature tees. Hole 7, stroke index 1 has a second shot over a large lake to the green so a straight drive is essential.
*18 holes, 6312yds, Par 71, SSS 70.*
*Club membership 500.*
**Visitors** restricted Sat & Sun mornings.
**Societies** telephone in advance.
**Green Fees** not confirmed.
**Facilities** ♀ ♨ 🏠 ↑ ℓ Derek Thomson.
**Leisure** sauna, 20 bay floodlit driving range.
**Location** On A36 between Bath/Warminster
**Hotel** ★★★ 62% Mendip Lodge Hotel, Bath Rd, FROME ☎ 01373 463223 40 ⇄

## CHIPPENHAM
Map 03 ST97

**Chippenham** Malmesbury Rd SN15 5LT
☎ 01249 652040
Easy walking on downland course. Testing holes at 1st and 15th.
*18 holes, 5559yds, Par 69, SSS 67, Course record 64.*
*Club membership 650.*
**Visitors** must contact in advance and have a handicap certificate.
**Societies** must contact in writing; handicap certificates required.
**Green Fees** not confirmed.
**Facilities** ♀ ♨ 🏠 ↑ ℓ Bill Creamer.
**Location** 1.5m N on A429
**Hotel** ★★★★(red)♨ Manor House Hotel, CASTLE COMBE ☎ 01249 782206 16 ⇄ ℞Annexe24 ⇄ ℞

## CRICKLADE
Map 04 SU09

**Cricklade Hotel & Country Club** Common Hill SN6 6HA
☎ 01793 750751
A challenging 9-hole course with undulating greens and beautiful views. Par 3 6th (128yds) signature hole from an elevated tee to a green protected by a deep pot bunker.
*9 holes, 1830yds, Par 62, SSS 57.*
*Club membership 140.*
**Visitors** welcome.
**Societies** apply in writing.
**Green Fees** not confirmed.
**Facilities** ⊗ 〼 ▙ ▆ ♀ ♨ ↑ 🛏 ℓ Ian Bolt.
**Leisure** hard tennis courts, heated indoor swimming pool, solarium, gymnasium, trolley for hire, snooker & pool table, croquet.
**Location** On the B4040 out of Cricklade, towards Malmesbury
**Hotel** ★★★ 70% Stanton House Hotel, The Avenue, Stanton Fitzwarren, SWINDON ☎ 01793 861777 86 ⇄ ℞

## ERLESTOKE                    Map 03 ST95

**Erlestoke Sands** SN10 5UA ☎ 01380 831069
The course is set on the lower slopes of Salisbury Plain with
distant views to the Cotswolds and Marlborough Downs. The
7th plunges from an elevated three-tiered tee, high in the
woods, to a large green with a spectacular backdrop of a
meandering river and hills. The course was built to suit every
standard of golfer from the novice to the very low
handicapper and its two tiers offer lakes and rolling
downland.
*18 holes, 6406yds, Par 73, SSS 71, Course record 69.*
*Club membership 706.*
**Visitors** phone for tee booking in advance 01380 831027.
**Societies** must book in advance.
**Green Fees** £14 per 18 holes (£18 weekends & bank
holidays).
**Facilities** ⊗ ⅲ ᴸ ♥ ♀ ⚎ 🏠 ⚐ ⟨ Tony Valentine.
**Leisure** motorised carts for hire, buggies for hire, trolley
for hire, driving range, putting green, practice
area.
**Location** On B3098 Devizes/Westbury road
**Hotel** ★★ 67% The Cedar Hotel, Warminster Rd,
WESTBURY
☎ 01373 822753 8 ⇆ ⟨Annexe8 ⇆ ⟨

## GREAT DURNFORD                Map 04 SU13

**High Post** SP4 6AT ☎ 01722 782356
An interesting downland course on Wiltshire chalk with
good turf and splendid views over the southern area of
Salisbury Plain. The par 3, 17th and the two-shot 18th
require good judgement.
*18 holes, 6297yds, Par 70, SSS 70, Course record 64.*
*Club membership 580.*
**Visitors** a handicap certificate is required at
weekends & bank holidays. Telephone
professional in advance 01722 782219.,
**Societies** apply by telephone to manager.
**Green Fees** £30 per day; £23 per round (£35/£28
weekends).
**Facilities** ⊗ ⅲ ᴸ ♥ ♀ ⚎ 🏠 ⟨ Ian Welding.
**Leisure** trolley for hire, driving range, putting green,
practice area.
**Location** 1.75m SE on A345
**Hotel** ★★★ 68% Rose & Crown Hotel, Harnham
Rd, Harnham, SALISBURY
☎ 01722 327908 28 ⇆ ⟨

## HIGHWORTH                     Map 04 SU29

**Highworth Community Golf Centre** Swindon Rd SN6 7SJ
☎ 01793 766014
Public downland course, situated in a high position affording
good views.
*9 holes, 3120yds, Par 35, SSS 35.*
*Club membership 150.*
**Visitors** no restrictions.
**Societies** advisable to contact in advance.
**Green Fees** £5 per 9 holes (£6 weekends).
**Facilities** ♥ 🏠 ⚐ ⟨ Mark Toombs.
**Leisure** trolley for hire, putting green, practice area, pitch
& putt.
**Location** Off A361 Swindon to Letchlade road

**Hotel** ★★★ 63% The Crest Hotel, Oxford Rd,
Stratton St Margaret, SWINDON
☎ 01793 831333 91 ⇆ ⟨

**Wrag Barn Golf & Country Club** Shrivenham Rd
SN6 7QQ ☎ 01793 861327
This course, designed by Hawtree, is some 6,500yards long. The
Par of 72 can be demanding as it maximises the natural features
of gentle contours, tess and water. The Par 3 5th is particularly
tricky. A long approach shot has to carry over a stream 5 yards in
front of the tree-protected green. The large greenside bunker to
the right attracts an alarming number of balls!
*18 holes, 6500yds, Par 72.*
*Club membership 600.*
**Visitors** no restrictions but may not play before noon at
weekends.
**Societies** contact in advance.
**Green Fees** £30 per day; £18 per round (£25 per round
weekends & bank holidays).
**Facilities** ⊗ ⅲ ᴸ ♥ ♀ 🏠 ⚐ ⟨ Barry Loughrey.
**Leisure** motorised carts for hire, buggies for hire, trolley
for hire, driving range, putting green, practice
area.
**Location** On B4000 Shrivenham Road
**Hotel** ★★★ 70% Stanton House Hotel, The Avenue,
Stanton Fitzwarren, SWINDON
☎ 01793 861777 86 ⇆ ⟨

## KINGSDOWN                     Map 03 ST86

**Kingsdown** SN13 8BS ☎ 01225 742530
Fairly flat, open downland course with very sparse tree cover
but surrounding wood.
*18 holes, 6445yds, Par 72, SSS 71, Course record 64.*
*Club membership 650.*
**Visitors** welcome except at weekends. Must contact in
advance & handicap certificate required.
**Societies** apply by letter.
**Green Fees** £22 per day.
**Facilities** ⊗ ⅲ ᴸ ♥ ♀ ⚎ 🏠 ⚐ ⟨ Andrew Butler.
**Leisure** trolley for hire, putting green, practice area.
**Location** W side of village
**Hotel** ★★ 68% Box House Hotel, London Rd, BOX
☎ 01225 744447 9 ⇆ ⟨

## LANDFORD                      Map 04 SU21

**Hamptworth Golf & Country Club** Hamptworth Rd,
Hamptworth SP5 2DU ☎ 01794 390155
Hamptworth enjoys ancient woodland and an abundance of
wildlife in a beautiful setting on the edge of the New Forest.
The 14th is one of its most challenging holes having a narrow
fairway guarded by established forest oaks. The 2nd is a
dogleg of 543yds and plays differently all year.
*18 holes, 6516yds, Par 72, SSS 71, Course record 68.*
*Club membership 450.*
**Visitors** telephone to check availability.
**Societies** weekdays only, write or telephone in advance.
**Green Fees** £28 per day; £17.50 per 18 holes (£33/22.50
weekends).
**Facilities** ⊗ ⅲ ᴸ ♥ ♀ ⚎ ⚐
**Leisure** buggies for hire, trolley for hire, practice area.
**Location** 1m NW
**Hotel** ★★★ 60% Bartley Lodge, Lyndhurst Rd,
CADNAM ☎ 01703 812248 20 ⇆ ⟨

## MARLBOROUGH                        Map 04 SU16

**Marlborough** The Common SN8 1DU ☎ 01672 512147
Downland course open to prevailing wind. Extensive views.
*18 holes, 6526yds, Par 72, SSS 71.*
*Club membership 920.*
**Visitors** restricted at certain times; must have a handicap
certificate at weekends. Must contact in advance.
**Societies** must telephone in advance.
**Green Fees** not confirmed.
**Facilities** ♀ ⅄ 🏠 𝓵 L Ross.
**Location** N side of town centre on A345
**Hotel** ★★★ 59% Castle & Ball Hotel, High St,
MARLBOROUGH
☎ 01672 515201 34 ⇄ 𝓻Annexe2 ⇄ 𝓻

## OAKSEY                               Map 03 ST99

**Oaksey Park Golf & Leisure** SN16 9SB
☎ 01666 577995
A testing nine-hole parkland course set on the west side of the
Cotswold Water Parks.
*9 holes, 3100yds, Par 70, SSS 69, Course record 66.*
*Club membership 250.*
**Visitors** no restrictions.
**Societies** telephone for details.
**Green Fees** £8 per 18 holes; £5 per 9 holes (£13/£8
weekends & bank holidays).
**Facilities** ⊗ ⅃ 💺 ♀ ⅄ 🍴𝓵 David Carroll.
**Leisure** fishing, driving range, putting green, practice
area, shooting, water sports, horse riding.
**Location** Between A419 & A429
**Hotel** ★★★ 68% Stratton House Hotel, Gloucester
Rd, CIRENCESTER
☎ 01285 651761 41 ⇄ 𝓻

## OGBOURNE ST GEORGE              Map 04 SU27

**Ogbourne Downs** SN8 1TB ☎ 01672 841327 & 841287
Downland turf and magnificent greens.
*18 holes, 6226yds, Par 71, SSS 70, Course record 65.*
*Club membership 890.*
**Visitors** welcome weekdays only, handicap certificate
required. Must contact in advance.
**Societies** must apply for booking form in advance.
**Green Fees** £20 per day/round (£30 weekends by prior
arrangement only).
**Facilities** ⊗ ⅃ 💺 ♀ ⅄ 🏠 𝓵 Colin Harraway.
**Leisure** motorised carts for hire, buggies for hire, trolley
for hire, driving range, putting green, practice area.
**Location** N side of village on A436
**Hotel** ★★★ 73% Ivy House Hotel & Garden
Restaurant, High St, MARLBOROUGH
☎ 01672 515333 12 ⇄ 𝓻Annexe16 ⇄ 𝓻

## SALISBURY                           Map 04 SU12

**Salisbury & South Wilts** Netherhampton SP2 8PR
☎ 01722 742645
Gently undulating and well drained parkland course in
country setting with panoramic views of the cathedral and
surrounding country. Any of the three 9-hole courses - Main,
Old and Drummony can be combined for a challenging 18-
hole round

*Main Course: 18 holes, 6528yds, Par 71, SSS 71, Course
record 61.*
*Old Course: 18 holes, 6177yds, Par 70, SSS 70.*
*Drummond: 18 holes, 6121yds, Par 69, SSS 69, Course
record 63.*
*Club membership 1000.*
**Visitors** must telephone in advance.
**Societies** telephone initially.
**Green Fees** £25 per day (£40 weekends & bank holidays).
£12 per day on 9 hole course of the day.
**Facilities** ⊗ ⅃ 💺 ♀ ⅄ 🏠 𝓵 Gary Emerson.
**Leisure** trolley for hire, driving range, putting green,
practice area.
**Location** 2m W on A3094
**Hotel** ★★★ 68% Rose & Crown Hotel, Harnham Rd,
Harnham, SALISBURY
☎ 01722 327908 28 ⇄ 𝓻

## SWINDON                             Map 04 SU18

**Broome Manor Golf Complex** Pipers Way SN3 1RG
☎ 01793 532403
Two courses and a 20-bay floodlit driving range. Parkland
with water hazards, open fairways and short cut rough.
Walking is easy on gentle slopes.
*18 holes, 6283yds, Par 71, SSS 70, Course record 62 or 9
holes, 2690yds, Par 66, SSS 66.*
*Club membership 800.*
**Visitors** casual times available but advisable to contact in
advance.
**Societies** must be prebooked.
**Green Fees** £8.50 per 18 holes; £5 per 9 holes (£10/£6
weekends).
**Facilities** ⊗ ⅃ 💺 ♀ ⅄ 🏠 𝓵 Barry Sandry.
**Leisure** trolley for hire, driving range, putting green,
practice area.
**Location** 1.75m SE of town centre off B4006
**Hotel** ★★★ 63% The Crest Hotel, Oxford Rd,
Stratton St Margaret, SWINDON
☎ 01793 831333 91 ⇄ 𝓻

## TIDWORTH                            Map 04 SU24

**Tidworth Garrison** Bulford Rd SP9 7AF
☎ 01980 842301
A breezy, dry downland course with lovely turf, fine
trees and views over Salisbury Plain and the surrounding
area. The 3rd and 12th holes are notable. The 564-yard
13th, going down towards the clubhouse, gives the big
hitter a chance to let fly.
*18 holes, 6101yds, Par 69, SSS 69, Course record 62.*
*Club membership 700.*
**Visitors** must contact in advance, weekend & bank
holiday bookings may not be made until
Thursday prior.
**Societies** Tue & Thu, bookings required 12-18 months
in advance.
**Green Fees** £18 per day.
**Facilities** ⊗ ⅃ 💺 ♀ ⅄ 🏠 𝓵 Terry Gosden.
**Leisure** trolley for hire, driving range, putting green,
practice area.
**Location** W side of village off A338
**Hotel** ★★ 61% Danebury Hotel, High St,
ANDOVER
☎ 01264 323332 23 ⇄ 𝓻

## UPAVON                                      Map 04 SU15

**Upavon** Douglas Av SN9 6BQ
☎ 01980 630787 & 630281
Downland course set on sides of infamous valley, with some
wind affecting play. The 2nd, 9th, 11th and 18th are all par 3
to small greens. A well-drained course.
*9 holes, 5601yds, Par 69, SSS 67, Course record 66.*
*Club membership 450.*
**Visitors**      must contact in advance and may not play before
              noon at weekends.
**Societies**     telephone in advance.
**Green Fees**    £18 per day; £12 per round (£24 weekends; £12
              after 4pm).
**Facilities**    ⊗ by prior arrangement 〗Ⅲ by prior arrangement
              ㄥ ▆ ♀ ﹅ 🏠 ⚐ ⎰ Richard Blake.
**Leisure**       hard tennis courts, trolley for hire, putting green,
              practice area.
**Location**      2m E on A342
**Hotel**         ★★★ 61%  Bear Hotel, Market Place,
              DEVIZES ☎ 01380 722444 24 ⇔ ੈ

## WARMINSTER                                 Map 03 ST84

**West Wilts** Elm Hill BA12 0AU
☎ 01985 212702 & 213133
A hilltop course among the Wiltshire downs without
trees and somewhat windswept. First-class springy turf
with many interesting holes.
*18 holes, 5709yds, Par 70, SSS 68, Course record 62.*
*Club membership 650.*
**Visitors**      must contact in advance.
**Societies**     apply by letter.
**Green Fees**    £24 per day/round in summer; £24 per day,
              £16 per round in winter (£35 weekends).
**Facilities**    ⊗ 〗Ⅲ ㄥ ▆ ♀ ﹅ 🏠 ⚐ ⎰ Andrew Lamb.
**Leisure**       trolley for hire, putting, practice area.
**Location**      N side of town centre off A350
**Hotel**         ★★★★ 70%  Bishopstrow House,
              WARMINSTER
              ☎ 01985 212312 30 ⇔ ੈ

## WOOTTON BASSETT                            Map 04 SU08

**Brinkworth** Longmans Farm, Brinkworth SN15 5DG
☎ 01666 510277
Fairly long and open course with ditches and water hazards
on the 2nd and 18th holes. Several testing par 3s with
crosswinds and three long and tricky par 5s, notably the 4th,
8th and 14th holes.
*18 holes, 5884yds, Par 70, SSS 70.*
*Club membership 70.*
**Visitors**      welcome any time no contact needed.
**Societies**     telephone in advance or apply in writing.
**Green Fees**    £6.50 per 18 holes (£8.50 weekends & bank
              holidays).
**Facilities**    ▆ ♀ ﹅ ⚐
**Leisure**       trolley for hire, putting green, practice area.
**Location**      Just off B4042 between Malmesbury/Wootton
              Bassett
**Hotel**         ★★★ 69%  Marsh Farm Hotel, Coped Hall,
              WOOTTON BASSETT
              ☎ 01793 848044 4 ⇔ ੈAnnexe24 ⇔ ੈ

**Wiltshire** Vastern SN4 7PB  ☎ 01793 849999
A Peter Alliss/Clive Clark design set in rolling Wiltshire
countryside. A number of lakes add a challenge for both low
and high handicappers.
*18 holes, 6496yds, Par 72, SSS 71.*
*Club membership 800.*
**Visitors**      must contact in advance.
**Societies**     contact in advance.
**Green Fees**    £25 per day; £20 per round (£30/£25 weekends).
**Facilities**    ⊗ 〗Ⅲ ㄥ ▆ ♀ ﹅ 🏠 ⚐ ⎰ Andy Gray.
**Leisure**       motorised carts for hire, buggies for hire, trolley
              for hire, putting green, practice area.
**Location**      Leave M4 at junc 16, on A3102
**Hotel**         ★★★ 69%  Marsh Farm Hotel, Coped Hall,
              WOOTTON BASSETT
              ☎ 01793 848044 4 ⇔ ੈAnnexe24 ⇔ ੈ

---

# YORKSHIRE, EAST RIDING OF

## BEVERLEY                                    Map 08 TA03

**Beverley & East Riding** The Westwood HU17 8RG
☎ 01482 869519
Picturesque parkland course with some hard walking and
natural hazards - trees and gorse bushes. Also cattle and
sheep (spring to autumn); horse-riders are an occasional
hazard in the early morning.
*18 holes, 6127yds, Par 69, SSS 69, Course record 65.*
*Club membership 500.*
**Visitors**      advised to contact pro shop 01482 869519.
**Societies**     telephone then written confirmation.
**Green Fees**    £16 per day; £12 per round (£21/£16 weekends
              & bank holidays).
**Facilities**    ⊗ 〗Ⅲ ㄥ ▆ ♀ ﹅ 🏠 ⚐ ⎰ Ian Mackie.
**Leisure**       trolley for hire, putting green, practice area.
**Location**      1m SW on B1230
**Hotel**         ★★★ 65%  Beverley Arms Hotel, North Bar
              Within, BEVERLEY
              ☎ 01482 869241 57 ⇔ ੈ

## BRANDESBURTON                              Map 08 TA14

**Hainsworth Park** Burton Holme YO25 8RT
☎ 01964 542362
A parkland course with easy walking.
*18 holes, 6003yds, Par 71, SSS 69, Course record 62.*
*Club membership 500.*
**Visitors**      contact in advance.
**Societies**     telephone initially.
**Green Fees**    £12 per round (£15 weekends & bank holidays).
**Facilities**    ⊗ 〗Ⅲ ㄥ ▆ ♀ ﹅ 🏠 ⚐ ⼻
**Leisure**       grass tennis courts, fishing, trolley for hire,
              putting green, practice area.
**Location**      SW side of village on A165
**Hotel**         ★★ 68%  Burton Lodge Hotel,
              BRANDESBURTON
              ☎ 01964 542847 8rm(7 ⇔ ੈ)Annexe2 ⇔ ੈ

## BRIDLINGTON                     Map 08 TA16

**Bridlington** Belvedere Rd YO15 3NA
☎ 01262 606367 & 672092
Clifftop, seaside course, windy at times, with hazards of
bunkers, ponds, ditches and trees.
*18 holes, 6294yds, Par 71, SSS 71, Course record 65.*
*Club membership 600.*
**Visitors** preferably book in advance, limited at weekends.
**Societies** telephone bookings in advance.
**Green Fees** £18 per day; £12 per round (£25/£20 weekends
& bank holidays).
**Facilities** ⊗ �𝄞 ⅃ ♨ ♀ ♨ 🏌 🏌 Anthony Howarth.
**Leisure** motorised carts for hire, trolley for hire, putting
green, practice area.
**Location** 1m S off A165
**Hotel** ★★★ 65% Expanse Hotel, North Marine Dr,
BRIDLINGTON ☎ 01262 675347 48 ⇌ 🐾

## BROUGH                          Map 08 SE92

**Brough** Cave Rd HU15 1HB ☎ 01482 667291 & 667374
Parkland course.
*18 holes, 6159yds, Par 68, SSS 69.*
*Club membership 800.*
**Visitors** with member only at weekends. Must have
handicap certificate and contact in advance.
**Societies** apply by letter.
**Green Fees** not confirmed.
**Facilities** ♀ ♨ 🏌 🏌 Gordon Townhill.
**Location** 0.5m N
**Hotel** B Forte Posthouse Hull, Ferriby High Rd,
NORTH FERRIBY ☎ 01482 645212 96 ⇌ 🐾

## DRIFFIELD (GREAT)               Map 08 TA05

**Driffield** Sunderlandwick YO25 9AD ☎ 01377 253116
An easy walking, parkland course.
*18 holes, 6199yds, Par 70, SSS 69, Course record 67.*
*Club membership 398.*
**Visitors** must adhere to club dress rule.
**Societies** apply in writing or telephone.
**Green Fees** £18 per day/round (£25 weekends).
**Facilities** ⊗ �𝄞 ⅃ ♨ ♀ ♨ 🏌 Ian Mackie.
**Leisure** fishing, trolley for hire, putting green, practice
area.
**Location** 2m S off A164
**Hotel** ★★★ 69% Bell Hotel, 46 Market Place,
DRIFFIELD ☎ 01377 256661 14 ⇌ 🐾

## FLAMBOROUGH                     Map 08 TA27

**Flamborough Head** Lighthouse Rd YO15 1AR
☎ 01262 850333 & 850417
Undulating seaside course.
*18 holes, 5483yds, Par 66, SSS 66, Course record 63.*
*Club membership 500.*
**Visitors** may not play before noon on Sun or Wed
between 10.30 and 1.30.
**Societies** must contact in advance.
**Green Fees** £15 per day; £12 per round (£18 weekends &
bank holidays).
**Facilities** ⊗ �𝄞 ⅃ ♨ ♀ ♨ 🏌
🏌 G Hutchinson (summer only).

**Leisure** trolley for hire, putting green, practice area.
**Location** 2m E off B1259
**Hotel** ★ 64% Flaneburg Hotel, North Marine Rd,
FLAMBOROUGH
☎ 01262 850284 13rm(8 🐾)

## HESSLE                          Map 08 TA02

**Hessle** Westfield Rd, Raywell HU16 5YL
☎ 01482 650171 & 650190
Well-wooded downland course, easy walking, windy.
*18 holes, 6638yds, Par 72, SSS 72, Course record 63.*
**Visitors** not Tue between 9-1 and may not play before
11am on Sat & Sun.
**Societies** by prior arrangement.
**Green Fees** £23 per day; £18 per round (£25 per round
weekends & bank holidays).
**Facilities** ⊗ �𝄞 ⅃ ♨ ♀ ♨ 🏌 Grahame Fieldsend.
**Leisure** trolley for hire, putting green, practice area.
**Location** 3m SW of Cottingham
**Hotel** B Forte Posthouse Hull, Ferriby High Rd,
NORTH FERRIBY ☎ 01482 645212 96 ⇌ 🐾

## HORNSEA                         Map 08 TA14

**Hornsea** Rolston Rd HU18 1XG
☎ 01964 532020 & 534989
Flat, parkland course with good greens.
*18 holes, 6685yds, Par 72, SSS 72, Course record 66.*
*Club membership 600.*
**Visitors** with member only at weekends & after 3pm.
Must contact in advance.
**Societies** contact Secretary in advance.
**Green Fees** £25 per day; £18 per round.
**Facilities** ⊗ ⁄⁄ ⅃ ♨ ♀ ♨ 🏌 🏌 Brian Thompson.
**Leisure** trolley for hire, putting green, practice area,
snooker.
**Location** 1m S on B1242, follow signs for Hornsea Pottery
**Hotel** ★★★ 65% Beverley Arms Hotel, North Bar
Within, BEVERLEY
☎ 01482 869241 57 ⇌ 🐾

## HULL                            Map 08 TA02

**Ganstead Park** Longdales Ln, Coniston HU11 4LB
☎ 01482 874754 & 811121
Parkland course, easy walking.
*18 holes, 6801yds, Par 72, SSS 73, Course record 67.*
**Visitors** contact in advance.
**Societies** telephone in advance.
**Green Fees** £15 (£24 weekends).
**Facilities** ⊗ ⁄⁄ ⅃ ♨ ♀ ♨ 🏌 Michael J Smee.
**Leisure** trolley for hire, putting green, practice area.
**Location** 6m NE off A165
**Hotel** ★★ 63% Waterfront Hotel, Dagger Ln, HULL
☎ 01482 227222 30 ⇌ 🐾

**Hull** The Hall, 27 Packman Ln HU10 7TJ ☎ 01482 658919
Parkland course.
*18 holes, 6242yds, Par 70, SSS 70.*
*Club membership 840.*
**Visitors** only weekdays. Contact professional
01482 653074.
**Societies** only on Tue and Thu by prior arrangement.
**Green Fees** £30 per day; £25 per round.                    ▶

**Facilities** ⊗ ⅢⅡ ⅡⅡ ♀ ⅄ ⅢⅡ ⅋ David Jagger.
**Leisure** trolley for hire, putting green, practice area.
**Location** 5m W of city centre off A164
**Hotel** ★★★ 69% Willerby Manor Hotel, Well Ln,
WILLERBY ☎ 01482 652616 34 ⇄ ↾

*Springhead Park* Willerby Rd HU5 5JE ☎ 01482 656309
Municipal parkland course with tight, tree-lined, undulating
fairways.
*18 holes, 6402yds, Par 71, SSS 71.*
*Club membership 667.*
**Visitors** welcome ex Sun (tee reserved).
**Green Fees** not confirmed.
**Facilities** ⅢⅡ ⅋⅋ Barry Herrington.
**Location** 5m W off A164
**Hotel** ★★★ 69% Willerby Manor Hotel, Well Ln,
WILLERBY ☎ 01482 652616 34 ⇄ ↾

*Sutton Park* Salthouse Rd HU8 9HF ☎ 01482 374242
Municipal parkland course.
*18 holes, 6251yds, Par 70, SSS 69, Course record 67.*
*Club membership 300.*
**Visitors** no restrictions.
**Societies** prior arrangement via club, telephone and
confirm in writing.
**Green Fees** £5.50 (£7.50 weekends).
**Facilities** ♀ ⅄ ⅢⅡ ⅋⅋ Paul Rushworth.
**Leisure** trolley for hire, putting green, practice area.
**Location** 3m NE on B1237 off A165
**Hotel** ★★ 63% Waterfront Hotel, Dagger Ln, HULL
☎ 01482 227222 30 ⇄ ↾

**SOUTH CAVE**       Map 08 SE93

*Cave Castle Golf Hotel* Church Hill, South Cave HU15 2EU
☎ 01430 421286
A young but challenging course at the foot of the Wolds with
superb views. There is a keen interest in ladies golf and
tuition and golf clinics are available.
*18 holes, 6500yds, Par 73, SSS 71.*
*Club membership 400.*
**Visitors** must contact in advance.
**Societies** by arrangement with Manager.
**Green Fees** £18 per day; £12.50 per round (£25/£18
weekends and bank holidays).
**Facilities** ⊗ ⅢⅡ ⅡⅡ ♀ ⅄ ⅢⅡ ⅋⅋ ↾ Karl Worby.
**Leisure** fishing, trolley for hire, putting green, practice
area.
**Hotel** ★★ 65% Fox & Coney Inn, Market Place,
South Cave ☎ 01430 422275 8 ⇄ ↾

**WITHERNSEA**       Map 08 TA32

*Withernsea* Chesnut Av HU19 2PG ☎ 01964 612078
Exposed seaside links with narrow, undulating fairways,
bunkers and small greens.
*9 holes, 5112yds, Par 66, SSS 64.*
*Club membership 550.*
**Visitors** with member only at weekends.
**Societies** apply in writing.
**Green Fees** not confirmed.
**Facilities** ⅄ ⅢⅡ ⅋ Graham Harrison.
**Location** S side of town centre off A1033
**Hotel** ★★ 64% Pearson Park Hotel, Pearson Park,
HULL ☎ 01482 343043 32 ⇄ ↾

---

# YORKSHIRE, NORTH

**ALDWARK**       Map 08 SE46

*Aldwark Manor* YO6 2NF ☎ 01347 838353
An easy walking, scenic 18-hole parkland course with holes
both sides of the River Ure. The course surrounds the
Victorian Aldwark Manor Golf Hotel.
*18 holes, 6171yds, Par 71, SSS 70, Course record 69.*
*Club membership 430.*
**Visitors** must contact in advance, restricted weekends.
**Societies** must telephone in advance.
**Green Fees** £20 per day; £16 per round (£24/£20 weekends
& bank holidays).
**Facilities** ⊗ ⅢⅡ ⅡⅡ ♀ ⅄ ⅢⅡ ⅋⅋ ⅍
**Leisure** fishing, trolley for hire, putting green, practice
area.
**Location** 5m SE of Boroughbridge off A1
**Hotel** ★★★⅓ 70% Aldwark Manor Hotel,
ALDWARK
☎ 01347 838146 17 ⇄ ↾Annexe3 ⇄ ↾

**BEDALE**       Map 08 SE28

*Bedale* Leyburn Rd DL8 1EZ ☎ 01677 422451
Secluded parkland course with many trees.
*18 holes, 6565yds, Par 72, SSS 71, Course record 68.*
*Club membership 600.*
**Visitors** welcome when course is free.
**Societies** must apply in advance.

# ALDWARK
# MANOR
# GOLF HOTEL
Aldwark, Alne, York YO6 2NF
Telephone: (01347) 838146/7
Golf Shop: (01347) 838353
Fax: (01347) 838867

Extensively refurbished Victorian Country
House Hotel – set in 110 acres of rural
Yorkshire. 20 luxury bedrooms –
Conference and Banqueting up to 90 persons
– excellent cuisine. Special breaks available.

The hotel is surrounded by its own 18 hole
6171 yd par 71 golf course, spanning both
sides of the river Ure. Located 12 miles
north of the historic city of York and the
spa town of Harrogate.

**Green Fees** £18 per day/round (£28 weekends & bank
holidays).
**Facilities** ⊗ �X ╚ ⬛ ♀ ⚒ ⛿ 𝑓 Tony Johnson.
**Leisure** trolley for hire, putting green, practice area.
**Location** 0.25 N of town on A684
**Hotel** ★★ 62% Motel Leeming, Great North Rd,
Leeming Bar ☎ 01677 422122 40 ⇶ 𝄢

---

BENTHAM Map 07 SD66

**Bentham** Robin Ln LA2 7AG ☎ 01524 262455
Moorland course with glorious views.
*9 holes, 5760yds, Par 70, SSS 69, Course record 69.*
*Club membership 480.*
**Visitors** no restrictions.
**Societies** must apply in advance.
**Green Fees** not confirmed.
**Facilities** ♀ ⚒
**Leisure** putting green,practice area.
**Location** N side of High Bentham
**Hotel** ★★ 67% The Traddock, AUSTWICK
☎ 015242 51224 11 ⇶ 𝄢

---

CATTERICK GARRISON Map 08 SE29

**Catterick Garrison** Leyburn Rd DL9 3QE
☎ 01748 833268
Scenic parkland/moorland course of Championship standard,
with good views of the Pennines and Cleveland hills. Testing
1st and 3rd holes.
*18 holes, 6313yds, Par 71, SSS 70, Course record 68.*
*Club membership 700.*
**Visitors** telephone professional shop for tee availability.
**Societies** by arrangement.
**Green Fees** £20 per day/round (£25 weekends).
**Facilities** ⊗ �X ╚ ⬛ ♀ ⚒ ⛿ 𝟄 𝑓 Andy Marshall.
**Leisure** motorised carts for hire, buggies for hire, trolley
for hire, putting green, practice area.
**Location** 0.5m W of Catterick Garrison Centre
**Hotel** ★★ 59% Bridge House Hotel, CATTERICK
BRIDGE ☎ 01748 818331 16rm(4 ⇶9 𝄢)

---

COPMANTHORPE Map 08 SE54

**Pike Hills** Tadcaster Rd YO2 3UW
☎ 01904 706566 & 700797
Parkland course surrounding nature reserve. Level terrain.
*18 holes, 6140yds, Par 71, SSS 69, Course record 67.*
*Club membership 800.*
**Visitors** with member only weekends & bank holidays.
**Societies** must apply in advance.
**Green Fees** £20 per day; £15 per round.
**Facilities** ⊗ �X ╚ ⬛ ♀ ⚒ ⛿ 𝟄 𝑓 Ian Gradwell.
**Leisure** motorised carts for hire, buggies for hire, trolley
for hire, 2 putting greens, practice area.
**Location** 3m SW of York on A64
**Hotel** ★★★★ 64% Swallow Hotel, Tadcaster Rd,
YORK ☎ 01904 701000 113 ⇶ 𝄢

---

EASINGWOLD Map 08 SE56

**Easingwold** Stillington Rd YO6 3ET ☎ 01347 821964
Parkland course with easy walking. Trees are a major feature
and on six holes water hazards come into play.

*18 holes, 6285yds, Par 72, SSS 70, Course record 65.*
*Club membership 600.*
**Visitors** prior enquiry essential.
**Societies** prior application in writing essential.
**Green Fees** £25 per day (£30 weekends).
**Facilities** ⊗ �X ╚ ⬛ ♀ ⚒ ⛿ 𝑓 John Hughes.
**Leisure** trolley for hire, putting green, practice area.
**Location** 1m S
**Hotel** ★★ 65% George Hotel, Market Place,
EASINGWOLD ☎ 01347 821698 14 ⇶ 𝄢

---

FILEY Map 08 TA18

**Filey** West Av YO14 9BQ ☎ 01723 513293 & 513134
Parkland course with good views, windy. Stream runs
through course. Testing 9th and 13th holes.
*18 holes, 6112yds, Par 70, SSS 69.*
*Club membership 900.*
**Visitors** must telephone to reserve tee time.
**Societies** contact by telephone.
**Green Fees** Apr-Oct: £20 per day (£25 weekends). Nov-Mar
£14 per day (£18 weekends).
**Facilities** ⊗ �X ╚ ⬛ ♀ ⚒ ⛿ 𝟄 𝑓
**Leisure** motorised carts for hire, buggies for hire, trolley
for hire, putting green, practice area.
**Location** 0.5m S of Filey
**Hotel** ★★ 63% Sea Brink Hotel, The Beach, FILEY
☎ 01723 513257 11 ⇶ 𝄢

---

GANTON Map 08 SE97

**Ganton** YO12 4PA ☎ 01944 710329
Championship course, heathland, gorse-lined fairways
and heavily bunkered; variable winds.
*18 holes, 6720yds, Par 73, SSS 74, Course record 65.*
*Club membership 500.*
**Visitors** by prior arrangement.
**Societies** prior arrangement in writing.
**Green Fees** not confirmed.
**Facilities** ⊗ �X ╚ ⬛ ♀ ⚒ ⛿ 𝟄 𝑓 Gary Brown.
**Leisure** motorised carts for hire, buggies for hire,
trolley for hire, putting green, practice area.
**Location** 0.25m NW off A64
**Hotel** ★★★ 63% East Ayton Lodge Country
House, Moor Ln, Forge Valley, EAST
AYTON
☎ 01723 864227 11 ⇶ 𝄢Annexe20 ⇶ 𝄢

---

HARROGATE Map 08 SE35

**Harrogate** Forest Ln Head, Starbeck HG2 7TF
☎ 01423 862999 & 862547
One of Yorkshire's oldest and best courses was designed
in 1897 by 'Sandy' Herd. A perfect example of golf
architecture, its greens and fairways offer an interesting
but fair challenge. The undulating parkland course once
formed part of the ancient Forest of Knaresborough.
Excellent clubhouse.
*18 holes, 6241yds, Par 69, SSS 70, Course record 64.*
*Club membership 650.*
**Visitors** advisable to contact professional in advance.
**Societies** must contact in writing or intially by
telephone.
**Green Fees** £32 per day; £28 per round (£40 day/round
weekends & bank holidays). ▶

**Facilities** ⊗ ⱦ ⓛ ♥ ♀ ⚲ 🏠 ⓕ Paul Johnson.
**Leisure** trolley for hire, putting green, practice area.
**Location** 2.25m N on A59
**Hotel** ★★★ 73% Balmoral Hotel & Henry's Restaurant, Franklin Mount, HARROGATE ☎ 01423 508208 20 ⇥ ⓕ

**Oakdale** Oakdale HG1 2LN
☎ 01423 567162 & 567188
A pleasant, undulating parkland course which provides a good test of golf for the low handicap player without intimidating the less proficient. A special feature is an attractive stream which comes in to play on four holes. Excellent views from the clubhouse which has good facilities.
*18 holes, 6456yds, Par 71, SSS 71.*
*Club membership 1034.*
**Visitors** no party bookings weekends.
**Societies** telephone followed by letter.
**Green Fees** £30 per day; £25 per round (£30 per round weekends and bank holidays).
**Facilities** ⊗ ⱦ ⓛ ♥ ♀ ⚲ 🏠 ⓕ ⓕ Clive Dell.
**Leisure** motorised carts for hire, buggies for hire, trolley for hire, putting green, practice area.
**Location** N side of town centre off A61
**Hotel** ★★★ 69% Grants Hotel, 3-13 Swan Rd, HARROGATE ☎ 01423 560666 42 ⇥ ⓕ

**Rudding Park** HG3 1DJ ☎ 01423 872100
Opened in Spring 1995, Rudding Park has been designed by Hawtree of Oxford as a parkland course with 5 water features to be operated on a Pay and Play basis.
*18 holes, 6871yds, Par 72, SSS 73, Course record 73.*
**Visitors** handicap certificate required, tee reservation available but not essential.
**Societies** apply by telephone in advance.
**Green Fees** £16 per round (£19 weekends and bank holidays).
**Facilities** ⊗ ⱦ ⓛ ♥ ♀ ⚲ 🏠 🎏 ⓕ Christopher Steele.
**Leisure** heated outdoor swimming pool, motorised carts for hire, buggies for hire, trolley for hire, driving range, putting green.
**Location** 2m SE of Harrogate town centre
**Hotel** ★★★ 64% Studley Hotel, Swan Rd, HARROGATE ☎ 01423 560425 36 ⇥ ⓕ

**HOWDEN** Map 08 SE72

**Boothferry** Spaldington Ln DN14 7NG ☎ 01430 430364
A heavily bunkered meadowland course with several dykes.
*18 holes, 6651yds, Par 73, SSS 72, Course record 64.*
*Club membership 650.*
**Visitors** must contact in advance.
**Societies** must contact for booking form.
**Green Fees** £8.50 per 18 holes; £5.50 per 9 holes (£12/£7.50 weekends).
**Facilities** ⊗ ⱦ ⓛ ♥ ♀ ⚲ 🏠 🎏 ⓕ Stewart Wilkinson.
**Leisure** trolley for hire, driving range, putting green, practice area.
**Location** 2.5m N of Howden off B1228
**Hotel** ★★ 66% Clifton Hotel, 1 Clifton Gardens, Boothferry Rd, GOOLE ☎ 01405 761336 9rm(5 ⇥3 ⓕ)

**KIRKBYMOORSIDE** Map 08 SE68

**Kirkbymoorside** Manor Vale YO6 6EG ☎ 01751 431525
Hilly parkland course with narrow fairways, gorse and hawthorn bushes. Beautiful views.
*18 holes, 6000yds, Par 69, SSS 69, Course record 65.*
*Club membership 650.*
**Visitors** are advised to contact in advance, may not play before 9.30 or between 12.30-1.30.
**Societies** must apply in advance.
**Green Fees** £17 per day (£25 weekends & bank holidays).
**Facilities** ⊗ ⱦ ⓛ ♥ ♀ ⚲ 🎏
**Leisure** trolley for hire, putting green, practice area.
**Location** N side of village
**Hotel** ★★★ 71% Appleton Hall Country House Hotel, APPLETON-LE-MOORS ☎ 01751 417227 & 417452 10 ⇥ ⓕ

**KNARESBOROUGH** Map 08 SE35

**Knaresborough** Boroughbridge Rd HG5 0QQ
☎ 01423 862690 & 864865
Undulating parkland course with mature trees.
*18 holes, 6496yds, Par 70, SSS 71.*
*Club membership 796.*
**Visitors** restricted start times summer weekends.
**Societies** apply by telephone or letter, no bookings for Sat, Sun or Tue.
**Green Fees** £25 per day; £18.50 per round (£30/£25 weekends).
**Facilities** ⊗ ⱦ ⓛ ♥ ♀ ⚲ 🏠 ⓕ Gary J Vickers.
**Leisure** buggies for hire, putting green, practice area.
**Location** 1.25m N on A6055
**Hotel** ★★★ 70% Dower House Hotel, Bond End, KNARESBOROUGH ☎ 01423 863302 28 ⇥ ⓕAnnexe4 ⇥ ⓕ

**MALTON** Map 08 SE77

**Malton & Norton** Welham Park, Norton YO17 9QE
☎ 01653 693882 & 697912
Parkland course with panoramic views of the moors. Very testing 1st hole (564 yds dog-leg, left).
*Welham Course: 18 holes, 6456yds, Par 72, SSS 71.*
*Park Course: 18 holes, 6242yds, Par 72, SSS 70.*
*Derwent Course: 18 holes, 6286yds, Par 72, SSS 70.*
*Club membership 825.*
**Visitors** anytime except during competitions.
**Societies** telephone and confirm in writing.
**Green Fees** £22 per day/round (£28 weekends & bank holidays).
**Facilities** ⊗ ⱦ ⓛ ♥ ♀ ⚲ 🏠 🎏 ⓕ S Robinson.
**Leisure** trolley for hire, putting green, practice area.
**Location** 1m S
**Hotel** ★★★ 70% Burythorpe House Hotel, Burythorpe, MALTON ☎ 01653 658200 11 ⇥ ⓕ

**MASHAM** Map 08 SE28

**Masham** Burnholme, Swinton Rd HG4 4HT
☎ 01765 689379
Flat parkland course crossed by River Burn, which comes into play on two holes.

*9 holes, 6102yds, Par 70, SSS 69.*
*Club membership 327.*
**Visitors**      must play with member at weekends & bank
              holidays.
**Societies**    write or telephone well in advance.
**Green Fees** £15 per day/round.
**Facilities**   ⊗ ᴸ ⬛ ♀ ᴸ
**Leisure**      putting green.
**Location**    1m SW off A6108
**Hotel**        ★ 67% Buck Inn, THORNTON WATLASS
              ☎ 01677 422461 7rm(5 ⇄ ℝ)

---

## MIDDLESBROUGH                    Map 08 NZ41

***Middlesbrough*** Brass Castle Ln, Marton TS8 9EE
☎ 01642 311515
Undulating parkland course, prevailing winds. Testing 9th,
16th and 17th holes.
*18 holes, 6167yds, Par 70, SSS 70.*
*Club membership 960.*
**Visitors**      restricted Tue & Sat.
**Societies**    Wed, Thu & Fri only. Must contact the club in
              advance.
**Green Fees** not confirmed.
**Facilities**   ♀ ᴸ 🏠 ℂ Don Jones.
**Leisure**      putting green,practice area,trolley hire.
**Location**    4m S off A172
**Hotel**        ★★ 62% Marton Way Toby Hotel, Marton Rd,
              MIDDLESBROUGH
              ☎ 01642 817651 53 ⇄ ℝ

***Middlesbrough Municipal*** Ladgate Ln TS5 7YZ
☎ 01642 315533
Parkland course with good views. The front nine holes have
wide fairways and large, often well-guarded greens while the
back nine demand shots over tree-lined water hazards and
narrow entrances to subtly contoured greens. Driving range.
*18 holes, 6333yds, Par 71, SSS 70, Course record 67.*
*Club membership 540.*
**Visitors**      book on the day weekdays, 7days in advance for
              weekends & bank holidays.
**Societies**    apply in writing giving at least 2 weeks in advance.
**Green Fees** £8.50 per round (£11.50 weekends).
**Facilities**   ⊗ ᴸ ⬛ ♀ ᴸ 🏠 ℂ Alan Hope.
**Leisure**      buggies for hire, trolley for hire, driving range,
              putting green, practice area.
**Location**    2m S of Middlesbrough on the A174
**Hotel**        ★★ 62% Marton Way Toby Hotel, Marton Rd,
              MIDDLESBROUGH
              ☎ 01642 817651 53 ⇄ ℝ

---

## PANNAL                             Map 08 SE35

***Pannal*** Follifoot Rd HG3 1ES  ☎ 01423 872628
Fine championship course. Moorland turf but well-
wooded with trees closely involved with play.
*18 holes, 6618yds, Par 72, SSS 72, Course record 62.*
*Club membership 780.*
**Visitors**      preferable to contact in advance, weekends
              limited.
**Societies**    apply in advance.
**Green Fees** £38 per day; £30 per round (£38 per round
              weekends).
**Facilities**   ⊗ ᴸ ⬛ ♀ ᴸ 🏠 ℂ Murray Burgess.
**Leisure**      trolley for hire, putting green, practice area.

**Location**    E side of village off A61
**Hotel**        ★★★★ 59% The Majestic, Ripon Rd,
              HARROGATE ☎ 01423 568972 156 ⇄ ℝ

---

## RAVENSCAR                         Map 08 NZ90

***Raven Hall Hotel Golf Course*** YO13 0ET
☎ 01723 870353
Opened by the Earl of Cranbrook in 1898, this 9-hole clifftop
course is sloping and with good quality small greens. Because
of its clifftop position it is subject to strong winds which
make it great fun to play, especially the 6th hole.
*9 holes, 1894yds, Par 32, SSS 32.*
*Club membership 120.*
**Visitors**      spikes essential, no jeans/T shirts, busy at
              weekends.
**Societies**    telephone in advance.
**Green Fees** not confirmed.
**Facilities**   ♀ ℂ 🏠
**Leisure**      hard tennis courts, heated indoor plus outdoor
              swimming pool, sauna, putting green.
**Location**    Situated on cliff top
**Hotel**        ★★★ 60% Raven Hall Hotel, RAVENSCAR
              ☎ 01723 870353 53 ⇄ ℝ

---

## REDCAR                            Map 08 NZ62

***Cleveland*** Queen St TS10 1BT  ☎ 01642 471798
Links championship course.
*18 holes, 6707yds, Par 72, SSS 72, Course record 67.*
*Club membership 820.*
**Visitors**      must contact in advance, may not play Sat.
**Societies**    must apply in writing.
**Green Fees** £20 per day/round (£30 weekends & bank
              holidays).
**Facilities**   ⊗ ℳ ᴸ ⬛ ♀ ᴸ 🏠 ℂ Stephen Wynn.
**Leisure**      putting green, practice area.
**Location**    8m E of Middlesborough
**Hotel**        ★★ 62% Marton Way Toby Hotel, Marton Rd,
              MIDDLESBROUGH
              ☎ 01642 817651 53 ⇄ ℝ

***Wilton*** Wilton Castle TS10 4QY  ☎ 01642 465265
Parkland course with some fine views.
*18 holes, 6104yds, Par 70, SSS 69.*
*Club membership 750.*
**Visitors**      restricted Sat.
**Societies**    must telephone in advance.
**Green Fees** not confirmed.
**Facilities**   ♀ ᴸ 🏠 ℂ R Smith.
**Location**    3m W on A174
**Hotel**        ★★ 62% Marton Way Toby Hotel, Marton Rd,
              MIDDLESBROUGH
              ☎ 01642 817651 53 ⇄ ℝ

---

## RICHMOND                          Map 07 NZ10

***Richmond*** Bend Hagg DL10 5EX
☎ 01748 823231(Secretary) & 825319
Parkland course.
*18 holes, 5769yds, Par 70, SSS 68, Course record 64.*
*Club membership 600.*
**Visitors**      may not play before 11.30am on Sun.
**Societies**    must contact in writing.                    ▶

Green Fees not confirmed.
Facilities � Paul Jackson.
Leisure putting green,trolley hire.
Location 0.75m N
Hotel ★★ 68% King's Head Hotel, Market Place, RICHMOND
☎ 01748 850220 24 ⇆ ⨿Annexe4 ⇆ ⨿

---

## RIPON Map 08 SE37

Ripon City Palace Rd HG4 3HH ☎ 01765 603640
Hard-walking on undulating parkland course; two testing par 3's at 5th and 7th.
*18 holes, 6120yds, Par 71, SSS 69.*
*Club membership 675.*
Visitors book with professional. Limited play Sat especially Apr-Aug.
Societies contact in writing or telephone.
Green Fees £18 per day (£25 weekends & bank holidays).
Facilities ⊗ flags S T Davis.
Leisure motorised carts for hire, buggies for hire, trolley for hire, putting green.
Location 1m NW on A6108
Hotel ★★★ 67% Ripon Spa Hotel, Park St, RIPON
☎ 01765 602172 40 ⇆ ⨿

---

## SALTBURN-BY-THE-SEA Map 08 NZ62

Saltburn by the Sea Hob Hill, Guisborough Rd TS12 1NJ
☎ 01287 622812
Undulating meadowland course surrounded by woodland. Particularly attractive in autumn. There are fine views of the Cleveland Hills and of Tees Bay.
*18 holes, 5846yds, Par 70, SSS 68, Course record 62.*
*Club membership 900.*
Visitors telephone in advance.
Societies apply in writing.
Green Fees £19 (£24 weekends).
Facilities ⊗ flags Alan Hope.
Leisure trolley for hire, putting green.
Location 0.5m out of Saltburn on Guisborough road
Hotel ★★ 62% Marton Way Toby Hotel, Marton Rd, MIDDLESBROUGH
☎ 01642 817651 53 ⇆ ⨿

---

## SCARBOROUGH Map 08 TA08

Scarborough North Cliff North Cliff Av YO12 6PP
☎ 01723 360786
Seaside parkland course begining on cliff top overlooking bay and castle. Good views.
*18 holes, 6425yds, Par 71, SSS 71, Course record 66.*
*Club membership 860.*
Visitors must be member of a club with handicap certificate. May not play before 10.30am Sun.
Societies prior booking with secretary for parties of 8-40.
Green Fees £25 per day; £18 per round (£28/ £22 weekends & bank holidays).
Facilities ⊗ flags Simon N Deller.
Leisure motorised carts for hire, trolley for hire, putting green, practice area.
Location 2m N of town centre off A165
Hotel ★★★ 63% Esplanade Hotel, Belmont Rd, SCARBOROUGH ☎ 01723 360382 73 ⇆ ⨿

---

Scarborough South Cliff Deepdale Av YO11 2UE
☎ 01723 374737
Parkland/seaside course designed by Dr Mackenzie.
*18 holes, 6039yds, Par 70, SSS 69, Course record 66.*
*Club membership 700.*
Visitors contact in advance may not play before 9.30am Mon-Fri, 10am Sat and 10.30am Sun.
Societies must contact Secretary in advance.
Green Fees not confirmed.
Facilities ⊗ flags A R Skingle.
Leisure putting green,practice area,trolley hire.
Location 1m S on A165
Hotel ★★ 64% Bradley Court, 7-9 Filey Rd, South Cliff, SCARBOROUGH
☎ 01723 360476 40 ⇆ ⨿

---

## SELBY Map 08 SE63

Selby Brayton Barff YO8 9LD ☎ 01757 228622
Mainly flat, links-type course; prevailing SW wind. Testing holes including the 3rd, 7th and 16th.
*18 holes, 6246yds, Par 70, SSS 70.*
*Club membership 840.*
Visitors contact professional on 01757 228785, members and guests only at weekends.
Societies welcome Wed-Fri, must apply in advance.
Green Fees £25 per day; £22 per round.
Facilities ⊗ flags Andrew Smith.
Leisure motorised carts for hire, buggies for hire, trolley for hire, putting green, practice area, snooker.
Location Off A19 at Brayton
Hotel ★★★ 68% Monk Fryston Hall, MONK FRYSTON ☎ 01977 682369 28 ⇆ ⨿

---

## SETTLE Map 07 SD86

Settle Buckhaw Brow, Giggleswick BD24 0DH
☎ 01729 825288
Picturesque parkland course.
*9 holes, 4400yds, Par 64, SSS 62, Course record 59.*
*Club membership 380.*
Visitors may not play before 4pm on Sun.
Societies apply in writing or telephone 4 weeks in advance.
Green Fees £10 per day.
Facilities ⨿
Location 1m N on A65
Hotel ★★★ 64% Falcon Manor Hotel, Skipton Rd, SETTLE
☎ 01729 823814 15 ⇆ ⨿Annexe5 ⇆ ⨿

---

## SKIPTON Map 07 SD95

Skipton Off North West By-Pass BD23 1LL
☎ 01756 795657 & 793257
Undulating parkland course with some water hazards and panoramic views.
*18 holes, 6049yds, Par 70, SSS 69, Course record 69.*
*Club membership 750.*
Visitors welcome by prior arrangement.
Societies must apply in writing.
Green Fees £18 (£22 Sun & bank holidays).
Facilities ⊗ flags Peter Robinson.
Leisure driving range, practice area.
Location 1m N on A65

Hotel　★★★(red) Devonshire Arms Country House Hotel, BOLTON ABBEY ☎ 01756 710441 41 ⇆ 👣

Location　2m N on A168
Hotel　★★ 62% Three Tuns Hotel, Market Place, THIRSK ☎ 01845 523124 11 ⇆ 👣

## STOCKTON-ON-THE-FOREST　　　Map 08 SE65

**Forest Park** YO3 9UW ☎ 01904 400425 & 400688
A parkland/meadowland course, opened in 1991, with natural features including a stream and mature and new trees.
*Old Foss Course: 18 holes, 6600yds, Par 71, SSS 72.*
*The West Course: 9 holes, 6384yds, Par 70, SSS 70.*
*Club membership 650.*
Visitors　welcome, subject to tee availability. Advisable to contact club in advance.
Societies　by prior arrangement.
Green Fees Old Foss: £14.50 per round (£20 weekends & bank holidays). West Course: £12 per 18 holes, £7 per 9 holes (£16/£9 weekends and bank holidays).
Facilities　⊗ �🝙 ⮾ 🍽 ♀ ⚘ 🏠 🎯
Leisure　trolley for hire, driving range, putting green, practice area.
Location　1.5m from end of A64, York bypass
Hotel　★★★ 69% York Pavilion Hotel, 45 Main St, Fulford, YORK
☎ 01904 622099 13 ⇆ 👣Annexe22 ⇆ 👣

## TADCASTER　　　　　　　　Map 08 SE44

**Cocksford** Cocksford, Stutton LS24 9NG ☎ 01937 834253
Three 9-hole courses; the old 18-hole combination set on undulating meadowland with the famous Cock Beck featuring on 8 of the original 18 holes. Whatever combination you choose the course is relatively short featuring a number of drivable par 4s, but beware danger surrounds many of the greens!
*Old Course: 18 holes, 5570yds, Par 71, SSS 69.*
*Plews Course: 18 holes, 5559yds, Par 70, SSS 68.*
*Quarry Hills Course: 18 holes, 4951yds, Par 67, SSS 65.*
*Club membership 450.*
Visitors　welcome.
Societies　telephone the secretary.
Green Fees £20 per day; £16 per round (£25/£22 weekends).
Facilities　⊗ �🝙 ⮾ 🍽 ♀ ⚘ 🏠 🎯 🏊
　　　　　🥂 Graham Thompson.
Leisure　outdoor swimming pool, motorised carts for hire, trolley for hire, putting green, practice area.
Location　Between York & Leeds, A162 from Tadcaster
Hotel　★★★🏨 71% Wood Hall Hotel, Trip Ln, Linton, WETHERBY
☎ 01937 587271 37 ⇆ 👣Annexe6 ⇆ 👣

## THIRSK　　　　　　　　　　Map 08 SE48

**Thirsk & Northallerton** Thornton-le-Street YO7 4AB
☎ 01845 522170 & 526216
The course has good views of the nearby Hambleton Hills. Testing course, mainly flat land.
*9 holes, 6342yds, Par 72, SSS 70, Course record 67.*
*Club membership 420.*
Visitors　no play on Sun, must have handicap certificate.
Societies　must apply in writing.
Green Fees £15 per day; £10 per 18 hole (£20 Sat & bank holidays).
Facilities　⊗ �🝙 ⮾ 🍽 ♀ ⚘ 🏠 🎯 🥂 Robert Garner.
Leisure　trolley for hire, putting green, practice area.

## WHITBY　　　　　　　　　　Map 08 NZ81

**Whitby** Low Straggleton, Sandsend Rd YO21 3SR
☎ 01947 600660
Seaside course on cliff top. Good views and fresh sea breeze.
*18 holes, 6134yds, Par 71.*
*Club membership 800.*
Visitors　may not play on competition days.
Societies　must contact in writing.
Green Fees £20 per day/round (£25 weekends and bank holidays).
Facilities　⊗ �🝙 ⮾ 🍽 ♀ ⚘ 🏠 🎯 🥂 Richard Wood.
Leisure　trolley for hire, putting green, practice area.
Location　1.5m NW on A174
Hotel　★★ 67% White House Hotel, Upgang Lane, West Cliff, WHITBY
☎ 01947 600469 12rm(7 ⇆4 👣)

## YORK　　　　　　　　　　　Map 08 SE65

**Forest of Galtres** Moorlands Rd, Skelton YO3 3RF
☎ 01904 766198
Level parkland course situated in the heart of the ancient Forest of Galtres with mature oak trees and interesting water hazards coming into play on the 5th, 6th, 14th and 17th holes. Views towards York Minster.
*18 holes, 6312yds, Par 72, SSS 70, Course record 66.*
*Club membership 400.*
Visitors　telephone to book, may play any time.
Societies　booking system, telephone for forms.
Green Fees £20 per day; £15 per round (£22.50/£18.50 weekends and bank holidays).
Facilities　⊗ �🝙 ⮾ 🍽 ♀ ⚘ 🏠 🎯 🥂 Neil Suckling.
Hotel　★★ 66% Jacobean Lodge Hotel, Plainville Ln, Wigginton, YORK
☎ 01904 762749 8 ⇆ 👣Annexe6 ⇆ 👣

**Fulford** Heslington Ln YO1 5DY ☎ 01904 413579
A flat, parkland/moorland course well-known for the superb quality of its turf, particularly the greens, and now famous as the venue for some of the best golf tournaments in the British Isles.
*18 holes, 6775yds, Par 72, SSS 72, Course record 62.*
*Club membership 700.*
Visitors　must contact in advance.
Societies　not Tue am, book with the manager.
Green Fees £35 per day; £25 per round (£40 per round weekends & bank holidays).
Facilities　⊗ �🝙 ⮾ 🍽 ♀ ⚘ 🏠 🎯 🥂 Bryan Hessay.
Leisure　trolley for hire, driving range, putting green, practice area.
Location　2m S of York off A19
Hotel　★★★★ 64% Swallow Hotel, Tadcaster Rd, YORK ☎ 01904 701000 113 ⇆ 👣

**Heworth** Muncaster House, Muncastergate YO3 9JX
☎ 01904 422389
11-hole parkland course, easy walking. Holes 3 to 9 played twice from different tees.
*11 holes, 6141yds, Par 70, SSS 69, Course record 67.*
*Club membership 550.*　　　　　　　　　　　　　▶

**Visitors** advisable to telephone the professional in advance.
**Societies** apply in writing.
**Green Fees** £14 per day; £10 per round (£17/£14 weekends & bank holidays).
**Facilities** ⊗ ⋙ �ቔ ⌷ ⏇ ♀ ⚲ ⛉ ⚑ ⵏ Gregg Roberts.
**Location** 1.5m NE of city centre on A1036
**Hotel** ★★★ 72% Dean Court Hotel, Duncombe Place, YORK ☎ 01904 625082 41 ⇆ ⋔

---

**Swallow Hall** Crockey Hill YO1 4SG
☎ 01904 448889
A small 18-hole, Par 3 course with 2 par 4s. Attached to a caravan park.
*18 holes, 3100yds, Par 56, SSS 56, Course record 61.*
*Club membership 100.*
**Visitors** no restrictions.
**Societies** must telephone in advance.
**Green Fees** £7 per 18 holes; £3.50 per 9 holes (£8/£4 weekends & bank holidays).
**Facilities** ⏇ ⚲ ⵏ ⛝
**Leisure** hard tennis courts, trolley for hire, driving range, putting green, practice area.
**Location** Off A19, signposted to Wheldrake
**Hotel** ★★★ 69% York Pavilion Hotel, 45 Main St, Fulford, YORK
☎ 01904 622099 13 ⇆ ⋔Annexe22 ⇆ ⋔

---

**York** Lords Moor Ln, Strensall YO3 5XF
☎ 01904 491840 & 490304
A pleasant, well-designed, heathland course with easy walking. The course is of good length but being flat the going does use not tire. There are two testing pond holes.
*18 holes, 6323yds, Par 70, SSS 70, Course record 66.*
*Club membership 700.*
**Visitors** with member only weekends, must contact in advance.
**Societies** more than 16 contact secretary, under 16 contact professional.
**Green Fees** £28 per day/£20 per round.
**Facilities** ⊗ ⋙ �ቔ ⏇ ♀ ⚲ ⛉ ⵏ A B Mason.
**Leisure** trolley for hire, driving range, putting green, practice area.
**Location** 6m NE, E of Strensall village
**Hotel** ★★★ 72% Dean Court Hotel, Duncombe Place, YORK
☎ 01904 625082 41 ⇆ ⋔

---

# YORKSHIRE, SOUTH

## BARNSLEY       Map 08 SE30

**Barnsley** Wakefield Rd, Staincross S75 6JZ
☎ 01226 382856
Undulating municipal parkland course with easy walking apart from last 4 holes. Testing 8th and 18th holes.
*18 holes, 6042yds, Par 69, SSS 69, Course record 64.*
*Club membership 450.*
**Visitors** no restrictions.
**Societies** by arrangement.

**Green Fees** not confirmed.
**Facilities** ♀ ⚲ ⛉ ⵏ ⵏ Mike Melling.
**Location** 3m N on A61
**Hotel** ★★★ 66% Ardsley House Hotel, Doncaster Rd, Ardsley, BARNSLEY
☎ 01226 309955 73 ⇆ ⋔

---

**Sandhill** Middlecliffe Ln, Little Houghton S72 0HW
☎ 01226 753444
Opened in 1993, the course is reasonably flat with generously wide fairways laid out between and amongst 25 acres of newly planted woodlands. Holes of note are the 4th which is a 311 yard Par 4 to a horseshoe green around a 9-foot deep bunker; the 7th Par 3 to blind reverse Mackenzie Green and the 11th 416 yard Par 4 dogleg where the brave can take on the out of bounds.
*18 holes, 6214yds, Par 71, SSS 70, Course record 69.*
*Club membership 275.*
**Visitors** welcome by prior booking.
**Societies** telephone for availability, write to confirm.
**Green Fees** not confirmed.
**Facilities** ♀ ⚲ ⛉
**Leisure** 18 bay floodlit driving range.
**Location** 5m E of Barnsley, off A635
**Hotel** ★★★ 66% Ardsley House Hotel, Doncaster Rd, Ardsley, BARNSLEY
☎ 01226 309955 73 ⇆ ⋔

---

## BAWTRY       Map 08 SK69

**Austerfield Park** Cross Ln, Austerfield DN10 6RF
☎ 01302 710841 & 710850
Long moorland course with postage stamp 8th and testing 618-yd 7th. Driving range attached.
*18 holes, 6854yds, Par 70, SSS 70, Course record 64.*
*Club membership 600.*
**Visitors** telephone in advance.
**Societies** must contact in advance.
**Green Fees** £19 per day; £15 per round (£23/£19 weekends).
**Facilities** ⊗ ⋙ �ቔ ⏇ ♀ ⚲ ⛉ ⵏ Peter Rothery.
**Leisure** trolley for hire, driving range, putting green, practice area, par 3 course, bowling green.
**Location** 2m from Bawtry on A614
**Hotel** ★★★ 65% The Crown Hotel, High St, BAWTRY
☎ 01302 710341 57 ⇆ ⋔

---

## CONISBROUGH       Map 08 SK59

**Crookhill Park Municipal** Carr Ln DN12 2BE
☎ 01709 862979
A rolling parkland course.
*18 holes, 5839yds, Par 70, SSS 68.*
*Club membership 500.*
**Visitors** restricted weekends before 9am. Must contact in advance.
**Societies** by arrangement.
**Green Fees** not confirmed.
**Facilities** ♀ ⚲ ⛉ ⵏ ⵏ Richard Swaine.
**Leisure** pool table.
**Location** 1.5m SE on B6094
**Hotel** ★★★ 62% Danum Swallow Hotel, High St, DONCASTER ☎ 01302 342261 66 ⇆ ⋔

## DONCASTER
Map 08 SE50

**Doncaster** 278 Bawtry Rd, Bessacarr DN4 7PD
☎ 01302 868316 & 865632
Pleasant undulating heathland course with wooded surroundings. Quick drying, ideal autumn, winter and spring.
*18 holes, 6220yds, Par 69, SSS 70, Course record 66.*
*Club membership 600.*
| | |
|---|---|
| **Visitors** | must contact in advance. Times restricted on Wed & weekends. |
| **Societies** | must contact in advance. |
| **Green Fees** | £25 per day; £20 per round (£30/25 weekends & bank holidays). |
| **Facilities** | ⊗ ⊪ ⅃ ⚑ ⅃ ⚑ ⅃ ⚑ ⅃ Graham Bailey. |
| **Leisure** | trolley for hire, putting green, practice area. |
| **Location** | 4m SE on A638 |
| **Hotel** | ★★★ 64% Mount Pleasant Hotel, Great North Rd, ROSSINGTON ☎ 01302 868696 & 868219 29 ⇆ ℝ |

**Doncaster Town Moor** Bawtry Rd, Belle Vue DN4 5HU
☎ 01302 535286 & 533167
Easy walking, but testing, heathland course with good true greens. Friendly club. Notable hole is 11th (par 4), 464 yds. Situated in centre of racecourse.
*18 holes, 6072yds, Par 69, SSS 69, Course record 66.*
*Club membership 520.*
| | |
|---|---|
| **Visitors** | may not play on Sun morning. |
| **Societies** | must contact in advance. |
| **Green Fees** | not confirmed. |
| **Facilities** | ⅃ ⚑ ⅃ Steven C Poole. |
| **Leisure** | practice area, trolley hire. |
| **Location** | 1.5m E,at racecourse,on A638 |
| **Hotel** | ★★★ 62% Danum Swallow Hotel, High St, DONCASTER ☎ 01302 342261 66 ⇆ ℝ |

**Owston Park** Owston Hall, Ownston DN6 9JF
☎ 01302 330821
A flat course surrounded by woodland. A lot of mature trees and a few ditches in play. A practice putting green and chipping area.
*9 holes, 3042yds, Par 36, SSS 71.*
| | |
|---|---|
| **Visitors** | no restrictions. |
| **Societies** | telephone in advance. |
| **Green Fees** | £3.90 per 9 holes. |
| **Facilities** | ⅃ ⚑ ⅃ Mike Parker. |
| **Leisure** | trolley for hire, putting green. |
| **Location** | 5m N of Doncaster off A19 |
| **Hotel** | ★★★ 62% Danum Swallow Hotel, High St, DONCASTER ☎ 01302 342261 66 ⇆ ℝ |

**Wheatley** Armthorpe Rd DN2 5QB
☎ 01302 831655
Fairly flat well-bunkered, lake-holed, parkland course.
*18 holes, 6169yds, Par 70, SSS 69.*
*Club membership 600.*
| | |
|---|---|
| **Visitors** | must contact in advance and have an introduction from own club. |
| **Societies** | must contact in advance. |
| **Green Fees** | not confirmed. |
| **Facilities** | ⅃ ⚑ ⅃ T C Parkinson. |
| **Location** | NE side of town centre off A18 |
| **Hotel** | ★★★ 62% Grand St Leger, Bennetthorpe, DONCASTER ☎ 01302 364111 20 ⇆ ℝ |

## HICKLETON
Map 08 SE40

**Hickleton** DN5 7BE ☎ 01709 896081
Undulating parkland course with stream running through; designed by Neil Coles and Brian Huggett.
*18 holes, 6403yds, Par 71, SSS 71.*
*Club membership 600.*
| | |
|---|---|
| **Visitors** | restricted weekends after 2.30pm. Must contact in advance. |
| **Societies** | must contact in advance on 01709 888436. |
| **Green Fees** | not confirmed. |
| **Facilities** | ⅃ ⚑ ⅃ ⚑ ⅃ Paul Shepherd. |
| **Location** | 0.5m W on B6411 |
| **Hotel** | ★★★ 62% Danum Swallow Hotel, High St, DONCASTER ☎ 01302 342261 66 ⇆ ℝ |

## HIGH GREEN
Map 08 SK39

**Tankersley Park** S30 4LG ☎ 0114 246 8247
Akin to an inland links, this parkland course is hilly, windy and has good views.
*18 holes, 6212yds, Par 69, SSS 70, Course record 65.*
*Club membership 634.*
| | |
|---|---|
| **Visitors** | must contact in advance. |
| **Societies** | must apply in writing. |
| **Green Fees** | £24.50 per day/weekends; £19.50 per round. |
| **Facilities** | ⊗ ⊪ ⅃ ⚑ ⅃ ⚑ ⅃ ⚑ ⅃ Ian Kirk. |
| **Leisure** | motorised carts for hire, trolley for hire, putting green, practice area. |
| **Location** | Off A61/M1 onto A616, Stocksbridge bypass |
| **Hotel** | ★★★ 68% Tankersley Manor, Church Ln, TANKERSLEY ☎ 01226 744700 40 ⇆ ℝ |

## RAWMARSH
Map 08 SK49

**Wath** Abdy Ln S62 7SJ ☎ 01709 872149 & 878677
Parkland course, not easy in spite of its length; 17th hole (par 3) is a difficult 244yds with narrow driving area.
*18 holes, 5857yds, Par 68, SSS 68.*
*Club membership 550.*
| | |
|---|---|
| **Visitors** | must play with member at weekends. Must contact in advance and have a handicap certificate. |
| **Societies** | must contact in writing, may not play at weekends. |
| **Green Fees** | not confirmed. |
| **Facilities** | ⅃ ⚑ ⅃ Chris Bassett. |
| **Leisure** | putting green,practice area,trolley hire. |
| **Location** | 2.5m N off A633 |
| **Hotel** | ★★ 66% Brentwood Hotel, Moorgate Rd, ROTHERHAM ☎ 01709 382772 33 ⇆ ℝ Annexe10 ⇆ ℝ |

## ROTHERHAM
Map 08 SK49

**Grange Park** Upper Wortley Rd S61 2SJ
☎ 01709 559497
Parkland/meadowland course, with panoramic views especially from the back nine. The golf is testing, particularly at the 1st, 4th and 18th holes (par 4), and 8th, 12th and 15th (par 5).
*18 holes, 6461yds, Par 71, SSS 70.*
*Club membership 325.*
▶

**Visitors** no restrictions.
**Societies** apply in writing.
**Green Fees** not confirmed.
**Facilities** ♀ ⚘ 🏠 ♈ ⌑ Eric Clark.
**Location** 3m NW off A629
**Hotel** ★★ 66% Brentwood Hotel, Moorgate Rd, ROTHERHAM
☎ 01709 382772 33 ⇄ ⬧Annexe10 ⇄ ⬧

**Phoenix** Pavilion Ln, Brinsworth S60 5PA
☎ 01709 363864 & 382624
Undulating meadowland course with variable wind.
*18 holes, 6182yds, Par 71, SSS 69, Course record 65.*
*Club membership 1100.*
**Visitors** must contact in advance.
**Societies** must apply in writing.
**Green Fees** £21 per day (£28 weekends & bank holidays).
**Facilities** ⊗ �🍽 ᒐ ♥ ♀ ⚘ 🏠 ⌑
**Leisure** hard tennis courts, squash, gymnasium, trolley for hire, driving range, putting green, practice green.
**Location** SW side of town centre off A630
**Hotel** ★★ 66% Brentwood Hotel, Moorgate Rd, ROTHERHAM
☎ 01709 382772 33 ⇄ ⬧Annexe10 ⇄ ⬧

**Rotherham Golf Club Ltd** Thrybergh Park, Doncaster Rd, Thrybergh S65 4NU
☎ 01709 850812 (Secretary) & 850480 (Pro)
Parkland course with easy walking along tree-lined fairways.
*18 holes, 6324yds, Par 70, SSS 70, Course record 65.*
*Club membership 500.*
**Visitors** must contact in advance.
**Societies** must contact secretary in advance.
**Green Fees** £26.50 per day/round (£31.50 weekends & bank holidays).
**Facilities** ⊗ ⍟ ᒐ ♥ ♀ ⚘ 🏠 ⌑ Simon Thornhill.
**Leisure** motorised carts for hire, buggies for hire, trolley for hire, putting green, practice area.
**Location** 3.5m E on A630
**Hotel** ★★ 66% Brentwood Hotel, Moorgate Rd, ROTHERHAM
☎ 01709 382772 33 ⇄ ⬧Annexe10 ⇄ ⬧

**Sitwell Park** Shrogswood Rd S60 4BY ☎ 01709 541046
Parkland course with easy walking.
*18 holes, 6209yds, Par 71, SSS 70, Course record 61.*
*Club membership 450.*
**Visitors** must contact in advance.
**Societies** must contact in advance.
**Green Fees** £27 per day; £23 per round (£31/£27 weekends & bank holidays).
**Facilities** ⊗ ⍟ ᒐ ♥ ♀ ⚘ 🏠 ♈ ⌑ Nic Taylor.
**Leisure** motorised carts for hire, trolley for hire, putting green, practice area.
**Hotel** ★★ 66% Brentwood Hotel, Moorgate Rd, ROTHERHAM
☎ 01709 382772 33 ⇄ ⬧Annexe10 ⇄ ⬧

## SHEFFIELD                                                            Map 08 SK38

*Abbeydale* Twentywell Ln, Dore S17 4QA
☎ 0114 236 0763
Parkland course, well-kept and wooded. Testing hole: 12th, par 3.
*18 holes, 6419yds, Par 72, SSS 71.*
*Club membership 750.*

**Visitors** restricted Wed 10am-1.30pm.
**Societies** must apply in writing.
**Green Fees** not confirmed.
**Facilities** ♀ ⚘ 🏠 ⌑
**Location** 4m SW of city centre off A621
**Hotel** B Forte Posthouse Sheffield, Manchester Rd, Broomhill, SHEFFIELD
☎ 0114 267 0067 135 ⇄ ⬧

**Beauchief Municipal** Abbey Ln S8 0DB ☎ 0114 236 7274
Municipal course with natural water hazards. The rolling land looks west to the Pennines and a 12th-century abbey adorns the course.
*18 holes, 5452yds, Par 67, SSS 66, Course record 65.*
*Club membership 450.*
**Visitors** are advised to book in advance in summer.
**Societies** weekdays only, must apply in writing to: Recreation Department, Tower Lodge, Firth Park Road, Sheffield S5 6WS.
**Green Fees** £8 per round (£8.70 weekends).
**Facilities** ⊗ ᒐ ♥ ♀ ⚘ 🏠 ⌑ A Highfield.
**Leisure** trolley for hire, putting green, practice area.
**Location** 4m SW of city centre off A621
**Hotel** ★★★ 72% Beauchief Hotel, 161 Abbeydale Rd South, SHEFFIELD
☎ 0114 262 0500 41 ⇄ ⬧

**Birley Wood** Birley Ln S12 3BP ☎ 0114 264 7262
Undulating meadowland course with well-varied features, easy walking and good views. Practice range and green.
*18 holes, 5100yds, Par 66, SSS 65, Course record 64.*
*Club membership 300.*
**Visitors** no restrictions.
**Societies** apply in advance.
**Green Fees** £4.20 (£8.10 weekends).
**Facilities** ⚘ ♈ ⌑ Peter Ball.
**Leisure** putting green, practice area.
**Location** 4.5m SE of city centre off A621
**Hotel** ★★★ 65% Mosborough Hall Hotel, High St, Mosborough, SHEFFIELD
☎ 0114 248 4353 23 ⇄ ⬧

**Concord Park** Shiregreen Ln S5 6AE ☎ 0114 234 9802
Hilly municipal parkland course with some fairways wood-flanked, good views, often windy. Eight par 3 holes.
*18 holes, 4321yds, Par 65, SSS 62, Course record 57.*
*Club membership 150.*
**Visitors** no restrictions.
**Green Fees** £9.75 per 36 holes; £6.50 per 18 holes. Prices under review..
**Facilities** ᒐ ♥ ♀ ⚘
**Leisure** hard tennis courts, heated indoor swimming pool, squash, solarium, gymnasium, practice area.
**Location** 3.5m N of city centre on B6086 off A6135
**Hotel** B Forte Posthouse Sheffield, Manchester Rd, Broomhill, SHEFFIELD
☎ 0114 267 0067 135 ⇄ ⬧

*Dore & Totley* Bradway Rd, Bradway S17 4QR
☎ 0114 236 0492
Flat parkland course.
*18 holes, 6265yds, Par 70, SSS 70, Course record 65.*
*Club membership 580.*
**Visitors** must contact in advance a handicap certificate may be requested, may not play 9.30am-noon & after 2.30pm.

| | |
|---|---|
| **Societies** | must apply in writing. |
| **Green Fees** | not confirmed. |
| **Facilities** | ♀ ⅄ 🛋 ( Neil Cheetham. |
| **Leisure** | putting green,practice area,trolley hire. |
| **Location** | 7m S of city centre on B6054 off A61 |
| **Hotel** | B Forte Posthouse Sheffield, Manchester Rd, |
| | Broomhill, SHEFFIELD |
| | ☎ 0114 267 0067 135 ➡ 🐾 |

**Hallamshire Golf Club Ltd** Sandygate S10 4LA
☎ 0114 230 2153 (Secretary) & 230 5222 (Pro)
Situated on a shelf of land at a height of 850 ft.
Magnificent views to the west. Moorland turf, long
carries over ravine. Good natural drainage.
*18 holes, 6359yds, Par 71, SSS 71, Course record 63.*
*Club membership 600.*

| | |
|---|---|
| **Visitors** | contact professional in advance. Tees reserved for members 8-9.30 and noon-1.30. |
| **Societies** | parties of 12+ should book in advance with secretary. |
| **Green Fees** | £31 per day (£36 weekends & bank holidays). |
| **Facilities** | ⊗ by prior arrangement 🎿 by prior arrangement ┗ 🛢 ♀ ⅄ 🛋 🌱 ( G R Tickell. |
| **Leisure** | trolley for hire, putting green, practice area. |
| **Location** | Off A57 at Crosspool onto Sandygate Rd, clubhouse 0.75m on right |
| **Hotel** | B Forte Posthouse Sheffield, Manchester Rd, Broomhill, SHEFFIELD ☎ 0114 267 0067 135 ➡ 🐾 |

**Hillsborough** Worrall Rd S6 4BE
☎ 0114 234 9151 (Secretary) & 233 2666 (Pro)
Beautiful moorland/woodland course 500 ft above sea-level,
reasonable walking. Challenging first four holes into a
prevailing wind and a tight, testing 14th hole.
*18 holes, 6216yards, Par 71, SSS 70, Course record 64.*
*Club membership 650.*

| | |
|---|---|
| **Visitors** | contact professional in advance. May not play Tue (Ladies Day), Thu and weekends before 2pm |
| **Societies** | must apply in writing to secretary. |
| **Green Fees** | £28 per day (£35 weekends & bank holidays); £20 per round Sun. |
| **Facilities** | ⊗ 🎿 ┗ 🛢 ♀ ⅄ 🛋 🌱 ( Graham Walker. |
| **Leisure** | trolley for hire, driving range, putting green, practice area. |
| **Location** | 3m NW of city centre off A616 |
| **Hotel** | ★★★ 59% Rutland Hotel, 452 Glossop Rd, Broomhill, SHEFFIELD ☎ 0114 266 4411 70 ➡ 🐾Annexe17 ➡ 🐾 |

**Lees Hall** Hemsworth Rd, Norton S8 8LL
☎ 0114 255 4402
Parkland/meadowland course with panoramic view of city.
*18 holes, 6137yds, Par 71, SSS 69, Course record 63.*
*Club membership 725.*

| | |
|---|---|
| **Visitors** | restricted Wed. |
| **Societies** | must apply in writing. |
| **Green Fees** | not confirmed. |
| **Facilities** | ♀ ⅄ 🛋 ( J R Wilkinson. |
| **Location** | 3.5m S of city centre off A6102 |
| **Hotel** | B Forte Posthouse Sheffield, Manchester Rd, Broomhill, SHEFFIELD ☎ 0114 267 0067 135 ➡ 🐾 |

*Tinsley Park Municipal Golf* High Hazels Park WN6 8EW
☎ 0114 256 0237
Undulating meadowland course with plenty of trees and
rough.
*18 holes, 6064yds, Par 71, SSS 69.*
*Club membership 420.*

| | |
|---|---|
| **Visitors** | no restrictions. |
| **Societies** | apply in writing to Sheffield City Council, Recreation Dept., Meersbrook Park, Sheffield. |
| **Green Fees** | not confirmed. |
| **Facilities** | ♀ ⅄ 🛋 🌱 ( A P Highfield. |
| **Leisure** | putting green,trolley hire. |
| **Location** | 4m E of city centre off A630 |
| **Hotel** | ★★★ 65% Mosborough Hall Hotel, High St, Mosborough, SHEFFIELD ☎ 0114 248 4353 23 ➡ 🐾 |

**SILKSTONE**                           Map 08 SE20

**Silkstone** Field Head, Elmhurst Ln S75 4LD
☎ 01226 790328
Parkland/downland course, fine views over the Pennines.
Testing golf.
*18 holes, 6069yds, Par 70, SSS 70, Course record 64.*
*Club membership 508.*

| | |
|---|---|
| **Visitors** | with member only at weekends. |
| **Societies** | contact in advance. |
| **Green Fees** | £25 per day/round. |
| **Facilities** | ⊗ 🎿 ┗ 🛢 ♀ ⅄ 🛋 ( Kevin Guy. |
| **Leisure** | trolley for hire, putting green, practice area, snooker. |
| **Location** | 1m E off A628 |
| **Hotel** | ★★★ 66% Ardsley House Hotel, Doncaster Rd, Ardsley, BARNSLEY ☎ 01226 309955 73 ➡ 🐾 |

**STOCKSBRIDGE**                       Map 08 SK29

**Stocksbridge & District** 30 Royd Ln, Townend, Deepcar
S30 5RZ ☎ 0114 288 2003
Hilly moorland course.
*18 holes, 5200yds, Par 65, SSS 65, Course record 64.*
*Club membership 300.*

| | |
|---|---|
| **Visitors** | contact the professional. |
| **Societies** | apply to professional. |
| **Green Fees** | £16 per day (£25 weekends & bank holidays). |
| **Facilities** | ⊗ 🎿 ┗ 🛢 ♀ ⅄ 🛋 ( Timothy Brookes. |
| **Leisure** | putting green, practice area. |
| **Location** | S side of town centre |
| **Hotel** | B Forte Posthouse Sheffield, Manchester Rd, Broomhill, SHEFFIELD ☎ 0114 267 0067 135 ➡ 🐾 |

**THORNE**                               Map 08 SE61

**Thorne** Kirton Ln DN8 5RJ ☎ 01405 812084 & 815173
Picturesque parkland course with 6000 newly planted trees.
*18 holes, 5366yds, Par 68, SSS 66, Course record 62.*
*Club membership 300.*

| | |
|---|---|
| **Visitors** | no restrictions. |
| **Societies** | telephone in advance. |
| **Green Fees** | £8.50 per round (£10 weekends & bank holidays). |
| **Facilities** | ⊗ 🎿 ┗ 🛢 ♀ ⅄ 🛋 🌱 ( Richard Highfield. |
| **Leisure** | trolley for hire, putting green, practice area. ▶ |

Location    14m SE of Pontefract off of M18
Hotel       ★★ 67% Belmont Hotel, Horsefair Green,
            THORNE ☎ 01405 812320 23 ⇆ ⥾

## WORTLEY                                    Map 08 SK39

**Wortley** Hermit Hill Ln S30 7DF
☎ 0114 288 8469 (Secretary) & 288 6490 (Pro)
Well-wooded, undulating parkland course sheltered from
prevailing wind.
*18 holes, 6028yds, Par 69, SSS 68, Course record 62.*
*Club membership 510.*
Visitors    may not play between 11.30am and 1pm. Must
            contact professional in advance.
Societies   telephone in advance and confirm in writing
            with deposit.
Green Fees  £24 (£30 weekends & bank holidays).
Facilities  ⊗ ⅏ ⅃ ⅃ ♀ ⅄ ⅂ ⤚⅊ ⅌ Ian Kirk.
Leisure     trolley for hire, putting green, practice area.
Location    0.5m NE of village off A629
Hotel       B Forte Posthouse Sheffield, Manchester Rd,
            Broomhill, SHEFFIELD
            ☎ 0114 267 0067 135 ⇆ ⥾

---

# YORKSHIRE, WEST

---

## ALWOODLEY                                  Map 08 SE24

**Alwoodley** Wigton Ln LS17 8SA ☎ 0113 268 1680
A fine heathland course with length, trees and abundant
heather. Many attractive situations - together a severe test
of golf.
*18 holes, 6686yds, Par 72, SSS 72, Course record 67.*
*Club membership 455.*
Visitors    must contact in advance,
Societies   must apply in advance.
Green Fees  £50 per day/round (£60 weekends & bank
            holidays).
Facilities  ⊗ ⅏ ⅃ ⅃ ♀ ⅄ ⤚⅊ ⅌ John Green.
Leisure     motorised carts for hire, trolley for hire,
            putting green, practice area.
Location    5m N off A61
Hotel       ★★★ 63% Harewood Arms Hotel,
            Harrogate Rd, HAREWOOD
            ☎ 0113 288 6566 13 ⇆ ⥾Annexe11 ⇆ ⥾

## BAILDON                                    Map 07 SE13

**Baildon** Moorgate BD17 5PP ☎ 01274 595162 & 584266
Moorland course with much bracken rough. The 5th is a hard
climb.
*18 holes, 6225yds, Par 70, SSS 70, Course record 64.*
*Club membership 500.*
Visitors    contact in advance, restricted Tue & weekends.
Societies   large numbers apply in writing, small numbers
            check with the professional.
Green Fees  £16 per day/round.
Facilities  ⊗ ⅏ ⅃ ⅃ ♀ ⅄ ⅂ ⤚⅊ ⅌ Richard Masters.
Leisure     trolley for hire, putting green, practice area.
Location    3m N of Bradford, off A6038

Hotel       ★★★ 70% Hollins Hall, Hollins Hill, Baildon,
            SHIPLEY
            ☎ 01274 530053 59 ⇆ ⥾

## BINGLEY                                    Map 07 SE13

**Bingley St Ives** Golf Club House, St Ives Estate, Harden
BD16 1AT ☎ 01274 562436 & 511788
Parkland/moorland course.
*18 holes, 6485yds, Par 71, SSS 71, Course record 69.*
*Club membership 450.*
Visitors    contact professional on 01274 562506, no green
            fees Sat.
Societies   telephone in advance, the professional 01274
            562506.
Green Fees  £27 per day, £25 per round.
Facilities  ⊗ ⅏ ⅃ ⅃ ♀ ⅄ ⅂ ⅌ Ray Firth.
Leisure     motorised carts for hire, buggies for hire, trolley
            for hire, putting green, practice area.
Location    0.75m W off B6429
Hotel       ★★★ 66% Oakwood Hall Hotel, Lady Ln,
            BINGLEY
            ☎ 01274 564123 & 563569 20 ⇆ ⥾

## BRADFORD                                   Map 07 SE13

**Bradford Moor** Scarr Hall, Pollard Ln BD2 4RW
☎ 01274 638313 & 626107
Parkland course, hard walking.
*9 holes, 5900yds, Par 70, SSS 68, Course record 66.*
*Club membership 330.*
Visitors    no visitors at weekends.
Societies   can book starting times by application in writing.
Green Fees  £12 per day/round.
Facilities  ⊗ ⅏ ⅃ ⅃ ♀ ⅄ ⅂ ⤚⅊ ⅌ Ron Hughes.
Leisure     trolley for hire, putting green, practice area.
Location    2m NE of city centre off A658
Hotel       ★★ 66% Park Drive Hotel, 12 Park Dr,
            BRADFORD ☎ 01274 480194 11 ⇆ ⥾

**Clayton** Thornton View Rd, Clayton BD14 6JX
☎ 01274 880047
Moorland course, difficult in windy conditions.
*9 holes, 5407yds, Par 68, SSS 67.*
*Club membership 350.*
Visitors    may not play after 4pm on Sun.
Societies   apply in writing to the Secretary or Captain.
Green Fees  not confirmed.
Facilities  ♀ ⅄
Leisure     putting green.
Location    2.5m SW of city centre on A647
Hotel       ★★★ 64% Novotel, Merrydale Rd,
            BRADFORD
            ☎ 01274 683683 127 ⇆ ⥾

**East Bierley** South View Rd, East Bierley BD4 6PP
☎ 01274 681023
Hilly moorland course with narrow fairways. Two par 3 holes
over 200 yds.
*9 holes, 4700yds, Par 64, SSS 63.*
*Club membership 200.*
Visitors    restricted Sat (am), Sun & Mon evening. Must
            contact in advance.
Societies   must apply in writing.
Green Fees  not confirmed.

**Facilities** ♀ ⚹
**Location** 4m SE of city centre off A650
**Hotel** ★★★ 64% Novotel, Merrydale Rd,
BRADFORD ☎ 01274 683683 127 ➟ ♟

**Headley** Headley Ln, Thornton BD13 3LX
☎ 01274 833481
Hilly moorland course, short but very testing, windy, fine views.
*9 holes, 4996yds, Par 64, SSS 64, Course record 61.*
*Club membership 300.*
**Visitors** must contact in advance, may not play weekends/BHs.
**Societies** must contact in advance.
**Green Fees** £11 weekdays.
**Facilities** ⊗ ⭤ ⭑ ♥ ♀ ⚹
**Leisure** putting green, practice area.
**Location** 4m W of city centre off B6145 at Thornton
**Hotel** ★★ 66% Park Drive Hotel, 12 Park Dr,
BRADFORD ☎ 01274 480194 11 ➟ ♟

**Phoenix Park** Phoenix Park, Thornbury BD3 7AT
☎ 01274 667573
Very short, tight, moorland course, rather testing.
*9 holes, 2491yds, Par 66, SSS 64, Course record 66.*
*Club membership 260.*
**Visitors** restricted weekends.
**Societies** must apply in advance.
**Green Fees** not confirmed.
**Facilities** ♀ ⚹ 🖻
**Location** E side of city centre on A647
**Hotel** ★★ 66% Park Drive Hotel, 12 Park Dr,
BRADFORD ☎ 01274 480194 11 ➟ ♟

**Queensbury** Brighouse Rd, Queensbury BD13 1QF
☎ 01274 882155 & 816864
Undulating woodland/parkland course.
*9 holes, 5024yds, Par 66, SSS 65, Course record 63.*
*Club membership 380.*
**Visitors** preferable to telephone in advance, restricted at weekends.
**Societies** apply in writing.
**Green Fees** £10 per day (£20 weekends & bank holidays).
**Facilities** ⊗ ⭤ by prior arrangement ⭑ ♥ ♀ ⚹ 🖻 ⭑
♟ Geoff Howard.
**Leisure** putting green, practice area.
**Location** 4m from Bradford on A647
**Hotel** ★★ 66% Park Drive Hotel, 12 Park Dr,
BRADFORD ☎ 01274 480194 11 ➟ ♟

**South Bradford** Pearson Rd, Odsal BD6 1BH
☎ 01274 679195
Hilly course with good greens, trees and ditches. Interesting short 2nd hole (par 3) 200 yds, well-bunkered and played from an elevated tee.
*9 holes, 6068yds, Par 70, SSS 68, Course record 65.*
*Club membership 300.*
**Visitors** must contact in advance.
**Societies** must apply in writing to the secretary.
**Green Fees** £10 (£22 weekends).
**Facilities** ⊗ ⭤ ⭑ ♥ ♀ ⚹ 🖻 ♟ Ian Marshall.
**Leisure** trolley for hire, putting green, practice area.
**Location** 2m S of city centre off A638
**Hotel** ★★★ 64% Novotel, Merrydale Rd,
BRADFORD ☎ 01274 683683 127 ➟ ♟

**West Bowling** Newall Hall, Rooley Ln BD5 8LB
☎ 01274 724449 & 728036
Undulating, tree-lined parkland course. Testing hole: 'the coffin' short par 3, very narrow.
*18 holes, 5763yds, Par 69, SSS 68, Course record 65.*
*Club membership 500.*
**Visitors** must contact in advance, weekend very limited.
**Societies** must apply in writing.
**Green Fees** £26 per round (£34 weekends). Handicap certificate £4 discount.
**Facilities** ⊗ ⭤ ⭑ ♥ ♀ ⚹ 🖻 ♟ Allan Swaine.
**Leisure** trolley for hire, putting green, practice area, snooker.
**Location** S side of city centre off A638
**Hotel** ★★★★ 63% Cedar Court Hotel Bradford,
Mayo Av, Off Pooley Ln, BRADFORD
☎ 01274 406606 & 406601 127 ➟ ♟

**West Bradford** Chellow Grange Rd BD9 6NP
☎ 01274 542767
Parkland course, windy, especially 3rd, 4th, 5th and 6th holes. Hilly but not hard.
*18 holes, 5741yds, Par 69, SSS 68.*
*Club membership 440.*
**Visitors** restricted Sat.
**Societies** must apply in writing.
**Green Fees** not confirmed.
**Facilities** ♀ (ex Mon) ⚹ 🖻 ♟ Nigel M Barber.
**Leisure** putting,trolley hire.
**Location** W side of city centre off B6269
**Hotel** ★★★ 70% Hollins Hall, Hollins Hill, Baildon,
SHIPLEY
☎ 01274 530053 59 ➟ ♟

## CLECKHEATON                    Map 08 SE12

**Cleckheaton & District** Bradford Rd BD19 6BU
☎ 01274 851266
Parkland course with gentle hills.
*18 holes, 5769yds, Par 71, SSS 68.*
*Club membership 550.*
**Visitors** must contact in advance and have an introduction from own club.
**Societies** weekdays only; must contact in advance.
**Green Fees** not confirmed.
**Facilities** ♀ ⚹ 🖻 ⭑ ♟ Mike Ingham.
**Location** 1.5m NW on A638 junc 26 M62
**Hotel** ★★★ 66% Gomersal Park Hotel, Moor Ln,
GOMERSAL
☎ 01274 869386 52 ➟ ♟

## DEWSBURY                       Map 08 SE22

**Hanging Heaton** White Cross Rd WF12 7DT
☎ 01924 461606
Arable land course, easy walking, fine views. Testing 4th hole (par 3).
*9 holes, 5400mtrs, Par 69, SSS 67.*
*Club membership 550.*
**Visitors** must play with member at weekends & bank holidays. Must contact in advance.
**Societies** must telephone in advance.
**Green Fees** not confirmed.
**Facilities** ♀ ⚹ 🖻 ♟ S Hartley.
**Location** 0.75m NE off A653                    ▶

**Hotel**    ★★ 70%  Healds Hall Hotel, Leeds Rd,
Liversedge, DEWSBURY
☎ 01924 409112 25 ⇔ ſ◌

## ELLAND                                    Map 07 SE12

**Elland** Hammerstones, Leach Ln HX5 0TA
☎ 01422 372505
Parkland course.
*9 holes, 2815yds, Par 66, SSS 66, Course record 64.*
*Club membership 450.*
**Visitors**    welcome.
**Societies**    must contact in writing.
**Green Fees** £14 per day/round (£25 weekends and bank
holidays).
**Facilities**    ⊗ ⵔ ⅃ ◪ ♀ ⏉ 🛆 ☎ ſ N Bell.
**Location**    1m SW
**Hotel**    ★★ 70% Rock Inn Hotel & Churchills,
HOLYWELL GREEN
☎ 01422 379721 18 ⇔ ſ◌

## FENAY BRIDGE                               Map 08 SE11

**Woodsome Hall** HD8 0LQ ☎ 01484 602739 & 602971
A parkland course with good views and an historic
clubhouse.
*18 holes, 6081yds, Par 69, SSS 69, Course record 65.*
*Club membership 800.*
**Visitors**    must contact in advance.
**Societies**    must apply in writing.
**Green Fees** £30 per day; £25 per round (£35/£30 weekends
& bank holidays).
**Facilities**    ⊗ ⵔ ⅃ ◪ ♀ 🛆 ☎ ſ M Higginbotton.
**Leisure**    trolley for hire, putting green, practice area.
**Location**    1.5m SW off A629
**Hotel**    ★★★ 70% Springfield Park Hotel, Penistone
Rd, KIRKBURTON
☎ 01484 607788 44 ⇔ ſ◌

## GARFORTH                                   Map 08 SE43

*Garforth* LS25 2DS ☎ 0113 286 2021
Parkland course with fine views, easy walking.
*18 holes, 6005yds, Par 69, SSS 69.*
*Club membership 500.*
**Visitors**    must contact in advance and have handicap
certificate. With member only weekends & bank
holidays.
**Societies**    must apply in advance.
**Green Fees** not confirmed.
**Facilities**    🛆 ☎ ☞ ſ
**Location**    1m N
**Hotel**    B Hilton National Leeds/Garforth, Wakefield
Rd, GARFORTH ☎ 0113 286 6556 144 ⇔ ſ◌

## GUISELEY                                   Map 08 SE14

**Bradford** Hawksworth Ln LS20 8NP ☎ 01943 875570
Moorland course with eight par 4 holes of 360 yds or more.
*18 holes, 6259yds, Par 71, SSS 71.*
*Club membership 600.*
**Visitors**    must have a handicap certificate. May not play
Sat.
**Societies**    make prior arrangements with secretary.

**Green Fees** £25 per day; £20 per round (£32/£25 weekends).
**Facilities**    ⊗ ⵔ ⅃ ◪ ♀ 🛆 ☎ ſ Sydney Weldon.
**Leisure**    trolley for hire, putting green, practice area.
**Location**    SW side of town centre off A6038
**Hotel**    ★★★ 56%  Cow & Calf Hotel, Moor Top,
ILKLEY ☎ 01943 607335 20 ⇔ ſ◌

## HALIFAX                                    Map 07 SE02

**Halifax** Bob Hall, Union Ln, Ogden HX2 8XR
☎ 01422 244171 & 240047
Hilly moorland course crossed by streams, natural hazards,
and offering fine views. Testing 172-yd 17th (par3).
*18 holes, 6037yds, Par 70, SSS 70, Course record 63.*
*Club membership 700.*
**Visitors**    contact professional for tee times.
**Societies**    contact manager for dates.
**Green Fees** £20 per day; £15 per round (£30 weekends).
**Facilities**    ⊗ ⵔ ⅃ ◪ ♀ 🛆 ☎ ☞ ſ Michael Allison.
**Location**    A629 Halifax/Keighley
**Hotel**    ★★★ 74%  Holdsworth House Hotel,
Holmfield, HALIFAX
☎ 01422 240024 40 ⇔ ſ◌

*Lightcliffe* Knowle Top Rd, Lightcliffe HX3 8SW
☎ 01422 202459
Heathland course.
*9 holes, 5388yds, Par 68, SSS 68.*
*Club membership 545.*
**Visitors**    must be a member of a recognised Golf Club.
**Societies**    must contact 21 days in advance.
**Green Fees** not confirmed.
**Facilities**    ♀ 🛆 ☎ ſ Robert Kershaw.
**Leisure**    putting green.
**Location**    3.5m E on A58
**Hotel**    ★★★ 74%  Holdsworth House Hotel,
Holmfield, HALIFAX
☎ 01422 240024 40 ⇔ ſ◌

**West End** Paddock Ln, Highroad Well HX2 0NT
☎ 01422 341878 & 363293
Semi-moorland course.
*18 holes, 5951yds, Par 69, SSS 69, Course record 62.*
**Visitors**    contact in advance.
**Societies**    must apply in writing to Secretary.
**Green Fees** £22 per day; £17 per round (£27/£20 weekends
& bank holidays).
**Facilities**    ⊗ ⵔ ⅃ ◪ ♀ 🛆 ☎ ſ David Rishworth.
**Leisure**    trolley for hire, putting green, practice area.
**Location**    W side of town centre off A646
**Hotel**    ★★★ 74%  Holdsworth House Hotel,
Holmfield, HALIFAX
☎ 01422 240024 40 ⇔ ſ◌

## HEBDEN BRIDGE                              Map 07 SD92

**Hebden Bridge** Mount Skip, Wadsworth HX7 8PH
☎ 01422 842896 & 842732
Moorland course with splendid views.
*9 holes, 5064yds, Par 68, SSS 65, Course record 64.*
*Club membership 300.*
**Visitors**    weekends after 4pm only.
**Societies**    apply in writing.
**Green Fees** £12 per day (£15 weekends).
**Facilities**    ♀ (evenings only) 🛆

**Leisure**    putting green.
**Location**   1.5m E off A6033
**Hotel**      ★★ 65%  Hebden Lodge Hotel, New Rd,
               HEBDEN BRIDGE ☎ 01422 845272 12 ⇋ ⓘ

## HOLYWELL GREEN                                     Map 07 SE01

**Halifax Bradley Hall** HX4 9AN ☎ 01422 374108
Moorland/parkland course, tightened by recent tree planting,
easy walking.
*18 holes, 6213yds, Par 70, SSS 70, Course record 65.*
*Club membership 500.*
**Visitors**     contact in advance.
**Societies**    must apply in writing.
**Green Fees** £20 per day; £16 per round (£35/£28 weekends
               & bank holidays).
**Facilities**   ⊗ ⅲ 🔔 ⚑ ♀ 📇 ⓘ Peter Wood.
**Leisure**      trolley for hire, putting green, practice area.
**Location**     S on A6112
**Hotel**        ★★ 70%  Rock Inn Hotel & Churchills,
                 HOLYWELL GREEN ☎ 01422 379721 18 ⇋ ⓘ

## HUDDERSFIELD                                       Map 07 SE11

**Bagden Hall** Wakefield Rd, Scissett HD8 9LE
☎ 01484 864839
Picturesque tree-lined course offering a challenging test of
golf for all levels of handicap. Lake guarded greens require
pin-point accuracy.
*9 holes, 3002, Par 56, SSS 55, Course record 60.*
*Club membership 150.*
**Visitors**     anytime.
**Societies**    company day packages available.
**Green Fees** £9 per 18 holes (£12 weekends).
**Facilities**   ⊗ ⅲ 🔔 ⚑ ♀ 📇 ⓘ Ian Darren.
**Leisure**      trolley for hire, putting green.
**Hotel**        ★★★ 69% Bagden Hall, Wakefield Rd,
                 Scissett, HUDDERSFIELD
                 ☎ 01484 865330 17 ⇋ ⓘ

**Bradley Park** Off Bradley Rd HD2 1PZ ☎ 01484 539988
Parkland course, challenging with good mix of long and short
holes. Also 14-bay floodlit driving range and 9-hole par 3
course, ideal for beginners. Superb views.
*18 holes, 6284yds, Par 70, SSS 70, Course record 65.*
*Club membership 300.*
**Visitors**     may book by phone for weekends from the
                 preceeding Thu.
**Societies**    welcome midweek only, apply in writing to
                 professional.
**Green Fees** £9.50 per round (£11.50 weekends).
**Facilities**   ⊗ ⅲ 🔔 ⚑ ♀ 📇 ⓘ Parnell E Reilly.
**Leisure**      motorised carts for hire, buggies for hire, trolley
                 for hire, driving range, putting greeen, practice
                 area, par 3 course.
**Location**     2.5m from junct 25 of M62
**Hotel**        ★★★ 65%  The George Hotel, St George's
                 Square, HUDDERSFIELD
                 ☎ 01484 515444 60 ⇋ ⓘ

**Crosland Heath** Felk Stile Rd, Crosland Heath HD4 7AF
☎ 01484 653216
Moorland course with fine views over valley.
*18 holes, 5972yds, Par 70, SSS 70.*
*Club membership 350.*

**Visitors**     welcome, but advisable to check with
                 professional. Must contact in advance and have
                 an introduction from own club.
**Societies**    must telephone in advance.
**Green Fees** not confirmed.
**Facilities**   ⚑ 📇 ⓘ Chris Gaunt.
**Location**     SW off A62
**Hotel**        ★★★ 65%  The George Hotel, St George's
                 Square, HUDDERSFIELD
                 ☎ 01484 515444 60 ⇋ ⓘ

**Huddersfield** Fixby Hall, Lightridge Rd, Fixby HD2 2EP
☎ 01484 426203
A testing heathland course of championship standard laid out
in 1891.
*18 holes, 6432yds, Par 71, SSS 71, Course record 64.*
*Club membership 500.*
**Visitors**     must book tee times with professional.
**Societies**    welcome Mon & Wed-Fri, prior arrangement
                 required.
**Green Fees** Summer:£40 per day; £30 per round (£50/£40
               weekends). Winter: £20 per day/round (£30
               weekends).
**Facilities**   ⊗ ⅲ 🔔 ⚑ ♀ 📇 ⓘ Paul Carman.
**Leisure**      trolley for hire, putting green, practice area.
**Location**     2m N off A641
**Hotel**        ★★★ 65%  The George Hotel, St George's
                 Square, HUDDERSFIELD
                 ☎ 01484 515444 60 ⇋ ⓘ

**Longley Park** Maple St, Off Somerset Rd HD5 9AX
☎ 01484 422304
Lowland course.
*9 holes, 5269yds, Par 66, SSS 66.*
*Club membership 440.*
**Visitors**     must contact in advance & have handicap
                 certificate, restricted Thu & weekends.
**Societies**    must apply in writing.
**Green Fees** not confirmed.
**Facilities**   ♀ 📇 ⓘ Paul Middleton.
**Leisure**      putting green,trolley hire.
**Location**     0.5m SE of town centre off A629
**Hotel**        ★★★ 65%  The George Hotel, St George's
                 Square, HUDDERSFIELD
                 ☎ 01484 515444 60 ⇋ ⓘ

## ILKLEY                                             Map 07 SE14

**Ben Rhydding** High Wood, Ben Rhydding LS29 8SB
☎ 01943 608759
Moorland/parkland course with splendid views over the
Wharfe valley.
*9 holes, 4711yds, Par 65, SSS 64, Course record 64.*
*Club membership 260.*
**Visitors**     contact in advance. May only play at weekend as
                 guest of member.
**Societies**    advance notice in writing. In view of limited
                 resources requests considered by monthly
                 committee meeting.
**Green Fees** £10 per day (£15 bank holidays).
**Facilities**   ♀ 📇
**Leisure**      putting green.
**Location**     SE side of town
**Hotel**        ★★ 74%  Rombalds Hotel & Restaurant, 11
                 West View, Wells Rd,  ILKLEY
                 ☎ 01943 603201 15 ⇋ ⓘ

**Ilkley** Nesfield Rd, Myddleton LS29 0BE
☎ 01943 600214
This beautiful parkland course is situated in Wharfedale and the Wharfe is a hazard on each of the first seven holes. In fact, the 3rd is laid out entirely on an island in the middle of the river.
*18 holes, 5953yds, Par 69, SSS 70, Course record 66.*
*Club membership 450.*
**Visitors** advisable to contact in advance.
**Societies** apply in writing.
**Green Fees** £35 per day/round (£40 weekends & bank holidays).
**Facilities** ⊗ ⅧⅬ ☕ ♀♨ 🏌️🏳️ John L Hammond.
**Leisure** fishing, trolley for hire, putting green, practice area.
**Location** W side of town centre off A65
**Hotel** ★★ 74% Rombalds Hotel & Restaurant, 11 West View, Wells Rd, ILKLEY
☎ 01943 603201 15 ⇔ 🐾

## KEIGHLEY        Map 07 SE04

**Branshaw** Branshaw Moor, Oakworth BD22 7ES
☎ 01535 643235
Picturesque moorland course with fairly narrow fairways and good greens. Extensive views.
*18 holes, 6000yds, Par 69, SSS 69.*
*Club membership 500.*
**Visitors** welcome most times, restrictions at weekends advisable to ring.
**Societies** apply in writing to the secretary.
**Green Fees** £15 per day; £12 per round (£20/£18 weekends).
**Facilities** ⊗ ⅧⅬ ☕ ♀♨ 🏳️🏌️
**Leisure** trolley for hire, practice area.
**Location** 2m SW on B6149
**Hotel** ★★ 66% Dalesgate Hotel, 406 Skipton Rd, Utley, KEIGHLEY ☎ 01535 664930 21 ⇔ 🐾

*Keighley* Howden Park, Utley BD20 6DH
☎ 01535 604778
Parkland course with good views down the Aire Valley.
*18 holes, 6149yds, Par 69, SSS 70, Course record 65.*
*Club membership 600.*
**Visitors** restricted Sat & Sun. Must contact in advance.
**Societies** must apply in advance.
**Green Fees** not confirmed.
**Facilities** ♀♨ 🏳️🏌️ Mike Bradley.
**Leisure** putting green, practice area, trolley hire.
**Location** 1m NW of town centre off B6143
**Hotel** ★★ 66% Dalesgate Hotel, 406 Skipton Rd, Utley, KEIGHLEY
☎ 01535 664930 21 ⇔ 🐾

## LEEDS        Map 08 SE33

**Brandon** Holywell Ln, Shadwell LS17 8EZ
☎ 0113 273 7471
An 18-hole links type course enjoying varying degrees of rough, water and sand hazards.
*18 holes, 3650yds, Par 56.*
**Visitors** pay & play course booking not usually necessary.
**Societies** telephone or write in advance.
**Green Fees** £5 per round (£6 weekend & bank holidays).

**Facilities** 🚩 🏠 🏳️
**Leisure** trolley for hire, putting, practice area.
**Hotel** ★★★ 79% Haley's Hotel & Restaurant, Shire Oak Rd, Headingley, LEEDS
☎ 0113 278 4446 22 ⇔ 🐾

*Gotts Park* Armley Ridge Rd LS12 2QX ☎ 0113 263 8232
Municipal parkland course; hilly and windy with narrow fairways. Some very steep hills to some greens. A challenging course requiring accuracy rather than length from the tees.
*18 holes, 4960yds, Par 65, SSS 64, Course record 63.*
*Club membership 300.*
**Visitors** no restrictions.
**Green Fees** not confirmed.
**Facilities** ♀ (evenings) 🏠 🏳️🏌️ John F Simpson.
**Location** 3m W of city centre off A647
**Hotel** ★★★★ 68% The Queen's, City Square, LEEDS ☎ 0113 243 1323 190 ⇔ 🐾

**Headingley** Back Church Ln, Adel LS16 8DW
☎ 0113 267 9573 0113 267 5100
An undulating course with a wealth of natural features offering fine views from higher ground. Its most striking hazard is the famous ravine at the 18th. Leeds's oldest course, founded in 1892.
*18 holes, 6298yds, Par 69, SSS 70, Course record 64.*
*Club membership 675.*
**Visitors** must contact in advance.
**Societies** must telephone in advance and confirm in writing.
**Green Fees** £30 per day; £25 per round (£36 per day/round weekends & bank holidays).
**Facilities** ⊗ ⅧⅬ ☕ ♀♨ 🏠 🏳️🏌️ Steven Foster.
**Leisure** trolley for hire, putting green, practice area.
**Location** 5.5m N of city centre off A660
**Hotel** B Forte Posthouse Leeds/Bradford, Leeds Rd, BRAMHOPE ☎ 0113 284 2911 124 ⇔ 🐾

*Horsforth* Layton Rise, Layton Rd, Horsforth LS18 5EX
☎ 0113 258 6819
Moorland course overlooking airport.
*18 holes, 6243yds, Par 71, SSS 70.*
*Club membership 750.*
**Visitors** restricted Sat & with member only Sun.
**Societies** must apply in writing.
**Green Fees** not confirmed.
**Facilities** ♀♨ 🏠 🏳️ Peter Scott.
**Leisure** putting green, trolley hire, practice area.
**Location** 6.5m NW of city centre off A65
**Hotel** B Forte Posthouse Leeds/Bradford, Leeds Rd, BRAMHOPE ☎ 0113 284 2911 124 ⇔ 🐾

*Leeds* Elmete Ln LS8 2LJ ☎ 0113 265 8775
Parkland course with pleasant views.
*18 holes, 6097yds, Par 69, SSS 69.*
*Club membership 600.*
**Visitors** with member only weekends, yellow tees only. Must contact in advance.
**Societies** must apply in writing.
**Green Fees** not confirmed.
**Facilities** ♀♨ 🏠 🏳️🏌️ Simon Longster.
**Location** 5m NE of city centre on A6120 off A58
**Hotel** ★★★ 79% Haley's Hotel & Restaurant, Shire Oak Rd, Headingley, LEEDS
☎ 0113 278 4446 22 ⇔ 🐾

**Leeds Golf Centre** Wike Ridge Ln, Shadwell LS17 9JW
☎ 0113 288 6000
Two courses - the 18-hole Wike Ridge, a traditional
heathland course designed by Donald Steele. The sand-based
greens are constructed to USGA specification and there are
an excellent variety of holes with some very challenging Par
5's. The 9-hole Oaks is complemented by a floodlit driving
range and other practice facilities. The course is the home of
the Leeds Golf Academy.
*Wike Ridge Course: 18 holes, 6482yds, Par 72, SSS 71.*
*Oaks: 9 holes, 1355yds, Par 27.*
*Club membership 500.*

| | |
|---|---|
| Visitors | no restrictions, telephone booking advisable. |
| Societies | tee reservation available in advance. |
| Green Fees | Wike Ridge: £20 per day; £12.50 per 18 holes, £6.50 per 9 holes. Oaks: £6.50 per 18 holes; £5 per 9 holes. |
| Facilities | ⊗ ℋ ⓛ ▬ ♀ ♉ 🏠 ♉ ℓ John Clapham. |
| Leisure | motorised carts for hire, buggies for hire, trolley for hire, driving range, putting green. |
| Location | 5m N,take A58 course on N side of Shadwell |
| Hotel | ★★★ 79% Haley's Hotel & Restaurant, Shire Oak Rd, Headingley, LEEDS ☎ 0113 278 4446 22 ⊨ ⋔ |

---

**Middleton Park Municipal** Middleton Park, Middleton LS10
3TN ☎ 0113 270 0449
Parkland course.
*18 holes, 5263yds, Par 68, SSS 66.*
*Club membership 300.*

| | |
|---|---|
| Visitors | may only use the club 6 times in one year. |
| Green Fees | not confirmed. |
| Facilities | ♀ ♉ 🏠 ♉ |
| Leisure | putting green,practice area. |
| Location | 3m S off A653 |
| Hotel | ★★★★ 68% The Queen's, City Square, LEEDS ☎ 0113 243 1323 190 ⊨ ⋔ |

---

**Moor Allerton** Coal Rd, Wike LS17 7EA
☎ 0113 266 1154
The Moor Allerton Club has 27 holes set in 220 acres of
undulating parkland, with magnificent views extending
across the Vale of York. The Championship Course was
designed by Robert Trent Jones, the famous American
course architect, and is the only course of his design in
the British Isles.
*Lakes Course: 18 holes, 6470yds, Par 71, SSS 72.*
*Blackmoor Course: 18 holes, 6673yds, Par 71, SSS 73.*
*High Course: 18 holes, 6841yds, Par 72, SSS 74.*
*Club membership 1200.*

| | |
|---|---|
| Visitors | contact professional (0113 266 5209). |
| Societies | must apply in advance. |
| Green Fees | £36 (£60 Sat, no casual visitors Sun). |
| Facilities | ⊗ ℋ ⓛ ▬ ♀ ♉ 🏠 ♉ ℓ Richard Lane. |
| Leisure | hard tennis courts, sauna, motorised carts for hire, buggies for hire, trolley for hire, covered driving range, putting green, practice field. |
| Location | 5.5m N of city centre on A61 |
| Hotel | ★★★ 63% Harewood Arms Hotel, Harrogate Rd, HAREWOOD ☎ 0113 288 6566 13 ⊨ ⋔Annexe11 ⊨ ⋔ |

---

**Moortown** Harrogate Rd, Alwoodley LS17 7DB
☎ 0113 268 6521
Championship course, tough but fair. Springy moorland
turf, natural hazards of heather, gorse and streams,
cunningly placed bunkers and immaculate greens.
*18 holes, 6782yds, Par 72, SSS 73, Course record 66.*
*Club membership 566.*

| | |
|---|---|
| Visitors | must contact in advance. |
| Societies | apply in writing in advance. |
| Green Fees | £45 per day; £40 per round (£50/£45 weekends). |
| Facilities | ⊗ ℋ ⓛ ▬ ♀ ♉ 🏠 ♉ ℓ Bryon Hutchinson. |
| Leisure | motorised carts for hire, buggies for hire, trolley for hire, putting green, practice area. |
| Location | 6m N of city centre |
| Hotel | ★★★ 63% Harewood Arms Hotel, Harrogate Rd, HAREWOOD ☎ 0113 288 6566 13 ⊨ ⋔Annexe11 ⊨ ⋔ |

---

**Oulton Park** Rothwell LS26 8EX ☎ 0113 282 3152
27-hole championship-length municipal course. Although
municipal, a dress rule is applied. 16-bay driving range.
*Main Course: 18 holes, 6450yds, Par 71, SSS 71, Course
record 65.*
*Short Course: 9 holes, 3250yds, Par 35, SSS 35.*
*Club membership 450.*

| | |
|---|---|
| Visitors | must apply 24hrs in advance. |
| Societies | Mon-Fri. Must contact in advance. |
| Green Fees | £20 per 18 holes; £7.50 per 9 holes. |
| Facilities | ⊗ ℋ ⓛ ▬ ♀ ♉ 🏠 ♉ ⌂ ℓ Stephen Gromett. |
| Leisure | heated indoor swimming pool, squash, sauna, solarium, gymnasium, motorised carts for hire, buggies for hire, trolley for hire, driving range. |
| Location | Junc 30 on M62 |
| Hotel | ★★★★★ 70% Oulton Hall Hotel, Rothwell Ln, Oulton, LEEDS ☎ 0113 282 1000 152 ⊨ ⋔ |

---

**Roundhay** Park Ln LS8 2EJ ☎ 0113 266 2695 & 249 2523
Attractive municipal parkland course, natural hazards, easy
walking.
*9 holes, 5223yds, Par 70, SSS 65, Course record 61.*
*Club membership 400.*

| | |
|---|---|
| Visitors | must contact professional at all times. |
| Societies | telephone or write to the professional. |
| Green Fees | £7 per round (£8 weekends & bank holidays). |
| Facilities | ♉ 🏠 ♉ ℓ James Pape. |
| Leisure | trolley for hire, putting green, practice area. |
| Location | 4m NE of city centre off A58 |
| Hotel | ★★★ 79% Haley's Hotel & Restaurant, Shire Oak Rd, Headingley, LEEDS ☎ 0113 278 4446 22 ⊨ ⋔ |

---

**Sand Moor** Alwoodley Ln LS17 7DJ ☎ 0113 268 5180
A beautiful, undulating course overlooking Lord
Harewood's estate and the Eccup Reservoir. The course
is wooded with some holes adjacent to water. The 12th is
perhaps the most difficult where the fairway falls away
towards the reservoir.
*18 holes, 6429yds, Par 71, SSS 71, Course record 63.*
*Club membership 553.*

| | |
|---|---|
| Visitors | restricted weekends & bank holidays. |
| Societies | must apply in advance. |
| Green Fees | not confirmed. |
| Facilities | ♀ ♉ 🏠 ℓ Peter Tupling. ▶ |

| Leisure | practice area. |
| Location | 5m N of city centre off A61 |
| Hotel | B Forte Posthouse Leeds/Bradford, Leeds Rd, BRAMHOPE ☎ 0113 284 2911 124 ⇌ ⋔ |

**South Leeds** Gipsy Ln, Beeston LS11 5TU
☎ 0113 277 1676
Parkland course, windy, hard walking, good views.
*18 holes, 5769yds, Par 69, SSS 68, Course record 64.*
*Club membership 500.*

| Visitors | probably difficult for weekend play. |
| Societies | must apply in advance. |
| Green Fees | £18 per round/day (£26 weekends). |
| Facilities | ⊗ ⋔ ⓑ ⚑ ♀ ♨ 🏠 ꞁ Mike Lewis. |
| Leisure | trolley for hire, putting green, practice area. |
| Location | 3m S of city centre off A653 |
| Hotel | ★★★★ 68% The Queen's, City Square, LEEDS ☎ 0113 243 1323 190 ⇌ ⋔ |

*Temple Newsam* Temple-Newsam Rd LS15 0LN
☎ 0113 264 5624
Two parkland courses. Testing long 13th (563 yds) on second course.
*Lord Irwin: 18 holes, 6460yds, Par 69, SSS 71.*
*Lady Dorothy: 18 holes, 6276yds, Par 70, SSS 70.*
*Club membership 520.*

| Visitors | no restrictions. |
| Societies | must apply in advance. |
| Green Fees | not confirmed. |
| Facilities | ♀ ♨ 🏠 ꞁ ꞁ David Bulmer. |
| Location | 3.5m E of city centre off A63 |
| Hotel | ★★★ 79% Haley's Hotel & Restaurant, Shire Oak Rd, Headingley, LEEDS ☎ 0113 278 4446 22 ⇌ ⋔ |

## MARSDEN            Map 07 SE01

*Marsden* Mount Rd, Hemplow HD7 6NN
☎ 01484 844253
Moorland course with good views, natural hazards, windy.
*9 holes, 5702yds, Par 68, SSS 68.*
*Club membership 200.*

| Visitors | must play with member at weekends. |
| Societies | Mon-Fri; must contact in advance. |
| Green Fees | not confirmed. |
| Facilities | ♀ ♨ 🏠 ꞁ A J Bickerdike. |
| Leisure | hard tennis courts. |
| Location | S side off A62 |
| Hotel | ★★★ 62% Briar Court Hotel, Halifax Rd, Birchencliffe, HUDDERSFIELD ☎ 01484 519902 47 ⇌ ⋔ |

## MELTHAM            Map 07 SE01

*Meltham* Thick Hollins Hall HD7 3DQ
☎ 01484 850227 & 851521
Parkland course with good views. Testing 548 yd, 13th hole (par 5).
*18 holes, 6305yds, Par 70, SSS 70, Course record 65.*
*Club membership 500.*

| Visitors | may not play Sat & Wed (Ladies Day), desirable to contact professional in advance. |
| Societies | must apply in writing. |

**Green Fees** £20 per day (£25 weekends & bank holidays).

| Facilities | ⊗ ⋔ ⓑ ⚑ ♀ ♨ 🏠 ꞁ ꞁ Paul Davies. |
| Leisure | trolley for hire, putting green, practice area. |
| Location | SE side of village off B6107 |
| Hotel | ★★★ 65% The George Hotel, St George's Square, HUDDERSFIELD ☎ 01484 515444 60 ⇌ ⋔ |

## MIRFIELD            Map 08 SE21

**Dewsbury District** Sands Ln WF14 8HJ
☎ 01924 492399
Heathland/parkland course with panoramic view from top, hard walking. Ponds in middle of 3rd fairway, left of 5th green and 17th green.
*18 holes, 6267yds, Par 71, SSS 71.*
*Club membership 650.*

| Visitors | weekends after 1pm, on non competition days. Telephone in advance. |
| Societies | telephone bookings. |
| Green Fees | £20 per day; £16 per round (£18 per round weekends after 1pm). |
| Facilities | ⊗ ⋔ ⓑ ⚑ ♀ ♨ 🏠 ꞁ Nigel P Hirst. |
| Leisure | trolley for hire, putting green, practice area. |
| Location | 1m S off A644 |
| Hotel | ★★★ 65% The George Hotel, St George's Square, HUDDERSFIELD ☎ 01484 515444 60 ⇌ ⋔ |

## MORLEY            Map 08 SE22

**Howley Hall** Scotchman Ln LS27 0NX
☎ 01924 478417 & 473852
Parkland course with easy walking and good views.
*18 holes, 6058yds, Par 71, SSS 69.*
*Club membership 700.*

| Visitors | standard course only, may not play Sat. |
| Societies | contact for details. |
| Green Fees | £25 per day; £21 per round (£30 day/round Sun & bank holidays). |
| Facilities | ⊗ ⋔ ⓑ ⚑ ♀ ♨ 🏠 ꞁ ꞁ Stephen Spinks. |
| Leisure | motorised carts for hire, trolley for hire, putting green, practice area. |
| Location | 1.5m S on B6123 |
| Hotel | ★★ 66% Alder House Hotel, Towngate Rd, off Healey Ln, BATLEY ☎ 01924 444777 22rm(21 ⇌ ⋔) |

## NORMANTON            Map 08 SE32

*Normanton* Snydale Rd WF6 1PN ☎ 01924 892943
A pleasant, flat course with tight fairways in places and an internal out-of-bounds requiring accuracy.
*9 holes, 5288yds, Par 66, SSS 66.*
*Club membership 250.*

| Visitors | may not play on Sun. |
| Societies | mid-week only. |
| Green Fees | not confirmed. |
| Facilities | ♀ ♨ 🏠 ꞁ ꞁ Martin Evans. |
| Location | 0.5m SE on B6133 |
| Hotel | ★★★ 68% Swallow Hotel, Queens St, WAKEFIELD ☎ 01924 372111 64 ⇌ ⋔ |

## OSSETT                                          Map 08 SE22

**Low Laithes** Parkmill Ln, Flushdyke WF5 9AP
☎ 01924 274667
Testing parkland course.
*18 holes, 6463yds, Par 72, SSS 71, Course record 65.*
*Club membership 600.*
**Visitors**      may not play weekends and bank holidays. Must
                  contact in advance.
**Societies**     by prior arrangement.
**Green Fees**    £22 per day; £18 per round.
**Facilities**    ⊗ ⅏ ⅃ ⬛ ♀ 🔥 📧 ℓ Paul Browning.
**Leisure**       trolley for hire, putting green, practice area.
**Location**      1.5m SE off A128
**Hotel**         B Forte Posthouse Northampton/Rugby, CRICK
                  ☎ 01788 822101 88 ⇄ 🐦

## OTLEY                                           Map 08 SE24

**Otley** Off West Busk Ln LS21 3NG
☎ 01943 465329
An expansive course with magnificent views across
Wharfedale. It is well-wooded with streams crossing the
fairway. The 4th is a fine hole which generally needs two
woods to reach the plateau green. The 17th is a good
short hole.
*18 holes, 6225yds, Par 70, SSS 70, Course record 66.*
*Club membership 700.*
**Visitors**      telephone to check tee time.
**Societies**     telephone enquiries welcome, bookings in
                  writing.
**Green Fees**    £30 per 36 holes; £24 per 27 holes (£35/£30
                  weekends and bank holidays).
**Facilities**    ⊗ ⅏ ⅃ ⬛ ♀ 🔥 📧 ʏ ℓ Simon Poot.
**Leisure**       trolley for hire, putting green, practice area.
**Location**      1.5m SW off A6038
**Hotel**         B Forte Posthouse Leeds/Bradford, Leeds
                  Rd, BRAMHOPE
                  ☎ 0113 284 2911 124 ⇄ 🐦

## OUTLANE                                         Map 07 SE01

**Outlane** Slack Ln HD3 3YL ☎ 01422 374762
Moorland course.
*18 holes, 6015yds, Par 71, SSS 70, Course record 67.*
*Club membership 600.*
**Visitors**      telephone in advance, must be correctly
                  equipped and attired.
**Societies**     apply in writing.
**Green Fees**    £18 per day (£27 weekends & bank holidays).
**Facilities**    ⊗ ⅏ ⅃ ⬛ ♀ 🔥 📧 ʏ ℓ David Chapman.
**Leisure**       trolley for hire, putting green, practice area.
**Location**      S side of village off A640
**Hotel**         ★★★ 69%  Old Golf House Hotel, New Hey
                  Rd, Outlane, HUDDERSFIELD
                  ☎ 01422 379311 50 ⇄ 🐦

## PONTEFRACT                                      Map 08 SE42

*Mid Yorkshire* Havercroft Ln, Darrington WF8 3BP
☎ 01977 704522
An 18-hole championship-standard course opened in 1992.
*18 holes, 6500yds, Par 72, SSS 72, Course record 68.*
*Club membership 500.*

**Visitors**      must contact in advance, with member only at
                  weekends.
**Societies**     apply in writing to the secretary.
**Green Fees**    not confirmed.
**Facilities**    ♀ 🔥 📧 ʏ 📧 ℓ Peter Scott.
**Leisure**       golf academy with 28 driving bays.
**Location**      2m SE
**Hotel**         ★★★ 68%  Wentbridge House Hotel,
                  WENTBRIDGE ☎ 01977 620444 16 ⇄ 🐦

*Pontefract & District* Park Ln WF8 4QS ☎ 01977 792241
Parkland course.
*18 holes, 6227yds, Par 72, SSS 70.*
*Club membership 800.*
**Visitors**      welcome except Wed & weekends. Must contact
                  in advance and have a handicap certificate.
**Societies**     welcome except Wed & weekends.
**Green Fees**    not confirmed.
**Facilities**    ♀ 🔥 📧 ℓ Nick Newman.
**Leisure**       putting green, trolley hire, practice area.
**Location**      1.5m W on B6134
**Hotel**         ★★★ 68%  Wentbridge House Hotel,
                  WENTBRIDGE ☎ 01977 620444 16 ⇄ 🐦

## PUDSEY                                          Map 08 SE23

**Calverley** Woodhall Ln LS28 5QY ☎ 0113 256 9244
Two parkland courses on top of a hill. The course was
established 10 years ago and has a few water hazards and
some bunkers.
*18 holes, 5567yds, Par 68, SSS 67, Course record 67.*
*Club membership 572.*
**Visitors**      must contact pro shop in advance.
**Societies**     contact in writing or telephone.
**Green Fees**    £18 per day; £12 per round (£17 per round
                  weekends). 9 hole course £6 at all times.
**Facilities**    ⊗ ⅏ ⅃ ⬛ ♀ 🔥 📧 ʏ ℓ Derek Johnson.
**Leisure**       trolley for hire, putting green, practice area.
**Hotel**         ★★ 66%  Park Drive Hotel, 12 Park Dr,
                  BRADFORD ☎ 01274 480194 11 ⇄ 🐦

**Fulneck** LS28 8NT ☎ 0113 256 5191
Picturesque, hilly parkland course. Compact but strenuous.
*9 holes, 5456yds, Par 66, SSS 67, Course record 65.*
*Club membership 250.*
**Visitors**      with member only weekends & bank holidays.
**Societies**     must apply in writing.
**Green Fees**    £14 per day.
**Facilities**    ⅃ ⬛ ♀ 🔥
**Leisure**       putting green.
**Location**      S side of town centre
**Hotel**         ★★★ 64%  Novotel, Merrydale Rd,
                  BRADFORD ☎ 01274 683683 127 ⇄ 🐦

**Woodhall Hills** Calverley LS28 5UN
☎ 0113 255 4594 & 256 2857
Meadowland course, prevailing SW winds, fairly hard
walking. Testing holes: 8th, 377 yd (par 4); 14th,
206 yd (par 3).
*18 holes, 6102yds, Par 71, SSS 69, Course record 63.*
*Club membership 570.*
**Visitors**      any day advise secretary/professional in
                  advance.
**Societies**     must apply in writing.
**Green Fees**    £20.50 per day/round (£25.50 weekends & bank
                  holidays).                                    ▶

**Facilities** ⊗ ⅢⓀ♨♥♀⚒🏠( Warren Lockett.
**Leisure** trolley for hire, putting green, practice area.
**Location** 2.5m NW off A647
**Hotel** ★★ 66% Park Drive Hotel, 12 Park Dr,
BRADFORD ☎ 01274 480194 11 ⇥ 🐾

## RAWDON            Map 08 SE23

*Rawdon Golf & Lawn Tennis Club* Buckstone Dr LS19 6BD
☎ 0113 250 6040
Undulating parkland course.
*9 holes, 5980yds, Par 72, SSS 69.*
*Club membership 700.*
**Visitors** must contact in advance & have handicap
certificate. With member only at weekends.
**Societies** must contact in advance.
**Green Fees** not confirmed.
**Facilities** ♀⚒🏠( Syd Wheldon.
**Leisure** hard and grass tennis courts.
**Location** S side of town off A65
**Hotel** ★★★ 65% Apperley Manor, Apperley Ln,
Apperley Bridge, BRADFORD
☎ 0113 250 5626 13 ⇥ 🐾

## RIDDLESDEN        Map 07 SE04

*Riddlesden* Howden Rough BD20 5QN ☎ 01535 602148
Undulating moorland course with prevailing west winds,
some hard walking and beautiful views. Ten par 3 holes and
spectacular 6th and 15th holes played over old quarry sites.
*18 holes, 4295yds, Par 63, SSS 61.*
*Club membership 350.*
**Visitors** restricted before 2pm weekends.
**Societies** apply by telephone or in writing.
**Green Fees** £10 per round (£15 weekends).
**Facilities** ⊗Ⓚ♥♀⚒
**Location** 1m NW
**Hotel** ★★ 66% Dalesgate Hotel, 406 Skipton Rd,
Utley, KEIGHLEY
☎ 01535 664930 21 ⇥ 🐾

## SCARCROFT         Map 08 SE34

*Scarcroft* Syke Ln LS14 3BQ ☎ 0113 289 2311
Undulating parkland course with prevailing west wind and
easy walking.
*18 holes, 6031yds, Par 71, SSS 69.*
*Club membership 667.*
**Visitors** must contact in advance.
**Societies** must contact in advance.
**Green Fees** not confirmed.
**Facilities** ♀⚒🏠🧵( Darren Tear.
**Leisure** putting green,practice area,trolley hire.
**Location** 0.5m N of village off A58
**Hotel** ★★★ 63% Harewood Arms Hotel, Harrogate
Rd, HAREWOOD
☎ 0113 288 6566 13 ⇥ 🐾Annexe11 ⇥ 🐾

## SHIPLEY           Map 07 SE13

*Northcliffe* High Bank Ln BD18 4LJ
☎ 01274 596731 & 587193
Parkland course with magnificent views of moors. Testing 1st
hole (18th green 100 feet below tee).

*18 holes, 6104yds, Par 71, SSS 69, Course record 65.*
*Club membership 700.*
**Visitors** no restrictions.
**Societies** book via secretary in advance, weekdays only.
**Green Fees** on application.
**Facilities** ⊗Ⅲ Ⓚ♥♀⚒🏠🧵( M Hillas.
**Leisure** motorised carts for hire, trolley for hire, putting
green, practice area.
**Location** 1.25m SW of Shipley, off A650
**Hotel** ★★★ 70% Hollins Hall, Hollins Hill, Baildon,
SHIPLEY ☎ 01274 530053 59 ⇥ 🐾

## SILSDEN           Map 07 SE04

*Silsden* High Brunthwaite BD20 0NH
☎ 01535 652998
Tight downland course which can be windy. Good views of
the Aire Valley.
*14 holes, 4870yds, Par 65, SSS 64, Course record 61.*
*Club membership 300.*
**Visitors** may not play before 11am on Sun.
**Societies** must apply in advance.
**Green Fees** not confirmed.
**Facilities** ♀⚒
**Location** 1m E
**Hotel** ★★ 66% Dalesgate Hotel, 406 Skipton Rd,
Utley, KEIGHLEY
☎ 01535 664930 21 ⇥ 🐾

## SOWERBY          Map 07 SE02

*Ryburn* The Shaw, Norland HX6 3QP
☎ 01422 831355
Moorland course, easy walking.
*9 holes, 4984yds, Par 66, SSS 64, Course record 64.*
*Club membership 200.*
**Visitors** must contact in advance.
**Societies** apply in writing.
**Green Fees** not confirmed.
**Facilities** ⊗Ⅲ Ⓚ♥♀⚒
**Location** 1m S of Sowerby Bridge off A58
**Hotel** ★★ 69% The Hobbit Hotel, Hob Ln, Norland,
SOWERBY BRIDGE
☎ 01422 832202 17 ⇥ 🐾Annexe5 ⇥ 🐾

## TODMORDEN        Map 07 SD92

*Todmorden* Rive Rocks, Cross Stone Rd OL14 8RD
☎ 01706 812986
Pleasant moorland course.
*9 holes, 5382yds, Par 68, SSS 68, Course record 67.*
*Club membership 240.*
**Visitors** restricted Thu & weekends. Advisable to contact
in advance.
**Societies** must apply in writing.
**Green Fees** £15 per day (£20 weekends & bank holidays).
**Facilities** ⊗ by prior arrangement Ⅲ by prior arrangement
Ⓚ♥♀⚒
**Leisure** putting green, practice area.
**Location** NE off A646
**Hotel** ★★★⚑ 64% Scaitcliffe Hall, Burnley Rd,
TODMORDEN
☎ 01706 818888 13 ⇥ 🐾

## WAKEFIELD      Map 08 SE32

**City of Wakefield** Lupset Park, Horbury Rd WF2 8QS
☎ 01924 367442 & 360282
Parkland course.
*18 holes, 6319yds, Par 72, SSS 70, Course record 67.*
*Club membership 600.*
**Visitors**    restricted weekends.
**Societies**    must apply in advance to stewardess 01924
367242.
**Green Fees** £7.90 per round (£9.90 weekends and bank
holidays).
**Facilities**    ⊗ ⅧⓁ ☐ ♀ ♨ 🏠 ✦ ⓒ Roger Holland.
**Leisure**    trolley for hire, putting green, practice area.
**Location**    1.5m W of city centre on A642
**Hotel**    B Forte Posthouse Wakefield, Queen's Dr,
Ossett, WAKEFIELD
☎ 01924 276388 99 ⊨ ⓡ

**Painthorpe House** Painthorpe Ln, Painthorpe, Crigglestone
WF4 3HE ☎ 01924 274527 & 255083
Undulating meadowland course, easy walking.
*9 holes, 4544yds, Par 62, SSS 62, Course record 64.*
*Club membership 150.*
**Visitors**    no visitors Sun.
**Societies**    must telephone in advance.
**Green Fees** £5 per 18 holes (£8 Sat & bank holidays).
**Facilities**    ⊗ ⅧⓁ ☐ ♀ ♨
**Leisure**    putting green, practice area.
**Location**    2m S off A636
**Hotel**    B Forte Posthouse Wakefield, Queen's Dr, Ossett,
WAKEFIELD ☎ 01924 276388 99 ⊨ ⓡ

**Wakefield** Woodthorpe Ln, Sandal WF2 6JH
☎ 01924 258778
A well-sheltered meadowland/heath course with easy walking
and good views.
*18 holes, 6613yds, Par 72, SSS 72, Course record 66.*
*Club membership 540.*
**Visitors**    contact must be made in advance.
**Societies**    must apply in writing.
**Green Fees** £27.50 per day; £22 per round (£30 weekends &
bank holidays).
**Facilities**    ⊗ ⅧⓁ ☐ ♀ ♨ 🏠 ⓒ Ian M Wright.
**Leisure**    trolley for hire, putting green, practice area.
**Location**    3m S off A61
**Hotel**    B Forte Posthouse Wakefield, Queen's Dr, Ossett,
WAKEFIELD ☎ 01924 276388 99 ⊨ ⓡ

## WETHERBY      Map 08 SE44

**Wetherby** Linton Ln LS22 4JF
☎ 01937 580089
Parkland course with fine views.
*18 holes, 6235yds, Par 71, SSS 70, Course record 66.*
*Club membership 650.*
**Visitors**    may not play Mon & Tues morning.
**Societies**    apply in writing or telephone in advance.
**Green Fees** £28 per day; £23 per round (£34 per day/round
weekends).
**Facilities**    ⊗ ⅧⓁ ☐ ♀ ♨ 🏠 ⓒ D Padgett.
**Leisure**    trolley for hire, putting green, practice area.
**Location**    1m W off A661
**Hotel**    ★★★ 57% Jarvis Wetherby Hotel, Leeds Rd,
WETHERBY ☎ 01937 583881 72 ⊨ ⓡ

# CHANNEL ISLANDS

# ALDERNEY

## ALDERNEY      Map 16

**Alderney** Route des Carrieres GY9 3YD
☎ 01481 822835
Undulating seaside course with sea on all sides and offering
magnificent views from its high tees and greens. Course
designed by Frank Pennink.
*9 holes, 5006yds, Par 64, SSS 65, Course record 65.*
*Club membership 400.*
**Visitors**    may not play before 10am at weekends.
Advisable to contact in advance.
**Societies**    must contact in advance.
**Green Fees** £12.50 per day (£17.50 weekends and bank
holidays).
**Facilities**    Ⓛ ☐ ♀ ♨ ✦
**Leisure**    trolley for hire, putting green, practice area,
bowling green.
**Location**    1m E of St Annes
**Hotel**    ★★ 73% Inchalla Hotel, St Anne,
ALDERNEY
☎ 01481 823220 10 ⊨ ⓡ

# GUERNSEY

## L'ANCRESSE VALE      Map 16

**Royal Guernsey** GY3 5BY
☎ 01481 46523
Not quite as old as its neighbour Royal Jersey, Royal
Guernsey is a sporting course which was re-designed
after World War II by Mackenzie Ross, who has many
fine courses to his credit. It is a pleasant links, well-
maintained, and administered by the States of Guernsey
in the form of the States Tourist Committee. The 8th
hole, a good par 4, requires an accurate second shot to the
green set amongst the gorse and thick rough. The 18th,
with lively tees, needs a strong shot to reach the green
well down below. The course is windy, with hard
walking. There is a junior section.
*18 holes, 6206yds, Par 70, SSS 70, Course record 64.*
*Club membership 934.*
**Visitors**    must have a handicap certificate; may not
play on Thu, Sat afternoons & Sun.
**Green Fees** £28 per day.
**Facilities**    ⊗ ⅧⓁ ☐ ♀ ♨ 🏠 ✦ ⓒ Norman Wood.
**Leisure**    trolley for hire, driving range, putting green.
**Location**    3m N of St Peter Port
**Hotel**    ★★★★ 71% St Pierre Park Hotel, Rohais,
ST PETER PORT
☎ 01481 728282 135 ⊨ ⓡ

## St Peter Port  Map 16

**St Pierre Park Golf Club** Rohais GY1 1FD
☎ 01481 728282
Par 3 parkland course with delightful setting, with lakes, streams and many tricky holes.
*9 holes, 2511yds, Par 54, SSS 50.*
*Club membership 200.*
**Visitors** contact in advance.
**Societies** must contact in advance.
**Green Fees** £14 per 18 holes (£16 weekends). Prices under review..
**Facilities** ⊗ ⫲ ⓛ ⬛ ♀ ⚘ 🏠 ⚑ 🍴
**Leisure** hard tennis courts, heated indoor swimming pool, sauna, solarium, gymnasium, trolley for hire, driving range, croquet, crazy golf, snooker.
**Location** 1m W off Rohais Rd
**Hotel** ★★★★ 71% St Pierre Park Hotel, Rohais, ST PETER PORT ☎ 01481 728282 135 ⇄ ᠺ

---

# JERSEY

---

## Grouville  Map 16

**Royal Jersey** JE3 9BD ☎ 01534 854416
A seaside links, historic because of its age: its centenary was celebrated in 1978. It is also famous for the fact that Britain's greatest golfer, Harry Vardon, was born in a little cottage on the edge of the course and learned his golf here.
*18 holes, 6059yds, Par 70, SSS 70, Course record 64.*
*Club membership 1364.*
**Visitors** restricted to 10am-noon & 2pm-4pm.
**Societies** welcome Mon-Fri. Must apply in writing.
**Green Fees** not confirmed.
**Facilities** ♀ ⚘ 🏠 ⚑ 🍴 Tommy Horton.
**Leisure** putting,trolley hire,practice area.
**Location** 4m E of St Helier off coast rd
**Hotel** ★★★ 65% Old Court House Hotel, GOREY ☎ 01534 854444 58 ⇄ ᠺ

## La Moye  Map 16

**La Moye** La Route Orange JE3 8GQ ☎ 01534 43401
Seaside championship links course (venue for the Jersey Open) situated in an exposed position on the south western corner of the island overlooking St Ouens Bay. Offers spectacular views, two start points, full course all year - no temporary greens.
*18 holes, 6664yds, Par 72, SSS 72, Course record 69.*
*Club membership 1300.*
**Visitors** must contact in advance.
**Societies** apply in writing.
**Green Fees** £40 per round (£45 weekends).
**Facilities** ⊗ ⫲ ⓛ ⬛ ⚘ 🏠 🍴 Mike Deeley.
**Leisure** practice ground.
**Location** W side of village off A13
**Hotel** ★★★★ 75% The Atlantic Hotel, La Moye, ST BRELADE ☎ 01534 44101 50 ⇄ ᠺ

## St Clement  Map 16

**St Clement** Jersey Recreation Grounds JE2 6PN
☎ 01534 21938
Very tight moorland course. Holes cross over fairways, impossible to play to scratch. Suitable for middle to high handicaps.
*9 holes, 2244yds, Par 30.*
*Club membership 500.*
**Visitors** must contact in advance.
**Green Fees** not confirmed.
**Facilities** ⚘
**Leisure** hard tennis courts.
**Location** E side of St Helier on A5
**Hotel** ★★★★(red)♨ Longueville Manor Hotel, ST SAVIOUR ☎ 01534 25501 32 ⇄ ᠺ

---

## St Ouen  Map 16

**Les Mielles Golf & Country Club** JE3 7PQ
☎ 01534 482787
Challenging American-style parkland course with bent grass greens, dwarf rye fairways and picturesque ponds situated in the Island's largest conservation area within St Ouen's Bay.
*18 holes, 5633yds, Par 70, SSS 68, Course record 62.*
*Club membership 1500.*
**Visitors** welcome all times, prior booking recommended.
**Societies** write in advance to avoid disappointment.
**Green Fees** £25 per day; £17 per 18 holes; £11.50 per 9 holes (£27.50/£19/£12.50 weekends).
**Facilities** ⊗ ⫲ ⓛ ⬛ ♀ ⚘ 🏠 ⚑ 🍴 Jeremy Philips.
**Leisure** motorised carts for hire, buggies for hire, trolley for hire, driving range, putting green, practice area.
**Hotel** ★★★ 67% Mermaid Hotel, ST PETER ☎ 01534 41255 68 ⇄ ᠺ

---

# ISLE OF MAN

---

## Castletown  Map 06 SC26

**Castletown Golf Links** Fort Island, Derbyhaven 1M9 1VA
☎ 01624 822201
Set on the Langness Peninsula, this superb Championship course is surrounded on three sides by the sea, and holds many surprises from its Championship tees. The hotel offers many leisure facilities.
*18 holes, 6750yds, Par 72, SSS 72, Course record 65.*
*Club membership 600.*
**Visitors** contact in advance. Sat reserved for hotel residents.
**Societies** must telephone in advance.
**Green Fees** £20 per day (£25 weekends & bank holidays).
**Facilities** ⊗ ⫲ ⓛ ⬛ ♀ ⚘ 🏠 ⚑ 🍴 Murray Crowe.
**Leisure** heated indoor swimming pool, fishing, sauna, solarium, motorised carts for hire, buggies for hire, trolley for hire, putting green, practice area.
**Hotel** ★★★ 67% Castletown Golf Links Hotel, Fort Island, CASTLETOWN ☎ 01624 822201 58 ⇄ ᠺ

## DOUGLAS                                    Map 06 SC37

*Douglas* IM2 1AE ☎ 01624 675952
Hilly, parkland and moorland course under the control of
Douglas Corporation.
*18 holes, 6080yds, Par 69, SSS 68.*
*Club membership 430.*
**Visitors** no restrictions.
**Societies** must apply in writing.
**Green Fees** not confirmed.
**Facilities** ♀⊥🛠🖚🏌️🍴 K Parry.
**Leisure** trolley hire.
**Location** 1m W off A1
**Hotel** ★★★ 72% The Empress Hotel, Central
Promenade, DOUGLAS
☎ 01624 661155 102 ⇆ 🐾

**Mount Murray Hotel & Country Club** Mount Murray,
Santon IM4 2HT ☎ 01624 661111
A moorland course with fantastic views of the island, the
course has some serious challenges. The 7th hole is a Par 5
but with 612yd drive, it is the longest on the island. The 18th
is 538yds ensuring there is no let up, especially as it has to
carry over a lake in front of the hotel.
*18 holes, 6664yds, Par 72, SSS 72.*
*Club membership 220.*
**Visitors** no restrictions.
**Societies** telephone in advance.
**Green Fees** £18 per day/round (£24 weekends).
**Facilities** ⊗🎚🍴♀⊥🖚🏌️🍴 Andrew Dyson.
**Leisure** hard tennis courts, heated indoor swimming
pool, squash, sauna, gymnasium, motorised carts
for hire, buggies for hire, trolley for hire, driving
range, putting green, practice area, crown green
bowling.
**Location** 4.5m W, on north side of A5
**Hotel** ★★★★ 71% Mount Murray Hotel & Country
Club, Santon, DOUGLAS
☎ 01624 661111 89 ⇆ 🐾

## ONCHAN                                    Map 06 SC47

*King Edward Bay Golf & Country Club* Howstrake,
Groudle Rd IM3 2JR ☎ 01624 620430
Club plays over King Edward Bay course. Hilly seaside links
course with natural hazards and good views.
*18 holes, 5457yds, Par 67, SSS 66.*
*Club membership 470.*
**Visitors** must have a handicap certificate.
**Societies** must contact in advance.
**Green Fees** not confirmed.
**Facilities** ♀⊥🖚🏌️🍴 Donald Jones.
**Leisure** sauna, solarium, caddy cars for hire, also buggies.
**Location** E side of town off A11
**Hotel** ★★★ 67% Sefton Hotel, Harris Promenade,
DOUGLAS ☎ 01624 626011 79 ⇆

## PEEL                                    Map 06 SC28

Peel Rheast Ln IM5 1BG ☎ 01624 842227
Moorland course, with natural hazards and easy walking.
Good views. 11th hole is a par 4, dog-leg.
*18 holes, 5914yds, Par 69, SSS 68.*
*Club membership 856.*

**Visitors** limited availability weekends.
**Societies** apply in writing.
**Green Fees** £15 per day (£18 weekends & bank holidays).
**Facilities** ⊗🎚🍴♀⊥🖚🍴 Murray Crowe.
**Leisure** trolley for hire, putting green, practice area.
**Location** SE side of town centre on A1
**Hotel** ★★★ 72% The Empress Hotel, Central
Promenade, DOUGLAS
☎ 01624 661155 102 ⇆ 🐾

## PORT ERIN                                    Map 06 SC16

**Rowany** Rowany Dr IM9 6LN
☎ 01624 834108 or 834072
Undulating seaside course with testing later holes.
*18 holes, 5840yds, Par 70, SSS 69, Course record 66.*
*Club membership 550.*
**Visitors** must contact in advance.
**Societies** telephone in advance.
**Green Fees** £15 per day; £10 per round.
**Facilities** ⊗🎚🍴♀⊥🖚🏌️
**Leisure** motorised carts for hire, trolley for hire, putting
green, practice area.
**Location** N side of village off A32
**Hotel** ★★★ 66% Cherry Orchard Hotel, Bridson St,
PORT ERIN ☎ 01624 833811 31 ⇆ 🐾

## PORT ST MARY                                    Map 06 SC26

**Port St Mary** Kallow Point Rd
☎ 01624 834932
Slightly hilly course with beautiful scenic views over Port St
Mary and the Irish Sea.
*9 holes, 5418yds, Par 68, SSS 66, Course record 62.*
*Club membership 432.*
**Visitors** anytime except between 8-10.30 weekends.
**Societies** contact for details.
**Green Fees** £9 daily (£11 weekends).
**Facilities** ⊗🎚🍴♀⊥🖚🏌️
**Leisure** hard tennis courts, trolley for hire, putting green,
practice area.
**Hotel** ★★★ 66% Cherry Orchard Hotel, Bridson St,
PORT ERIN
☎ 01624 833811 31 ⇆ 🐾

## RAMSEY                                    Map 06 SC49

**Ramsey** Brookfield IM8 2AH
☎ 01624 812244 & 813365
Parkland course, with easy walking. Windy. Good views.
Testing holes: 1st, par 5; 18th, par 3.
*18 holes, 5960yds, Par 70, SSS 69, Course record 64.*
*Club membership 960.*
**Visitors** contact in advance, visitors may not play before
10am weekdays.
**Societies** must apply in advance.
**Green Fees** £16 (£20 weekends & bank holidays).
**Facilities** ⊗🎚🍴♀⊥🖚🍴 Calum Wilson.
**Leisure** trolley for hire, putting green, practice area.
**Location** SW side of town
**Hotel** ★★★ 72% The Empress Hotel, Central
Promenade, DOUGLAS
☎ 01624 661155 102 ⇆ 🐾

# SCOTLAND

*"Golf's big prize is an invitation to play*
*Royal Dornoch, or Muirfield!"*

Most true golfers, by the nature of things, must have had at least one drop of Scottish blood bestowed on them. How else can you account for the quickening of the pulse as the border is reached? Some of us feel that if we haven't been to Scotland at least once in the year, irritation sets in. The lure of the people, the tartan, heather and the history is compelling. No wonder Keith Prowse, the travel agents, now offer a special package to pilgrims wishing to tee off at St Andrews.

Although this northern city, made of grey stone and exposed to a harsh winter climate, is the acknowledged Home of Golf, the Old Course there is overplayed and deserves Sundays off, which it duly gets! Undoubtedly a monument to our royal and ancient game, newcomers depart with private views about the experience they enjoyed, and assess the value of the £60 green fee they paid to walk across those hallowed humps and hollows.

But Scotland, wall-to-wall with courses and seaside links of incredible calibre, is sadly taken for granted by locals who seem not to appreciate what they have. Again, we must nominate favourites or mention known jewels, such as the Royal Dornoch, the second oldest place where golf began, with a club that opened in 1880. Senior professional John Panton, once dubbed the laird of the Highlands, rates this course, and Muirfield (near Edinburgh) among Scotland's finest. Receiving an invitation to play either is something akin to winning golf's premier prize

## SWEET-SMELLING PINE

If planning a golf invasion of Scotland my advice would be to seek out the established tests, even though some speak highly of newer creations, designed by others than ancient Britons. When I teed off at Gleneagles with the late Henry Longhurst for a pre-dinner friendly, there was nowhere else in the world to compare. Affectionately called 'The Glen', the pure air is filled with sweet-smelling pine, heather, bracken and wildlife abounds, and the scenery is breathtaking.

Good motor transport is essential to prise open the best of Scotland. In the old days the railways chose to buy several Scottish courses with Cruden Bay, 23 miles north of

Aberdeen being, like Gleneagles, a prime example of past railway ownership. Founded at the end of the 19th century, Cruden Bay was designed by Tom Simpson and is hailed as one of the nations finest links - and nearby there is an additional 9-holer, St Olaf, for the ladies who, some reckon, are not always treated too well by elite clubs, although times may be changing.

While motoring in the Aberdeen area, the A92 takes a wise player to Murcar which further adds glitter to this part of the north-east. Although I have not played there, friends say it has views of the sea, rolling duneland, streams and fine turf and, at only 6219 yards in length, must be on my list since I don't hit the ball vast lengths.

## TURNBERRY; CROWN JEWEL

My favourite Scottish links is Turnberry (Ayrshire) and if the wind off the sea isn't too fierce, and the sun shines, the place sparkles out by that lighthouse and everone feels almost turbo-charged. It's true that to play Turnberry today as a visitor is expensive and to enjoy a meal at the deeply impressive hotel is a somewhat costly experience.

Although now owned by overseas investors, the injection of foreign money has improved every aspect of Turnberry, underlining its status as one of the world's finest links. Whatever happens to the world economy in the future this is now one upgraded, king-size jewel in the crown of British sport, on par with Muirfield, the oldest course which defends its private status and old-world elegance against all predators, and, sometimes, against visitors, too! According to an American list of the world's 100 greatest courses, Muirfield is rated at number two, behind Pine Valley.

## UNTAMED AND NATURAL

Scotland is home to the Loch Ness Monster and that golfing monster known as Carnoustie. Ben Hogan won on this whopping links - and never returned. I don't know why this legend chose to stay home, but can guess. While the last few holes, over the Barry Burn that winds across fairways like an angry serpent, are indeed memorable, the whole challenge is too much like hard work in the wind.

While Prestwick, founded in 1851, may have been left behind by modern wonders such as Loch Lomond or Peter de Savary's course at Skibo Castle, it stays in my mind as highly desirable. There are some 14 blind shots you must hit over the sandhills and wherever you walk, you feel the spirits of champions past.

Anywhere else? Oh yes. We flew in a small aircraft to the Isle of Islay. The island folk were very special, as was their hospitality! I failed to hit a decent, or sober, shot. But for pure, untamed natural golf, there is nothing better. If life is kind, I shall return, and use my own clubs before sipping a drop.

# SCOTLAND

The directory which follows has been divided into three geographical regions. Counties have not been shown against individual locations as recent legislation has created a number of smaller counties which will be unfamiliar to the visitor. The postal authorities have confirmed that it is no longer necessary to include a county name in addresses, provided a post code is shown. All locations appear in the atlas section at the end of this guide in their appropriate counties.

## HIGHLANDS & ISLANDS

This region includes the counties of Aberdeen City, Aberdeenshire, Highland, Moray, Orkney, Shetland and Western Isles which reflect the recent national changes.

### ABERDEEN                                           Map 15 NJ90

**Auchmill** Bonnyview Rd, West Heatheryfold AB2 7FQ
☎ 01224 715214
This course is definitely not for beginners - the fairways are tree-lined and very tight on most holes. Three holes are quite hilly and although the remainder is flat there are nice views over Aberdeen. The course is not recommended for anyone over 22 handicap unless they have plenty of golf balls!
*18 holes, 5123metres, Par 68, SSS 67, Course record 67.*
*Club membership 300.*
**Visitors**        members have priority Sat & Wed for club competitions.
**Societies**     apply in writing to Leisure and Recreation Dept, Aberdeen District Council.
**Green Fees** £7 per round.
**Facilities**    ⊗ by prior arrangement ⅷ by prior arrangement ⌷ ♥ ♀ ♨
**Leisure**        putting green, practice area.
**Location**     Outskirts Aberdeen, A96 Aberdeen/Inverness
**Hotel**           ★★★ 66% The Craighaar, Waterton Rd, Buucksburn, ABERDEEN
                        ☎ 01224 712275 55 ⇄ ♞

**Balnagask** St Fitticks Rd AB1 3QT
☎ 01224 876407 & 01224 871286
Links course. Used by the Nigg Bay Club.
*18 holes, 5986ydss, SSS 69.*
**Visitors**        no restrictions.
**Societies**     apply to council.
**Facilities**    ♨
**Location**     2m E of city centre
**Hotel**           ★★★ 69% Caledonian Thistle, 10 Union Ter, ABERDEEN ☎ 01224 640233 80 ⇄ ♞

**Deeside** Golf Rd, Bieldside AB1 9DL
☎ 01224 869457
An interesting riverside course with several tree-lined fairways. A stream comes into play at 9 of the 18 holes on the main course. There is a subsidiary 9-hole course.
*18 holes, 5971yds, Par 71, SSS 69, Course record 63.*
*Club membership 800.*
**Visitors**        must contact in advance.
**Societies**     apply in writing.
**Green Fees** £25 per day (£30 weekends & bank holidays). 9 hole £8 per day..
**Facilities**    ⊗ ⅷ ♥ ♥ ♀ ♨ ♒ ♪ Frank J Coutts.
**Leisure**        trolley for hire, putting green, practice area.
**Location**     3m W of city centre off A93
**Hotel**           ★★★★ 70% Ardoe House, Blairs, South Deeside Rd, ABERDEEN
                        ☎ 01224 867355 71 ⇄ ♞

**Hazelhead Public** Hazelhead AB1 8BD
☎ No telephone
A tree-lined course.
*18 holes, 6595yds, Par 70, SSS 70.*
**Visitors**        no restrictions.
**Societies**     must contact in advance.
**Green Fees** not confirmed.
**Facilities**    ♨ ♒ ♪
**Location**     4m W of city centre off A944
**Hotel**           ★★★★ 70% Ardoe House, Blairs, South Deeside Rd, ABERDEEN
                        ☎ 01224 867355 71 ⇄ ♞

**Kings Links** AB2 1NR ☎ 01224 632269
A typical links course with no tree lines and plenty of bunkers.The 14th hole is tricky - a long par 4 with a raised green and not much fairway round the green. The course is playable all year. Nearby there is a 6-hole course. The Bon Accord Club, Caledonian Club and Northern Club play over this course.
*18 holes, 6384yds, Par 72, SSS 71.*
**Visitors**        contact starters on 01224 632269 regarding booking of tee times.
**Societies**     write to the Arts & Recreation Dept, St Nicholas House, Broad Street, Aberdeen.
**Green Fees** municipal rates.
**Facilities**    ♨
**Location**     0.75m NE of city centre
**Hotel**           ★★★ 69% Caledonian Thistle, 10 Union Ter, ABERDEEN ☎ 01224 640233 80 ⇄ ♞

**Murcar** Bridge of Don AB23 8BD
☎ 01224 704345
Seaside links course, prevailing NE wind, hard-walking. Testing 4th and 14th holes.
*18 holes, 6241yds, Par 71, SSS 71, Course record 65.*
*Club membership 800.*
**Visitors**        must contact in advance.
**Societies**     advance booking required.
**Green Fees** £35 per day; £25 per round (£40 per day/round weekends & bank holidays).
**Facilities**    ⊗ ⅷ ♥ ♥ ♀ ♨ ♒ ♪ Alan White.
**Leisure**        trolley for hire, putting green, practice area.
**Location**     5m NE of city centre off A92
**Hotel**           ★★★ 66% The Craighaar, Waterton Rd, Buucksburn, ABERDEEN
                        ☎ 01224 712275 55 ⇄ ♞

**Royal Aberdeen** Balgownie, Bridge of Don AB23 8AT
☎ 01224 702571
Championship links course. Windy, easy walking.
*Balgownie Course: 18 holes, 6372yds, Par 71, SSS 71,*
*Course record 63.*
*Silverburn Course: 18 holes, 4066yds, Par 64, SSS 60.*
*Club membership 500.*
Visitors     times for visitors 10-11.30 and 2-3.30pm
                 weekdays, after 3.30pm weekends.
Societies   apply in writing.
Green Fees £48 per day; £37 per round (£48 per round
                 weekends).
Facilities  ⊗ ▥ ▙ ☟ ♀ ♨ 🏠 🍴 🥂 Ronnie MacAskill.
Leisure    trolley for hire, putting green, practice area.
Location   2.5m N of city centre off A92
Hotel      ★★★ 69% Caledonian Thistle, 10 Union Ter,
            ABERDEEN ☎ 01224 640233 80 ⇆ 🐾

**Westhill** Westhill Heights, Westhill, Skene AB32 6RY
☎ 01224 742567
A highland course.
*18 holes, 5921yds, Par 69, SSS 69, Course record 65.*
*Club membership 800.*
Visitors     must contact in advance.
Societies   telephone in advance.
Green Fees £16 per day; £12 per round (£22/18 weekends
                 and bank holidays).
Facilities  ⊗ ▥ ▙ ☟ ♀ ♨ 🏠 🍴 🥂 Ronnie McDonald.
Leisure    motorised carts for hire, buggies for hire, trolley
            for hire, putting green, practice area.
Location   6m NW of city centre off A944
Hotel      ★★★ 63% Westhill Hotel, WESTHILL
            ☎ 01224 740388 37 ⇆ 🐾Annexe13 ⇆ 🐾

## COUNTRY HOTEL AND RESTAURANT

### Return to the Quality of Life

Varied à la carte menu
including vegetarian
dishes.
Seafood our speciality.
Only 10 minutes from
Royal Aberdeen
Murcar and Cruden
Bay courses.
A warm welcome
awaits you from the
Craig Family.

## NEWBURGH, ABERDEENSHIRE
## Tel: (01358) 789444

---

**ABOYNE**                            Map 15 NO59

**Aboyne** Formaston Park AB34 5HP ☎ 013398 86328
Beautiful parkland with outstanding views. Two lochs on
course.
*18 holes, 5975yds, Par 69, SSS 68, Course record 62.*
*Club membership 906.*
Visitors     no restrictions. Advisable to contact in advance.
Societies   prior booking essential.
Green Fees £21 per day; £16 per round (£25/£20 weekends).
Facilities  ⊗ ▥ ▙ ☟ ♀ ♨ 🏠 🍴 🥂 Innes Wright.
Leisure    trolley for hire, putting green, practice area.
Location   E side of village, N of A93
Hotel      ★★ 70% Birse Lodge Hotel, Charleston Rd,
            ABOYNE ☎ 013398 86253 12 ⇆ 🐾

---

**ALFORD**                              Map 15 NJ51

**Alford** Montgarrie Rd AB33 8AE ☎ 019755 62178
A flat parkland course in scenic countryside. Divided into
sections by a road, a railway and a burn.
*18 holes, 5290yds, Par 69, SSS 65, Course record 64.*
*Club membership 600.*
Visitors     advisable to contact in advance.
Societies   telephone in advance.
Green Fees £15 per day; £11 per round (£22/£17 weekends).
Facilities  ⊗ ▥ ▙ ☟ ♀ ♨ 🏠 🍴
Leisure    trolley for hire, trolley hire.
Hotel      ★★★(red)⚜ Kildrummy Castle Hotel,
            KILDRUMMY ☎ 019755 71288 16 ⇆ 🐾

---

**ALNESS**                            Map 14 NH66

**Alness** Ardross Rd IV17 0PQ ☎ 01349 883877
A short, but testing, parkland course with beautiful views
over the Cromarty Firth and the Black Isle.
*9 holes, 2606yds, Par 66, SSS 64.*
*Club membership 220.*
Visitors     telephone in advance for weekend play.
Societies   must contact in advance.
Green Fees £7 per day (£9 weekends).
Facilities  ▙ ☟ ♀ ♨ 🍴
Leisure    fishing, practice area.
Location   0.5m N off A9
Hotel      ★★★ 68% Morangie House Hotel, Morangie
            Rd, TAIN ☎ 01862 892281 26 ⇆ 🐾

---

**ARISAIG**                           Map 13 NM68

**Traigh** PH39 4NT ☎ 01687 450645
According to at least one newspaper Traigh is 'probably the
most beautifully sited nine-hole golf course in the world'.
Whether that is true or not, Traigh lies by the sea alongside
sandy beaches with views to Skye and the Inner Hebrides.
The feature of the course is a line of grassy hills, originally
sand dunes, that rise to some 60 feet. The nine-hole course
was completely redesigned for the 1995 season.
*9 holes, 2405yds, Par 68, SSS 65, Course record 67.*
*Club membership 125.*
Visitors     no restrictions.
Societies   contact in advance.
Green Fees £40 per week; £10 per day.
Facilities  ☟ 🏠 🍴
Leisure    trolley for hire, putting green, practice area.  ▶

## BANFF SPRINGS HOTEL

Overlooking the golden sands of the Moray Firth. Superb choice of golf courses nearby. Close to whisky and castle trails. Banff enjoys lower than average rainfall levels and reasonable green fees – what a boost to the avid golfer! Superb restaurant and bar facilities, 30 ensuite bedrooms.
*Come, relax and enjoy!*
**Banff Springs Hotel, Golden Knowes Road, Banff AB45 2JE.**
**Tel: (01261) 812881. Fax: (01261) 815546**

Location   6m S of Malling on A830
Hotel   ★★ 65% Arisaig Hotel, ARISAIG
      ☎ 01687 450210 15rm(6 ⇄)

### AUCHENBLAE       Map 15 NO77

*Auchenblae* AB30 1BU ☎ 01561 378869
Picturesque, small, undulating parkland course offering good views.
*9 holes, 2174yds, Par 32, SSS 30, Course record 60.*
*Club membership 78.*
**Visitors**   restricted Wed & Fri evenings.
**Societies**   must telephone in advance.
**Green Fees** not confirmed.
**Location**   0.5m NE
**Hotel**   ★★ 61% County Hotel, Arduthie Rd,
      STONEHAVEN ☎ 01569 764386 14 ⇄ ♟

### BALLATER       Map 15 NO39

*Ballater* Victoria Rd AB35 5QX ☎ 013397 55567
Moorland course with testing long holes and beautiful scenery.
*18 holes, 5638yds, Par 67, SSS 67, Course record 62.*
*Club membership 650.*
**Visitors**   must contact in advance.
**Societies**   prior booking recommended.
**Green Fees** £26 per 2 rounds; £17 per round (£30/£20 weekends).
**Facilities**   ⊗ ℍ ♚ ♨ ♀⚒ 🏠 ⚒ ♟ Frank Smith.
**Leisure**   hard tennis courts, fishing, motorised carts for hire, trolley for hire, putting green, practice area.
**Location**   W side of town
**Hotel**   ★★★ 72% Darroch Learg Hotel, Braemar Rd,
      BALLATER
      ☎ 013397 55443 14 ⇄ ♟Annexe5 ⇄ ♟

### BANCHORY       Map 15 NO69

*Banchory* Kinneskie Rd AB31 3TA ☎ 01330 822365
Sheltered parkland course situated beside the River Dee, with easy walking and woodland scenery. 11th and 12th holes are testing.
*18 holes, 5522yds, Par 67, SSS 65, Course record 60.*
*Club membership 975.*
**Visitors**   telephone for details on 01330 822447
**Societies**   must book in advance, no parties Thu & weekends.
**Green Fees** £22 per day, £16 per round (£25/£20 weekends). Weekly £70..
**Facilities**   ⊗ ℍ ♚ ♨ ♀⚒ 🏠 ⚒ ♟ J Charles Dernie.
**Location**   A93, 300 yds from W end of High St
**Hotel**   ★★★(red)⚘ Banchory Lodge Hotel,
      BANCHORY ☎ 01330 822625 22 ⇄ ♟

### BANFF       Map 15 NJ66

*Duff House Royal* The Barnyards AB45 3SX
☎ 01261 812062
Well-manicured flat parkland, bounded by woodlands and River Deveron. Well bunkered and renowned for its large, two-tier greens.
*18 holes, 6161yds, Par 68, SSS 69, Course record 63.*
*Club membership 1000.*
**Visitors**   a handicap certificate is preferred. Some time restrictions.
**Societies**   must apply in writing.
**Green Fees** not confirmed.
**Facilities**   ♀⚒ 🏠 ⚒ ♟ Bob Strachan.
**Location**   0.5m S on A98
**Hotel**   ★★★ 61% Banff Springs Hotel, Golden Knowes Rd, BANFF
      ☎ 01261 812881 30 ⇄ ♟

**THE BOAT HOTEL**

★★★ AA

Overlooking the beautiful but challenging Boat of Garten Golf Course – the 'Gleneagles' of the Highlands – the Boat Hotel offers you superb value Tee Break holidays with golf on any of 9 local courses. Special Rates for Golf Societies and all golf reserved in advance. All 32 rooms en-suite

*For Golf Brochure Contact:*
*Suzanne MacLean, Golf Desk,*
*The Boat Hotel, Boat of Garten,*
*Inverness-shire. PH24 3BH*
*Tel: 01479 831258  Fax: 01479 831414*

## BOAT OF GARTEN
Map 14 NH91

**Boat of Garten** PH24 3BQ ☎ 01479 831282
This parkland course was cut out from a silver birch
forest though the fairways are adequately wide. There are
natural hazards of broom and heather, good views and
walking is easy. A round provides great variety.
*18 holes, 5866yds, Par 69, SSS 69, Course record 64.*
*Club membership 600.*
**Visitors**   must contact in advance.
**Societies**   must telephone in advance.
**Green Fees** £20 per day (£23 weekends).
**Facilities**   ⊗ ⅋ ⅃ ⚑ ♀ ♨ 🏮 ⚐
**Leisure**   hard tennis courts, trolley for hire, putting
   green.
**Location**   E side of village
**Hotel**   ★★★ 65% Boat Hotel, BOAT OF
   GARTEN ☎ 01479 831258 32 ⇥ 🐾

## BONAR BRIDGE
Map 14 NH69

**Bonar Bridge-Ardgay** Migdale Rd IV24 3EJ
☎ 01863 766375
Wooded moorland course with picturesque views of hills and
loch.
*9 holes, 4640yds, Par 66, SSS 63, Course record 63.*
*Club membership 250.*
**Visitors**   restricted during competitions.
**Societies**   apply in writing.
**Green Fees** £10 per day; £50 per week.
**Facilities**   ⅃ ♨ ♨
**Location**   0.5m E
**Hotel**   ★★ 66% Dornoch Castle Hotel, Castle St,
   DORNOCH
   ☎ 01862 810216 4 ⇥ 🐾 Annexe13 ⇥ 🐾

## BRAEMAR
Map 15 NO19

**Braemar** Cluniebank Rd AB35 5XX ☎ 013397 41618
Flat course, set amid beautiful countryside on Royal Deeside,
with River Clunie running through several holes. The 2nd
hole is one of the most testing in the area.
*18 holes, 5000yds, Par 65, SSS 64, Course record 61.*
*Club membership 450.*
**Visitors**   are advised to book 24 hours in advance to play
   at weekends.
**Societies**   must contact secretary in advance 01224
   704471.
**Green Fees** £16 per day; £12 per round (£20 per day; £15
   per round weekends).
**Facilities**   ⊗ ⅃ ♀ ♨ 🏮 ⚐
**Leisure**   trolley for hire.
**Location**   0.5m S
**Hotel**   ★★★ 68% Invercauld Arms, BRAEMAR
   ☎ 013397 41605 68 ⇥ 🐾

## BRORA
Map 14 NC90

**Brora** Golf Rd KW9 6QS ☎ 01408 621417
Typical seaside links with little rough and fine views. Some
testing holes.
*18 holes, 6110yds, Par 69, SSS 69, Course record 61.*
*Club membership 704.*
**Visitors**   advisable to book in advance May-Oct.

**Societies**   advisable to book in advance.
**Green Fees** £16 per day.
**Facilities**   ⊗ ⅋ ⅃ ♀ ♨ 🏮 ⚐
**Leisure**   trolley for hire, putting green, practice area.
   limited fishing.
**Location**   E side of village
**Hotel**   ★★★ 64% The Links Hotel, Golf Rd, BRORA
   ☎ 01408 621225 23 ⇥ 🐾

## BUCKIE
Map 15 NJ46

**Buckpool** Barhill Rd, Buckpool AB56 1DU
☎ 01542 832933
Windy, seaside course, with easy walking. Overlooking
Moray Firth, its fairways are lined by whin and broom.
*18 holes, 6257yds, Par 70, SSS 70, Course record 64.*
*Club membership 430.*
**Visitors**   apply in advance.
**Societies**   apply in advance.
**Green Fees** £12 per day; £8 per round (£18/£10 weekends).
**Facilities**   ⊗ ⅋ ♀ ♨ ♀
**Leisure**   squash, trolley for hire, putting green.
**Location**   Off A98
**Hotel**   ★★ 68% Marine Hotel, Marine Place,
   BUCKIE ☎ 01542 832249 12 ⇥ 🐾

**Strathlene** Strathlene Rd AB56 1DJ ☎ 01542 831798
Windy seaside links course with magnificent view. A special
feature of the course is approach shots to raised greens (holes
4,5,6 & 13).
*18 holes, 5980yds, Par 69, SSS 69, Course record 65.*
*Club membership 370.*
**Visitors**   booking essential at weekends.
**Societies**   telephone for Mon-Fri & apply in writing for
   weekends.
**Green Fees** £14 per day; £10 per round (£18/£14 weekends).
**Facilities**   ⊗ ⅃ ♀ ♨ ♨ 🏮
**Leisure**   trolley for hire, putting green.
**Location**   3m E on A942
**Hotel**   ★★ 64% Mill House Hotel, Tynet, BUCKIE
   ☎ 01542 850233 15 ⇥ 🐾

## CAIRNBULG
Map 15 NK06

**Inverallochy** AB43 5YL ☎ 01346 582000
Windy seaside links course with natural hazards, tricky par 3s
and easy walking. Panoramic views of North Sea at every hole.
*18 holes, 5137yds, Par 64, SSS 65, Course record 60.*
*Club membership 300.*
**Visitors**   restricted at weekends and competition days.
**Societies**   apply in writing.
**Green Fees** not confirmed.
**Facilities**   ♨
**Leisure**   practice area.
**Location**   E side of village off B9107
**Hotel**   ★★ 65% Tufted Duck Hotel, ST COMBS
   ☎ 01346 582481 & 582482/3 18 ⇥ 🐾

## CARRBRIDGE
Map 14 NH92

**Carrbridge** Inverness Rd PH23 3AU ☎ 01479 841623
Short part-parkland, part-moorland course with magnificent
views of the Cairngorms.
*9 holes, 5402yds, Par 71, SSS 68, Course record 64.*
*Club membership 650.*   ▶

**AA ★★**
Les Routiers
Highly Recommended
01542 840432

## *Cullen Bay Hotel*
### *Banffshire AB56 2XA*

STB ●●●●
Commended
Fax: 840900

Central on the Moray/Banff golf course coastal belt, next to Cullen links (early tee-off?), our family run hotel offers a warm homely atmosphere. 18 courses within 20 miles, most on inclusive ticket to uncrowded greens.
Panoramic hilltop views of rocky coastline provide backdrop to our award winning chefs cuisine. Relax by lounge bars' log fire with Scotlands finest malts. 14 newly refurbished ensuite bedrooms, most with sea views.
**Parties of 8+ play for trophy and special incentive to win!**

---

**Visitors** during May-Sep, course open to visitors after 5pm Wed & 4pm Sun.
**Societies** small parties welcome, apply in writing.
**Green Fees** £10-£11 per day (£12 weekends). Evening (after 6.30pm) £5-£7.
**Facilities** ⓑ ☕ ⚑ ⚐
**Leisure** trolley for hire, putting green.
**Location** N side of village
**Hotel** ★★★★ 71% Dalrachney Lodge, CARRBRIDGE ☎ 01479 841252 11 ⇥ ⋔

### CRUDEN BAY                        Map 15 NK03

**Cruden Bay** AB42 7NN ☎ 01779 812285
A seaside links which provides golf of a high order. It was designed by a master architect, Tom Simpson, and although changed somewhat from his original design it is still a great golf course. Magnificent views.
*Main Course: 18 holes, 6395yds, Par 70, SSS 72, Course record 63.*
*St Olaf Course: 9 holes, 2553yds, Par 64, SSS 65.*
*Club membership 1100.*
**Visitors** welcome on weekdays, at weekends only when there are no competitions.
**Societies** weekdays only telephone in advance.
**Green Fees** Main Course £30 per day (£40 weekends); St Olaf £10 per day (£15 weekends).
**Facilities** ⊗ ⅏ ⓑ ☕ ♀ ⚐ ⚑ ⚐ Robert Stewart.
**Leisure** trolley for hire, driving range, putting green, practice area.
**Location** SW side of village on A975
**Hotel** ★★ 65% Red House Hotel, Aulton Rd, CRUDEN BAY ☎ 01779 812215 6rm(5 ⇥ ⋔)
**Additional hotel** ★★ 68% Udny Arms Hotel, Main St, NEWBURGH ☎ 01358 789444 26 ⇥ ⋔

### CULLEN                            Map 15 NJ56

**Cullen** The Links AB56 2UU ☎ 01542 840685
Interesting links on two levels with rocks and ravines offering some challenging holes. Spectacular scenery.
*18 holes, 4610yds, Par 63, SSS 62, Course record 58.*
*Club membership 600.*
**Visitors** no restrictions but during summer club medal matches given preference on Mon/Wed/Sat.
**Societies** advance applications advisable.
**Green Fees** £12 per day; £7 per round (£15/£9 weekends).
**Facilities** ⊗ ⅏ by prior arrangement ⓑ ☕ ♀ ⚐
**Leisure** trolley for hire, putting green, practice area.
**Location** 0.5m W off A98
**Hotel** ★★ 63% Cullen Bay Hotel, Cullen, BUCKIE ☎ 01542 840432 14 ⇥ ⋔

### DORNOCH                           Map 14 NH78

**Royal Dornoch** Golf Rd IV25 3LW
☎ 01862 810219 & 811220
Very challenging seaside championship links, designed by Tom Morris and John Sutherland.
*Championship: 18 holes, 6514yds, Par 70, SSS 73, Course record 65.*
*Struie Course: 18 holes, 5438yds, Par 69, SSS 66.*
*Club membership 1150.*
**Visitors** must have a handicap of 24 for gentlemen (ladies 35) on Championship Course. Must contact in advance and have a handicap certificate.
**Societies** must apply in advance.
**Green Fees** Championship course: £40 per round summer; £27 winter (£45/30 weekends). Struie course £16 per day; £11 per round (£8/£5.50 winter).
**Facilities** ⊗ ⅏ ⓑ ☕ ♀ ⚐ ⚑ ⚐ ⚑ W E Skinner.
**Leisure** hard tennis courts, fishing, motorised carts for hire, trolley for hire, putting green, practice area.
**Location** E side of town
**Hotel** ★★ 66% Dornoch Castle Hotel, Castle St, DORNOCH ☎ 01862 810216 4 ⇥ ⋔Annexe13 ⇥ ⋔

---

**Skibo Castle** The Carnegie Club, Skibo Castle IV25 3RG ☎ 01862 894600
Set within the grounds of an enchanting castle, with the sea on three sides and the hills of Sutherland and Ross-shire all around, this splendid course enjoys a magnificent position. Although not long by modern standards, strong and fickle winds will test even the most experienced golfer. Excellent leisure facilities.
*18 holes, 6403yds, Par 71, SSS 71.*
*Club membership 350.*
**Visitors** weekdays only by written application to the secretary.
**Green Fees** £50 per 18 holes.
**Facilities** ⊗ ☕ ♀ ⚐ ⚑ ⚐ ⚑ ⚐ ⚑ William Milne.
**Leisure** hard tennis courts, heated indoor swimming pool, fishing, sauna, solarium, gymnasium, trolley for hire, driving range, putting green, practice area.
**Location** Off A9 3m before Dornoch
**Hotel** ★★ 66% Dornoch Castle Hotel, Castle St, DORNOCH ☎ 01862 810216 4 ⇥ ⋔Annexe13 ⇥ ⋔

**★★**
# Dornoch Castle

DORNOCH,
SUTHERLAND
IV25 3SD
Tel. (01862) 810216
Fax: (01862) 810981

Play GOLF on the famous Royal Dornoch Championship Course, and stay at the charming Dornoch Castle. All rooms have private facilities: those in the new wing have modern decor, while those in the Castle enjoy the highest level of traditional atmosphere and elegance. Beaches and golf courses are within walking distance. Superb food ("Taste of Scotland" recommended) in one of the finest Restaurants of the area with a cellar to match will make your visit an experience not to be forgotten.

STB ☗☗☗☗ COMMENDED

---

## DUFFTOWN                    Map 15 NJ33

**Dufftown** Methercluny, Tomintoul Rd AB55 4BX
☎ 01340 820325
A short and undulating inland course with good views. Highest hole over 1000 ft above sea level.
*18 holes, 5308yds, Par 67, SSS 67, Course record 67.*
*Club membership 250.*
**Visitors** tee reserved Tue & Wed 4.30-6.30 & Sun 7.30-9 & 12.30-2.
**Societies** apply in writing.
**Green Fees** £15 per day; £10 per round.
**Facilities** ♀⚲↑
**Leisure** trolley for hire, putting green.
**Location** 0.75m SW off B9009
**Hotel** ★★★ 72% Craigellachie Hotel, CRAIGELLACHIE ☎ 01340 881204 30 ⇋ ৎ

## DURNESS                     Map 14 NC46

**Durness** Balnakeil IV27 4PG ☎ 01971 511364 & 511262
A 9-hole course set in tremendous scenery overlooking Balnakeil Bay. Part links and part inland with water hazards. Off alternative tees for second 9 holes giving surprising variety. Tremendous last hole played across the sea to the green over 100 yards away.
*9 holes, 5555yds, Par 70, SSS 69, Course record 72.*
*Club membership 150.*
**Visitors** restricted 10am-12.30 on Sun during Jun-Sep.
**Societies** must telephone in advance 01971 511364 (ex Sun).
**Green Fees** £11 per day.
**Facilities** ⊗⚲⚲↑
**Leisure** fishing, trolley for hire, putting green, practice area.
**Location** 1m W of village
**Guesthouse** QQQ Port-Na-Con House, Loch Eriboll, By Altnaharra ☎ 01971 511367 4rm(1 ৎ)

## ELGIN                       Map 15 NJ26

**Elgin** Hardhillock, Birnie Rd, New Elgin IV30 3SX
☎ 01343 542338
Possibly the finest inland course in the north of Scotland, with undulating greens and compact holes that demand the highest accuracy. There are thirteen par 4's and one par 5 hole on its parkland layout.
*18 holes, 6411yds, Par 69, SSS 71, Course record 64.*
*Club membership 1000.*
**Visitors** must contact in advance, weekend play only by prior arrangement.
**Societies** telephone secretary for details.

**Green Fees** £25 per day; £19 per round (£32/£26 weekends).
**Facilities** ⊗⚲⚲⚲♀⚲⚲↑ Ian P Rodger.
**Leisure** trolley for hire, driving range, putting green, practice area.
**Location** 1m S on A941
**Hotel** ★★★ 70% Mansefield House Hotel, Mayne Rd, ELGIN ☎ 01343 540883 17 ⇋ ৎ

## ELLON                       Map 15 NJ93

**McDonald** Hospital Rd AB41 9AW ☎ 01358 720576
Tight, parkland course with streams and a pond.
*18 holes, 5986yds, Par 70, SSS 69.*
*Club membership 710.*
**Visitors** no restrictions.
**Green Fees** not confirmed.
**Facilities** ♀⚲
**Location** 0.25m N on A948
**Hotel** ★ 66% Meldrum Arms Hotel, The Square, OLDMELDRUM ☎ 01651 872238 7 ৎ

## FORRES                      Map 14 NJ05

**Forres** Muiryshade IV36 0RD ☎ 01309 672250
An all-year parkland course laid on light, well-drained soil in wooded countryside. Walking is easy despite some hilly holes. A test for the best golfer.
*18 holes, 6240yds, Par 70, SSS 70, Course record 64.*
*Club membership 950.*
**Visitors** welcome although club competitions take priority. Weekends may be restricted in summer.
**Societies** must telephone 2-3 weeks in advance.
**Green Fees** not confirmed.
**Facilities** ♀⚲⚲↑ৎ Sandy Aird.
**Leisure** putting green,cart/buggy/trolley hire.
**Location** SE side of town centre off B9010
**Hotel** ★★ 69% Ramnee Hotel, Victoria Rd, FORRES ☎ 01309 672410 20 ⇋ ৎ

## FORT AUGUSTUS               Map 14 NH30

**Fort Augustus** Markethill PH32 4AU ☎ 01320 366660
Moorland course, with narrow fairways and good views. Bordered by the tree-lined Caledonian Canal.
*9 holes, 5454yds, Par 67, SSS 67, Course record 67.*
*Club membership 170.*
**Visitors** may not play Sat 1.30-4 & occasional Sun.
**Societies** telephone in advance.                          ▶

**Green Fees** £10 per day.
**Facilities** ♀ᴧ ⛳
**Location** 1m SW on A82
**Hotel** ★★ 67% Lovat Arms Hotel, FORT
AUGUSTUS
☎ 01320 366206 & 366204 21 ⇔ ♞

### FORTROSE                                      Map 14 NH75

**Fortrose & Rosemarkie** Ness Rd East IV10 8SE
☎ 01381 620529
Seaside links course, set on a peninsula with sea on three
sides. Easy walking, good views. Designed by James Braid;
the club was formed in 1888.
*18 holes, 5858yds, Par 71, SSS 69, Course record 64.*
*Club membership 770.*
**Visitors** restricted 8.45-10.15am & 1-2.15 then 4.45-
6.30pm.
**Societies** must telephone in advance.
**Green Fees** £21 per day; £15 per round (£30/£21 weekends
& bank holidays).
**Facilities** ⊗ ♠ ♥ ♀ᴧ ⛬ ⛳
**Leisure** trolley for hire, putting green, practice area.
**Location** E side of town centre
**Hotel** ★★ 67% Royal Hotel, Marine Ter,
CROMARTY ☎ 01381 600217 10 ⇔ ♞

### FORT WILLIAM                                      Map 14 NN17

**Fort William** Torlundy PH33 7SN ☎ 01397 704464
Spectacular moorland location looking onto the cliffs of Ben
Nevis. Tees and greens are in excellent condition and major
drainage improvements to the fairways were implemented in
1995.
*18 holes, 6500yds, Par 72, SSS 71, Course record 67.*
*Club membership 230.*
**Visitors** no restrictions.
**Societies** must contact in writing.
**Green Fees** £14 per day; £12 per round.
**Facilities** ♥ ♀ᴧ ⛳
**Leisure** trolley for hire, putting green.
**Location** 3m NE on A82
**Hotel** ★★★ 75% Moorings Hotel, Banavie, FORT
WILLIAM
☎ 01397 772797 21 ⇔ ♞Annexe3 ♞

### FRASERBURGH                                      Map 15 NJ96

**Fraserburgh** Philorth AB43 5TL ☎ 01346 516616
Testing seaside course.
*Corbie: 18 holes, 6278yds, Par 70, SSS 70, Course record
64.*
*Rosehill: 9 holes, 3380yds, Par 70, SSS 71.*
*Club membership 750.*
**Visitors** no restrictions but advised to check availability.
**Societies** must contact in advance.
**Green Fees** £14 per day; £11 per round (£20/£15 weekends).
9 hole course £10 per day.
**Facilities** ⊗ ⅷ ♠ ♥ ♀ᴧ ⛬ ⛳
**Leisure** trolley for hire, putting green, practice area.
**Location** 1m SE on B9033
**Hotel** ★★ 65% Tufted Duck Hotel, ST COMBS
☎ 01346 582481 & 582482/3 18 ⇔ ♞

### GAIRLOCH                                      Map 14 NG87

**Gairloch** IV21 2BE ☎ 01445 712407
Fine seaside links course running along Gairloch Sands with
good views over the sea to Skye. In windy conditions each
hole is affected.
*9 holes, 4514yds, Par 62, SSS 64, Course record 61.*
*Club membership 250.*
**Visitors** handicap certificate required.
**Societies** apply in writing to secretary.
**Green Fees** £12 per day; £45 per week.
**Facilities** ♥ ᴧ ⛬ ⛳
**Leisure** trolley for hire, practice area.
**Location** 1m S on A832
**Hotel** ★★ 63% The Old Inn, Flowerdale,
GAIRLOCH ☎ 01445 712006 14 ⇔ ♞

### GARMOUTH                                      Map 15 NJ36

**Garmouth & Kingston** Spey St IV32 7NJ
☎ 01343 870388
Seaside course with several parkland holes and tidal waters.
Naturally flat.
*18 holes, 5616yds, Par 67, SSS 67, Course record 62.*
*Club membership 450.*
**Visitors** must contact in advance for weekend play.
**Societies** advisable to phone in advance.
**Green Fees** £17 per day; £11 per round (£22/£16 weekends).
**Facilities** ⊗ ⅷ ♠ ♥ ♀ᴧ
**Leisure** fishing, trolley for hire, practice area.
**Location** In village on B9015
**Hotel** ★★★ 70% Mansefield House Hotel, Mayne
Rd, ELGIN ☎ 01343 540883 17 ⇔ ♞

### GOLSPIE                                      Map 14 NH89

**Golspie** Ferry Rd KW10 6ST ☎ 01408 633266
Founded in 1889, Golspie's seaside course offers easy
walking and natural hazards including beach heather and
whins. Spectacular scenery.
*18 holes, 5800yds, Par 68, SSS 68, Course record 64.*
*Club membership 300.*
**Visitors** contact in advance.
**Societies** contact in advance.
**Green Fees** £15 per day/round (£20 weekends & bank
holidays).
**Facilities** ⊗ by prior arrangement ⅷ by prior arrangement
♠ by prior arrangement ♥ by prior arrangement
♀ᴧ ⛬ ⛳
**Leisure** trolley for hire, putting green, practice area.
**Location** 0.5m S off A9
**Hotel** ★★ 61% Golf Links Hotel, GOLSPIE
☎ 01408 633408 9 ⇔ ♞

### GRANTOWN-ON-SPEY                                      Map 14 NJ02

**Grantown-on-Spey** Golf Course Rd PH26 3HY
☎ 01479 872079 (Apr-Oct)
Parkland and woodland course. Part easy walking, remainder
hilly. The 7th to 13th really sorts out the golfers.
*18 holes, 5517yds, Par 69, SSS 68.*
*Club membership 650.*
**Visitors** advisable to contact in advance. No visitors
before 10am weekends.

**Societies** clubhouse open Apr-Oct, apply in advance to secretary.
**Green Fees** £15 per day (£20 weekends). Evenings after 6pm £10.
**Facilities** ⊗ )Ⅲ by prior arrangement ⓛ 🍺 ♀ 👥 🏠 ⚐ Ⓕ Bill Mitchell.
**Leisure** trolley for hire, putting green, practice area.
**Location** SE side of town centre
**Hotel** ★★★ 67% Garth Hotel, Castle Rd, GRANTOWN-ON-SPEY
☎ 01479 872836 & 872162 17 ⇆ ℟

---

## HELMSDALE             Map 14 ND01

*Helmsdale* Golf Rd KW8 6JA ☎ 01431 821339
Sheltered, undulating course following the line of the Helmsdale River.
*9 holes, 1860yds, Par 62, SSS 61.*
*Club membership 90.*
**Visitors** no restrictions.
**Societies** apply in writing.
**Green Fees** not confirmed.
**Facilities** 👥
**Location** NW side of town on A896
**Hotel** ★★★ 64% The Links Hotel, Golf Rd, BRORA
☎ 01408 621225 23 ⇆ ℟

---

## HOPEMAN             Map 15 NJ16

**Hopeman** IV30 2YA ☎ 01343 830578
Links-type course with beautiful views over the Moray Firth. The 12th hole, called the Priescach, is a short hole with a drop of 100 feet from tee to green. It can require anything from a wedge to a wood depending on the wind.
*18 holes, 5531yds, Par 67, SSS 67, Course record 64.*
*Club membership 600.*
**Visitors** must contact in advance, restricted tee times at weekend.
**Societies** contact in advance.
**Green Fees** £12 per day (£17 weekends).
**Facilities** ⊗ )Ⅲ ⓛ 🍺 ♀ 👥 🏠 ⚐
**Leisure** trolley for hire, practice area.
**Location** E side of village off B9040
**Hotel** ★★★ 62% Stotfield Hotel, Stotfield Rd, LOSSIEMOUTH ☎ 01343 812011 45 ⇆ ℟

---

## HUNTLY             Map 15 NJ53

**Huntly** Cooper Park AB54 4SH ☎ 01466 792643
A parkland course lying between the Rivers Deveron and Bogie.
*18 holes, 5399yds, Par 67, SSS 66.*
*Club membership 800.*

**Visitors** may not play before 8am.
**Societies** must contact the secretary.
**Green Fees** £13 per day (£20 weekends); weekly ticket £65.
**Facilities** ⊗ )Ⅲ ⓛ 🍺 ♀ 👥 🏠
**Leisure** trolley for hire, driving range, putting green, practice area.
**Location** N side of Huntly, turn off A96 at bypass roundabout
**Hotel** ★★🌺 64% Castle Hotel, HUNTLY
☎ 01466 792696 20 ⇆ ℟

---

## INSCH             Map 15 NJ62

*Insch* Golf Ter AB52 6XN ☎ 01464 820363
A challenging 9-hole course soon be extended to 18. With the prevailing westerly winds the Par 5 1st and Par 4 4th play into the wind and are particularly challenging.
*9 holes, 5632yds, Par 70, SSS 67, Course record 66.*
*Club membership 400.*
**Visitors** restricted during club conpetitions and Tee times.
**Societies** apply in writing or telephone, bookings accepted.
**Green Fees** not confirmed.
**Facilities** ♀ 👥 🏠
**Hotel** ★★ 63% Lodge Hotel, OLD RAYNE
☎ 01464 851205 3 ℟Annexe4 ⇆ ℟

---

## INVERGORDON          Map 14 NH76

**Invergordon** King George St IV18 0BD ☎ 01349 852715
Fairly easy but windy 18-hole parkland course, with woodland, wide fairways and good views over Cromarty Firth. Very good greens and a fair challenge, especially if the wind is from the west..
*18 holes, 6030yds, Par 69, SSS 69.*
*Club membership 240.*
**Visitors** visitors advised to avoid Tue & Thu 4.30-6, Mon & Wed 5-6 and Sat 8.30-10 & 1-2pm.
**Societies** must contact in advance.
**Green Fees** £10 per day Mon-Fri/per round weekends.
**Facilities** ⓛ ♀ 👥 ⚐
**Leisure** trolley for hire, putting green, practice area.
**Location** W side of town centre on B817
**Hotel** ★★★ 68% Morangie House Hotel, Morangie Rd, TAIN ☎ 01862 892281 26 ⇆ ℟

---

## INVERNESS          Map 14 NH64

*Inverness* Culcabock IV2 3XQ ☎ 01463 239882
Fairly flat parkland course with burn running through it. Windy in winter. The 14th is one of the most difficult Par 4's in the north of Scotland. ▶

*The Castle Hotel*

Set in our own grounds we offer peace and tranquillity along with comfortable accommodation and good food. Huntly Golf Club is on our doorstep and there are numerous others all within an hours drive. We are happy to assist in making bookings at most courses.

Telephone: (01466) 792696 • Fax (01466) 792641
HUNTLY • ABERDEENSHIRE • AB54 4SH

18 holes, 6226yds, Par 69, SSS 70.
*Club membership 1100.*
**Visitors** restricted at weekends.
**Societies** must telephone in advance.
**Green Fees** not confirmed.
**Facilities** ♀ ⅄ 🏠 ⚑ 🍴 Alistair P Thomson.
**Leisure** putting green,practice area,trolley hire.
**Hotel** ★★★★ 67% Kingsmills Hotel, Culcabock Rd,
INVERNESS
☎ 01463 237166 78 ⇌ 🐾Annexe6 ⇌ 🐾

**Torvean** Glenurquhart Rd IV3 6JN ☎ 01463 711434
Municipal parkland course, easy walking, good views.
*18 holes, 5784yds, Par 69, SSS 68, Course record 64.*
*Club membership 415.*
**Visitors** must contact in advance.
**Societies** advance bookings through Inverness District
Council, Town House, Inverness.
**Green Fees** £11.90 per day; £8.90 per round (£13.40/£10.30
weekends).
**Facilities** ⊗ by prior arrangement 🍴 ♥ ♀ ⅄ 🏠 ⚑
**Leisure** trolley for hire, putting green.
**Location** 1.5m SW on A82
**Hotel** ★★(red)⚤ Dunain Park Hotel, INVERNESS
☎ 01463 230512 14rm(10 ⇌ 🐾)

---

## INVERURIE
Map 15 NJ72

**Inverurie** Blackhall Rd AB51 5JB ☎ 01467 624080
Parkland course, part of which is exposed and windy, and
part through wooded area.
*18 holes, 5711yds, Par 69, SSS 68, Course record 64.*
*Club membership 700.*
**Visitors** book tee time through shop up to 24 hrs in
advance 01467 620207.
**Societies** telephone administrator.
**Green Fees** £18 per day (£24 weekends).
**Facilities** ⊗ 🍴 🏠 ♥ ♀ ⅄ 🏠 ⚑ 🍴 Howard Ferguson.
**Leisure** trolley for hire, putting green, practice area.
**Location** W side of town off A96
**Hotel** ★★★ 68% Strathburn Hotel, Burghmuir Dr,
INVERURIE ☎ 01467 624422 25 ⇌ 🐾

---

## KEITH
Map 15 NJ45

**Keith** Fife Park AB55 3DF ☎ 01542 882469
Parkland course, with natural hazards over first 9 holes.
Testing 7th hole, 232 yds, par 3.
*18 holes, 5767yds, Par 69, SSS 68.*
*Club membership 500.*
**Visitors** no restrictions except competitions.
**Societies** by arrangement with outings secretary.
**Green Fees** £12 per day; £10 per round (£15/£12 weekends).
**Facilities** 🍴 ♥ ♀ ⅄
**Leisure** trolley for hire, putting green, practice area.
**Location** NW side of town centre off A96
**Hotel** ★★★ 72% Craigellachie Hotel,
CRAIGELLACHIE ☎ 01340 881204 30 ⇌ 🐾

---

## KEMNAY
Map 15 NJ71

**Kemnay** Monymusk Rd AB51 5RA
☎ 01467 642225 shop & 643746 office
Undulating parkland course with superb views. A stream
crosses four holes.

---

18 holes, 5903yds, Par 70, SSS 69, Course record 69.
*Club membership 800.*
**Visitors** telephone shop for booking.
**Societies** must telephone in advance.
**Green Fees** £18 per day; £14 per round (£20/£16 weekends).
**Facilities** ⊗ 🍴 🍴 ♥ ♀ ⅄ 🏠 ⚑
**Leisure** trolley for hire, practice area.
**Location** W side of village on B993
**Hotel** ★★★ 63% Westhill Hotel, WESTHILL
☎ 01224 740388 37 ⇌ 🐾Annexe13 ⇌ 🐾

---

## KINGUSSIE
Map 14 NH70

**Kingussie** Gynack Rd PH21 1LR
☎ 01540 661600
Hilly upland course with natural hazards and magnificent
views. Stands about 1000ft above sea level at its highest
point, and the River Gynack comes into play on five holes.
*18 holes, 5500yds, Par 66, SSS 68, Course record 63.*
*Club membership 800.*
**Visitors** must contact in advance.
**Societies** must contact in advance.
**Green Fees** £16 per day; £13 per round (£20/£15 weekends).
**Facilities** ⊗ 🍴 🍴 ♥ ♀ ⅄ 🏠 ⚑
**Leisure** motorised carts for hire, buggies for hire, trolley
for hire, putting green.
**Location** 0.25m N off A86
**Hotel** ★★ 71% Columba House Hotel, Manse Rd,
KINGUSSIE
☎ 01540 661402 7 ⇌ 🐾

# Columba House
# Hotel & Restaurant

Manse Road, Kingussie, Invernesshire PH21 1JF
Phone: 01540 661402    Fax 01540 661652

A former Manse now completely refurbished to a
country House Hotel with friendly atmosphere, Taste
of Scotland Restaurant overlooking large walled
garden. Coal fire in elegant but homely lounge.
Luxurious bedrooms, all en-suite, (four-posters
available) with mini-bar, television, tea/coffee,
telephone. Ample private parking. Golfing holidays
can be arranged on 7 excellent nearby courses.

**Please call for colour brochure**
*Resident proprietor: Myra Shearer*

## KINTORE
Map 15 NJ71

**Kintore** Balbithan Rd AB51 0UR ☎ 01467 632631
The course covers a large area of ground from the Don Basin, near the clubhouse, to mature woodland at the far perimeter. One of the main attractions is the excellent drainage which results in very few days of lost play.
*18 holes, 5997yds, Par 70, SSS 69, Course record 64.*
*Club membership 700.*

| | |
|---|---|
| **Visitors** | during season booking system is in operation & slots for visitors are available. Other times can be booked 24 hours in advance. |
| **Societies** | apply in writing or telephone. |
| **Green Fees** | £13 per day; £10 per round (£18/£15 weekends). |
| **Facilities** | ⊗ ⅃ ☗ ♀ ⅄ |
| **Leisure** | putting green, practice area. |
| **Location** | 1m from village centre on B977 |
| **Hotel** | ★★ 60% Torryburn Hotel, School Rd, KINTORE ☎ 01467 632269 9rm(8 ♄) |

## LEWIS, ISLE OF
Map 13 NB43

## STORNOWAY
Map 13 NB43

**Stornoway** Lady Lever Park HS2 0XP ☎ 01851 702240
Picturesque, tree-lined parkland course, fine views. The 11th hole, 'Dardanelles' - most difficult par 5.
*18 holes, 5252yds, Par 68, SSS 67, Course record 62.*
*Club membership 400.*

| | |
|---|---|
| **Visitors** | no golf on Sun. |
| **Societies** | apply in writing. |
| **Green Fees** | £10 per day/round. |
| **Facilities** | ⅃ ☗ ♀ ⅄ ☖ ♄ |
| **Leisure** | trolley for hire, putting green, practice area. |
| **Location** | N side of town centre off A857 |
| **Hotel** | ★★★ 66% Caberfeidh Hotel, STORNOWAY ☎ 01851 702604 46 ➪ ♄ |

## LOCHCARRON
Map 14 NG83

**Lochcarron** East End ☎ 01520 2257
Seaside links course with some parkland with an interesting 2nd hole. A short course but great accuracy is required. There are plans to extend to 18-holes on an additional 500 acres.
*9 holes, 1750yds, SSS 60.*
*Club membership 150.*

| | |
|---|---|
| **Visitors** | restricted Fri evening & Sat 2-5pm. |
| **Societies** | welcome but restricted Fri evening & Sat 2-5pm. |
| **Green Fees** | not confirmed. |
| **Facilities** | ♄ |
| **Location** | 1m E |
| **Hotel** | ★★ 66% Lochcarron Hotel, Main St, LOCHCARRON ☎ 01520 722226 10rm(9 ➪ ♄) |

## LOSSIEMOUTH
Map 15 NJ27

**Moray** IV31 6QS ☎ 01343 812018
Two fine Scottish Championship links courses, known as Old and New (Moray), and situated on the Moray Firth where the weather is unusually mild.
*Old Course: 18 holes, 6643yds, Par 71, SSS 73.*
*New Course: 18 holes, 6005yds, Par 69, SSS 69.*

| | |
|---|---|
| **Visitors** | must contact in advance. |
| **Societies** | must contact in advance. |
| **Green Fees** | Old Moray course £32 per day; £22 per round (£43/33 weekends). New Moray course £22 per day; £17 per round (£27/£22 weekends). |
| **Facilities** | ☍ Alistair Thomson. |
| **Leisure** | putting green, practice area. |
| **Location** | N side of town |
| **Hotel** | ★★★ 62% Stotfield Hotel, Stotfield Rd, LOSSIEMOUTH ☎ 01343 812011 45 ➪ ♄ |

## LYBSTER
Map 15 ND23

**Lybster** Main St KW3 6AE
Picturesque, short heathland course, easy walking.
*9 holes, 1896yds, Par 62, SSS 62.*
*Club membership 80.*

| | |
|---|---|
| **Visitors** | no restrictions. |
| **Societies** | must contact in advance. |
| **Green Fees** | not confirmed. |
| **Facilities** | ⅄ ♄ |
| **Location** | E side of village |
| **Hotel** | ★★ 65% Portland Arms, LYBSTER ☎ 01593 721208 19 ➪ ♄ |

## MACDUFF
Map 15 NJ76

**Royal Tarlair** Buchan St AB44 1TA
☎ 01261 832897
Seaside clifftop course, can be windy. Testing 13th, 'Clivet' (par 3).
*18 holes, 5866yds, Par 71, SSS 68.*
*Club membership 576.*

| | |
|---|---|
| **Visitors** | no restrictions. |
| **Societies** | apply in writing. |
| **Green Fees** | not confirmed. |
| **Facilities** | ♀ ⅄ ☖ |
| **Leisure** | trolley hire. |
| **Location** | 0.75m E off A98 |
| **Hotel** | ★★ 58% The Highland Haven, Shore St, MACDUFF ☎ 01261 832408 20 ➪ ♄ |

## MUIR OF ORD
Map 14 NH55

**Muir of Ord** Great North Rd IV6 7SX
☎ 01463 870825
Old established (1875), heathland course with tight fairways and easy walking. Testing 11th, 'Castle Hill' (par 3).
*18 holes, 5202yds, Par 67, SSS 66, Course record 61.*
*Club membership 750.*

| | |
|---|---|
| **Visitors** | may not play before 11am weekends without prior agreement and during club competitions. |
| **Societies** | telephone followed by letter of confirmation. |
| **Green Fees** | £14.50 per day; £12.50 per round (£18.50/£16.50 weekends). |
| **Facilities** | ⊗ ⅏ by prior arrangement ⅃ ☗ ♀ ⅄ ☖ ♄ ☍ Graham Vivers. |
| **Leisure** | trolley for hire, putting green, practice area. |
| **Location** | S side of village on A862 |
| **Hotel** | ★★★ 68% Priory Hotel, The Square, BEAULY ☎ 01463 782309 22 ➪ ♄ |

## NAIRN                                      Map 14 NH85

**Nairn** Seabank Rd IV12 4HB ☎ 01667 453208
Championship, seaside links founded in 1887 and created
from a wilderness of heather and whin. Designed by A.
Simpson, old Tom Morris and James Braid. Opening
holes stretch out along the shoreline with the turn for
home at the 10th. Regularly chosen for national
championships.
*18 holes, 6452yds, Par 71, SSS 73, Course record 65.*
*Club membership 1150.*
**Visitors**     book in advance through secretary, may not
                 play between 8-10.30 & 12-2.30.
**Societies**    subject to availability bookings through
                 secretary's office.
**Green Fees** £35 per round (£42 weekends).
**Facilities**   ⊗ ⅏ ﳞ ■ ♀ ⚎ 🖻 ⚑ ℓ Robin P Fyfe.
**Leisure**      trolley for hire, driving range, putting green,
                 practice area, 9 hole juniors/beginners
                 course.
**Hotel**        ★★★★ 62% Golf View Hotel & Leisure
                 Club, Seabank Rd, NAIRN
                 ☎ 01667 452301 47 ⇆ 🐾

**Nairn Dunbar** Lochloy Rd IV12 5AE
☎ 01667 452741
Links course with sea views and testing gorse-and whin-lined
fairways. Breezy at holes 6, 7 and 8. Testing hole: 'Long
Peter' (527 yds).
*18 holes, 6712yds, Par 72, SSS 73.*
*Club membership 700.*
**Visitors**     must contact in advance.
**Societies**    must contact in advance.
**Green Fees** £25 per day; £20 per round (£30/£25 weekends).
**Facilities**   ⊗ ⅏ ﳞ ■ ♀ ⚎ 🖻 ⚑ ℓ Brian Mason.
**Leisure**      motorised carts for hire, trolley for hire, putting
                 green, practice area.
**Location**     E side of town off A96
**Hotel**        ★★ 62% Alton Burn Hotel, Alton Burn Rd,
                 NAIRN
                 ☎ 01667 452051 19rm(14 ⇆3 🐾)Annexe7 ⇆ 🐾

## NETHY BRIDGE                               Map 14 NJ02

**Abernethy** PH25 3EB ☎ 01479 821305
Picturesque moorland course.
*9 holes, 2551yds, Par 33, SSS 33.*
*Club membership 350.*
**Visitors**     contact in advance.
**Societies**    must contact in advance.
**Green Fees** £9 per day (£12 weekends).
**Facilities**   ⊗ ﳞ ■ ⚎ ⚑
**Leisure**      trolley for hire, putting green.
**Location**     N side of village on B970
**Hotel**        ★★★⚎ 68% Muckrach Lodge Hotel,
                 DULNAIN BRIDGE
                 ☎ 01479 851257 10 ⇆ 🐾Annexe4 ⇆ 🐾

## NEWBURGH ON YTHAN                          Map 15 NJ92

**Newburgh on Ythan** Newburgh Links AB41 0FD
☎ 01358 789058 & 789436
This seaside coursewas founded in 1888 and is adjacent to
bird sanctuary. Testing 550-yd dog leg (par 5).

*18 holes, 6162yds, Par 72, SSS 69.*
*Club membership 400.*
**Visitors**     must contact in advance.
**Societies**    apply in advance.
**Green Fees** £13 per day (£15 weekends).
**Facilities**   ﳞ ■ ⚎
**Leisure**      practice area.
**Location**     E side of village on A975
**Hotel**        ★★ 68% Udny Arms Hotel, Main St,
                 NEWBURGH ☎ 01358 789444 26 ⇆ 🐾

## NEWMACHAR                                  Map 15 NJ81

*Newmachar* Swailend AB2 0UU
☎ 01651 863002
Championship-standard parkland course designed by Dave
Thomas and opened in 1991. Several lakes affect five of the
holes and there are well developed birch and Scots pine trees.
*Hawkshill Course: 18 holes, 6623yds, Par 72, SSS 74,*
*Course record 68.*
*Club membership 750.*
**Visitors**     must contact in advance & have handicap
                 certificate, restricted at weekends.
**Societies**    apply in writing.
**Green Fees** not confirmed.
**Facilities**   ♀ ⚎ 🖻 ℓ Glenn Taylor.
**Leisure**      putting, cart/buggy/trolley hire.
**Location**     2m N of Dyce, off A947
**Hotel**        ★★★ 68% Strathburn Hotel, Burghmuir Dr,
                 INVERURIE ☎ 01467 624422 25 ⇆ 🐾

## NEWTONMORE                                 Map 14 NN79

**Newtonmore** Golf Course Rd PH20 1AT
☎ 01540 673328 & 673878
Inland course beside the River Spey. Beautiful views and
easy walking. Testing 17th hole (par 3).
*18 holes, 6029yds, Par 70, SSS 68, Course record 68.*
*Club membership 420.*
**Visitors**     contact in advance.
**Societies**    apply in writing to secretary.
**Green Fees** £15 per day; £10 per round (£20/£14 weekends).
**Facilities**   ⊗ ⅏ ﳞ ■ ♀ ⚎ 🖻 ⚑ ℓ Robert Henderson.
**Leisure**      motorised carts for hire, buggies for hire, trolley
                 for hire, putting green, practice area.
**Location**     E side of town off A9
**Hotel**        ★★ 75% The Scot House Hotel, Newtonmore
                 Rd, KINGUSSIE
                 ☎ 01540 661351 9 ⇆ 🐾

## OLDMELDRUM                                 Map 15 NJ82

**Old Meldrum** Kirkbrae AB51 0DJ
☎ 01651 872648
Parkland course with tree-lined fairways and superb views.
Challenging 196 yard, Par 3, 11th over two ponds to a green
surrounded by bunkers.
*18 holes, 5988yds, Par 70, SSS 69, Course record 67.*
*Club membership 800.*
**Visitors**     may not play during Club competitions. Must
                 contact in advance. To book tee time tel: 01651
                 873555.
**Societies**    apply in writing to secretary
**Green Fees** £12 per day (£18 weekends).
**Facilities**   ⊗ ⅏ ﳞ ■ ♀ ⚎ 🖻

**Leisure**    trolley for hire, putting green, practice area.
**Location**    E side of village off A947
**Hotel**    ★ 66% Meldrum Arms Hotel, The Square, OLDMELDRUM ☎ 01651 872238 7 ▐▘

## ORKNEY      Map 16

### KIRKWALL      Map 16 HY41

**Orkney** Grainbank KW15 1RB ☎ 01856 872457
Open parkland course with few hazards and superb views over Kirkwall and Islands.
*18 holes, 5411yds, Par 70, SSS 67, Course record 65.*
*Club membership 376.*
**Visitors**    may not play on competition days.
**Societies**    write or telephone if possible.
**Green Fees** £10 per day; £35 per week; £50 per fortnight.
**Facilities**    ┗ ■ ♀ ⚲ ♈
**Leisure**    trolley for hire, putting green, practice area.
**Location**    0.5m W off A965
**Hotel**    ★★★ 62% Ayre Hotel, Ayre Rd, KIRKWALL ☎ 01856 873001 33 ⇆ ▐▘

### STROMNESS      Map 16 HY20

**Stromness** KW16 3DW ☎ 01856 850772
Testing parkland/seaside course with easy walking. Beautiful holiday course with magnificent views of Scapa Flow.
*18 holes, 4762yds, Par 65, SSS 63, Course record 61.*
*Club membership 275.*
**Visitors**    no restrictions except during major competitions.
**Societies**    no restrictions.
**Green Fees** £12 per day/round.
**Facilities**    ♀ ⚲
**Leisure**    hard tennis courts, putting green, bowling green.
**Location**    S side of town centre off A965
**Hotel**    ★★★ 62% Ayre Hotel, Ayre Rd, KIRKWALL ☎ 01856 873001 33 ⇆ ▐▘

### WESTRAY      Map 16 HY44

**Westray** Rosevale KW17 2DH ☎ 01857 677373
Interesting, picturesque seaside course, easy walking.
*9 holes, 2405yds, Par 33.*
*Club membership 60.*
**Visitors**    No restrictions.
**Green Fees** not confirmed.
**Facilities**    ♈
**Location**    1m NW of Pierowall off B9066
**Hotel**    ★★★ 62% Ayre Hotel, Ayre Rd, KIRKWALL ☎ 01856 873001 33 ⇆ ▐▘

### PETERCULTER      Map 15 NJ80

**Peterculter** Oldtown, Burnside Rd AB1 0LN ☎ 01224 734994
The course is a tight Par 68 (from Yellow tees) with a beautiful Par 2 2nd and two Par 5 holes in excess of 500 yards. Surrounded by wonderful scenery and bordered by the River Dee, there is a variety of birds, deer and foxes on the course, which also has superb views up the Dee Valley.
*18 holes, 5947yds, Par 68, SSS 68, Course record 68.*
*Club membership 1035.*

**Visitors**    welcome after 2.30pm weekdays & 4pm weekends.
**Societies**    contact up to 7 days in advance.
**Green Fees** £16 per day; £11 per round after 2pm (£21 per day; £15 per round after 4pm weekends).
**Facilities**    ⊗ ⅏ ┗ ■ ♀ ⚲ 🖰 ♈ ▐ Dean Vannet.
**Leisure**    motorised carts for hire, buggies for hire, trolley for hire, putting green, practice area.
**Location**    On A93
**Hotel**    ★★★ 63% Westhill Hotel, WESTHILL ☎ 01224 740388 37 ⇆ ▐▘Annexe13 ⇆ ▐▘

### PETERHEAD      Map 15 NK14

**Peterhead** Craigewan Links AB42 6LT ☎ 01779 472149
Natural links course bounded by the sea and the River Ugie.
*Old Course: 18 holes, 6173yds, Par 70, SSS 71, Course record 64.*
*New Course: 9 holes, 2228yds.*
*Club membership 800.*
**Visitors**    telephone for details. Competition day Sat.
**Societies**    apply in writing, not weekends.
**Green Fees** Old Course: £22 per day; £16 per round (£27/£20 weekends). New Course: £9 per day/round.
**Facilities**    ┗ ■ ♀ ⚲
**Leisure**    practice area.
**Location**    N side of town centre off A952
**Hotel**    ★★★ 67% Waterside Inn, Fraserburgh Rd, PETERHEAD ☎ 01779 471121 70 ⇆ ▐▘Annexe40 ⇆ ▐▘

### PORTLETHEN      Map 15 NO99

**Portlethen** Badentoy Rd AB1 4YA ☎ 01224 782575 & 781090
Set in pleasant parkland, this new course features mature trees and a stream which affects a number of holes.
*18 holes, 6707yds, Par 72, SSS 72, Course record 63.*
*Club membership 1000.*
**Visitors**    may not play Sat. Contact in advance.
**Societies**    apply in advance.
**Green Fees** £20 per day; £13 per round (£20 per round weekends).
**Facilities**    ⊗ ⅏ ┗ ■ ♀ ⚲ 🖰 ♈ ▐ Muriel Thomson.
**Leisure**    trolley for hire, putting green, practice area.
**Location**    Off A90 S of Aberdeen
**Hotel**    ★★ 61% County Hotel, Arduthie Rd, STONEHAVEN ☎ 01569 764386 14 ⇆ ▐▘

### PORTMAHOMACK      Map 14 NH98

**Tarbat** IV20 1YQ ☎ 01862 871236
Picturesque links course with magnificent views.
*9 holes, 5046yds, Par 66, SSS 65.*
*Club membership 180.*
**Visitors**    no restrictions.
**Societies**    must telephone in advance.
**Green Fees** not confirmed.
**Facilities**    ⚲
**Location**    E side of village
**Hotel**    ★★★ 68% Morangie House Hotel, Morangie Rd, TAIN ☎ 01862 892281 26 ⇆ ▐▘

## REAY

Map 14 NC96

**Reay** KW14 7RE ☎ 01847 811288
Picturesque seaside links with natural hazards, following the
contours of Sandside Bay. Tight and testing.
*18 holes, 5884yds, Par 69, SSS 68, Course record 64.*
*Club membership 450.*

**Visitors** restricted competition days
**Societies** apply in writing.
**Green Fees** £12 per day/round.
**Facilities** ♀ ♣
**Leisure** practice area.
**Location** 0.5m E off A836
**Hotel** ★★ 64% Melvich Hotel, MELVICH
☎ 01641 531206 14 ♠

## ROTHES

Map 15 NJ24

**Rothes** Blackhall AB38 7AN ☎ 01340 831443
A hilly course opened in 1990 on an elevated site overlooking
the remains of Rothes castle and the Spey valley. The 2nd
fairway and most of the 3rd are sheltered by woodland. The
ground alongside the 5th & 6th falls away steeply.
*9 holes, 4972yds, Par 68, SSS 65.*
*Club membership 280.*

**Visitors** course reserved Mon 5-6.30 & Tue 5-7.30.
**Societies** apply in writing to secretary.
**Green Fees** £8 per 18 holes (£10 weekends).
**Facilities** ♀ ♣
**Location** 9m S of Elgin on A941
**Hotel** ★★★ 61% Rothes Glen Hotel, ROTHES
☎ 01340 831254 16 ♠ ♠

## SHETLAND

Map 16

## LERWICK

Map 16 HU44

**Shetland** PO Box 18 ZE1 0YW ☎ 01595 84369
Challenging moorland course, hard walking. A burn runs the
full length of the course and provides a natural hazard.
Testing holes include the 3rd (par 4), 5th (par 4).
*Dale Course: 18 holes, 5800yds, Par 68, SSS 68, Course
record 68.*
*Club membership 450.*

**Visitors** advisable to contact in advance.
**Societies** telephone in advance.
**Green Fees** £10 per day.
**Facilities** ♣ ♥ ♀ ♣ ♦
**Leisure** putting green.
**Location** 4m N on A970
**Hotel** ★★★ 62% Lerwick Hotel, 15 South Rd,
LERWICK ☎ 01595 692166 35 ♠ ♠

## WHALSAY, ISLAND OF

Map 16 HU56

**Whalsay** Skaw Taing ZE2 9AA
☎ 01806 566450 & 566481
The most northerly golf course in Britain, with a large part of
it running round the coastline, offering spectacular holes in an
exposed but highly scenic setting. There are no cut fairways
as yet, these are defined by marker posts, with preferred lies
in operation all year round.

*18 holes, 6009yds, Par 70, SSS 68, Course record 65.*
*Club membership 134.*

**Visitors** are advised to telephone, and on arrival on
Whalsay call at the shop by the harbour.
**Societies** telephone in advance.
**Green Fees** £5 per day; £20 per week.
**Facilities** ♥ ♀ ♣
**Location** N end of Island
**Hotel** ★★★♣ 66% Busta House Hotel, BRAE
☎ 01806 522506 20 ♠ ♠

## SKEABOST BRIDGE

Map 13 NG44

**Skeabost** Skeabost House Hotel IV51 9NP
☎ 01470 532202
Short woodland and seaside course featuring some very tight
fairways and greens.
*9 holes, 3056yds, Par 62, SSS 60, Course record 58.*
*Club membership 80.*

**Visitors** must contact in advance.
**Societies** contact in advance.
**Green Fees** £6 per day.
**Facilities** ⊗ ♥ ♣ ♥ ♀ ♣ ♦ ♦ ♦
**Leisure** fishing, trolley for hire, putting green, practice
area.
**Hotel** ★★★♣ 64% Skeabost House Hotel,
SKEABOST BRIDGE
☎ 01470 532202 21 ♠ ♠Annexe5 ♠ ♠

## SKYE, ISLE OF

Map 13 NG53

## SCONSER

Map 13 NG53

**Isle of Skye** IV48 8TD ☎ 01478 650351
Seaside course, often windy, splendid views.
*9 holes, 4798yds, Par 66, SSS 64, Course record 64.*
*Club membership 220.*

**Visitors** contact in advance to avoid competition times.
**Societies** apply in advance.
**Green Fees** £10 per day; £40 per week.
**Facilities** ♣ ♦
**Location** 0.5m E of village on A850
**Hotel** ★★ 71% Rosedale Hotel, PORTREE
☎ 01478 613131 20 ♠ ♠Annexe3 ♠ ♠

## SOUTH UIST, ISLE OF

Map 13 NF72

## ASKERNISH

Map 13 NF72

**Askernish** Lochboisdale PA81 5SY
☎ No telephone
Golfers play on machair (hard-wearing short grass), close to
the Atlantic shore.
*9 holes, 5042yds, Par 68, SSS 67, Course record 64.*
*Club membership 15.*

**Visitors** no restrictions.
**Societies** welcome.
**Green Fees** £5 per day; £3.50 per round.
**Facilities** ⊗ ♥ ♣ ♥ ♀ ♦
**Location** 5m NW of Lochboisdale off A865 via ferry

## SPEY BAY
Map 15 NJ36

**Spey Bay** IV32 7PJ ☎ 01343 820424
Seaside links course over gently undulating banks and well-drained ground. Good views along Moray coast. Driving range.
*18 holes, 6092yds, Par 70, SSS 69, Course record 66.*
*Club membership 350.*
**Visitors** telephone for details.
**Societies** book by telephone.
**Green Fees** £15 per day; £10 per round (£18/£13 weekends).
**Facilities** ⊗ ⅏ ⻏ 🛈 ♀ 🛆 ⛳ 🗃 ⻏ Hamish MacDonald.
**Leisure** hard tennis courts, trolley for hire, driving range, putting green, practice area.
**Location** 4.5m N of Fochabers on B9104
**Hotel** ★★ 64% Mill House Hotel, Tynet, BUCKIE ☎ 01542 850233 15 ⇄ ⻏

## STONEHAVEN
Map 15 NO88

**Stonehaven** Cowie AB3 2RH ☎ 01569 762124
Challenging meadowland course overlooking sea with three gullies and splendid views.
*18 holes, 5103yds, Par 66, SSS 65, Course record 61.*
*Club membership 850.*
**Visitors** prefer prior booking, may not play before 4pm Sat.
**Societies** must contact in advance for booking form.
**Green Fees** £15 per day (£20 weekends).
**Facilities** ⊗ ⅏ ⻏ 🛈 ♀ 🛆 🗃
**Leisure** trolley for hire, putting green, practice area.
**Location** 1m N off A92
**Hotel** ★★ 61% County Hotel, Arduthie Rd, STONEHAVEN ☎ 01569 764386 14 ⇄ ⻏

## STRATHPEFFER
Map 14 NH45

**Strathpeffer Spa** IV14 9AS ☎ 01997 421219
Upland course with many natural hazards (no sand bunkers), hard walking and fine views. Testing 3rd hole (par 3) across loch.
*18 holes, 4792yds, Par 65, SSS 64, Course record 60.*
*Club membership 550.*
**Visitors** advisable to contact in advance.
**Societies** apply in writing.
**Green Fees** £16 per day; £12 per round. Weekly ticket (Mon-Fri) £50.
**Facilities** ⊗ ⻏ 🛈 ♀ 🛆 🗃 ⛳
**Leisure** trolley for hire, practice area.
**Location** 0.25m N of village off A834
**Hotel** ★★ 69% Brunstane Lodge Hotel, Golf Rd, STRATHPEFFER ☎ 01997 421261 7rm(6 ⇄ ⻏)

## TAIN
Map 14 NH78

**Tain** Chapel Rd IV19 1PA ☎ 01862 892314
Heathland/links course with river affecting 3 holes; easy walking, fine views.
*18 holes, 6246yds, Par 70, SSS 70, Course record 62.*
*Club membership 500.*
**Visitors** no restrictions.
**Societies** must book in advance.

**Green Fees** £22 per 36 holes; £15 per round (£24/£18 weekends).
**Facilities** ⊗ ⅏ by prior arrangement ⻏ 🛈 ♀ 🛆 🗃 ⛳
**Leisure** motorised carts for hire, buggies for hire, putting green, practice area.
**Location** E side of town centre off B9174
**Hotel** ★★★ 68% Morangie House Hotel, Morangie Rd, TAIN ☎ 01862 892281 26 ⇄ ⻏

## TARLAND
Map 15 NJ40

**Tarland** Aberdeen Rd AB3 4YN ☎ 013398 81413
Difficult upland course, but easy walking.
*9 holes, 5888yds, Par 67, SSS 68, Course record 66.*
*Club membership 350.*
**Visitors** must contact in advance.
**Societies** must telephone in advance.
**Green Fees** prices under review.
**Facilities** ⻏ 🛈 ♀ 🛆
**Location** 6E side of village off B9119)
**Hotel** ★★ 70% Birse Lodge Hotel, Charleston Rd, ABOYNE ☎ 013398 86253 12 ⇄ ⻏

## THURSO
Map 15 ND16

**Thurso** Newlands of Geise KW14 7XF ☎ 01847 63807
Parkland course, windy, but with fine views of Dunnet Head and the Orkney Islands.
*18 holes, 5828yds, SSS 69, Course record 63.*
*Club membership 252.*
**Visitors** no restrictions.
**Societies** contact in advance.
**Green Fees** £11 per day; £35 per week.
**Facilities** ♀ 🛆 🗃 ⛳
**Leisure** trolley for hire, practice area.
**Location** 2m SW on B874
**Hotel** ★★ 63% Pentland Hotel, Princes St, THURSO ☎ 01847 893202 53rm(28 ⇄ 11 ⻏)

## TORPHINS
Map 15 NJ60

**Torphins** Bog Rd AB31 4JU ☎ 013398 82115
Heathland/parkland course built on a hill with views of the Cairngorms.
*9 holes, 4800yds, Par 64, SSS 64, Course record 63.*
*Club membership 380.*
**Visitors** must contact in advance. Restricted on competition days.
**Societies** apply in advance.
**Green Fees** £10 per day (£12 weekends).
**Facilities** ⻏ 🛈 🛆
**Leisure** trolley for hire, putting green.
**Location** 0.25m W of village off A980
**Hotel** ★★★ 66% Tor-na-Coille Hotel, BANCHORY ☎ 01330 822242 24 ⇄ ⻏

## TURRIFF
Map 15 NJ74

*Turriff* Rosehall AB53 7HB ☎ 01888 562982
A well-maintained parkland course alongside the River Deveron in picturesque surroundings. 6th and 12th particularly challenging in a testing course.
*18 holes, 6145yds, Par 69, SSS 68, Course record 63.*
*Club membership 860.*

▶

| | |
|---|---|
| Visitors | may not play before 10am weekends. Must contact in advance. |
| Societies | apply in writing to the secretary. |
| Green Fees | not confirmed. |
| Facilities | ♀⅄📧🍴☏ Robin Smith. |
| Leisure | putting green,practice area,trolley hire. |
| Location | 1m W off B9024 |
| Hotel | ★★★ 61% Banff Springs Hotel, Golden Knowes Rd, BANFF ☎ 01261 812881 30 ⇆ ♙ |

---

### WICK                                                   Map 15 ND35

*Wick* Reiss KW1 4RW ☎ 01955 602726
Typical seaside links course, windy, easy walking.
*18 holes, 5976yds, Par 69, SSS 69, Course record 63.*
*Club membership 352.*

| | |
|---|---|
| Visitors | no restrictions. |
| Societies | apply in writing or telephone in advance. |
| Green Fees | not confirmed. |
| Facilities | ♀ |
| Location | 3.5m N off A9 |
| Hotel | ★★ 60% Mackay's Hotel, Union St, WICK ☎ 01955 602323 26 ⇆ ♙ |

---

# CENTRAL SCOTLAND

This region includes the counties of Angus, Argyll & Bute, Clackmannanshire, City of Edinburgh, Dundee City, East Lothian, Falkirk, Fife, Inverclyde, Midlothian, Perthshire & Kinross, Stirling and West Lothian which reflect the recent national changes.

---

### ABERDOUR                                               Map 11 NT18

*Aberdour* Seaside Place KY3 0TX ☎ 01383 860080
Parkland course with lovely views over Firth of Forth.
*18 holes, 5460yds, Par 67, SSS 66, Course record 63.*
*Club membership 800.*

| | |
|---|---|
| Visitors | must contact in advance. |
| Societies | telephone secretary in advance. |
| Green Fees | £28 per day; £17 per round. |
| Facilities | ⊗ 𝍐 ⅃ 📧 ♀⅄📧🍴☏ Gordon McCallum. |
| Leisure | motorised carts for hire, trolley for hire, putting green, practice area. |
| Location | S side of village |
| Hotel | ★★ 66% Woodside Hotel, High St, ABERDOUR ☎ 01383 860328 20 ⇆ ♙ |

---

### ABERFELDY                                              Map 14 NN84

*Aberfeldy* Taybridge Rd PH15 2BH ☎ 01887 820535
Founded in 1895, this flat, parkland course is situated by River Tay near the famous Wade Bridge and Black Watch Monument and enjoys some splendid scenery. The new layout will test the keen golfer.
*18 holes, 4907yds, Par 68, SSS 66.*
*Club membership 333.*

| | |
|---|---|
| Visitors | are advised to book in advance especially at weekends. |
| Societies | must contact in advance. |
| Green Fees | £22 per day; £14 per round (Weekly £55). |
| Facilities | ⊗ 𝍐 ⅃ 📧 ♀⅄📧🍴 |
| Leisure | fishing, trolley for hire. |
| Location | N side of town centre |
| Hotel | ★★ 63% The Weem, Weem, ABERFELDY ☎ 01887 820381 12 ⇆ ♙ |

---

### ABERFOYLE                                              Map 11 NN50

*Aberfoyle* Braeval FK8 3UY ☎ 01877 382493
Scenic heathland course with mountain views.
*18 holes, 5210yds, Par 66, SSS 66.*
*Club membership 665.*

| | |
|---|---|
| Visitors | may not tee off before 10.30am Sat & Sun. |
| Societies | must contact in advance. |
| Green Fees | not confirmed. |
| Facilities | ♀⅄ |
| Leisure | putting green,trolley hire. |
| Location | 1m E on A81 |
| Hotel | ★★ 75% Lake Hotel, PORT OF MENTEITH ☎ 01877 385258 15 ⇆ ♙ |

---

### ABERLADY                                               Map 12 NT47

*Kilspindie* EH32 0QD ☎ 01875 870358
Seaside course, short but tight and well-bunkered. Testing holes: 2nd, 3rd, 4th and 7th.
*18 holes, 5471yds, Par 69, SSS 66, Course record 62.*
*Club membership 750.*

AA ★★

# The Woodside Hotel
### High Street, Aberdour, Fife

You enjoy **FREE GOLF** when you stay with us!
Book your Tee-time with the hotel for Aberdour's scenic 18 hole course.
You will enjoy our warm hospitality and excellent food.
You must visit our unique bar! –
Taken from the RMS Orontes.
Conveniently located for Edinburgh.
St. Andrew's Golf Course is within easy driving distance.
**Tel: 01383 860328 for brochure and tariff.**

**Visitors** must contact in advance.
**Societies** contact secretary in advance.
**Green Fees** £30 per day; £20 per round (£35/£25 weekends).
**Facilities** ⊗ ⓛ ᵂ ♀ ♨ 🏠 ⌁ ℓ Graham J Sked.
**Leisure** trolley for hire, putting green, practice area.
**Location** W side of village off A198
**Hotel** ★★ 67% Kilspindie House Hotel, Main St, ABERLADY ☎ 01875 870682 26 ⇄ ⌁

---

**Luffness New** EH32 0QA ☎ 01620 843114 & 843336
Seaside course.
*18 holes, 6122yds, Par 69, SSS 69, Course record 62.*
*Club membership 700.*
**Visitors** must contact in advance but may not play at weekends & bank holidays.
**Societies** must contact in writing.
**Green Fees** £40 per day; £27 per round.
**Facilities** ♀ ♨ 🏠
**Leisure** putting,practice area,trolleys,caddies.
**Location** 1m E on A198
**Hotel** ★★★(red)♨♨ Greywalls Hotel, Muirfield, GULLANE ☎ 01620 842144 17 ⇄ ⌁Annexe5 ⇄ ⌁

---

## ALLOA Map 11 NS89

**Alloa** Schawpark, Sauchie FK10 3AX
☎ 01259 722745 & 724476
Undulating, wooded parkland course.
*18 holes, 6229yds, Par 69, SSS 71, Course record 63.*
*Club membership 910.*
**Visitors** 7 day booking system through professional.
**Societies** apply in writing.
**Green Fees** £25 per day; £16 per round (£30/£20 weekends).
**Facilities** ⊗ ⅷ ⓛ ᵂ ♀ ♨ 🏠 ⌁ ℓ Bill Bennett.
**Leisure** trolley for hire, practice area.
**Location** 1.5m NE on A908
**Hotel** ★★★♨♨ 73% Gean House, Gean Park, Tullibody Rd, ALLOA ☎ 01259 219275 7 ⇄ ⌁

---

**Braehead** Cambus FK10 2NT ☎ 01259 722078 & 725766
Attactive parkland course at the foot of the Ochil Hills, and offering spectacular views.
*18 holes, 6041yds, Par 70, SSS 69, Course record 64.*
*Club membership 800.*
**Visitors** advisable to telephone in advance.
**Societies** must contact the clubhouse manager in advance tel 01259 725766.
**Green Fees** £22 per day; £14 per round (£30/£22 weekends).
**Facilities** ⊗ ⅷ ⓛ ᵂ ♀ ♨ 🏠 ⌁ ℓ Paul Brookes.
**Leisure** motorised carts for hire, trolley for hire, putting green, practice area.
**Location** 1m W on A907
**Hotel** ★★★♨♨ 73% Gean House, Gean Park, Tullibody Rd, ALLOA ☎ 01259 219275 7 ⇄ ⌁

---

## ALVA Map 11 NS89

**Alva** Beauclerc St FK12 5LH ☎ 01259 760431
A 9-hole course at the foot of the Ochil Hills which gives it its characteristic sloping fairways and fast greens.
*9 holes, 2423yds, Par 66, SSS 64, Course record 62.*
*Club membership 314.*

**Visitors** may not play during medal competitions or Thu evening (Ladies night).
**Societies** apply in writing or telephone in advance.
**Green Fees** £15 per day; £9 per round (£12 per round weekends). Weekly ticket (weekdays) £30.
**Facilities** ♀ ♨
**Location** 7m from Stirling,A91 Stirling/St Andrews rd
**Hotel** ★★ 64% Harviestoun Country Inn, Dollar Rd, TILLICOULTRY ☎ 01259 752522 10 ⇄ ⌁

---

## ALYTH Map 15 NO24

**Alyth** Pitcrocknie PH11 8HF
☎ 01828 632268 & 632241
Windy, heathland course with easy walking.
*18 holes, 6205yds, Par 71, SSS 71, Course record 65.*
*Club membership 1000.*
**Visitors** advance booking advisable
**Societies** must telephone in advance.
**Green Fees** £30 per day; £18 per round (£35/£23 weekends).
**Facilities** ⊗ ⅷ ⓛ ᵂ ♀ ♨ 🏠 ⌁ ℓ Tom Melville.
**Leisure** motorised carts for hire, trolley for hire, driving range, putting green, practice area.
**Location** 1m E on B954
**Hotel** ★★ 61% Alyth Hotel, ALYTH ☎ 01828 632447 8 ⇄ ⌁

---

**Strathmore Golf Centre** Leroch PH11 8NZ
☎ 01828 633322
The course is set on rolling parkland and heath with splendid views over Strathmore. The course is laid out in two loops of nine which both start and finish at the clubhouse. Among the challenging holes is the 480yard 5th with a 180yard carry over water from a high tee position (a cop out route available!).
*Rannaleroch Course: 18 holes, 6490yds, Par 72, SSS 71.*
*Leitfie Course: 9 holes, 1719yds, Par 29.*
*Club membership 200.*
**Visitors** no restrictions.
**Societies** phone enquiry recommended.
**Green Fees** Rannaleroch: £20 per day; £12 per round (£25/£16 weekends). Leitfie: £8 per day; £5 per round (£10/£6 weekends).
**Facilities** ⊗ ⅷ ⓛ ᵂ ♀ ♨ 🏠 ⌁
**Leisure** motorised carts for hire, buggies for hire, trolley for hire, driving range, putting, practice area.
**Location** 5m SE of Alyth,off B954 at Meigle onto A926
**Hotel** ★★ 61% Alyth Hotel, ALYTH ☎ 01828 632447 8 ⇄ ⌁

---

## ANSTRUTHER Map 12 NO50

**Anstruther** Shore Rd, "Marsfield" KY10 3DZ
☎ 01333 310956 & 312283
Seaside links course with some excellent par 3 holes; always in good condition.
*9 holes, 4144mtrs, Par 62, SSS 63.*
*Club membership 600.*
**Visitors** advised to phone in advance.
**Societies** welcome except Jun-Aug. Must apply in writing.
**Green Fees** not confirmed.
**Facilities** ♀ Jun-Aug ♨
**Location** SW off A917
**Hotel** ★★ 60% Smugglers Inn, High St, ANSTRUTHER ☎ 01333 310506 8 ⇄ ⌁

## ARBROATH
Map 12 NO64

**Arbroath** Elliot DD11 2PE
☎ 01241 872069
Municipal seaside links course, with bunkers guarding greens. Played upon by Arbroath Artisan Club.
*18 holes, 6185yds, Par 70, SSS 69.*
*Club membership 550.*
**Visitors**   contact professional 01241 875837.
**Societies**   contact professional 01241 875837.
**Green Fees** £18 per day; £13 per round (£30/£18 weekends).
**Facilities**   ⊗ ⅲ ⅉ ⚑ ♀ ⚑ Lindsay Ewart.
**Leisure**   trolley for hire, driving range, putting green, practice area.
**Location**   2m SW on A92
**Hotel**   ★★ 62% Hotel Seaforth, Dundee Rd, ARBROATH
☎ 01241 872232 20 ⇔ ℟

**Letham Grange** Colliston DD11 4RL
☎ 01241 890373
Often referred to as the 'Augusta of Scotland', the Old Course provides championship standards in spectacular surroundings with attractive lochs and burns. The New Course is less arduous and shorter using many natural features of the estate.
*Old Course: 18 holes, 6632yds, Par 73, SSS 73, Course record 69.*
*New Course: 18 holes, 5528yds, Par 68, SSS 68, Course record 63.*
*Club membership 750.*
**Visitors**   no visitors weekends before 9.30am, Old Course before 10am Tue & New Course before 10am Fri.
**Societies**   telephone in advance.
**Green Fees** Old Course: £35 per day; £23 per round (£64/£32 weekends). New Course: £21 per day; £14.50 per roun d (£27/£17 weekends).
**Facilities**   ⊗ ⅲ ⅉ ⚑ ♀ ⚑ ⌂
**Leisure**   motorised carts for hire, buggies for hire, trolley for hire, putting green, practice area, curling rink (winter).
**Location**   4m N on A933
**Hotel**   ★★★ 69% Letham Grange Hotel & Golf Course, Colliston, ARBROATH
☎ 01241 890373 19 ⇔ ℟

## AUCHTERARDER
Map 11 NN91

**Auchterarder** Orchil Rd PH3 1LS
☎ 01764 662804 (Secretary) & 663711 (Pro)
Parkland course with easy walking.
*18 holes, 5775yds, Par 69, SSS 68, Course record 64.*
*Club membership 715.*
**Visitors**   must contact professional in advance.
**Societies**   must contact in advance.
**Green Fees** £25 per day; £16 per round (£35/£22 weekends).
**Facilities**   ⊗ ⅲ ⅉ ⚑ ♀ ⚑ ⌂ ⚑ Gavin Baxter.
**Leisure**   trolley for hire, putting green, practice area.
**Location**   0.75m SW on A824
**Hotel**   ★★★★★(red) The Gleneagles Hotel, AUCHTERARDER
☎ 01764 662231 234 ⇔ ℟

## THE GLENEAGLES HOTEL   See page 279

## BARRY
Map 12 NO53

**Panmure** Burnside Rd DD7 7RT
☎ 01241 855120
A nerve-testing, adventurous course set amongst sandhills - its hazards belie the quiet nature of the opening holes. This tight links has been used as a qualifying course for the Open Championship, and features Ben Hogan's favourite hole, the dog-leg 6th, which heralds the toughest stretch, around the turn.
*18 holes, 6317yds, Par 70, SSS 70, Course record 62.*
*Club membership 700.*
**Visitors**   may not play Sat. Parties of 6 or more must contact in advance.
**Societies**   must contact secretary in advance.
**Green Fees** not confirmed.
**Facilities**   ⅉ ⚑ ⌂ ⚑ ⌂ Andew Cullen.
**Leisure**   buggy, caddy cars, caddies.
**Location**   S side of village off A930
**Hotel**   ★★ 64% Glencoe Hotel, Links Pde, CARNOUSTIE
☎ 01241 853273 7 ⇔ ℟

## BATHGATE
Map 11 NS96

**Bathgate** Edinburgh Rd EH48 1BA
☎ 01506 630553 & 652232
Moorland course. Easy walking. Testing 11th hole, par 3.
*18 holes, 6250yds, Par 71, SSS 70.*
*Club membership 750.*
**Visitors**   must contact in advance & may not play at weekends.
**Societies**   apply in writing.
**Green Fees** £20 per day; £15 per round.
**Facilities**   ⊗ ⅲ ⅉ ⚑ ♀ ⚑ ⌂ ⚑ ⌂ Sandy Strachan.
**Leisure**   motorised carts for hire, buggies for hire, trolley for hire, putting green, practice area.
**Location**   E side of town off A89
**Hotel**   ★★ 56% Dreadnought Hotel, 17/19 Whitburn Rd, BATHGATE
☎ 01506 630791 19rm(18 ⇔ ℟)

## BLAIR ATHOLL
Map 14 NN86

**Blair Atholl** PH18 5TG ☎ 01796 481407
Parkland course, river runs alongside 3 holes, easy walking.
*9 holes, 5710metres, Par 69, SSS 70, Course record 64.*
*Club membership 400.*
**Visitors**   apply in advance to avoid competition times.
**Societies**   apply in writing.
**Green Fees** £11 per day (£14 weekends). Weekly ticket £50.
**Facilities**   ⊗ ⅉ ⚑ ♀ ⚑ ⌂ ⚑
**Leisure**   trolley for hire, practice area.
**Location**   0.5m S off B8079
**Hotel**   ★★ 64% Atholl Arms Hotel, BLAIR ATHOLL
☎ 01796 481205 30 ⇔ ℟

---

Entries with a shaded background identify courses that are considered to be particularly interesting

# THE GLENEAGLES HOTEL

## AUCHTERARDER *Perthshire & Kinross*
☏ 01764 662231                    Map 11 NN91

*John Ingham writes:* Between Perth and Stirling you'll find those delightful courses, the King's and Queen's designed by James Braid and opened in 1919 to universal acclaim. There is nothing better – anywhere! They represent the best in beautiful, undulating moorland golf set alongside the massive and famous hotel – once the Caledonian Railway Hotel. The splendid Gleneagles Hotel courses are loved by its residents and for very good reasons – they are the stuff of dreams, of springy fairways, heather, bracken and pheasants that dart away when a shot misses the short grass and plunges into the wild life.

The motto there 'High Above the High' is apt as the 395 yard twelfth on the King's, named Tappit Hen (maybe it should be 'tap it in') is more than 600 feet above sea level with magnificent panoramas providing, of course, that mellow Scottish mists allow.

Only visitors to the hotel can play the courses. Years ago I stayed at the Glen with the late Henry Longhurst. 'We'll just have a quick 18 before dinner' he had said and delighted in showing me round the superb course. Since those days Jack Nicklaus has built his type of course there, the Monarch, in an American style. So now all tastes are catered for at this 5-star escape,

Without doubt the Gleneagles experience will impress any golfer and if the weather is fine, there is no better place to be. I used to go there every autumn for the Gleneagles Foursomes and at that time of the year, with the leaves golden, you feel that anything is possible.

| | |
|---|---|
| **Visitors** | must be resident in the hotel. A handicap certificate is not required but advance booking is essential |
| **Societies** | must be resident in the hotel |
| **Green fees** | Kings, Queens, Monarchs: resident rate £65 per round. Wee: £15 per round |
| **Facilities** | ⊗ ⩩ ᴸ ☷ � Ŷ ⌒ ♨ ☖  ᵀ driving range, putting greens, practice area, ᶜ (Greg Schofield) motor carts (Monarch only), buggies, trollies. Golf academy |
| **Leisure** | tennis, squash, swimming, gymnasuim, riding, fishing, shooting etc |
| **Location** | Perthshire PH3 1NF 2 miles SW of A823 |

63 holes. Kings: 18 holes, 6125yds, Par 68, SSS 71
Queens: 18 holes, 5660 yds, Par 68, SSS 68
Monarch: 18 holes, 6551yds, Par 72, SSS 73
Wee: 9 holes, 1481yds, Par 27

### WHERE TO STAY AND EAT NEARBY

**HOTELS:**

**AUCHTERARDER**
★★★★★ (Red) ☸☸ The Gleneagles Hotel
☏ 01764 662231 234 ⇆ ℾ

# KINLOCH HOUSE HOTEL

AA ★★★ (red) ❀❀❀

By Blairgowrie, Perthshire, PH10 6SG
Telephone: Blairgowrie (01250) 884 237 Fax: (01250) 884 333

Kinloch House is an award winning, family run, Country house hotel in the heart of
Sporting Perthshire. Located approximately 1½ hours from Glasgow, Edinburgh, Inverness
and Aberdeen, the hotel has 30 golf courses within an hour's drive, including many
Championship ones. Full drying facilities for clothes and equipment are available, we
would be delighted to help plan your golf and book your tee times.
**Please write or telephone for a brochure.** *DAVID AND SARAH SHENTALL*

---

## BLAIRGOWRIE
Map 15 NO14

*Blairgowrie* Rosemount PH10 6LG ☎ 01250 872622
Two 18-hole heathland courses, also a 9-hole course.
*Rosemount Course: 18 holes, 6588yds, Par 72, SSS 72.*
*Lansdowne Course: 18 holes, 6895yds, Par 72, SSS 73.*
*Wee Course: 9 holes, 4654yds, Par 64, SSS 63.*
*Club membership 1200.*
Visitors    must contact in advance & have handicap
     certificate, restricted Wed, Fri & weekends.
Societies    must contact in writing.
Green Fees   not confirmed.
Facilities   ♀ ♣ 🏠 🖥 ℓ Gordon Kinnoch.
Location    2m S off A93
Hotel     ★★★(red)♨ Kinloch House Hotel,
     BLAIRGOWRIE
     ☎ 01250 884237 21 ⇋ 🏕

## BONNYBRIDGE
Map 11 NS88

*Bonnybridge* Larbert Rd FK4 1NY ☎ 01324 812822
Testing heathland course, with tightly guarded greens. Easy
walking.
*9 holes, 6060yds, Par 72, SSS 69.*
*Club membership 325.*
Visitors    must contact in advance and be accompanied by
     member.
Societies    must contact in advance.
Green Fees   not confirmed.
Facilities   ♣ 🏠
Location    1m NE off A883
Hotel     ★★★ 68% Inchyra Grange Hotel, Grange Rd,
     POLMONT ☎ 01324 711911 43 ⇋ 🏕

## BONNYRIGG
Map 11 NT36

*Broomieknowe* 36 Golf Course Rd EH19 2HZ
☎ 0131 663 9317
Easy walking mature parkland course laid out by Ben Sayers
and extended by James Braid. Elevated site with excellent
views.
*18 holes, 6150yds, Par 70, SSS 69, Course record 65.*
Visitors    must contact in advance.
Societies    contact for details.
Green Fees   £25 two rounds; £17 per round (£20 per round
     weekends).
Facilities   ⊗ 🍴 🍺 🍷 ♀ ♣ 🏠 🖥 ℓ Mark Patchett.
Leisure    trolley for hire, putting green, practice area.
Location    0.5m NE off B704
Hotel     ★★ 62% Eskbank Hotel, 29 Dalhousie Rd,
     DALKEITH ☎ 0131 663 3234 16 ⇋ 🏕

---

## BRECHIN
Map 15 NO56

Brechin Trinity DD9 7PD
☎ 01356 622383 & 01356 625270 (Pro)
Rolling parkland course, with easy walking and good views
of Strathmore Valley and Grampian Mountains. The course
was extended in 1993.
*18 holes, 6092yds, Par 72, SSS 70, Course record 66.*
*Club membership 620.*
Visitors    contact in advance.
Societies    must contact club steward in advance.
Green Fees   £19 per day; £14 per round (£27/£18 weekends).
     5 day ticket £45.
Facilities   ⊗ 🍴 🍺 🍷 ♀ ♣ 🏠 🖥 ℓ Stephen Rennie.
Leisure    squash, motorised carts for hire, buggies for hire,
     trolley for hire, putting green, practice area.
Location    1m N on B966
Hotel     ★★ 58% Northern Hotel, Clerk St, BRECHIN
     ☎ 01356 622156 & 625505 20rm(4 ⇋ 12 🏕)

## BRIDGE OF ALLAN
Map 11 NS79

*Bridge of Allan* Sunnylaw FK9 4LY ☎ 01786 832332
Parkland course, very hilly with good views of Stirling Castle
and beyond to the Trossachs. Testing 1st hole, 221 yds (par 3)
uphill 6 ft wall 25 yds before green.
*9 holes, 4932yds, Par 66, SSS 65, Course record 62.*
*Club membership 400.*
Visitors    restricted Sat.
Societies    must contact in advance.
Green Fees   not confirmed.
Facilities   ♀ ♣
Leisure    pool table.
Location    0.5m N off A9
Hotel     ★★★ 65% Royal Hotel, Henderson St,
     BRIDGE OF ALLAN
     ☎ 01786 832284 32 ⇋ 🏕

## BROXBURN
Map 11 NT07

*Niddry Castle* Castle Rd, Winchburgh EH52 6RQ
☎ 01506 891097
A 9-hole parkland course. While not very long, it requires
accurate golf to score well.
*9 holes, 5514yds, Par 70, SSS 67.*
*Club membership 320.*
Visitors    advisable to contact at weekends, restricted
     during competition time.
Societies    must contact in advance.
Green Fees   not confirmed.
Facilities   ♣
Location    9m W of Edinburgh off junc 1

**Hotel**   ★★★ 60% Forth Bridges Hotel, Forth Bridge, SOUTH QUEENSFERRY ☎ 0131 331 1199 108 ⇆ ⋒

---

## BURNTISLAND            Map 11 NT28

**Burntisland Golf House Club** Dodhead, Kirkcaldy Rd KY3 9EW ☎ 01592 874093 (Manager) & 873247 (Pro)
This hill course has fine sea views.
*18 holes, 5965yds, Par 70, SSS 69, Course record 62.*
*Club membership 800.*
**Visitors**   weekend play restricted. Book by telephoning professional.
**Societies**   apply in writing to manager.
**Green Fees** £25 per day; £15 per round (£35/£23 weekends).
**Facilities**   ⊗ ⅊ ᗷ ☕ ♀ ⚲ 🖼 ⚑ ⫞ Jacky Montgomery.
**Leisure**   trolley for hire, driving range, putting green, practice area.
**Location**   1m E on B923
**Hotel**   ★★ 65% Inchview Hotel, 69 Kinghorn Rd, BURNTISLAND ☎ 01592 872239 12 ⇆ ⋒

---

## BUTE, ISLE OF            Map 10 NS05

---

## KINGARTH               Map 10 NS05

*Bute* Kingarth, Rothesay PA20 9HN
☎ 01700 831648
Flat seaside course with good fenced greens.
*9 holes, 2497yds, Par 68, SSS 64, Course record 65.*
*Club membership 120.*
**Visitors**   restricted Sat until after 12.30pm.
**Societies**   apply in advance.
**Green Fees** not confirmed.
**Facilities**   ⚲
**Location**   1m W off A844
**Hotel**   ★★⚘ 72% Armory House Hotel, Ardmory Rd, ARDBEG ☎ 01700 502346 5 ⇆ ⋒

---

## PORT BANNATYNE        Map 10 NS06

*Port Bannatyne* Bannatyne Mains Rd PA20 0PH
☎ 01700 505223
Seaside hill course with panoramic views. Difficult hole: 4th (par 3).
*13 holes, 5085yds, Par 68, SSS 65, Course record 66.*
*Club membership 200.*
**Visitors**   no restrictions.
**Societies**   must telephone in advance.
**Green Fees** not confirmed.
**Facilities**   ⚲
**Location**   W side of village off A844
**Hotel**   ★★⚘ 72% Armory House Hotel, Ardmory Rd, ARDBEG ☎ 01700 502346 5 ⇆ ⋒

---

## ROTHESAY             Map 10 NS06

*Rothesay* Canada Hill PA20 9HN ☎ 01700 502244
A scenic island course designed by James Braid and Ben Sayers. The course is fairly hilly, with views of the Firth of Clyde, Rothesay Bay or the Kyles of Bute from every hole. Winds are a regular feature which makes the two par 5 holes extremely challenging.

---

*18 holes, 5043yds, Par 69, SSS 65, Course record 62.*
*Club membership 350.*
**Visitors**   pre-booking essential for weekends, telephone professional.
**Societies**   contact in advance, booking essential at weekends.
**Green Fees** not confirmed.
**Facilities**   ♀ ⚲ 🖼 ⚑ ⫞ James M Dougal.
**Leisure**   caddy cars,putting green,trolley hire,practice area.
**Location**   Off road to Kingarth
**Hotel**   ★★⚘ 72% Armory House Hotel, Ardmory Rd, ARDBEG ☎ 01700 502346 5 ⇆ ⋒

---

## CALLANDER           Map 11 NN60

**Callander** Aveland Rd FK17 8EN
☎ 01877 330090 & 330975
Parkland course, with fairly tightly guarded greens. Designed by Tom Morris Snr and overlooked by the Trossachs.
*18 holes, 5151yds, Par 66, SSS 66, Course record 61.*
*Club membership 750.*
**Visitors**   prior booking 24-48 hrs is advised in the playing season.
**Societies**   write or telephone for booking form.
**Green Fees** £22.50 per day; £17 per round (£28/£22.50 weekends).
**Facilities**   ⊗ ⅊ by prior arrangement ᗷ ⯛ ♀ ⚲ 🖼 ⚑ ⫞ William Kelly.
**Leisure**   trolley for hire.
**Location**   E side of town off A84
**Hotel**   ★★★⚘ 69% Roman Camp Hotel, CALLANDER ☎ 01877 330003 14 ⇆ ⋒

---

## CARDENDEN           Map 11 NT29

*Auchterderran* Woodend Rd KY5 0NH
☎ 01592 721579
This is a relatively flat course requiring a lot of thought. There are two or three holes to test the best.
*9 holes, 5250yds, Par 66, SSS 66, Course record 63.*
*Club membership 120.*
**Visitors**   no visitors between 7-11am & 1-3pm Sat, also some Sun in season.
**Societies**   apply in writing.
**Green Fees** not confirmed.
**Facilities**   ♀ ⚲
**Location**   N end Cardenden, Kirkcaldy/Glenrothes road
**Hotel**   ★★★ 57% Dean Park Hotel, Chapel Level, KIRKCALDY ☎ 01592 261635 20 ⇆ ⋒Annexe12 ⋒

---

## CARDROSS            Map 10 NS37

**Cardross** Main Rd G82 5LB ☎ 01389 841754
Undulating parkland course, testing with good views.
*18 holes, 6469yds, Par 71, SSS 72, Course record 65.*
*Club membership 800.*
**Visitors**   may not play at weekends unless introduced by member. Contact professional in advance 01359 841350
**Societies**   must contact in writing.
**Green Fees** £32 per day; £22 per round.
**Facilities**   ⊗ ⅊ by prior arrangement ᗷ ⯛ ♀ ⚲ 🖼 ⚑ ⫞ Robert Farrell.     ▶

| | |
|---|---|
| **Leisure** | motorised carts for hire, buggies for hire, trolley for hire, putting green, practice area. |
| **Location** | In centre of village on A814 |
| **Hotel** | ★★ 68% Commodore Toby Hotel, 112 West Clyde St, HELENSBURGH ☎ 01436 676924 45 ⇔ ℝ |

## CARNOUSTIE
Map 12 NO53

**CARNOUSTIE GOLF LINKS** See page 283

## CARRADALE
Map 10 NR83

**Carradale** PA28 6SG ☎ 01583 431643
Pleasant seaside course built on a promontory overlooking the Isle of Arran. Natural terrain and small greens are the most difficult natural hazards. Described as the most sporting 9-hole course in Scotland. Testing 7th hole (240 yds), par 3.
*9 holes, 2392yds, Par 62, SSS 64.*
*Club membership 320.*

| | |
|---|---|
| **Visitors** | no restrictions |
| **Societies** | contact in advance. |
| **Green Fees** | £7 per day also weekly and monthly rates available. |
| **Facilities** | ⚐ |
| **Leisure** | trolley for hire, putting green. |
| **Location** | S side of village |
| **Hotel** | ★★ 65% Seafield Hotel, Kilkerran Rd, CAMPBELTOWN ☎ 01586 554385 3 ℝAnnexe6 ℝ |

## COLONSAY, ISLE OF
Map 10 NR39

## SCALASAIG
Map 10 NR39

**Colonsay** PA61 7YP ☎ 01951 200316
Traditional links course on natural machair (hard wearing short grass), challenging, primitive. Colonsay Hotel, 2 miles away, is the headquarters of the club, offering accommodation and facilities.
*18 holes, 4775yds, Par 72, SSS 72.*
*Club membership 120.*

| | |
|---|---|
| **Visitors** | no restrictions. |
| **Societies** | apply in writing. |
| **Green Fees** | not confirmed. |
| **Facilities** | ⚐ |
| **Location** | 2m W on A870 |
| **Hotel** | ★ 75% Colonsay Hotel, SCALASAIG ☎ 01951 200316 10rm(1 ⇔7 ℝ)Annexe1rm |

## COMRIE
Map 11 NN72

**Comrie** PH6 2LR ☎ 01764 760055 & 760941
Scenic highland course.
*9 holes, 6040yds, Par 70, SSS 69, Course record 62.*
*Club membership 315.*

| | |
|---|---|
| **Visitors** | apply in advance. |
| **Societies** | must contact in advance. |
| **Green Fees** | £10 per day (£15 per day/£12 per round weekends). |
| **Facilities** | ⊗ ⬛ ⚐ ⚑ |
| **Leisure** | fishing, buggies for hire, trolley for hire, practice area. |
| **Location** | E side of village off A85 |
| **Guesthouse** | QQQ Mossgiel Guest House, Burrell St, COMRIE ☎ 01764 670567 5rm |

## COWDENBEATH
Map 11 NT19

**Cowdenbeath** Seco Place KY4 8PD ☎ 01383 511918
A parkland-based 9-hole golf course.
*Dora Course: 9 holes, 6552yds, Par 72, SSS 71, Course record 68.*
*Club membership 400.*

| | |
|---|---|
| **Visitors** | no restrictions. |
| **Societies** | must contact at least 2 weeks in advance. |
| **Green Fees** | not confirmed. |
| **Facilities** | ♀ |
| **Leisure** | putting green,practice area. |
| **Location** | 6m E of Dunfermline |
| **Hotel** | ★★ 66% Woodside Hotel, High St, ABERDOUR ☎ 01383 860328 20 ⇔ ℝ |

## CRAIL
Map 12 NO60

**Crail Golfing Society** Balcomie Clubhouse, Fifeness KY10 3XN ☎ 01333 450686 & 450416
Perched on the edge of the North Sea on the very point of the golfing county of Fife, the Crail Golfing Society's course at Balcomie is picturesque and sporting. And here again golf history has been made for Crail Golfing Society began its life in 1786. The course is highly thought of by students of the game both for its testing holes and the standard of its greens.
*18 holes, 5922yds, Par 69, SSS 69.*
*Club membership 950.*

| | |
|---|---|
| **Visitors** | must contact in advance, restricted 10am-noon & 2-4.30pm. |
| **Societies** | must contact in advance, as much notice as possible for weekend play. |
| **Green Fees** | £26 per day; £18 per round (£34/£23 weekends). ▶ |

## Pittenweem Road, Anstruther, Fife KY10 3DT
### Telephone/Fax: 01333 310573

Personally run accommodation offering the highest standards of hospitality in an immaculate setting. An ideal base for exploring the East Neuk with 40 golf courses within an hour drive – St Andrews only 9 miles away.

AA
QQQQ

Logis of Great Britain

HIGHLY COMMENDED

# CARNOUSTIE GOLF LINKS

**CARNOUSTIE** *Angus* ☎ **01241 853789**     **Map 12 NO53**

*John Ingham writes:* You love it, or hate it - but you respect it. Carnoustie can be a graveyard. Simply standing up to the buffeting is bad enough, but those closing holes, across the Barry Burn (or into it) are a prospect which can gnaw at the mind. The burn twists through the links like an angry serpent and has to be crossed no fewer than seven times.

Back in 1953 they came to see Ben Hogan play in the Open Championship. This little man from Texas had a magic about him, and the huge terrifying links, the dread of any short hitter, certainly promised to be a platform on which to examine the finest golfer of his day, and maybe of any day.

Not since 1860 had any golfer won the Open on his first attempt. Certainly Hogan hadn't come to this awesome place for the money which, in those days, was a pittance. He had come to prove he was the best player in the world. That was pressure!

When Mr Hogan saw the 'Stone Age' course, dating back to the birth of the game, he was shocked because it lacked trees and colour, and looked drab. But he beat the 7200-yard monster course for the 1953 Championship, which was, as they say, something else.

'Winning the British Open at Carnoustie gave me my greatest pleasure' he told the *Fort Worth Star-Telegram*. 'Certainly the other victories were pleasurable, but none gave me the feeling, the desire to perform, that gripped me in Scotland'.

Sadly, Hogan never returned and then the great links was taken from the Open Championship rota. Today there are hopes it may be re-instated.

**Visitors** must contact golf links in advance.Restricted hours. Must have a handicap certificate for Championship course

**Societies** prior arrangement required either in writing or by telephone

**Green fees** Championship: £78 per day; £45 per round Burnside: £26 per day; £17 per round; Buddon Links: £18 per day; £12 per round. Combination day tickets: Championship & Burnside £54; Championship & Buddon Links £50; Burnside & Buddon Links £22

**Facilities** ⛄

**Location** Carnoustie DD7 7JE Links Parade (SW side of town, off A930)

54 holes. Championship Course: 18 holes, 6936 yds, Par 72, SSS 74, Course record 68 (Colin Montgomerie) Burnside Course: 18 holes, 6020 yds, Par 68, SSS 69 Buddon Links: 18 holes, 5420 yds, Par 66, SSS 66

## WHERE TO STAY AND EAT NEARBY

**HOTELS:**

**ARBROATH**
★★ 62% Hotel Seaforth, Dundee Rd, ☎ 01241 872232. 20 (14 ⇆ 6 ⇆ 🐾)

**CARNOUSTIE**
★★ 67% Carlogie House, Carlogie Rd ☎ 01241 853185. 12 (10 🐾 1 ⇆ 1 ⇆ 🐾) Annexe 1 🐾

★★64% Glencoe, Links Pde. ☎ 01241 853273. 7 (4 🐾 3 ⇆ 🐾)

**RESTAURANT:**
**INVERKEILOR**
🏵 Gordon's, Homewood House, Main St. ☎ 01241 830364

**Facilities** ⊗ ⅷ ㊑ 💺 ♀ ⚑ 🏌 ⚐ Graheme Lennie.
**Leisure** trolley for hire, driving range, putting green, practice area.
**Location** 2m NE off A917
**Hotel** ★★ 63% Balcomie Links Hotel, Balcomie Rd, CRAIL ☎ 01333 450237 11 ⇆ ⋒
**Additional hotel** QQQQ The Spindrift, Pittenweem Rd, ANSTRUTHER ☎ 01333 310573 8 ⇆ ⋒

## CRIEFF                                    Map 11 NN82

**Crieff** Ferntower, Perth Rd PH7 3LR
☎ 01764 652909 & 652397 bookings
This course is what you might call 'up and down' but the turf is beautiful and the highland air fresh and invigorating. There are views from the course over Strathearn. Of the two courses the Ferntower is the more challenging. Both parkland, the Dornock has one water hazard.
*Ferntower Course: 18 holes, 6402yds, SSS 71, Course record 65.*
*Dornock Course: 9 holes, 4772yds, Par 64, SSS 63.*
*Club membership 720.*
**Visitors** must contact professional in advance.
**Societies** must contact professional in advance.
**Green Fees** Ferntower: £30 per day, £18 per round (£40/£25 weekends). Dornock: £12/£15.
**Facilities** ⊗ ⅷ ㊑ 💺 ♀ ⚑ ⚐ 🏌 ⚐ David Murchie.
**Location** 0.5m NE on A85
**Hotel** ★★ 69% Murraypark Hotel, Connaught Ter, CRIEFF ☎ 01764 653731 20 ⇆ ⋒

## CUPAR                                    Map 11 NO31

*Cupar* Hilltarvit KY15 5NZ ☎ 01334 53549
Hilly parkland course with fine views over north east Fife.5th/14th hole is most difficult - uphill and into the prevailing wind.
*9 holes, 5500yds, Par 68, SSS 65, Course record 62.*
*Club membership 450.*
**Visitors** welcome except Sat.
**Societies** must contact in advance.
**Green Fees** not confirmed.
**Facilities** ♀ ⚐
**Leisure** practice putting green.
**Location** 0.75m S off A92
**Hotel** ★★ 67% Eden House Hotel, 2 Pitscottie Rd, CUPAR ☎ 01334 652510 9 ⇆ ⋒Annexe2 ⇆ ⋒

## DALKEITH                                    Map 11 NT36

**Newbattle** Abbey Rd EH22 3AD
☎ 0131 663 2123 & 0131 660 1631
Undulating parkland course on three levels, surrounded by woods.
*18 holes, 6005yds, Par 69, SSS 70, Course record 61.*
*Club membership 700.*
**Visitors** Mon-Fri ex public holidays, before 4pm.
**Societies** welcome weekdays ex public holidays, before 4pm.
**Green Fees** £24 per day; £16 per round.
**Facilities** ⊗ ⅷ ㊑ 💺 ♀ ⚑ ⚐ David Torrance.
**Leisure** trolley for hire, putting green, small practice area.

**Location** SW side of town off A68
**Hotel** ★★ 62% Eskbank Hotel, 29 Dalhousie Rd, DALKEITH ☎ 0131 663 3234 16 ⇆ ⋒

## DALMALLY                                    Map 10 NN12

**Dalmally** Old Saw Mill PA33 1AE ☎ 01838 200370
A 9-hole flat parkland course alongside the River Orchy. The course is surrounded by mountains and there are plenty of water hazards.
*9 holes, 2257yds, Par 64, SSS 63, Course record 64.*
*Club membership 100.*
**Visitors** no visitors on Sun between 9-10 & 1-2.
**Societies** telephone in advance.
**Green Fees** £8 per day.
**Facilities** ♀ by prior arrangement ♀ by arrangement ⚑ ⚐
**Leisure** fishing, practice area.
**Location** On A85, 1.5m W of Dalmally
**Hotel** ★★ 57% Polfearn Hotel, TAYNUILT ☎ 01866 2251 16rm(3 ⇆ 11 ⋒)

## DOLLAR                                    Map 11 NS99

**Dollar** Brewlands House FK14 7EA ☎ 01259 742400
Compact hillside course.
*18 holes, 5242yds, Par 69, SSS 66, Course record 62.*
*Club membership 470.*
**Visitors** weekdays course available but restricted Wed ladies day, weekends must contact in advance.
**Societies** write or telephone in advance.
**Green Fees** £14 per day; £10 per round (£18.50 per day/round).
**Facilities** ⊗ ⅷ ㊑ 💺 ♀ ⚑ ⚐
**Leisure** trolley for hire, practice area.
**Location** 0.5m N off A91
**Hotel** ★★★ 65% Royal Hotel, Henderson St, BRIDGE OF ALLAN ☎ 01786 832284 32 ⇆ ⋒

## DRYMEN                                    Map 11 NS48

*Buchanan Castle* G63 0HY ☎ 01360 660307
Parkland course, with easy walking and good views.
*18 holes, 6086yds, Par 70, SSS 69.*
*Club membership 830.*
**Societies** must contact in advance.
**Green Fees** not confirmed.
**Facilities** ♀ ⚑ ⚐ 🏌 ⚐ Keith Baxter.
**Leisure** putting, trolley hire, practice area.
**Location** 1m W
**Hotel** ★★★ 67% Buchanan Arms Hotel, DRYMEN ☎ 01360 660588 51 ⇆ ⋒

## DUNBAR                                    Map 12 NT67

**Dunbar** East Links EH42 1LT ☎ 01368 862317
Another of Scotland's old links. It is said that it was some Dunbar members who first took the game of golf to the North of England. The club dates back to 1856. The wind, if blowing from the sea, is a problem.
*18 holes, 6426yds, Par 71, SSS 71, Course record 64.*
*Club membership 1000.*                                    ▶

| | |
|---|---|
| **Visitors** | may not play Thu, between 12.30-2 weekdays, 12-2 weekends or before 9.30am any day. |
| **Societies** | telephone in advance. |
| **Green Fees** | £30 per day (£40 weekends). |
| **Facilities** | ⊗ ⓑ 🍺 ♀ ♨ 🏠 ⚑ ( Derek Small. |
| **Leisure** | trolley for hire, putting green, practice area. |
| **Location** | 0.5m E off A1087 |
| **Hotel** | ★★ 61% Bayswell Hotel, Bayswell Park, DUNBAR ☎ 01368 862225 13 ⇄ ⋒ |

*Winterfield* North Rd EH42 1AY ☎ 01368 863562
Seaside course with superb views.
*18 holes, 5220yds, SSS 64.*
*Club membership 200.*

| | |
|---|---|
| **Visitors** | must contact in advance. |
| **Green Fees** | not confirmed. |
| **Facilities** | ♀ ♨ 🏠 ⚑ |
| **Location** | W side of town off A1087 |
| **Hotel** | ★★ 61% Bayswell Hotel, Bayswell Park, DUNBAR ☎ 01368 862225 13 ⇄ ⋒ |

## DUNBLANE                               Map 11 NN70

*Dunblane New Golf Club* Perth Rd FK15 0LJ
☎ 01786 823711
Well maintained parkland course, with reasonably hard walking. Testing 6th and 9th holes.
*18 holes, 5876yds, Par 69, SSS 68.*
*Club membership 800.*

| | |
|---|---|
| **Visitors** | may play 9.30am-noon & 2.30-4pm Mon-Fri. Must contact in advance. |
| **Societies** | welcome Mon, Wed-Fri, contact in advance. |
| **Green Fees** | not confirmed. |
| **Facilities** | ♀ ♨ 🏠 ⚑ ( |
| **Leisure** | putting,trolley hire,practice area. |
| **Location** | E side of town on A9 |
| **Hotel** | ★★★(red)▲▲ Cromlix House Hotel, Kinbuck, DUNBLANE ☎ 01786 822125 14 ⇄ ⋒ |

## DUNDEE                                 Map 11 NO43

*Caird Park* Mains Loan DD4 9BX ☎ 01382 453606
Municipal parkland course.
*18 holes, 5494yds, Par 69, SSS 68.*
*Club membership 400.*

| | |
|---|---|
| **Visitors** | no restrictions. |
| **Societies** | must contact Dundee District Council on 01382 223141 in advance. |
| **Green Fees** | not confirmed. |
| **Facilities** | ♀ 🏠 ⚑ ( J Black. |
| **Location** | 1.5m N of city centre off A972 |
| **Hotel** | ★★★ 62% The Queen's Hotel, 160 Nethergate, DUNDEE ☎ 01382 322515 47 ⇄ ⋒ |

*Camperdown* Camperdown House, Camperdown Park DD2 4TF ☎ 01382 621145
Parkland course. Testing 2nd hole.
*18 holes, 5999yds, Par 71, SSS 69.*
*Club membership 600.*

| | |
|---|---|
| **Visitors** | must contact in advance. |
| **Societies** | must contact in advance. |
| **Green Fees** | not confirmed. |
| **Facilities** | ♨ 🏠 ( |

| | |
|---|---|
| **Leisure** | hard tennis courts. |
| **Location** | 3m NW of city centre off A923 |
| **Hotel** | ★★★ 63% The Angus Thistle, 101 Marketgait, DUNDEE ☎ 01382 226874 58 ⇄ ⋒ |

**Downfield** Turnberry Av DD2 3QP
☎ 01382 825595
A fine inland course of recent Championship rating set in undulating woodland to the north of Dundee. The Gelly burn provides a hazard for several holes.
*18 holes, 6822yds, Par 73, SSS 73, Course record 65.*
*Club membership 750.*

| | |
|---|---|
| **Visitors** | must contact in advance, no visitors at weekends. |
| **Societies** | must contact in advance. |
| **Green Fees** | £39 per day; £27 per round. |
| **Facilities** | ⊗ ⅷ ⓑ 🍺 ♀ ♨ 🏠 ⚑ ( Kenny Hutton. |
| **Leisure** | trolley for hire, putting green, practice area. |
| **Location** | N of city centre off A923 |
| **Hotel** | ★★★ 63% The Angus Thistle, 101 Marketgait, DUNDEE ☎ 01382 226874 58 ⇄ ⋒ |

## DUNFERMLINE                           Map 11 NT08

*Canmore* Venturefair Av KY12 0PF
☎ 01383 724969
Undulating parkland course affording excellent views.
*18 holes, 5474yds, Par 67, SSS 66.*
*Club membership 620.*

| | |
|---|---|
| **Visitors** | no restrictions. Sat not usually available. |
| **Societies** | apply in writing to secretary. |
| **Green Fees** | not confirmed. |
| **Facilities** | ♀ ♨ 🏠 ( |
| **Location** | 1m N on A823 |
| **Hotel** | ★★★ 62% King Malcolm Thistle, Queensferry Rd, Wester Pitcorthie, DUNFERMLINE ☎ 01383 722611 48 ⇄ ⋒ |

*Dunfermline* Pitfirrane, Crossford KY12 8QV
☎ 01383 723534
Gently undulating parkland course with interesting contours. Sixteenth-century clubhouse.
*18 holes, 6237yds, Par 72, SSS 70, Course record 65.*
*Par 3 course: 9 holes, 1144yds, Par 27.*
*Club membership 690.*

| | |
|---|---|
| **Visitors** | may not play Sat. Contact to check times. |
| **Societies** | must contact in advance. |
| **Green Fees** | not confirmed. |
| **Facilities** | ♀ ♨ 🏠 ( Steve Craig. |
| **Leisure** | putting,trolley hire,practice area. |
| **Location** | 2m W on A994 |
| **Hotel** | ★★★ 62% King Malcolm Thistle, Queensferry Rd, Wester Pitcorthie, DUNFERMLINE ☎ 01383 722611 48 ⇄ ⋒ |

*Pitreavie* Queensferry Rd KY11 5PR
☎ 01383 722591
Picturesque woodland course with panoramic view of the River Forth Valley. Testing golf.
*18 holes, 6086yds, Par 70, SSS 69, Course record 65.*
*Club membership 700.*

| | |
|---|---|
| **Visitors** | welcome except for competition days. |
| **Societies** | must write or telephone in advance. |
| **Green Fees** | not confirmed. |
| **Facilities** | ♀ ♨ 🏠 ⚑ ( Jim Forrester. ▶ |

**Leisure**   putting green,practice area,trolley hire.
**Location**   SE side of town on A823
**Hotel**   ★★★ 62% King Malcolm Thistle, Queensferry Rd, Wester Pitcorthie, DUNFERMLINE
☎ 01383 722611 48 ⇦ ⋒

## DUNKELD                                 Map 11 NO04

**Dunkeld & Birnam** Fungarth PH8 0HU
☎ 01350 727524
Interesting heathland course with spectacular views of surrounding countryside.
*9 holes, 5322yds, Par 68, SSS 66, Course record 64.*
*Club membership 430.*
**Visitors**   must contact in advance.
**Societies**   apply in writing.
**Green Fees** on application.
**Facilities** ⊗ ⅲ ⮾ ⚐ ♀ ⚐ ⚑
**Leisure**   trolley for hire, driving range, putting green, practice area.
**Location**   1m N of village on A923
**Hotel**   ★★★(red)⚌ Kinnaird, Kinnaird Estate, DUNKELD ☎ 01796 482440 9 ⇦ ⋒

## DUNNING                                 Map 11 NO01

**Dunning** Rollo Park PH2 0RH
☎ 01764 684372 & 684747
Parkland course.
*9 holes, 4836yds, Par 66, SSS 64.*
*Club membership 580.*
**Visitors**   may not play on Sat before 4pm or Sun before 1pm. With member only after 5pm Mon-Fri.
**Societies**   must contact in advance in writing.
**Green Fees** not confirmed.
**Facilities** ⚐
**Location**   Off A9 NW
**Hotel**   ★★★⚌ 70% Duchally House Hotel, AUCHTERARDER
☎ 01764 663071 13rm(12 ⇦ ⋒)

## DUNOON                                  Map 10 NS17

**Cowal** Ardenslate Rd PA23 8LT ☎ 01369 705673
Moorland course. Panoramic views of Clyde Estuary and surrounding hills.
*18 holes, 6063yds, Par 70, SSS 70, Course record 63.*
*Club membership 700.*
**Visitors**   advisable to book in advance.
**Societies**   must telephone in advance.
**Green Fees** £24 per day; £16 per round (£35/£24 weekends).
**Facilities** ⊗ ⅲ ⮾ ⚐ ♀ ⚐ ⚑ ⚐
**Leisure**   trolley for hire, putting green, practice area.
**Location**   1m N
**Hotel**   ★★ 76% Enmore Hotel, Marine Pde, Kirn, DUNOON ☎ 01369 702230 11 ⇦ ⋒

## EDINBURGH                               Map 11 NT27

**Baberton** 50 Baberton Av, Juniper Green EH14 5DU
☎ 0131 453 4911
Parkland course.
*18 holes, 6123yds, Par 69, SSS 70, Course record 64.*
*Club membership 900.*

**Visitors**   may not play at weekends or after 3.30pm weekdays. Contact in advance.
**Societies**   must contact in advance.
**Green Fees** £28.50 per day; £18.50 per round.
**Facilities** ⊗ ⅲ ⮾ ⚐ ♀ ⚐ ⚐ ⚑ Ken Kelly.
**Leisure**   trolley for hire, putting green, practice area.
**Location**   5m W of city centre off A70
**Hotel**   ★★★ 67% Bruntsfield Hotel, 69/74 Bruntsfield Place, EDINBURGH
☎ 0131 229 1393 50 ⇦ ⋒

**Braid Hills** Braid Hills Approach EH10 6JZ
☎ 0131 447 6666
Municipal heathland course with good views of Edinburgh and the Firth of Forth.
*Course No 1: 18 holes, 6172yds, Par 70, SSS 68, Course record 62.*
*Course No 2: 18 holes, 4832yds, Par 65, SSS 63.*
**Visitors**   may not play on Sat mornings.
**Societies**   apply in writing to Leisure Management Unit, Edinburgh District Council, 141 London Road, Edinburgh.
**Green Fees** not confirmed.
**Facilities** ⚐ ⚐ ⚑ ⚐
**Leisure**   putting green,trolley hire,practice area.
**Location**   2.5m S of city centre off A702
**Hotel**   ★★★ 67% Braid Hills Hotel, 134 Braid Rd, Braid Hills, EDINBURGH
☎ 0131 447 8888 68 ⇦ ⋒

**Bruntsfield Links Golfing Society** 32 Barnton Av EH4 6JH
☎ 0131 336 1479
Parkland course with good views of Forth Estuary. 4th and 14th holes testing.
*18 holes, 6407yds, Par 71, SSS 71, Course record 67.*
*Club membership 1100.*
**Visitors**   Must contact in advance.
**Societies**   apply in writing.
**Green Fees** £45 per day; £35 per round (£50/£40 weekends).
**Facilities** ⊗ ⚐ ♀ ⚐ ⚐ ⚑ ⚐ Brian Mackenzie.
**Leisure**   motorised carts for hire, buggies for hire, trolley for hire, driving range, putting green. practice area.
**Location**   4m NW of city centre off A90
**Hotel**   ★★★ 64% The Barnton Thistle, Queensferry Rd, Barnton, EDINBURGH
☎ 0131 339 1144 50 ⇦ ⋒

**Carrick Knowe** Carrick Knowe Municipal, Glendevon Park EH12 5UZ ☎ 0131 337 1096
Flat parkland course. Played over by two clubs, Carrick Knowe and Carrick Vale.
*18 holes, 6299yds, Par 71, SSS 70.*
*Club membership 450.*
**Visitors**   may be restricted at weekends.
**Societies**   apply in writing to: Leisure Management Unit, Meadowbank Sports Centre, London Road, Edinburgh.
**Green Fees** not confirmed.
**Facilities** ⚑
**Leisure**   trolley hire,practice area.
**Location**   3m W of city centre, S of A8
**Hotel**   B Forte Posthouse Edinburgh, Corstorphine Rd, EDINBURGH
☎ 0131 334 0390 204 ⇦ ⋒

*Craigentinny* Fillyside Rd, Lochend
☎ 0131 554 7501
To the north east of Edinburgh, Craigentinny course is between Leith and Portobello. It is generally flat although there are some hillocks with gentle slopes. The famous Arthur's Seat dominates the southern skyline.
*18 holes, 5418yds, Par 67, SSS 65.*

| | |
|---|---|
| Societies | must apply in writing to: Leisure Management Unit,Meadowbank Sports Centre, London Road, Edinburgh. |
| Green Fees | not confirmed. |
| Facilities | ⚐ |
| Leisure | trolley hire, practice area. |
| Location | NE side of city, between Leith & Portobello |
| Hotel | ★★★ 70% King James Thistle, 107 Leith St, EDINBURGH ☎ 0131 556 0111 147 ⇆ ⁿ |

---

**Craigmillar Park** 1 Observatory Rd EH9 3HG
☎ 0131 667 0047
Parkland course, with good views.
*18 holes, 5851yds, Par 70, SSS 69, Course record 63.*
*Club membership 750.*

| | |
|---|---|
| Visitors | must contact in advance, may not play weekends and after 3.30pm weekdays. |
| Societies | must contact in writing. |
| Green Fees | £25 per day; £17 per round. |
| Facilities | ⊗ ❬ ⤨ ⬙ ♀ ♨ 🏠 ⚐ ⁿ B McGhee. |
| Leisure | trolley for hire, putting green, practice area. |
| Location | 2m S of city centre off A7 |
| Hotel | ★★★ 59% Donmaree Hotel, 21 Mayfield Gardens, EDINBURGH ☎ 0131 667 3641 15 ⇆ ⁿAnnexe2 ⇆ ⁿ |

---

*Dalmahoy Hotel Golf & Country Club* Kirknewton EH27 8EB ☎ 0131 333 1845
Two upland courses, one Championship.
*East Course: 18 holes, 6677yds, Par 72, SSS 72, Course record 64.*
*West Course: 18 holes, 5185yds, Par 68, SSS 66, Course record 62.*
*Club membership 700.*

| | |
|---|---|
| Visitors | weekend by application. |
| Societies | telephone or write for information. |
| Green Fees | not confirmed. |
| Facilities | ♀ ♨ 🏠 ⚐ 🏌 ⁿ Brian Anderson/Stuart Callan. |
| Leisure | hard tennis courts, heated indoor swimming pool, squash, sauna, solarium, gymnasium, range, putting, cart/buggy/trolley hire. |
| Location | 7m W of city centre on A71 |
| Hotel | ★★★★ 71% Dalmahoy Hotel, Country Club Resort, Kirknewton, EDINBURGH ☎ 0131 333 1845 43 ⇆ ⁿAnnexe108 ⇆ ⁿ |

---

*Duddingston* Duddingston Rd West EH15 3QD
☎ 0131 661 7688
Parkland, semi-seaside course with burn as a natural hazard. Testing 11th hole. Easy walking and windy.
*18 holes, 6647yds, Par 72, SSS 72.*
*Club membership 700.*

| | |
|---|---|
| Visitors | may not play at weekends. |
| Societies | Tue & Thu only. Must contact in advance. |
| Green Fees | not confirmed. |
| Facilities | ♀ ♨ 🏠 ⚐ ⁿ Alastair McLean. |
| Location | 2.5m SE of city centre off A1 |

---

| | |
|---|---|
| Hotel | ★★★ 59% Donmaree Hotel, 21 Mayfield Gardens, EDINBURGH ☎ 0131 667 3641 15 ⇆ ⁿAnnexe2 ⇆ ⁿ |

---

**Kingsknowe** 326 Lanark Rd EH14 2JD ☎ 0131 441 1145
Hilly parkland course with prevailing SW winds.
*18 holes, 5979ydss, Par 69, SSS 69, Course record 69.*
*Club membership 800.*

| | |
|---|---|
| Visitors | contact in advance and subject to availability of tee times. |
| Societies | apply in writing or telephone to secretary. |
| Green Fees | £21 per day; £17 per round (£25 per round weekends). |
| Facilities | ⊗ ⬙ ⤨ ♀ ♨ 🏠 ⁿ Andrew Marshall. |
| Leisure | trolley for hire, putting green, practice area. |
| Location | 4m SW of city centre on A70 |
| Hotel | ★★★ 67% Bruntsfield Hotel, 69/74 Bruntsfield Place, EDINBURGH ☎ 0131 229 1393 50 ⇆ ⁿ |

---

*Liberton* 297 Gilmerton Rd EH16 5UJ ☎ 0131 664 3009
Undulating, wooded parkland course.
*18 holes, 5299yds, Par 67, SSS 67.*
*Club membership 650.*

| | |
|---|---|
| Visitors | may only play before 5pm on Tue & Thu Apr-Sep. Must contact in advance. |
| Societies | must contact in writing. |
| Green Fees | not confirmed. |
| Facilities | ♨ 🏠 ⁿ |
| Location | 3m SE of city centre on A7 |
| Hotel | ★★ 62% Eskbank Hotel, 29 Dalhousie Rd, DALKEITH ☎ 0131 663 3234 16 ⇆ ⁿ |

---

**Lothianburn** 106A Biggar Rd, Fairmilehead EH10 7DU
☎ 0131 445 2206 & 0131 445 5067
Hillside course with a 'T' shaped wooded-area, situated in the Pentland foothills. Sheep on course. Testing in windy conditions.
*18 holes, 5750yds, Par 71, SSS 68, Course record 66.*
*Club membership 850.*

| | |
|---|---|
| Visitors | weekends after 3.30pm contact professional, weekdays up to 4pm. |
| Societies | apply to the secretary or telephone in the first instance. |
| Green Fees | £20 per day; £14 per round (£25/£20 weekends). |
| Facilities | ⊗ ⬙ ⤨ ⬙ ♀ ♨ 🏠 ⚐ ⁿ Kurt Mungall. |
| Leisure | trolley for hire, putting green, practice area. |
| Location | 4.5m S of city centre on A702 |
| Hotel | ★★★ 67% Braid Hills Hotel, 134 Braid Rd, Braid Hills, EDINBURGH ☎ 0131 447 8888 68 ⇆ ⁿ |

---

**Merchants of Edinburgh** 10 Craighill Gardens EH10 5PY
☎ 0131 447 1219
Testing hill course.
*18 holes, 4889mtrs, Par 65, SSS 64, Course record 59.*
*Club membership 750.*

| | |
|---|---|
| Visitors | must play with member at weekends. |
| Societies | must contact with secretary in writing. |
| Green Fees | £15 per day/round. |
| Facilities | ⊗ ⬙ ⤨ ⬙ ♀ ♨ 🏠 ⚐ ⁿ Neil Colquhoun. |
| Leisure | trolley for hire, putting green. |
| Location | 2m SW of city centre off A702 |
| Hotel | ★★★ 67% Braid Hills Hotel, 134 Braid Rd, Braid Hills, EDINBURGH ☎ 0131 447 8888 68 ⇆ ⁿ |

**Mortonhall** 231 Braid Rd EH10 6PB
☎ 0131 447 6974
Moorland course with views over Edinburgh.
*18 holes, 6557yds, Par 72, SSS 72, Course record 66.*
*Club membership 500.*
Visitors     advisable to contact by phone.
Societies     may not play at weekends. Must contact in writing.
Green Fees £28 per day; £23 per round (£38/£28 weekends).
Facilities    ⊗ ⅏ by prior arrangement ⬟ ⬛ ♀ ⬥ ⌂ ⚲
         ( Douglas Horn.
Leisure     trolley for hire, putting green, practice area.
Location     3m S of city centre off A702
Hotel      ★★★ 67% Braid Hills Hotel, 134 Braid Rd,
         Braid Hills, EDINBURGH
         ☎ 0131 447 8888 68 ⇆ ⁊

**Murrayfield** 43 Murrayfield Rd EH12 6EU
☎ 0131 337 3478
Parkland course on the side of Corstorphine Hill, with fine views.
*18 holes, 5725yds, Par 70, SSS 69.*
*Club membership 750.*
Visitors     contact in advance, may not play at weekends.
Green Fees £28 per day; £22 per round.
Facilities    ⊗ ⬟ ⬛ ♀ ⬥ ⌂ ⚲ ( J J Fisher.
Leisure     trolley for hire, putting green, practice area.
Location     2m W of city centre off A8
Hotel      B Forte Posthouse Edinburgh, Corstorphine Rd,
         EDINBURGH
         ☎ 0131 334 0390 204 ⇆ ⁊

*Portobello* Stanley St EH15 1JJ
☎ 0131 669 4361
Public parkland course, easy walking.
*9 holes, 2400yds, Par 32, SSS 32.*
*Club membership 70.*
Visitors     may not play Sat 8.30-10am & 12.30-2pm and on competition days.
Societies     must contact in advance.
Green Fees not confirmed.
Facilities    ⚲
Leisure     trolley hire.
Location     3m E of city centre off A1
Hotel      ★★★ 59% Donmaree Hotel, 21 Mayfield
         Gardens, EDINBURGH
         ☎ 0131 667 3641 15 ⇆ ⁊Annexe2 ⇆ ⁊

**Prestonfield** Priestfield Rd North EH16 5HS
☎ 0131 667 9665
Parkland course with beautiful views.
*18 holes, 6212yds, Par 70, SSS 70, Course record 62.*
*Club membership 850.*
Visitors     contact secretary in advance.
Societies     must contact secretary.
Green Fees £30 per day; £20 per round (£40 per day; £30 per round weekends & bank holidays).
Facilities    ⊗ ⅏ ⬟ ⬛ ♀ ⬥ ⌂ ⚲ ( Graham MacDonald.
Leisure     trolley for hire, putting green, practice area.
Location     1.5m S of city centre off A68
Hotel      ★★★ 59% Donmaree Hotel, 21 Mayfield
         Gardens, EDINBURGH
         ☎ 0131 667 3641 15 ⇆ ⁊Annexe2 ⇆ ⁊

**Ravelston** 24 Ravelston Dykes Rd EH4 5NZ
☎ 0131 315 2486
Parkland course.
*9 holes, 5200yds, Par 66, SSS 65, Course record 64.*
*Club membership 610.*
Visitors     must contact in advance but may not play at weekends & bank holidays.
Green Fees £15 per round.
Facilities    ⬛ ⬥
Leisure     practice nets.
Location     3m W of city centre off A90
Hotel      B Forte Posthouse Edinburgh, Corstorphine Rd,
         EDINBURGH
         ☎ 0131 334 0390 204 ⇆ ⁊

*Royal Burgess* 181 Whitehouse Rd, Barnton EH4 6BZ
☎ 0131 339 2075
No mention of golf clubs would be complete without mention of the Royal Burgess, which was instituted in 1735, thus being the oldest golfing society in the world. Its course is a pleasant parkland, and one with very much variety. A club which all those interested in the history of the game should visit.
*18 holes, 6111yds, Par 71, SSS 71, Course record 66.*
*Club membership 620.*
Visitors     must contact in advance. Gentlemen only.
Societies     must contact in advance.
Green Fees not confirmed.
Facilities    ♀ ⬥ ⌂ ⚲ ( George Yuille.
Location     5m W of city centre off A90
Hotel      ★★★ 64% The Barnton Thistle,
         Queensferry Rd, Barnton, EDINBURGH
         ☎ 0131 339 1144 50 ⇆ ⁊

*Silverknowes* Silverknowes, Parkway EH4 5ET
☎ 0131 336 3843
Public links course on coast overlooking the Firth of Forth.
*18 holes, 6216yds, Par 71, SSS 70.*
*Club membership 500.*
Visitors     restricted Sat & Sun.
Societies     must apply in writing to: Leisure Management Unit, Meadowbank Sports Centre, London Road, Edinburgh.
Green Fees not confirmed.
Facilities    ⌂ ⚲
Leisure     putting,trolley hire,practice area.
Location     4m NW of city centre N of A902
Hotel      ★★ 65% Murrayfield Hotel, 18 Corstorphine
         Rd, EDINBURGH
         ☎ 0131 337 1844 23 ⇆ ⁊Annexe10 ⁊

**Swanston** 111 Swanston Rd, Fairmilehead EH10 7DS
☎ 0131 445 2239
Hillside course with steep climb at 12th & 13th holes.
*18 holes, 5024yds, Par 66, SSS 65.*
Visitors     contact in advance. Must contact in advance.
Societies     telephone for details.
Green Fees £18 per day; £12 per round (£22/£17 weekends & public holidays).
Facilities    ⊗ ⅏ ⬟ ⬛ ♀ ⬥ ⌂ (
Location     4m S of city centre off B701
Hotel      ★★★ 67% Braid Hills Hotel, 134 Braid Rd,
         Braid Hills, EDINBURGH
         ☎ 0131 447 8888 68 ⇆ ⁊

**Torphin Hill** Torphin Rd, Colinton EH13 0PG
☎ 0131 441 1100
Beautiful hillside, heathland course, with fine views of
Edinburgh and the Forth Estuary.
*18 holes, 4580mtrs, Par 67, SSS 66, Course record 64.*
*Club membership 550.*
**Visitors**   must contact in advance.
**Societies**   must contact in advance.
**Green Fees** £15 per day (£25 weekends).
**Facilities**   ⊗ ⅢⅢ ⅃ ⊑ ♀ ⅄ 🏠 ( Jamie Browne.
**Leisure**   putting green, practice area.
**Location**   5m SW of city centre S of A720
**Hotel**   ★★★ 67% Braid Hills Hotel, 134 Braid Rd,
   Braid Hills, EDINBURGH
   ☎ 0131 447 8888 68 ⇄ ╟

**Turnhouse** 154 Turnhouse Rd EH12 0AD
☎ 0131 339 1014
Hilly, parkland/heathland course, good views.
*18 holes, 5622yds, Par 69, SSS 70, Course record 63.*
*Club membership 800.*
**Visitors**   may not play at weekends or Wed.
**Societies**   must contact in writing.
**Green Fees** not £24 per day, £16 per round.
**Facilities**   ⊗ ⅢⅢ ⅃ ⊑ ♀ ⅄ 🏠 ( John Murray.
**Leisure**   buggies for hire, trolley for hire, putting green,
   practice area.
**Location**   6m W of city centre N of A8
**Hotel**   ★★★ 64% The Barnton Thistle, Queensferry
   Rd, Barnton, EDINBURGH
   ☎ 0131 339 1144 50 ⇄ ╟

**EDZELL**                                              Map 15 NO66

**Edzell** High St DD9 7TF
☎ 01356 647283 (Secretary) & 648462 (Pro)
This delightful course is situated in the foothills of the
Scottish Highlands and provides good golf as well as
conveying to everyone who plays there a feeling of peace
and quiet. The village of Edzell is one of the most
picturesque in Scotland.
*18 holes, 6348yds, Par 71, SSS 71, Course record 65.*
*Club membership 650.*
**Visitors**   may not play 4.45-6.15 weekdays & 7.30-
   10, 12-2 weekends. Not before 2pm on 1st
   Sat each month.
**Societies**   must contact secretary at least 14 days in
   advance.
**Green Fees** £25.50 per day; £19 per round (£37.50 per
   day; £25 per round weekends & bank
   holidays). Weekday rates after 4pm
   weekends.
**Facilities**   ⊗ ⅢⅢ ⅃ ⊑ ♀ ⅄ 🏠 ( A J Webster.
**Leisure**   trolley for hire, putting green, practice area.
**Location**   S side of village on B966
**Hotel**   ★★★ 62% Glenesk Hotel, High St,
   EDZELL
   ☎ 01356 648319 25rm(23 ⇄ ╟)

Entries with a shaded background identify
courses that are considered to be particularly
interesting

**ELIE**                                                Map 12 NO40

**Golf House Club** KY9 1AS ☎ 01333 330301
One of Scotland's most delightful holiday courses with
panoramic views over the Firth of Forth. Some of the
holes out towards the rocky coastline are splendid. This
is the course which has produced many good
professionals, including the immortal James Braid.
*18 holes, 6273yds, Par 70, SSS 69, Course record 62.*
*Club membership 600.*
**Visitors**   advisable to contact in advance, limited
   availability at weekends May-Sep.
**Societies**   must contact in advance.
**Green Fees** £40 per day; £28.50 per round (£50/£36
   weekends).
**Facilities**   ⊗ ⅢⅢ ⅃ ⊑ ♀ ⅄ 🏠 ⋔ ( Robin Wilson.
**Leisure**   hard tennis courts, trolley for hire, driving
   range, putting green, practice area.
**Location**   W side of village off A917
**Hotel**   ★★★ 69% Old Manor Hotel, Leven Rd,
   LUNDIN LINKS
   ☎ 01333 320368 19 ⇄ ╟

**FALKIRK**                                            Map 11 NS88

**Falkirk** 136 Stirling Rd, Camelon FK2 7YP
☎ 01324 611061
Parkland course with trees, gorse and streams.
*18 holes, 6230yds, Par 71, SSS 70, Course record 66.*
*Club membership 800.*
**Visitors**   telephone starter 01324 612219, visiting parties
   only on Sun.
**Societies**   telephone 01324 612219 in advance.
**Green Fees** £20 per day; £15 per round (weekdays). £30 per
   day on Sun..
**Facilities**   ⊗ ⅢⅢ ⅃ ⊑ ♀ ⅄ 🏠 ( Colin Gillies.
**Leisure**   trolley for hire, putting green, practice area.
**Location**   1.5m W on A9
**Hotel**   ★★★ 68% Inchyra Grange Hotel, Grange Rd,
   POLMONT ☎ 01324 711911 43 ⇄ ╟

**FALKLAND**                                           Map 11 NO20

**Falkland** The Myre KY7 7AA ☎ 01337 857404
A flat, well kept course with excellent greens and views of
East Lomond Hill and Falkland Palace.
*9 holes, 5216yds, Par 68, SSS 65, Course record 62.*
*Club membership 325.*
**Visitors**   parties must make prior arrangements.
**Societies**   must contact in advance.
**Green Fees** not confirmed.
**Facilities**   ♀ ⅄
**Location**   N side of town on A912
**Hotel**   ★★ 65% Lomond Hills Hotel, Parliament
   Square, FREUCHIE
   ☎ 01337 857329 & 857498 25 ⇄ ╟

**FAULDHOUSE**                                         Map 11 NS96

**Greenburn** 6 Greenburn Rd EH47 9HG ☎ 01501 770292
Exposed rolling course with sparse tree cover. Water hazards
from a pond and a burn.
*18 holes, 6045yds, Par 71, SSS 70, Course record 65.*
*Club membership 800.*                                    ▶

**Visitors** contact for details.
**Societies** by prior arrangement.
**Green Fees** £19 per day; £13 per round (£23/£16 weekends).
**Facilities** ⊗ �𝕀𝕀 ⓛ 🛒 ♀ ⚲ 🏠 ( Malcolm Leighton.
**Leisure** trolley for hire, putting green, practice area.
**Location** 3m SW of Whitburn
**Hotel** ★★ 56% Dreadnought Hotel, 17/19 Whitburn Rd, BATHGATE
☎ 01506 630791 19rm(18 ⇄ ℝ)

## FORFAR                                          Map 15 NO45

**Forfar** Cunninghill, Arbroath Rd DD8 2RL
☎ 01307 463773 & 462120
Moorland course with wooded, undulating fairways and fine views.
*18 holes, 6053yds, Par 69, SSS 70, Course record 61.*
*Club membership 820.*
**Visitors** no restrictions.
**Societies** must contact in advance.
**Green Fees** £24 per day; £16 per round (£32 weekends & bank holidays £20 after 3pm).
**Facilities** ⊗ �𝕀𝕀 ⓛ 🛒 ♀ ⚲ 🏠 ( Peter McNiven.
**Leisure** trolley for hire, putting green, practice area.
**Location** 1.5m E of Forfar on A932
**Hotel** ★★★⚤ 64% Idvies House Hotel, Letham, FORFAR ☎ 01307 818787 10 ⇄ ℝ

## GIFFORD                                          Map 12 NT56

**Gifford** Edinburgh Rd EH41 4QN ☎ 01620 810267
Parkland course, with easy walking.
*9 holes, 6243yds, Par 71, SSS 70, Course record 64.*
*Club membership 470.*
**Visitors** restricted weekends, not after 4pm Sat & noon Sun.
**Societies** telephone in advance.
**Green Fees** £10 per day (£10 per round weekends).
**Facilities** ⚲
**Leisure** trolley for hire, putting green, practice area.
**Location** 1m SW off B6355
**Hotel** ★★ 69% Tweeddale Arms Hotel, GIFFORD
☎ 01620 810240 16 ⇄ ℝ

## GIGHA ISLAND                                          Map 10 NR64

**Gigha** PA41 7AA ☎ 01583 505287
A 9-hole course with scenic views of the Sound of Gigha to the east and to the north the Kilberry Hills. The 9th hole is a good par 3, especially with a strong blow of wind from the west.
*9 holes, 5042 yds, Par 66, SSS 65.*
*Club membership 40.*

**Visitors** no restrictions.
**Societies** telephone for details.
**Green Fees** £10 per day; £7 per 18 holes.
**Facilities** ⇤
**Location** 0.5m N of Druimeonbeg farm shop

## GLENROTHES                                          Map 11 NO20

**Glenrothes** Golf Course Rd KY6 2LA
☎ 01592 754561 & 758686
Testing and hilly parkland course with burn crossed four times. Good views.
*18 holes, 6444yds, Par 71, SSS 71, Course record 67.*
*Club membership 770.*
**Visitors** no restrictions.
**Societies** write to secretary.
**Green Fees** £17 per day; £10 per round (£19/£12.50 weekends). Prices under review.
**Facilities** ⊗ �𝕀𝕀 ⓛ 🛒 ♀ ⚲
**Leisure** putting green, practice area.
**Location** W side of town off B921
**Hotel** ★★★ 69% Balgeddie House Hotel, Balgeddie Way, GLENROTHES
☎ 01592 742511 18 ⇄ ℝ

## GLENSHEE (SPITTAL OF)                                          Map 15 NO16

**Dalmunzie** Dalmunzie Estate PH10 7QG
☎ 01250 885226
Well maintained Highland course with difficult walking. Testing 5th hole. Small but good greens.
*9 holes, 2035yds, Par 30, SSS 30.*
*Club membership 70.*
**Visitors** restricted Sun 10.30-11.30am.
**Societies** advance contact preferred.
**Green Fees** £8.50 per day; £5 per round; £34 weekly.
**Facilities** ⊗ ⟐ 🛒 ♀ 🏠 ⼞ ⇤
**Leisure** hard tennis courts, fishing, stalking & clay pigeon shooting.
**Location** 2m NW of Spittal of Glenshee
**Hotel** ★★⚤ 65% Dalmunzie House Hotel, SPITTAL OF GLENSHEE
☎ 01250 885224 18rm(16 ⇄ ℝ)

## GOREBRIDGE                                          Map 11 NT36

**Vogrie** Vogrie Estate Country Park EH23 4NU
☎ 01875 821716
A 9-hole municipal course located with a country park. The wide fairways are particularly suited to beginners.
*9 holes, 2530yds, Par 33.*
**Visitors** book by telephone 24 hrs in advance.
**Green Fees** not confirmed.

*Dalmunzie House*
*the hotel in the hills*

**Spittal o' Glenshee, Blairgowrie, Perthshire PH10 7QG**
**Telephone: 01250 885224 Fax: 01250 885225**
Family run country house with its own 9 hole golf course offers 16 bedrooms with private bathroom, log fire, personal service and 'Taste of Scotland' cooking. Many golf courses within 1 hours drive such as Blairgowrie, Alyth, Pitlochry, Kirriemuir, Aboyne and Ballater.

**STB 3 CROWNS COMMENDED**

**Facilities** ⌂
**Location** Off B6372
**Hotel** ★★★⚜ 62% Johnstounburn House, HUMBIE
☎ 01875 833696 11rm(10 ⇄ ℕ)Annexe9 ⇄ ℕ

## GOUROCK

Map 10 NS27

*Gourock* Cowal View PA19 6HD
☎ 01475 631001
Moorland course with hills and dells. Testing 8th hole, par 5.
Magnificent views over Firth of Clyde.
*18 holes, 6492yds, Par 73, SSS 73, Course record 64.*
*Club membership 720.*
**Visitors** by introduction or with member.
**Societies** welcome weekdays, must contact in advance.
**Green Fees** not confirmed.
**Facilities** ⚲⌂🏠ϒℂ A M Green.
**Leisure** putting,trolley hire,practice area.
**Location** SW side of town off A770
**Hotel** ★★★⚜ 63% Manor Park Hotel, LARGS
☎ 01475 520832 10 ⇄ ℕAnnexe13 ⇄ ℕ

## GREENOCK

Map 10 NS27

*Greenock* Forsyth St PA16 8RE
☎ 01475 720793
Testing moorland course with panoramic views of Clyde
Estuary.
*18 holes, 5838yds, Par 69, SSS 69.*
*Club membership 730.*
**Visitors** may not play Sat. Must contact in advance and
have a handicap certificate.
**Societies** must telephone in advance.
**Green Fees** not confirmed.
**Facilities** ⚲⌂🏠ℂ Graham Ross.
**Leisure** Putting green,trolley hire.
**Location** SW side of town off A770
**Hotel** ★★★⚜ 63% Manor Park Hotel, LARGS
☎ 01475 520832 10 ⇄ ℕAnnexe13 ⇄ ℕ

*Whinhill* Beith Rd PA16 9LN
☎ 01475 724694 evenings & weekends only
Picturesque heathland public course.
*18 holes, 5454yds, Par 66, SSS 68, Course record 64.*
*Club membership 270.*
**Visitors** may only use club facilities with member.
**Green Fees** not confirmed.
**Facilities** ⚲⌂
**Leisure** putting green.
**Location** 1.5m SW off B7054
**Hotel** ★★★⚜ 63% Manor Park Hotel, LARGS
☎ 01475 520832 10 ⇄ ℕAnnexe13 ⇄ ℕ

## GULLANE

Map 12 NT48

**Gullane** EH31 2BB ☎ 01620 842255
Gullane is a delightful village and one of Scotland's great
golf centres. Gullane club was formed in 1882. There are
three Gullane courses and the No 1 is of championship
standard. It differs from most Scottish courses in as much
as it is of the downland type and really quite hilly. The
first tee is literally in the village. The views from the top
of the course are magnificent and stretch far and wide in
every direction - in fact, it is said that 14 counties can be
seen from the highest spot.

*Course No 1: 18 holes, 6466yds, Par 71, SSS 72, Course*
*record 65.*
*Course No 2: 18 holes, 6244yds, Par 71, SSS 70.*
*Course No 3: 18 holes, 5251yds, Par 68, SSS 66.*
*Club membership 1200.*
**Visitors** advance booking recommended.
**Societies** advance booking advised.
**Green Fees** Course No 1: £63 per day; £42 per round
(£53 per round weekends). Course No. 2;
£31.50 per day; £21 per round (£40/£26.50
weekends). Course No. 3: £19 per round;
£12.50 per round (£24/£16 weekends).
**Facilities** ⊗🎦⌂☕⚲⌂🏠ϒℂ Jimmy Hume.
**Leisure** motorised carts for hire, buggies for hire,
trolley for hire, putting green, practice area.
**Location** At west end of village on A198
**Hotel** ★★★(red)⚜ Greywalls Hotel, Muirfield,
GULLANE
☎ 01620 842144 17 ⇄ ℕAnnexe5 ⇄ ℕ

---

**MUIRFIELD**
(Honourable Company of Edinburgh Golfers)   See page 293

## HADDINGTON

Map 12 NT57

*Haddington* Amisfield Park EH41 4PT ☎ 01620 823627
Inland course, tree-lined and bunkered, but not hilly.
*18 holes, 6280yds, Par 71, SSS 70.*
*Club membership 600.*
**Visitors** may not play between 7am-10am & noon-2pm at
weekends. Must contact in advance.
**Societies** must contact in advance; deposits required.
**Green Fees** not confirmed.
**Facilities** ⚲⌂🏠ℂ John Sandilands.
**Leisure** pool table.
**Location** E side off A613
**Hotel** ★★ 69% Tweeddale Arms Hotel, GIFFORD
☎ 01620 810240 16 ⇄ ℕ

## HELENSBURGH

Map 10 NS28

*Helensburgh* 25 East Abercromby St G84 9JD
☎ 01436 674173
Sporting moorland course with superb views of Loch
Lomond and River Clyde.
*18 holes, 6104yds, Par 69, SSS 70, Course record 64.*
*Club membership 880.*
**Visitors** may not play at weekends.
**Societies** must contact in writing.
**Green Fees** £23.50 per day; £15.50 per round.
**Facilities** ⊗🎦⌂☕⚲⌂🏠ϒℂ David Fotheringham.
**Leisure** trolley for hire, driving range, putting green,
practice area.
**Location** NE side of town off B832
**Hotel** ★★ 68% Commodore Toby Hotel, 112 West
Clyde St, HELENSBURGH
☎ 01436 676924 45 ⇄ ℕ

## INNELLAN

Map 10 NS17

*Innellan* Knockamillie Rd PA23 7SG
☎ 01369 830242 & 703327
Situated above the village of Innellan, this undulating hilltop
course has extensive views of the Firth of Clyde.   ▶

*9 holes, 4683yds, Par 64, SSS 64, Course record 63.*
*Club membership 199.*

| | |
|---|---|
| Visitors | welcome but may not play after 5pm on Mondays. |
| Societies | telephone initially. |
| Green Fees | £8 (£10 weekends). |
| Facilities | ┗ ♊ ♀ |
| Location | 4m S of Dunoon |
| Hotel | ★★ 76% Enmore Hotel, Marine Pde, Kirn, DUNOON ☎ 01369 702230 11 ⇥ ▶ |

## INVERARAY                                    Map 10 NN00

**Inveraray** Lochgilphead Rd ☎ 01499 302508
Testing parkland course with beautiful views overlooking Loch Fyne.
*9 holes, 5790yds, Par 70, SSS 68.*
*Club membership 130.*

| | |
|---|---|
| Visitors | welcome. |
| Societies | write or telephone to the secretary. |
| Green Fees | £10 per 18 holes. |
| Facilities | △ |
| Leisure | practice area. |
| Location | 1m S of Inveraray |
| Hotel | ★ 64% Fernpoint Hotel, INVERARAY ☎ 01499 302170 7 ⇥ ▶ |

## ISLAY, ISLE OF                              Map 10 NR34

## PORT ELLEN                                   Map 10 NR34

**Machrie Hotel** Machrie PA42 7AN ☎ 01496 302310
Championship links course opened in 1891, where golf's first £100 Open Championship was played in 1901. Fine turf and many blind holes. Par 4.
*18 holes, 6226yds, Par 71, SSS 71, Course record 65.*
*Club membership 250.*

| | |
|---|---|
| Visitors | no restrictions. |
| Societies | apply in writing. |
| Green Fees | £25 per day; £16.50 per round. |
| Facilities | ⊗ ⬚ ┗ ♊ ♀ △ 🖾 ⍮ 🖼 |
| Leisure | fishing, buggies for hire, trolley for hire, putting green, practice area. |
| Location | 4m N off A846 |
| Hotel | ★★ 57% Lochside Hotel, 19 Shore St, BOWMORE ☎ 01496 810244 8 ⇥ ▶ |

## KENMORE                                      Map 14 NN74

**Kenmore** PH15 2HN ☎ 01887 830226
Testing course in mildly undulating natural terrain. Beautiful views in tranquil setting by Loch Tay.
*9 holes, 6052yds, Par 70, SSS 69, Course record 71.*
*Club membership 100.*

| | |
|---|---|
| Visitors | advance booking advisable. |
| Societies | telephone in advance. |
| Green Fees | £16 per day; £10 per 18 holes; £7 per 9 holes (£18/£12/£8 weekends). |
| Facilities | ⊗ ⬚ ┗ ♊ ♀ △ 🖾 ⍮ 🖼 |
| Leisure | fishing, motorised carts for hire, buggies for hire, trolley for hire, putting green, practice area. |
| Location | On A827 |

| | |
|---|---|
| Hotel | ★★ 59% Fortingall Hotel, FORTINGALL ☎ 01887 830367 & 830368 9 ⇥ ▶ |

**Taymouth Castle** PH15 2NT ☎ 01887 830228
Parkland course set amidst beautiful mountain and loch scenery. Easy walking. Fishing.
*18 holes, 6066yds, Par 69, SSS 69, Course record 62.*
*Club membership 250.*

| | |
|---|---|
| Visitors | must book in advance. |
| Societies | must contact in advance. |
| Green Fees | £26 per day; £16 round (£36/£20 weekends). |
| Facilities | ⊗ ⬚ ┗ ♊ ♀ △ 🖾 ⍮ 🖼 |
| Leisure | fishing, motorised carts for hire, buggies for hire, trolley for hire, putting green, practice area. |
| Location | 1m E on A827 |
| Hotel | ★★ 59% Fortingall Hotel, FORTINGALL ☎ 01887 830367 & 830368 9 ⇥ ▶ |

## KILLIN                                       Map 11 NN53

**Killin** FK21 8TX ☎ 01567 820312
Parkland course with good views. Glorious setting.
*9 holes, 2600yds, Par 66, SSS 65, Course record 61.*
*Club membership 250.*

| | |
|---|---|
| Visitors | may not play competition days. |
| Societies | previous record of courses visited required. |
| Green Fees | £14 per day; £11 per round; £40 per week 5 days. |
| Facilities | ⊗ ⬚ ┗ ♊ ♀ △ 🖾 ⍮ |
| Leisure | motorised carts for hire, buggies for hire, trolley for hire, putting green, practice area. |
| Location | 1m N on A827 |
| Hotel | ★★★ 59% Dall Lodge Country House Hotel, Main St, KILLIN ☎ 01567 820217 10 ⇥ ▶ |

## KILMACOLM                                    Map 10 NS36

**Kilmacolm** Porterfield Rd PA13 4PD ☎ 01505 872139
Moorland course, easy walking, fine views. Testing 7th, 13th and 14th holes.
*18 holes, 5961yds, Par 69, SSS 69, Course record 64.*
*Club membership 850.*

| | |
|---|---|
| Visitors | must contact in advance. |
| Societies | apply in writing. |
| Green Fees | £30 per day; £20 per round. |
| Facilities | ⊗ ┗ ♊ ♀ △ 🖾 ⍮ David Stewart. |
| Leisure | trolley for hire, driving range, putting green, practice area. |
| Location | SE side of town off A761 |
| Hotel | ★★★★⚑ 72% Gleddoch House Hotel, LANGBANK ☎ 01475 540711 39 ⇥ ▶ |

## KINCARDINE                                   Map 11 NS98

**Tulliallan** Alloa Rd FK10 4BB ☎ 01259 730396
Partially hilly parkland course with testing 3rd hole (par 4).
*18 holes, 5982yds, Par 69, SSS 69.*
*Club membership 525.*

| | |
|---|---|
| Visitors | restricted at weekends. |
| Societies | may not play on Sat; must contact in advance. |
| Green Fees | not confirmed. |
| Facilities | ♀ △ 🖾 ⍮ ⍮ Steven Kelly. |
| Location | 1m NW on A977 |
| Hotel | ★★★ 59% Dall Lodge Country House Hotel, Main St, KILLIN ☎ 01567 820217 10 ⇥ ▶ |

# MUIRFIELD
## (Honourable Company of Edinburgh Golfers)

**GULLANE** *East Lothian* ☎ 01620 842123   Map 12 NT 48

*John Ingham writes:* Ask an American superstar to name the best golf course in Great Britain, or maybe even in the entire world, and the likely answer will be Muirfield. It certainly features in the top ten of any meaningful selection.

Purely on shape and balance, the course has everything. Ask competitors in the Open Championship what they think of the last nine holes, and they will tell you it can wreck the stoutest heart. But ask Isoa Aoki of Japan what he thinks, and he will smile and maybe tell of his course record 63 here.

Established in 1744, it is just ten years older than the Royal & Ancient itself but not as old as Royal Blackheath. However, these dates show that Muirfield certainly has seniority and tradition. Quite simply, it is exclusive and entirely excellent. Muirfield has staged some outstanding Open Championships with one, I suspect, standing out in people's minds more than any other.

Back in 1972, Tony Jacklin was Europe's best player and looked set to prove it again at Muirfield when he had appeared to wear down Lee Trevino, the defending champion. At the 71st hole, Trevino seemed to be frittering away strokes as he mis-hit a shot downwind through the dry, fast, green. The next few minutes were truly hair-raising 'I was mad' recalled Trevino. 'My next shot from the bank was strictly a give-up one. And the ball went straight in the hole.' Jacklin had chipped up, well short. Then he missed his putt, turned for the return putt, and missed again. We all did mental arithmetic. Jacklin had blown it and when he bogeyed the last, furious at himself, he suddenly wasn't the winner - Trevino was.

Those of us who were there recall Trevino had holed one bunker shot, and chipped in three times. Muirfield looked on his brilliance with favour and sad Jacklin never won an Open again.

| | |
|---|---|
| **Visitors** | Tue & Thur only; contact in advance and have handicap certificate |
| **Societies** | telephone in advance. But restricted to Tue and Thur |
| **Green fees** | £77 per day; £57 per round |
| **Facilities** | ⊗ 🍺 ⚲ ⚽ 🏌<br>practice area, putting green |
| **Location** | Duncur Rd, Muirfield, Gullane EH31 2EG (off A198 on NE side of village) |

18 holes, 6601 yards, Par 70, SSS 73, Course record 63 (R Davies, Isoa Aoki).

## WHERE TO STAY AND EAT NEARBY

**HOTELS:**

**ABERLADY**
★★ 67% Kilspindie House, Main St.
☎ 01875 870682.  26 (8 🐾 18 ⇄ 🐾)

**GULLANE**
★★★(Red)🏵🏵 ⚍ Greywalls, Muirfield. ☎ 01620 842144. 17 ⇄ 🐾 Annexe 5 ⇄ 🐾

**NORTH BERWICK**
★★★ 65% The Marine, Cromwell Rd.
☎ 01620 892406.  83 (3 ⇄ 80 ⇄ 🐾)

★★ 62% Nether Abbey, 20 Dirleton Ave. ☎ 01620 892802.  16 (6 🐾 4 ⇄)

★★ 64% Point Garry, West Bay Rd.
☎ 01620 892380. 15(8 🐾 2 ⇄ 5 ⇄ 🐾)

**RESTAURANT:**

**GULLANE**
🏵🏵🏵  La Potinière, Main St.
☎ 01620 843214.

## KINGHORN

Map 11 NT28

*Kinghorn* Macduff Cres KY3 9RE ☎ 01592 890345
Municipal course, 300 ft above sea level with views over
Firth of Forth and North Sea. Undulating and quite testing.
Facilities shared by Kinghorn Ladies.
*18 holes, 5269yds, Par 65, SSS 67.*
*Club membership 190.*
**Visitors** no restrictions.
**Societies** must contact in writing.
**Green Fees** not confirmed.
**Facilities** ♀⅄
**Location** S side of town on A921
**Hotel** ★★★ 57% Dean Park Hotel, Chapel Level,
KIRKCALDY
☎ 01592 261635 20 ➡ ℟Annexe12 ℟

## KINROSS

Map 11 N010

**Green Hotel** 2 The Muirs KY13 7AS ☎ 01577 863407
Two interesting and picturesque parkland courses, with easy
walking.
*Red Course: 18 holes, 6257yds, Par 72, SSS 70.*
*Blue Course: 18 holes, 6456yds, Par 71, SSS 71.*
*Club membership 600.*
**Visitors** must contact in advance.
**Societies** must contact in advance.
**Green Fees** £25 per day; £15 per round (£35/£25 weekends).
**Facilities** ⊗ ℳ ⅃ ⬛ ♀⅄ 🏠 ⊶ ⋈ ℟ Stuart Geraghty.
**Leisure** hard tennis courts, heated indoor swimming
pool, squash, fishing, sauna, solarium, trolley for
hire, putting green, practice area.

**THE IDEAL**
**GREEN**
**FOR GOLFERS**

JUST A SHORT IRON FROM THE FRONT DOOR YOU WILL
FIND THE FIRST TEES OF OUR OWN TWO SCENIC GOLF
COURSES. BOTH OFFER AN ENJOYABLE AND STIMULATING
CHALLENGE WHETHER YOU'RE A HOLIDAY GOLFER OR LOW
HANDICAP PLAYER.
OUR 47 MODERN SPACIOUS BEDROOMS ARE ALL WELL
APPOINTED AND INCLUDE SATELLITE TV. INDOOR LEISURE
COMPLEX FEATURES INDOOR POOL, SAUNA, SOLARIUM,
SQUASH COURT AND FITNESS AREA. OVER 50 OTHER
GREAT COURSES WITHIN AN HOUR'S EASY DRIVE
INCLUDING ST. ANDREWS, GLENEAGLES AND CARNOUSTIE.

**THE GREEN**
**H O T E L**
**2 The Muirs, Kinross, Scotland KY13 7AS.**
**Tel: (01577) 863467. Fax: (01577) 863180**

**Location** NE side of town on B996
**Hotel** ★★★ 70% Green Hotel, 2 The Muirs,
KINROSS ☎ 01577 863467 47 ➡ ℟

*Kinross Beeches Park* KY13 7EU ☎ 01577 862237
Parkland course on the banks of Loch Leven.
*Blue Course: 18 holes, 6456yds, Par 71, SSS 71.*
*Red Course: 18 holes, 6257yds, Par 72, SSS 70.*
*Club membership 540.*
**Visitors** no restrictions.
**Green Fees** not confirmed.
**Facilities** ♀⅄ 🏠 ⊶ ℟ Stuart Geraghty.
**Leisure** caddy cars.
**Location** NE side of town on B996
**Hotel** ★★★ 70% Green Hotel, 2 The Muirs,
KINROSS ☎ 01577 863467 47 ➡ ℟

## KIRKCALDY

Map 11 NT29

**Dunnikier Park** Dunnikier Way KY1 3LP
☎ 01592 261599
Parkland, rolling fairways, not heavily bunkered, views of
Firth of Forth.
*18 holes, 6036metres, Par 72, SSS 72, Course record 65.*
*Club membership 660.*
**Visitors** visitors must contact course starter in person.
**Societies** apply in writing.
**Green Fees** £18 per day; £11 per round (£20/£15 weekends).
**Facilities** ⊗ ℳ ⅃ ⬛ ♀⅄ 🏠 ℟ Gregor Whyte.
**Leisure** trolley for hire, practice area.
**Location** 2m N on B981
**Hotel** ★★★ 57% Dean Park Hotel, Chapel Level,
KIRKCALDY
☎ 01592 261635 20 ➡ ℟Annexe12 ℟

*Kirkcaldy* Balwearie Rd KY2 5LT ☎ 01592 205240
Parkland course.
*18 holes, 6004yds, Par 71, SSS 69, Course record 65.*
*Club membership 700.*
**Visitors** may not play Sat. Must contact in advance.
**Societies** apply in writing.
**Green Fees** £20 per day; £15 per round (£30/£20 Sun).
**Facilities** ⊗ ℳ ⅃ ⬛ ♀⅄ 🏠 ⊶ ℟ Scott McKay.
**Leisure** trolley for hire, putting green, practice area.
**Location** SW side of town off A910
**Hotel** ★★★ 57% Dean Park Hotel, Chapel Level,
KIRKCALDY
☎ 01592 261635 20 ➡ ℟Annexe12 ℟

## KIRRIEMUIR

Map 15 NO35

*Kirriemuir* Shielhill Rd, Northmuir DD8 4LN
☎ 01575 573317
Parkland and heathland course set at the foot of the Angus
glens, with good view.
*18 holes, 5553yds, Par 68, SSS 67, Course record 62.*
*Club membership 750.*
**Visitors** must play with member at weekends.
**Societies** must apply in advance, may not play weekends.
**Green Fees** £19 per day; £14 per round.
**Facilities** ⊗ ℳ ⅃ ⬛ ♀⅄ 🏠 ⊶ ℟ A Caira.
**Leisure** trolley for hire, putting green.
**Location** 1m N off B955
**Hotel** ★★★⬩⬩ 73% Castleton House Hotel,
GLAMIS ☎ 01307 840340 6 ➡ ℟

## LADYBANK
Map 11 NO30

**Ladybank** Annsmuir KY15 7RA ☎ 01337 830814
Picturesque parkland/heathland course, popular with visitors.
Qualifying course for the British Open.
*18 holes, 6641yds, Par 71, SSS 72, Course record 63.*
*Club membership 900.*
**Visitors**   advance booking essential.
**Societies**   must telephone or write in advance.
**Green Fees** £35 per day; £26 per round.
**Facilities**   ⊗ ⅲ ⅙ ⬛ ♀ ⚖ ⬒ ⫪ ℓ Martin Gray.
**Leisure**   motorised carts for hire, buggies for hire, trolley
for hire, putting green, practice area.
**Location**   N side of village off B9129
**Hotel**   ★★ 65% Lomond Hills Hotel, Parliament
Square, FREUCHIE
☎ 01337 857329 & 857498 25 ⇆ ☞

## LARBERT
Map 11 NS88

**Falkirk Tryst** 86 Burnhead Rd FK5 4BD
☎ 01324 562054 & 562091
Moorland course, fairly level with trees and broom, well-
bunkered. Winds can affect play.
*18 holes, 6053yds, Par 70, SSS 69.*
*Club membership 850.*
**Visitors**   must contact in advance no play at weekends.
**Societies**   visitors welcome Mon-Fri must book or phone
depending on numbers.
**Green Fees** £25 per day; £15 per round.
**Facilities**   ⊗ ⅲ ⅙ ⬛ ♀ ⬒ ⫪ ℓ Steven Dunsmore.
**Leisure**   trolley for hire, putting green, practice area.
**Location**   1m NE off A88/B905
**Hotel**   ★★★ 68% Inchyra Grange Hotel, Grange Rd,
POLMONT ☎ 01324 711911 43 ⇆ ☞

*Glenbervie Clubhouse* Stirling Rd FK5 4SJ
☎ 01324 562605
Parkland course with good views.
*18 holes, 6469yds, Par 70, SSS 70, Course record 65.*
*Club membership 600.*
**Visitors**   must contact in advance. May not play at
weekends.
**Societies**   Tue & Thu only. Apply in writing.
**Green Fees** not confirmed.
**Facilities**   ♀ ⬒ ⬒ ℓ John Chillas.
**Location**   2m NW on A9
**Hotel**   ★★★ 68% Inchyra Grange Hotel, Grange Rd,
POLMONT ☎ 01324 711911 43 ⇆ ☞

## LESLIE
Map 11 NO20

**Leslie** Balsillie Laws KY6 3EZ ☎ 01592 620040
Challenging parkland course.
*9 holes, 4686yds, Par 63, SSS 64, Course record 63.*
*Club membership 230.*
**Visitors**   contact secretary in writing.
**Societies**   letter to the Secretary.
**Green Fees** £8 per day (£10 weekends).
**Facilities**   ⊗ by prior arrangement ⅲ by prior arrangement
⅙ by prior arrangement ⬛ by prior arrangement
⬒
**Location**   N side of town off A911

**Hotel**   ★★★ 69% Balgeddie House Hotel, Balgeddie
Way, GLENROTHES
☎ 01592 742511 18 ⇆ ☞

## LEUCHARS
Map 12 NO42

**St Michael's** KY16 0DX ☎ 01334 839365
Parkland course with open views over Fife and Tayside. The
undulating course weaves its way through tree plantations.
The short Par 4 7th, parallel to the railway and over a pond to
a stepped green, poses an interesting challenge.
*18 holes, 5802yds, Par 70.*
*Club membership 550.*
**Visitors**   may not play on Sun before noon.
**Societies**   must apply in writing, limited weekends
**Green Fees** £22.50 per day; £15 per round.
**Facilities**   ⊗ ⅲ ⅙ ⬛ ♀ ⬒
**Leisure**   trolley for hire, putting green.
**Location**   NW side of village on A919
**Hotel**   ★★ 65% St Michaels Inn, LEUCHARS
☎ 01334 839220 7 ⇆ ☞

## LEVEN
Map 11 NO30

**Leven Links** The Promenade KY8 4HS
☎ 01333 428859
Leven has the classic ingredients which make up a golf
links in Scotland; undulating fairways with hills and
hallows, out of bounds and a 'burn' or stream. A top
class championship links course used for British Open
final qualifying stages, it has fine views over Largo Bay.
*18 holes, 6436yds, Par 71, SSS 70, Course record 63.*
*Club membership 500.*
**Visitors**   contact in advance. Limited availability Fri
pm & Sat, contact for these times no more
than 5 days in advance.
**Societies**   apply in advance.
**Green Fees** £30 per day; £20 per round (£36/£24
weekends).
**Facilities**   ⊗ ⅲ ⅙ ⬛ ♀ ⬒ ⬒ ⫪
**Leisure**   trolley for hire, putting green, practice area.
**Hotel**   ★★★ 56% Caledonian Hotel, 81 High St,
LEVEN ☎ 01333 424101 24 ⇆ ☞

*Scoonie* North Links KY8 4SP ☎ 01333 27057
A pleasant inland links course suitable for all ages.
*18 holes, 4967mtrs, SSS 66.*
*Club membership 150.*
**Visitors**   no restrictions.
**Societies**   apply in writing.
**Green Fees** not confirmed.
**Facilities**   ♀ ⬒ ⫪
**Hotel**   ★★★ 56% Caledonian Hotel, 81 High St,
LEVEN ☎ 01333 424101 24 ⇆ ☞

## LINLITHGOW
Map 11 NS97

*Linlithgow* Braehead EH49 6QF ☎ 01506 842585
Slightly hilly parkland course in beautiful setting.
*18 holes, 5800yds, Par 70, SSS 68.*
*Club membership 400.*
**Visitors**   may not play Sat. Must book in advance Sun.
**Societies**   must contact in writing.
**Green Fees** not confirmed.
**Facilities**   ♀ ⬒ ⬒ ℓ Derek Smith.   ▶

| | |
|---|---|
| **Location** | 1m S off Bathgate Road off A803 |
| **Hotel** | ★★★ 63% The Earl O'Moray Inn, Bonsyde, LINLITHGOW ☎ 01506 842229 8 ⇄ ♠ |

**West Lothian** Airngath Hill EH49 7RH ☎ 01506 826030
Hilly parkland course with superb views of River Forth.
*18 holes, 6406yds, Par 71, SSS 71, Course record 64.*
*Club membership 800.*
**Visitors**     Weekends by arrangement. Advisable to contact in high season.
**Societies**     apply in writing.
**Green Fees** £20 day ; £15 per round (£28/20 weekends).
**Facilities**     ⊗ ⓑ ▆ ♀ ♨ 🏠 🕈 ℃ Neil Robertson.
**Leisure**     trolley for hire, putting green, practice area.
**Location**     1m S off A706
**Hotel**     ★★★ 63% The Earl O'Moray Inn, Bonsyde, LINLITHGOW ☎ 01506 842229 8 ⇄ ♠

## LIVINGSTON                                          Map 11 NT06

**Deer Park Golf & Country Club** Golfcourse Rd EH54 9EG
☎ 01506 431037
Long testing course, fairly flat, championship standard.
*18 holes, 6688yds, Par 72, SSS 72, Course record 65.*
*Club membership 650.*
**Visitors**     must book in advance, Sun after 10am.
**Societies**     telephone or write
**Green Fees** £22 per day; £16 per round (£36.50/£26 weekends).
**Facilities**     ⊗ 🏮 ⓑ ▆ ♀ ♨ 🏠 🕈 ℃ William Yule.
**Leisure**     heated indoor swimming pool, squash, sauna, solarium, gymnasium, motorised carts for hire, buggies for hire, trolley for hire, putting green, practice area.
**Location**     N side of town off A809
**Hotel**     ★★ 56% Dreadnought Hotel, 17/19 Whitburn Rd, BATHGATE ☎ 01506 630791 19rm(18 ⇄ ♠)

**Pumpherston** Drumshoreland Rd, Pumpherston EH53 0LF
☎ 01506 432122
Undulating parkland course with testing 6th hole (par 3), and view of Pentland Hills.
*9 holes, 5434yds, Par 66, SSS 67.*
*Club membership 430.*
**Visitors**     must be accompanied by a member.
**Societies**     apply in writing to the secretary.
**Green Fees** £10 per 18 holes with member.
**Facilities**     ⓑ ▆ ♀ ♨
**Leisure**     puttimg green, practice area.
**Location**     1m E between A71 & A89
**Hotel**     ★★ 56% Dreadnought Hotel, 17/19 Whitburn Rd, BATHGATE ☎ 01506 630791 19rm(18 ⇄ ♠)

## LOCHGELLY                                          Map 11 NT19

**Lochgelly** Cartmore Rd KY5 9PB ☎ 01592 780174
Parkland course with easy walking and often windy.
*18 holes, 5491yds, Par 68, SSS 67.*
*Club membership 650.*
**Visitors**     no restrictions.
**Societies**     must apply in writing.
**Green Fees** not confirmed.
**Facilities**     ⊗ 🏮 ⓑ ▆ ♀ ♨
**Leisure**     putting green.

| | |
|---|---|
| **Location** | W side of town off A910 |
| **Hotel** | ★★★ 57% Dean Park Hotel, Chapel Level, KIRKCALDY ☎ 01592 261635 20 ⇄ ♠Annexe12 ♠ |

**Lochore Meadows** Lochore Meadows Country Park, Crosshill KY5 8BA ☎ 01592 860086
Lochside course with natural stream running through, and woodland nearby. Country park offers many leisure facilities.
*9 holes, 5554yds, Par 72, SSS 71.*
*Club membership 200.*
**Visitors**     no restrictions.
**Societies**     must contact in advance.
**Green Fees** not confirmed.
**Facilities**     ♨
**Leisure**     fishing, putting green,practice area.
**Location**     2m N off B920
**Hotel**     ★★★ 70% Green Hotel, 2 The Muirs, KINROSS ☎ 01577 863467 47 ⇄ ♠

## LOCHGILPHEAD                                          Map 10 NR88

**Lochgilphead** Blarbuie Rd PA31 8LE ☎ 01546 602340
A varied course with short but interesting holes. Some elevated greens and tees and some tight fairways.
*9 holes, 2242yds, Par 64, SSS 63, Course record 58.*
*Club membership 250.*
**Visitors**     restricted during weekend club competitions. apply in advance, restricted wekends.
**Green Fees** £10 per day; £30 per week. Winter £5 per day.
**Facilities**     ⓑ by prior arrangement ▆ ♀ ♨ 🏠
**Leisure**     putting green, practice area.
**Hotel**     ★★ 63% The Stag Hotel, Argyll St, LOCHGILPHEAD ☎ 01546 602496 17 ⇄ ♠

## LONGNIDDRY                                          Map 12 NT47

**Longniddry** Links Rd EH32 0NL ☎ 01875 852141
Undulating seaside links and partial parkland course. One of the numerous courses which stretch east from Edinburgh right to Dunbar. The inward half is more open and less testing than the wooded outward half.
*18 holes, 6219yds, Par 69, SSS 70, Course record 63.*
*Club membership 1000.*
**Visitors**     may book tee times up to 7 days in advance, welcome most times except during competitions.
**Societies**     Mon-Thu, apply in writing, handicap certificate required.
**Green Fees** £35 per day; £25 per round (£35 per round weekends).
**Facilities**     ⊗ 🏮 ⓑ ▆ ♀ ♨ 🏠 🕈 ℃ John Gray.
**Leisure**     trolley for hire, putting green, practice area.
**Location**     W side of village off A198
**Hotel**     ★★ 67% Kilspindie House Hotel, Main St, ABERLADY ☎ 01875 870682 26 ⇄ ♠

## LUNDIN LINKS                                          Map 12 NO40

**Lundin** Golf Rd KY8 6BA ☎ 01333 320202
The Leven Links and the course of the Lundin Club adjoin each other. The course is part seaside and part inland. The holes are excellent but those which can be described as seaside holes have a very different nature from the inland style ones.

*18 holes, 6387yds, Par 71, SSS 71, Course record 63.*
*Club membership 820.*
| | |
|---|---|
| Visitors | visitors welcome weekdays 9-3.30 (3pm Fridays) and Sat after 2.30pm, no vistors Sun. Book well in advance. |
| Societies | book well in advance by telephoning Secretary. |
| Green Fees | Mon-Fri £35 per day; £25 per round. Sat after 2.30pm £35 per round (Winter£15/£10/£15). |
| Facilities | ⊗ �𝍬 ⓘ ⯑ ♀ ⯑ ⯑ 𝆕 David Webster. |
| Leisure | trolley for hire, putting green, practice area. |
| Location | W side of village off A915 |
| Hotel | ★★★ 69% Old Manor Hotel, Leven Rd, LUNDIN LINKS ☎ 01333 320368 19 ⇥ 𝆕 *See advertisement on page 302.* |

**Lundin Ladies** Woodielea Rd KY8 6AR
☎ 01333 320832
Short, lowland course with Roman stones on the second fairway, and coastal views.
*9 holes, 2365yds, Par 68, SSS 67, Course record 67.*
*Club membership 350.*
| | |
|---|---|
| Visitors | contact in advance. Competition days Wed and some weekends. |
| Societies | telephone secretary. |
| Green Fees | £7.50 per day (£9.50 weekends). |
| Facilities | ⯑ 𝆕 |
| Leisure | trolley for hire, putting green. |
| Location | W side of village off A915 |
| Hotel | ★★★ 69% Old Manor Hotel, Leven Rd, LUNDIN LINKS ☎ 01333 320368 19 ⇥ 𝆕 |

## LUSS                                        Map 10 NS39

**Loch Lomond** Rossdhu House G83 8NT
☎ 01436 860223
This is a Members Only club. Visitors are not permitted to play on this Tom Weiskopf/Jay Morrish designed course except as guest of members.
*18 holes, 6698yds, Par 72, SSS 72, Course record 69.*
*no visitors strictly private.*
| | |
|---|---|
| Facilities | ⯑ 𝆕 𝆕 Colin Campbell. |

## MACHRIHANISH                          Map 10 NR62

**Machrihanish** PA28 6PT
☎ 01586 810213
Magnificent seaside links of championship status. The 1st holes is the famous drive across the Atlantic. Sandy soil allows for play all year round. Large greens, easy walking, windy. Fishing.
*18 holes, 6228yds, Par 70, SSS 70.*
| | |
|---|---|
| Visitors | no restrictions. |
| Societies | apply in writing. |
| Green Fees | £28 per day; £20 per round (£35 per day Sat). Winter £20 per day. |
| Facilities | ⊗ ⯑ ⓘ ⯑ ♀ ⯑ 𝆕 𝆕 |
| Location | 5m W of Campbeltown on B843 |
| Hotel | ★★ 65% Seafield Hotel, Kilkerran Rd, CAMPBELTOWN ☎ 01586 554385 3 𝆕Annexe6 𝆕 |

## MARKINCH                                Map 11 NO20

**Balbirnie Park** Balbirnie Park KY7 6NR
☎ 01592 752006
Scenic parkland course with several interesting holes.
*18 holes, 6214yds, Par 71, SSS 70, Course record 65.*
*Club membership 900.*
| | |
|---|---|
| Visitors | must contact in advance. Numbers restricted weekends and visitors must play from yellow tees. |
| Societies | booking forms sent out on request by asst secretary. |
| Green Fees | £28 per day; £20 per round (£36/£28 weekends). |
| Facilities | ⊗ ⯑ ⓘ ⯑ ♀ ⯑ 𝆕 |
| Leisure | trolley for hire, putting green. |
| Location | 2m E of Glenrothes |
| Hotel | ★★★★(red)⚘ Balbirnie House, Balbirnie Park, MARKINCH ☎ 01592 610066 30 ⇥ 𝆕 |

## MILNATHORT                             Map 11 NO10

**Milnathort** South St KY13 7XA ☎ 01577 864069
Undulating parkland course.
*9 holes, 5969yds, Par 71, SSS 69, Course record 65.*
*Club membership 600.*
| | |
|---|---|
| Visitors | must contact in advance. |
| Societies | advisable to book in advance. |
| Green Fees | £10 per day (£15 weekends). |
| Facilities | ⯑ ♀ ⯑ |
| Leisure | driving range, putting green, practice area. |
| Location | S side of town on A922 |
| Hotel | ★★★ 70% Green Hotel, 2 The Muirs, KINROSS ☎ 01577 863467 47 ⇥ 𝆕 |

## MONIFIETH                               Map 12 NO43

**Monifieth** The Links DD5 4AW ☎ 01382 532767
The chief of the two courses at Monifieth is the Medal Course. It has been one of the qualifying venues for the Open Championship on more than one occasion. A seaside links, but divided from the sand dunes by a railway which provides the principal hazard for the first few holes. The 10th hole is outstanding, the 17th is excellent and there is a delightful finishing hole. The other course here is the Ashludie, and both are played over by a number of clubs who share the links.
*Medal Course: 18 holes, 6655yds, Par 71, SSS 72, Course record 63.*
*Ashludie Course: 18 holes, 5123yds, Par 68, SSS 66.*
*Club membership 1750.*
| | |
|---|---|
| Visitors | must contact in advance. Restricted to after 2pm Sat & 10am Sun. |
| Societies | must contact in advance by telephone or writing to Medal Starter's Box, Princes St, Monifieth. |
| Green Fees | Medal Course: £32 per day, £22 per round (£38/£26 weekends). Ashludie Course: £20 per day, £14 per round (£22/£15 weekends). |
| Facilities | ⊗ ⯑ ⓘ ⯑ ♀ ⯑ 𝆕 𝆕 Ian McLeod. |
| Leisure | trolley for hire, putting green, practice area. |
| Location | NE side of town on A930 |
| Hotel | ★★ 67% Carlogie House Hotel, Carlogie Rd, CARNOUSTIE ☎ 01241 853185 12 ⇥ 𝆕Annexe1 𝆕 |

## MONTROSE GOLF COURSES

(Montrose Links Trust)

Medal Course, generally recognised as one of the oldest sites of golf in the world – ranked 5th.

INDIVIDUAL ROUND AND DAY TICKETS AVAILABLE ON BOTH COURSES . . . OR

**GOLFERS – How's this for a great day out?**

**TWO LINKS COURSES:** Medal Course Par 71, SSS 72
Broomfield Course Par 66, SSS 63

Available throughout the year for clubs, societies, parties and casual visitors.

### Prices for 1997 range from £28.00 to £49.00 per day

This includes: 1 day's golf (36 holes), morning coffee and bacon roll, light lunch (soup and sandwiches), high tea.

**Special packages available in conjunction with local hotels**

*Great Scottish Golf Tour ticket welcome here*

**Enquiries to:**   Mrs M Stewart, Secretary,
Montrose Links Trust, Traill Drive,
Montrose DD10 8SW.
Tel: 01674 672932
Fax: 01674 671800

---

**MONTROSE**                   Map 15 NO75

Montrose Links Trust Traill Dr DD10 8SW
☎ 01674 672932
The links at Montrose like many others in Scotland are on commonland and are shared by three clubs. The Medal course at Montrose - the fifth oldest in the world - is typical of Scottish seaside links, with narrow, undulating fairways and problems from the first hole to the last. The Broomfield course is flatter and easier.
*Medal Course: 18 holes, 6470yds, Par 71, SSS 72, Course record 64.*
*Broomfield Course: 18 holes, 4765yds, Par 66, SSS 63.*
*Club membership 1300.*
Visitors   may not play on the Medal Course on Sat & before 10am on Sun. Must have a handicap certificate for Medal Course. Contact in advance.
Societies   must contact secretary in advance.
Green Fees not confirmed.
Facilities  ⊗ ⽧ ⽫ ⽪ ♀ ⼈ 🏠 ⼲ ℂ Kevin Stables.
Leisure   trolley for hire, putting green, practice area.
Location  NE side of town off A92
Hotel   ★★★ 61% Park Hotel, 61 John St, MONTROSE
☎ 01674 673415 59rm(48 ⇌5 ℝ)

---

**MUCKHART**                  Map 11 NO00

Muckhart FK14 7JH ☎ 01259 781423
Scenic heathland/downland course.
*18 holes, 6034yds, Par 71, SSS 70.*

---

*Club membership 750.*
Visitors   telephone to book - steward 01259 781423 or professional 01259 781493.
Societies   booking by prior arrangement.
Green Fees £20 per 36 holes; £14 per round (£28/£20 weekends).
Facilities  ⊗ ⽧ ⽫ ⽪ ♀ ⼈ 🏠 ⼲ ℂ Keith Salmoni.
Leisure   trolley for hire, putting green, practice area.
Location  SW of village off A91
Hotel   ★★★ 66% Whinsmuir Country Inn, POWMILL
☎ 01577 840595 13 ⇌ ℝ

---

**MULL, ISLE OF**             Map 10 NM73

---

**CRAIGNURE**             Map 10 NM73

Craignure Scallastle PA65 6PB
A flat links course, overlooking the sea.
*9 holes, 5072yds, Par 70, SSS 65, Course record 72.*
*Club membership 100.*
Visitors   may not play on competition days.
Societies   write to the secretary in advance.
Green Fees £9 per day; £40 per week.
Facilities  ⼈ ⼲
Location  0.5m N of Craignure A849
Hotel   ★★★ 72% Western Isles Hotel, TOBERMORY ☎ 01688 302012 26 ⇌ ℝ

---

**TOBERMORY**             Map 13 NM55

Tobermory PA75 6PE ☎ 01688 302020 & 302493
A physically demanding, hilly seaside cliff-top course. No sand-bunkers, superb views over the Sound of Mull. Testing 3rd hole (par 3) and interesting 7th much affected by the winds.
*9 holes, 4890yds, Par 64, SSS 64, Course record 65.*
*Club membership 150.*
Visitors   no restrictions except competition days.
Societies   prefrable to contact in advance.
Green Fees £12 per day/round; £40 per week.
Facilities  ⼲
Leisure   practice area.
Location  0.5m N off A848
Hotel   ★★★ 72% Western Isles Hotel, TOBERMORY ☎ 01688 302012 26 ⇌ ℝ

---

**MUSSELBURGH**           Map 11 NT37

Musselburgh Monktonhall EH21 6SA ☎ 0131 665 2005
Testing parkland course with natural hazards including trees and a burn, easy walking.
*18 holes, 6614yds, Par 71, SSS 73, Course record 65.*
*Club membership 900.*
Visitors   must contact in advance.
Societies   must contact in advance.
Green Fees £25 per day; £17 per round (£30/£21 weekends).
Facilities  ⊗ ⽧ ⽫ ⽪ ♀ ⼈ 🏠 ⼲ ℂ Fraser Mann.
Leisure   motorised carts for hire, buggies for hire, trolley for hire, putting green, practice area.
Location  1m S on B6415
Hotel   ★★★ 59% Donmaree Hotel, 21 Mayfield Gardens, EDINBURGH
☎ 0131 667 3641 15 ⇌ ℝAnnexe2 ⇌ ℝ

**Musselburgh Old Course** Millhill EH21 7RP
☎ 0131 665 6981
A links type course.
*9 holes, 2371yds, Par 33, SSS 33, Course record 67.*
*Club membership 70.*
**Visitors** may not play at weekends.
**Societies** must contact in advance.
**Green Fees** not confirmed.
**Facilities** ♀⚲
**Location** 1m E of town off A1
**Hotel** ★★★ 59% Donmaree Hotel, 21 Mayfield
Gardens, EDINBURGH
☎ 0131 667 3641 15 ➡ ♠Annexe2 ➡ ♠

## MUTHILL Map 11 NN81

**Muthill** Peat Rd PH5 2DA ☎ 01764 681523
Parkland course with fine views. Not too hilly, tight with
narrow fairways.
*9 holes, 4700yds, Par 66, SSS 63.*
*Club membership 500.*
**Visitors** no restrictions.
**Societies** book in advance.
**Green Fees** £12 per day (£15 weekends). 5 day ticket £40.
**Facilities** ⊗♠⚲⚲♠
**Leisure** trolley for hire, putting green.
**Location** W side of village off A822
**Hotel** ★★ 69% Murraypark Hotel, Connaught Ter,
CRIEFF ☎ 01764 653731 20 ➡ ♠

## NORTH BERWICK Map 12 NT58

**Glen** East Links, Tantallon Ter EH39 4LE
☎ 01620 895288 & 892726
An interesting course with a good variety of holes. The views
of the town, the Firth of Forth and the Bass Rock are
breathtaking.
*18 holes, 6089yds, Par 69, SSS 69, Course record 64.*
*Club membership 650.*
**Visitors** booking advisable.
**Societies** advance booking recommended.
**Green Fees** £23 per day; £15.50 per round (£28/£20
weekends).
**Facilities** ⊗♨♠⚲⚲♠♠⚓
**Leisure** buggies for hire, trolley for hire, putting green,
practice area.
**Location** 1m E of B198
**Hotel** ★★ 62% Nether Abbey Hotel, 20 Dirleton Av,
NORTH BERWICK
☎ 01620 892802 16rm(4 ➡6 ♠)

**North Berwick** Beach Rd EH39 4BB ☎ 01620 892135
Another of East Lothian's famous courses, the links at
North Berwick is still popular. A classic championship
links, it has many hazards including the beach, streams,
bunkers, light rough and low walls. The great hole on the
course is the 15th, the famous 'Redan', selected for
televisions best 18 in the UK. Used by both the Tantallon
and Bass Rock Golf Clubs.
*18 holes, 6420yds, Par 71, SSS 71, Course record 64.*
*Club membership 730.*
**Visitors** must contact in advance.
**Societies** must contact in advance.
**Green Fees** £40 per day; £22 per round (£55/£40
weekends).

**Facilities** ⊗♨♠⚲⚲♠♠⚓ ♂ 〔 D Huish.
**Leisure** trolley for hire, putting green, practice area.
**Location** W side of town on A198
**Hotel** ★★★ 63% The Marine Hotel, Cromwell
Rd, NORTH BERWICK
☎ 01620 892406 83 ➡ ♠
**Additional** Q Castle Inn, DIRLETON
**hotel** ☎ 01620 850221 4 ➡ ♠Annexe4rm

## OBAN Map 10 NM83

**Glencruitten** Glencruitten Rd PA34 4PU
☎ 01631 62868
There is plenty of space and considerable variety of hole
on this downland course - popular with holidaymakers. In
a beautiful, isolated situation, the course is hilly and
testing, particularly the 1st and 12th, par 4's, and 10th
and 15th, par 3's.
*18 holes, 4452yds, Par 61, SSS 63, Course record 55.*
*Club membership 600.*
**Visitors** restricted Thu & weekends
**Societies** must contact in writing.
**Green Fees** £15.50 per day; £12.50 per round
(£16.50/£14.50 weekends).
**Facilities** ⊗♨♠⚲⚲♠♠
**Leisure** trolley for hire, practice area.
**Location** NE side of town centre off A816
**Hotel** ★★★ 55% Caledonian Hotel, Station
Square, OBAN
☎ 01631 563133 70 ➡

## The Castle Inn
### Dirleton, North Berwick,
### East Lothian EH39 5EP

Fully licensed hotel with 8 bedrooms,
4 en suite. Accommodates 14. Cask
conditioned ales. Bar lunches & suppers.

Warm, friendly atmosphere. Surrounded
by many well known golf courses –
North Berwick, Muirfield, Gullane
and Luffness

Open all year.
**Telephone: (01620) 850221**

## PENICUIK      Map 11 NT25

**Glencorse** Milton Bridge EH26 0RD
☎ 01968 677189 & 676481
Picturesque parkland course with burn affecting ten holes.
Testing 5th hole (237 yds) par 3.
*18 holes, 5217yds, Par 64, SSS 66, Course record 60.*
*Club membership 700.*
**Visitors**     contact professional.
**Societies**    contact secretary for details.
**Green Fees** £24 per day; £18 per round (£24 per round weekends and bank holidays).
**Facilities**    ⊗ ⅢⅡ ⅃ ⅃ ⅃ ⅃ ⅃ Cliffe Jones.
**Leisure**     trolley for hire, driving range, practice area.
**Location**    1.5m N of Penicuik on A701
**Hotel**      ★★ 60% Roslin Glen Hotel, 2 Penicuik Rd, ROSLIN
           ☎ 0131 440 2029 7 ⇌ 🛏

## PERTH      Map 11 NO12

**Craigie Hill** Cherrybank PH2 0NE
☎ 01738 620829 & 622644
Slightly hilly, parkland course. Good views over Perth.
*18 holes, 5386yds, Par 66, SSS 67, Course record 60.*
*Club membership 560.*
**Visitors**     restricted access Sat. Telephone up to 3 days in advance.
**Societies**    must contact in writing.
**Green Fees** £20 per day; £15 per round (£25 Sun).
**Facilities**    ⊗ ⅢⅡ ⅃ ⅃ ⅃ ⅃ ⅃ Steven Harrier.
**Leisure**     trolley for hire, putting green, practice area.
**Location**    1m SW of city centre off A952
**Hotel**      ★★★ 61% The Royal George, Tay St, PERTH
           ☎ 01738 624455 42 ⇌ 🛏

**King James VI** Moncreiffe Island PH2 8NR
☎ 01738 445132 (Secretary) & 632460 (Pro)
Parkland course, situated on island in the middle of River Tay. Easy walking.
*18 holes, 6038yds, Par 70, SSS 69, Course record 62.*
*Club membership 650.*
**Visitors**     visitors restricted on competition days. Contact professional for bookings.
**Societies**    book by telephone.
**Green Fees** £22 per day; £15 per round (£28/£18 weekends). Winter £9 per round..
**Facilities**    ⊗ ⅢⅡ ⅃ ⅃ ⅃ ⅃ ⅃ Tom Coles.
**Leisure**     buggies for hire, trolley for hire, putting green, practice area.
**Location**    SE side of city centre
**Hotel**      ★★★ 61% Queens Hotel, Leonard St, PERTH
           ☎ 01738 442222 51 ⇌ 🛏

**Murrayshall Country House Hotel** Murrayshall, Scone PH2 7PH ☎ 01738 552784
This course is laid out in 130 acres of parkland with tree-lined fairways. Hotel and driving range.
*18 holes, 6446yds, Par 73, SSS 71.*
*Club membership 350.*
**Visitors**     no restrictions.
**Societies**    telephone in advance.
**Green Fees** £30 per day; £20 per round (£40 per day; £25 per round weekends).
**Facilities**    ⊗ ⅢⅡ ⅃ ⅃ ⅃ ⅃ ⅃ ⅃ ⅃ George Finlayson.
**Leisure**     hard tennis courts, motorised carts for hire, buggies for hire, trolley for hire, driving range, putting green, practice area.
**Location**    E side of village off A94
**Hotel**      ★★★⚐ 74% Murrayshall Country House Hotel & Golf Course, New Scone, PERTH
           ☎ 01738 551171 19 ⇌ 🛏
**Additional** ★★ 65% The Tayside Hotel, Mill St, Stanley
**hotel**        ☎ 01738 828249 16rm(4 ⇌ 10 🛏)

**North Inch** North Inch, off Hay St PH1 5PH
☎ 01738 636481
An enjoyable short and often testing course incorporating mature trees, open parkland with fine views and attractive riverside.
*18 holes, 5178yds, Par 65, Course record 60.*
*Club membership 476.*
**Visitors**     advisable to telephone in advance.
**Green Fees** £3.20-£7.40.
**Facilities**    ⊗ ⅃ ⅃ ⅃ ⅃
**Leisure**     squash, gymnasium, trolley for hire, putting green.
**Hotel**      ★★★ 61% The Royal George, Tay St, PERTH
           ☎ 01738 624455 42 ⇌ 🛏

## PITLOCHRY      Map 14 NN95

**Pitlochry** Pitlochry Estate Office PH16 5QY
☎ 01796 472792
A varied and interesting heathland course with fine views and posing many problems. Its SSS permits few errors in its achievement.
*18 holes, 5811yds, Par 69, SSS 68.*
*Club membership 400.*
**Visitors**     may not play before 9.30am.
**Societies**    must contact in writing.
**Green Fees** not confirmed.
**Facilities**    ⅃ ⅃ ⅃ ⅃ ⅃ George Hampton.
**Location**    N side of town off A924
**Hotel**      ★★★⚐ 72% Pine Trees Hotel, Strathview Ter, PITLOCHRY
           ☎ 01796 472121 20rm(19 ⇌ 🛏)

**To Cover The Whole Region**

PERTHSHIRE
'ALL OF SCOTLAND'

Centrally situated
Play a different course daily
Tee-off times pre-booked
Inclusive golfing tariff

**THE TAYSIDE HOTEL**
Stanley, near Perth
AA ◉    AA ★★
STB ❧❧❧ Commended
Tel: (01738) 828249
Fax: (01738) 827216

## POLMONT

Map 11 NS97

***Grangemouth*** Polmont Hill FK2 0YE
☎ 01324 711500
Windy parkland course. Testing holes: 3rd, 4th (par 4's); 5th
(par 5); 7th (par 3) 216 yds over reservoir (elevated green);
8th, 9th, 18th (par 4's).
*18 holes, 6314yds, Par 71, SSS 71.*
*Club membership 700.*
**Visitors** must contact in advance.
**Societies** must contact in writing.
**Green Fees** not confirmed.
**Facilities** ♀♨☎ℓ
**Leisure** pool tables.
**Location** On unclass rd 0.5m N of M9 junc 4
**Hotel** ★★★ 68% Inchyra Grange Hotel, Grange Rd,
POLMONT
☎ 01324 711911 43 ⇄ ℝ

**Polmont** Manuelrigg, Maddiston FK2 0LS
☎ 01324 711277
Parkland course, hilly with few bunkers. Views of the River
Forth and Ochil Hills.
*9 holes, 3073yds, Par 72, SSS 69, Course record 71.*
*Club membership 300.*
**Visitors** no visitors on Sat, Mon-Fri must tee of before 5pm.
**Societies** apply in writing to club secretary.
**Green Fees** £7 per 18 holes (£12 Sun).
**Facilities** ⊗ 𝕏 ▐ ☟ ♨
**Leisure** putting green.
**Location** E side of village off A803
**Hotel** ★★★ 68% Inchyra Grange Hotel, Grange Rd,
POLMONT
☎ 01324 711911 43 ⇄ ℝ

## PORT GLASGOW

Map 10 NS37

***Port Glasgow*** Devol Rd PA14 5XE ☎ 01475 704181
A moorland course set on a hilltop overlooking the Clyde,
with magnificent views to the Cowal hills.
*18 holes, 5712yds, Par 68, SSS 68.*
*Club membership 390.*
**Visitors** may not play on Sat.
**Societies** apply in writing.
**Green Fees** not confirmed.
**Facilities** ♀♨☎
**Leisure** putting green.
**Location** 1m S
**Hotel** ★★★♨♨ 72% Gleddoch House Hotel,
LANGBANK
☎ 01475 540711 39 ⇄ ℝ

## PRESTONPANS

Map 11 NT37

**Royal Musselburgh** Prestongrange House EH32 9RP
☎ 01875 810276
Tree-lined parkland course overlooking Firth of Forth.
*18 holes, 6237yds, Par 70, SSS 70, Course record 64.*
*Club membership 970.*
**Visitors** must contact professional in advance, restricted
Fri afternoons & weekends.
**Societies** must contact in advance,
**Green Fees** £35 per day; £20 per round (£35 per round
weekends).

**Facilities** ⊗ 𝕏 ▐ ☟ ♀♨☎ 🏴 ℓ John Henderson.
**Leisure** trolley for hire, putting green, practice area,
snooker.
**Location** W side of town centre off A59
**Hotel** ★★ 67% Kilspindie House Hotel, Main St,
ABERLADY
☎ 01875 870682 26 ⇄ ℝ

## RATHO

Map 11 NT17

***Ratho Park*** EH28 8NX
☎ 0131 333 2566 0131 333 1752
Flat parkland course.
*18 holes, 5900yds, Par 69, SSS 68, Course record 62.*
*Club membership 850.*
**Visitors** must contact in advance.
**Societies** must contact in writing.
**Green Fees** not confirmed.
**Facilities** ♀♨☎ℓ Alan Pate.
**Leisure** putting green,practice area,trolley hire.
**Location** 0.75m E, N of A71
**Hotel** B Forte Posthouse Edinburgh, Corstorphine Rd,
EDINBURGH
☎ 0131 334 0390 204 ⇄ ℝ

## ST ANDREWS

Map 12 NO51

**British Golf Museum**
☎ 01334 478880 (Situated opposite Royal &
Ancient Golf Club). The museum which tells the
history of golf from its origins to the present day, is
of interest to golfers and non-golfers alike. Themed
galleries and interactive displays explore the history
of the major championships and the lives of the
famous players, and trace the development of golfing
equipment and costume. An audio-visual theatre
shows historic golfing moments. **Open**: mid April-
mid Oct 10-5.30pm. **Admission**: There is a charge.
☎ for details.

ST ANDREWS LINKS    See page 303

## ST FILLANS

Map 11 NN62

**St Fillans** South Loch Earn Rd PH6 2NJ
☎ 01764 685312
Fairly flat, beautiful parkland course. Wonderfully rich in
flora, animal and bird life.
*9 holes, 5796yds, Par 68, SSS 67, Course record 73.*
*Club membership 400.*
**Visitors** advisable to contact in advance.
**Societies** Apr-Oct, apply to starter.
**Green Fees** £10 per day (£15 per day weekends & bank
holidays).
**Facilities** ▐ ☟ ♨☎
**Leisure** fishing, trolley for hire.
**Location** E side of village off A85
**Hotel** ★★★ 67% The Four Seasons Hotel, Loch Earn,
ST FILLANS
☎ 01764 685333 12 ⇄ ℝ

# GOLFING BREAKS FOR INDIVIDUALS OR SOCIETIES

A most comfortable, privately owned
3 Star Hotel with an excellent
restaurant and superb cellar.
We tailor holidays to your particular
requirements using St. Andrews and
other local Championship courses.

*S.T.B  4 Crowns Highly Commended*
*A.A 3 Stars 73%*

**SEND FOR OUR GOLF BROCHURE**
**40 THE SCORES, ST. ANDREWS KY16 9AS**
**TEL: (01334) 472611 FAX: (01334) 472188**

# ON THE VERY DOORSTEP OF THE HOME OF GOLF

This famous 30 bedroom hotel is literally only
yards from the R & A clubhouse and the first tee
of the Old Course. Enjoying magnificent views of
the Bay, and only minutes walk from the historic
town centre, this is the ideal choice for your
golfing holiday in St. Andrews.

Facilities include a coffee shop, two bars and a
highly regarded restaurant.

We are happy to assist in making bookings at
most local courses.

**SCORES HOTEL**
**ST ANDREWS**

*The Scores Hotel St. Andrews, Fife, KY16 9BB, Scotland*
*Tel: (01334) 472451     Fax: (01334) 473947*

## The Old Manor Hotel
### Near St Andrews

AA ★★★ ֎

Family owned Country House
overlooking Lundin and Leven
Championship Courses. St. Andrews,
Crail, Elie, Ladybank, close by, and
over 30 courses within a half hour
drive. Twenty-five en-suite rooms,
2 Restaurants. Excellent food, fine
wine and real ale.
Golf Breaks for individuals
and Societies.

**Lundin Links, Fife KY8 6AJ**
**Tel: 01333 320368 Fax: 01333 320911**

**SALINE** Map 11 NT09

**Saline** Kinneddar Hill KY12 9LT
☎ 01383 852591
Hillside course with panoramic view of the Forth Valley.
*9 holes, 5302yds, SSS 66, Course record 68.*
*Club membership 420.*
**Visitors** advisable to contact in advance and may not play Sat, some restrictions Sun.
**Societies** contact in advance.
**Green Fees** £9 per day (£11 Sun).
**Facilities** ⊗ by prior arrangement ⶅ by prior arrangement 🖥♥♀⚘
**Leisure** driving range, putting green, practice area.
**Location** 0.5m E at junc B913/914
**Hotel** ★★★ 62% King Malcolm Thistle, Queensferry Rd, Wester Pitcorthie, DUNFERMLINE ☎ 01383 722611 48 ⇄ 🐾

**SOUTHEND** Map 10 NR60

**Dunaverty** PA28 6RW
☎ 01586 830677
Undulating, seaside course.
*18 holes, 4799yds, Par 66, SSS 63, Course record 59.*
*Club membership 400.*
**Visitors** limited Sat, contact in advance.
**Societies** apply in advance.
**Green Fees** £18 per day; £12 per round; £45 per week.
**Facilities** ⊗ by prior arrangement ⶅ by prior arrangement 🖥♥⚘🏠

▶

# ST ANDREWS LINKS

**ST ANDREWS** *Fife* ☏ 01334 475757          Map 12  N051

*John Ingham writes:* If golf has a mother, then without doubt it is St Andrews, the most famous links in all the world. Sir Winston Churchill is said to have claimed golf was invented by the Devil, and if this is so then the famous Old Course must be the Devil's playground. How can one reconcile these two thoughts; the birthplace and mother of the game - and yet the very Devil of a test?

The great Bobby Jones started by hating St Andrews and shredded his card into a hundred pieces, letting it blow in the wind. But eventually he came to love the place, and earn the affection of all golf. However you view St Andrews, you cannot ignore it. That master shot-maker from America, Sam Snead, took one look and claimed they should plant cattle fodder on the bumpy acres. Gary Player once said it should be towed out to sea, and sunk. But Jack Nicklaus loved it so much that when he won an Open title here, he threw his putter into the air. And he went away, and copied several of the St Andrews features in other courses that now decorate this earth.

St Andrews is much more than an 18-hole test. It is a whole experience and a walk in history. Name the famous players of yesteryear, and they played here, taking divots from the very spot that you can also take divots - merely by paying for a ticket. You too can wander out with your clubs to conquer some holes, maybe, and to be brought to a humbling halt by others.

Jack Nicklaus won his most remarkable victory on this course, thanks to an historic missed putt of just 3 feet 6 inches by Doug Sanders, who had needed a final hole par 4 to win the 1970 Open Championship. The all-time course record is 62, shot by Curtis Strange in the 1987 Dunhill Cup. Surely nobody can ever beat that?

| Visitors | must telephone in advance |
| --- | --- |
| Societies | must book at least a month in advance. |
| Green fees | Old course: £60; New Course £25; Jubilee £25, Eden £18; Strathtyrum £14, Balgove £6 (18 holes) |
| Facilities | ⊗ ⅷ ⅃ ⅃ ☕ ♀ ⅃ 🛍 ⌁ driving range, putting green, practice area, trolleys. |
| Location | St. Andrews KY16 9SF NW of town off the A91 |

**Old Course: 18 holes, 6566yds, Par 72, SSS 72**

**New (West Sands Rd): 18 holes, 6604yds, Par 71, SSS 72**

**Jubilee (West Sands Rd): 18 holes, 6805yds, Par 72, SSS 73**

**Eden (Dundee Rd): 18 holes, 6112yds, Par 70, SSS 69**

**Strathtyrum): 18 holes, 5195yds, Par 69**

**Balgove 9 holes  3060 yds**

## WHERE TO STAY AND EAT NEARBY

**HOTELS:**

**ST ANDREWS**

★★★★★ ❀❀ 63% Old Course St Andrews, Old Station Rd. ☎ 01334 474371. 125 ⇄ ♠

★★★❀ 73% St Andrews Golf, 40 The Scores. ☎ 01334 472611. 23 (3 ♠ 20 ⇄ ♠)

★★★67% Scores, 76 The Scores ☎ 01334 472451. 30  (2 ♠ 28 ⇄ ♠)

**RESTAURANTS:**

**CUPAR**

❀❀❀ Ostlers Close, Bonnygate ☎ 01334 655574

| | |
|---|---|
| Leisure | fishing, putting green, practice area. |
| Location | 10m S of Campbeltown on B842 |
| Hotel | ★★ 65% Seafield Hotel, Kilkerran Rd, CAMPBELTOWN ☎ 01586 554385 3 ↝Annexe6 ↝ |

## SOUTH QUEENSFERRY      Map 11 NT17

*Dundas Parks* c/o Secretary, 3 Stewart Clark Av EH30 9QF
☎ 0131 331 2363 (evenings only)
Parkland course situated on the estate of Lady Jane Stewart-Clark, with excellent views. For 18 holes, the 9 are played twice.
*9 holes, 6024yds, Par 70, SSS 69, Course record 66.*
*Club membership 500.*

| | |
|---|---|
| Visitors | must contact in advance. |
| Societies | must contact in advance. |
| Green Fees | not confirmed. |
| Facilities | ⚐ |
| Leisure | putting green, practice ground, bunker & driving bay. |
| Location | 1m S on A8000 |
| Hotel | ★★★ 60% Forth Bridges Hotel, Forth Bridge, SOUTH QUEENSFERRY ☎ 0131 331 1199 108 ↝ ↝ |

## STIRLING      Map 11 NS79

*Stirling* Queens Rd FK8 3AA ☎ 01786 464098
Undulating parkland course with magnificent views. Testing 15th, 'Cotton's Fancy', 384 yds (par 4).
*18 holes, 6438yds, Par 72, SSS 71, Course record 65.*
*Club membership 1100.*

| | |
|---|---|
| Visitors | may reserve tee off times mid week 9-4.30pm. At weekends tee off times may be reserved on day of play subject to availability. |
| Societies | must apply in writing or telephone. |
| Green Fees | £26 per day; £18 per round (£10 per day/round Nov-Mar). |
| Facilities | ⊗ ⅢL ↝ ⚐ ♀⚐ ⚐ ↝ ↝ Ian Collins. |
| Leisure | trolley for hire, driving range, putting green, practice area. |
| Location | W side of town on B8051 |
| Hotel | ★★ 64% Terraces Hotel, 4 Melville Ter, STIRLING ☎ 01786 472268 18 ↝ ↝ |

## STRATHTAY      Map 14 NN95

*Strathtay* PH15 ☎ 01350 727797
A wooded mainly hilly course with pleasing panoramic views. 5th hole 'Spion Kop' is especially difficult. It is steep, with heavy rough on both sides of the hilly fairway and an unsighted green of the back of the hill which is affected by winds.
*9 holes, 4082yds, Par 63, SSS 63, Course record 61.*
*Club membership 158.*

| | |
|---|---|
| Visitors | restricted May-Sep; Sun 12.30-5pm & Mon 6-8pm. Also some Wed & Thu evenings. |
| Societies | by letter or telephone to Secretary T D Lind, Lorne Cottage, Dalguise, Dunkeld, Perthshire PH8 0JX. |
| Green Fees | not confirmed. |
| Facilities | ⚐ |
| Location | Eastern end of minor rd to Weem, off A827 |
| Hotel | ★★ 63% The Weem, Weem, ABERFELDY ☎ 01887 820381 12 ↝ ↝ |

## TARBERT      Map 10 NR86

*Tarbert* PA29 6XX ☎ 01880 820536
Beautiful moorland course. Four fairways crossed by streams.
*9 holes, 4460yds, Par 66, SSS 63, Course record 62.*

| | |
|---|---|
| Visitors | may not play Sat pm. |
| Societies | apply in writing. |
| Green Fees | £15 per day; £10 per 18 holes; £5 per 9 holes. |
| Location | N1m W on B8024) |
| Hotel | ★★★⚐⚐ 64% Stonefield Castle Hotel, TARBERT ☎ 01880 820836 33 ↝ ↝ |

## TAYPORT      Map 12 NO42

*Scotscraig* Golf Rd DD6 9DZ ☎ 01382 552515
A rather tight course on downland-type turf with an abundance of gorse. The sheltered position of this Open qualifying course ensures good weather throughout the year.
*18 holes, 6550yds, Par 71, SSS 72, Course record 69.*
*Club membership 750.*

| | |
|---|---|
| Visitors | restricted at weekends. Must contact in advance. |
| Societies | advance booking. |
| Green Fees | £36 per day; £25 per round (£42/£30 weekends). |
| Facilities | ⊗ Ⅲ L ↝ ⚐ ♀⚐ ⚐ ↝ ↝ |
| Leisure | trolley for hire, driving range, putting green, practice area. |
| Location | S side of village off B945 |
| Hotel | ★★★ 62% The Queen's Hotel, 160 Nethergate, DUNDEE ☎ 01382 322515 47 ↝ ↝ |

## THORNTON      Map 11 NT29

*Thornton* Station Rd KY1 4DW ☎ 01592 771111
Undulating and fairly difficult parkland course.
*18 holes, 6177yds, Par 70, SSS 69, Course record 64.*
*Club membership 700.*

| | |
|---|---|
| Visitors | restricted at weekends before 10am & between 12.30-2pm, also Tue 1-1.30 & Thu 9-10. Booking in advance recommended. |
| Societies | apply in advance. |
| Green Fees | £20 per day; £14 per round (£30/£20 weekends). |
| Facilities | ⊗ Ⅲ L ↝ ⚐ ♀⚐ |
| Leisure | trolley for hire, putting green, practice area. |
| Location | 1m E of town off A92 |
| Hotel | ★★★ 69% Balgeddie House Hotel, Balgeddie Way, GLENROTHES ☎ 01592 742511 18 ↝ ↝ |

## TIGHNABRUAICH      Map 10 NR97

*Kyles of Bute* PA21 2EE ☎ 01700 811603
Moorland course which is hilly and exposed to wind. Good views of the Kyles of Bute.
*9 holes, 4778yds, Par 66, SSS 64, Course record 62.*
*Club membership 150.*

| | |
|---|---|
| Visitors | may not play Wed pm or Sun am. |
| Societies | telephone in advance. |
| Green Fees | £6 per day/round. |
| Facilities | ⚐ ⚐ ↝ |
| Leisure | trolley for hire. |
| Location | 1.25m S off B8000 |
| Hotel | ★★ 76% Kilfinan Hotel, KILFINAN ☎ 01700 821201 11 ↝ |

## TILLICOULTRY                    Map 11 NS99

**Tillicoultry** Alva Rd FK13 6BL ☎ 01259 750124
Parkland course at foot of the Ochil Hills entailing some hard walking.
*9 holes, 4904metres, Par 68, SSS 66, Course record 61.*
*Club membership 400.*
**Visitors** must contact in advance.
**Societies** apply to the secretary.
**Green Fees** £10 per round before 4pm, £12 after 4pm (£15 weekends).
**Facilities** ⊗ ⍵ ⏻ ⍙ ⛳ ♀ ⩘
**Location** A91, 9m E of Stirling
**Hotel** ★★ 64% Harviestoun Country Inn, Dollar Rd, TILLICOULTRY ☎ 01259 752522 10 ⇋ ℝ

## UPHALL                          Map 11 NT07

**Uphall** EH52 6JT ☎ 01506 856404 & 855553 (Pro)
Windy parkland course, easy walking.
*18 holes, 5567yds, Par 69, SSS 67, Course record 62.*
*Club membership 500.*
**Visitors** restricted weekends.
**Societies** must contact in advance.
**Green Fees** not confirmed.
**Facilities** ♀ ⩘ 🖰 ⌁ ℓ Gordon Law.
**Location** W side of village on A899
**Hotel** ★★ 56% Dreadnought Hotel, 17/19 Whitburn Rd, BATHGATE ☎ 01506 630791 19rm(18 ⇋ ℝ)

## WEST CALDER                     Map 11 NT06

**Harburn** EH55 8RS ☎ 01506 871131
Moorland, reasonably flat.
*18 holes, 5921yds, Par 69, SSS 69, Course record 62.*
*Club membership 870.*
**Visitors** contact secretary, limited weekends.
**Societies** must contact in writing.
**Green Fees** £21 two rounds; £16 per round (£26/£19 Fri, £32/£21 weekends & bank holidays).
**Facilities** ⊗ ⍙ ⛳ ♀ ⩘ 🖰 ℓ Tom Stangoe.
**Leisure** motorised carts for hire, buggies for hire, trolley for hire, putting green, practice area.
**Location** On B7008
**Hotel** ★★★ 61% The Hilcroft Hotel, East Main St, WHITBURN ☎ 01501 740818 30 ⇋ ℝ

## WHITBURN                        Map 11 NS96

**Polkemmet Country Park** EH47 0AD ☎ 01501 743905
Public parkland course surrounded by mature woodland and rhododendron bushes. 15-bay floodlit driving range.
*9 holes, 2969mtrs, Par 37.*
**Visitors** no restrictions.
**Green Fees** per 9 holes summer £2.85 (£3.60 Sun) prices due to be reviewed.
**Facilities** ⊗ ⍵ ⍙ ⛳ ♀
**Leisure** trolley for hire, driving range, practice area.
**Location** 2m W off B7066
**Hotel** ★★★ 61% The Hilcroft Hotel, East Main St, WHITBURN ☎ 01501 740818 30 ⇋ ℝ

---

# SOUTHERN LOWLANDS & BORDERS

This region includes the counties of City of Glasgow, Dumbarton & Clydebank, Dumfries & Galloway, East Ayrshire, East Dunbartonshire, East Renfrewshire, North Ayrshire, North Lanarkshire, Renfrewshire, Scottish Borders, South Ayrshire and South Lanarkshire which reflect the recent national changes..

## AIRDRIE                         Map 11 NS76

**Airdrie** Rochsoles ML6 0PQ ☎ 01236 762195
Picturesque parkland course with good views.
*18 holes, 6004yds, Par 69, SSS 69, Course record 64.*
*Club membership 450.*
**Visitors** must contact in advance. With member only weekends & bank holidays.
**Societies** apply in writing.
**Green Fees** not confirmed.
**Facilities** ♀ ⩘ 🖰 ℓ A McCloskey.
**Leisure** putting green,practice area,trolley hire.
**Location** 1m N on B802
**Hotel** ★★★★ 64% Westerwood Hotel Golf & Country Club, 1 St Andrews Dr, Westerwood, CUMBERNAULD ☎ 01236 457171 47 ⇋ ℝ

**Easter Moffat** Mansion House, Plains ML6 8NP
☎ 01236 842878
Moorland/parkland course.
*18 holes, 6221yds, Par 72, SSS 70.*
*Club membership 450.*
**Visitors** may only play on weekdays.
**Societies** must contact in advance.
**Green Fees** not confirmed.
**Facilities** ♀ ⩘ 🖰 ℓ Brian Dunbar.
**Location** 2m E on old Edinburgh-Glasgow road
**Hotel** ★★★★ 64% Westerwood Hotel Golf & Country Club, 1 St Andrews Dr, Westerwood, CUMBERNAULD ☎ 01236 457171 47 ⇋ ℝ

## ARRAN, ISLE OF                  Map 10 NR94

## BLACKWATERFOOT                  Map 10 NR82

**Shiskine** Shore Rd KA27 8AH ☎ 01770 860226
Unique 12-hole links course with gorgeous outlook to the Mull of Kintyre.
*12 holes, 2990yds, Par 41, SSS 42.*
*Club membership 520.*
**Visitors** must contact in advance.
**Societies** must contact in writing in advance. Jul and Aug no parties.
**Green Fees** £12 per 2 rounds; £8 per round.
**Facilities** ⊗ ⍵ ⍙ ⛳ ⩘ 🖰
**Leisure** hard tennis courts, buggies for hire, trolley for hire, putting green, outdoor all weather bowling green.
**Location** W side of village off A841                    ▶

**Hotel**       ★★ 64%  The Lagg Hotel, Kilmory,  BRODICK
            ☎ 01770 870255 15 ⇄ ℝ

## BRODICK                                   Map 10 NS03

***Brodick*** KA27 8DL  ☎ 01770 302349 & 302513
Short seaside course, very flat.
*18 holes, 4405yds, Par 62, SSS 62, Course record 60.*
*Club membership 552.*
**Visitors**    must contact in advance but may not play on
            competition days.
**Societies**   must contact in advance.
**Green Fees**  not confirmed.
**Facilities**  ♀ ☖ ⌂ ℓ  Peter McCalla.
**Leisure**     caddy cars, practice area.
**Location**    N side of village
**Hotel**       ★★★ 76%  Auchrannie Country House Hotel,
            BRODICK ☎ 01770 302234 28 ⇄ ℝ

## CORRIE                                    Map 10 NS04

**Corrie** Sannox KA27 8JD  ☎ 01770 810223
A heathland course on the coast with beautiful mountain
scenery. An upward climb to 6th hole, then a descent from the
7th. All these holes are subject to strong winds in bad weather.
*9 holes, 1948yds.*
*Club membership 280.*
**Visitors**    welcome except Sat pm and two first Thu
            afternoons of the month.
**Societies**   maximum size of party 16, apply in advance.
**Green Fees**  £7 per day.
**Facilities**  ⊗ ⽱ ▙ ♟ ☖ ⌁
**Location**    2m N on A841
**Hotel**       ★★★ 76%  Auchrannie Country House Hotel,
            BRODICK ☎ 01770 302234 28 ⇄ ℝ

## LAMLASH                                   Map 10 NS03

**Lamlash** KA27 8JU  ☎ 01770 600296 & 600196 (Starter)
Undulating heathland course with magnificent views of the
mountains and sea.
*18 holes, 4640yds, Par 64, SSS 64, Course record 62.*
*Club membership 400.*
**Visitors**    contact in advance.
**Societies**   must contact in writing.
**Green Fees**  £12 per day (£15 weekends).
**Facilities**  ⊗ ⽱ ▙ ♟ ♀ ☖ ⌂
**Leisure**     trolley for hire, putting green, trolley hire.
**Location**    0.75m N of Lamlash on A841
**Hotel**       ★★★ 76%  Auchrannie Country House Hotel,
            BRODICK ☎ 01770 302234 28 ⇄ ℝ

## LOCHRANZA                                 Map 10 NR95

**Lochranza** KA27 8HL  ☎ 01770 830273
This course opened in 1991 is mainly on the level, set amid
spectacular scenery where the fairways are grazed by wild red
deer, while overhead buzzards and golden eagles may be
seen. There are water hazards including the river which is
lined by mature trees. The final three holes are nicknamed the
Bermuda Triangle provide an absorbing finish right to the
18th hole - a 530 yard dogleg through trees and over the
river.The nine large greens are played off 18 tees. The course
is closed during the winter from 1 November to mid April.

*9 holes, 5033mtrs, Par 70, SSS 70, Course record 74.*
**Visitors**    no restrictions; course closed Nov-mid Apr.
**Societies**   advance booking preferred.
**Green Fees**  £15 per day; £10 per 18 holes; £5 per 9 holes.
**Facilities**  ♟ ☖ ⌂ ⌁
**Leisure**     trolley for hire, putting green.
**Hotel**       ★★ 64%  The Lagg Hotel, Kilmory,  BRODICK
            ☎ 01770 870255 15 ⇄ ℝ

## MACHRIE                                   Map 10 NR83

**Machrie Bay** KA27 8DZ  ☎ 01770 850232
Fairly flat seaside course. Designed at turn of century by
William Fernie.
*9 holes, 4396yds, Par 66, SSS 66, Course record 56.*
*Club membership 315.*
**Visitors**    no restrictions.
**Societies**   write in advance.
**Green Fees**  £5 per day.
**Facilities**  ⊗ ♟ ☖
**Leisure**     hard tennis courts, fishing, putting green.
**Location**    9m W of Brodick via String Rd
**Hotel**       ★★ 64%  The Lagg Hotel, Kilmory,  BRODICK
            ☎ 01770 870255 15 ⇄ ℝ

## WHITING BAY                               Map 10 NS02

***Whiting Bay*** KA27 8QT  ☎ 01770 700347
Heathland course.
*18 holes, 4405yds, Par 63, SSS 63, Course record 59.*
*Club membership 350.*
**Visitors**    tee reserved 8.45-9.30am, also Sun 11.45-1pm.
**Societies**   apply by telephone and confirm in writing with
            deposit.
**Green Fees**  not confirmed.
**Facilities**  ♀ ☖ ⌂
**Leisure**     putting green, motor cart, buggy/trolley hire.
**Location**    NW side of village off A841
**Hotel**       ★★ 64%  The Lagg Hotel, Kilmory,  BRODICK
            ☎ 01770 870255 15 ⇄ ℝ

## AYR                                       Map 10 NS32

***Belleisle*** Belleisle Park KA7 4DU  ☎ 01292 441258
Parkland course with beautiful sea views. First-class conditions.
*Belleisle Course: 18 holes, 6540yds, Par 70, SSS 72.*
*Seafield Course: 18 holes, 5498yds, Par 68, SSS 67.*
*Club membership 300.*
**Visitors**    advised to contact in advance.
**Societies**   advised to contact in advance.
**Green Fees**  not confirmed.
**Facilities**  ♀ ☖ ⌂ ⌁ ⌘ ℓ  David Gemmell.
**Leisure**     putting,cart/trolley hire.
**Location**    2m S on A719
**Hotel**       ★★★ 59%  Quality Friendly Hotel, Burns
            Statue Square,  AYR
            ☎ 01292 263268 75 ⇄ ℝ
**Additional**  ★★★ 62%  Jarvis Caledonian, Dalblair Rd,
**hotel**       AYR ☎ 01292 269331 114 ⇄ ℝ

Entries with a shaded background identify
courses that are considered to be particularly
interesting

# Golfing Breaks in Ayr

Visitors to Scotland's beautiful west coast are at the heart of golf when they stay in Ayrshire. The Jarvis Caledonian Hotel is situated in the heart of the town. Yet only a short stroll to Ayr's sandy beaches. The hotel offers you comfortable bedrooms all with own private bathroom. You'll have complimentary use of the Leisure Club & Swimming Pool during your stay. Hudson's Bar & Grill is a "lively place to meet and eat" 22 Golf Courses within 1 hours drive from the Hotel.

*To find out more call:*
**The Jarvis Caledonian Hotel**
**Dalblair Road**
**Ayr KA7 1UG**
**(01292) 269331**

*Dalmilling* Westwood Av KA8 0QY ☎ 01292 263893
Meadowland course, with easy walking.
*18 holes, 5724yds, Par 69, SSS 68.*
*Club membership 140.*
**Visitors** must contact in advance.
**Societies** must contact in advance.
**Green Fees** not confirmed.
**Facilities** ♀ ⚑ 🏌 ☂ 🍴 Philip Cheyney.
**Leisure** caddy cars for hire.
**Location** 1.5m E of town centre off A719
**Hotel** ★★ 65% Carlton Toby Hotel, 187 Ayr Rd, PRESTWICK
☎ 01292 476811 39 ➡ 🐾

---

## BALLOCH                                    Map 10 NS38

*Cameron House Hotel & Country Estate* Loch Lomond
G83 8QZ ☎ 01389 757211
Only available for residents of the hotel or a party booked in advance. A challenging 9-hole course with water hazards.
*The Wee Demon Course: 9 holes, 2266yds, Par 32.*
*Club membership 200.*
**Visitors** must be residents or party booked in advance.
**Societies** apply in writing.
**Green Fees** not confirmed.
**Facilities** ♀ ⚑ 🏌 🍴
**Leisure** hard tennis courts, heated indoor swimming pool, squash, fishing, sauna, solarium, gymnasium, practice nets, trolley hire.
**Hotel** ★★★★ 75% Cameron House Hotel and Country Estate, BALLOCH
☎ 01389 755565 68 ➡ 🐾

---

## BALMORE                                    Map 11 NS57

**Balmore** Golf Course Rd G64 4AW ☎ 01360 620240
Parkland course with fine views.
*18 holes, 5530yds, Par 66, SSS 67, Course record 63.*
*Club membership 700.*
**Visitors** must contact in advance and be accompanied by member.
**Societies** apply in writing.
**Green Fees** not confirmed.
**Facilities** ⊗ 🍴 🏌 ☂ ⚑ ⛳
**Leisure** putting green, practice area.
**Location** N off A807
**Hotel** ★★★ 65% Black Bull Thistle, Main St, MILNGAVIE ☎ 0141 956 2291 27 ➡ 🐾

---

## BARASSIE                                    Map 10 NS33

**Kilmarnock (Barassie)** 29 Hillhouse Rd KA10 6SY
☎ 01292 313920
A magnificent seaside course, relatively flat with much heather. The turf and greens are quite unequalled. The 15th is a testing par 3 at 220 yards.
*18 holes, 6473yds, Par 71, SSS 72, Course record 63.*
*Club membership 600.*
**Visitors** with member only Wed & weekends. May not play Fri am. Contact secretary in advance.
**Societies** must telephone in advance and confirm in writing.
**Green Fees** £40 per day; £30 per round (£28.50/£21.50 winter).
**Facilities** ⊗ 🍴 🏌 ☂ ♀ ⛳ 🍴 🏌 ☂ W R Lockie.
**Leisure** trolley for hire, putting green, practice area.
**Location** E side of village on B746
**Hotel** ★★★★ 65% Marine Highland Hotel, TROON ☎ 01292 314444 72 ➡ 🐾

---

## BARRHEAD                                    Map 11 NS45

*Fereneze* Fereneze Av G78 1HJ
☎ 0141 881 1519
Hilly moorland course, with a good view at the end of a hard climb to the 3rd, then levels out.
*18 holes, 5821yds, Par 70, SSS 68.*
*Club membership 700.*
**Visitors** must contact in advance but may not play at weekends.
**Societies** apply in writing.
**Green Fees** not confirmed.
**Facilities** ♀ ⚑ 🏌 ☂ 🍴 Darren Robinson.
**Leisure** putting green, practice area, pool table.
**Location** NW side of town off B774
**Hotel** ★★★ 60% Dalmeny Park Country House, Lochlibo Rd, BARRHEAD
☎ 0141 881 9211 19 ➡ 🐾

---

## BEARSDEN                                    Map 11 NS57

**Bearsden** Thorn Rd G61 4BP ☎ 0141 942 2381
Parkland course, with 16 greens and 11 teeing grounds. Easy walking and views over city.
*9 holes, 6014yds, Par 68, SSS 69, Course record 67.*
*Club membership 450.*

▶

**Visitors** must be accompanied by and play with member.
**Societies** apply by writing.
**Green Fees** no fees given as must be with member.
**Facilities** ⊗ 〒 🏌 ☂ ♀ ⚲
**Leisure** putting green, practice area.
**Location** 1m W off A809
**Hotel** ★★★ 65% Black Bull Thistle, Main St, MILNGAVIE ☎ 0141 956 2291 27 ⇌ ⋔

---

*Douglas Park* Hillfoot G61 2TJ ☎ 0141 942 2220
Parkland course with wide variety of holes.
*18 holes, 5957yds, Par 69, SSS 69.*
*Club membership 900.*
**Visitors** Must be accompanied by member and must contact in advance.
**Societies** Wed & Thu. Must telephone in advance.
**Green Fees** not confirmed.
**Facilities** ♀ ⚲ 🏠 ⋔ David Scott.
**Leisure** caddy cars.
**Location** E side of town on A81
**Hotel** ★★★ 65% Black Bull Thistle, Main St, MILNGAVIE ☎ 0141 956 2291 27 ⇌ ⋔

---

*Glasgow* Killermont G61 2TW ☎ 0141 942 2011
One of the finest parkland courses in Scotland.
*18 holes, 5968yds, Par 70, SSS 69.*
*Club membership 800.*
**Visitors** must contact in advance & have handicap certificate.
**Green Fees** not confirmed.
**Facilities** ♀ (members guest only) ⚲ 🏠 ⋔ ⋔ J Steven.
**Location** SE side off A81
**Hotel** ★★★ 65% Black Bull Thistle, Main St, MILNGAVIE ☎ 0141 956 2291 27 ⇌ ⋔

---

**Windyhill** Baljaffray Rd G61 4QQ
☎ 0141 942 2349 & 0141 942 7157 pro
Hard walking parkland/moorland course; testing 12th hole.
*18 holes, 6254yds, Par 71, SSS 70, Course record 64.*
*Club membership 520.*
**Visitors** may not play at weekends. Must contact professional in advance.
**Societies** must apply in writing.
**Green Fees** £20 per day.
**Facilities** ⊗ 〒 🏌 ☂ ♀ ⚲ 🏠 ⋔ ⋔ G Collinson.
**Leisure** trolley for hire, putting green, practice area.
**Location** 2m NW off B8050
**Hotel** ★★★ 65% Black Bull Thistle, Main St, MILNGAVIE ☎ 0141 956 2291 27 ⇌ ⋔

---

## BEITH
Map 10 NS35

**Beith** Threepwood Rd KA15 2JR ☎ 01505 503166
Hilly course, with panoramic views over 7 counties.
*18 holes, 5616yds, Par 68, SSS 68.*
*Club membership 420.*
**Visitors** contact for details.
**Societies** apply in writing to secretary at least 1 month in advance.
**Green Fees** contact for details.
**Facilities** 🏌 ☂ ♀ ⚲
**Location** 1.5m NE off A737
**Hotel** ★★★ 65% Bowfield Hotel & Country Club, HOWWOOD ☎ 01505 705225 12 ⇌ ⋔

---

## BELLSHILL
Map 11 NS76

**Bellshill** Community Rd, Orbiston ML4 2RZ
☎ 01698 745124
Parkland course.
*18 holes, 5900yds, Par 69, SSS 69.*
*Club membership 500.*
**Visitors** apply in writing in advance, may not play on competition Sat & Sun.
**Societies** apply in writing in advance.
**Green Fees** £18 per day (£25 weekends).
**Facilities** ⊗ 〒 🏌 ☂ ♀ ⚲
**Leisure** putting green, practice area.
**Location** 1m SE off A721
**Hotel** ★★ 62% Silvertrees Hotel, Silverwells Crescent, BOTHWELL ☎ 01698 852311 7 ⇌ ⋔Annexe19 ⇌ ⋔

---

## BIGGAR
Map 11 NT03

**Biggar** The Park, Broughton Rd ML12 6AH
☎ 01899 220319
Flat parkland course, easy walking and fine views.
*18 holes, 5600yds, Par 67, SSS 66, Course record 61.*
*Club membership 340.*
**Visitors** Must contact in advance. Smart casual wear required.
**Societies** must book in advance, observe dress code.
**Green Fees** £9 per day (£14 weekends & bank holidays).
**Facilities** ⊗ 〒 🏌 ☂ ♀ ⚲ 🏠
**Leisure** hard tennis courts, motorised carts for hire, buggies for hire, trolley for hire, putting green, practice area.
**Location** S side of town
**Hotel** ★★★🏌 70% Shieldhill Hotel, Quothquan, BIGGAR ☎ 01899 220035 11 ⇌ ⋔

---

## BISHOPBRIGGS
Map 11 NS67

*Bishopbriggs* Brackenbrae Rd G64 2DX
☎ 0141 772 1810
Parkland course with views to Campsie Hills.
*18 holes, 6041yds, Par 69, SSS 69, Course record 63.*
*Club membership 600.*
**Visitors** must be accompanied by member, contact in advance and have an introduction from own club.
**Societies** apply in writing to the Committee one month in advance.
**Green Fees** not confirmed.
**Facilities** ♀ ⚲ 🏠
**Location** 0.5m NW off A803
**Hotel** ★★★ 65% Black Bull Thistle, Main St, MILNGAVIE ☎ 0141 956 2291 27 ⇌ ⋔

---

*Cawder* Cadder Rd G64 3QD
☎ 0141 772 5167
Two parkland courses; Cawder Course is hilly, with 5th, 9th, 10th, 11th-testing holes. Keir Course is flat.
*Cawder Course: 18 holes, 6295yds, Par 70, SSS 71.*
*Keir Course: 18 holes, 5877yds, Par 68, SSS 68.*
*Club membership 1150.*
**Visitors** must contact in advance & may play on weekdays only.

**Societies** must contact in writing.
**Green Fees** not confirmed.
**Facilities** ♀ ⅄ 🏠 ⚑ ℓ
**Location** 1m NE off A803
**Hotel** ★★★ 65% Black Bull Thistle, Main St,
MILNGAVIE ☎ 0141 956 2291 27 ⇄ ↾

## BISHOPTON
Map 10 NS47

*Erskine* PA7 5PH ☎ 01505 862302
Parkland course.
*18 holes, 6287yds, Par 71, SSS 70.*
*Club membership 700.*
**Visitors** must be accompanied by member and must have
a handicap certificate.
**Societies** apply in writing.
**Green Fees** not confirmed.
**Facilities** ♀ ⅄ 🏠 ℓ Peter Thomson.
**Location** 0.75 NE off B815
**Hotel** B Forte Posthouse Glasgow Erskine, North Barr,
ERSKINE ☎ 0141 812 0123 166 ⇄ ↾

## BONHILL
Map 10 NS37

*Vale of Leven* North Field Rd G83 9ET
☎ 01389 52351
Hilly moorland course, tricky with many natural hazards -
gorse, burns, trees. Overlooks Loch Lomond.
*18 holes, 5162yds, Par 67, SSS 66, Course record 61.*
*Club membership 640.*
**Visitors** may not play Sat Apr-Sep.
**Societies** apply to the secretary.
**Green Fees** not confirmed.
**Facilities** ♀ ⅄ 🏠 ⚑
**Location** E side of town off A813
**Hotel** ★★ 61% Dumbuck Hotel, Glasgow Rd,
DUMBARTON ☎ 01389 734336 22 ⇄ ↾

## BOTHWELL
Map 11 NS75

**Bothwell Castle** Blantyre Rd G71 8PJ ☎ 01698 853177
Flat parkland course in residential area.
*18 holes, 6200yds, Par 71, SSS 70, Course record 63.*
*Club membership 1000.*
**Visitors** may only play Mon-Fri 9.30-10.30am & 2-3pm.
**Green Fees** £28 per day; £20 per round.
**Facilities** ⊗ ⅢⅢ ⅃ 📖 ♥ ♀ ⅄ 🏠 ⚑ ℓ Gordon Niven.
**Leisure** trolley for hire, putting green, practice area.
**Location** NW of village off B7071
**Hotel** ★★ 62% Silvertrees Hotel, Silverwells
Crescent, BOTHWELL
☎ 01698 852311 7 ⇄ ↾Annexe19 ⇄ ↾

## BRIDGE OF WEIR
Map 10 NS36

**Ranfurly Castle** The Clubhouse, Golf Rd PA11 3HN
☎ 01505 612609
A highly challenging, 240 acre, picturesque moorland course.
*18 holes, 6284yds, Par 70, SSS 71, Course record 65.*
*Club membership 825.*
**Visitors** contact in advance.
**Societies** apply in writing.
**Green Fees** £35 per day; £25 per round.
**Facilities** ⅢⅢ ⅃ 📖 ♥ ♀ ⅄ 🏠 ⚑ ℓ Tom Eckford.

**Leisure** buggies for hire, trolley for hire, putting green,
practice area.
**Location** 5m NW of Johnstone
**Hotel** ★★★ 65% Bowfield Hotel & Country Club,
HOWWOOD ☎ 01505 705225 12 ⇄ ↾

## BURNSIDE
Map 11 NS66

**Blairbeth** Fernbrae Av, Fernhill G73 4SF
☎ 0141 634 3355
Parkland course.
*18 holes, 5518yds, Par 70, SSS 68, Course record 64.*
*Club membership 600.*
**Visitors** must contact in advance & may not play
weekends.
**Societies** apply in advance.
**Green Fees** £16 per day Mon-Fri.
**Facilities** ⊗ ⅢⅢ ⅃ 📖 ♥ ♀ ⅄
**Leisure** putting green.
**Location** S off A749
**Hotel** ★★★ 64% Macdonald Thistle, Eastwood Toll,
GIFFNOCK ☎ 0141 638 2225 56 ⇄ ↾

*Cathkin Braes* Cathkin Rd G73 4SE
☎ 0141 634 6605
Moorland course, prevailing westerly wind, small loch hazard
at 5th hole.
*18 holes, 6208yds, Par 69, SSS 69.*
*Club membership 890.*
**Visitors** must contact in advance & have handicap
certificate but may not play at weekends.
**Societies** apply in writing.
**Green Fees** not confirmed.
**Facilities** ♀ ⅄ 🏠 ℓ Stephen Bree.
**Leisure** putting green, practice area, trolley hire.
**Location** 1m S on B759
**Hotel** ★★★ 64% Macdonald Thistle, Eastwood Toll,
GIFFNOCK ☎ 0141 638 2225 56 ⇄ ↾

## CARLUKE
Map 11 NS85

**Carluke** Mauldslie Rd, Hallcraig ML8 5HG
☎ 01555 771070
Parkland course with views over the Clyde Valley. Testing
11th hole, par 3.
*18 holes, 5853yds, Par 70, SSS 68, Course record 63.*
*Club membership 750.*
**Visitors** must contact in advance & may not play
weekends.
**Societies** prior arrangement required.
**Green Fees** £25 per day; £18 per round.
**Facilities** ⊗ ⅢⅢ ⅃ 📖 ♥ ♀ ⅄ 🏠 ℓ Richard Forrest.
**Leisure** putting green.
**Location** 1m W off A73
**Hotel** ★★★ 66% Popinjay Hotel, Lanark Rd,
ROSEBANK
☎ 01555 860441 36 ⇄ ↾Annexe5 ⇄ ↾

## CARNWATH
Map 11 NS94

*Carnwath* 1 Main St ML11 8JX ☎ 01555 840251
Picturesque parkland course slightly hilly, with small greens
calling for accuracy. Panoramic views.
*18 holes, 5953yds, Par 70, SSS 69.*
*Club membership 470.* ▶

| | |
|---|---|
| **Visitors** | restricted after 5pm, no visitors Sat. |
| **Societies** | apply in writing or telephone. |
| **Green Fees** | not confirmed. |
| **Facilities** | ♀ ♣ 🏠 |
| **Location** | W side of village on A70 |
| **Hotel** | ★★★ 67% Cartland Bridge Hotel, Glasgow Rd, LANARK ☎ 01555 664426 18 ⇄ ℝ |

## CASTLE DOUGLAS                 Map 11 NX76

**Castle Douglas** Abercromby Rd DG7 1BB
☎ 01556 502180 or 502099
Parkland course, one severe hill.
*9 holes, 2704yds, Par 68, SSS 66.*
*Club membership 500.*

| | |
|---|---|
| **Visitors** | welcome except Tue & Thu after 4pm & during competitions. Must contact secretary in advance. |
| **Societies** | apply by writing to secretary. |
| **Green Fees** | £12 per day/round. |
| **Facilities** | ⊗ ⓑ ■ ♀ ♣ ✠ |
| **Leisure** | trolley for hire, putting green, practice area. |
| **Location** | W side of town |
| **Hotel** | ★★ 66% Douglas Arms, King St, CASTLE DOUGLAS ☎ 01556 502231 20rm(15 ⇄ ℝ) |

## CLARKSTON                 Map 11 NS55

***Cathcart Castle*** Mearns Rd G76 7YL
☎ 0141 638 0082
Tree-lined parkland course, with undulating terrain.
*18 holes, 5832yds, Par 68, SSS 68.*
*Club membership 990.*

| | |
|---|---|
| **Visitors** | must have a letter of introduction from own club. |
| **Societies** | Tue & Thu only; must apply in writing. |
| **Green Fees** | not confirmed. |
| **Facilities** | ♀ ♣ 🏠 ℂ David Naylor. |
| **Location** | 0.75m SW off A726 |
| **Hotel** | ★★★ 64% Macdonald Thistle, Eastwood Toll, GIFFNOCK ☎ 0141 638 2225 56 ⇄ ℝ |

## CLYDEBANK                 Map 11 NS56

**Clydebank & District** Glasgow Rd, Hardgate G81 5QY
☎ 01389 873289
An undulating parkland course established in 1905 overlooking Clydebank.
*18 holes, 5823yds, Par 68, SSS 68, Course record 64.*
*Club membership 889.*

| | |
|---|---|
| **Visitors** | Round only, weekdays only. Must tee off before 4pm. Apply to professional 01389 878686. |
| **Societies** | must apply in writing. |
| **Green Fees** | £13 per round. |
| **Facilities** | ⊗ ⅷ ⓑ ■ ♀ ♣ 🏠 ℂ David Pirie. |
| **Leisure** | putting green, practice area. |
| **Location** | 2m E of Erskine Bridge |
| **Hotel** | ★★★ 65% Patio Hotel, 1 South Av, Clydebank Business Park, CLYDEBANK ☎ 0141 951 1133 80 ⇄ ℝ |

***Clydebank Municipal*** Overtoun Rd, Dalmuir G81 3RE
☎ 0141 941 1331
Hilly, compact parkland course with tough finishing holes.
*18 holes, 5349yds, Par 67, SSS 67.*

| | |
|---|---|
| **Visitors** | no restrictions. |

---

| | |
|---|---|
| **Societies** | contact in advance. |
| **Green Fees** | not confirmed. |
| **Facilities** | ♣ 🏠 ✠ ℂ Stewart Savage. |
| **Leisure** | trolley hire. |
| **Location** | 2m NW of town centre |
| **Hotel** | ★★★ 65% Patio Hotel, 1 South Av, Clydebank Business Park, CLYDEBANK ☎ 0141 951 1133 80 ⇄ ℝ |

## COATBRIDGE                 Map 11 NS76

**Drumpellier** Drumpellier Av ML5 1RX
☎ 01236 424139 & 428723
Parkland course.
*18 holes, 6227yds, Par 71, SSS 70, Course record 60.*
*Club membership 827.*

| | |
|---|---|
| **Visitors** | must contact in advance. |
| **Societies** | apply in advance. |
| **Green Fees** | not confirmed. |
| **Facilities** | ⊗ ⅷ ⓑ ■ ♀ ♣ 🏠 ✠ ℂ David Ross. |
| **Leisure** | trolley for hire, putting green, practice area. |
| **Location** | 0.75m W off A89 |
| **Hotel** | ★★★ 63% Bothwell Bridge Hotel, 89 Main St, BOTHWELL ☎ 01698 852246 74 ⇄ ℝ |

## COLDSTREAM                 Map 12 NT83

**Hirsel** Kelso Rd TD12 4NJ
☎ 01890 882678 & 883052
Parkland course, with hard walking and sheltered trees.
Testing 3rd and 6th holes. A further 9 holes have been developed.
*18 holes, 6092yds, Par 70, SSS 69.*
*Club membership 680.*

| | |
|---|---|
| **Visitors** | contact for details. |
| **Societies** | write or telephone the secretary in advance. |
| **Green Fees** | £15 per day (£20 weekends & bank holidays). |
| **Facilities** | ⊗ ⅷ ⓑ ■ ♀ ♣ 🏠 ✠ |
| **Leisure** | motorised carts for hire, trolley for hire, putting green, practice area. |
| **Location** | At W end of Coldstream on A697 |
| **Hotel** | ★★★⚜ 69% Tillmouth Park Hotel, CORNHILL-ON-TWEED ☎ 01890 882255 12 ⇄ ℝ Annexe2 ⇄ ℝ |

## COLVEND                 Map 11 NX85

**Colvend** Sandyhills DG5 4PY
☎ 01556 630398
Picturesque and challenging course on Solway coast. Superb views.
*9 holes, 4480yds, Par 66, SSS 62, Course record 63.*
*Club membership 490.*

| | |
|---|---|
| **Visitors** | restricted Apr-Sep on Tue at 2pm, Thu at 5.30pm and some weekends for members competitions. |
| **Societies** | must telephone in advance. |
| **Green Fees** | £12 per day. |
| **Facilities** | ⊗ ⅷ ⓑ ■ ♀ ♣ ✠ |
| **Leisure** | trolley for hire, putting green, practice area. |
| **Location** | 6m from Dalbeattie on A710 Solway Coast Rd |
| **Hotel** | ★★ 65% Clonyard House Hotel, COLVEND ☎ 01556 630372 15 ⇄ ℝ |

## CUMBERNAULD   Map 11 NS77

**Dullatur** 1A Glen Douglas Dr G68 0DW ☎ 01236 723230
Parkland course, with natural hazards and wind. Testing 17th
hole, par 5.
*18 holes, 6219yds, Par 70, SSS 70, Course record 65.*
*Club membership 700.*
**Visitors**  telephone for availability. May not play weekends.
**Societies** must apply in writing to secretary.
**Green Fees** £25 per day; £15 per round.
**Facilities** ⊗ ⅲ ⓑ ♨ ♀ ⚘ 🛢 🏌 ℓ Duncan Sinclair.
**Leisure**  tennis courts, sauna, solarium, gymnasium,
     motorised carts for hire, buggies for hire, trolley
     for hire, putting green, practice area.
**Location**  1.5m N
**Hotel**   ★★★★ 64% Westerwood Hotel Golf &
     Country Club, 1 St Andrews Dr, Westerwood,
     CUMBERNAULD ☎ 01236 457171 47 ⇌ ℝ

**Palacerigg** Palacerigg Country Park G67 3HU
☎ 01236 734969
Parkland course.
*18 holes, 6444yds, Par 72, SSS 71, Course record 66.*
*Club membership 400.*
**Visitors**  anytime except club competitions, advance
     booking advisable.
**Societies** apply in writing to the Secretary.
**Green Fees** £8 per round.
**Facilities** ⊗ ⅲ ⓑ ♨ ♀ ⚘ 🛢
**Leisure**  driving range, putting green, practice area.
**Location**  2m S
**Hotel**   ★★★★ 64% Westerwood Hotel Golf &
     Country Club, 1 St Andrews Dr, Westerwood,
     CUMBERNAULD ☎ 01236 457171 47 ⇌ ℝ

**Westerwood Hotel Golf & Country Club** 1 St Andrews Dr,
Westerwood G68 0EW ☎ 01236 457171
Undulating parkland/woodland course designed by Dave
Thomas and Seve Ballesteros. Holes meander through silver
birch, firs, heaths and heathers, and the spectacular 15th, 'The
Waterfall', has its green set against a 40ft rockface. Buggie
track. Hotel facilities.
*18 holes, 6721yds, Par 73, SSS 73, Course record 65.*
*Club membership 1500.*
**Visitors**  advised to book in advance.
**Societies** all bookings through golf coordinator on 01256
     457171 ext 215.
**Green Fees** £22.50 (£27.50 weekends).
**Facilities** ⊗ ⅲ ⓑ ♨ ♀ ⚘ 🛢 🏌 ℓ Steven Killen.
**Leisure**  hard tennis courts, heated indoor swimming
     pool, sauna, solarium, gymnasium, motorised
     carts for hire, buggies for hire, trolley for hire,
     driving range, putting green, practice area, golf
     school.
**Location**  Adjacent to A80
**Hotel**   ★★★★ 64% Westerwood Hotel Golf &
     Country Club, 1 St Andrews Dr, Westerwood,
     CUMBERNAULD
     ☎ 01236 457171 47 ⇌ ℝ

## CUMMERTREES   Map 11 NY16

**Powfoot** DG12 5QE ☎ 01461 700276
The hills of Cumbria, away beyond the Solway Firth, and
from time to time a sight of the Isle of Man, make

playing at this delightfully compact semi-links seaside
course a scenic treat. Lovely holes include the 2nd, the
8th and the 11th.
*18 holes, 6283yds, Par 71, SSS 70.*
*Club membership 820.*
**Visitors**  contact in advance. May not play 8.45-10 &
     noon-1.30 weekdays and until after 2pm
     weekends.
**Societies** must book in advance.
**Green Fees** £27 per day; £20 per round (£20 Sun after
     2pm).
**Facilities** ⊗ ⅲ ⓑ ♨ ♀ ⚘ 🛢 ℓ Gareth Dick.
**Leisure**  trolley for hire, putting green, practice area.
**Location**  0.5m off B724
**Hotel**   ★★ 64% Golf Hotel, Links Av,
     POWFOOT
     ☎ 01461 700254 19rm(14 ⇌ ℝ)

## DUMBARTON   Map 10 NS37

**Dumbarton** Broadmeadow G82 2BQ ☎ 01389 732830
Flat parkland course.
*18 holes, 5992yds, Par 71, SSS 69, Course record 64.*
*Club membership 700.*
**Visitors**  may not play weekends & public holidays.
**Societies** advance booking with secretary.
**Green Fees** not confirmed.
**Facilities** ♀ ⚘
**Leisure**  putting green,practice area.
**Location**  0.25m N off A814
**Hotel**   ★★ 61% Dumbuck Hotel, Glasgow Rd,
     DUMBARTON ☎ 01389 734336 22 ⇌ ℝ

AA ★★★
Let the tranquillity and splendour of the
region entice you to spend a few days at
**HETLAND HALL.**
Explore the Solway Coast, the Galloway
Forest and the Borders. Hetland Hall is
situated by the main A75 Euro route,
8 miles from Dumfries and 22 miles
from Carlisle.
Besides the many fitness facilities offered
within the hotel and its extensive grounds,
Dumfries & Galloway offers 24 Golf courses
all in different glorious scenery.

# Hetland Hall Hotel
**CARRUTHERSTOWN,**
**DUMFRIES DG1 4JX**
**TEL: 01387 840201  FAX: 01387 8402**

Best
Western

## DUMFRIES                                         Map 11 NX97

**Dumfries & County** Nunfield, Edinburgh Rd DG1 1JX
☎ 01387 253585
Parkland course alongside River Nith, with views over the
Queensberry Hills.
*18 holes, 5928yds, Par 69, SSS 68.*
*Club membership 800.*
**Visitors**  must contact in advance but may not play most
              weekends between 9.30-11 & 2-3.30.
**Societies** apply in writing.
**Green Fees** £22 per day/round (£25 weekends).
**Facilities** ⊗ ⅷ ⓛ ♟ ♀ ⚑ 👜 ⚐ ℓ Gordon Gray.
**Leisure**   trolley for hire, putting green, practice area.
**Location**  1m NE off A701
**Hotel**     ★★★ 63% Station Hotel, 49 Lovers Walk,
              DUMFRIES ☎ 01387 254316 32 ⇋ ℝ
**Additional** ★★★ 69% Hetland Hall Hotel,
**hotel**      CARRUTHERSTOWN
              ☎ 01387 840201 27 ⇋ ℝ
              *See advert on page 311*

**Dumfries & Galloway** 2 Laurieston Av DG2 7NY
☎ 01387 263848
Parkland course.
*18 holes, 5803yds, Par 68, SSS 68.*
*Club membership 800.*
**Visitors**  may not play on competition days.
**Societies** apply in writing.
**Green Fees** not confirmed.
**Facilities** ♀ ⚑ 👜 ⚐ ℓ Joe Fergusson.
**Leisure**   putting green,practice area,trolley hire.
**Location**  W side of town centre on A75
**Hotel**     ★★★ 63% Station Hotel, 49 Lovers Walk,
              DUMFRIES
              ☎ 01387 254316 32 ⇋ ℝ

## DUNS                                            Map 12 NT75

**Duns** Longformacus Rd TD11 3NR
☎ 01361 882717 & 882194
Interesting upland course, with natural hazards of water and
hilly slopes. Views south to the Cheviot Hills.
*9 holes, 5864yds, Par 68, SSS 68, Course record 65.*
*Club membership 340.*
**Visitors**  welcome except competition days and Mon, Tue
              and Wed after 3pm.
**Societies** write or telephone the secretary in advance for
              booking details.
**Green Fees** £10 per day/round ( 50% reduction Nov-15
              Mar).
**Facilities** ⓛ ♟ ♀ (evenings) ⚑
**Leisure**   trolley for hire, putting green, practice area.
**Location**  1m W off A6105
**Hotel**     ★★★ 69% Marshall Meadows Country House
              Hotel,  BERWICK-UPON-TWEED
              ☎ 01289 331133 18 ⇋ ℝ

## EAGLESHAM                                       Map 11 NS55

**Bonnyton** Kirktonmoor Rd G76 0QA ☎ 01355 302781
Windy, moorland course.
*18 holes, 6255yds, Par 72, SSS 71.*
*Club membership 960.*

**Visitors**  welcome weekdays only (ex Tue), must contact
              in advance.
**Societies** must telephone in advance.
**Green Fees** £30 per 2 rounds; £20 per round.
**Facilities** ⊗ ⅷ ⓛ ♟ ♀ ⚑ 👜 ⚐ ℓ Kendal McWade.
**Leisure**   buggies for hire, trolley for hire, putting green,
              practice area.
**Location**  0.25m SW off B764
**Hotel**     ★★★ 63% Bruce Swallow Hotel, Cornwall St,
              EAST KILBRIDE ☎ 013552 29771 78 ⇋ ℝ

## EAST KILBRIDE                                   Map 11 NS65

**East Kilbride** Chapelside Rd, Nerston G74 4PF
☎ 013552 20913
Parkland and hill course. Very windy. Testing 7th, 9th and
14th holes.
*18 holes, 6419yds, Par 71, SSS 71.*
*Club membership 800.*
**Visitors**  by appointment. Must be a member of
              recognised golfing society.
**Societies** must telephone in advance & submit formal
              application.
**Green Fees** not confirmed.
**Facilities** ♀ ⚑ 👜 ⚐ ℓ A Taylor.
**Location**  0.5m N off A749
**Hotel**     ★★★ 63% Bruce Swallow Hotel, Cornwall St,
              EAST KILBRIDE
              ☎ 013552 29771 78 ⇋ ℝ

**Torrance House** Calderglen Country Park, Strathaven Rd
G75 0QZ ☎ 013552 48638
A parkland course.
*18 holes, 6415yds, Par 72, SSS 69, Course record 71.*
*Club membership 1000.*
**Visitors**  welcome, may book up to six days in advance.
**Societies** Mon-Fri. Apply in writing to John Dunlop, East
              Kilbride District Council, Civic Centre, East
              Kilbride.
**Green Fees** not confirmed.
**Facilities** ♀ ⚑ ⚐ ℓ John Dunlop.
**Leisure**   practice area, caddy cars.
**Location**  1.5m SE of Kilbride on A726
**Hotel**     ★★★ 63% Bruce Swallow Hotel, Cornwall St,
              EAST KILBRIDE
              ☎ 013552 29771 78 ⇋ ℝ

## EYEMOUTH                                        Map 12 NT96

**Eyemouth** Gunsgreen House TD14 5SF
☎ 01890 750551
With the exception of a steep climb to the 1st tee, this is a
compact, flat and popular seaside course. Fast smooth greens
and fine views are typified by the 15th, played from an
elevated tee to a green on a peninsula over a North Sea inlet.
*9 holes, 4608mtrs, Par 66, SSS 65, Course record 60.*
*Club membership 250.*
**Visitors**  may not play before 10.30am Sat or noon Sun.
**Societies** apply in writing.
**Green Fees** not confirmed.
**Facilities** ♀ (evenings) ⚑ 👜 ℓ Craig Maltman.
**Location**  E side of town
**Hotel**     ★★★ 69% Marshall Meadows Country House
              Hotel,  BERWICK-UPON-TWEED
              ☎ 01289 331133 18 ⇋ ℝ

## GALASHIELS
Map 12 NT43

**Galashiels** Ladhope Recreation Ground TD1 2NJ
☎ 01896 753724
Hillside course, superb views from the top; 10th hole very steep.
*18 holes, 5185yds, Par 67, SSS 66, Course record 61.*
*Club membership 343.*
**Visitors** must contact the secretary in advance especially for weekends.
**Societies** arrangements with secretary especially for weekends.
**Green Fees** £16 per day; £12 per round (£20/£14 weekends).
**Facilities** ⊗ ⅷ ⅙ Ⅼ ♎ ♀
**Leisure** trolley for hire, changing room being built, clubhouse.
**Location** N side of town centre off A7
**Hotel** ★★★ 64% Kingsknowes Hotel, Selkirk Rd, GALASHIELS
☎ 01896 758375 11rm(10 ⇄ ▮)

---

**Torwoodlee** TD1 2NE ☎ 01896 752260
Parkland course with natural hazards designed by James Braid. Testing 3rd hole (par 3).
*18 holes, 6200yds, Par 70, SSS 69, Course record 65.*
*Club membership 550.*
**Visitors** restricted Thu - ladies day and Sat - mens competitions.
**Societies** letter to secretary.
**Green Fees** £20 per day; £12 5er round (£25/£20 weekends).
**Facilities** ⊗ ⅷ ⅙ Ⅼ ♀ ♎ 🖻
**Leisure** trolley for hire, putting green, practice area.
**Location** 1.75m NW off A7
**Hotel** ★★★ 65% Woodlands House Hotel & Restaurants, Windyknowe Rd, GALASHIELS
☎ 01896 754722 9 ⇄ ▮

## GALSTON
Map 11 NS53

**Loudoun** Edinburgh Rd KA4 8PA ☎ 01563 821993
Pleasant, testing parkland course.
*18 holes, 5844yds, Par 67, SSS 68, Course record 61.*
*Club membership 750.*
**Visitors** must contact in advance. No play at weekends.
**Societies** telephone in advance.
**Green Fees** £29 per day; £17 per round.
**Facilities** ⊗ ⅷ ⅙ Ⅼ ♀ ♎ 🖻
**Leisure** trolley for hire, putting green, practice area.
**Location** NE side of town on A71
**Hotel** ★★★ 66% Strathaven Hotel, Hamilton Rd, STRATHAVEN ☎ 01357 521778 10 ⇄ ▮

## GARTCOSH
Map 11 NS66

**Mount Ellen** G69 8EY ☎ 01236 872277 & 872421
Downland course with 73 bunkers. Testing hole: 10th ('Bedlay'), 156 yds, par 3.
*18 holes, 5525yds, Par 68, SSS 68.*
*Club membership 500.*
**Visitors** may play Mon-Fri 9am-4pm. Must contact in advance.
**Societies** must contact in advance.
**Green Fees** not confirmed.
**Facilities** ♀ ♎ 🖻 ▮ Gerry Rielly.

**Leisure** putting green, cart/buggy/trolley hire.
**Location** 0.75m N off A752
**Hotel** ★★★★ 60% The Copthorne, George Square, GLASGOW ☎ 0141 332 6711 141 ⇄ ▮

## GATEHOUSE-OF-FLEET
Map 11 NX55

**Gatehouse** Laurieston Rd DG7 2PW ☎ 01644 450263
Set against a background of rolling hills with scenic views of Fleet Bay and the Solway Firth.
*9 holes, 2398yds, Par 66, SSS 64, Course record 60.*
*Club membership 315.*
**Visitors** restricted Sun before 11.30am.
**Societies** telephone in advance.
**Green Fees** £10 per day/round.
**Facilities** ♎
**Leisure** putting green.
**Location** 0.25m N of town
**Hotel** ★★★★♨ 67% Cally Palace Hotel, GATEHOUSE OF FLEET
☎ 01557 814341 56 ⇄

## GIRVAN
Map 10 NX19

**Brunston Castle** Bargany, Dailly KA26 9RH
☎ 01465 811471
Sheltered inland parkland course. A championship design by Donald Steel, the course is bisected by the River Girvan and shaped to incorporate all the natural surroundings. It finishes with the 17th 185 yards over a man made lake. Driving range.
*Burns: 18 holes, 6858yds, Par 72, SSS 73, Course record 69.*
*Club membership 400.* ▶

# The Cally Palace Hotel & Golf Course

**Gatehouse of Fleet, Dumfries & Galloway DG7 2DL**

AA ★★★★

Set in its own grounds within 500 acres of Fleet Forest, The Cally Palace is one of the most beautiful locations in Scotland. 56 luxurious bedroom suites. Fine food and friendly, professional service. Within the grounds there is an 18 hole par 70 golf course much of it in mature wooded areas and around Cally Lake. As a private course it is for the exclusive use of the hotel residents. Also, there is an indoor leisure centre, outdoor tennis, putting, croquet and boating.

**– everything one could wish for –**

Discounts are offered for 'over 60's' and non golfers

**Telephone 01557 814341 for brochure**

**Visitors**    reserved for members at weekends 8-10 &
                12.30-1.30.
**Societies**   telephone to book.
**Green Fees**  £35 per day; £22.50 per round (£39/£27.50
                weekends).
**Facilities**  ⊗ ⅢⅬ ⚑ ♀ ⚖ 🏠 ⚑ 🏌 ⚑ Derek J McKenzie.
**Leisure**     motorised carts for hire, buggies for hire, trolley
                for hire, driving range, putting green, practice
                area.
**Location**    6m SE of Turnberry
**Hotel**       ★★★ 73% Malin Court, TURNBERRY
                ☎ 01655 331457 17 ⇌ ℞

*Girvan* Golf Course Rd KA26 9HW
☎ 01465 714272
Municipal seaside and parkland course. Testing 17th hole
(223-yds) uphill, par 3. Good views.
*18 holes, 5098yds, Par 64, SSS 65.*
*Club membership 175.*
**Visitors**    no restrictions.
**Societies**   may not play Jul & Aug.
**Green Fees**  not confirmed.
**Facilities**  ♀ ⚖
**Location**    N side of town off A77
**Hotel**       ★★★ 73% Malin Court, TURNBERRY
                ☎ 01655 331457 17 ⇌ ℞

## GLASGOW                                        Map 11 NS56

**Alexandra** Alexandra Park, Alexandra Pde G31 8SE
☎ 0141 552 1294
Parkland course, hilly with some woodland.
*9 holes, 2800yds, Par 31, Course record 25.*
*Club membership 85.*
**Visitors**    no restrictions.
**Societies**   telephone 24 hrs in advance or by writing one
                week in advance.
**Green Fees**  prices under review.
**Facilities**  ⚖
**Leisure**     practice area.
**Location**    2m E of city centre off M8/A8
**Hotel**       ★★★ 68% The Town House Hotel, 54 West
                George St, GLASGOW
                ☎ 0141 332 3320 34 ⇌ ℞

*Cowglen* Barrhead Rd G43 1AU
☎ 0141 632 0556
Parkland course with good views over Clyde valley to
Campsie Hills.
*18 holes, 5976yds, Par 69, SSS 69, Course record 63.*
*Club membership 775.*
**Visitors**    play on shorter course. Must contact in advance
                and have a handicap certificate. No visitors at
                weekends.
**Societies**   must telephone in advance.
**Green Fees**  not confirmed.
**Facilities**  ♀ ⚖ 🏠 ⚑ John McTear.
**Leisure**     putting,practice area,driving range.
**Location**    4.5m SW of city centre on B762
**Hotel**       ★★★ 64% Macdonald Thistle, Eastwood Toll,
                GIFFNOCK
                ☎ 0141 638 2225 56 ⇌ ℞

**Haggs Castle** 70 Dumbreck Rd, Dumbreck G41 4SN
☎ 0141 427 1157
Wooded, parkland course where Scottish National
Championships and the Glasgow and Scottish Open have
been held. Quite difficult.
*18 holes, 6464yds, Par 73, SSS 72.*
*Club membership 900.*
**Visitors**    may not play at weekends. Must contact in
                advance.
**Societies**   apply in writing.
**Green Fees**  £38 per day; £27 per round.
**Facilities**  ⊗ ⅢⅬ ⚑ ♀ ⚖ 🏠 ⚑ 🏌 ⚑ Jim McAlister.
**Leisure**     buggies for hire, trolley for hire, putting
                green, practice area.
**Location**    2.5m SW of city centre on B768
**Hotel**       ★★★ 59% Sherbrooke Castle Hotel, 11
                Sherbrooke Av. Pollokshields, GLASGOW
                ☎ 0141 427 4227 10 ⇌ ℞Annexe11 ⇌ ℞

*Kirkhill* Greenless Rd, Cambuslang G72 8YN
☎ 0141 641 8499
Meadowland course designed by James Braid.
*18 holes, 5889yds, Par 69, SSS 69, Course record 63.*
*Club membership 650.*
**Visitors**    must play with member at weekends. Must
                contact in advance.
**Societies**   must contact in advance.
**Green Fees**  not confirmed.
**Facilities**  ♀ ⚖
**Location**    5m SE of city centre off A749
**Hotel**       ★★★ 59% Stuart Hotel, 2 Cornwall Way,
                EAST KILBRIDE ☎ 013552 21161 39 ⇌ ℞

*Knightswood* Lincoln Av G71 5QZ
☎ 0141 959 2131
Parkland course within easy reach of city. Two dog-legs.
*9 holes, 2700yds, Par 33, SSS 33.*
*Club membership 60.*
**Visitors**    no restrictions.
**Societies**   welcome.
**Green Fees**  not confirmed.
**Location**    4m W of city centre off A82
**Hotel**       ★★★ 64% Jurys Glasgow Hotel, Great
                Western Rd, GLASGOW
                ☎ 0141 334 8161 133 ⇌ ℞

*Lethamhill* 1240 Cumbernauld Rd, Millerston G33 1AH
☎ 0141 770 6220
Municipal parkland course.
*18 holes, 5859yds, Par 70, SSS 68.*
**Visitors**    must have an introduction from own club.
**Societies**   must contact in advance.
**Facilities**  ⚖
**Location**    3m NE of city centre on A80
**Hotel**       ★★★★ 60% The Copthorne, George Square,
                GLASGOW ☎ 0141 332 6711 141 ⇌ ℞

*Linn Park* Simshill Rd G44 5EP ☎ 0141 637 5871
Municipal parkland course with six par 3's in outward half.
*18 holes, 4952yds, Par 65, SSS 65, Course record 61.*
*Club membership 80.*
**Visitors**    no restrictions.
**Green Fees**  not confirmed.
**Facilities**  ⚖
**Location**    4m S of city centre off B766

**Hotel**   ★★★ 63% Bruce Swallow Hotel, Cornwall St, EAST KILBRIDE ☎ 013552 29771 78 ⇥ ฿

**Pollok** 90 Barrhead Rd G43 1BG ☎ 0141 632 4351
Parkland course with woods and river.
*18 holes, 6254yds, Par 71, SSS 70, Course record 62.*
*Club membership 620.*
**Visitors**     no ladies. Must play with member at weekends. Must contact in advance.
**Societies**   must contact in writing.
**Green Fees** £33 per day; £26 per round.
**Facilities**   ⊗ 爪 ﾑ ■ ♀ 👐 🖻
**Leisure**    putting green, practice area.
**Location**   4m SW of city centre on A762
**Hotel**     ★★★ 63% Tinto Firs Thistle, 470 Kilmarnock Rd, GLASGOW ☎ 0141 637 2353 28 ⇥ ฿

**Williamwood** Clarkston Rd G44 3YR ☎ 0141 637 4311
Inland course, fairly hilly with wooded areas, a small lake and pond.
*18 holes, 5878yds, SSS 69, Course record 61.*
*Club membership 800.*
**Visitors**     apply in writing to secretary, no weekend play.
**Societies**   midweek bookings only, apply in writing to secretary.
**Green Fees** not confirmed.
**Facilities**   ⊗ 爪 ﾑ ■ ♀ 👐 🖻 ℓ Jack Gardner.
**Leisure**    trolley for hire, practice area.
**Location**   5m S of city centre on B767
**Hotel**     ★★★ 64% Macdonald Thistle, Eastwood Toll, GIFFNOCK ☎ 0141 638 2225 56 ⇥ ฿

## GLENLUCE                     Map 10 NX15

**Wigtownshire County** Mains of Park DG8 0NN
☎ 01581 300420
Seaside links course on the shores of Luce Bay, easy walking but affected by winds. The 12th hole, a dogleg with out of bounds to the right,is named after the course's designer, Gordon Cunnigham.
*18 holes, 5847yds, Par 70, SSS 68, Course record 67.*
*Club membership 450.*
**Visitors**     may play any day by prior arrangement ex competition days.
**Societies**   must contact in advance.
**Green Fees** £20 per day ; £16 per round (£22/£18 weekends).
**Facilities**   ⊗ 爪 ﾑ ■ ♀ 👐 🖻 ⌐
**Leisure**    trolley for hire, putting green, practice area.
**Location**   1.5m W off A75
**Hotel**     ★★★★ 68% North West Castle Hotel, STRANRAER ☎ 01776 704413 71 ⇥ ฿

## GREAT CUMBRAE ISLAND
## (MILLPORT)                 Map 10 NS15

**Millport** Golf Rd KA28 0HB ☎ 01475 530305 & 530311
Pleasantly situated on the west side of Cumbrae looking over Bute to Arran and the Mull of Kintyre. Exposure means conditions may vary according to wind strength and direction. A typical seaside resort course welcoming visitors.
*18 holes, 5828yds, Par 68, SSS 69, Course record 64.*
*Club membership 470.*
**Visitors**     advisable to phone and book tee times especially in summer months.
**Societies**   telephone or write in advance.

**Green Fees** £15 per day; £11 per round (£20/£15 weekends and bank holidays) Due to be reviewed..
**Facilities**   ⊗ 爪 ﾑ ■ ♀ 👐 🖻 ℓ Kenneth Docherty.
**Leisure**    trolley for hire, putting green, practice area.
**Location**   Approx 4m from ferry slip
**Hotel**     ★★★ 66% Brisbane House, 14 Greenock Rd, Esplanade, LARGS ☎ 01475 687200 23 ⇥ ฿

## GRETNA                     Map 11 NY36

**Gretna** Kirtle View DG16 5HD ☎ 01461 338464
A nice parkland course on gentle hills. Opened in 1991, it offers a good test of skill.
*9 holes, 3214yds, Par 72, SSS 71, Course record 71.*
*Club membership 250.*
**Visitors**     no restrictions.
**Societies**   telephone in advance.
**Green Fees** £8 per day (£10 weekends & bank holidays).
**Facilities**   ⊗ by prior arrangement 爪 by prior arrangement ﾑ by prior arrangement ■ ♀ 👐
**Leisure**    trolley for hire, driving range.
**Location**   0.5m W of Gretna on B721,signposted
**Hotel**     ★★ 66% Solway Lodge Hotel, Annan Rd, GRETNA
          ☎ 01461 338266 3 ⇥ ฿Annexe7 ⇥ ฿

## HAMILTON                 Map 11 NS75

**Hamilton** Carlisle Rd, Ferniegair ML3 7TU
☎ 01698 282872
Beautiful parkland course.
*18 holes, 6243yds, Par 70, SSS 71, Course record 62.*
**Visitors**     must contact in advance, may not play weekends. Must be accompanied by member.
**Societies**   apply in writing.
**Green Fees** not confirmed.
**Facilities**   ⊗ 爪 ﾑ ■ ♀ 👐 🖻 ℓ Maurice Moir.
**Location**   1.5m SE on A72
**Hotel**     ★★ 62% Silvertrees Hotel, Silverwells Crescent, BOTHWELL
          ☎ 01698 852311 7 ⇥ ฿Annexe19 ⇥ ฿

**Strathclyde Park** Mote Hill ML3 6BY
☎ 01698 266155
Municipal parkland course.
*9 holes, 3128yds, Par 36, SSS 70, Course record 64.*
*Club membership 200.*
**Visitors**     same day booking system in operation, telephone above number (Regional Authority).
**Societies**   must contact in advance on above telephone number.
**Green Fees** £2.50 per round.
**Facilities**   ■ ♀ 👐 🖻 ℓ William Walker.
**Leisure**    driving range, putting green, practice area.
**Location**   N side of town off B7071
**Hotel**     ★★ 62% Silvertrees Hotel, Silverwells Crescent, BOTHWELL
          ☎ 01698 852311 7 ⇥ ฿Annexe19 ⇥ ฿

## HAWICK                   Map 12 NT51

**Hawick** Vertish Hill TD9 0NY ☎ 01450 372293
Hill course with good views.
*18 holes, 5929yds, Par 68, SSS 69, Course record 63.*
*Club membership 600.*               ▶

# Tweed Valley Hotel

As a centre for golf the Tweed Valley is a natural choice. Quiet, friendly and well appointed, with a noteworthy reputation for good food. Including its own smokehouse, fine wines and huge selection of whiskies at the bar. Special rates throughout the year. Enjoy countryside golf on 17 scenic courses. All arranged for you.

**Tweed Valley Hotel, Walkerburn, Peeblesshire EH43 6AA**
Tel: 01896 870636    Fax: 01896 870639

---

**Visitors** must contact in advance.
**Societies** write or telephone for booking arrangement.
**Green Fees** £24 per day; £16 per round (£24 day/round).
**Facilities** ⊗ ⅷ ℔ ♥ ♀ ♨ 🖻
**Leisure** trolley for hire, putting green, practice area.
**Location** SW side of town
**Hotel** ★★ 71% Kirklands Hotel, West Stewart Place, HAWICK
☎ 01450 372263 5 ➾ ♔Annexe7 ➾ ♔

---

## INNERLEITHEN                    Map 11 NT33

**Innerleithen** Leithen Water, Leithen Rd EH44 6NL
☎ 01896 830951
Moorland course, with easy walking. Burns and rivers are natural hazards. Testing 5th hole (100 yds) par 3.
*9 holes, 6056yds, Par 70, SSS 69, Course record 65.*
*Club membership 240.*
**Visitors** advisable to check for availability for weekends.
**Societies** by prior booking.
**Green Fees** £15 per day; £10 per round (£18/£12 weekends).
**Facilities** ⊗ by prior arrangement ⅷ by prior arrangement ℔ ♥ by prior arrangement ♀ ♨
**Leisure** putting green, practice area.
**Location** 1.5m N on B709
**Hotel** ★★★♨ 61% Tweed Valley Hotel & Restaurant, Galashiels Rd, WALKERBURN
☎ 01896 870636 16 ➾ ♔

---

## IRVINE                    Map 10 NS33

**Glasgow** Gailes KA11 5AE ☎ 0141 942 2011
A lovely seaside links. The turf of the fairways and all the greens is truly glorious and provides tireless play. Established in 1787, this is the ninth oldest course in the world and is a qualifying course for the Open Championship.
*18 holes, 6510yds, Par 71, SSS 72, Course record 64.*
*Club membership 1100.*
**Visitors** must contact in advance but may not play weekends & bank holidays before 2.30pm.
**Societies** initial contact by telephone.
**Green Fees** £37 per day; £30 per round (£33 afternoon round weekends).
**Facilities** ⊗ ⅷ by prior arrangement ℔ ♥ ♀ ♨ 🖻 ♔ ℓ J Steven.
**Leisure** trolley for hire, putting green, practice area.
**Location** 2m S off A737
**Hotel** ★★★★ 52% Hospitality Inn, 46 Annick Rd, IRVINE ☎ 01294 274272 128 ➾ ♔

---

**Irvine** Bogside KA12 8SN ☎ 01294 275626
Testing links course; only two short holes.
*18 holes, 6400yds, Par 71, SSS 71, Course record 65.*
*Club membership 450.*
**Visitors** may not play before 3pm Sat & Sun. Must contact in advance.
**Societies** are welcome weekdays, telephone 01294 275979 to book in advance.
**Green Fees** not confirmed.
**Facilities** ♀ ♨ 🖻 ℓ Keith Erskine.
**Location** N side of town off A737
**Hotel** ★★★★ 52% Hospitality Inn, 46 Annick Rd, IRVINE ☎ 01294 274272 128 ➾ ♔

---

**Irvine Ravenspark** 13 Kidsneuk Ln KA12 8SR
☎ 01294 271293
Parkland course.
*18 holes, 6702yds, Par 71, SSS 71, Course record 65.*
*Club membership 600.*
**Visitors** may not play Sat before 2pm.
**Societies** not allowed Sat, contact club steward in advance.
**Green Fees** £11 per day; £7 per round (£17/£11 weekends).
**Facilities** ⊗ ⅷ ℔ ♥ ♀ ♨ 🖻 ℓ Peter Bond.
**Leisure** putting green, practice ground.
**Location** N side of town on A737
**Hotel** ★★★♨ 71% Montgreenan Mansion House Hotel, Montgreenan Estate, KILWINNING
☎ 01294 557733 21 ➾ ♔

---

**Western Gailes** Gailes by Irvine KA11 5AE
☎ 01294 311649
A magnificent seaside links with glorious turf and wonderful greens. The view is open across the Firth of Clyde to the neighbouring islands. It is a well-balanced course crossed by 3 burns. There are 2 par 5's, the 6th and 14th, and the 11th is a testing 445-yd, par 4, dog-leg.
*18 holes, 6664yds, Par 71, SSS 73, Course record 65.*
**Visitors** welcome Mon, Tue, Wed & Fri. Must contact in advance and have a handicap certificate.
**Societies** must contact in advance.
**Green Fees** not confirmed.
**Facilities** ♀ ♨
**Leisure** caddies & caddy cars for hire.
**Location** 2m S off A737
**Hotel** ★★★♨ 71% Montgreenan Mansion House Hotel, Montgreenan Estate, KILWINNING ☎ 01294 557733 21 ➾ ♔

---

## JEDBURGH                    Map 12 NT62

**Jedburgh** Dunion Rd TD8 6DQ ☎ 01835 863587
Undulating parkland course, windy, with young trees.
*9 holes, 5760yds, Par 68, SSS 67.*
*Club membership 265.*

**Visitors**    restricted at weekends during competitions.
**Societies**    must contact at least one month in advance.
**Green Fees** not confirmed.
**Facilities**    ♀ (Apr-Sep) ⛳ 🏠
**Location**    1m W on B6358
**Hotel**    L Larkhall Burn, JEDBURGH
           ☎ 01835 862040 6 ⇄ ♞

## JOHNSTONE          Map 10 NS46

**Cochrane Castle** Scott Av, Craigstone PA5 0HF
☎ 01505 320146
Fairly hilly parkland course, wooded with two small streams
running through it.
*18 holes, 6223yds, Par 71, SSS 71, Course record 65.*
*Club membership 660.*
**Visitors**    may not play at weekends. Must contact in
           writing.
**Societies**    apply in writing.
**Green Fees** £25 per day; £17 per round.
**Facilities**    ⊗ �🍴 ฿ ☕ ♀ ⛳ 🏠 ( Stuart Campbell.
**Leisure**    trolley for hire, putting green, practice area.
**Location**    0.5m W off A737
**Hotel**    ★★★ 64% Lynnhurst Hotel, Park Rd,
           JOHNSTONE ☎ 01505 324331 21 ⇄ ♞

*Elderslie* 63 Main Rd, Elderslie PA5 9AZ ☎ 01505 322835
Parkland course, undulating, with good views.
*18 holes, 6175yds, Par 70, SSS 70.*
*Club membership 940.*
**Visitors**    may not play at weekends & bank holidays.
           Must contact club in advance and preferably
           have a handicap certificate.
**Societies**    must telephone in advance.
**Green Fees** not confirmed.
**Facilities**    ♀ ⛳ 🏠 ( Richard Bowman.
**Leisure**    putting green, trolley hire, practica area.
**Location**    E side of town on A737
**Hotel**    ★★★ 64% Lynnhurst Hotel, Park Rd,
           JOHNSTONE ☎ 01505 324331 21 ⇄ ♞

## KELSO          Map 12 NT73

**Kelso** Racecourse Rd TD5 7SL ☎ 01573 223009
Parkland course. Easy walking.
*18 holes, 6046yds, Par 70, SSS 69, Course record 64.*
*Club membership 500.*
**Visitors**    advisable to telephone in advance.
**Societies**    apply in writing.
**Green Fees** £20 per day; £12 per round (£27/£18 weekends).
**Facilities**    ⊗ ⍟ ฿ ☕ ♀ ⛳ 🏠 ♈
**Leisure**    trolley for hire, putting green, practice area.
**Location**    N side of town centre off B6461
**Hotel**    ★★★ 61% Cross Keys Hotel, 36-37 The
           Square, KELSO ☎ 01573 223303 24 ⇄ ♞

## KILBIRNIE          Map 10 NS35

*Kilbirnie Place* Largs Rd KA25 7AT ☎ 01505 683398
Easy walking parkland course.
*18 holes, 5400yds, Par 69, SSS 67.*
*Club membership 450.*
**Visitors**    no restrictions.
**Societies**    must apply in writing in advance.
**Green Fees** not confirmed.

**Facilities**    ♀ ⛳
**Leisure**    putting green, practice area.
**Location**    1m W on A760
**Hotel**    ★★ 69% Elderslie Hotel, John St, Broomfields,
           LARGS ☎ 01475 686460 26rm(9 ⇄ 5 ♞)

## KILMARNOCK          Map 10 NS43

**Annanhill** Irvine Rd KA1 2RT ☎ 01563 521644
Municipal, tree-lined parkland course played over by private
clubs.
*18 holes, 6269yds, Par 71, SSS 70, Course record 66.*
*Club membership 394.*
**Visitors**    book at starters office.
**Societies**    apply in writing.
**Green Fees** £14.25 per day; £9 per round (£17.50/£14.25
           weekends).
**Facilities**    ⊗ by prior arrangement ⍟ by prior arrangement
           ฿ by prior arrangement ☕ by prior arrangement
           ♀ ⛳
**Leisure**    putting green, practice area.
**Location**    1m W on A71
**Hotel**    ★★★☚ 75% Chapeltoun House Hotel,
           STEWARTON ☎ 01560 482696 8 ⇄ ♞

*Caprington* Ayr Rd KA1 4UW ☎ 01563 23702
Municipal parkland course.
*18 holes, 5718yds, Par 69, SSS 68.*
*Club membership 400.*
**Visitors**    may not play on Sat.
**Societies**    must contact in advance.
**Green Fees** not confirmed.
**Facilities**    ♀ ⛳ 🏠
**Location**    1.5m S on B7038
**Hotel**    ★★★☚ 75% Chapeltoun House Hotel,
           STEWARTON ☎ 01560 482696 8 ⇄ ♞

## KILSYTH          Map 11 NS77

**Kilsyth Lennox** Tak Ma Doon Rd G65 0RS
☎ 01236 824115 & 823089
Hilly moorland course, hard walking. Course and facilities
revamped with 18-holes after a serious fire early in 1993.
*18 holes, 5912yds, Par 70, SSS 70, Course record 66.*
*Club membership 500.*
**Visitors**    advisable to contact in advance. No restrictions
           weekdays up to 5pm, may play Sun on
           application but not Sat.
**Societies**    must contact in advance.
**Green Fees** £16 per day; £10 per round (£18/£12 weekends).
**Facilities**    ⊗ ⍟ ฿ ☕ ♀ ⛳ 🏠 ( R Abercrombie.
**Leisure**    buggies for hire, putting green.
**Location**    N side of town off A803
**Hotel**    ★★★ 64% Kirkhouse Inn, STRATHBLANE
           ☎ 01360 770621 15 ⇄ ♞

## KIRKCUDBRIGHT          Map 11 NX65

**Kirkcudbright** Stirling Crescent DG6 4EZ
☎ 01557 330314
Parkland course. Hilly, with hard walking. Good views.
*18 holes, 5598yds, Par 68, SSS 68, Course record 63.*
*Club membership 500.*
**Visitors**    advisable to contact in advance.
**Societies**    contact in advance.           ▶

**Green Fees** £20 per day/round (£15 per round).
**Facilities** ⊗ ⅲ ⅃ 🍴 ♀ ♨
**Leisure** trolley for hire, driving range, putting green.
**Location** NE side of town off A711
**Hotel** ★★ 72% Selkirk Arms Hotel, Old High St, KIRKCUDBRIGHT
🕿 01557 330402 15 ⇆ 🕻Annexe1 ⇆ 🕻

## KIRKINTILLOCH
Map 11 NS67

**Hayston** Campsie Rd G66 1RN
🕿 0141 776 1244
An undulating, tree-lined course with a sandy subsoil.
*18 holes, 6042yds, Par 70, SSS 70, Course record 62.*
*Club membership 800.*
**Visitors** must apply in advance, may not play weekends,
**Societies** Tue & Thu, apply in writing
**Green Fees** £25 per day; £18 per round.
**Facilities** ⊗ ⅲ ⅃ 🍴 ♀ ♨ 🏠🕻 Steven Barnett.
**Leisure** trolley for hire, putting green, practice area.
**Location** 1m NW off A803
**Hotel** ★★★ 64% Kirkhouse Inn, STRATHBLANE
🕿 01360 770621 15 ⇆ 🕻

*Kirkintilloch* Campsie Rd G66 1RN
🕿 0141 776 1256
Parkland course in rural setting.
*18 holes, 5269yds, Par 70, SSS 66.*
*Club membership 650.*
**Visitors** must be introduced by member.
**Societies** apply in writing.
**Green Fees** not confirmed.
**Facilities** ♨ 🏠
**Location** 1m NW off A803
**Hotel** ★★★ 64% Kirkhouse Inn, STRATHBLANE
🕿 01360 770621 15 ⇆ 🕻

## LANARK
Map 11 NS84

**Lanark** The Moor, Whitelees Rd ML11 7RX
🕿 01555 663219
Chosen as one of the pre-qualifying tests for the Open Championship held at Lanark from 1977 to 1983. The address of the club, 'The Moor', gives some indication as to the kind of golf to be found there. Golf has been played at Lanark for well over a century and the Club dates from 1851.
*Old Course: 18 holes, 6423yds, Par 70, SSS 71, Course record 62.*
*9 Hole: 9 holes, 2980yds, Par 56.*
*Club membership 880.*
**Visitors** must contact in advance, no visitors weekends,
**Societies** apply in advance.
**Green Fees** £35 per day; £23 per round. 9 hole course £4 per day.
**Facilities** ⊗ ⅲ ⅃ 🍴 ♀ ♨ 🏠 🍴🕻 Ron Wallace.
**Leisure** motorised carts for hire, buggies for hire, trolley for hire, putting green, practice area.
**Location** E side of town centre off A73
**Hotel** ★★★ 67% Cartland Bridge Hotel, Glasgow Rd, LANARK
🕿 01555 664426 18 ⇆ 🕻

## LANGBANK
Map 10 NS37

*Gleddoch Golf and Country Club* PA14 6YE
🕿 01475 540304
Parkland and heathland course with other sporting facilities available to temporary members. Good views over Firth of Clyde.
*18 holes, 5661yds, Par 68, SSS 67.*
*Club membership 600.*
**Visitors** must contact in advance.
**Societies** must contact in advance.
**Green Fees** not confirmed.
**Facilities** ♀ ♨ 🏠 🍴 ⋈🕻 Keith Campbell.
**Leisure** grass tennis courts, heated indoor swimming pool, squash, sauna, archery, clay pigeon shooting.
**Location** B789-Old Greenock Road
**Hotel** ★★★♨ 72% Gleddoch House Hotel, LANGBANK 🕿 01475 540711 39 ⇆ 🕻

## LANGHOLM
Map 11 NY38

**Langholm** Whiteside DG13 0JR 🕿 013873 80673
Hillside course with fine views, hard walking.
*9 holes, 5744yds, Par 70, SSS 68, Course record 63.*
*Club membership 200.*
**Visitors** restricted Sat & Sun.
**Societies** apply in writing to secretary.
**Green Fees** £10 per day/round.
**Facilities** ⊗ by prior arrangement ⅲ by prior arrangement ⅃ by prior arrangement 🍴 by prior arrangement ♀
**Leisure** putting green, practice area.
**Location** E side of village off A7
**Hotel** ★★ 57% Eskdale Hotel, Market Place, LANGHOLM
🕿 013873 80357 & 81178 15rm(11 ⇆ 🕻)

## LARGS
Map 10 NS25

*Largs* Irvine Rd KA30 8EU 🕿 01475 673594
A parkland, tree-lined course with views to the Clyde coast and Arran Isles.
*18 holes, 6220yds, Par 70, SSS 71, Course record 64.*
*Club membership 850.*
**Visitors** may not play weekends & competition days. Must contact in advance.
**Societies** apply in writing.
**Green Fees** not confirmed.
**Facilities** ♀ ♨ 🏠 🍴🕻
**Location** 1m S of town centre on A78
**Hotel** ★★ 69% Elderslie Hotel, John St, Broomfields, LARGS 🕿 01475 686460 26rm(9 ⇆5 🕻)

*Routenburn* Routenburn Rd KA30 8QA
🕿 01475 673230
Heathland course with fine views over Firth of Clyde.
*18 holes, 5675yds, Par 68, SSS 68.*
*Club membership 500.*
**Visitors** no restrictions.
**Societies** apply in writing.
**Green Fees** not confirmed.
**Facilities** ♀ ♨ 🏠🕻 J Grieg McQueen.
**Leisure** caddy car for hire.

**Location** 1m N off A78
**Hotel** ★★★♨ 63% Manor Park Hotel, LARGS
☎ 01475 520832 10 ⇆ ⛏Annexe13 ⇆ ⛏

## LARKHALL
Map 11 NS75

*Larkhall* Burnhead Rd ML9 3AB ☎ 01698 881113
Small, inland parkland course.
*9 holes, 6700yds, Par 72, SSS 71, Course record 69.*
*Club membership 250.*
**Visitors** restricted Tue & Sat.
**Green Fees** not confirmed.
**Facilities** ♀
**Location** E side of town on B7019
**Hotel** ★★★ 66% Popinjay Hotel, Lanark Rd,
ROSEBANK
☎ 01555 860441 36 ⇆ ⛏Annexe5 ⇆ ⛏

## LAUDER
Map 12 NT54

*Lauder* Galashiels Rd TD2 6RS ☎ 01578 722526
Inland course and practice area on gently sloping hill.
*9 holes, 3001yds, Par 72, SSS 70, Course record 70.*
*Club membership 200.*
**Visitors** restricted Wed 4.30-5.30pm and Sun before
noon.
**Societies** telephone in advance.
**Green Fees** not confirmed.
**Facilities** ⛌
**Location** On Galashiels Rd, off A68, 0.5m from Lauder
**Hotel** ★★ 63% Lauderdale Hotel, 1 Edinburgh Rd,
LAUDER ☎ 01578 722231 9 ⇆ ⛏

## LEADHILLS
Map 11 NS81

*Leadhills* ML12 6XR ☎ no telephone
A testing, hilly course with high winds. At 1500ft above sea
level it is the highest golf course in Scotland.
*9 holes, 4354yds, Par 66, SSS 64.*
*Club membership 80.*
**Visitors** no restrictions.
**Societies** must contact in advance.
**Green Fees** not confirmed.
**Location** E side of village off B797
**Hotel** ★★ 61% Mennockfoot Lodge Hotel, Mennock,
SANQUHAR
☎ 01659 50382 & 50477 1 ⇆Annexe8 ⇆ ⛏

## LENNOXTOWN
Map 11 NS67

*Campsie* Crow Rd G65 7HX ☎ 01360 310244
Scenic hillside course.
*18 holes, 5507yds, Par 70, SSS 67, Course record 65.*
*Club membership 640.*
**Visitors** contact professional 1360 310920.
**Societies** wrtten application.
**Green Fees** £20 per day; £12 per round (£15 per round
weekends).
**Facilities** ⊗ �X ⛟ ⛊ ♀ ⛐ ⛨ ⛏ Mark Brennan.
**Leisure** putting green, practice area.
**Location** 0.5m N on B822
**Hotel** ★★★ 64% Kirkhouse Inn, STRATHBLANE
☎ 01360 770621 15 ⇆ ⛏

## LENZIE
Map 11 NS67

*Lenzie* 19 Crosshill Rd G66 5DA
☎ 0141 776 1535 & 0141 776 6020
Pleasant moorland course.
*18 holes, 5984yds, Par 69, SSS 69, Course record 64.*
*Club membership 890.*
**Visitors** must contact in advance and may not play
weekends.
**Societies** apply in writing.
**Green Fees** £24 per day; £16 per round.
**Facilities** ⊗ �X ⛟ ⛊ ♀ ⛐ ⛨ Jim McCallum.
**Leisure** motorised carts for hire, trolley for hire, putting
green, practice area.
**Location** S side of town on B819
**Hotel** ★★★ 64% Kirkhouse Inn, STRATHBLANE
☎ 01360 770621 15 ⇆ ⛏

## LESMAHAGOW
Map 11 NS83

*Holland Bush* Acretophead ML11 0JS
☎ 01555 893484 & 893646
Fairly difficult, tree-lined municipal parkland and moorland
course. 1st half is flat, while 2nd half is hilly. No bunkers.
*18 holes, 6110yds, Par 71, SSS 69, Course record 63.*
*Club membership 500.*
**Visitors** no restrictions.
**Societies** contact the professional in advance.
**Green Fees** £12 per day (£15 weekends) under review.
**Facilities** ⊗ �X ⛟ ⛊ ♀ ⛐ ⛨ ⛏ Ian Rae.
**Leisure** trolley for hire, practice area.
**Hotel** ★★★ 66% Strathaven Hotel, Hamilton Rd,
STRATHAVEN ☎ 01357 521778 10 ⇆ ⛏

## LOCHMABEN
Map 11 NY08

*Lochmaben* Castlehillgate DG11 1NT
☎ 01387 810552
Comfortable-walking parkland course between two lochs
with fine old trees and fast greens all year round.
*18 holes, 5357yds, Par 67, SSS 66, Course record 60.*
*Club membership 850.*
**Visitors** advised to contact in advance.
**Societies** must contact in advance.
**Green Fees** £16 per day; £14 per round (£20/£16 weekends).
**Facilities** ⊗ �X ⛟ ⛊ ♀ ⛐
**Leisure** fishing, putting green, practice area.
**Location** S side of village off A709
**Hotel** ★★★ 69% Dryfesdale Hotel, LOCKERBIE
☎ 01576 202427 15 ⇆ ⛏

## LOCHWINNOCH
Map 10 NS35

*Lochwinnoch* Burnfoot Rd PA12 4AN ☎ 01505 842153
Parkland course, slightly hilly in middle, with testing golf.
Overlooks bird sanctuary and boating loch.
*18 holes, 6243yds, Par 71, SSS 70.*
*Club membership 650.*
**Visitors** may not play at weekends and bank holidays
unless accompanied by member. Restricted
during competition days.
**Societies** apply in writing to club administrator.
**Green Fees** not confirmed.
**Facilities** ♀ ⛐ ⛨ ⛏ Gerry Reilly. ▶

**Location** W side of town off A760
**Hotel** ★★★ 65% Bowfield Hotel & Country Club, HOWWOOD ☎ 01505 705225 12 ⇋ ƒ

## LOCKERBIE                                Map 11 NY18

**Lockerbie** Corrie Rd DG11 2ND
☎ 01576 202462 & 203363
Parkland course with fine views and featuring the only pond hole in Dumfriesshire.
*18 holes, 5614yds, Par 68, SSS 67, Course record 64.*
*Club membership 620.*
**Visitors** restricted Sun. Advisable to book in advance.
**Societies** must contact secretary in advance.
**Green Fees** £18 per day (£22 per day Sat; £18 per round Sun).
**Facilities** ⊗ ⅦⅡ ⅃ ⅊ ⅄
**Leisure** trolley for hire, putting green, practice area.
**Location** E side of town centre off B7068
**Hotel** ★★★ 69% Dryfesdale Hotel, LOCKERBIE ☎ 01576 202427 15 ⇋ ƒ

## MAUCHLINE                                Map 11 NS42

**Ballochmyle** Catrine Rd KA5 6LE ☎ 01290 550469
Wooded parkland course.
*18 holes, 5952yds, Par 70, SSS 69, Course record 65.*
*Club membership 730.*
**Visitors** no visitors on Mon from Oct-Mar except with member.
**Societies** apply in writing.
**Green Fees** £25 per day; £18 per round (£30 per day weekends).
**Facilities** ⊗ Ⅶ by prior arrangement ⅃ ⅊ ⅄ ⌂
**Leisure** trolley for hire, putting green, practice area.
**Location** 1m SE on B705
**Hotel** ★★ 57% Royal Hotel, 1 Glaisnock St, CUMNOCK
☎ 01290 420822 11rm(6 ⇋ ƒ)

## MAYBOLE                                  Map 10 NS20

**Maybole Municipal** Memorial Park KA19 7DX
Hilly parkland course.
*9 holes, 2635yds, Par 33, SSS 65, Course record 64.*
*Club membership 100.*
**Visitors** no restrictions.
**Societies** must contact in advance.
**Green Fees** not confirmed.
**Hotel** ★★(red)⚘ Ladyburn, MAYBOLE ☎ 01655 740585 8rm(4 ⇋3 ƒ)

## MELROSE                                  Map 12 NT53

**Melrose** Dingleton TD6 9HS
☎ 01896 822855 & 822391
Undulating tree-lined fairways with spendid views.
*9 holes, 5579yds, Par 70, SSS 68, Course record 61.*
*Club membership 380.*
**Visitors** competitions all Sats and many Suns Apr-Oct, ladies priority Tue, junior priority Wed am in holidays.
**Societies** apply in writing.
**Green Fees** £15 per round/day.

**Facilities** ⊗ by prior arrangement Ⅶ by prior arrangement ⅃ by prior arrangement ⅊ ⅄
**Leisure** practice area.
**Location** S side of town centre on B6359
**Hotel** ★★★ 64% Burt's Hotel, The Square, MELROSE ☎ 01896 822285 21 ⇋ ƒ

## MILNGAVIE                                Map 11 NS57

**Clober** Craigton Rd G62 7HP ☎ 0141 956 1685 & 6963
Parkland course. Testing 5th hole, par 3.
*18 holes, 5042yds, Par 65, SSS 65, Course record 61.*
*Club membership 600.*
**Visitors** may not play after 4.30pm Mon-Thu and after 4pm Fri & last Tue in month (Mar-Sep). Must play with member weekends and bank holidays.
**Societies** must contact in advance.
**Green Fees** not confirmed.
**Facilities** ⅊ ⅄ ⌂
**Leisure** putting green, trolley hire.
**Location** NW side of town
**Hotel** ★★★ 65% Black Bull Thistle, Main St, MILNGAVIE ☎ 0141 956 2291 27 ⇋ ƒ

**Dougalston** Strathblane Rd G62 8HJ ☎ 0141 956 5750
Tree-lined with water features.
*18 holes, 6683yds, Par 72, SSS 71.*
*Club membership 500.*
**Visitors** are restricted at weekends.
**Societies** weekdays only.
**Green Fees** £15 per round; £20 per 36 holes.
**Facilities** ⊗ Ⅶ ⅃ ⅊ ⅄ ⅂
**Leisure** trolley for hire, putting green, practice area.
**Location** NE side of town on A81
**Hotel** ★★★ 65% Black Bull Thistle, Main St, MILNGAVIE ☎ 0141 956 2291 27 ⇋ ƒ

**Hilton Park** Auldmarroch Estate, Stockiemuir Rd G62 7HB
☎ 0141 956 4657
Moorland courses set amidst magnificent scenery.
*Hilton Course: 18 holes, 6054yds, Par 70, SSS 70, Course record 65.*
*Allander Course: 18 holes, 5374yards, Par 69, SSS 66, Course record 66.*
*Club membership 1100.*
**Visitors** must contact in advance but may not play at weekends.
**Societies** apply in advance to secretary.
**Green Fees** £26 per day; £18 per round.
**Facilities** ⊗ Ⅶ ⅃ ⅊ ⅄ ⌂ ⅂ ⅂ William Condichie.
**Leisure** buggies for hire, trolley for hire, putting green, practice area.
**Location** 3m NW on A809
**Hotel** ★★★ 65% Black Bull Thistle, Main St, MILNGAVIE ☎ 0141 956 2291 27 ⇋ ƒ

**Milngavie** Laigh Park G62 8EP ☎ 0141 956 2073
Moorland course, hard walking, sometimes windy, good views. Testing 1st and 4th holes (par 4).
*18 holes, 5818yds, Par 68, SSS 68, Course record 59.*
*Club membership 700.*
**Visitors** must contact in advance, may not play weekends.
**Societies** apply in writing.
**Green Fees** £25 per day; £15 per round.
**Facilities** ⊗ Ⅶ ⅃ ⅊ ⅊ ⅄

**Leisure**     putting green, practice area.
**Location**    1.25m N
**Hotel**      ★★★ 65% Black Bull Thistle, Main St,
MILNGAVIE
☎ 0141 956 2291 27 ⇋ ⋔

## MINTO                 Map 12 NT52

**Minto** Denholm TD9 8SH
☎ 01450 870220
Pleasant, undulating parkland course featuring mature trees and panoramic views of Scottish Border country. Short but quite testing.
*18 holes, 5460yds, Par 68, SSS 67, Course record 65.*
*Club membership 670.*
**Visitors**    advisable to telephone in advance, and essential for weekends.
**Societies**   telephone or write.
**Green Fees** £20 per day; £15 per round (£30/£25 weekends & bank holidays).
**Facilities**   ⊗ ⅷ ⮯ 🏌 ♀ ♨
**Leisure**     motorised carts for hire, buggies for hire, trolley for hire, practice area.
**Location**    5m from Hawick, 1.25m off A698 at Denholm
**Hotel**      ★★ 71% Kirklands Hotel, West Stewart Place, HAWICK
☎ 01450 372263 5 ⇋ ⋔Annexe7 ⇋ ⋔

## MOFFAT             Map 11 NT00

**Moffat** Coatshill DG10 9SE ☎ 01683 220020
Scenic moorland course overlooking the town, with panoramic views.
*18 holes, 5218yds, Par 69, SSS 67, Course record 60.*
*Club membership 350.*
**Visitors**    advised to contact in advance.
**Societies**   apply in writing to the clubmistress.
**Green Fees** £17.50 per day (£25.50 weekends & bank holidays). Weekdays (ex Wed) £12.50 per round after 3pm.
**Facilities**   ⊗ ⅷ ⮯ 🏌 ♀ ♨ 🖻 ⋔
**Leisure**     trolley for hire, putting green, games room.
**Location**    1m SW off A701
**Hotel**      ★★★ 63% Moffat House Hotel, High St, MOFFAT
☎ 01683 220039 16 ⇋ ⋔Annexe4 ⇋ ⋔

## MONREITH          Map 10 NX34

**St Medan** DG8 8NJ ☎ 01988 700358
Links course with panoramic views of the Solway and Isle of Man.
*9 holes, 4608yds, Par 64, SSS 63, Course record 60.*
*Club membership 300.*
**Visitors**    no restrictions.
**Societies**   apply in advance.
**Green Fees** £15 per day; £12 per 18 holes; £7 per 9 holes.
**Facilities**   ⊗ ⅷ ⮯ 🏌 ♀ ♨ ⋔
**Leisure**     trolley for hire, putting green.
**Location**    1m SE off A747
**Hotel**      ★★★⚌ 65% Corsemalzie House Hotel, PORT WILLIAM
☎ 01988 860254 14 ⇋ ⋔

## MOTHERWELL        Map 11 NS75

**Colville Park** New Jerviston House, Jerviston Estate, Merry St ML1 4UG ☎ 01698 265779
Parkland course. First nine, tree-lined, second nine, more exposed. Testing 10th hole par 3, 16th hole par 4.
*18 holes, 6250yds, Par 71, SSS 70, Course record 63.*
*Club membership 800.*
**Visitors**    must contact in advance in writing.
**Societies**   apply in writing.
**Green Fees** not confirmed.
**Facilities**   ⊗ ⅷ ⮯ 🏌 ♀ ♨
**Leisure**     putting green, practice area.
**Location**    1.25m NE on A723
**Hotel**      ★★ 62% Silvertrees Hotel, Silverwells Crescent, BOTHWELL
☎ 01698 852311 7 ⇋ ⋔Annexe19 ⇋ ⋔

## MUIRHEAD          Map 11 NS66

**Crow Wood** Garnkirk House, Cumbernauld Rd G69 9JF
☎ 0141 779 4954 & 0141 779 2011
Parkland course.
*18 holes, 6261yds, Par 71, SSS 71, Course record 62.*
*Club membership 800.*
**Visitors**    must contact in advance but may not play weekends & bank holidays.
**Societies**   apply in advance.
**Green Fees** £25 per day; £17 per round.
**Facilities**   ⊗ ⅷ ⮯ 🏌 ♀ ♨ 🖻 ⌁ Brian Moffat.
**Leisure**     trolley for hire, putting green, practice area.
**Location**    0.5m W on A80
**Hotel**      ★★★ 68% Malmaison Hotel, 278 West George St, GLASGOW ☎ 0141 221 6400 21 ⇋ ⋔

## NEWCASTLETON      Map 12 NY48

**Newcastleton** Holm Hill TD9 0QD ☎ 01387 375257
Hill course.
*9 holes, 5748yds, Par 70, SSS 68.*
*Club membership 100.*
**Visitors**    contact in advance.
**Societies**   contact by telephone or in writing in advance.
**Green Fees** £7 per day/round (£8 weekends).
**Facilities**   ♨ ⋔
**Leisure**     fishing, putting green.
**Location**    W side of village
**Hotel**      ★★ 57% Eskdale Hotel, Market Place, LANGHOLM
☎ 013873 80357 & 81178 15rm(11 ⇋ ⋔)

## NEW CUMNOCK       Map 11 NS61

**New Cumnock** Lochhill, Cumnock Rd KA18 4PN
☎ 01290 338848
Parkland course.
*9 holes, 5176yds, Par 68, SSS 68, Course record 68.*
*Club membership 280.*
**Visitors**    restricted on Sun competition days.
**Societies**   apply in writing.
**Green Fees** £7 per day.
**Facilities**   ♨ ⇋
**Leisure**     fishing, practice area.
**Location**    0.75m N on A76                ▶

**Hotel**  ★★ 57%  Royal Hotel, 1 Glaisnock St,
CUMNOCK ☎ 01290 420822 11rm(6 ➡ ♠)

## NEW GALLOWAY                    Map 11 NX67

**New Galloway** DG7 3RN
☎ 01644 420737 & 01644 430455
Set on the edge of the Galloway Hills and overlooking Loch
Ken, the course has excellent tees and first class greens.
*9 holes, 5006yds, Par 68, SSS 67, Course record 63.*
*Club membership 350.*
**Visitors**    restricted on Sun (competition days).
**Societies**   contact secretary in advance.
**Green Fees** £10 per day.
**Facilities**  ♥ ♀ ⅄
**Leisure**     putting green, practice area,.
**Location**    S side of town on A762
**Hotel**       ★★ 66%  Douglas Arms, King St, CASTLE
DOUGLAS ☎ 01556 502231 20rm(15 ➡ ♠)

## NEWTON MEARNS                    Map 11 NS55

**East Renfrewshire** Pilmuir G77 8PS ☎ 01355 500258
Undulating moorland with loch; prevailing SW wind.
*18 holes, 6097yds, Par 70, SSS 70, Course record 64.*
*Club membership 900.*
**Visitors**    telephone for details.
**Societies**   must contact in advance.
**Green Fees** not confirmed.
**Facilities**  ♀ ⅄ ⬠ ♪ Gordon Clarke.
**Leisure**     driving range, putting green, practice area,trolley
hire.
**Location**    3m SW on A77
**Hotel**       ★★★ 64%  Macdonald Thistle, Eastwood Toll,
GIFFNOCK ☎ 0141 638 2225 56 ➡ ♠

**Eastwood** Muirshield, Loganswell G77 6RX
☎ 01355 500280
Moorland course.
*18 holes, 5864yds, Par 68, SSS 69, Course record 62.*
*Club membership 900.*
**Visitors**    contact in advance, may only play with member
at weekends.
**Societies**   must contact in advance.
**Green Fees** £30 per day; £20 per round.
**Facilities**  ⊗ ⅢⅢ ℔ ♥ ♀ ⅄ ⬠ ♪ Alan McGinness.
**Leisure**     trolley for hire, putting green, practice area.
**Location**    2.5m S on A77
**Hotel**       ★★★ 64%  Macdonald Thistle, Eastwood Toll,
GIFFNOCK ☎ 0141 638 2225 56 ➡ ♠

**Whitecraigs** 72 Ayr Rd G46 6SW
☎ 0141 639 4530 & 0141 639 2140 pro
Beautiful parkland course.
*18 holes, 6230yds, Par 70, SSS 70, Course record 65.*
*Club membership 1078.*
**Visitors**    must contact professional in advance and have a
handicap certificate. With member only
weekends and bank holidays.
**Green Fees** £35 per day; £28 per round.
**Facilities**  ⊗ ⅢⅢ ℔ ♥ ♀ ⅄ ⬠ ♪ ♪ Alistair Forrow.
**Leisure**     trolley for hire, putting green, practice area.
**Location**    1.5m NE on A77
**Hotel**       ★★★ 64%  Macdonald Thistle, Eastwood Toll,
GIFFNOCK ☎ 0141 638 2225 56 ➡ ♠

## NEWTON STEWART                    Map 10 NX46

**Newton Stewart** Kirroughtree Av, Minnigaff DG8 6PF
☎ 01671 402172
Parkland course in picturesque setting. Short but quite tight.
*18 holes, 5970yds, Par 69, SSS 69.*
*Club membership 300.*
**Visitors**    must contact in advance.
**Societies**   must contact in advance.
**Green Fees** £19 per day; £16 per round (£23/£19 weekends
& bank holidays).
**Facilities**  ⊗ ⅢⅢ ℔ ♥ ♀ ⅄ ⬠ ♪
**Leisure**     trolley for hire, practice area.
**Location**    0.5m N of town centre
**Hotel**       ★★ 67%  Creebridge House Hotel, NEWTON
STEWART ☎ 01671 402121 20 ➡ ♠

## PAISLEY                    Map 11 NS46

**Barshaw** Barshaw Park PA1 3TJ ☎ 0141 889 2908
Municipal parkland course.
*18 holes, 5703yds, Par 68, SSS 67, Course record 63.*
*Club membership 100.*
**Visitors**    no restrictions.
**Societies**   by prior arrangement with Parks Manager, Dept
of Sports & Leisure, Renfrewshire Council,
Mirren House, 6 Maxwell St, Paisley PA3 2AB.
**Green Fees** £6 per round.
**Facilities**  ♥ ⅄ ⬠ ♪ ♪ John Scott.
**Leisure**     putting green.
**Location**    1m E off A737
**Hotel**       ★★★ 68%  Glynhill Hotel & Leisure Club,
Paisley Rd, RENFREW
☎ 0141 886 5555 125 ➡ ♠

**Paisley** Braehead PA2 8TZ
☎ 0141 884 3903 & 884 4114
Moorland course, windy but with good views.
*18 holes, 6466yds, Par 71, SSS 72, Course record 66.*
*Club membership 800.*
**Visitors**    must contact in advance. Visitors may not play
weekends or public holidays.
**Societies**   weekdays only, excluding bank holidays.
Contact in advance.
**Green Fees** £28 per day; £20 per round.
**Facilities**  ⊗ ⅢⅢ ℔ ♥ ♀ ⅄ ⬠ ♪ Grant Gilmour.
**Leisure**     trolley for hire, putting green, practice area.
**Location**    S side of town off B774
**Hotel**       ★★★ 68%  Glynhill Hotel & Leisure Club,
Paisley Rd, RENFREW
☎ 0141 886 5555 125 ➡ ♠

**Ralston** Strathmore Av, Ralston PA1 3DT
☎ 0141 882 1349
Parkland course.
*18 holes, 6071yds, Par 71, SSS 69.*
*Club membership 750.*
**Visitors**    must be accompanied by member.
**Green Fees** not confirmed.
**Facilities**  ♀ ⅄
**Location**    2m E off A737
**Hotel**       ★★★ 66%  Swallow Hotel, 517 Paisley Rd
West, GLASGOW
☎ 0141 427 3146 117 ➡ ♠

## PATNA
Map 10 NS41

**Doon Valley** Hillside Park KA6 7JT
☎ 01292 531607 & 550411
Established parkland course located on an undulating hillside.
*9 holes, 5654yds, Par 70, SSS 68.*
*Club membership 90.*
**Visitors** mid week tee times available any time, advisable to contact for weekends.
**Societies** telephone to arrange.
**Green Fees** £13.80 per day; £9 per round.
**Facilities** ⚒
**Leisure** fishing.
**Location** 10m S of Ayr on the A713
**Hotel** ★★(red)⚌ Ladyburn, MAYBOLE
☎ 01655 740585 8rm(4 ⇄3 ⋒)

## PEEBLES
Map 11 NT24

**Peebles** Kirkland St EH45 8EU ☎ 01721 720197
Parkland course with fine views.
*18 holes, 6160yds, Par 70, SSS 70, Course record 63.*
*Club membership 690.*
**Visitors** must contact in advance, may not play Sat.
**Societies** apply by telephone or in writing in advance.
**Green Fees** £23 per day; £17 per round (£30/£23 weekends).
**Facilities** ⊗ ⅏ ⚏ ⚑ ♀ ⚒ 🖰 ⚲
**Leisure** motorised carts for hire, buggies for hire, trolley for hire, putting green, practice area.
**Location** W side of town centre off A72
**Hotel** ★★★ 71% Peebles Hydro Hotel, PEEBLES
☎ 01721 720602 137 ⇄ ⋒

## PORTPATRICK
Map 10 NX05

**Portpatrick** Golf Course Rd DG9 8TB ☎ 01776 810273
Seaside links-type course, set on cliffs overlooking the Irish Sea, with magnificent views.
*Dunskey Course: 18 holes, 5882yds, Par 70, SSS 68, Course record 65.*
*Dinvin Course: 9 holes, 1504yds, Par 27, SSS 27.*
*Club membership 720.*
**Visitors** must contact in advance.
**Societies** must contact in advance.
**Green Fees** 18 holes: £25 per day; £17 per round (£30/£20 weekends) 9 holes: £12 per day; £6 per round.
**Facilities** ⊗ ⅏ ⚏ ⚑ ♀ ⚒ 🖰 ⚲
**Leisure** trolley for hire, putting green, practice area.
**Location** 300 yds right from war memorial
**Hotel** ★★★ 66% Fernhill Hotel, PORTPATRICK
☎ 01776 810220 14 ⇄ ⋒Annexe6 ⇄ ⋒

## PRESTWICK
Map 10 NS32

**Prestwick** 2 Links Rd KA9 1QG ☎ 01292 477404
Seaside links with natural hazards and fine views.
*18 holes, 6544yds, Par 71, SSS 72.*
*Club membership 575.*
**Visitors** restricted Thu; may not play at weekends. Must contact in advance and have a handicap certificate.
**Societies** must contact in writing.
**Green Fees** not confirmed.
**Facilities** ⚒ 🖰 ⚲ ⓕ F C Rennie.

---

**Location** In town centre off A79
**Hotel** ★★ 62% Parkstone Hotel, Esplanade, PRESTWICK ☎ 01292 477286 15 ⇄ ⋒

**Prestwick St Cuthbert** East Rd KA9 2SX
☎ 01292 477101
Parkland course with easy walking, natural hazards and sometimes windy.
*18 holes, 6470yds, Par 71, SSS 71, Course record 64.*
*Club membership 880.*
**Visitors** must contact in advance but may not play at weekends & bank holidays.
**Societies** Mon-Fri, apply in writing.
**Green Fees** £27 per day; £20 per round.
**Facilities** ⊗ ⅏ ⚏ ⚑ ♀ ⚒
**Leisure** trolley for hire, putting green, practice area.
**Location** 0.5m E of town centre off A77
**Hotel** ★★ 61% St Nicholas Hotel, 41 Ayr Rd, PRESTWICK ☎ 01292 479568 17rm(12 ⇄ ⋒)

**Prestwick St Nicholas** Grangemuir Rd KA9 1SN
☎ 01292 477608
Seaside links course with whins, heather and tight fairways. It provides easy walking and has an unrestricted view of the Firth of Clyde.
*18 holes, 5952yds, Par 69, SSS 69, Course record 63.*
*Club membership 650.*
**Visitors** except weekends & public holidays. Must contact in advance.
**Societies** must contact in advance.
**Green Fees** £35 per day; £22 per round.
**Facilities** ⊗ ⅏ ⚏ ⚑ ♀ ⚒ 🖰
**Leisure** putting green.
**Location** S side of town off A79
**Hotel** ★★ 62% Parkstone Hotel, Esplanade, PRESTWICK ☎ 01292 477286 15 ⇄ ⋒

## RENFREW
Map 11 NS46

**Renfrew** Blythswood Estate, Inchinnan Rd PA4 9EG
☎ 0141 886 6692
Tree-lined parkland course.
*18 holes, 6818yds, Par 72, SSS 73.*
*Club membership 800.*
**Visitors** restricted to Mon, Tue & Thu, apply in advance.
**Societies** apply in writing in advance.
**Green Fees** not confirmed.
**Facilities** ♀ ⚒ 🖰 ⓕ Stuart Kerr.
**Leisure** putting green,trolley hire.
**Location** 0.75m W off A8
**Hotel** ★★★ 68% Glynhill Hotel & Leisure Club, Paisley Rd, RENFREW
☎ 0141 886 5555 125 ⇄ ⋒

## RIGSIDE
Map 11 NS83

**Douglas Water** Old School, Ayr Rd ML11 9NP
☎ 01555 880361
A 9-hole course of 3,000 yards with good variety and some hills and spectacular views. An interesting course with a challenging longest hole of 564 yards but, overall, not too testing for average golfers.
*9 holes, 5890yds, Par 72, SSS 69.*
*Club membership 250.* ▶

**Visitors** no restrictions weekdays or Sun, competitions on Sat normal restrictions.
**Societies** apply in writing/telephone in advance.
**Green Fees** not confirmed.
**Facilities** ⚲ (prior arrangement) ⌂
**Location** Ayr rd A70
**Hotel** ★★★ 67% Tinto Hotel, Symington, BIGGAR
☎ 01899 308454 29 ⇔ ℮

## ST BOSWELLS                                Map 12 NT53

**St Boswells** Braeheads TD6 0DE
☎ 01835 823527
Attractive parkland course by the banks of the River Tweed; easy walking.
*9 holes, 5250yds, Par 66.*
*Club membership 320.*
**Visitors** contact in advance.
**Societies** booking by writing to secretary.
**Green Fees** £15 per day; £10 per round (£15 per day/round weekends).
**Facilities** ▬ ⚲ ⌂
**Leisure** fishing.
**Location** 500yds off A68 east end of village
**Hotel** ★★★⚑ 76% Dryburgh Abbey Hotel, ST BOSWELLS
☎ 01835 822261 25 ⇔ ℮Annexe1 ⇔ ℮

## SANQUHAR                                   Map 11 NS70

**Sanquhar** Euchen Golf Course, Blackaddie Rd DG4 6JZ
☎ 01659 50577
Moorland course, fine views.
*9 holes, 5594yds, Par 70, SSS 68 or 55 holes.*
*Club membership 200.*
**Visitors** no restrictions.
**Societies** must pre-book.
**Green Fees** £10 per day (£12 weekends).
**Facilities** ⊗ by prior arrangement �📶 by prior arrangement ▬ ⚲ ⌂
**Leisure** putting green, practice area.
**Location** 0.5m SW off A76
**Hotel** ★★ 61% Mennockfoot Lodge Hotel, Mennock, SANQUHAR
☎ 01659 50382 & 50477 1 ⇔Annexe8 ⇔ ℮

## SELKIRK                                    Map 12 NT42

**Selkirk** Selkirk Hill TD7 4NW
☎ 01750 22508
Pleasant moorland course set around Selkirk Hill. Unrivalled views.
*9 holes, 5620yds, Par 68, SSS 67, Course record 61.*
*Club membership 364.*
**Visitors** may not play Mon evening, competition/match days.
**Societies** must telephone in advance.
**Green Fees** not confirmed.
**Facilities** ⌂
**Location** 1m S on A7
**Hotel** ★★ 62% Heatherlie House Hotel, Heatherlie Park, SELKIRK
☎ 01750 21200 7rm(6 ℮)

## SHOTTS                                     Map 11 NS86

**Shotts** Blairhead ML7 5BJ ☎ 01501 820431 & 826628
Moorland course.
*18 holes, 6205yds, Par 70, SSS 70, Course record 63.*
*Club membership 500.*
**Visitors** may not play weekends.
**Societies** apply in writing.
**Green Fees** £17 per day.
**Facilities** ⊗ 📶 ⚏ ▬ ⚲ ⌂ ℓ
**Leisure** buggies for hire, trolley for hire, putting green, practice area.
**Location** 2m from M8 off Benhar Road
**Hotel** ★★★ 61% The Hilcroft Hotel, East Main St, WHITBURN ☎ 01501 740818 30 ⇔ ℮

## SKELMORLIE                                 Map 10 NS16

**Skelmorlie** Beithglass PA17 5ES ☎ 01475 520152
Parkland/moorland course with magnificent views over Firth of Clyde. Designed by James Braid, the club celebrated its centenary in 1991. The first five holes are played twice.
*13 holes, 5056yds, Par 64, SSS 65.*
*Club membership 385.*
**Visitors** no visitors before 4pm Sat.
**Societies** apply by telephone.
**Green Fees** £16 per day; £12 per 18 holes (£18/£13 weekends).
**Facilities** ▬ ⚲ ⌂ ⛳
**Leisure** fishing.
**Location** E side of village off A78
**Hotel** ★★★⚑ 63% Manor Park Hotel, LARGS
☎ 01475 520832 10 ⇔ ℮Annexe13 ⇔ ℮

## SOUTHERNESS                                Map 11 NX95

**Southerness** DG2 8AZ ☎ 01387 880677
Natural links, Championship course with panoramic views. Heather and bracken abound.
*18 holes, 6566yds, Par 69, SSS 73, Course record 65.*
*Club membership 830.*
**Visitors** must contact in advance.
**Societies** must contact in advance.
**Green Fees** £25 per day (£35 weekends & bank holidays).
**Facilities** ⊗ 📶 ⚏ ▬ ⚲ ⌂ 🏠
**Leisure** trolley for hire, putting green, practice area.
**Location** 3.5m S of Kirkbean off A710
**Hotel** ★★ 65% Clonyard House Hotel, COLVEND
☎ 01556 630372 15 ⇔ ℮

## STEVENSTON                                 Map 10 NS24

**Ardeer** Greenhead KA20 4JX ☎ 01294 464542
Parkland course with natural hazards.
*18 holes, 6500yds, Par 72, SSS 72, Course record 64.*
*Club membership 560.*
**Visitors** may not play Sat.
**Societies** must contact in advance.
**Green Fees** not confirmed.
**Facilities** ⚲ ⌂ 🏠
**Location** 0.5m N off A78
**Hotel** ★★★⚑ 71% Montgreenan Mansion House Hotel, Montgreenan Estate, KILWINNING
☎ 01294 557733 21 ⇔ ℮

# ROYAL TROON

**TROON** *South Ayrshire* ☎ **01292 311555**    **Map 10 NS33**

*John Ingham writes:* When Jack Nicklaus first played Royal Troon in the 1962 Open, he was 22 and hit the ball a long way. At that time Nicklaus told me 'There are only two holes that I might not reach with my second shot. My favourite shot is the drive, which I hit up to 350 yards. Just before I swing,' he said, 'all my concentration is directed on one thing and that is to give the ball as big a hit - and as square a hit - as I physically can.'

While sheer length from the back tees at Royal Troon is a great advantage, bearing in mind the full course measures 7097 yards, where you hit the ball is more important than how far. The reason is that this championship links-type course is peppered with bunkers not visible from the tee.

That particular Open was won by Arnold Palmer, in those days a longish hitter as well. However, Palmer also had a delightful putting touch, essential for Royal Troon greens, which can prove hard to read.

Royal Troon is one of the finest links in the world and in an American list appears at number 36. Created in 1878, it was then mercifully free of jumbo jets from nearby Prestwick and has provided entertaining and testing golf for players from all over the world. Greg Norman holds the record with a 10-under-par round of 64. A round which put him in a tie for the 1989 Open which he lost to Mark Calcavecchia.

In the 1960s I played a round at this grand links with the late Henry Longhurst, a good club single figure man who had once won the German Amateur championship. To my best drives, lashed in the breeze, he would just hiss 'Wrong line' and, sure enough, when we got up the fairway, the ball would be submerged in soft sand. In fact I'm told there are 365 bunkers, one for every day of the year!

The Marine Higland hotel is on the edge of the course and, as there are 22 other courses in the area, this makes a great place for a holiday.

So great is Royal Troon, in fact, that the Royal and Ancient has announced that the 1997 Open will again be staged there - for the seventh time since 1923!

| | |
|---|---|
| **Visitors** | may not play Wed, Fri, weekends. Must write in advance and have a letter of introduction from own club and a handicap certificate of under 20. Ladies and under 18s may only play on the Portland |
| **Societies** | apply in writing |
| **Green fees** | £90 per day (Portland only £55) inc lunch. |
| **Facilities** | ⊗ ⑪ 🍴 ♥ ♀ 👤 🏠 ⚐ ( (J D Montgomerie) |
| **Location** | Craigend Rd Troon KA10 6EP ( S side of town on B749) |

36 holes. Old Course: 18 holes, 7097yds, Par 73, SSS 74, course record 64 (Greg Norman)
Portland: 18 holes, 6274yds, Par 71, SSS 71

## WHERE TO STAY AND EAT NEARBY

**HOTELS:**
**TROON**
★★★⚜⚜ ♨ 81% Lochgreen House, Monktenhill Rd, Southwood ☎ 01292 313343. 7 ⇋ ♠

★★★★⚜ 65% Marine Highland. ☎ 01292 314444, 72 ⇋ ♠

★★★⚜⚜ 74% Highgrove House ☎ 01292 312511. 9 (2 ♠ 7 ⇋ ♠)

★★★⚜ 66% Piersland House, Craigend Rd. ☎ 01292 314747. 15 (1 ⇋ 14 ⇋ ♠) Annexe 8 ⇋ ♠

**Auchenharvie** Moor Park Rd West KA20 3HU
☎ 01294 603103
Long and flat municipal course with narrow greens and a
pond affecting the 3rd and 12th holes. Easy walking.
*9 holes, 5048yds, Par 65, SSS 65.*

| | |
|---|---|
| Visitors | municipal course 6 day advance booking system. |
| Societies | apply to professional. |
| Green Fees | £3.30 per 9 holes (£5.50 weekends). |
| Facilities | ⊗ ⓛ 🍷 🖢 🚶 🏠 ⚑ 🎖 Bob Rogers. |
| Leisure | trolley for hire, driving range, putting green, practice area. |
| Hotel | ★★★🏅 71% Montgreenan Mansion House Hotel, Montgreenan Estate, KILWINNING ☎ 01294 557733 21 ⇄ 📷 |

## STRANRAER
Map 10 NX06

**Stranraer** Creachmore by Stranraer DG9 0LF
☎ 01776 870245
Parkland course with beautiful view of Lochryan.
*18 holes, 6308yds, Par 70, SSS 71, Course record 66.*
*Club membership 596.*

| | |
|---|---|
| Visitors | must contact in advance. Members times reserved throughout year. |
| Societies | must telephone in advance. |
| Green Fees | £24 per day; £17.50 per round (£30/£23 weekends). |
| Facilities | 🍷 🚶 🏠 |
| Leisure | trolleys, practice area. |
| Location | 2.5m NW on A718 |
| Hotel | ★★★★ 68% North West Castle Hotel, STRANRAER ☎ 01776 704413 71 ⇄ 📷 |

## STRATHAVEN
Map 11 NS64

**Strathaven** Glasgow Rd ML10 6NL ☎ 01357 520421
Gently undulating, tree-lined, Championship parkland course
with panoramic views over town and Avon valley.
*18 holes, 6224yds, Par 71, SSS 71, Course record 63.*
*Club membership 950.*

| | |
|---|---|
| Visitors | welcome weekdays up to 4pm only. Must contact in advance. |
| Societies | apply in writing to general manager. |
| Green Fees | £30 per day; £20 per round. |
| Facilities | ⊗ 🍴 ⓛ 🍷 🖢 🚶 🏠 🎖 Matt McCrorie. |
| Leisure | trolley for hire, putting green, practice area. |
| Location | NE side of town on A726 |
| Hotel | ★★★ 66% Strathaven Hotel, Hamilton Rd, STRATHAVEN ☎ 01357 521778 10 ⇄ 📷 |

## THORNHILL
Map 11 NX89

**Thornhill** Blacknest DG3 5DW
☎ 01848 330546 & 331779
Moorland/parkland course with fine views.
*18 holes, 6011yds, Par 71, SSS 70.*
*Club membership 700.*

| | |
|---|---|
| Visitors | apply in advance, restricted competition days. |
| Societies | apply in writing. |
| Green Fees | £18 per day (£22 weekends & bank holidays). |
| Facilities | ⊗ 🍴 ⓛ 🍷 🖢 🚶 |
| Leisure | trolley for hire, putting green, practice area. |
| Location | 1m E of town off A92 |
| Hotel | ★★ 72% Trigony House Hotel, Closeburn, THORNHILL ☎ 01848 331211 8 ⇄ 📷 |

## TROON
Map 10 NS33

**ROYAL TROON** See page 325

**Troon Municipal** Harling Dr KA10 6NE
☎ 01292 312464
Three links courses, two Championship.
*Lochgreen Course: 18 holes, 6785yds, Par 74, SSS 73.*
*Darley Course: 18 holes, 6501yds, Par 71, SSS 71.*
*Fullarton Course: 18 holes, 4822yds, Par 64, SSS 63.*
*Club membership 3000.*

| | |
|---|---|
| Visitors | no restrictions. |
| Societies | apply in writing. |
| Green Fees | not confirmed. |
| Facilities | 🍷 🚶 🏠 🎖 Gordon McKinley. |
| Leisure | putting, trolley hire, practice area. |
| Location | 100yds from railway station |
| Hotel | ★★ 62% Craiglea Hotel, South Beach, TROON ☎ 01292 311366 20rm(10 ⇄ 📷) |

## TURNBERRY
Map 10 NS20

**TURNBERRY HOTEL GOLF COURSES** See page 327

## UDDINGSTON
Map 11 NS66

**Calderbraes** 57 Roundknowe Rd G71 7TS
☎ 01698 813425
Parkland course with good view of Clyde Valley. Testing 4th
hole (par 4), hard uphill.
*9 holes, 5046yds, Par 66, SSS 67, Course record 65.*
*Club membership 230.*

| | |
|---|---|
| Visitors | weekdays before 5pm. |
| Societies | welcome. |
| Green Fees | not confirmed. |
| Facilities | 🍷 🚶 |
| Leisure | putting green, practice area. |
| Location | 1.5m NW off A74 |
| Hotel | ★★ 67% Redstones Hotel, 8-10 Glasgow Rd, UDDINGSTON ☎ 01698 813774 & 814843 18rm(16 ⇄ 📷) |

## UPLAWMOOR
Map 10 NS45

**Caldwell** G78 4AU
☎ 01505 850366 (Secretary) & 850616 (Pro)
Parkland course.
*18 holes, 6294yds, Par 71, SSS 70, Course record 63.*
*Club membership 600.*

| | |
|---|---|
| Visitors | must be with member at weekends & bank holidays. Must contact professional in advance. |
| Societies | writing to professional. |
| Green Fees | £28 per day; £20 per round. |
| Facilities | ⊗ 🍴 ⓛ 🍷 🖢 🚶 🏠 🎖 Stephen Forbes. |
| Leisure | trolley for hire, putting green, practice area. |
| Location | 0.5m SW A736 |
| Hotel | ★★★ 60% Dalmeny Park Country House, Lochlibo Rd, BARRHEAD ☎ 0141 881 9211 19 ⇄ 📷 |

# TURNBERRY HOTEL GOLF COURSES

**TURNBERRY** *South Ayrshire*

☎ **01655 331000**                    **Map 10 NS20**

*John Ingham writes:* The hotel is sumptuous, the Ailsa and Arran courses beneath it are total magic. The air reaches down into your inner lung and of all places in Scotland, Turnberry has to be among the finest.

Tunberry is delightfully off the beaten track and, although the courses are principally for residents of the hotel, if you wish to fly in, then Prestwick Airport is only seventeen miles from the first tee. What makes the place so desirable is the warmness of the welcome and, course professional Brian Gunson will tell you, this is literally so on occasions, as the links is on the friendliest of gulf streams.

The Ailsa course has been the venue for the Open in 1977 and 1986 and hosted it again in 1994. It was here in the 1977 Open, that Jack Nicklaus put up such a brave fight against Tom Watson. Then, in 1986, we had a wondrous victory from Greg Norman. He has fond memories of Turnberry, where a few hours after the prize-giving he was able to sit with his wife on the edge of the great links, drinking champagne, and watching the moon roll round the pure white lighthouse out by the 9th green.

Without any doubt, Turnberry is the stuff of dreams and you must go there if you possibly can.

| | |
|---|---|
| **Visitors** | The golf courses are principally for residents of the hotel, so must contact in advance |
| **Societies** | contact in advance as courses are for residents of the hotel |
| **Green fees** | Arran £30, Ailsa £60 fees include a round on Arran if played on same day |
| **Facilities** | ⊗ ⍟ ⮭ ⬚ ⚲ 🛏 ⛳ 🖼 ⚲ ⟍ ⛳ (Brian Gunson) practice area, putting green, trollies |
| **Leisure** | tennis (hardcourt), swimming pool, squash, snooker, health spa |
| **Location** | Turnberry KA26 9LT. On A719 N side of village |

**36 holes. Ailsa Course: 18 holes, 6440 yds, Par 69, SSS 72, Course record 63 (Greg Norman & Maric Hayes) Arran Course: 18 holes, 6014yds, Par 68, SSS 69. Course record 65 (E Macintosh/C Ronald/S McGregor)**

## WHERE TO STAY AND EAT NEARBY

**HOTELS:**

**MAYBOLE**
★★(Red)⚜ ♨ Ladyburn
☎ 01655 740585. 8(7 ⇥ ⋔)

**TURNBERRY**
★★★★★(Red) ❀❀ Turnberry Hotel, Golf Courses & Spa.
☎ 01655 331000. 132 ⇥ ⋔

★★★ ❀ 73%Malin Court.
☎ 01655 31457. 17 ⇥ ⋔

327

## WEST KILBRIDE

Map 10 NS24

**West Kilbride** 33-35 Fullerton Dr, Seamill KA23 9NQ
☎ 01294 823911
Seaside links course on Firth of Clyde, with fine views of Isle of Arran from every hole.
*18 holes, 5974yds, Par 70, SSS 70, Course record 63.*
*Club membership 840.*
**Visitors** may not play at weekends, must contact in advance.
**Societies** Tue & Thu only; must contact in advance.
**Green Fees** £35 per day; £21 per round.
**Facilities** ⊗ ⅶ ⅃ ♥ ♀ ⅄ ⅋ ⅌ Gregor Howie.
**Leisure** trolley for hire, driving range, putting green, practice area.
**Location** W side of town off A78
**Hotel** ★★ 69% Elderslie Hotel, John St, Broomfields, LARGS
☎ 01475 686460 26rm(9 ⇄5 ↾)

## WEST LINTON

Map 11 NT15

**West Linton** EH46 7HN
☎ 01968 660256 & 660970
Moorland course with beautiful views of Pentland Hills.
*18 holes, 6132yds, Par 69, SSS 70, Course record 63.*
*Club membership 725.*
**Visitors** weekdays anytime, weekends not before 1pm.
**Societies** contact the secretary in writing.
**Green Fees** £24 per day; £16 per round (£25 per round weekends). Five day ticket (Mon-Fri) £75.
**Facilities** ⊗ ⅶ ⅃ ♥ ♀ ⅄ ⅋ ⅌ Ian Wright.
**Leisure** motorised carts for hire, trolley for hire, putting green, practice area.
**Location** NW side of village off A702
**Hotel** ★★★ 71% Peebles Hydro Hotel, PEEBLES
☎ 01721 720602 137 ⇄ ↾

## WIGTOWN

Map 10 NX45

**Wigtown & Bladnoch** Lightlands Ter DG8 9EF
☎ 01988 403354 & 403209
Slightly hilly parkland course with fine views over Wigtown Bay to Galloway Hills.
*9 holes, 5462yds, Par 68, SSS 67, Course record 62.*
*Club membership 150.*
**Visitors** advisable to contact in advance for weekend play.
**Societies** contact secretary in advance.
**Green Fees** £15 per day; £10 per round.
**Facilities** ⊗ ⅃ ♥ ♀ ⅄
**Leisure** putting green, practice area.
**Location** SW on A714
**Hotel** ★★ 67% Creebridge House Hotel, NEWTON STEWART
☎ 01671 402121 20 ⇄ ↾

## WISHAW

Map 11 NS75

**Wishaw** 55 Cleland Rd ML2 7PH ☎ 01698 372869
Parkland course with many tree-lined areas. Bunkers protect 17 of the 18 greens.
*18 holes, 6073yds, Par 69, SSS 69, Course record 64.*
*Club membership 940.*
**Visitors** may not play Sat.
**Societies** apply in writing.
**Green Fees** £20 per day; £12 per round (Sun £25 per day/round).
**Facilities** ⊗ ⅶ ⅃ ♥ ♀ ⅄ ⅋ ⅌ John Campbell.
**Leisure** motorised carts for hire, buggies for hire, trolley for hire, putting green, practice area.
**Location** NW side of town off A721
**Hotel** ★★★ 66% Popinjay Hotel, Lanark Rd, ROSEBANK
☎ 01555 860441 36 ⇄ ↾Annexe5 ⇄ ↾

## GOLFING BREAKS IN SCOTLAND. PAR EXCELLENCE.

Enjoy the beauty of Scotland and guaranteed tee-off times at some of Scotland's finest golf courses. Centred around ten of our top grade hotels, our Golfing Breaks are the ideal way to spend 3, 5 or 7 days away on an inclusive package.

*Prices including Dinner, Bed and Breakfast, start at £195 for a 3 night "Hole in One" break, to £495 for the "Par Excellence" 7 night break with discounted rates for non-golfers.*

FOR BROCHURES AND FURTHER INFORMATION CONTACT
Golfing Co-Ordinator, Scottish Golfing Breaks,
Hospitality Inn, 46 Annick Road, Irvine, KA11 4LD.
Telephone: 01294 274272 Fax: 01294 277287

## THISTLE HOTELS
AND
MOUNT CHARLOTTE HOTELS

# WALES

*'Dai was a Welsh winner; so is every visitor'*

D ai Rees once told me to hit down on the ball, and get the hands 'here' to drive shots low into the wind. For me this advice led to a powerful hook! But he knew the secrets for sure because Welshman Dai led the British Ryder Cup team to that 1957 victory, and collected titles all over the world. Ian Woosnam is, without doubt, the great modern-day 'Taffie' and could pocket our premier title soon to add to his US Masters. So Wales, you see, can produce stars other than rugby players.

Wales can be proud, too, about certain excellent courses. Sometimes wild and exposed, they provide a wholesome day out for us, and a friendly welcome to 'foreigners' from over the border. Some of the great tests started in a humble way. During the last century, for instance, a fellow called Tony Ruck collected flower pots from a lady in the village, sank them into fairly basic greens and created the Aberdovey course in Merioneth, at the mouth of the Dovey estuary.

To return to Dai Rees, he won the PGA Close Championship at Ashburnham (Burry Port) in 1959 and when I went there to see him win, I found the holes near the clubhouse not too impressive.Further out the course shows itself in great colours. Well worth a trip back, we decided.

### PORTHCAWL RATED TOP

It's pointless to say which is the best course in Wales. We tend to judge this on how we played, and whether we won! But Royal Porthcawl (near Bridgend) is a top rated course by our American researchers. I love the place, and not just because you can have a view of the sea from every single hole. Go there, but with an introduction from someone significant.

In 1893, an Honourable Finch-Hatton, just back from Australia, was showing chums the boomerang on the Morfa, a low-lying piece of land beneath the famous castle at Harlech. Great place for golf, thought Finch-Hatton and thus the splendid St David's course was created. Edward VII became club patron and the Duke of Windsor was captain in 1935. St David's welcomes everyone, even into the clubhouse and no travel agents have set money-making traps. Try it.

The St Pierre clubhouse, just across the Severn Bridge, is as ancient as the country. It is a fine, lush parkland course with a large lake and magnificent trees. Why haven't we mentioned Southerndown (Bridgend). Downland, above the sea with views across the Bristol Channel, and if you look over there, that is the direction to Ireland...... where yet another golf feast awaits.

# WALES

The directory which follows has been divided into three geographical regions. Counties have not been shown against individual locations as recent legislation has created a number of smaller counties which will be unfamiliar to the visitor. The postal authorities have confirmed that it is no longer necessary to include a county name in addresses, provided a post code is shown. All locations appear in the atlas at the end of this guide in their appropriate counties.

## NORTH WALES

This region includes the counties of Aberconwy & Colwyn, Anglesey, Denbighshire, Flintshire, Gwynedd and Wrexham which reflect the recent national changes.

### ABERDOVEY (ABERDYFI)          Map 06 SN69

**Aberdovey** LL35 0RT ☎ 01654 767493
A beautiful championship course at the mouth of the Dovey estuary, Aberdovey has all the true characteristics of a seaside links. It has some fine holes among them the 3rd, the 12th, an especially good short hole, and the 15th. There are some striking views to be had from the course.
*18 holes, 6445yds, Par 71, SSS 71, Course record 66.*
*Club membership 1000.*
**Visitors** must contact in advance, restrictions at weekends.
**Societies** prior arrangement essential.
**Green Fees** £34 per day; £22 per round (£40/£27 weekends).
**Facilities** ⊗ ⅲ ⅃ ♭ ☕ ♀ ☖ ☎ ℓ John Davies.
**Leisure** motorised carts for hire, buggies for hire, trolley for hire, putting green, practice area.
**Location** 0.5m W on A493
**Hotel** ★★★ 69% Trefeddian Hotel, ABERDOVEY ☎ 01654 767213 46 ⇋ ℝ

### ABERGELE          Map 06 SH97

**Abergele & Pensarn** Tan-y-Gopa Rd LL22 8DS
☎ 01745 824034
A beautiful parkland course with views of the Irish Sea and Gwyrch Castle. There are splendid finishing holes, a testing par 5, 16th; a 185 yd, 17th to an elevated green, and a superb par 5 18th with out of bounds just behind the green.
*18 holes, 6520yds, Par 72, SSS 71, Course record 66.*
*Club membership 1250.*
**Visitors** must contact in advance. Limited play weekends.

**Societies** must contact in advance.
**Green Fees** £22 per day (£28 weekends & bank holidays).
**Facilities** ⊗ ⅲ ⅃ ♭ ☕ ♀ ☖ ☎ ℓ Iain R Runcie.
**Leisure** trolley for hire, putting green, practice area.
**Location** 0.5m W off A547/A55
**Hotel** ★★★ 63% Kinmel Manor Hotel, St Georges Rd, ABERGELE ☎ 01745 832014 42 ⇋ ℝ
**Additional hotel** ★★★ 60% Colwyn Bay Hotel, Penmaenhead, COLWYN BAY ☎ 01492 516555 43 ⇋ ℝ

### ABERSOCH          Map 06 SH32

**Abersoch** LL53 7EY ☎ 01758 712622
Seaside links, with five parkland holes.
*18 holes, 5819yds, Par 69, SSS 68.*
*Club membership 650.*
**Visitors** must contact in advance. Competition days Sun & Thu.
**Societies** must apply in advance.
**Green Fees** £18 per day (£20 weekends).
**Facilities** ⊗ ⅲ ⅃ ♭ ☕ ♀ ☖ ☎ ℓ A D Jones.
**Leisure** trolley for hire, driving range.
**Location** S side of village
**Hotel** ★★★ 64% Abersoch Harbour Hotel, ABERSOCH ☎ 01758 712406 9 ⇋ ℝAnnexe5 ⇋ ℝ

### ANGLESEY, ISLE OF          Map 06

*Golf Courses on the island of Anglesey are listed below.*

### AMLWCH          Map 06 SH49

**Bull Bay** LL68 9RY ☎ 01407 830960
Wales's northernmost course,Bull Bay is a pleasant coastal, heathland course with natural meadow, rock, gorse and wind hazards. Views from all tees across Irish Sea to Isle of Man.
*18 holes, 6217yds, Par 70, SSS 70, Course record 65.*
*Club membership 825.*
**Visitors** advisable to contact in advance.
**Societies** advance booking essential.
**Green Fees** £20 per day; £15 per round (£25/£20 Fri & weekends). Winter £13/£10 (£16/£13 Fri & weekends).
**Facilities** ⊗ ⅲ ⅃ ♭ ☕ ♀ ☖ ☎ ⅋ ℓ
**Leisure** trolley for hire, putting green, practice area, snooker.
**Location** 1m W on A5025
**Hotel** ★★ 60% Trecastell Hotel, Bull Bay, AMLWCH ☎ 01407 830651 12rm(8 ⇋3 ℝ)

### BEAUMARIS          Map 06 SH67

**Baron Hill** LL58 8YW ☎ 01248 810231
Undulating course with natural hazards of rock and gorse. Testing 3rd and 4th holes (par 4's). Nole 5/14 plays into the prevailing wind with an elevated tee across two streams. The hole is between two gorse covered mounds.
*9 holes, 5062mtrs, Par 68, SSS 69, Course record 62.*
*Club membership 400.*
**Visitors** ladies have priority on Tue & club competitions Sun.
**Societies** apply in writing to secretary.
**Green Fees** £14 per day, £40 weekly.

**Facilities** ⊗ ⫟ ⓛ ▬ ♀ ⅄
**Location** 1m SW off A545
**Hotel** ★★ 70% Bishopsgate House Hotel, 54 Castle
St, BEAUMARIS
☎ 01248 810302 9 ⇆ ⋔ Annexe2rm

## HOLYHEAD                 Map 06 SH28

**Holyhead** Lon Garreg Fawr, Trearddur Bay LL65 2YG
☎ 01407 763279
Treeless, undulating seaside course which provides a
varied and testing game, particularly in a south wind. The
fairways are bordered by gorse, heather and rugged
outcrops of rock. Accuracy from most tees is paramount
as there are 43 fairway and greenside bunkers and lakes.
Designed by James Braid. Indoor driving range.
*18 holes, 6058yds, Par 70, SSS 70, Course record 64.*
*Club membership 1000.*
**Visitors** must contact in advance.
**Societies** must contact in advance.
**Green Fees** £20 per day; £15 per round (£25/£20
weekends & bank holidays).
**Facilities** ⊗ ⫟ ⓛ ▬ ♀ ⅄ ⌂ ⅌ ⋈ ⋔ Stephen Elliot.
**Leisure** trolley for hire, covered driving range,
putting green, practice area.
**Location** 1.25m S on B4545
**Hotel** ★★★ 71% Trearddur Bay Hotel,
TREARDDUR BAY
☎ 01407 860301 31 ⇆ ⋔

## LLANGEFNI                Map 06 SH47

*Llangefni (Public)* LL77 7LJ
☎ 01248 722193
Picturesque parkland course designed by Hawtree & Son.
*9 holes, 1342yds, Par 28, SSS 28.*
**Visitors** no restrictions.
**Societies** must contact in advance.
**Facilities** ⅄ ⌂ ⅌ ⋔
**Location** 1.5m off A5
**Hotel** ★★★(red) Tre-Ysgawen Hall, Capel Coch,
LLANGEFNI
☎ 01248 750750 19 ⇆ ⋔

## RHOSNEIGR              Map 06 SH37

*Anglesey* Station Rd LL64 5QX
☎ 01407 811202
Links course, low and fairly level with sand dunes and tidal
river.
*18 holes, 6300yds, Par 68, SSS 68.*
*Club membership 400.*
**Visitors** phone in advance, some times are reserved for
members.
**Societies** telephone & confirm in writing.
**Green Fees** not confirmed.
**Facilities** ♀ ⅄ ⌂ ⋔ Mark Harrison.
**Leisure** putting green, trolley hire, practice area.
**Location** NE side of village on A4080
**Hotel** ★★★ 71% Trearddur Bay Hotel,
TREARDDUR BAY
☎ 01407 860301 31 ⇆ ⋔

## BALA                      Map 06 SH93

**Bala** Penlan LL23 7YD ☎ 01678 520359 & 521361
Mountainous course with natural hazards. All holes except
first and last affected by wind.
*10 holes, 4962yds, Par 66, SSS 64, Course record 64.*
*Club membership 200.*
**Visitors** book in advance.
**Societies** must contact in advance.
**Green Fees** £12 per day (£15 weekends & bank holidays).
**Facilities** ⊗ by prior arrangement ⫟ by prior arrangement
ⓛ by prior arrangement ▬ by prior arrangement
♀ ⅄ ⌂ ⋔
**Leisure** trolley for hire, putting green, practice area,
snooker, pool.
**Location** 0.5m SW off A494
**Hotel** ★★ 63% Plas Coch Hotel, High St, BALA
☎ 01678 520309 10 ⇆ ⋔

## BANGOR                  Map 06 SH57

**St Deiniol** Penybryn LL57 1PX ☎ 01492 353098
Elevated parkland course with panoramic views of
Snowdonia, Menai Straits, and Anglesey.
*18 holes, 5068mtrs, Par 68, SSS 67, Course record 61.*
*Club membership 700.*
**Visitors** must contact in advance.
**Societies** must contact in advance.
**Green Fees** £12 per week (£16 weekends).
**Facilities** ⊗ by prior arrangement ⫟ by prior arrangement
ⓛ ▬ ♀ ⅄ ⌂ ⋔
**Leisure** trolley for hire, putting green.
**Location** E side of town centre off A5122
**Hotel** ★★★ 68% Menai Court Hotel, Craig y Don Rd,
BANGOR ☎ 01248 354200 13 ⇆ ⋔

## BETWS-Y-COED         Map 06 SH75

*Betws-y-Coed* LL24 0AL ☎ 01690 710556
Attractive flat meadowland course set between two rivers in
Snowdonia National Park.
*9 holes, 4996yds, Par 64, SSS 64.*
*Club membership 350.*
**Visitors** no restrictions.
**Societies** must telephone in advance.
**Green Fees** not confirmed.
**Facilities** ♀ ⅄
**Location** NE side of village off A5
**Hotel** ★★★ 69% The Royal Oak Hotel, Holyhead Rd,
BETWS-Y-COED ☎ 01690 710219 27 ⇆ ⋔

## BODELWYDDAN        Map 06 SJ07

**Kinmel Park** LL18 5SR ☎ 01745 833548
Flat parkland pay and play course that is suitable for
beginners.
*9 holes, 3100, Par 58, SSS 58.*
**Visitors** no restrictions.
**Societies** telephone for details.
**Green Fees** £3 for 18 holes.
**Facilities** ⊗ ⓛ ▬ ♀ ⅄ ⋔ ⋔ Peter Stebbings.
**Leisure** driving range.
**Hotel** ★★★ 64% Oriel House Hotel, Upper Denbigh
Rd, ST ASAPH ☎ 01745 582716 19 ⇆ ⋔

## BRYNFORD
Map 07 SJ17

**Holywell** Brynford CH8 8LQ ☎ ℓ 01352 713937 & 710040
Exposed moorland course, with bracken and gorse flanking
undulating fairways. 720 ft above sea level.
*18 holes, 6100yds, Par 70, SSS 70, Course record 69.*
*Club membership 505.*
**Visitors**    must contact in advance.
**Societies**   by prior arrangement with the secretary.
**Green Fees**  £15 per round (£20 weekends & bank holidays).
**Facilities**  ⊗ ⅲ ⅃ ⬛ ♀ ⌷ ⌸ ℓ Saen O'Conner.
**Leisure**     trolley for hire, putting green, practice area.
**Location**    1.25m SW off B5121
**Hotel**       ★★ 67% Stamford Gate Hotel, Halkyn Rd,
                HOLYWELL ☎ 01352 712942 12 ⇄ ℝ

## CAERNARFON
Map 06 SH46

**Caernarfon** Llanfaglan LL54 5RP
☎ 01286 673783 & 678359
Parkland course with gentle gradients.
*18 holes, 5891yds, Par 69, SSS 68.*
*Club membership 730.*
**Visitors**    must contact in advance.
**Societies**   must apply in advance.
**Green Fees**  £18 per day; £15 per round (£22/£20 weekends
                & bank holidays).
**Facilities**  ⊗ ⅲ ⅃ ⬛ ♀ ⌷ ⌸ ℓ Aled Owen.
**Leisure**     motorised carts for hire, buggies for hire, trolley
                for hire, putting green, practice area.
**Location**    1.75m SW
**Hotel**       ★★ 63% Stables Hotel, LLANWNDA
                ☎ 01286 830711 & 830935 Annexe14 ⇄ ℝ

## CAERWYS
Map 06 SJ17

**Caerwys Nine Of Clubs** CH7 5AQ ☎ 01352 720692
Following the natural contours of the land and with a south-
west aspect, this course could be considered a litle gem. Each
approach to every green is different and there are many
interesting and challenging holes.
*9 holes, 3080yds, Par 60, Course record 61.*
*Club membership 150.*
**Visitors**    no restrictions.
**Societies**   telephone then confirm in writing.
**Green Fees**  £8.50 per day; £4.50 per 18 holes (£10.50/£5.50
                weekends & bank holidays).
**Facilities**  ⊗ ⅃ ⌷ ⌸ ⌶
**Leisure**     trolley for hire, putting green, practice area,
                snooker.
**Location**    1.5m SW of A55, midway between St Asaph
                and Holywell
**Hotel**       ★★ 65% Bryn Awel Hotel, Denbigh Rd, MOLD
                ☎ 01352 758622 7 ⇄ ℝAnnexe10 ⇄ ℝ

## CHIRK
Map 07 SJ23

**Chirk Golf & Country Club** LL14 5AD ☎ 01691 774407
Overlooked by the National Trust's Chirk Castle, is a
championship-standard 18-hole course with a 664 yard, par 5
at the 9th - one of the longest in Europe. Also a 9-hole course,
driving range and golf academy.
*Manor Course: 18 holes, 7045yds, Par 72, SSS 73, Course
record 72.*
*Mine Rock: 9 holes, 1141yds, Par 27.*
*Club membership 750.*
**Visitors**    advisable to contact in advance. May not play in
                members preferred tee times 7-11 daily.
**Societies**   must telephone for provisonal booking.
**Green Fees**  £22 per day; £15 per round (£28/£22 weekends).
                9 holes: £4 per round (£5 weekends).
**Facilities**  ⊗ ⅲ ⅃ ⬛ ♀ ⌷ ⌸ ⌶ ℓ James Waugh.
**Leisure**     squash, fishing, buggies for hire, trolley for hire,
                driving range, putting green, practice area, clay
                pigeon shotingby arrangement.
**Location**    5m N of Oswestry
**Hotel**       ★★★ 67% Hand Hotel, Church St, CHIRK
                ☎ 01691 772479 14 ⇄ ℝ

## COLWYN BAY
Map 06 SH87

**Old Colwyn** Woodland Av, Old Colwyn LL29 9NL
☎ 01492 515581
Hilly, meadowland course with sheep and cattle grazing on it
in parts.
*9 holes, 5243yds, Par 68, SSS 66, Course record 63.*
*Club membership 267.*
**Visitors**    welcome ex Sat. Contact in advance.
**Societies**   must contact in advance.
**Green Fees**  £10 per day (£15 weekends and bank holidays).
                May-Sep 9 holes after 7pm £5.
**Facilities**  ♀ (weekends/evenings) ⌷
**Leisure**     practice area.
**Location**    E side of town centre on B5383
**Hotel**       ★★★ 64% Hopeside Hotel, Princes Dr, West
                End, COLWYN BAY
                ☎ 01492 533244 19 ⇄ ℝ

**★★★**
**THE**
**COLWYN**
**BAY**
**HOTEL**

*Penmaenhead*
*Old Colwyn*
*Colwyn Bay*
*Clwyd LL29 9LD*
*Tel: 01492 516555*
*Fax: 01492 515565*
*Previously called Hotel 70°*

Occupying an enviable position commanding panoramic
views of the Irish Sea, Colwyn Bay and the dramatic
mountains of Snowdonia.
This splendid modern Hotel offers a very high standard of
comfort, service and luxury through-out. All bedrooms en
suite with full facilities and sea views.
Elegant restaurants serving excellent cuisine in superb
surroundings.
Ideally located for touring Snowdonia National Park and
Conwy. Numerous golf courses nearby for the discerning
golf enthusiast.
Excellent conference and banqueting facilities available
for up to 200 persons.

## CONWY

Map 06 SH77

**Conwy (Caernarvonshire)** Beacons Way, Morfa
LL32 8ER ☎ 01492 592423
Founded in 1890, Conwy has hosted national and
international championships since 1898. Set among
sandhills, possessing true links greens and a profusion of
gorse on the latter holes, especially the 16th, 17th and
18th. This course provides the visitor with real golfing
enjoyment against a background of stunning beauty.
*18 holes, 6647yds, Par 72, SSS 72, Course record 69.*
*Club membership 1050.*
**Visitors** must contact secretary in advance.
**Societies** must contact in advance.
**Green Fees** £23 per day (£28 weekends & bank
holidays).
**Facilities** ⊗ ⅢⓁ ♨ ♀ ♨ 🏠 🐾 ⓕ Peter Lees.
**Leisure** motorised carts for hire, buggies for hire,
trolley for hire, putting green, practice area.
**Location** 1m W of town centre on A55
**Hotel** ★★★ 58% Sychnant Pass Hotel, Sychnant
Pass Rd, CONWY
☎ 01492 596868 10 ➪ ⋔

## CRICCIETH

Map 06 SH43

**Criccieth** Ednyfed Hill LL52 0PH ☎ 01766 522154
Hilly course on Lleyn Peninsula. Good views.
*18 holes, 5787yds, Par 69, SSS 68.*
*Club membership 350.*
**Visitors** must contact in advance.
**Societies** telephone in advance.
**Green Fees** £12 per day Mon-Sat (£15 Sun and bank
holidays).
**Facilities** ⊗ Ⅲ Ⓛ ♨ ♀ ♨ 🏠
**Leisure** trolley for hire, putting green.
**Location** 1m NE
**Hotel** ★★★⚤ 70% Bron Eifion Country House
Hotel, CRICCIETH ☎ 01766 522385 19 ➪ ⋔

## DENBIGH

Map 06 SJ06

*Bryn Morfydd Hotel* Llanrhaedr LL16 4NP
☎ 01745 890280
In a beautiful setting in the Vale of Clwyd, the original 9-hole
Duchess course was designed by Peter Alliss in 1982. In
1992, the 18-hole Dukes course was completed: a parkland
course designed to encourage use of finesse in play.
*Dukes Course: 18 holes, 5650yds, Par 70, SSS 67.*
*Duchess Course: 9 holes, 2098yds, Par 54.*
*Club membership 450.*
**Visitors** advance reservation advisable.
**Societies** apply in writing.
**Green Fees** not confirmed.
**Facilities** ♀ ♨ 🏠 🐾 🖾
**Leisure** heated outdoor swimming pool, putting green,
practice area, trolley hire.
**Location** On A525 between Denbigh and Ruthin

**Denbigh** Henllan Rd LL16 5AA ☎ 01745 814159
Parkland course, giving a testing and varied game. Good
views.
*18 holes, 5712yds, Par 69, SSS 68, Course record 64.*
*Club membership 725.*

**Visitors** must contact in advance.
**Societies** apply in writing.
**Green Fees** £19 per day (£25 Sun, round only Sat).
**Facilities** ⊗ Ⅲ Ⓛ ♨ ♀ ♨ 🏠 ⓕ Mike Jones.
**Leisure** trolley for hire, putting green, practice area.
**Location** 1.5m NW on B5382
**Hotel** ★★★ 65% Talardy Park Hotel, The Roe,
ST ASAPH
☎ 01745 584957 18 ➪ ⋔

## DOLGELLAU

Map 06 SH71

**Dolgellau** Pencefn Rd LL40 2ES
☎ 01341 422603
Undulating parkland course. Good views of mountains and
Mawddach estuary.
*9 holes, 4671yds, Par 66, SSS 63, Course record 62.*
*Club membership 280.*
**Visitors** may not play on Sat.
**Societies** must contact in advance.
**Green Fees** £13 (£16 weekends & bank holidays).
**Facilities** ⊗ Ⅲ Ⓛ ♨ ♀ ♨
**Location** 0.5m N
**Hotel** ★★ 64% Royal Ship Hotel, Queens Square,
DOLGELLAU
☎ 01341 422209 24rm(18 ➪ ⋔)

## EYTON

Map 07 SJ34

**Plassey** LL13 0SP
☎ 01978 780028
Plesant 9-hole course set in naturally contoured parkland with
water hazards. It is within Plassey Leisure Park and Craft
Centre and all park facilities are available to golfers.
*9 holes, 2300yds.*
*Club membership 200.*
**Visitors** must contact in advance,
**Societies** telephone then confirm in writing.
**Green Fees** £5 (£6 weekends & bank holidays).
**Facilities** ⊗ Ⅲ Ⓛ ♨ ♀ ♨ 🏠 🐾 ⓕ Richard Hughes.
**Leisure** heated indoor swimming pool, fishing, sauna,
solarium, trolley for hire, putting green, practice
area.
**Location** 2.5m off A483 Chester/Oswestry
**Hotel** ★★ 65% Cross Lanes Hotel & Restaurant,
Cross Lanes, Bangor Rd, MARCHWIEL
☎ 01978 780555 16 ➪ ⋔

## FFESTINIOG

Map 06 SH74

*Ffestiniog* Y Cefn LL41 4LS
☎ 01766 762637
Moorland course set in Snowdonia National Park.
*9 holes, 4570yds, Par 68, SSS 66.*
*Club membership 150.*
**Visitors** welcome except during competitions.
**Societies** must telephone in advance.
**Green Fees** not confirmed.
**Facilities** ♨
**Location** 1m E on B4391
**Hotel** ★★(red)⚤ Maes y Neuadd Hotel,
TALSARNAU
☎ 01766 780200 12 ➪ ⋔Annexe4 ➪ ⋔

## FLINT                                           Map 07 SJ27

**Flint** Cornist Park CH6 5HJ ☎ 01352 732327 & 812974
Parkland course incorporating woods and streams. Excellent
views of Dee estuary.
*9 holes, 6984yds, Par 69, SSS 69, Course record 65.*
*Club membership 260.*
**Visitors**    must contact in advance.
**Societies**   not weekends.
**Green Fees** £10 per round.
**Facilities**  ⊗ ⅏ ⅊ 👤 ⚑ ♀ ⛳
**Leisure**     hard tennis courts, practice area.
**Location**    1m W
**Hotel**       ★★ 67%  Stamford Gate Hotel, Halkyn Rd,
                HOLYWELL ☎ 01352 712942 12 ⇋ ♘

## HARLECH                                         Map 06 SH53

**Royal St Davids** LL46 2UB ☎ 01766 780361
Championship links, with easy walking and natural
hazards.
*18 holes, 6427yds, Par 69, SSS 72.*
*Club membership 700.*
**Visitors**    pre booking essential, must hold current
                handicap certificate.
**Societies**   telephone secretary in advance. Handicap
                certificates required.
**Green Fees** £26 per day (£32 weekends & bank
                holidays).
**Facilities**  ⊗ ⅏ ⅊ 👤 ⚑ ♀ ⛳ ☖ ♘ John Barnett.
**Leisure**     motorised carts for hire, buggies for hire,
                trolley for hire, putting green, practice area.
**Location**    W side of town on A496
**Hotel**       ★★ 64%  Ty Mawr Hotel, LLANBEDR
                ☎ 01341 241440 10 ⇋ ♘

## HAWARDEN                                        Map 07 SJ36

**Hawarden** Groomsdale Ln CH5 3EH
☎ 01244 531447 & 520809
Parkland course with comfortable walking and good views.
*18 holes, 5842yds, Par 69, SSS 69.*
*Club membership 550.*
**Visitors**    arrange visit with the professional.
**Societies**   by prior arrangement.
**Green Fees** £12 (£15 weekends).
**Facilities**  ⊗ ⅏ ⅊ 👤 ⚑ ♀ ⛳ ☖ ♘ Chris Hope.
**Leisure**     putting green, practice area.
**Location**    W side of town off B5125
**Hotel**       ★★★ 72%  The Gateway To Wales Hotel,
                Welsh Rd, Sealand, Deeside, CHESTER
                ☎ 01244 830332 39 ⇋ ♘

## LLANDUDNO                                       Map 06 SH78

**Llandudno (Maesdu)** Hospital Rd LL30 1HU
☎ 01492 876450
Part links, part parkland, this championship course starts
and finishes on one side of the main road, the remaining
holes, more seaside in nature, being played on the other
side. The holes are pleasantly undulating and present a
pretty picture when the gorse is in bloom. Often windy,
this varied and testing course is not for beginners.
*18 holes, 6545yds, Par 72, SSS 72, Course record 66.*
*Club membership 1045.*
**Visitors**    must book in advance.
**Societies**   must apply in advance to secretary.
**Green Fees** £22 per day (£30 weekends & bank
                holidays). £16 per round after 3pm (£20
                weekends & bank holidays).
**Facilities**  ⊗ ⅏ ⅊ 👤 ⚑ ♀ ⛳ ☖ ♘ Simon Boulden.
**Leisure**     motorised carts for hire, buggies for hire,
                trolley for hire, putting green, practice area.
**Location**    S side of town centre on A546
**Hotel**       ★★★ 67%  Imperial Hotel, The Promenade,
                LLANDUDNO
                ☎ 01492 877466 100 ⇋ ♘
**Additional**  ★★ 60%  Esplanade Hotel, Glan-y-Mor
**hotel**       Pde, Promenade, LLANDUDNO
                ☎ 01492 860300 59 ⇋ ♘

**North Wales** 72 Bryniau Rd, West Shore LL30 2DZ
☎ 01492 875325 & 876878
Challenging seaside links with superb views of Anglesey
and Snowdonia.
*18 holes, 6247yds, Par 71, SSS 71, Course record 65.*
*Club membership 525.*
**Visitors**    must contact in advance.
**Societies**   must contact in advance.
**Green Fees** £22 per day (£28 weekends & bank
                holidays).
**Facilities**  ⊗ ⅏ ⅊ 👤 ⚑ ♀ ⛳ ☖ ♘ ♟ Richard Bradbury.
**Leisure**     motorised carts for hire, buggies for hire,
                trolley for hire, practice ground, practice
                area.
**Location**    W side of town on A546
**Hotel**       ★★(red) St Tudno Hotel, Promenade,
                LLANDUDNO ☎ 01492 874411 21 ⇋ ♘

**Rhos-on-Sea** Penrhyn Bay LL30 3PU
☎ 01492 549641 & 549100
Seaside course, with easy walking and panoramic views.
*18 holes, 6064yds, Par 69, SSS 69.*
*Club membership 400.*
**Visitors**    advised to telephone beforehand to guarantee tee
                times.

# ESPLANADE HOTEL ★★

Glan-y-Mor Parade, Promenade, Llandudno LL30 2LL
Tel: (01492) 860300  Fax: (01492) 860418
SPECIAL ATTENTION GIVEN TO GOLFING PARTIES
MEMBERSHIP FOR NORTH WALES GOLF CLUB
Premier seafront position. Ideally situated for town and leisure facilities. 60 rooms all with
bathroom and toilet en-suite, tea/coffee making facilities, colour TV, intercom and baby listening
service, direct plane telephone. Central heating throughout. Car park. Fully licensed. Lift. Small
ballroom. Open all year. Christmas and New Year festivities. Spring and Autumn breaks.

**Societies**  booking essential, telephone in advance.
**Green Fees** £10 per day (£20 weekends).
**Facilities** ⊗ Ⅷ ⓛ ♥ ♀ ♨ ⊜ ⋈ ⓕ
**Leisure** trolley for hire, putting green.
**Location** 0.5m W off A546
**Hotel** ★★★ 62% Gogarth Abbey Hotel, West Shore,
LLANDUDNO ☎ 01492 876211 40 ⇄ ſ✶

---

## LLANFAIRFECHAN                        Map 06 SH67

**Llanfairfechan** Llannerch Rd LL33 0ES ☎ 01248 680144
Hillside course with panoramic views of coast.
*9 holes, 3119yds, Par 54, SSS 57, Course record 53.*
*Club membership 189.*
**Visitors** booking necessay for Sun play.
**Societies** apply in writing.
**Green Fees** £10 per day (£15 weekends & bank holidays).
**Facilities** ⓛ ♀ ♨
**Leisure** putting green.
**Location** W side of town on A55
**Hotel** ★★★ 58% Sychnant Pass Hotel, Sychnant Pass
Rd, CONWY ☎ 01492 596868 10 ⇄ ſ✶

---

## LLANGOLLEN                              Map 07 SJ24

**Vale of Llangollen** Holyhead Rd LL20 7PR
☎ 01978 860906
Parkland course, set in superb scenery by the River Dee.
*18 holes, 6661yds, Par 72, SSS 72, Course record 67.*
*Club membership 760.*
**Visitors** must contact in advance. Restricted club
competition days.
**Societies** apply in writing to the secretary.
**Green Fees** £20 per day (£25 weekends & bank holidays).
**Facilities** ⊗ Ⅷ ⓛ ♥ ♀ ♨ ⊜ ⓕ David Vaughan.
**Leisure** motorised carts for hire, buggies for hire, trolley
for hire, putting green, practice area.
**Location** 1.5m E on A5
**Hotel** ★★★⚌ 69% Bryn Howel Hotel & Restaurant,
LLANGOLLEN ☎ 01978 860331 36 ⇄ ſ✶

---

## MOLD                                     Map 07 SJ26

**Old Padeswood** Station Rd, Padeswood CH7 4JL
☎ 01244 547401 & 550414
Meadowland course, undulating in parts.
*18 holes, 6685yds, Par 72, SSS 72, Course record 66.*
*Club membership 600.*
**Visitors** welcome, subject to tee availability.
**Societies** telephone in advance.
**Green Fees** £16 (£20 weekends & bank holidays).
**Facilities** ⊗ Ⅷ ⓛ ♥ ♀ ♨ ⊜ ⋈ ⓕ Tony Davies.
**Leisure** buggies for hire, trolley for hire, putting green,
practice area.
**Location** 3m SE off A5118
**Hotel** ★★ 65% Bryn Awel Hotel, Denbigh Rd,
MOLD
☎ 01352 758622 7 ⇄ ſ✶Annexe10 ⇄ ſ✶

---

**Padeswood & Buckley** The Caia, Station Ln CH7 4JD
☎ 01244 550537
Gently undulating parkland course, with natural hazards and
good views of the Welsh Hills.
*18 holes, 5982yds, Par 70, SSS 69, Course record 66.*
*Club membership 700.*

**Visitors** weekdays only, contact secretary in advance
**Societies** apply in writing.
**Green Fees** £25 per day, £20 per round (£25 bank holiday).
**Facilities** ⊗ Ⅷ ⓛ ♥ ♀ ♨ ⊜ ⋈ ⓕ David Ashton.
**Leisure** motorised carts for hire, buggies for hire, trolley
for hire, driving range, putting green, practice
area, snooker.
**Location** 3m SE off A5118
**Hotel** ★★ 65% Bryn Awel Hotel, Denbigh Rd,
MOLD
☎ 01352 758622 7 ⇄ ſ✶Annexe10 ⇄ ſ✶

---

## MORFA NEFYN                             Map 06 SH24

**Nefyn & District** LL53 6DA
☎ 01758 720966
A 27-hole course played as two separate 18's, Neffyn is a
cliff top links where you never lose sight of the sea. A
well-maintained course which will be a very tough test
for the serious golfer, is still user friendly for the casual
visitor. Every hole has a different challenge and the old
13th fairway is approximately 30 yards arcross from sea-
to-sea. The course has an added bonus of a pub on the
beach roughly halfway round for those whose golf may
need some bolstering!
*Old Course: 18 holes, 6201yds, Par 71, SSS 71, Course
record 67.*
*New Course: 18 holes, 6548yds, Par 71, SSS 71, Course
record 67.*
*Club membership 800.*
**Visitors** advisable to contact in advance.
**Societies** apply by telephone.
**Green Fees** £25 per day; £20 per round (£35/£25
weekends & bank holidays).
**Facilities** ⊗ Ⅷ ⓛ ♥ ♀ ♨ ⊜ ⋈ ⓕ John Froom.
**Leisure** motorised carts for hire, buggies for hire,
trolley for hire, putting green, practice area.
**Location** 0.75m NW
**Hotel** ★★★ 64% Riverside Hotel, ABERSOCH
☎ 01758 712419 12 ⇄ ſ✶

---

## NORTHOP                                  Map 07 SJ26

**Northop Country Park** CH7 6WA
☎ 01352 840440
Designed by former British Ryder Cup captain, John Jacobs,
the parkland course gives the impression of having been
established for many years. No two holes are the same and
designed to allow all year play.
*18 holes, 6750yds, Par 72, SSS 73, Course record 65.*
*Club membership 500.*
**Visitors** advisable to prebook.
**Societies** apply in writing or by telephone in advance.
**Green Fees** £28 per round (£35 weekends & bank holidays).
**Facilities** ⊗ Ⅷ ⓛ ♥ ♀ ♨ ⊜ ⋈ ⓕ David Llewllyn.
**Leisure** hard tennis courts, heated indoor swimming
pool, sauna, solarium, gymnasium, motorised
carts for hire, buggies for hire, trolley for hire,
driving range, putting green, practice area.
**Location** 150 yds from Connahs Quay turnoff on A55
**Hotel** ★★★★ 69% St Davids Park Hotel, St Davids
Park, EWLOE
☎ 01244 520800 121 ⇄ ſ✶

## PANTYMWYN                                    Map 07 SJ16

**Mold** Cilcain Rd CH7 5EH ☎ 01352 740318 & 741513
Meadowland course with some hard walking and natural
hazards. Fine views.
*18 holes, 5528yds, Par 67, SSS 67, Course record 64.*
*Club membership 600.*
**Visitors**     contact in advance.
**Societies**    provisional booking by telephone.
**Green Fees** £16 per day (£21 per day, £18 per round
              weekends & bank holidays).
**Facilities**   ⊗ ⅢⅡ ㅂ ♣ ♀ ♨ ☎ ❙ ▮ Martin Carty.
**Leisure**      motorised carts for hire, trolley for hire, putting
              green, practice area.
**Location**     E side of village
**Hotel**        ★★ 65% Bryn Awel Hotel, Denbigh Rd,
              MOLD
              ☎ 01352 758622 7 ➡ ⋔Annexe10 ➡ ⋔

## PENMAENMAWR                                 Map 06 SH77

**Penmaenmawr** Conway Old Rd LL34 6RD
☎ 01492 623330
Hilly course with magnificent views across the bay to
Llandudno and Anglesey. Dry-stone wall natural hazards.
*9 holes, 5350yds, Par 67, SSS 66, Course record 64.*
*Club membership 600.*
**Visitors**     advisable to contact in advance. May not play
              Sat.
**Societies**    must contact in advance.
**Green Fees** £12 per day (£18 Sun & bank holidays).
**Facilities**   ⊗ ⅢⅡ ㅂ ♣ ♀ ♨
**Leisure**      putting green, practice area.
**Location**     1.5m NE off A55
**Hotel**        ★★★ 62% The Castle, High St, CONWY
              ☎ 01492 592324 29 ➡ ⋔

## PORTHMADOG                                  Map 06 SH53

**Porthmadog** Morfa Bychan LL49 9TP
☎ 01766 514124 & 513828
Seaside links,very interesting but with easy walking and good
views.
*18 holes, 6350yds, Par 71, SSS 71.*
*Club membership 900.*
**Visitors**     must contact in advance.
**Societies**    apply telephone initially.
**Green Fees** £18 per day (£25 weekends & bank holidays).
**Facilities**   ⊗ ⅢⅡ ㅂ ♣ ♀ ♨ ☎ ▮ Peter L Bright.
**Leisure**      trolley for hire, putting green, practice area.
**Location**     1.5m SW
**Hotel**        ★★ 62% Plas Isa Hotel, Porthmadog Rd,
              CRICCIETH ☎ 01766 522443 14 ➡ ⋔

## PRESTATYN                                   Map 06 SJ08

**Prestatyn** Marine Rd East LL19 7HS ☎ 01745 854320
Very flat seaside links exposed to stiff breeze. Testing holes:
9th, par 4, bounded on 3 sides by water; 10th, par 4; 16th, par
4.
*18 holes, 6564yds, Par 72, SSS 72, Course record 66.*
*Club membership 660.*
**Visitors**     welcome except Sat & Tue mornings. Must
              contact in advance.

**Societies**    prior booking required.
**Green Fees** £20 per day (£25 weekends & bank holidays).
**Facilities**   ⊗ ⅢⅡ ㅂ ♣ ♀ ♨ ☎ ❙ ▮ Malcolm Staton.
**Leisure**      trolley for hire, putting green, practice area.
**Location**     0.5m N off A548
**Hotel**        ★★ 61% Hotel Marina, Marine Dr, RHYL
              ☎ 01745 342371 26rm(20 ➡2 ⋔)

*St Melyd* The Paddock, Meliden Rd LL19 8NB
☎ 01745 854405
Parkland course with good views of mountains and Irish Sea.
Testing 1st hole (423 yds) par 4. 18 tees.
*9 holes, 5829yds, Par 68, SSS 68, Course record 65.*
*Club membership 400.*
**Visitors**     must contact in advance.
**Societies**    must telephone in advance.
**Green Fees** not confirmed.
**Facilities**   ♀ ♨ ☎ ▮ Richard Bladbury.
**Location**     0.5m S on A547
**Hotel**        ★★ 61% Hotel Marina, Marine Dr, RHYL
              ☎ 01745 342371 26rm(20 ➡2 ⋔)

## PWLLHELI                                    Map 06 SH33

*Pwllheli* Golf Rd LL53 5PS ☎ 01758 701644
Easy walking on flat seaside course with outstanding views of
Snowdon, Cader Idris and Cardigan Bay.
*18 holes, 6091yds, Par 69, SSS 69.*
*Club membership 880.*
**Visitors**     restricted Tue,Thu & weekends.
**Societies**    must telephone in advance.
**Green Fees** not confirmed.
**Facilities**   ♀ ♨ ☎ ▮
**Leisure**      putting green, practice area, trolley hire.
**Location**     0.5m SW off A497
**Hotel**        ★★★ 64% Riverside Hotel, ABERSOCH
              ☎ 01758 712419 12 ➡ ⋔

## RHUDDLAN                                    Map 06 SJ07

**Rhuddlan** Meliden Rd LL18 6LB ☎ 01745 590217
Attractive, gently undulating parkland course with good
views. Well bunkered with trees and water hazards. The 476
yard 8th and 431 yard 11th require both length and accuracy.
The clubhouse has been refurbished.
*18 holes, 6482yds, Par 71, SSS 71, Course record 67.*
*Club membership 1060.*
**Visitors**     must contact in advance. Sun with member only.
**Societies**    telephone to book reservation.
**Green Fees** £24 per day (£30 per round Sat).
**Facilities**   ⊗ ⅢⅡ ㅂ ♣ ♀ ♨ ☎ ❙ ▮ Andrew Carr.
**Leisure**      trolley for hire, putting green, practice area.
**Location**     E side of town on A547
**Hotel**        ★★★ 64% Oriel House Hotel, Upper Denbigh
              Rd, ST ASAPH ☎ 01745 582716 19 ➡ ⋔

## RHYL                                        Map 06 SJ08

**Rhyl** Coast Rd LL18 3RE ☎ 01745 353171
Seaside course.
*9 holes, 6165yds, Par 70, SSS 70, Course record 65.*
*Club membership 350.*
**Visitors**     must contact in advance. Limited availability at
              weekends due to club competitions.
**Societies**    must contact in advance.

# Hotel Marina

AA★★ WTB ♛♛♛ Commended

## MARINE DRIVE, RHYL, LL18 3AU

## TELEPHONE: (01745) 342371

## SET ON THE LOVELY EAST PARADE

Situated near Sun Centre on Rhyl's lovely East Parade, the hotel has 26 bedrooms all en suite. The hotel also has a late night Piano Bar and a recently refurbished night club called Quaffers Place and its own Steak Bar. We can cater for large or small parties either requiring accommodation or food only. Discounts available for organised groups. Large car park and lift.

**Green Fees** £10 per 18 holes (£15 weekends & bank holidays).
**Facilities** ⊗ ⅲ ⓛ ▮ ♀ ⚘ ⬚ ⓕ ⓕ Tim Leah.
**Leisure** trolley for hire, putting green, practice area.
**Location** 1m E on A548
**Hotel** ★★ 61% Hotel Marina, Marine Dr, RHYL ☎ 01745 342371 26rm(20 ⇄2 ⏃)

### RUABON     Map 07 SJ34

**Penycae** Ruabon Rd, Penycae LL14 1TP
☎ 01978 810108
An architecturally designed and built 9-hole course with an opening hole from an elevated tee wooded to one side and backed by trees and a river. The 2nd at 262 yards crosses water twice as the river meanders down the fairway. Th 5th is very narrow being wooded on either side and with a slight dogleg. The 6th also a par 3, needs a high shot to clear the mature birch in the path.
*9 holes, 2140yds, Par 64, SSS 62, Course record 62.*
*Club membership 200.*
**Visitors** advisable to book in advance.
**Societies** telephone or write in advance.
**Green Fees** £6 per 18 holes; £4 per 9 holes (£8/£5 weekends & bank holidays).
**Facilities** ⊗ ⅲ by prior arrangement ⓛ ▮ ♀ ⚘ ⬚ ⓕ ⓕ Nick Rothe.
**Leisure** trolley for hire, putting green.
**Location** 1m off A5
**Hotel** ★★★ 67% Hand Hotel, Church St, CHIRK ☎ 01691 772479 14 ⇄ ⏃

### RUTHIN     Map 06 SJ15

**Ruthin-Pwllglas** Pwllglas LL15 2PE ☎ 01824 703427
Hilly parkland course in elevated position with panoramic views. Stiff climb to 3rd and 9th holes.
*10 holes, 5362yds, Par 66, SSS 66.*
*Club membership 380.*
**Visitors** welcome except for competition days.
**Societies** apply in writing.
**Green Fees** not confirmed.
**Facilities** ♀ ⚘
**Location** 2.5m S off A494
**Hotel** ★★★ 63% Ruthin Castle, RUTHIN ☎ 01824 702664 58 ⇄ ⏃

### ST ASAPH     Map 06 SJ07

**Llannerch Park** North Wales Golf Range, Llannerch Park LL17 0BD ☎ 01745 730805
*9 holes, 1587yds, Par 30.*
**Visitors** pay & play.
**Societies** telephone in advance.
**Green Fees** £2 per 9 holes.
**Facilities** ▮ ⬚ ⓕ
**Leisure** driving range.
**Location** 1.5m S off A525

### WREXHAM     Map 07 SJ35

**Clays Farm Golf Centre** Bryn Estyn Rd, Llan-y-Pwll LL13 9UB ☎ 01978 661406 & 661416
Parkland course in a rural setting with views of the Welsh mountains and noted for the difficulty of its par 3s.
*18 holes, 5624yds, Par 69, SSS 69, Course record 70.*
*Club membership 420.*
**Visitors** must contact in advance.
**Societies** at busy times prior arrangement required by telephone.
**Green Fees** £11 per round (£14 weekends).
**Facilities** ⊗ ⅲ ⓛ ▮ ♀ ⚘ ⬚ ⓕ ⓕ Paul Williams.
**Leisure** motorised carts for hire, buggies for hire, trolley for hire, driving range, putting green, practice area.
**Hotel** ★★★⚘ 65% Llwyn Onn Hall Hotel, Cefn Rd, WREXHAM ☎ 01978 261225 13 ⇄ ⏃

**Wrexham** Holt Rd LL13 9SB ☎ 01978 351476
Inland, sandy course with easy walking. Testing dog-legged 7th hole (par 4), and short 14th hole (par 3) with full carry to green.
*18 holes, 6233yds, Par 70, SSS 70, Course record 64.*
*Club membership 600.*
**Visitors** may not play competition days, and are advised to contact in advance. A handicap certificate is required.
**Societies** welcome except for Tue, Wed & weekends. Apply in writing
**Green Fees** £20 (£25 weekends).
**Facilities** ⊗ ⅲ ⓛ ▮ ♀ ⚘ ⬚ ⓕ David Larvin.
**Leisure** trolley for hire, putting green, practice area.
**Location** 2m NE on A534
**Hotel** ★★★⚘ 65% Llwyn Onn Hall Hotel, Cefn Rd, WREXHAM ☎ 01978 261225 13 ⇄ ⏃

# MID WALES

This region includes the counties of
Cardiganshire, Carmarthenshire,
Pembrokeshire and Powys which reflect
the recent national changes.

## ABERYSTWYTH          Map 06 SN58

**Aberystwyth** Brynymor Rd SY23 2HY
☎ 01970 615104
Undulating meadowland course. Testing holes: 16th (The
Loop) par 3; 17th, par 4; 18th, par 3. Good views over
Cardigan Bay.
*18 holes, 6109yds, Par 71, SSS 71, Course record 67.*
*Club membership 450.*

| | |
|---|---|
| **Visitors** | must contact in advance. |
| **Societies** | write or telephone in advance. |
| **Green Fees** | £18 per day; £15 per round (£20/£18 weekends and bank holidays). |
| **Facilities** | ⊗ ⅢⅢ ⅃ ⅃ ♀ ⅄ 🖼 ⅀ Ⅽ Kevin Bayliss. |
| **Leisure** | trolley for hire, driving range, putting green, practice area. |
| **Location** | N side of town |
| **Hotel** | ★★★ 66% Belle Vue Royal Hotel, Marine Ter, ABERYSTWYTH ☎ 01970 617558 36 ⇥ ⅀ |

# The Mill
# at Glynhir AA ★ ★

Ashley Courtenay
Hotel of Distinction

BWRDD CROESO CYMRU
WALES TOURIST BOARD

👑 👑 👑 👑

LLANDYBIE,
NR.
AMMANFORD,
DYFED
SA18 2TE
Tel/Fax:
(01269) 850672

Originally a XVIIth-century mill tastefully
converted to a luxury 11 bedroom country house
hotel idyllic situation overlooking Brecon National
Park yet convenient for Gower and Pembrokeshire
coast. All en suite rooms have spa baths. Fish from
our grounds. Free golf next door and at 9 other
courses in area, indoor swimming pool.
**Golf, D B&B from £27.50.**

## AMMANFORD          Map 03 SN61

**Glynhir** Glynhir Rd, Llandybie SA18 2TF
☎ 01269 850472 & 851365
Parkland course with good views, latter holes close to Upper
Loughor River. The 14th is a 394-yd dog leg.
*18 holes, 5986yds, Par 69, SSS 69, Course record 66.*
*Club membership 700.*

| | |
|---|---|
| **Visitors** | no visitors Sun. Contact professional in advance (01269 851010). |
| **Societies** | welcome weekdays only. Contact in advance. |
| **Green Fees** | £15 per day (£20 Sat & bank holidays). |
| **Facilities** | ⊗ ⅢⅢ ⅃ ⅃ ♀ ⅄ ⅀ Ⅽ ⅀ Ⅽ Ian Roberts. |
| **Leisure** | trolley for hire, putting green. |
| **Location** | 2m N of Ammanford |
| **Hotel** | ★★ 67% Mill at Glynhir, Glyn-Hir, Llandybie, AMMANFORD ☎ 01269 850672 11 ⇥ ⅀ |

## BORTH          Map 06 SN69

**Borth & Ynyslas** SY24 5JS ☎ 01970 871202
Seaside links, over 100 years old, with strong winds at times.
Some narrow fairways.
*18 holes, 6116yds, Par 70, SSS 70, Course record 65.*
*Club membership 625.*

| | |
|---|---|
| **Visitors** | must contact in advance, may play weekends ring to check no competitions in progress. |
| **Societies** | telephone in advance. |
| **Green Fees** | £18 per day (£22 weekends & bank holidays). |
| **Facilities** | ⊗ ⅢⅢ ⅃ ⅃ ♀ ⅄ 🖼 ⅀ Ⅽ J G Lewis. |
| **Leisure** | trolley for hire, practice area. |
| **Location** | 0.5m N on B4353 |
| **Hotel** | ★★ 65% Four Seasons Hotel, 50-54 Portland St, ABERYSTWYTH ☎ 01970 612120 14rm(13 ⇥ ⅀) |

## BRECON          Map 03 SO02

**Brecon** Newton Park LD3 8PA ☎ 01874 622004
Parkland course, with easy walking. Natural hazards include
two rivers on its boundary. Good river and mountain scenery.
*9 holes, 5256yds, Par 66, SSS 66, Course record 61.*
*Club membership 420.*

| | |
|---|---|
| **Visitors** | advisable to contact in advance, limited availability at weekends. |
| **Societies** | apply in writing. |
| **Green Fees** | £10 per day. |
| **Facilities** | ⅃ ♀ ⅄ |
| **Leisure** | practice area. |
| **Location** | 0.75m W of town centre on A40 |
| **Hotel** | ★★ 62% Castle of Brecon Hotel, Castle Square, BRECON ☎ 01874 624611 33 ⇥ ⅀Annexe12 ⅀ |

**Cradoc** Penoyre Park, Cradoc LD3 9LP ☎ 01874 623658
Parkland with wooded areas, lakes and spectacular views
over the Brecon Beacons. Challenging golf.
*18 holes, 6301yds, Par 71, SSS 71, Course record 65.*
*Club membership 700.*

| | |
|---|---|
| **Visitors** | must contact secretary in advance. |
| **Societies** | apply in writing or telephone in advance to secretary. |
| **Green Fees** | £18 per day (£22 weekends & bank holidays). |
| **Facilities** | ⊗ ⅢⅢ ⅃ ⅃ ♀ ⅄ 🖼 ⅀ Richard Davies. |

| | |
|---|---|
| **Leisure** | trolley for hire, putting green, practice area. |
| **Location** | 2m N on B4520 |
| **Hotel** | ★★ 62% Castle of Brecon Hotel, Castle Square, BRECON |
| | ☎ 01874 624611 33 ⇆ ᚛Annexe12 ᚛ |

## BUILTH WELLS                                    Map 03 SO05

**Builth Wells** The Clubhouse, Golf Links Rd LD2 3NF
☎ 01982 553296
Well guarded greens and a stream running thorough the
centre of the course add interest to this 18-hole undulating
parkland course. The clubhouse is a converted 16th-century
Welsh long house.
*18 holes, 5386yds, Par 66, SSS 67, Course record 65.*
*Club membership 380.*

| | |
|---|---|
| **Visitors** | contact secretary. |
| **Societies** | by prior arrangement. |
| **Green Fees** | £16 per day; £12 per round (£22/ £18 weekends and bank holidays). |
| **Facilities** | ⊗ ᛗ ᛒ ᛞ ♀ ⅄ ᚛ ᚛ ᚛ Roy Truman. |
| **Location** | N of A483 |
| **Hotel** | ★★★⚌ 64% Caer Beris Manor Hotel, BUILTH WELLS |
| | ☎ 01982 552601 22 ⇆ ᚛ |

## BURRY PORT                                      Map 02 SN40

**Ashburnham** Cliffe Ter SA16 0HN
☎ 01554 832269 & 833846
This course has a lot of variety. In the main it is of the
seaside type although the holes in front of the clubhouse
are of an inland character. They are, however, good holes
which make a very interesting finish. Course record
holder, Sam Torrance.
*18 holes, 6916yds, Par 72, SSS 74, Course record 70.*
*Club membership 730.*

| | |
|---|---|
| **Visitors** | must be bona fide member of affiliated golf club and produce handicap certificate, very limited weekend times. |
| **Societies** | telephone for initial enquiry. |
| **Green Fees** | £30 per day; £25 per round (£40/£30 weekends). |
| **Facilities** | ⊗ ᛗ ᛒ ᛞ ♀ ⅄ ᚛ ᚛ ᚛ Robert Ryder. |
| **Leisure** | trolley for hire, putting green, practice area. |
| **Location** | 5m W of Llanelli, A484 road |
| **Hotel** | ★★★ 64% Diplomat Hotel, Felinfoel, LLANELLI |
| | ☎ 01554 756156 23 ⇆ ᚛Annexe8 ⇆ ᚛ |

## CAERSWS                                         Map 06 SO09

**Mid-Wales Golf Centre** SY17 5SB ☎ 01686 688303
A 9-hole, Par 3 course with sand bunkers and three ponds.
*9 holes, 2554yds, Par 54, SSS 54.*
*Club membership 95.*

| | |
|---|---|
| **Visitors** | welcome, restricted during competitions on Sun am. |
| **Societies** | telephone in advance. |
| **Green Fees** | £6 per day (£8 weekends & bank holidays). |
| **Facilities** | ⊗ by prior arrangement ᛗ by prior arrangement ᛒ ᛞ ♀ ⅄ ᚛ ᚛ |
| **Leisure** | trolley for hire, driving range, putting green, practice area. |
| **Location** | 0.75m off A470 out of Caersws |

| | |
|---|---|
| **Hotel** | ★★ 64% Elephant & Castle, Broad St, NEWTOWN |
| | ☎ 01686 626271 25 ⇆ ᚛Annexe11 ⇆ ᚛ |

## CARDIGAN                                        Map 02 SN14

**Cardigan** Gwbert-on-Sea SA43 1PR ☎ 01239 612035
A links course, very dry in winter, with wide fairways, light
rough and gorse. Every hole overlooks the sea.
*18 holes, 6641yds, Par 72, SSS 72.*
*Club membership 500.*

| | |
|---|---|
| **Visitors** | may not play between 1-2pm. Must have a handicap certificate. |
| **Societies** | must telephone in advance. |
| **Green Fees** | not confirmed. |
| **Facilities** | ♀ ⅄ ᚛ ᚛ ᚛ Colin Parsons. |
| **Leisure** | squash, putting,cart/buggy/trolley hire. |
| **Location** | 3m N off B4548 |
| **Hotel** | ★★★ 65% Cliff Hotel, GWBERT |
| | ☎ 01239 613241 70 ⇆ ᚛ |

## CARMARTHEN                                      Map 02 SN42

**Carmarthen** Blaenycoed Rd SA33 6EH
☎ 01267 281588 & 281214
Hilltop course with good views.
*18 holes, 6210yds, Par 71, SSS 70, Course record 68.*
*Club membership 700.*

| | |
|---|---|
| **Visitors** | must have a handicap certificate, telephone for times at weekends. |
| **Societies** | apply in writing minimum of ten days in advance. |
| **Green Fees** | £18 per round (£25 weekends & bank holidays). |
| **Facilities** | ⊗ ᛗ ᛒ ᛞ ♀ ⅄ ᚛ ᚛ ᚛ Pat Gillis. |
| **Leisure** | trolley for hire, putting green, practice area. |
| **Location** | 4m N of town |
| **Hotel** | ★★★ 60% The Ivy Bush Royal, Spilman St, CARMARTHEN |
| | ☎ 01267 235111 73 ⇆ ᚛ |

**Derllys Court** Llysonnen Rd SA33 5DT ☎ 01267 211575
Gently undulating parkland course with challenging par 3s
(5th and 8th) and a testing par 5 involving a shot across a
lake.
*9 holes, 2859yds, Par 35, SSS 66, Course record 33.*
*Club membership 60.*

| | |
|---|---|
| **Visitors** | welcome at all times. |
| **Societies** | telephone in advance. |
| **Green Fees** | £9 per 18 holes; £5 per 9 holes. |
| **Facilities** | ⊗ ᛒ ᛞ ⅄ ᚛ ᚛ ᚛ |
| **Leisure** | trolley for hire, practice area. |
| **Location** | Just off A40 between Carmarthen/St Clears |
| **Hotel** | ★★★ 60% The Ivy Bush Royal, Spilman St, CARMARTHEN |
| | ☎ 01267 235111 73 ⇆ ᚛ |

## GWBERT-ON-SEA                                    Map 02 SN15

**Cliff Hotel** SA43 1PP ☎ 01239 613241
This is a short course with 2 Par 4's and the remainder are
challenging Par 3's. Particularly interesting holes are played
across the sea on to a small island.
*9 holes, 1545yds, Par 29.*

| | |
|---|---|
| **Visitors** | telephone to book in advance. |
| **Societies** | telephone in advance. |

▶

# Cliff Hotel
### GWBERT, CARDIGAN, WEST WALES
### TEL: CARDIGAN (01239) 613241

AA ★★★ Hotel in breathtaking position on cliffs overlooking Cardigan Bay. Outdoor pool, Squash, Gym, Snooker, Sauna. FREE Golf on hotel's own 9-hole course. Cardigan Golf Course (18 holes) only ½ mile away. Bargain breaks available. Also self-catering in Gate House.

**Green Fees** £5.50 per 9 holes (£6.75 weekends and bank holidays).
**Facilities** ⊗ ⅏ ⅃ 🍺 ♀ ⚘ ⚐ 🛏
**Leisure** heated outdoor swimming pool, squash, fishing, sauna, solarium, gymnasium, motorised carts for hire, putting green, snooker table.
**Hotel** ★★★ 65% Cliff Hotel, GWBERT
☎ 01239 613241 70 ⇆ ⌀

---

## HAVERFORDWEST         Map 02 SM91

**Haverfordwest** Arnolds Down SA61 2XQ
☎ 01437 764523
Parkland course in attractive surroundings.
*18 holes, 6005yds, Par 70, SSS 69.*
*Club membership 770.*
**Visitors** restricted at weekends.
**Societies** apply in writing or telephone for booking form.
**Green Fees** £16 per day (£20 weekends).
**Facilities** ⊗ ⅏ ⅃ 🍺 ♀ ⚘ ⚐ ⚐ ⌀ Alex Pile.
**Leisure** motorised carts for hire, buggies for hire, trolley for hire, putting green, practice area.
**Location** 1m E on A40
**Hotel** ★★ 65% Hotel Mariners, Mariners Square, HAVERFORDWEST
☎ 01437 763353 30 ⇆ ⌀

---

Entries with a shaded background identify courses that are considered to be particularly interesting

---

## HAY-ON-WYE         Map 03 SO24

**Rhosgoch** Rhosgoch, Builth Wells LD2 3JY
☎ 01497 851251
The course is parkland, quite challenging, with beautiful scenery.
*9 holes, 4842yds, Par 68, SSS 64, Course record 68.*
*Club membership 165.*
**Visitors** no restrictions.
**Societies** please telephone in advance.
**Green Fees** not confirmed.
**Facilities** ♀ ⚘ ⚐
**Location** 5m N of Hay-on-Wye
**Hotel** ★★★ 67% The Swan-at-Hay Hotel, Church St, HAY-ON-WYE
☎ 01497 821188 15 ⇆ ⌀Annexe3 ⇆ ⌀

**Summerhill** Hereford Rd, Clifford HR3 5EW
☎ 01497 820451
Undulating parkland course set deep in the Wye Valley on the Welsh Border overlooking the Black Mountains.
*9 holes, 2929yds, Par 70, SSS 67.*
**Visitors** welcome anytime.
**Societies** contact for information.
**Green Fees** £8 per round (£10 weekends and bank holidays).
**Facilities** ⊗ ⅏ ⅃ 🍺 ♀ ⚘ ⚐ ⌀ ⌀
**Location** B4350 Whitney toll bridge road
**Hotel** ★★★ 67% The Swan-at-Hay Hotel, Church St, HAY-ON-WYE
☎ 01497 821188 15 ⇆ ⌀Annexe3 ⇆ ⌀

---

## KIDWELLY         Map 02 SN40

**Pontnewydd Golf Centre** Trimsaran SA17 4LB
☎ 01554 810278
In the Gwendraeth valley, a new 18-hole parkland course with greens well protected by the planting of 35,000 trees. There is a covered practice area and 9-hole course under construction.
*18 holes, 6173yds, Par 70, SSS 69, Course record 68.*
*Club membership 300.*
**Visitors** advisable to book for weekends.
**Societies** must contact in advance.
**Green Fees** not confirmed.
**Facilities** ♀ ⚘ ⚐ ⌀
**Leisure** covered practice area.
**Location** 4.5m E, off B4317
**Hotel** ★★★ 60% The Ivy Bush Royal, Spilman St, CARMARTHEN
☎ 01267 235111 73 ⇆ ⌀

---

## KNIGHTON         Map 07 SO27

**Knighton** Frydd Wood LD7 1EF ☎ 01547 528646
Hill course with hard walking.
*9 holes, 5320yds, Par 68, SSS 66, Course record 65.*
*Club membership 150.*
**Visitors** may not play on Sun until after 4.30pm.
**Societies** must contact in advance.
**Green Fees** not confirmed.
**Facilities** ♀ ⚘
**Location** 0.5m S off B4355
**Hotel** ★★★ 60% The Knighton Hotel, Broad St, KNIGHTON ☎ 01547 520530 15 ⇆ ⌀

## LETTERSTON
Map 02 SM92

**Priskilly Forest** Castlemorris SA62 5EH
☎ 01348 840276
Testing parkland course surrounded by rhododendrons.
Challenging dog-leg 4th with hazards both sides.
*9 holes, 5712yds, Par 70, SSS 68, Course record 76.*
**Visitors** advance booking advisable at weekends during summer.
**Societies** telephone in advance.
**Green Fees** £10 per day; £8per 18 holes; £5 per 9 holes.
**Facilities** ⊗ 🍺 🛂 🖆 🍴 🏠
**Leisure** fishing, motorised carts for hire, buggies for hire, trolley for hire.
**Hotel** ★★ 63% Abergwaun Hotel, The Market Square, FISHGUARD
☎ 01348 872077 11rm(7 ➡ 📯)

## LLANDRINDOD WELLS
Map 03 SO06

*Llandrindod Wells LD1 5NY*
☎ 01597 822010 & 823873 (sec)
Moorland course, designed by Harry Vardon, with easy walking and panoramic views. One of the highest courses in Wales. (1,100 ft above sea level).
*18 holes, 5759yds, Par 68, SSS 67, Course record 65.*
*Club membership 650.*
**Visitors** no restrictions.
**Societies** must telephone in advance.
**Green Fees** not confirmed.
**Facilities** 🍺 🛂 🖆 🍴
**Leisure** putting green,practice area,trolley hire.
**Location** 1m SE off A483
**Hotel** ★★★ 65% Hotel Metropole, Temple St, LLANDRINDOD WELLS
☎ 01597 823700 121 ➡ 📯

## LLANDYSSUL

**Saron** Saron SA44 5EL ☎ 01559 370705
Set in 50 acres of mature parkland with large trees and magnificent Teifi Valley views. Numerous water hazards and bunkers.
*9 holes, 2400yds, Par 32, Course record 34.*
**Visitors** may play at all times no arrangements required.
**Societies** telephone for details.
**Green Fees** £6 per 18 holes; £4.50 per 9 holes.
**Facilities** 🍴
**Leisure** trolley for hire.
**Location** Off A484 at Saron
**Hotel** ★★ 72% Ty Mawr Country Hotel & Restaurant, BRECHFA
☎ 01267 202332 5rm(4 ➡ 📯)

## LLANGATTOCK
Map 03 SO21

**Old Rectory** NP8 1PH ☎ 01873 810373
Sheltered course with easy walking.
*9 holes, 2200yds, Par 54, SSS 59, Course record 53 or 53yds.*
*Club membership 180.*
**Visitors** telephone for information.
**Societies** telephone for booking.
**Green Fees** £10 per day; £5 per 18 holes.
**Facilities** ⊗ 🎄 🛂 🍺 🛂 🖆 🍴 🏠

**Leisure** outdoor swimming pool.
**Location** SW of village
**Hotel** ★★🏌 71% Gliffaes Country House Hotel, CRICKHOWELL
☎ 01874 730371 19 ➡ 📯Annexe3 ➡ 📯

## LLANGYBI
Map 02 SN65

**Cilgwyn** SA48 8NN ☎ 01570 493286
Picturesque parkland course in secluded valley, with natural hazards of ponds, stream and woodland.
*9 holes, 5309yds, Par 68, SSS 66.*
*Club membership 300.*
**Visitors** no restrictions, apart from Sun when advisable to telephone.
**Societies** apply in advance by letter or telephone.
**Green Fees** £15 per day; £10 per round (£20/£15 weekends & bank holidays).
**Facilities** ⊗ 🎄 🛂 🍺 🍷 🛂 🖆 🍴 🏠
**Leisure** trolley for hire, putting green, practice area.
**Location** 5m N of Lampeter on A485
**Hotel** ★★★🏌 69% Falcondale Country House Hotel, LAMPETER ☎ 01570 422910 19 ➡ 📯

## LLANIDLOES
Map 06 SN98

**St Idloes** Penrallt SY18 6LG ☎ 01686 412559
Hill-course, slightly undulating but walking is easy. Good views.
*9 holes, 2755yds, Par 66, SSS 66, Course record 61.*
*Club membership 300.*
**Visitors** may not play on Sun mornings.
**Societies** apply in writing to the secretary at least one month in advance.
**Green Fees** £10 (£12 weekends).
**Facilities** ⊗ 🎄 🛂 🍺 🍷 🛂 🖆 🍴 🍷 Phillip Parkin.
**Leisure** trolley for hire, putting green, practice area.
**Location** 1m N off B4569
**Hotel** ★★ 67% Glansevern Arms Hotel, Pant Mawr, LLANGURIG ☎ 0686 440240 7 ➡ 📯

## LLANRHYSTUD
Map 06 SN56

**Penrhos Golf & Country Club** SY23 5AY
☎ 01974 202999
Beautifully scenic course incorporating five lakes and spectacular coastal and inland views. Many leisure facilities.
*Penrhos: 18 holes, 6641yds, Par 72, SSS 73, Course record 71.*
*Academy: 9 holes, 1827yds, Par 31.*
*Club membership 300.*
**Visitors** must telephone, no jeans allowed on main course.
**Societies** must telephone in advance.
**Green Fees** £15 per round plus £5 per extra round (£18 per round weekends & bank holidays).
**Facilities** ⊗ 🎄 🛂 🍺 🍷 🛂 🖆 🍴 🍷 Paul Diamond.
**Leisure** hard tennis courts, heated indoor swimming pool, sauna, solarium, gymnasium, motorised carts for hire, buggies for hire, trolley for hire, driving range, putting green, practice area.
**Location** Turn off A487 onto B4337 in Llanrhystud
**Hotel** ★★★🏌 67% Conrah Hotel, Ffosrhydygaled, Chancery, ABERYSTWYTH
☎ 01970 617941 11 ➡ 📯Annexe9 ➡ 📯

## LLANSTEFFAN    Map 02 SN31

*Llansteffan* SA33 5LU ☎ 01267 241526
A Pay and Play downland course with superb views of the sea
and Gower Coast. Quite challenging in a sea breeze!
*9 holes, 2165yds, Par 30.*
**Visitors**   no restrictions, visitors welcome at all times.
**Societies**   contact in advance for bank holidays.
**Green Fees** not confirmed.
**Facilities**   🖬 ⚑
**Leisure**   putting green,practice area,trolley hire.
**Location**   S of Carmarthen off B4312
**Hotel**   ★★ 66% Forge Restaurant & Motel, ST
  CLEARS ☎ 01994 230300 Annexe18 ⇥ 🐾

## MACHYNLLETH    Map 06 SH70

**Machynlleth** Ffordd Drenewydd SY20 8UH
☎ 01654 702000
Lowland course with mostly natural hazards.
*9 holes, 5726yds, Par 68, SSS 67, Course record 65.*
*Club membership 250.*
**Visitors**   Thur ladies day, Sun morning mens competition.
**Societies**   telephone in advance.
**Green Fees** £12 per day (£15 weekends & bank holidays).
**Facilities**   ⊗ 🖴 ⚑ ♀ ⚘
**Leisure**   trolley for hire, putting green, practice area.
**Location**   0.5m E off A489
**Hotel**   ★★ 65% Wynnstay Arms Hotel, Maengwyn St,
  MACHYNLLETH ☎ 01654 702941 20 ⇥ 🐾

## MILFORD HAVEN    Map 02 SM90

*Milford Haven* Woodbine House, Hubberstone SA73 3RX
☎ 01646 692368
Parkland course with excellent greens and views of the
Milford Haven waterway.
*18 holes, 6030yds, Par 71, SSS 70.*
*Club membership 450.*
**Visitors**   no restrictions, advisable to contact in advance.
**Societies**   telephone to book.
**Green Fees** not confirmed.
**Facilities**   ♀ ⚘ 🖬 ⚑ ♪
**Leisure**   putting green,practice area,trolley hire.
**Location**   1.5m W
**Hotel**   ★★ 63% Lord Nelson Hotel, Hamilton Ter,
  MILFORD HAVEN
  ☎ 01646 695341 32 ⇥ 🐾

## NEWPORT    Map 02 SN03

**Newport (Pemb)** The Golf Club SA42 0NR
☎ 01239 820244
Seaside links course, with easy walking and good view of the
Preselli Hills and Newport Bay.
*9 holes, 5815yds, Par 70, Course record 61.*
*Club membership 350.*
**Visitors**   telephone in advance.
**Societies**   must telephone in advance.
**Green Fees** £15 per 18 holes; £10 per 9 holes.
**Facilities**   ⊗ 🎵 🖴 ⚑ ♀ ⚘ 🖬 ⚑ ⋈ ⫟ Colin Parsons.
**Leisure**   motorised carts for hire, buggies for hire, trolley
  for hire, driving range, putting green, practice
  area.

**Location**   1.25m N
**Hotel**   ★★ 65% Trewern Arms, NEVERN
  ☎ 01239 820395 9 ⇥ 🐾

## NEWTOWN    Map 06 SO19

**St Giles** Pool Rd SY16 3AJ
☎ 01686 625844
Inland country course with easy walking. Testing 2nd hole,
par 3, and 4th hole, par 4. River Severn skirts four holes.
*9 holes, 5936yds, Par 70, SSS 69, Course record 67.*
*Club membership 350.*
**Visitors**   may not play at weekends.
**Societies**   must contact in advance.
**Green Fees** £12.50 per day (£15 weekends and bank
  holidays).
**Facilities**   ⊗ 🎵 🖴 ⚑ ♀ ⚘ 🖬 ⚑ ⫟ ⫟ D P Owen.
**Leisure**   fishing, trolley for hire, putting green, practifce
  area.
**Location**   0.5m NE on A483
**Hotel**   ★★ 64% Elephant & Castle, Broad St,
  NEWTOWN
  ☎ 01686 626271 25 ⇥ 🐾Annexe11 ⇥ 🐾

## PEMBROKE DOCK    Map 02 SM90

**South Pembrokeshire** Defensible Barracks SA72 6SE
☎ 01646 621453
Parkland course overlooking the Cleddau River.
*9 holes, 5804yds, Par 70, SSS 69, Course record 65.*
*Club membership 350.*
**Visitors**   must contact in advance, especially during
  season.
**Societies**   apply in advance.
**Green Fees** £10 per day to be reviewed when 18 hole course
  is open.
**Facilities**   ⊗ 🎵 🖴 ⚑ ♀ ⚘
**Leisure**   practice area.
**Location**   SW side of town centre off B4322
**Hotel**   ★★ 60% Old Kings Arms, Main St,
  PEMBROKE
  ☎ 01646 683611 21 ⇥ 🐾

## ST DAVID'S    Map 02 SM72

**St David's City** Whitesands Bay SA62 6PT
☎ 01437 720312 & 721751
Links course with alternative tees for 18 holes. Panoramic
views of St David's Head and Ramsey Island.
*9 holes, 6117yds, Par 70, SSS 70, Course record 67.*
*Club membership 200.*
**Visitors**   prior booking with secretary is encouraged but
  no always necessary, please check for weekends,
  Ladies Day Fri pm.
**Societies**   book with the secretary in advance.
**Green Fees** £14 per day.
**Facilities**   ⚑ ⚘
**Leisure**   trolley for hire, putting green, practice net.
**Location**   2m W overlooking Whitesands Bay
**Hotel**   ★★★ 68% Warpool Court Hotel, ST
  DAVID'S
  ☎ 01437 720300 25 ⇥ 🐾

# PENALLY ABBEY ★★ ⊛⊛ 81%
## Penally, Tenby, Dyfed SA70 7PY
## Telephone: (01834) 843033 Fax: (01834) 844714

Penally Abbey, one of Pembrokeshire's loveliest country houses, is a 12 bedroom, gothic style, stone built mansion. Situated in an elevated position overlooking the golf course, adjacent to the church, on the village green in the picturesque floral village of Penally, 2 miles from Tenby.

---

TENBY                           Map 02 SN10

*Tenby* The Burrows SA70 7NP
☎ 01834 844447
The oldest club in Wales,this fine old seaside links, with sea views and natural hazards provides good golf.
*18 holes, 6232yds, Par 69, SSS 71.*
*Club membership 750.*
| | |
|---|---|
| Visitors | subject to competition & tee reservation. Must produce handicap certificate. |
| Societies | must apply in advance. |
| Green Fees | not confirmed. |
| Facilities | ♀ ♿ 🏠 ♟ T Mountford. |
| Leisure | putting,trolley hire,practice area. |
| Hotel | ★★★ 70% Atlantic Hotel, Esplanade, TENBY ☎ 01834 842881 & 844176 40 ➡ 🐾 |
| Additional hotel | ★★ 80% Penally Abbey Country House, Penally, TENBY ☎ 01834 843033 8 ➡ 🐾Annexe4 ➡ |

WELSHPOOL                    Map 07 SJ20

*Welshpool* Golfa Hill SY21 9AQ
☎ 01938 83249
Undulating, hilly, heathland course with bracing air. Testing holes are 2nd (par 5), 14th (par 3), 17th (par 3) and a memorable 18th.
*18 holes, 5708yds, Par 70, SSS 69, Course record 68.*
*Club membership 550.*
| | |
|---|---|
| Visitors | restricted at weekends. |
| Societies | must book in advance. |
| Green Fees | not confirmed. |
| Facilities | ♀ ♿ 🏠 |
| Location | 3m W off A458 |
| Hotel | ★★ 67% Royal Oak Hotel, WELSHPOOL ☎ 01938 552217 24 ➡ 🐾 |

---

Entries with a shaded background identify courses that are considered to be particularly interesting

---

A golf course name printed in *bold italics* means we have been unable to verify information with the club's management for the current year

---

●
## SOUTH WALES
●

This region includes the counties of Blaenau Gwent, Bridgend, Caerphilly, Cardiff, Merthyr Tydfil, Monmouthshire, Neath Port Talbot, Newport, Rhondda Cynon Taff, Swansea, Torfaen and Vale of Glamorgan which reflect the recent national changes.

ABERDARE                     Map 03 SO00

Aberdare Abernant CF44 0RY
☎ 01685 872797 & 878735
Mountain course with parkland features overlooking Cynon Valley.
*18 holes, 5767yds, Par 69, SSS 69, Course record 65.*
*Club membership 550.*
| | |
|---|---|
| Visitors | must contact in advance, may only play on Sat with member, Sun by arrangement with secretary. |
| Societies | apply in writing in advance to the secretary. |
| Green Fees | £14 per day (£18 weekends & bank holidays). |
| Facilities | ⊗ 🍴 ♭ 🍺 ♀ ♿ 🏠 ♟ A Palmer. |
| Leisure | trolley for hire, putting green, practice area. |
| Location | 0.75m E |
| Hotel | ★★★ 59% The Baverstock Hotel, The Heads Of Valley Rd, MERTHYR TYDFIL ☎ 01685 386221 53 ➡ 🐾 |

ABERGAVENNY               Map 03 SO21

*Monmouthshire* Gypsy Ln, LLanfoist NP7 9HE
☎ 01873 853171
This parkland course is very picturesque, with the beautifully wooded River Usk running alongside. There are a number of par 3 holes and a testing par 4 at the 15th.
*18 holes, 5961yds, Par 72, SSS 70.*
*Club membership 700.*
| | |
|---|---|
| Visitors | must play with member at weekends. Must contact in advance & have handicap certificate. |
| Societies | must contact in writing. |
| Green Fees | not confirmed. |
| Facilities | ♿ 🏠 ♟✝ ♟ |
| Leisure | fishing. |
| Location | 2m S off B4269 |
| Hotel | ★★ 70% Llanwenarth Arms Hotel, Brecon Rd, ABERGAVENNY ☎ 01873 810550 18 ➡ 🐾 |

**Wernddu Golf Centre** Old Ross Rd NP7 8NG
☎ 01873 856223
Two 9-hole parkland courses. The old course is an ideal starter course with wind hazards on the 4th; the new course in longer and more challenging with winds hazards on the 3rd and 9th holes and water affecting the 5th and 7th holes. There is also a 26-bay floodlit driving range and a practice putting green.
*Old Course: 9 holes, 2001yds, Par 31, SSS 30.*
*New Course: 9 holes, 3564yds, Par 36, SSS 35.*
*Club membership 300.*
**Visitors** ring in advance for details.
**Societies** telephone in advance.
**Green Fees** £12 per 18 holes; £8 per 9 holes.
**Facilities** ⊗ ⅢⅢ ⅛ ⅌ ♀ ⅄ 🏠 ⚐ ⅃ Alan Ashmead.
**Leisure** trolley for hire, driving range, putting green, practice area.
**Location** 1.5m NE on B4521
**Hotel** ★★ 70% Llanwenarth Arms Hotel, Brecon Rd, ABERGAVENNY
☎ 01873 810550 18 ⇆ ↾

---

### BARGOED                              Map 03 ST19

*Bargoed* Heolddu CF8 9GF ☎ 01443 830143
Mountain parkland course, testing par 4, 13th hole.
*18 holes, 5836yds, Par 70, SSS 70, Course record 65.*
*Club membership 500.*
**Visitors** must play with member at weekends.
**Societies** must contact in advance.
**Green Fees** not confirmed.
**Facilities** ♀ ⅄
**Leisure** putting green.
**Location** NW side of town
**Hotel** ★★★ 67% Maes Manor Hotel, BLACKWOOD
☎ 01495 224551 & 220011 8 ⇆ Annexe14 ⇆

---

### BARRY                               Map 03 ST16

**Brynhill** Port Rd CF62 8PN
☎ 01446 720277 & 735061
Meadowland course with some hard walking. Prevailing west wind.
*18 holes, 5947yds, Par 70, SSS 68.*
*Club membership 750.*
**Visitors** must contact in advance. May not play on Sun.
**Societies** phone secretary for details.
**Green Fees** £20 per round (£25 Sat).
**Facilities** ⊗ ⅢⅢ ⅛ ⅌ ♀ ⅄ ⅃ Peter Fountain.
**Leisure** trolley for hire, putting green, practice area.
**Location** 1.25m N on B4050
**Hotel** ★★★ 60% Mount Sorrel Hotel, Porthkerry Rd, BARRY ☎ 01446 740069 43 ⇆ ↾

---

**RAF St Athan** St Athan CF62 4WA
☎ 01446 797186 & 751043
This is a very windy course with wind straight off the sea to make all holes interesting. Further interest is added by this being a very tight course with lots of trees.
*9 holes, 6452yds, Par 71, SSS 71.*
*Club membership 450.*
**Visitors** contact in advance.
**Societies** apply in advance.
**Green Fees** £10 (£15 weekends & bank holidays).

**Facilities** ⊗ ⅢⅢ ⅛ ⅌ ♀ ⅄ 🏠
**Leisure** trolley for hire, putting green, practice area.
**Location** Between Barry & Llantwit Major
**Hotel** ★★ 67% West House Country Hotel & Restaurant, West St, LLANTWIT MAJOR
☎ 01446 792406 & 793726 21 ⇆ ↾

---

**St Andrews Major** Coldbrook Rd, Argae Ln, Cadoxton CF6 3BB ☎ 01446 722227
A new 9-hole, Pay and Play course with 6 Par 4s and 1 Par 5.
*9 holes, 3000yds, Par 70, SSS 68.*
*Club membership 520.*
**Visitors** must contact in advance.
**Societies** contact in advance.
**Green Fees** £8 per 9 holes; £13 per 18 holes.
**Facilities** ⊗ ⅢⅢ ⅛ ⅌ ♀ ⅄ 🏠 ⚐ ⅃
**Leisure** trolley for hire, putting green.
**Location** Off Barry new link road
**Hotel** ★★★⚲ 74% Egerton Grey Country House Hotel, Porthkerry, BARRY
☎ 01446 711666 10 ⇆ ↾

---

### BETTWS NEWYDD                       Map 03 SO30

*Alice Springs* NP5 1JY
☎ 01873 880772 & 880708
Two 18-hole undulating parkland courses set back to back with magnificent views of the Usk Valley. The Queen's course has testing 7th and 15th holes. The King's Course which opened in summer 1992, is 6662yds long.
*Queens Course: 18 holes, 6041yds, Par 67, SSS 69.*
*Kings Course: 18 holes, 6662yds, Par 72, SSS 71.*
*Club membership 350.*
**Visitors** should contact the club in advance for weekend play.
**Societies** must telephone in advance.
**Green Fees** not confirmed.
**Facilities** ♀ ⅄ 🏠 ⅃ Jim Howard.
**Leisure** caddy cars.
**Hotel** ★★★ 73% Glen-yr-Afon House Hotel, Pontypool Rd, USK
☎ 01291 672302 & 673202 27 ⇆ ↾

---

### BLACKWOOD                           Map 03 ST19

**Blackwood** Cwmgelli NP2 1EL
☎ 01495 222121 & 223152
Heathland course with sand bunkers. Undulating, with hard walking. Testing 2nd hole par 4. Good views.
*9 holes, 5332yds, Par 66.*
*Club membership 310.*
**Visitors** contact club or turn up and pay greens staff, may not play at weekends & bank holidays unless with member.
**Societies** by prior arrangement for members of a recognised golf club.
**Green Fees** £13 weekdays.
**Facilities** ⊗ by prior arrangement ⅢⅢ by prior arrangement ⅛ by prior arrangement ⅌ by prior arrangement ♀ ⅄
**Leisure** putting green, practice area.
**Location** 0.25m N of Blackwood, off A4048
**Hotel** ★★★ 67% Maes Manor Hotel, BLACKWOOD
☎ 01495 224551 & 220011 8 ⇆ Annexe14 ⇆

## BRIDGEND
Map 03 SS97

**Coed-Y-Mwstwr** The Clubhouse, Coychurch CF35 6AF
☎ 01656 862121
Challenging holes on this 9-hole course include the par 3 3rd
(142yds) involving a drive across a lake and the par 4 5th
(448yds) which is subject to strong prevailing winds.
*9 holes, 5758yds, Par 70, SSS 68.*
*Club membership 260.*
**Visitors**  must have handicap certificate, advisable to
contact in advance.
**Societies**  by prior application.
**Green Fees** £15 per 18 holes; £10 per 9 holes.
**Facilities**  ⊗ ⫪ ⓑ ▆ ♀ ⚒ 🎣 𝆑 Peter Evans.
**Leisure**  trolley for hire, putting green, practice area.
**Location**  1m out of Coychurch turn at village garage
**Hotel**  ★★★ 74% Coed-y-Mwstwr Hotel, Coychurch,
BRIDGEND ☎ 01656 860621 23 ⇥ 📞

**Southerndown** Ewenny CF32 0QP
☎ 01656 880476 & 880326
Downland championship course with rolling fairways
and fast greens. The par-3 5th is played across a valley
and the 18th, with its split level fairway, is a demanding
finishing hole. Superb views.
*18 holes, 6417yds, Par 70, SSS 72, Course record 64.*
*Club membership 710.*
**Visitors**  must contact in advance & have handicap
certificate.
**Societies**  on Tue & Thu by arrangement with
secretary.
**Green Fees** £30 (£36 weekends and bank holidays).

**Facilities**  ⊗ ⫪ ⓑ ▆ ♀ ⚒ 🎣 𝆑 D G McMonagle.
**Leisure**  trolley for hire, putting green, practice area.
**Location**  3m SW on B4524
**Hotel**  ★★★ 74% Coed-y-Mwstwr Hotel,
Coychurch, BRIDGEND
☎ 01656 860621 23 ⇥ 📞

## CAERLEON
Map 03 ST39

**Caerleon** NP6 1AY ☎ 01633 420342
Parkland course.
*9 holes, 2900yds, Par 34, SSS 34, Course record 29.*
*Club membership 120.*
**Visitors**  contact for details.
**Societies**  telephone.
**Green Fees** £5.15 per 18 holes; £3.45 per 9 holes
(£6.50/£4.30 weekends).
**Facilities**  ⓑ ▆ ♀ 🎣 𝆑 Alex Campbell.
**Leisure**  trolley for hire, driving range, putting green.
**Location**  3m from M4 turn off for Caerleon
**Hotel**  ★★★★ 65% Celtic Manor Hotel, Golf &
Country Club, Coldra Woods, NEWPORT
☎ 01633 413000 72 ⇥ 📞

## CAERPHILLY
Map 03 ST18

**Caerphilly** Penchapel, Mountain Rd CF8 1HJ
☎ 01222 883481 & 863441
Undulating mountain course with woodland affording good
views especially from 10th hole, 700 ft above sea level.
Recently upgraded to 18 holes.  ▶

★ ★ ★

# St. Mary's Hotel, Golf & Country Club

A luxury country hotel converted from a 17th
century farmhouse, we offer elegance and
comfort with first class friendly service. Set in
picturesque surroundings on a privately
owned 150 acre 27 hole golf complex 2 mins
from M4, making it the perfect location for
business or pleasure.

• 18 hole St Mary's Course
• 9 hole Sevenoaks Course
• 15 bay floodlit driving range
• Tennis court
• Equestrian centre

All rooms fitted with:
• Whirlpool baths
• Satellite TV
• Coffee & tea facilities
• Direct dial telephone

*Golf, Equestrian and Weekend Breaks available.*

🏁 *Please call us for a FREE video and brochure and sample for
yourselves "The Magic of St. Mary's".*

Best Western

**St. Mary's Golf Club Ltd. St. Mary's Hill Pencoed,
South Glamorgan CF35 5EA.**
**Hotel Reservation: Tel: (01656) 861100 Fax: (01656) 863400**

*14 holes, 6032yds, Par 73, SSS 71.*
*Club membership 750.*

**Visitors**  telephone in advance, must produce a current
handicap certificate or letter from club
secretary,may not play at weekends except with
member, no visitors bank holidays.
**Societies**  apply in writing in advance to the secretary.
**Green Fees** £20 (weekly tickets available).
**Facilities**  ⊗ ⫻ by prior arrangement ⬛ ♥ ♀ ⚥ ⌂
ℓ Richard Barter.
**Leisure**  trolley for hire, putting green, practice area.
**Location**  0.5m S on A469
**Hotel**  ★★★ 73% Manor Parc Country Hotel &
Restaurant, Thornhill Rd, Thornhill, CARDIFF
☎ 01222 693723 12 ⇆ ⫿

---

**Mountain Lakes & Castell Heights** Blaengwynlais
CF8 31NG ☎ 01222 861128 & 886666
The 9-hole Castell Heights course within the Mountain Lakes
complex was established in 1982 on a 45-acre site. In 1988 a
further 18-hole course was designed by Bob Sandow to take
advantage of 150-acres of mountain heathland, combining
both mountain top golf and parkland. Most holes are tree
lined and there are 16 'lakes' as hazards. Host of major PGA
tournaments.
*Mountain Lakes Course: 18 holes, 6046mtrs, Par 74, SSS 73,*
*Course record 69.*
*Castell Heights Course: 9 holes, 2688mtrs, Par 34, SSS 32.*
*Club membership 500.*

**Visitors**  advisable to check availability, Castell Heights is
pay as you play.
**Societies**  written or telephone notice in advance.
**Green Fees** Mountain Lakes: £20 per day; £15 per round.
Castell Heights: £5 (£5.50 weekends).
**Facilities**  ⊗ ⬛ ♥ ♀ ⚥ ⌂ ℓ Sion Bebb.
**Leisure**  motorised carts for hire, buggies for hire, trolley
for hire, driving range, putting green, practice
area.
**Location**  Near Black Lock Inn, Caerphilly Mountain
**Hotel**  ★★★ 73% Manor Parc Country Hotel &
Restaurant, Thornhill Rd, Thornhill, CARDIFF
☎ 01222 693723 12 ⇆ ⫿

---

**Virginia Park Golf Club** Virginia Park CF38 3SW
☎ 01222 863919 & 585368
Beside Caerphilly leisure centre, the course is totally flat but
with plenty of trees and bunkers and 2 lakes. It is a tight,
challenging course with 6 par 4 and 3 par 3 holes. Also a 20-
bay flodlit driving range.
*9 holes, 2566yds, Par 33.*
*Club membership 250.*

**Visitors**  telephone in advance.
**Societies**  telephone then write to confirm.
**Green Fees** £11 per 18 holes; £6 per 9 holes.
**Facilities**  ⬛ ♥ ♀ ⚥ ⌂ ⫿
**Leisure**  trolley for hire, driving range, leisure centre
adjacent.
**Location**  Off Pontyewindy Rd
**Hotel**  ★★★ 73% Manor Parc Country Hotel &
Restaurant, Thornhill Rd, Thornhill, CARDIFF
☎ 01222 693723 12 ⇆ ⫿

## CAERWENT                                          Map 03 ST49

**Dewstow** NP6 4AH
☎ 01291 430444
A newly-established, picturesque parkland course with
spectacular views over the Severn estuary towards Bristol.
Testing holes include the Par three 7th, which is approached
over water, some 50 feet lower than the tee. There is also a
26-bay floodlit driving range.
*Valley Course: 18 holes, 6123yds, Par 72, SSS 70, Course*
*record 69.*
*Park Course: 18 holes, 6147yds, Par 69, SSS 69, Course*
*record 72.*
*Club membership 850.*

**Visitors**  may book two days in advance (six days in
advance in winter).
**Societies**  apply in writing or telephone for details.
**Green Fees** £18 per day; £11 per 18 holes; £7 per 9 holes
(£15 per round; £9 per 9 holes weekends & bank
holidays).
**Facilities**  ⊗ ⫻ ⬛ ♥ ♀ ⚥ ⌂ ⫿ ℓ Gareth Bebb.
**Leisure**  motorised carts for hire, buggies for hire, trolley
for hire, driving range, putting green.
**Location**  0.5m S of A48 at Caerwent
**Hotel**  ★★★★ 72% St Pierre Hotel, Country Club
Resort, St Pierre Park, CHEPSTOW
☎ 01291 625261 143 ⇆ ⫿

## CARDIFF                                           Map 03 ST17

**Cardiff** Sherborne Av, Cyncoed CF2 6SJ
☎ 01222 753320
Parkland course, where trees form natural hazards. Interesting
variety of holes, mostly bunkered.
*18 holes, 6016yds, Par 70, SSS 70, Course record 66.*
*Club membership 900.*

**Visitors**  contact in advance.
**Societies**  Thu only, pre-booking essential.
**Green Fees** £30 per day summer (£20 winter).
**Facilities**  ⊗ ⫻ ⬛ ♥ ♀ ⚥ ⌂ ℓ Terry Hanson.
**Leisure**  trolley for hire, putting green, practice area.
**Location**  3m N of city centre
**Hotel**  B Forte Posthouse Pentwyn, Pentwyn Rd,
Pentwyn, CARDIFF
☎ 01222 731212 142 ⇆ ⫿

---

**Llanishen** Cwm Lisvane CF4 5UD
☎ 01222 755078
Mountain course, with hard walking overlooking the Bristol
Channel.
*18 holes, 5296yds, Par 68, SSS 66, Course record 63.*
*Club membership 600.*

**Visitors**  must play with member at weekends & bank
holidays. Must contact in advance.
**Societies**  contact in advance.
**Green Fees** £24 per weekday.
**Facilities**  ⊗ ⫻ ⬛ ♥ ♀ ⚥ ⌂ ℓ Adrian Jones.
**Leisure**  trolley for hire, putting green, practice area.
**Location**  5m N of city centre off A469
**Hotel**  B Forte Posthouse Pentwyn, Pentwyn Rd,
Pentwyn, CARDIFF
☎ 01222 731212 142 ⇆ ⫿

**Peterstone** Peterstone, Wentloog CF3 8TN
☎ 01633 680009
Parkland course with abundant water features and several
long drives (15th, 601yds).
*18 holes, 6555yds, Par 72, SSS 71, Course record 67.*
*Club membership 709.*
**Visitors**      contact in advance suggested.
**Societies**     telephone enquiries welcome.
**Green Fees**    £20 per day; £15 per round (£27.50/£22.50
                  weekends).
**Facilities**    ⊗ ⍾ ⓚ ⬛ ♀ ⚲ 🖻 🖾 🅕 Mike Pycroft.
**Leisure**       motorised carts for hire, buggies for hire, trolley
                  for hire, putting green, practice area.
**Location**      3m from Castleton off A48
**Hotel**         B Forte Posthouse Pentwyn, Pentwyn Rd,
                  Pentwyn, CARDIFF
                  ☎ 01222 731212 142 ⇔ 🅟

**Radyr** Drysgol Rd, Radyr CF4 8BS
☎ 01222 842408
Hillside, parkland course which can be windy. Good views.
*18 holes, 6031yds, Par 69, SSS 70, Course record 63.*
*Club membership 870.*
**Visitors**      must play with member at weekends. Must
                  contact in advance and have an introduction
                  from own club.
**Societies**     must contact in advance.
**Green Fees**    not confirmed.
**Facilities**    ♀ ⚲ 🖻 🅕 Steve Gough.
**Location**      4.5m NW of city centre off A4119
**Hotel**         ★★★★ 62% Park Thistle, Park Place,
                  CARDIFF ☎ 01222 383471 119 ⇔ 🅟

**St Mellons** St Mellons CF3 8XS
☎ 01633 680408
This parkland course comprises quite a few par-3 holes
and provides some testing golf. It is indeed a challenge to
the single handicap golfer. The 12th hole runs over a
stream, making an accurate drive virtually essential.
*18 holes, 6275yds, Par 70, SSS 70, Course record 63.*
*Club membership 700.*
**Visitors**      must contact in advance. With member only
                  at weekends.
**Societies**     must contact in advance.
**Green Fees**    £25 per day.
**Facilities**    ⊗ ⍾ ⓚ ⬛ ♀ ⚲ 🖻 🅕 Barry Thomas.
**Leisure**       buggies for hire, trolley for hire, putting
                  green, practice area.
**Location**      5m NE off A48
**Hotel**         B Forte Posthouse Pentwyn, Pentwyn Rd,
                  Pentwyn, CARDIFF
                  ☎ 01222 731212 142 ⇔ 🅟

**Whitchurch** Pantmawr Rd, Whitchurch CF4 6XD
☎ 01222 620985 sec & 614660 pro
Well manicured parkland course, with easy walking.
*18 holes, 6321yds, Par 71, SSS 71, Course record 62.*
*Club membership 750.*
**Visitors**      contact secretary/professional in advance.
**Societies**     Thu only. Must contact in advance.
**Green Fees**    £30 per day (£35 weekends & bank holidays).
**Facilities**    ⊗ ⍾ ⓚ ⬛ ♀ ⚲ 🖻 🅕 Eddie Clark.
**Leisure**       trolley for hire, putting green, practice area.
**Location**      4m N of city centre on A470
**Hotel**         ★★★★ 62% Park Thistle, Park Place,
                  CARDIFF ☎ 01222 383471 119 ⇔ 🅟

---

**Marriott**

# ST. PIERRE

## HOTEL & COUNTRY CLUB

## St Pierre Park Chepstow Gwent NP6 6YA

### Telephone: (01291) 625261

---

**CHEPSTOW**                                    Map 03 ST59

**ST PIERRE HOTEL, COUNTRY CLUB RESORT**
See page 349

**CLYDACH**                                     Map 03 SN60

**Inco** SA6 5PQ ☎ 01792 844216
Flat meadowland course.
*12 holes, 6303yds, Par 71, SSS 70.*
*Club membership 300.*
**Visitors**      no restrictions.
**Societies**     must contact in advance.
**Green Fees**    not confirmed.
**Facilities**    ♀ ⚲
**Location**      0.75m SE on B4291
**Hotel**         ★★ 62% Oak Tree Parc Hotel, Birchgrove Rd,
                  BIRCHGROVE ☎ 01792 817781 10 ⇔ 🅟

**CREIGIAU (CREIYIAU)**                         Map 03 ST08

**Creigiau** Llantwit Rd CF4 8NN ☎ 01222 890263
Downland course, with small greens.
*18 holes, 6015yds, Par 71, SSS 69.*
*Club membership 1020.*
**Visitors**      must contact in advance.
**Societies**     Wed only min number 20, must book in
                  advance.
**Green Fees**    £26 per day/round.
**Facilities**    ⊗ ⍾ ⓚ ⬛ ♀ ⚲ 🖻 🅕 Iain Luntz.       ▶

| | |
|---|---|
| **Leisure** | trolley for hire, practice area. |
| **Location** | 6m NW of Cardiff on A4119 |
| **Hotel** | ★★★★ 65% Miskin Manor Hotel, MISKIN ☎ 01443 224204 32 ⇥ ♠ |

## CWMBRAN
Map 03 ST29

**Green Meadow Golf & Country Club** Treherbert Rd, Croesyceiliog NP44 2BZ
☎ 01633 869321 & 860655
Undulating parkland course with panoramic views. The 7th hole is played partly down hill with the front half of the green enclosed with water; the 13th is exposed to winds with large mature trees along righthand side of green.
*18 holes, 6029yds, Par 71, SSS 72.*
*Club membership 400.*

| | |
|---|---|
| **Visitors** | by prior arrangement advised especially at weekends, tel 01633 862626. Correct standard of dress compulsory. |
| **Societies** | telephone for brochure, Golf Shop 01633 862626. |
| **Green Fees** | £15 per day; £12 per 18 holes (£18/£15 weekends). |
| **Facilities** | ⊗ ⅲ ⓑ ♥ ♀ ⚎ ☎ ⚑ ⚐ Dave Woodman. |
| **Leisure** | hard tennis courts, motorised carts for hire, buggies for hire, trolley for hire, driving range, driving range, practice area. |
| **Location** | 5m N of junct 26 M4, off A4042 |
| **Hotel** | ★★★★ 63% Parkway Hotel, Cwmbran Dr, CWMBRAN ☎ 01633 871199 70 ⇥ ♠ |

*Pontnewydd* Maesgwyn Farm, West Pontnewydd NP44 1AB
☎ 01633 482170
Mountainside course, with hard walking. Good views across the Severn Estuary.
*10 holes, 5353yds, Par 68, SSS 67, Course record 63.*
*Club membership 250.*

| | |
|---|---|
| **Visitors** | must play with member weekends & bank holidays. |
| **Green Fees** | not confirmed. |
| **Facilities** | ♀ ⚎ |
| **Location** | N side of town centre |
| **Hotel** | ★★★★ 63% Parkway Hotel, Cwmbran Dr, CWMBRAN ☎ 01633 871199 70 ⇥ ♠ |

## DINAS POWIS
Map 03 ST17

**Dinas Powis** Old High Walls CF64 4AJ
☎ 01222 512727
Parkland/downland course with views over the Bristol Channel and the seaside resort of Barry.
*18 holes, 5486yds, Par 67, SSS 67, Course record 60.*
*Club membership 550.*

| | |
|---|---|
| **Visitors** | must contact in advance. No visitors during weekends. |
| **Societies** | telephone in advance. |
| **Green Fees** | £22.50 per day (with member only weekends). |
| **Facilities** | ⊗ ⅲ ⓑ ♥ ♀ ⚎ ☎ ⚐ Gareth Bennett. |
| **Leisure** | trolley for hire, putting green, practice area. |
| **Location** | NW side of village |
| **Hotel** | ★★★ 60% Mount Sorrel Hotel, Porthkerry Rd, BARRY ☎ 01446 740069 43 ⇥ ♠ |

## GLYNNEATH
Map 03 SN80

**Glynneath** Pen-y-graig, Pontneathvaughan SA11 5UH
☎ 01639 720452
Attractive hillside golf overlooking the Vale of Neath in the foothills of the Brecon Beacons National Park. Reasonably level farmland/wooded course.
*18 holes, 5533yds, Par 68, SSS 67, Course record 66.*
*Club membership 600.*

| | |
|---|---|
| **Visitors** | restricted starting times at weekend. |
| **Societies** | apply in writing in advance. |
| **Green Fees** | £15 per day (£20 weekends and bank holidays). |
| **Facilities** | ⊗ ⓑ ♥ ♀ ⚎ ☎ |
| **Leisure** | buggies for hire, trolley for hire, snooker. |
| **Location** | 2m NE on B4242 |
| **Hotel** | ★★ 62% Oak Tree Parc Hotel, Birchgrove Rd, BIRCHGROVE ☎ 01792 817781 10 ⇥ ♠ |

## LLANWERN
Map 03 ST38

**Llanwern** Tennyson Av NP6 2DY
☎ 01633 412029 & 412380
Parkland Course.
*New Course: 18 holes, 6115yds, Par 70, SSS 69, Course record 63.*
*Club membership 650.*

| | |
|---|---|
| **Visitors** | welcome, but with member only at weekends. |
| **Societies** | telephone and confirm in writing. |
| **Green Fees** | £20 per day (£25 weekends). |
| **Facilities** | ⊗ ⅲ ⓑ ♥ ♀ ⚎ ☎ ⚐ Stephen Price. |
| **Leisure** | putting green, practice area, snooker room. |
| **Location** | 0.5m S off A455 |
| **Hotel** | ★★★★ 65% Celtic Manor Hotel, Golf & Country Club, Coldra Woods, NEWPORT ☎ 01633 413000 72 ⇥ ♠ |

## MAESTEG
Map 03 SS89

**Maesteg** Mount Pleasant, Neath Rd CF34 9PR
☎ 01656 734106 & 732037
Reasonably flat hill-top course with scenic views.
*18 holes, 5929yds, Par 70, SSS 69, Course record 69.*
*Club membership 720.*

| | |
|---|---|
| **Visitors** | must be a member of a recognised golf club & have a handicap certificate. |
| **Societies** | apply in writing. |
| **Green Fees** | £17 per day (£20 weekends & bank holidays). |
| **Facilities** | ⊗ ⓑ ♥ ♀ ⚎ ☎ ⚐ John Black. |
| **Leisure** | trolley for hire, putting green,practice area. |
| **Location** | 0.5m W off B4282 |
| **Hotel** | ★★★ 60% Aberavon Beach Hotel, PORT TALBOT ☎ 01639 884949 52 ⇥ |

## MAESYCWMMER
Map 03 ST19

*Bryn Meadows Golf & Country Hotel* The Bryn CF8 7SM
☎ 01495 225590 or 224103
A heavily wooded parkland course with panoramic views of the Brecon Beacons.
*18 holes, 6132yds, Par 72, SSS 69, Course record 68.*
*Club membership 540.*

| | |
|---|---|
| **Visitors** | may not play Sun mornings. Must contact in advance. ▶ |

# ST PIERRE

## ST PIERRE PARK, CHEPSTOW *Monmouthshire*
☎ 01291 625261                          Map 03 ST59

*John Ingham writes:* Just over the Severn Bridge, and a mile down the old Newport road, is St Pierre, the parkland course where huge trees stand in the way of any golf shot not hit on the perfect line!

Set in 400 yards of glorious deer park, with a lake preserved as a wild life sanctuary, a clubhouse which was once a great mansion and the 800-year-old church of St Pierre nearby, you cannot help but be impressed by the place, and the atmosphere.

There are two courses to sample. The Old was designed by C K Cotton in 1962 while the Mathern was created by Bill Graham, a Geordie businessman who snapped up the place after driving past in his car after World War II. He immediately saw the potential as the fast motorway link with London and the south was being created.

The courses have staged several successful tournaments including the old Dunlop Masters which I used to cover for a London newspaper. Competitors would get pretty cross when they found their towering drives achieved nothing because the ball, when they got up to it, was 'snookered' by huge trees, several hundred years old. Among other hazards there was none more fearsome than the lake that guards the short 18th hole - a 'mere' 245 yards across water. Television cameras here filmed Tony Jacklin and Peter Oosterhuis almost holing in one, But they missed Arwyn Griffiths who arrived on the last tee needing a par-3 for an amazing course record 63. Unhappily, Mr Griffiths found the ordeal too much and took a ghastly 11 shots, although he still won the amateur event and was thus able to celebrate at the very excellent 19th hole!

Accommodation is sumptuous within the historic buildings, making it a very special place for a few days away from it all.

While there are stories of spirits walking in the night I suspect they had something to do with the tough Old course which at 6785yards cannily sorts out even the best players while the shorter Mathern, at 5732 yards with a par 68 can also throw up a few nightmare situations if you become stymied behind a whopping oak tree!

| | |
|---|---|
| Visitors | must contact in advance and on the Old Course play to a proficient standard so as not to restrict play apply in writing. Handicap certificate required |
| Societies | Monday to Friday only. Must make an advance reservation |
| Green fees | Midweek only Old Course £40, Mathern Course £30. Day ticket (both courses) £55 |
| Facilities | ⊗ 〼 ╚ ╩ ♀ ⇔ ᗱ 🖾 ⚵ putting green, practice area, ⌁ (Renton Doig) buggies, trolleys |
| Leisure | hard tennis courts, indoor swimming, squash, snooker, crown bowling, croquet, jacuzzi, health spa |
| Location | Chepstow NP6 6YA 3m SW off A48 |

36 holes. Old Course: 18 holes, 6785yds, Par71 SSS 73
Mathern Course: 18 holes, 5732yds, Par 68, SSS 67

## WHERE TO STAY AND EAT NEARBY

**HOTELS:**

**CHEPSTOW**

★★★★✿ 72% Marriott St Pierre Hotel & Country Club ☎ 01291 625261 143 ⇔ ᖆ

★★ 66% The George Hotel, Moor St ☎ 01291 625363. 14 ⇔ ᖆ

★★65% Castle View, 16 Bridge St ☎ 01291 620349. 9(8 ⇔ 1 ᖆ ) Annexe 4 ⇔

**RESTAURANTS:**

**TINTERN**
✿ Royal George Hotel (★★) ☎ 01291 689205

**WHITEBROOK**
✿✿✿ The Crown at Whitebrook (★★) ☎ 01600 860254

| | |
|---|---|
| Societies | Tue & Thu only. |
| Green Fees | not confirmed. |
| Facilities | ♀♣ ☎ ⚲ ⌗ ℓ Bruce Hunter. |
| Leisure | heated indoor swimming pool, sauna, gymnasium, buggy/trolley hire,practice area. |
| Location | On the A4048 Blackwood to Ystrad Mynach rd |
| Hotel | ★★★ 67% Maes Manor Hotel, BLACKWOOD ☎ 01495 224551 & 220011 8 ⇆Annexe14 ⇆ |

## MARGAM                                    Map 03 SS78

**Lakeside** Water St SA13 2PA
☎ 01639 899959
A nine hole course with four Par 4's and five Par 3's.
*Old Course: 9 holes, 2500yds, Par 31, SSS 31, Course record 63.*
*New Course: 9 holes, 2500yds, Par 34.*
*Club membership 250.*

| | |
|---|---|
| Visitors | no restrictions. New course due to open June 96. |
| Societies | apply in advance by letter or telephone. |
| Green Fees | £8 per 18 holes; £5 per 9 holes. |
| Facilities | ⊗ ⅢⅢ ⓑ ♥ ♀♣ ☎ ⚲ ℓ Mathew Wootton. |
| Leisure | trolley for hire, driving range. |
| Location | Off junct 38 of M4 |
| Hotel | ★★★ 60% Aberavon Beach Hotel, PORT TALBOT ☎ 01639 884949 52 ⇆ |

## MERTHYR TYDFIL                              Map 03 SO00

**Merthyr Tydfil (Cilanws)** Cilsanws, Cefn Coed CF48 2NU
☎ 01685 723308
Mountain-top course with good views and water hazards.
Requires accuracy off the tee.
*11 holes, 5956yds, Par 70, SSS 69, Course record 65.*
*Club membership 210.*

| | |
|---|---|
| Visitors | may not play on Sun. |
| Societies | by prior arrangement. |
| Green Fees | £12 per day (£16 weekends & bank holidays). |
| Facilities | ♣ |
| Location | Off A470 at Cefn Coed |
| Hotel | ★★ 66% Nant Ddu Lodge Hotel, Cwm Taf, Merthyr Tydfil ☎ 01685 379111 12 ⇆ ♞Annexe4 ⇆ |

**Morlais Castle** Pant, Dowlais CF48 2UY
☎ 01685 722822
Beautiful moorland course in National Park adjacent to
Brecon Beacons. Rocky terrain off the fairways makes for a
testing game.
*18 holes, 6320yds, Par 71, SSS 71.*
*Club membership 450.*

| | |
|---|---|
| Visitors | must contact in advance for weekends. |
| Societies | apply in writing. |
| Green Fees | £14 per day (£16 weekends & bank holidays). |
| Facilities | ⊗ by prior arrangement ⅢⅢ by prior arrangement ⓑ ♥ ♀♣ ☎ ℓ P Worthing. |
| Leisure | practice area. |
| Location | 2.5m N off A465 |
| Hotel | ★★ 66% Nant Ddu Lodge Hotel, Cwm Taf, Merthyr Tydfil ☎ 01685 379111 12 ⇆ ♞Annexe4 ⇆ |

## MONMOUTH                                   Map 03 SO51

**Monmouth** Leasebrook Ln NP5 3SN
☎ 01600 712212
Parkland course in scenic setting. High, undulating land with
good views. Testing 1st and 4th holes.
*18 holes, 5689yds, Par 69, SSS 69, Course record 68.*
*Club membership 600.*

| | |
|---|---|
| Visitors | advisable to contact in advance, bank holidays only with member. |
| Societies | advance notice advisable, write or telephone secretary. |
| Green Fees | £15 per day. |
| Facilities | ⊗ ⅢⅢ ⓑ ♥ ♀♣ ☎ |
| Leisure | motorised carts for hire, trolley for hire, putting green, practice area. |
| Location | 1.5m NE off A40 |
| Hotel | ★★ 68% Riverside Hotel, Cinderhill St, MONMOUTH ☎ 01600 715577 & 713236 17 ⇆ ♞ |

**Rolls of Monmouth** The Hendre NP5 4HG
☎ 01600 715353
A hilly and challenging parkland course encompassing
several lakes and ponds and surrounded by woodland. Set
within a beautiful private estate complete with listed
mansion.
*18 holes, 6733yds, Par 72, SSS 73.*
*Club membership 200.*

| | |
|---|---|
| Visitors | telephone in advance. |
| Societies | must contact in advance. |
| Green Fees | £30 per day (£35 weekends & bank holidays). Monday special £25 per 18 holes,lunch & coffee. |
| Facilities | ⊗ ⅢⅢ ⓑ ♥ ♀♣ ☎ ⚲ |
| Leisure | motorised carts for hire, buggies for hire, trolley for hire, putting green, practice area. |
| Location | 4m W on B4233 |
| Hotel | ★★ 68% Riverside Hotel, Cinderhill St, MONMOUTH ☎ 01600 715577 & 713236 17 ⇆ ♞ |

## MOUNTAIN ASH                                Map 03 ST09

**Mountain Ash** Cefnpennar CF45 4DT ☎ 01443 479459
Mountain course.
*18 holes, 5553yds, Par 69, SSS 67, Course record 63.*
*Club membership 600.*

| | |
|---|---|
| Visitors | contact in advance for details. |
| Societies | must contact in writing. |
| Green Fees | £15 per day (£18 weekends). |
| Facilities | ⊗ ⅢⅢ ⓑ ♥ ♀♣ ☎ ℓ Ceri Hiscox. |
| Leisure | trolley for hire, putting green. |
| Location | 1m NW off A4059 |
| Hotel | ★★★ 59% The Baverstock Hotel, The Heads Of Valley Rd, MERTHYR TYDFIL ☎ 01685 386221 53 ⇆ ♞ |

A golf course name printed in ***bold italics***
means we have been unable to verify
information with the club's management for
the current year

## NANTYGLO
Map 03 SO11

**West Monmouthshire** Golf Rd, Winchestown NP3 4QT
☎ 01495 310233
Established in 1906, this mountain and heathland course was officially designated in 1994 by the Guiness Book of Record as being the highest above sea level, with the 14th tee at a height of 1513ft. The course has plenty of picturesque views, hard walking and natural hazards. Testing 3rd hole, par 5, and 7th hole, par 4.
*18 holes, 6013yds, Par 71, SSS 69, Course record 65.*
*Club membership 350.*
**Visitors** welcome, must be guest of member for play on Sun.
**Societies** apply in writing or contact golf shop 01495 313052.
**Green Fees** £18 per day (Mon-Sat).
**Facilities** ⊗ ⅋⅏ ⅃ ⅌ ⅗ ⅘ ☎
**Leisure** trolley for hire, putting green, practice area,.
**Location** 0.25m W off A467
**Hotel** ★★★ 54% Angel Hotel, Cross St, ABERGAVENNY
☎ 01873 857121 29 ⇌ ℞

## NEATH
Map 03 SS79

**Earlswood** Jersey Marine SA10 6JP ☎ 01792 812198
Earlswood is a hillside course offering spectacular scenic views over Swansea Bay. The terrain is gently undulating parkland with natural hazards and is designed to appeal to both the new and the experienced golfer.
*18 holes, 5084yds, Par 68, SSS 68.*
**Visitors** no restrictions.
**Societies** advisable to contact in advance.
**Green Fees** £8 per 18 holes.
**Facilities** ⅌ ⅗ ☎ ⅗ ℰ Mike Day.
**Leisure** trolley for hire, catering can be arranged at Swansea Bay Golf Club.
**Location** Approx 4m E of Swansea, off A483
**Hotel** ★★ 65% Castle Hotel, The Parade, NEATH
☎ 01639 641119 & 643581 28 ⇌ ℞

**Neath** Cadoxton SA10 8AH
☎ 01639 643615 & 632759
Mountain course, with spectacular views. Testing holes: 10th par 4; 12th par 5; 15th par 4.
*18 holes, 6492yds, Par 72, SSS 72, Course record 66.*
*Club membership 700.*
**Visitors** with member only at weekends & bank holidays.
**Societies** should either telephone or write in advance.
**Green Fees** not confirmed.
**Facilities** ⅌ ⅗ ☎ ⅗ ℰ E M Bennett.
**Leisure** putting green,trolley hire.
**Location** 2m NE off A4230
**Hotel** ★★ 65% Castle Hotel, The Parade, NEATH
☎ 01639 641119 & 643581 28 ⇌ ℞

**Swansea Bay** Jersey Marine SA10 6JP
☎ 01792 812198 & 814153
Fairly level seaside links with part-sand dunes.
*18 holes, 6605yds, Par 72, SSS 72.*
*Club membership 500.*
**Visitors** welcome.
**Societies** telephone enquiry or letter stating requirements.
**Green Fees** £16 per day (£22 weekends & bank holidays).

**Facilities** ⊗ ⅋⅏ by prior arrangement ⅃ ⅌ ⅗ ⅗ ☎ ⅗
ℰ Mike Day.
**Leisure** trolley for hire, putting green, practice area.
**Location** 4m SW off A48
**Hotel** ★★ 65% Castle Hotel, The Parade, NEATH
☎ 01639 641119 & 643581 28 ⇌ ℞

## NELSON
Map 03 ST19

**Whitehall** The Pavilion CF46 6ST ☎ 01443 740245
Windy hilltop course. Testing 4th hole (225 yds) par 3, and 6th hole (402 yds) par 4. Pleasant views.
*9 holes, 5666yds, Par 69, SSS 68, Course record 63.*
*Club membership 300.*
**Visitors** must be a member of a recognised golf club & have a handicap certificate. Must contact in advance to play at weekends.
**Societies** must contact in writing 4 weeks in advance.
**Green Fees** not confirmed.
**Facilities** ⅌ ⅗
**Location** Turn off A470 to Nelson and take A4054 S
**Hotel** ★★★ 63% Llechwen Hall Hotel, Llanfabon, PONTYPRIDD
☎ 01443 742050 & 740305 11 ⇌ ℞

## NEWPORT
Map 03 ST38

**Newport** Great Oak, Rogerstone NP1 9FX
☎ 01633 896794 & 892643
An undulating parkland course, part-wooded. The 2nd hole is surrounded by bunkers - a difficult hole. The 11th hole is a bogey 4 and the fairway runs through an avenue of trees, making a straight drive preferable. Set 300ft above sea level, it offers fine views.
*18 holes, 6431yds, Par 72, SSS 71, Course record 64.*
*Club membership 800.*
**Visitors** must contact in advance & have handicap certificate. With member only on Sat.
**Societies** must contact in writing.
**Green Fees** not confirmed.
**Facilities** ⅌ ⅗ ☎ ⅗ ℰ Roy Skuse.
**Leisure** putting green,practice area,trolley hire.
**Location** 3m NW of city centre off B4591
**Hotel** ★★★★ 65% Celtic Manor Hotel, Golf & Country Club, Coldra Woods, NEWPORT
☎ 01633 413000 72 ⇌ ℞

**Parc** Church Ln, Coedkernew NP1 9TU
☎ 01633 680933
A challenging but enjoyable 18-hole course with water hazards and accompanying wildlife. The 38-bay driving range is floodlit until 10pm.
*18 holes, 5512yds, Par 70, SSS 70, Course record 71.*
*Club membership 400.*
**Visitors** book in advance 01633 680933.
**Societies** telephone in advance.
**Green Fees** £10 per round (£12 weekends and bank holidays).
**Facilities** ⊗ ⅋⅏ ⅃ ⅌ ⅗ ⅗ ☎ ⅗ ℰ B Thomas/L Bond.
**Leisure** trolley for hire, driving range, putting green, practice area.
**Location** 3m SW of Newport, off A48
**Hotel** ★★★ 60% Jarvis Wentloog Hotel, CASTLETON
☎ 01633 680591 55 ⇌ ℞

# THE CELTIC MANOR

- *Luxurious Bedrooms*
- *Award Winning Restaurant*
- *Health & Leisure Centre*
- *Beauty Therapy Suites*
- *Ian Woosnam Golf Academy*
- *Two 18 Hole Courses*

*Designed by Robert Trent Jones*

## *The Complete Resort*

AA ★ ★ ★ ★

*"Both our courses are a golfer's dream; challenging, interesting and set in beautiful Welsh countryside."*

*IAN WOOSNAM MBE, TOURING PROFESSIONAL*

THE CELTIC MANOR HOTEL,
GOLF & COUNTRY CLUB
Coldra Woods, Newport, Gwent NP6 2YA
Tel: 01633 413000 Fax: 01633 412910/410284

---

**Tredegar Park** Bassaleg Rd NP9 3PX
☎ 01633 894433 & 894517
A parkland course with River Ebbw and streams as natural hazards. The ground is very flat with narrow fairways and small greens. The 17th hole (par 3) is played on to a plateau where many players spoil their medal round.
*18 holes, 6095yds, Par 71, SSS 70.*
*Club membership 750.*
**Visitors** must be a member of a golf club affiliated to a national golf union, please contact in advance.
**Societies** apply to secretary.
**Green Fees** £23 per day; £15 in winter (£30 weekends & bank holidays).
**Facilities** ⊗ ⅷ ⅃ ♨ ♀ ♨ 🏠 ⚑ ⟨ M L Morgan.
**Leisure** trolley for hire, putting green, practice area.
**Location** 2m SW off A467 exit 27 of M4
**Hotel** ★★★ 62% Kings Hotel, High St, NEWPORT ☎ 01633 842020 47 ⇄ ⓡ

## OAKDALE                                          Map 03 ST19

**Oakdale** Llwynon Ln NP2 0NF ☎ 01495 220044
*9 holes, 1344yds, Par 28, Course record 27.*
**Visitors** no restrictions pay & play.
**Societies** telephone for further information and arrangements.
**Green Fees** £3.75 per 9 holes; £2.25 additional round.
**Facilities** ♨ 🏠 ⚑ ⟨ Clive Coombs.
**Leisure** trolley for hire, driving range.
**Location** B4251 E of Blackwood

---

## PENARTH                                          Map 03 ST17

**Glamorganshire** Lavernock Rd CF64 5UP
☎ 01222 701185
Parkland course, overlooking the Bristol Channel.
*18 holes, 6181yds, Par 70, SSS 70, Course record 64.*
*Club membership 1000.*
**Visitors** contact professional in advance.
**Societies** must contact in advance.
**Green Fees** £24 per day (£30 weekends & bank holidays).
**Facilities** ⊗ ⅷ ⅃ ♨ ♀ ♨ 🏠 ⚑ ⟨ Andrew Kerr-Smith.
**Leisure** squash, motorised carts for hire, buggies for hire, trolley for hire, driving range, putting green, practice area.
**Location** S side of town centre on B4267
**Hotel** ★ 66% Walton House Hotel, 37 Victoria Rd, PENARTH ☎ 01222 707782 13rm(11 ⇄ ⓡ)

## PENCOED                                          Map 03 SS98

*St Mary's Hotel Golf & Country Club* St Mary Hill
CF35 5EA ☎ 01656 861100
A parkland course with many American style features. The Par 3 13th called 'Alcatraz' has a well deserved reputation.
*St Mary's Course: 18 holes, 5120yds, Par 67, SSS 66, Course record 67.*
*Sevenoaks Course: 9 holes, 2426yds, Par 35, SSS 34.*
*Club membership 1100.*
**Visitors** must produce a handicap certificate.
**Societies** telephone Kay Brazell.
**Green Fees** not confirmed.
**Facilities** ♀ ♨ 🏠 ⚑ ⟨ ⋈ ⟨ Jason Harris.
**Leisure** hard tennis courts, 15 bay driving range.
**Hotel** ★★★ 70% St Mary's Hotel & Country Club, St Marys Golf Club, PENCOED ☎ 01656 861100 24 ⇄ ⓡ
*See advertisement on page 345.*

## PENRHYS                                          Map 03 ST09

**Rhondda** Golf Club House CF43 3PW ☎ 01443 441384
Mountain course with good views.
*18 holes, 6205yds, Par 70, SSS 70, Course record 67.*
*Club membership 600.*
**Visitors** contact secretary for weekend play.
**Societies** contact for details.
**Green Fees** £15 (£20 weekends & bank holidays).
**Facilities** ⊗ ⅷ ⅃ ♨ ♀ ♨ 🏠 ⟨ Rhys Davies.
**Leisure** motorised carts for hire, buggies for hire, trolley for hire, putting green, practice area.
**Location** 0.5m W off B4512
**Hotel** ★★ 64% Wyndham Hotel, Dunraven Place, BRIDGEND ☎ 01656 652080 & 657431 24 ⇄ ⓡ

## PONTARDAWE                                       Map 03 SN70

**Pontardawe** Cefn Llan SA8 4SH
☎ 01792 830041 & 830977
Meadowland course situated on plateau 600 ft above sea-level with good views over Bristol Channel and Brecon Beacons.
*18 holes, 6038yds, Par 70, SSS 70, Course record 64.*
*Club membership 500.*

**Visitors**   must contact in advance, but may not play on weekends.
**Societies**   apply in writing.
**Green Fees** £19 per day.
**Facilities**   ⊗ � 🏌 ▆ ♀ 🏌 🏠 ℓ Gary Hopkins.
**Leisure**   trolley for hire, putting green, practice area.
**Location**   N side of town centre M4 junc 45 off A4067
**Hotel**   ★★ 62% Oak Tree Parc Hotel, Birchgrove Rd, BIRCHGROVE
      ☎ 01792 817781 10 ⇥ 🏌

---

## PONTLLIW                         Map 02 SS69

**Allt-y-Graban** Allt-y-Graban Rd SA4 1DT
☎ 01792 885757
A new course opened for 1994. It is a 9-hole course but with plans for 12 holes. There are 6 par-4 holes and 3 par-3 holes. The 4th is a challenging hole with a blind tee shoot into the valley and a dogleg to the left onto an elevated green.
*9 holes, 2210yds, Par 66, SSS 66.*
*Club membership 158.*
**Visitors**   no restrictions,
**Societies**   telephone in advance.
**Green Fees** £12 per day; £9 per 18 holes; £6 per 9 holes (£8 per 18 holes; £5 per 9 holes in winter).
**Facilities**   ▆ ▆ ♀ 🏌 🏠 🚩 ℓ Steven Rees.
**Leisure**   trolley for hire, putting green, practice area.
**Hotel**   ★★★ 61% Fforest Hotel, Pontardulais Rd, Fforestfach, SWANSEA
      ☎ 01792 588711 34 ⇥ 🏌

---

## PONTYPOOL                    Map 03 SO20

**Pontypool** Trevethin NP4 8TR
☎ 01495 763655
Undulating, mountain course with magnificent views.
*18 holes, 6046yds, Par 69, SSS 69.*
*Club membership 638.*
**Visitors**   must have a handicap certificate.
**Societies**   apply in writing or by phone, deposit payable.
**Green Fees** £18 per day; £24 weekends and bank holidays.
**Facilities**   ⊗ � 🏌 ▆ ♀ 🏌 🏠 🚩 ℓ James Howard.
**Leisure**   motorised carts for hire, buggies for hire, trolley for hire, putting green, practice area.
**Location**   1.5m N off A4043
**Hotel**   ★★★ 73% Glen-yr-Afon House Hotel, Pontypool Rd, USK
      ☎ 01291 672302 & 673202 27 ⇥ 🏌

**Woodlake Park Golf & Country Club** Glascoed NP4 0TE
☎ 01291 673933
Undulating parkland course with magnificent views over Llandegfedd Reservoir. Superb green constructed to USGA specification. Holes 4, 7 & 16 are Par 3's which are particularly challenging. Holes 6 & 17 are long Par 4's which can be wind affected. An indoor golf centre with chipping/pitching & 4 bunker positions, plus an indoor driving range ensure golf can be played whatever the weather!
*18 holes, 6278yds, Par 71, SSS 72, Course record 68.*
*Club membership 350.*
**Visitors**   book in advance.
**Societies**   telephone or write for society package.
**Green Fees** £27.50 per day; £20 per round.
**Facilities**   ⊗ � 🏌 ▆ ♀ 🏌 🏠 🚩 ℓ Adrian Pritchard.

**Leisure**   fishing, motorised carts for hire, buggies for hire, trolley for hire, putting green, practice area.
**Location**   Overlooking Llandegfedd Reservoir
**Hotel**   ★★★ 73% Glen-yr-Afon House Hotel, Pontypool Rd, USK
      ☎ 01291 672302 & 673202 27 ⇥ 🏌

---

## PONTYPRIDD                   Map 03 ST09

**Pontypridd** Ty Gwyn Rd CF37 4DJ
☎ 01443 409904 & 402359
Well-wooded mountain course with springy turf. Good views of the Rhondda Valleys and coast.
*18 holes, 5721yds, Par 69, SSS 68.*
*Club membership 850.*
**Visitors**   must play with member on weekends & bank holidays. Must have a handicap certificate.
**Societies**   weekdays only. Must apply in writing.
**Green Fees** not confirmed.
**Facilities**   ♀ 🏌 🏠 ℓ Wade Walters.
**Location**   E side of town centre off A470
**Hotel**   ★★★ 66% Heritage Park Hotel, Coed Cae Rd, Trehafod, PONTYPRIDD
      ☎ 01443 687057 50 ⇥ 🏌

---

## PORT TALBOT                 Map 03 SS78

**British Steel Port Talbot** Sports & Social Club, Margam SA13 2NF ☎ 01639 814182 & 871111
A 9 hole course with two lakes. All the holes are affected by crosswinds and the 7th, Par 3, is alongside a deep stream, so is very tight.
*9 holes, 4726yds, Par 62, SSS 63, Course record 60.*
*Club membership 250.*
**Visitors**   contact in advance, may not play at weekends.
**Societies**   by prior arrangement.
**Green Fees** £8 per 18 holes.
**Facilities**   ⊗ ▆ ▆ ♀ 🏌
**Leisure**   hard tennis courts, practice area.
**Hotel**   ★★★ 60% Aberavon Beach Hotel, PORT TALBOT
      ☎ 01639 884949 52 ⇥

---

## PORTHCAWL                   Map 03 SS87

**Royal Porthcawl** CF36 3UW
☎ 01656 782251
This championship-standard heathland/downland links course is always in sight of the sea, and has hosted many major tournaments.
*18 holes, 6406yds, Par 72, SSS 73.*
*Club membership 800.*
**Visitors**   must contact in advanced & produce handicap certificate limit men 20, ladies 30. Restricted at weekends & bank holidays.
**Societies**   apply in writing.
**Green Fees** £45 per day (£50 weekends if available).
**Facilities**   ⊗ � 🏌 ▆ ♀ 🏌 🏠 🚩 🍴 ℓ Peter Evans.
**Leisure**   trolley for hire, driving range, putting green, practice area.
**Location**   1.5m NW of town centre
**Hotel**   ★★★ 61% Seabank Hotel, The Promenade, PORTHCAWL
      ☎ 01656 782261 61 ⇥ 🏌

## PYLE                                    Map 03 SS88

**Pyle & Kenfig** Waun-Y-Mer CF33 4PU
☎ 01656 783093 & 771613
Links and downland course, with sand-dunes. Easy walking.
Often windy.
*18 holes, 6081mtrs, Par 71, SSS 73, Course record 68.*
*Club membership 1010.*
**Visitors**       by arrangement midweek, guests of members
                   only at weekends.
**Societies**      for large numbers apply in writing, small
                   numbers telephone booking accepted.
**Green Fees** £30 per day/round.
**Facilities**   ⊗ ⅷ ᒪ ♥ ♀ ᐃ 🏠 ᵀ ⸀ Robert Evans.
**Leisure**        motorised carts for hire, buggies for hire, trolley
                   for hire, driving range, putting green, practice
                   area.
**Location**       S side of Pyle off A4229
**Hotel**          ★★★ 61% Seabank Hotel, The Promenade,
                   PORTHCAWL ☎ 01656 782261 61 ⇄ ℟

## RAGLAN                                  Map 03 SO40

**Raglan Park** Park Lodge NP5 2ER ☎ 01291 690077
New parkland course with well laid greens and a mature back
9 that are already the source of local praise. Several testing
holes where a combination of wind and water make golf
challenging. Easy walking.
*18 holes, 6391yds, Par 72, SSS 72.*
*Club membership 300.*
**Societies**      advance arrangement required.
**Green Fees** £15 per day.
**Facilities**   ⊗ ⅷ ᒪ ♥ ♀ ᐃ 🏠
**Leisure**        buggies for hire, putting green under
                   construction, practice area.
**Hotel**    -     ★★★ 66% Llansantffraed Court, Llanvihangel
                   Gobion, ABERGAVENNY
                   ☎ 01873 840678 21 ⇄ ℟

## SOUTHGATE                              Map 02 SS58

**Pennard** 2 Southgate Rd SA3 2BT
☎ 01792 233131 & 233451
Undulating, cliff-top seaside links with good coastal views.
*18 holes, 6265yds, Par 71, SSS 71, Course record 69.*
*Club membership 912.*
**Visitors**       advisable to contact in advance.
**Societies**      by prior arrangement, telephone in advance.
**Green Fees** £24 (£30 weekends & bank holidays).
**Facilities**   ⊗ ⅷ ᒪ ♥ ♀ ᐃ 🏠 ᵀ ⸀ M V Bennett.
**Leisure**        squash, trolley for hire.
**Location**       8m W of Swansea by A4067 and B4436
**Hotel**          ★★ 61% Nicholaston House Hotel,
                   Nicholaston, PENMAEN
                   ☎ 01792 371317 13 ⇄ ℟

## SWANSEA                                 Map 03 SS69

**Clyne** 120 Owls Lodge Ln, The Mayals, Blackpyl SA3 5DP
☎ 01792 401989
Moorland course, very open to the wind and with grazing
rights for local commoners.
*18 holes, 6334yds, Par 70, SSS 71, Course record 64.*
*Club membership 800.*

**Visitors**       must be member of a club with handicap
                   certificate and contact in advance.
**Societies**      must telephone in advance.
**Green Fees** not confirmed.
**Facilities**   ♀ ᐃ 🏠 ⸀ Mark Bevan.
**Leisure**        range, putting, practice area, trolley hire.
**Location**       3.5m SW on B4436 off A4067
**Hotel**          ★★ 69% Langland Court, Langland Court Rd,
                   LANGLAND
                   ☎ 01792 361545 16 ⇄ ℟Annexe5 ⇄ ℟

*Langland Bay* Langland Bay SA3 4QR
☎ 01792 366023
Parkland course overlooking Gower coast. The par 4, 6th is
an uphill dog-leg open to the wind, and the par 3, 16th (151
yds) is aptly named 'Death or Glory'.
*18 holes, 5857yds, Par 70, SSS 69.*
*Club membership 850.*
**Visitors**       no restrictions.
**Societies**      must telephone in advance.
**Green Fees** not confirmed.
**Facilities**   ♀ ᐃ 🏠 ⸀
**Location**       6m W on A4067
**Hotel**          ★★ 69% Langland Court, Langland Court Rd,
                   LANGLAND
                   ☎ 01792 361545 16 ⇄ ℟Annexe5 ⇄ ℟

*Morriston* 160 Clasemont Rd SA6 6AJ
☎ 01792 796528 & 772335
Pleasant parkland course.
*18 holes, 5891yds, Par 68, SSS 68, Course record 64.*
*Club membership 700.*
**Visitors**       may not play at weekends.
**Societies**      apply in writing.
**Green Fees** £21 per day.
**Facilities**   ⊗ ⅷ ᒪ ♥ ♀ ᐃ 🏠 ᵀ ⸀ D A Rees.
**Leisure**        trolley for hire, putting green, practice area.
**Location**       5m N on A48
**Hotel**          ★★ 62% Oak Tree Parc Hotel, Birchgrove Rd,
                   BIRCHGROVE ☎ 01792 817781 10 ⇄ ℟

## TALBOT GREEN                            Map 03 ST08

*Llantrisant & Pontyclun* Llanelry Rd CF7 8HZ
☎ 01443 222148
Parkland course.
*12 holes, 5712yds, Par 68, SSS 68.*
*Club membership 600.*
**Visitors**       must have a club membership card & handicap
                   certificate and should be accompanied by a
                   member.
**Societies**      apply in writing.
**Green Fees** not confirmed.
**Facilities**   ᐃ 🏠 ᵀ ⸀
**Location**       N side of village off A473
**Hotel**          ★★★★ 65% Miskin Manor Hotel, MISKIN
                   ☎ 01443 224204 32 ⇄ ℟

## TREDEGAR                               Map 03 SO10

*Tredegar and Rhymney* Cwmtysswg, Rhymney NP2 3BQ
☎ 01685 840743 & 843400
Mountain course with lovely views.
*9 holes, 5504yds, Par 68, SSS 68, Course record 69.*
*Club membership 194.*

**Visitors** no restrictions.
**Societies** must contact in writing.
**Green Fees** not confirmed.
**Facilities** ♀ (by arrangement) ⚫
**Location** 1.75m SW on B4256
**Hotel** ★★ 68% Tregenna Hotel, Park Ter,
MERTHYR TYDFIL
☎ 01685 723627 & 382055 24 ⇄ ↖

---

## UPPER KILLAY                    Map 02 SS59

*Fairwood Park* Blackhills Ln SA2 7JN
☎ 01792 203648 & 297849
Championship parkland course on Gower coast with good
views and easy walking.
*18 holes, 6741yds, Par 72, SSS 72.*
*Club membership 720.*
**Visitors** welcome except when championship or club
matches are being held. Must contact in advance.
**Societies** must contact in advance.
**Green Fees** not confirmed.
**Facilities** ♀ ⚫ 🏠 ⚑ ⚫
**Location** 1.5m S off A4118
**Hotel** ★ 76% Windsor Lodge Hotel, Mount Pleasant,
SWANSEA
☎ 01792 642158 & 652744 18 ⇄ ↖

---

## WENVOE                         Map 03 ST17

*Wenvoe Castle* CF5 6BE ☎ 01222 594371
Parkland course which is hilly for first 9 holes. Lake, situated
280 yds from tee at 10th hole, is a hazard.
*18 holes, 6422yds, Par 72, SSS 71, Course record 64.*
*Club membership 600.*

**Visitors** must be a member of a recognised golf club &
have a handicap certificate. Must play with
member at weekends.
**Societies** must contact in writing.
**Green Fees** not confirmed.
**Facilities** ♀ ⚫ 🏠 ⚫ Robin Day.
**Leisure** carts/buggy/trolley hire,practice area.
**Location** 1m S off A4050
**Hotel** ★★★⚫ 74% Egerton Grey Country House
Hotel, Porthkerry, BARRY
☎ 01446 711666 10 ⇄ ↖

---

## YSTALYFERA                     Map 03 SN70

*Palleg* Lower Cwm-twrch SA9 1QT
☎ no telephone
Heathland course liable to become heavy going after winter
rain.
*9 holes, 6400yds, Par 72, SSS 72.*
*Club membership 200.*
**Visitors** restricted Sat (Apr-Sep) & Sun mornings in
winter.
**Societies** must contact two months in advance.
**Green Fees** not confirmed.
**Facilities** ♀ (ex Mon) ⚫
**Location** 1.5m N off A4068
**Hotel** ★★ 62% Oak Tree Parc Hotel, Birchgrove Rd,
BIRCHGROVE
☎ 01792 817781 10 ⇄ ↖

# IRELAND

*The Irish welcome is overwhelming. Few clubs circle the waggons to keep visiors out...'*

Picturesque public houses in Cork are irrisistible. This particular bar, no bigger than our kitchen, had a lino floor, former church pews against unpainted walls and a dozen customers, all telling farmer's yarns, and taking no notice of intruders, namely two American girls (one my wife) asking to sample a glass of the black stuff. We had been to Killarney Golf Club where the parkland grass is lush green, the scenery too dramatic to keep your head down and where the clubhouse is vast and modern. So, obviously, we had to recapture the non-tourist atmosphere at a Ballingeary watering-hole, and plan to take Christy O'Connor's advice and go to Dingle, another day. Nothing had changed since previous visits....

Previous visits. Odd, how one recalls every one so vividly. We flew into Dublin, checked in at Ryans for a hire car and were playing Royal Dublin (Dollymount), just four miles away, the same afternoon. The first nine holes go outwards, away from the clubhouse and, down a fierce breeze, I reached the turn in 34. On the inward nine, against the gale (well, that's the excuse) I took 43 back!

Royal Dublin is a grand course, but so is the mighty Portmarnock which we played the following day. It is giant-sized and I recall the old Canada Cup there with Arnold Palmer and Sam Snead winning. While it has none of the beauty of the Killarney course, it is a proper links, created in 1893 with a shack as its clubhouse. South African Bobby Locke, who used to play down the road at Woodbrook, near Bray, said Portmarnock was the finest links in Europe. Off the back tees in a wind, it's unplayable for such as me, although I did start with a birdie before blowing up and mentally quitting. Anyone who plays this test is qualified to talk about it for the rest of time - which we tend to do!

### EUROPE'S FINEST

The West Coast of Ireland means Shannon Airport to some, and Ballybunion Golf Course to seasoned golfers. I know top Americans who love the place and rate it number one in Europe. The official list of the world's 100 Greatest Courses has it in there at number eight. Designed in 1906 by someone called Murphy, it overlooks the ocean. Point out to sea and the next stop is

America! When the wind howls and the white horses, dolphins and what have you are in full flight, you aim your teeshot wide of the fairway and watch it curve back - you hope.

Your next stop in County Clare (because that's where we are) must be the Lahinch Golf Club. Played over in 1891 by members of the Black Watch, it was designed by Tom Morris and later upgraded by Dr A Mackenzie. Why anyone is allowed to mess about with the classics of golf is beyond me, but there is usually someone on the committee who has a 'bright' idea. Happily, this one remains true and at 6,300 yards, you'll take the road via Ennis with a great deal to look forward to - and that Irish welcome.

Usually, I never admit that Newcastle's Royal County Down Golf Course is somewhere I have never played. Shame overpowers me, because I know for a fact, that it is a magnificent course. In 1889 Tom Morris was instructed to lay the place out 'at a cost not exceeding £4'. Today, someone like Jack Nicklaus instructs committees that he will require not less than £1 million! Played beneath the shadow of Slieve Donard, the highest of the Mourne Mountains, the views are said to be the finest from any course in the British Isles.

## FAULKNER'S FAVOURITE

Since we are now in Northern Ireland, I can confirm that Royal Portrush Golf Course is etched in my mind. I reported an Amateur Championship win by Ireland's Joe Carr and as we all looked out towards the sea, wild and raging as it was, with bright sunshine illuminating the scene, folk talked of the day England's Max Faulkner had won the Open Championship in 1951 on this superb links. And they recall that Harry Colt, the man who designed it, claimed it was the best example of his work.

There are views of the Giant's Causeway, the Paps of Jura can be seen on a clear day and, if you don't hit your drives dead straight, you can end in 'Purgatory' at the hole that follows one called 'Calamity Corner'. And at the end of it all, you will hope they can bring the Open back here again, then you will enjoy sinking into a chair to recall that, although you went into the rough here and there, at least it was adorned with briar roses and wild flowers. And you will find it difficult to go home......

## THE NEXT 50 YEARS

So that's our Round Britain trip. In my lifetime, golf in the United Kingdom has changed from a middle-class club game for those with disposable income, to a sport for the masses. Because of this, certain clubs have circled waggons, and limit visitors. In the next 50 years, we shall see popular golf emerge, and clubhouses may return to what they were - basic, plank pavilions with an ordinary course, unpretentious and available, like a seat in the cinema. A dream?

# NORTHERN IRELAND

## CO ANTRIM

### ANTRIM                                    Map 01 D5

**Massereene** 51 Lough Rd BT41 4DQ ☎ 01849 428096
The first nine holes are parkland, while the second,
adjacent to the shore of Lough Neagh, have more of a
links character with sandy ground.
*18 holes, 6559yds, Par 72, SSS 71, Course record 66.*
*Club membership 969.*
**Visitors** must contact in advance.
**Societies** book in advance.
**Green Fees** £20 (£25 weekends & bank holidays).
**Facilities** ⊗ ⅷ ⻭ ⚑ ♀ ♨ 🛏 ⚐ Jim Smyth.
**Leisure** trolley for hire, putting green.
**Location** 1m SW of town
**Hotel** ★★★★ 71% Galgorm Manor,
BALLYMENA ☎ 01266 881001 23 ⇄ ⟰

### BALLYCASTLE                              Map 01 D6

**Ballycastle** Cushendall Rd BT54 6QP
☎ 01265 762536
An unusual mixture of terrain beside the sea, with
magnificent views from all parts. The first five holes are
inland type; the middle holes on the Warren are links type
and the rest, on high ground, are heath type.
*18 holes, 5201mtrs, Par 71, SSS 68, Course record 64.*
*Club membership 950.*
**Visitors** are welcome during the week.
**Societies** apply in writing.
**Green Fees** £17 per day (£22 per round weekends).
**Facilities** ⊗ ⅷ ⻭ ⚑ ♀ ♨ 🛏 ⚐ Ian McLaughlin.
**Leisure** trolley for hire.
**Location** Between Portrush & Cushendall (A2)
**Hotel** ★★ 57% Thornlea Hotel, 6 Coast Rd,
CUSHENDALL ☎ 012667 71223 13 ⇄ ⟰

### BALLYCLARE                              Map 01 D5

**Ballyclare** 23 Springdale Rd BT39 9JW
☎ 01960 322696 & 342352
Parkland course with lots of trees and shrubs and water
hazards provided by the river, streams and lakes.
*18 holes, 5745mtrs, Par 71, SSS 71, Course record 67.*
*Club membership 580.*
**Visitors** no restrictions.
**Societies** must contact in advance.
**Green Fees** £15 (£20 weekends & bank holidays).
**Facilities** ⊗ ⅷ ⻭ ⚑ ♀ ♨
**Leisure** buggies for hire, trolley for hire, driving range,
putting green, practice area.
**Location** 1.5m N
**Hotel** ★★★★ 63% Stormont Hotel, 587 Upper
Newtonards Rd, BELFAST
☎ 01232 658621 109 ⇄ ⟰

### BALLYGALLY                              Map 01 D5

**Cairndhu** 192 Coast Rd BT40 2QG ☎ 01574 583324
Built on a hilly headland, this course is both testing and
scenic, with wonderful coastal views.
*18 holes, 561mtrs, Par 70, SSS 69, Course record 64.*
*Club membership 830.*
**Visitors** may not play on Sat.
**Societies** must apply in writing.
**Green Fees** £25 per day; £17 per round (£30/£22 Sun &
bank holidays).
**Facilities** ⊗ ⅷ ⻭ ⚑ ♀ ♨ 🛏 ⚐ Robert Walker.
**Leisure** trolley for hire, putting green, practice area.
**Location** 4m N of Larne on coast road
**Hotel** ★★★ 61% Ballygally Castle Hotel, 274 Coast
Rd, BALLYGALLY
☎ 01574 583212 30 ⇄ ⟰

### BALLYMENA                              Map 01 D5

**Ballymena** 128 Raceview Rd BT42 4HY ☎ 01266 861487
Parkland course of level heathland with plenty of bunkers.
*18 holes, 5654yds, Par 68, SSS 67.*
**Visitors** may not play on Tue or Sat.
**Societies** must contact in advance.
**Green Fees** not confirmed.
**Facilities** ♀ ⚐ James Gallagher.
**Leisure** bowling green.
**Location** 2m E on A42
**Hotel** ★★★★ 71% Galgorm Manor, BALLYMENA
☎ 01266 881001 23 ⇄ ⟰

**Galgorm Castle Golf & Country Club** Galgorm Rd
BT42 1HL ☎ 01266 46161
Challenging, American-style championship course scheduled
to open in the summer of 1997. Set in 240 acres of mature,
undulating parkland within the estate of one of Ireland's
unique 17th-century castles, it will feature two rivers and five
beautifully positioned lakes.
*18 holes, 6800mtrs, Par 72.*
*Club membership 400.*
**Visitors** scheduled to open summer 1997. Contact for
details
**Societies** apply in writing or telephone in advance.
**Green Fees** not confirmed.
**Facilities** ⊗ ⅷ ⻭ ⚑ ♀ ♨ 🛏 ⚐
**Leisure** fishing, trolley for hire, driving range, putting
green, practice area.
**Location** S from Ballymena

### CARRICKFERGUS                          Map 01 D5

**Carrickfergus** 25 North Rd BT38 8LP
☎ 019603 363713 & 351803
Parkland course, fairly level but nevetheless demanding, with
a notorious water hazard at the 1st. Well maintained and with
nice views.
*18 holes, 5759yds, Par 68, SSS 68.*
*Club membership 815.*
**Visitors** restrictions at weekends.
**Societies** must contact in advance.
**Green Fees** not confirmed.
**Facilities** ♀ ♨ 🛏 ⚐ Raymond Stevenson.
**Leisure** caddy cars.

**Location**    9m NE of Belfast on A2
**Hotel**    ★★★ 58% Chimney Corner Hotel, 630 Antrim Rd, NEWTOWNABBEY
☎ 01232 844925 & 844851 63 ⇄ ♠

---

**Greenisland** 156 Upper Rd, Greenisland
☎ 01232 862236
*9 holes, 5536mtrs, Par 71, SSS 68.*
**Visitors**    welcome, may be restricted on Sat.
**Societies**    by prior arrangement.
**Green Fees** not confirmed.
**Facilities**
**Hotel**    ★★★ 58% Chimney Corner Hotel, 630 Antrim Rd, NEWTOWNABBEY
☎ 01232 844925 & 844851 63 ⇄ ♠

---

## CUSHENDALL            Map 01 D6

**Cushendall** 21 Shore Rd ☎ 01266 771318
Scenic course with spectacular views over the Sea of Moyle and Red Bay to the Mull of Kintyre. The River Dall winds through the course, coming into play in seven of the nine holes.
*9 holes, 4386mtrs, Par 66, SSS 63.*
*Club membership 714.*
**Visitors**    restricted on Sun.
**Societies**    must contact in writing.
**Green Fees** not confirmed.
**Facilities**    ♀ ♿
**Hotel**    ★★ 57% Thornlea Hotel, 6 Coast Rd, CUSHENDALL
☎ 012667 71223 13 ⇄ ♠

---

## LARNE            Map 01 D5

**Larne** 54 Ferris Bay Rd, Islandmagee BT40 3RT
☎ 01960 382228
An exposed part links, part heathland course offering a good test, particularly on the last three holes along the sea shore.
*9 holes, 6686yds, Par 70, SSS 69, Course record 64.*
*Club membership 430.*
**Visitors**    may not play on Sat.
**Societies**    apply in writing or telephone in advance.
**Green Fees** £8 per round (£15 weekends & bank holidays).
**Facilities**    ⊗ by prior arrangement ♨ by prior arrangement ♥ by prior arrangement ♀ ♿
**Leisure**    putting green, practice area, snooker room.
**Location**    6m N of Whitehead on Browns Bay rd
**Hotel**    ★★★ 61% Ballygally Castle Hotel, 274 Coast Rd, BALLYGALLY
☎ 01574 583212 30 ⇄ ♠

---

## LISBURN            Map 01 D5

**Aberdelghy** Bell's Ln, Lambeg BT27 4QH
☎ 01846 662738
This parkland course has no bunkers but the par-3 3rd high on the hill and the 5th hole over the dam provide a challenge. The par-4 6th hole is a long dog leg.
*9 holes, 2192mtrs, Par 33, SSS 65.*
*Club membership 150.*
**Visitors**    restricted Sat 8-11am.
**Societies**    telephone in advance.
**Green Fees** not confirmed.
**Facilities**    ♿ 🏠 ♟ ♪ Ian Murdoch.

---

**Leisure**    practice area, lessons, trolley hire.
**Location**    1.5m N of Lisburn off A1
**Hotel**    B Forte Posthouse Belfast, Kingsway, Dunmurry, BELFAST
☎ 01232 612101 82 ⇄ ♠

---

**Lisburn** Blaris Lodge, 68 Eglantine Rd BT27 5RQ
☎ 01846 677216
Meadowland course, fairly level, with plenty of trees and shrubs. Challenging last three holes.
*18 holes, 6647yds, Par 72, SSS 72, Course record 67.*
*Club membership 1421.*
**Visitors**    must play with member at weekends. Must tee off before 3pm weekdays.
**Societies**    must contact in writing.
**Green Fees** £25 per round (£30 weekends & bank holidays).
**Facilities**    ⊗ ♨ ♀ ♿ 🏠 ♟ ♪ Blake Campbell.
**Leisure**    trolley for hire, putting.
**Location**    2m from town on A1
**Hotel**    ★★★★ 63% Stormont Hotel, 587 Upper Newtonards Rd, BELFAST
☎ 01232 658621 109 ⇄ ♠

---

## MAZE            Map 01 D5

**Down Royal Park** Dunygarton Rd BT27 5RT
☎ 01846 621339
The 9-hole Valley course and the 18-hole Down Royal Park are easy walking, undulating heathland courses. Down Royal's 2nd hole is 628yards and thought to be among the best par 5 holes in Ireland.
*Down Royal Park Course: 18 holes, 6824yds, Par 72, Course record 73.*
*Valley Course: 9 holes, 2500yds, Par 33.*
**Visitors**    no restrictions.
**Societies**    reservations in advance.
**Green Fees** not confirmed.
**Facilities**    ♀ ♿ 🏠
**Leisure**    putting green.
**Location**    Inside Down Royal Race Course
**Hotel**    ★★★ 62% Dukes Hotel, 65 University St, BELFAST
☎ 01232 236666 21 ⇄ ♠

---

## NEWTOWNABBEY            Map 01 D5

**Ballyearl Golf & Leisure Centre** 585 Doagh Rd, Mossley BT36 8RZ ☎ 01232 848287
*9 holes, 2520yds, Par 27.*
**Visitors**    no restrictions.
**Societies**    telephone in advance.
**Green Fees** £4 (£5 weekends).
**Facilities**    ♥ ♿ 🏠 ♟ ♪ Jim Robinson.
**Leisure**    squash, gymnasium, driving range, practice area.

---

**Mallusk** Antrim Rd BT36 ☎ 01232 843799
Attractive 9-hole parkland course featuring 3 small par 4s and several water hazards, notably on the tricky, dog-leg 7th hole.
*9 holes, 4444yds, Par 62, SSS 62, Course record 62.*
*Club membership 150.*
**Visitors**    no restrictions.
**Societies**    contact for details.
**Green Fees** £5.50 (£7.50 weekends).
**Facilities**    ♥ ♀ ♿ ⋈
**Leisure**    hard tennis courts, sauna, putting green.      ▶

## PORTBALLINTRAE                    Map 01 C6

**Bushfoot** 50 Bushfoot Rd, Portballintrae BT57 8RR
☎ 01265 731317
A seaside links course with superb views in an area of
outstanding beauty. A challenging par-3 7th is ringed by
bunkers with out-of-bounds beyond, while the 3rd has a blind
approach. Also a putting green and pitch & putt course.
*9 holes, 5876yds, Par 70, SSS 67, Course record 68.*
*Club membership 850.*
**Visitors**      must contact in advance.
**Societies**     must contact in advance.
**Green Fees** £13 per round (£16 weekends & bank holidays).
**Facilities**   ⊗ ⅲ ㄅ ⚑ ♀ ᇫ ⚐
**Leisure**       trolley for hire, putting green, practice area.
**Location**     Off Ballaghmore rd
**Hotel**          ★★ 60%  Beach House Hotel, The Sea Front,
                         PORTBALLINTRAE
                         ☎ 012657 31214 32 ⇆ ⋒

## PORTRUSH                         Map 01 C6

**ROYAL PORTRUSH**  See page 361

## WHITEHEAD                        Map 01 D5

**Bentra Municipal** Slaughterford Rd BT38 9TG
☎ 01960 378996
A well matured course designed with the experienced golfer
and novice in mind with wide fairways and some particularly
long holes.
*9 holes, 2885mtrs, Par 37, SSS 35.*
**Green Fees** £6.75 per 18 holes (£10.50 weekends & bank
                    holidays).
**Facilities**   ⊗ ⅲ ㄅ ⚑ ♀ ⒢ ⚐
**Leisure**       trolley for hire, driving range, putting green.
**Hotel**          ★★★ 58%  Chimney Corner Hotel, 630 Antrim
                         Rd, NEWTOWNABBEY
                         ☎ 01232 844925 & 844851 63 ⇆ ⋒

*Whitehead* McCrae's Brae
☎ 01960 353631
Undulating parkland course with magnificent sea views.
*18 holes, 6426yds, Par 72, SSS 71, Course record 67.*
*Club membership 850.*
**Visitors**      may not play on Sat. Must play with member on
                    Sun.
**Societies**     must contact in advance.
**Green Fees** not confirmed.
**Facilities**   ♀ ᇫ ⒢ ⚐
**Leisure**       putting green.
**Location**     0.5m N
**Hotel**          ★★★ 58%  Chimney Corner Hotel, 630 Antrim
                         Rd, NEWTOWNABBEY
                         ☎ 01232 844925 & 844851 63 ⇆ ⋒

Entries with a shaded background identify
courses that are considered to be particularly
interesting

# CO ARMAGH

## ARMAGH                           Map 01 C5

**County Armagh** The Demesne, Newry Rd BT60 1EN
☎ 01861 525861
Mature parkland course with excellent views of Armagh city
and its surroundings.
*18 holes, 5649mtrs, Par 70, SSS 69, Course record 63.*
*Club membership 1000.*
**Visitors**      time sheet operates at weekends.
**Societies**     must contact in writing.
**Green Fees** £12 per round (£18 weekends & bank holidays).
**Facilities**   ⊗ ⅲ ㄅ ⚑ ♀ ᇫ ⒢ ⚐ Alan Rankin.
**Leisure**       trolley for hire, putting green, practice area.
**Location**     On the Newry road
**Hotel**          ★★★★ 63%  Stormont Hotel, 587 Upper
                         Newtonards Rd,  BELFAST
                         ☎ 01232 658621 109 ⇆ ⋒

## LURGAN                           Map 01 D5

**Craigavon Golf & Ski Centre** Turmoyra Ln, Silverwood
BT66 6NG ☎ 01762 326606
Parkland course with a lake and stream providing water
hazards.
*18 holes, 6496yds, Par 72, SSS 72.*
*Club membership 400.*
**Visitors**      restricted Sat am.
**Societies**     telephone in advance.
**Green Fees** £10 per day (£13 weekends & bank holidays).
**Facilities**   ⊗ ⅲ ⚑ ᇫ ⚐
**Leisure**       trolley for hire, floodlit driving range, putting
                    green, practice area.
**Location**     2m N at Silverwood off the M1
**Hotel**          ★★★★ 63%  Stormont Hotel, 587 Upper
                         Newtonards Rd,  BELFAST
                         ☎ 01232 658621 109 ⇆ ⋒

*Lurgan* The Demesne BT67 9BN ☎ 01762 322087
Testing parkland course bordering Lurgan Park Lake with a
need for accurate shots. Drains well in wet weather and suits
a long straight hitter.
*18 holes, 6382yds, Par 70, SSS 70, Course record 66.*
*Club membership 800.*
**Visitors**      may not play Sat, contact in advance.
**Societies**     must contact in advance, not Sat.
**Green Fees** £15 per round (£20 weekends & bank holidays).
**Facilities**   ⊗ ⅲ ㄅ ⚑ ♀ ᇫ ⒢ ⚐ Des Paul.
**Leisure**       putting green, practice area.
**Location**     0.5m from town centre near Lurgan Park
**Hotel**          ★★★★ 63%  Stormont Hotel, 587 Upper
                         Newtonards Rd,  BELFAST
                         ☎ 01232 658621 109 ⇆ ⋒

## PORTADOWN                        Map 01 D5

**Portadown** 192 Gilford Rd BT63 5LF
☎ 01762 355356
Well wooded parkland course on the banks of the River
Bann, which features among the water hazards.
*18 holes, 5649mtrs, Par 70, SSS 70, Course record 65.*
*Club membership 1004.*                                 ▶

# ROYAL PORTRUSH

**PORTRUSH** *Co Antrim* ☎ 01265 822311     **Map 01 D4**

*John Ingham writes:* It was more than thirty years ago that I first saw Royal Portrush, but the memory lingers on. That week in 1960, the great Joe Carr won the British Amateur Championship for his third, and last, time. But everyone there was a winner; the sun shone, and the course glistened as the foaming ocean was almost blown inland on to the briar roses that dotted the rough.

What a splendid seaside paradise this is, I wrote in a London evening newspaper, whose readers were keen to follow players such as Joe Carr and Michael Bonallack. There among the gallery was the late Fred Daly, winner of the 1947 Open and the only Irishman ever to win.

The man who designed this course was Harry S Colt, a name that appears as a creator of many fine courses. This one is considered among the six best in the United Kingdom. It is spectacular, breathtaking, but one of the tightest driving tests known to man because, if you get in the long stuff, you may stay there. On a clear day, you have a fine view of Islay and the Paps of Jura - seen from the 3rd tee. Then there's the Giant's Causeway, from the 5th, as good a downhill dogleg hole as you'll find anywhere.

While the greens have to be 'read' from the start, there are fairways up and down valleys, and holes called Calamity Corner and Purgatory for good reason. The second hole, called Giant's Grave, is 509 yards but there's an even longer one waiting for you at the 17th, while the last hole, a 479-yarder, nearly cost Max Faulkner his 1951 Open title. He hit a crooked drive, and had to bend his second shot with a wooden club. Dressed in primrose-coloured slacks, his colourful plumage and out-going attitude attracted most of the small crowd.

The Open did not return to Portrush and championship golf is the loser because the place is a gem. Founded in 1888, it was also the venue of the first professional golf event held in Ireland, when in 1895, Sandy Herd beat Harry Vardon in the final.

You'll love it.

**Visitors** must contact in advance, have a letter of introduction from their own club and a handicap certificate. Restricted Saturday and Sunday morning

**Societies** must apply in writing.

**Green fees** Dunluce Links £45 per day (£55 weekends) Valley Links £20 per day (£30 weekends)

**Facilities** ⊗ ⅺ Ⅱ ⅃ ☕ ♀ (all day) ♨ 🏠 ✈ 2 practice grounds, caddies & caddy cars ℓ (Dai Stevenson)

**Leisure** snooker

**Location** Bushmills Rd Portrush BT56 8JQ (0.5m from Portrush on main road to Bushmills)

45 holes. **Dunluce Links: 18 holes, 6794 yds, Par 72, SSS 73, course record 66**
**Valley Links: 18 holes, 6273 yds, Par 70, SSS 70, course record 65**
**Skerries Course: 9 holes, 1187 yds**

## WHERE TO STAY AND EAT NEARBY

**HOTELS:**
**PORTRUSH**
★★★ 61% Causeway Coast, 36 Ballyreagh Rd.
☎ 01265 822435.  21 ⇆ ♖

**RESTAURANT:**
**PORTRUSH**
働働 Ramore, The Harbour.
☎ 01265 824313.

**Visitors** may not play on Tue & Sat.
**Societies** apply in writing.
**Green Fees** £16 per round (£20 weekends & bank holidays).
**Facilities** ⊗ ⅢⅢ ⓛ 🍴 ♀ 🏌 🏧 ⚑ ℓ Paul Stevenson.
**Leisure** squash, motorised carts for hire, trolley for hire, putting green, practice area.
**Location** SE via A59
**Hotel** ★★★★ 63% Stormont Hotel, 587 Upper Newtonards Rd, BELFAST
☎ 01232 658621 109 ⇔ ℞

---

## TANDRAGEE                                      Map 01 D5

**Tandragee** Markethill Rd BT62 2ER
☎ 01762 841272
Pleasant hilly parkland with mature trees.
*18 holes, 5446mtrs, Par 69, SSS 69, Course record 62.*
*Club membership 1175.*
**Visitors** contact in advance.
**Societies** must contact in advance.
**Green Fees** £15 per round (£21 weekends & bank holidays).
**Facilities** ⊗ ⅢⅢ ⓛ 🍴 ♀ 🏌 🏧 ⚑ ℓ Paul Stevenson.
**Leisure** sauna, gymnasium, trolley for hire, driving range, putting green, practice area.
**Location** On B3 out of Tandragee towards Markethill
**Farmhouse** QQQQ Brook Lodge Farmhouse, 79 Old Ballynahinch Rd, Cargacroy, LISBURN
☎ 01846 638454 6rm(4 ℞)

---

## CO BELFAST

---

## BELFAST                                        Map 01 D5

*See also* The Royal Belfast, Hollywood, Co Down.

**Balmoral** 518 Lisburn Rd BT9 6GX
☎ 01232 381514
Parkland course, mainly level, with tree-lined fairways and a stream providing a water hazard.
*18 holes, 6238yds, Par 69, SSS 70.*
**Visitors** preferred Mon & Thu.
**Societies** must contact in advance.
**Green Fees** not confirmed.
**Facilities** ♀ ⚑ ℓ Geoff Bleakley.
**Location** 3m SW
**Hotel** ★★★★ 63% Stormont Hotel, 587 Upper Newtonards Rd, BELFAST
☎ 01232 658621 109 ⇔ ℞

---

**Cliftonville** 44 Westland Rd BT14 6NH
☎ 01232 744158 & 746595
Parkland course with rivers bisecting two fairways.
*9 holes, 6242yds, Par 70, SSS 70, Course record 66.*
*Club membership 430.*
**Visitors** may not play: after 5pm unless with member, on Sat or on Sun mornings.
**Societies** must contact in writing.
**Green Fees** £12 (£15 weekends & bank holidays).
**Facilities** ⊗ ⅢⅢ ⓛ 🍴 ♀ 🏌 🏧
**Leisure** trolley for hire, putting green, practice area.

**Location** Between Cavehill Rd & Cliftonville Circus
**Hotel** ★★★★ 63% Stormont Hotel, 587 Upper Newtonards Rd, BELFAST
☎ 01232 658621 109 ⇔ ℞

---

**Dunmurry** 91 Dunmurry Ln, Dunmurray BT17 9JS
☎ 01232 610834
Maturing very nicely, this tricky parkland course has several memorable holes which call for skilful shots.
*18 holes, 5832yds, Par 69, SSS 69, Course record 64.*
*Club membership 900.*
**Visitors** telephone in advance. May only play Sat after 5pm, restricted Fri (Ladies Day).
**Societies** must contact in writing.
**Green Fees** £17 per round (£26.50 weekends & bank holidays).
**Facilities** ⊗ ⅢⅢ ⓛ 🍴 ♀ 🏌 🏧 ⚑ ℓ Paul Leonard.
**Leisure** trolley for hire, putting green, practice area, snooker.
**Hotel** ★★★★ 63% Stormont Hotel, 587 Upper Newtonards Rd, BELFAST
☎ 01232 658621 109 ⇔ ℞

---

**Fortwilliam** Downview Ave BT15 4EZ
☎ 01232 370770 (Office) & 770980 (Pro)
Parkland course in most attractive surroundings. The course is bisected by a lane.
*18 holes, 5789yds, Par 70, SSS 68, Course record 65.*
*Club membership 1000.*
**Visitors** contact professional in advance.
**Societies** must contact in advance.
**Green Fees** £19 per round (£25 weekends & bank holidays). Ladies £17 (£21 Sun & bank holidays, no play Sat).
**Facilities** ⊗ ⅢⅢ ⓛ 🍴 ♀ 🏌 🏧 ⚑ ℓ Peter Hanna.
**Leisure** trolley for hire, putting green, practice area.
**Location** Off Antrim road
**Hotel** ★★★★ 63% Stormont Hotel, 587 Upper Newtonards Rd, BELFAST
☎ 01232 658621 109 ⇔ ℞

---

**Malone** 240 Upper Malone Rd, Dunmurry BT17 9LB
☎ 01232 612758 (Office) & 614917 (Pro)
Two parkland courses, extremely attractive with a large lake, mature trees and flowering shrubs and bordered by the River Lagan. Very well maintained and offering a challenging round.
*Main Course: 18 holes, 6654yds, Par 71, SSS 71, Course record 68.*
*Edenderry: 9 holes, 6402yds, Par 72, SSS 71.*
*Club membership 1300.*
**Visitors** advisable to contact pro-shop in advance.
**Societies** apply in writing or fax to club manager. Large group normally Mon & Thu only.
**Green Fees** £30 (£35 weekends). Ladies £20/£28. 9 hole course: £15 (£20 weekends). Ladies £12/£15.
**Facilities** ⊗ ⅢⅢ ⓛ 🍴 ♀ 🏌 🏧 ⚑ ℓ Michael McGee.
**Leisure** squash, trolley for hire, putting green, practice area.
**Location** 4.5m S
**Hotel** ★★★★ 63% Stormont Hotel, 587 Upper Newtonards Rd, BELFAST
☎ 01232 658621 109 ⇔ ℞

*Mount Ober Golf, Ski & Leisure* 24 Ballymaconaghy Rd
BT8 4QZ ☎ 01232 401811
Inland parkland course which has recently been refurbished.
*18 holes, 5391yds, Par 67, SSS 68, Course record 67.*
*Club membership 400.*
Visitors     must contact in advance at weekends & bank
             holidays.
Societies    must contact in writing.
Green Fees   not confirmed.
Facilities   ♀ ♣ 🖼 ⚑ ℓ Geoff Loughrey/Chris Spence.
Leisure      driving ranges,putting,buggy etc. hire.
Hotel        ★★★★ 63% Stormont Hotel, 587 Upper
             Newtonards Rd, BELFAST
             ☎ 01232 658621 109 ⇔ 🐾

---

*Ormeau* Ravenshill Rd
☎ 01232 641069 & 640999
Parkland.
*9 holes, 2653mtrs, Par 68, SSS 65.*
*Club membership 520.*
Visitors     welcome weekdays except Tue after 2pm. May
             play Sat after 5.30pm & Sun by arrangement.
Societies    contact in advance.
Green Fees   not confirmed.
Facilities   ♀ ♣ 🖼 ⚑ ℓ Bertie Wilson.
Leisure      putting green,trolley hire,practice area.
Location     S of city centre
Hotel        ★★★ 62% Dukes Hotel, 65 University St,
             BELFAST
             ☎ 01232 236666 21 ⇔ 🐾

---

*Shandon Park* 73 Shandon Park BT5 6NY
☎ 01232 401856
Fairly level parkland offering a pleasant challenge.
*18 holes, 6261yds, Par 70, SSS 70.*
*Club membership 1100.*
Visitors     may not play on competition days. Must contact
             in advance and have a handicap certificate.
Societies    may play Mon & Fri only, applications to club.
Green Fees   not confirmed.
Facilities   ♀ ♣ 🖼 ⚑ ℓ Barry Wilson.
Leisure      putting green,trolley hire,practice area.
Location     Off Knock road
Hotel        ★★★★ 63% Stormont Hotel, 587 Upper
             Newtonards Rd, BELFAST
             ☎ 01232 658621 109 ⇔ 🐾

## DUNDONALD                                     Map 01 D5

*Knock* Summerfield BT16 0QX
☎ 01232 483251 & 482249
Parkland course with huge trees, deep bunkers and a river
cutting across several fairways. This is a hard but fair course
and will test the best of golfers.
*18 holes, 6435yds, Par 70, SSS 71, Course record 66.*
*Club membership 890.*
Visitors     with member only on Sat.
Societies    must contact in advance.
Green Fees   £20 per day (£25 weekends & bank holidays).
Facilities   ⊗ ⅺ ⓛ 🖤 ♀ ♣ 🖼 ⚑ ℓ Gordon Fairweather.
Leisure      buggies for hire, trolley for hire, putting green,
             practice area.
Hotel        ★★★★ 71% Culloden Hotel, Bangor Rd,
             Holywood, BELFAST
             ☎ 01232 425223 87 ⇔ 🐾

## NEWTOWNBREDA                                  Map 01 D5

**The Belvoir Park** 73 Church Rd BT8 4AN
☎ 01232 491693
This undulating parkland course is not strenuous to walk,
but is certainly a test of your golf, with tree-lined
fairways and a particularly challenging finish at the final
four holes.
*18 holes, 6516yds, Par 71, SSS 71, Course record 65.*
*Club membership 1000.*
Visitors     must contact in advance, may not play Sat.
Societies    must contact in writing.
Green Fees   £30 per day (£35 Wed, weekends &
             holidays).
Facilities   ⊗ ⅺ ⓛ 🖤 ♀ ♣ 🖼 ⚑ ℓ Maurice Kelly.
Leisure      motorised carts for hire, buggies for hire,
             trolley for hire, putting green, practice area.
Location     3m from centre off Saintfield/Newcastle rd
Hotel        ★★★★ 63% Stormont Hotel, 587 Upper
             Newtonards Rd, BELFAST
             ☎ 01232 658621 109 ⇔ 🐾

# CO DOWN

## ARDGLASS                                      Map 01 D5

*Ardglass* Castle Pl BT30 7TP ☎ 01396 841219
A scenic cliff-top seaside course with spectacular views and
some memorable holes.
*18 holes, 5498mtrs, Par 70, SSS 69, Course record 65.*
*Club membership 800.*
Visitors     must contact in advance.
Societies    must contact in advance, welcome weekdays &
             restricted times Sun.
Green Fees   £17 per day (£22 per round weekends & bank
             holidays).
Facilities   ⊗ ⅺ ⓛ 🖤 ♀ ♣ 🖼 ⚑ ℓ Philip Farrell.
Leisure      trolley for hire, putting green, practice area.
Hotel        ★★★ 65% Slieve Donard Hotel, Downs Rd,
             NEWCASTLE ☎ 013967 23681 118 ⇔ 🐾

## ARDMILLAN                                     Map 01 D5

*Mahee Island* 14 Mahee Island, Comber BT23 6EP
☎ 01238 541234
An undulating parkland course, almost surrounded by water,
with magnificent views of Strangford Lough and its islands,
with Scrabo Tower in the background.
*9 holes, 5590yds, Par 68, SSS 67, Course record 63.*
*Club membership 450.*
Visitors     may not play on Wed after 5pm or Sat before
             5pm.
Societies    apply in writing.
Green Fees   £10 per round (£15 weekends & public
             holidays).
Facilities   ♣ 🖼
Leisure      trolley for hire, putting green, practice area.
Location     On Comber/Killyleagh road 0.5m from Comber
Hotel        ★★★★ 63% Stormont Hotel, 587 Upper
             Newtonards Rd, BELFAST
             ☎ 01232 658621 109 ⇔ 🐾

## BALLYNAHINCH                                      Map 01 D5

**Spa** 20 Grove Rd BT24 8PN
☎ 01238 562365
Parkland course with tree-lined fairways and scenic views of
the Mourne Mountains.
*18 holes, 6003mtrs, Par 72, SSS 72, Course record 67.*
*Club membership 877.*
**Visitors**     must contact in advance.
**Societies**    must contact in advance.
**Green Fees** £14 (£18 weekends & bank holidays).
**Facilities**   ⊗ ⅏ ⅃ ☂ ♀ ⅄ 🛍 ⅌
**Leisure**      buggies for hire, trolley for hire, putting green,
                 practice area.
**Location**     1m S on the Grove Rd
**Hotel**        ★★★ 65% Slieve Donard Hotel, Downs Rd,
                 NEWCASTLE
                 ☎ 013967 23681 118 ⇥ ⅋

## BANBRIDGE                                         Map 01 D5

*Banbridge* 116 Huntly Rd BT32 3UR
☎ 01820 662211
A picturesque course with excellent views of the Movene
mountains. The holes are not long, but are tricky, and six new
holes opened in 1992 completed the 18.
*18 holes, 5003mtrs, Par 69, SSS 67, Course record 66.*
*Club membership 700.*
**Visitors**     may not play Tue, Sat or before 11am on Sun.
**Societies**    must contact in writing.
**Green Fees** not confirmed.
**Facilities**   ♀ ⅄
**Leisure**      putting green, driving range, trolley hire,
                 practice area.
**Location**     0.5m along Huntly road
**Hotel**        ★★★ 65% Slieve Donard Hotel, Downs Rd,
                 NEWCASTLE
                 ☎ 013967 23681 118 ⇥ ⅋

## BANGOR                                            Map 01 D5

**Bangor** Broadway BT20 4RH
☎ 01247 270922
Undulating parkland course in the town. It is well maintained
and pleasant and offers a challenging round, particularly at
the 5th.
*18 holes, 6424yds, Par 71, SSS 71, Course record 62.*
*Club membership 1147.*
**Visitors**     may not play Sat & weekdays 1-2. Wed
                 unrestricted before 4.45pm.
**Societies**    Must contact in advance, Mon/Wed by
                 telephone, Fri by letter.
**Green Fees** £17.50 per round (£25 Sun ). Winter: £15 (£20
                 Sun).
**Facilities**   ⊗ ⅏ ⅃ ☂ ♀ ⅄ 🛍 ⅌ ⅌ Norman V Drew.
**Leisure**      trolley for hire, putting green, practice area.
**Location**     1m from town on Donaghadee road
**Hotel**        ★★★ 63% Royal Hotel, Seafront, BANGOR
                 ☎ 01247 271866 34 ⇥ ⅋

---

Entries with a shaded background identify
courses that are considered to be particularly
interesting

---

**Blackwood Golf Centre** 150 Crawfordsburn Rd, Clandeboye
BT19 1GB ☎ 01247 852706
The golf centre is a pay and play development with a
computerised booking system for the 18-hole championship-
standard Hamilton course. The course is built on mature
woodland with man-made lakes that come into play on 3
holes. The Temple course is an 18-hole Par 3 course with
holes ranging from the 75yd 1st to the 'hit it out of your
boots' 185yd 10th, which has a lake on the right of the green.
Banked by gorse with streams crossing throughout, this Par 3
course is no pushover.
*Hamilton Course: 18 holes, 6304yds, Par 71, SSS 70.*
*Temple Course: 18 holes, 2492yds, Par 54.*
**Visitors**     pay as you play, computerized booking system
                 for the Hamilton Course.
**Societies**    telephone in advance.
**Green Fees** Hamilton: £12 per 18 holes (£16 weekends &
                 bank holidays). Temple: £7 per 18 holes (£9
                 weekends).
**Facilities**   ⊗ ⅏ ⅃ ☂ ♀ ⅄ 🛍 ⅌ ⅌ ⅃ Tony White.
**Leisure**      trolley for hire, driving range, putting green,
                 practice area.
**Location**     2m from Bangor, off A2 to Belfast
**Hotel**        ★★★ 74% Clandeboye Lodge Hotel, 10 Estate
                 Rd, Clandeboye, BANGOR
                 ☎ 01247 852500 43 ⇥ ⅋

**Carnalea** Station Rd BT19 1EZ
☎ 01247 270368
A scenic course on the shores of Belfast Lough.
*18 holes, 5574yds, Par 68, SSS 67, Course record 63.*
*Club membership 1200.*
**Visitors**     restricted Sat.
**Societies**    must contact in advance.
**Green Fees** £11 (£15 weekends & bank holidays).
**Facilities**   ⊗ ⅏ ⅃ ☂ ♀ ⅄ 🛍 ⅌
**Leisure**      trolley for hire, putting green, practice area.
**Location**     2m W adjacent to railway station
**Hotel**        ★★★ 66% Old Inn, 15 Main St,
                 CRAWFORDSBURN
                 ☎ 01247 853255 33 ⇥ ⅋

*Clandeboye* Tower Rd, Conlig, Newtownards BT23 3PN
☎ 01247 271767
Parkland/heathland courses. The Dufferin is the
championship course and offers a tough challenge.
Nevertheless, the Ava has much to recommend it, with a
notable 2nd hole.
*Dufferin Course: 18 holes, 6469yds, Par 71, SSS 71.*
*Ava Course: 18 holes, 5656yds, Par 70, SSS 68.*
*Club membership 1200.*
**Visitors**     must play with member at weekends.
**Societies**    Mon-Wed & Fri, Apr-Sep; Mon & Wed, Oct-
                 Mar. Must contact in advance.
**Green Fees** not confirmed.
**Facilities**   ♀ ⅄ 🛍 ⅌ ⅃ Peter Gregory.
**Location**     2m S on A21
**Hotel**        ★★★ 63% Royal Hotel, Seafront, BANGOR
                 ☎ 01247 271866 34 ⇥ ⅋

**Helen's Bay** Golf Rd, Helen's Bay
☎ 01247 852815
A parkland course on the shores of Belfast Lough. The 4th
hole Par 3 is particularly challenging as the green is screened
by high trees.
*9 holes, 5168mtrs, Par 68, SSS 67.*

| | |
|---|---|
| **Visitors** | welcome Sun, Mon, Wed, Thu (before 1.30pm); Fri (after 11.30am during Jul & Aug) & Sat after 6pm. Book in advance with secretary. |
| **Societies** | welcome Mon, Wed, Thu (before 1.30pm) & Fri. Telephone secretary in advance. |
| **Green Fees** | £13 per day (£15 Sun & bank holidays). Sat after 6pm £6.50. |
| **Facilities** | ⊗ ⫩ ⫪ 🍴 ⚲ ⚒ ⚑ |
| **Leisure** | trolley for hire. |
| **Location** | A2 from Belfast |
| **Hotel** | ★★★ 66% Old Inn, 15 Main St, CRAWFORDSBURN ☎ 01247 853255 33 ⇆ ⋔ |

## CLOUGHEY · · · · · · · · · · · · · · · · · · · · · · · · · Map 01 D5

**Kirkistown Castle** 142 Main Rd, Cloughey BT22 1JA
☎ 012477 71233
A seaside semi-links popular with visiting golfers because of its quiet location. The course is exceptionally dry and remains open when others in the area have to close. The Par 4 10th is particularly distinctive with a long drive and a slight dogleg to a raised green with a gorse covered motte waiting for the wayward approach shot.
*18 holes, 6167yds, Par 69, SSS 70, Course record 65.*
*Club membership 920.*

| | |
|---|---|
| **Visitors** | must contact in advance, restricted weekends. |
| **Societies** | apply in writing. |
| **Green Fees** | £13 (£25 weekends & bank holidays). |
| **Facilities** | ⊗ ⫩ ⫪ 🍴 ⚲ ⚒ ⚑ ⋔ Jonathan Peden. |
| **Leisure** | trolley for hire, driving range, putting green, practice area. |
| **Hotel** | ★★★ 66% Old Inn, 15 Main St, CRAWFORDSBURN ☎ 01247 853255 33 ⇆ ⋔ |

## DONAGHADEE · · · · · · · · · · · · · · · · · · · · · · · Map 01 D5

**Donaghadee** Warren Rd BT21 0PQ
☎ 01247 883624
Undulating seaside course requiring a certain amount of concentration. Splendid views.
*18 holes, 5570mtrs, Par 71, SSS 69, Course record 65.*
*Club membership 1190.*

| | |
|---|---|
| **Visitors** | contact in advance. |
| **Societies** | telephone in advance. |
| **Green Fees** | £14 per round (£18 Sat after 4pm, Sun & bank holidays). |
| **Facilities** | ⊗ ⫩ ⫪ 🍴 ⚲ ⚒ ⚑ ⋔ Gordon Drew. |
| **Leisure** | trolley for hire, putting green, practice area. |
| **Hotel** | ★★★ 66% Old Inn, 15 Main St, CRAWFORDSBURN ☎ 01247 853255 33 ⇆ ⋔ |

## DOWNPATRICK · · · · · · · · · · · · · · · · · · · · · · · Map 01 D5

*Bright Castle* 14 Coniamstown Rd, Bright BT30 8LU
☎ 01396 841319
Parkland course in elevated position with views of the Mountains of Mourne. A good challenge for the energetic golfer.
*18 holes, 7300yds, Par 74, SSS 74.*

| | |
|---|---|
| **Visitors** | no restrictions. |
| **Societies** | must contact in advance. |
| **Green Fees** | not confirmed. |

| | |
|---|---|
| **Facilities** | |
| **Location** | 5m S |
| **Hotel** | ★★★ 65% Slieve Donard Hotel, Downs Rd, NEWCASTLE ☎ 013967 23681 118 ⇆ ⋔ |

**Downpatrick** 43 Saul Rd BT30 6PA
☎ 01396 615947 & 615167
This undulating parkland course has recently been extended, with Hawtree & Son as architects. It provides a good challenge.
*18 holes, 6100yds, Par 70, SSS 69, Course record 66.*
*Club membership 800.*

| | |
|---|---|
| **Visitors** | must contact in advance. |
| **Societies** | must telephone in advance. |
| **Green Fees** | £15 per day (£20 weekends & bank holidays). |
| **Facilities** | ⊗ ⫩ ⫪ 🍴 ⚲ ⚒ ⚑ ⋔ |
| **Leisure** | motorised carts for hire, buggies for hire, trolley for hire, putting green, practice area. |
| **Location** | 1.5m from town centre |
| **Hotel** | ★★ 64% Enniskeen House Hotel, 98 Bryansford Rd, NEWCASTLE ☎ 013967 22392 12 ⇆ ⋔ |

## HOLYWOOD · · · · · · · · · · · · · · · · · · · · · · · · · Map 01 D5

**Holywood** Nuns Wall, Demesne Rd
☎ 01232 423135
Hilly parkland course with some fine views and providing an interesting game.
*18 holes, 5480mtrs, Par 69, SSS 68, Course record 64.*
*Club membership 1100.*

| | |
|---|---|
| **Visitors** | must contact in advance. |
| **Societies** | must contact in writing. |
| **Green Fees** | £15 per round (£21 weekends). |
| **Facilities** | ⊗ ⫩ ⫪ 🍴 ⚲ ⚒ ⚑ ⋔ Michael Bannon. |
| **Leisure** | trolley for hire, driving range, putting green, practice area. |
| **Hotel** | ★★ 74% Rayanne Country House & Restaurant, 60 Desmesne Rd, HOLYWOOD ☎ 01232 425859 6 ⇆ ⋔ |

*The Royal Belfast* Station Rd, Craigavad BT18 0BP
☎ 01232 428165
On the shores of Belfast Lough, this attractive course consists of wooded parkland on undulating terrain which provides a pleasant, challenging game.
*18 holes, 5963yds, Par 70, SSS 69.*
*Club membership 1200.*

| | |
|---|---|
| **Visitors** | may not play on Wed or Sat before 4.30pm; must be accompanied by a member or present a letter of introduction from their own golf club. |
| **Societies** | must contact in writing. |
| **Green Fees** | not confirmed. |
| **Facilities** | ⚲ ⚒ ⚑ ⋔ |
| **Leisure** | hard tennis courts, squash, caddy cars. |
| **Location** | 2m E on A2 |
| **Hotel** | ★★★★ 71% Culloden Hotel, Bangor Rd, Holywood, BELFAST ☎ 01232 425223 87 ⇆ ⋔ |

## KILKEEL                                    Map 01 D5

**Kilkeel** Mourne Park BT34 4LB ☎ 016937 65095
Picturesquely situated at the foot of the Mourne Mountains,
Kilkeel was recently upgraded to an 18-hole course. Eleven
holes now have tree-lined fairways with the remainder in
open parkland. The 13th hole is testing and a well positioned
tee shot is essential.
*18 holes, 6615yds, Par 72, SSS 72.*
*Club membership 650.*
**Visitors**     May not play Sat. Must contact in advance.
**Societies**    must contact in writing.
**Green Fees**   £16 (£18 weekends & bank holidays).
**Facilities**   ⊗ ⅏ ﾑ ♥ ♀ ﾑ
**Leisure**      fishing, trolley for hire, driving range, putting
                 green, practice area.
**Location**     On Newry road
**Hotel**        ★★(red) Glassdrumman Lodge, 85 Mill Rd,
                 ANNALONG
                 ☎ 013967 68451 8 ⇌ ⋔Annexe2 ⇌ ⋔

## MAGHERALIN                                Map 01 D5

**Edenmore** Edenmore House, 70 Drumnabreeze Rd BT67
0RH ☎ 01846 611310 & 619199
Set in mature parkland with gently rolling slopes. There are 9
well-established holes and an additional 9 holes opened in the
summer of 1994. The original Par 5 4th is played across a
lake and between two large oak trees. The Par 3 8th has an
elevated tee and a green nestled among lime trees.
*18 holes, 6244yds, Par 71, SSS 70.*
*Club membership 300.*
**Visitors**     telephone in advance, may not play until after
                 2pm Sat or Sun.
**Societies**    telephone in advance.
**Green Fees**   £8 per 18 holes; £5 per 9 holes (£10/£7
                 weekends & bank holidays).
**Facilities**   ⊗ ⅏ ♥ ﾑ 🏠 ⋔
**Leisure**      trolley for hire, putting green, practice area.
**Hotel**        B Forte Posthouse Belfast, Kingsway, Dunmurry,
                 BELFAST ☎ 01232 612101 82 ⇌ ⋔

## NEWCASTLE                                 Map 01 D5

**ROYAL COUNTY DOWN**   See page 367

## NEWRY                                     Map 01 D5

**Newry** 11 Forkhill Rd BT35 8LZ ☎ 01693 63871
Short 18-hole course enjoying panoramic views of the
Mourne Mountains and across Newry.
*18 holes, 3000mtrs, Par 53, SSS 52, Course record 51.*
*Club membership 150.*
**Visitors**     welcome anytime.
**Societies**    apply in writing or telephone.
**Green Fees**   £3.50 (£4.50 weekends & bank holidays).
**Facilities**   ⊗ ⅏ ﾑ ♥ ♀ ﾑ 🏠
**Leisure**      motorised carts for hire, buggies for hire,
                 practice area.
**Hotel**        ★★ 64% Enniskeen House Hotel, 98
                 Bryansford Rd, NEWCASTLE
                 ☎ 013967 22392 12 ⇌ ⋔

## NEWTOWNARDS                              Map 01 D5

**Scrabo** 233 Scrabo Rd BT23 4SL ☎ 01247 812355
Hilly and picturesque, this course offers a good test of golf.
*18 holes, 5722mtrs, Par 71, SSS 71, Course record 65.*
*Club membership 956.*
**Visitors**     may not play on Sat or Sun before 11.30am.
                 Contact in advance.
**Societies**    must contact in advance.
**Green Fees**   £15 per round (£20 Sun).
**Facilities**   ⊗ ⅏ ﾑ ♥ ♀ ﾑ 🏠 ⋔ Alistair Cardwell.
**Leisure**      trolley for hire, putting green, practice area.
**Hotel**        ★★★★ 63% Stormont Hotel, 587 Upper
                 Newtonards Rd, BELFAST
                 ☎ 01232 658621 109 ⇌ ⋔

## WARRENPOINT                              Map 01 D5

**Warrenpoint** Lower Dromore Rd BT34 3LN
☎ 016937 53695
Parkland course with marvellous views and a need for
accurate shots.
*18 holes, 6108yds, Par 71, SSS 70.*
*Club membership 1100.*
**Visitors**     must contact in advance.
**Societies**    must contact in advance.
**Green Fees**   £17 (£23 weekends & bank holidays).
**Facilities**   ⊗ ⅏ ﾑ ♥ ♀ ﾑ 🏠 ⋔ ⋔ Nigel Shaw.
**Leisure**      squash, trolley for hire, putting green, practice
                 area.
**Location**     1m W
**Hotel**        ★★★ 65% Slieve Donard Hotel, Downs Rd,
                 NEWCASTLE ☎ 013967 23681 118 ⇌ ⋔

---

# CO FERMANAGH

## ENNISKILLEN                              Map 01 C5

***Ashwoods Golf Centre*** Sligo Rd BT74 7JY
☎ 01365 325321 & 322908
Only 1 mile from Lough Erne, this course is open
meadowland. It has been well planted with many young trees.
*9 holes, 1290yds, Par 27.*
**Visitors**     no restrictions.
**Societies**    must book in advance.
**Green Fees**   not confirmed.
**Facilities**   ﾑ 🏠 ⋔ ⋔ Pat Trainor.
**Leisure**      putting, trolley hire, practice area.
**Hotel**        ★★★ 54% Killyhevlin Hotel, ENNISKILLEN
                 ☎ 01365 323481 44 ⇌ ⋔Annexe26rm

**Castle Hume** Castle Hume BT93 7ED ☎ 01365 327077
Castle Hulme is a particularly scenic and challenging course.
Set in undulating parkland with large rolling greens, rivers,
lakes and water hazards all in play on a championship
standard course.
*18 holes, 6400yds, Par 72, SSS 70, Course record 69.*
*Club membership 150.*
**Visitors**     advisable to telephone in advance.
**Societies**    telephone in advance.                    ▶

# ROYAL COUNTY DOWN

NEWCASTLE *Co Down* ☎ 013967 23314          Map 01 D5

*C*harlie Mulqueen writes: Where the mountains of Mourne sweep down to the sea – that's the location for one of the game's most beautiful and challenging golf courses, Royal Co Down alongside the lovely seaside town of Newcastle. There can be few grander places when the sun shines on the Mournes and on the Irish Sea and on the furze bushes that dot the sides of almost every fairway, turning the whole scene into one of riotous colour in early summer.

The most prestigious Championships, including the British Amateur, men's and ladies', and the Curtis Cup have come to Newcastle where the game began in 1889. Legend has it that Old Tom Morris was commissioned to lay out a course at a cost not exceeding £4. Another of golf's early greats, Harry Vardon, reconstructed the links in 1908, the same year it was made 'Royal' by Edward VII. Slight changes here and there over the decades have served only to make Newcastle a finer and fairer challenge.

Most people's favourite hole at Newcastle is the 9th, a none too difficult par five of less than 500 yards, but it has been suggested that the chief hazards of the hole are the distracting views of the sea and Slieve Donard, the highest of the Mourne Mountains – a breathtaking sight perhaps unrivalled in all of golf. .

However, nobody should run away with the idea that this is anything other than an outstanding test of golf where length, accuracy and a sure touch on the many fiercely undulating greens are all essential attributes. The 13th is such a beautiful hole that it was copied at a course in Cincinatti, Ohio…Newcastle is that kind of place, a jewel among golf courses.

| | |
|---|---|
| **Visitors** | may not play No 2 course on Saturdays. May not play on Championship Course on Sun am or Wed pm |
| **Societies** | must contact in advance |
| **Green fees** | Championship: wkdays Winter £35, Summer £50. W/e Winter £45, Summer £60. Add £12 for full day. No 2: summer£15 w/e £25. winter £10 w/e £18 |
| **Facilities** | ⊗ ▙ ♥ ♀ ♣ 🏠 ⛳ ☏ (Kevan Whitson) practice area, putting green, driving range trollies |
| **Location** | Newcastle BT33 0AN |

**36 holes.**
**Championship Course 18 holes,**
**6692yds, Par71 SSS 72**
**No 2 Course 18 holes, 4681yds, Par 66**
**SSS 65**

## WHERE TO STAY AND EAT NEARBY

**HOTELS:**
**NEWCASTLE**
★★★ 65% Slieve Donard Hotel
☎ 013967 23681.  118 ⇄ ℝ

★★ 64% Enniskeen Hotel, 98
Bryansford Rd ☎ 013967 22392
12 (3 ℝ 8 ⇄  1 ⇄  ℝ)

**Green Fees** £12 per round (£18 weekends & bank holidays).
**Facilities** ⊗ ⅺ ⅼ ⬛ ♀ 🏃 🏠 ⛳
**Leisure** fishing, motorised carts for hire, buggies for hire, trolley for hire, putting green, practice area.
**Location** 4m from Enniskillen on the Belleek Rd
**Hotel** ★★★ 54% Killyhevlin Hotel, ENNISKILLEN
🕿 01365 323481 44 ⇄ ⏴Annexe26rm

---

***Enniskillen*** Castlecoole BT74 6HZ
🕿 01365 325250
Meadowland course in Castle Coole estate.
*18 holes, 5588mtrs, Par 71, SSS 69, Course record 67.*
*Club membership 500.*
**Visitors** restricted Tue and weekends.
**Societies** must contact club steward in advance.
**Green Fees** not confirmed.
**Facilities** ♀ 🏃 ⛳
**Location** 1m E
**Hotel** ★★★ 54% Killyhevlin Hotel, ENNISKILLEN
🕿 01365 323481 44 ⇄ ⏴Annexe26rm

---

# CO LONDONDERRY

---

## AGHADOWEY                              Map 01 C6

---

**Brown Trout Golf & Country Inn** 209 Agivey Rd
BT51 4AD 🕿 01265 868209
A challenging course with two par 5s. During the course of
the 9 holes, players have to negotiate water 7 times and all the
fairways are lined with densely packed fir trees.
*9 holes, 5510yds, Par 70, SSS 68, Course record 70.*
*Club membership 150.*
**Visitors** no restrictions.
**Societies** must contact by telephone, restricted tee-off times Sun.
**Green Fees** £8 per day (£12 weekends & bank holidays).
**Facilities** ⊗ ⅺ ⅼ ⬛ ♀ 🏃 ⛳ 🏮🔔 Ken Revie.
**Leisure** fishing, gymnasium, practice area.
**Location** Junc of A54 & B66
**Hotel** ★★ 67% Brown Trout Golf & Country Inn, 209
Agivey Rd, AGHADOWEY
🕿 01265 868209 17 ⇄ ⏴

---

## CASTLEDAWSON                           Map 01 C5

---

**Moyola Park** 15 Curran Rd BT45 8DG
🕿 01648 468468
Parkland course with some difficult shots, calling for length
and accuracy. The Moyola River provides a water hazard at
the 8th.
*18 holes, 6522yds, Par 71, SSS 70, Course record 67.*
*Club membership 1000.*
**Visitors** contact professional in advance. May not play weekends until late afternoon.
**Societies** must contact in advance, preferably in writing
**Green Fees** £12 per day (£17 weekends & bank holidays).
**Facilities** ⊗ ⅺ ⅼ ⬛ ♀ 🏃 🏠 ⛳ 🔔 Vivian Teague.
**Leisure** trolley for hire, putting green, practice area.
**Location** 3m NE of Magherafelt
**Hotel** ★★★★ 71% Galgorm Manor, BALLYMENA
🕿 01266 881001 23 ⇄ ⏴

---

## CASTLEROCK                             Map 01 C6

---

**Castlerock** 65 Circular Rd BT51 4TJ 🕿 01265 848314
A most exhilarating course with three superb par 4s, four
testing short holes and two par 5s. After an uphill start,
the hazards are many, including the river and a railway,
and both judgement and accuracy are called for. A
challenge in calm weather, any trouble from the elements
will test your golf to the limits.
*Mussenden Course: 18 holes, 6499yds, Par 73, SSS 72,
Course record 67.*
*Bann Course: 9 holes, 2457mtrs, Par 35, SSS 33.*
*Club membership 960.*
**Visitors** contact in advance.
**Societies** Mon-Thu only, must contact in advance.
**Green Fees** Mussenden: £17 per round (£25 weekends &
bank holidays). Bann: £7 per 18 holes (£10
weekends & bank holidays).
**Facilities** ⊗ ⅺ ⅼ ⬛ ♀ 🏃 🏠 ⛳ 🔔 Robert Kelly.
**Leisure** trolley for hire, putting green, practice area.
**Location** 6m from Coleraine on A2
**Hotel** ★★★ 61% Causeway Coast Hotel, 36
Ballyreagh Rd, PORTRUSH
🕿 01265 822435 21 ⇄ ⏴

---

## KILREA                                  Map 01 C5

---

**Kilrea** Drumagarner Rd
A relatively short undulating inland course with tight
fairways and small greens. The opening hole is a long par 3,
particularly into the wind.
*9 holes, 3956mtrs, Par 62, SSS 62, Course record 61.*
*Club membership 300.*
**Visitors** welcome but restricted Tue am, Wed pm during summer and Sat all year.
**Societies** contact D P Clark (Sec), 37 Townhill Rd,
Portglenope, Co Antrim BT44 8AD.
**Green Fees** £10 per round (£12.50 weekends & bank holidays).
**Facilities** 🏃
**Hotel** ★★ 67% Brown Trout Golf & Country Inn, 209
Agivey Rd, AGHADOWEY
🕿 01265 868209 17 ⇄ ⏴

---

## LIMAVADY                                Map 01 C6

---

**Benone** 53 Benone Ave BT49 0LQ 🕿 015047 50555
*9 holes, 1458yds, Par 27.*
**Visitors** no reservations.
**Societies** telephone in advance.
**Green Fees** £3.75 per day (£4.50 weekends & public
holidays). Prices under review.
**Facilities** ⬛ 🏃 ⛳
**Leisure** hard tennis courts, heated outdoor swimming
pool, driving range, putting green, bowling green.
**Location** Between Coleraine/Limavady on A2

---

**Radisson Roe Park Hotel & Golf Resort** Roe Park
BT49 9LB 🕿 015047 22222
A parkland course opened in 1992 on an historic Georgian
estate. The course surrounds the original buildings and a
driving range has been created in the old walled garden. Final
holes 15-18 are particularly memorable with water, trees, out-
of-bounds, etc to provide a testing finish.

*18 holes, 6318yds, Par 70, SSS 71.*
*Club membership 300.*
**Visitors**  advance booking recommended.
**Societies**  contact in advance.
**Green Fees** £16 per round (£20 weekends & bank holidays) reduced fees for hotel guests.
**Facilities** ⊗ ⏐⏐ ⓑ ⏐ ♀ ⏏ ⑮ ⚏ ⏁ ⏁ Seamus Duffy.
**Leisure**  heated indoor swimming pool, fishing, sauna, solarium, gymnasium, motorised carts for hire, buggies for hire, trolley for hire, driving range, putting green, practice area.
**Location**  On Ballykelly rd A2

---

## LONDONDERRY      Map 01 C5

*City of Derry* 49 Victoria Rd BT47 2PU ☎ 01504 46369
Two parkland courses on undulating parkland with good views and lots of trees. The 9-hole course will particularly suit novices.
*Prehen Course: 18 holes, 6406yds, Par 71, SSS 71, Course record 68.*
*Dunhugh Course: 9 holes, 4708yds, Par 63.*
*Club membership 732.*
**Visitors**  must make a booking to play on Prehen Course at weekends or before 4.30pm on weekdays.
**Societies**  must contact in advance.
**Green Fees** not confirmed.
**Facilities** ♀ ⏏ ⑮ ⏁ Michael Doherty.
**Location**  2m S
**Hotel**  ★★★ 65% Everglades Hotel, Prehen Rd, LONDONDERRY ☎ 01504 46722 52 ⇌ ⏅

---

## PORTSTEWART      Map 01 C6

*Portstewart* 117 Strand Rd BT55 7PG ☎ 01265 832015
Three links courses with spectacular views, offering a testing round on the Strand course in particular.
*Strand Course: 18 holes, 6784yds, Par 72, SSS 72.*
*Town Course: 18 holes, 4733yds, Par 64, SSS 62.*
*3: 9 holes, 2622yds, Par 32.*
**Visitors**  preferred on weekdays.
**Societies**  must contact in advance.
**Green Fees** not confirmed.
**Facilities** ♀ ⏁ ⏁ Alan Hunter.
**Leisure**  indoor bowling.
**Hotel**  ★★★ 61% Causeway Coast Hotel, 36 Ballyreagh Rd, PORTRUSH ☎ 01265 822435 21 ⇌ ⏅

---

# CO TYRONE

## COOKSTOWN      Map 01 C5

*Killymoon* 200 Killymoon Rd BT80 8TW
☎ 016487 63762 & 62254
Parkland course on elevated, well drained land.
*18 holes, 5481mtrs, Par 70, SSS 69, Course record 64.*
*Club membership 950.*
**Visitors**  booking essential through proshop on 016487 63460.
**Societies**  must contact in advance.

**Green Fees** £15 per round (£18 Sun & bank holidays).
**Facilities** ⊗ ⏐⏐ ⓑ ⏐ ♀ ⏏ ⑮ ⏁ Gary Chambers.
**Leisure**  trolley for hire, putting green, practice area.
**Hotel**  ★★ 63% Royal Arms Hotel, 51 High St, OMAGH ☎ 01662 243262 19 ⇌ ⏅

---

## DUNGANNON      Map 01 C5

*Dungannon* 34 Springfield Ln BT70 1QX
☎ 01868 722098 or 727338
Parkland course with five par 3s and tree-lined fairways.
*18 holes, 5950yds, Par 71, SSS 68, Course record 62.*
*Club membership 600.*
**Visitors**  contact in advance, may not play before 4pm Sat.
**Societies**  apply in writing to secretary.
**Green Fees** £15 per day (£18 weekends & bank holidays).
**Facilities** ⊗ ⓑ ⏐ ♀ ⏏ ⑮
**Leisure**  trolley for hire, putting green.
**Location**  0.5m outside town on Donaghmore road
**Hotel**  L The Cohannon Inn, 212 Ballynakilly Rd, DUNGANNON ☎ 01868 724488 Annexe22 ⇌ ⏅

---

## FINTONA      Map 01 C5

*Fintona* Ecclesville Demesne BT78 2AF ☎ 01662 841480
Attractive 9-hole parkland course with a notable water hazard - a trout stream that meanders through the course causing many problems for badly executed shots.
*9 holes, 5765mtrs, Par 72, SSS 70.*
*Club membership 365.*
**Societies**  apply in writing well in advance, weekends not advisable as competitions played.
**Green Fees** £10 per 18 holes.
**Facilities** ⓑ ⏐ ♀ ⏏
**Hotel**  ★★ 66% Mahons Hotel, IRVINESTOWN ☎ 013656 21656 18 ⇌ ⏅

---

## NEWTOWNSTEWART      Map 01 C5

*Newtownstewart* 38 Golf Course Rd BT78 4HU
☎ 016626 61466
Parkland course bisected by a stream.
*18 holes, 5468mtrs, Par 70, SSS 69, Course record 66.*
*Club membership 700.*
**Visitors**  contact in advance.
**Societies**  must contact secretary in advance.
**Green Fees** £10 per round (£15 weekends & bank holidays).
**Facilities** ⊗ ⏐⏐ by prior arrangement ⓑ ⏐ ♀ ⏏ ⑮ ⏁
**Leisure**  hard tennis courts, motorised carts for hire, buggies for hire, trolley for hire, putting green, practice area.
**Location**  2m SW on B84
**Hotel**  ★★ 63% Royal Arms Hotel, 51 High St, OMAGH ☎ 01662 243262 19 ⇌ ⏅

---

## OMAGH      Map 01 C5

*Omagh* 83a Dublin Rd BT78 1HQ ☎ 01662 243160
Undulating parkland course beside the River Drumnagh.
*18 holes, 5636mtrs, Par 71, SSS 70.*
**Visitors**  play restricted Sat.
**Societies**  must contact in advance. ▶

**Green Fees** £10 (£15 weekends & bank holidays).
**Facilities** ⬟
**Leisure** putting green.
**Location** On S outskirts of town
**Hotel** ★★ 63% Royal Arms Hotel, 51 High St,
OMAGH ☎ 01662 243262 19 ⇥ ☏

---

## STRABANE                                    Map 01 C5

*Strabane* Ballycolman Rd ☎ 01504 382271 & 382007
Testing parkland course with the River Mourne running
alongside and creating a water hazard.
*18 holes, 5552mtrs, Par 69, SSS 69.*
*Club membership 550.*
**Visitors** may not play on Sat.
**Societies** must contact in writing.
**Green Fees** not confirmed.
**Facilities** ⚲⬟
**Hotel** ★★ 63% Royal Arms Hotel, 51 High St,
OMAGH ☎ 01662 243262 19 ⇥ ☏

# REPUBLIC OF IRELAND

## CO CARLOW

### BORRIS
Map 01 C3

**Borris** Deerpark ☎ 0503 73143 & 73310
Testing parkland course with tree-lined fairways situated within the McMorrough Kavanagh Estate at the foot of Mount Leinster.
*9 holes, 6096yds, Par 70, SSS 69, Course record 66.*
*Club membership 350.*
**Visitors**    advisable to contact in advance, weekends very restricted.
**Societies**    applications in writing.
**Green Fees** IR£12 per 18 holes.
**Facilities**    ㅣ ♥ ♀ ♨
**Leisure**    trolley for hire, putting green, practice area.
**Hotel**    ★★★★(red)♨ Mount Juliet Hotel, THOMASTOWN
     ☎ 056 24455 32 ⇔ ⋔Annexe21 ⇔ ⋔

### CARLOW
Map 01 C3

**Carlow** Deerpark ☎ 0503 31695
Created in 1922 to a design by Tom Simpson, this testing and enjoyable course is set in a wild deer park, with beautiful dry terrain and a varied character. With sandy sub-soil, the course is playable all year round. There are water hazards at the 2nd, 10th and 11th and only two par 5s, both offering genuine birdie opportunities.
*18 holes, 5599mtrs, Par 70, SSS 69, Course record 62.*
*Club membership 1100.*
**Visitors**    are welcome, although play is limited on Tue and difficult on Sat & Sun. Must contact in advance.
**Societies**    must book in advance.
**Green Fees** IR£20 per day (IR£25 per round weekends & bank holidays).
**Facilities**    ⊗ ㅣ ㅣ ♥ ♀ ♨ ⊞ ⚑ ⋔ Andrew Gilbert.
**Leisure**    trolley for hire, putting green, practice area.
**Location**    2m N of Carlow
**Guesthouse** QQQQ Barrowville Town House, Kilkenny Rd, CARLOW ☎ 0503 43324 7 ⇔ ⋔

## CO CAVAN

### BALLYCONNELL
Map 01 C4

**Slieve Russell Hotel Golf & Country Club**
☎ 049 26444 & 26474
An 18-hole course with a new 9-hole Par 3 to complement it. On the main course, the 2nd plays across water while the 16th has water surrounding the green. The course finishes with a 519 yard, Par 5 18th.

*18 holes, 6650yds, Par 72, SSS 72, Course record 68.*
*Club membership 770.*
**Visitors**    must book in advance.
**Societies**    write or telephone in advance, not allowed Sat.
**Green Fees** IR£25 per day (IR£30 Sat). Reduced rate for hotel residents.
**Facilities**    ⊗ ㅣ ㅣ ♥ ♀ ♨ ⊞ ⚑ ⋔ ⋔ Liam McCool.
**Leisure**    hard tennis courts, heated indoor swimming pool, squash, sauna, solarium, gymnasium, buggies for hire, trolley for hire, practice area.
**Location**    1.5m E of Ballyconnell
**Hotel**    ★★★★ 66% Slieve Russell Hotel & Country Club, BALLYCONNELL
     ☎ 049 26444 151 ⇔ ⋔

### BELTURBET
Map 01 C4

**Belturbet** Erne Hill ☎ 049 22287
Beautifully maintained parkland course with predominantly family membership and popular with summer visitors.
*9 holes, 5480yds, Par 68, SSS 65, Course record 64.*
*Club membership 150.*
**Visitors**    restrictions the same as for members.
**Societies**    must contact secretary or captain in advance.
**Green Fees** not confirmed.
**Facilities**    ♀ ♨
**Hotel**    ★★★★ 66% Slieve Russell Hotel & Country Club, BALLYCONNELL
     ☎ 049 26444 151 ⇔ ⋔

### BLACKLION
Map 01 C5

**Blacklion** Toam ☎ 072 53024
Parkland course established in 1962, with coppices of woodland and mature trees. The lake comes into play on two holes and there are some magnificent views of the lake, islands and surrounding hills. It has been described as one of the best maintained nine-hole courses in Ireland.
*9 holes, 5614mtrs, Par 72, SSS 69.*
*Club membership 250.*
**Visitors**    no restrictions.
**Societies**    must contact in advance.
**Green Fees** IR£8 per day (IR£10 weekends & bank holidays).
**Facilities**    ㅣ ♥ ♀ ♨
**Leisure**    fishing, trolley for hire, putting green, small practice area.
**Hotel**    ★★★ 70% Sligo Park Hotel, Pearse Rd, SLIGO ☎ 071 60291 89 ⇔ ⋔

### CAVAN
Map 01 C4

**County Cavan** Drumelis ☎ 049 31541 & 31283
Parkland course.
*18 holes, 5519mtrs, Par 70, SSS 69, Course record 66.*
*Club membership 830.*
**Visitors**    welcome but restricted at weekends.
**Societies**    contact for details.
**Green Fees** not confirmed.
**Facilities**    ♀ ♨
**Leisure**    putting green, practice area.
**Location**    On Killeshandra rd    ▶

**Hotel**    ★★★ 64% Kilmore Hotel, Dublin Rd,
CAVAN
☎ 049 32288 39 ⇌ ℉

---

## VIRGINIA                                        Map 01 C4

**Virginia** ☎ 049 47235 & 40223
*9 holes, 4139mtrs, Par 64, SSS 62.*
*Club membership 400.*
**Visitors**     may not play Thu & Sun.
**Societies**    must apply in writing to secretary.
**Green Fees** IR£10.
**Facilities**   ⚲ ⌂
**Location**     By Lough Ramor
**Hotel**        ★★ 60% Conyngham Arms Hotel, SLANE
☎ 041 24155 16rm(15 ⇌ ℉)

---

# CO CLARE

---

## CLONLARA                                        Map 01 B3

*Clonlara Golf & Leisure*
☎ 061 354141
A 9-hole parkland course, Par 35, on the banks of the River
Shannon with views of Clare Hills. Set in grounds of 63 acres
surrounding the 17th century Landscape House, there is also
a leisure complex for self-catering holidays.
*9 holes, 5328mtrs, Par 70, SSS 68.*
*Club membership 70.*
**Visitors**     players only no accompanying persons.
**Societies**    welcome subject to availability prior notice
required.
**Green Fees** not confirmed.
**Facilities**   ♀ ⚲ ⫞ ⌂
**Leisure**      hard tennis courts, sauna, games room.
**Location**     7m NE of Limerick
**Hotel**        ★★★★ 68% Castletroy Park Hotel, Dublin Rd,
LIMERICK
☎ 061 335566 107 ⇌ ℉

---

## ENNIS                                        Map 01 B3

**Ennis** Drumbiggle ☎ 065 24074
On rolling hills, this immaculately manicured course presents
an excellent challenge to both casual visitors and aspiring
scratch golfers, with tree-lined fairways and well protected
greens.
*18 holes, 5275mtrs, Par 69, SSS 68, Course record 65.*
*Club membership 1000.*
**Visitors**     advisable to contact in advance, course available
Mon-Sat at most times.
**Societies**    apply in writing.
**Green Fees** IR£16 per day.
**Facilities**   ⊗ ⫞ ⓛ ⫟ ♀ ⚲ ⌂ ⫞ ⫞ Martin Ward.
**Leisure**      trolley for hire, putting green, practice area.
**Hotel**        ★★★ 68% Auburn Lodge Hotel, Galway Rd,
ENNIS
☎ 065 21247 100 ⇌ ℉

---

## KILKEE                                        Map 01 B3

**Kilkee** East End ☎ 065 56048
Well established course on the cliffs of Kilkee Bay, with
beautiful views.
*18 holes, 6500yds, Par 72, SSS 71, Course record 68.*
*Club membership 390.*
**Visitors**     must book in advance.
**Societies**    apply in writing.
**Green Fees** IR£15 per round.
**Facilities**   ⊗ ⫞ ⓛ ⫟ ♀ ⚲ ⌂ ⫞
**Leisure**      squash, sauna, buggies for hire, trolley for hire,
putting green, practice area.
**Hotel**        ★★ 60% Halpin's Hotel, Erin St, KILKEE
☎ 065 56032 12 ⇌ ℉

---

## KILRUSH                                        Map 01 B3

**Kilrush** Parknamoney ☎ 065 51138
Parkland course that was extended to 18 holes in the summer
of 1994.
*18 holes, 5986yds, Par 70, SSS 70, Course record 68.*
*Club membership 375.*
**Visitors**     welcome, contact for details.
**Societies**    by prior arrangement.
**Green Fees** IR£15 per day.
**Facilities**   ⊗ ⫞ ⓛ ⫟ ♀ ⚲ ⌂ ⫞
**Leisure**      trolley for hire, putting green, small practice
area.
**Hotel**        ★★ 60% Halpin's Hotel, Erin St, KILKEE
☎ 065 56032 12 ⇌ ℉

---

## LAHINCH                                        Map 01 B3

**Lahinch** ☎ 065 81003
Originally designed by Tom Morris and later modified by
Dr Alister MacKenzie, Lahinch has hosted every
important Irish amateur fixture and the Home
Internationals. The par five 5th - The Klondike - is
played along a deep valley and over a huge dune; the par
three 6th may be short, but calls for a blind shot over the
ridge of a hill to a green hemmed in by hills on three
sides.
*Old Course: 18 holes, 6696yds, Par 72, SSS 73.*
*Castle Course: 18 holes, 5619yds, Par 70, SSS 70.*
*Club membership 1840.*
**Visitors**     must contact in advance.
**Societies**    apply in writing
**Green Fees** Old Course IR£40; Castle Course IR£25.
**Facilities**   ⊗ ⫞ ⓛ ⫟ ♀ ⚲ ⌂ ⫞ ⫞ R McCavery.
**Location**     2m W of Ennistymon on N67
**Hotel**        ★★ 70% Sheedy's Spa View Hotel &
Orchid Restaurant, LISDOONVARNA
☎ 065 74026 11 ⇌ ℉

---

## MILLTOWN MALBAY                                        Map 01 B3

**Spanish Point** ☎ 065 84198
A 9-hole links course with 3 elevated greens and 4 elevated
tees. The 8th hole is a 75-metre par 3, locally known as 'the
Terror'.
*9 holes, 4600mtrs, Par 64, SSS 62, Course record 63.*
*Club membership 250.*
**Visitors**     contact in advance.

**Societies** apply in writing to the secretary 065 84219
**Green Fees** IR£10 per day.
**Facilities** ⛳ 💼 ♀ 👤 ♈
**Hotel** ★★★ 65% West County Inn Hotel, Clare Rd,
ENNIS ☎ 065 28421 110 ➡ ♞

### NEWMARKET-ON-FERGUS Map 01 B3

**Dromoland Castle** ☎ 061 368444 & 368144
Set in 200 acres of parkland, the course is enhanced by
numerous trees and a lake. Three holes are played around the
lake which is in front of the castle.
*18 holes, 6098yds, Par 71, SSS 72, Course record 67.*
*Club membership 500.*
**Visitors** must contact in advance.
**Societies** contact in writing.
**Green Fees** IR£22 per day (IR£27 weekends & bank
holidays).
**Facilities** ⊗ ⅷ ⛳ 💼 ♀ 👤 🏠 ♈ ℂ Philip Murphy.
**Leisure** hard tennis courts, fishing, motorised carts for
hire, buggies for hire, trolley for hire, driving
range, putting green, practice area.
**Location** 2m N, on main Limerick/Galway rd
**Hotel** ★★★ 64% Clare Inn Hotel, NEWMARKET-
ON-FERGUS
☎ 061 368161 121 ➡ ♞

### SCARRIFF Map 01 B3

**East Clare** Bodyke ☎ 061 921322
Beside Lough Derg, East Clare was opened in June 1992 as a
9-hole course in 148 acre site with natural trees and water on
well-drained land. An 18-hole championship course deigned
by Arthur Spring is in preparation.
*9 holes, 52yds, Par 70, SSS 70 or 32 holes.*
*Club membership 130.*
**Visitors** no restrictions unless there is a club competition
or a society playing.
**Societies** apply in writing, deposit required.
**Green Fees** not confirmed.
**Facilities** 👤 ♈
**Hotel** ★★★ 65% West County Inn Hotel, Clare Rd,
ENNIS
☎ 065 28421 110 ➡ ♞

### SHANNON AIRPORT Map 01 B3

**Shannon** ☎ 061 471849
Superb parkland course with tree-lined fairways, strategically
placed bunkers, water hazards and excellent greens, offering
a challenge to all levels of players - including the many
famous golfers who have played here.
*18 holes, 6874yds, Par 72, SSS 74.*
*Club membership 800.*
**Visitors** must contact in advance & have handicap
certificate. Restricted play at certain times.
**Societies** must contact in writing.
**Green Fees** not confirmed.
**Facilities** ♀ 👤 🏠 ♈ ℂ Artie Pyke.
**Leisure** putting green, practice area, motorised carts,
buggy & trolley hire.
**Location** 2m from Shannon Airport
**Hotel** ★★★ 63% Fitzpatrick Bunratty Shamrock
Hotel, BUNRATTY
☎ 061 361177 115 ➡ ♞

## CO CORK

### BANDON Map 01 B2

**Bandon** Castlebernard ☎ 023 41111
Lovely parkland course in pleasant rural surroundings.
*18 holes, 5663mtrs, Par 70, SSS 69, Course record 66.*
*Club membership 800.*
**Visitors** welcome but may not play during club
competitions. Must contact in advance.
**Societies** must apply in writing.
**Green Fees** not confirmed.
**Facilities** ♀ 👤 🏠 ♈ ℂ Paddy O'Boyle.
**Leisure** hard tennis courts, caddy cars.
**Hotel** ★★ 70% Inishannon House Hotel,
INISHANNON
☎ 021 775121 13 ➡ ♞Annexe1 ➡ ♞

### BANTRY Map 01 B2

**Bantry Park** Donemark ☎ 027 50579
An undulating 9-hole course with some magnificent sea views.
*9 holes, 5946mtrs, Par 72, SSS 72.*
*Club membership 300.*
**Visitors** contact in advance.
**Societies** must apply in writing.
**Green Fees** IR£13 per day.
**Facilities** ⊗ ⅷ ⛳ 💼 ♀ 👤 ♈
**Leisure** trolley for hire, putting green.
**Hotel** ★★★⚓ 70% Sea View Hotel,
BALLYLICKEY
☎ 027 50073 & 50462 17 ➡ ♞

### BLARNEY Map 01 B2

**Muskerry** Carrigrohane ☎ 021 385297
An adventurous game is guaranteed at this course, with
its wooded hillsides and the meandering Shournagh River
coming into play at a number of holes. The 15th is a
notable hole - not long, but very deep - and after that all
you need to do to get back to the clubhouse is stay out of
the water.
*18 holes, 6327yds, Par 71, SSS 71.*
*Club membership 706.*
**Visitors** may not play Wed afternoon & Thu
morning. Some limited opportunities at
weekends.
**Societies** must telephone in advance and then confirm
in writing.
**Green Fees** not confirmed.
**Facilities** ♀ 👤 🏠 ♈ ℂ
**Leisure** practice area,trolley hire.
**Location** 7.5m NW of Cork
**Hotel** ★★★ 66% Blarney Park Hotel,
BLARNEY
☎ 021 385281 76 ➡ ♞

### CASTLETOWNBERE Map 01 A2

**Berehaven** Millcove ☎ 027 70700
Seaside links founded in 1902.
*9 holes, 2398mtrs, Par 68, SSS 66, Course record 63.* ▶

**Visitors** no restrictions ex first week June.
**Societies** apply to J J McLaughlin, Main St,
Castletownbere.
**Green Fees** IR£8 per day (IR£10 weekends & bank
holidays).
**Facilities** ⊗ ⅃ℎ ▆ ♀ ᪐ ⑂
**Leisure** hard tennis courts, sauna, trolley for hire,
practice area, camp site.
**Location** 2m E on Glen Garriff Rd
**Hotel** ★★★⚌ 70% Sea View Hotel,
BALLYLICKEY
☎ 027 50073 & 50462 17 ⇄ 🐾

---

## CHARLEVILLE                                        Map 01 B2

**Charleville** ☎ 063 81257
Wooded parkland course offering not too strenuous walking.
*18 holes, 6212yds, Par 71, SSS 69, Course record 65.*
*Club membership 1000.*
**Visitors** only prebooked at weekends.
**Societies** contact in advance.
**Green Fees** IR£12 (IR£15 weekends & bank holidays).
**Facilities** ⊗ ⅁⅃ℎ ▆ ♀ ᪐ 🏠 ⑂
**Leisure** trolley for hire, putting green, practice area.
**Hotel** ★★★(red)⚌ Longueville House Hotel,
MALLOW
☎ 022 47156 & 47306 16 ⇄ 🐾

---

## CLONAKILTY                                        Map 01 B2

**Dunmore** Dunmore, Muckross ☎ 023 33352
A hilly, rocky 9-hole course overlooking the Atlantic.
*9 holes, 4464yds, Par 64, SSS 61, Course record 57.*
*Club membership 250.*
**Visitors** must contact in advance, may not play
weekends.
**Societies** apply in writing.
**Green Fees** IR£10 per 18 holes.
**Facilities** ⊗ ⅁⅃ℎ ▆ ♀ ᪐ ⑂ 🏠
**Leisure** trolley for hire.
**Location** 3.5m S of Clonakilty
**Hotel** ★★ 64% Courtmacsherry,
COURTMACSHERRY
☎ 023 46198 13rm(9 ⇄1 🐾)

---

## CORK                                               Map 01 B2

**Cork** Little Island ☎ 021 353451
This championship-standard course is always kept in
superb condition and is playable all year round. It has
many memorable and distinctive features including holes
at the water's edge and holes in a disused quarry.
*18 holes, 5910mtrs, Par 72, SSS 70.*
*Club membership 750.*
**Visitors** may not play 12.30-2pm or on Thu (Ladies
Day), and only after 2pm Sat & Sun.
**Societies** must contact in advance.
**Green Fees** IR£30 (IR£35 weekends).
**Facilities** ⊗ ⅁⅃ℎ ▆ ♀ ᪐ 🏠 ⑂ ℓ Peter Hickey.
**Leisure** trolley for hire, putting green, practice area.
**Location** 5m E, on N25
**Hotel** ★★★★ 70% Jurys Hotel, Western Rd,
CORK ☎ 021 276622 185 ⇄ 🐾

---

**Fitzpatrick Silver Springs** Tivoli
☎ 021 507533 & 505128
Five Par 4s and 4 Par3s make up this short 9-hole course. The
4th has a 189 metre drive with out of bounds on the righthand
side.
*9 holes, 1786mtrs, Par 32, Course record 26.*
*Club membership 70.*
**Visitors** no restrictions.
**Societies** apply by telephone.
**Green Fees** IR£5 (IR£7 weekends and bank holidays).
**Facilities** ⅃ℎ ▆ ♀ ᪐ ⑂ 🏠 ℓ Freddy Twomey.
**Leisure** hard tennis courts, heated indoor swimming
pool, squash, sauna, solarium, gymnasium,
buggies for hire, trolley for hire, putting green.
**Location** 1m E of city centre
**Hotel** ★★★★ 66% Fitzpatrick Silver Springs Hotel,
Tivoli, CORK
☎ 021 507533 109 ⇄ 🐾

---

**Fota Island** Carrigtwohill ☎ 021 883700 & 883710
Fota Island Golf Club is in the heart of the 780 acre island in
Cork Harbour which is recognised as one of Ireland's most
outstanding landscapes. The course is gently undulating
parkland routed among mature woodlands with occasional
views of the harbour. The overall design is very traditional,
featuring pot bunkers, a double green and undulating putting
surfaces. The 10th and 18th holes are narrow Par 5's that
require great accuracy and shotmaking skills.
*18 holes, 6500yds, Par 72, SSS 72, Course record 67.*
*Club membership 300.*
**Visitors** advisable to contact in advance.
**Societies** contact in advance.
**Green Fees** IR£27 per round (IR£30 weekends). Extra 18
Holes IR£10.
**Facilities** ⊗ ⅁⅃ℎ ▆ ♀ ᪐ 🏠 ⑂ ℓ Kevin Morris.
**Leisure** motorised carts for hire, buggies for hire, trolley
for hire, driving range, putting green, practice
area.
**Location** Off N25 E of Cork City
**Hotel** ★★★ 66% Midleton Park, MIDLETON
☎ 021 631767 40 ⇄ 🐾

---

*Mahon Municipal* Blackrock ☎ 021 362480
Municipal course which stretches alongside the river estuary,
with some holes across water.
*18 holes, 4818mtrs, Par 67, SSS 66.*
*Club membership 380.*
**Visitors** may not play mornings at weekends.
**Green Fees** not confirmed.
**Facilities** ♀ ᪐ 🏠 ⑂
**Location** 2m from city centre
**Hotel** ★★★★ 66% Fitzpatrick Silver Springs Hotel,
Tivoli, CORK ☎ 021 507533 109 ⇄ 🐾

---

## DONERAILE                                          Map 01 B2

*Doneraile* ☎ 022 24137
Parkland.
*9 holes, 5528yds, SSS 66.*
**Visitors** no restrictions
**Societies** welcome.
**Green Fees** not confirmed.
**Location** Off T11
**Hotel** ★★★(red)⚌ Longueville House Hotel,
MALLOW
☎ 022 47156 & 47306 16 ⇄ 🐾

## DOUGLAS

Map 01 B2

**Douglas** ☎ 021 895297
Level inland course overlooking the city of Cork. Suitable for golfers of all ages and abilities.
*18 holes, 5383mtrs, Par 70, SSS 68.*
*Club membership 810.*
**Visitors** advisable to play Mon & Wed-Fri, contact in advance.
**Societies** must contact in writing, dates allocated early Feb.
**Green Fees** IR£20 (IR£22 weekends).
**Facilities** ⊗ ⅷ ⅃ ⅃ ♀ ⅃ 🖻 ⅋ ℓ Gary Nicholson.
**Leisure** trolley for hire, putting green, practice area.
**Hotel** ★★★★ 70% Jurys Hotel, Western Rd, CORK ☎ 021 276622 185 ⇄ ℟

## FERMOY

Map 01 B2

**Fermoy** Corrin Cross ☎ 025 31472
Rather exposed heathland course, bisected by a road.
*18 holes, 5586mtrs, Par 70, SSS 69.*
*Club membership 1000.*
**Visitors** contact in advance.
**Societies** advisable to write in advance.
**Green Fees** IR£13 (IR£16 weekends).
**Facilities** ⊗ ⅷ ⅃ ⅃ ♀ ⅃ 🖻 ⅋ ℓ John Savage.
**Leisure** buggies for hire, trolley for hire, putting green, practice area.
**Location** 2m SW
**Hotel** ★★★(red)⚌ Longueville House Hotel, MALLOW ☎ 022 47156 & 47306 16 ⇄ ℟

## GLENGARRIFF

Map 01 B2

**Glengarriff** ☎ 027 63150
Founded 1935.
*9 holes, 2042mtrs, SSS 62.*
*Club membership 300.*
**Visitors** welcome, details not supplied
**Societies** apply to club.
**Green Fees** not confirmed.
**Facilities** ♀ ⅃ ⅋
**Leisure** practice area,trolley hire.
**Location** On N71
**Hotel** ★★★ 58% Westlodge Hotel, BANTRY ☎ 027 50360 90 ⇄ ℟

## KINSALE

Map 01 B2

**Kinsale** Farrangalway ☎ 021 772197
In addition to the existing 9-hole (Ringenane) course, a new 18-hole (Farrangalway) course was opened in 1994. Set in unspoilt farmland and surrounded by peacefull rolling countryside, it offers a stiff yet fair challenge to be enjoyed by all standards of golfers. New putting green.
*Farrangalway: 18 holes, 6608yds, Par 71, SSS 71, Course record 70.*
*Ringenane: 9 holes, 2552yds, Par 70, SSS 66, Course record 63.*
*Club membership 740.*
**Visitors** must contact in advance.
**Societies** apply in writing.

**Green Fees** Farrangalway: IR£15 per round (IR£20 weekends). Ringenane: IR£10 per 18 holes.
**Facilities** ⅃ ⅋
**Leisure** trolley for hire, putting green, practice area.
**Location** On main Cork/Kinsale rd
**Hotel** ★★★ 68% Trident Hotel, Worlds End, KINSALE ☎ 021 772301 58 ⇄ ℟

## LITTLE ISLAND

Map 01 B2

**Harbour Point** Clash Rd ☎ 021 353094
A new championship-standard course in rolling countryside on the banks of the River Lee at Cork's scenic harbour. A distinctive and testing course for every standard of golfer.
*18 holes, 5883metres, Par 72, SSS 71, Course record 71.*
**Visitors** must contact in advance.
**Societies** telephone for bookings.
**Green Fees** IR£10 per round before 11am Mon, Wed, Thu & Fri; IR£20 other times.
**Facilities** ⊗ ⅷ ⅃ ⅃ ♀ ⅃ 🖻 ⅋
**Leisure** motorised carts for hire, buggies for hire, trolley for hire, driving range, putting green, practice area.
**Location** 5m E of Cork
**Hotel** ★★★★ 66% Fitzpatrick Silver Springs Hotel, Tivoli, CORK ☎ 021 507533 109 ⇄ ℟

## MACROOM

Map 01 B2

**Macroom** Lackaduve ☎ 026 41072
A particularly scenic parkland course located on undulating ground along the banks of the River Sullane. Bunkers and mature trees make a variable and testing course and the 18th has a 50 yards carry over the river to the green.
*18 holes, 5574mtrs, Par 72, SSS 70.*
*Club membership 550.*
**Visitors** restricted some weekends, contact in advance.
**Societies** apply in writing.
**Green Fees** IR£12 (IR£15 weekends & bank holidays).
**Facilities** ⊗ ⅃ ⅃ ⅃ ⅋
**Leisure** trolley for hire, putting green.
**Location** Through castle entrance in town square
**Hotel** ★★ 70% Castle Hotel, Main St, MACROOM ☎ 026 41074 26 ⇄ ℟

## MALLOW

Map 01 B2

**Mallow** Ballyellis ☎ 022 21145
A well wooded parkland course overlooking the Blackwater Valley, Mallow is straightforward, but no less of a challenge for it. The front nine is by far the longer, the back nine is demanding in its call for accuracy and the par 3 18th provides a tough finish.
*18 holes, 5769metres, Par 72, SSS 71, Course record 67.*
*Club membership 1400.*
**Visitors** must contact in advance.
**Societies** apply in advance.
**Green Fees** IR£17 per round (IR£20 weekends & bank holidays).
**Facilities** ⊗ ⅷ ⅃ ⅃ ♀ ⅃ 🖻 ⅋ ℓ Sean Conway.
**Leisure** hard tennis courts, squash, sauna, trolley for hire, putting green, practice area.
**Hotel** ★★★(red)⚌ Longueville House Hotel, MALLOW ☎ 022 47156 & 47306 16 ⇄ ℟

## MIDLETON Map 01 C2

**East Cork** Gortacrue ☎ 021 631687
A well wooded course calling for accuracy of shots.
*18 holes, 5207mtrs, Par 69, SSS 67.*
*Club membership 511.*
**Visitors** may not play Sun mornings.
**Societies** must apply in writing or telephone.
**Green Fees** not confirmed.
**Facilities** ♀ ⅄ ⚐
**Leisure** squash, fishing, driving range, putting green, practice area, trolley hire.
**Location** On the A626
**Hotel** ★★★ 66% Midleton Park, MIDLETON ☎ 021 631767 40 ⇄ 🐾

## MITCHELSTOWN Map 01 B2

**Mitchelstown** Limerick Rd, Gurrane ☎ 025 24072
Attractive, gently undulating parkland course set in the Golden Vale, noted for the quality of the greens, the magnificent views of the Galtee Mountains and its friendly atmosphere. Ideal for golfers seeking tranquility and a golfing challenge.
*18 holes, 5160mtrs, Par 67, SSS 68, Course record 65.*
*Club membership 400.*
**Visitors** advisable to book for weekend play.
**Societies** apply in writing.
**Green Fees** IR£10 per day.
**Facilities** ⓑ 🕮 ♀ ⅄
**Leisure** trolley for hire, putting green, practice area.
**Location** 0.75m on Limerick rd from Mitchelstown
**Hotel** ★★★(red)♨ Longueville House Hotel, MALLOW ☎ 022 47156 & 47306 16 ⇄ 🐾

## MONKSTOWN Map 01 B2

**Monkstown** Parkgariffe, Monkstown ☎ 021 841376
Undulating parkland course with five tough finishing holes.
*18 holes, 5441mtrs, Par 70, SSS 68, Course record 66.*
*Club membership 960.*
**Visitors** restricted weekends, must contact in advance.
**Societies** apply in writing or telephone. Large groups (24+) should book before Xmas.
**Green Fees** IR£23 Mon-Thu; IR£26 Fri-Sun & bank holidays.
**Facilities** ⊗ 🕮 ⓛ 🎔 ♀ ⅄ ⋒ ⚐ ⅌ Batt Murphy.
**Leisure** motorised carts for hire, trolley for hire, putting green, practice area.
**Location** 0.5m SE of Monkstown village
**Hotel** ★★★★ 70% Jurys Hotel, Western Rd, CORK ☎ 021 276622 185 ⇄ 🐾

## OVENS Map 01 B2

**Lee Valley Golf & Country Club** Clashanure ☎ 021 331721
An undulating test of all golfing abilities designed by Ryder Cup star Christy O'Connor Junior. Seven of the 18 holes have water and the unusual feature of two fairy forts which are over 300 years old - can they be blamed for errors on the testing Par 5 8th and 12th holes?! The 508yard, Par 5 8th is already regarded as one of the best holes in Ireland with its spectacular lake a feature from tee to green.

*18 holes, 6434mtrs, Par 72, SSS 70, Course record 68.*
*Club membership 400.*
**Visitors** telephone in advance.
**Societies** telephone in advance.
**Green Fees** IR£30 per 36 holes, IR£20 per round (IR£35/IR£25 weekends & bank holidays).
**Facilities** ⊗ 🕮 ⓛ 🎔 ♀ ⅄ ⋒ ⚐ ⅌ ⅌ Brendan McDaid.
**Leisure** motorised carts for hire, buggies for hire, trolley for hire, driving range, putting green, practice area.
**Location** 8m from Cork on Cork/Killarney road N22
**Hotel** ★★ 57% Vienna Woods Hotel, Glanmire, CORK ☎ 021 821146 20 ⇄ 🐾

## SKIBBEREEN Map 01 B2

**Skibbereen & West Carbery** Licknavar ☎ 028 21227
Expanded to an 18-hole course in May 1993. Slightly hilly course in scenic locatio.
*18 holes, 6004yds, Par 71, SSS 69, Course record 68.*
*Club membership 640.*
**Visitors** advisable to contact in advance, may be restricted Sun for competitions.
**Societies** apply in writing.
**Green Fees** IR£12 per day (IR£15 July/Aug).
**Facilities** ⊗ 🕮 ⓛ 🎔 ♀ ⅄
**Leisure** trolley for hire, putting green, practice area.
**Location** 20m S of Bantry, off N71
**Hotel** ★★★ 68% Liss Ard Lake Lodge, SKIBBEREEN

## YOUGHAL Map 01 C2

**Youghal** Knockaverry ☎ 024 92787
For many years the host of various Golfing Union championships, Youghal offers a good test of golf and is well maintained for year-round play. There are panoramic views of Youghal Bay and the Blackwater estuary.
*18 holes, 5700mtrs, Par 70, SSS 70, Course record 67.*
*Club membership 600.*
**Visitors** may not play Wed (Ladies Day) and should contact in advance for weekends.
**Societies** must apply in writing a few months in advance.
**Green Fees** not confirmed.
**Facilities** ♀ ⅄ ⋒ ⚐ ⅌ Liam Burns.
**Leisure** putting green,trolley hire,practice area.
**Hotel** ★★ 64% Devonshire Arms Hotel and Restaurant, Pearse Square, YOUGHAL ☎ 024 92827 & 92018 10 ⇄ 🐾

---

# ● CO DONEGAL ●

---

## BALLINTRA Map 01 B5

**Donegal** Murvagh, Laghy ☎ 073 34054
This massive links course was opened in 1973 and provides a world-class facility in peaceful surroundings. It is a very long course with some memorable holes, including five par 5s, calling for some big hitting. Donegal is the home club of former Curtis Cup captain, Maire O'Donnell.

*18 holes, 6243mtrs, Par 73, SSS 73, Course record 68.*
*Club membership 750.*
**Visitors**    must contact in advance, limited availability at weekends.
**Societies**    must contact in advance.
**Green Fees**   IR£17 per day (IR£22.50 per round weekends & bank holidays).
**Facilities**    ⊗ �X ⅃ ▟ ❦ ♀ ♨
**Leisure**    buggies for hire, trolley for hire, putting green, practice area.
**Location**    6m S of Donegal on Ballyshannon road
**Hotel**    ★★★ 73% Sand House Hotel, ROSSNOWLAGH
   ☎ 072 51777 46 ⇥ ↑

## BALLYBOFEY      Map 01 C5

***Ballybofey & Stranorlar*** Stranorlar ☎ 074 31093
A most scenic course incorporating pleasant valleys backed by mountains with three of its holes bordered by a lake. There are three Par 3s on the first nine and two on the second. The most difficult hole is the long uphill Par 4 16th. The only Par 5 is the 7th.
*18 holes, 5366mtrs, Par 68, SSS 68, Course record 64.*
*Club membership 450.*
**Visitors**    may play on weekdays. Advisable to book in advance
**Green Fees**   not confirmed.
**Facilities**    ♀ ♨
**Leisure**    squash.
**Location**    0.25m from Stranorlar
**Hotel**    ★★★ 62% Kee's Hotel, Stranolar, BALLYBOFEY
   ☎ 074 31018 36 ⇥ ↑

## BALLYLIFFEN      Map 01 C6

***Ballyliffin*** ☎ 077 76119
The Old course is a links course with rolling fairways, surrounded by rolling hills and bounded on one side by the ocean. Nick Faldo said 'This is the most natural golf links I have ever played.' It has an old-fashioned charm with its uniquely contoured fairways. The new 18-hole course, the Glaslady (opened summer 1995), offers a modern (and arguably 'fairer') championship test.
*Old Links: 18 holes, 6384yds, Par 72, SSS 70, Course record 68.*
*Glashedy Links: 18 holes, 6982yds, Par 71, SSS 72.*
*Club membership 903.*
**Visitors**    telephone in advance.
**Societies**    telephone in advance.
**Green Fees**   not confirmed.
**Facilities**    ♀ ♨ 🏠
**Leisure**    putting green,practice area,trolley hire.
**Guesthouse**   QQQQ Mount Royd Country Home, CARRIGANS ☎ 074 40163 4 ↑

## BUNCRANA      Map 01 C6

***Buncrana Municipal*** Ballmacarry ☎ 077 62279
A 9-hole course with a very challenging Par-3 3rd with all carry out of bounds on either side.
*9 holes, 2125yds, Par 62, SSS 60, Course record 59.*
*Club membership 100.*

**Visitors**    during open competitions only visitors with club handicaps.
**Societies**    write in advance.
**Green Fees**   not confirmed.
**Facilities**    ♀ ♨ 🏠
**Guesthouse**   QQQQ Mount Royd Country Home, CARRIGANS ☎ 074 40163 4 ↑

**North West** Lisfannon, Fahan ☎ 077 61027
A traditional-style links course on gently rolling sandy terrain with some long par 4s. Good judgement is required on the approaches and the course offers a satisfying test coupled with undemanding walking.
*18 holes, 5968yds, Par 69, SSS 68, Course record 64.*
*Club membership 580.*
**Visitors**    contact in advance for weekends. Wed - Ladies Day
**Societies**    telephone in advance.
**Green Fees**   IR£12 (IR£17 weekends).
**Facilities**    ⊗ ⅃ ⅃ ▟ ❦ ♀ ♨ 🏠 ┌ Seamus McBriarty.
**Leisure**    motorised carts for hire, buggies for hire, trolley for hire, practice area, putting green.
**Guesthouse**   QQQQ Mount Royd Country Home, CARRIGANS ☎ 074 40163 4 ↑

## BUNDORAN      Map 01 B5

**Bundoran** ☎ 072 41302
This popular course, acknowledged as one of the best in the country, runs along the high cliffs above Bundoran beach and has a difficult par of 69. Designed by Harry Vardon, it offers a challenging game of golf in beautiful surroundings and has been the venue for a number of Irish golf championships.
*18 holes, 5599mtrs, Par 69, SSS 70, Course record 66.*
*Club membership 560.*
**Visitors**    must contact in advance.
**Societies**    must contact in advance.
**Green Fees**   IR£14 (IR£16 weekends & bank holidays) + VAT.
**Facilities**    ▟ ⅃ ♀ ♨ 🏠 ┐ ┌ David T Robinson.
**Leisure**    trolley for hire, putting green, practice area.
**Hotel**    ★★★ 73% Sand House Hotel, ROSSNOWLAGH
   ☎ 072 51777 46 ⇥ ↑

## CRUIT ISLAND      Map 01 B5

***Cruit Island*** Kincasslagh ☎ 075 43296
A links course on a small island. It is perched along the cliffs overlooking the Atlantic. The course is short but always challenging as the wind blows 90% of the time. It is crowned by a magnificent 6th hole which is played across a cove to an island green. With the prevailing wind in your face and the Atlantic waves crashing in front, it is not for the fainthearted.
*9 holes, 4833mtrs, Par 68, SSS 66, Course record 62.*
*Club membership 200.*
**Visitors**    restricted Sun & Thu mornings for Club competitions.
**Societies**    apply in writing to secretary.
**Green Fees**   not confirmed.
**Facilities**    ♀ (all day in summer) ♨
**Hotel**    ★★ 70% Arnold's Hotel, DUNFANAGHY
   ☎ 074 36208 & 36142 34 ⇥ ↑

## DUNFANAGHY                                    Map 01 C6

**Dunfanaghy** Kill ☎ 074 36335 & 36488
Overlooking Sheephaven Bay, the course has a flat central
area with three difficult streams to negotiate. At the Port-na-
Blagh end there are five marvellous holes, including one
across the beach, while at the Horn Head end, the last five
holes are a test for any golfer.
*18 holes, 5066mtrs, Par 68, SSS 66, Course record 64.*
*Club membership 395.*
**Visitors**     must book in advance, Jun-Aug time sheet in
                 operation.
**Societies**    must telephone in advance.
**Green Fees**   IR£12.50 per round (IR£14.50 weekends).
**Facilities**   ᒪ ☖ ♀ ⚐ 🏳
**Leisure**      motorised carts for hire, buggies for hire, trolley
                 for hire, putting green, practice area.
**Location**     On N56
**Hotel**        ★★ 70% Arnold's Hotel, DUNFANAGHY
                 ☎ 074 36208 & 36142 34 ⇌ 🐾

## GREENCASTLE                                   Map 01 C6

**Greencastle** Moville ☎ 077 81013
A typical links course along the shores of Lough Foyle,
surrounded by rocky headlands and sandy beaches. In 1992 to
celebrate its centenary, the club increased its size from 9 to
18 holes.
*18 holes, 5118mtrs, Par 69, SSS 67.*
*Club membership 600.*
**Visitors**     no restrictions.
**Societies**    telephone in advance.
**Green Fees**   not confirmed.
**Facilities**   ♀ ⚐
**Leisure**      putting green.
**Hotel**        ★★★ 65% Everglades Hotel, Prehen Rd,
                 LONDONDERRY
                 ☎ 01504 46722 52 ⇌ 🐾

## GWEEDORE                                      Map 01 B6

**Gweedore** Derrybeg ☎ 075 31140
This 9-hole links course provides plenty of challenge with
two subtle Par 3s and the Par 5 5th/14th at 556yards into the
prevailing west wind is a monster.
*9 holes, 6201yds, Par 71, SSS 69.*
*Club membership 150.*
**Visitors**     no restrictions.
**Societies**    telephone in advance.
**Green Fees**   not confirmed.
**Facilities**   ⚐
**Hotel**        ★★ 65% Carrig Rua Hotel, DUNFANAGHY
                 ☎ 074 36133 22 ⇌ 🐾

## LETTERKENNY                                   Map 01 C5

**Letterkenny** Barnhill ☎ 074 21150
The fairways are wide and generous, but the rough, when you
find it, is short, tough and mean. The flat and untiring terrain
on the shores of Lough Swilly provides good holiday golf.
Many interesting holes include the intimidating 1st with its
high tee through trees and the tricky dog-leg of the 2nd hole.
*18 holes, 6239yds, Par 70, SSS 71, Course record 67.*
*Club membership 500.*

**Visitors**     preferred Mon-Fri. Advisable to contact in
                 advance for weekends and bank holidays.
**Societies**    apply by writing or telephone.
**Green Fees**   not confirmed.
**Facilities**   ♀ ⚐ 🏳
**Leisure**      table tennis.
**Location**     2m from town on Rathmelton road
**Hotel**        ★★★ 62% Kee's Hotel, Stranolar,
                 BALLYBOFEY
                 ☎ 074 31018 36 ⇌ 🐾

## NARIN                                         Map 01 B5

**Narin & Portnoo** ☎ 075 45107
Seaside links with every hole presenting its own special
feature. The Par 4 5th, for instance, demands a perfectly
placed drive to get a narrow sight of the narrow entrance to
the elevated green. Cross winds from the sea can make some
of the Par 4s difficult to reach with two woods.
*18 holes, 5322mtrs, Par 69, SSS 68, Course record 63.*
*Club membership 420.*
**Visitors**     weekends by arrangement.
**Societies**    telephone in advance.
**Green Fees**   IR£12 per day (IR£15 weekends & bank
                 holidays).
**Facilities**   ᒪ ☖ ♀ ⚐ 🏠
**Leisure**      trolley for hire, putting green.
**Location**     6m from Ardara
**Hotel**        ★★★ 63% Abbey Hotel, The Diamond,
                 DONEGAL
                 ☎ 073 21014 49 ⇌ 🐾

## PORTSALON                                     Map 01 C6

**Portsalon** ☎ 074 59459
Another course blessed by nature. The three golden beaches
of Ballymastocker Bay lie at one end, while the beauty of
Lough Swilly and the Inishowen Peninsula beyond is a
distracting but pleasant feature to the west. Situated on the
Fanad Peninsula, this lovely links course provides untiring
holiday golf at its best.
*18 holes, 5878yards, Par 69, SSS 68, Course record 66.*
*Club membership 400.*
**Visitors**     telephone in advance.
**Societies**    telephone in advance.
**Green Fees**   IR£12 (IR£14 weekends).
**Facilities**   ⊗ 🍴 ᒪ ☖ ♀ ⚐
**Leisure**      trolley for hire, putting green.
**Hotel**        ★ 61% Pier Hotel, RATHMULLAN
                 ☎ 074 58178 & 58115 10 ⇌ 🐾

## RATHMULLAN                                    Map 01 C6

**Otway** Saltpans ☎ 074 58319
*9 holes, 4234yds, Par 64, SSS 60.*
**Visitors**     welcome.
**Societies**    contact for details.
**Green Fees**   not confirmed.
**Location**     W shore of Loch Swilly
**Hotel**        ★★★🏵 69% Fort Royal Hotel, Fort Royal,
                 RATHMULLAN
                 ☎ 074 58100 11 ⇌ 🐾Annexe4 ⇌

## ROSAPENNA
Map 01 C6

*Rosapenna* Downings ☎ 074 55301
Dramatic links course offering a challenging round.
Originally designed by Tom Morris and later modified by
James Braid and Harry Vardon, it includes such features as
bunkers in mid fairway. The best part of the links runs in the
low valley along the ocean.
*18 holes, 6271yds, Par 70, SSS 71.*
*Club membership 200.*
**Visitors** no restrictions.
**Societies** must contact in advance.
**Green Fees** not confirmed.
**Facilities** ♀ ⛏ 🏠 ⚑ ⛳ ⌂ ℂ Simon Byrne.
**Leisure** hard tennis courts.
**Hotel** ★★ 70% Arnold's Hotel, DUNFANAGHY
☎ 074 36208 & 36142 34 ⇆ ℅

---

# CO DUBLIN

---

## BALBRIGGAN
Map 01 D4

*Balbriggan* Blackhall ☎ 01 8412229 & 01 8412173
A parkland course with great variations and good views of
the Mourne and Cooley mountains.
*18 holes, 5881mtrs, Par 71, SSS 71.*
*Club membership 650.*
**Visitors** must contact in advance. With member only at
weekends.
**Societies** must apply in writing.
**Green Fees** IR£14 per round. Early bird before 10am IR£8
(ex Tue).
**Facilities** ⊗ 🍳 🥄 ▆ ♀ ⛏
**Leisure** trolley for hire, putting green, practice area.
**Hotel** ★★★ 65% Boyne Valley Hotel, DROGHEDA
☎ 041 37737 35 ⇆ ℅

---

## BRITTAS
Map 01 D4

*Slade Valley* Lynch Park ☎ 01 4582183 & 4582739
This is a course for a relaxing game, being fairly easy and in
pleasant surroundings.
*18 holes, 5388mtrs, Par 69, SSS 68, Course record 65.*
*Club membership 800.*
**Visitors** must contact in advance.
**Societies** telephone in advance.
**Green Fees** IR£17 per round (afternoons); IR£15 (before
noon).
**Facilities** ⊗ 🍳 🥄 ▆ ♀ ⛏ 🏠 ⚑ ⌂ ℂ John Dignam.
**Leisure** trolley for hire, putting green.
**Location** 9m SW of Dublin on N81
**Hotel** ★★★ 56% Downshire House Hotel,
BLESSINGTON
☎ 045 865199 14 ⇆ ℅Annexe11 ⇆ ℅

---

## CLOGHRAN
Map 01 D4

*Forrest Little* ☎ 01 8401183
Testing parkland course.
*18 holes, 5865mtrs, Par 70, SSS 70.*

---

**Visitors** preferred weekday mornings.
**Green Fees** not confirmed.
**Facilities** ♀ 🏠 ⚑ ℂ Tony Judd.
**Location** 6m N of Dublin on N1
**Hotel** ★★★ 68% Marine Hotel, Sutton Cross,
DUBLIN ☎ 01 8390000 26 ⇆ ℅

---

## CLONSILLA
Map 01 D4

*Luttrellstown Castle* ☎ 01 8208210
*18 holes, 6032mtrs, Par 72, SSS 73, Course record 66.*
*Club membership 400.*
**Visitors** welcome.
**Societies** must phone in advance.
**Green Fees** IR£34 per 18 holes (IR£39 weekends).
**Facilities** ⊗ 🍳 🥄 ▆ ♀ ⛏ 🏠 ⚑ ⌂ ℂ Graham Campbell.
**Leisure** hard tennis courts, heated outdoor swimming
pool, fishing, sauna, buggies for hire, trolley for
hire, driving range, putting green, practice area,.
**Location** Porterstown rd
**Hotel** ★★★ 66% Finnstown Country House Hotel &
Golf Course, Newcastle Rd, LUCAN
☎ 01 6280644 25 ⇆ ℅Annexe20 ⇆ ℅

---

## DONABATE
Map 01 D4

*Balcarrick* Corballis
☎ 01 8436228 & 8436957
Splendid 18-hole parkland course located close to the sea. A
strong prevailing wind often plays a big part on every hole.
Many challenging holes, notably the 7th - nicknamed 'Amen
Corner'.
*18 holes, 6273mtrs, Par 73, SSS 71.*
*Club membership 480.*
**Visitors** advisable to contact for weekend play.
**Societies** telephone in advance.
**Green Fees** IR£10 (IR£15 weekends & bank holidays).
**Facilities** 🥄 ▆ ♀ ⛏ 🏠
**Leisure** putting green.
**Hotel** B Forte Posthouse Dublin, Cloghran, DUBLIN
☎ 01 8444211 188 ⇆ ℅

---

*Beaverstown* Beaverstown
☎ 01 8436439 & 8436721
Well wooded course with water hazards at more than half of
the holes.
*18 holes, 5855mtrs, Par 71, SSS 71, Course record 69.*
*Club membership 800.*
**Visitors** may not play 12.30-1.30pm daily & must contact
in advance to play on Wed, Sat or Sun.
**Societies** must contact in writing.
**Green Fees** not confirmed.
**Facilities** ♀ ⛏
**Leisure** caddy cars.
**Location** 5m from Dublin Airport
**Hotel** B Forte Posthouse Dublin, Cloghran, DUBLIN
☎ 01 8444211 188 ⇆ ℅

---

*Corballis Public* Corballis ☎ 01 8436583
Well maintained coastal course with excellent greens.
*18 holes, 4971yds, Par 65, SSS 64.*
**Visitors** no restrictions.
**Societies** apply in writing or telephone.
**Green Fees** IR£7 per round (IR£8 weekends).
**Facilities** ▆ ⛏ 🏠 ⚑ ▶

**Leisure** buggies for hire, trolley for hire, putting green.
**Hotel** B Forte Posthouse Dublin, Cloghran, DUBLIN
☎ 01 8444211 188 ⇌ ↻

---

**Donabate** Balcarrick ☎ 01 8436346 & 8436001
Level parkland course.
*18 holes, 5704yds, Par 70, SSS 69, Course record 67.*
*Club membership 900.*
**Visitors** welcome, weekdays & late Sunday afternoon.
**Societies** must apply in writing.
**Green Fees** IR£18 (IR£24 Sunday).
**Facilities** ⊗ 爪 և 里 ♀ ⚐ ☎ ☂ ⓣ Hugh Jackson.
**Leisure** buggies for hire, trolley for hire, practice green,
putting green.
**Hotel** B Forte Posthouse Dublin, Cloghran, DUBLIN
☎ 01 8444211 188 ⇌ ↻

---

*The Island* Corballis ☎ (01) 8436104 & 8436205
Links course on a promontory, with sea inlets separating
some of the fairways. Accuracy as well as length of shots
are required on some holes and sand hills provide an
additional challenge.
*18 holes, 6078mtrs, Par 71, SSS 72.*
*Club membership 800.*
**Visitors** preferred on Mon, Tue & Fri.
**Societies** must apply in advance.
**Green Fees** not confirmed.
**Facilities** ♀ ⚐
**Leisure** putting green,practice area,trolley hire.
**Hotel** B Forte Posthouse Dublin, Cloghran,
DUBLIN ☎ 01 8444211 188 ⇌ ↻

---

# DUBLIN Map 01 D4

*Carrickmines* Carrickmines ☎ 01 2955972
Meadowland course.
*9 holes, 6100yds, Par 71, SSS 69.*
*Club membership 500.*
**Visitors** with member only Sat, Sun & bank holidays.
**Societies** contact for details.
**Green Fees** not confirmed.
**Location** 7m S of Dublin
**Hotel** ★★★ 61% Royal Marine Hotel, Marine Rd,
DUN LAOGHAIRE ☎ 01 2801911 104 ⇌ ↻

---

**Castle** Woodside Dr, Rathfarnham
☎ 01 4904207 & 4905835
A tight, tree-lined parkland course which is very highly
regarded by all who play there.
*18 holes, 5732mtrs, Par 70, SSS 68, Course record 63.*
*Club membership 1200.*
**Visitors** welcome but may not play at weekends.
**Societies** must apply in writing 6 months in advance.
**Green Fees** IR£27 per round.
**Facilities** ⊗ 爪 և 里 ♀ ⚐ ☎ ⓣ David Kinsella.
**Leisure** trolley for hire, putting green, practice area.
**Hotel** ★★★★ 70% Jurys Hotel, Pembroke Rd,
Ballsbridge, DUBLIN 4 ☎ 01 6605000 292 ⇌ ↻

---

**Clontarf** Donnycarney House, Malahide Rd
☎ 01 8331892 & 8331520
The nearest golf course to Dublin city, with a historic
building as a clubhouse, Clontarf is a parkland type course
bordered on one side by a railway line. There are several
testing and challenging holes including the 12th, which
involves playing over a pond and a quarry.

*18 holes, 5459mtrs, Par 69, SSS 68, Course record 66.*
*Club membership 1100.*
**Visitors** welcome daily but advisable to contact in
advance.
**Societies** Tue & Fri. Must contact in advance.
**Green Fees** Apr-Oct IR£23 per round. Nov-Mar IR£15..
**Facilities** ⊗ 爪 և 里 ♀ ⚐ ☎ ⓣ Joe Craddock.
**Leisure** buggies for hire, trolley for hire, practice area,
putting green, bowling green.
**Location** 2.5m N via Fairview
**Hotel** ★★★ 65% Doyle Skylon Hotel, Drumcondra
Rd, DUBLIN 9 ☎ 01 8379121 92 ⇌ ↻

---

*Corrstown* Kilsallaghan ☎ 01 8640533
A new course with the first 9 holes in play - a pleasant
parkland setting well sheltered by mature trees. An additional
18-hole championship standard course is due to open in
Spring 1995. It has been designed by Eddie B. Connaughton
to test the best golfers.
*River: 18 holes, 6885yds, Par 72, SSS 73.*
*Orchard: 9 holes, 3053yds, Par 70, SSS 69.*
*Club membership 900.*
**Visitors** welcome to play 9 hole course but with member
only on weekdays. Further 18 Holes open by
mid Sep 1995.
**Societies** by arrangement.
**Green Fees** not confirmed.
**Facilities** ⚐ ☎ ☂ ⓣ Pat Gittens.
**Leisure** motorised carts, practice area, buggy & trolley
hire.
**Location** W of Dublin Airport via St Margarets
**Hotel** ★★★ 65% Doyle Skylon Hotel, Drumcondra
Rd, DUBLIN 9 ☎ 01 8379121 92 ⇌ ↻

---

*Deer Park Hotel & Golf Course* Howth ☎ 01 8322624
Claiming to be Irelands largest golf/hotel complex, be warned
that its popularity makes it extremely busy at times and only
hotel residents can book tee-off times.
*St Fintans: 9 holes, 3373yds, Par 37.*
*Deer Park: 18 holes, 6678yds, Par 72.*
*Grace O'Malley: 9 holes, 3105yds, Par 35.*
*Short Course: 12 holes, 1810yds, Par 36.*
*Club membership 200.*
**Visitors** no restrictions. There may be delays especially
Sun mornings.
**Societies** must contact by telephone.
**Green Fees** not confirmed.
**Facilities** ♀ ⚐ ☂ ⋈
**Leisure** putting green,practice area,trolley hire.
**Location** On right 0.5m before Howth Harbour
**Hotel** ★★★ 66% Howth Lodge Hotel, HOWTH
☎ 01 8321010 46 ⇌ ↻

---

**Edmonstown** Edmondstown Rd, Edmondstown
☎ 01 4931082
A popular and testing parkland course situated at the foot of
the Dublin Mountains in the suburbs of the city. An attractive
stream flows in front of the 4th and 6th greens calling for an
accurate approach shot.
*18 holes, 5663mtrs, Par 70, SSS 69.*
*Club membership 750.*
**Visitors** must contact in advance as there are daily times
reserved for members.
**Societies** must contact in advance.
**Green Fees** IR£24 per round (IR£28 weekends) summer.
IR£18 per round (IR£24 weekends) winter.

**Facilities** ⊗ 〉Ⅲ ㅣ ■ ♀ ♣ 🏠 ⚑ ⚑ Andrew Crofton.
**Leisure** trolley for hire, putting green, practice area.
**Hotel** ★★★ 68% Doyle Montrose Hotel, Stillorgan Rd, DUBLIN ☎ 01 2693311 179 ⇔ ☏

---

**Elm Park Golf & Sports Club** Nutley House, Nutley Ln, Dennybrook ☎ 01 2693438
Interesting parkland course requiring a degree of accuracy, particularly as half of the holes involve crossing the stream.
*18 holes, 5355mtrs, Par 69, SSS 68, Course record 64.*
*Club membership 1750.*
**Visitors** must contact in advance.
**Societies** apply in advance.
**Green Fees** IR£40 per round (IR£45 weekends).
**Facilities** ⊗ 〉Ⅲ ㅣ ■ ♀ ♣ 🏠 ⚑ ⚑ Seamus Green.
**Leisure** grass tennis courts, trolley for hire, putting green.
**Location** 3m from city centre
**Hotel** ★★★★ 70% Jurys Hotel, Pembroke Rd, Ballsbridge, DUBLIN 4 ☎ 01 6605000 292 ⇔ ☏

---

*Foxrock* Torquay Rd, Foxrock
☎ 01 2895668 & 2893992
A well-treed parkland course.
*9 holes, 5667mtrs, Par 70, SSS 69.*
*Club membership 650.*
**Visitors** welcome but contact in advance, no green fees Tue & weekends.
**Societies** apply in writing to William Daly.
**Green Fees** not confirmed.
**Facilities** ♀ ♣ 🏠 ⚑ ⚑ David Walker.
**Leisure** practice area, trolley hire.
**Hotel** ★★★ 61% Royal Marine Hotel, Marine Rd, DUN LAOGHAIRE ☎ 01 2801911 104 ⇔ ☏

---

*Grange* Rathfarnham ☎ 01 932889
Wooded parkland course which provides both interest and challenge.
*18 holes, 5517mtrs, Par 68, SSS 69.*
**Visitors** preferred on weekdays.
**Green Fees** not confirmed.
**Facilities** ♀ 🏠 ⚑ W Sullivan.
**Location** 6m from city centre
**Hotel** ★★★ 68% Doyle Montrose Hotel, Stillorgan Rd, DUBLIN ☎ 01 2693311 179 ⇔ ☏

---

**Hollywood Lakes** Hollywood ☎ 01 8433406 & 8433407
A parkland course opened in 1992 with large USGA-type, sand-based greens and tees. There are water features on seven holes. The front nine requires accuracy while the second nine includes a 636yard Par 5.
*18 holes, 6246mtrs, Par 72, SSS 72, Course record 67.*
*Club membership 380.*
**Visitors** welcome but may not play weekends & bank holidays.
**Societies** telephone then write in advance.
**Green Fees** IR£16 per day (IR£20 weekends).
**Facilities** ⊗ 〉Ⅲ ㅣ ■ ♀ ♣
**Leisure** trolley for hire, practice area.
**Location** 3m off main Dublin/Belfast road
**Hotel** ★★★ 68% Marine Hotel, Sutton Cross, DUBLIN ☎ 01 8390000 26 ⇔ ☏

---

**Howth** St Fintan's, Carrickbrack Rd, Sutton ☎ 01 8323055
A moorland course with scenic views of Dublin Bay. It is very hilly and presents a good challenge for the athletic golfer.
*18 holes, 5618mtrs, Par 71, SSS 69.*
*Club membership 1200.*
**Visitors** contact in advance.
**Societies** must contact in advance.
**Green Fees** not confirmed.
**Facilities** ⊗ 〉Ⅲ ㅣ ■ ♀ ♣ 🏠 ⚑ John McGuirk.
**Leisure** trolley for hire, practice area.
**Hotel** ★★★ 68% Marine Hotel, Sutton Cross, DUBLIN ☎ 01 8390000 26 ⇔ ☏

---

**Milltown** Lower Churchtown Rd ☎ 01 4976090
Level parkland course on the outskirts of the city.
*18 holes, 5638mtrs, Par 71, SSS 69, Course record 64.*
*Club membership 1400.*
**Visitors** must contact in advance but may not play weekends.
**Societies** apply in writing.
**Green Fees** IR£30 Mon-Fri.
**Facilities** ⊗ 〉Ⅲ ㅣ ■ ♀ ♣ 🏠 ⚑ ⚑ John Harnett.
**Leisure** trolley for hire, putting green, practice area.
**Hotel** ★★★★ 70% Jurys Hotel, Pembroke Rd, Ballsbridge, DUBLIN 4 ☎ 01 6605000 292 ⇔ ☏

---

*Newlands* Clondalkin 22 ☎ 01 4593157
Mature parkland course offering a testing game.
*18 holes, 5714mtrs, Par 71, SSS 70.*
*Club membership 1000.*
**Visitors** must contact in advance and may play Mon, Thu, Fri and Wed mornings only.
**Societies** must contact in writing.
**Green Fees** not confirmed.
**Facilities** ♀ ♣ 🏠 ⚑ ⚑ Karl O'Donnell.
**Leisure** putting green, practice area, trolley hire.
**Hotel** ★★★ 61% Doyle Green Isle Hotel, Naas Rd, DUBLIN 12 ☎ 01 4593406 48 ⇔ ☏Annexe35 ⇔ ☏

---

**The Open Golf Centre** Newton House, St Margaret's ☎ 01 8640324
A 27-hole Pay and Play parkland course that is testing for the low handicap golfer but not too intimidating for high handicapper.
*18 holes, 5973yds, Par 71, SSS 71, Course record 66.*
**Visitors** no restrictions. Booking essential.
**Societies** telephone for booking form.
**Green Fees** IR£7.60 per 18 holes (IR£11.50 weekends & bank holidays).
**Facilities** ■ ♣ 🏠 ⚑ ⚑ Roger Yates.
**Leisure** trolley for hire, indoor driving range, video tuition, putting green.
**Location** Adjacent to Dublin airport
**Hotel** ★★★ 68% Marine Hotel, Sutton Cross, DUBLIN ☎ 01 8390000 26 ⇔ ☏

---

**Rathfarnham** Newtown ☎ 01 4931201 & 4931561
Parkland course designed by John Jacobs in 1962.
*9 holes, 2921mtrs, Par 36, SSS 70, Course record 69.*
*Club membership 624.*
**Visitors** must contact in advance but may not play weekends.
**Societies** restricted to Mon, Wed & Fri.  ▶

Green Fees IR£20 per round.
Facilities 🏌 🍽 ♀ ⛳ 🏠 ☏ Brian O'Hara.
Leisure buggies for hire, putting green, practice area.
Hotel ★★★★ 70% Jurys Hotel, Pembroke Rd, Ballsbridge, DUBLIN 4
☎ 01 6605000 292 ⇆ ☏

---

**Royal Dublin** North Bull Island, Dollymount
☎ 01 8336346
A popular course with visitors, for its design subtleties, for the condition of the links and the friendly atmosphere. Founded in 1885, the club moved to its present site in 1889 and received its Royal designation in 1891. A notable former club professional was Christie O'Connor, who was appointed in 1959 and immediately made his name. Along with its many notable holes, Royal Dublin has a fine and testing finish. The 18th is a sharply dog-legged par 4, with out of bounds along the right-hand side. The decision to try the long carry over the 'garden' is one many visitors have regretted.
*18 holes, 6030mtrs, Par 72, SSS 71, Course record 65.*
*Club membership 800.*
Visitors must contact in advance & have handicap certificate.
Societies must book one year in advance.
Green Fees IR£45 per round (IR£55 weekends).
Facilities ⊗ 🎏 🏌 🍽 ♀ ⛳ 🏠 ⛳ ☏ Leonard Owens.
Leisure practice ground & nets, putting green.
Hotel ★★★ 66% Howth Lodge Hotel, HOWTH
☎ 01 8321010 46 ⇆ ☏

---

*St Anne's* North Bull Island, Dollymount ☎ 01 8336471
Links course, recently extended from 9 holes to 18.
*18 holes, 5652mtrs, Par 70, SSS 69.*
*Club membership 500.*
Visitors telephone for restrictions.
Societies must apply in writing.
Green Fees not confirmed.
Facilities ♀ ⛳ ☏
Leisure putting green,trolley hire,practice area.
Hotel ★★★ 66% Howth Lodge Hotel, HOWTH
☎ 01 8321010 46 ⇆ ☏

---

**St Margaret's Golf & Country Club** St Margaret's
☎ 01 8640400
A championship standard course which measures nearly 7,000 yards off the back tees, but flexible teeing offers a fairer challenge to the middle and high handicap golfer. The modern design makes wide use of water hazards and mounding. The Par 5 8th hole is set to become notorious - featuring lakes to the left and right of the tee and a third lake in front of the green. Ryder Cup player,Sam Torrance, has described the 18th as 'possibly the strongest and most exciting in the world'.
*18 holes, 6917yds, Par 73, SSS 73, Course record 69.*
*Club membership 200.*
Visitors telephone in advance.
Societies apply in writing.
Green Fees IR£40 per round.
Facilities ⊗ 🎏 🏌 🍽 ♀ ⛳ 🏠 ⛳ 🍴
☏ Ciaran Monaghan.
Leisure buggies for hire, trolley for hire, driving range, putting green, practice area.
Location 3m NW
Hotel ★★★ 68% Marine Hotel, Sutton Cross, DUBLIN ☎ 01 8390000 26 ⇆ ☏

---

## Finnstown
## Country House Hotel
## & Golf Course ★★★

### Newcastle Road, Lucan, Co Dublin
### Tel: 00 3531 628044    Fax: 00 3531 6281088

Finnstown Country House is only eight miles from Dublin city centre. Situated off the main road and on 50 acres of mature woodlands, guests may relax and enjoy the friendly atmosphere and service of a small grade A country house hotel together with the amenities of today and a fine Restaurant. The hotel has its own wooded walks, 9 hole golf course, hard tennis courts, outdoor pool, gymnasium, saunas and Turkish bath.

*A beautiful place in a great location.*

---

*Stackstown* Kellystown Rd, Rathfarnham
☎ 01 4942338 & 4941993
Pleasant course in scenic surroundings.
*18 holes, 5925mtrs, Par 72, SSS 72, Course record 70.*
*Club membership 1042.*
Visitors preferred Mon-Fri.
Societies telephone in advance and confirm in writing.
Green Fees not confirmed.
Facilities ♀ ⛳ 🏠 ☏ Michael Kavanach.
Leisure sauna.
Location 9m S of city centre
Hotel ★★★ 68% Doyle Montrose Hotel, Stillorgan Rd, DUBLIN ☎ 01 2693311 179 ⇆ ☏

---

*Sutton* Cush Point, Burrow Rd, Sutton
☎ 01 8324875
Founded in 1890.
*9 holes, 5226mtrs, Par 70, SSS 67.*
Visitors welcome except for competition days, contact for further details.
Societies by prior arrangement.
Green Fees not confirmed.
Facilities ☏ Nicky Lynch.
Leisure lessons can be arranged.
Location Approx 7m NE of city
Hotel ★★★ 66% Howth Lodge Hotel, HOWTH
☎ 01 8321010 46 ⇆ ☏

---

## DUN LAOGHAIRE

Map 01 D4

**Dun Laoghaire** Eglinton Park, Tivoli Rd
☎ 01 2803916 & 2805116
This is a well wooded parkland course, not long, but

requiring accurate club selection and placing of shots. The course was designed by Harry Colt in 1918.
*18 holes, 5197mtrs, Par 69, SSS 67, Course record 63.*
*Club membership 1040.*
**Visitors**   may not play Sat.
**Societies**   must apply in writing.
**Green Fees** IR£26 per day.
**Facilities**   ⊗ 〣 ⅃ ⬛ ♀ ♨ 🏠 ⚑ ʈ Owen Mulhall.
**Leisure**   trolley for hire, putting green.
**Hotel**   ★★★ 61% Royal Marine Hotel, Marine Rd, DUN LAOGHAIRE ☎ 01 2801911 104 ⇆ 🐾

## KILLINEY         Map 01 D4

**Killiney** Ballinclea Rd ☎ 01 2852823 & 2851983
The course is on the side of Killiney Hill with picturesque views over south Dublin and the Wicklow Mountains.
*9 holes, 5430mtrs, Par 70, SSS 68.*
*Club membership 450.*
**Visitors**   welcome Mon, Wed, Fri & Sun afternoons.
**Green Fees** IR£20.
**Facilities**   ⊗ 〣 ⅃ ⬛ ♀ ♨ 🏠 ⚑ ʈ P O'Boyle.
**Leisure**   buggies for hire, trolley for hire, putting green, practice area.
**Hotel**   ★★★ 66% Fitzpatrick Castle Hotel, KILLINEY ☎ 01 2840700 90 ⇆ 🐾

## KILTERNAN         Map 01 D4

**Kilternan Golf & Country Club Hotel** ☎ 01 2955559
Interesting and testing course overlooking Dublin Bay.
*18 holes, 4914mtrs, Par 68, SSS 67, Course record 69.*
*Club membership 789.*
**Visitors**   may not play before 1.30pm at weekends.
**Societies**   apply in writing/telephone in advance.
**Green Fees** not confirmed.
**Facilities**   ♀ ♨ 🏠 ⚑ ⋈ ʈ
**Leisure**   hard tennis courts, heated indoor swimming pool, fishing, sauna, solarium, gymnasium, dry ski slope, indoor tennis, night club.
**Hotel**   ★★★ 66% Fitzpatrick Castle Hotel, KILLINEY ☎ 01 2840700 90 ⇆ 🐾

## LUCAN         Map 01 D4

**Finnstown Fairways** Newcastle Rd
☎ 01 6280644
A flat parkland 9-hole course based in grounds originally laid out in the 18th century. Very challenging 6th and 7th holes among many mature trees.
*9 holes, 2695yds, Par 66, SSS 66.*
*Club membership 200.*
**Visitors**   time sheet in use, must reserve in advance.
**Societies**   must reserve in advance.
**Green Fees** IR£10 per day (IR£12 weekends).
**Facilities**   ⊗ 〣 ⅃ ⬛ ♀ ♨ ⚑ 🏠
**Leisure**   hard tennis courts, heated outdoor swimming pool, sauna, solarium, gymnasium, buggies for hire, trolley for hire, driving range, practice area, turkish bath.
**Location**   Off N4
**Hotel**   ★★★ 66% Finnstown Country House Hotel & Golf Course, Newcastle Rd, LUCAN ☎ 01 6280644 25 ⇆ 🐾Annexe20 ⇆ 🐾

**Hermitage** Ballydowd
☎ 01 6265049 & 6268491
Part level, part undulating course bordered by the River Liffey and offering some surprises.
*18 holes, 6034mtrs, Par 71, SSS 70.*
*Club membership 1100.*
**Visitors**   contact for details
**Societies**   must telephone well in advance.
**Green Fees** not confirmed.
**Facilities**   ♀ ♨ 🏠 ⚑ ʈ Ciaran Carroll.
**Leisure**   putting green,trolley hire.
**Hotel**   ★★★ 66% Finnstown Country House Hotel & Golf Course, Newcastle Rd, LUCAN ☎ 01 6280644 25 ⇆ 🐾Annexe20 ⇆ 🐾

**Lucan** Celbridge Rd ☎ 01 6282106
Founded in 1902 as a 9-hole course and only recently extended to 18 holes, Lucan involves playing across both the main road and a lane which bisects the course.
*18 holes, 5958mtrs, Par 71, SSS 71.*
*Club membership 780.*
**Visitors**   with member only Sat & Sun, after 1pm Wed.
**Societies**   must apply in writing.
**Green Fees** not confirmed.
**Facilities**   ♀ ♨
**Leisure**   putting green,trolley hire,practice area.
**Hotel**   ★★★ 55% Lucan Spa Hotel, LUCAN ☎ 01 6280494 50 ⇆ 🐾

## MALAHIDE         Map 01 D4

**Malahide** Beechwood, The Grange
☎ 01 8461611
Splendid parkland course with raised greens and water hazards affecting many of the holes, demanding accuracy from tee to green.
*Blue Course: 18 holes, 5372mtrs, Par 69, SSS 68.*
*Red Course: 18 holes, 5708mtrs, Par 71, SSS 71, Course record 67.*
*Yellow Course: 18 holes, 5304mtrs, Par 69, SSS 68.*
*Club membership 1100.*
**Visitors**   must contact in advance.
**Societies**   must contact in advance.
**Green Fees** IR£25 per 18 holes (IR£35 weekends & bank holidays).
**Facilities**   ⊗ 〣 ⅃ ⬛ ♀ ♨ 🏠 ⚑ ʈ David Barton.
**Leisure**   trolley for hire, putting green, practice area.
**Location**   1m from coast road at Portmarnock
**Hotel**   ★★★ 66% Howth Lodge Hotel, HOWTH ☎ 01 8321010 46 ⇆ 🐾

## PORTMARNOCK         Map 01 D4

**PORTMARNOCK**   See page 387

## RATHCOOLE         Map 01 D4

**Beech Park** Johnstown
☎ 01 580100
Relatively flat parkland with heavily wooded fairways.
*18 holes, 5730mtrs, Par 72, SSS 70, Course record 67.*
*Club membership 750.*
**Visitors**   restricted on some days, telephone in advance. ▶

**Societies**   apply in writing.
**Green Fees** not confirmed.
**Facilities**  ♀♿
**Hotel**       ★★★ 66%  Finnstown Country House Hotel &
                Golf Course, Newcastle Rd, LUCAN
                ☎ 01 6280644 25 ➷ ⬧Annexe20 ➷ ⬧

## RUSH                                        Map 01 D4

*Rush* ☎ 01 8438177
Seaside borders three fairways on this links course. There are
28 bunkers and undulating fairways to add to the challenge of
the variable and strong winds that blow at all times and
change with the tides. There are no easy holes!
*9 holes, 5598mtrs, Par 70, SSS 69.*
*Club membership 350.*
**Visitors**    restricted Wed, Thu, weekends & bankholidays.
**Societies**   apply in writing.
**Green Fees** not confirmed.
**Facilities**  ♀♿
**Hotel**       B Forte Posthouse Dublin, Cloghran, DUBLIN
                ☎ 01 8444211 188 ➷ ⬧

## SKERRIES                                     Map 01 D4

**Skerries** Hacketstown
☎ 01 8491567
Tree-lined parkland course on gently rolling countryside,
with sea views from some holes. The 1st and 18th are
particularly challenging. The club can be busy on some days,
but is always friendly.
*18 holes, 6081mtrs, Par 73, SSS 72.*
*Club membership 800.*
**Visitors**    must contact in advance but may not play at
                weekends.
**Societies**   must contact well in advance in writing.
**Green Fees** IR£18 per round (IR£22.50 weekends).
**Facilities**  ⊗ ♍ ♌ ♥ ♀♿ 🏠 ⌂ ⌁ Jimmy Kinsella.
**Leisure**     buggies for hire, trolley for hire, putting green,
                practice area.
**Hotel**       ★★★ 65%  Boyne Valley Hotel, DROGHEDA
                ☎ 041 37737 35 ➷ ⬧

## TALLAGHT                                     Map 01 D4

*Ballinascorney* Ballinascorney
☎ 01 4516430
A meadowland course founded in 1971.
*18 holes, 5465yds, Par 71, SSS 67.*
*Club membership 500.*
**Visitors**    welcome weekdays. Weekends after 4pm.
**Societies**   contact for details.
**Green Fees** not confirmed.
**Facilities**  ♀♿
**Leisure**     putting green,practice area,trolley hire.
**Location**    10m SW of Dublin
**Hotel**       ★★★ 61%  Doyle Green Isle Hotel, Naas Rd,
                DUBLIN 12
                ☎ 01 4593406 48 ➷ ⬧Annexe35 ➷ ⬧

> Entries with a shaded background identify
> courses that are considered to be particularly
> interesting

# CO GALWAY

## BALLINASLOE                                  Map 01 B4

**Ballinasloe** Rosglos ☎ 0905 42126
Well maintained parkland course, recently extended from a
par 68 to a par 72.
*18 holes, 5868metres, Par 72, SSS 70.*
*Club membership 840.*
**Visitors**    contact in advance.
**Societies**   contact in advance.
**Green Fees** IR£14 daily.
**Facilities**  ⊗ ♍ ♌ ♥ ♀♿
**Leisure**     trolley for hire, putting green, practice area.
**Hotel**       ★★★ 67%  Hayden's Hotel, BALLINASLOE
                ☎ 0905 42347 50 ➷ ⬧

## BALLYCONNEELY                                Map 01 A4

**Connemara** ☎ 095 23502 & 23602
This championship links course is situated on the verge
of the Atlantic Ocean in a most spectacular setting, with
the Twelve Bens Mountains in the background.
Established as recently as 1973, it is a tough challenge,
due in no small part to its exposed location, with the back
9 the equal of any in the world. The last six holes are
exceptionally long.
*18 holes, 6173mtrs, Par 72, SSS 73, Course record 68.*
*Club membership 700.*
**Visitors**    advisable to book in advance.
**Societies**   telephone in advance.
**Green Fees** May-Sep IR£25 (other times IR£16).
**Facilities**  ⊗ ♍ ♌ ♥ ♀♿ 🏠 ⌁
**Leisure**     motorised carts for hire, buggies for hire,
                trolley for hire, putting green, practice area.
**Location**    9m SW of Clifton
**Hotel**       ★★★ 69%  Abbeyglen Castle Hotel, Sky
                Rd, CLIFDEN ☎ 095 21201 40 ➷ ⬧

## GALWAY                                       Map 01 B4

*Galway* Blackrock, Salthill ☎ 091 22033
Designed by Dr Alister MacKenzie, this course is inland
by nature, although some of the fairways run close to the
ocean. The terrain is of gently sloping hillocks with plenty
of trees and furze bushes to catch out the unwary.
Although not a long course, it provided a worthy challenge
as the venue of the Celtic International Tournament in
1984 and continues to delight the visiting golfer.
*18 holes, 6376yds, Par 70, SSS 70.*
*Club membership 1050.*
**Visitors**    preferred on weekdays, except Tue.
**Societies**   must apply in writing.
**Green Fees** not confirmed.
**Facilities**  ♀♿ 🏠 ⌁ ⌁ Don Wallace.
**Leisure**     trolley hire.
**Location**    2m W in Salthill
**Hotel**       ★★ 58%  Lochlurgain Hotel, 22 Monksfield,
                Upper Salthill, GALWAY
                ☎ 091 22122 due to change to 529595 13 ➷ ⬧
**Additional**  ★★★★ 64%  Ardilaun House Hotel, Taylor's
**hotel**       Hill, GALWAY ☎ 091 21433 90 ➷ ⬧
                *See advertisement on page 388.*

# PORTMARNOCK

## PORTMARNOCK *Co Dublin* ☎ 01 8462968  Map 01 D4

*John Ingham writes:* The night before our fourball tackled Portmarnock was spent, as I recall, in Dublin. Guinness in that city seems smoother, while the conversation with locals, ranged from why no southern Irish player ever won the Open to how such a small nation can boast so many great writers, wits and actors.

I can thoroughly recommend this preparation, prior to facing one of the world's great golfing challenges - providing you only intend playing eighteen holes in one day! Frankly, you will have to reach into the base of your golf bag to pull out every shot if you want to play to your handicap on this superb links.

An opening birdie, downwind, made me wonder what the fuss was about. Two hours later, with a backswing too fast and the breeze now something near a gale, I decided that a test of 7182 yards off the back tees was too man-size for me. Maybe it would be more enjoyable on a calm, summer evening!

I remember the course not for the way it humiliated me, but for the 1960 Canada Cup where I watched Sam Snead and Arnold Palmer winning with such skillful play. Even so, both took 75 in one round while scores by the mighty Gary Player ranged from 65 to 78.

There are no blind shots, unless you drive into sandhills. This is natural golf with no unfair carries off the tee and the only damage to your card is self-inflicted. True, there are a couple of holes of 560 yards and the 522-yard 16th is frightening as you tee up in a fierce wind.

It's incredible to think that Portmarnock was 'discovered' almost by accident in 1893 by a Mr Pickeman and the course architect, Ross. They had rowed a boat from Sutton to the peninsula where they came across a wilderness of bracken, duneland and natural-looking bunkers made by God. They were inspired to create the course, built a shack for a clubhouse and talked about the only real hazard left - a cow that devoured golf balls.

Today it's so very different - with a modern clubhouse filled with members delighted to belong to such an internationally well-known establishment.

| | |
|---|---|
| Visitors | contact in advance and confirm in writing. Restricted Saturday, Sunday and public holidays. Handicap certificate required |
| Societies | must contact in advance |
| Green fees | Monday-Friday (excluding public holidays) £IR60: Saturday, Sunday & public holidays – Men only £IR70 per day |
| Facilities | ⊗ ⅀ ⅃ ♀ (all day) ♣ 🖙 ⚑ ⌇ (Joey Purcell) |
| Location | 12m from Dublin. 1m from village down Golf Rd |

27 holes. Old Course: 18 holes, 7182 yds, Par 72, SSS 75, course record 64 (Sandy Lyle)
New Course: 9 holes, 3478yds, Par 37

### WHERE TO STAY AND EAT NEARBY

**HOTELS:**
**HOWTH**
★★★ 66% Howth Lodge.
☎ 01 8321010.  46 (5 🖙 3 ⇥ 38 ⇥ ⋒)

## Taylors Hill, Galway
### Telephone: 00 353 91 521433  Fax: 0035 91 521546

Originally a country mansion located in it's own 5 acres of Private grounds, 5 minutes from Galway city. The hotel has luxurious accommodation with 89 bedrooms, an award winning restaurant and leisure centre. Choose from six superb golf courses within close proximity, including the renowned Galway Bay Golf and Country Club. *Discounted group and midweek rates available.* Ample car parking.

Internet   http://www.iol.ie/ardilaun      Email   ardilaun@iol.ie

---

*Glenlo Abbey* Bushy Park ☎ 091 26666
A championship course overlooking the magnificent Lough Corrib but only 10 minutes from the centre of Galway city. Nine fairways but large double green with two flags and four tee postions allows 18 diffent holes. The Par 3, 4th hole is on an island-like green extending into the lough.
*9 holes, Par 72, SSS 72.*

| | |
|---|---|
| **Visitors** | no restrictions. |
| **Societies** | telephone in advance. |
| **Green Fees** | not confirmed. |
| **Facilities** | ♀ ♨ 🏠 🍴 🏨 |
| **Leisure** | fishing, sauna, gymnasium. |
| **Location** | On N59 Galway/Clifden rd |
| **Hotel** | ★★★★♨ 69% Glenlo Abbey, Bushypark, GALWAY ☎ 091 526666 45 ⇆ 🐾 |

---

### GORT      Map 01 B3

**Gort** Laughtyshaughnessy ☎ 091 31336
Replacing the original 9-hole course, this new 18-hole course, opened in June 1996, offers golfers a real challenge. The 564yd 9th and the 516yd 17th are played into a prevailing wind and the par 4 gog-leg 7th will test the best.
*18 holes, 6538yds, Par 71.*
*Club membership 350.*

| | |
|---|---|
| **Visitors** | telephone in advance. |
| **Societies** | must contact in advance. |
| **Green Fees** | £10 per day. |
| **Facilities** | ♨ 🍴 ♀ ♨ |
| **Leisure** | putting green, practice area. |
| **Hotel** | ★★★ 67% Galway Ryan Hotel, Dublin Rd, GALWAY ☎ 091 753181 96 ⇆ 🐾 |

---

### LOUGHREA      Map 01 B3

**Loughrea** Bullaun Rd, Graigue ☎ 091 841049
An excellent parkland course with good greens and extended in 1992 to 18-holes. The course has an unusual feature in that it incorporates a historic souterrain (underground shelter/food store).
*9 holes, 5261metres, Par 69, SSS 67, Course record 68.*
*Club membership 615.*

| | |
|---|---|
| **Visitors** | contact in advance, may not generally play Sun. |
| **Societies** | written application required. Anytime weekdays, 9-11.30 Sat, no play Sun. |
| **Green Fees** | IR£10 per day (IR£12 weekends and bank holidays). |
| **Facilities** | ♨ 🍴 ♀ ♨ |
| **Leisure** | trolley for hire, putting green, practice area. |
| **Hotel** | ★★★ 67% Hayden's Hotel, BALLINASLOE ☎ 0905 42347 50 ⇆ 🐾 |

---

### MOUNTBELLEW      Map 01 B4

*Mountbellew* Ballinasloe ☎ 0905 79259
A 9-hole wooded parkland course with 2 quarries and penalty drains to provide hazards.
*9 holes, 5143mtrs, Par 69, SSS 66.*

| | |
|---|---|
| **Visitors** | welcome. |
| **Societies** | by prior arrangement. |
| **Green Fees** | not confirmed. |
| **Facilities** | |
| **Location** | Of N63 midway between Roscommon/Galway |
| **Hotel** | ★★★ 67% Hayden's Hotel, BALLINASLOE ☎ 0905 42347 50 ⇆ 🐾 |

---

### ORANMORE      Map 01 B3

**Athenry** Palmerstown ☎ 091 794466
Wooded parkland course, recently extended to 18 holes.
*18 holes, 5552metres, Par 70, SSS 69, Course record 70.*
*Club membership 800.*

| | |
|---|---|
| **Visitors** | advisable to telephone in advance, may not play Sun. |
| **Societies** | must apply in writing for booking to the secretary. |
| **Green Fees** | IR£15 per day. |
| **Facilities** | ⊗ ⅏ ♨ ♀ ♀ ♨ 🏠 🍴 ⌇ Declan Cummingham. |
| **Leisure** | buggies for hire, trolley for hire, putting green, practice area. |
| **Hotel** | ★★★ 67% Galway Ryan Hotel, Dublin Rd, GALWAY ☎ 091 753181 96 ⇆ 🐾 |

---

**Galway Bay Golf & Country Club** Renville
☎ 091 790500
A championship golf course surrounded on three sides by the Atlantic Ocean and featuring water hazards on a number of holes. Each hole has its own characteristics made more obvious by the everchanging seaside winds.
*18 holes, 6091mtrs, Par 72, SSS 71.*
*Club membership 400.*

| | |
|---|---|
| **Visitors** | contact in advance. |
| **Societies** | contact in advance. |
| **Green Fees** | IR£25 per round (IR£30 weekends & bank holidays). |
| **Facilities** | ⊗ ⅏ ♨ ♀ ♀ ♨ 🏠 🍴 ⌇ Eugene O'Connor. |
| **Leisure** | sauna, motorised carts for hire, buggies for hire, trolley for hire, driving range, putting green, practice area. |
| **Hotel** | ★★★★♨ 69% Glenlo Abbey, Bushypark, GALWAY ☎ 091 526666 45 ⇆ 🐾 |

## OUGHTERARD
Map 01 B4

**Oughterard** ☎ 091 82131
Well maintained parkland course with mature trees and shrubs. Some very challenging holes.
*18 holes, 6150yds, Par 70, SSS 69, Course record 67.*
*Club membership 630.*
**Visitors** contact secretary in advance.
**Societies** must apply in writing, 12 mths notice required for weekend play
**Green Fees** IR£15 per day; married couple IR£25.
**Facilities** ⊗ ⅢⅢ ⌸ ♥ ♀ ♨ ⌂ ⚐ ℓ Michael Ryan.
**Leisure** motorised carts for hire, buggies for hire, trolley for hire, driving range, putting green, practice area.
**Location** 1m from town on Galway road
**Hotel** ★★★ 65% Connemara Gateway Hotel, OUGHTERARD ☎ 091 82328 62 ⇆ ℀

## PORTUMNA
Map 01 B3

**Portumna** ☎ 0509 41059
Parkland course with mature trees.
*18 holes, 5474mtrs, Par 68, SSS 67, Course record 68.*
*Club membership 650.*
**Visitors** restricted Sun & public holidays.
**Societies** must contact in writing.
**Green Fees** IR£12 per day.
**Facilities** ⊗ by prior arrangement ⅢⅢ by prior arrangement ⌸ ♥ ♀ ♨ ⚐
**Leisure** trolley for hire, putting green, practice area.
**Location** 2.5m from town on Woodford/Ennis road
**Hotel** ★★ 66% County Arms Hotel, BIRR ☎ 0509 20791 & 20193 18 ⇆ ℀

## RENVYLE
Map 01 A4

**Renvyle House Hotel** ☎ 095 43511
Pebble Beach course at Renvyle House is an exceptionally demanding Par 3. Exposed to Atlantic winds, crosswinds are a regular feature. A lake comes into play on 3 holes on one of which is a drive over water. On 4 holes pebble beach and the sea demand precision.
*9 holes, 2000yds, Par 32.*
**Visitors** must contact in advance.
**Societies** contact in advance.
**Green Fees** IR£10 per day.
**Facilities** ⊗ ⅢⅢ ⌸ ♥ ♀ ⚐ ⌂ ℓ Gus Murphy.
**Leisure** hard tennis courts, heated outdoor swimming pool, fishing, trolley for hire, putting green, croquet, bowling.
**Hotel** ★★★ 68% Renvyle House Hotel, RENVYLE ☎ 095 43511 65 ⇆ ℀

## TUAM
Map 01 B4

**Tuam** Barnacurragh ☎ 093 28993
Interesting course with plenty of trees and bunkers.
*18 holes, 6377yds, Par 73, SSS 70.*
**Visitors** preferred Mon-Fri.
**Green Fees** not confirmed.
**Facilities** ♀ ⌂ ⚐
**Location** 0.5m from town on Athenry road
**Hotel** ★★★★ 64% Ardilaun House Hotel, Taylor's Hill, GALWAY ☎ 091 21433 90 ⇆ ℀

# CO KERRY

## BALLYBUNION
Map 01 A3

**BALLYBUNION** See page 391

## BALLYFERRITER
Map 01 A2

**Ceann Sibeal** ☎ 066 56255 & 56408
This most westerly golf course in Europe has a magnificent scenic location. It is a traditional links course with beautiful turf, many bunkers, a stream that comes into play on 14 holes and, usually, a prevailing wind.
*18 holes, 6700yds, Par 72, SSS 71, Course record 72.*
*Club membership 432.*
**Visitors** telephone in advance.
**Societies** must contact in advance.
**Green Fees** IR£27 per day; IR£21 per round.
**Facilities** ⊗ ⅢⅢ ⌸ ♥ ♀ ♨ ⌂ ⚐ ℓ Dermot O'Connor.
**Leisure** trolley for hire, putting green, practice area.
**Hotel** ★★★ 70% Skellig Hotel, DINGLE ☎ 066 51144 115 ⇆ ℀

## CASTLEGREGORY
Map 01 A2

**Castlegregory** Stradbally
☎ 066 39444
A links course sandwiched between the sea and a freshwater lake and mountains on two sides. The 3rd hole is visually superb with a 365yard drive into the wind.
*9 holes, 2569mtrs, Par 68, SSS 68, Course record 67.*
*Club membership 200.*
**Visitors** advisable to contact in advance.
**Societies** apply in advance.
**Green Fees** IR£12 per 18 holes.
**Facilities** ⊗ ⅢⅢ ⌸ ♥ ♨ ⚐
**Leisure** fishing, trolley for hire, putting green.
**Hotel** ★★★ 64% The Brandon Hotel, TRALEE ☎ 066 23333 160 ⇆ ℀

## GLENBEIGH
Map 01 A2

**Dooks** ☎ 066 68205
Old-established course on the sea shore between the Kerry mountains and Dingle Bay. Sand dunes are a feature (the name Dooks is a derivation of the Gaelic word for sand bank) and the course offers a fine challenge in a superb Ring of Kerry location.
*18 holes, 6010yds, Par 70, SSS 68.*
*Club membership 750.*
**Visitors** must contact in advance.
**Societies** contact in advance.
**Green Fees** IR£18 per round.
**Facilities** ⊗ ⅢⅢ ⌸ ♥ ♀ ♨ ⌂
**Leisure** trolley for hire, putting green.
**Hotel** ★★★ 64% Gleneagle Hotel, KILLARNEY ☎ 064 31870 177 ⇆ ℀

## KENMARE                                    Map 01 B2

**Kenmare** Kilgarvan Rd ☎ 064 41291
Extended to a championship 18-hole course in 1993 this
challenging parkland course enjoys a magnificent setting
where the cascading waters of the Sheen and Roughty rivers
join the Atlantic. Although it can be exacting on a good
golfer, it is never unfair to the weak or the novice golfer.
*18 holes, 5615yds, Par 71.*
*Club membership 400.*
**Visitors**    enquire for weekends.
**Societies**   contact in advance.
**Green Fees** IR£12.50 per 18 holes.
**Facilities**  Ꮭ ᒃ ᒥᐧᒥᏝᐧᒥ
**Leisure**     trolley for hire, putting green, practice area.
**Hotel**       ★★★★(red)⚌ Park Hotel Kenmare,
                KENMARE ☎ 064 41200 49 ⇄ ↾

## KILLARNEY                                  Map 01 B2

**Beaufort** Churchtown, Beauford
☎ 064 44440
A championship standard Par 71 parkland course designed by
Dr Arthur Spring. This relatively new course is in the centre
of south-west Ireland's golfing mecca. Old ruins of an 11th
century castle dominate the back nine and the whole course is
overlooked by the MacGillycuddy Reeks. The Par 3 8th and
Par 4 11th are two of the most memorable holes.
*18 holes, 6149yds, Par 71, SSS 72.*
*Club membership 150.*
**Visitors**    booking advisable for weekends.
**Societies**   advance booking essential.

★★★

# Gleneagle Hotel
## KILLARNEY, CO. KERRY
TEL. 00 353 64 - 31870.
FAX. 00 353 64 - 32646

Located in 25 acres of landscaped parkland, on the
banks of the river Flesk, adjacent to the 25,000 acre
National Park – the Gleneagle is ideally situated for
a wide range of leisure holidays and general and
special activities.

With 3 bars, 3 restaurants, 3 conference rooms and
170 en-suite bedrooms, it is the ideal choice for
meetings, seminars with a full business and social
programme. Swimming pool, sauna, gym, jacuzzi,
steam room, pitch and putt, tennis, squash,
children's playground plus new activity play area,
creche – all on site. Lake cruises, coach tours,
fishing, golf, pony trekking, cycle hire etc. are all
arranged by the hotel.    Email  gleneagle@iol.ie

*Free colour brochure available.*

# IRELAND'S LEADING
# LEISURE HOTEL

**Green Fees** IR£25 per round,IR£10 second round (IR£28,
                IR£12 weekends).
**Facilities**  ⊗ �␀ ᒃ ᒥᐧᒥᏝᐧᒥ
**Leisure**     motorised carts for hire, buggies for hire, trolley
                for hire, putting green, practice area.
**Location**    7m W of Killarney, off R562
**Hotel**       ★★★ 64% Castlerosse Hotel, KILLARNEY
                ☎ 064 31144 110 ⇄ ↾

---

**Killarney Golf & Fishing Club** Mahony's Point
☎ 064 31034
Both of the courses are parkland with tree-lined fairways,
many bunkers and small lakes which provide no mean
challenge. Mahony's Point Course has a particularly
testing par 5, 4, 3 finish and both courses call for great
skill from the tee. Killarney has been the venue for many
important events, including the Irish Open in 1991, and is
a favourite of many famous golfers
*Mahony's Point: 18 holes, 5826mtrs, Par 72, SSS 72,*
*Course record 68.*
*Killeen: 18 holes, 6474mtrs, Par 72, SSS 73, Course*
*record 65.*
*Club membership 1300.*
**Visitors**    must contact in advance & have a handicap
                certificate.
**Societies**   must telephone in advance.
**Green Fees** IR£33 per round.
**Facilities**  ⊗ ᐧᒃ ᒥᐧᒥᏝᐧᒥ ᒥ Tony Coveney.
**Leisure**     sauna, gymnasium, trolley for hire, putting
                green, practice area.
**Location**    On Ring of Kerry road
**Hotel**       ★★★★ 76% Aghadoe Heights Hotel,
                KILLARNEY
                ☎ 064 31766 60 ⇄ ↾
**Additional**  ★★★ 64% Gleneagle Hotel,
**hotel**       KILLARNEY
                ☎ 064 31870 177 ⇄ ↾

## KILLORGLIN                                 Map 01 A2

**Killorglin** Stealroe ☎ 066 61979
A parkland course designed by Eddie Hackett as a
challenging but fair test of golf.
*18 holes, 6497yds, Par 72, SSS 71, Course record 68.*
*Club membership 200.*
**Visitors**    pre booking of tee time advisable.
**Societies**   apply in writing.
**Green Fees** IR£12 per 18 holes (IR£14 weekends & bank
                holidays).
**Facilities**  ⊗ ᐧᒃ ᒥᐧᒥᏝᐧᒥ
**Leisure**     fishing, trolley for hire.
**Location**    3km from Killorglin, on N70 to Tralee
**Hotel**       ★★★ 64% The Brandon Hotel, TRALEE
                ☎ 066 23333 160 ⇄ ↾

## PARKNASILLA                                Map 01 A2

*Parknasilla* ☎ 064 45122
Short, tricky 9-hole course, with 18 different tees which make
the second 9 more interesting.
*9 holes, 2447yds, Par 70, SSS 65.*
*Club membership 90.*
**Visitors**    may not play on competition days.
**Societies**   must contact in advance.
**Green Fees** not confirmed.                          ▶

# BALLYBUNION

**BALLYBUNION** *Co Kerry* ☎ **068 27146**　　　　**Map 01 A3**

*John Ingham writes:* Since golf is a state of mind over muscle and a great day on the links is exhilarating, it is my view that memorable fairways tend not to be decorated with artificial lakes that are fun only for ducks and golf ball manufacturers.

Some of the best courses look natural, even though they may have been helped along by skilful architects such as Colt, Hawtree or Mackenzie. And in the Emerald Isle, it is entirely appropriate that, back in 1906, a Mr Murphy built Ballybunion on the West Coast of Ireland. Believe me, there are few greater adventures waiting to be tackled and not to play this old course is a crime.

In an American list of the world's top 100 courses, Ballybunion is in there at number eight and the reason is simple: it probably represents the ultimate links on as wild a stretch as you will find. The Atlantic waves crash into the shore and no golfer will ever feel closer to nature as he hunts his ball and flights it through crosswinds and breathtaking views. This course is a star even in a part of Ireland that is wall-to-wall golf courses of the highest calibre. The experience of taking on this classic will be remembered as long as you live.

There are now two courses at Ballybunion, separated only by a 19th hole that has heard all the wondrous stories before, as well as hosting such great names as Tom Watson, five times winner of the Open. Likeable Tom can't speak highly enough of the place and claims that before anyone builds a golf course, they should play Ballybunion.

**Visitors** must contact in advance, preferred Mon-Fri

**Societies** must book in advance

**Green fees** Old Course: £IR45 per round; Cashen Course: £IR30 per round. Both courses IR£65

**Facilities** ⊗ ✕ ⑂ ▟ ☂ ♀ ⚐ ⌂ ⚑ ℾ caddy cars, putting green, practice area, trollies

**Leisure** private fishing, sauna

**Location** Sandhill Rd

36 holes. Old Course: 18 holes, 6603 yds, Par 71, SSS 72 Carshen Course: 18 holes, 6477 yds, Par 72

## WHERE TO STAY AND EAT NEARBY

**HOTELS:**
**BALLYHEIGE**
★★★✿ 58% The White Sands
☎: 066 33102 75. ⇥ ℾ

| | |
|---|---|
| **Facilities** | ♀ ⚲ 🏠 ⚐ 🍴 ♟ Charles McCarthy. |
| **Leisure** | hard tennis courts, heated indoor swimming pool, sauna, trolley hire, clay pigeon shooting. |
| **Hotel** | ★★★★ 74% Great Southern Hotel, PARKNASILLA ☎ 064 45122 25 ⇆ ⚐Annexe59 ⇆ ⚐ |

## TRALEE                                          Map 01 A2

*Tralee* West Barrow ☎ 066 36379
The first Arnold Palmer designed course in Europe, the magnificent 18-hole links are set in spectacular scenery on the Barrow peninsula. Perhaps the most memorable hole is the par four 17th which plays from a high tee, across a deep gorge to a green perched high against a backdrop of mountains.
*18 holes, 5961mtrs, Par 73.*
*Club membership 1000.*

| | |
|---|---|
| **Visitors** | may play before 4.30pm on weekdays but only 10.30am-12.15pm on Wed & 11am-12.30pm at weekends & bank holidays. Must have a handicap certificate. |
| **Societies** | weekdays only; must contact in writing. |
| **Green Fees** | not confirmed. |
| **Facilities** | ♀ ⚲ 🏠 |
| **Leisure** | buggy/trolley hire. |
| **Location** | 8m W of Tralee on Spa-Fenit road |
| **Hotel** | ★★★ 64% The Brandon Hotel, TRALEE ☎ 066 23333 160 ⇆ ⚐ |

## WATERVILLE                                    Map 01 A2

Waterville House & Golf Links ☎ 066 74102
On the western tip of the Ring of Kerry, this course is highly regarded by many top golfers. The feature holes are the par five 11th, which runs along a rugged valley between towering dunes, and the par three 17th, which features an exceptionally elevated tee. Needless to say, the surroundings are beautiful.
*18 holes, 6549yds, Par 72.*

| | |
|---|---|
| **Visitors** | must contact in advance. |
| **Societies** | must contact secretary/manager in advance. |
| **Green Fees** | IR£40 per round. |
| **Facilities** | ⊗ ⚒ ⚑ ♟ ♀ ⚲ 🏠 ⚐ 🍴 ♟ Liam Higgins. |
| **Leisure** | heated outdoor swimming pool, fishing, sauna, motorised carts for hire, buggies for hire, trolley for hire, driving range, putting green, practice area. |
| **Hotel** | ★★★ 57% Derrynane Hotel, CAHERDANIEL ☎ 066 75136 75 ⇆ |

# CO KILDARE

## ATHY                                          Map 01 C3

*Athy* Geraldine ☎ 0507 31729
A meadowland course approaching its centenary year having been founded in 1906.
*18 holes, 5500mtrs, Par 72, SSS 69, Course record 69.*
*Club membership 400.*

| | |
|---|---|
| **Visitors** | welcome weekdays. |
| **Societies** | contact for infromation. |
| **Green Fees** | not confirmed. |
| **Facilities** | ♀ ⚲ |
| **Leisure** | putting, trolley hire, practice area. |
| **Location** | 2m N of Athy |
| **Hotel** | ★★ 60% Hotel Montague, Portlaoise, EMO ☎ 0502 26154 75 ⇆ ⚐ |

## CARBURY                                        Map 01 C4

**Highfield** Highfield House ☎ 0405 31021
A relatively flat parkland course but with interesting undulations, especially by the fast flowing stream which runs through many holes. The 7th doglegs over the lake, the 10th is a great Par 5 with a challenging green, the 14th Par 3 is over rushes onto a plateau green (out of bounds on lift) and the 18th Par 3 green is tucked between bunkers and a huge chestnut tree.
*18 holes, 5707mtrs, Par 72, SSS 69.*
*Club membership 400.*

| | |
|---|---|
| **Visitors** | welcome, must contact in advance for weekend play. |
| **Societies** | telephone or apply in writing. |
| **Green Fees** | IR£7 per day (IR£10 weekends & bank holidays). |
| **Facilities** | ⚑ ♀ ⚲ 🍴 |
| **Leisure** | trolley for hire, driving range, practice area, putting green. |
| **Location** | 9m from Enfield |
| **Hotel** | ★★ 59% Curryhills House Hotel, PROSPEROUS ☎ 045 868150 10 ⇆ ⚐ |

## CASTLEDERMOT                                   Map 01 C3

*Kilkea Castle* ☎ 0503 45156
A beautiful new course opened in the summer of 1994 in the grounds of a 12th-century castle - visible from all over the course. The River Griese and two lakes create numerous water hazards.
*18 holes, 6200mtrs, Par 71.*

| | |
|---|---|
| **Visitors** | welcome contact for details. |
| **Societies** | welcome, contact for details. |
| **Green Fees** | not confirmed. |
| **Facilities** | ♀ ⚲ 🏠 |

## DONADEA                                        Map 01 C4

*Knockanally Golf & Country Club* ☎ 045 69322
Home of the Irish International Professional Matchplay championship, this parkland course is set in a former estate, with a Palladian-style clubhouse.
*18 holes, 6485yds, Par 72, SSS 72.*
*Club membership 500.*

| | |
|---|---|
| **Visitors** | may not play on Sun 8.30am-noon. |
| **Societies** | must contact in writing or telephone. |
| **Green Fees** | not confirmed. |
| **Facilities** | ♀ ⚲ 🏠 ⚐ 🍴 ♟ Peter Hickey. |
| **Leisure** | fishing, putting green, practice area, trolley hire. |
| **Location** | 3m off main Dublin-Galway road |
| **Hotel** | ★★ 59% Curryhills House Hotel, PROSPEROUS ☎ 045 868150 10 ⇆ ⚐ |

## KILDARE — Map 01 C3

*Cill Dara* Cill Dara, Little Curragh
☎ 045 21295
Only 1 mile from the famous Curragh racecourse, this 9-hole parkland course is unusual in having links type soil as well as plenty of trees.
*9 holes, 5738mtrs, Par 71, SSS 70, Course record 64.*
*Club membership 450.*
**Visitors** welcome.
**Societies** apply in writing to Mr J Commins, Society Secretary.
**Green Fees** not confirmed.
**Facilities** ♀♿🏌🛅🏌 J Bulger.
**Leisure** putting green,trolley hire.
**Location** 1m E of Kildare
**Hotel** ★★ 60% Hotel Montague, Portlaoise, EMO ☎ 0502 26154 75 ⇌ 🐾

*Curragh* Curragh ☎ 045 41238
A particularly challenging course, well wooded and with lovely scenery all around.
*18 holes, 6003mtrs, Par 72, SSS 71.*
*Club membership 900.*
**Visitors** preferred on Mon, Thu & Fri.
**Societies** apply in writing.
**Green Fees** not confirmed.
**Facilities** ♀♿🏌🛅🏌 Phil Lawlor.
**Leisure** putting green,practice area,trolley hire.
**Location** Off N7 between Newbridge & Kildare
**Hotel** ★★ 59% Curryhills House Hotel, PROSPEROUS ☎ 045 868150 10 ⇌ 🐾

## KILL — Map 01 D4

*Killeen* ☎ 045 866003 & 866045
Set in pleasant countryside, the attractive course is characterised by its many lakes. It provides a challenge to test the skills of the moderate enthusiast and the more experienced golfer.
*18 holes, 5561mtrs, Par 71, SSS 70.*
**Visitors** please ring for tee-times
**Societies** must contact in advance.
**Green Fees** IR£13 per round (IR£15 weekends & bank holidays).
**Facilities** ⊗)🏌🛅💺♀♿🛅🏌
**Leisure** trolley for hire, putting green, practice area.
**Location** Off N7 at Kill signposted
**Hotel** ★★★ 75% Barberstown Castle, STRAFFAN ☎ 01 6288157 & 6288206 10 ⇌ 🐾

## NAAS — Map 01 D4

*Bodenstown* Sallins ☎ 045 897096
The old course in Bodenstown has ample fairways and large greens, some of which are raised, providing more than a fair test of golf. The Ladyhill course is a little shorter and tighter, but still affords a fair challenge.
*Bodenstown: 18 holes, 6132mtrs, Par 71, SSS 71.*
*Ladyhill: 18 holes, 5428mtrs, Par 71, SSS 68.*
*Club membership 700.*
**Visitors** may not play on Bodenstown course at weekends.
**Societies** must contact by telephone.
**Green Fees** £10 per round; £8 weekends (Ladyhill Course).
**Facilities** ⊗🏌🛅💺♀♿
**Leisure** trolley for hire, putting green, practice area.
**Location** 4m from town near Bodenstown graveyard
**Hotel** ★★★ 56% Downshire House Hotel, BLESSINGTON ☎ 045 865199 14 ⇌ 🐾Annexe11 ⇌ 🐾

*Naas* Kerdiffstown ☎ 045 897509
Scenic parkland course with different tees for the return 9.
*9 holes, 3000mtrs, Par 36, SSS 70, Course record 68.*
*Club membership 800.*
**Visitors** may not play on Sun, Tue or Thu.
**Societies** must contact in advance.
**Green Fees** not confirmed.
**Facilities** ♀♿
**Location** 1m from town on Sallins-Johnstown road
**Hotel** ★★★ 56% Downshire House Hotel, BLESSINGTON ☎ 045 865199 14 ⇌ 🐾Annexe11 ⇌ 🐾

*Woodlands* Cooleragh, Coill Dubh ☎ 045 860777
Interesting 9-hole course currently undergoing reconstruction. The orientation of play will change to clockwise from its present anti-clockwise direction, with new greens, tees and additional ground coming into play, making it a more challenging round in 1997.
*9 holes, 5292yds, Par 68, SSS 66, Course record 71.*
*Club membership 325.*
**Visitors** must contact in advance.
**Societies** telephone in advance for details.
**Green Fees** IR£6 per 18 holes (IR£7 weekends).
**Facilities** ⊗🛅💺♀♿
**Leisure** trolley for hire, putting green, practice area.
**Location** Off the Clane/Edenderry road
**Hotel** ★★★ 68% Keadeen Hotel, NEWBRIDGE ☎ 045 431666 37 ⇌ 🐾

## STRAFFAN — Map 01 D4

*Castlewarden* ☎ 01 4588218 & 4589254
Founded in 1990, Castlewarden is maturing into a delightful parkland course.
*18 holes, 6452ydss, Par 72, SSS 70.*
*Club membership 646.*
**Visitors** welcome contact for details.
**Societies** by prior application.
**Green Fees** IR£12 (IR£16 weekends).
**Facilities** ⊗🏌🛅💺♀♿🛅🏌 Gerry Egan.
**Leisure** trolley for hire, putting green, practice area.
**Location** Between Naas/Newlands Cross
**Hotel** ★★★★★(red)🏌 The Kildare Hotel & Country Club, STRAFFAN ☎ 01 6273333 36 ⇌ 🐾Annexe7 ⇌ 🐾

**Kildare Hotel & Country Club** ☎ 01 6273333
Known as The K-Club, this course is growing in reputation. Designed by Arnold Palmer, its 6,456 metre length is a challenge to even the best golfers. Covering 177 acres of prime Kildare woodland there are 14 man-made lakes as well as the River Liffey to create water hazards. There is the promise of a watery grave at the monster 7th (Par 5, 520 metres) and at the 17th the tee shot is to the green on the water's edge. There is also a practise area and driving range. ▶

18 holes, 6163mtrs, Par 72, SSS 72, Course record 68.
Club membership 390.
**Visitors**     contact in advance, restricted at members
                times.
**Societies**    telephone & write in advance, societies not
                allowed on weekends & Wed afternoon.
**Green Fees** IR£100.
**Facilities**   ⊗ Ⅲ ᴸ ᴸ ᴸ ᴸ Ernie Jones.
**Leisure**      hard tennis courts, heated indoor swimming
                pool, squash, fishing, sauna, solarium,
                gymnasium, buggies for hire, trolley for
                hire, driving range, practice area, driving
                range, tuition, horseriding,.
**Hotel**        ★★★★★(red)🏌 The Kildare Hotel &
                Country Club, STRAFFAN
                ☎ 01 6273333 36 ⇨ ᴿAnnexe7 ⇨ ᴿ

18 holes, 5857mtrs, Par 71, SSS 70, Course record 65.
Club membership 1000.
**Visitors**     must contact in advance.
**Societies**    must contact in advance.
**Green Fees** IR£20 per day (IR£22 weekends & bank
                holidays).
**Facilities**   ⊗ Ⅲ ᴸ ᴸ ᴸ ᴸ ᴸ Noel Leahy.
**Leisure**      buggies for hire, trolley for hire, driving
                range, putting green, practice area.
**Location**     1m from centre on Castlecomer road
**Hotel**        ★★★ 68% Hotel Kilkenny, College Rd,
                KILKENNY ☎ 056 62000 80 ⇨ ᴿ

## THOMASTOWN                                   Map 01 C3

**MOUNT JULIET HOTEL GOLF COURSE** See page 395

# CO KILKENNY

## CALLAN                                        Map 01 C3

**Callan** Geraldine ☎ 056 25136 & 25949
Meadowland.
*9 holes, 5722mtrs, Par 72, SSS 70, Course record 67.*
*Club membership 500.*
**Visitors**     welcome. Weekend play by prior arrangement.
**Societies**    must apply in writing.
**Green Fees** IR£11 per round.
**Facilities**   ⊗ Ⅲ ᴸ ᴸ ᴸ ᴸ ᴸ
**Leisure**      fishing, trolley for hire, putting green.
**Hotel**        ★★★ 68% Hotel Kilkenny, College Rd,
                KILKENNY ☎ 056 62000 80 ⇨ ᴿ

## CASTLECOMER                                   Map 01 C3

*Castlecomer* Drumgoole ☎ 056 41139
*9 holes, 5923mtrs, Par 71, SSS 71, Course record 65.*
*Club membership 500.*
**Visitors**     welcome Mon-Sat book in advance.
**Societies**    welcome Mon-Sat.
**Green Fees** not confirmed.
**Facilities**   ᴸ ᴸ
**Leisure**      practice area.
**Location**     10m N of Kilkenny
**Hotel**        ★★★ 68% Newpark Hotel, KILKENNY
                ☎ 056 22122 84 ⇨ ᴿ

## KILKENNY                                      Map 01 C3

**Kilkenny** Glendine ☎ 056 65400 & 22125
One of Ireland's most pleasant inland courses, noted for
its tricky finishing holes and its par threes. Features of
the course are its long 11th and 13th holes and the
challenge increases year by year as thousands of trees
planted over the last 30 years or so are maturing. As host
of the Kilkenny Scratch Cup annually, the course is
permanently maintained in championship condition. The
Irish Dunlop Tournament and the Irish Professional
Matchplay Championship have also been held here.

# CO LAOIS

## ABBEYLEIX                                     Map 01 C3

**Abbeyleix** Rathmoyle ☎ 0502 31450 & 31229
*9 holes, 5626mtrs, Par 70, SSS 68.*
*Club membership 300.*
**Visitors**     welcome.
**Societies**    apply in writing.
**Green Fees** not confirmed.
**Facilities**   ⊗ by prior arrangement Ⅲ ᴸ ᴸ ᴸ ᴸ
**Leisure**      putting green, practice area.
**Hotel**        ★★★ 62% Killeshin Hotel, Dublin Rd,
                PORTLAOISE ☎ 0502 21663 44 ⇨ ᴿ

## MOUNTRATH                                     Map 01 C3

*Mountrath* Knockanina ☎ 0502 32558
Small picturesque course at the foot of the Slieve Bloom
Mountains in central Ireland. The course is in the process of
being extended to 18 holes, due to be completed by summer
1994.
*9 holes, 4634mtrs, Par 68, SSS 66.*
*Club membership 300.*
**Visitors**     no restrictions.
**Societies**    must contact in advance.
**Green Fees** not confirmed.
**Facilities**   ᴸ ᴸ
**Location**     1.5m from town on Dublin-Limerick road
**Hotel**        ★★★ 62% Killeshin Hotel, Dublin Rd,
                PORTLAOISE ☎ 0502 21663 44 ⇨ ᴿ

## PORTARLINGTON                                 Map 01 C3

**Portarlington** Garryhinch ☎ 0502 23115
Lovely parkland course designed around a pine forest. It is
bounded on the 16th and 17th by the River Barrow which
makes the back 9 very challenging.
*18 holes, 5673mtrs, Par 71, SSS 69.*
*Club membership 562.*                                ▶

# MOUNT JULIET

THOMASTOWN *Co Kilkenny*

☎ 056 24455                     Map 01 C3

*Charlie Mulqueen writes:* Nick Faldo and David Leadbetter are just two of the game's luminaries to have fallen in love with Mount Juliet, the only Jack Nicklaus designed golf course in Ireland. Faldo, perhaps, is somewhat biased given that he completed a hat-trick of Irish Open successes there in 1993.

Mount Juliet stands as a monument to the architectural ability of Nicklaus. The estate was acquired in the late '80s by Tim Mahony, who gave the Golden Bear a free hand. In return, Nicklaus delivered a 7100 yards, par 72 course of great quality and considerable charm. The hundreds of mature trees help to give the impression that the course has been here for centuries rather than just since 1991 - an occasion marked by a memorable exhibition between Nicklaus and Ireland's own great Christy O'Connor Senior. Since 1993 it has hosted the Murphy's Irish Open.

Mount Juliet's 'signature hole' arrives as early as the third, played from an elevated tee across an awesome lake to an island green. The golfer confronts a lot more water as the round progresses, especially at the perilous 13th, which has certainly proved unlucky for many of the contestants in each of the last three Irish Opens. Nor can even the best relax until they have completed the 470 yards, par four 18th. Again a lake comes into play all the way down the left and very frequently it requires two full woods to reach the long, narrow green. South African David Frost took 10 here in the opening round of the 1993 Irish Open and still hit back to finish third!

When the golf is over, the 1500 acres of the Mount Juliet estate offers many more attractions; horse riding, clay pigeon shooting or archery, fishing in the delightful River Nore or dinner in the superb 18th-century mansion transformed into a luxury hotel. And if the golf hasn't been up to requirements, up you get bright and early the following morning for a lesson on the magnificent David Leadbetter academy. Mount Juliet has it all - it's a must!

| | |
|---|---|
| Visitors | no restrictions |
| Societies | book in advance by telephone |
| Green fees | Week days £IR65 (residents £IR35). Weekends £IR70 (residents £IR45) |
| Facilities | ⊗ ⪦ ⌱ ⬤ ♀ ⬠ ⪨ ⌂ ⫪ ⌭ (David Leadbetter Golf Academy) driving range, putting green, motor carts, practice area, trollies, caddy cars, caddies |
| Leisure | tennis, indoor swimming pool, private fishing, clay target shooting, archery, full leisure centre |
| Location | Dublin/Waterford rd Off the N9 |

18 holes, 7100yds, Par72 SSS 74
Course record 65 (Nick Faldo/John Daly)

## WHERE TO STAY AND EAT NEARBY

**HOTELS:**

**THOMASTOWN**
★★★★ (Red) ⬤⬤ ⬤ Mount Juliet Hotel, ☎ 056 24455. 32 ⇌ ☀ Annexe 21 ⇌ ☀

**KILKENNY**
★★★ 68% Newpark Hotel
☎ 056 22122. 84 (25 ⇌ 59 ⇌ ☀)

★★★ 68% Hotel Kilkenny, College Rd
☎ 056 62000. 80 ⇌ ☀

**Visitors** welcome but restricted Tue-Ladies Day, Sat & Sun societies and club competitions.
**Societies** must apply in writing.
**Green Fees** IR£12 per round (IR£14 weekends & bank holidays).
**Facilities** ⊗ 〗🍴 ᴸ 💺 ♀ ⛳
**Leisure** trolley for hire, putting green, practice area.
**Location** 4m from town on Mountmellick road
**Hotel** ★★ 60% Hotel Montague, Portlaoise, EMO ☎ 0502 26154 75 ⇄ �});

---

## PORTLAOISE                                    Map 01 C3

**The Heath** ☎ 0502 46533 & 46622 (Pro shop)
One of the oldest clubs in Ireland. The course is set in pretty countryside and offers a good challenge.
*18 holes, 5736mtrs, Par 71, SSS 69, Course record 69.*
*Club membership 800.*
**Visitors** contact in advance, preferred on weekdays.
**Societies** apply in advance.
**Green Fees** IR£16 per round (IR£10 weekends and bank holidays).
**Facilities** ⊗ 〗🍴 ᴸ 💺 ♀ ⛳ 🏠 ⛳ 𝄢 Eddie Doyle.
**Leisure** trolley for hire, driving range, putting green, practice area.
**Location** 3m N on N7
**Hotel** ★★★ 62% Killeshin Hotel, Dublin Rd, PORTLAOISE ☎ 0502 21663 44 ⇄ 🌩

---

## RATHDOWNEY                                    Map 01 C3

**Rathdowney** ☎ 0505 46170
A pleasant 9-hole course. 1st is difficult with out-of-bounds along the right. 5th, Par 3 has out-of-bounds very close to left. Plans are in hand for conversion to 18-holes.
*9 holes, 6196yds, Par 70, SSS 69, Course record 70.*
*Club membership 230.*
**Visitors** welcome. Ladies have priority on Wed, Sat & Sun mornings are reserved for member & societies.
**Societies** must apply in writing and pay deposit to confirm booking.
**Green Fees** IR£6 per day.
**Facilities** ⊗ by prior arrangement 〗 by prior arrangement ᴸ by prior arrangement 💺 by prior arrangement ♀ ⛳
**Location** 0.5m SE
**Hotel** ★★★ 68% Hotel Kilkenny, College Rd, KILKENNY ☎ 056 62000 80 ⇄ 🌩

---

# CO LEITRIM

---

## BALLINAMORE                                    Map 01 C4

**Ballinamore** ☎ 078 44346
A very dry and very testing 9-hole parkland course along the Ballinamore/Ballyconnell Canal.
*9 holes, 5680yds, Par 68, SSS 66, Course record 66.*
*Club membership 100.*
**Visitors** restricted occasionally.
**Societies** must contact in writing.

**Green Fees** not confirmed.
**Facilities** ♀ ⛳
**Leisure** fishing.
**Hotel** ★★ 64% Royal Hotel, BOYLE ☎ 079 62016 16 ⇄ 🌩

---

# CO LIMERICK

---

## ADARE                                    Map 01 B3

*Adare Manor* ☎ 061 396204
An 18-hole parkland course, Par 69, in an unusual setting. In the grounds of an ancient monastery, the course surrounds the ruins of a castle, a friary and an abbey.
*18 holes, 5800yds, Par 69, SSS 69.*
*Club membership 600.*
**Visitors** for weekends it is adviable to contact in advance.
**Societies** by prior arrangement, preferably in writing.
**Green Fees** not confirmed.
**Facilities** ⛳ 🏠 ⛳
**Leisure** caddy cars & caddies available.
**Hotel** ★★★★(red)♨ Adare Manor, ADARE ☎ 061 396566 28 ⇄ 🌩Annexe36 ⇄ 🌩

---

## LIMERICK                                    Map 01 B3

*Castletroy* Castletroy
☎ 061 335753 & 335261
Parkland course with out of bounds on the left of the first two holes. The long par five 10th features a narrow entrance to a green guarded by a stream. The par three 13th has a panoramic view of the course and surrounding countryside from the tee and the 18th is a daunting finish, with the drive played towards a valley with the ground rising towards the green which is protected on both sides by bunkers. In recent years the club has hosted the finals of the Irish Mixed Foursomes and the Senior Championships.
*18 holes, 5793mtrs, Par 69, SSS 71.*
*Club membership 1066.*
**Visitors** must contact in advance & have handicap certificate but may not play Sun or 1-2.30pm weekdays.
**Societies** must contact in advance.
**Green Fees** not confirmed.
**Facilities** ♀ ⛳ 🏠 ⛳ 𝄢 Noel Cassidy.
**Leisure** caddy cars & motorised buggy for hire.
**Location** 3m from city on Dublin road
**Hotel** ★★★★ 68% Castletroy Park Hotel, Dublin Rd, LIMERICK ☎ 061 335566 107 ⇄ 🌩

---

*Limerick* Ballyclough ☎ 061 415146 & 414083
Tree-lined parkland course which hosted the 1991 Ladies Senior Interprovincial matches. The club are the only Irish winners of the European Cup Winners Team Championship.
*18 holes, 5938mtrs, Par 72, SSS 71, Course record 67.*
*Club membership 1300.*
**Visitors** may not play after 4pm or on Tue & weekends.
**Societies** must contact in writing.
**Green Fees** IR£22.50 per round.
**Facilities** ⊗ 〗🍴 ᴸ 💺 ♀ ⛳ 🏠 ⛳ 𝄢 John Cassidy.

**Leisure**   trolley for hire, putting green, practice area.
**Location**  3m S on Fedamore Road
**Hotel**     ★★★ 69% Jurys Hotel, Ennis Rd, LIMERICK
              ☎ 061 327777 94 ⇥ ☏

---

**Limerick County Golf & Country Club** Ballyneety
☎ 61 351881
Limerick County was designed by Des Smyth and presents beautifully because of the strategic locaton of the main features. It stretches over undulating terrain with one elevated section providing views of the surrounding countryside. It features over 70 bunkers with six lakes and several unique design features.
*18 holes, 6712yds, Par 72, SSS 74, Course record 70.*
*Club membership 300.*
**Visitors**  welcome but prebooking essential.
**Societies** book by telephone or in writing.
**Green Fees** IR£20 per round; IR£12.50 before 9.30am Mon-Fri..
**Facilities** ⊗ ⅢI ᛒ ♨ ♀ ⚲ 🏠 ⛟ 🗲 ☏ Philip Murphy.
**Leisure**   sauna, buggies for hire, trolley for hire, driving range, golf school, jacuzzi.
**Location**  5m SE of Limerick on R512
**Hotel**     ★★★ 66% Limerick Inn Hotel, Ennis Rd, LIMERICK
              ☎ 061 326666 153 ⇥

---

## NEWCASTLE WEST                          Map 01 B3

**Killeline** Cork Rd
☎ 069 61600
Set in 160 acres of gently contoured parkland in the heart of the Golden Vale with views to the Galtee Mountains. Because of its design and many mature trees, accuracy in playing is the key to good scoring.
*18 holes, 5800yds, Par 70.*
*Club membership 400.*
**Visitors**  welcome weekdays, by arrangement weekends.
**Societies** telephone in advance.
**Green Fees** IR£11 per 18 holes.
**Facilities** ⊗ ᛒ ♨ ♀ ⚲ 🏠 ⛟
**Leisure**   trolley for hire, practice area.
**Location**  0.25m off main Limerick/Killarney route
**Hotel**     ★★★ 76% Dunraven Arms Hotel, ADARE
              ☎ 061 396633 66 ⇥ ☏

---

**Newcastle West** Ardagh
☎ 069 76500
A new course set in 150 acres of unspoilt countryside, built to the highest standards on sandy free draining soil. A practice ground and driving range are included. Hazards on the course include lakes, bunkers, streams and trees. A signature hole is likely to be the Par 3 6th playing 185 yards over a lake.
*18 holes, 6041yds, Par 71, SSS 73.*
*Club membership 620.*
**Visitors**  advisable to contact in advance.
**Societies** contact in advance.
**Green Fees** IR£15 per day.
**Facilities** ⊗ ⅢI ᛒ ♨ ♀ ⚲ 🏠 ⛟
**Leisure**   trolley for hire, driving range, putting green, practice area.
**Location**  2m off N21 between Limerick & Killarney
**Hotel**     ★★★★(red)⚑ Adare Manor, ADARE
              ☎ 061 396566 28 ⇥ ☏Annexe36 ⇥ ☏

---

## CO LONGFORD

### LONGFORD                              Map 01 C4

**County Longford** Glack, Dublin Rd ☎ 043 46310
A lovely 18-hole parkland course with lots of trees.
*18 holes, 6044yds, Par 70, SSS 69, Course record 69.*
*Club membership 739.*
**Visitors**  very welcome, but advisable to telephone in advance for Tue and Sun play.
**Societies** by prior arrangement.
**Green Fees** not confirmed.
**Facilities** ♀ ⚲
**Leisure**   buggy/trolley hire.
**Location**  E of town
**Hotel**     ★★★ 58% Abbey Hotel, Galway Rd, ROSCOMMON ☎ 0903 26240 & 26505 25 ⇥ ☏

---

## CO LOUTH

### ARDEE                                 Map 01 D4

**Ardee** Townparks ☎ 041 53227
Pleasant parkland course with mature trees and a stream.
*18 holes, 6100yds, Par 69, SSS 69.*
**Visitors**  may normally play on weekdays (except Wed).
**Green Fees** not confirmed.
**Facilities** ♀
**Hotel**     ★★★ 65% Ballymascanlon House Hotel, DUNDALK ☎ 042 71124 36 ⇥

---

### BALTRAY                               Map 01 D4

**County Louth** ☎ 041 22329
Generally held to have the best greens in Ireland, this links course was designed by Tom Simpson to have well guarded and attractive greens without being overly dependant on bunkers. It provides a good test for the modern champion, notably as the annual venue for the East of Ireland Amateur Open.
*18 holes, 6613yds, Par 73, SSS 71.*
*Club membership 1100.*
**Visitors**  must contact in advance.
**Societies** by prior arrangement.
**Green Fees** IR£35 (IR£40 weekends).
**Facilities** ⊗ ⅢI ᛒ ♨ ♀ ⚲ 🏠 ⛟ ☏
              🗲 Paddy McGuirk.
**Leisure**   hard tennis courts, buggies for hire, trolley for hire.
**Location**  5m NE of Drogheda
**Hotel**     ★★ 60% Conyngham Arms Hotel, SLANE ☎ 041 24155 16rm(15 ⇥ ☏)

---

### DUNDALK                               Map 01 D4

**Ballymascanlon House Hotel** ☎ 042 71124
Now a testing 18-hole parkland course with numerous water hazards and two difficult holes through woodland, this very scenic course is set at the edge of the Cooley Mountains. ▶

*18 holes, 5512yds, Par 68.*

| | |
|---|---|
| **Visitors** | must telephone in advance to check availability. |
| **Societies** | booking by telephone or letter. |
| **Green Fees** | IR£10 per 18 holes (IR£14 weekends & bank holidays). |
| **Facilities** | ⊗ 〗ﬃ ﬁ ▮ ⌾ ♨ 巫 |
| **Leisure** | a complete new complex is due to open October 1996. |
| **Location** | 3m N of Dundalk on the Carlingford road |
| **Hotel** | ★★★ 65% Ballymascanlon House Hotel, DUNDALK ☎ 042 71124 36 ⇄ |

---

***Dundalk*** Blackrock ☎ 042 21731
A tricky course with extensive views.
*18 holes, 6115mtrs, Par 72, SSS 72.*
*Club membership 1000.*

| | |
|---|---|
| **Visitors** | must contact in advance and may not play Tue or Sun. |
| **Societies** | must apply in writing in advance. |
| **Green Fees** | not confirmed. |
| **Facilities** | ⌾ 巫 ⌾ ♙ ⓕ James Cassidy. |
| **Leisure** | sauna, putting green,practice area,trolley hire. |
| **Location** | 2.5m S on coast road |
| **Hotel** | ★★★ 65% Ballymascanlon House Hotel, DUNDALK ☎ 042 71124 36 ⇄ |

---

***Killinbeg*** Killin Park ☎ 042 39303
Opened in 1991 and designed by Eddie Hackett, this undulating 12-hole parkland course has mature woodland and river features.
*12 holes, 3322yds, Par 72, SSS 69.*
*Club membership 100.*

| | |
|---|---|
| **Visitors** | no restrictions. |
| **Societies** | apply by telephone or in writing in advance. |
| **Green Fees** | not confirmed. |
| **Facilities** | ⌾ 巫 ♙ |
| **Location** | Bridge-a-Crinn |
| **Hotel** | ★★★ 65% Ballymascanlon House Hotel, DUNDALK ☎ 042 71124 36 ⇄ |

---

### GREENORE        Map 01 D4

***Greenore*** ☎ 042 73212 & 73678
Situated amidst beautiful scenery on the shores of Carlingford Lough, the trees here are an unusual feature on a links course. There are quite a number of water facilities, tight fairways and very good greens.
*18 holes, 6506mtrs, Par 71, SSS 71.*
*Club membership 500.*

| | |
|---|---|
| **Visitors** | must contact in advance at weekends. A letter of introduction is desirable, but not essential. |
| **Societies** | must contact well in advance. |

---

| | |
|---|---|
| **Green Fees** | not confirmed. |
| **Facilities** | ⌾ 巫 |
| **Leisure** | trolley hire. |
| **Hotel** | ★★★ 65% Ballymascanlon House Hotel, DUNDALK ☎ 042 71124 36 ⇄ |

---

### TERMONFECKIN        Map 01 D4

**Seapoint** ☎ 041 22333
A very long championship links course of 7,000 yards with a particularly interesting 17th hole.
*18 holes, 5904mtrs, Par 72, SSS 71.*
*Club membership 330.*

| | |
|---|---|
| **Visitors** | phone in advance for restrictions. |
| **Societies** | apply in writing or telephone in advance. |
| **Green Fees** | IR£22.50 per 18 holes (IR£27.50 weekends & bank holidays). |
| **Facilities** | ⊗ 〗ﬃ ﬁ ▮ ⌾ 巫 ﬁ 巫 ⓕ David Carroll. |
| **Leisure** | trolley for hire, putting green, practice area. |
| **Hotel** | ★★ 60% Conyngham Arms Hotel, SLANE ☎ 041 24155 16rm(15 ⇄ ♞) |

---

## CO MAYO

---

### BALLINA        Map 01 B4

**Ballina** Mossgrove, Shanaghy ☎ 096 21050
Undulating but mostly flat inland course. Planned to be extended to 18 holes during 1995.
*18 holes, 5700yds, Par 70, SSS 68 or 5933yds.*
*Club membership 478.*

| | |
|---|---|
| **Visitors** | welcome but may not play Sun before 3.30pm. Restrictions apply depending on competitions/society visits. |
| **Societies** | apply in writing or telephone in advance. |
| **Green Fees** | IR£16 per day. |
| **Facilities** | ﬁ ▮ ⌾ 巫 ♙ |
| **Leisure** | trolley hire, putting green. |
| **Location** | 1m outside town on Bonnocolon Rd |
| **Hotel** | ★★★ 57% Downhill Hotel, BALLINA ☎ 096 21033 50 ⇄ ♞ |

---

### BALLINROBE        Map 01 B4

**Ballinrobe** Cloonagashel ☎ 092 41118
Mainly flat terrain with some very interesting features. Although no other club plays on the course, its landlords, The Ballinrobe Race Company, hold races there five or six times a year.

*Downhill Hotel* ★★★

Ballina, Co Mayo
Tel: 00 353 96 21033
Fax: 00 353 96 21338

**THE VENUE THAT LEADS THE WAY**
- Hushaway weekend and mid week breaks
- Eagles Health & Leisure Club
- Luxury accommodation
- Superb cuisine with fresh local meats and fish
- Six 18 hole golf courses all nearby
- Family owned, personally supervised
- Renowned for its hospitality and friendly staff

*18 holes, 4300mtrs, Par 73, SSS 73, Course record 69 or 60 holes.*
*9 holes, 5540yds, Par 72, SSS 68.*
*Club membership 420.*

| | |
|---|---|
| **Visitors** | welcome daily, telephone to reserve Tee-time. |
| **Societies** | must telephone or write to Secretary in advance. |
| **Green Fees** | IR£17.50 per day; 9-hole course IR£10. |
| **Facilities** | ⊗ ㏒ ☎ ♀ ♨ ♏ |
| **Leisure** | buggies for hire, trolley for hire, driving range, putting green, practice area. |
| **Hotel** | ★★★ 62% Breaffy House Hotel, CASTLEBAR ☎ 094 22033 38 ➡ ♞ |

## BALLYHAUNIS      Map 01 B4

**Ballyhaunis** Coolnaha ☎ 0907 30014
Undulating parkland course with 9 holes, 10 greens and 18 tees.
*18 holes, 5413mtrs, Par 70, SSS 68.*
*Club membership 340.*

| | |
|---|---|
| **Visitors** | welcome all times but must avoid members competitions on Sun & Thu. |
| **Societies** | must apply in writing or telephone. |
| **Green Fees** | IR£10 per day. |
| **Facilities** | by prior arrangement by prior arrangement ㏒ ☎ ♀ ♨ |
| **Leisure** | trolley for hire, putting green. |
| **Hotel** | ★★★ 62% Breaffy House Hotel, CASTLEBAR ☎ 094 22033 38 ➡ ♞ |

## BELMULLET      Map 01 A5

**Carne** Carne ☎ 097 82292 & 81051
*18 holes, 6042mtrs, Par 72.*
*Club membership 350.*

| | |
|---|---|
| **Visitors** | welcome, booking essential to guarantee tee-time. |
| **Societies** | booking advisable. |
| **Green Fees** | IR£17 per day (Mar-Oct); IR£11.50 (Nov-Feb). |
| **Facilities** | ⊗ ⍸ ㏒ ☎ ♀ ♨ ♏ |
| **Leisure** | buggies for hire, trolley for hire. |
| **Hotel** | ★★★ 57% Downhill Hotel, BALLINA ☎ 096 21033 50 ➡ ♞ |

## CASTLEBAR      Map 01 B4

**Castlebar** Hawthorn, Rocklands ☎ 094 21649
Pleasant parkland course with a particularly interesting 9th hole.
*18 holes, 5698mtrs, Par 71, SSS 70, Course record 67.*
*Club membership 800.*

| | |
|---|---|
| **Visitors** | very welcome weekdays, must contact in advance for weekend play. |
| **Societies** | must contact in advance. |
| **Green Fees** | IR£12 per day (IR£15 weekends). |
| **Facilities** | ⊗ ㏒ ☎ ♀ ♨ ☒ ♏ |
| **Leisure** | trolley for hire, putting green, practice area. |
| **Location** | 1m from town on Belcarra road |
| **Hotel** | ★★★ 62% Breaffy House Hotel, CASTLEBAR ☎ 094 22033 38 ➡ ♞ |

## CLAREMORRIS      Map 01 B4

**Claremorris** Castlemagarrett ☎ 094 71527
A 9-hole parkland course on hilly terrain. There are plenty of trees and a drain across the course.
*9 holes, 5600mtrs, Par 70, SSS 69, Course record 66.*
*Club membership 300.*

| | |
|---|---|
| **Visitors** | no restrictions. |
| **Societies** | welcome weekdays, contact 094 71868 for details. |
| **Green Fees** | not confirmed. |
| **Facilities** | ♀ ♨ |
| **Leisure** | putting green,practice area. |
| **Location** | 1.5m from town |
| **Hotel** | ★★★ 62% Breaffy House Hotel, CASTLEBAR ☎ 094 22033 38 ➡ ♞ |

## KEEL      Map 01 A4

**Achill** Achill Island, Westport ☎ 098 43456
Seaside links in a scenic location on the edge of the Atlantic Ocean.
*9 holes, 2723yds, Par 70, SSS 66, Course record 69.*
*Club membership 170.*

| | |
|---|---|
| **Visitors** | welcome but cannot play on some Sundays |
| **Societies** | must write or telephone in advance. |
| **Green Fees** | IR£5 per round. |
| **Facilities** | ♏ |
| **Leisure** | trolley for hire, practice area. |
| **Hotel** | ★★★ 59% Hotel Westport, The Demesne, Newport Rd, WESTPORT ☎ 098 25122 49 ➡ ♞ |

## SWINFORD      Map 01 B4

**Swinford** Brabazon Park ☎ 094 51378
A pleasant parkland course with good views of the beautiful surrounding countryside.
*9 holes, 5542mtrs, Par 70, SSS 68.*
*Club membership 420.*

| | |
|---|---|
| **Visitors** | must contact in advance in peak season. |
| **Societies** | must apply in writing or telephone in advance. |
| **Green Fees** | IR£7 per day. |
| **Facilities** | ㏒ ☎ ♀ ♨ |
| **Leisure** | squash, fishing, trolley for hire, putting green, practice area. |
| **Hotel** | ★★★ 62% Breaffy House Hotel, CASTLEBAR ☎ 094 22033 38 ➡ ♞ |

## WESTPORT      Map 01 B4

**Westport** Carrowholly ☎ 098 28262 & 27070
This is a beautiful course with wonderful views of Clew Bay, with its 365 islands, and the holy mountain called Croagh Patrick, famous for the annual pilgrimage to its summit. Golfers indulge in a different kind of penance on this challenging course with many memorable holes. Perhaps the most exciting is the par five 15th, 580 yards long and featuring a long carry from the tee over an inlet of Clew Bay.
*18 holes, 6667yds, Par 73, SSS 71, Course record 65.*
*Club membership 750.*

| | |
|---|---|
| **Visitors** | must contact in advance. ▶ |

| | |
|---|---|
| Societies | apply in writing or telephone well in advance. |
| Green Fees | IR£15-IR£18 (IR£15-IR£22.50 weekends & bank holidays). |
| Facilities | ⊗ ⵣ ᴌ ➍ ♀ ⅄ ➔ ⊶ ℸ Alex Mealia. |
| Leisure | buggies for hire, trolley for hire, putting, practice area. |
| Location | 2.5m from town |
| Hotel | ★★★ 59% Hotel Westport, The Demesne, Newport Rd, WESTPORT ☎ 098 25122 49 ⊨ ↜ |

---

# CO MEATH

---

## BETTYSTOWN                    Map 01 D4

**Laytown & Bettystown** ☎ 041 27170
A very competitive and trying links course, home of famous golfer, Des Smyth.
*18 holes, 5652mtrs.*
*Club membership 950.*

| | |
|---|---|
| Visitors | may not play 1-2pm. Must contact in advance. |
| Societies | must contact in writing. |
| Green Fees | not confirmed. |
| Facilities | ⅄ ➔ ⊶ ℸ |
| Leisure | tennis courts. |
| Hotel | ★★ 60% Conyngham Arms Hotel, SLANE ☎ 041 24155 16rm(15 ⊨ ↜) |

---

## DUNSHAUGHLIN                    Map 01 D4

**Black Bush** Thomastown ☎ 01 8250021
Three 9-hole courses, giving three possible 18-hole combinations, set in lovely parkland, with a lake providing a hazard at the 1st. Recently added creeks, trees and bunkers make for challenging and accurate shot-making.
*Course 1: 18 holes, 6930yds, Par 73, SSS 72.*
*Course 2: 18 holes, 6559yds, Par 71, SSS 71.*
*Course 3: 18 holes, 6647yds, Par 72, SSS 71.*
*Club membership 900.*

| | |
|---|---|
| Visitors | must contact in advance but cannot play 1-2pm weekdays. |
| Societies | advance booking by letter. |
| Green Fees | IR£13 per round (IR£15 weekends). |
| Facilities | ⊗ by prior arrangement ⵣ by prior arrangement ᴌ ➍ ♀ ⅄ ➔ ⊶ ℸ Shane O'Grady. |
| Leisure | trolley for hire, driving range, putting green, practice area. |
| Location | 1.5m from village on Dublin-Navan road |
| Hotel | ★★★ 66% Finnstown Country House Hotel & Golf Course, Newcastle Rd, LUCAN ☎ 01 6280644 25 ⊨ ↜Annexe20 ⊨ ↜ |

---

## KELLS                    Map 01 C4

**Headfort** ☎ 046 40857 & 40639
A delightful parkland course which is regarded as one of the best of its kind in Ireland. There are ample opportunities for birdies, but even if these are not achieved, Headfort provides for a most pleasant game.

*18 holes, 6007mtrs, Par 72, SSS 71, Course record 67.*
*Club membership 680.*

| | |
|---|---|
| Visitors | restricted Tues Ladies Day. Must contact in advance. |
| Societies | must apply in writing. |
| Green Fees | IR£17 (IR£20 weekends and bank holidays). |
| Facilities | ⊗ ⵣ ᴌ ➍ ♀ ⅄ ➔ ⊶ ℸ Brendan McGovern. |
| Leisure | trolley for hire, putting green, practice area. |
| Hotel | ★★ 62% Headfort Arms Hotel, Ceanannus, KELLS ☎ 046 40063 & 40121 18 ⊨ ↜ |

---

## NAVAN                    Map 01 C4

**Royal Tara** Bellinter ☎ 046 25508 & 25244
Pleasant parkland course offering plenty of variety. Situated close to the Hill of Tara, the ancient seat of the Kings of Ireland.
*New Course: 18 holes, 5757mtrs, Par 71, SSS 70.*
*Old Course: 9 holes, 3184yds, Par 35, SSS 35.*
*Club membership 1000.*

| | |
|---|---|
| Visitors | prior arrangement is advisable. Tue is ladies day. |
| Societies | apply in writing or telephone. |
| Green Fees | IR£15 per round (IR£20 weekends & bank holidays). |
| Facilities | ⊗ ⵣ ᴌ ➍ ♀ ⅄ ➔ ⊶ ℸ Adam Whiston. |
| Leisure | trolley for hire, putting green, practice area. |
| Location | 6m from town on N3 |
| Hotel | ★★ 60% Conyngham Arms Hotel, SLANE ☎ 041 24155 16rm(15 ⊨ ↜) |

---

## TRIM                    Map 01 C4

**Trim** Mewtownmoynagh ☎ 046 31463
Extended in 1990 to form a big 18-hole parkland course. The new part blends well with the old and is only distinguished by a plentiful planting of young trees. Four very challenging Par 5's.
*18 holes, 6720mtrs, Par 73, SSS 72.*

| | |
|---|---|
| Visitors | welcome some restrictions telephone for details. |
| Societies | not Sun, enquiries welcome. |
| Green Fees | not confirmed. |
| Facilities | ♀ |
| Location | 3m outside Trim on Trim/Longwood rd |
| Hotel | ★★ 60% Conyngham Arms Hotel, SLANE ☎ 041 24155 16rm(15 ⊨ ↜) |

---

# CO MONAGHAN

---

## CARRICKMACROSS                    Map 01 C4

**Mannan Castle** Donaghmoyne ☎ 042 63308
Parkland and picturesque, the course starts with a dogleg, then a Par 4 Index 1, next a Par 5 with majestic cypress trees as a back drop to the green. The 4th needs a good tee shot to the green. The long Par 5 5th requires a straight hitter; the 6th doglegs left and the 7th overlook the whole course. Downhill to the 8th with trouble on the right and straight and long into the 9th.
*9 holes, 5900mtr, Par 72, SSS 70.*
*Club membership 340.*

**Visitors** may play anytime except competition times Sat, Sun & Mon from 2-2.30pm.
**Societies** apply in writing to the secretary.
**Green Fees** IR£8 per day.
**Facilities** ⓑ ♚ ♀ ⚲
**Location** 4m N
**Hotel** ★★★ 65% Ballymascanlon House Hotel, DUNDALK ☎ 042 71124 36 ⇌

**Nuremore** ☎ 042 61438 & 64016
Picturesque parkland course of championship length incorporating the drumlins and lakes which are a natural feature of the Monaghan countryside. Precision is required on the 10th to drive over a large lake and between a narrow avenue of trees.
*18 holes, 6400yds, Par 72, SSS 70, Course record 67.*
*Club membership 150.*
**Visitors** welcome all times but must contact Maurice Cassidy in advance.
**Societies** must contact in advance.
**Green Fees** IR£16 per day (IR£20 weekends & bank holidays).
**Facilities** ⊗ ⍟ ⓑ ♚ ♀ ⚲ 🖿 ⚑ ⇥ ꕤ Maurice Cassidy.
**Leisure** hard tennis courts, heated indoor swimming pool, squash, fishing, sauna, gymnasium, buggies for hire, trolley for hire, putting green, practice area.
**Location** S on Dublin road N7
**Hotel** ★★★★ 69% Nuremore Hotel, CARRICKMACROSS ☎ 042 61438 69rm

**CASTLEBLAYNEY** Map 01 C4

*Castleblayney* Onomy ☎ 042 46356
Scenic course on Muckno Park estate, adjacent to Muckno Lake and Blayney Castle.
*9 holes, 5378yds, Par 68, SSS 66, Course record 68.*
*Club membership 275.*
**Visitors** may not play during competitions.
**Societies** must contact in advance.
**Green Fees** not confirmed.
**Facilities** ♀ ⚲
**Leisure** hard tennis courts, fishing.
**Hotel** ★★★ 65% Ballymascanlon House Hotel, DUNDALK ☎ 042 71124 36 ⇌

**CLONES** Map 01 C5

**Clones** Hilton Park ☎ 047 56017
Parkland course set in Drumlin country. Due to limestone belt, the course is very dry and playable all year round. There is a timesheet in operation on Sundays.
*9 holes, 5880yds, Par 68, SSS 67.*
*Club membership 329.*
**Visitors** must contact in advance.
**Societies** apply in writing.
**Green Fees** IR£6 per day (IR£10 weekends).
**Facilities** ⊗ ⓑ ♚ ♀ ⚲
**Leisure** putting green, practice area.
**Location** 3m from Clones on Scotshouse rd
**Hotel** ★★★ 65% Ballymascanlon House Hotel, DUNDALK ☎ 042 71124 36 ⇌

**MONAGHAN** Map 01 C5

**Rossmore** Rossmore Park, Cootehill Rd ☎ 047 81316
An undulating 18-hole parkland course amidst beautiful countryside.
*18 holes, 5534mtrs, Par 70, SSS 68.*
*Club membership 700.*
**Visitors** must contact in advance.
**Societies** must apply in writing.
**Green Fees** IR£13 per day.
**Facilities** ⊗ ⓑ ♚ ♀ ⚲ 🖿
**Leisure** driving range, putting green.
**Location** 2m S on Cootehill road
**Hotel** ★★★ 65% Ballymascanlon House Hotel, DUNDALK ☎ 042 71124 36 ⇌

---

# CO OFFALY

**BIRR** Map 01 C3

**Birr** The Glenns ☎ 0509 20082
The course has been laid out over undulating parkland utilising the natural contours of the land, which were created during the ice age. The sandy subsoil means that the course is playable all year round.
*18 holes, 5700mtrs, Par 70, SSS 70, Course record 64.*
*Club membership 750.*
**Visitors** contact in advance.
**Societies** advance contact to secretary.
**Green Fees** IR£12 per round (IR£14 weekends).
**Facilities** ⊗ ⍟ ⓑ ♚ ♀ ⚲ 🖿 ⚑
**Leisure** motorised carts for hire, trolley for hire, driving range, putting green, practice area.
**Hotel** ★★ 66% County Arms Hotel, BIRR ☎ 0509 20791 & 20193 18 ⇌ ꕤ

**EDENDERRY** Map 01 C4

*Edenderry* ☎ 0405 31072
A most friendly club which offers a relaxing game in pleasant surroundings. In 1992 the course was extended to 18 holes.
*18 holes, 6121mtrs, Par 73, SSS 72.*
*Club membership 700.*
**Visitors** restricted Thu & weekends.
**Societies** may not play on Thu & Sun; must contact the secretary in writing.
**Green Fees** not confirmed.
**Facilities** ♀ ⚲
**Leisure** putting, trolley hire, practice area.
**Hotel** ★★ 59% Curryhills House Hotel, PROSPEROUS ☎ 045 868150 10 ⇌ ꕤ

**TULLAMORE** Map 01 C4

*Tullamore* Brookfield ☎ 0506 21439
Well wooded parkland course.
*18 holes, 6322yds, Par 71, SSS 70, Course record 65.*
*Club membership 989.*
**Visitors** must contact in advance, restricted on Tue & at weekends. ▶

**Societies**  must contact in writing.
**Green Fees**  not confirmed.
**Facilities**  ♀ ♨ 🏠 ⛳ ☏ Donagh McArdle.
**Leisure**  putting green,practice area,trolley hire.
**Location**  2.5m SW on Kinnity road
**Hotel**  ★★★ 64% Prince Of Wales Hotel, ATHLONE
☎ 0902 72626 73 ⇄ ╞

---

# CO ROSCOMMON

---

## ATHLONE                                 Map 01 C4

**Athlone** Hodson Bay
☎ 0902 92073
A picturesque course with a panoramic view of Lough Ree.
Overall, it is a tight, difficult course with some outstanding
holes and is noted for its magnificent greens.
*18 holes, 5935mtrs, Par 71, SSS 70.*
*Club membership 1000.*
**Visitors**  must contact in advance.
**Societies**  apply in writing.
**Green Fees**  IR£15 (IR£18 weekends).
**Facilities**  ⊗ ⅏ ⅃ ♣ ♀ ♨ 🏠 ⛳ 🎏 ☏ Martin Quinn.
**Leisure**  trolley for hire, driving range, putting green,
practice area.
**Location**  4m from town beside Lough Ree
**Hotel**  ★★★ 69% Hodson Bay Hotel, Hodson Bay,
Kiltoom, ATHLONE
☎ 0902 92444 46 ⇄ ╞

---

## BALLAGHADERREEN                          Map 01 B4

*Ballaghaderreen* ☎ 0907 60295
Mature 9-hole course with an abundance of trees. Accuracy
off the tee is vital for a good score. Small protected greens
require a good short-iron plan. The Par 3, 2nd hole at 178
yards has ruined many a good score.
*9 holes, 5727yds, Par 70, SSS 66.*
*Club membership 150.*
**Visitors**  no restrictions.
**Societies**  apply in writing or telephone Sec 0907 60029
during office hours.
**Green Fees**  not confirmed.
**Facilities**  ♀ ♨
**Leisure**  putting,practice area,trolley hire.
**Location**  3m W of town
**Hotel**  ★★ 64% Royal Hotel, BOYLE
☎ 079 62016 16 ⇄ ╞

---

## BOYLE                                    Map 01 B4

*Boyle* Roscommon Rd ☎ 079 62594
Situated on a low hill and surrounded by beautiful scenery,
this is an undemanding course where, due to the generous
fairways and semi-rough, the leisure golfer is likely to finish
the round with the same golf ball.
*9 holes, 5324yds, Par 67, SSS 66, Course record 65.*
*Club membership 260.*
**Visitors**  no restrictions.

**Societies**  must contact in writing.
**Green Fees**  not confirmed.
**Facilities**  ♀ ♨ ⛳
**Leisure**  putting green,practice area.
**Hotel**  ★★ 64% Royal Hotel, BOYLE
☎ 079 62016 16 ⇄ ╞

---

## CARRICK-ON-SHANNON                       Map 01 C4

**Carrick-on-Shannon** Woodbrook
☎ 079 67015
A pleasant 9-hole course overlooking the River Shannon.
*9 holes, 5571mtrs, Par 70, SSS 68.*
*Club membership 500.*
**Visitors**  contact in advance.
**Societies**  must contact in advance.
**Green Fees**  IR£10 per day.
**Facilities**  ⊗ ⅃ ♣ ♀ ♨ ⛳
**Leisure**  trolley for hire, driving range, putting green,
practice area.
**Location**  4m W beside N4
**Hotel**  ★★ 64% Royal Hotel, BOYLE
☎ 079 62016 16 ⇄ ╞

---

## CASTLEREA                                Map 01 B4

*Castlerea* Clonalis ☎ 0907 20068
The clubhouse is virtually at the centre of Castlerea course
with 7 tees visible. A pleasant parkland very near the centre
of town.
*9 holes, 4974mtrs, Par 68, SSS 66.*
*Club membership 200.*
**Visitors**  welcome.
**Societies**  contact for details.
**Green Fees**  not confirmed.
**Facilities**  ♀ ♨
**Leisure**  putting,driving range,practice area.
**Location**  On Dublin/Castlebar road
**Hotel**  ★★★ 58% Abbey Hotel, Galway Rd,
ROSCOMMON
☎ 0903 26240 & 26505 25 ⇄ ╞

---

## ROSCOMMON                               Map 01 B4

**Roscommon** Mote Park
☎ 0903 26382 & 26927
Located on the rolling pastures of the old Mote Park estate,
this recently extended 18-hole course successfully blends the
old established nine holes with an exciting and equally
demanding new 9-hole lay-out. Numerous water hazards,
notably on the tricky 13th, multi-tiered greens and an
excellent irrigation to give an all-weather surface.
*18 holes, 6290mtrs, Par 72, SSS 70, Course record 64.*
*Club membership 500.*
**Visitors**  contact in advance.
**Societies**  apply in writing.
**Green Fees**  IR£15 per day.
**Facilities**  ⊗ ⅏ ⅃ ♣ ♀ ♨
**Leisure**  trolley for hire, putting green, practice ground.
**Location**  0.5m S of Roscommon town
**Hotel**  ★★★ 58% Abbey Hotel, Galway Rd,
ROSCOMMON
☎ 0903 26240 & 26505 25 ⇄ ╞

# CO SLIGO

## BALLYMOTE
Map 01 B4

**Ballymote** Ballinascarrow ☎ 071 83158 & 83089
Although Ballymote was founded in 1940, it has a new
course only opened in July 1993. This is a 9-hole parkland
course with some trees.
*9 holes, 5302mtrs, Par 68, SSS 67.*
*Club membership 250.*
Visitors welcome except for club competitions.
Societies telephone in advance.
Green Fees IR£5 per day.
Facilities ⚒
Location 1m N
Hotel ★★ 64% Royal Hotel, BOYLE
☎ 079 62016 16 ⇄ ☂

## ENNISCRONE
Map 01 B5

*Enniscrone* ☎ 096 36297
In a magnificent situation with breathtaking views of
mountain, sea and rolling countryside, this course offers
some unforgettable golf. It has been designated by the
Golfing Union of Ireland as suitable for major national
and provincial championships and offers an exciting
challenge among its splendid sandhills. A particularly
favourite hole is the tenth, with a marvellous view from
the elevated tee and the chance of a birdie with an
accurate drive.
*18 holes, 6620yds, Par 72, SSS 72.*
*Club membership 900.*
Visitors may not play before 10.30am or between
1.30 & 3pm on Sun.
Societies must telephone in advance.
Green Fees not confirmed.
Facilities ⚒⚒⚒
Leisure driving range, putting green, practice area,
trolley & buggy hire.
Location 0.5m S on Ballina road
Hotel ★★★ 57% Downhill Hotel, BALLINA
☎ 096 21033 50 ⇄ ☂

## SLIGO
Map 01 B5

*County Sligo* Rosses Point ☎ 071 77134 or 77186
Now considered to be one of the top links courses in
Ireland, County Sligo is host to a number of
competitions, including the West of Ireland

Championships and internationals. Set in an elevated
position on cliffs above three large beaches, the
prevailing winds provide an additional challenge.
*18 holes, 6003mtrs, Par 71, SSS 72.*
*Club membership 1069.*
Visitors must contact in advance. Must play on
medal course (white tee markers).
Societies must contact in writing & pay a deposit.
Green Fees not confirmed.
Facilities ⚒⚒ Leslie Robinson.
Leisure putting,practice area,buggy/trolley hire.
Location Off N15 to Donegal
Hotel ★★ 60% Ballincar House Hotel, Rosses
Point Rd, Ballincar, SLIGO
☎ 071 45361 25 ⇄ ☂

**Strandhill** Strandhill ☎ 071 68188
This scenic course is situated between Knocknarea Mountain
and the Atlantic, offering golf in its most natural form amid
the sand dunes of the West of Ireland. The 1st, 16th and 18th
are Par 4 holes over 364 metres in length; the 2nd and 17th
are testing Par 3s which vary according to the prevailing
wind; the Par 4 13th is a testing dogleg right. This is a course
where accuracy will be rewarded.
*18 holes, 5516mtrs, Par 69, SSS 68.*
*Club membership 450.*
Visitors must contact in advance.
Societies apply in advance.
Green Fees IR£14 (IR£17 weekends).
Facilities ⚒⚒⚒
Leisure motorised carts for hire, buggies for hire, trolley
for hire, putting green, practice area.
Location 5m from town
Hotel ★★ 60% Ballincar House Hotel, Rosses Point
Rd, Ballincar, SLIGO ☎ 071 45361 25 ⇄ ☂

## TOBERCURRY
Map 01 B4

**Tobercurry** ☎ 071 85849
A 9-hole parkland course designed by Edward Hackett. The
8th hole, a Par 3, is regarded as being one of the most testing
in the west of Ireland.
*9 holes, 2745mtrs, Par 35, SSS 35.*
*Club membership 300.*
Visitors restricted on Sun.
Societies telephone in advance on 071 85770.
Green Fees IR£10 per day.
Facilities ⚒⚒⚒
Leisure trolley for hire, putting green.
Location 0.25m from Tobercurry
Hotel ★★★ 57% Downhill Hotel, BALLINA
☎ 096 21033 50 ⇄ ☂

**Rosses Point Road – Sligo**
**Tel: 00 353 71 45361**
**Fax: 00 353 71 44198**

Your Secret Hideaway in Beautiful and Peaceful Surroundings!
Ideally located near Rosses Point (3 miles) and Strandhill
(7 miles) in the heart of the Glorious Yeats Country.
*Distinctively Different*

# CO TIPPERARY

## CAHIR
Map 01 C3

**Cahir** Kilcommon ☎ 052 41474
Parkland course dissected by the River Suir which adds a challenge to the par 4 8th and par 3 16th.
*18 holes, 5740mtrs, Par 71, SSS 71.*
*Club membership 350.*

| | |
|---|---|
| **Visitors** | may play any time except during competitions. |
| **Societies** | by prior arrangement, apply in writing. |
| **Green Fees** | IR£12 per round or part of round.. |
| **Facilities** | ⊗ by prior arrangement ⅲ by prior arrangement ╚ ♨ ♀ ♨ ╒ Dominic Foran. |
| **Leisure** | trolley for hire, putting green, practice area. |
| **Location** | 1m from Cahir on the Clogheen road |
| **Hotel** | ★★★ 63% Clonmel Arms, Sarsfield Rd, CLONMEL ☎ 052 21233 31 ⇆ ☂ |

## CARRICK-ON-SUIR
Map 01 C2

**Carrick-on-Suir** Garvonne ☎ 051 40047
*9 holes, 5948yds, Par 70, SSS 68.*

| | |
|---|---|
| **Visitors** | may not play on Sun. |
| **Societies** | contact for details. |
| **Green Fees** | not confirmed. |
| **Facilities** | |
| **Location** | 2m SW |
| **Hotel** | ★★★ 72% Minella Hotel, CLONMEL ☎ 052 22388 70 ⇆ ☂ |

## CLONMEL
Map 01 C2

**Clonmel** Lyreanearla, Mountain Rd
☎ 052 24050
Set in the scenic, wooded slopes of the Comeragh Mountains, this is a testing course with lots of open space and plenty of interesting features. It provides an enjoyable round in exceptionally tranquil surroundings.
*18 holes, 5785mtrs, Par 71, SSS 70.*
*Club membership 850.*

| | |
|---|---|
| **Visitors** | may not play at weekends & bank holidays. Must contact in advance. |
| **Societies** | must contact in writing. |
| **Green Fees** | not confirmed. |
| **Facilities** | ♀ ♨ 🖼 ╒ Robert Hayes. |
| **Leisure** | bowls, pool table, table tennis. |
| **Hotel** | ★★★ 72% Minella Hotel, CLONMEL ☎ 052 22388 70 ⇆ ☂ |

## NENAGH
Map 01 B3

**Nenagh** Beechwood ☎ 067 31476
Interesting gradients call for some careful approach shots. Some magnificent views.
*18 holes, 5491mtrs, Par 69, SSS 68, Course record 64.*
*Club membership 820.*

| | |
|---|---|
| **Visitors** | must contact in advance. |
| **Societies** | must apply in writing. |
| **Green Fees** | IR£15 per day. |
| **Facilities** | ⊗ ⅲ ╚ ♨ ♀ ♨ 🖼 ╒ |
| **Leisure** | trolley for hire, driving range, putting green, |

practice area.

| | |
|---|---|
| **Location** | 3m from town on old Birr rd |
| **Hotel** | ★★★ 65% Castle Oaks House Hotel, CASTLECONNELL ☎ 061 377666 11 ⇆ ☂ |

## ROSCREA
Map 01 C3

**Roscrea Golf Club** Derryvale ☎ 0505 21130
An 18-hole parkland course.
*18 holes, 5750mtrs, Par 71, SSS 70, Course record 69.*
*Club membership 420.*

| | |
|---|---|
| **Visitors** | on Sun by arrangement. |
| **Societies** | apply in writing to Hon Secretary. |
| **Green Fees** | not confirmed. |
| **Facilities** | ♀ ♨ ╒ |
| **Leisure** | caddy car/trolley hire,practice area. |
| **Location** | N7, Dublin side of Roscrea |
| **Hotel** | ★★ 66% County Arms Hotel, BIRR ☎ 0509 20791 & 20193 18 ⇆ ☂ |

## TEMPLEMORE
Map 01 C3

**Templemore** Manna South ☎ 0504 31400
Parkland course with newly planted trees which offers a pleasant test to visitors without being too difficult. Walking is level too.
*9 holes, Par 68, SSS 67, Course record 68.*
*Club membership 220.*

| | |
|---|---|
| **Visitors** | may not play on Sun during Special Events & Open weeks. |
| **Societies** | must contact in advance. |
| **Green Fees** | not confirmed. |
| **Facilities** | ♀ ♨ |
| **Location** | 0.5m S |
| **Hotel** | ★★ 66% County Arms Hotel, BIRR ☎ 0509 20791 & 20193 18 ⇆ ☂ |

## THURLES
Map 01 C3

**Thurles** Turtulla ☎ 0504 21983 & 22466
Superb parkland course with a difficult finish at the 18th.
*18 holes, 5904mtrs, Par 72, SSS 71, Course record 65.*
*Club membership 800.*

| | |
|---|---|
| **Visitors** | welcome, limited availability at weekends, Tuesday is Ladies day. |
| **Societies** | apply in writing to Hon Secretary. |
| **Green Fees** | IR£16 per round. |
| **Facilities** | ⊗ ⅲ ╚ ♨ ♀ ♨ 🖼 ╒ Sean Hunt. |
| **Leisure** | squash, sauna, gymnasium, trolley for hire, driving range, putting green, practice area. |
| **Location** | 1m from town on Cork road |
| **Hotel** | ★ 57% Royal Hotel, Bridge St, TIPPERARY ☎ 062 33244 16 ⇆ ☂ |

## TIPPERARY
Map 01 C3

**County Tipperary** Dundrum House Hotel, Dundrum
☎ 062 71116
The course had been built into a mature Georgian estate using the features of woodland and parkland adorned by the Multeen River. Designed by Philip Walton. The 4th hole is one of the most testing Par 5's in Ireland.
*18 holes, 6709yds, Par 72, SSS 72, Course record 70.*

*Club membership 190.*
**Visitors**    booking is advisable especially at weekends.
**Societies**    apply in writing.
**Green Fees** IR£18 per round (IR£20-IR£22 weekends).
**Facilities** ⊗ ⅢⅢ ▙ ♥ ♀ ⚁ 🏠 ⍓ ⊨
**Leisure**    hard tennis courts, fishing, buggies for hire,
     trolley for hire, driving range, putting green,
     practice area.
**Location**    7m W of Cashel off N8
**Hotel**    ★ 57% Royal Hotel, Bridge St, TIPPERARY
     ☎ 062 33244 16 ⇄ ⎰

---

**Tipperary** Rathanny ☎ 062 51119
Recently extended to 18-holes, this parkland course has
plenty of trees and bunkers and water at three holes to
provide additional hazards.
*18 holes, 5761mtrs, Par 71, SSS 71, Course record 69.*
*Club membership 700.*
**Visitors**    advisable to contact by phone, weekend play
     available but limited on Sun.
**Societies**    apply in writing.
**Green Fees** IR£12 per day.
**Facilities** ⊗ ▙ ♥ ♀ ⚁ 🏠 ⍓
**Leisure**    buggies for hire, trolley for hire, putting green.
**Location**    1m S
**Hotel**    ★ 57% Royal Hotel, Bridge St, TIPPERARY
     ☎ 062 33244 16 ⇄ ⎰

---

# CO WATERFORD

---

## DUNGARVAN      Map 01 C2

---

**Dungarvan** Knocknagrannagh ☎ 058 41605 & 43310
Opened in June 1993. A championship-standard course
beside Dungarvan Bay, with seven lakes and hazards placed
to challenge all levels of golfer.
*18 holes, 6487yds, Par 72, SSS 71, Course record 66.*
*Club membership 575.*
**Visitors**    welcome weekdays, booking advisable
     weekends.
**Societies**    telephone then write to confim booking.
**Green Fees** IR£14 per round (IR£18 weekends & bank
     holidays).
**Facilities** ⊗ ⅢⅢ ▙ ♥ ♀ ⚁ 🏠 ⍓ ⎰ David Hayes.
**Leisure**    trolley for hire, driving range, putting green,
     practice area.
**Location**    Off N25 between Waterford & Youghal
**Hotel**    ★★★ 59% Lawlors Hotel, DUNGARVAN
     ☎ 058 41122 & 41056 89 ⇄ ⎰

---

**Gold Coast Golf & Leisure** Ballinacourty ☎ 058 42249
A parkland course bordered by the Atlantic Ocean.
*9 holes, 5659mtrs, Par 72, SSS 69, Course record 67.*
*Club membership 400.*
**Visitors**    book in advance, times available throughout the
     week.
**Societies**    apply by telephone in advance.
**Green Fees** IR£12 per day.
**Facilities** ⊗ ⅢⅢ ▙ ♥ ♀ ⚁ ⍓ ⊨
**Leisure**    hard tennis courts, heated indoor swimming
     pool, sauna, gymnasium, trolley for hire, driving
     range, putting green, practice area.

**Hotel**    ★★★ 59% Lawlors Hotel, DUNGARVAN
     ☎ 058 41122 & 41056 89 ⇄ ⎰

---

**West Waterford** Coolcormack ☎ 058 43216 & 41475
Designed by Eddie Hackett, the course is on 150 acres of
rolling parkland by the Brickey River with a backdrop of the
Comeragh Mountains, Knockmealdowns and Drum Hills.
The first nine holes are laid out on a large plateau featuring a
stream which comes into play at the 3rd and 4th holes. The
river at the southern boundary affects several later holes.
*18 holes, 6004mtrs, Par 72, SSS 74, Course record 70.*
*Club membership 175.*
**Visitors**    pre book for tee times.
**Societies**    telephone or write in advance.
**Green Fees** IR£15 per 18 holes (IR£20 weekends & bank
     holidays).
**Facilities** ⊗ ⅢⅢ ▙ ♥ ♀ ⚁ 🏠 ⍓
**Leisure**    buggies for hire, 5 acre practice area.
**Location**    Approx 3m W of Dungarvan, off N25
**Hotel**    ★★★ 59% Lawlors Hotel, DUNGARVAN
     ☎ 058 41122 & 41056 89 ⇄ ⎰

---

## DUNMORE EAST      Map 01 C2

---

**Dunmore East** ☎ 051 383151
Challenging golf for low and high handicappers. The 6th hole
requires a tee shot that carries 150yards over the sea. The
course overlooks the village of Dunmore East and the sea so
many holes are affected by crosswinds.
*18 holes, 6655yds, Par 72, SSS 70.*
*Club membership 300.*
**Visitors**    welcome, no restrictions.
**Societies**    telephone in advance.
**Green Fees** IR£10 per day (IR£12 weekends & bank holidays).
**Facilities** ⊗ ⅢⅢ ▙ ♥ ♀ ⚁ 🏠 ⍓
**Leisure**    trolley for hire, putting green, practice area.
**Hotel**    ★★ 66% Dooley's Hotel, 30 The Quay,
     WATERFORD ☎ 051 73531 35rm(34 ⇄ ⎰)

---

## LISMORE      Map 01 C2

---

**Lismore** Ballyin ☎ 058 54026
Picturesque tree-dotted sloping course on the banks of the
Blackwater River. Rothwell's is a diffiuclt hole with a
sloping green and trees to either side.
*9 holes, 5790yds, Par 69, SSS 67, Course record 67.*
*Club membership 350.*
**Visitors**    may not play Sun before noon. Restricted Wed,
     Thu & weekends.
**Societies**    must apply in writing.
**Green Fees** IR£8 per day (IR£10 weekends & bank holidays).
**Facilities** ▙ ♥ ♀ ⚁
**Leisure**    trolley for hire, putting green, practice area.
**Hotel**    ★★★ 59% Lawlors Hotel, DUNGARVAN
     ☎ 058 41122 & 41056 89 ⇄ ⎰

---

## TRAMORE      Map 01 C2

---

**Tramore** Newtown Hill ☎ 051 386170
This course has matured nicely over the years to become a
true championship test and has been chosen as the venue for
the Irish Professional Matchplay Championship and the Irish
Amateur Championship. Most of the fairways are lined with
evergreen trees, calling for accurate placing of shots, and the
course is continuing to develop.      ▶

*18 holes, 5918mtrs, Par 72, SSS 72, Course record 65.*
*Club membership 1200.*
**Visitors**    pre-booking required.
**Societies**    apply in writing.
**Green Fees** IR£22 per round (IR£25 weekends & bank holidays).
**Facilities**   ⊗ ⅷ ⓛ ⓛ ♀ ⚥ 🏠 ⚐ 🖾 ⓣ Derry Kiely.
**Leisure**    squash, trolley for hire, putting green, practice area.
**Hotel**     ★★★★ 75% Waterford Castle Hotel, The Island, WATERFORD ☎ 051 78203 19 ⇄ 🕅

---

## WATERFORD        Map 01 C2

**Faithlegg House** Dunmore East ☎ 051 382241
Some wicked slopes and borrows on the immaculate greens, a huge 432yard 17th what has a host of problems and a doglegged approach to the two-tier 18th green are just some of the novel features on this course. Set on the banks of the River Suir, the course has been integrated into a landscape textured with mature trees,flowing parkland and five lakes.
*18 holes, 6057mtrs, Par 72, SSS 72, Course record 69.*
*Club membership 65.*
**Visitors**    no restrictions.
**Societies**   apply in writing or telephone at least a month in advance.
**Green Fees** not confirmed.
**Facilities**   ♀ ⚥ 🏠 ⚐ ⓣ Ted Higgins.
**Hotel**     ★★★ 66% Jurys Hotel, Ferrybank, WATERFORD ☎ 051 32111 98 ⇄ 🕅

---

**Waterford** Newrath ☎ 051 76748 & 74182
Undulating parkland course in pleasant surroundings.
*18 holes, 5722mtrs, Par 71, SSS 70, Course record 66.*
*Club membership 931.*
**Visitors**    must contact in advance.
**Societies**   must apply in writing.
**Green Fees** IR£20 (IR£22 weekdays & bank holidays).
**Facilities**   ⊗ ⅷ ⓛ ⓛ ♀ ⚥ 🏠 ⚐ ⓣ Eamonn Condon.
**Location**   1m N
**Hotel**     ★★★ 66% Jurys Hotel, Ferrybank, WATERFORD ☎ 051 32111 98 ⇄ 🕅

---

**Waterford Castle** The Island, Ballinakill ☎ 051 71633
*18 holes, 5810mtrs, Par 72, SSS 71.*
*Club membership 300.*
**Visitors**    must contact in advance.
**Societies**   apply in advance.
**Green Fees** IR£20 (IR£22 weekends).
**Facilities**   ⓛ ⓛ ♀ ⚥ 🏠 ⚐
**Location**   2m E on Island approached by private ferry
**Hotel**     ★★★★ 75% Waterford Castle Hotel, The Island, WATERFORD ☎ 051 78203 19 ⇄ 🕅

---

# CO WESTMEATH

## ATHLONE        Map 01 C4

**Glasson Golf & Country Club** Glasson ☎ 0902 85120
An 18-hole championship standard course designed by Christy O'Connor Jnr. There are a number of outstanding holes including the Par 3 15th which has both tee and green

situated in Killiure Bay. As Christy said 'Although only 185 yards off the back tee there is no room for error whatsoever'.
*18 holes, 6653yds, Par 72, Course record 65.*
*Club membership 240.*
**Visitors**    no restrictions.
**Societies**   telephone in advance.
**Green Fees** not confirmed.
**Facilities**   ♀ ⚥ 🏠 ⚐ ⓣ
**Leisure**    caddy cars & buggies, caddies available.
**Location**   6m N of Athlone on N55
**Hotel**     ★★★ 64% Prince Of Wales Hotel, ATHLONE ☎ 0902 72626 73 ⇄ 🕅

---

## DELVIN        Map 01 C4

**Delvin Castle** Clonyn ☎ 044 64315
Only opened in 1991, Delvin is a developing course. The design of the course is built around the prevailing wind.
*18 holes, 5800mtrs, Par 70, SSS 68.*
*Club membership 400.*
**Visitors**    no restrictions.
**Societies**   apply in writing in advance.
**Green Fees** not confirmed.
**Facilities**   ⚥ 🏠 ⚐ ⓣ David Keenaghan.
**Leisure**    trolleys for hire.
**Hotel**     ★★ 62% Headfort Arms Hotel, Ceanannus, KELLS ☎ 046 40063 & 40121 18 ⇄ 🕅

---

## MOATE        Map 01 C4

**Moate** ☎ 0902 81271
Extended in 1994 to 18 holes, the course is parkland with trees. Although the original 9-holes did not have water hazards the new section has a lake.
*18 holes, 5642mtrs, Par 72, SSS 70, Course record 67.*
*Club membership 550.*
**Visitors**    welcome, advisable to telephone in advance.
**Societies**   welcome, prior arrangement not needed.
**Green Fees** IR£10 (IR£13 weekends).
**Facilities**   ⓛ ⓛ ♀ ⚥
**Leisure**    buggies for hire, trolley for hire, putting green, practice area.
**Location**   1m N
**Hotel**     ★★★ 64% Prince Of Wales Hotel, ATHLONE ☎ 0902 72626 73 ⇄ 🕅

---

**Mount Temple** Mount Temple Village
☎ 0902 81841 & 81545
A traditionally built, highly-rated, all year round course with parkland and unique links-type greens and natural undulating fairways.A challenge for all levels of golfers as the wind plays a major part in the scoring on this course.
*18 holes, 5950mtrs, Par 71, SSS 71, Course record 73.*
*Club membership 150.*
**Visitors**    welcome but must book for weekends.
**Societies**   telephone in advance.
**Green Fees** IR£10 per round (IR£14 weekends & bank holidays).
**Facilities**   ⊗ ⓛ ⓛ ♀ ⚥ 🏠 ⚐
**Leisure**    putting green.
**Hotel**     ★★★ 64% Prince Of Wales Hotel, ATHLONE ☎ 0902 72626 73 ⇄ 🕅

## MULLINGAR
Map 01 C4

**Mullingar** ☎ 044 48366
The wide rolling fairways between mature trees provide parkland golf at its very best. The course, designed by the great James Braid, offers a tough challenge and annually hosts one of the most important amateur events in the British Isles - the Mullingar Scratch Cup. It has also been the venue of the Irish Professional Championship. One advantage of the layout is that the clubhouse is never far away.
*18 holes, 6406yds, Par 72, SSS 71, Course record 63.*
*Club membership 1000.*

| | |
|---|---|
| **Visitors** | preferred if booked in advance, Sundays are Medal days, Wednesday Ladies day. |
| **Societies** | apply in writing. |
| **Green Fees** | IR£18 per round (IR£26 weekends & bank holidays). |
| **Facilities** | ⊗ Ⅲ ⓑ 🏌 🖤 ♀ ⚲ 🛍 🍴 John Burns. |
| **Leisure** | buggies for hire, trolley for hire, driving range, putting green, practice area. |
| **Location** | 3m S |
| **Hotel** | ★★★ 64% Prince Of Wales Hotel, ATHLONE ☎ 0902 72626 73 ⇆ 🐾 |

---

# CO WEXFORD

---

## COURTOWN HARBOUR
Map 01 D3

*Courtown* Kiltennel, Gorey ☎ 055 25166
Treelined fairways and views of the sea make this 18-hole parkland course attractive. There are 4 excellent Par 3's, one of which is the 18th played over a large pond.
*18 holes, 5852mtrs, Par 71, SSS 70.*

| | |
|---|---|
| **Visitors** | may not play on competition days. |
| **Societies** | contact for details. |
| **Green Fees** | not confirmed. |
| **Facilities** | ♀ 🍴 John Coone. |
| **Hotel** | ★★ 69% Courtown Hotel, COURTOWN HARBOUR ☎ 055 25210 & 25108 21 ⇆ 🐾 |

---

## ENNISCORTHY
Map 01 D3

**Enniscorthy** Knockmarshall ☎ 054 33191
A pleasant course suitable for all levels of ability.
*18 holes, 5697mtrs, Par 70, SSS 68.*
*Club membership 800.*

| | |
|---|---|
| **Visitors** | must telephone for booking. |
| **Societies** | must book in advance. |
| **Green Fees** | IR£14 per day (IR£16 weekends & bank holidays). |
| **Facilities** | ⊗ Ⅲ ⓑ 🏌 🖤 ♀ ⚲ |
| **Leisure** | trolley for hire, putting green, practice area. |
| **Location** | 1m from town on New Ross road |
| **Hotel** | ★ 56% Murphy-Flood's Hotel, Market Square, ENNISCORTHY ☎ 054 33413 21rm(5 ⇆13 🐾) |

---

## GOREY
Map 01 D3

**Courtown** Kiltennel ☎ 055 25166
A pleasant parkland course which is well wooded and enjoys views across the Irish Sea near Courtown Harbour.
*18 holes, 5898mtrs, Par 71, SSS 71, Course record 65.*
*Club membership 1200.*

| | |
|---|---|
| **Visitors** | must contact in advance. |
| **Societies** | advisable to contact in advance. |
| **Green Fees** | IR£14-IR£18 (IR£18-IR£23 weekends). |
| **Facilities** | ⊗ Ⅲ ⓑ 🏌 🖤 ♀ ⚲ 🛍 🍴 John Coone. |
| **Leisure** | trolley for hire, putting green, practice area. |
| **Location** | 3m from town, off Courtown Road |
| **Hotel** | ★★★(red)▲ Marlfield House Hotel, GOREY ☎ 055 21124 19 ⇆ 🐾 |

---

## NEW ROSS
Map 01 C3

**New Ross** Tinneranny ☎ 051 21433
Recently extended to 18-holes, this well kept parkland course has an attractive backdrop of hills and mountains. Straight hitting and careful placing of shots is very important, especially on the 2nd, 6th, 10th and 15th, all of which are challenging holes.
*18 holes, 5751yds, Par 71, SSS 70.*
*Club membership 700.*

| | |
|---|---|
| **Visitors** | welcome, booking required for weekend play. |
| **Societies** | apply to secretary/manager. |
| **Green Fees** | IR£13 (IR£16 weekends & bank holidays). |
| **Facilities** | ⓑ 🖤 ♀ ⚲ |
| **Leisure** | trolley for hire, putting green, practice area. |
| **Location** | 3m from town centre |
| **Hotel** | ★★ 59% The Old Rectory Hotel, Rosbercon, NEW ROSS ☎ 051 21719 12 ⇆ 🐾 |

---

## ROSSLARE
Map 01 D2

*Rosslare* Rosslare Strand ☎ 053 32203 & 32238
This traditional links course is within minutes of the ferry terminal at Rosslare, but its popularity is not confined to visitors from Fishguard or Le Havre. It is a great favourite with the Irish too. Many of the greens are sunken and are always in beautiful condition, but the semi-blind approaches are among features of this course which provide a healthy challenge.
*Old Course: 18 holes, 6577yds, Par 72, SSS 71, Course record 68.*
*New Course: 9 holes, 3153yds, Par 70, SSS 70.*
*Club membership 900.*

| | |
|---|---|
| **Visitors** | book in advance. |
| **Societies** | apply in writing/telephone. |
| **Green Fees** | not confirmed. |
| **Facilities** | ♀ ⚲ 🛍 🍴 Austin Skerritt. |
| **Leisure** | putting, buggy/trolley hire, practice area. |
| **Location** | 6m N of Rosslare Ferry Terminal |
| **Hotel** | ★★★★ 76% Kelly's Resort Hotel, ROSSLARE ☎ 053 32114 Annexe99 ⇆ 🐾 |

**St Helen's Bay Golf & Country Club** St Helens, Kilrane
☎ 053 33234 & 33669
A championship-standard golf course designed by Philip Walton. Parkland with water hazards, bunkers and trees incorporated generously.
*18 holes, 5813mtrs, Par 72, SSS 72, Course record 69.*
*Club membership 180.*
**Visitors** contact in advance.
**Societies** telephone in advance.
**Green Fees** IR£15-IR£18 per 18 holes (IR£19-IR£20 weekends). IR£10-IR£12 per 9 holes (IR£12-IR£14 weekends).
**Facilities** ⊗ ⅢⅡ ᴸ ♨ ♀ ⚐ 🛆 ⛳ 🏌 ⚑
**Leisure** hard tennis courts, sauna, gymnasium, buggies for hire, trolley for hire, driving range, putting green, practice area.
**Hotel** ★★★ 58% Hotel Rosslare, ROSSLARE HARBOUR
☎ 053 33110 25rm(22 ⇆ ℕ)

---

**WEXFORD** Map 01 D3

*Wexford* Mulgannon ☎ 053 42238
Parkland course with panoramic view of the Wexford coastline and mountains.
*18 holes, 6100yds, Par 71, SSS 69.*
*Club membership 800.*
**Visitors** must contact in advance but may not play Thu & weekends.
**Societies** must contact in writing.
**Green Fees** not confirmed.
**Facilities** ♀ 🛆 ⚐ ᴸ G Ronayne.
**Leisure** pool table.
**Hotel** ★★★ 72% Talbot Hotel, Trinity St, WEXFORD
☎ 053 22566 100 ⇆ ℕ

---

# CO WICKLOW

---

**ARKLOW** Map 01 D3

*Arklow* Abbeylands ☎ 0402 32492
Scenic links course.
*18 holes, 5404mtrs, Par 68, SSS 67, Course record 66.*
*Club membership 450.*
**Visitors** may play Mon-Fri.
**Societies** must apply in writing.
**Green Fees** not confirmed.
**Facilities** ♀ 🛆 ⚐
**Location** 0.5m from town centre
**Hotel** ★★★(red)🍴 Marlfield House Hotel, GOREY
☎ 055 21124 19 ⇆ ℕ

---

**BALTINGLASS** Map 01 D3

**Baltinglass** Dublin Rd
☎ 0508 81350
On the banks of the River Slaney, the 9-hole course has 4 Par-4s over 400 yards which have to be played twice. Reputed to be one of the hardest 9-hole courses in the Republic.
*9 holes, 5554mtrs, Par 68, SSS 69, Course record 68.*
*Club membership 400.*
**Visitors** advisable to check availability for weekends.
**Societies** apply in writing.
**Green Fees** IR£10 (IR£12 weekends & bank holidays).
**Facilities** ⊗ ⅢⅡ ᴸ ♨ ♀ 🛆
**Leisure** putting green, practice area.

---

**Rathsallagh** ☎ 045 403316
Designed by Peter McEvoy and Christy O'Connor Jnr, this is a spectacular course which will test the pro's without intimidating the club golfer. Set in 252 acres of lush parkland with thousands of mature treesn naturalwater hazards and gently rolling landscape.
*18 holes, 6916yds, Par 72, SSS 74.*
*Club membership 180.*
**Visitors** must have appropriate attire & book in advance. Restricted weekends.
**Societies** telephone in advance.
**Green Fees** IR£25 Sun pm/Mon; Tue-Fri am IR£29; Fri pm-Sun am & holidays IR£35. Early Bird before 9.30am Mon-Fri.
**Facilities** ⊗ ⅢⅡ ᴸ ♨ ♀ 🛆 ⚐ 🏌 ⚑
**Leisure** hard tennis courts, heated indoor swimming pool, sauna, motorised carts for hire, buggies for hire, trolley for hire, driving range, putting green, practice area, riding.
**Location** 15m SE of Naas
**Hotel** ★★★ 56% Downshire House Hotel, BLESSINGTON
☎ 045 865199 14 ⇆ ℕAnnexe11 ⇆ ℕ

---

**BLAINROE** Map 01 D3

**Blainroe** ☎ 0404 68168
Parkland course overlooking the sea on the east coast, offering a challenging round to golfers of all abilities.
*18 holes, 6068mtrs, Par 72, SSS 72, Course record 71.*
*Club membership 868.*
**Visitors** must contact in advance.
**Societies** must telephone in advance.
**Green Fees** IR£20 (IR£28 weekends and bank holidays).
**Facilities** ⊗ ⅢⅡ ᴸ ♨ ♀ 🛆 ⚐ 🏌 ᴸ John McDonald.
**Leisure** trolley for hire, putting green, practice area.
**Location** S of Wicklow, on coast road
**Hotel** ★★★(red)🍴 Tinakilly Country House & Restaurant, RATHNEW
☎ 0404 69274 29 ⇆ ℕ

---

**BLESSINGTON** Map 01 D3

*Tulfarris Hotel & Country Club*
☎ 045 64574 & 51219
Designed by Eddie Hachett, this course is on the Blessington lakeshore with the Wicklow Mountains as a backdrop.
*9 holes, 2806mtrs, Par 36, SSS 69, Course record 74.*
*Club membership 150.*
**Visitors** tee booking advisable; may not play Sun 8-12.30pm.
**Societies** must contact in writing or telephone in advance.
**Green Fees** not confirmed.
**Facilities** ♀ 🛆 ⚐ 🏌 ⚑
**Leisure** hard tennis courts, heated indoor swimming pool, fishing, sauna, gymnasium, caddy cars.

| | |
|---|---|
| Location | Via N81, 2m from Blessington village |
| Hotel | ★★★ 56% Downshire House Hotel, |
| | BLESSINGTON |
| | ☎ 045 865199 14 ⇆ ⋔Annexe11 ⇆ ⋔ |

## BRAY          Map 01 D4

**Bray** Ravenswell Rd ☎ 01 2862484
A 9-hole parkland course with plenty of trees and bunkers.
*9 holes, 5761mtrs, Par 70, SSS 70, Course record 65.*
*Club membership 500.*
**Visitors** restricted Mon, Sat & Sun.
**Societies** contact in advance.
**Green Fees** IR£17 per day.
**Facilities** ♥ ♀ ♨ 🛍 ⋔ ⋔ Michael Walby.
**Leisure** trolley for hire, putting green, practice area.
**Hotel** ★★★ 58% Royal Hotel, Main St, BRAY
   ☎ 01 2862935 91 ⇆ ⋔

**Old Conna** Ferndale Rd ☎ 01 2826055 & 2826766
Fairly young but interesting course with a number of shots across water.
*18 holes, 6550yds, Par 72, SSS 71, Course record 70.*
*Club membership 900.*
**Visitors** advisable to contact in advance but may not play weekends. Smart dress essential on course & in clubhouse.
**Societies** must telephone well in advance.
**Green Fees** IR£22.50 per round. Early bird before 9.30am IR£13.50.
**Facilities** ⊗ ⋔ ♭ ♥ ♀ ♨ 🛍 ⋔ ⋔ Paul McDaid.
**Leisure** trolley for hire, putting green, practice area.
**Hotel** ★★★ 58% Royal Hotel, Main St, BRAY
   ☎ 01 2862935 91 ⇆ ⋔

***Woodbrook*** Dublin Rd ☎ 01 2824799
Pleasant parkland with magnificent views and bracing sea breezes which has hosted a number of events, including the Irish Close and the Irish Open Championships. A testing finish is provided by an 18th hole with out of bounds on both sides.
*18 holes, 5996mtrs, Par 72, SSS 71, Course record 65.*
*Club membership 960.*
**Visitors** must contact in advance and have a handicap certificate.
**Societies** must contact in advance.
**Green Fees** not confirmed.
**Facilities** ♀ ♨ 🛍 ⋔ ⋔ Billy Kinsella.
**Location** 11m S of Dublin on N11
**Hotel** ★★★ 58% Royal Hotel, Main St, BRAY
   ☎ 01 2862935 91 ⇆ ⋔

## BRITTAS BAY       Map 01 D3

**The European Club** ☎ 0404 47415
A major new links course 30 miles south of Dublin, the course runs through a large dunes system with great views of Arklow Bay. It was ranked no 7 in Ireland's 30 greatest golf courses by the Irish Golf Institute in 1994.
*18 holes, 6800yds, Par 71, SSS 71.*
*Club membership 100.*
**Visitors** pre-booking advised especially for weekends.
**Societies** must book in advance.
**Green Fees** IR£25 (IR£30 weekends). Oct-Feb: £20/£25.
**Facilities** ⊗ ⋔ ♭ ♥ ♨ ⋔

| | |
|---|---|
| Leisure | trolley for hire, putting green, practice area. |
| Hotel | ★★★(red)♨ Tinakilly Country House & |
| | Restaurant, RATHNEW |
| | ☎ 0404 69274 29 ⇆ ⋔ |

## DELGANY        Map 01 D3

**Delgany** ☎ 01 2874536
An undulating parkland course amidst beautiful scenery.
*18 holes, 5474mtrs, Par 69, SSS 68, Course record 63.*
*Club membership 850.*
**Visitors** may play Mon, Wed (until 11am), Thu & Fri. Contact in advance.
**Societies** contact in advance.
**Green Fees** IR£20 weekdays (IR£24 weekends & bank holidays).
**Facilities** ⊗ ⋔ ♭ ♥ ♀ ♨ 🛍 ⋔ ⋔ Gavin Kavanagh.
**Leisure** motorised carts for hire, buggies for hire, trolley for hire, putting green, practice area.
**Location** 0.75m from village
**Hotel** ★★★ 58% Royal Hotel, Main St, BRAY
   ☎ 01 2862935 91 ⇆ ⋔

## GREYSTONES      Map 01 D3

**Charlesland Golf & Country Club Hotel** ☎ 01 2876764
Championship lenght, Par 72 course with a double dog-leg at the 9th and 18th. Water hazards at the 3rd and 11th.
*18 holes, 5907mtrs, Par 72, SSS 72.*
*Club membership 744.*
**Visitors** must contact in advance.
**Societies** must apply in advance.
**Green Fees** IR£23 per round (IR£28 weekends & bank holidays).
**Facilities** ♭ ♥ ♀ ♨ 🛍 ⋔ ⋔ ⋔ Paul Heeney.
**Leisure** sauna, motorised carts for hire, buggies for hire, driving range, putting green.
**Hotel** ★★★(red)♨ Tinakilly Country House & Restaurant, RATHNEW
   ☎ 0404 69274 29 ⇆ ⋔

***Greystones*** ☎ 01 2876624 & 2874136
A part level and part hilly parkland course.
*18 holes, 5401mtrs, Par 69, SSS 68.*
*Club membership 941.*
**Visitors** may only play Mon, Tue & Fri morning. Must contact in advance.
**Societies** must contact in writing.
**Green Fees** not confirmed.
**Facilities** ♀ ♨ 🛍 ⋔ ⋔
**Hotel** ★★★(red)♨ Tinakilly Country House & Restaurant, RATHNEW ☎ 0404 69274 29 ⇆ ⋔

## KILCOOLE        Map 01 D3

***Kilcoole*** Ballyfillop ☎ 01 2872066
*9 holes, 5506mtrs, Par 70, SSS 69.*
*Club membership 250.*
**Visitors** restricted Sat & Sun 8-10am.
**Societies** apply in writing or telephone.
**Green Fees** not confirmed.
**Facilities** ♀ ♨ 🛍
**Leisure** caddy cars.
**Location** N11 Kilcoole/Newcastle    ▶

Hotel      ★★ 65%  Hunter's Hotel,  RATHNEW
           ☎ 0404 40106 16 ⇄ 📷

## RATHDRUM                                            Map 01 D3

Glenmalure Greenane  ☎  0404 46679
A moorland course with elevated tees and greens. The 12th,
known as the Helicopter Pad, is difficult.
*18 holes, 5300yds, Par 71, SSS 67, Course record 73.*
*Club membership 200.*
Visitors      no restrictions.
Societies     telephone at least 3 days in advance..
Green Fees   IR£12 per day (IR£18 weekends & bank
             holidays).
Facilities   ⊗ ⅢⅢ ⓛ ⬛ ♀ ⚒ ⚐
Leisure      buggies for hire, trolley for hire, putting green.
Hotel        ★★ 64%  Woodenbridge Hotel,  WOODEN
             BRIDGE ☎ 0402 35146 12 ⇄ 📷

## SHILLELAGH                                          Map 01 D3

*Coollattin* Coollattin ☎  055 26302
Plenty of trees provide features on this 9-hole parkland
course.
*9 holes, 5672mtrs, Par 70, SSS 70.*
Visitors      may not play weekends.
Societies     contact for details.
Green Fees   not confirmed.
Facilities   ♀
Hotel        ★★★(red)⚜ Marlfield House Hotel,  GOREY
             ☎ 055 21124 19 ⇄ 📷

## WICKLOW                                             Map 01 D3

Wicklow Dunbur Rd  ☎  0404 67379
Partly links, partly meadow, the Wicklow course does not
have any trees. It was extended to 18-holes in spring 1994 by
adding 11 new holes.
*18 holes, 5556mtrs, Par 71.*
*Club membership 475.*
Visitors      welcome, no restrictions.
Societies     contact for details.
Green Fees   IR£15 (IR£18 weekends).
Facilities   ⊗ ⅢⅢ ⓛ ⬛ ⚒ 🗄 ⚐ David Daly.
Leisure      trolley for hire, putting green, practice area.
Hotel        ★★★(red)⚜ Tinakilly Country House &
             Restaurant,  RATHNEW
             ☎ 0404 69274 29 ⇄ 📷

## WOODENBRIDGE                                        Map 01 D3

*Woodenbridge* Arklow ☎  0402 35202
Expanded to 18 holes in summer of 1994, this course is in a
lovely wooded valley - the Vale of Avoca.
*9 holes, 5582mtrs, Par 70, SSS 68.*
Visitors      welcome.
Societies     no details given.
Green Fees   not confirmed.
Facilities
Hotel        ★★ 64%  Woodenbridge Hotel,  WOODEN
             BRIDGE ☎ 0402 35146 12 ⇄ 📷

# GOLF DRIVING RANGES

## ENGLAND

### BEDFORDSHIRE
Bedford, Mowsbury Driving Range ( 01234 216374) 14 bays covered floodlit 9am-9pm

Ivinghoe, Ivinghoe Driving Range ( 01296 662720) 30 bays open floodlit 9.30am-9.30pmWD 7.30pmWE

Leighton Buzzard, Aylesbury Vale (01525 240196) 10 bays covered floodlit 8am-9pm

Luton, Stockwood Park Golf Centre ( 01582 413704) 20 bays covered floodlit 6am-9.30pmWD5.30am-8pmWE

Tilsworth, Tilsworth Golf Centre (01525 210721/2) 30 bays covered floodlit 10am-10pm

Wyboston, Wyboston Lakes Range (01480 223004) 14 bays covered floodlit 7am-10pm

### BERKSHIRE
Ascot, Lavender Park Golf Centre (01344 884074 / 886096) 29 bays floodlit 9am-10.30pmWD 9am-10pmSUN

Binfield, Blue Mountain Golf Centre (01344 300200) 33 bays covered floodlit 7.15am-9pm

Maidenhead, Bird Hill Golf Range (01628 771030 / 75588) 38 bays covered floodlit 8am-10pm

Wokingham, Downshire Golf Range (01344 422708) 30 bays covered floodlit 7.30am-10pmWD 6am- 10pmWE

### BUCKINGHAMSHIRE
Bletchley, Windmill Hill Golf Complex (01908 378623) 23 bays covered floodlit + 5 bays open 8am-9pmWD 8am-8pmWE

Colnbrook, Colnbrook Driving Range (01753 682670/685127) 15 bays covered floodlit + 10 bays open 9.am-10.30pm

Loudwater, Wycombe Heights Golf Range (01494 812862) 24 bays covered floodlit 10am-10pm

Wavendon, Wavendon Golf Centre (01908 281811) 36 bays covered floodlit 7am(Mon.10am) - 10pm

### CAMBRIDGESHIRE
Hemingford Abbots, Hemingford Golf Centre (01480 492939) 30 bays floodlit 10am-9.30pmWD(Fri.10am-8.30pm) 9am-8.30pmWE

Thorney, Thorney Golf Centre (01733 270570) 13 bays covered floodlit 8am-dusk

Pidley, Lakeside Lodge (01487 740540) 6 bays covered floodlit + 17 bays open 7am-11pm

Ramsey, Edrich Golf Driving Range (01487 813519) 12 bays covered floodlit + 12 bays open 7am-9pmWD 7am-7pmWE

St Neots, Abbotsley Golf & Squash Club (01480 215153) 22 bays floodlit covered 7.30am-10pm

### CHESHIRE
Hartford, Hartford Golf Range(01606 871162) 30 bays covered floodlit 10am-9pm exc. Sat 10am-7pm

Heaton Mersey, Cranford Golf Driving Range (0161 432 8242) 43 bays covered floodlit 10.am-11pm

Knutsford, Mere Golf & Country Club (01565 830219) 6 bays open (floating ball) 8am-7pm

Warrington, Drive Time Golf Range (01925 234800) 60 bays covered floodlit 9am-10pm

### CORNWALL
Lostwithiel, Lostwithiel Golf & Country Club (01208 873822 / 873550) 6 bays floodlit 7.30am-9pm

St. Austell, Porthpean (01726 64613) 9 bays covered floodlit 9am-9pm

Redruth, Treleigh, Radnor Golf Centre (01209 211059) 12 bays covered floodlit + 6 bays open 8.30am-8.30pmWD 8.30am-6pmWE

Truro, Killiow Park (01872 70246) 8 bays indoor floodlit + 4 bays open 9.30am-9pmWD 9.30am-6pmWE

### CUMBRIA
Crosby-on-Eden, Eden (01228 573003) 16 bays floodlit 8am-8.30pmWD 8am-6pmWE

### DERBYSHIRE
Chesterfield, Grassmoor Golf Centre (01246 856044) 26 bays floodlit covered 8am-9pm

Horsley, Horsley Lodge Golf Range (01332 780838) 10 bays covered floodlit Dawn-10.pm

Long Eaton, Trent Lock (0115 9464398/9461184) 24 bays covered floodlit 8am-10pm

### DEVON
High Bicklington, Libbaton (01769 560269) 7 bays covered floodlit 8.am-10pm

Ilfracombe, Ilfracombe & Woolacombe Golf Range (01271 866222) 12 bays covered (not floodlit) + 6 open tees 8am-8pm summer 6pm winter

Ivybridge, Dinnaton (01752 892512/892452) 6 tee driving net 10am-9pm

Tedburn St. Mary, Fingle Glen Golf Range (01647 61817) 12-bays covered floodlit 9am- 9.pmWD 9am-8.30pmWE

### DORSET
Christchurch, Iford Bridge Golf Range (01202 473817) 14 bays open 8am-6pm

Wareham, Hyde, East Dorset Golf Centre (01929 472272) 22 bays floodlit (12 indoor) 8am-9pmWD 8am-6pmWE (Sum. 7.30am WD/WE)

Verwood, Crane Valley Golf Range (01202 814088) 10 bays covered + 2 bays open floodlit 7.30am-9pmWD 5pmWE)

Weymouth, Wessex Golf Centre (01305 784737) 20 bays open 9am-7pm

### CO. DURHAM
Chester-le-Street, Roseberry Grange (0191 370 0660) 17 bays covered floodlit 8am-9pmWD 7am-9pm Sat 7pm Sun

Durham, Ramside Hall (0191 386 9514) 16 bays covered floodlit 8am-8.45pm

Newton Aycliffe, Aycliffe Driving Range (01325 310820) 18 bays covered floodlit 7am-8.30pmWD-8pmWE

Stockton-on-Tees, Knotty Hill Golf Centre (01740 620320) 14 bays covered floodlit +12 bays open 8am-9pm

### ESSEX
Bulphan, Langdon Hills Driving Range (01268 548444) 22 bays covered floodlit 7am-9.30pmWD/9pmWE

Canvey Island, Castle Point (01268 510830) 21 bays covered floodlit 7am-9pmWD 8pmWE

Colchester, Colchester Golf Range (01206 230974) 12 bays covered floodlit + 2 open bays 10am-9pmWD 10am-6pmWE

Chelmsford, Chanels (01245 361100) 13 bays covered floodlit 7am-10pmWD 6.30am-10pmWEr

Earls Colne, Earls Colne (01787 224466) 20 bays covered floodlit 9am-10pmWD 8am-9pmWE

Epping, Nazeing Golf Club (01992 893798) 16 mats open air driving area (buckets of balls available) 7.30am-8pm

Leigh-on-Sea, Leigh Driving Range (01702 710586) 18 bays covered floodlit 9am-9.30pmWD/ 9pmWE

Maldon, Woodham Mortimer (01245 222276) 15 bays covered floodlit + 6 open tees 10am-9pm

## GLOUCESTERSHIRE

Gloucester, Gloucester Hotel & CC (01452 525653) 12 bays covered floodlit 10am-8.45pm

## GREATER LONDON

Addiscombe, Croydon Golf Centre (0181 656 1690) 24 bays covered floodlit 9am-10pmWD 9am-8pmWE

Arkley, A1 Golf Range (0181 447 1411) 47 bays covered floodlit (10 open) 8am-10pm

Bushey, Bushey Golf Range (0181 950 2215) 27 bays covered floodlit 9am-10pm

Carshalton, Oaks Sports Centre (0181 643 8363) 16 bays covered floodlit 9am-10pm

Chadwell Heath, Warren Park (0181 597 1120) 30 bays covered floodlit 9am-10pmWD/Sun. 9am-9pmSat.

Chessington, Chessington Golf Centre (0181 391 0948) 17 bays covered floodlit 9am-10pmWD 9am-9pmWE

Elstree, Elstree Golf Range (0181 953 6115) 62 bays covered floodlit 7am-10pm

Greenford, Lime Trees Park (0181 842 0442) 24 bays covered floodlit 8am-10pm

Hounslow, Airlinks (0181 561 1418) 36 bays covered floodlit 10am-10.30pm

Ilford, Barkingside, Fairlop Waters (0181 500 9911) 36 bays covered floodlit 9am-10pm

Kingston, Beverley Park (0181 949 9200) 60 bays covered floodlit summer 8.am-10pmWD9pmWE winter 9am-10pmWD 8am-9pmWE

Northolt, Ealing Golf Range (0181 845 4967) 36 bays covered floodlit + 4 bays open floodlit 10am-10pm

Northolt, London Golf Centre (0181 845 3180) 19 bays covered floodlit 9am-10pm

Orpington, Lullingstone Park (01959 533793) 15 bays covered 7am-darkWD 5am-darkWE

Orpington, Ruxley Park Golf Centre (01689 871490) 28 bays covered floodlit summer5am-10pm winter7.30am-10pm

Richmond, Richmond Driving Range (0181 332 9200) 23 bays covered floodlit 9.30am-9.30pm

Ruislip, Ruislip Driving Range (01895 638081) 40 bays covered floodlit 10am-10pm

Twickenham, Twickenham (0181 783 1748) 12 bays covered floodlit 9.30am-10pm

## GREATER MANCHESTER

Altrincham, Altrincham (0161 927 7504) 27 bays covered floodlit 9am-9.30WD/-7pmWE

Bardsley, Bardsley Park Golf Centre (0161 627 2463) 18 bays covered floodlit 10am-9pmWD 9.30am-6pmWE

Castleton, Castle Hawk Golf Range (01706 59995) 20 bays covered floodlit 9.am-8pmWD 9.am-6pmWE

Wigan, Up Holland, Beacon Park Driving Range (01695 622700) 24 bays covered floodlit 9am-9pm

## HAMPSHIRE

Alton, Worldham Park (01420 543151) 6 bays covered + 7 bays open 9am-8pmWD 8am-7pmWE

Basingstoke, Basingstoke Golf Centre (01256 50054) 24 bays covered floodlit 8.30amWD/8amWE-9.30pm

Botley, Botley Park Hotel & Country Club (01489 780888) 7bays open +6 bays covered daylight hours

Crondall, Oak Park (01252 8500660) 16 bays floodlit covered summer 6.30am-9pm winter7am-7pm

Dibden, Dibden Golf Centre (01703 845596) 20 bays floodlit 8am-8pm

Ower, Paulton's Golf Centre(01703 813992) 24 covered floodlit 8am-8,30pmWD 7am-6.30pmWE

Liphook, Old Thorns (01428 724555) 7 bays covered 8am-6pm

Portsmouth, Portsmouth Golf Centre (01705 664549) 22 bays covered floodlit 8am-9pmWD 7am-8pmWE

Southampton,Chilworth, Southampton Golf Range (01703 733166) 24 bays covered + 10 bays open floodlit 7.30am-9pmWD 6pmWE

Tadley, Tadley Driving Range (01734 815213) 12 bays covered floodlit summer8am-9pmWD 7.30am-6WE winter 8am-8pmWD 6pmWE

## HEREFORD & WORCESTER

Bishampton, The Vale Driving Range (01386 462781) 20 bays floodlit 8am-10pm

Bransford, Bank House Hotel (Pine Lakes) (01886 833551) 20 bays (5covered) summer8am-dark winter8am-4pm 9pmTuie & Thu

Ombersley, Ombersley Golf Range (01905 620747) 30 bays open daylight hours

Redditch, Abbey Park (01527 63918) 10 bays covered summer 7am-9pm winter7am-dark

Worcester, Worcester Golf Range (01905 421213) 26 bays covered floodlit 9.30am-9.45WD 5.30pmWE/BH

## HERTFORDSHIRE

Berkhamsted, Shooters Golf Centre (01442 872048) 25 bays covered floodlit 9am-10pm

Bishop's Stortford, Great Hadham (01279 843558) 15 bays covered floodlit 7.30am-dusk

Graveley, Chesfield Downs (01462 482929) 21-bays covered floodlit + 3 open 7am-10pm (9am-10pm Tue & Thu)

Hemel Hempstead, Little Hay Golf Range (01442 833798) 23 bays covered floodlit 10am-8pmWD 7.30pmWE/BH

Royston, Kingsway (01763 262727/262943) 36 bays covered floodlit 8.30am-10pmWD 7.30am-9.30pmWE

Royston, Whaddon Golf Centre (01223 207325) 14 bays covered floodlit 8am-dusk

Stevenage, Stevenage Golf Range (01438 880424) 24 bays covered floodlit 7.30am-10pm

Ware, Whitehill Golf Centre (01920 438495) 25 bays covered floodlit + open range 7am-9.30Mon Wed Thu Fri 10am-9.30pm Tue 7am-duskWE

Welwyn Garden City, Gosling Sports Park (01707 331056) 22bays covered floodlit 10am-10pm(Mon-Thu)10am-9pm(Fri.) 9am-8pmWE

## KENT

Ashford, Homelands Bettergolf Centre (01233 661620) 15 bays covered floodlit 8am-10pm

Biddenden, Chart Hills (01580 292148 pro shop)Chatham, Chatham Golf Centre practice area 30 bays summer 8am-8pm winter 8am-1hr before dusk

Chelmsfield, Chelmsfield LakesGolf Centre (01689 896266) 40 bays covered floodlit 6.30am-9.30pm

Dartford, Birchwood Park (01322 660554) 38 bays covered floodlit 7.30am-10pm

Dartford, Swanley, Olympic Golf Centre (01322 669201) 18 bays covered +9 bays open floodlit 10am-10pm

Edenbridge, Edenbridge Golf Range (01732 865202) 16 bays floodlit 8am-10pm

Folkestone, Etchinghill Golf Course (01303 863863) 11 bays covered floodlit 8am-9pmWD 7pmWE

Herne Bay, Herne Bay Golf Range (01227 742742) 15 bays covered floodlit 9am-10pm

Maidstone, Langley Park Driving Range (01622 863163) 25 bays covered floodlit 10am-10pmWD 10am-9pmWE

Orpington, St. Paul's Cray, Ruxley Park Golf Centre(see under Greater London)

Sittingbourne, The Oast Golf Centre (01795 473527) 17 bays covered floodlit 9am-9.30pm

Sittingbourne, Upchurch, RiverValley Golf Range (01634 379592) 16 bays covered floodlit 7am-9pmWD 6am-8pmWE

## LANCASHIRE

Blackburn, Blackburn Driving Range (01254 581996) 27 bays covered floodlit 9am-9pmWD /7pmWE

Blackpool, Heron's Reach, de Vere Hotel (01253 838866) 18 open7am-9pm

Blackpool, Phoenix Driving Range (01253 854846) 27 bays covered floodlit 9.30am-10pmWD 9am-10pmWE

Bolton, Kearsley Golf Range (01204 575726) 10 covered floodlit +30 grass tees 11am-10pmWD 11am-5pmWE

Chorley, Euxton Park Golf Centre (012572 61601) 11 bays covered floodlit + grass tees 11am-10pmWD 11am-5pmWE

Preston, Preston Driving Range (01772 861827) 23 bays covered floodlit 9.30am-9pmWD 9am-6pmWE (Sun. 1.30pm 6pm Winter)

Tarleton, Leisure Lakes Golf Range (01772 815842) 20 bays covered floodlit 9am-8.30pmWD 6pm0WE

Upholland, Beacon Park (01695 622700) 24 bays covered floodlit 9am-9pm

## LEICESTERSHIRE

Botcheston, Leicestershire Forest (01455 824800) 20 covered 7am-dusk

Greetham, Greetham Valley (01780 460666) 16 bays covered floodlit +5 open 8am-9pmWD 7.30am-7amWE/Bank Hols.

Leicester, Humberstone Heights (0116 2764674) 25 bays covered floodlit 8.30am-9.30pmWD 7am-7pmWE

Leicester, Whetstone Golf Range (0116 2861424) 20 bays open 8am-dusk

Loughborough, Charnwood Golf Centre (01509 610022) 24 bays covered floodlit 8.30am-10.30pm

Wilson, Breedon Priory Golf Course (01332 863081) 2 bays covered 20 bays open summer 8am-8pm approx. winter 8am-dusk

## LINCOLNSHIRE

Belton, DeVere Belton Woods (01476 593200) 24 bays covered floodlit 8am-10pm(Summer) 8am-9pm(Winter)

Gainsborough, Thonock Driving Range (01427 613088) 25 bays covered floodlit 9am-8pmWD 8am-duskWE

Holbeach, Gedney Hill (01406 330922) 10 bays covered floodlit

Horncastle, Horncastle (01507 526800) 25 bays covered floodlit 9am-9.30pm

Lincoln, Lincoln Bowls (01522 522059) 20 bays covered floodlit 9am-late

Scunthorpe, Messingham, Grange Park (01724 764478) 20 bays covered floodlit 9am-9.30pmWD /8.30pmWE

Skegness, The Elms Golf Centre (01754 881230) 20 bays covered floodlit 10am-10pm

## LONDON SEE ALSO GREATER LONDON

N9 Edmonton, Lea Valley Leisure Centre (0181 345 6666) 20 bays covered floodlit 8am-9.30pmWD/-8.30pmWE

N14 Southgate, Trent Park (0181 366 7432) 24 bays floodlit 9am-10pmWD 7.30am-9.30pmWE

E4 Chingford, Chingford Golf Range (0181 529 2409) 18 covered floodlit 9.30am-10pm

## MERSEYSIDE

Formby, Formby Golf Centre (017048 75952) 14 bays covered floodlit + 7bays open summer9.30am-9.30pm winter8.30pm

Moreton, Wirral Golf & Drive Centre (0151 677 6606) 20 bays covered floodlit +10 bays open 8am-9pm

## NORFOLK

Norwich, Bawburgh, Norwich Golf Centre (01603 742323) 14 bays covered floodlit 8am-8.30pmWD 5pmWE

King's Lynn, Eagles Golf Centre (01553 827147) 20 bays covered floodlit 8am-9pmWD/-8pmWE

King's Lynn, Middleton Hall (01553 841800) 6 bays covered floodlit 8am-10pm

Norwich, Sprowston Park (01603 410657) 27 bays covered floodlit 7.30am-8.30pmWD 6.30WE

Norwich, Wensum Valley (01603 261012) 4 bays covered + 2 bays open floodlit 7.30am-dusk

## NORTHAMPTONSHIRE

Daventry, Staverton Park (01327 302000) 16 bays covered floodlit 7.30am-10pm

Northampton, Collingtree Park (01604 700000) 16 bays covered floodlit 8am-9pm

Northampton, Delapre Golf Complex (01604 764036) 40 bays covered floodlit 9am-10pm

## NOTTINGHAMSHIRE

Newark, John Lee Golf Centre (01636 702161) 24 bays covered floodlit 9.am-10pmWD/-6pmWE

Nottingham, Richard Harrod Leisure Centre (0115 961 2949) 28 bays covered floodlit 9.30am-10pm exc. Mon 12-10pm

Nottingham, Cotgrave Place Golf Range(0115 933 4686) 10 bays covered floodlit 8am-8.45pm

Nottingham, Ramsdale Park Golf Centre (0115 965 5600) 25 bays covered floodlit + 1 video training bay 7.30am-10pmWD 6am-10pmWE

Nottingham, Riverside Golf Centre (0115 986 2179) 24 bays closed floodlit 9.30am-9.30pm

Oxton, Oakmere Park (0115 965 3545) 33 bays covered floodlit 7.30am-9.30pmWD 7am-7pmWE

## OXFORDSHIRE

**Abingdon**, Drayton Park (01235 550607) 21 bays covered floodlit 8am-8.30pmWD 7am-8.30pmWE

**Oxford**, Oxford Golf Centre (01865 721592) 19 bays covered floodlit + 8 bays open 10am-9pmWD 8pmWE.

## SHROPSHIRE

**Oswestry**, Mile End (01691 670580) 12 bays covered floodlit 8.30am-dusk(Summer) 8.30am-6pm(Winter)

**Telford**, Telford Hotel Golf & Country Club (01952 586052) 8 bays covered floodlit dawn-10pm

## SOMERSET

**Congresbury**, Mendip Spring (01934 852322) 11 bays covered floodlit 8am-9pm

**Farrington Gurney**, Farrington Golf Range (01761 241274) 18 bays floodlit +10 open grass 8am-9am

**Langport**, Long Sutton Golf Range (01458 241017) 10 bays covered floodlit 8am-9.30pm(Sun-9pm)

**Monkton Combe**, Combe Grove Manor Golf Range (01225 835533) 19 bays (9 covered) 10am-7.45pmWD 6.30pmWE

**Taunton**, Swingrite Golf Range, Holway (01823 442600) 12 bays covered + 7 bays open floodlit 9am-9pmWD/-7pmWE

**Taunton**, Oake Manor (01823 461993) 11-bays covered dawn-dusk

**Taunton**, Taunton Vale, West Monkton (01823 412220) 8 bays floodlit 80am-9pm

**Tickenham**, Golf Drive-In (01275 856626) 24 covered floodlit 8.30am-8.30pmWD 8am-6.30pmWE

**Yeovil**, Halstock Driving Range (01935 891689) 12 bays covered floodlit 8.30am-7.30pm(-7pm Winter)

## STAFFORDSHIRE

**Burton-upon-Trent**, Craythorne (01283 564329) 13 bays covered floodlit 8am-9.30pm

**Litchfield**, Seedy Mill Golf Range (01543 417333) 27 bays covered floodlit 7am-10pm

**Newcastle-under-Lyme**, Keele Golf Centre (01782 717417) 26 bays covered floodlit 9am-10pm

## SUFFOLK

**Halesworth**, St. Helena (01986 875567) 10 bays covered floodlit + 8 bays open 8.30am-9.30pm

**Ipswich**, Fynn Valley (01473 785463) 10 bays covered floodlit + 13 bays open 8am-8.30pmWD -7pmWE

**Ipswich**, Ipswich Golf Centre (01473 726821) 15 bays open + 2 bay covered 9am-7pmWD 6.30pmWE

## SURREY

**Camberly**, Pine Ridge (01276 20770) 36 bays covered floodlit 8am-10pm

**Cobham**, Silvermere Driving Range (01932 867275) 34 bays covered floodlit 8am-9.30pmWD 8pmWE

**Esher**, Sandown Golf Centre (01372 461234) 33 bays floodlit 10am-10pmWD/-9pmWE (closed during race meetings)

**Farnham**, Blacknest Golf Club (01420 22888) 24 bays covered 7.30am-9pm

**Godalming**, Broadwater Park (01483 429955) 16 bays covered floodlit 8am-10pm

**Old Woking**, Hoebridge Golf Centre (01483 722611) 25 bays covered floodlit 7.30am-10pmWD dawn-10pmWE

**Woking**, Windlemere Golf Range (01276 858727) 12 bays covered floodlit 9am-10pm

## SUSSEX (EAST)

**Ditchling**, Mid Sussex Golf Course (01273 846567) 20 bays open summer 7.30am-9.30pm winter 9am-4/5pm

**Eastbourne**, Eastbourne Golfing Park (01323 520400) 24 bays covered floodlit 10amm-10pm

**Hellingly**, Wellshurst Golf Range (01435 813456) 16 bays covered floodlit 7.30am-9.30pm

**Horam**, Horam Park (01435 813477) 16 bays covered floodlit 10am-9pm (approx.)

**Ticehurst**, Dale Hill (01580 200112) 10 open bays 7.30am-7pm

## SUSSEX (WEST)

**Chichester**, Chichester Golf Range (01243 533833) 27 bays covered floodlit 8.30am-8.830pm

**Crawley**, Pease Pottage Driving Range(01293 521706) 30 bays covered floodlit 8am-10pm

**Crawley**, Tilgate Driving Centre (01293 530103) 35 bays covered floodlit 7am-10pmWD/-8.30pmWE

**Horsham**, Horsham Golf Park (01403 271525) 30 bays open 7.30am-dusk

**Petworth**, Osiers Farm (01798 344097) 6 bays open 8am-dusk

**Pulborough**,West Chiltington Driving Range (01798 812115) 8 bays covered floodlit + 8 bays ope 7.30am-dusk

**Rustington**, Rustington Golf Centre (01903 850790) 30 bays covered floodlit +10 bays open 9am-9pm

**Slinfold**, Slinfold Park (01403 791555) 14 bays covered + 5 bays open floodlit 8am-9pmWD/-7pmWE

## TYNE & WEAR

**Newcastle-upon-Tyne**, Parklands (0191 236 4480) 45 bays two-tier covered floodlit 8am-10pm

**Washington**, Washington Moat House (0191 4029988) 21 bays covered floodlit 9am-9pm

## WARWICKSHIRE

**Coventry**, Brandon Wood (01203 543141) 11 bays covered + 8 bays open floodlit 9am-8.30pmWD 8am-9pmWE

**Lea Marston**, Lea Marston Driving Range (01675 470707) 30 bays covered floodlit 9am-10pmWD 8.30am-10pmWE

**Nuneaton**, Purley Chase (01203 395348) 13 bays covered floodlit 8am-9.30pm

**Stratford on-Avon**, Stratford Oaks Golf Range (01789 731571) 23 bays covered floodlit 8am-9pm

**Warwick**, Warwick Golf Centre (01926 494316) 24 bays covered floodlit 8am-9pmWD 6pmWE

## WEST MIDLANDS

**Bromsgrove**, Bromsgrove Golf Centre (01527 575886) 41 bays covered floodlit 9am-10pmWD 6pmSat.10am-6pmSun

**Coventry**, John Reay Golf Centre (01 203 333920 /333405) 30 bays covered floodlit 9am-10pm

**Dudley**, Sedgley Driving Range (01902 880503) 16 bays covered floodlit 9.30am-9pmWD 9am-6pmWE

**Dudley**, Swindon Ridge (01902 896191) 23 bays covered + 5 bays open floodlit 9am-9.30pmWD 10am-6pmWE

Halesowen, Halesowen Golf Range (0121 550 2920) 4 bays closed + 11 bays open 9.30am-dusk 7.30pmWE

Solihull, Four Ashes Golf Centre (01564 779055) 28 bays covered floodlit 10am-10pmWD 10am-6pmWE

Wishaw, The Belfry (01675 470301) 16 bays covered floodlit 7.30am-9.30pm

Wolverhampton, Three Hammers (01902 790940) 23 bays covered floodlit 9.30am-10pmWD 9am-9pmWE

Wolverhampton, Perton Park Golf Range (01902 380103) 12 bays covered + 6 bays open 7am-dusk

## WILTSHIRE

Calne, Bowood (01249 822228) 10 bays covered floodlit 7.30am-10pm

Westbury, Thoulstone Park (01373 832825) 24 bays covered floodlit 8am-7.30pmMon.-Thu. 8am-6.30pmSun.

Swindon, Broome Manor Golf Complex (01793 532403) 34 bays covered + 6 bays open floodlit 8am-9.30pmWD 7am-9pmWE

Swindon, Wrag Barn Golf Range (01793 766027) 12 bays covered floodlit 8am-7.30pm

Trowbridge, Wingfield Golf Range (01225 776365) 28 bays covered floodlit 9.30am-9.30pm-6pm Sun

## YORKSHIRE EAST RIDING

Hull, Hull Golf Centre (01482 492720) 24 bays covered floodlit 9am-9pmWD 8pmWE

## YORKSHIRE (NORTH)

Middlesborough, Middlesborough Driving Range (01642 300720) 20 bays covered floodlit 9am-9pmWD 9am-6pmWE

York, York Driving Range (01904 690421) 20 bays floodlit 10am-5pmWD 7am-10pmWE

## YORKSHIRE (SOUTH)

Bawtry, Austerfield Park (01302 710841) 10 bays covered floodlit 9am-10pm

Barnsley, Sandhill Golf Range (01226 751775) 18 bays covered floodlit 9am-9.WD 9am-6.pmWE

## YORKSHIRE (WEST )

Huddersfield, Bradley Park (01484 223772) 14 bays covered floodlit 9am-9.30pm

Knaresborough, Scotton Golf Range (01423 868943) 12 bays covered + 6 bays open 10am-dusk

Leeds, Leeds Golf Centre (0113 288 6000) 21 covered floodlit 7am-9.30pm

Leeds, Oulton Park (01132 823152) 22 bays covered floodlit 9am-9pm

Pontefract, Mid Yorkshire (01977 704522) 28 bays covered floodlit 8am-dusk

## CHANNEL ISLANDS
## GUERNSEY

L'Ancresse Vale, Royal Guernsey (01481 45070) 12 bays open dawn-dusk

## JERSEY

St. Ouens Bays, Les Mielles Golf & Country Club (01534 482787) 20 bays covered + 10 open 7am-dark

## ISLE OF MAN

Douglas, Mount Murray (01624 661111) 20 bays covered + 4 bays open floodlit 8am-10pmWD 9am-10pmWE

## SCOTLAND

## HIGHLANDS & ISLANDS

Inverness, Fairways Golf Range (01463 713334) 22 bays covered floodlit 8am-10pm

Spey Bays, Spey Bays Hotel (01343 820424) 16 bays covered floodlit 10am-10.30pm

## CENTRAL

Bathgate, Whitburn, Polkemmet Country Park (01501 743905) 15 bays covered floodlit 9am-9pm

Edinburgh, Port Royal (0131 333 4377) 24 bays covered + 13 bays open floodlit 10am- 10.pm

Edinburgh, Lasswade, Melville (0131 663 8038) 22 bays covered + 12 bays open floodlit 9am-10pmWD 9am-8pmWE

Errol, Middlebank Golf Range (01821 670320) 7 bays covered + 21 bays open floodlit 9am-9pm

Glenrothes, Glenrothes Golf Range (01592 775374) 20 bays covered floodlit 10am-8.30pmWD 5.30pmWE

Perth, Murrayshall Country House Hotel (01738 551171) 10 bays covered + 8 open floodlit + indoor facility 7.30am-dusk

## SOUTHERN LOWLANDS & BORDERS

Cumbernauld, Cumbernauld Golf Range (01236 737000) 20 bays covered floodlit 9am-10.30pm (Summer) 9.30am-9.30pm(Winter)

Cumbernauld, Westerwood (01236 457171) 8 bays open 7.30am-dusk

Glasgow, Bishopbriggs Golf Range (0141 762 4883) 20 bays covered + 2 bays open floodlit 10am-10pm(closed5pm-6pm)

Glasgow, Renfrew, Normandy Golf Range (0141886 7477) 20 bays covered + 5 bays open floodlit 9.30am-10pm

Glasgow, Uddingston, Clydeway Golf Centre (0141 641 8899) 25 bays covered floodlit 9am-9pmWD 10am-6.30pmWE

Stevenston, Auchenharvie Driving Range (01294 603103) 18 bays covered floodlit 8am-3pm 4pm-8.30pmWD 8am-5pmWE

## WALES

## NORTH

Penymynydd, Bannel Golf Range (01244 544639) 10 bays closed floodlit + 3 bays open 10am-9pmWD 10am-6pmWE

Bodelwyddan, Kinmel Park Golf Complex (01745 833548) 24 bays covered floodlit 10am 10pmWD 6pmSat 8pmSun(

St. Asaph, North Wales Golf Range (01745 730805) 14 bays covered floodlit 10am-9pm (close earlier Winter)

Wrexham, Clays Farm Golf Centre ((01978 661406/661416) 16 bays covered floodlit 8am-9pmWD 6pmWE

## CENTRAL

Caersws, Mid-Wales (01686 688303) 12 bays covered floodlit 8.30am-9.30pm (8.30-6pmWE Winter)

Haverfordwest, Mayfield Golf Range (01437 890308) 12 bays covered floodlit 10am-9.pmWD 10am-9pmWE

Middletown, Welsh Border Golf Range (01743 884247) 10 bays covered floodlit 9am-8.30pm winter 6pmWE

Newport, Parc (01633 680933) 30 bays covered + 8 open floodlit 7.30am-10pmWD 8pmWE

## SOUTH

**Abergavenny,** Wernddu Golf Centre (01873 856223) 26 bays covered floodlit 8am-9.30pm

**Barry,** South Wales Golf Range (01446 742434) 16 bays covered floodlit 9am-8pmWD 9am-5pmWE

**Bridgend,** Pencoed, St. Mary's Driving Range (01656 860280) 15 bays covered floodlit 8am-9pm

**Caerleon,** Carleon Driving Range (01633 420342) 12 bays covered floddlit+ 3 open 7.30-8am-9pm

**Caerphilly,** Mountain Lakes (01222 861128) 20 bays covered floodlit 8am-9pm

**Caerwent,** Dewstow (01291 430444) 20 bays covered floodlit 9am-9pm

**Cwmbran,** Green Meadow (01633 862626) 26 bays covered floodlit 8am-10pm


## NORTHERN IRELAND

### CO ANTRIM

**Whitehead,** Whitehead Driving Range (01960 353159) 18 bays covered 18 bays open floodlit 10am-9pmWD 6pmWE

### CO ARMAGH

**Lurgan,** Craigavon Golf Centre (01762 326606) 10 bays covered + 10 bays open all floodlit 9am-9.30pmWD 9am-8pmWE

### CO BELFAST

**Belfast,** Knockbracken Golf Centre (01232 792108) 30 bays covered floodlit + 60 grass baysopen 9am-11pm

**Belfast,** Newtonabbey, Ballyearl Golf Centre (01232 848287) 27 bays covered floodlit 9am-10pm

### CO DOWN

**Bangor,** Blackwood (01247 852706) 20 bays covered floodlit 8am-10pm

**Warrenpoint,** Newry & Mourne Golf Centre (016937 73247) 10 bays closed floodlit 10am-10pmWD 10am-8pmWE

### CO TYRONE

**Omagh,** Clanabogan Driving Range (01662 245409) 10 covered floodlit 9am-9.30pm 10am-10pmSun.

## REPUBLIC OF IRELAND

(From UK dial 00353 and ignore first digit of numbers below)

### CO CORK

**Little Island,** Harbour Point (021 353094) 21 bays covered floodlit 9.30am-9.30pm

### CO DUBLIN

**Dublin,** Leopardstown Golf Centre (01 289 5341 / 895671) 40 bays covered floodlit + 50(approx.) bays open 9am-9.30pmWD 7.30am-9.30pmWE

**Dublin,** Ward Golf Centre (01 834 8711) 30 bays covered + 20 bays open floodlit 10am-10pm

### CO GALWAY

**Galway,** Galway Range (091 526737 / 26753) 24 bays floodlit 10am-10pmWD 10am-9pmWE 9.30pmWD WE Summer only-call first

### CO KILDARE

**Celbridge,** Celbridge Golf Centre (01 628 8833) 40 bays covered floodlit + 20 bays open 8.30am-10pm summer 10am-10pm winter

### CO LAIOS

**Portlaoise,** The Heath (0502 46533) 10 bays covered floodlit 10.30am-10.30pm

1

© The Automobile Association 1996

Point of Ayre
Seascale

Isle of Man
Ramsey
Maughold Head
ISLE
OF
MAN
Peel
Onchan
DOUGLAS

I r i s h
S e a

Port St Mary
Port Erin
Castletown
Dreswick Point

SC

Carmel Head
Amlwch
Great
Ormes
Head
Llandudno
COLWYN
BAY
Rhyl
Prest
Holyhead
ANGLESEY
R
S
Holy Island
Llangefni
Beaumaris
Conwy
Abergele
Rhosneiger
Llanfairfechan
Penmaenmawr
Bodelwyddan
Anglesey
Bangor
Denbigh
Caernarfon
ABERCONWY
AND COLWYN
DENE
Caernarfon
Bay
SH
Betws-y-coed

Morfa
Nefyn
Ffestiniog
Lleyn Peninsula
Criccieth
Porthmadog
Pwllheli
Bala
Abersoch
Harlech
GWYNEDD
Bardsey
Island
Dolgellau

○ Town Names
● Golf Course

POW
Machynlleth
Cae
Cardigan  Bay
Aberdyfi
Borth
0    10    20 miles
0   10   20   30 kilometres
SN  Aberystwyth
Llanidloes

CARDIGANSHIRE
Llanrhystud

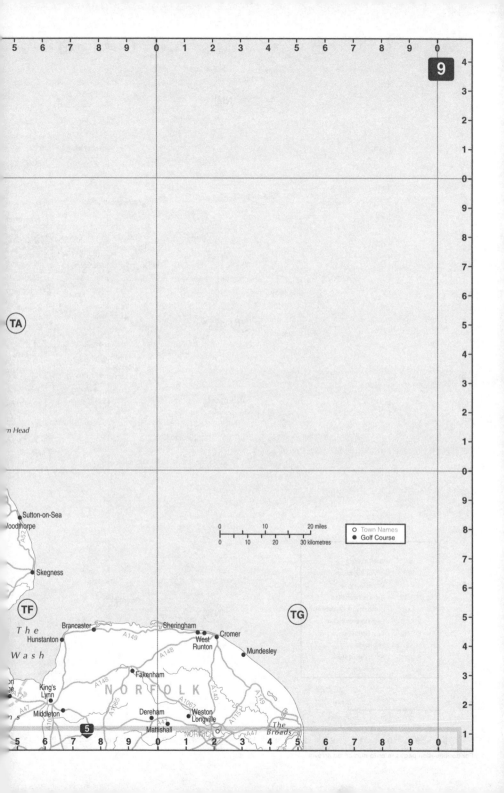

**9**

5 6 7 8 9 0 1 2 3 4 5 6 7 8 9 0

4
3
2
1
0

9
8
7
6

**TA**

5
4
3
2

*n Head*

1

0

9

Sutton-on-Sea
*Woodthorpe*

8

Skegness

7
6

**TF**

5

*The*
Brancaster
Sheringham
Cromer

Hunstanton
West
Runton
Mundesley

4

*Wash*

Fakenham

3

King's
Lynn

**N O R F O L K**

2

Middleton
Dereham
Weston
Longville

Mattishall
**NORWICH**
*The
Broads*

1

**5**

5 6 7 8 9 0 1 2 3 4 5 6 7 8 9 0

0      10      20 miles
0    10    20    30 kilometres

○ Town Names
● Golf Course

**TG**

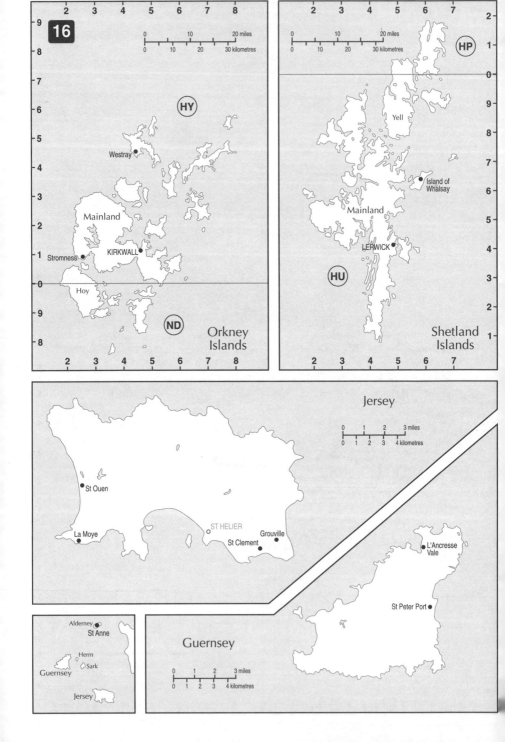

**16**

20 miles
30 kilometres

HY

Westray

Mainland

Stromness
KIRKWALL

Hoy

ND

Orkney Islands

20 miles
30 kilometres

HP

Yell

Island of Whalsay

Mainland

LERWICK

HU

Shetland Islands

Jersey

3 miles
4 kilometres

St Ouen

La Moye

ST HELIER

Grouville
St Clement

L'Ancresse Vale

St Peter Port

Alderney
St Anne

Herm
Guernsey   Sark

Jersey

Guernsey

3 miles
4 kilometres

# INDEX